CONFLICT OF LAWS: AMERICAN, COMPARATIVE, INTERNATIONAL

CASES AND MATERIALS

Second Edition

By

Symeon C. Symeonides
Dean & Professor of Law
Willamette University College of Law

Wendy Collins Perdue
Associate Dean & Professor of Law
Georgetown University Law Center

and

Arthur T. von Mehren
Joseph Story Professor of Law Emeritus
Harvard Law School

AMERICAN CASEBOOK SERIES®

THOMSON
WEST

Mat #40059242

American Casebook Series and West Group are trademarks
registered in the U.S. Patent and Trademark Office.

COPYRIGHT © 1998 WEST GROUP

© 2003 By West, a Thomson business
        610 Opperman Drive
        P.O. Box 64526
        St. Paul, MN 55164–0526
        1–800–328–9352

Printed in the United States of America

ISBN 0–314–26473–6

 *TEXT IS PRINTED ON 10% POST CONSUMER RECYCLED PAPER*

To
Christopher and Marianna
of two generations
S.C.S.

To
William and Benjamin
W.C.P.

To the third generation
Mack, Page, Tika, Frank, Reed, Edward
Colin, Will, and Ben
A.v.M.

Preface

This casebook is designed for use in a typical three-credit course on Conflict of Laws. We begin with choice of law (Part I), continue with jurisdiction (Part II), and conclude with recognition of judgments (Part III).

We know that opinions differ on the proper sequence for teaching this course and we respect the view that logically one should begin with jurisdiction. However, because most students already have a basic understanding of jurisdiction from courses taken earlier, one can defer coverage of jurisdiction until completion of the discussion of the choice-of-law problem. At that point, one can teach jurisdiction at both an accelerated pace and a more sophisticated level.

In selecting cases for this book, we tried to include as many recent cases as possible so as to give the student a more realistic picture of contemporary conflicts law and practice. At the same time, we retained those of the old cases that have influenced the shaping American conflicts law.

In recognition of the increasing frequency and importance of international conflicts, we have included one chapter on such conflicts in each of the three Parts of the book. We have also included at the end a chapter on conflicts in cyberspace and conflicts involving the Indian Tribes, which we believe will provide an opportunity for some concluding reflections on the nature, function, and limits of sovereignty and territoriality. Finally, throughout the book, we have provided extensive information about the law and practice of other--mostly civil-law--countries so as to provide an opportunity for instructive comparative discussion.

In order to keep the length of the book within manageable limits, we edited the cases as severely as we could, while preserving the essence and flavor of the original. All deletions, in cases and other materials, are indicated by three asterisks (* * *). All deletions of citations are indicated by the bracketed word [cit.]. Most footnotes have been omitted without indication. Those that remain retain the original numbering. We have also abbreviated the titles of, and citations to, most secondary sources. An extensive bibliography appearing at the end of the book shows the abbreviations we used.

Principal responsibility for the various chapters was divided as follows: Symeonides authored chapters 1-4, 7 and 12; Perdue authored chapters 5-6, 8, 10-11, and 13; and von Mehren authored chapter 9 and contributed to other chapters. Although we did not attempt to reconcile our varying writing styles, we did try to reconcile our pedagogical differences and to present a unified, versatile book that addresses the needs of the teachers and students who use it. They will judge whether we succeeded.

Symeon C. Symeonides   *Salem, OR*
Wendy Collins Perdue   *Washington, D.C.*
Arthur T. von Mehren   *Cambridge, MA*

Acknowledgments

We gratefully acknowledge the permission granted by the following publishers and individuals to reprint excerpts from the works indicated below in parentheses:

The *American Law Institute* (Complex Litigation: Statutory Recommendations and Analysis (1994); Project on International Jurisdiction and Judgments (Tent. Draft 4/14/2003); Restatement of the Law: Conflict of Laws (1934); Restatement of the Law Second: Conflict of Laws 2d (1971); Restatement of the Law Second: Judgments 2d (1980); and Restatement (Third) of Foreign Relations Law of the United States (1986));

The *California Western Law Review* (William Vetter, "Of Tribal Courts and 'Territories': Is Full Faith and Credit Required," 23 *Cal. W. L. Rev.* 219 (1987));

The *University of Chicago Law Review* (Lea Brilmayer, "How Contacts Count: Due Process Limitations on State Court Jurisdiction," 1980 *Sup. Ct. Rev.* 77); Brainerd Currie, "Full Faith and Credit to Foreign Land Decrees," 21 *U. Chi. L. Rev.* 620 (1954); and J. Goldsmith, "Against Cyberanarchy," 65 *U. Chi. L. Rev.* 1199 (1998));

The *University of Colorado Law Review* (Margaret Stewart, "A New Litany of Personal Jurisdiction," 60 *U. Colo. L. Rev.* 5 (1989));

The *Columbia Law Review* (Douglas Laycock, "Equal Citizens of Equal and Territorial States: The Constitutional Foundations of Choice of Law," 92 *Colum. L. Rev.* 249 (1992))

Professor David P. Currie and the *Foundation Press* (Summary of Brainerd Currie's Choice-of-Law Theory (1963));

The *Harvard Law Review* (Mary Twitchell, "The Myth of General Jurisdiction," 101 *Harv. L. Rev.* 610 (1988));

Juris Publishing, Inc. (Andreas Lowenfeld, "Lex Mercatoria: An Arbitrator's View," in *Lex Mercatoria and Arbitration* 56 (T. Carbonneau, ed. 1990));

The *Mercer Law Review* (Luther L. McDougal, "Toward Application of the Best Rule of Law in Choice of Law Cases," 35 *Mercer L. Rev.* 483 (1984));

The *University of Michigan Press* (David F. Cavers, *The Choice-of-Law Process* (1965));

The New York State Bar Association (New York State Bar Assoc., *Service of Process Abroad: A Nuts and Bolts Guide*, 122 F.R.D. 63 (1989)); and

The Board of Trustees of the *Leland Stanford Junior University* (William F. Baxter, "Choice of Law and the Federal System," 16 *Stan. L. Rev.* 1 (1963); and David Johnson & David Post, "Law and Borders -- The Rise of Law in Cyberspace," 48 *Stan. L. Rev.* 1367 (1996)).

In writing textual material for this book, we have drawn freely on--and in a few instances reproduced excerpts from–works we published elsewhere. In this regard, we wish to acknowledge and thank the following:

The Curatorium of the Hague Academy of International Law and Martinus Nijhoff Publishers (for Arthur T. von Mehren, *Theory and Practice of Adjudicatory Authority in Private International Law: A Comparative Study of the Doctrine, Policies and Practices of Common- and Civil Law Systems*, 295 Recueil des Cours 9 (2003)), and Symeon C. Symeonides, *The American Choice-of-Law Revolution in the Courts: Today and Tomorrow*, 298 Recueil des Cours (2003));

Kluwer Law International (for Symeon C. Symeonides, *Private International Law at the End of the 20th Century: Progress or Regress?* (2000);

T.M.C. Asser Press (for Symeon C. Symeonides, "Territoriality and Personality in Tort Conflicts," in *Intercontinental Cooperation Through Private International Law: Essays in Memory of Peter Nygh*, (T. Einhorn & K. Siehr, eds) 405 (2003);

Yearbook of Private International Law (for Symeon C. Symeonides, "Resolving Punitive Damages Conflicts," 5 *Ybk. Priv. Int'l L.*, ___ (2003);

Willamette Law Review (Symeon C. Symeonides, "American Choice of Law at the Dawn of the 21st Century," 37 *Willamette L. Rev.* 1 (2000);

Tulane Law Review Association (Symeon C. Symeonides, "Louisiana's New Law of Choice of Law for Tort Conflicts: An Exegesis," 66 *Tul. L. Rev.* 677 (1992)); and

The American Society of Comparative Law, Inc. (for the twelve annual choice-of-law surveys and other articles published in the *American Journal of Comparative Law* by Symeon C. Symeonides)

Our gratitude also goes to our research assistants for both the first and the second edition: Tanya Martinez Shively of Louisiana State University, Erica Hashimoto of Georgetown, and Jan von Hein of Harvard (for the first edition); and Evan Hansen and Aaron Young of Willamette, Ann Nash and Amber Smith of Georgetown, and Moritz Bälz of Harvard (for the second edition).

Last but not least, we want to acknowledge the support and encouragement of our families: To Haroula, Christopher and Marianna, to David, Bill, and Ben, and to Joan–Thanks for enduring with grace and understanding the pains of another book.

S.C.S.   *W.C.P.*   *A.v.M.*

Summary of Contents

PART IV: A FINAL LOOK AT CONFLICTS

Table of Contents

PART II: JURISDICTION

Chapter 8. Personal Jurisdiction in Interstate Cases

Chapter 9. Jurisdiction in International Cases

PART III: RECOGNITION OF JUDGMENTS

Chapter 10. Recognition of Sister State Judgments

Chapter 11. Federal-State Recognition of Judgments

PART IV: A FINAL LOOK AT CONFLICTS

Chapter 13. A Final Look at Conflict of Laws: Cyberspace and Indian Tribes

CONFLICT OF LAWS: AMERICAN, COMPARATIVE, INTERNATIONAL

CASES AND MATERIALS

Second Edition

Chapter 1

INTRODUCTION

A. ABOUT THE SUBJECT

1. Conflict of Laws: A Tentative Definition. The law of *Conflict of Laws* is that branch of the law that aspires to provide solutions to international or interstate legal disputes between persons or entities other than countries or states *as such*.

A dispute is considered international or interstate if one or more of its constituent elements are connected with more than one country or state.[1] These elements may be the events that give rise to the dispute, the location of its object, or the nationality, citizenship, domicile, residence, or other affiliation of the parties. Thus, a contract dispute between citizens of different countries, or domiciliaries or residents of different states, or a property dispute between residents of one state regarding assets situated in another state, or a tort resulting from conduct occurring in one state and causing injury in another state are all examples of disputes that fall within the scope of this subject. A brief description of four cases contained in this book illustrates the types of problems that will be studied in this course.

2. Some Examples. a. The Disaster at Sioux City. While on a flight from Denver to Chicago, an airplane crashed in a cornfield in Sioux City, Iowa, causing the death of 112 of the 296 passengers. The victims were domiciled in thirty states of the United States and two foreign countries. The airplane was owned and operated by United Airlines, a Delaware corporation that had its principal place of business in Illinois. United had maintained the plane in California and had trained its flight crew in Colorado. The plane had been manufactured in California by McDonnell Douglas, a Maryland corporation that had its principal place of business in Missouri. There is suspicion that engine malfunction contributed to the accident. The plane's engines were manufactured in Ohio by General Electric, a New York corporation that had its principal place of business in New York. The above states differ, *inter alia*, on whether the three corporations are subject to punitive damages. See In re Air Crash Disaster at Sioux City, Iowa, 734 F.Supp. 1425, (N.D.Ill.1990), *infra* at 305.

b. An Environmental Disaster. A different disaster, long in the making, was

---

1. Hereafter the word "state" is used to denote any country or a territorial subdivision of a country, such as a state or province, that has its own system of private law. Thus, the United States, a state of the United States, a Canadian province, or France are "states" within the meaning of this definition. Cases involving the laws of more than one state are referred to hereafter as "multistate" cases.

the cause of a dispute between a Pennsylvania insured and its Pennsylvania insurer. Since the early 1970s, the insured's paint manufacturing plant, situated in Pennsylvania, has been producing waste that was deposited in New Jersey. Perhaps unbeknownst to everybody involved, the deposited materials caused gradual soil contamination, which New Jersey authorities discovered in the late 1980s and charged the insured with the clean-up costs. Seeking to recoup these costs, the insured sued the insurer in New Jersey, under an insurance policy purchased in Pennsylvania in the early 1970s. The laws of the two states differ on whether the policy provides coverage for accidental yet gradual contamination. See Gilbert Spruance Co. v. Pennsylvania Mfrs. Ass'n Ins. Co., 629 A.2d 885 (N.J.1993), infra at 363. Other similar cases involve many more parties, insurance policies, states, and contaminated sites. See, e.g., Carrier Corp. v. Home Ins. Co., 648 A.2d 665 (Conn.Super.Ct.1994) (400 insurance policies issued in at least ten states by 19 insurance companies over a period of 30 years and covering 44 environmental sites located in several states).

c. The Hong Kong Connection. Two Dutch companies, a British corporation, an Oregon corporation, three California domiciliaries, and a resident of Singapore entered into a contract with a Hong Kong shipping company headquartered in California, by which they acquired shares in the stock of the shipping company and set up a joint venture for international maritime transportation. The contract provided that it "shall be governed by and construed in accordance with Hong Kong law and each party hereby irrevocably submits to the non-exclusive jurisdiction and service of process of the Hong Kong courts." The joint venture was less than successful and litigation ensued. The involved states differ, *inter alia*, on whether the parties owed each other a fiduciary duty and on what constitutes a breach of that duty. See Nedlloyd Lines B.V. v. Superior Court, 834 P.2d 1148 (Cal.1992), infra at 351.

d. The French Will. A French domiciliary and dual citizen of the United States and France, executed in France a testament by which she left all of her money in a New York bank account to persons other than her son and only heir, a California domiciliary. The testament is valid under New York law, but not under French law, which reserves for children a certain minimum portion of their parent's estate. See Estate of Renard, 437 N.Y.S.2d 860 (N.Y.Sur.Ct.1981), infra at 414.

3. The Three Questions or Divisions of Conflicts Law. The fact that the above cases ended up in court should not give the impression that litigation is the only means of resolving multistate disputes. Negotiation, mediation, or arbitration are as available--if not more appropriate--for these disputes as for other legal disputes. Although "casebooks" like this one tend to focus on judicial resolutions, one should not overlook the benefits of alternative means of dispute resolution or the critical role of careful pre-dispute or pre-litigation planning. By studying the judicial mode of dispute resolution, the student can learn how best to avoid litigation, or at least how to make it more predictable.

In this planning, either in preparation for litigation or in efforts to avoid it, the parties involved in multistate activity should keep in mind three major questions: (1) Where can or should litigation take place? (2) Which law will the court apply? and (3) Where can one enforce the resulting judgment? These three questions correspond to the three consecutive phases that comprise the process of judicial resolution of most multistate disputes, namely: (1) jurisdiction; (2) choice of law; and (3) recognition and enforcement of judgments. This book explores all three phases.

a. Jurisdiction. From the plaintiff's perspective, the question of jurisdiction can be divided into two parts: (a) Where *can* we file? and (b) Where *should* we file? From the court's perspective, one can divide the question into more parts: (a) Do we have jurisdiction, i.e., are we empowered and authorized to adjudicate this action? (b) If so, do we have discretion to abstain from exercising this power? If so, should we decline to hear this case? Chapters 8 and 9 explore these questions.

Obviously, the choice of a forum can have a decisive bearing on the outcome of a case. A successful choice not only presupposes familiarity with the jurisdictional rules of all involved states, but also requires investigation of all the advantages and disadvantages of litigating in a particular state and court. Besides litigational convenience, the inquiry should encompass the all-important question of which law the court will likely apply to the merits, and whether the resulting judgment can be enforced in the forum state. The fact that the forum state has a substantive law that favors the plaintiff should not end the inquiry, unless the plaintiff correctly concludes that the court will apply that law.

b. Choice of Law. Whether the court will, or will not, apply its own law to the merits of a multistate case is often a complicated question, but its answer is not prejudged by the fact that the court has and assumes jurisdiction. With minor exceptions in its formative period (see infra B.5), private international law adopted the premise that, in appropriate cases, the courts of one sovereign should be prepared to apply the law of another sovereign.[2] Thus, jurisdiction and choice of law have become two independent inquiries which may or may not lead to the same state.[3] Chapters 2-7 focus on the latter inquiry. They examine the criteria and methods for determining how one should choose the law that governs multistate cases.

c. Recognition and Enforcement of Judgments. Once the court renders a judgment, the judgment debtor will either voluntarily comply with the judgment or, if not, the judgment creditor will proceed to enforce the judgment. If the debtor has sufficient assets in the forum state, the judgment will be satisfied out of those assets and the matter will end there. If not, then the creditor will proceed to enforce the judgment in another state in which the debtor has sufficient assets. Must the latter state recognize the judgment, or does it have a choice on the matter? To what extent can the latter state inquire into the rendering court's jurisdiction, the law applied, or other matters that the rendering court had or could have decided? What differences exist between the requirements for recognizing a sister-state judgment and a foreign-country judgment? These are some of the questions explored in chapters 10–12.

---

2. This remains true today in the United States, even if certain modern choice-of-law methodologies or practices appear to unduly favor the law of the forum state.

3. In the United States, this principle is subject exceptions in certain cases, such as divorce and workers' compensation. In these cases the choice-of-law question is merged into the jurisdictional question in the sense that a court that assumes jurisdiction over these cases generally applies its own law to the merits.

4. Categories of Conflicts. *a. Vertical, Interstate, and International Conflicts.* The United States Constitution allocates law making-powers between the federal government and the constituent states by assigning to the federal government certain enumerated powers on matters of national concern (see U.S. Const. Art. 1§8) and reserving to the states the remaining powers, including the great bulk of private law (see U.S. Const. Amend. X). Thus, by establishing and preserving a plurilegal federal union, the Constitution creates the conditions for the occurrence of conflicts of laws, of both the vertical and the horizontal type.

"Vertical" conflicts are those that occur between federal law and state law. "Horizontal" conflicts are those that occur between or among:

    (a) the laws of the states of the United States (intra-national "interstate" conflicts); or

    (b) the laws of foreign countries, on the one hand, and, on the other hand,

        (i) the laws of the United States (international "federal" conflicts), or

        (ii) the laws of a state of the United States (international "state" conflicts).

The following diagram depicts these categories of conflicts.

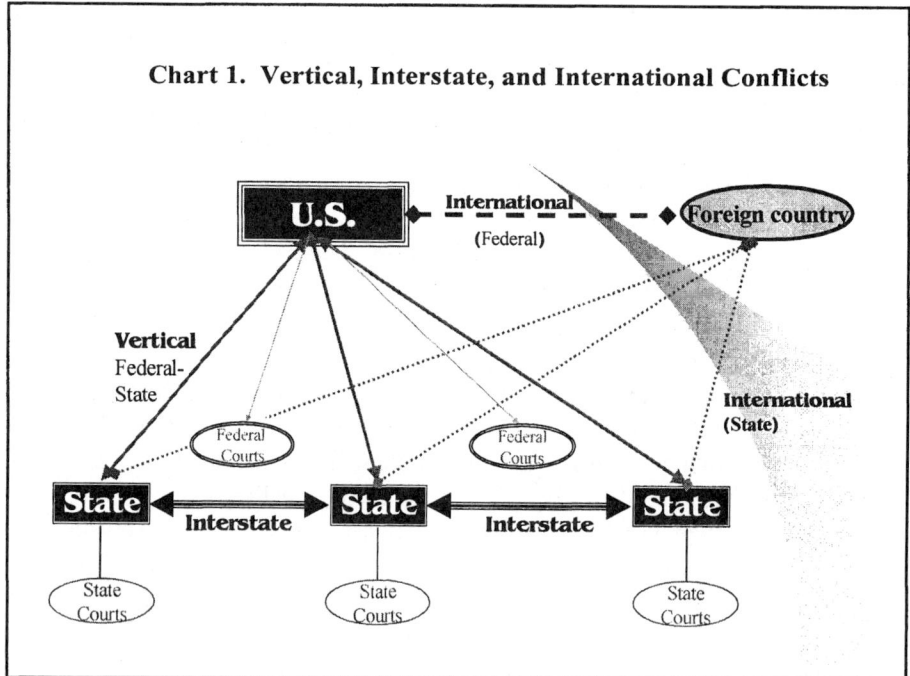

Chart 1. Vertical, Interstate, and International Conflicts

Every year American courts decide approximately 1,500 conflicts cases, of which interstate conflicts are by far the most numerous.[4] This book examines all of the above categories of conflicts from the perspective of American federal and state law, but also periodically looks at the experiences of other nations. In this field, more

---

4. See Symeonides, *Choice of Law in 2002*, 3.

than in any other, the comparative approach is both necessary and rewarding.

b. The Sources of American Conflicts Law. In theory, the resolution of all three categories of conflicts is a matter of federal law. In practice, this is true only with regard to vertical conflicts. Under the Constitution's supremacy clause (see U.S. Const. Art. VI), principles of federal law govern conflicts between federal and state law. Federal principles also govern conflicts between federal and foreign law, but these principles have grown out of, and continue to draw from, the states' experience with interstate conflicts.

The Constitution also addresses horizontal interstate conflicts by enunciating the obligation of each state to give "full faith and credit" to the laws and judgments of sister states, and by assigning to Congress the power to enact laws governing the manner in which each state will discharge this obligation.[5] For better or worse, however, Congress has exercised this power very sparingly.[6] Thus, by default, the power and the initiative for resolving interstate conflicts remain with the states,[7] subject only to mild restraints imposed by the Constitution as interpreted by the United States Supreme Court. These restraints are explored in chapter 5, which focuses primarily on the Due Process and Full Faith and Credit clauses, but also examines the role of the Privileges and Immunities, Equal Protection, and Commerce clauses.

The states possess the same power with regard to international conflicts between state law and foreign law, subject to some but not all of the same constitutional restraints as interstate conflicts,[8] as well as a rarely utilized admonition that, in addressing these conflicts, states should not interfere with the federal government's conduct of foreign affairs. Chapter 7 explores these issues.

c. State and Federal Courts. Under the American system of dual sovereignty, conflicts cases can be adjudicated either by state or federal courts. The applicable choice-of-law principles depend not on whether the adjudicating court is state or federal, but rather on the category in which the particular conflict belongs. For example, if state choice-of-law principles govern a particular case, then those principles govern even if a federal court adjudicates the case. Chapter 6 focuses on federal courts and explores the history of and reasons for this practice. Conversely, when a state court encounters a case that is governed by federal choice-of-law principles, such as a conflict between federal maritime law and foreign law, the court must follow the federal principles. Finally, because of the supremacy of the federal

---

5. See U.S. Const. Art. IV § 1 (providing that "Full Faith and Credit shall be given in each State" to the "laws and judgments of every other State" and authorizing Congress to enact laws prescribing "the Effect" of such laws and judgments.)

6. See, e.g. 28 U.S.C.A. § 1738A (Federal Parental Kidnapping Prevention Act); 28 U.S.C.A. §1738C ("Defense of Marriage Act").

7. Although each state legislature has the inherent power to enact choice-of-law legislation, very few states have exercised this power. Only one state has a comprehensive conflicts codification. See Book IV of the Louisiana Civil Code, enacted in 1991, (hereinafter referred to as the "Louisiana codification"). Although many other states have piecemeal, narrowly-drawn statutes, the great bulk of American conflicts law is found in the law reports, not the statute books. It has been created judicially through the pronouncements of the courts in adjudicating conflicts cases and through the operation of the doctrine of stare decisis.

8. The Full Faith and Credit clause does not apply to international conflicts, and the Privileges and Immunities clause does not apply to non-U.S. citizens.

constitution, both state and federal courts must be mindful of the federal constitutional restraints, even when adjudicating a case that is otherwise governed by state choice-of-law principles. See chapters 5 and 7.

5. Nomenclature. The use of the term *Conflict of Laws* to describe our subject seems to assume that, in all multistate cases, each involved state has an active or passive desire, claim, or "interest" to apply its law, and that these claims "conflict" in the sense of being of roughly equal validity and intensity. As we shall see later, both of these assumptions have been questioned throughout history. For example, even if one accepts the propriety of using anthropomorphic terms to describe states objectives, one can question whether or why a state would be "interested" in the outcome of disputes between private persons. Similarly, one can question whether such a state "interest" is implicated in each case connected with that state, or whether the application of that state's law indeed effectuates that interest. Nevertheless, for better or worse, the term *Conflict of Laws*, which was coined in Europe in the middle ages, has prevailed in the United States and a few other common law jurisdictions, and is used throughout this book.

Ironically, the term *Private International Law*, which was coined in the United States, has prevailed in Europe and the rest of the world. This term is more descriptive, but also more idealistic than the term Conflict of Laws. The word *international* describes an important attribute of the disputes that fall within the scope of this subject--they are international (or interstate) in that they have contacts with more than one country or state. The word *private* echoes the civil-law division between private and public law and signifies that only private-law disputes fall within the scope of this subject. These are disputes arising from relations between persons other than a state or its subdivisions acting in the exercise of governmental authority. In contrast, public-law disputes of an international character, such as those between sovereign countries or international entities, fall within the scope of *Public International Law* or simply *International Law*.

However, the term private international law may be misleading if it gives the impression that there exists a distinct body of law universally or even uniformly observed by most nations that provides solutions to multistate disputes. Reality is much different. Besides the few international conventions that avoid or resolve conflicts through substantive or conflicts rules, international law provides little guidance on the subject. Thus, for the most part, the task of resolving multistate disputes is left to individual states or countries, subject to certain mild restraints imposed by international law. Accordingly, conflicts law is essentially *national* law. Moreover, as noted earlier, within the United States, conflicts law is, *de facto* and for the most part, *state* law rather than federal law.

B. A BRIEF HISTORY OF CHOICE–OF–LAW DOCTRINE

1. From Ancient Greece to Medieval Italy. According to most western authors, the history of choice of law begins in the 12th century in Northern Italy. Yet conflicts problems existed and solutions to them were devised in much earlier times. Although the historical record is incomplete, some evidence of those solutions has survived. For example, in addressing a court in the Greek island-state of Aegina, the Athenian orator Isocrates (436–358 B.C.) argued that the court should uphold his client's testament because it conformed to both the law of the testator's "fatherland" and the law of the forum. See Isocrates, *Aegineticus* 19.16. A compact between two Greek city-states signed *circa* 100 B.C., provided that tort claims should be adjudicated by the courts of the state in which the tortfeasor was domiciled, and should be governed by the law of the forum. See Evrigenis, *PIL*, 50–51. Similarly, a decree issued in Hellenistic Egypt *circa* 120 B.C. provided that contracts written in Greek were subject to the jurisdiction of the Greek courts and governed by Greek law, whereas contracts written in the Egyptian language were subject to the jurisdiction of the Egyptian courts and governed by Egyptian law. See Juenger, *Multistate Justice* 7–8.

Notice that both the Greek compact and the Egyptian decree attached the choice-of-law question to the jurisdictional question and answered both questions through a pre-established rule. In contrast, the Romans detached the two questions and addressed only the question of jurisdiction. Roman law vested a special official-- the *praetor peregrinus*--with jurisdiction over cases with foreign elements, or at least disputes between non-Roman citizens, but was silent on the question of which law should govern those disputes. Left to his own devices, the praetor came up with the idea that, rather than choosing the law of one of the involved states, he would draw from their laws to craft an ad hoc substantive rule for the case at hand. Thus, for the first time, multistate disputes were resolved not through a *choice* of law, but rather through the *creation* of new substantive law applicable only to those disputes. This law, later called *jus gentium*, was gradually incorporated into the *jus civile* (the law that governed relations between Roman citizens), and both were eventually "codified" by Emperor Justinian in his *Digest* (533 A.D.). Although the Digest was an exceedingly long document, it was silent on the whole choice-of-law question, perhaps because in the meantime and for a variety of reasons, conflicts between Roman and non-Roman laws had become far less frequent.

By the 12th century, when the Italian scholars known as Glossators (1100–1250) "re-discovered" Justinian's Digest, the social and economic environment had changed dramatically. Although the Digest--supplemented by the new *jus commune* or common law that was based on it--was the overarching "general" law for all of Italy, the city-states of Northern Italy began to develop their own diverging local customs and laws (*statuta*). The increase of trade among these city-states began to generate new "interstate" conflicts of laws. For example, "[i]f a merchant from Bologna was sued in Modena, should he be judged by the statutes of the former or the latter city?" asked the famous Glossator Accursius (1228?). The need to address such questions became increasingly pressing.

2. Bartolus and the Statutists. For more than a century, several Glossators and their successors, the Commentators (1250-1400), wrestled with conflicts questions.[9]

---

9. One Glossator, Magister Aldricus (1170–1200), argued that conflicts problems should be resolved through the application of that law which is *potior et utilior* (better and more useful). Eight centuries later, a "better-law" approach was proposed in the United States. See infra Ch. 3.

One Commentator, Bartolus of Sassoferrato (1313–1357), attempted to provide the answers. However, as a loyal and careful Romanist, Bartolus recognized that, for these answers to have any authority, they had to be grounded on Justinian's law. Although Justinian had said virtually nothing on the subject, Bartolus found a way to make it appear that these answers were implicit in Justinian's Code, in fact in the very first sentence of it. This sentence provided: "*Cunctos populos, quos clementiae nostrae regit temperamentum, in tali volumus religione versari, quam divinum Petrum apostolum traditisse Romanis[.]*" Codex 1.1.1. Literally translated, this sentence states: "All peoples who are subject to our merciful sway, we desire them to live under that religion which the divine apostle Peter has delivered to the Romans."

Obviously, this sentence had nothing to do with secular law, much less conflicts law. It simply expressed the emperor's desire for all peoples under his power to adhere to the Christian religion. But notice, the emperor spoke only of people *under his power*, his "merciful sway," or his jurisdiction, as we would say today. Bartolus read this sentence as an acknowledgment by the emperor/law-giver of a limitation to his own power, and thus as an implicit delineation of the scope of Roman law *vis a vis* foreign law. If Roman law governs only those under the emperor's sway, then those who are not subject to his authority must be governed by the law of their own sovereign.[10] From this elementary proposition, Bartolus began to construct principles for delineating the reach of Roman and non-Roman laws, and for resolving conflicts between these laws or between the laws of the Italian city-states.[11]

Bartolus and later scholars collectively known as *statutists* developed a method of resolving conflicts that was based on a simplistic classification of local laws (*statuta*) into two categories: real or personal. Real statutes were those that operated only within the territory of the enacting state, but not beyond. In contrast, personal statutes operated beyond the territory of the enacting state and bound all persons that owed allegiance to it.[12] The statutists thought that this classification could resolve all potential conflicts because all statutes, both domestic and foreign, belonged to either the one or the other category, leaving neither gaps nor doubts.

Obviously, this was too optimistic, but worse than that was the fact that the statutists' criteria for classifying a statute as real or personal were completely mechanical--they were based solely on the statute's wording. For example, the

---

10. See Bartolus, *Commentarii in Lex Cunctos Populos* (transl. by Clarence Smith), in 14 *Am. J. Leg. Hist.* 154, 174–83, 247–75 (1970).

11. These "intra-Roman" conflicts presented a more difficult problem for Bartolus. First, he had to answer the question of whether the Digest even permitted city-states to adopt laws that diverged from the general law of the Digest. He answered the question affirmatively by stretching the meaning of a provision of the Digest (D.1.3.32) that recognized the authority of local *customs* and--Bartolus postulated--local *statutes*. He then proposed that conflicts between these statutes be resolved through the same principles of conflicts resolution that he enunciated in discussing the *Cunctos populos* clause. See Bartolus, *Commentarii in Lex de Quibus*, supra n. 10 at 163–74. By so doing, Bartolus tacitly subscribed to the notion that, by and large, the same principles under which one can resolve "international conflicts" can also resolve inter-city or interstate conflicts.

12. A third category of statutes, called "mixed," was added later. However, contrary to what this term might connote, it did not really describe a new category of statutes. Rather it encompassed all those personal statutes which, on closer examination, were thought to operate territorially.

statutists argued that, if the statute's first words referred to a person, such as saying that "the first-born son shall succeed to the property," then the statute was personal. If the words referred to a thing, such as by saying that "the property shall pass to the first-born son," then the statute was real. This logic, or lack of it, explains the ridicule with which subsequent authors treated the statutists commentaries. This criticism was justified to the extent it referred to the statutists' mechanical classification of statutes. However, such criticism should not obscure the statutists' impact, positive or negative, on the future direction of private international law. In particular, the following features of statutist methodology are relevant to contemporary American conflicts law:

a. The statutists re-introduced the "conflictual method," a method by which multistate disputes are resolved by choosing the law of one of the involved states rather than by blending those laws and crafting a new substantive rule as the *praetor peregrinus* had done. The conflictual method has remained the dominant method ever since;

b. The statutists introduced the "unilateral" conflictual method, as distinguished from the "bilateral" method, which appeared later in history. The bilateral method postulates a system of *a priori* choice-of-law rules that designate the cases that fall within the scope of domestic and foreign law. In contrast, the unilateral method approaches the matter from the other end. It focuses on the conflicting domestic and foreign laws themselves, and tries to determine whether the case at hand falls within the intended scope of the one or the other law. After surviving the subsequent onslaught of the bilateral method, the unilateral method reappeared later in Europe as well as in the United States, where it formed the basis of one of the most influential approaches--Brainerd Currie's interest analysis. See infra, chapter 3;

c. In trying to ascertain the intended scope of conflicting laws, the statutists committed a serious error by unduly relying on the wording of the statutes. In light of the fact that at least the first statutists were more grammarians than lawyers, this error was understandable. However, this was simply an error in interpretative *technique*, which could be easily corrected through the use of more enlightened interpretative methods that rely on teleology rather than on grammar. Eventually this correction occurred when a later Commentator, Guy de Coquille, proposed that the classification of statutes into real or personal should not depend on the wording of the statute but rather on the presumed and apparent *purpose* of those who enacted it. This is no different from examining the *policy* of a law, and this notion is now an integral part of many modern choice-of-law methodologies. See infra chapter 3;

d. The statutists' classification of statutes was the first comprehensive--and predictably unsuccessful--attempt to delineate the legislative competence of states. Bartolus, of course, pretended that his delineation was implicit in the supranational law of Justinian's Digest. Yet, by basing his delineation on the wording of city-state statutes, Bartolus subconsciously subscribed to the opposite and somewhat circular premise, namely: that a state's legislative competence depends on the words that state unilaterally chooses to express its assertion of legislative competence, rather than on any super-arching law that assigns to all states their respective spheres of competence. Eventually, this premise led to the understanding that private international law is primarily national law. Moreover, this premise also led to the notion that a state's "claim" or "interest" to apply its law, as that claim is expressed in the words or the content of its statutes, is an acceptable criterion for resolving conflicts of laws. The similarity of this line of thinking with contemporary American approaches, especially "interest analysis," is obvious. See infra chapter 3.

3. The Dutch Contribution; Comity. During the 15th and 16th centuries, other Italian and especially French scholars, like Dumoulin and d'Argentré,[13] refined and modified Bartolus' method, but without departing from the basic tenets of statutist thinking. By the 17th century, the leadership of conflicts literature moved to the Netherlands, which by that time was one of the major trading nations in the world. In the meantime, Europe had witnessed the emergence of modern nation-states and Jean Bodin's works on territorial sovereignty (*Six livres de la république* (1576)) had become a "best-seller."

It is therefore no surprise that the Dutch authors became intensely preoccupied with explaining *why* courts apply foreign law, in other words, reconciling the application of foreign law with the principle of territorial sovereignty. The Dutch answer can be synopsized in one henceforth famous word--*comity*. Comity was defined as something between mere courtesy and a legal duty, as derived from the tacit consent of nations and based on mutual forbearance and enlightened self-interest. In a ten page essay, the most famous of these authors, Ulricus Huber (1624–1694),[14] postulated the following three axioms:

(1) The laws of each state have force within its territory but not beyond.

(2) These laws bind all those who are found within the territory, whether permanently or temporarily.

(3) Out of comity, foreign laws may be applied so that rights acquired under them can retain their force, provided that they do not prejudice the state's powers or rights.

The first two axioms elevate territorialism into the main operating principle of private international law, a position that remained unchallenged for many generations. The third axiom attempts to explain *why* the forum state will apply the law of another sovereign, but not *when*. Neither the vague notion of comity nor the less vague but equally problematic notion of "acquired rights" provide concrete guidance as to the circumstances in which the forum will or will not apply the law of another state.

---

13. Dumoulin (1500–1566) resurrected the idea of party autonomy (namely the notion that a contract should be governed by the law chosen by the parties) and extended that notion to cases in which the parties did not make an express choice. D'Argentré (1519–1590) modified Bartolus' classification of statutes by creating a third category, called "mixed" statutes (see supra n.12), and thus expanded the category of statutes that operated territorially. He also advocated the primacy of the *lex fori*.

14. Huber's essay, entitled *De conflictu legum diversarum in diversis imperiis*, was contained in a larger work entitled *Praelectiones Juris Romani et hodierni* (1689). This essay, which was the first work to use the term "conflict of laws," is reputed to be the most widely read document on our subject. It is translated into English in E. Lorenzen, *Selected Articles on the Conflict of Laws*, 162–80 (1947).

Huber's axioms exerted a strong influence on both English and American conflicts law, described infra, but had little influence in continental Europe which remained faithful to statutist teachings until the middle of the 19th century.

4. The German Contribution: Wächter and Savigny. In the mid 19th century, two German authors published their views which, although diametrically opposed, changed the course and direction of European private international law. The first author was Carl Georg von Wächter, and his contribution was rather destructive. "He debunked statutist learning, exposed the vested rights theory's circular reasoning and disparaged the comity doctrine," Juenger, *Multistate Justice*, 32. In the place of these discarded internationalist doctrines, Wächter proposed an ethnocentric unilateral approach that was based on the primacy of the law of the forum (*lex fori*). Describing the judge as an instrument of state legislative will, Wächter argued that, in resolving conflicts disputes, the judge should keep in mind the policies and interests of the forum state, rather than notions of comity and other multistate considerations.[15] Although Wächter's approach had no followers in Europe, it bears remarkable resemblance to approaches developed in the second half of the 20th century in the United States, especially Ehrenzweig's *lex fori* approach and Currie's interest analysis. See infra, chapter 3.

The second German author was the great Romanist Friedrich Carl von Savigny (1779–1861).[16] His contribution was both constructive and decisive. Like Wächter, Savigny rejected the statutist doctrine but, unlike Wächter, he rejected both the unilateral approach and the primacy of the *lex fori*. Instead, Savigny adopted and perfected the bilateral choice-of-law approach, which had previously lost the competition with the unilateral approach. Rather than focusing on the conflicting laws and trying to ascertain their intended spatial reach, Savigny began his analysis from the opposite end. He focused on disputes or "legal relationships" and sought to identify the state in which each relationship had its "seat" or in whose legislative jurisdiction it "belonged." He divided private international law into broad categories corresponding to the major divisions of private law (family law, successions, property, contracts, torts, etc.) and then, through "connecting factors" (such as domicile, situs, or the place of the transaction or event) identified those inherent characteristics of each legal relationship that placed its seat in one state rather another.

The result of this classificatory approach was a network of neutral, even-handed, bilateral choice-of-law rules that assigned each legal relationship to one particular state, regardless of that state's actual or imputed "wish" to apply its law and regardless of that law's content. These rules also placed foreign law on parity with forum law. Indeed, in Savigny's cosmopolitan and universalist milieu, there was

---

15. See Wächter, Über die Collision der Privatrechtsgesetze verschiedener Staaten (pt. 1), 24 *Archiv für die zivilistiche Praxis*, 230 (1841), (pts. 2–4) 25 *Archiv für die zivilistiche Praxis*, 1, 161, 361 (1842). For an English commentary and partial translation, see Nadelmann, Wächter's Essay on the Collision of Private Laws of Different States, 13 *Am. J. Comp. L.* 414 (1963).

16. Savigny's contribution to conflicts is contained in the 8th volume of his treatise on Roman law entitled *System des heutigen Römischen Rechts* (1849). This volume was translated into English by William Guthrie, under the title *Private International Law, A Treatise on the Conflict of Laws and the Limits of their Operation in Respect of Place and Time* (1869).

no room for forum protectionism. He argued forcefully that the objective of private international law should not be to promote the forum's interests as such, but rather to produce "international uniformity of decisions"--a regime that would eliminate forum shopping because all involved states would apply the same law to a particular case, regardless of which state's courts adjudicate the case.

Savigny's dream did not materialize, but his approach to conflicts is still considered as the classic approach in Europe. It resembles both the traditional and some modern approaches followed in the United States today.

5. The Dearth of English Conflicts Doctrine. Up until the mid-1700s, the English common law courts did not assert jurisdiction over cases that arose outside England.[17] This had less to do with judicial self-restraint and more to do with the English jury system. Jurors were drawn from the vicinage (i.e., the locale of the events giving rise to the dispute) and, since the court could not impanel foreign jurors, foreign cases could not be tried in England. Later on, the courts developed the legal fiction that the foreign locale was somehow situated in England, and thus assumed jurisdiction over cases arising abroad. Consistently with this fiction, however, the courts applied English law to these cases.

Eventually, English courts dropped this fiction, openly asserted jurisdiction over cases with foreign elements, and for the first time confronted the conflicts question. Faced with a dearth of indigenous doctrine, English courts and writers turned to continental doctrine and borrowed copiously from it. Since Huber's doctrine was in vogue at the time, they imported it wholesale. His passing reference to "rights acquired" under foreign law evolved into a full-fledged doctrine of "vested rights,"[18] which later found its way to the United States in the early 20th century writings of Professor Joseph Beale. See infra chapter 2.

6. Early American Conflicts Law. Until Beale's time, however, American conflicts law had remained virtually immune from English influence. Indeed, the relative dearth of mature English doctrine during the formative period of American conflicts law, coupled with the existence at that time of a rich continental tradition, explains why American conflicts law is one of the few branches of American law that owes its origins to civilian sources.

The author most responsible for this development was Joseph Story who, for all practical purposes, is the intellectual father of American conflicts law. In 1834, Story published his seminal *Commentaries on the Conflict of Laws*, which--though not the first American conflicts book--[19] was the first *comprehensive* conflicts treatise

---

17. In contrast, the special courts for commercial and maritime matters did have jurisdiction over disputes arising abroad. However, rather than resolving those disputes through a choice of law, these courts applied the pan-european law merchant and the multinational or a-national maritime law, respectively. See Juenger, *Multistate Justice* 23–24.

18. See A. Dicey, *A Digest of the Law of England with Reference to the Conflict of Laws* (1896).

19. A few years earlier, Samuel Livermore, a Louisiana civil law lawyer published his *Dissertations on the Questions Which Arise from the Contrariety of the Positive Laws of Different States and Nations* (1828). For the influence of this book on American conflicts law, see de Nova, The First American Book on Conflict of Laws, 8 *Am. J. Leg. Hist.* 136 (1964). The book was a concerted effort to import to the United States the doctrine of the Italian statutists. Although this effort failed, Livermore indirectly influenced the course of American conflicts law by making available the otherwise inaccessible continental conflicts literature to Joseph Story. In addition to providing a thorough English summary of this literature in his own

(continued...)

in the English language. Story synthesized and recast in a systematic fashion the writings of dozens of continental authors as well as several judicial decisions from England and especially Scotland. However, Story was decidedly influenced by Huber's axioms and his comity principle. Story reformulated these axioms as follows:

[1.] [E]very nation possesses an exclusive sovereignty and jurisdiction within its territory * * * [and its laws] affect, and bind directly all property, whether real or personal, within its territory and all persons, who are residents within it, * * * and also all contracts made, and acts done within it. * * *

[2.] [N]o state or nation can, by its laws, directly affect, or bind property out of its own territory, or bind persons not resident therein * * *.

[3.] [W]hatever force and obligation the laws of one country have in another, depend solely upon the laws, and municipal regulations of the latter, that is to say, upon its own proper jurisprudence and polity, and upon its own express or tacit consent. A state may prohibit the operation of all [or of some] foreign laws, and the rights growing out of them, within its own territories. * * * When [its law is] silent, then, and then only, can the question properly arise, what law is to govern in the absence of a clear declaration of the sovereign will. * * *

[4.] The real difficulty is to ascertain, what principles in point of public convenience ought to regulate the conduct of nations on this subject in regard to each other * * *. [T]he phrase 'comity of nations' * * * is the most appropriate phrase to express the true foundation and extent of the obligation of the laws of one nation within the territories of another. It is derived altogether from the voluntary consent of the latter; and is inadmissible, when it is contrary to its known policy, or prejudicial to its interests. * * *[20]

Unlike Huber, Story took the next step of erecting around these general parameters a comprehensive system of bilateral choice-of-law rules which American courts followed until the beginning of the 20th century.

At that time, Professor Joseph H. Beale succeeded Story in the stewardship of American conflicts doctrine. In a three-volume work[21] dedicated to Story, Beale rejected Story's cosmopolitan perspective, discarded the notion of comity, and adopted the English doctrine of vested rights. Around this doctrine, Beale erected a rigid, Prussian-like system of bilateral choice-of-law rules that purported to reflect the current American judicial practice. These rules were etched in stone in the *Restatement of the Law, Conflict of Laws* (hereinafter "Restatement") which Beale drafted in 1934 under the auspices of the American Law Institute. The Restatement was the basis of what is referred to hereinafter and elsewhere as the "traditional" American approach. This approach is the focus of the next chapter.

---

19. (...continued)
book, Livermore donated his entire library of continental writings to the Harvard Law School, his alma mater, where Justice Story, then professor, was teaching. Story made good use of these writings in his *Commentaries.*

20. Joseph Story, *Commentaries on the Conflict of Laws*, 19, 21, 24–25, 37 (1834).

21. Joseph H. Beale, *A Treatise on the Conflict of Laws*, 3 vols. (1935)

Part I

CHOICE OF LAW

Chapter 2

THE TRADITIONAL AMERICAN APPROACH TO THE CHOICE-OF-LAW PROBLEM

A. INTRODUCTION

This chapter focuses on what is usually referred to as the *traditional* American choice-of-law approach, which has had an almost universal following in the United States until the early 1960s. The word "traditional" usually has negative connotations, especially when used in juxtaposition with "modern." Nevertheless, the study of the traditional approach is necessary and valuable, for at least two reasons: First, this approach remains in force in most states in areas other than torts and contracts (where it has given way to other "modern" approaches, which will be studied in Chapter 3). Thus, "traditional" in this context does not necessarily mean *passé*, especially since, even in torts and contract, the traditional approach retains its following in about a dozen states. See pp. 299 *et seq*. Second, regardless of its current viability, the traditional approach remains the best vehicle for introducing the elementary questions, basic syllogism, and fundamental objectives of the choice-of-law process. Since the modern approaches grew out of a reaction to the traditional approach, the study of the traditional approach provides a valuable frame of reference within which to compare, contrast, understand, and critique the modern approaches.

B. THE TRADITIONAL AMERICAN APPROACH TO TORT AND CONTRACT CONFLICTS

1. TORTS

Alabama Great Southern R.R. Co. v. Carroll
Supreme Court of Alabama, 1892.
97 Ala. 126, 11 So. 803.

McCLELLAN, J. The plaintiff, W. D. Carroll, is, and was at the time of entering into the service of the defendant, the Alabama Great Southern Railroad Company, and at the time of being injured in that service, a citizen of Alabama. The defendant is an Alabama corporation, operating a railroad extending from Chattanooga, in the state of Tennessee, through Alabama to Meridian, in the state of Mississippi. At the time of the casualty complained of plaintiff was in the service of the defendant in the capacity of brakeman on freight trains running from Birmingham, Ala., to Meridian, Miss., under a contract which was made in the state of Alabama. The injury was caused by the breaking of a link between two cars in a freight train which was proceeding from Birmingham to Meridian. The point at which the link broke and the injury was suffered was in the state of Mississippi. The evidence tended to show that the link which broke was a defective link, and that it was in a defective condition when the train left Birmingham. * * * It was shown to be the duty of certain employees of defendant stationed along its line to inspect the links attached to cars to be put in trains, or forming the couplings between cars in trains at Chattanooga, Birmingham, and some points between Birmingham and the place where this link broke, and also that it was the duty of the conductor of freight trains, and the other train men, to maintain such inspection as occasion afforded throughout the runs or trips of such trains; and the evidence affords ground for inference that there was a negligent omission on the part of such employees to perform this duty, or, if performed, the failure to discover the defect in, and to remove, this link was the result of negligence * * *

This was the negligence, not of the master, the defendant, but of fellow servants of the plaintiff, for which at common law the defendant is not liable. * * * [T]he decisions of the supreme court of Mississippi * * * apply * * * the doctrine of fellow-servants to the exemption of railway companies from liability to one servant for injuries resulting from the negligence of another[.] * * *

It is, however, further contended that the plaintiff, if his evidence be believed, has made out a case for the recovery sought under the employers' liability act of Alabama, it being clearly shown that there is no such or similar law of force in the state of Mississippi. Considering this position in the abstract,—that is, disassociated from the facts of this particular case, which are supposed to exert an important influence upon it,—there cannot be two opinions as to its being unsound and untenable. So looked at, we do not understand appellee's counsel even to deny either the proposition or its application to this case,—that there can be no recovery in one state for injuries to the person sustained in another, unless the infliction of the injuries is actionable under the law of the state in which they were received. Certainly this is the well-established rule of law, subject, in some jurisdictions, to the qualification that the infliction of the injuries would also support an action in the state where the suit is brought had they been received within that state. [cit.]

But it is claimed that the facts of this case take it out of the general rule which the authorities cited above abundantly support, and authorize the courts of Alabama to subject the defendant to the payment of damages under section 2590 of the Code, although the injuries counted on were sustained in Mississippi under circumstances which involved no liability on the defendant by the laws of that state. This insistence is, in the first instance, based on that aspect of the evidence which goes to show that the negligence which produced the casualty transpired in Alabama, and the theory that, wherever the consequences of that negligence manifested itself, a recovery can be had in Alabama. We are referred to no authority in support of this proposition, and exhaustive investigation on our part has failed to disclose any. * * *

It is admitted, or at least cannot be denied, that negligence of duty unproductive of damnifying results will not authorize or support a recovery. Up to the time this train passed out of Alabama no injury had resulted. For all that occurred in Alabama, therefore, no cause of action whatever arose. The fact which created the right to sue,—the injury,—without which confessedly no action would lie anywhere, transpired in the state of Mississippi. It was in that state, therefore, necessarily that the cause of action, if any, arose; and whether a cause of action arose and existed at all, or not, must in all reason be determined by the law which obtained at the time and place when and where the fact which is relied on to justify a recovery transpired. Section 2590 of the Code of Alabama had no efficacy beyond the lines of Alabama. It cannot be allowed to operate upon facts occurring in another state, so as to evolve out of them rights and liabilities which do not exist under the law of that state, which is of course paramount in the premises. Where the facts occur in Alabama, and a liability becomes fixed in Alabama, it may be enforced in another state having like enactments, or whose policy is not opposed to the spirit of such enactments; but this is quite a different matter. This is but enforcing the statute upon facts to which it is applicable, all of which occurred within the territory for the government of which it was enacted. Section 2590 of the Code, in other words, is to be interpreted in the light of universally recognized principles of private, international, or interstate law, as if its operation had been expressly limited to this state, and as if its first line read as follows: "When a personal injury is received in Alabama by a servant or employee," etc. The negligent infliction of an injury here, under statutory circumstances, creates a right of action here, which, being transitory, may be enforced in any other state or country the comity of which admits of it; but for an injury inflicted elsewhere than in Alabama our statute gives no right of recovery, and the aggrieved party must look to the local law to ascertain what his rights are. Under that law this plaintiff had no cause of action, as we have seen, and hence he has no rights which our courts can enforce, unless it be upon a consideration to be presently adverted to. We have not been inattentive to the suggestions of counsel in this connection, which are based upon that rule of the statutory and common criminal law under which a murderer is punishable where the fatal blow is delivered, regardless of the place where death ensues. Green v. State, 66 Ala. 40 [(1880)]. This principle is patently without application here. There would be some analogy if the plaintiff had been stricken in Alabama, and suffered in Mississippi, which is not the fact. There is, however, an analogy which is afforded by the criminal law, but which points away from the conclusion appellee's counsel desires us to reach. This is found in that well-established doctrine of criminal law that where the unlawful act is committed in one jurisdiction or state, and takes effect—produces the result which it is the purpose of the law to prevent, or, it having ensued, punish for—in another jurisdiction or state, the crime is deemed to have been committed and is punished in that jurisdiction or state in which the result is manifested, and not where the act was committed. [cit.]

* * * It is the purpose of the statute, and must be the limit of its operation, to

govern persons standing in the relation of master and servants to each other, in respect of their conduct in certain particulars within the state of Alabama. Mississippi has the same right to establish governmental rules for such persons within her borders as Alabama, and she has established rules which are different from those of our law; and the conduct of such person towards each other is, when its legality is brought in question, to be adjudged by the rules of the one or the other state, as it falls territorially within the one or the other. * * * For the error in refusing to instruct the jury to find for the defendant, if they believed the evidence, the judgment is reversed, and the cause will be remanded.

Notes and Questions

1. *Territoriality*. Read again the following statements from *Carroll*:

(a) "[W]hether a cause of action arose and existed at all, or not, must * * * be determined by the law which obtained at the time and place when and where the fact which is relied on to justify a recovery transpired."

(b) "Section 2590 of the Code of Alabama had no efficacy beyond the lines of Alabama. It cannot be allowed to operate upon facts occurring in another state * * * [but] is to be interpreted * * * as if its operation had been expressly limited to this state."

Through these two statements the court purports to explain why Mississippi's law should and Alabama's law could not apply to this case. Leaving aside for now the cross-border nature of this case, is statement (a) as logically inevitable as the court suggests? Does statement (b) coincide with your intuitive understanding of how laws operate "in space"? What, if anything, would prevent the application of Alabama law to a dispute between an Alabama domiciliary, hired by an Alabama employer in Alabama for work primarily in Alabama, and injured while acting within the scope and course of his employment?

2. *Territoriality and Vested Rights*. Many years after *Carroll*, Professor Joseph Beale, one of the chief spokesmen for the traditional theory in the United States, echoed the views espoused in that case by stating that "[t]he law of a state prevails throughout its boundaries and, generally speaking, not outside them," 1 Beale, *Conflict of Laws* 308 (1935), and that:

Law operates by extending its power over acts done throughout the territory within its jurisdiction and creating out of those acts new rights and obligations. * * * It follows also that not only must the law extend over the whole territory subject to it and apply to every act done there, but only one law can so apply. * * * By its very nature law must apply to everything and must exclusively apply to everything within the boundary of its jurisdiction.

Id. at 45–46.

These postulates found their way into the *Restatement of the Law, Conflict of Laws* (1934) (hereinafter "Restatement"), drafted by Beale under the auspices of the American Law Institute:

§ 1. (1) No state can make a law which by its own force is operative in another state; the only law in force in the sovereign state is its own law, but by the law of each state rights or other interests in that state may, in certain cases, depend upon the law in force in some other state or states. * * *

§ 377. The place of wrong is in the state where the last event necessary to make an actor liable for an alleged tort takes place.

§ 378. The law of the place of wrong determines whether a person has sustained a legal injury.

§ 384. (1) If a cause of action in tort is created at the place of wrong, a cause of action will be recognized in other states.

(2) If no cause of action is created at the place of wrong, no recovery in tort can be had in any other state.

§ 386. The law of the place of wrong determines whether a master is liable in tort to a servant for a wrong caused by a fellow servant.[1]

The *Carroll* court based its holding that the plaintiff could not recover in Alabama on the supposedly undeniable "proposition" that "there can be no recovery in one state for injuries to the person sustained in another, unless the infliction of the injuries is actionable under the law of the state in which they were received." The corollary of this "proposition" is that, had plaintiff's injuries been actionable under Mississippi law, plaintiff would have been entitled to recover in Alabama because Mississippi would have "vested" him with a right that Alabama was bound to recognize. This is what the "vested rights" school taught. See Restatement § 384, supra. For the origins of this doctrine, see supra 12.

3. *The Local Law Theory*. Professor Walter W. Cook, one of the first American critics of the vested rights theory and of the traditional theory in general, thought he had a better insight when he advanced his "local law theory." He said:

The forum, when confronted by a case involving foreign elements, always applies its own law to the case, but in doing so adopts and enforces as its own law a rule of decision identical, or at least highly similar, though not identical, in scope with a rule of decision found in the system in force in another state with which some or all of the foreign elements are connected. * * * The rule thus "incorporated" into the law of the forum, * * * the forum * * * enforces not a foreign right but a right created by its own law.

Cook, *The Logical Bases* 20–21. Thus, in a case like *Carroll*, the Alabama court did not really apply Mississippi's fellow-servant rule but rather a newly-fashioned rule modeled after the Mississippi fellow-servant rule. Is this explanation any better? Which problems, if any, does it help you to resolve?

4. *Localizing the Tort*. The *Carroll* court rejected plaintiff's argument that the tort had occurred in Alabama, where the injurious conduct occurred, on the ground that "negligence of duty unproductive of damnifying results will not authorize or support a recovery." Is the converse also true? The court reasoned that, because the injury occurred in Mississippi, "[i]t was in that state, therefore, necessarily that the cause of action, if any, arose." The Restatement adopted this reasoning in § 377, which defines the place of tort as "the state where the last event necessary to make an actor liable for an alleged tort takes place." A Note under that section further

---

1. Quoted with the permission of the copyright owner, The American Law Institute.

defines this place as the place of impact by providing that, in cases of bodily harm, the place of the tort is where the harmful force or "deleterious" substance "takes effect upon the body."

Consider the following scenario. While flying over Alabama airspace on a flight from Miami to Seattle, the passengers of a commercial airplane are served a chicken dinner that is infected with salmonella bacteria. Before the flight is over, the salmonella bacteria "takes effect upon the bod[ies]" of all 200 passengers, but at different times as the plane flies over the airspace of fifteen or so states between Miami and Seattle. Where is the place of the tort in this case? In Philip Morris, Inc. v. Angeletti, 752 A.2d 200 (Md.2000), a class action filed against cigarette manufacturers, the deleterious substance was nicotine, which had harmed thousands of smokers in several states over a period of many years. Relying on the Restatement, the court held that the place of the tort was wherever "the harmful force [of nicotine] took effect upon the body" or, as the plaintiffs facetiously commented, the state in which "the magical moment of addiction" occurred. Id. at 230.

The same Restatement Note provides that "[w]here harm is done to the reputation of a person, the place of wrong is where the defamatory statement is communicated." Where is that place in a case in which the statement is broadcast by CNN all over the world?

Do the above cases suggest that a "place-of-conduct" rule is better than the "place-of-impact" rule? Before you answer, suppose that in the last case, the statement was not broadcast by CNN, but rather by a television station that operates from a country that does not allow a defamation action or any other similar action. Would you then prefer a place-of-conduct rule?

Finally, are the states that adhere to the *lex loci delicti* rule better off by defining or by not defining *a priori* and in detail the *locus delicti*? Consider, for example, article 10(9) of the Spanish Civil Code, which provides that torts are governed by the law of "the place where the event from which they derive has occurred." Where is that place in a case like *Carroll*? In contrast, the European Union's new Draft Regulation on the Law Applicable to Non-Contractual Obligations of 2002 provides that torts are to be governed by "the law of the country in which the loss is sustained, irrespective of the country or countries in which the harmful event occurred and irrespective of the country in which the indirect consequences of the harmful event are sustained." In a case like *Carroll*, would this provision lead to Mississippi or Alabama law?

5. *Territoriality, Cross-Border Torts, and Interstate Boundaries*. In an oft-quoted statement made more than seventy years after *Carroll*, the Illinois Supreme Court observed that "[a]dvanced methods of distribution and other commercial activity * * * [and] modern methods of doing business * * * have largely effaced the economic significance of State lines." Gray v. American Radiator & Standard Sanitary Corp., 176 N.E.2d 761, 766 (Ill.1961). What was beginning to be true then is unquestionably true today, and the new word "internet" is simply the latest manifestation of this reality. State boundaries are even less important within the United States than international boundaries in the rest of the world. For, although state lines divide the United States into more than fifty jurisdictions each with its

own system of law, these lines generally have little effect on the economic, political, and cultural unity of the country. It is not simply that people travel and goods circulate freely and constantly throughout the country, that many people live in one state and work in another,[2] or that, as in the movies, a police car chase may begin in one state and end abruptly in another.[3] It is also that, in their everyday lives, people cross state lines with little awareness of doing so.[4] Many large population centers spread across state boundaries. City names like Texarkana, or Kansas City (Missouri)/Kansas City (Kansas) amply illustrate this American phenomenon of "economically and socially integrated greater metropolitan area[s]"[5] that defy state boundaries.

While cross-border torts are also common around the world, it is doubtful that courts in other countries encounter cases in which the tort occurs literally *at* the boundary line. Yet one finds such cases in the United States. One recent example is Pittman v. Maldania, Inc., 2001 WL 1221704 (Del.Super.2001), a case in which the defendant's rental office was located squarely on the Delaware/Maryland border. The building was on the Delaware side of the border, but its door opened into Maryland. The plaintiff, a Pennsylvania resident, rented water skis inside the building in Delaware, and then used them a few feet away in Maryland waters, where he was injured. Predictably, the laws of the two states differed, thus producing a conflict of laws.

In Sacra v. Sacra, 426 A.2d 7 (Md.App.1981), two cars collided in Delaware, but the impact of the collision pushed one car across the border into Maryland, where it struck a Maryland utility pole and exploded. Invoking the "last event" rule, one of the parties argued that the tort occurred in Maryland, and thus Maryland law should govern. The court rejected the argument, reasoning that this was "a single, integrated accident, which occurred in Delaware and * * * [t]he fact that the state line intervened between the impact and death was merely a fortuitous situation." Id. at 9.

In Judge Trucking Co. Inc. v. Cooper, 1994 WL 750369 (Del.Super.Ct. 1994),

---

2. See, e.g., Allstate Insurance v. Hague, 449 U.S. 302 (1981) (infra 455, victim lived in Wisconsin and worked in Minnesota); Bledsoe v. Crowley, 849 F.2d 639 (D.C.1988) (plaintiff lived in the District of Columbia and worked in Maryland); Foster v. Legget, 484 S.W.2d 827 (Ky.1972) (infra 192, defendant lived in Ohio but worked in Kentucky); Cipolla v. Shaposka, 267 A.2d 854 (Pa.1970) (infra 196, plaintiff lived in Pennsylvania but attended school in Delaware); Kaiser-Georgetown Community Health Plan, Inc. v. Stutsman, 491 A.2d 502 (D.C.1985) (infra 248, plaintiff lived in Virginia but worked in the District of Columbia); Biscoe v. Arlington County, 738 F.2d 1352 (D.C.Cir.1984) (plaintiff lived in Maryland but worked in the District of Columbia).

3. See, e.g., Lommen v. The City of East Grand Forks, 522 N.W.2d 148 (Minn.Ct.App. 1994) (chase began in Minnesota and ended in North Dakota, injuring a North Dakota resident); Biscoe v. Arlington County, 738 F.2d 1352 (D.C.Cir.1984) (chase began in Virginia and ended in the District of Columbia, injuring a Maryland resident); Skipper v. Prince George's County, 637 F.Supp. 638 (D.D.C.1986) (chase began in Maryland and ended in the District of Columbia, injuring a D.C. resident); Bays v. Jenks, 573 F.Supp. 306 (W.D.Va.1983) (chase began in West Virginia and ended in Virginia); Tribe v. Borough of Sayre, 562 F.Supp. 419 (W.D.N.Y.1983) (chase began in Pennsylvania and ended in New York, injuring a New York resident).

4. For example, in many cases, a drive between two points in state A may go through state B. See, e.g., District of Columbia v. Coleman, 667 A.2d 811 (D.C.1995) (defendant lived in Maryland, worked as policeman in the District of Columbia, and, while driving between two points in D.C., drove through Maryland where he committed a tort).

5. Gaither v. Myers, 404 F.2d 216, 223 (D.C.Cir.1968) ("It is a commonplace that residents of Maryland [and Virginia] are part of the Washington metropolitan trading area, and that District residents and businesses have an interest in the well-being of the[ ] citizens of [those] State[s].").

the state of the accident was in dispute because the very location of the border was in dispute. The two-car collision occurred on the northern lane of US Route 54, which runs East-West along the Delaware/Maryland border (with Delaware to the North and Maryland to the south). The plaintiffs argued that the accident occurred in Delaware, because "people in the area consider the state line to run down the centerline of Route 54." Id. at *2. After a long discussion of the history of the Delaware/Maryland boundary, which included detailed description of geodetic surveys and boundary agreements, the court concluded that the boundary was actually located at the northern shoulder of Route 54, and thus the accident had occurred in Maryland.

None of the above implies that state boundaries are irrelevant. As one commentator observed, "Maine has a different character than Texas, Nevada emphasizes different values than South Carolina, and * * * Northern and Southern Californians joke about dividing the state in two precisely because it is thought that statehood appropriately reflects value choices, and two such different cultures are incongruously joined into a single state." Brilmayer, *Shaping and Sharing*, 408. Even so, however, do these observations support the proposition that territoriality should be the inexorable governing principle for tort conflicts? Even if the answer is yes, does territoriality point in a clear direction in cases involving cross-border torts? For example, in a case like *Pittman* or *Sacra*, supra, does territoriality point to Delaware (place of conduct) or Maryland (place of injury)?

6. ***The Reasons for and "Virtues" of the Lex Loci Delicti Rule.*** This chapter contains many cases that apply the *lex loci delicti* rule, and a few that avoid it. Before reading these cases, consider the following potential advantages of this rule.

(a) *Ease of application.* The *lex loci* rule is easy to apply. All the court needs to do is to identify the state where the tort occurred. That is easy, is it not? Was it easy in *Carroll*? Even if one accepts the Restatement's view that a tort occurs at the place of "the last event necessary to make an actor liable," where is that place in a products liability case in which a product is distributed in all fifty states and causes injury to users in each state? Can complex problems such as these be resolved adequately by simple rules? Are simplicity and - administrability of the law of such importance as to justify sacrificing for their sake the need to obtain rational and fair results?

(b) *A common ground.* The *locus delicti* may be the only geographic factor that is common to both parties in a tort dispute. For example, unlike the parties' domiciles, which may be in different states, the *locus delicti* cannot be in two different states. Was this true in *Carroll*? Accepting for the moment the view that equates the *locus delicti* with the place of the injury, and leaving aside the case of multistate injury, is it not true that in single-injury cases the *locus delicti* is the place in which the defendant's conduct "reaches out and touches" the victim? Is this a good reason for an inexorable *lex loci delicti* rule?

(c) *A neutral rule.* The *lex loci delicti* rule is a neutral rule in that it does not, *a priori*, favor either plaintiffs or defendants as a class. In contrast, a rule that, for example, applies the law of the forum *qua* forum favors plaintiffs as a class. This is because the rules of jurisdiction allow plaintiffs considerable latitude in selecting a forum, and plaintiffs oblige by suing in a favorable forum. But is the *lex loci delicti* rule as neutral as it seems to be? At least in intentional torts, does not the rule potentially favor defendants? (Would this rule be more or less neutral, with regard to both intentional and non-intentional torts, if the *locus delicti* were equated with the locus of the injurious conduct?) Should neutrality be an independent goal of the choice-of-law process? And, incidentally, is forum shopping *necessarily* evil? One judge has called it "a national legal pastime." Skelly Wright, *The Federal Courts* 333. For an interesting debate on the pros and cons of forum shopping, see Juenger, *What's Wrong with Forum Shopping?*; Opeskin, *The Price of Forum Shopping: A Reply*; Juenger, *Forum Shopping: A Rejoinder*.

(d) *Party expectations.* According to the Supreme Court of Canada, the application of the law of the place of the tort is consistent with the parties' expectations because "[o]rdinarily people expect their activities to be governed by the law of the place where they happen to be and expect that concomitant legal benefits and responsibilities will be defined accordingly. The government of that place is the only one with power to deal with these activities." Tolofson v. Jensen; Lucas (Litigation Guardian of) v. Gagnon, 120 D.L.R. 4th 289 [1994], 3 S.C.R. 1022. The Court noted that, although the substantive laws of the *locus delicti* may appear to outsiders to be unwise, or unfavorable to plaintiffs, "one does not ordinarily ignore the law of the land in favour of those who visit. * * * [S]uch differences are a concomitant of the territoriality principle. While, no doubt * * * the underlying principles of private international law are order and fairness, order comes first." Id. at 1058. What do you think of these statements? Do they accurately describe reality in the United States?

(e) *The locus state's "interests."* According to Judge Posner, the state where the tort occurs "has the greatest interest in striking a reasonable balance among safety, cost, and other factors pertinent to the design and administration of a system of tort law. Most people affected whether as victims or as injurers by accidents and other injury-causing events are residents of the jurisdiction in which the event takes place. So if law can be assumed to be generally responsive to the values and preferences of the people who live in the community that formulated the law, the law of the place of the accident can be expected to reflect the values and preferences of the people most likely to be involved in accidents--can be expected, in other words, to be responsive and responsible law, law that internalizes the costs and benefits of the people affected by it." Spinozzi v. ITT Sheraton Corp., 174 F.3d 842, 845 (7th Cir.1999). Does this statement support the application of Mississippi law or Alabama law in *Carroll*?

(f) *Uniformity of result and avoidance of forum shopping.* The *lex loci* rule ensures interstate or international uniformity of result: if all states followed this rule and IF they all applied it in the same manner and without exceptions, then each multistate tort would be resolved in the same way, regardless of where litigation occurs. Thus forum shopping would be eliminated. (In Section C of this chapter, you will learn that the latter "if" is much bigger than it sounds.) But is uniformity alone a good reason for the *lex loci* rule? If yes, could not the same uniformity be attained through a rule that chooses between states in alphabetical order? Is the uniform resolution of multistate tort disputes throughout the United States an important national goal? If yes, should the implementation of this goal be left to the individual states? Should Congress address this problem through legislation imposing either uniform substantive rules or uniform choice-of-law rules? If Congress does not do so, should the Supreme Court develop choice-of-law rules and ensure compliance by state courts? Keep these questions in mind as you proceed through this book, especially Chapters 5 and 6. If uniformity of result is or should be an important goal of the choice-of-law process in interstate conflicts, is the same true for international conflicts? The classical theory of private international law has always assumed that international uniformity of decisions should be one of the main objectives of the choice-of-law process. See supra 11-12. But how can one achieve such uniformity?

7. ***"Jurisdiction–Selecting" Rules.*** In contrast to the name *Private International Law* by which this subject is known in Europe (supra 6), the American name *Conflict of Laws* presupposes that there is at least a potential conflict of laws in every case with foreign elements. If this is true, should not a proper analysis of such cases begin by examining whether in fact there is a conflict in the particular case? If so, could a court answer this question without looking into the content of the substantive laws of the involved states? For example, would there have been a conflict in *Carroll* if Mississippi and Alabama had adopted an identical Employers Liability Act? The traditional method did not ask these questions. The content (and much less the purpose and policy of the supposedly conflicting laws) was not *officially* a factor in the court's choice of the applicable law. In fact, this choice was perceived not as one between laws, but rather as one between states (or "jurisdictions"), regardless of what their laws on the subject provided. This is why one of the major critics of traditional choice-of-law rules, Professor David F. Cavers, called them "jurisdiction-selecting" rules. Cavers, *Critique* 173.

8. ***The Purposes of the Conflicting Laws.*** What was the purpose of the Mississippi fellow-servant rule? Was it to "punish" injured employees such as W.D. Carroll by denying them recovery from the employer (who was more likely to be solvent than the culpable fellow-servant)? Was it to "punish," or to cause to be more careful, employees such as Carroll's fellow-servants by not relieving them of liability for injury they caused to other fellow servants? Was it to protect employers by not imposing on them the burden of employment accidents caused by one employee to another? Whatever the purpose underlying this rule, would its application promote that purpose in *Carroll*?

What was the purpose of the Alabama rule that imposed liability on the employer? Was it to protect victims of industrial accidents and their families from the economic consequences of such accidents? To place such costs on employers rather than employees or fellow servants because employers are in a better position to bear and to spread those costs? To make employers more careful and to ensure safe conditions at the workplace? Whatever the purpose underlying this rule, would its application promote that purpose in *Carroll*?

9. ***"Conflicts Justice" versus "Substantive Justice."*** Suppose that the same

negligence that caused Carroll's injury also caused injury to another of his fellow servants, a few moments before the train crossed the Alabama-Mississippi border. Would this case be sufficiently different from *Carroll* as to justify an entirely different result on the merits? Is such a difference in result an inevitable and fair price for having a federal system in which each state has different substantive laws? Is this merely another case of having to "draw the line somewhere"? Should conflicts law aspire to achieve the same quality of justice in multistate situations as is pursued in fully domestic situations? Is this possible or appropriate? Consider the following two lines of argument:

(a) By definition, multistate cases are qualitatively different from analogous fully domestic cases, precisely because the former are not entirely confined within a single state and thus involve a potential conflict between the value judgments of two or more societies. This is why, in multistate cases, we do not automatically apply the law of the forum but instead we are prepared to consider the possibility of applying the law of another state. For cases that, under the forum's choice-of-law rules, are thus referred to the law of another state, the question of whether the result is fair to the individuals involved is one that depends entirely upon whether the chosen law itself is fair, which is something over which we have no control. Considerations of justice should play a role in formulating the rules by which the choice is made but not in deciding whether or not to follow those rules. Our obligation is to select the proper law fairly, not to guarantee that that law itself is fair. Our aspiration is to attain "conflicts justice," not "substantive or material justice."

(b) A judge's duty is to resolve disputes *justly and fairly*, under the law. This duty does not disappear the moment the judge encounters a case with foreign elements. Resolving such disputes in a manner that is substantively fair and equitable to the litigants should be an objective of conflicts law as much as it is of substantive law. Conflicts law should not be content with a different or lesser quality of justice, so-called "conflicts justice," but should aspire to attain "material or substantive justice."

What do you think? For further discussion of these concepts, see Symeonides, *Material Justice*, 125 *et seq.*

Fitts v. Minnesota Min. & Mfg. Co.
Supreme Court of Alabama, 1991.
581 So.2d 819.

SHORES, J. Dr. William Gafford, his wife Susan, and their three children were killed in August 1983 when the plane he was piloting crashed shortly after takeoff near Ebro, Florida. All five family members were residents of Tuscaloosa, Alabama, and were returning home from a Florida vacation.

Two separate wrongful death/product liability actions were filed in the Circuit Court of Jefferson County, Alabama, in 1985. One was brought by William F. Gafford, Sr., as administrator of the estate of Dr. Gafford, and one was brought by Floyd O. Fitts, the father of Susan Fitts Gafford, on behalf of her and the children.

Both suits were against Gulfstream Aerospace Corporation (formerly North American Rockwell) as the designer and manufacturer of the plane, and Minnesota Mining & Manufacturing Company ("3M") as the designer and manufacturer of a flight instrument called a "Stormscope."

Gulfstream and 3M maintain that their products were not defectively designed and were not causally related to the crash. They contend that Dr. Gafford was contributorily negligent in flying into known adverse weather conditions. They assert that his negligence was the proximate cause of the accident.

On the eve of trial, the plaintiffs filed a motion requesting that the trial court make a pretrial determination that Alabama's substantive law (rather than Florida's) applied to this case, or, in the alternative, to certify the choice-of-law issue for an appeal to this Court pursuant to Rule 5, A. R. App. P.

The appeal on behalf of the estate of Dr. William F. Gafford, Jr. was dismissed upon the motion of the administrator. Apparently, he was satisfied with the trial court's choice of Florida law for Dr. Gafford's case. This leaves the wife and children's case before us on appeal. Apparently, Alabama law was preferred for their case.

Lex loci delicti has been the rule in Alabama for almost 100 years. Under this principle, an Alabama court will determine the substantive rights of an injured party according to the law of the state where the injury occurred. [cit.]; *Alabama Great Southern R. R. v. Carroll* [supra]. The plaintiff contends that the doctrine of *lex loci delicti* is outmoded and unfair. He urges Alabama to adopt the approach of the *Restatement (Second) of Conflict of Laws (1971).*[2]

We therefore consider the question of whether Alabama should retain the traditional conflict of laws principle of *lex loci delicti* in tort cases or embrace the "most significant relationship" approach of §§ 6, 145, 146, and 175 of the *Restatement (Second) of Conflict of Laws*[.] * * *

Our review of the state of the law today shows us that a change in our choice of law rules is not the simple decision that the plaintiff would have us believe. Professor Herma Hill Kay of the University of California at Berkeley, has noted: "Courts willing to consider the adoption of new choice of law theory in the United State today are faced with a bewildering array of academic theories, many with loyal judicial adherents." Kay, *Theory Into Practice: Choice of Law in the Courts*, 34 Mercer L. Rev. 521, 523 (1983). The approach of the *Restatement (Second)*, which the plaintiffs urge us to adopt, is only one of many. * * *

Many states join Alabama in adhering to the traditional view of the first *Restatement*, which looks to the *lex loci delicti* in tort cases. [The court cited cases from sixteen states.]

After careful consideration, we are not convinced that we should abandon the *lex loci delicti* rule for the approach of the *Restatement (Second)* on the facts of the present case. Professor Kay and other commentators tell us that the adoption of the

---

2. The defendants argue that the motivation of the plaintiff in seeking to change the law is not to enhance the state of the law in Alabama, but to attempt to increase the damages recoverable in the case. They note that under the Florida wrongful death law, the only compensatory damages allowed for the death of the wife and children would be funeral expenses, because they had no income.

approach of the *Restatement (Second)* has not brought certainty or uniformity to the law:

"* * * This review of the cases suggests that, if the original Restatement was unsuccessful because of its dogmatic rigidity and its insistence on the uncritical application of a few specific rules, the Restatement Second may fail to provide enough guidance to the courts to produce even a semblance of uniformity among the states following its method. In the drafters' attempt to mollify their critics, they have created an umbrella for traditionalist and modern theorist alike: a fragile shelter that may prove itself unable to survive any but the most gentle of showers."

We find that we agree with the Supreme Court of Georgia. The newer approaches to choice of law problems are neither less confusing nor more certain than the traditional approach. "Until it becomes clear that a better rule exists, we will adhere to our traditional approach." [cit.]

We also see no need for any special exception in this particular case on public policy grounds, as the plaintiff requests. The plaintiff knew the law of Alabama at the time he filed the suits, and chose to file in Alabama. The judgment of the trial court is due to be Affirmed.

HOUSTON, J. (concurring specially). "I think the *desideratum of predictability* must be kept in proper perspective." [cit.]. * * * It is true that in a lawsuit predictability of result is not readily achievable, even in a case involving no choice-of-law problem. However, predictability of the law to be applied by the trial and appellate courts is something needed and desired. The rule of *lex loci delicti* has been consistently applied in Alabama for almost 100 years. [cit.] Predictability in regard to the rule of law that will be applied by the courts of a particular jurisdiction is essential, except as to a rule of law that would not be consented to today by the conscience and feeling of justice of the majority of those whose obedience is required. [cit.] I am not persuaded that the doctrine of *lex loci delicti* would not be consented to by the conscience and feeling of justice of the majority of Alabamians; therefore, I will not depart from the doctrine of *stare decisis*.

Notes and Questions

1. The *Fitts* court cites cases from sixteen other states that adhered to the *lex loci delicti* rule. In fact, two of those states (Indiana and Utah), had already abandoned this rule before *Fitts*, and five states (Delaware, South Dakota, Tennessee, Vermont, and Montana) have done so since then, thus reducing to ten the states that still follow the *lex loci* rule. For a list, see infra, 299 *et seq*. As late as 2003, Alabama was among those states.

2. The majority opinion in *Fitts* states: "The plaintiff knew the law of Alabama at the time he filed the suits, and chose to file in Alabama." Apparently, the court is referring to Alabama conflicts law, not substantive law. It seems that plaintiff's attorney thought that he could easily persuade Alabama courts to abandon the *lex loci* rule and to apply Alabama's substantive law, which was more generous to the wife and children than was Florida's law. The gamble did not pay off. Was it worth

taking? Consider the following information. Ten years before *Fitts*, Florida had abandoned the *lex loci delicti* rule in favor of the flexible choice-of-law formula contained in the 1971 Restatement (Second) of Conflict of Laws, which applies the law of the state that has "the most significant relationship" with the parties and the dispute. You will study the Restatement (Second) in Chapter 3. Assume for now that, under this formula, a Florida court would have applied Alabama tort law because that state had a more significant relationship with the parties and the dispute than did Florida. With this information, where would you file suit today if you represented the plaintiff in a case identical to *Fitts*?

Do you see anything wrong with a system in which, when faced with an identical case, Florida courts apply Alabama law, while Alabama courts apply Florida law? If yes, how would you remedy it? If Alabama courts are unwilling to abandon the *lex loci* rule because it "has been the rule in Alabama for almost 100 years" (*Fitts*), should not these courts consider Florida's desire not to have its law applied because Florida does not have a sufficiently significant relationship with the parties and the dispute? This is a version of the famous *renvoi* question, which is explored in Section C.2(a), infra.

3. The *Fitts* court referred to the two actions as "wrongful death/product liability actions" and adhered to the localization rule adopted in *Carroll* that the *locus delicti* is at the place of the injury rather than at the place of the negligence. But where is the place of the injury in a wrongful death action? Before you answer this question, consider the fact that today many states differentiate between a "survival action" (which is designed to compensate the decedent for his or her loss) and a wrongful death action (which is designed to compensate the decedent's survivors for their losses). Is it sensible to contend that, with regard to the latter action, the injury occurs at the survivors' home state? The Restatement rejects this contention by providing expressly that "the place of wrong * * * means the place of wrong to the decedent, not where pecuniary loss is caused to his relatives." Restatement § 391, cmt. (a). Apparently this is the reason for which the *Fitts* court made no reference to the place of domicile, or even the existence, of the survivors. The Restatement does not contain a separate provision for products liability actions and thus these actions also are subject to the place-of-injury rule. This may explain why the *Fitts* court did not consider it necessary to mention the state where the airplane and the "stormscope" were designed, manufactured, tested, or sold. Is the place-of-injury rule more or less objectionable in products liability actions than in other tort actions?

4. Although *Fitts* dos not provide more facts, one could surmise that the Gafford family spent considerable time in Florida, and probably owned or rented a summerhouse there. In addition, the Gafford plane "crashed shortly after takeoff" in Florida. *Fitts*, supra. Given these facts, and considering that most airplane crashes occur during takeoff or landing, Florida's contacts with the case were not entirely negligible or fortuitous.

Consider this variation, however. Suppose that the Gaffords were flying back from a vacation in the American Virgin Islands when their plane crashed in Haiti. Suppose further that under Haitian law, Dr. Gafford's survivors would recover no more than 50,000 *gourdes* ($10,000) in damages because that law allows the recovery of future monetary losses only, estimated by the yearly earnings and the life expectancy of a Haitian doctor of the same age. Do you think that the Alabama court would be as adamant in applying Haitian law in this case as it was in applying Florida law in *Fitts*?

5. Assume now that the Alabama court remains firm in its refusal to abandon the *lex loci delicti* rule because it "has been the rule in Alabama for almost 100 years." (*Fitts*). In representing the Gaffords, your only hope of getting more than the 50,000 Haitian *gourdes* is to convince the Alabama court to make an exception "for *this case only*" and to apply the more generous Alabama law. Consider the following line of arguments: Haitian law should not apply *in this case* because: (a) the *locus delicti* was entirely fortuitous; or (b) the issue at stake is one of damages which is a remedial and thus a procedural, not substantive, matter that should be governed by the law of the forum; or (c) Haitian compensation standards are so minimal as to amount to almost no compensation, and thus the application of such law is repugnant to the forum's fundamental notions of justice and fairness. Arguments (b) and (c) are patterned after two traditional exceptions to the *lex loci delicti* rule, namely, the substance versus procedure dichotomy and the public policy exception, respectively, both of which you will study later in this chapter. Notice, however, that the *Fitts* court, which in a footnote barely mentioned that the issue was one of damages, showed no willingness to characterize this issue as procedural, and appeared to be totally unconcerned with the fact that the wife and children would recover substantially less under Florida law than under Alabama law. The court was equally unconcerned with the potential fortuity of the *locus delicti*.

2. CONTRACTS

Milliken v. Pratt

Supreme Court of Massachusetts, 1878.
125 Mass. 374.

[Daniel Pratt, a Massachusetts merchant wanted to buy goods on credit from plaintiffs, Deering, Milliken & Co, a Maine partnership. To that effect, plaintiffs required Daniel to procure from his wife, Sarah A. Pratt, defendant here, a guaranty in the amount of five hundred dollars. Sarah signed in her Massachusetts home the following document:

"Portland, January 29, 1870. In consideration of one dollar paid by Deering, Milliken & Co., receipt of which is hereby acknowledged, I guarantee the payment to them by Daniel Pratt of the sum of five hundred dollars, from time to time as he may want—this to be a continuing guaranty. Sarah A. Pratt."

The document was mailed by Daniel from Massachusetts and received by plaintiffs in Maine in early 1870. The one dollar mentioned in the guaranty was not paid, and the only consideration moving to the defendant therefor was the giving of credit by the plaintiffs to her husband. The plaintiffs subsequently sold on credit and delivered goods to Daniel from time to time until October 7, 1871. Some of the goods were selected personally by Daniel at the plaintiffs' store in Portland, others were ordered by letters mailed by Daniel from Massachusetts to the plaintiffs at Portland, and all were sent by the plaintiffs by express from Portland to Daniel in Massachusetts, who paid all express charges. This action is brought for goods sold from September 1, 1871, to October 7, 1871, inclusive, amounting to $860.12, upon which Daniel paid $300, leaving a balance due of $560.12. The lower court ordered judgment for the defendant; and the plaintiffs appealed.]

GRAY, C. J. The general rule is that the validity of a contract is to be determined by the law of the state in which it is made; if it is valid there, it is deemed valid everywhere, and will sustain an action in the courts of a state whose laws do not permit such a contract. *Scudder v. Union National Bank*, 91 U.S. 406 [1875]. Even a contract expressly prohibited by the statutes of the state in which the suit is brought, if not in itself immoral, is not necessarily nor usually deemed so invalid that the comity of the state, as administered by its courts, will refuse to entertain an action on such a contract made by one of its own citizens abroad in a state the laws of which permit it. [cit.]

If the contract is completed in another state, it makes no difference in principle whether the citizen of this state goes in person, or sends an agent, or writes a letter, across the boundary line between the two states. [cit.] So if a person residing in this state signs and transmits, either by a messenger or through the post-office, to a person in another state, a written contract, which requires no special forms or solemnities in its execution, and no signature of the person to whom it is addressed, and is assented to and acted on by him there, the contract is made there, just as if the writer personally took the executed contract into the other state, or wrote and signed it there; and it is no objection to the maintenance of an action thereon here, that such a contract is prohibited by the law of this Commonwealth. [cit.]

The guaranty, bearing date of Portland, in the State of Maine, was executed by the defendant, a married woman, having her home in this Commonwealth, as collateral security for the liability of her husband for goods sold by the plaintiffs to him, and was sent by her through him by mail to the plaintiffs at Portland. The sales of the goods ordered by him from the plaintiffs at Portland, and there delivered by them to him in person, or to a carrier for him, were made in the State of Maine. [cit.] The contract between the defendant and the plaintiffs was complete when the guaranty had been received and acted on by them at Portland, and not before. [cit.] It must therefore be treated as made and to be performed in the State of Maine.

The law of Maine authorized a married woman to bind herself by any contract as if she was unmarried.[cit.] The law of Massachusetts, as then existing, did not allow her to enter into a contract as surety or for the accommodation of her husband or of any third person. [cit.] Since the making of the contract sued on, and before the bringing of this action, the law of this Commonwealth has been changed, so as to enable married women to make such contracts. [cit.]

The question therefore is, whether a contract made in another state by a married woman domiciled here, which a married woman was not at the time capable of making under the law of this Commonwealth, but was then allowed by the law of that state to make, and which she could now lawfully make in this Commonwealth, will sustain an action against her in our courts.

It has been often stated by commentators that the law of the domicil, regulating the capacity of a person, accompanies and governs the person everywhere. But this statement, in modern times at least, is subject to many qualifications; and the opinions of foreign Jurists upon the subject * * * are too varying and contradictory to control the general current of the English and American authorities in favor of holding that a contract, which by the law of the place is recognized as lawfully made by a capable person, is valid everywhere, although the person would not, under the law of his domicil, be deemed capable of making it. * * *

Mr. Justice Story, in his Commentaries on the Conflict of laws, after elaborate consideration of the authorities, arrives at the conclusion that * * * "although foreign jurists generally hold that the law of the domicil ought to govern in regard to the capacity of persons to contract; yet the common law holds a different doctrine, namely, that the *lex contractus* is to govern." Story Confl. §§ 103, 24. [cit.]

In *Pearl v. Hansborough*, 9 Humph. 426, the rule was carried so far as to hold that where a married woman domiciled with her husband in the State of Mississippi, by the law of which a purchase by a married woman was valid and the property purchased went to her separate use, bought personal property in Tennessee, by the law of which married women were incapable of contracting the contract of purchase was void and could not be enforced in Tennessee. Some authorities, on the other hand, would uphold a contract made by a party capable by the law of his domicil, though incapable by the law of the place of the contract. [cit.] But that alternative is not here presented. * * *

The principal reasons on which continental jurists have maintained that personal laws of the domicil, affecting the status and capacity of all inhabitants of a particular class, bind them wherever they may go, appear to have been that each state has the rightful power of regulating the status and condition of its subjects, and, being best acquainted with the circumstances of climate, race, character, manners and customs, can best judge at what age young persons may begin to act for themselves, and whether and how far married women may act independently of their husbands; that laws limiting the capacity of infants or of married women are intended for their protection, and cannot therefore be dispensed with by their agreement; that all civilized states recognize the incapacity of infants and married women; and that a person, dealing with either, ordinarily has notice by the apparent age or sex, that the person is likely to be of a class whom the laws protect, and is thus put upon inquiry how far, by the law of the domicil of the person, the protection extends.

On the other hand, it is only by the comity of other states that laws can operate beyond the limit of the state that makes them. In the great majority of cases, especially in this country, where it is so common to travel, or to transact business through agents, or to correspond by letter, from one state to another, it is more just, as well as more convenient, to have regard to the law of the place of the contract, as a uniform rule operating on all contracts of the same kind, and which the contracting parties may be presumed to have in contemplation when making their contracts, than to require them at their peril to know the domicil of those with whom they deal, and to ascertain the law of that domicil, however remote, which in many cases could not be done without such delay as would greatly cripple the power of contracting abroad at all. * * *

It is possible also that in a state where the common law prevailed in full force, by which a married woman was deemed incapable of binding herself by any contract whatever, it might be inferred that such an utter incapacity, lasting throughout the joint lives of husband and wife, must be considered as so fixed by the settled policy of the state, for the protection of its own citizens, that it could not be held by the courts of that state to yield to the law of another state in which she might undertake to contract.

But it is not true at the present day that all civilized states recognize the absolute incapacity of married women to make contracts. The tendency of modern legislation is to enlarge their capacity in this respect, and in many states they have nearly or quite the same powers as if unmarried. In Massachusetts, even at the time of the making of the contract in question, a married woman was vested by statute with a very extensive power to carry on business by herself, and to bind herself by contracts with regard to her own property, business and earnings; and before the bringing of the present action, the power had been extended so as to include the making of all kinds of contracts, with any person but her husband, as if she were unmarried. There is therefore no reason of public policy which should prevent the maintenance of this action.

Judgments for the plaintiffs.

Linn v. Employers Reinsurance Corp.
Supreme Court of Pennsylvania, 1958.
392 Pa. 58, 139 A.2d 638.

COHEN, J. Plaintiff insurance brokers brought this action in law to require the defendant insurance company to account and pay to them commissions on insurance premiums received since 1953 from a New Jersey company. At the close of plaintiff's evidence, the trial judge entered a nonsuit which the court *en banc* refused to remove, and this appeal followed.

From the undisputed evidence it appears that in 1926 the plaintiffs [a Pennsylvania corporation] were engaged in the insurance brokerage business in Philadelphia. In that year plaintiffs offered to place with the defendant contracts for the reinsurance of certain risks undertaken by the Selected Risks Insurance Company of New Jersey for a consideration of five per cent of all premiums collected by the defendant on such policies. Plaintiff Linn went to New York City to negotiate an agreement with one William Ehmann, an agent of the defendant. Ehmann stated that he would first have to obtain authority to accept the offer from the defendant's home office in Kansas City. He promised that he would communicate with the plaintiff "as soon as he could get word from Kansas City." Linn then returned to Philadelphia, and subsequently received a telephone call from Ehmann accepting the offer.

The defendant entered into the required treaty with the New Jersey company which, as modified and renewed, continues in effect. From 1926 until 1953 the defendant paid the plaintiffs the agreed upon commissions. But in 1953, the defendant notified the plaintiffs that it did not consider itself obligated further under the contract and that it would discontinue accounting to the plaintiffs for the premiums received from the New Jersey company.

On this evidence the trial judge found that the contract was made in New York, and applying the New York Statute of Frauds, held that the agreement was unenforcible thereunder because it was not to be performed within one year from the date it was entered into. Wherefore, the court concluded that the defendant was under no duty to account.

We recognize that the formal validity of a contract is determined by the law of the state in which the contract was made. [cit.] Since the provisions of the Statute of Frauds relate to formal validity, it is to the statute of the place of contracting that we must refer.[3] It is therefore necessary for us to determine in which state the contract was made.

When a principal authorizes an agent to accept an offer made by a third party, as the defendant authorized Ehmann in the present case, the place of contracting is where the agent accepts the offer. Rodman v. Thalheimer, 1874, 75 Pa. 232, 238; Restatement, Conflict of Laws § 330 (1934); 2 Beale, Conflict of Laws, §§ 325.1, 328.1 (1935). In the case of acceptance by mail or telegraph, the act of acceptance is held to be effective where the acceptance was posted, [cit.], or received by the telegraph company for transmission. [cit.]

This Court has not heretofore been required to determine the place where an acceptance spoken over the telephone is effective.

Professor Williston and the Restatement of Contracts take the position that a contract made over the telephone is no different from a contract made where the parties orally address one another in each other's presence. In the latter case the offeror does not have the risk of hearing an acceptance addressed to him, and a contract is formed only if the acceptance is heard. Consequently, the place of contracting is where the acceptance is heard and not where the acceptance is spoken. [cit.] While we agree that this analysis represents a sound theoretical view, the reported cases which consider this issue are uniform in holding that by analogy to the situations in which acceptance is mailed or telegraphed, an acceptance by telephone is effective, and a contract is created at the place where the acceptor speaks. [cit.] See also 2 Beale, op. cit. supra, § 326.2; Restatement, Conflict of Laws, *supra* § 326, comment (c). In fact, where the federal courts are charged with the duty of applying Pennsylvania law they have reached this conclusion. [cit.]

We believe that in this day of multistate commercial transactions it is particularly desirable that the determination of the place of contracting be the same regardless of the state in which suit is brought. The absence of uniformity makes the rights and liabilities of parties to a contract dependent upon the choice of the state in which suit is instituted and thus encourages "forum-shopping." For this reason we chose to follow the established pattern of decisions and hold that acceptance by telephone of an offer takes place where the words are spoken.

Applying this principle to the facts before us, we conclude that the state where

---

3. The rules embodied in the Pennsylvania Statute of Frauds are matters of substance not procedure, and apply only to contracts made in Pennsylvania. [cit.]

the contract was made is the state from which Ehmann telephoned the defendant's acceptance to Linn. However, contrary to the trial court's determination, there is no evidence in the record to indicate from which state Ehmann spoke. It is likely that he telephoned from his New York office, but it is also possible that he called from Kansas City or even Philadelphia; we cannot substitute speculation for evidence. The record of this case, therefore, must be remitted to the court below for determination of this question.

Judgment reversed and record remanded for further proceedings in accordance with this opinion. Costs to abide the event.

Notes and Questions

1. According to the Restatement: (a) the law of the place of the making of the contract (*lex loci contractus*) determines the contract's validity with respect to such matters as contractual capacity, necessary form, mutual assent or consideration, fraud, illegality and any other circumstances that make a promise voidable (§ 332); and (b) the law of the place of performance (*lex loci solutionis*) determines matters such as the manner, time, place, and sufficiency of performance, and the permissible excuses for non-performance. (§ 358). *Milliken* and *Linn* involved issues of capacity and form, respectively. Is the *lex loci contractus* rule equally satisfactory or unsatisfactory for each of the above issues?

2. In defending the *lex loci contractus* rule, the *Milliken* court spoke of the advantages of "a uniform rule operating on all contracts * * * which the contracting parties may be presumed to have in contemplation when making their contracts, [rather] than to require them at their peril to know the domicil of those with whom they deal, and to ascertain the law of that domicil, however remote."

(a) Is this not a good reason for adhering to the *lex loci contractus* rule? If yes, was this reason applicable to the *Milliken* facts? Did the Milliken partners not know that Ms. Pratt was a domiciliary of Massachusetts? Should they also have known that she lacked capacity under Massachusetts' law?

(b) Does the above-quoted reason for adhering to the *lex loci contractus* rule apply when the contract is made: (i) in the home state of the incapable party; or (ii) in a state with which neither party has any contacts, such as a state through whose airspace the parties pass at the time they close the deal?

3. The above-quoted statement from *Milliken* was made in response to an argument in favor of the rule followed in most European countries that capacity is governed by the law of a person's domicile. The court's understanding of the European rule, however, was incomplete. Most European systems begin with the principle that capacity is governed by one's "personal law" (which is defined in some countries as the law of the domicile and in others as the law of the nationality of that person), but also provide several exceptions to this principle. For example, even traditional systems provided that an alien who, while in the forum country, enters into a contract for which he lacks capacity under his personal law, is deemed capable of contracting if he would have such capacity under the law of the forum. See Greek Civ. Code art. 9; Spanish Civ. Code art. 10(8). What do you think is the

rationale underlying these rules? Are they directly applicable to a case like *Milliken*? Article 2 of the Benelux Treaty on Private International Law (1969) provides that "a person declared incapable by his law may not invoke his incapacity against one who * * * has in good faith and in conformity with the law of the place of the act considered him to be capable." Article 11 of the E.E.C. Convention on Contractual Obligations (1980) (hereafter "Rome Convention") provides that a party that has capacity under the law of the place of the making "may invoke his incapacity resulting from another law only if the other party to the contract was aware of this incapacity at the time of the conclusion of the contract or was not aware thereof as a result of negligence." Would these rules resolve the *Milliken* problem in a satisfactory manner? If not, why? If yes, do these rules suggest that a system of rules need not be irrational?

4. What was the basis for the court's conclusion in *Milliken* that the contract had been made in Maine? Apparently the court considered this contract to be *unilateral*, that is, one formed by an act of the promisee made in reliance upon the promise. If so, then under traditional conflicts rules the contract was deemed formed when and where such act took place. See Restatement §§ 323–24. Here this act was the sale of the goods to Mr. Pratt, which were "delivered * * * to him in person, or to a carrier for him, * * * in the State of Maine." *Milliken*. Apparently, a different conclusion would follow had the goods been delivered in Massachusetts by plaintiff's truck. In contrast, if the contract were bilateral, as in *Linn*, then the place of contracting would be "where the second promise is made in consideration of the first promise," Restatement § 325, or the place from which the acceptance of an offer was sent. Restatement § 326. Could the contract in *Milliken* be characterized as a bilateral contract in which the second promise was made in Massachusetts?

5. In *Linn*, the parties conceded that the offer had been made by Linn and the acceptance by Ehmann. In oral contracts, is it always as easy to establish which party made the offer and which the acceptance? Even if the parties have the best intentions, how can one remember who spoke the magic words? Suppose that, after his trip to New York, Linn got cold feet about the deal he had discussed with Ehmann. In a subsequent critical telephone conversation with Ehmann, Linn was lukewarm and evasive until Ehmann said: "I spoke to the home office and they authorized me to offer you this deal and to throw in a free three-year membership in our golf club." Linn, an avid golfer, immediately said: "I accept, we have a deal." Should the outcome of such an important transaction turn on who said the magic words, almost thirty years earlier? Would it not make better sense to focus instead on the parties' relationship during those years?

6. Should the place from which a party spoke the magic words have any relevance, especially in the era of internet, mobile phones, and telephones on airplanes? Upon remand, the *Linn* jury found that Ehmann's critical telephone call was not made from New York, and thus the trial court entered a judgment for plaintiff. On appeal, the Supreme Court affirmed, holding:

> [D]efendant's contention as to the applicability of New York law has not been sustained by the evidence. * * * While it is true that plaintiffs have the ultimate burden of proof in convincing the jury that a valid contract was entered into, the

burden of producing evidence to show that this contract was made in New York was alleged and necessarily assumed by defendant. This burden was not met. Since it was not established that the laws of New York are applicable, the laws of the forum, Pennsylvania, are presumed to apply. Unlike the New York Statute of Frauds the various provisions in the Pennsylvania statute do not require that an agreement of this sort be in writing even if it is not to be performed within a year. It has been said that the Statute of Frauds, where applicable, is not a mere rule of evidence, but rather, is a limitation of judicial authority to afford a remedy. [cit.] Our statutes do not so limit the authority of this court to grant a remedy in this case.

Linn v. Employers Reinsurance Corp., 397 Pa. 153, 153 A.2d 483, 485 (Pa.1959). Is this holding consistent with the *lex loci contractus* rule or is it a graceful cop out?

7. Are contracts formed through correspondence less problematical than oral contracts? What if the involved states differ as to when an acceptance becomes effective? What about all those mail order solicitations that promise you the world for $19.99 and provide in fine print that "contract not completed until approved by headquarters in Nebraska"? Is this an attempt to artificially place the "last act" in Nebraska in hopes of ensuring the application of its law to the contract? If so, should the consumer's home state countenance such an attempt?

8. In contracts in which both parties are present in the same state at the time of offer and acceptance, the *lex loci contractus* rule encounters none of the above practical problems. But does it guarantee rational results? Suppose that the critical conversation between Linn and Ehmann had taken place while they were independently vacationing in Aruba, where they had never been before or since. Should Aruban law apply in this case? Should it matter whether the issue in question is one of formal or substantive validity, or whether Aruban law validates or invalidates the contract? See Rome Convention Art. 9(1); Hague Sales Convention Art. 11(1).

9. Suppose that on the same day Mrs. Pratt signed the guaranty for the Milliken partners' benefit, she also signed an identical guaranty for a Massachusetts merchant. Would the latter guaranty be enforceable? If not, does this difference bother you?

10. Notice that, between the time of the making of the contract and the time of trial, the Massachusetts legislature had repealed the rule declaring married women to be incapable of entering into the type of contracts involved in *Milliken*. Do you think the repeal influenced the court's decision? Should it?

11. What policies underlie a rule that declares certain people to be incapable of entering into certain contracts? What policies underlie a rule that requires certain contracts to conform to a certain form? Do the answers to these questions help resolve conflicts like those in *Milliken* and *Linn* in a rational manner?

12. Is it fair to say that in both *Milliken* and *Linn*, the court reached the right result but for the wrong reasons? In *Milliken*, the court refused to apply, at the expense of an out-of-state merchant, a forum rule that no longer reflected the forum's current public policy. In *Linn*, the court applied the law of the forum state to uphold a contract that had been performed in that state for 26 years.

C. THE TRADITIONAL APPROACH TO CONFLICTS IN OTHER AREAS

In areas other than torts and contracts, the traditional theory was equally dominated by "jurisdiction-selecting," territorially-based, and usually inexorable choice-of-law rules. Most of these rules will be studied in Chapter 4, in juxtaposition with contemporary judicial practice in areas other than torts and contracts. A good sample of these rules can be obtained by perusing Chapter 7 of the first Restatement, entitled "Property." Besides providing for all subjects normally covered in a typical Property course, this chapter encompasses marital property and successions, and is divided into two large units entitled "Immovables" and "Movables." This division, which is of civil-law origin, parallels the common-law distinction between real and personal property, except that the term immovables also encompasses certain interests in land such as leaseholds that in other areas of the law usually are regarded as personalty. Whether a thing is a movable or an immovable is determined according to the law of the situs of the thing (Restatement § 208).

1. *Immovables*. With respect to immovables, the Restatement requires the application of the law of the place where the immovable is situated (*lex rei sitae*), for almost all issues and virtually without any exceptions. Thus, the law of the situs applies to: (a) the substantive and formal validity of a conveyance of an interest in land (§§ 215, 217), the effect and interpretation of the conveyance (§§ 220, 214), and the capacity of the grantor and the grantee (§§ 216, 219); (b) to transfers by operation of law and acquisition through adverse possession or prescription (§§ 223–24); (c) to the validity, effect, and enforcement of mortgages (§§ 225–31); (d) to the effect of marriage upon immovables owned by a spouse at the time of marriage (§ 237) or acquired by either or both spouses during the marriage (§ 238); and the effect of a divorce or the death of either spouse upon such immovables (§ 248); (e) to all issues of intestate succession to land (§ 245), including the right of illegitimate and adopted children to inherit and the extent of their share (§§ 246–47); and (f) to most issues of testate succession to land, including the validity, effect, and revocation of a will (§§ 249–50).

Why is the situs rule given such a vast scope, and why is it subject to virtually no exceptions? Consider these reasons:

(a) the situs state has exclusive de jure and de facto power over land situated within its borders;

(b) certainty and clarity of title are universally shared objectives of property law and cannot be accomplished if land in one state is subject to diverse and potentially conflicting laws;

(c) the situs state has the strongest interest in regulating land situated within its borders; and,

(d) the situs rule is easy to apply and hard to manipulate because usually there is little question as to whether a thing is an immovable or where it is situated, and because immovables do not move.

Are these reasons sufficient to retain the situs rule? Consider the first reason, the power rationale. Professor Beale explained this rationale bluntly by saying that "[the] laws [of the situs] alone can apply to the land since any contrary provision [by non-situs courts or legislatures] would be given no effect by the courts and the executive officers of the state of situs." 2 Beale, *Conflict of Laws* 938–39. In other words, the situs courts may refuse to enforce a foreign judgment on the ground that the rendering court had failed to apply situs law. In Chapter 10, you will see that this assumption is not necessarily true with regard to sister-state *judgments*. Under the Full Faith and Credit Clause of the Constitution, an otherwise valid judgment rendered by a court with proper jurisdiction is entitled to enforcement in all sister states, without regard to which law the court applied. While it is true that a state has no jurisdiction *directly* to affect land situated outside its borders, it may do so indirectly (if it has jurisdiction over the parties) by ordering them to pay money or to execute the necessary conveyances. Such judgments are entitled to recognition in the situs state.

The second reason, certainty and clarity of title, can be broken into two parts. The first part relates to the need to ensure the certainty and integrity of the situs' recording system, to protect good faith purchasers who rely upon this system, and to facilitate the task of the title examiner who should not have to interpret foreign laws. But is this reason, although a good one, somewhat overstated? Is the application of foreign law necessarily inimical to the above objectives? After all, like domestic judgments, a foreign judgment is not effective against third parties until it is recognized by the situs courts *and* is recorded in the situs' land records. The second part of this reason relates to interstate and international uniformity of result, namely, ensuring that similar issues are treated alike regardless of where they are litigated. The situs rule is capable of accomplishing such uniformity, perhaps more than any other traditional rule, even though it is not immune from escape devices, such as characterization and *renvoi*, which are studied later in this chapter. But, again, should uniformity of result be the exclusive goal of the choice-of-law process? What about other goals, such as protecting justified party expectations and accommodating the legitimate interests of other states?

The third reason, pertaining to the interests of the situs state, though also valid in principle, is equally overstated. Indeed, a state has a strong interest in ensuring the most efficient, productive, commercially sound, and environmentally prudent utilization of land within its borders. Few people would question the interest of the situs state in matters such as adverse possession, boundary disputes, easements, rules against perpetuities, zoning, or environmental regulations. But does the situs state *qua* situs really have an interest in regulating matters such as: (a) whether a non-domiciliary has the proper age or mental capacity to make a testament, or whether he was subject to undue influence at the time he made the testament? (b) whether children or spouses should be guaranteed a certain minimum share of the decedent's estate (forced heirship, statutory share), or whether illegitimate children can inherit and how much, or whether an adopted child also can inherit from her biological parents? or (c) whether land acquired by a foreign spouse should be classified as community property or as separate property? The rules that regulate these matters embody certain societal value judgments. If all the affected parties are domiciled in one state and the land is situated in another, to which state's legislative competence do these value judgments belong?

What about questions such as whether a testament should be handwritten by the testator, attested by three rather than two witnesses, or whether a testament is revoked by a certain word written on its face? As noted earlier, the Restatement requires the application of situs law to the formal and substantive validity of a "conveyance of an interest in land" (§§ 215, 217) and the application of the *lex loci contractus* to the formal and substantive validity of contracts (§ 332). Why is it that a system that assigned such a large role to the *lex loci contractus* rule for *inter vivos* transactions assigned no role to the law of the place of the making with regard to testaments? Of course there are substantial differences between contracts and testaments, but are these differences sufficient to justify such disparate treatment? Incidentally, this contract/conveyance distinction, which also is made in domestic law, often provides courts with expedient ways of avoiding the rigidity of the situs rule. But are the situs rule and the *lex loci contractus* rule consistent with each other?

2. ***Movables.*** Under the Restatement, the situs rule also applies to movables, but only with regard to *inter vivos* transactions. Thus, the formal and substantive validity of a conveyance of an interest in a chattel is governed by "the law of the state where the chattel is at the time of the conveyance." (§§ 255–57). Are any of the reasons advanced in support of the situs rule for immovables applicable here?

In the area of marital property and successions, the Restatement shifts gears and resorts to the law of the domicile. Thus, the law of the husband's domicile at the time of marriage determines the rights of both spouses to movables then owned by either spouse (§ 289), while the law of the spouses' common domicile determines their respective rights in movables acquired during marriage (§ 290).

In successions, both testate and intestate, the pertinent domicile is the decedent's domicile at the time of death. This rule is thought to be consistent with the decedent's expectations and allows all of her movables to be treated as a single unit, regardless of where they are situated. But why should unity of treatment be confined to movables only? Why not include immovables, as is done in most civil law countries? Can you think of any reason other than the "situs taboo"? As to the decedent's expectations, consider § 306 of the Restatement, which provides: "The validity * * * of a will of movables is determined by the law of the state in which the deceased died domiciled." What if the decedent was domiciled in state A when she made the testament, and in state B when she died? Would it be more consistent with her expectations to apply the law of state A *or* B, whichever upholds the testament?

3. ***Domicile.*** The Restatement devotes more than thirty sections to the concept of domicile. While many of these sections are now clearly outdated or unconstitutional (such as those defining the domicile of a married woman as that of her husband's, see §§ 27–28), the remaining sections contain principles that, with some updating, remain valid today. Among them are the principles that: (a) "[e]very person has at all times one domicil, and no person has more than one domicil at a time" (§ 11) (at least for the same purpose); (b) once established, a domicile continues until another one is acquired (§ 23); and (c) in order to acquire a new domicile, "a person must establish a dwelling-place with the intention of making it his home" (§ 15), and the physical and mental elements must coexist at the same time. (Id.)

D. THE STRUCTURE, OPERATION, AND ESCAPE MECHANISMS OF THE TRADITIONAL APPROACH

As we have seen, the traditional approach was based on pre-conceived choice-of-law rules formulated around broad categories borrowed from domestic law, such as torts, contracts, conveyances, successions, status, etc. This section focuses on the structure and operation of these rules and the various escapes from them.

A typical traditional rule, such as the rule that torts are to be governed by the *lex loci delicti*, or that contracts are to be governed by the *lex loci contractus*, consists of three ingredients: (1) the legal category (tort, contract, etc.) that is the object of the rule; (2) the applicable law (*lex loci delicti, lex loci contractus*); and (3) the connecting factor (*locus delicti, locus contractus*) which "connects" the legal category or problem with the state that supplies the applicable law.

The process of employing these rules was also divided into three distinct mental steps, described below and explored in this section.

(a) Characterization. The first step was to determine *which* rule was applicable to the problem by fitting that problem into the legal category of tort, contract, and so forth. This step, known as characterization, classification, or qualification, is the focus of the next subsection.

(b) Localization. The second step was to "localize" the connecting factor, to place it on the map, by determining *where* the tort occurred or the contract was made. Although this is largely a factual inquiry, it is aided by certain localization sub-rules, such as that a contract is deemed made at the place of acceptance (as in *Linn* and *Milliken*), or that a tort occurs at the place of the injury (as in *Carroll*) rather than the place of conduct.

(c) Application. The third step consited of ascertaining the content of the law of the state in which the connecting factor was located, determining "how much" of that law was applicable to the case, examining whether any exceptions to its application are operable, and, if they were not, applying that law to the case at hand. Subsection 2 of this section focuses on this step.

(d) Escapes. Each of these three steps offered different opportunities for "escapes" or manipulations. As will be seen in this section, judges who were dissatisfied with the results that an orthodox application of the traditional theory would produce frequently utilized these escapes. This casuistic and thus unpredictable practice inflicted a serious blow to the traditional theory's claim of certainty and predictability. A question worth asking while reading the cases in this section is whether the source of the problem was bad cases, bad rules, bad judges, or a combination of all of the above.

1. CHARACTERIZATION

Alabama Great Southern R.R. Co. v. Carroll

Supreme Court of Alabama, 1892.
97 Ala. 126, 11 So. 803.
(For the main body of the opinion, see supra at 16.)

MCCLELLAN, J. * * * Another consideration, * * * it is insisted, entitles this plaintiff to recover here under the employers' liability act for an injury inflicted beyond the territorial operation of that act. This is claimed upon the fact that at the time plaintiff was injured he was in the discharge of duties which rested on him by the terms of a contract between him and the defendant, which had been entered into in Alabama, and hence was an Alabama contract, in connection with the facts that plaintiff was and is a citizen of this state, and the defendant is an Alabama corporation. These latter facts—of citizenship and domicile, respectively, of plaintiff and defendant—are of no importance in this connection, it seems to us, further than this: they may tend to show that the contract was made here, which is not controverted, and, if the plaintiff has a cause of action at all, he, by reason of them, may prosecute it in our courts. They have no bearing on the primary question of the existence of a cause of action, and, as that is the question before us, we need not further advert to the fact of plaintiffs citizenship or defendant's domicile.

* * * The [plaintiff's] theory is that the employers' liability act became a part of this contract, that the duties and liabilities which it prescribes became contractual duties and liabilities or duties and liabilities springing out of the contract, and that these duties attended upon the execution whenever its performance was required, in Mississippi as well as in Alabama, and that the liability prescribed for a failure to perform any of such duties attached upon such failure and consequent injury wherever it occurred, and was enforceable here, because imposed by an Alabama contract, notwithstanding the remission of duty and the resulting injury occurred in Mississippi, under whose laws no liability was incurred by such remission. * * * If this argument is sound, and it is sound if the duties and liabilities prescribed by the act can be said to be contractual duties and obligations at all, it would lead to conclusions, the possibility of which has not hitherto been suggested by any court or law writer, and which, to say the least, would be astounding to the profession. * * *

[T]he duties and liabilities incident to the relation between the plaintiff and the defendant, which are involved in this case, are not imposed by, and do not rest in or spring from, the contract between the parties. The only office of the contract, under section 2590 of the Code, is the establishment of a relation between them,—that of master and servant; and it is upon that relation, that incident or consequence of the contract, and not upon the rights of the parties under the contract, that our statute operates. The law is not concerned with the contractual stipulations, except in so far as to determine from them that the relation upon which it is to operate exists. Finding this relation, the statute imposes certain duties and liabilities on the parties to it, wholly regardless of the stipulations of the contract as to the rights of the parties under it, and, it may be, in the teeth of such stipulations. It is the purpose of the statute, and must be the limit of its operation, to govern persons standing in the relation of master and servants to each other, in respect of their conduct in certain particulars within the state of Alabama. Mississippi has the same right to establish governmental rules for such persons within her borders as Alabama, and she has established rules which are different from those of our law; and the conduct of such person toward each other is, when its legality is brought in question, to be adjudged by the rules of the one or the other state, as it falls territorially within the one or the other. * * *

Levy v. Daniels' U–Drive Auto Renting Co.

Supreme Court of Connecticut, 1928.
108 Conn. 333, 143 A. 163.

WHEELER, C.J. The complaint alleged these facts: The defendant, Daniels' U–Drive Auto Renting Company, Incorporated, rented in Hartford to Sack an automobile, which he operated, and in which Levy, the plaintiff [a Connecticut domiciliary], was a passenger. During the time the automobile was rented and operated, the defendant renting company was subject to section 21 of chapter 195 of the Public Acts of Connecticut, 1925, which provides:

"Any person renting or leasing to another any motor vehicle owned by him shall be liable for any damage to any person or property caused by the operation of such motor vehicle while so rented or leased."

While the plaintiff was a passenger, Sack brought the car to a stop on the main highway at Longmeadow, Mass., and negligently allowed it to stand directly in the path of automobiles proceeding southerly in the same direction his automobile was headed, without giving sufficient warning to automobiles approaching from his rear, and without having a tail light in operation, and when, due to inclement weather, the visibility was reduced to an exceedingly low degree. At this time the defendant Maginn negligently ran into and upon the rear end of the car Sack was operating, and threw plaintiff forcibly forward, causing him serious injuries. The specific acts of Maginn's negligence are set up at length in the complaint; it is not essential at this time to recite them. The plaintiff suffered his severe injuries in consequence of the concurrent negligence of both defendants.

The defendant demurred to the complaint upon several grounds, upon only one of which the trial court rested its decision [granting the demurrer]; namely, that the liability of the defendant must be determined by the law of Massachusetts, which did not impose upon persons renting automobiles any such obligation as the Connecticut act did. * * *

It is the defendant's contention in support of this ground of demurrer that the action set forth in the complaint is one of tort, and, since Massachusetts has no statute like, or substantially like, the Connecticut act, it must be determined by the common law of that state, under which the plaintiff must prove, to prevail, the negligence of the defendant in renting a defective motor vehicle and in failing to disclose the defect. If this were the true theory of the complaint, the conclusion thus reached must have followed. "The locus delicti determined the existence of the cause of action." [cit.] Under the law of Massachusetts, the plaintiff concededly would have a cause of action against Sack and Maginn for their tortious conduct in the operation of the cars they were driving. The plaintiff concedes the correctness of this. His counsel, however, construe the complaint as one in its nature contractual. The act makes him who rents or leases any motor vehicle to another liable for any damage to any person or property caused by the operation of the motor vehicle while so rented or leased. Liability for "damage caused by the operation of such motor vehicle" means caused by its tortious operation. This was undoubtedly the legislative intent; otherwise the act would be invalid. The plaintiff concedes this to be the true construction of these words, and the defendant acquiesces in this construction.

The complaint alleges a tortious operation of the automobile rented to Sack by the defendant, causing the injuries to the plaintiff as alleged, and constituting an action ex delicto. The statute gives, in terms, the injured person a right of action against the defendant which rented the automobile to Sack, though the injury occurred in Massachusetts. It was a right which the statute gave directly, not derivatively, to the injured person as a consequence of the contract of hiring. The purpose of the statute was not primarily to give the injured person a right of recovery against the tortious operator of the car, but to protect the safety of the traffic upon highways by providing an incentive to him who rented motor vehicles to rent them to competent and careful operators, by making him liable for damage resulting from the tortious operation of the rented vehicles. The common law would not hold the defendant liable upon the facts recited in the complaint for the negligence of Sack in the operation of this automobile. [cit.] The rental of motor vehicles to any but competent and careful operators, or to persons of unknown responsibility, would be liable to result in injury to the public upon or near highways, and this imminent danger justified, as a reasonable exercise of the police power, this statute, which requires all who engage in this business to become responsible for any injury inflicted upon the public by the tortious operation of the rented motor vehicle. * * *

The statute made the liability of the person renting motor vehicles a part of every contract of hiring a motor vehicle in Connecticut. A liability ex delicto is created by the law of the place of the delict. [cit.] A liability arising out of a contract depends upon the law of the place of contract, "unless the contract is to be performed or to have its beneficial operation and effect elsewhere, or it is made with reference to the law of another place." [cit.] We will enforce rights of action on contracts arising in other jurisdictions unless these contravene our own law, or our own fundamental and important public policy imperatively requires their nonenforcement. [cit.] It is a general rule subject to the exceptions we have noted, that rights ex contractu may be enforced anywhere. [cit.]

If the liability of this defendant under this statute is contractual, no question can arise as to the plaintiff's right to enforce this contract, provided the obligation imposed upon this defendant was for the "direct, sole and exclusive benefit" of the plaintiff. The contract was made in Connecticut; at the instant of its making the statute made a part of the contract of hiring the liability of the defendant which the plaintiff seeks to enforce. The law inserted in the contract this provision. The statute did not create the liability; it imposed it in case the defendant voluntarily rented the automobile. Whether the defendant entered into this contract of hiring was his own voluntary act; if he did he must accept the condition upon which the law permitted the making of the contract. The contract was for the "direct, sole, and exclusive benefit" of the plaintiff, who is alleged to have been injured through the tortious operation of the automobile rented by the defendant to Sack. The right of the plaintiff as a beneficiary of this contract to maintain this action is no longer an open question in this state. [cit.] The contract was made for him and every other member of the public. That the beneficiary was undetermined because each of the public was a beneficiary is of no consequence. His injury determines his identity and right of action. [cit.] The assent of the beneficiary, if required, is manifested in his action upon the contract. The demurrer should have been overruled. * * *

Notes and Questions

1. The characterization process is not peculiar to conflicts law. It is encountered in applying any legal rule, foreign or domestic. When domestic law provides a different limitations period for contract actions than for tort actions, or a different rule for movables than for immovables, or for tangibles than intangibles, the court must determine within which category the action or the thing fits. In turn, this determination pinpoints the applicable rule and the corresponding result. The same is true in conflicts cases under the traditional method. As we have seen, the traditional choice-of-law rules point in different directions for torts, contracts, conveyances, successions, family law, and so forth. Determining whether the problem at hand is one of tort, contract, or something else, determined which choice-of-law rule was applicable and hence which state's law governed the case. Characterization in multistate cases differs from characterization in domestic cases only with regard to the degree of the involved difficulty. In domestic cases, characterization is easier because it is conducted exclusively under a single law and usually is facilitated by readily available precedent. In multistate cases, characterization is more difficult due to the involvement of foreign law or laws and the relative paucity of precedent.

2. A preliminary question one faces in multistate cases, but not in domestic cases, is which state's standards should control the characterization process--the substantive law of the forum (*lex fori*)? the law that the forum's choice-of-law rule designates applicable to the case (*lex causae*); or a combination of the two laws? How did *Carroll* and *Levy* answer this question? The Restatement assigns the matter to the *lex fori*. (§ 7). The Restatement (Second) provides that, with some exceptions, "[t]he classification and interpretation of Conflict of Laws concepts and terms are determined in accordance with the law of the forum," while the classification and interpretation of concepts and terms employed by the applicable law (*lex causae*) are determined in accordance with that law. Restatement (Second) § 7. Although

legislators rarely address this question,[1] academic authors have debated it for more than a century. Their views can be synopsized as follows: (a) apply the *lex fori* (Kahn, Bartin); (b) apply the *lex causae* (Clunet, Wolff); (c) apply the concepts and categories derived through a comparative analysis of several legal systems, including but not limited to the *lex fori* and the *lex causae* (Rabel); (d) apply the categories of the *lex fori* to determine which of the forum's choice-of-law rules is applicable, and thus identify the *lex causae*, and then apply the categories of the *lex causae* to delimit the scope of the *lex causae* (Robertson); and (e) begin with the categories of the *lex fori* but also consider the categories of any other potentially applicable law (Falconbridge). See generally Robertson, *Characterization*; 1 Ehrenzweig, *PIL* 111–119; Rigaux, *La théorie des qualifications*; von Overbeck, *Cour général* 91–126. Which of the above views do you prefer? Why?

3. Compare the characterization outcomes in *Carroll* and *Levy*. Can you reconcile them? In *Levy*, a person not contractually related to the defendant convinced the court to characterize his cause of action as being contractual. In *Carroll*, a person contractually related to the defendant through a contract of employment sued his employer for an injury he received while acting in the scope and course of his employment. Yet, the court thought "astounding" the plaintiff's argument that his cause of action was contractual. What was astounding about this argument? How do you explain the difference?

4. The reason Mr. Levy had a cause of action was because he was the victim of a tort committed by Mr. Sack, the driver of the rented car, but the reason Levy had an action *against the rental company* was because that company had entered into a lease contract with Sack. Is there an easy way to characterize Levy's action? Do you think the answer to the characterization question would have been different had this been a domestic case in which the issue was which statute of limitation (e.g., three years for contracts, one year for torts) to apply?

5. The *Levy* court eventually agreed with the plaintiff's characterization of "the complaint as one in its nature contractual," but only after examining "[t]he purpose of the statute" on which the complaint was based. The words last quoted show the court stumbling onto something important and meaningful, at least for those who believe that conflicts between laws cannot be resolved intelligently without first examining their content and underlying purpose. But did the court make good use of this important discovery? What purpose did the court ascribe to the Connecticut statute? If the court were correct in identifying that purpose, was the court also correct in assuming that that statute was intended to regulate contracts? If the statute's purpose was to "protect the safety of the traffic upon highways," then which highways was the statute intended to regulate? Connecticut highways? Massachusetts highways? What about Canadian and Mexican highways? In Matteis v. National Car

---

1. Among codifications that address this question, see, e.g., Spanish Civ. Code Art. 12(1) (*lex fori*); U.K. codif. § 9(2) ("The characterisation * * * is a matter for the courts of the forum."); Quebec Civ. Code Art. 3078 and Hungarian codif. § 3 (*lex fori* except where the foreign "legal institution" at stake is unknown to the *lex fori*); Argentine Draft Code of PIL, art. 2 (*lex causae*), but if this "does not lead to a reasonable solution," then the *lex fori* applies; Puerto Rico Draft Code, art. 5 (subject to some exceptions, characterization is to be conducted under the *lex fori*, but that "the legal categories and terms of [the applicable] foreign law * * * shall be interpreted and applied in accordance with that law").

Rental Systems, Inc., 1993 WL 28828 (Conn.Sup.1993), a Connecticut plaintiff attempted to take this statute with him all the way to Louisiana, which, like Massachusetts in *Levy*, did not have a similar statute. The court refused to apply the Connecticut statute to a Louisiana accident involving a car rented in that state because such application "would require a party, such as [the rental company], to be exposed for damage liability in accordance with [the law of] any jurisdiction in which the plaintiff resides * * * [and] would * * * not provide protection for the justified expectations of the parties." Id. at *3.

6. Does the above-quoted statement mean that the state in which the car was rented is more important than the state in which the plaintiff is domiciled? In Bosler v. National Car Rental, 1993 WL 44341 (Conn.Sup.1993), the car was rented in Massachusetts, the accident occurred in Rhode Island, and Connecticut's only connection was that the plaintiff was domiciled there when the accident occurred, though not when the action was filed. The court thought this connection to be "significant" and applied the Connecticut statute, because that statute "is presumably designed to allow individuals to secure relief for accidents involving rented vehicles from the lessor." Id. at *9. Is this statement consistent with *Levy*? Does this statement mean that the place of the accident has become an inconsequential factor? In Brunow v. Burnett, 1994 WL 149334 (Conn.Sup.1994), neither the plaintiff nor the defendant were domiciled in Connecticut, the car had been rented in Massachusetts, but the accident occurred in Connecticut. The court found the last contact to be most significant and applied the Connecticut statute. After all, the court reasoned, that statute "was enacted 'to protect the safety of traffic upon highways.'" 1994 WL 149334 at *3 (citing *Levy*).

Matteis, *Bosler* and *Brunow* all were decided after Connecticut had abandoned the *lex loci delicti* and had adopted the flexible approach of the Restatement (Second). See O'Connor v. O'Connor, 519 A.2d 13 (Conn.1986), reproduced infra at 145. *O'Connor* criticized *Levy*'s characterization as an "evasive device." Id. at 20. True enough. As you will see in studying the modern approaches in Chapter 3, their inherent flexibility obviates the need to use "evasive" characterizations or other "escape devices." *Matteis*, *Bosler* and *Brunow* resolved the characterization question in a "non-evasive" manner by uniformly concluding that the actions filed against the rental company under Connecticut's lessor's liability statute were tort actions. Nevertheless, the basic question still remains: Has the abandonment of the traditional theory and the more rational resolution of the characterization question enabled the Connecticut courts to reach more rational, fair, or predictable results?

7. Several other states, such as New York, Michigan, Iowa, and Minnesota have statutes similar to the Connecticut statute involved in *Levy*. All of those states have abandoned the *lex loci* rule in favor of modern flexible approaches. In employing these approaches, these states have uniformly characterized these statutes as tort statutes but have encountered a new characterization question--whether the purpose of those statutes is to regulate the car owner's conduct ("conduct-regulating" rules) or rather to ensure recovery compensation for the victim ("loss-allocating" rules). See Symeonides, *The Choice-of-Law Revolution*, §§ 172, 175, 180. This new distinction of tort rules is studied in chapter 3, infra, but its very existence is a

reminder that characterization problems have not disappeared with the advent of modern theories.

8. Returning to *Levy*, suppose Connecticut law allows the rental company to sue the driver, Sack, for indemnity and the company does so. Sack invokes a Massachusetts "guest statute," which prevents gratuitous guest passengers from suing the host driver. Sack argues that, because he is immune from a suit by Levy, Sack also should be immune from an indemnity suit by the rental company. Which law should answer the question of whether the company may sue Sack for indemnity?

9. Suppose that: Sack, the driver, was a Massachusetts domiciliary but he rented the car in Connecticut; his passenger was not Mr. Levy, but rather Mrs. Sack; and Massachusetts had a rule of interspousal immunity which prohibited Mrs. Sack from suing Mr. Sack. As in *Levy*, the accident occurred in Massachusetts. Mrs. Sack sues the rental company in Connecticut. The company argues that under Massachusetts law a wife may not sue her husband and hence she may not sue her husband's lessor. What now? See Zelinger v. State Sand & Gravel Co., 156 N.W.2d 466 (Wis.1968).

Haumschild v. Continental Cas. Co.
Supreme Court of Wisconsin, 1959.
7 Wis.2d 130, 95 N.W.2d 814.

CURRIE, J. This appeal presents a conflict of laws problem with respect to interspousal liability for tort growing out of an automobile accident. Which law controls, that of the state of the forum, the state of the place of wrong, or the state of domicile? Wisconsin is both the state of the forum and of the domicile while California is the state where the alleged wrong was committed. Under Wisconsin law a wife may sue her husband in tort. Under California law she cannot. [cit.] [The trial court, applying California law, granted summary judgment for defendant driver and his insurer and dismissed the suit by the passenger, the driver's ex wife.]

This court was first faced with this question in Buckeye v. Buckeye, 234 N.W. 342 [(Wis.1931)]. In that case Wisconsin was the state of the forum and domicile, while Illinois was the state of the place of wrong. It was there held that the law governing the creation and extent of tort liability is that of the place where the tort was committed, citing Goodrich, Conflict of Laws (1st ed.), p. 188. From this premise it was further held that interspousal immunity from tort liability necessarily is governed by the law of the place of injury. * * *

The principle enunciated in the *Buckeye* case and followed in subsequent Wisconsin cases, that the law of the place of wrong controls as to whether one spouse is immune from suit in tort by the other, is the prevailing view in the majority of jurisdictions in this country. * * * However, criticism of the rule of the *Buckeye* case, by legal writers, some of them recognized authorities in the field of conflict of laws, and recent decisions by the courts of California, New Jersey, and Pennsylvania, have caused us to re-examine the question afresh. * * *

The first case to break the ice and flatly hold that the law of domicile should be applied in determining whether there existed an immunity from suit for tort based upon family relationship is Emery v. Emery, 289 P.2d 218 [(Cal.1955)]. In that case two unemancipated minor sisters sued their unemancipated minor brother and their father to recover for injuries sustained in an automobile accident that occurred in the state of Idaho, the complaint alleging wilful misconduct in order to come within the provisions of the Idaho "guest" statute. All parties were domiciled in California. The opinion by Mr. Justice Traynor recognized that the California court, in passing on the question of whether an unemancipated minor child may sue the parent or an unemancipated brother, had a choice to apply the law of the place of wrong, of the forum, or of the domicile. It was held that the immunity issue was not a question of tort but one of capacity to sue and be sued, and rejected the law of the place of injury as "both fortuitous and irrelevant." In deciding whether to apply the law of the forum, or the law of the domicile, the opinion stated this conclusion (289 P.2d at pages 222–223):

> " * * * We think that disabilities to sue and immunities from suit because of a family relationship are more properly determined by reference to the law of the state of the family domicile. That state has the primary responsibility for establishing and regulating the incidents of the family relationship and it is the only state in which the parties can, by participation in the legislative processes, effect a change in those incidents. Moreover, it is undesirable that the rights, duties, disabilities, and immunities conferred or imposed by the family relationship should constantly change as members of the family cross state boundaries during temporary absences from their home." * * *

The two reasons most often advanced for the common law rule, that one spouse may not sue the other, are the ancient concept that husband and wife constitute in law but one person, and that to permit such suits will be to foment family discord and strife. The Married Women's Acts of the various states have effectively destroyed the "one person" concept thereby leaving as the other remaining reason for the immunity the objective of preventing family discord. This is also the justification usually advanced for denying an unemancipated child the capacity to sue a parent, brother or sister. Clearly this policy reason for denying the capacity to sue more properly lies within the sphere of family law, where domicile usually controls the law to be applied, than it does tort law, where the place of injury generally determines the substantive law which will govern. * * *

We are convinced that, from both the standpoint of public policy and logic, the proper solution of the conflict of laws problem, in cases similar to the instant action, is to hold that the law of the domicile is the one that ought to be applied in determining any issue of incapacity to sue based upon family relationship.

However, in order to adopt such a conflict of laws rule it will be necessary to overrule at least six prior decisions of this court, and to partially overrule two others. If it ever is proper for a court to depart from *stare decisis* we scarcely can perceive of a more justifiable situation in which to do so. In the first place, the rule being discarded is one lying in the field of conflict of laws as applied to torts so that there can hardly have been any action taken by the parties in reliance upon it. Secondly, strong reasons of public policy exist for supplanting such rule by a better one which does not unnecessarily discriminate against the citizens of our own state.

The most compelling argument against taking such step is that it departs from the rule of the Restatement, and disturbs the sought after ideal of establishing some uniformity in the conflict of laws field. However, as well appears from the cases hereinbefore cited, there is a clearly discernible trend away from the rule of the Restatement insofar as it requires that the law of the place of wrong is to be applied in determining questions of incapacity to sue based on family status. Furthermore, it must be recognized that, in the field of the conflict of laws, absolutes should not be made the goal at the sacrifice of progress in furtherance of sound public policy.

After most careful deliberation, it is our considered judgment that this court should adopt the rule that, whenever the courts of this state are confronted with a conflict of laws problem as to which law governs the capacity of one spouse to sue the other in tort, the law to be applied is that of the state of domicile. We, therefore, expressly overrule the cases of Buckeye v. Buckeye, supra; [and five other cases]. * * *

It is interesting to note that, if the rule now adopted had been applied in the first six cited overruled automobile accident cases, the result in four of such cases would have been to hold that there was no interspousal immunity from suit, because the parties were domiciled in Wisconsin. * * *

Judgment reversed and case remanded for further proceedings not inconsistent with this opinion. * * *

Folk v. York–Shipley, Inc.
Supreme Court of Delaware, 1968.
239 A.2d 236.

WOLCOTT, C.J. This is an appeal from the grant of partial summary judgment against Donna G. Folk, a plaintiff with her husband, Robert P. Folk, in an action in the Superior Court against York–Shipley, Inc., a Delaware corporation. The complaint asserts two separate causes of action, that of Mrs. Folk for loss of her husband's consortium, and that of Mr. Folk for personal injury.[1]

The basic facts are that a head-on collision took place in Pennsylvania between a tractor-trailer driven by Mr. Folk and a tractor-trailer owned by York–Shipley and driven by its employee. Mr. Folk suffered serious injury. Mr. and Mrs. Folk are domiciled in Delaware, and York–Shipley is a Delaware corporation.

The parties agree that by reason of Friday v. Smoot, 211 A.2d 594 [Del. 1965], a decision of this Court, the accident having taken place in Pennsylvania, the substantive law of Pennsylvania applies and governs the tort. The parties also are agreed that the substantive law of Pennsylvania * * * denies a wife the right to sue for loss of consortium [while the law of Delaware permits such an action].

Mrs. Folk makes three alternate arguments in support of her contention that her claim for loss of consortium may be asserted in an action in the Superior Court of Delaware.

First, it is argued that her cause of action for loss of consortium is separate and

---

1. The husband's action is still pending, undisposed of, before the Superior Court.

distinct from her husband's action for personal injury. It is argued that her claim is for injury to her marriage relationship and, since her marriage domicile is in Delaware, that injury took place in Delaware and not in Pennsylvania. * * *

Analysis of the asserted right of action demonstrates that it is the personal injury to the husband which is also the injury to the marriage of which the wife complains. The argument of Mrs. Folk that the injury she complains of is the subsequent inability of her husband to perform part of his marital duties, and that therefore the injury took place in Delaware, fails to recognize the distinction between injury and damage.

In this case, the injury to the marriage was the injury to the husband in Pennsylvania. From this injury flowed the damage of which she complains. That this is necessarily so becomes apparent when we consider that York–Shipley, or its employee, committed no other allegedly negligent act to which the damage to the Folk marriage could be related. The alleged negligence of York–Shipley, which is the basis for Mrs. Folk's claim, took place in Pennsylvania. We are therefore dealing with a Pennsylvania tort. * * * Since we are dealing with a Pennsylvania tort, under *Friday v. Smoot*, supra, that law governs. The *Newberg* case, a decision of the Pennsylvania Supreme Court, holds that a wife has no cause of action under these circumstances. Since Mrs. Folk has no cause of action in the jurisdiction in which the tort was committed, it follows that it may not be enforced in a Delaware court. [cit.]

Next, Mrs. Folk argues that loss of consortium is so intimately associated with the family relationship in a marriage that a matter of family law is involved, which, as a matter of policy, should be decided in accordance with the law of the matrimonial domicile, which, of course, is Delaware.

Cited in support of the argument is *Haumschild v. Continental Casualty Co.*, [*supra*], but we think the case is not in point. * * * In the instant case, we are not concerned with interspousal immunity to suit. Mrs. Folk seeks to sue a stranger to the marriage for damages resulting from a negligent act which took place in Pennsylvania. The two cases are entirely dissimilar. Indeed, the Haumschild case is further distinguishable on the ground that the wife in it was seeking to assert a cause of action unenforceable in California because of the defense of interspousal immunity, but enforceable in Wisconsin. The distinction is clear for * * * a wife may have a cause of action in tort against her husband which is nevertheless unenforceable against him.

We are of the opinion that the case before us does not present a question of family law but of tort law. It follows, therefore, that Delaware as the matrimonial domicile will not, as a matter of policy, apply its family law to permit the maintenance of this lawsuit. * * * The judgment below is affirmed.

Notes and Questions

1. What exactly was the object of characterization in *Carroll*, *Levy*, *Haumschild*, and *Folk*? The plaintiff's cause of action, the statute or rule on which the action was based, the statute or rule that was invoked as a bar to the action, the whole dispute,

or something else? For example, was there any doubt that Mrs. Haumschild's action was one in tort? What then did the court characterize as a matter of family law? The Restatement describes characterization as "determining the quality and character of legal ideas." (§ 7). What does this mean? The Restatement (Second) speaks of "classification and interpretation * * * of concepts and terms." (§ 7). Foreign codes speak of the characterization of "facts or relationships," (Hungarian codif. Art. 3); or of "a legal or factual issue" (Puerto Rico Draft Code, Art. 5). Which of the above formulations best describes the courts' characterizations in the above cases? Which one do you think is best? Why?

2. Rather than asking whether the dispute was one of tort, the *Haumschild* court narrowly formulated the question as one of "capacity to sue." This narrowing of broad categories into smaller questions or "issues" is another small breakthrough in traditional conflicts thinking. From now on, the word "issue" will become one of the most often-used words in your conflicts lexicon. The other breakthrough was the court's examination of the "reasons" or "policies" underlying the rule that impeded the plaintiff's capacity to sue. The *Levy* court did likewise, although it examined a forum rule (rather than a foreign rule) which empowered (rather than prevented) the plaintiff to sue the particular defendant.

3. Compare *Haumschild* with *Folk*. Are these cases so "entirely dissimilar" as the *Folk* court assumed? If they are, which of the two sounds more like a tort dispute? After all, *Haumschild* involved physical injuries directly sustained by the wife, while *Folk* involved injury "to the marriage." Regardless of how one characterizes Mrs. Folk's action, should not the law of the marital domicile have as much of a say in *Folk* as in *Haumschild*? Furthermore, even accepting the tort characterization, did Mrs. Folk make a good point when she argued that the "injury to her marriage relationship" had occurred in Delaware rather than in Pennsylvania?

4. In both *Levy* and *Haumschild*, the re-characterization of the issues as one of contract and family law, respectively, removed those cases from the scope of the *lex loci delicti* rule but placed them into the scope of another traditional and equally mechanical choice-of-law rule: *lex loci contractus* and *lex domicilii*, respectively. What implications does this re-characterization have for future cases? Suppose that a Connecticut domiciliary rents a car in Massachusetts and drives to Connecticut, where he injures a Connecticut domiciliary. If a Connecticut court follows *Levy*'s characterization, the court must apply Massachusetts law and deny recovery to a Connecticut domiciliary injured in that state. (Compare with *Bosler v. National Car Rental*, supra 47).) Anything wrong with this? Suppose that two California spouses drive into Wisconsin and have an accident there. Under *Haumschild*, a Wisconsin court would have to apply California law and deny recovery. Anything wrong with this? See Wilcox v. Wilcox, 133 N.W.2d 408 (Wis.1965); Zelinger v. State Sand & Gravel Co., 156 N.W.2d 466 (Wis.1968).

Would it not be preferable if the *Haumschild* court were to abandon the *lex loci delicti* rule rather than to retain and evade it? A few years after *Haumschild*, other states began using cases involving the *Haumschild* pattern as the opportunity to abandon the *lex loci* rule. Six of those cases involved interspousal immunity. See Armstrong v. Armstrong, 441 P.2d 699 (Ala. 1968) (Alaska spouses, accident in

Yukon territory); Schwartz v. Schwartz, 447 P.2d 254 (Ariz.1968) (New York spouses, Arizona accident); Pevoski v. Pevoski, 358 N.E.2d 416 (Mass.1976) (Massachusetts spouses, New York accident); and Forsman v. Forsman, 779 P.2d 218 (Utah 1989) (California spouses, Utah accident). Two cases involved intrafamily immunity. See Balts v. Balts, 142 N.W.2d 66 (Minn.1966) (Minnesota parent and child, Wisconsin accident); Jagers v. Royal Indem. Co., 276 So.2d 309 (La.1973) (Louisiana parent and child, Mississippi accident).

5. Notice that the real defendant in *Haumschild* was the husband's insurer. Obviously, the only reason the insurer could be sued in this case was the existence of an insurance contract between the insurer and Mr. Haumschild. Should the court have taken the next step of saying that Mrs. Haumschild's action against the insurer was contractual?

This is exactly what the court did in Sturiano v. Brooks, 523 So.2d 1126 (Fla.1988). Mrs. Sturiano was injured in an accident in Florida while riding in the family car driven by Mr. Sturiano, who was killed. She sued his estate (i.e., the car's insurer). The Sturianos were lifelong domiciliaries of New York, where they had purchased their insurance policy, but also had spent the six previous winters in Florida. They did not notify the insurer of their "migration" to Florida. After assuming without discussion that Florida law governed the plaintiff's capacity to sue her husband's estate, the court concluded that the issue of whether the plaintiff could recover from the insurer was contractual, and thus was governed by New York law. Under that law, the insurer was not liable for claims between spouses unless the policy contained a special clause expressly covering such claims. Although several years earlier the Florida Supreme Court had abandoned the *lex loci delicti* rule, the court rejected plaintiff's plea also to abandon the *lex loci contractus*. The court reasoned:

> While it is true that *lex loci contractus* is an inflexible rule, we believe that this inflexibility is necessary to ensure stability in contract arrangements. When parties come to terms in an agreement, they do so with the implied acknowledgment that the laws of that jurisdiction will control absent some provision to the contrary. This benefits both parties, not merely an insurance company. * * * Although *lex loci contractus* is old, it is not yet outdated. The very reason Sturiano gives as support for discarding *lex loci contractus*, namely that we live in a migratory, transitory society, provides support for upholding that doctrine. Parties have a right to know what the agreement they have executed provides. To allow one party to modify the contract simply by moving to another state would substantially restrict the power to enter into valid, binding, and stable contracts.

> * * * [W]e believe that the reasoning controlling those decisions [in which the court abandoned the *lex loci delicti* rule] does not apply in the instant case. With tort law, there is no agreement, no foreseen set of rules and statutes which the parties had recognized would control the litigation. In the case of an insurance contract, the parties enter into that contract with the acknowledgment that the laws of that jurisdiction control their actions. In essence, that jurisdiction's laws are incorporated by implication into the agreement. The parties to

this contract did not bargain for Florida's or any other state's laws to control. We must presume that the parties did bargain for, or at least expected, New York law to apply.

523 So. 2d at 1129–30.

Do you agree with the court's characterization of the *Sturiano* action as contractual? Would it have made a difference if the insurance policy had been purchased by and in the name of Mr. Sturiano, or Mrs. Sturiano, or both spouses? The court does not discuss this question but states that "*the Sturianos* purchased automobile insurance" (emphasis added). Accepting the court's conclusion that the action was contractual (and its unwillingness to abandon the *lex loci contractus* rule), does characterization end there? As noted earlier, the first Restatement had two rules for contracts--*lex loci contractus* for matters of validity, and *lex loci solutionis* for matters of performance. Was the issue before the court one of validity or one of performance? Finally, do you agree with the court's description of the virtues of the *lex loci contractus* rule? In general? In this case? Suppose that Mr. Sturiano had applied for and had received his policy while he attended a convention in Connecticut. Should Connecticut law apply? Based on the above quoted excerpt from *Sturiano*, did the court apply the law of New York because the contract had been made there, or because of New York's other contacts to the case? As to the insurer's expectations, in this day and age, is one who insures an auto*mobile* entitled to rely on the law of a single state? Suppose that during the winter months Sturiano sent his payments for the insurance premium from his Florida address. Should this fact alter the insurer's expectations?

6. Conflicts casebooks are replete with examples of cases in which courts applying the traditional theory characterized identical issues in irreconcilable ways. Indeed, one does not have to look hard to find such cases. These cases demonstrate that distinguishing between torts or contracts, contracts or conveyances, movables or immovables, successions or marital property, has given much more trouble to courts in conflicts cases than in domestic cases. What does this prove? Critics of the traditional theory charge that, because courts inconsistently characterized identical issues, it was impossible to predict the outcome of a conflicts case because it was impossible to predict how the court would characterize the issue. Thus, the traditional theory was said to be unable to deliver one of its most important promises: predictability of choice-of-law decisions.

But what is meant by predictability? Intrastate or interstate predictability? It may be difficult to predict how the courts of different states will characterize the same issue, but is it as difficult to predict how the courts of a *single* state will characterize that issue? The defendants in *Haumschild* and *Levy* might have been surprised by the court's characterization, as any other litigant is "surprised" by an unfavorable decision overruling clear settled precedent or addressing a new issue. Thereafter, however, litigants in similar cases should have little difficulty in predicting how the court will characterize the same issue, at least until the court overrules *Haumschild* and *Levy*. (Eventually, these cases were essentially overruled in 1967 and 1986, respectively, but only after Wisconsin and Connecticut had abandoned the traditional theory in favor of more flexible approaches.) See Heath v. Zellmer, 151

N.W.2d 664 (Wis.1967); and *O'Connor v. O'Connor*, supra 47. A question worth asking in studying Chapter 3 is whether these newer approaches have produced the predictability that has eluded the traditional theory. For now see the Connecticut cases described supra at 46-47.

The critics have a stronger case when they charge that:

(a) because of wide divergence in the characterization of identical issues by the courts of various states, the traditional theory failed to attain another of its most important goals--*interstate* uniformity of result;

(b) because of its inherent manipulability, characterization became a substitute for more candid and direct analysis of conflicts cases. For example, by manipulating the characterization process, the *Levy* and *Haumschild* courts were able to produce good substantive results in those two cases, but they also prolonged the life of a bad choice-of-law rule, the *lex loci delicti*, without articulating why this rule should not apply in similar future cases; and

(c) the frequent utilization of characterization as a means of avoiding the results of the traditional rules demonstrates the inherent deficiencies of these rules. In other words, had these rules been more rational, the temptation to evade them would not have been as strong.

These points are well taken. But which would you prefer: (1) a system of bad rules that do not allow escapes, such as characterization? (2) abandoning all rules and replacing them with flexible ad hoc approaches? or (3) applying to the Omniscient Being for a system of "perfect" rules that need no escapes? If you choose (2), as have most American states, you may be able to apply these approaches without first needing to characterize the issue at hand. But should you expect either more intrastate predictability or more interstate uniformity? Remember this question as you study Chapter 3. For now see the recent Connecticut cases at 46-47, supra. If you choose (3) and your relationship with the Omniscient Being is good enough as to be blessed with those perfect rules, do you think that they can be applied without first characterizing the issue? Can you guarantee that all the courts will believe in the same Omniscient Being, in exactly the same way, every day of the week? If not, with what choices are you left?

2. SUBSTANCE VS. PROCEDURE

It has been said that "one of the eternal truths of every system of private international law is that a distinction must be made between substance and procedure, between right and remedy." Cheshire & North, *PIL*, 74–75. Indeed, the distinction between substance and procedure is ancient, necessary, and unavoidable in domestic, federal, and conflicts law. For example, you are already familiar with the rule that, unlike substantive statutes, procedural statutes may apply retroactively; or the rule that, for *Erie* purposes, state law governs substantive matters while federal law governs procedural matters. In conflicts law, the distinction between substance and procedure was important under the traditional theory because, unlike substantive matters which may be governed by foreign law, "[a]ll matters of procedure are governed by the law of the forum." Restatement § 585. The reasons the Restatement offered for this rule were practicality, convenience, and cost avoidance. If the forum were required to apply the procedural rules of another state,

> [t]he difficulties involved would be very great; so great as to be impossible in many instances. A heavy burden would be thrown upon the courts of the forum and the orderly administration of justice there would be hampered and delayed. A limitation upon the scope of the reference to the foreign law is thus necessary. Such limitation excludes those phases of the case which make administration of the foreign law by the local tribunal impracticable, inconvenient, or violative of local policy. In these instances, the local rules at the forum are applied and are classified as matters of procedure.

Restatement, Intro. Note to Chapter 12, at 700–701 (1934). Professor Beale offered a balancing test that might have been implicit in the Restatement: "If the practical convenience to the court in adopting the local rule of law is great, and the effect of so doing upon the rights of the parties is negligible, the law of the forum will be held to be controlling." 3 Beale, *Conflict of Laws*, 1599–1600.

From a methodological perspective, the substance/procedure distinction can appear either in the first step of the choice-of-law process, as a sub-species of characterization, or in the third step of the process, as a question of "how much" of the foreign law to apply. Either way, the chief question is where to "draw the line" between substance and procedure in actual cases, especially along the interface between the two. This is a difficult question in domestic, federal, and conflicts law. As Cook observed, "the substantive shades off by imperceptible degrees into the procedural." Cook, *Logical Bases*, 166.

Undaunted by such difficulties, the Restatement offers what purports to be an exhaustive list of subjects classified as procedural. Among them are: which court can entertain the action (§ 586); the form of the action (§ 587); who may and who must be sued (§ 588); methods of serving process (§ 589); methods of securing obedience to the court (§ 590); at what moment the action began (§ 591); all matters of pleading and the conduct of proceedings in court (§ 592); whether a claim of a defendant may be pleaded by way of setoff or counterclaim (§ 593); whether an issue of fact shall be tried by the court or by a jury (§ 594); the proof in court of a fact alleged as well as presumptions and inferences to be drawn from evidence (§ 595); the competency and credibility of witnesses (§ 596); admissibility of a particular piece of evidence (§ 597); matters pertaining to the execution of judgments (§ 600); whether the plaintiff must be free of fault in order to maintain an action (§ 601); whether compliance with a certain form is a prerequisite for filing an action (statute of frauds) (§ 602); statutes of limitation (§§ 603–605); limitations by forum law on the amount of recovery (§ 606); and access to courts (§§ 607–620).

This subsection offers samples of how courts following the traditional theory have used or abused the substance/procedure distinction. Noticeably absent from this subsection are cases involving statutes of limitation. These cases are good pedagogical tools to illustrate both good and bad applications of this distinction, but they also are good examples of *contemporary* judicial practice in this very important area of the law. For this reason, the study of these cases is deferred until Chapter 4. Suffice it to say for now that, subject to few exceptions, the traditional approach characterized questions of statutes of limitation as procedural questions which, therefore, were governed by the law of the forum. See Restatement §§ 603–04.

Grant v. McAuliffe
Supreme Court of California, 1953.
41 Cal.2d 859, 264 P.2d 944.

TRAYNOR, J. [Grant and two other Californians were injured in Arizona when the car in which they were riding collided with a car driven by Pullen, also a Californian. A few days later, Pullen died as a result of injuries received in the collision and defendant McAuliffe was appointed administrator of his estate by a California court. Grant and his co-passengers filed actions against Pullen's estate to recover damages for the injuries caused by Pullen's alleged negligence. The trial court granted defendant's motion to dismiss. Each plaintiff appealed and the appeals have been consolidated.] * * * The basic question is whether plaintiffs' causes of action against Pullen survived his death and are maintainable against his estate. The statutes of this state provide that causes of action for negligent torts survive the death of the tort feasor and can be maintained against the administrator or executor of his estate. [cit.] Defendant contends, however, that the survival of a cause of action is a matter of substantive law, and that the courts of this state must apply the law of Arizona governing survival of causes of action. There is no provision for survival of causes of action in the statutes of Arizona, although there is a provision that in the event of the death of a party to a pending proceeding his personal representative can be substituted as a party to the action [cit.] if the cause of action survives. [cit.] The Supreme Court of Arizona has held that if a tort action has not been commenced before the death of the tort feasor a plea in abatement must be sustained. [cit.]

Thus, the answer to the question whether the causes of action against Pullen survived and are maintainable against his estate depends on whether Arizona or California law applies. In actions on torts occurring abroad, the courts of this state determine the substantive matters inherent in the cause of action by adopting as their own the law of the place where the tortious acts occurred, unless it is contrary to the public policy of this state. * * * But the forum does not adopt as its own the procedural law of the place where the tortious acts occur. It must, therefore, be determined whether survival of causes of action is procedural or substantive for conflict of laws purposes.

This question is one of first impression in this state. The precedents in other jurisdictions are conflicting. In many cases it has been held that the survival of a cause of action is a matter of substance and that the law of the place where the tortious acts occurred must be applied to determine the question. [cit.] The Restatement of the Conflict of Laws, section 390, is in accord. It should be noted, however, that the majority of the foregoing cases were decided after drafts of the Restatement were first circulated in 1929. Before that time, it appears that the weight of authority was that survival of causes of action is procedural and governed by the domestic law of the forum. [cit.] Many of the cases, decided both before and after the Restatement, holding that survival is substantive and must be determined by the law of the place where the tortious acts occurred, confused the problems involved in survival of causes of action with those involved in causes of action for wrongful death. [cit.] The problems are not analogous. [cit.] A cause of action for wrongful death is statutory. It is a new cause of action vested in the widow or next of kin, and arises on the death of the injured person. Before his death, the injured person himself has a separate and distinct cause of action and, if it survives, the same cause of action can be enforced by the personal representative of the deceased against the tort feasor. The survival statutes do not create a new cause of action, as do the wrongful death statutes. [cit.] * * * They merely prevent the abatement of the cause of action of the injured person, and provide for its enforcement by or against the personal representative of the deceased. They are analogous to statutes of limitation, which are procedural for conflict of laws purposes and are governed by the domestic law of the forum. [cit.] Thus, a cause of action arising in another state, by the laws of which an action cannot be maintained thereon because of lapse of time, can be enforced in California by a citizen of this state, if he has held the cause of action from the time it accrued. [cit.]

Defendant contends, however, that the characterization of survival of causes of action as substantive or procedural is foreclosed by Cort v. Steen, 224 P.2d 723 [(1950)], where it was held that the California survival statutes were substantive and therefore did not apply retroactively. The problem in the present proceeding, however, is not whether the survival statutes apply retroactively, but whether they are substantive or procedural for purposes of conflict of laws. "'Substance' and 'procedure' ... are not legal concepts of invariable content." W. W. Cook, *The Logical and Legal Bases of the Conflict of Laws* (1942), c. 6: "Substance and Procedure", and a statute or other rule of law will be characterized as substantive or procedural according to the nature of the problem for which a characterization must be made.

Defendant also contends that a distinction must be drawn between survival of causes of action and revival of actions, and that the former are substantive but the latter procedural. On the basis of this distinction, defendant concludes that many of the cases cited above as holding that survival is procedural and is governed by the domestic law of the forum do not support this position, since they involved problems of "revival" rather than "survival." The distinction urged by defendant is not a valid one. Most of the statutes involved in the cases cited provided for the "revival" of a pending proceeding by or against the personal representative of a party thereto should he die while the action is still pending. But in most "revival" statutes, substitution of a personal representative in place of a deceased party is expressly conditioned on the survival of the cause of action itself. If the cause of action dies with the tort feasor, a pending proceeding must be abated. A personal representative cannot be substituted in the place of a deceased party unless the cause of action is still subsisting. In cases where this substitution has occurred, the courts have looked to the domestic law of the forum to determine whether the cause of action survives as well as to determine whether the personal representative can be substituted as a party to the action. [cit.] Defendant's contention would require the courts to look to their local statutes to determine "revival" and to the law of the place where the tort occurred to determine "survival," but we have found no case in which this procedure was followed.

Since we find no compelling weight of authority for either alternative, we are free to make a choice on the merits. We have concluded that survival of causes of action should be governed by the law of the forum. Survival is not an essential part of the cause of action itself but relates to the procedures available for the enforcement of the legal claim for damages. Basically the question is one of the administration of decedents' estates, which is a purely local proceeding. The problem here is whether the causes of action that these plaintiffs had against Pullen before his death survive as liabilities of his estate. Section 573 of the [California] Probate Code provides that "all actions founded ... upon any liability for physical injury, death or injury to property, may be maintained by or against executors and administrators in all cases in which the cause of action ... is one which would not abate upon the death of their respective testators or intestates...." Civil Code, section 956, provides that "A thing in action arising out of a wrong which results in physical injury to the person ... shall not abate by reason of the death of the wrongdoer ...," and causes of action for damage to property are maintainable against executors and administrators under section 574 of the Probate Code. [cit.] Decedent's estate is located in this state, and letters of administration were issued to defendant by the courts of this state. The responsibilities of defendant, as administrator of Pullen's estate, for injuries inflicted by Pullen before his death are governed by the laws of this state. This approach has been followed in a number of well-reasoned cases. [cit.] It retains control of the administration of estates by the local Legislature and avoids the problems involved in determining the administrator's amenability to suit under the laws of other states. The common law doctrine *actio personalis moratur cum persona* had its origin in a penal concept of tort liability. [cit.] Today, tort liabilities of the sort involved in these actions are regarded as compensatory. When, as in the present case, all of the parties were residents of this state, and the estate of the deceased tort feasor is being administered in this state, plaintiff's right to prosecute their causes of action is governed by the laws of this state relating to administration of estates.

The orders granting defendant's motions to abate are reversed, and the causes remanded for further proceedings.

Gibson, C.J., Shenk, J., and Carter, J., concurred.

SCHAUER, J. I dissent. In Cort v. Steen (1950), 224 P.2d 723, this court held that under the doctrine of nonsurvivability the abatement of an action by the death of the injured person through the tort feasor's act or otherwise, or by the death of the tort feasor, abates the wrong as well; that the effect of a survival statute is to create a right or cause of action rather than to either continue an existing right or revive or extend a remedy theretofore accrued for the redress of an existing wrong; and that consequently a survival statute enacted after death of the tort feasor did not apply to the tort or cause of action involved. * * * [E]ven more regrettable than the failure to either follow or unequivocally overrule the cited cases is the character of the "rule" which is now promulgated: the majority assert that henceforth "a statute or other rule of law will be characterized as substantive or procedural according to the nature of the problem for which a characterization must be made," thus suggesting that the court will no longer be bound to consistent enforcement or uniform application of "a statute or other rule of law" but will instead apply one "rule" or another as the untrammeled whimsy of the majority may from time to time dictate, "according to the nature of the problem" as they view it in a given case. This concept of the majority strikes deeply at what has been our proud boast that ours was a government of laws rather than of men.

Although any administration of an estate in the courts of this state is local in a procedural sense, the rights and claims both in favor of and against such an estate are substantive in nature, and vest irrevocably at the date of death. [cit.] Since this court has clearly held that a right or cause of action created by a survival statute is likewise substantive, rather than procedural, we should hold, if we would follow the law, that the trial court properly granted defendant's motions to abate. * * *

Kilberg v. Northeast Airlines, Inc.
Court of Appeals of New York, 1961.
9 N.Y.2d 34, 211 N.Y.S.2d 133, 172 N.E.2d 526.

DESMOND, C.J. Defendant is a common carrier of passengers by air. Plaintiff's intestate, a passenger on one of defendant's planes, was killed in August, 1958 when the airship crashed and burned at Nantucket, Massachusetts, in the course of a flight from a New York airport. * * * There was in effect at the time of this disaster section 2 of chapter 229 of the General Statutes of Massachusetts which gave a cause of action against a common carrier for negligently causing a passenger's death but limited to not less than $2,000 or more than $15,000 the damages to be awarded therefor. * * *

* * * Modern conditions make it unjust and anomalous to subject the traveling citizen of this State to the varying laws of other States through and over which they move. The number of States limiting death case damages has become smaller over the years but there are still 14 of them [cit.] An air traveler from New York may in a flight of a few hours' duration pass through several of those commonwealths. His plane may meet with disaster in a State he never intended to cross but into which the plane has flown because of bad weather or other unexpected developments, or an airplane's catastrophic descent may begin in one State and end in another. The place of injury becomes entirely fortuitous. Our courts should if possible provide protection for our own State's people against unfair and anachronistic treatment of the lawsuits which result from these disasters. There is available, we find, a way of accomplishing this conformably to our State's public policy and without doing violence to the accepted pattern of conflict of law rules.

Since both Massachusetts [cit.] and New York [cit.] authorize wrongful death suits against common carriers, the only controversy is as to amount of damages recoverable. New York's public policy prohibiting the imposition of limits on such damages is strong, clear and old. * * * We will still require plaintiff to sue on the Massachusetts statute but we refuse on public policy grounds to enforce one of its provisions as to damages.

Actually, we have in Wooden v. Western N. Y. & Pa. R. R. Co., 26 N.E. 1050,

1051 [1891] a flat holding by our court that, in an action brought for causing a wrongful death in Pennsylvania, the New York courts would enforce our limitation of damages (as it then existed) although Pennsylvania had no such limitation. The reason, equally pertinent here, is that the "restriction pertains to the remedy rather than the right" ([id.]) and "does not strictly affect the rule of damages, but rather the extent of damages, and that extent, as limited or unlimited, does not enter into any definition of the right enforced or the cause of action permitted to be prosecuted."
* * *

As to conflict of law rules it is of course settled that the law of the forum is usually in control as to procedures including remedies [cit.]. However, as Professor Leflar says (Conflict of Laws, § 60), remedial and substantive "shade into each other constantly" and "the law of the forum normally determines for itself" whether a given question is one of substance or procedure. This is the conventional approach and was the one used in the only New York appellate decision on the subject. [cit.]. As to whether the measure of damages should be treated as a procedural or a substantive matter in wrongful death cases, there is authority both ways [cit.] and no controlling New York decision except the statements quoted in an earlier paragraph of this opinion from the *Wooden* decision. [cit.] It is open to us, therefore, particularly in view of our own strong public policy as to death action damages, to treat the measure of damages in this case as being a procedural or remedial question controlled by our own State policies. * * *

From all of this it follows that while plaintiff's second or contract cause of action is demurrable, his first count declaring under the Massachusetts wrongful death action is not only sustainable but can be enforced, if the proof so justifies, without regard to the $15,000 limit. Plaintiff, therefore, may apply if he be so advised for leave to amend his first cause of action accordingly.

The judgment appealed from should be affirmed, with costs. * * *

Notes and Questions

1. Are you convinced by the court's procedural characterization of the Arizona survival rule in *Grant* and the Massachusetts rule limiting the amount of recoverable damages in *Kilberg*? Would it be "inconvenient" or "burdensome" for California or New York, respectively, to apply Arizona's or Massachusetts' rule, respectively? Was "the effect of [not applying those rules] upon the rights of the parties * * * negligible"? Beale, supra.

2. Notice that survival of actions is not among the issues the Restatement classified as procedural. In fact, § 390 of the Restatement expressly assigned this issue to the *lex loci delicti*. The prevailing opinion throughout the United States, both before and after *Grant*, considered this to be a substantive issue. With regard to the amount of recoverable damages, the Restatement took a curious, but not surprising, position. It provided that the *lex loci delicti* determines "the measure of damages" (§ 417) (apparently because this issue is substantive), but that a statutory ceiling imposed *by the law of the forum* prevails over the measure of recoverable damages provided by the *lex loci delicti* (§ 606) (apparently on the assumption that such a

ceiling was procedural). Thus, neither *Grant* nor *Kilberg* followed the Restatement's classifications of these issues. Were the results, nevertheless, good? In *Grant*? In *Kilberg*? If the results were good, was there another way to reach them while remaining within the confines of the traditional system?

3. Read again the second-to-last sentence in the majority opinion in *Grant*, and the second paragraph of *Kilberg*. Do they offer better explanations of the real reasons behind the court's decisions than those offered by the substance/procedure gymnastics? For an affirmative and authoritative answer with regard to *Grant*, see Traynor, *Is this Conflict Really Necessary?* 670. Why then did good judges like Traynor and Desmond find it necessary to go through such strenuous and unconvincing reasoning to apply forum law?

4. What possible reasons underlie the Arizona non-survival rule in *Grant*? Could it be a notion, from the time penal law was not clearly separated from tort law, that a dead person cannot be punished? Could it be a mechanism for protecting the tortfeasor's heirs and creditors? Whatever the reason, would applying the rule in *Grant* serve that reason?

What possible reasons underlie the California survival rule? Could it be a notion that the function of tort law is to compensate rather than to punish, and that such compensation must be extracted from the tortfeasor's pocket, be he alive or dead, before providing for his heirs or creditors? If so, would applying the rule in *Grant* promote this policy?

5. Is a Statute of Frauds a procedural or a substantive rule? The Restatement classified it as procedural. See § 602, supra. In *Linn*, supra 33, the court said in footnote 3 that the forum's Statute of Frauds was substantive and thus applicable "only to contracts made in [the forum state]." Ultimately, the court applied that statute and upheld the contract under it, because the defendant was unable to prove that the contract had not been made in the forum state.

In Marie v. Garrison, 13 Abb. N.Cas. 210 (N.Y.Super.Ct.1883), the contract was unenforceable under the Statute of Frauds of both the forum state, New York, and the state in which the contract was made, Missouri. Yet, in what is widely regarded as a classic (ab)use of the substance/procedure distinction, a court appointed Referee managed to find that the contract fell between the cracks of both statutes. He found the New York statute of frauds inapplicable, because it was substantive and the contract had not been made in New York. The statute provided that "[e]very contract" of the type in question "shall be *void* unless the contract * * * be in writing." (emphasis added). The Referee asked:

> Can it fairly be said that a contract declared "void" by statute still subsists *as a contract*, and that the only effect of the statute is to deprive a party of a remedy? Is such a word as "void" a mere word of *evidence*?

> I think not. I regard the word "void" as a word of substance, and not as a mere word of procedure. In that view, the statute cannot, by accepted rules under the "Conflict of Laws," be applied to contracts made in other States, and accordingly not to the present case.

Marie, 13 Abb. N. Cas. at 257. On the other hand, the Missouri Statute of Frauds was procedural, the Referee opined, since that statute provided that "no 'action shall be brought[.]' * * * [T]he remedy *in Missouri only* is affected by these words." Id. at 279. Since the plaintiff had not sought a remedy in a Missouri forum, the Referee held that the Missouri statute of frauds was also inapplicable. *Voila!* The contract was held enforceable, although it would not have been enforceable under the statute of frauds of either state.

Vest v. St. Albans Psychiatric Hospital, Inc.
Supreme Court of Appeals of West Virginia, 1989.
182 W.Va. 228, 387 S.E.2d 282.

NEELY, J. The appellants, Otis and Pauline Vest, citizens of West Virginia, brought this action in the circuit court of Raleigh County, West Virginia, charging the defendant, a Virginia corporation, with medical malpractice occurring in the Commonwealth of Virginia. The action was dismissed because the appellants failed to comply with a notice provision of Virginia's statute on medical malpractice review panels. * * *

The Virginia legislature has established a system of medical malpractice review panels that are available to either party in a potential medical-malpractice lawsuit. *Va. Code*, 8.01–581.1 *et seq.* [1984]. A plaintiff may not bring suit against a "health-care provider" registered in Virginia without first notifying the defendant of the claim and allowing time for the case to be reviewed by a medical review panel. * * * The panel hears evidence and issues a non-binding opinion on the issues of liability and extent of injury. The panel's opinion is admissible as evidence if the matter goes to a full civil trial.

* * * The appellants seek relief here, on the ground that the notice provisions of the Virginia statute are procedural only, not substantive law, and cannot be applied to bar their action in a West Virginia court.

We now reverse the judgment below, and hold that, in a West Virginia court, a citizen of West Virginia suing a Virginia hospital for injuries sustained in Virginia need not comply with the medical review panel provisions of Virginia law.

* * * In tort cases, West Virginia courts apply the traditional choice-of-law rule, *lex loci delicti*; that is, the substantive rights between the parties are determined by the law of the place of injury. [cit.] There is no dispute that the substantive law to be applied in this case is the law of Virginia. It is just as clear that West Virginia procedure applies in all cases before West Virginia state courts, and a merely procedural rule of Virginia law would be ignored here.

A leading commentator on conflict of laws writes:

[One] type of rule often called procedural actually is designed to govern access to courts, and necessarily governs access only to courts of the state having the rule. A state can control access to its own courts but it cannot prevent courts of another state, if they have jurisdiction, from proceeding to exercise it.

R. Leflar, *American Conflicts Law*, 243–44 (3d ed. 1977). *See also* Crider v. Zurich Insurance Co., 380 U.S. 39 (1965) (Federal court in Alabama may hear action based on Georgia worker's compensation act, even though Georgia limits enforcement to its own administrative board; the Court found it compelling that the worker was an

Alabama resident, injured in Alabama, merely employed by a Georgia corporation).

* * * The decision of the Virginia legislature to close the doors of its courts to medical-malpractice plaintiffs, unless they notify the defendant before filing suit and give the defendant a chance to have a medical review panel convened, must also close the doors to the federal courts sitting in Virginia, because for that purpose they are both courts of the same sovereign, the Commonwealth of Virginia, and exercise the same personal jurisdiction. * * *

The courts of West Virginia, on other hand, are never under the sovereignty of the Commonwealth of Virginia. A defendant in a West Virginia state court, over whom this state has personal jurisdiction, is subject to the sovereignty of this state. This state may choose, under principles of comity and the broad limits of the U.S. *Constitution*, to apply in its courts the substantive law of another jurisdiction, in accord with this state's choice-of-law rules. Another state may deny plaintiffs access to its own courts, but may not by that act deny access to the courts of West Virginia. When there is a living cause of action (even though itself a creature of Virginia law), venue is proper in a West Virginia state court, and West Virginia has personal jurisdiction over the defendant, the plaintiff may bring his claim before the state courts of West Virginia and be heard. * * *

If a defendant has subjected himself to suit in West Virginia under this state's long-arm statute, and the plaintiff is a resident of West Virginia, we refuse to require the plaintiff to litigate his tort claim first before any tribunal in another state. On the other hand, in consideration of our own public policy and principles of comity, we would not permit Virginia citizens with few contacts in this state to sue Virginia "health care providers" here simply to avoid the review panel procedures required in the Commonwealth of Virginia. * * *

The basic principle in this case is that a state can control access only to its own courts. Nonetheless, the particulars of another state's alternatives to the traditional civil trial are bound to influence this Court's decision to defer to that process or not. Virginia's medical malpractice review process, we conclude, is so complicated and expensive that, once it was in motion, a plaintiff would have little choice but to remain in the Virginia courts.

For the reasons set out above, we reverse the judgment of the Circuit Court of Raleigh County and remand the case for further proceedings consistent with this opinion.

BROTHERTON, C. J., dissenting: * * * It is undisputed that the alleged injury took place in Radford, Virginia. It is also undisputed that the Fourth Circuit Court of Appeals has held that the Virginia statute requiring a medical review panel be convened to review medical malpractice suits is the *substantive* law of that state. [cit.] Consequently, the majority's decision * * * is nothing short of blatant protectionism of West Virginia residents in direct contravention of the *lex loci delicti* theory of conflicts of law. * * *

The question is not controlling "access to the courts of sister states," as the majority so coyly phrases the issue. It is a question of maintaining the integrity and predictability of the internal laws of the sister state as well as avoiding the dreaded specter of "forum shopping" to obtain the most favorable law. In this case, the plaintiff voluntarily availed himself of the benefits of the Commonwealth of Virginia, much as if he was involved in an automobile accident on Virginia roads. It is not only fitting, but legally correct, that he be subjected to the substantive law of the state where the injury occurred. * * *

I can only speculate that if the situation was reversed, and a Virginia court ignored a similar statute in our State, the majority would be appalled at the disregard for comity between two sister states. In this case, however, the majority essentially proclaims: All ye citizens of this great State who stray from the friendly confines of its boundaries and are injured in a foreign state, return home, cast out your nets, and if in the casting, the net reaches far enough to snare the corporate defendant that caused the injury, reel in the net and we will give to you "the most favored citizen" interpretation of our substantive law. Foreign defendants will know to beware of causing harm to our citizens! * * *

Notes and Questions

1. What was the purpose of the Virginia medical-review rule in *Vest*? Consider the following possibilities: (a) to facilitate the court's task by making available to it the review panel's assessment (but note that the findings of the panel are not binding on the court and that the medical-review rule has not reduced the use of medical expert testimony at trial); (b) to weed out frivolous claims (but note that the panel has no power to dismiss a claim); and (c) by delaying litigation to discourage certain plaintiffs from going to court, and thus: (i) reduce the courts' workload; and/or (ii) protect health care providers; and/or (iii) reduce medical insurance costs and overall health-care costs. Does the answer to the above question help determine whether this rule should be applied in West Virginia?

2. If Virginia's medical-review rule was procedural, as the *Vest* court held, then why would that rule prevent a Virginia plaintiff from suing in *West* Virginia, as the court opined?

3. Reverse the laws of the two states in *Vest*, so that West Virginia, the forum, has a medical-review rule but Virginia, the *locus delicti*, does not. Would, or should, the court apply this rule in this case?

4. Both the Restatement and the Restatement (Second) provide that the *lex fori* determines whether an issue shall be tried by the court or by a jury. See §§ 594 and 129, respectively. (For an application of this rule, see Vanier v. Ponsoldt, 833 P.2d 949 (Kan.1992).) What are the reasons for this rule? Practicality and convenience is one. For example, if (as in most civil-law jurisdictions) the forum state has no jury system for civil cases, it would be highly impractical, inconvenient, and perhaps dangerous to require the forum state to set up such a system for one foreign case, would it not? But if practicality and convenience were the only reasons for this rule, what about the converse case in which the forum has a jury system, but the foreign state does not. It is not impractical to try the foreign case without a jury, is it? Then why *must* such a case be tried by the jury? Does the forum have a right, or perhaps an obligation, to ensure that its proceedings are conducted according to its own notions of fair adjudication and to use its own mechanisms for discovering the truth?

If yes, should it matter whether the litigants are foreign or domestic or whether or not the case contains foreign elements?

5. The Restatement also provides that the *lex fori* governs "presumptions and inferences to be drawn from evidence," the "competency of witnesses," and the "admissibility of a particular piece of evidence." See §§ 595, 596 and 597, respectively. The Federal Rules of Evidence provide that, in diversity cases, matters of evidence are governed by the Federal Rules, except with regard to presumptions, privileges, and the competency of witnesses, which the Federal Rules expressly relegate to state law. In Barron v. Ford Motor Co. of Canada Ltd., 965 F.2d 195 (7th Cir.1992), *cert. denied*, 506 U.S. 1001 (1992), the issue was whether a North Carolina rule that prohibited evidence of a plaintiff's failure to wear a seat belt at the time of the accident was "procedural" (and thus governed by the Federal Rules) or whether it was "substantive" (and thus governed by state law). In ruling on this issue, Judge Posner said:

> A pure rule of evidence, like a pure rule of procedure, is concerned solely with accuracy and economy in litigation and should therefore be tailored to the capacities and circumstances of the particular judicial system, here the federal one; while a substantive rule is concerned with the channeling of behavior outside the courtroom, and where as in this case the behavior in question is regulated by state law rather than by federal law, state law should govern even if the case happens to be in federal court. [cit.] The North Carolina rule could be either. It is a rule of evidence if it is motivated by concern that jurors attach too much weight to a plaintiff's failure to wear his seatbelt. It is a substantive rule if it is designed not to penalize persons who fail to fasten their seatbelts. Many rules mix procedural or evidentiary with substantive policy concerns, examples being the parol evidence rule, the "mend the hold" doctrine. * * * The more broadly the North Carolina rule is interpreted, the stronger the inference that its predominant character is that of a rule of evidence. * * *

965 F.2d at 199. Judge Posner concluded that the rule was substantive because, according to North Carolina precedents, "it is founded on the desire of the North Carolina courts not to penalize the failure to fasten one's seatbelt, because nonuse is so rampant in the state that the average person could not be thought careless for failing to fasten his seatbelt." Id. at 200. Do Judge Posner's pronouncements offer a more promising basis from which to articulate the criteria for distinguishing between substance and procedure?

3. THE APPLICATION OF THE DESIGNATED LAW

a. Renvoi

In the previous subsection we saw the distinction between substantive and procedural law for conflicts purposes. In this subsection we look at the distinction between substantive (or domestic, local, or internal) law, on the one hand, and conflicts law on the other. The former is the law that applies to fully domestic cases, while the latter is the law that applies to multistate cases.

When confronted with a multistate case, the court looks to its own conflicts law and identifies the applicable statutory or judicial choice-of-law rule. This rule may refer the matter to the internal law of the forum or to the law of another state, State X. In the latter case, a question arises as to whether the reference to the law of State X is a reference to the internal law of that state or to its "whole law," that is, to *both* its substantive and its conflicts law. This is the famous *renvoi* question. This question is answered by the forum's choice-of-law rule. If the reference is to include the whole law of the other state, then it is said that the forum adheres to the doctrine of renvoi.[1]

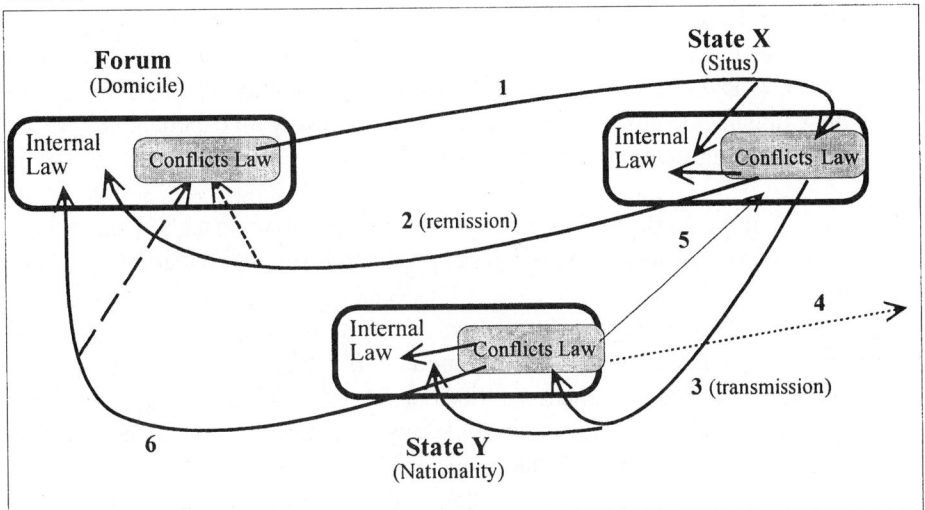

Once the forum decides to look to the conflicts law of State X, then a number of possibilities arise, depending on what that law provides. The above diagram illustrates some of these possibilities. It uses a scenario involving the succession of a domiciliary of the forum state whose estate encompasses, *inter alia*, immovables situated in State X. Suppose, as is usually the case in the Anglo–American world, that the forum's choice-of-law rule provides that succession to immovables is governed by the "whole law" of the situs state, State X. In such a case, the initial reference (see vector #1, supra) is to State X's conflicts law.

One resulting possibility is that the conflicts law of State X may refer the matter to its own internal law. If so, that law applies and the matter ends there.

A second possibility is that State X may refer the matter back to the forum state (vector #2), if, for example, State X's choice-of-law rule provides that succession is governed by the law of the decedent's last domicile. This reference back is called *remission*. Theoretically, one should ask at this point whether this remission is meant to be a reference to the internal law of the forum or to its conflicts law. If the reference is to the latter, then the possibility of the perpetually-enclosed or never-ending circle exists. In practice, however, no court, in any country, has found itself entrapped in this circle. The forum simply accepts the reference back, and

---

1. The word is French and derives from the verb *renvoyer*, which means to refer back or to refer further. The corresponding English term is *remission* or *transmission*. Their inelegance may explain why the French term has prevailed in the literature.

applies its internal law.[2]

A third possibility (vector #3) is that State X may refer the matter to the law of a third state, if, for example, State X's choice-of-law rule provides that succession is governed by the law of the decedent's last nationality and the decedent was a national of State Y, although he was domiciled in the forum state. (This reference to the third state is called *transmission*.) The question then is whether this transmission points to the internal or the conflicts law of State Y. Ordinarily, this question is answered by the conflicts law of State X, the transmitting state. If the transmission is to the conflicts law of State Y, then that law may refer the matter to its own internal law, or to the internal or conflicts law of: another state, State Z (vector #4); State X (vector #5); or the forum state (vector #6). If the reference points to the conflicts law of any of these states, then the possibility of the never-ending circle arises again, but only in the abstract. In practice, every time there is a reference back to the sending state, the internal law of that state applies and the matter ends there.

Article 5 of the Austrian conflicts codification (1978) offers a good example of these possibilities and how modern codifications handle them. That article provides in part:

> If the foreign legal order refers back, Austrian internal rules (rules excepting conflicts rules) shall be applied; if reference is made to a third jurisdiction, further references shall be considered, but the internal rules of the legal order which itself does not refer to any other law or to which another law refers back for the first time shall be determinative.

Underneath all the apparent complexity of the renvoi doctrine lies a very important philosophical question: *Should the forum resolve conflicts problems based exclusively on its own notions about which is the proper law, or should the forum consider in principle the corresponding notions of other states?* Each state's conflicts rules embody that state's notions as to which law should govern a given multistate situation. When the forum's conflicts rule designates State X as the state of the governing law, it is because: (a) the forum considers itself to be "uninterested" in the case; and (b) the forum considers State X to be more "interested."[3] In such a case, should the forum ask whether State X considers itself interested? If State X considers itself disinterested and State Y or the forum state more interested, should not the forum take into account X's disinterest? Should the forum be more Roman than the Romans?

Traditional conflicts systems, like the Greek and Spanish, take a negative stance towards renvoi.[4] The Restatement likewise rejected renvoi (§ 7) except in two areas: all questions of title to land, and matters of divorce. § 8. Apparently the Restate-

---

2. All conflicts codifications that adhere to *renvoi* provide expressly that a remission to the law of the forum is accepted and the internal law of the forum applies. See, e.g., Austrian codif. Art. 5(2); German codif. Art. 4(1)(b); Italian codif. Art. 13(1)(b); Hungarian codif., Art. 4; Swiss codif., Art. 14(1); Portuguese Civ. Code, Art. 18(1).

3. The anthropomorphic terms "interested" or "uninterested" state have a specific meaning in governmental interest analysis, which will be studied in Chapter 3. It may be argued that traditional choice-of-law rules are based on mechanical factors and do not reflect a state's genuine interest in applying its law. Nevertheless, traditional rules reflect a state's judgment, good or bad, as to how its law should operate in multistate cases.

4. See, e.g., Greek Civ. Code, art. 32; Spanish Civ. Code, art. 12(2); and Peruvian Civ. Code, art. 2048. For recent codifications that reject renvoi, see U.K. codif. § 9(5); Quebec Civ. Code Art. 3080.

ment's drafters thought that the complexities associated with renvoi would disrupt the simplicity of the system they had tried to establish. Nevertheless, as some of the cases in this subsection exemplify, courts following the Restatement have ignored its proscription of renvoi in order to avoid the results that the Restatement's rules dictated. This is why in the United States renvoi came to be viewed as an "escape device," rather than as a useful tool for attaining rational and uniform results.

The drafters of the Restatement (Second) understood the potential of renvoi in helping to attain uniformity. They put it to use, albeit in hortatory language. Section 8 of the Restatement (Second) provides in part:

> (2) When the objective of the particular choice-of-law rule is that the forum reach the same result on the very facts involved as would the courts of another state, the forum will apply the choice-of-law rules of the other state, subject to considerations of practicability and feasibility.

> (3) When the state of the forum has no substantial relationship to the particular issue or the parties and the courts of all interested states would concur in selecting the local [substantive] law rule applicable to this issue, the forum will usually apply this rule.

The Restatement (Second) implements the uniformity *desideratum* in the area of successions by providing that succession to land is governed by "the law that would be applied by the courts of the situs," see, e.g., Rest. 2d §§ 236, 239–42, and that succession to movables is governed by "the law that would be applied by the courts of the state where the decedent was domiciled at the time of death." See, e.g., Rest. 2d §§ 260, 261, 263–65.

Modern conflicts codifications in countries such as Germany, Italy, and Portugal, employ renvoi in a way that is designed to attain certain substantive results considered *a priori* to be desirable, such as favoring the validity of juridical acts or according a person the status of legitimacy.[5] In the United States, the Louisiana conflicts codification utilizes renvoi in certain cases (involving foreign immovables, status, and limitations), prohibits renvoi in all cases in which the forum legislature provides dispositive choice-of-law rules, and permits renvoi in all cases in which the legislature relegates the choice to the courts.[6] Thus, renvoi need not be an all-or-nothing proposition. Furthermore, acceptance of renvoi in principle does not entail the surrender of the choice-of-law process to the wishes of other states. The forum retains full control of this process and the freedom to decide when and how much of renvoi to accept.

Estate of Wright
Supreme Judicial Court of Maine, 1994.
637 A.2d 106.

COLLINS, J. * * * The Testator [a U.S. citizen] executed his Last Will and Testament on January 11, 1992 which provided that Maine law was to apply to the

---

5. See, e.g., German codif., Art. 4; Swiss codif., Art. 14; Italian codif., Art. 13(3); Portuguese Civ. Code, Arts. 17–19.

6. See La. Civ. Code Art. 3517 (1992), and pertinent discussion in Symeonides, *PIL Codification in a Mixed Jurisdiction*, 477–78.

administration of his estate. The Testator died on January 18, 1992 in Maine. The will did not provide for any distribution to the Children (who were the issue of a previous marriage), although it did provide for distributions to the Testator's wife and to the Testator's other children. The Children who were not provided for in the will were the beneficiaries of trusts set up by the Testator in 1960. The Testator's estate included interests in property located in France and Switzerland. The focus of the Children's argument is that they are entitled to forced shares as provided by Swiss law. Contrary to the initial assertion of the Estate, the Probate Court determined that the Testator was domiciled in Switzerland, not in Maine. Thus, Swiss law determines the validity of the choice-of-law provision. The Children argue that Swiss law would not give effect to a choice-of-law provision of a U.S. citizen domiciled in Switzerland. The Estate took the counter argument--that Swiss law would give effect to such a choice-of-law provision. The Probate Court determined that a Swiss court would give effect to such a provision. In addition, the Probate Court awarded attorney fees and expenses to the Children pursuant to 18-A M.R.S.A. § 1-601 (1981).

Swiss Law. * * * The issues presented in this appeal are determined by an 1850 Swiss–United States treaty (the "Treaty") and a Swiss federal law enacted in 1988. The Treaty, which deals partly with probate issues, provides:

> Any controversy that may arise among the claimants to the same succession, as to whom the property shall belong, *shall be decided according to the laws and by the judges of the country in which the property is situated.* (emphasis added).

At the time the Treaty was entered into, Swiss law did not allow foreigners domiciled in Switzerland to adopt a choice-of-law provision in their wills. Sometime after 1850, Swiss law began to allow such provisions. This allowance of choice-of-law provisions currently appears in Article 90 of the Swiss Federal Law on Private International Law ("Article 90"), enacted in 1988, which provides:

> The estate of a person whose last domicile is in Switzerland is subject to Swiss law. *A foreigner can nevertheless through a last will and testament * * * subject his estate to one of his national laws.* This stipulation becomes ineffective if at the time of death he is no longer a citizen of this State or has become a Swiss citizen. (emphasis added).

The Children argue that "laws" in the Treaty refers to substantive law and not to conflict-of-law rules. As such, they argue that Article 90, which is a conflict-of-law rule, cannot be applied to this case through the Treaty. Thus, the Children conclude that the substantive Swiss Civil Code, which imposes forced shares in their favor, is applicable. The Estate claims that the Treaty includes conflict-of-law rules. Both parties agree that if the Treaty incorporates Article 90, the Testator would be lawfully permitted to choose Maine law to govern the distribution of his Estate. Thus, the main issue is whether the Treaty refers to conflict-of-law rules, therefore allowing Article 90 to validate the Testator's choice-of-law provision.

Two decisions of Swiss cantonal courts hold that the Treaty applies to "substantive" law and not to conflict-of-law rules.[3] Both decisions found choice-of-law provisions in wills of U.S. citizens domiciled in Switzerland to be invalid. However, these holdings are not dispositive since they are decisions of cantonal courts, not federal courts. In Switzerland, federal courts have final authority and are not bound by cantonal decisions when ruling on federal law. Further, the persuasiveness of these cantonal decisions is undermined because Switzerland, a civil law country, does not recognize the concept of *stare decisis*, by the fact that the cantonal decisions are not recent pronouncements, and by the fact that two decisions of the New York Surrogate Court have held differently.[4]

In the absence of *stare decisis*, a Swiss federal court, in attempting to interpret the Treaty, would give some consideration to the opinions expressed in legal commentary. The Estate's expert, to whom the Probate Court attached the better reasoning and greater credibility, testified that most modern Swiss scholars and governmental authorities believe that the Treaty should be interpreted to include Swiss conflict of law rules. After reviewing the testimony and credentials of both party's experts, we also find the testimony of the Estate's expert most persuasive.

Finally, we recognize that "[t]he primary purpose of the treaty was to assure to the citizens of each country equality of treatment with the nationals of the country in which they might reside...." *In re Estate of Prince*, 267 N.Y.S.2d [138] at 141-42 [(1964)]. A finding that a U.S. citizen domiciled in Switzerland is not entitled to adopt a choice-of-law provision, which Swiss law enacted subsequent to the Treaty's adoption allows to all other foreign domiciliaries, would run counter to this purpose.

After reviewing the evidence that was presented to the Probate Court, we find that a Swiss federal court would hold that the Treaty includes conflict-of-law rules and that Article 90 applies to U.S. citizens who are domiciled in Switzerland. Thus, we find that a Swiss court would give effect to the Testator's choice-of-law provision. * * *

Judgment affirmed. All concurring.

Notes and Questions

1. As noted earlier, in cases involving succession to land, both the Restatement and the Restatement (Second) authorize the application of the "whole law" of the situs state. When the situs state is a foreign country that, like most civil-law

---

3. Kirk, 109 J.T. III 72 (1961) (relying on Rougeron); Rougeron, 81 S.J. 598 (1959) * * *; Although Article 90 was not enacted until 1988, at the time of both of these decisions there was a similar provision in Swiss law that allowed foreign citizens domiciled in Switzerland to utilize choice-of-law provisions.

4. In re Schneider's Estate, 96 N.Y.S.2d 652 (1950), * * * held that the Treaty included Swiss conflict-of-law rules. * * * Note, however, that the court made its decision based, in part, on the fact that no Swiss case had yet ruled on this issue. Id. at 661.; In re Estate of Prince, 267 N.Y.S.2d 138 (1964) allowed a U.S. citizen domiciled in Switzerland to provide that property located in the U.S. be disposed of according to N.Y. law. The court, which noted its disapproval of the Swiss Rougeron decision, stated: ...
the Swiss court's [in Rougeron] interpretation of the treaty is restrictive in character and would tend to take away from American citizens the right to freely dispose of their property. This was not the objective of the treaty and its purpose was not to deny or destroy rights possessed by citizens of either country. The primary purpose of the treaty was to assure to the citizens of each country equality of treatment with the nationals of the country in which they might reside.... It must be recognized that it is the prerogative of the Swiss courts to control personal property within their jurisdiction if they do not choose to recognize the ruling of this decision and this court does not intend its ruling to apply to any real property having a situs in Switzerland.
267 N.Y.S.2d at 141–42 (citations omitted).

countries, assigns succession issues to the law of the decedent's last domicile or nationality, and the decedent is a domiciliary or citizen of the forum state, a renvoi to the law of the forum is inevitable. Cases involving this scenario are quite common and non-controversial. See, e.g., *In re Schneider's Estate*, described in footnote 4 of the above case. *Estate of Wright* differs from these cases in that: (a) in this case the decedent was domiciled in the situs state rather than in the forum state; and (b) the case was decided not under either of the Restatements but under the Swiss-USA treaty which, as federal law, preempts state choice-of-law rules. The treaty does not *expressly* authorize renvoi. Whether the treaty is susceptible to a reading that would authorize renvoi is a much closer question than the court assumed it to be. For example, it is rather unlikely that the drafters of that treaty intended to authorize renvoi, if only because in 1850, when the treaty was drafted, renvoi was an unknown concept in judicial or legislative practice and even in conflicts literature.[1] Furthermore, treaties drafted since the time renvoi became a known concept, such as most of the conventions drafted during the 20th century under the auspices of the Hague Conference on Private International Law, typically contain an express anti-renvoi provision.[2] Such provisions make perfect sense because the very purpose of conflicts conventions is to resolve conflicts problems directly through the rules set forth in the conventions, rather than to relegate these problems to the courts of the contracting countries.

2. According to which law should one answer the question of whether the word "laws" in the treaty was meant to encompass the conflicts rules of the situs? (a) the law of the forum *qua* forum? (b) the law of the situs *qua* situs? (c) "American" law, including forum law, as the law of one of the contracting countries? or (d) Swiss law as the law of the other contracting country? Which of these options did the *Wright* court adopt?

3. Having concluded that the word "laws" in the Treaty was meant to encompass the conflicts law of Switzerland, and having correctly concluded that Article 90 of the Swiss conflicts statute is indeed a conflicts rule, the next question the *Wright* court had to consider was whether in fact a Swiss court would have applied Article 90 to a case such *Wright*. Should not this question be answered under Swiss conflicts law? How did the *Wright* court answer it? Are you persuaded by the court's conclusion? Consider the following information. Civil law systems which, like the Swiss system, adhere to the institution of forced heirship do so out of a belief that the principle that a testator should be free to dispose of his estate as he wishes should be subordinated in part to the need to ensure that children receive a certain percentage ("forced share") of their parent's estate. To the extent that the very notion of forced heirship is antithetical to the principle of honoring the testator's wishes, it is also antithetical to the notion that the testator should be allowed to evade forced heirship merely by inserting a choice-of-law clause in his testament. This is why

---

1. The French jurist Froland was the first author to have discussed this concept in connection with two French judicial decisions rendered in 1652 and 1663, but his discussion was virtually ignored for more than two centuries. The first serious discussion of this concept was provoked by the famous *Forgo* case, decided by the French *Cour de Cassation* in 1879. See Wolff, *PIL* 189–91.

2. See, e.g., art. 17 of the Hague Convention on the Law Applicable to the Estates of Deceased Persons (1989); art. 15 of the Hague Convention on the Law Applicable to Contracts for the International Sale of Goods (1986); art. 17 of the Hague Convention on the Law Applicable to Trusts and their Recognition (1985).

these systems do not honor such clauses. Switzerland does not expressly prohibit such clauses and Article 90, if read in isolation, would seem to permit them. However, Article 90 should be read together with Articles 17 and 18 of the same statute which provide, respectively, that "[t]he application of provisions of foreign law is excluded if it leads to a result that is incompatible with the Swiss public policy (*ordre public*)," and that "[t]he present statute does not prejudice those mandatory provisions of Swiss law, which, in light of their particular purpose, are applicable irrespective of the law designated by the present statute." You will study the "public policy exception" in Section C, infra, but even without knowing much about that concept, would you not suspect that the Swiss forced heirship provision could be considered a rule of public policy or a "mandatory provision"? Would it make a difference whether or not the children were domiciled in Switzerland? In any event, if you represented the children would you have invoked Articles 17-18, or would you have placed all your eggs in the renvoi basket and concede that, "if the Treaty incorporates Article 90, the Testator would be lawfully permitted to choose Maine law to govern the distribution of his Estate"?

American Motorists Ins. Co. v. ARTRA Group, Inc.
Court of Appeals of Maryland, 1995.
338 Md. 560. 659 A.2d 1295.

CHASANOW, J. [American Motorists Insurance Company ("American Motorists"), an Illinois corporation, brought an action for a declaratory judgment seeking a declaration that certain insurance policies issued by it to the ARTRA Group, Inc. ("ARTRA"), also an Illinois corporation, did not provide coverage for soil and groundwater contamination caused by the operation of ARTRA's paint-manufacturing factory. The factory was situated in Maryland and the policies insuring it were issued in Illinois between 1976 and 1985. Under the internal law of Illinois, but not Maryland, these policies would be interpreted as requiring American Motorists to provide coverage.] * * * ARTRA asserted that, under the doctrine of *lex loci contractus*, Illinois law controlled the substantive issues * * *. In response, American Motorists moved for summary judgment and argued that the court should apply the principle of renvoi and that a Maryland court should look to the entire body of Illinois law, including Illinois conflict of law principles and determine whether Illinois would apply Maryland law for a decision on the coverage issues presented. American Motorists argued that, in the instant case, Illinois would apply the law of Maryland to the underlying dispute since Illinois conflict of law rules apply the "most significant contacts" test of Restatement (Second) Conflict of Laws §§ 188 and 193 (1971). * * * Thus, American Motorists argued because, under § 193, the validity of and rights created by an insurance policy are determined by the law of the state where the risk is located and because the risk of pollution was located in Maryland, Illinois choice-of-law rules would dictate the application of Maryland law to the substantive issues in the case. * * *

[The trial court agreed with American Motorists but the Court of Special Appeals, Maryland's intermediate court, reversed, finding that the doctrine of renvoi was not accepted in Maryland and that under the *lex loci contractus* rule followed in Maryland the case was governed by "the substantive law of Illinois but not * * * Illinois's choice-of-law rules." American Motorists petitioned for a writ of certiorari, which was granted by Maryland's highest court, the Court of Appeals.]

I. In determining the issues presented in the instant case, we initially point out that, for the purpose of this opinion, we must assume that Illinois choice-of-law rules would dictate the application of Maryland law to the substantive issues in the present case. * * *

American Motorists's first suggestion is that we recognize that the rule of *lex loci contractus* is antiquated and should be abandoned in favor of some form of the more modern approaches to choice of law such as the one advocated by Restatement (Second) Conflict of Laws. * * * Based on our holding on the *renvoi* issue, we need not give any consideration to the intriguing question of whether Maryland's traditional *lex loci contractus* test should be abandoned in favor of one of the "modern" most significant relationship tests. American Motorists's second suggestion is that we engraft the doctrine of *renvoi* to our body of conflict of law rules. We need not determine today how far we should go in incorporating the doctrine of *renvoi*, but we do adopt a limited form of *renvoi* * * * which permits us to apply Maryland law where the application of *lex loci contractus* indicates that the foreign jurisdiction would apply Maryland law to the substantive issues of the controversy.

* * * It has been suggested that *renvoi* could have the danger of creating an endless cycle. In the instant case, Maryland choice-of-law rules apply the doctrine of *lex loci contractus* and, pursuant thereto, apply Illinois law. In applying Illinois law, we also adopt Illinois choice of law, which would apply Maryland law, which applies Illinois law, and back and forth. What breaks the endless cycle? As shall be seen, we adopt a limited form of *renvoi* in the instant case that does not have the endless cycle.

* * * Where the forum would apply the law of the foreign jurisdiction and the foreign jurisdiction would apply the law of the forum, it would seem that the balance should tip in favor of the jurisdiction with the most significant contacts or, if not to the jurisdiction with the most significant contacts, then for ease of application and to prevent forum shopping, the law of the forum should be applied. In the instant case, Maryland is apparently the jurisdiction with the most significant contacts as well as the forum. Maryland courts should, in applying Illinois law, apply Illinois' most significant relationship choice-of-law rule and follow the law an Illinois court would follow if the case was instituted in Illinois—Maryland law. Thus, whether suit was filed in Maryland or Illinois, Maryland law would govern the contract.

In our situation, there may not even be a real "conflict." In the absence of some reason to apply foreign law, Maryland courts would ordinarily apply Maryland substantive law, and there is no reason to apply the substantive law of a foreign state if that foreign state recognizes that Maryland has the most significant interest in the issues and that Maryland substantive law ought to be applied to the contract issues. * * *

ARTRA contends that failure to apply a strict *lex loci contractus* test in the instant case would be unfair because ARTRA allegedly had some expectation that Illinois law would govern these insurance contracts. This contention is unpersuasive, at best, because if American Motorists had filed its declaratory judgment action in

Illinois then, as was held below, Maryland law would have been applied to the coverage issues, since Illinois applies the law of the state with the most significant contacts and the location of the risk, i.e., Maryland. For consistency and to prevent forum shopping when the action is filed in Maryland, our courts also ought to apply Maryland substantive law when the place of contracting would apply Maryland law to resolve the dispute had suit been filed in that jurisdiction.

It is axiomatic that Maryland law is Maryland law because our courts and legislature believe the rules of substantive law we apply are the best of the available alternatives. From this fundamental principle, it is safe to assume our courts would prefer to follow Maryland law unless there is some good reason why Maryland law should yield to the law of a foreign jurisdiction. Our own substantive law is not only more familiar to and easier for Maryland judges to apply, but there has been a legislative or judicial determination that it is preferable to the available alternatives. Sometimes, however, there are good reasons why our courts should, and do, apply the law of a foreign jurisdiction. First, if Maryland does not defer to other states when they have a significant interest, they might not defer to Maryland when we have a significant interest. Second, we should discourage forum shopping and strive for some uniformity and predictability in resolving conflict of law issues regardless of where suit is filed. For simplicity, predictability, and uniformity in contract law, Maryland courts have, as have a majority of other state courts, followed the rule of *lex loci contractus* and have applied the substantive law of the place of contracting. In declining to apply Maryland law to a contract made in another state, we do so not because we deem the law of the other state preferable to Maryland law, but because our preference for Maryland law is outweighed by considerations of simplicity, predictability and uniformity. Where, however, the place of contracting applies Maryland law, then simplicity, predictability, and uniformity would be better achieved if Maryland courts followed the conflict of law rule of the place of contracting and apply Maryland law. In that case, there would be uniformity in choice of law regardless of in which jurisdiction suit was filed, and where, as in the instant case, suit was filed in Maryland, then Maryland courts would be applying Maryland law.

The limited *renvoi* exception which we adopt today will allow Maryland courts to avoid the irony of applying the law of a foreign jurisdiction when that jurisdiction's conflict of law rules would apply Maryland law. Under this exception, Maryland courts should apply Maryland substantive law to contracts entered into in foreign states jurisdictions [sic] in spite of the doctrine of *lex loci contractus* when:

    1) Maryland has the most significant relationship, or, at least, a substantial relationship with respect to the contract issue presented; and

    2) The state where the contract was entered into would not apply its own substantive law, but instead would apply Maryland substantive law to the issue before the court.

Our holding that Maryland's adherence to *lex loci contractus* must yield to a test such as Restatement (Second) Conflict of Laws § 188 when the place of contracting would apply Maryland law pursuant to that test is not a total jettisoning of *lex loci* *contractus.*[5] * * *

* * * *Lex loci contractus* is still the law in the majority of jurisdictions, although there is a significant modern erosion of the rule. If that erosion continues, however, this Court may, in the proper case, have to reevaluate what the best choice-of-law rules ought to be to achieve simplicity, predictability, and uniformity.

[The court then applied Maryland substantive law and held that under that law American Motors was not required to provide coverage.]

Judgement of the Court of Special Appeals Reversed. Case remanded to that court with instructions to affirm the judgment of the Circuit Court. * * *

RAKER, J., dissenting: * * * Today, the majority fails to shed new "light" on the murky maze of Conflict of Laws. Instead, in an unwarranted departure from the bedrock of Maryland choice of law in contract cases—*lex loci contractus*—the majority adopts a "limited *renvoi* exception." [cit.] In so doing, it unwisely qualifies a solid, predictable rule in favor of the often criticized and rejected doctrine of *renvoi*. In my view, it makes no "sense" in the instant case to curtail Maryland's well-established rule. * * *

I believe that today's decision will lead to uncertainty, confusion, and unpredictability. Accordingly, I respectfully dissent.

Braxton v. Anco Electric, Inc.
Supreme Court of North Carolina, 1991.
330 N.C. 124, 409 S.E.2d 914.

MARTIN, J. [The plaintiff, a resident of North Carolina, was injured in a construction site accident in Virginia, while working for a North Carolina corporation that was a subcontractor of another North Carolina corporation. After receiving worker's compensation benefits under North Carolina law, the plaintiff brought this negligence action against defendant, another North Carolina corporation, that was also a subcontractor of the same general contractor as plaintiff's employer. Under North Carolina law, the defendant would not be considered to be the plaintiff's "statutory employer" and thus would not be shielded from liability by the "exclusive remedy bar" of that state's workers' compensation statute. In contrast, under Virginia law, the defendant would be immune from a negligence suit by plaintiff because that state's workers' compensation statute extends the definition of "statutory employer" to include all subcontractors working under the general contractor's umbrella. Following the *lex loci delicti* rule, the district court dismissed plaintiff's action. The intermediate court reversed, holding that North Carolina law should apply because of that state's "overriding state interests and public policy reasons."] * * * We affirm, but for partially different and additional reasons.

---

5. At least one author has recognized that a jurisdiction may maintain its adherence to the rule of *lex loci contractus* while nonetheless recognizing the choice-of-law rules of an interested jurisdiction: "Many states using the traditional rules simply have not switched over to a more modern approach. By looking at the choice-of-law rule of another concerned jurisdiction, a court adhering to the traditional approach may be enlightened. Even if a state has recently reaffirmed its commitment to a traditional approach, giving some deference to how the case would have been decided in another concerned court improves interstate relations by demonstrating respect for the foreign jurisdiction's whole law." (Footnote omitted). Rhoda S. Barish, Comment, Renvoi and the Modern Approaches to Choice-of-Law, 30 Am. U. L. Rev. 1049, 1075–76 (1981).

* * * We do not hesitate in holding that as to the tort law controlling the rights of the litigants in the lawsuit allowed by this decision, the long-established doctrine of *lex loci delicti commissi* applies, and Virginia law controls. [cit.] But in regard to the "exclusive remedy bar" imposed by statute, we turn to our own statute for an answer.

We hold that plaintiff, as a North Carolina worker covered by its workers' compensation statute, is entitled to the protections afforded by our statute with regard to the question of whether his cause of action is eliminated by a particular workers' compensation plan. The question we decide arises in the context of the "mutual concessions" inherent in the workers' compensation design wherein an employee trades off his common law right of recovery in tort for the assurance that any work-related injury, regardless of fault, will be compensated. In this regard we view plaintiff as a beneficiary of the particular bargain which North Carolina has struck between the rights of employees as potential plaintiffs seeking to recover in tort for work-related injuries and the rights of employers and third-parties as potential tortfeasors seeking to escape liability by virtue of the blanket provision of compensation for such injuries. To determine whether the law says that plaintiff, in return for collecting workers' compensation benefits, has traded away his right to sue in this situation, we look to the law which guarantees his receipt of those benefits, which is the law of North Carolina.

Public policy considerations point to the same result. All the parties are North Carolina citizens; the plaintiff's contract of employment and the contracts giving rise to the workers' compensation coverage were signed here; and the plaintiff was receiving benefits under our workers' compensation statute. Under these circumstances, North Carolina's interests in implementing the protections afforded by our statute are paramount. Mr. Braxton's temporary presence in Virginia so as to carry out his employment contract does not strip him of the rights he otherwise enjoys under the North Carolina workers' compensation statute with regard to the breadth of our state's exclusive remedy bar on common law actions in tort. * * *

[T]he Supreme Court of Virginia has actually ruled on a case like the one at bar. Our holding is also consistent with that ruling. In *Solomon v. Call*, 166 S.E. 467 (Va.1932), a traveling salesman from Pennsylvania was injured due to the negligence of certain third-parties in an automobile accident while on assignment in Virginia. Mr. Solomon received workers' compensation benefits from Pennsylvania. The same conflict of laws arose between Virginia's bar of suits against third-party tortfeasors and Pennsylvania's adherence to common law in this regard. Although the accident occurred in Virginia, the Virginia court decided to apply Pennsylvania law and allow the claim, based on the facts that, "[t]he plaintiff's employment was under a Pennsylvania contract, with a Pennsylvania employer and embraced within the terms of the Workmen's Compensation Act of that state. His contract of employment was entirely foreign to the state of Virginia and clearly outside of the Virginia Workmen's Compensation Act." *Solomon* [supra]. The same is true in the present case. * * *

Thus, the workers' compensation law of North Carolina governs the question of whether this action has been precluded by statute; it has not. The Court of Appeals was correct in reversing the judgment of the trial court dismissing the plaintiff's case.

We also arrive at the same conclusion when applying classic conflict of laws *renvoi.* [cit.]

We begin with the traditional doctrine of *lex loci delicti commissi*, which takes us to Virginia law. Taking into consideration the whole law of Virginia, including its conflict of laws jurisprudence, we inquire as to what Virginia's court of last resort would do when faced with the question of an injured employee's ability to sue a third-party tortfeasor in a case in which the injury occurred in one state but the employment contract(s), the residences of the parties, and the workers' compensation benefits were associated with another jurisdiction. To resolve this issue, Virginia's conflict of laws policy looks to the workers' compensation law of the state in which the plaintiff was covered by the act and in which he received benefits. *Solomon v. Call*, [supra]. In so doing, the Virginia court would find that in the present case, the law of North Carolina under which the plaintiff became covered by workers' compensation and under which he received benefits, would allow the suit against an allegedly negligent third-party tortfeasor. Applying *renvoi*, we hold that plaintiff stated a cause of action under N.C.R.Civ.P. 12(b)(6), and we affirm the decision of the Court of Appeals. AFFIRMED.

MEYER, J., dissenting. * * * It is indeed ironic that the majority rushes to embrace this anachronistic and much-criticized doctrine [of renvoi], while at the same time renouncing the well-settled body of law surrounding *lex loci*. Surely the majority cannot escape the irony of its application of *renvoi* insofar as it reinforces the importance of the law of the situs, requiring as it does that Virginia's conflict of laws policy deserves deference, but not its substantive law. The majority places itself in the shoes of the Virginia court and prophesies that, because of plaintiff's eligibility for and receipt of North Carolina workers' compensation benefits, that court would apply North Carolina law rather than the law of Virginia. This convenient remission to North Carolina law by the majority cannot be taken as anything less than result-oriented. * * *

Notes and Questions

1. What are the best theoretical arguments the *ARTRA* court offers in favor of adopting renvoi? What counter-arguments do you have?

2. The *ARTRA* court states that renvoi "will allow Maryland courts to avoid the irony of applying the law of a foreign jurisdiction when that jurisdiction's conflict of law rules would apply Maryland law." Is it also ironic that, under *ARTRA*, the decision whether to apply Maryland law depends in large part on Illinois' rather than Maryland's choice-of-law rules? Would it not be preferable if Maryland's highest court were itself to reform Maryland's judicially-adopted choice-of-law rule rather than to depend on the "enlightenment" provided by "'the choice-of-law rule of another concerned jurisdiction'"? *ARTRA*, fn. 5. Does the *ARTRA* court explain why it chose to adopt this limited exception to the *lex loci contractus* rule rather than to "jettison" the rule altogether? Is the explanation convincing? Why? Suppose that rather than adopting a "modern" approach, Illinois had retained the *lex loci contractus* rule but somehow would have applied Maryland law? Do you think that the *ARTRA* court would have adopted the renvoi exception in such a case? Incidentally, slightly more than a month before the Maryland Court of Appeals decided *ARTRA*, the Supreme Court of Illinois had held that an environmental

insurance policy that (like the policy involved in *ARTRA*) was issued in Illinois to an Illinois insured by an insurer doing business in that state, was governed by Illinois law, even with regard to risks situated in other states. See Lapham-Hickey Steel Corp. v. Protection Mutual Ins. Co., 655 N.E.2d 842, 845 (Ill.1995). Apparently this decision was not brought to the *ARTRA* court's attention. On another matter, the court's statement that "[*l*]ex loci contractus is still the law in the majority of jurisdictions" was erroneous, at least if the court was referring to United States jurisdictions. In 1995, only ten such jurisdictions followed the *lex loci contractus* rule. See Symeonides, *Choice of Law in 1995*, at 198.

3. The *ARTRA* court stated that under its renvoi exception, a Maryland court should apply Maryland substantive law to contracts entered into in another state when: "1) Maryland has the most significant * * * or, at least, a substantial relationship with respect to the contract issue presented; and 2) The state where the contract was entered into * * * would apply Maryland substantive law to the issue before the court." Is the Maryland court to make its own determination of whether Maryland has a significant relationship or should that determination be made according to the other state's choice-of-law rules? If the court is to make its own determination and it concludes that Maryland has the most significant relationship then why shouldn't that determination suffice for applying Maryland substantive law? If that determination is to be made according to the other state's choice-of-law rules and those rules refer to Maryland law, then why should it matter whether that reference is based on the existence of a significant relationship, significant interests, or any other factor, such as a difference in localizing the *locus contractus*?

4. Does *ARTRA* prove that exceptions or "escapes" such as renvoi help to prolong the life of bad choice-of-law rules? If bad rules are to be retained, however, does renvoi also help to improve them in the meantime?

Does *ARTRA* justify the perception prevailing in the United States that renvoi is merely an "escape device" to be employed whenever the traditional choice-of-law rules produce substantively undesirable results? What was so desirable about the *ARTRA* result? Did the use of renvoi in that case relieve an Illinois insurer from defending and indemnifying an Illinois insured who thus might be unable to indemnify a Maryland manufacturer for cleaning up a contaminated site in Maryland? Did the court's holding make it more or less likely that, if the site is to be cleaned up at all, Maryland parties would bear the costs? Was the *ARTRA* court oblivious to these considerations, or did the court consciously subordinate them to the interest of being substantively neutral to all parties?

5. Compare the use of renvoi in *Estate of Wright*, *ARTRA*, and *Braxton*. From the perspective of choice-of-law methodology, what differences do you see between the two cases? In which of these cases did renvoi have more of a bearing on the outcome? Which case reached the better result? Why?

6. Leaving aside renvoi, compare *Braxton* with *Carroll*. Which of the two cases reached the better result? Which of the two cases offered better reasoning?

7. What do you think of Justice Meyer's dissenting argument in *Braxton* that renvoi "reinforces the importance of the law of the situs [of the tort], requiring as it does that [the situs]'s conflict of laws policy deserves deference, but not its substantive law"? Does *ARTRA* provide a good response to this argument? What do you think of Justice Meyer's accusation that "[t]his convenient remission to [forum]

law by the majority cannot be taken as anything less than result-oriented"?

8. At the time *Haumschild*, supra 48, was decided, both Wisconsin and California adhered to the *lex loci delicti* rule. They differed only in characterizing the intrafamily immunity issue as one of tort in Wisconsin, and one of status in California. Inspired mostly by the California case of Emery v. Emery, 289 P.2d 218 (Cal.1955), Justice Currie, writing for the majority in *Haumschild*, re-characterized the issue as one of status. Yet the majority explicitly disassociated itself from renvoi because of the "never ending circle" problem. The majority thought that adopting renvoi would require the court to go back and forth between Wisconsin and California law: "Applying such principle the court is referred back to Wisconsin law * * *. Again the court applies Wisconsin law and * * * would have to again refer to California law." *Haumschild*, 95 N.W.2d at 820. Is renvoi a train that aimlessly goes back and forth between the various states? Does not *ARTRA* prove that nothing prohibits Justice Currie from getting off when the train returns to Wisconsin?

Justice Fairchild, who concurred in *Haumschild*, found the majority's re-characterization problematic, because, *inter alia*, it would require Wisconsin's courts to apply the law of the spouses' domicile in the converse case in which the spouses are domiciled in an immunity state and have an accident in Wisconsin. Id. at 821. To avoid such a result, Fairchild would dispose of *Haumschild* "upon the theory that California law governs the existence of the alleged cause of action and that in California the immunity question cannot be decided by resort to the law of torts but rather the law of status." Id. at 822. Is Fairchild's formula a form of renvoi, or is it simply characterization according to the *lex causae* rather than the *lex fori*? Whatever it is, is this formula better for future cases than that of the majority? If yes, how? If not, why?

9. You recall that in *Folk*, supra 50, the plaintiff, invoking *Haumschild*, argued strenuously that her action for loss of consortium was "so intimately associated with the family relationship that it involves a matter of family law to which the law of the marriage domicile [Delaware] should be applied," rather than the law of Pennsylvania, where her husband's injury had occurred. After the court rejected this argument, the plaintiff used the renvoi argument. She argued that "if the law of Pennsylvania governs as to whether or not she has a cause of action, then all the law of Pennsylvania, including its rule as to conflicts of law, should govern. Since Pennsylvania in its conflicts law applies the 'most significant contact' rule [cit.], it would apply Delaware law since Delaware is the place with the most significant contacts." Relying on Beale and the Restatement, the *Folk* majority rejected this argument as well, because the adoption of renvoi would "effectively emasculate" the *lex loci delicti* rule which the court then followed. See *Folk*, 239 A.2d at 240. Did the adoption of renvoi in *ARTRA* also "emasculate" the *lex loci contractus* rule Maryland followed? What about the *Braxton* court's reliance on renvoi?

10. Compare *Haumschild* with *Folk*. Their facts and issues are almost identical. Both cases rejected renvoi, but they reached opposite results. Which of the two cases was better reasoned? Why?

11. At the time *Carroll* was decided, both Alabama, the forum, and Mississippi, the place of the injury, followed the *lex loci delicti* rule. *Carroll* followed a localization sub-rule that placed the tort at the place of impact, and applied the law of Mississippi, where the impact had occurred. Suppose that Mississippi followed

a different localization sub-rule, e.g., the place-of-conduct rule. If *Carroll* were to follow this rule, would this be a form of renvoi?

12. Recall *Fitts*, supra 26, in which an Alabama court applied Florida law to a wrongful death/product liability action arising from a Florida air crash, even though, under its "most significant relationship" approach, a Florida court would have likely applied Alabama law. In Nailen v. Ford Motor Co., 690 F.Supp. 552 (S.D.Miss. 1988), the wrongful death occurred in Mississippi, which, like Florida, had adopted the "most significant relationship" approach. Plaintiff's mother, an Alabama domiciliary, was killed in a traffic accident in Mississippi, while driving from Alabama to Texas. More than two years after the accident and more than a year after he had been discharged as administrator of his mother's estate, plaintiff, also an Alabama domiciliary, filed a wrongful death action in Mississippi against Ford , the manufacturer of his mother's car. The action would be timely under Mississippi's six-year limitation period for tort actions but would be untimely under Alabama's two-year limitation for wrongful death actions and Alabama's one-year limitation for tort actions in general. The plaintiff argued that the court should apply Mississippi law, either independently through Mississippi's most-significant-relationship approach or through a renvoi via Alabama's choice-of-law rules. He contended that, under those rules, an Alabama court would apply Mississippi law, both because Alabama is a *lex loci delicti* state, and because Alabama's wrongful death statute is expressly made inapplicable to deaths occurring outside Alabama. Following Mississippi's most significant relationship approach, the trial court applied Alabama law and dismissed the action as untimely. The court rejected plaintiff's renvoi argument, including his invocation of Subsections (2) and (3) of § 8 of the Restatement (Second) (quoted supra at 69), which authorize renvoi when the forum's objective is to "reach the same result as the courts of another state" or when the forum has "no substantial relationship to the particular issue or the parties." The court found both subsections inapplicable, reasoning as follows:

> Subsection 2 says essentially that if the objective is for all interested courts to reach the same result then the choice-of-law rules of the other state will be applied by the forum court. An examination of *Mitchell v. Craft*, 211 So.2d 509 (Miss.1968) [the case in which Mississippi abandoned the *lex loci* rule], and its progeny, suggests that the objective of a Mississippi court in applying Mississippi's conflict of laws rules is not necessarily uniformity with other courts but rather so that all relevant facts can be considered, and that government interests can be protected. In fact, in *Mitchell* it was repeatedly stated that the application of the *lex loci delicti* analysis, as used in Alabama, bears little relationship to any relevant considerations for choosing one law against another in a torts-conflicts case. [cit.] There can be no doubt but that Mississippi adopted the "center of gravity" or "most substantial contacts" analysis to avoid reaching the same result as would a state bound by conflict of laws rules which require applying the substantive law of the place whereof [sic.] the injury occurred and nowhere else.

> Subsection 3 has no application to the case at bar because it is invoked only where the forum state has no substantial relationship to the particular issues or parties and where all interested states would concur in selecting the applicable local law. Although under Mississippi's conflicts analysis the "center of gravity"

or "most substantial contacts" in this case requires the application of Alabama's substantive law, that does not mean to imply that Mississippi does not have a substantial interest, as the forum state, in applying its conflict of laws rules. To that end Mississippi becomes an "interested state" and, as previously discussed, will not permit, under its conflict of laws rules, the application of its local or substantive law to this action.

Id. at 557. What do you think of each of the above quoted paragraphs? Is renvoi appropriate when the non-forum state follows a mechanical rule, such as the *lex loci delicti*? Most experts answer this question in the negative. See, e.g., von Mehren, *Renvoi*. What about the converse situation in which, as in *ARTRA*, the forum adheres to a mechanical rule? Is renvoi more appropriate in that case?

13. On appeal, Mr. Nailen re-urged his renvoi argument, but the Court of Appeals rejected it rather summarily and affirmed the dismissal of his action. See Nailen v. Ford Motor Co., 873 F.2d 94 (5th Cir.1989). Was *Nailen* a case in which renvoi was invoked as an "escape device" by the plaintiff rather than by the court? Was the court correct in not playing this game? Since the plaintiff wanted to have the *lex loci delicti* applied to his case and since Alabama was a *lex loci delicti* state, why did the plaintiff not file in Alabama, which was also his home state? Would his action have been time-barred had he filed in Alabama? As mentioned above, the traditional view is that statutes of limitation are procedural and thus the forum applies its own statute of limitation even to actions governed by foreign law. See Restatement §§ 603–04. Both Alabama and Mississippi adhere to this view (although Mississippi has abandoned the traditional theory in tort conflicts). In one instance, however, the traditional theory requires the application of the shorter limitation of the foreign state, if that period qualifies as being "substantive." A time limitation that is "built-in" a wrongful death statute is a typical example of such a "substantive" limitation. The Alabama Supreme Court has so held with regard to the two-year limitation contained in the Alabama wrongful death statute. See Downtown Nursing Home, Inc. v. Pool, 375 So.2d 465, 466 (Ala.1979), *cert. denied* 445 U.S. 930 (1980). The Mississippi wrongful death statute contains no time limitation (built-in or otherwise), but the Mississippi Supreme Court has, under the above rationale, applied the shorter built-in limitation of the wrongful death statutes of the state of the *locus delicti*. See Louisville & Nashville R.R. Co. v. Dixon, 150 So. 811, 812 (Miss.1933). In light of the above information, if Mr. Nailen were to file his action in Alabama, would that state apply: (a) its own two-year statute of limitation for wrongful death actions; (b) Mississippi's six-year statute of limitation; or (c) Alabama's one-year general statute of limitation for torts in general?

b. The Ordre Public Reservation

Loucks v. Standard Oil Co. of New York
Court of Appeals of New York, 1918.
224 N.Y. 99, 120 N.E. 198.

CARDOZO, J. The action is brought to recover damages for injuries resulting in death. The plaintiffs are the administrators of the estate of Everett A. Loucks. Their intestate, while traveling on a highway in the state of Massachusetts, was run down and killed through the negligence of the defendant's servants then engaged in its business. He left a wife and two children, residents of New York. A statute of Massachusetts [cit.] provides that "if a person * * * causes the death of a person who is in the exercise of due care, * * * he * * * shall be liable in damages in the sum of not less than $500, nor more than $10,000, to be assessed with reference to the degree of his * * * culpability, * * *." The question is whether a right of action under that statute may be enforced in our courts. * * *

A tort committed in one state creates a right of action that may be sued upon in another unless public policy forbids. That is the generally accepted rule in the United States. (Huntington v. Attrill, 146 U.S. 657, 670 [1903]) * * *.

A foreign statute is not law in this state, but it gives rise to an obligation, which, if transitory, "follows the person and may be enforced wherever the person may be found." [cit.]. "No law can exist as such except the law of the land; but ... it is a principle of every civilized law that vested rights shall be protected," Beale, supra, § 51. The plaintiff owns something, and we help him to get it. [cit.] We do this unless some sound reason of public policy makes it unwise for us to lend our aid. "The law of the forum is material only as setting a limit of policy beyond which such obligations will not be enforced there." Sometimes, we refuse to act where all the parties are non-residents. [cit.] That restriction need not detain us: in this case all are residents. If aid is to be withheld here, it must be because the cause of action in its nature offends our sense of justice or menaces the public welfare. [cit.].

Our own scheme of legislation may be different. We may even have no legislation on the subject. That is not enough to show that public policy forbids us to enforce the foreign right. A right of action is property. If a foreign statute gives the right, the mere fact that we do not give a like right is no reason for refusing to help the plaintiff in getting what belongs to him. We are not so provincial as to say that every solution of a problem is wrong because we deal with it otherwise at home. Similarity of legislation has indeed this importance: its presence shows beyond question that the foreign statute does not offend the local policy. But its absence does not prove the contrary. It is not to be exalted into an indispensable condition. The misleading word "comity" has been responsible for much of the trouble. It has been fertile in suggesting a discretion unregulated by general principles (Beale, Conflict of Laws, § 71).

The sovereign in its discretion may refuse its aid to the foreign right. [cit.]. From this it has been an easy step to the conclusion that a like freedom of choice has been confided to the courts. But that, of course, is a false view. [cit.]. The courts are not free to refuse to enforce a foreign right at the pleasure of the judges, to suit the individual notion of expediency or fairness. They do not close their doors unless help would violate some fundamental principle of justice, some prevalent conception of good morals, some deep-rooted tradition of the common weal.

This test applied, there is nothing in the Massachusetts statute that outrages the public policy of New York. We have a statute which gives a civil remedy where death is caused in our own state. We have thought it so important that we have now imbedded it in the Constitution Const. art. 1, § 18. The fundamental policy is that there shall be some atonement for the wrong. Through the defendant's negligence, a resident of New York has been killed in Massachusetts. He has left a widow and children who are also residents. The law of Massachusetts gives them a recompense for his death. It cannot be that public policy forbids our courts to help in collecting what belongs to them. We cannot give them the same judgment that our law would give if the wrong had been done here. Very likely we cannot give them as much. But that is no reason for refusing to give them what we can. We shall not make things better by sending them to another state, where the defendant may not be found, and where suit may be impossible. Nor is there anything to shock our sense of justice in the possibility of a punitive recovery. The penalty is not extravagant. It conveys no hint of arbitrary confiscation. [cit.]. It varies between moderate limits according to the defendant's guilt. We shall not feel the pricks of conscience if the offender pays the survivors in proportion to the measure of his offense.

We have no public policy that prohibits exemplary damages or civil penalties.

We give them for many wrongs. To exclude all penal actions would be to wipe out the distinction between the penalties of public justice and the remedies of private law. Finally, there are no difficulties of procedure that stand in the way. We have a statute authorizing the triers of the facts, when statutory penalties are sued for, to fit the award to the offense (Code Civ. Pro. § 1898). The case is not one where special remedies established by the foreign law are incapable of adequate enforcement except in the home tribunals. [cit.].

We hold, then, that public policy does not prohibit the assumption of jurisdiction by our courts, and that this being so, mere differences of remedy do not count. * * * The fundamental public policy is perceived to be that rights lawfully vested shall be everywhere maintained. At least, that is so among the states of the Union. [cit.]. There is a growing conviction that only exceptional circumstances should lead one of the states to refuse to enforce a right acquired in another. * * *

The judgment of the Appellate Division should be reversed, and the order of the Special Term affirmed, with costs in the Appellate Division and in this court.

Kilberg v. Northeast Airlines, Inc.

Court of Appeals of New York, 1961.
9 N.Y.2d 34, 211 N.Y.S.2d 133, 172 N.E.2d 526.
(For the main body of the opinion, see supra at 60).

DESMOND, C.J. * * * Our courts should if possible provide protection for our own State's people against unfair and anachronistic treatment of the lawsuits which result from these disasters. There is available, we find, a way of accomplishing this conformably to our State's public policy and without doing violence to the accepted pattern of conflict of law rules.

Since both Massachusetts [cit.] and New York [cit.] authorize wrongful death suits against common carriers, the only controversy is as to amount of damages recoverable. New York's public policy prohibiting the imposition of limits on such damages is strong, clear and old. Since the Constitution of 1894, our basic law has been (N. Y. Const., art. I, § 16; N. Y. Const. [1894], art. I, § 18) that "The right of action now existing to recover damages for injuries resulting in death shall never be abrogated; and the amount recoverable shall not be subject to any statutory limitation." Each later revision of the State Constitution has included this same prohibition against limitations of death action damages. The reasons for its adoption are set forth in the proceedings of the 1894 Constitutional Convention [cit.]. New York's original wrongful death law (L. 1847, ch. 450), passed very soon after Lord Campbell's Act became law in Great Britain, had like the latter no restriction as to damages. The Legislature later imposed such limits but the convention which drew the 1894 Constitution rejected and forbade them. "The argument which evidently controlled the convention in its action consisted of the claim that the arbitrary limitation was absurd and unjust in measuring the pecuniary values of all lives to the next of kin by the same arbitrary standard" (Justice Hatch in Medinger opinion, supra, p. 46). The absurdity and injustice have become increasingly apparent in the six decades that have followed. For our courts to be limited by this damage ceiling (at least as to our own domiciliaries) is so completely contrary to our public policy that we should refuse to apply that part of the Massachusetts law. [cit.] The Massachusetts cases likewise say that Massachusetts will enforce the *lex loci delicti* in wrongful death suits unless Massachusetts public policy forbids [cit.].

* * * We will still require plaintiff to sue on the Massachusetts statute but we refuse on public policy grounds to enforce one of its provisions as to damages. * * *

Owen v. Owen
Supreme Court of South Dakota, 1989.
444 N.W.2d 710.

MORGAN, J. [Vicki Owen was a passenger in a car driven by her husband Ronald when he lost control of the car and hit a utility pole in Indiana. At the time of the accident, both parties were domiciled in South Dakota but were temporarily residing in Indiana. Vicki sued Ronald in South Dakota seeking damages for the injuries she sustained at the accident. Unlike South Dakota, Indiana had a "guest statute" which prevented an injured guest passenger from recovering compensation from a negligent host driver in the absence of a showing of "wanton or willful misconduct" on the part of the driver. Following the *lex loci delicti* rule, the trial court applied the Indiana statute and dismissed Vicki's action. After reaffirming its adherence to the *lex loci* rule because of its " 'built-in virtues of certainty, simplicity, and ease of application'," the Supreme Court of South Dakota proceeded as follows to "create a limited public policy exception to *lex loci delicti*."]

* * * First, we note that the *lex loci delicti* rule in the field of torts has long admitted two exceptions:

(1) The law of the forum, lex fori, was applied to procedural matters, and
(2) the law of the forum was controlling whenever the law of the place of the wrong was contrary to an extraordinarily strong public policy of the forum state.
16 Am.Jur.2d *Conflicts of Law* § 101 (1979).

The reasons that a foreign jurisdiction's law would be contrary to public policy were succinctly explained by the Supreme Court of Tennessee in *Whitlow v. Nashville C. & St. L.R. Co.*, 84 S.W. 618, 621 (Tenn.1904):

To justify a court in refusing to enforce a right of action which occurred under the law of another state, because it is against the policy of our laws, it must appear that it is against good morals or natural justice, or that, for some other such reason, the enforcement of it would be prejudicial to the general interest of our citizens.

Accord Winters v. Maxey, 481 S.W.2d 755, 756 (Tenn.1972).[2] * * *

[E]nforcing Indiana's guest statute against citizens of this state runs contrary to the strong public policy established by our legislature, thereby lowering a standard of protection it intended for injured passengers.

To understand our reasoning, it is necessary to retrace the demise of the South Dakota guest statute. For many years, this court noted injured plaintiffs' displeasures with the guest statute, SDCL 32-34-1 (repealed in 1978), but held that it was up to the legislature, not the court, to change the law. *Behrns v. Burke*, 229 N.W.2d 86, 90 (S.D.1975).

Reacting to our decisions, the legislature, in 1978, repealed the guest statute, * * * The new standard of care owed injured passengers by a host became "want of ordinary care or skill." SDCL 20-9-1.

And while Indiana is free to enforce its guest statute against its own citizens, South Dakota is certainly not obligated to follow a statute that runs so contrary to its public policy. The legislature intended that an injured passenger be allowed to recover against a host under a theory of simple negligence. To enforce Indiana's guest statute in an action between two of our own citizens, who were only temporarily in Indiana, is against "natural justice" as well as "prejudicial to the general interest of our citizens." *Whitlow*, 84 S.W. at 621.

Further, we believe the parties' contacts with this state warrants applying South Dakota law. Other than the fortuitous event of the accident occurring in Indiana, the parties' contacts are with South Dakota. Both parties are long-time residents of this state; they owned a home in South Dakota and paid property taxes in this state; they registered their vehicles in South Dakota and held South Dakota drivers licenses; they voted in South Dakota elections; they both intended to return to South Dakota to live and in fact have returned after the accident. All of these factors convince us that Vicki is not a plaintiff who is forum shopping, but, rather, a life-long resident entitled to the protection of this state's law.

Indiana's interests in this matter are minimal. This is not an issue of enforcing Indiana's rules of the road. Instead, this court must decide whether Vicki, because she is a guest, is barred from seeking redress for a wrong committed. The accident may have occurred in Indiana, but it has no interest in seeing its guest statute applied to our citizens.

Allowing this limited public policy exception to *lex loci delicti* maintains the certainty, simplicity, and ease of application we discussed earlier, while providing a means to avoid applications that are repugnant to the public policy of our state.

Having ruled that Indiana's guest statute violates our public policy and will not be enforced, it is not necessary to address Vicki's constitutional objection.

We reverse and remand.

MILLER, J. (concurring specially). I am pleased to see an erosion of the *lex loci*

---

2. This court is aware that the *Winters* decision found that an Alabama guest statute did not violate Tennessee's public policy. We, however, are not bound by that holding and do not agree with its reasoning.

delicti rule but strongly assert that the majority does not go far enough. By adopting the public policy exception, the majority brings South Dakota's conflicts of law approach out of the middle ages. I believe we should now enter the twentieth century by joining the vast majority of states in abolishing *lex loci* completely and adopting an approach which best suits these modern times. * * *

Certainly [the majority's used of the public policy exception] is preferred to blindly applying *lex loci*. We must remember, however, that it does not cure the weaknesses inherent in the rigid rule. Like the rule itself, it lacks analytical focus. It has been characterized as "an escape hatch to avoid absurd results." Sprague, [Choice of Law: A Fond Farewell to Comity and Public Policy, 74 Cal. L. Rev. 1477 (1986)] *supra*, at 1451. It is said to have arisen "not because of analytical accuracy, nor because it provided for principled decision, but as an alternative to the rigid and inappropriate requirements of vested rights." *Id*. It has been criticized as "too easy to use without hard legal thinking," *Id*. at 1452, "a substitute for the intellectual exertion necessary to find appropriate factors," *Id*., and as "purely duplicative, and therefore obsolete, because the 'public policies' employed defensively in earlier times are already an integral part of the modern analysis." *Id*. at 1458. * * *

I am authorized to state that Justices Henderson and Sabers' join in this special concurrence.

Notes and Questions

1. Buried towards the end of the first Restatement (section 612 of the Restatement's 625 sections), is the following statement: "No Action can be maintained upon a cause of action created in another state the enforcement of which is contrary to the strong public policy of the forum." The statement's location perhaps symbolized the traditional theory's view of the public policy exception as being almost an afterthought in the choice-of-law process. In principle, the choice of the applicable law was made without regard to its content, flowing automatically from the application of the traditional theory's territorially focused, jurisdiction-selecting rules. Once the choice was made, however, the court was permitted to examine the content of the chosen law and to entertain certain limited defenses or exceptions to its application. One such exception was the public policy exception, described in section 612, and intended to serve as a corrective mechanism in extraordinary cases. Two other exceptions, the penal and the tax exceptions, are discussed in the next two Subsections.

2. Justice Cardozo's description in *Loucks* of the conditions for deploying the public policy exception remains classic. The exception applies only if the foreign law "offends our sense of justice or menaces the public welfare," "shock[s] our sense of justice," or "violate[s] some fundamental principle of justice, some prevalent conception of good morals, some deep-rooted tradition of the common weal." Mere difference between the two laws "is not enough to show that public policy forbids us to enforce the foreign right." Id. The first Restatement did not endorse this particular phraseology (which the Second Restatement endorses) but seemed to enunciate a similar test:

The application of this [exception] * * * is *extremely limited*. * * * There is a strong public policy favoring the enforcement of duties validly created by the law governing their creation. * * * The desirability of uniform enforcement of rights acquired in other states is especially strong among the states of the United States. Differences in policy among them are of minor nature * * *. The social interest in uniform enforcement regardless of state lines is particularly great. Restatement § 612 cmt. (c), (emphasis added).

Foreign legal systems adopt a similar conception of the *ordre public* exception, with certain refinements, such as the concept of *ordre public international*, as distinguished from the *ordre public interne*. Only the former may be invoked as a defense to the application of foreign law. See Audit, *Droit international privé* §§ 300 et seq.; Loussouarn & Bourel, *Droit international privé*, 304 et seq.. The underlying concept is that the forum should be more tolerant of certain results in multistate cases than in domestic cases. Furthermore, it is not the foreign law as such that must be examined, but rather *the result* of its application *in the particular case*. A court may refuse to apply a provision of foreign law only if the application of that provision would produce a result that is "manifestly incompatible" with the forum's *ordre public international*. See, e.g., Quebec Civ. Code Art.3081 (a court may refuse to apply "provisions" of a foreign law "if their application is manifestly inconsistent with public order as understood in international relations."; German codif. Art. 6 ("manifestly incompatible with essential principles of German law * * * [or] with fundamental rights").

Thus, in all traditional systems, a mere difference between forum and foreign law is not sufficient to trigger deployment of the public policy exception. Only a clear conflict in fundamental policy can do so. As one judge observed, "The test is a matter of degree. The public policy exception * * * necessarily refers to a high degree of public policy; otherwise, differences between the laws of sister states would always result in applying the law of the forum[.]" Bethlehem Steel Corp. v. G.C. Zarnas & Co., Inc., 498 A.2d 605, 613 (Md.1985), Rodowski, J. dissenting.

Did either *Kilberg* or *Owen* correctly apply the above test? In Cooney v. Osgood Machinery, Inc., 612 N.E.2d 277 (N.Y.1993), the New York Court of Appeals, reiterated Cardozo's classic test and, without even mentioning *Kilberg*, stated: "[N]ot every difference between foreign and New York law threatens our public policy. Indeed, if New York statutes or court opinions were routinely read to express fundamental policy, choice of law principles would be meaningless. Courts invariably would be forced to prefer New York law over conflicting foreign law on public policy grounds." 612 N.E.2d at 284.

3. *Loucks* and *Kilberg* involved the same Massachusetts statute except that, by the time *Kilberg* was decided, the ceiling on recoverable damages was raised from $10,000 to $15,000. How do you explain the difference in outcome between these two cases?

In 1961, the year *Kilberg* was decided, fourteen states imposed a ceiling on the amount of wrongful death damages. Was the *Kilberg* court correct to characterize such ceilings "anachronistic." Are such ceilings anachronistic today?

In 1989, the year *Owen* was decided, only two states had a guest statute, compared with over thirty in the 1930s. South Dakota repealed its guest statute eleven years before *Owen*. Was it credible for the *Owen* court to suggest that a statute that had been in force in the forum state as late as eleven years earlier was "against 'natural justice'"?

4. In all three cases in this subsection, the party who would be adversely affected by the application of the foreign rule was a domiciliary of the forum state. The party who would benefit from the application of that rule was an interstate carrier in *Loucks* and *Kilberg*, and an interstate insurer in *Owen*. How relevant are these affiliations? Should the forum's sensitivity to offensive foreign laws depend on who will suffer or benefit from their application?

5. Both the Restatement and Justice Cardozo phrased the public policy exception in jurisdictional terms ("[n]o action can be maintained;" "public policy does not prohibit the assumption of jurisdiction by our courts"), and both spoke of a "cause of action" as being potentially repugnant to the forum's public policy. Clearly, if the court finds that the cause of action is repugnant to the forum's public policy, the court will "not maintain" the action. But what if it is a *defense* or a *limitation* to an action that is claimed to be repugnant? Dismissing the action would be self-defeating, would it not? How did *Kilberg* and *Owen* handle this issue?

6. When a court refuses on public policy grounds to apply a certain part of the otherwise applicable foreign law, how is the court to fill the resulting void? For foreign solutions to this problem, see, e.g., Hungarian codif. § 7(3) (forum law replaces the rejected foreign law); Austrian codification § 6 (accord); But see, Portuguese Civ. Code Art. 22(2) (apply "the most appropriate rules of the competent foreign law or, residually, [forum law]"); Italian codif. Art. 16(2) (choose another law "on the basis of other connecting factors possibly provided" and in the absence of such factors apply forum law). How did *Kilberg* and *Owen* handle this question? Did *Kilberg* apply forum law *in toto*, or Massachusetts law but without its ceiling on damages? Did *Owen* apply forum law *in toto*, or Indiana law but without its guest statute? To the extent *Kilberg* and *Owen* applied the law of the forum, did they apply it *qua* forum law, or because of the forum's substantive contacts with the case? If it is the latter, then why did these cases retain the *lex loci* rule?

7. Both *Kilberg* and *Owen* professed adherence to the *lex loci delicti* rule while piercing a big hole in it. In both cases the hole proved to be fatal. Both states abandoned the *lex loci* rule, two and three years later, respectively. See *Babcock v. Jackson,* infra 127, and Chambers v. Dakotah Charter, Inc., 488 N.W.2d 63 (S.D. 1992). In contrast, the supreme courts of the ten states that continue to follow the *lex loci* rule have managed avoid its results by routinely employing the public policy exception. See Symeonides, *The Choice-of-Law Revolution*, §§ 46-51. Boone v. Boone, 546 S.E.2d 191 (S.C.2001), is a typical example. *Boone* was an interspousal-immunity conflict like *Haumschild*, in which two spouses domiciled in South Carolina, which allowed interspousal tort suits, were involved in an accident in Georgia, which barred such suits. The court acknowledged its past adherence to the *lex loci* rule, which in this case would dictate the application of the Georgia immunity rule. However, the court noted with relief, "foreign law may not be given effect in this State if it is 'against good morals or natural justice.'" 546 S.E.2d at 193. The court opined that it would be "contrary to 'natural justice,'" id. at 194, to preclude one spouse from suing the other, as the Georgia rule did, and hence the court declined to apply it. Do you agree with this reasoning? See also Alexander v. General Motors Corp., 478 S.E.2d 123 at 124 (Ga.1996) (holding that a Virginia rule that did not impose strict liability on manufacturers was so "radically dissimi-

lar," id. at 124, to Georgia's strict-liability rule as to justify its rejection on public policy grounds); Mills v. Quality Supplier Trucking, Inc., 510 S.E.2d 280 (W.Va.1998)(refusing on public policy grounds to apply the contributory negligence rule of the *lex loci* and applying instead the comparative negligence rule of the *lex fori*). Do these cases meet Cardozo's classic public policy test, or do they lend credence to the prevailing opinion that public policy is just a convenient escape device?

8. Under the traditional theory, public policy was not a rule of choice of law but rather was an exception to all choice-of-law rules. As such, it was supposed to function only *negatively*, by repelling obnoxious foreign laws, rather than affirmatively, by justifying the application of forum law. *Owen* clearly belies this description, as do many other cases decided in the ten states that retain the *lex loci* rule. See Symeonides, *The Choice-of-Law Revolution*, §§ 46-51. For example, in Torres v. State, 894 P.2d 386 (N.M. 1995), the New Mexico court applied the law of the forum without even looking at the law of the state of injury because, the court reasoned, the *lex loci* rule "is not utilized if [its] application would violate New Mexico public policy." Id. at 390. This use of public policy differs little from its use by modern approaches under which the forum's public policy is an integral *affirmative* factor in the court's decision to apply or not to apply the law of the forum.

c. The Penal-Law Exception

Loucks v. Standard Oil Co. of New York
Court of Appeals of New York, 1918.
224 N.Y. 99, 120 N.E. 198.
(For the main body of the opinion, see supra 82).

CARDOZO, J. * * * "The courts of no country execute the penal laws of another" (The Antelope, [23 U.S. 66 (1825)]). The defendant invokes that principle as applicable here. Penal in one sense, the statute indisputably is. The damages are not limited to compensation; they are proportioned to the offender's guilt. A minimum recovery of $500 is allowed in every case. But the question is not whether the statute is penal in some sense. The question is whether it is penal within the rules of private international law. A statute penal in that sense is one that awards a penalty to the state, or to a public officer in its behalf, or to a member of the public, suing in the interest of the whole community to redress a public wrong (Huntington v. Attrill, 146 U.S. 657, 668 [1903]; [cit.]). The purpose must be, not reparation to one aggrieved, but vindication of the public justice. *Huntington v. Attrill*; [cit.]. The Massachusetts statute has been classified in some jurisdictions as penal, and in others as remedial. Connecticut, Rhode Island and Vermont put it in the first category. [cit.] New Hampshire and some of the Federal courts put it in the second. [cit.] The courts of Massachusetts have said that the question is still an open one. [cit.]. No matter how they may have characterized the act as penal, they have not meant to hold that it is penal for every purpose [cit.]. Even without that reservation by them, the essential purpose of the statute would be a question for our courts. *Huntington v. Attrill*; [cit.].

We think the better reason is with those cases which hold that the statute is not penal in the international sense. On that branch of the controversy, indeed, there is no division of opinion among us. It is true that the offender is punished, but the purpose of the punishment is reparation to those aggrieved by his offense. [cit.]. The common law did not give a cause of action to surviving relatives. [cit.]. In the light of modern legislation, its rule is an anachronism. Nearly everywhere, the principle is now embodied in statute that the next of kin are wronged by the killing of their kinsman. The family becomes a legal unit, invested with rights of its own, invested with an interest in the continued life of its members, much as it was in primitive law. [cit.]. The damages may be compensatory or punitive according to the statutory scheme. [cit.]. In either case, the plaintiffs have a grievance above and beyond any that belongs to them as members of the body politic. They sue to redress an outrage peculiar to themselves.

We cannot fail to see in the history of the Massachusetts statutes a developing expression of this policy and purpose. The statutes have their distant beginnings in the criminal law. To some extent the vestiges of criminal forms survive. But the old forms have been filled with a new content. The purpose which informs and vitalizes them is the protection of the survivors. They are moods and phases, the particular and varying expression, of a tendency in legislation as general as the common law. They are not to be viewed in isolation, apart from the stream of events. At first, the remedy was given only when the wrongdoer was a common carrier. That statute goes back to 1840, antedating Lord Campbell's Act in England (1846). The remedy was by indictment and fine, the fine being payable to the widow and next of kin. If there were no survivors of the prescribed class, there could be no indictment. [cit.]. The reason was that even then the dominant purpose was reparation to the family. But later an alternative remedy by civil action at the suit of the executor or administrator became available even against carriers. [cit.]. Then other statutes gave a civil remedy against other wrongdoers, and a civil remedy exclusively. Some statutes were confined to cases where the defendant was the employer of the decedent. [cit.]. Finally there came one which gave a remedy against all persons who had not otherwise been made liable. [cit.]. That is the statute sued on. The remedy is civil; it is an action of tort.

Through all this legislation there runs a common purpose. [cit.]. It is penal in one element and one only: the damages are punitive. The courts of Massachusetts do not give punitive damages even for malicious torts except by force of statute. [cit.]. That may have led them to emphasize unduly the penal element in such recoveries. But the punishment of the wrongdoer is not designed as atonement for a crime; it is solace to the individual who has suffered a private wrong. This is seen in many tokens. The employer may be innocent himself. Smart money will still be due in proportion to his servant's negligence. That is a distribution of burdens more characteristic of torts than crimes. But even more significant is the distribution of benefits. All the statutes are in pari materia. All or none are penal in the international sense. [cit.]. Under all, liability is conditioned upon the existence of a widow or of next of kin. Under some, there must be proof also that the next of kin were dependent on the decedent's wages for support. That restriction brings the dominant purpose into clear relief as reparation to those aggrieved. Other purposes may be served at the same time. It is easy to cite dicta that seem to give them prominence.

[cit.]. They are dicta only. Nor are all the dicta on one side. [cit.]. There are crosscurrents and eddies in the stream. We follow the main course. The executor or administrator who sues under this statute is not the champion of the peace and order and public justice of the commonwealth of Massachusetts. He is the representative of the outraged family. He vindicates a private right.* * *

Notes and Questions

1. "The courts of no country execute the penal laws of another," said the United States Supreme Court in The Antelope, 23 U.S. (10 Wheat) 66, 123, 6 L.Ed. 268 (1825). This principle holds true today, even as among the states of the United States. Strictly speaking, in the area of criminal law there is not a choice-of-law question--it is merged into the jurisdictional question. A state either has jurisdiction, in which case it applies its own law, or it does not have jurisdiction, in which case it ordinarily would extradite the defendant to the state that has jurisdiction. But as *Loucks* demonstrates, the question of whether a statute of another state is or is not penal is not free from ambiguity. To fall outside the scope of the choice-of-law process, the foreign statute must be "penal in the international sense;" that is, it must be designed primarily for the "vindication of the public justice," rather than the "vindicat[ion of] a private right." *Loucks*.

2. What about rules that impose exemplary or punitive damages? As the adjective "punitive" suggests, these rules are penal to the extent they are designed to punish the defendant, rather than to compensate the victim who *ex hypothesi* is made whole through compensatory damages. Does the fact that punitive damages are paid to the victim (and her attorney) mean that punitive-damages rules are not "penal in the international sense"? According to *Loucks*, a statute fits this definition if it "awards a penalty * * * to a member of the public, suing in the interest of the whole community to redress a public wrong." Although punitive-damages rules are partly based on such a rationale, American courts have never utilized the penal-law exception as the basis for refusing to award punitive damages under another state's law. However, as a result of recent "tort reforms," nine states enacted statutes providing that a portion of punitive damages awards is to be paid to a public fund (see Symeonides, *Punitive Damages,* §1.1). According to *Loucks*, a statute that "awards a penalty to the state" *is* "penal in the international sense." Do these new statutes fit this definition?

3. The penal-law exception means that a state does not *directly* apply, i.e. "*execute*" (*The Antelope*, supra) the penal laws of another state. However, a state may rely, for its own purposes, on the penal laws or judgments of another state. For example, a state may declare ineligible for political office a person convicted of a criminal offense in another state or country. Even in the context of a criminal trial, the criminal laws of another state become relevant in, for example, determining the legality of evidence collected in that state. Whether the admissibility of such evidence will be determined under the law of that state, or instead under the law of the forum state, is a veritable choice-of-law question. Section 138 of Restatement (Second)--which does not purport to apply to criminal cases--provides that (subject to exceptions regarding privileged communications, parol evidence rule, and the statute of frauds), "the local law of the forum determines the admissibility of

evidence," apparently on the assumption that this is a procedural question. Many courts have taken the same position in a criminal trial.[1]

One such case is State v. Lynch, 969 P.2d 920 (Mont.1998), which involved the admissibility of wiretap evidence obtained in Nevada and used to prosecute a Nevada domiciliary in Montana, for a crime committed in Montana. The evidence would have been admissible in Nevada, but not in Montana. The lower court allowed the use of that evidence, and convicted the defendant for deliberate homicide. The Montana Supreme Court reversed, holding that the admissibility of the evidence was a procedural question and thus should be governed by the law of the forum. The court noted that "the objective of the exclusionary rule is to punish illegal police conduct," id. at 924, and acknowledged that "the efficacy of the rule may be attenuated when applied in Montana to evidence obtained in another jurisdiction by authorities over which Montana has no control." Id. Nonetheless, said the Court:

> Montana's paramount interest in affording defendants the fullest protection of Montana law when appearing in its courts and this State's clear prohibition against non-consensual electronic surveillance of oral and wire communications, must prevail. The rights and protections under Montana law enjoyed by persons accused of and prosecuted for crimes committed in this State would be significantly diminished if evidence, clearly inadmissible if obtained in Montana, could nevertheless be used against the defendant simply because it was fortuitously gathered in some other jurisdiction where Montana's evidentiary laws did not apply. The *character* of the evidence is what is fundamentally at issue, not where or how it was obtained. And, the *character* of the evidence is not changed simply because it was obtained in a different jurisdiction under different laws.

Id.

Commonwealth v. Sanchez, 716 A.2d 1221 (Pa.1998), involved a scenario similar to *Lynch*, but reached the opposite result. Based on information collected by California police after a "canine sniff" of a Federal Express package in California, Pennsylvania police obtained a Pennsylvania search warrant, resulting in the arrest and conviction of the addressee of the package, a Pennsylvania domiciliary. Under California law, a canine sniff is not considered a search, and thus it need not be supported by probable cause. Under Pennsylvania law, a canine sniff is considered a search, and thus must be supported by probable cause. Characterizing the question as procedural, the trial court applied forum law, held the canine sniff to be illegal, and suppressed all of the evidence obtained subsequent to it. The intermediate court

---

1. See Washington v. Brown, 940 P.2d 546 (Wash.1997), cert. denied, 503 U.S. 1007 (1998) (holding that defendant's statements recorded by California police without defendant's knowledge, as permitted by California law, were admissible in a Washington murder, even though similar action in Washington might have violated Washington law); State v. Briggs, 756 A.2d 731 (R.I. 2000) (holding that the law of Rhode Island, where the murder occurred and the trial was conducted, governed the voluntariness and thus admissibility of statements made by defendant to police in New Hampshire, as well as the admissibility of the contents of a trash can seized by police in New Hampshire. New Hampshire law was more favorable to defendant than Rhode Island law.); Davidson v. State, 25 S.W.3d 183 (Tex. Crim. App. 2000), on remand 42 S.W.3d 165 (Tex.App. 2001) (holding that incriminating oral statement made by defendant to a customs officer in Montana, which would be admissible in Montana, was not admissible in Texas because it was not electronically recorded as required by Texas law.); Vega v. State, 32 S.W.3d 897 (Tex.App. 2000) (holding that evidence obtained from defendant's interrogation in Illinois, which would have been admissible in Illinois, was not admissible in Texas).

reversed, concluding that the question was one of substantive law, and that it should be decided under California law. The Pennsylvania Supreme Court affirmed the substantive characterization and held that California law should govern, because California "possessed the greater interest in the validity of the canine sniff in question," id. at 1223, since the sniff took place there and involved California police officers. Said the Court:

> While [Pennsylvania] has an interest in protecting its citizens from police misconduct and searches that are not supported by probable cause, the courts of [Pennsylvania] have no power to control the activities of a sister state or to punish conduct occurring within that sister state. No Pennsylvania state interest would be advanced by analyzing the propriety of the canine sniff under Pennsylvania law because the canine sniff did not occur in Pennsylvania and no Pennsylvania state officer was involved in the canine sniff. * * * Pennsylvania has no interest in a canine sniff search conducted within California's borders, even if the results are later used in the Pennsylvania Courts.

Id. A dissenting Justice challenged the majority's substantive characterization of the question, questioned the importation of choice-of-law analysis into criminal law, and disputed the majority's reading of the forum's interests. He concluded as follows:

> [Pennsylvania] has a strong interest in ensuring that the authority of Pennsylvania law, especially that law which stands to safeguard individual rights, is not weakened or undermined in any way. * * * By importing California law into this jurisdiction, the Majority empowers the Commonwealth to circumvent Pennsylvania's Constitutional and procedural safeguards and introduce otherwise inadmissible evidence through the back door. Unlike the Majority, I believe that Pennsylvania has an undeniable and unrivaled interest in preventing this from occurring.

Id. at 1227, Nigro, J., dissenting (footnotes omitted).

4. In all of the above cases, the evidence was lawfully obtained in one state, but was inadmissible in another case in which the trial was held. What about the converse scenario, namely situations in which the evidence is unlawfully collected in one state but is presented in trial in another state in which the evidence is admissible? Should the court admit the evidence? If this is always a procedural question, as many courts assume, then the answer would have to be affirmative, would it not? For cases so holding, see Commonwealth v. Dennis, 618 A.2d 972 (Pa.Super.1992) (applying Pennsylvania standards for determining sufficiency of application for New Jersey search warrant). People v. Benson, 454 N.Y.S.2d 155 (N.Y.A.D.1982) (confession obtained in Texas was admitted in New York, although it would be inadmissible in Texas; however, the confession was obtained by a New York police officer and complied with New York standards.)

Do you see anything wrong with the above cases? Is the purpose of the exclusionary rule to: (a) deter police misconduct; (b) protect the rights of defendants; (c) weed out unreliable evidence; or (d) accomplish some or all of the above? Do the answers to these questions provide a better starting point for resolving the above conflicts than an a priori characterization of the exclusionary rule as being procedural?

5. Similar questions of evidence admissibility arise in civil trials. For example, Larrison v. Larrison, 750 A.2d 895 (Pa.Super.2000), a child custody case, involved

the admissibility of a taped telephone call made across state lines. The call was made from Pennsylvania, the law of which required consent of both parties before recording the conversation, and was recorded by the recipient in New York, the law of which did not require such consent. The court concluded that the pertinent rules of the two states were substantive rather than procedural, and resolved the conflict by applying New York law, under which the recording was admissible. The court reasoned that New York had the greater interest in allowing its citizens to lawfully record telephone conversations within its borders and that, while Pennsylvania also had an interest in protecting its citizens from having telephone conversations recorded without proper consent, Pennsylvania courts "have no power to control the activities that occur within a sister state." Id. at 898. The court concluded that "Pennsylvania has no state interest in a recording of a telephone conversation placed to New York, even if the recording is later used in the Pennsylvania Courts." Id. Should the expectations of the Pennsylvania caller play a role in such a case?

6. What about the admissibility of "privileged" communications, such as those between spouses, patient and doctor, penitent and priest, and client and attorney? Unlike many other rules of evidence, the rules that establish these privileges subordinate the goal of truth-seeking to broader societal interests of protecting certain relationships and encouraging socially desirable confidences. For these reasons, the Restatement (Second) regards the admissibility of such communications as substantive, and assigns it in principle to the law of the state that has "the most significant relationship" to the communication--usually the state in which the communication occurred. Section 139 provides that a communication that is not privileged under the law of that state, but is privileged under the law of the forum, is admissible unless admission would be "contrary to the strong public policy of the forum." §139(1). In Gonzalez v. State, 45 S.W.3d 1001 (Tex.Crim.App.2001), the defendant confided to a pastor in California for a crime committed in Texas. This communication would be privileged under Texas law, but not under California law. The Texas court held that California had the most significant relationship to the communication and allowed the evidence, after finding that Texas did not have a strong public policy against admission. See also State v. Donahue, 18 P.3rd 608 (Wash.App.2001) (reaching the same result in a case involving physician-patient privilege).

The same Restatement section provides that a communication that is not privileged under the law of the forum, but is privileged under the law of the state that has the most significant relationship, will be admitted "unless there is some special reason why the forum policy favoring admission should not be given effect." § 139(2). For a case applying this provision, see Kos v. State, 15 S.W.3d 633 (Tex.App.2000) (holding that statements made by defendant to a physician in New Mexico, which would be privileged under New Mexico law but not under Texas law, were admissible in Texas).

d. The Foreign Tax Exception

Attorney General of Canada
v. R.J. Reynolds Tobacco Holdings, Inc.
United States Court of Appeals, Second Circuit.
268 F.3d 103 (2nd Cir. 2001).

KATZMANN, J. This action was brought by the Attorney General of Canada ("Canada") on behalf of the government of Canada for damages based on lost tax revenue and additional law enforcement costs. Canada alleges that these damages resulted from a scheme facilitated by defendants to avoid various Canadian cigarette taxes by smuggling cigarettes across the United States Canadian border for sale on the Canadian black market. Under the Racketeer Influenced and Corrupt Organizations Act ("RICO"), 18 U.S.C. § 1961 *et seq.,* Canada seeks revenue that it lost "from the evasion of tobacco duties and taxes," and from "[d]efendants' conduct [that] compelled [Canada] to rollback duties and taxes," as well as monies spent "seeking to stop the smuggling and catch the wrongdoers."[1]

This case involves the construction of RICO in light of the common law doctrine known as the "revenue rule," a long established feature of the law of the United States and other nations including Canada, which holds that the courts of one sovereign will not enforce the tax judgments or claims of another sovereign. RICO broadly created a civil treble damages remedy for any person injured in its business or property by reason of a violation of the statute. Canada's action proceeds on the premise that the taxes it allegedly lost as a result of defendants' alleged RICO violations fall within RICO's damages provision. As the relief Canada seeks would be foreclosed by the revenue rule in the absence of RICO, and as there is no indication that Congress intended RICO to abrogate the revenue rule with respect to claims brought by foreign sovereigns under the statute, we have no choice but to conclude that RICO may not be used by Canada to seek recovery of lost tax revenues and tax enforcement costs as RICO damages. We therefore affirm. Although the judiciary can do no more, we note that Canada can seek recourse through the political branches--the executive and Congress. * * *

* * * RICO is a broadly worded statute that "has as its purpose the elimination of the infiltration of organized crime and racketeering into legitimate organizations operating in interstate commerce." [cit.] "RICO provides that '[a]ny person injured in his business or property by reason of' a RICO violation may bring a civil action to recover treble damages." [cit.] * * * Canada alleges that defendants violated RICO by "conduct[ing] or participat[ing] ... in the conduct of [an] enterprise's affairs through a pattern of racketeering activity," namely repeated instances of mail fraud, 18 U.S.C. § 1341, and wire fraud, 18 U.S.C. § 1343, in violation of 18 U.S.C. § 1962(c). * * * Canada explains that these RICO violations were the proximate cause

---

1. [Editors' note. The defendants were accused of falsely declaring that cigarettes they exported from Canada to the U.S. were not intended for the Canadian market (and thus avoiding the payment of Canadian sales taxes) and then smuggling the cigarettes back into Canada for sale on the black market. When Canada imposed a tax on exported cigarettes, the Canadian defendants shipped raw Canadian tobacco to Puerto Rico and North Carolina, where their affiliates U.S. companies manufactured Canadian-style cigarettes made to look as if they had been made in Canada, and then smuggled them into Canada for sale on the black market.]

of injury to its "property" because it was deprived of revenue from tobacco duties and taxes and was forced to spend money to stop defendants' illegal activity. * * *

[The district court granted defendants' motion to dismiss the complaint, holding that the revenue rule barred Canada's lost revenue claims.] Canada appeals the dismissal, arguing that the revenue rule is inapplicable * * *. Defendants oppose the appeal, arguing that the revenue rule precludes an action for the enforcement of foreign tax claims * * *.

I. THE VITALITY OF THE REVENUE RULE. The revenue rule is a longstanding common law doctrine providing that courts of one sovereign will not enforce final tax judgments or unadjudicated tax claims of other sovereigns. It has been defended on several grounds, including respect for sovereignty, concern for judicial role and competence, and separation of powers. Examination of both the policies underlying the revenue rule, and the rule's congruence with the international tax policies pursued by the political branches of our government, supports the conclusion that the revenue rule is applicable to the particular facts of the case at hand.

Although the United States Supreme Court and this Circuit have not ruled on the precise scope of the rule, they have acknowledged its continuing vitality in the international context. *See* * * * *Banco Nacional de Cuba v. Sabbatino,* 376 U.S. 398 (1964) (noting the view that many courts in the United States have adhered to the principle that "a court need not give effect to the penal or revenue laws of foreign countries") * * *.

The rule has its origin in eighteenth-century English court decisions seeking to protect British trade from the oppressiveness of foreign customs. In *Boucher v. Lawson,* 95 Eng. Rep. 53 (K.B.1734) (Lord Hardwicke, C.J.), the court specifically acknowledged that its concerns with promoting British trade led it to uphold a transaction that violated Portuguese export laws. * * * Since then, the rule has entered United States common law, international law and the national law of other common law jurisdictions. We note that the international acceptance of the revenue rule extends to Canada's Supreme Court and provincial courts.

A. Respect for Sovereignty. Tax laws embody a sovereign's political will. They create property rights and affect each individual's relationship to his or her sovereign. They mirror the moral and social sensibilities of a society. Sales taxes, for example, may enforce political and moral judgments about certain products. Import and export taxes may reflect a country's ideological leanings and the political goals of its commercial relationships with other nations.

In defense of the revenue rule, some courts have observed that the rule prevents foreign sovereigns from asserting their sovereignty within the borders of other nations, thereby helping nations maintain their mutual respect and security. * * *

Other courts have suggested that it is too sensitive and difficult for courts to determine whether such foreign revenue laws should be enforced by another sovereign. * * * In part, the reluctance of courts to delve into such matters is based on the "desire to avoid embarrassing another state by scrutinizing its penal and revenue laws." *Sabbatino,* 376 U.S. at 437; [cit.]. Similarly, in *Peter Buchanan L.D. v. McVey,* [1955] A.C. 516, 529 (Ir.H.Ct.1950), *aff'd,* [1955] A.C. 530 (Ir.S.C.1951), relied on by the United States Supreme Court in *Sabbatino,* the Irish High Court noted that courts had traditionally exercised the right to reject foreign law that conflicted with the public policy or morality of the domestic court, and stated:

[M]odern history [is not] without examples of revenue laws used for purposes which would not only affront the strongest feelings of neighbouring communities but would run counter to their political aims and vital interests.... So long as these possibilities exist it would be equally unwise for the courts to permit the enforcement of the revenue claims of foreign States or to attempt to discriminate between those claims which they would and those which they would not enforce. Safety lies only in universal rejection.

The case before us illustrates the point. Canada asserts that the revenue laws at issue were the product of an assessment of its public health priorities. * * *

The tenor of the times, at least among many people in the states of this judicial circuit, is anti-smoking. It is unlikely that enforcing a foreign tax regime aimed at deterring smoking would offend most citizens of New York, Connecticut or Vermont, whatever our personal habits or vices. (Of course, citizens of United States tobacco-growing states might vehemently object to Canada's taxation scheme.) But consider, for example, other possibilities involving a foreign sovereign's taxes. How would we respond if a foreign sovereign asked us to help enforce a tax designed to render it very expensive to sell United States newspapers in that nation? Or to make the inclusion of United States-made content in machinery built in that foreign country prohibitively expensive? Suppose it were a tax that had been raised to deter the sale of United States pharmaceuticals in that country? Or if a foreign nation imposed an immigration tax on members of a particular religious group or racial minority? It is much less likely that United States citizens would be kindly disposed towards tolerating such taxes, let alone providing judicial resources to enforce them. These hypotheticals--and we do not suggest that they are anything but hypotheticals--demonstrate the sensitive nature of the issues that can be raised through a foreign sovereign's exercise of its taxation powers. * * * Addressing the public policy concerns raised by the imposition of such foreign taxes could embroil United States courts in delicate issues in which they have little expertise or capacity.

We do not suggest that the revenue rule always bars United States courts from furthering the tax policies of foreign sovereigns. This circuit has held the revenue rule "inapplicable" to a United States criminal action premised on violations of foreign tax laws. *United States v. Trapilo*, 130 F.3d 547, 551 (2d Cir.1997), *cert. denied*, 525 U.S. 812 (1998); *see also United States v. Pierce*, 224 F.3d 158 (2d Cir.2000). These concerns about sovereignty and extraterritorially are therefore not absolute, and are not implicated in every case involving foreign tax laws. However, as explained below in Section I.B, the particular facts of this case--most notably, the fact that a foreign sovereign plaintiff is directly seeking to enforce its tax laws, and that our government has negotiated and signed a treaty with this sovereign providing for limited extraterritorial tax enforcement assistance but stopping well short of the assistance requested here--lead us to be wary in this instance of becoming the enforcer of foreign tax policy.

B. Judicial Role and Competence. 1. General Principles. Concern about institutional role and competence provides particularly compelling support for the application of the revenue rule in this particular case. Our Constitution provides the framework for interaction and dialogue among the branches of our government. "The conduct of foreign relations is committed largely to the Executive Branch, with power in the Legislative Branch to, *inter alia,* ratify treaties with foreign sovereigns.

The doctrine of separation of powers prohibits the federal courts from excursions into areas committed to the Executive Branch or the Legislative Branch." [cit.] * * *

Extraterritorial tax enforcement directly implicates relations between our country and other sovereign nations. When a foreign nation appears as a plaintiff in our courts seeking enforcement of its revenue laws, the judiciary risks being drawn into issues and disputes of foreign relations policy that are assigned to--and better handled by--the political branches of government. * * * Again, Judge Hand put it well:

> To pass [judgment] upon the provisions for the public order of another state is, or at any rate should be, beyond the powers of a court; it involves the relations between the states themselves, with which courts are incompetent to deal, and which are intrusted to other authorities.... Revenue laws fall within the same reasoning; they affect a state in matters as vital to its existence as its criminal laws.

Moore, 30 F.2d at 604 (L.Hand, J., concurring); * * *.

2. The Leading Role of the Political Branches. Indeed, with regard to the domestic collection of foreign taxes and the enforcement of United States taxes abroad, the political branches of our government have consistently acted on behalf of the United States in establishing and managing the nation's relationships with other countries. * * *

We believe that the political branches of our government have clearly expressed their intention to define and limit the parameters of any assistance given with regard to the extraterritorial enforcement of a foreign sovereign's tax laws. Thus, that version of the revenue rule under which United States courts abstain from assisting foreign sovereign plaintiffs with extraterritorial tax enforcement is fully consistent with our broader legal, political and institutional framework. * * *

3. The United States-Canada Treaty Framework. Significantly, we have fairly recently [1995] negotiated a tax convention with Canada providing for assistance with the enforcement of certain fully adjudicated foreign tax judgments. * * * [This treaty] bars Canada from asking the United States for collection assistance with regard to a Canadian revenue claim arising when a person was a United States citizen or corporation, which includes many of the defendants and revenue claims in this case. * * * [T]he treaty does not abrogate the rule that courts of one nation should not adjudicate the unresolved tax claims of another. That is particularly significant, because in this case Canada is not asking for the enforcement of a fully adjudicated Canadian tax judgment, but rather for a United States court to assess and adjudicate the application of Canadian tax laws to the wrongdoing alleged in its complaint. * * * By permitting such a claim to go forward, we would be ignoring and undermining the treaty negotiation process and the clearly expressed views of the political branches of the United States government and instead engaging in *ad hoc* judicial policymaking in the delicate realm of foreign affairs. * * *

II. RICO AND THE REVENUE RULE. Canada argues that the revenue rule is not relevant here because it brings this action under a United States statute--civil RICO-- rather than under Canadian tax law. * * * Because we find that the revenue rule is a doctrine with continuing force in the particular context of this case, Canada cannot succeed unless it can show that RICO bars the application of the revenue rule. We ultimately conclude that Canada's arguments, though ably made, are unavailing.

Notwithstanding Canada's assertion that Congress was not aware of the broad scope of the revenue rule at the time of RICO's enactment, it is clear that the revenue rule was well established by that date. Therefore, * * * Congress is presumed to have legislated with knowledge of the rule. * * * Congress was and is aware of the revenue rule, the precise extent of extraterritorial enforcement assistance available under our tax treaties, and the existence of cigarette smuggling in violation of foreign tax laws. In spite of the extensive Congressional attention to these areas, we are not cognizant of any manifestation of Congressional intent that civil RICO and the United States courts should be available to a foreign sovereign seeking to recover lost tax revenues.

III. DIRECT AND INDIRECT ENFORCEMENT UNDER THE REVENUE RULE. * * * Canada argues to this Court that "[n]othing in the revenue rule, ... prohibits a foreign nation from bringing a suit in the United States to enforce rights established *under United States law.* This is not an attempt by Canada to assert its sovereignty extraterritorially; it is not a claim to enforce Canadian tax law or any other Canadian law." We are not persuaded by Canada's arguments that this is an action brought solely under United States law, and not a claim for Canadian taxes. On the contrary, Canada seeks to use the United States law to enforce, both directly and indirectly, its tax laws.

As to direct enforcement, * * * we must look to the "object" of the claim [and] [w]hen we do so, we see that, at bottom, Canada would have a United States court require defendants to reimburse Canada for its unpaid taxes, plus a significant penalty due to RICO's treble damages provision. Thus, Canada's object is clearly to recover allegedly unpaid taxes.

We also conclude that Canada's claim for damages based on law enforcement costs is in essence an indirect attempt to have a United States court enforce Canadian revenue laws, an exercise barred by the revenue rule. * * * The primary purpose identified by Canada for using its police forces to stop the smuggling was to enforce its customs and excise taxes. In effect, Canada is requesting that defendants pay the salary of the tax enforcers; such police costs are thus derivative of the taxes Canada sought to enforce. * * * Particularly in light of the separation of powers and foreign relations concerns discussed above, we must decline to allow Canada to indirectly enforce its revenue laws simply by pleading tort damages based on the costs of enforcing those laws.

* * * Law enforcement costs incurred to secure taxes for the sovereign are qualitatively different from the damages suffered by a private individual; they fall within the class of acts that are *"jure imperii,"* that is, that are expressions of a foreign sovereign's will or are carried out by virtue of that sovereign authority. [cit.] United States courts have traditionally been reluctant to enforce foreign laws that are *"jure imperii."*

Additional considerations reinforce our determination that Canada's claim for law enforcement costs must be dismissed. To proceed with the law enforcement costs claim, we would have to examine the tax laws at issue in order to assess the causation aspect of this claim. For example, we would have to assess whether the law enforcement costs were in fact spent on achieving the cessation of cigarette smuggling. So doing, we would have to examine whether, when and to what extent the smuggling existed, which would require a determination that tax laws were applicable to defendants. These inquiries could draw the courts into troubled waters. * * *

CONCLUSION. To the extent that the allegations set forth in Canada's complaint are correct, we understand Canada's frustration that it cannot recoup its lost revenue and law enforcement costs against defendants that allegedly committed most of their wrongdoing on our side of the common border with Canada. No court wishes to find itself in the position of being unable to right an alleged wrong. [cit.] Nonetheless, we are without license to abandon unilaterally the centuries-old, albeit sharply-attacked, revenue rule. "The hard fact is that sometimes we must make decisions we do not like" because the laws "compel the result." [cit.] "When and if the [revenue] rule is changed, it is a more proper function of the policy-making branches of our government to make such a change." [cit.] Recourse, to the degree it is warranted and available, lies with the executive and legislature. ˙

Because the judgment is affirmed based on the revenue rule, we need not address the other grounds discussed by the district court or raised by the parties on appeal.

CALABRESI, J. (dissenting). On its face, and despite the considerable confusion created by defendants' able arguments, the revenue rule has nothing to do with this case. * * * It is manifest that the suit before us in no way requires our courts to enforce foreign judgments or claims; it simply is an action for damages provided for and brought under federal law. Nevertheless, the majority invokes the revenue rule to bar the suit. Because I do not think the rule applies and because none of the possible rationales for the rule supports its extension to the facts in this case, I respectfully dissent.

The majority's description of Canada's suit makes clear that this action arises from a violation of a United States statute, namely the civil enforcement provision of RICO, 18 U.S.C. § 1964(c), which itself creates the cause of action. * * * The Canadian tax laws come into play only indirectly, as a factor to be used in the calculation of damages, and do so entirely because the RICO statute itself makes the Canadian laws relevant to that calculation. * * * It follows that Canada, in suing for damages resulting from the violation of a United States statute, neither is seeking to have non-Canadian courts enforce Canadian judgments, laws, or policies, nor is basing this action on the violation of the Canadian statute. * * *

* * * Th[e] concern for extra-territoriality * * * has no meaning whatever when what is enforced by imposing damages or penalties is, in fact, a domestic law, that is, a law enacted by the legislative and executive branches of our country. And, what Canada alleges in this suit is a violation of the RICO statute.

The * * * separation of powers, foreign policy, and court competency concerns * * * [are] once again misplaced whenever the legislative and executive branches have created the cause of action. Under the circumstances, the courts cannot be said to be formulating foreign policy, they are simply implementing the policy established by the other branches. * * * [W]hen American law renders an activity--including the violations of foreign tax laws--an American tort or crime, the issues of whether our foreign policy favors or disfavors the particular form of taxation involved or the choice of items to be taxed must disappear. As the Supreme Court has explained, the purpose of civil RICO is "not merely to compensate victims but to turn them into prosecutors, "private attorneys general," dedicated to eliminating racketeering activity." [cit.] "The aim is to divest the association of the fruits of its ill-gotten gains." [cit.] To reject the application of civil RICO to the case at hand is to hamper this congressional objective. * * *

* * * I cannot * * * join an opinion that applies an old and dubious common law rule, in ways that have nothing to do with its roots or rationales, in order to limit an act of Congress that the Supreme Court has repeatedly applied in the broadest possible ways.

For these reasons, I, regretfully and respectfully, dissent.

Notes and Questions

1. Although the obligation to pay taxes is not penal, the revenue-law exception resembles the penal-law exception in the sense that both function as effective defenses to the application of otherwise governing foreign law and both involve laws of another sovereign that are enacted in *jure imperii*, that is, in the exercise of direct sovereign authority. Nevertheless, as early as the 19th century, notable scholars have criticized the revenue-law exception as "laying down an exceedingly lax morality," 3 Kent, *Commentaries on American Law* 265 (14th ed., 1896) and as being "inconsistent with good faith and moral duties of nations." Story, *Commentaries on the Conflict of Laws* 338-39 (8th ed. 1883). Do you agree with these criticisms? The *R.J. Reynolds* court acknowledged these criticisms, but concluded that the revenue-law exception should apply in this case because it was impliedly sanctioned by a US-Canada treaty that "strictly limited the extent to which each government can pursue its tax claims using the other's domestic administrative and judicial processes." *R.J. Reynolds*, 263 F.3d at 125.

2. *R.J. Reynolds* is only the second case so far in this book that involved an *international* conflict, the first being *Estate of Wright*, supra 69. Unlike *Estate of Right*, however, the international dimension of *R.J. Reynolds* had a decisive bearing on both the court's analysis and the outcome. Besides the presence of an international treaty, this dimension brought into play doctrines such as the Foreign Affairs and Act of State doctrines, which appear only in international cases. These doctrines will be studied in chapter 7, infra, which focuses on international conflicts. As for the outcome, suffice it to say that it would have been completely different had *R.J. Reynolds* been an interstate case. For, despite old dicta to the contrary, American courts have not squarely applied the revenue-law exception to sister state tax claims and eventually abandoned the rule because it "encourage[d] willful, dishonest tax evasion. * * * [and] offer[ed] a legally respectable asylum to the tax dodger." Oklahoma Tax Commission v. Neely, 282 S.W.2d 150, 152 (Ark.1955). Today, most American states have statutes that expressly authorize the application of the tax laws of sister states on the condition of reciprocity. (Sister-state tax judgments have always been enforceable under the Constitution's Full Faith and Credit clause.) Thus, tax evaders from one state no longer can expect to find an asylum in a sister state of the United States. However, as *R.J. Reynolds* illustrates, the same is not true of foreign tax evaders.

3. What do you think of Canada's and Judge Calabresi's arguments that Canada's lawsuit sought to enforce a U.S. statute (RICO), rather than to collect

Canadian taxes? Consider the following hypotheticals:

(a) Suppose that the illegal activities of the *R.J.Reynolds* defendants also caused injury to one of their competitors, a Canadian tobacco company. If that company were to bring a civil RICO action, would the revenue-law exception bar that action? If not, would not that company be entitled to treble damages under RICO?

(b) Suppose that, rather than filing a civil RICO action, Canada had filed an ordinary tort action seeking simple (not treble) damages for the tax revenues it lost and the expenses it incurred because of defendants' activities? Would the revenue-law exception bar such an action?

(c) Suppose that *the United States* brought criminal RICO charges against the same defendants as in *R.J. Reynolds* premised on the violation of the same Canadian tax laws. Under established case law (see *United States v. Trapilo,* 130 F.3d 547, 551 (2d Cir.1997), *cert. denied,* 525 U.S. 812 (1998), the revenue-law exception would not bar the prosecution of these charges. What then is the difference between such a case and *R.J. Reynolds*? The *R.J. Reynolds* court distinguished the two cases on the ground that while in criminal RICO actions "the United States Attorney acts in the interest of the United States, and his or her conduct is subject to the oversight of the Executive Branch," 268 F.3d at 123. In contrast, there is no such oversight over a civil action plaintiff, especially "a foreign sovereign [suing] to further its own interest [which] may be, but is not necessarily consistent with the policies and interests of the United States." Id.

4. As a result of violating both Canadian and United States laws, the *R.J. Reynolds* defendants "made several hundred million dollars in profits," *R.J. Reynolds,* 268 F.3d at 107, at the expense of Canadian taxpayers. Is it not true that the *R.J. Reynolds* decision allowed the defendants to keep these illegal profits? Does the United States have an "interest" in condoning this phenomenon?

5. Suppose that the Canadian government had obtained a Canadian judgment ordering defendants to pay the taxes they evaded, and then sued to have that judgment enforced in the United States. As *R.J. Reynolds* states, the revenue-law exception encompasses *both* tax claims and tax judgments of foreign countries. However, treaties between the United States and a few foreign countries, including Canada, allow limited U.S. assistance in the collection of certain tax judgments of those countries against tax debtors who are *not* U.S. citizens. See *R.J. Reynolds,* 268 F.3d 115–122. Thus, the judgment would not be enforceable against the American defendants. Even as to the Canadian defendants, however, enforcement of the judgment would be subject to the discretion of the executive branch.

E. JUDICIAL NOTICE AND PROOF OF FOREIGN LAW

Geller v. McCown

Supreme Court of Nevada, 1947.
64 Nev. 102, 177 P.2d 461, Reh. denied 64 Nev. 102, 178 P.2d 380.

EATHER, C.J. * * * The action was commenced by Alice B. McCown, the divorced wife of deceased, Malcolm S. McCown, against Charles Geller, as administrator with the will annexed of the estate of said deceased, Malcolm S.

McCown, on her rejected claim for $15,143.75, arising out of her claim to alleged dower and community property now claimed as a portion of the property of the said deceased's estate. * * * [Plaintiff-]Respondent alleges that decedent, Malcolm S. McCown, * * * owned undescribed realty in Yukon Territory, Canada, at the time of the marriage of the decedent and respondent * * * in which respondent alleges in the amended complaint "that plaintiff is entitled to a one-third share by virtue of downer [sic] under the laws of said Yukon Territory." * * *

There is no law governing the allotment of dower rights in Yukon Territory pleaded in said amended complaint so that the trial court might known what laws existed in Yukon Territory governing such matters. The law of Yukon Territory or of the Dominion of Canada was nowhere pleaded in said amended complaint.

In Wickersham v. Johnson, 38 P. 89 [1894], the court said:

There was no evidence at all tending to show what the law was in the foreign country touching any of the questions which are raised here, and it must therefore be assumed that the law with respect to those matters was the same there as in California,

citing Norris v. Harris, 15 Cal. 226, 254 [1860], in which it was stated:

It is a well settled rule, founded on reason and authority, that the lex fori, or, in other words, the laws of the country to whose courts a party appeals for redress, furnish in all cases, prima facie, the rule of decision; and if either party wishes the benefit of a different rule or law, as for instance, the lex domicilii, lex loci contractus, or lex loci rei sitae, he must aver and prove it. The courts of a country are presumed to be acquainted only with their own laws; those of other countries are to be averred and proved, like other facts of which courts do not take judicial notice, and the mode of proving them, whether they be written or unwritten, has been long established.

See also cases cited therein.

The courts do not take judicial notice of either the written or unwritten laws of a foreign country.

In view of the rule that courts will not take judicial notice of the laws of a foreign country, such laws must be pleaded and proved the same as any other question of fact. [cit.].

Section 3361, N.C.L.1929, provides as follows: "No estate is allowed the husband as tenant by courtesy, upon the death of his wife, nor is any estate in dower allotted to the wife upon the death of her husband."

* * * Where the existence of a foreign law is ingredient of cause of action, formal allegation and proof of it is necessary. [cit.].

It is elementary that a statute of another state, if essential to the action or defense, must be pleaded. It is regarded as fact, not law. [cit.].

The law of Yukon Territory not being adequately pleaded it would be assumed that the law applicable to respondent's claim would be the Nevada rule of law which is provided by the statute, Section 3361, N.C.L.1929, supra, that there is no dower law in Nevada. This rule is sustained also in *Wickersham v. Johnson*, supra, and cases therein cited.

The judgment is therefore reversed and the cause remanded to the district court with directions to set aside the judgment; respondent to be allowed to amend her pleadings. Costs to appellant. * * *

Walton v. Arabian American Oil Co.

United States Court of Appeals, Second Circuit, 1956.
233 F.2d 541, *cert. denied*, 352 U.S. 872, 77 S.Ct. 97, 1 L.Ed.2d 77.

FRANK, Circuit Judge. Plaintiff is a citizen and resident of Arkansas, who, while temporarily in Saudi Arabia, was seriously injured when an automobile he was driving collided with a truck owned by defendant, driven by one of defendant's employees. Defendant is a corporation incorporated in Delaware, licensed to do business in New York, and engaged in extensive business activities in Saudi Arabia. Plaintiff's complaint did not allege pertinent Saudi Arabian "law," nor at the trial did he prove or offer to prove it. Defendant did not, in its answer, allege such "law," and defendant did not prove or offer to prove it. There was evidence from which it might have been inferred, reasonably, that, under well-established New York decisions, defendant was negligent and therefore liable to plaintiff. The trial judge, saying he would not take judicial notice of Saudi–Arabian "law," directed a verdict in favor of the defendant and gave judgment against the plaintiff.

1. As jurisdiction here rests on diversity of citizenship, we must apply the New York rules of conflict of laws. It is well settled by the New York decisions that the "substantive law" applicable to an alleged tort is the "law" of the place where the alleged tort occurred. [cit.] * * *.

2. The general federal rule is that the "law" of a foreign country is a fact which must be proved. However, under Fed. Rules Civ.Proc. rule 43(a), 28 U.S.C.A., a federal court must receive evidence if it is admissible according to the rules of evidence of the state in which the court sits. At first glance, then, it may seem that the judge erred in refusing to take judicial notice of Saudi Arabian "law" in the light of New York Civil Practice Act, § 344–a. [This Act provides in part that "[t]he failure of either party to plead any matter of [foreign] law * * * shall not be held to preclude either the trial or appellate court from taking judicial notice thereof."] In Siegelman v. Cunard White Star, 2 Cir., 221 F.2d 189, 196–197 [1955], applying that statute, we took judicial notice of English "law" which had been neither pleaded nor proved. Our decision, in that respect, has been criticized; but it may be justified on the ground that an American court can easily comprehend, and therefore, under the statute, take judicial notice of, English decisions, like those of any state in the United States.[9] However, where, as here, comprehension of foreign "law" is, to say the least, not easy, then, according to the somewhat narrow interpretation of the New York statute by the New York courts, a court "abuses" its discretion under that statute perhaps if it takes judicial notice of foreign "law" when it is not pleaded, and surely does so unless the party, who would otherwise have had the burden of proving that "law," has in some way adequately assisted the court in judicially learning it.

3. Plaintiff, however, argues thus: The instant case involves such rudimentary

---

9. * * * An American court may go astray even in taking judicial notice of English "law." The similarity in language may be deceptive by concealing significant differences. Indeed, just because the English language appears the same as the American language (although it is not), an American may understand the former less adequately than he understands German or French, which is more obviously "foreign" and different. * * * Moreover, the taken-for-granted, unexpressed, background assumptions of English judges and lawyers differ from the unspoken assumptions of American judges and lawyers, and thus may well induce serious misunderstandings. * * *

tort principles, that the judge, absent a contrary showing, should have presumed that those principles are recognized in Saudi Arabia; therefore the burden of showing the contrary was on the defendant, which did not discharge that burden. But we do not agree that the applicable tort principles, necessary to establish plaintiff's claim, are "rudimentary": In countries where the common law does not prevail, our doctrines relative to negligence, and to a master's liability for his servant's acts, may well not exist or be vastly different. Consequently, here plaintiff had the burden of showing, to the trial court's satisfaction, Saudi Arabian "law."

This conclusion seems unjust for this reason: Both the parties are Americans. The plaintiff was but a transient in Saudi Arabia when the accident occurred and has not been there since that time. The defendant company engages in extensive business operations there, and is therefore in a far better position to obtain information concerning the "law" of that country. But, under the New York decisions which we must follow, plaintiff had the burden. As he did not discharge it, a majority of the court holds that the judge correctly gave judgment for the defendant.

4. In argument, plaintiff's counsel asserted that Saudi Arabia has "no law or legal system", and no courts open to plaintiff, but only a dictatorial monarch who decides according to his whim whether a claim like plaintiff's shall be redressed, i.e., that Saudi Arabia is, in effect, "uncivilized." According to Holmes, J.--in Slater v. Mexican National R. Co., 194 U.S. 120, 129 [(1904)],--the *lex loci* does not apply "where a tort is committed in an uncivilized country" or in one "having no law that civilized countries would recognize as adequate." If such were the case here, we think the New York courts would apply (and therefore we should) the substantive "law" of the country which is most closely connected with the parties and their conduct—in this case, American "law." But plaintiff has offered no data showing that Saudi Arabia is thus "uncivilized." We are loath to and will not believe it, absent such a showing.

5. The complaint in this action was filed on May 10, 1949. * * * At [pre-trial] hearings the question of proving Saudi-Arabian law was discussed. When the case came on for trial on November 7, 1953 Judge Bicks indicated that in his view the burden was on the plaintiff to prove the foreign "law". When the plaintiff's counsel said that he was not prepared to prove the "law" of Saudi-Arabia, Judge Bicks proposed that the case be adjourned long enough to allow the plaintiff to prepare such proof. It was agreed that the case be put over for two days to enable the plaintiff to decide whether to request an adjournment for that purpose.

When the hearing resumed on November 9, plaintiff's counsel unequivocally took the position that he did not wish to prove the foreign "law" and wanted no adjournment. He chose to rely on the applicability of New York "law". To that end he proposed that he proceed to present his case in order to make a record for appeal. The plaintiff's evidence as to liability was presented and on a proper motion the judge dismissed the complaint. He specifically ruled that he would not take judicial notice of the "law" of Saudi-Arabia and that the plaintiff's failure to prove that "law" required dismissal.

Since the plaintiff deliberately refrained from establishing an essential element of his case, the complaint was properly dismissed. The majority of the court thinks that, for the following reasons, it is inappropriate to remand the case so that the plaintiff may have another chance: He had abundant opportunity to supply the missing element and chose not to avail himself of it. It does not appear whether Judge Bicks or counsel for the parties considered the application of Section 344–a of the New York Civil Practice Act. Since Judge Bicks specifically determined that he would not take judicial notice of the Arabian "law", he must have considered that in some circumstances he might take judicial notice of foreign "law". But in any event, as we have pointed out, it would have been an abuse of discretion under the New York cases to take notice of the foreign "law" here. The judgment of dismissal must therefore be affirmed.

The writer of the opinion thinks we should remand for this reason: Apparently neither the trial judge nor the parties were aware of New York Civil Practice Act, § 344–a; consequently, in the interests of justice, we should remand with directions to permit the parties, if they so desire, to present material which may assist the trial judge to ascertain the applicable "law" of Saudi-Arabia.[16]

Affirmed.

Notes and Questions

1. *Jus novit curia* ("the court knows the law"), is an ancient and widely accepted maxim in both the civil-law world and the common-law world. Theoretically, a litigant does not need to prove to the court the existence of the law on which her remedy is based. If such a law exists, the court ought to know about it, take judicial notice of it *sua sponte*, and apply it to the case, whether or not that party pleaded it or proved its content. Should this maxim also apply when the law upon which the remedy is based is foreign? Civil-law systems always have affirmatively answered this question.[1] Common-law systems began with a negative answer but have slowly moved towards the middle. *Geller* reflects the original common law position of treating foreign law as a question of fact, with all the attending consequences with regard to pleading, proof, and appellate review.

Is the treatment of foreign law as "fact" consistent with the vested-rights theory? Does that theory not require the forum to recognize certain rights vested by foreign law? For example, section 384 of the Restatement (quoted after *Carroll*, supra at 20) provides that "[i]f a cause of action in tort is created at the place of wrong, a cause of action *will* be recognized in other states." (Emphasis added). If the forum, statutorily or judicially, adopts this rule and yet refuses to recognize such an action because the plaintiff is unable or unwilling to prove the law of the place of the wrong, is not the court violating its own law and the vested-rights theory? Are the forum's choice-of-law rules "waivable" by the parties?

2. If foreign law is a question of fact, and its content is not proven, then how should the court proceed? If the plaintiff's action is based upon such a law, then one option is to dismiss the action. The trial court in *Walton* followed this option. The

---

16. Or that it has no "civilized" legal system; see point 4 of the text, supra. * * *

1. See, e.g., Austrian codif., Art. 3 ("If foreign law is determinative, it shall be applied ex officio and as it would be in its original jurisdiction."); Peruvian Civ. Code Art. 2051 ("Foreign law which is declared applicable under the Peruvian conflict rules law must be applied ex officio."); Swiss codif., Art. 16 ("The content of [the applicable] foreign law is established ex officio."); Italian codif., Art. 14.

second option is to apply the *lex fori*, on the basis of varying rationales or fictions.

One such rationale is that the law of the forum is the basic or residual law that applies in all cases unless one demonstrates a good for its displacement. *Norris v. Harris*, the California case upon which *Geller* relied, echoed this rationale when it stated that "the lex fori * * * furnish[es] in all cases, prima facie, the rule of decision; and if either party wishes the benefit of a different rule or law * * *, he must aver and prove it. The courts of a country are presumed to be acquainted only with their own laws." 15 Cal. at 254 (quoted in *Geller*, supra).

Another rationale, also used in *Geller*, was that the unproven foreign law was the same as the law of the forum. This fiction is sufficiently realistic when applied to the common law, or even the statutory law, of sister states, or when the case "involves such rudimentary * * * [legal] principles" which can be presumed to be the same in all "civilized" legal systems (*Walton*). It is less realistic when applied to the law of foreign non-common-law countries, or when the case involves less rudimentary principles such as dower rights (*Geller*). Yet one case applied the presumption to the law of Costa Rica and another to the law of China. Was the *Walton* court correct in not indulging this fiction? Could the court have assumed that the principle of respondeat superior, which has been part of western law for centuries, was also recognized in Saudi Arabia? More than 30 years after *Walton*, in Chadwick v. Arabian American Oil Co., 656 F.Supp. 857 (D.Del.1987), the same defendant company, Aramco, proved that Saudi Arabia did not recognize respondeat superior. Said the court:

> Under Saudi Arabian law, vicarious liability is not recognized unless it is proven that an actor's free will is obliterated by the person directing the actor to act. [cit.] The Shari'a, the common law of Saudi Arabia, "has a strict rule that responsibility for human action is individual and not vicarious." [cit.].

656 F.Supp. at 861. Does the above excerpt help explain why the plaintiff in *Walton* refused to supply the court with information regarding Saudi Arabia law?

3. Eleven years after *Geller*, the Nevada Supreme Court had the opportunity to revisit the issue of notice and proof of foreign law. In Choate v. Ransom, 323 P.2d 700 (Nev.1958), the court decided that "it is time that we recognize that the statutes and reported court opinions of our sister states are a proper subject for judicial notice." Id. at 703–04. The court quoted at length from Professor Wigmore who complained against "'the needless expenditure of effort involved in compelling formal proof of what was in most instances virtually indisputable'" and the "'absurd * * * insistence on treating the states of the Union as foreign to each other.'" Id. at 704.

4. But what about the law of foreign countries? As Wigmore observed, "'[n]o one would demand that a court take judicial notice of foreign systems of law in foreign languages.'" Id. Indeed, no one has so demanded, and very few courts take judicial notice of foreign-country law. One such court was the same court that decided *Walton*. In Siegelman v. Cunard White Star, 221 F.2d 189 (2d Cir.1955), the court took judicial notice of English law, which plaintiff had neither pleaded nor proved. Are you surprised that the same court took such a different approach one year later in *Walton*? When the foreign law is so different from forum law and as inaccessible as in *Walton*, most American courts would take the same stance.

One example is provided by Banque Libanaise Pour Le Commerce v. Khreich,

915 F.2d 1000 (5th Cir.1990), *reh'g denied* (5th Cir. 1990), in which the plaintiff bank invoked the law of Abu Dhabi but offered what the court considered to be insufficient proof of its contents. The trial court applied forum law, and the bank appealed and offered supplementary evidence of Abu Dhabi law. The court of appeals was not sympathetic:

> While it is true that an appellate court is free to review questions of foreign law on appeal, this argument does not, however, negate the Bank's burden of proof of the foreign law at trial. The law clearly states that absent sufficient proof to establish with reasonable certainty the substance of the foreign principles of law, the district court should apply the law of the forum. [cit.]. In this case, the fact that the Bank provided extensive supplements on appeal, containing translations of Abu Dhabi law and a statement from an Abu Dhabi lawyer explaining applicable law, is further evidence that better evidence could and should have been made available to the district court. The district court should not be asked to decide a case based on incomplete and frequently confusing explanations of foreign law, and the Bank should not be entitled to a second chance to meet his burden of proof on appeal.

> It was the Bank's burden to provide the legal pigment and then paint the district court a clear portrait of the relevant Abu Dhabi law. The Bank failed to provide a pallet, a painter with a usable brush, and paint possessing distinct visibility. The resultant picture contains neither abstract nor realistic exposition. Given this state of the art, the district court was well within its discretionary realm to refuse to accept this virtually barren canvas when it was within the Bank's power to present a canvas upon which it had etched a clear and visible statement of the applicable Abu Dhabi law. Therefore we affirm the district court's application of the law of the forum.

915 F.2d at 1006-1007.

In *Chadwick*, supra, the defendant Aramco, seasoned by three decades of experience in defending lawsuits like the one in *Walton*, provided the district court with a "clear portrait" of Saudi Arabia law. This portrait enabled the court to explain in a very erudite fashion why Saudi Arabia did not recognize the concept of third party beneficiary:

> According to Saudi law, only parties to a contract can enforce the terms thereof, and third party beneficiary rights do not exist. The reason * * * is deeply rooted in Saudi history. Prior to the revelations received by Mohammad in the Seventh Century A.D., and codified in the Qur'an, Saudi Arabia was inhabited by a collection of warring tribes. The time period prior to the Qur'an is known as the Period of Ignorance before Islam. During this period, if one member of a tribe killed a member of a second tribe, the entire membership of the first tribe was deemed responsible for the death. This rule of collective and vicarious responsibility was finally ended with the words of God as transmitted by the Prophet. So, too, was the perpetual feuding and bloodshed amidst tribes. Saudi Arabia thus follows the "relativity rule" with respect to contractual obligations. One neither profits from nor is obligated by contracts to which he is not a party. As a result, this cause of action does not lie against Aramco. "Contractual rights belong to the contracting party only...." [cit.]

Chadwick, 656 F.Supp. at 861. In contrast, the plaintiff's evidence on Saudi law consisted of an "unsupported affidavit" by "an American who worked in Saudi Arabia for over two years" and who was "neither a lawyer nor an expert in Saudi law." Id. The court, while noting its freedom to do otherwise, decided to "give no probative value to th[is] affidavit." Id. Are your surprised by this decision? What conclusions and lessons do you draw from it?

5. Most states have enacted statutes on judicial notice of foreign law, and most of those statutes differentiate between sister-state law and foreign country law. Judicial notice is compulsory with regard to the former ("shall"), and discretionary with regard to the latter ("may"). Many of these statutes followed the Uniform Judicial Notice of Foreign Law Act of 1936, which was adopted by 24 states. Recent statutes are modelled after the Act's successor, the Uniform Interstate and International Procedure Act of 1962, which was adopted by six states before it was officially withdrawn. This Act blurred the distinction between sister-state and foreign country law. It provides in part:

§ 4.01 [Notice]. A party who intends to raise an issue concerning the law of any jurisdiction or governmental unit thereof outside this state shall give reasonable notice in his pleadings or other reasonable notice.

§ 4.02 [Materials to be considered]. In determining the law of any jurisdiction or governmental unit thereof outside this state, the court may consider any relevant material or source, including testimony, whether or not submitted by a party or admissible under the rules of evidence.

§ 4.03 [Court Decision and Review]. The court, not jury, shall determine the law of any governmental unit outside this state and its determination shall be subject to review on appeal as a ruling on a question of law.

6. Since 1966, federal courts follow Federal Rule of Civil Procedure 44.1, which provides:

Determination of foreign law. A party who intends to raise an issue concerning the law of a foreign country shall give notice by pleadings or other reasonable written notice. The court, in determining foreign law, may consider any relevant material or source, including testimony, whether or not submitted by a party or admissible under the federal rules of evidence. The court's determination shall be treated as a question of law.

7. Notice that in all the cases in this subsection, one party raised the issue of the applicability of a foreign law, although that party was unable or unwilling to prove its content. What if none of the parties raise the issue of foreign law? In the United States, most courts will adjudicate the case under the law of the forum, even though under the forum's choice-of-law rules the case would be governed by foreign law. An amazingly high number of conflicts cases thus goes undetected. Here the fiction is one of tacit acquiescence by the parties to the application of forum law. In Chapter 4, you will study the principle of party autonomy, which allows a party to a contract or other juridical act to choose in advance the law applicable to the contract or other act. This freedom, however, is subject to certain limitations imposed by the law that would be applicable in the absence of choice by the parties. The fiction of tacit acquiescence to the law of the forum wipes out those limitations and *de facto* extends the principle of party autonomy to cases other than contracts. Do you see anything wrong with this phenomenon? In an adversarial system, should one blame the court for not looking after the parties' interests, especially when they are

represented by counsel? Assuming that foreign law is more favorable to one party than forum law, why do you think that party chooses not to invoke that law? What tactical, practical, or other reasons may explain counsel's decision not to invoke foreign law? Is such a decision always motivated by the client's best interests?

8. From the extensive literature on the subject of judicial notice and proof of foreign law in American courts, see Schlesinger, Baade, Damaska & Herzog, *Comparative Law,* 43-228 (5th ed.1988); Scoles, Hay, Borchers & Symeonides, *Conflict of Laws*, §§ 12.15-12.19; 9 Wright & Miller, *Federal Practice and Procedure* §§ 2441-2447.

Chapter 3

CONTEMPORARY APPROACHES
TO THE CHOICE-OF-LAW PROBLEM

I. INTRODUCTION

In Chapter 2 we have seen the American courts' discontent with, and evasion from, the dictates of the system of the first Restatement. By the early 1960s, evasion became open dissension and then defiance, which, though isolated at first, soon acquired the appearance and intensity of a figurative rebellion against the established system. This movement came to be known as the American conflicts "revolution," a term that was both hyperbolic and simplistic at the same time. Nevertheless, this term has prevailed in the literature and it is used hereafter without quotation marks as a shorthand description of the American search for new ways of resolving conflicts problems. This chapter focuses on this movement.

In order to build on, and provide a contrast to, the materials in the previous chapter, the focus of this chapter will remain on tort and contract conflicts, the two areas to which the revolution has been largely confined.

II. THE SCHOLASTIC "REVOLUTION":
THE EARLY PROTAGONISTS

The bulk of this chapter consists of judicial decisions. This is only proper, since they are the primary ingredients of the "living" conflicts law in this country. However, academic writers have had a much greater role in influencing judicial opinion in this field than in other fields. Whether this is due to the perceived esoteric nature of the subject matter, the dearth of English precedent or doctrine during the formative period of American conflicts law, or the relatively infrequent occurrence of conflicts cases in general--which retards the accumulation of judicial expertise on the subject--is beside the point. The fact remains that it is academic writers like Story and later Beale who provided the theoretical underpinnings of the traditional choice-of-law system; and again, it is academic writers of a later generation who have pinpointed and articulated that system's deficiencies and have instigated dissension from it.

For this reason, it is appropriate to begin this chapter with a presentation of the views of a few of those writers, the early protagonists, whose writings served as both the motor and the compass of the revolution during its early years. Along the way, we shall consider the views of other commentators who have provided support, or suggested new directions, for the revolution.

1. Walter Wheeler Cook (1873–1943)

The roots of the revolution may be traced to Professor Walter Wheeler Cook, one of the earliest and most outspoken critics of the established choice-of-law orthodoxy. Together with Judge Learned Hand, Cook is usually remembered as the author of the "local law" theory, which is no more memorable than the theory Cook intended to displace--the vested rights theory. The local law theory was Cook's attempt to reconcile the application of foreign law with the sovereignty of the forum state. He resolved the ostensible tension by proclaiming that in adjudicating multistate cases, the forum neither applies foreign law as such, nor enforces a foreign vested right. Rather the forum fashions a local-law remedy that is modeled after the pertinent foreign rule. Cook, *Logical Bases*, 20–21. While this theory was of dubious validity, it had the effect of placing the *lex fori* at the center of choice-of-law thinking. Cook's subliminal message was that the function of conflicts law is not to preserve the international or interstate order, but rather to carry out local law and policy. This was a drastic departure from the universalistic conception of private international law that characterized earlier generations of American conflicts scholars, including Story and Beale.

Cook's main contribution to American conflicts law lies not in enunciating a new theory, but in deconstructing the traditional theory and thus, in his words, freeing the "intellectual garden" of conflict of laws of "rank weeds" so that useful vegetables could grow and flourish. Cook argued that: the first Restatement's professed goals of certainty, predictability, and uniformity were illusory because of the many escape devices that judges could and did use at will; the Restatement's seemingly simple but excessively broad principles were "inadequate," both in describing what the courts were doing and in directing what courts should do; and a simplistic, static system based on prefabricated rules could not provide functional solutions to inherently complex conflicts problems. See Cook, *An Unpublished Chapter*, 422. He advocated for a "a set of guiding principles, which make provision for as much certainty as may reasonably be hoped for in a changing world, and at the same time provide for not only needed flexibility but also continuity of growth." Cook, *Logical Bases*, 97. This statement was an early harbinger of a notion that later prevailed in American conflicts thought--that an "approach" is preferable to a system of rules.

Although Cook fell short of articulating an alternative approach of his own, his writings contained many of the seeds of modern approaches. For example, on the basic question of how the forum court should select the foreign law on which to "model" its rule of decision in multistate cases, Cook simply said that "the problem involved is that of legal thinking in general," and that the forum should use "the same method actually used in deciding cases involving purely domestic torts, contracts, property, etc." Id. at 43. This resort to the "domestic method" for handling conflicts cases anticipated Brainerd Currie's perception of the choice-of-law process as being based on the "ordinary process of construction and interpretation." See Currie, *Selected Essays*, 183-84, discussed infra at 126, 137. Cook's reference to "socially useful" solutions to conflicts problems also anticipated the result-selectivism of many judicial decisions and academic commentators, and the notion that one should not sacrifice "material justice" to the pursuit of "conflicts justice." (See infra 165 *et seq.*) Moreover, Cook's admonition that one should consider legislative purposes and policies "before a wise choice *between conflicting rules* can be made," Cook, *Logical Bases*, 46 (emphasis added) reveals that, like many modern American scholars, Cook thought of the choice-of-law problem as one of choosing between conflicting rules, not competing states or "jurisdictions" in the abstract.

2. David F. Cavers (1902–1986)

Professor David F. Cavers, who at the time shared many of Cook's legal-realist convictions, continued the attack on the traditional theory. In a pioneering law review article published in 1933, Cavers further exposed the mechanistic, "jurisdiction-selecting" nature of the traditional methodology by comparing it to a slot-machine programmed to select the applicable law in a "blindfold" fashion, without regard to the content of that law. See Cavers, *Critique*, 178. This was not a choice *of law*, much less a rational one, he argued, but rather a pre-selection of a "jurisdiction" *regardless* of law and based exclusively on territorial contacts. He argued that such a content-blind selection not only prevented a more individualized treatment of conflicts cases, but also prevented intelligent choices. After all, Cavers reminded us, "[t]he court is not idly choosing a law; it is deciding a controversy. How can it choose wisely without considering how that choice will affect that controversy?" Id. at 189.

For these reasons, Cavers argued, the jurisdiction-selecting, content-blind rules of the traditional theory should be discarded and replaced with a true *process* of direct choice of *law*. Rather than choosing between states without regard to the outcome their laws would produce, this process should focus directly on the content of these states' laws, their underlying policies, and the result their application would produce in the case at hand. The choice of one law over another should be a content-targeted choice that produces "justice in the individual case." Id., *passim*.

Although this early version of Cavers's proposed process fell short of articulating a complete methodology, it provided useful markers on the path on which the quest for alternative methodologies should proceed. More than thirty years later, Cavers returned to the conflicts scene with a set of "principles of preference" for the solution of tort and contract conflicts. These principles are discussed later in this chapter.

3. Brainerd Currie (1912–1965) and Interest Analysis

With their incisive and pioneering work, Cook and Cavers demonstrated the deficiencies of the traditional approach and helped to discredit the first Restatement in its infancy. Professor Brainerd Currie inflicted the decisive blow. Building on the works of Cook, Cavers, Freund, and Justice Stone, Currie enunciated his approach in a series of law review articles published in the 1950s, and eventually provided the following summary of his "governmental interest analysis" for publication in Cheatham, Griswold, Reese & Rosenberg, Conflict of Laws, 477-78 (5th ed. 1964):

1. Normally, even in cases involving foreign elements, the court should be expected, as a matter of course, to apply the rule of decision found in the law of the forum.

2. When a court is asked to apply the law of a foreign state different from the law of the forum, it should inquire into the policies expressed in the respective laws, and into the circumstances in which it is reasonable for the respective states to assert an interest in the application of those policies. In making these determinations the court should employ the ordinary process of construction and interpretation.

3. If the court finds that one state has an interest in the application of its policy in the circumstances of the case and the other has none, it should apply the law of the only interested state.

4. If the court finds an apparent conflict between the interests of the two states it should reconsider. A more moderate and restrained interpretation of the policy or interest of one state or the other may avoid conflict.

5. If, upon reconsideration, the court finds that a conflict between the legitimate interests of the two states is unavoidable, it should apply the law of the forum.

6. If the forum is disinterested, but an unavoidable conflict exists between the interests of two other states, and the court cannot with justice decline to adjudicate the case, it should apply the law of the forum, at least if that law corresponds with the law of one of the other states. Alternatively, the court might decide the case by a candid exercise of legislative discretion, resolving the conflict as it believes it would be resolved by a supreme legislative body having power to determine which interest should be required to yield.

7. The conflict of interest between states will result in different dispositions of the same problem, depending on where the action is brought. If with respect to a particular problem this appears seriously to infringe a strong national interest in uniformity of decision, the court should not attempt to improvise a solution sacrificing the legitimate interest of its own state, but should leave to Congress, exercising its powers under the Full Faith and Credit Clause, the determination of which interest shall be required to yield.[1]

Each of the above points will be discussed later in this chapter, which is structured around some of the major working concepts and categories of Currie's analysis.

Currie's theory was greeted with enthusiasm and quickly dominated choice-of-law thinking in the United States. His "seductive style" of writing has "hypnotized a whole generation of American lawyers," Korn, *Critique*, 812, perhaps in the same way Beale's teachings had indoctrinated the previous generation. In recent years, judicial support for Currie's approach has decreased dramatically. See infra 303. Although academic support has also declined and Currie's "new critics" seem to

---

1. Reprinted with permission of David P. Currie and The Foundation Press.

outnumber the old and new defenders,[2] his analysis "still controls the academic conflicts agenda." Juenger, *Critique*, 4. The new critics seem to concur with the old ones and among themselves that interest analysis is "chaotic," "unpredictable," "parochial," "chauvinistic," and possibly unconstitutional.[3]

These and other criticisms will be considered later in this chapter, at which time you will have the opportunity to form your own opinion. Even if you find these criticisms to be justified, however, you should still try to separate the tenable from the untenable elements in Currie's analysis. Moreover, even if you conclude that the latter elements outnumber the former, you should not hasten to make assumptions about Currie's overall contribution to the advancement of American conflicts law. That contribution is a decidedly positive one.

III. THE JUDICIAL REVOLUTION

A. INTRODUCTION

The scholastic dissent against the established conflicts system described in the preceding section would have been practically inconsequential had it not been followed by a similar dissent in the judicial ranks. The previous chapter contains several examples of such dissent, albeit a disguised one. For example, *Levy* and *Haumschild*, supra 43, 48, are examples of manipulative characterization, but they were also harbingers of things to come in that each case spoke of the policies or purposes of the substantive rules involved in the conflict. Similarly, *Grant v. McAuliffe*, and *Kilberg*, supra 57, 60, are examples of a misuse of the substance/procedure dichotomy, but they also exemplified the courts' increasing impatience with the fortuitous way in which the *lex loci delicti* rule operated.

The first court to move from covert dissent to overt defiance was the New York Court of Appeals. In 1954, it decided *Auten v. Auten*, reproduced infra 119, which abandoned the *lex loci contractus* rule. In 1963, the same court decided the seminal case *Babcock v. Jackson*, reproduced infra at 127, which openly abandoned the *lex loci delicti* rule and launched what came to be known as the judicial conflicts revolution.

Courts in other states moved in the same direction, and by 1977 half of the states had abandoned the *lex loci delicti* rule. By 2003, a total of forty-two jurisdictions (including the District of Columbia and the Commonwealth of Puerto Rico) had

---

2. For early criticisms see, *inter alia*, Hill, *A Reply to Currie*; Rosenberg, *Comments on Reich v. Purcell*; von Mehren, *Book Review*; Evrigenis, *Tendances Doctrinales*; Kegel, *Crisis*. In recent years, criticisms of interest analysis have multiplied. See, e.g, Bodenheimer, *Reorientation*; Brilmayer, *Methods*; Ely, *The State's Interest*; Hay, *Reflections*; Juenger, *Critique*; Trautman, *Reflections*. For old and new defenders of interest analysis, see, e.g., Kay, *A Defense*; Posnak, *"New Crits"*; Sedler, *Reformulation*; Weinberg, *On Departing from Forum Law*; Weintraub, *Interest Analysis*.

3. For a much kinder assessment, see Kay, *A Defense*, 38–167.

Chart 2. The Erosion of the Lex Loci Delicti Rule

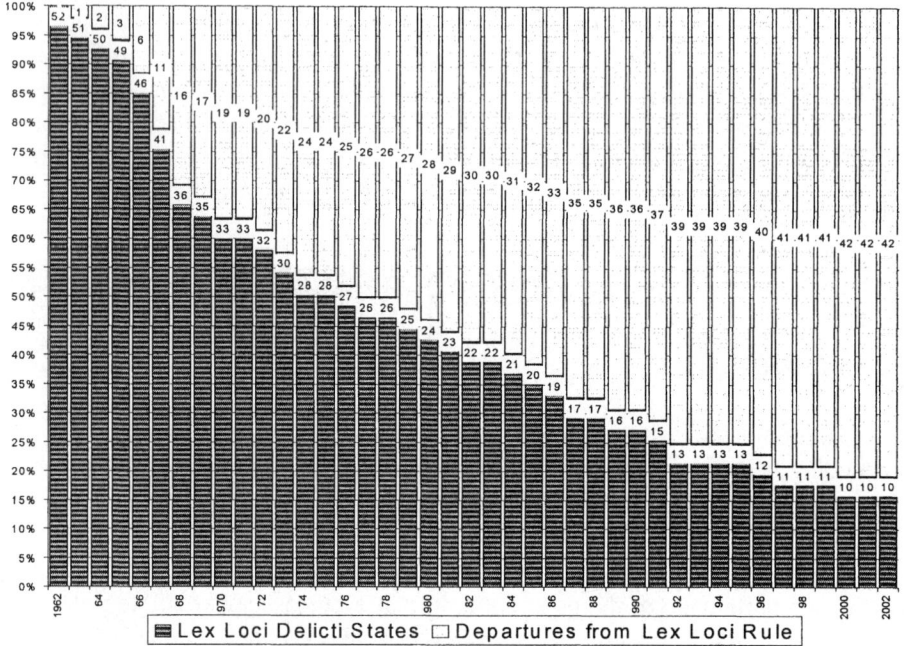

Chart 3. The Erosion of the Lex Loci Contractus Rule

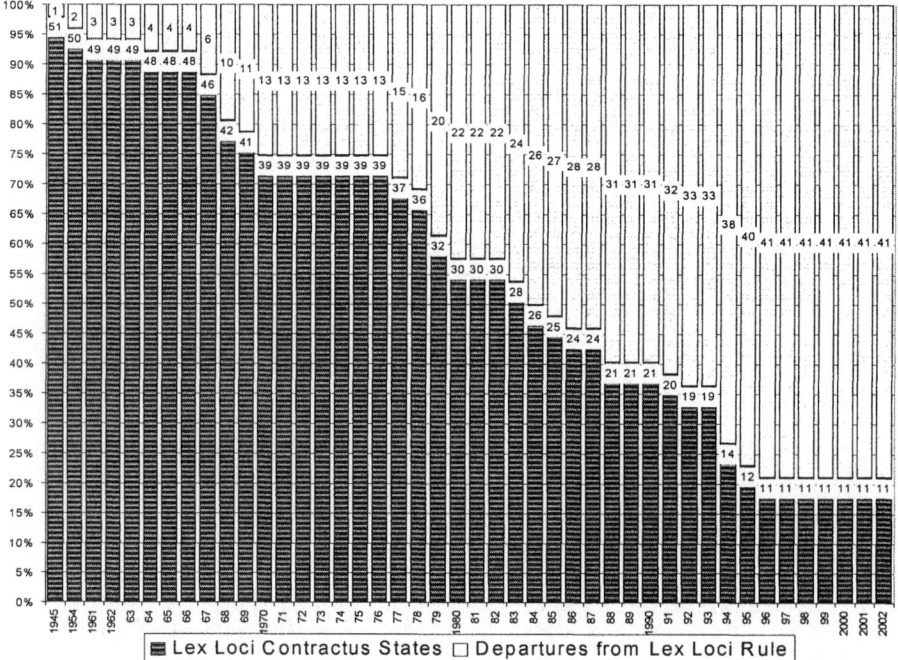

done likewise. The chronology of this movement is shown in Chart 1, supra, and documented in Symeonides, *The Revolution Today*, §§ 41-42

In contract conflicts, the abandonment of the traditional theory was slower than in torts. Besides *Auten*, a 1945 Indiana case, W.H. Barber Co. v. Hughes, 63 N.E.2d 417 (Ind.1945), employed "a method used by modern teachers of Conflict of Laws in rationalizing the results obtained by the courts in decided cases [and called the] center of gravity" approach. Id. at 423. However, neither *Barber* nor *Auten* garnered any following until the 1960s. Even then, dissension against the *lex loci contractus* rule was slow and, as late as 1985, half of the states continued to follow the rule. By 2003, that number was down to 11 states. Chart 2, supra, depicts this movement. For documentation, see Symeonides, *The Revolution Today*, §§ 43-44.

B. EARLY GROPINGS: "CENTER OF GRAVITY"

Auten v. Auten
Court of Appeals of New York, 1954.
308 N.Y. 155, 124 N.E.2d 99.

FULD, J. [Plaintiff and defendant were married in England in 1917 and continued to live there with their two children until 1931, at which time defendant deserted his wife, obtained an *ex parte* Mexican divorce, and settled in New York. In 1933 plaintiff came to New York City where she and defendant signed a separation agreement which obligated defendant to pay to a trustee, for the "account of" plaintiff the sum of 50 pounds a month for the support of herself and the children. In addition, the agreement provided that the parties were to continue to live separate and apart, that neither should sue "in any action relating to their separation" and that the wife should not "cause any complaint to be lodged against * * * [the husband], in any jurisdiction, by reason of the said alleged divorce or remarriage." Defendant made a few payments and then stopped paying. In 1934, plaintiff filed an action for separation in an English court, charging defendant with adultery. She also obtained an order for alimony *pendente lite*, but never prosecuted her action to trial. She claimed that she filed the action in order to "to enforce" the 1931 agreement, and not with any thought or intention of repudiating it. In 1947, plaintiff filed the present action to recover $26,564 of arrearages due her under that agreement. One of defendant's defenses was that plaintiff's filing of the separation action in England operated as a repudiation of the agreement and effected a forfeiture of her right to any payments under it.]

* * * Both of the courts below, concluding that New York law was to be applied, held that under such law plaintiff's commencement of the English action and the award of temporary alimony constituted a rescission and repudiation of the separation agreement, requiring dismissal of the complaint. Whether that is the law of this state, or whether something more must be shown to effect a repudiation of the agreement [cit.], need not detain us, since in our view it is the law of England, not that of New York, which is here controlling.

Choosing the law to be applied to a contractual transaction with elements in different jurisdictions is a matter not free from difficulty. The New York decisions evidence a number of different approaches to the question. [cit.] * * * [Some of those] decisions, including the most recent one in this court, have resorted to a method--first employed to rationalize the results achieved by the courts in decided cases [cit.]--which has come to be called the "center of gravity" or the "grouping of contacts" theory of the conflict of laws. Under this theory, the courts, instead of regarding as conclusive the parties' intention or the place of making or performance, lay emphasis rather upon the law of the place "which has the most significant contacts with the matter in dispute". [cit.]

Although this "grouping of contacts" theory may, perhaps, afford less certainty and predictability than the rigid general rules [cit.] the merit of its approach is that it gives to the place "having the most interest in the problem" paramount control over the legal issues arising out of a particular factual context, thus allowing the forum to apply the policy of the jurisdiction "most intimately concerned with the outcome of [the] particular litigation" [cit.]. Moreover, by stressing the significant contacts, it enables the court, not only to reflect the relative interests of the several jurisdictions involved [cit.], but also to give effect to the probable intention of the parties and consideration to "whether one rule or the other produces the best practical result". [cit.]

Turning to the case before us, examination of the respective contacts with New York and England compels the conclusion that it is English law which must be applied to determine the impact and effect to be given the wife's institution of the separation suit. It hardly needs stating that it is England which has all the truly significant contacts, while this state's sole nexus with the matter in dispute--entirely fortuitous, at that--is that it is the place where the agreement was made and where the trustee, to whom the moneys were in the first instance to be paid, had his office. The agreement effected a separation between British subjects, who had been married in England, had children there and lived there as a family for fourteen years. It involved a husband who, according to the papers before us, had willfully deserted and abandoned his wife and children in England and was in the United States, when the agreement was signed, merely on a temporary visa. And it concerned an English wife who came to this country at that time because it was the only way she could see her husband to discuss their differences. The sole purpose of her trip to New York was to get defendant to agree to the support of his family, and she returned to England immediately after the agreement was executed. While the moneys were to be paid through the medium of a New York trustee, such payments were "for account of" the wife and children, who, it was thoroughly understood, were to live in England. The agreement is instinct with that understanding; not only does it speak in terms of English currency in providing for payments to the wife, not only does it recite that the first payment be made to her "immediately before sailing for England", but it specifies that the husband may visit the children "if he should go to England".

In short, then, the agreement determined and fixed the marital responsibilities of an English husband and father and provided for the support and maintenance of the allegedly abandoned wife and children who were to remain in England. It merely substituted the arrangements arrived at by voluntary agreement of the parties for the duties and responsibilities of support that would otherwise attach by English law. There is no question that England has the greatest concern in prescribing and governing those obligations, and in securing to the wife and children essential support and maintenance. And the paramount interest of that country is not affected by the fact that the parties separate and provide for such support by a voluntary agreement. It is still England, as the jurisdiction of marital domicile and the place where the wife and children were to be, that has the greatest concern in defining and regulating the rights and duties existing under that agreement, and, specifically, in determining the circumstances that effect a termination or repudiation of the agreement.

Nor could the parties have expected or believed that any law other than England's would govern the effect of the wife's institution of a separation action. It is most unlikely that the wife could have intended to subject her rights under English law to the law of a jurisdiction several thousand miles distant, with which she had not the slightest familiarity. On the contrary, since it was known that she was returning to England to live, both parties necessarily realized that any action which she took, whether in accordance with the agreement or in violation of it, would have to occur in England. If any thought was given to the matter at all, it was that the law of the place where she and the children would be should determine the effect of acts performed by her.* * *

Since, then, the law of England must be applied, and since, at the very least, an issue exists as to whether the courts of that country treat the commencement of a separation action as a repudiation of an earlier-made separation agreement, summary judgment should not have been granted.[2] * * *

[J]udgment * * * reversed, * * * and * * * remitted for further proceedings in accordance with this opinion. * * *

Haag v. Barnes

Court of Appeals of New York, 1961.

9 N.Y.2d 554, 216 N.Y.S.2d 65, 175 N.E.2d 441.

FULD, J. This appeal is concerned with the effect in New York of an agreement made in another State for the support of a child born out of wedlock. [The agreement between plaintiff and defendant had been signed in 1956 in Chicago, Illinois, and provided that it "shall in all respects be interpreted, construed and governed by the laws of the State of Illinois." In the agreement, defendant expressed his willingness to support plaintiff and her child on condition that such support "shall not constitute an admission" that he was the child's father. The amount of support was to be $275 per month, until the child reached sixteen. In exchange, plaintiff "released and forever discharged" defendant "from all manner of actions ... which [she] now has

---

2. In point of fact, the English lawyers, whose affidavits have been submitted by plaintiff, unequivocally opine that the institution of a separation suit and the award of alimony *pendente lite* did not, under the law of England, constitute a repudiation of the separation agreement or bar the present action to recover amounts due under it.

against [him] or ever had or which she ... hereafter can, shall or may have, for, upon
or by reason of any matter, ... including ... the support of [the child]." According to
the plaintiff, the child was the product of a sexual relation she and defendant had had
in New York, when she worked for him as a temporary secretary during one of his
business trips there, in 1954. The child was born in Chicago in 1955 and, after two
years in California, she and plaintiff have since been living in New York. Since the
1956 agreement, defendant paid plaintiff a total of $30,000, which was far in excess
of what he was required to pay under the agreement. Plaintiff filed the present action
in 1959 seeking child support under New York law.]

* * * The traditional view was that the law governing a contract is to be
determined by the intention of the parties. [cit.] The more modern view is that "the
courts, instead of regarding as conclusive the parties' intention or the place of
making or performance, lay emphasis rather upon the law of the place 'which has the
most significant contacts with the matter in dispute'". See *Auten v. Auten*, [supra].
Whichever of these views one applies in this case, however, the answer is the same,
namely, that Illinois law applies.

The agreement, in so many words, recites that it "shall in all respects be
interpreted, construed and governed by the laws of the State of Illinois" and, since
it was also drawn and signed by the complainant in Illinois, the traditional conflicts
rule would, without doubt, treat these factors as conclusive and result in applying
Illinois law. But, even if the parties' intention and the place of the making of the
contract are not given decisive effect, they are nevertheless to be given heavy weight
in determining which jurisdiction "'has the most significant contacts with the matter
in dispute'". *Auten v. Auten*, [supra]. And, when these important factors are taken
together with other of the "significant contacts" in the case, they likewise point to
Illinois law. Among these other Illinois contacts are the following: (1) both parties
are designated in the agreement as being "of Chicago, Illinois", and the defendant's
place of business is and always has been in Illinois; (2) the child was born in Illinois;
(3) the persons designated to act as agents for the principals (except for a third
alternate) are Illinois residents, as are the attorneys for both parties who drew the
agreement; and (4) all contributions for support always have been, and still are being,
made from Chicago.

Contrasted with these Illinois contacts, the New York contacts are of far less
weight and significance. Chief among these is the fact that child and mother
presently live in New York and that part of the "liaison" took place in New York.
When these contacts are measured against the parties' clearly expressed intention to
have their agreement governed by Illinois law and the more numerous and more
substantial Illinois contacts, it may not be gainsaid that the "center of gravity" of this
agreement is Illinois and that, absent compelling public policy to the contrary [cit.],
Illinois law should apply.

As to the question of public policy, we would emphasize that the issue is *not*
whether the New York statute reflects a different public policy from that of the
Illinois statute, but rather whether enforcement of the particular agreement before us
under Illinois law represents an affront to our public policy. Cf. *Loucks v. Standard
Oil Co.*, [supra Ch. 2]. It is settled that the New York Paternity Law requires

something more than the provision of "the bare necessities otherwise required to be supplied by the community", that, "although providing for indemnification of the community, [it] is chiefly concerned with the welfare of the child". [cit.] In our judgment, enforcement of the support agreement in this case under Illinois law and the refusal to allow its provisions to be reopened in the present proceeding does not do violence to this policy.

As matter of fact, the agreement before us clearly goes beyond "indemnification of the community" and the provision of "bare necessities". Whether we read it as a whole, or look only to the financial provisions concerned ($275 a month until the child reaches the age of 16), we must conclude that "the welfare of the child" is fully protected. [cit.] The public policy of this State having been satisfied, there is no reason why we should not enforce the provisions of the parties' support agreement under Illinois law and treat the agreement as a bar to the present action for support.

The order of the Appellate Division should be affirmed.

Notes and Questions

1. *Auten* and *Haag* followed the "center of gravity" or "grouping of contacts" approach, which was a transitional stage in the development of American conflicts law from the traditional to the modern approaches. Unlike the traditional approach which based its selection of the applicable law on a single connecting factor or contact (e.g., the *locus delicti* or the *locus contractus*), *Auten* and *Haag* speak of contac*ts* in the plural, and purport to apply the law of the state that has "the most significant contacts." This was an important development in choice-of-law methodology. A method that relies on multiple factors or contacts may be less predictable, but it is also more likely to produce rational results than is a method that relies on a single contact, is it not?

But how is one to locate the center of gravity or to group the contacts? Is one to look for the state with the *most* contacts or the most *significant* contacts? If it is the former, why would a state with more contacts have a better claim to apply its law? If it is the latter, how is one to determine the significance of contacts?

Auten states that the grouping of contacts theory "gives to the place 'having the *most interest* in the problem' paramount control * * * thus allowing the forum to apply the policy of the jurisdiction '*most intimately concerned* with the outcome of [the] particular litigation'." (Emphasis added.) Does it necessarily follow that a state with the most, or most significant, contacts also has the "most interest" in applying its law? For example, let us assume (as *Auten*, but not *Haag*, assumed) that in a case involving a child-support agreement, State A, which is the domicile of both the child and the obligee mother as well as the parents' former matrimonial domicile, has more significant contacts than does State B, which is the domicile of the obligor father or the *locus contractus*. Suppose, however, that State A has a law that exhibits utter disregard for the rights of children and mothers and scandalously favors absconding debtor fathers. In such a case, would State A be "most intimately concerned" or have the "most interest" in applying its law? Can one determine whether a state is interested in applying its law without first asking *what* its law provides for the particular issue? See Cavers, supra 115.

2. Are you persuaded that Illinois' contacts in *Haag* were more significant than New York's contacts? What about the court's statement that "both parties are designated in the agreement as being of Chicago Illinois"? (Did the court not know that Ms. Haag was not "of Chicago"?) What about the statement that Chicago was Mr. Barnes' place of business? Was this a business-related dispute? Was the fact that Mr. Barnes sent his payments from Chicago any more "significant" than the fact that Ms. Haag received them in New York? What about the fact that Mr. Barnes attended a Chicago high school, a Chicago college, or a Chicago law school? That he had played football for a Chicago team? That he belonged to a Chicago Rotary Club? Are these not factual "contacts"? Are they relevant? Why not?

3. Read again the second-to-last paragraph in *Haag*. Does it help explain the result?

4. Compare *Haag* with *Auten*. Then compare the center of gravity approach with the traditional approach. Which one is more susceptible to manipulation?

5. In 1953, one year before *Auten*, the U.S. Supreme Court decided Lauritzen v. Larsen, 345 U.S. 571 (1953), an international maritime tort conflict reproduced infra 538, Ch. 7. The Court adopted an approach consisting of "ascertaining and valuing *points of contact* between the transaction and the states or governments whose competing laws are involved * * * [and] weighing of the significance of one or more connecting factors between the shipping transaction regulated and the national interest served by the assertion of authority." Id. at 539 (emphasis added). Notice the use of plural in "points of contact" and "connecting factors." Indeed, *Lauritzen* eschewed reliance on a single connecting factor in favor of a list of *seven* factors or contacts, which will be discussed in Chapter 7.

C. POLICY-BASED APPROACHES

The balance of this chapter contains cases decided under modern choice-of-law approaches other than the center of gravity. These approaches are referred to hereinafter by their common denominator as "policy-based" because, to a lesser or greater extent, they examine the policies underlying the competing substantive laws before choosing one of them. The use of the word "policy" is also symbolic of the philosophical origins of most of these approaches in the "policy" school of thought, which succeeded American Legal Realism and sociological jurisprudence in the period after World War II. See Symeonides, *An Outsider's View*, 208-34.

As you will soon discover, few cases rely exclusively on a single policy-based approach. Courts tend to be less interested in theoretical purity and more interested in reaching what they perceive to be the proper result. The majority of cases that abandoned the traditional approach tend to use modern approaches interchangeably and often as *a posteriori* rationalizations for results reached on other grounds. For this reason, this chapter groups cases not by the approach they ostensibly follow, but rather by fact/law pattern each case presents.

At the same time, this chapter recognizes that Currie's interest analysis remains the best pedagogical vehicle for exploring and debating the issues and dilemmas of the choice-of-law process. For this reason, the arrangement of cases follows in part the categories that interest analysis has established, namely, "false" conflicts, "true" conflicts, and "no-interest" or "unprovided for" conflicts. These terms are explained infra at 127. (For now let us say that they correspond to "easy," "difficult," and "not so easy" conflicts.) As you read these cases, remember that the placement of a case under these categories does not necessarily imply that the court deciding the case subscribes to these categories or to interest analysis.

A PRELIMINARY NOTE ON CURRIE'S INTEREST ANALYSIS

1. *Rejection of all choice-of-law rules in favor of the "domestic" process.* Brainerd Currie's contempt for the traditional theory was so intense that it led him to reject not only the particular choice-of-law rules of the first Restatement but also all choice-of-law rules. He said:

> The rules [of the traditional theory] * * * have not worked and cannot be made to work * * * . But the root of the trouble goes deeper. In attempting to use rules we encounter difficulties that stem not from the fact that the particular rules are bad, * * * but rather from the fact that we have such rules at all * * * . We would be better off without choice-of-law rules.

Currie, *Selected Essays*, 180, 183.

To fill the vacuum left by his rejection of choice-of-law rules, Currie resorted, like Cook, to the method of statutory construction and interpretation that courts employ in fully domestic cases. In Currie's words, "[j]ust as we determine by that process how a statute applies in time, and how it applies to marginal cases, so we may determine how it should be applied to cases involving foreign elements." Id. at 184.

Although this was not a new notion, it carried several interrelated implications, including the following:

(a) a rejection of the theretofore prevailing assumption that multistate cases are so different from fully domestic cases as to require a distinctive mode of refereeing that draws from principles superior, or at least external, to the involved states. Indeed, Currie rejected the existence of an overarching legal order that delineates affirmatively and a priori the legislative jurisdiction of each state. He believed that in searching for solutions to conflicts problems, the forum should look inward rather than upward. His approach to conflicts placed him squarely into the "unilateralist" camp (see supra 9);

(b) the rejection of pre-established choices in favor of an *ad hoc* judicial choice of the applicable law;

(c) a rejection of the notion that the choice of law could be made on the basis of territorial contacts alone and without regard to the content of the substantive laws of the states that have those contacts.

In short, rather than selecting the applicable law through pre-ordained choice-of-law rules that were oblivious to the content of the substantive laws of the involved states, Currie, like Cavers, focused directly on the content of these laws. He argued that the "ordinary process of construction and interpretation" would reveal the policies underlying those laws and would, in turn, determine their intended sphere of operation in terms of space.

2. *The Concept of Governmental Interests.* According to Currie, whenever a case falls within a law's spatial reach as delineated by the interpretative process, the state from which that law emanates has a "governmental interest" in applying that law so as to effectuate its underlying purposes. In Currie's words:

> [T]he court should * * * inquire whether the relationship of the forum state to the case at bar--that is, to the parties, to the transaction, to the subject matter, to the litigation–is such as to bring the case within the scope of the state's governmental concern, and to provide a legitimate basis for the assertion that the state has an interest in the application of its policy in this instance.

Currie, *Selected Essays*, 189.

Despite what the term might imply, a "governmental" or state interest is not the unilateral wish of a state to apply its law in a given case. Rather it is the result of the judge's evaluation of the reasonableness of this wish in light of the factual elements that connect that state with the case at hand. In Currie's words, an "interest * * * is the product of (a) a governmental policy and (b) the concurrent existence of an appropriate relationship between the state having the policy and the transaction, the parties, or the litigation." Id. at 621. In the words of one of Currie's followers, a state's interest consists in making "effective, in all situations involving persons as to whom it has responsibility for legal ordering, that resolution of contending private interests the state has made for local purposes." Baxter, *Choice of Law*, 17. Thus Currie projected his legal-realist view of law as "an instrument of social control" (Currie, *Selected Essays*, 64) at the interstate level by postulating that states do have an interest in the outcome of litigation between private persons.

3. *False, True, and In-Between Conflicts.* Whether states in fact have such interests, and Currie's particular assumptions about those interests, are important questions that are explored later in this chapter. Suffice it to say for now that the introduction of the notion of state interests created some new possibilities for choice-of-law thinking and allowed categorization of conflicts cases into three categories, depending on which of the states involved in the conflict possess such an interest. The possibilities are that:

> (a) only one of the involved states would be interested in applying its law--the "*false conflict*" pattern;
>
> (b) more than one state would be interested--the "*true conflict*" pattern; or
>
> (c) none of the states are interested--the "no-interest" pattern or "*unprovided-for* case."

These are the three well-known, if not well-accepted, categories of conflicts under Currie's analysis. In his later work, Currie recognized a fourth category, placed between a false and a true conflict, which he called an "*apparent conflict*." In Currie's words, an apparent conflict is present in cases which "each state would be constitutionally justified in asserting an interest, but on reflection the conflict is avoided by a moderate definition of the policy or interest of one state or the other," or "a case in which reasonable men may disagree on whether a conflicting interest should be asserted." Currie, *The Disinterested Third State*, 763, 764.

Obviously, none of the above terms or categories are either self-evident or dispositive. For example, determining whether or not a state is "interested" is something about which reasonable people may disagree. Nevertheless, from a pedagogical perspective, these terms are useful for providing a proper framework for analysis and discussion, and this is why and how this section employs them.

1. False Conflicts

One of Currie's uncontested contributions to American conflicts theory was his articulation of the concept of *false conflicts*. According to Currie, a multistate case presents a false conflict when of the two or more states involved in the case only one is interested in applying its law.[1] As explained earlier, a state is considered to be interested when the application of its law to the particular case would promote the policies or purposes underlying that law.

Although the concept of false conflict is meaningful only in approaches such as interest analysis that subscribe to the notion of state interests, the term false conflict is used widely, even by courts or commentators that do not subscribe to the specifics of Currie's analysis. As one commentator observed, this concept "enjoys protean facility for justifying everyman's choice-of-law theory. Members of the choice-of-law guild who discover a rational solution for a conflicts problem tend to characterize the problem as a 'false conflict.'" Comment, *False Conflicts*, 78. This Section contains cases that, under interest analysis, *could be* characterized as false conflicts, regardless of whether the court deciding the case recognizes this concept or subscribes to interest analysis.

a. COMMON-DOMICILE CASES

Babcock v. Jackson
Court of Appeals of New York, 1963.
12 N.Y.2d 473, 240 N.Y.S.2d 743, 191 N.E.2d 279.

FULD, J. On Friday, September 16, 1960, Miss Georgia Babcock and her friends, Mr. and Mrs. William Jackson, all residents of Rochester, left that city in Mr. Jackson's automobile, Miss Babcock as guest, for a week-end trip to Canada. Some hours later, as Mr. Jackson was driving in the Province of Ontario, he apparently lost control of the car; it went off the highway into an adjacent stone wall, and Miss Babcock was seriously injured. Upon her return to this State, she brought the present action against William Jackson, alleging negligence on his part in operating his automobile.

At the time of the accident, there was in force in Ontario a statute providing that "the owner or driver of a motor vehicle, other than a vehicle operated in the business

---

1. False conflicts also include cases in which the laws of the involved states are: (a) identical; or (b) different, but produce identical results.

of carrying passengers for compensation, is not liable for any loss or damage resulting from bodily injury to, or the death of any person being carried in * * * the motor vehicle" [cit.] Even though no such bar is recognized under this State's substantive law of torts [cit.] the defendant moved to dismiss the complaint on the ground that the law of the place where the accident occurred governs and that Ontario's guest statute bars recovery. The court at Special Term, agreeing with the defendant, granted the motion and the Appellate Division, over a strong dissent by Justice Halpern, affirmed the judgment of dismissal without opinion.

The question presented is simply drawn. Shall the law of the place of the tort *invariably* govern the availability of relief for the tort or shall the applicable choice of law rule also reflect a consideration of other factors which are relevant to the purposes served by the enforcement or denial of the remedy?

The traditional choice of law rule, embodied in the original Restatement of Conflict of Laws (§ 384), and until recently unquestioningly followed in this court, [cit.] has been that the substantive rights and liabilities arising out of a tortious occurrence are determinable by the law of the place of the tort. [cit.] It had its conceptual foundation in the vested rights doctrine, namely, that a right to recover for a foreign tort owes its creation to the law of the jurisdiction where the injury occurred and depends for its existence and extent solely on such law. [cit.] Although espoused by such great figures as Justice Holmes [cit.] and Professor Beale, [cit.] the vested rights doctrine has long since been discredited because it fails to take account of underlying policy considerations in evaluating the significance to be ascribed to the circumstance that an act had a foreign situs in determining the rights and liabilities which arise out of that act. "The vice of the vested rights theory", it has been aptly stated, "is that it affects to decide concrete cases upon generalities which do not state the practical considerations involved". (Yntema, 37 Yale L. J. 468, 482-83.) More particularly, as applied to torts, the theory ignores the interest which jurisdictions other than that where the tort occurred may have in the resolution of particular issues. It is for this very reason that, despite the advantages of certainty, ease of application and predictability which it affords, [cit.] there has in recent years been increasing criticism of the traditional rule by commentators and a judicial trend towards its abandonment or modification.

Significantly, it was dissatisfaction with "the mechanical formulae of the conflicts of law" [cit.] which led to judicial departure from similarly inflexible choice of law rules in the field of contracts, grounded, like the torts rule, on the vested rights doctrine. * * * In Auten v. Auten, [supra], however, this court abandoned such rules and applied what has been termed the "center of gravity" or "grouping of contacts" theory of the conflict of laws. "Under this theory," we declared in the Auten case, "the courts, instead of regarding as conclusive the parties' intention or the place of making or performance, lay emphasis rather upon the law of the place 'which has the most significant contacts with the matter in dispute'" [*Auten*, supra]. The "center of gravity" rule of Auten has not only been applied in other cases in this State, as well as in other jurisdictions, but has supplanted the prior rigid and set contract rules in the most current draft of the Restatement of Conflict of Laws. (See Restatement, Second, Conflict of Laws, § 332b [Tentative Draft No. 6, 1960].)

Realization of the unjust and anomalous results which may ensue from application of the traditional rule in tort cases has also prompted judicial search for a more satisfactory alternative in that area. In the much discussed case of Kilberg v. Northeast Airlines [supra], this court declined to apply the law of the place of the tort as respects the issue of the quantum of the recovery in a death action arising out of an airplane crash, where the decedent had been a New York resident and his relationship with the defendant airline had originated in this State. * * *

The emphasis in *Kilberg* was plainly that the merely fortuitous circumstance that the wrong and injury occurred in Massachusetts did not give that State a controlling concern or interest in the amount of the tort recovery as against the competing interest of New York in providing its residents or users of transportation facilities there originating with full compensation for wrongful death. Although the *Kilberg* case did not expressly adopt the "center of gravity" theory, its weighing of the contacts or interests of the respective jurisdictions to determine their bearing on the issue of the extent of the recovery is consistent with that approach. [cit.]

The same judicial disposition is also reflected in a variety of other decisions, some of recent date, others of earlier origin, relating to workmen's compensation, tortious occurrences arising out of a contract, issues affecting the survival of a tort right of action and intrafamilial immunity from tort and situations involving a form of statutory liability. These numerous cases differ in many ways but they are all similar in two important respects. First, by one rationale or another, they rejected the inexorable application of the law of the place of the tort where that place has no reasonable or relevant interest in the particular issue involved. And, second, in each of these cases the courts, after examining the particular circumstances presented, applied the law of some jurisdiction other than the place of the tort because it had a more compelling interest in the application of its law to the legal issue involved.

The "center of gravity" or "grouping of contacts" doctrine adopted by this court in conflicts cases involving contracts impresses us as likewise affording the appropriate approach for accommodating the competing interests in tort cases with multi-State contacts. Justice, fairness and "the best practical result" [cit.] may best be achieved by giving controlling effect to the law of the jurisdiction which, because of its relationship or contact with the occurrence or the parties, has the greatest concern with the specific issue raised in the litigation. The merit of such a rule is that "it gives to the place 'having the most interest in the problem' paramount control over the legal issues arising out of a particular factual context" and thereby allows the forum to apply "the policy of the jurisdiction 'most intimately concerned with the outcome of [the] particular litigation.'" (Auten v. Auten, supra)

Such, indeed, is the approach adopted in the most recent revision of the Conflict of Laws Restatement in the field of torts. According to the principles there set out, "The local law of the state which has the most significant relationship with the occurrence and with the parties determines their rights and liabilities in tort" (Restatement, Second, Conflict of Laws, § 379 [1]; also Introductory Note to Topic 1 of Chapter 9, p. 3 [Tentative Draft No. 8, 1963]), and the relative importance of the relationships or contacts of the respective jurisdictions is to be evaluated in the light of "the issues, the character of the tort and the relevant purposes of the tort rules involved" (§ 379 [2], [3]).

Comparison of the relative "contacts" and "interests" of New York and Ontario in this litigation, vis-a-vis the issue here presented, makes it clear that the concern of New York is unquestionably the greater and more direct and that the interest of Ontario is at best minimal. The present action involves injuries sustained by a New York guest as the result of the negligence of a New York host in the operation of an automobile, garaged, licensed and undoubtedly insured in New York, in the course of a week-end journey which began and was to end there. In sharp contrast, Ontario's sole relationship with the occurrence is the purely adventitious circumstance that the accident occurred there.

New York's policy of requiring a tort-feasor to compensate his guest for injuries caused by his negligence cannot be doubted--as attested by the fact that the Legislature of this State has repeatedly refused to enact a statute denying or limiting recovery in such cases (see, e.g., 1930 Sen. Int. No. 339, Pr. No. 349; 1935 Sen. Int. No. 168, Pr. No. 170; 1960 Sen. Int. No. 3662, Pr. No. 3967)--and our courts have neither reason nor warrant for departing from that policy simply because the accident, solely affecting New York residents and arising out of the operation of a New York based automobile, happened beyond its borders. Per contra, Ontario has no conceivable interest in denying a remedy to a New York guest against his New York host for injuries suffered in Ontario by reason of conduct which was tortious under Ontario law. The object of Ontario's guest statute, it has been said, is "to prevent the fraudulent assertion of claims by passengers, in collusion with the drivers, against insurance companies" (Survey of Canadian Legislation, 1 U. Toronto L. J. 358, 366) and, quite obviously, the fraudulent claims intended to be prevented by the statute are those asserted against Ontario defendants and their insurance carriers, not New York defendants and their insurance carriers. Whether New York defendants are imposed upon or their insurers defrauded by a New York plaintiff is scarcely a valid legislative concern of Ontario simply because the accident occurred there, any more so than if the accident had happened in some other jurisdiction.

It is hardly necessary to say that Ontario's interest is quite different from what it would have been had the issue related to the manner in which the defendant had been driving his car at the time of the accident. Where the defendant's exercise of due care in the operation of his automobile is in issue, the jurisdiction in which the allegedly wrongful conduct occurred will usually have a predominant, if not exclusive, concern. In such a case, it is appropriate to look to the law of the place of the tort so as to give effect to that jurisdiction's interest in regulating conduct within its borders, and it would be almost unthinkable to seek the applicable rule in the law of some other place.

The issue here, however, is not whether the defendant offended against a rule of the road prescribed by Ontario for motorists generally or whether he violated some standard of conduct imposed by that jurisdiction, but rather whether the plaintiff, because she was a guest in the defendant's automobile, is barred from recovering damages for a wrong concededly committed. As to that issue, it is New York, the place where the parties resided, where their guest-host relationship arose and where the trip began and was to end, rather than Ontario, the place of the fortuitous occurrence of the accident, which has the dominant contacts and the superior claim for application of its law. Although the rightness or wrongness of defendant's conduct may depend upon the law of the particular jurisdiction through which the automobile passes, the rights and liabilities of the parties which stem from their guest-host relationship should remain constant and not vary and shift as the automobile proceeds from place to place. Indeed, such a result, we note, accords with "the interests of the host in procuring liability insurance adequate under the applicable law, and the interests of his insurer in reasonable calculability of the premium." (Ehrenzweig, Guest Statutes in the Conflict of Laws, 69 Yale L.J. 595, 603.)

Although the traditional rule has in the past been applied by this court in giving controlling effect to the guest statute of the foreign jurisdiction in which the accident occurred [cit.] it is not amiss to point out that the question here posed was neither raised nor considered in those cases and that the question has never been presented in so stark a manner as in the case before us with a statute so unique as Ontario's. Be that as it may, however, reconsideration of the inflexible traditional rule persuades us, as already indicated, that, in failing to take into account essential policy considerations and objectives, its application may lead to unjust and anomalous results. This being so, the rule, formulated as it was by the courts, should be discarded. [cit.]

In conclusion, then, there is no reason why all issues arising out of a tort claim must be resolved by reference to the law of the same jurisdiction. Where the issue involves standards of conduct, it is more than likely that it is the law of the place of the tort which will be controlling but the disposition of other issues must turn, as does the issue of the standard of conduct itself, on the law of the jurisdiction which has the strongest interest in the resolution of the particular issue presented.

The judgment appealed from should be reversed, with costs, and the motion to dismiss the complaint denied.

VAN VOORHIS, J. (Dissenting) * * * Attempts to make the law or public policy of New York State prevail over the laws and policies of other States where citizens of New York State are concerned are simply a form of extraterritoriality which can be turned against us wherever actions are brought in the courts of New York which involve citizens of other States.... Undoubtedly ease of travel and communication, and the increase in interstate business have rendered more awkward discrepancies between the laws of the States in many respects. But this is not a condition to be cured by introducing or extending principles of extraterritoriality, as though we were living in the days of the Roman or British Empire, when the concepts were formed that the rights of a Roman or an Englishman were so significant that they must be enforced throughout the world even where they were otherwise unlikely to be honored by "lesser breeds without the law." Importing the principles of extraterritoriality into the conflicts of laws between the States of the United States can only make confusion worse confounded. If extraterritoriality is to be the criterion, what would happen, for example, in case of an automobile accident where some of the passengers came from or were picked up in States or countries where causes of action against the driver were prohibited, others where gross negligence needed to be shown, some, perhaps, from States where contributory negligence and others where comparative negligence prevailed? In the majority opinion it is said that "Where the defendant's exercise of due care in the operation of his automobile is in issue, the jurisdiction in which the allegedly wrongful conduct occurred will usually have a predominant, if not exclusive, concern." This is hardly consistent with the statement in the footnote that gross negligence would not need to be established in an action by a passenger if the accident occurred in a State whose statute so required. If the status of the passenger as a New Yorker would prevent the operation of a statute in a sister State or neighboring country which granted immunity to the driver in suits by passengers, it is said that it would also prevent the operation of a statute which instead of granting immunity permits recovery only in case of gross negligence. There are passenger statutes or common-law decisions requiring gross negligence or its substantial equivalent to be shown in 29 States. One wonders what would happen if contributory negligence were eliminated as a defense by statute in another jurisdiction? Or if comparative negligence were established as the rule in the other State?

In my view there is no overriding consideration of public policy which justifies or directs this change in the established rule or renders necessary or advisable the confusion which such a change will introduce.

The judgment dismissing the complaint should be affirmed. * * *

Notes and Questions

1. If *Auten* represents the transition from the traditional approach to the modern approaches, *Babcock* represents the transition from the center of gravity to the modern policy-based approaches. In fact, one can see the transition occurring between the eleventh and the twelfth paragraphs of the majority opinion, at which point the court shifts to an examination of the policies underlying the pertinent substantive rules of the two states. The second part of *Babcock* is claimed by the proponents of all modern policy-based approaches. For the purposes of this discussion, let us assume that this part followed interest analysis.

2. Read again this part of *Babcock* (beginning at paragraph 12). Can you detect the following two steps? (a) identifying the policies or purposes underlying the pertinent rules of Ontario and New York; and (b) examining whether the application of each rule to the particular case will effectuate that policy or purpose.

3. If one accepts the *Babcock* court's reading of the policies of the two states, then *Babcock* is as easy a case as they come, since only one of the two states would have an interest in applying its law. This is why *Babcock* is considered a classic false conflict. If this is true, then the *Babcock* result may also demonstrate the superiority of interest analysis over the traditional theory, at least with regard to false conflicts-- the court applied the law of the interested state without sacrificing any policies of the uninterested state. In contrast, at least according to Currie, the traditional theory's failure to recognize state interests resulted in randomly sacrificing the interests of one state without promoting the interests of the other state, or a common interest of both states. See Currie, *Selected Essays*, 191. See also id. at 589-90. Does the above

statement accurately describe the result reached in *Carroll*, supra at 16?

4. However, even a case like *Babcock* leaves room for arguing that the conflict involved therein may not be totally false. For example, the court assumed that the policy underlying the Ontario guest statute was "to prevent the fraudulent assertion of claims by passengers, in collusion with the drivers, against insurance companies." Accepting for now this assumption, why did the court conclude that Ontario was not interested in applying this statute? If its purpose was to protect insurers, which factor should determine whether Ontario would be interested in applying it? The insurer's domicile or place of business? The place of the insurance contract? Why would Ontario not be interested in protecting the insurer in *Babcock*? Suppose for example that the insurer conducted business in Ontario. Should this change the court's conclusion? Does the insurer's liability depend on the law of the place where the insurance policy is sold or the insured is domiciled, even if the object of the insurance contract is something as mobile as an automobile? If so, what if the laws of New York and Ontario were reversed so that New York's law is more protective of the insurer than Ontario's? In such a case, should one accept the application of New York law as being inevitable?

Was the purpose of the Ontario guest statute to protect the insurer, as the court assumed, or to protect the driver from the burden and aggravation of litigation initiated by his gratuitous guest? Would the answer to this question affect the calculus of interests? Could it be that the purpose of the Ontario statute was to punish the guest's potential ungratefulness? The statute's history seems to suggest such a possibility, at least if one considers the experience of the bill's sponsor--he had been sued by two hitchhikers to whom he had offered a ride on a snowy winter night and who had been injured in an accident during that ride. See Reese, *Choice of Law*, 558; Trautman, *Two Views on Kell*, 469. If the purpose of the Ontario statute was to protect good samaritans, would Ontario have had an interest in applying it?

5. *Issue-by-Issue Analysis*. Notice how the *Babcock* court phrased the question in the third paragraph of the opinion: whether the *lex loci delicti* will "*invariably* govern the availability of relief." The italicized word suggests that the court did not envision a wholesale abandonment of the *lex loci* rule, but rather a narrowing of its scope depending on the *particular issue* with regard to which the laws of the two states differed. In *Babcock* these laws differed on only one issue--the driver's immunity from suit because of the Ontario guest-statute, and the absence of such a statute in New York. The court focused on that issue and wisely assumed that it would be neither necessary nor productive to determine what law would govern other issues in the case or the case *as a whole*.

Although it may appear self-evident, this *issue-by-issue analysis* is one of the major breakthroughs of modern policy-based approaches. Rather than thinking in broad global terms, such as whether the problem at hand should be characterized as one of tort or contract, or which law should apply to the tort or contract as a whole, one isolates the particular issue with regard to which a conflict may exist and proceeds accordingly. This mode of analysis is a return to the familiar schemes of common-law adjudication--that Beale's system had submerged--which avoids deductive methods of reasoning and prefers small, cautious steps of inductive reasoning. At least in the abstract, is not such an analysis more conducive to a nuanced, individualized, and thus more rational, resolution of conflicts problems?

6. ***Dépeçage.*** *Babcock* was an easy case because it involved a conflict on a single issue. When a case involves conflicts with regard to more than one issue, then issue-by-issue analysis requires a separate analysis of each issue. Depending on the circumstances, the court may conclude that on one issue State X is the only interested state, while on another issue State Y is the only interested state. If the court applies the laws of the two states to the two issues, respectively, the resulting phenomenon is called *dépeçage*.[1] This seemingly strange phenomenon and the problems it may create will be revisited later in this chapter. See infra 259.

7. ***The distinction between issues of loss distribution and issues of conduct regulation.*** Because *Babcock* was a single-issue conflict, the court did not need to engage in *dépeçage* in the sense of actually applying the laws of two different states. However, the court clearly signaled its readiness to engage in *dépeçage* by stating in dictum that it would have reached a different conclusion with regard to Ontario's interest "had the issue related to the manner in which the defendant had been driving his car at the time of the accident * * * [or to] the defendant's exercise of due care."

At the same time, through this dictum, the court enunciated an important distinction between, on the one hand, issues of conduct regulation, such as "whether the defendant offended against a rule of the road prescribed by Ontario for motorists generally or whether he violated some standard of conduct imposed by that jurisdiction," and, on the other hand, issues such as the one actually involved in *Babcock*, namely, "whether the plaintiff, because she was a guest in the defendant's automobile, is barred from recovering damages for a wrong concededly committed." The latter issues are hereafter referred to as issues of "loss distribution," or "loss allocation."

In 1994, the same court provided a more succinct definition by describing as conduct-regulating those tort rules that "have the prophylactic effect of governing conduct to prevent injuries from occurring" and as loss-distributing those rules that "prohibit, assign, or limit liability after the tort occurs." Padula v. Lilarn Props. Corp. 644 N.E.2d 1001, 1002 (N.Y.1994), reproduced infra 279. This distinction is discussed in detail later in this chapter. As we shall see then, this distinction is often difficult to apply in practice because many rules of law may both regulate conduct and effect or affect loss distribution. *Babcock* assumed that a guest statute did not affect conduct in that a driver does not drive differently depending on whether the state in which she drives has a guest statute. If this assumption is correct, then this is another reason that *Babcock* was an easy case. Remember this as you read the other cases in this chapter.

Babcock also stated that in conduct-regulating conflicts, the state in which the conduct occurred "will usually have a predominant, if not exclusive, concern," and

---

1. The word is French and literally means the "dismemberment" of the case. This French term has come to prevail in American legal literature, although most French writers use the term *morcellement*. See 2 Batiffol & Lagarde, *DIP*, 273. The English term is *scission*, see Morris, *Conflict of Laws*, 544, while some Americans prefer the more colloquial term "picking-and-choosing." See Wilde, *Dépeçage*, 329.

that "it would be almost unthinkable to seek the applicable rule in the law of some other place." Thus, according to *Babcock*, conduct-regulating rules operate territorially. In contrast, loss-distributing rules (such as Ontario's guest statute or New-York's opposite common-law rule, rules eliminating or limiting the defendant's liability, such as rules of intrafamily immunity or rules imposing a ceiling on the amount of recovery) *do not necessarily operate territorially*. As in *Babcock*, in cases involving conflicting loss-distribution rules, the focus turns on the parties' contacts (e.g., domicile) with the involved states, although territorial contacts continue to be relevant, and as we shall see later, often function as tie-breakers.

Rong Yao Zhou v. Jennifer Mall Restaurant, Inc.
District of Columbia Court of Appeals, 1987.
534 A.2d 1268.

NEWMAN, J. * * * At approximately 11:30 p.m. on the evening of May 28, 1982, Rong Yao Zhou and Xiu Juan Wu, husband and wife, were seriously injured when they were struck by a car operated by a drunk driver on Connecticut Avenue in Chevy Chase, Maryland. The driver, Peter Joray, was returning from the Brittany Restaurant (trade name of appellee Jennifer Mall Restaurant, Inc.) in Washington, D.C. Employees of the restaurant had unlawfully served alcohol to Joray after he had become intoxicated and after his intoxication had become apparent. It was in this impaired condition that Joray entered his car and drove into Maryland, soon thereafter injuring Zhou and Wu. * * *

II. We are confronted at the outset by the question of whether to apply District of Columbia law or Maryland law to a personal injury action arising from an accident occurring in Maryland, near the District of Columbia boundary, where the defendant's allegedly negligent conduct occurred in the District of Columbia by a corporation doing business here, and where plaintiffs are District of Columbia residents. We note that the choice of law issue has not been raised by the parties to this suit, who have assumed that District of Columbia law applies. Under Maryland law, a tavern keeper would not be liable in tort under the facts alleged in this case. [cit.]

The District of Columbia has long followed the "governmental interests analysis" approach to choice of law. [cit.] Therefore, it is not the place of the injury that necessarily determines which law is to be applied. Rather, our jurisdiction, and others, [cit.] have recognized that the place of the injury may be a mere "fortuity" in light of the fact that the relationship of the parties to the litigation is centered elsewhere. [cit.] An automobile or other vehicular accident occurring close to the border between two states presents a classic case of such a fortuity. [cit.]

In applying governmental interests analysis to the facts of this case, we consider the interests, respectively, of Maryland and the District of Columbia. From the ruling of Maryland's highest court in *Felder* [v. Butler, 438 A.2d 494 (1981)], *supra*, we understand that state to adhere to a policy of protecting negligent bar owners from civil liability, although they remain subject to the criminal penalties that attach for serving a person who is "visibly under the influence," [cit.]. By contrast, a District of Columbia rule that would make tavern keepers answerable in tort, as well as under the criminal sanctions of D.C. Code § 25-121 (b) (1981), would signify interests of this jurisdiction in compensating victims for resulting injuries, as well as in deterring harmful conduct.

The apparent clash of policies between Maryland and the District of Columbia presents a "false conflict" in the context of this case. A "false conflict" occurs when the policy of one state would be advanced by application of its law, while that of the other state would not be advanced by application of its law. In such a situation, the law of the interested jurisdiction prevails. [cit.] Here, Maryland's interest in protecting tavern owners from tort liability is not implicated where the negligent restaurant is situated in the District of Columbia and the unlawful conduct occurred therein. Hence we apply the law of the interested jurisdiction, the District of Columbia.[1]

Should there remain any question whether District of Columbia law applies in this case, *Gaither* [*v. Myers* 404 F.2d 216 (D.C.Cir.1968)], furnishes the answer. *Gaither* is binding precedent that District of Columbia law applies when a cause of action is cognizable under District of Columbia tort law on the basis of a violation within the District of Columbia of a District of Columbia statute or regulation, even though the injury occurs nearby in Maryland where a similar statute has been interpreted by Maryland's highest court as not supporting civil liability. In *Gaither*, the District of Columbia regulation at issue required car owners to remove their keys from their vehicles when leaving them unattended. The negligent conduct occurred in the District of Columbia. The car was subsequently stolen and driven into Maryland, where it struck and injured plaintiff five miles from the District of Columbia border.

Finally, we observe that other jurisdictions that have confronted the question of tavern keeper liability arising in a multi-state context have concluded that "the place where the liquor was unlawfully sold is of greater significance than the location of the accident because, when an intoxicated person is driving, the actual site of the crash is largely fortuitous," [cit.] and, accordingly, have applied the rule of liability of the state in which the vendor committed the unlawful act. * * *

Notes and Questions

1. As in *Babcock*, the plaintiff and the defendant in *Zhou* were domiciled in the same state. Unlike *Babcock*, however, the parties in *Zhou* did not have any pre-existing relationship between them. Moreover, the fact that they happened to be residents of the same state was as fortuitous as was the fact that the accident had occurred in Maryland rather than in Virginia or the District of Columbia. Did the court apply the law of the District of Columbia because the District was: (a) the domicile of both parties; (b) the domicile of the plaintiff; (c) the domicile of the

---

1. The only interest of Maryland that is implicated in this litigation, an interest in protecting public safety which we infer from its statutory prohibition on serving persons under the influence, is consistent with rather than in conflict with applying a District of Columbia rule of civil liability.

defendant; or (d) the place where the defendant had acted? (Incidentally, who was the defendant in *Zhou*?)

2. Is the District of Columbia rule that makes negligent tavern keepers answerable in tort ("dram shop act") a rule of conduct regulation or a rule of loss distribution? If it is the former, then which District of Columbia contact would justify the rule's application in *Zhou*? If it is the latter, then which District of Columbia contact would justify the rule's application in this case? Gaither v. Myers 404 F.2d 216 (D.C.Cir.1968), on which *Zhou* relied, involved a conduct-regulating rule. *Gaither* is reproduced infra at 286.

SECOND NOTE AND QUESTIONS ON INTEREST ANALYSIS

1. *Is the "domestic method" capable of pinpointing the policies underlying the competing rules of law?* How did the *Babcock* and *Zhou* courts identify the policies underlying the conflicting rules of the two states? Did they employ Currie's "domestic method of construction and interpretation"? Many commentators dispute that this method is capable of pinpointing the policies underlying the conflicting rules. See, inter alia, Bodenheimer, *Reorientation*, 737; Brilmayer, *The Myth*, 399, 424; Hay, *Reflections*, 1661; Juenger, *Critique*, 33–35; Reese, *Chief Judge Fuld*, 559–60; Rosenberg, *Two Views on Kell*, 463–64.

To the extent it pertains to the ascertainment of *forum* policies, is such skepticism justified? "The most important lesson taught in the first year of law school is that an intelligent decision to apply or not to apply a legal rule depends upon knowing the reasons for the rule." Weintraub, *Interest Analysis*, 631. "Governmental interest analysis is merely one of the many applications of teleological interpretation. It seeks to determine the pertinence of rules of law to multiple-contact cases through an analysis of the purposes behind these rules." Baade, *Counter-Revolution*, 149. Ascertaining the *telos* or purpose of a law is not always easy, but is it so much more difficult in conflicts cases than it is in ordinary domestic cases?

On the other hand, does *teleology* not have its limits when the rule in question is that of another state, especially a foreign country? A common legal tradition, language, and terminology facilitate the ascertainment of the policies underlying a sister state's law, but what about the laws of a foreign countries? See *Walton v. Arabian American Oil Co.*, supra 105, and accompanying Note. How did the *Babcock* court identify the policy of the Ontario guest statute? Are you satisfied with the court's interpretive method and conclusion?

2. *Can the policies underlying a rule of law help to delineate its intended territorial reach?* What about Currie's notion that, to the extent they can be established through the interpretative process, legislative purposes or policies can help delineate the intended spatial operation of the particular rule of law? Many commentators criticized this notion. "[L]egislatures *have* no actual intent on territorial reach," said one commentator (Brilmayer, *The Myth*, 393), "policies do not come equipped with labels proclaiming their spatial dimension," said another (Juenger, *Critique*, 35), and a third commentator asked rhetorically: "Has any state

legislature declared it important that its substantive law be chosen in some defined category of cases having multistate contacts?" (Gottesman, *Sea of Indeterminacy*, 531). (For defenses, see Kay, *A Defense*, 117-29; Sedler, *Forum Preference*, 606-20; Sedler, *Reflections*, 1632-35; and Weintraub, *Interest Analysis*, 630-34.)

The answer to the latter question is "yes." A perusal of state statutes reveals the existence of numerous provisions that contain precisely such declarations. They proclaim that the law of the enacting state shall apply to transactions or events that have certain enumerated contacts with the enacting state. Some of these statutes even expressly prohibit the contractual choice of another state's law. For documentation and discussion, see Symeonides, *American Choice of Law*, 29-32. True enough, like the guest statute in *Babcock*, the majority of statutes do not contain language declaring their intended extraterritorial reach. However, does the lack of such express declarations imply lack of legislative intent? (and incidentally is the phrase "legislative intent" confined to "actual" intent?) How do courts handle similar questions in domestic cases, for example in resolving conflicts between overlapping statutes, determining whether a statute is "remedial" or "procedural," or whether it should apply prospectively only or retrospectively as well? What then is different about multistate cases? As you read the cases in this chapter, see if you are satisfied with the way in which the courts have answered the questions of the extraterritorial reach of statutes. See, e.g., Justice Traynor's decisions in *Bernkrant v. Fowler* and *People v. One Ford Victoria*, infra 189, 187.

3. ***Do states really have an interest in the outcome of litigation between private parties***? Currie's assertion that a state has an interest in how a court resolves conflicts of laws was not new in American law. For example, this notion had figured prominently in a cluster of U.S. Supreme Court decisions in the 1930s interpreting the Full Faith and Credit clause of the Constitution.[1] Yet this notion continues to encounter criticism. Many commentators have argued that, aside from public-law matters such as taxation or currency regulation, states do not have an interest in the outcome of litigation between private persons.[2] Do you agree? Leaving aside the unfortunate qualifier "governmental" and Currie's rather awkward personification of states, would you agree that: a state like Michigan, the home of the three large auto makers, would be adversely affected if they are subjected to punitive damages under the law of another state;[3] or that the tax base of a state like Nevada, which

---

1. See Bradford Electric Light Co. v. Clapper, 286 U.S. 145 (1932); Alaska Packers Ass'n v. Industrial Accident Comm'n, 294 U.S. 532 (1935), reproduced infra 447; Pacific Employers Ins. Co. v. Industrial Accident Comm'n, 306 U.S. 493 (1939). See also Watson v. Employers Liability Assur. Corp. Limited, 348 U.S. 66 (1954).

2. See Ehrenzweig, *PIL*, 63; Hay, *Reflections*, 1660; Juenger, *Interstate Torts*, 206; Kegel, *Crisis*, 180–82; Rheinstein, *Festschrift*, 664. For responses, see Baade, *Counter-Revolution*, 148–49; Cavers, *Process*, 100; Kay, *A Defense* 133; Shapira, *Interest Approach*, 72–73; Sedler, *Reformulation*, 191–92.

3. See, e.g., Kelly v. Ford Motor Co., 933 F.Supp. 465, 470 (E.D.Pa.1996) (stating that Michigan had "a very strong interest" in applying its law denying punitive damages so as to ensure that "its domiciliary defendants are protected from excessive financial liability," and that by protecting from punitive damages companies such as Ford, "Michigan hopes to promote corporate migration into its economy . . . [which] will enhance the economic climate and well being of the state . . . by generating revenues."); Ness v. Ford Motor Co., 1993 U.S. Dist. Lexis 9938 at *5 (N.D.Ill.1993) ("Michigan has an interest in seeing that product-liability plaintiffs are not overcompensated, resulting in higher insurance premiums for Michigan manufacturers, higher costs, and lost jobs."; In re Air Crash Disaster Near Chicago, 644 F.2d 594 (7th

(continued...)

depends heavily on the casino industry, would be adversely affected if that industry is subjected to civil liability under another state's dram-shop act;[4] or that a country like Greece, which depends heavily on its shipping industry, would be adversely affected if it is subjected to American operating costs and compensation standards?[5]

If the answers to the above questions are affirmative, then these states would much prefer to avoid those *adverse consequences*, would they not? If so, *that* is the essence of a state "interest" here under discussion--it is a shorthand way of describing the notion that the policies, values, and objectives embodied in a state's law *can* be adversely affected when that law is *not* applied to a case the law was intended to reach. Unfortunately, in articulating this notion, Currie used terms that implied an *active desire* on the part of a "government" to apply its law and, worse, a proclivity to assert that desire in an aggressive, imperialistic fashion so as to accrue gains at the expense of other states, rather to avoid impairment of its own strongly held policies. Currie's exaggerations, or errors, however, do not nullify the idea that a state is not indifferent to the way a court resolves a conflicts case, even if the dispute is exclusively between private persons, and even if the state does not formally take a position by filing an *amicus curiae* brief.[6]

But does this emphasis on state interests entail the possibility of neglecting the interests of the individuals caught in the conflict? Indeed, Currie admitted that he found "no place in conflict-of-laws analysis for a calculus of private interests [because] [b]y the time the interstate plane is reached the resolution of conflicting private interests has been achieved; it is subsumed in the statement of the laws of the respective states."[7] What about the poor litigant whose interest is not so "subsumed"?

4. *How or where are state interests expressed?* If states have an interest in the outcome of litigation between private parties, where are those interests to be found? Obviously, the substantive legal rules involved in the particular conflict are the primary source of such interests, but are they the only source? Currie thought so. He was unwilling to recognize interests other than those reflected in the domestic rules implicated in the particular conflict, or to concede that these interests may acquire a different tenor or intensity in multistate cases. Accordingly, he refused to include in his calculus a state's "multistate interests," namely, interests that, though not

---

3. (...continued)
Cir.1981), *cert. denied* 454 U.S. 878 (1981) (emphasizing California's "substantial interest in the economic health of corporations [such as McDonnell Douglas Corp.] which do business within its borders" and the ability of such corporations to "enhance[] the economic well-being of the state." 644 F.2d at 614). For Michigan's protectionism of the three major auto makers, see Symeonides, *Choice of Law in 1998*, 375-76.

4. See *Bernhard v. Harrah's Club*, reproduced infra 215; *Hoeller v Riverside Resort Hotel*, discussed infra 222.

5. In practically every major international maritime conflicts case that has reached the United States Supreme Court, at least one foreign government, and occasionally the United States government as well, filed amicus curiae briefs bringing to the court's attention the country's respective interests in the outcome of litigation between shipowners and seamen. See Symeonides, *Maritime Conflicts*, 224–25, 228, 247; infra Ch. 7.

6. States have submitted such briefs in several interstate conflicts states, in state or federal courts. In international conflicts, briefs by foreign governments are even more common. For documentation, see Symeonides, *American Choice of Law*, 23-24.

7. Currie, *Selected Essays*, 610. But see Currie's letter to Cavers in Cavers, *Correspondence with Currie*, 488: "I shall not admit that I am unwilling to consider the claims of human beings to justice unless I can fit them into the conception of state interests."

directly reflected in a state's domestic law, stem from that state's membership in a broader community of states.[8] Despite his statement that "[t]he short-sighted, selfish state is nothing more than an experimental mode [and that] [n]o such state exists, at least in this country," Currie, *Selected Essays*, 616, Currie specifically dismissed the view that a state should be guided in its choice-of-law decisions by the "needs of the interstate and international system." Id. at 614. The only restraints he recognized were those imposed by the federal constitution. See infra 140-01.

5. *Currie's "personal-law principle."* Is a state always interested in protecting only its own residents and not similarly situated non-residents? For example, *Babcock* assumed that Ontario was interested in protecting only Ontario insurers, and *Zhou* assumed that Maryland was interested in protecting only Maryland tavern owners. Although Currie was not the first to subscribe to this motion, he articulated it in almost uncompromising terms. For example, in discussing *Kilberg v. Northeast Airlines (*supra, at 60) Currie was quite explicit that New York's pro-plaintiff "no damages ceiling" rule was reserved for the benefit of New York plaintiffs only: "New York's policy is not for the protection of all who buy tickets in New York, or board planes there. It is for the protection of New York people." Currie, *Selected Essays*, 705. See also id. at 691-721. Similarly, Currie thought that a state with a defendant-protecting rule, such as the guest statute involved in *Babcock* or the rule of contractual incapacity involved in *Milliken v. Pratt (*supra at 30) has an interest in applying such a rule to benefit resident defendants only. See id. at 724, 85–86, respectively.[9] Currie's notion that a state is interested in protecting its domiciliaries but not similarly situated out-of-staters has become known as his "personal-law principle." What do you think of this principle? Are Currie's critics correct when they charge that his approach "amounts to little more than a complicated way of saying that the law of the domicile governs"? Juenger, *Critique*, 39.

6. *Constitutional objections.* Some constitutional law scholars have argued that Currie's personal-law principle, which postulates that states are interested in "generat[ing] victories for their own people in a way that they are not interested in generating victories for others," violates the Privileges and Immunities clause of the Constitution.[10] Anticipating these charges, Currie proclaimed that his principle is "not vitiated, but rather vindicated" by the Constitution and that his approach, which "counsels the rational, moderate and controlled pursuit of self-interest[,] * * * also counsels that self-interest should be subordinated freely, and even gladly, to the constitutional restraints required and made possible by the federal union." Currie, *Selected Essays*, 525.[11] In essence, Currie argued that his approach was not

---

8. See the criticisms of Hill, *Reply to Currie*, 489–90; Kegel, *Crisis*, 180–82; Rosenberg, *Two Views on Kell*, 464; von Mehren, *Recent Trends*, 938; von Mehren, *Book Review*, 92–93. For Currie's response, see Currie, *Selected Essays*, 186–87. See also Kay, *A Defense*, 131–33.

9. Currie expressed this notion only with regard to what he called compensatory and defendant-protecting laws. In contrast, he thought that conduct-regulating laws, such as traffic laws, operate territorially and bind or benefit everyone within the territory regardless of his or her domicile. See id. at 58–61.

10. Ely, *The State's Interest*, 173-178. See Laycock, *Equal Citizens*.

11. Currie also returned the criticism to supporters of the traditional theory who "because of the compulsion of internationalist and altruist ideals, have guiltily suppressed the natural instincts of community self-interest." Id. He argued that "[the traditional theory's] impersonal choice-of-law rules * * * [were]

(continued...)

unconstitutional because the Constitution would not allow it to be--the Equal Protection and Privileges and Immunities clauses would control undue protectionism (id. at 123-26, 185, 191, 280, 285), while the Due Process and Full Faith and Credit clauses would control excessive forum favoritism (id. at 271, 280-81, 191). Is it good policy first to instigate and nurture protectionism and favoritism and then to depend on constitutional compulsion to curtail it? We shall return to these constitutional law issues in Chapter 5.

7. *Policy objections.* Currie also anticipated policy objections to his personal-law principle when he stated that his approach did "not imply the ruthless pursuit of self-interest by the states" (id. at 185)[12] and did not preclude what he called "rational altruism." Id. at 186. He strongly condemned, however, what he called the "irrational altruism" of the traditional approach, which "often require[d] a state to sacrifice its own interest even though the interest of no other state is thereby advanced." Id. at 191. But Currie never retreated from his basic premise that a state is interested in protecting its own citizens only. Again, is it good policy to elevate protectionism into a choice-of-law principle and then to depend on "rational altruism" to curtail the inevitable excesses? Leaving aside constitutional restraints, are Currie's prescriptions consistent with the basic social and moral principles underlying American federalism? Professor Cavers, one of Currie's friends and co-revolutionaries, charged that some of Currie's prescriptions are "more appropriate to a tribal system of law than to that prevailing in the American Union."[13] Do you agree?

THE FIRST SYNTHESIS: THE RESTATEMENT (SECOND)

In 1953, the American Law Institute (ALI) began drafting the Restatement (Second) of Conflicts, partly in response to the challenge of the conflicts revolution. The Reporter's task was assigned to Professor Willis L. Reese, who was a member of the new school of conflicts thought, although not of its revolutionary branch. Reese agreed with many of the criticisms leveled against the first Restatement, but more importantly, he was receptive to the criticisms of his own drafts of the second Restatement. A cursory look at the successive versions of what eventually became §6 of the Restatement (Second) reveals this evolution in the Reporter's own thinking, as well as the gradual gains of the new school over the old. The final version of the Restatement (Second) promulgated in 1969, did not join the revolution, but was a conscious compromise and synthesis between the old and the new schools, as well as among the various branches of the new schools.

1. *Section 6.* The cornerstone of the Restatement (Second) is § 6. It sets forth the guiding principles of the choice-of-law process, as follows:

---

11. (...continued)
discriminatory at times, and at other times enforce[d] a purposeless self-denial, or an unwarranted intrusion into the concerns of other states." Id.

12. See also id. at 549: "In a federal union such as ours there is no room for the cycle of discrimination, retaliation, and reciprocity. Each state may and should extend the benefits of its laws to foreigners, not merely with the hope but with the assurance that all other states will reciprocate as a matter of course."

13. Cavers, *Process*, 151 n. 29. See also Bodenheimer, *Reorientation*, 738; Trautman, *Reflections*, 1615; Brilmayer, *The Myth*, 416.

(1) A court, subject to constitutional restrictions, will follow a statutory directive of its own state on choice of law.

(2) When there is no such directive, the factors relevant to the choice of the applicable rule of law include (a) the needs of the interstate and international systems, (b) the relevant policies of the forum, (c) the relevant policies of other interested states and the relative interests of those states in the determination of the particular issue, (d) the protection of justified expectations, (e) the basic policies underlying the particular field of law, (f) certainty, predictability and uniformity of result, and (g) ease in the determination and application of the law to be applied.[1]

From a philosophical viewpoint, § 6, and specifically the policies listed in its subsection 2, is important in that it establishes the ideology of the Restatement (Second), which distinguishes it from other modern theories such as Professor Leflar's "better-law" approach (described infra at 165) or Currie's interest analysis. Similarly, the list of subsection 2 is broader and qualitatively different from the policies relied upon by interest analysis which disregards, de-emphasizes, or expressly rejects most of the policies listed in subsection 2, and relies mostly on policies like those mentioned in clauses (b), (c), and (e) of that subsection. The contrast between Currie's interest analysis and the Restatement (Second) is most manifest in their varying degrees of sensitivity towards "the needs of the interstate and international systems" and the need for "uniformity of result." To Currie's ethnocentric attitude toward both these goals, the Restatement juxtaposes a universalistic perception of private international law reflected in the statement that "the most important function of choice-of-law rules is to make the interstate and international systems work well[,] * * * to further harmonious relations between states and to facilitate commercial intercourse between them." § 6 cmt. d. The contrast is hardly surprising, since, unlike interest analysis, which Currie conceived from the perspective of the forum judge confined to the role of the "handmaiden" of the forum legislature, the Restatement (Second) was drafted from the perspective of a neutral forum, under the auspices of the American Law Institute, a body that strives for national uniformity.

From a methodological viewpoint, § 6 is important in that it provides a guiding, as well as a validating, test for applying almost all other sections of the Restatement, most of which incorporate § 6 by reference.[2] Because the § 6 factors are not listed in a hierarchical order, and in fact they may point in different directions in a given case (Restatement (Second) § 6, cmt. (c)), they fall short of providing the court with an actual choice of law. Nevertheless, these factors can help steer courts away from a jurisdiction-selecting choice that is based solely on factual contacts. Although the specific sections of the Restatement call for the application of the law of the state with the "most significant relationship"--a term that evokes jurisdiction-selecting

---

1. Quoted with the permission of the copyright owner, The American Law Institute.

2. See, e.g., Restatement (Second) § 145, which provides that a tort issue is governed by the law of the state that, with respect to that issue, has the most significant relationship to the occurrence and the parties "under the principles stated in § 6."

notions--the choice of that state is to be made "under the principles stated in §6,"[3] and by taking into account the contacts listed in the specific sections. This constantly repeated cross-reference to § 6 also helps supplement the multilateral approach of the specific Restatement sections with elements from a unilateral approach.

2. *The "most-significant-relationship" formula* is the other cornerstone of the Restatement (Second). While § 6 articulates the principles and policies that should guide the choice-of-law process, the ubiquitous most-significant-relationship formula describes the objective of that process--to apply the law of the state that, with regard to the particular issue, has the most significant relationship with the parties and the dispute.

3. *Rules.* In relatively few cases, the Restatement identifies *a priori* the state of the most significant relationship through black-letter rules. This is the case with most of the sections devoted to property and successions issues.[4] See infra Chapter 4 at 395-96 and 418 *et seq.* In cases involving land, the applicable law is almost invariably the "law that would be applied by the courts of the situs."[5] This is as close as the Restatement (Second) comes to prescribing black-letter rules. These rules are subject to the traditional escape mechanisms of the generic type, such as *ordre public* and *renvoi.* For example, the above-quoted phrase regarding land is an explicit authorization for *renvoi,* which occasionally may lead to the application of non-situs law.

4. *Presumptive rules.* In other cases, the Restatement identifies the state of the most significant relationship only tentatively, through presumptive rules that instruct the judge to apply the law of a certain state, unless it appears that in the particular case another state has a more significant relationship. For example, all ten of the Restatement sections that designate the law governing different types of torts conclude with the following escape clause: "unless, with respect to the particular issue, some other state has a more significant relationship under the principles stated in § 6 to the occurrence and the parties, in which event the local law of the other state will be applied"[6] This clause is one of the most repeated phrases in the entire Restatement. See, e.g., §§ 146-51, 153-55, 175. In the area of contract conflicts, the "unless" clause appears in most of the sections devoted to particular contracts. See, e.g., §§ 189-93, 196.

5. *Pointers.* In some instances, the presumptive rules are even more equivocal and amount to no more than mere pointers in the direction of the likely applicable law. The pertinent sections provide that the state with the "most significant relationship" will "usually" be one particular state. For example, in the area of tort conflicts, eleven of the nineteen sections devoted to specific tort issues conclude with

---

3. Restatement (Second) § 145, supra n.2.

4. For succession to movables, see §§ 260-65; For inter-vivos transactions involving movables, see §§ 245-55. See also the unilateral choice-of-law rules contained in Restatement (Second) §§ 285 (divorce); 286 (nullity of marriage); and 289 (adoption).

5. For inter vivos transactions involving land, see §§ 223, 225-32. For succession to land, see §§ 236, 239-42. This phrase is often accompanied by the prediction that these courts "usually" will apply their own law.

6. For example, in an action for an invasion of privacy, the applicable law is the local law of the state where the invasion occurred, "unless, with respect to the particular issue, some other state has a more significant relationship." § 152.

the adage that "[t]he applicable law will usually be the local law of the state where the injury occurred." (See § 156, tortious character of conduct; § 157, standard of care; § 158, interest entitled to legal protection; § 159, duty owed to plaintiff; § 160, legal cause; § 162, specific conditions of liability; § 164, contributory fault; § 165, assumption of risk; § 166, imputed negligence; and § 172, joint torts); one section, § 169, provides that for intrafamily immunity the applicable law "will usually be the local law of the state of the parties' domicil;" and only the remaining seven sections (161, 163, 168, 170-71, and 173-74) are unaided by such a presumption.

In contract conflicts, § 188 provides that, subject to some exceptions, "[i]f the place of negotiating the contract and the place of performance are in the same state, the local law of this state will usually be applied." Similarly, § 198 provides that "[t]he capacity of a party to contract will usually be upheld if he has such capacity under the local law of the state of his domicil," while § 199 provides that contractual "[f]ormalities which meet the requirements of the place where the parties execute the contract will usually be acceptable." Similar language is found in many other sections of the Restatement (Second).

6. **Ad hoc *analysis.*** Finally, in the remaining and most difficult cases, the Restatement provides neither presumptive rules nor pointers. It simply provides a non-exclusive, non-hierarchical list of the factual contacts that should be "taken into account" by the judge in choosing the applicable law. On this point the Restatement (Second) differs drastically from the first Restatement, which made the choice of the applicable law dependent on a single physical contact. The contacts to be taken into account in applying the Restatement (Second) vary from one subject matter to another. In torts, these contacts include the place of the injury, the place of the conduct causing the injury, the domicile, residence, nationality and place of business of the parties, and the place where the relationship, if any, between the parties is centered. See § 145(2). In contracts, these contacts include the places of contracting, negotiation and performance of the contract, the location of the subject matter, and the domicile, residence, nationality, or place of business of the parties. See § 188(2).

The determination of the state with the most significant relationship is to be made "under the principles stated in § 6" by "taking into account" the above factual contacts "according to their relative importance with respect to the particular issue." See, e.g. §§ 145, 188. This language suggests that the policy part of this analysis should carry more weight than the evaluation of the factual contacts. Yet, courts have tended to do it the other way around, by first focusing on the factual contacts listed in the pertinent section of the Restatement (Second) and then, if ever, on the policies of § 6. When the contacts of state A are clearly more numerous than are those of state B, some courts tend to assume that state A is the one that has the more significant relationship, without testing that assumption under the principles of § 6. In contrast, when the factual contacts are evenly divided between the two states, courts look to the policies of § 6, but many courts pay lip service to most of the policies listed therein, and confine themselves to examining "the relative policies of the forum [and] of other interested states." § 6. It seems that cases that follow the first type of practice differ little from cases that follow a "grouping of contacts" approach, while cases that follow the latter type of practice differ little from cases that follow a pure interest analysis.

7. *Judicial Acceptance of the Restatement (Second)*. After a slow start, the Restatement (Second) has managed to gain judicial acceptance in a plurality of states. In 2003, 21 states followed the Restatement in tort conflicts and 24 did likewise in contract conflicts. These states are listed at the end of this chapter. See infra 299 *et seq*. In addition, the Restatement (Second) is followed in part by several other states that have adopted a "mixed" approach (see id.), as well as by many federal courts in federal question cases. See Symeonides, *The Revolution Today*, §§ 80-87 (also discussing the reasons for the Restatement's wide following and the various gradations of commitment to it). Thus, three decades after its official promulgation, the Restatement (Second) appears close to dominating the American methodological landscape.

O'Connor v. O'Connor

Supreme Court of Connecticut, 1986.
201 Conn. 632, 519 A.2d 13.

PETERS, J. The sole issue on this appeal is whether, under the circumstances of this case, an injured person may pursue a cause of action under Connecticut law to recover for allegedly tortious conduct that occurred in a jurisdiction where such a cause of action would not be permitted. The plaintiff, Roseann O'Connor, brought an action against the defendant, Brian O'Connor, seeking damages for injuries that she suffered as a result of an automobile accident in Quebec.[1] * * *

At the time of the accident, the defendant was operating the automobile and the plaintiff was his sole passenger. The parties, both of whom were Connecticut domiciliaries, were on a one day pleasure trip that began, and was intended to end, in Vermont. The plaintiff underwent hospital treatment for her injuries in Quebec and has suffered continuing physical disabilities while residing in Connecticut.

The plaintiff brought an action against the defendant on August 17, 1983, alleging that she had suffered serious and permanent injuries as a result of the defendant's negligent operation of the automobile. The plaintiff's complaint stated a cause of action permitted by General Statutes § 38-323, part of Connecticut's No-fault Motor Vehicle Insurance Act, General Statutes §§ 38-319 through 38-350. Section 38-323 permits the victim of serious physical or economic injury caused by an automobile accident to sue the tortfeasor for damages. The defendant, however, moved to strike the complaint, on the ground that the applicable law in the case was the law of Quebec. Quebec law would not permit the plaintiff's tort action because Quebec Revised Statutes, chapter A-25, title II, §§ 3 and 4, provides instead for government funded compensation for victims of bodily injury caused by automobile accidents.

* * * [T]he plaintiff urges this court to reexamine the propriety of our continued adherence to the doctrine of lex loci delicti in cases of personal injury. In the

---

1. The parties were not related at the time of the accident. They subsequently married each other.

particular circumstances of this case, the plaintiff maintains, we should no longer adhere rigidly to the doctrine of lex loci but should instead seek to discern and to apply the law of the jurisdiction that has the most significant relationship to the controversy, in accordance with the principles of the Restatement (Second) of Conflict of Laws. Under the Restatement, according to the plaintiff, the jurisdiction that has the most significant relationship to this tort action is not Quebec but Connecticut. Quebec, although it was the place of injury, has no significant interest in applying its statutory compensation scheme to the controversy because the location of the automobile accident in Quebec was purely fortuitous. Connecticut, by contrast, has a substantial interest in applying its law to the case because: (1) both parties are domiciled and employed in Connecticut; (2) both parties are subject to the requirements and entitled to the benefits of Connecticut's no-fault insurance law, and that law embodies a policy of providing access to the courts for persons with serious bodily injuries; and (3) aside from her initial treatment after the accident, the plaintiff has received all of her post-accident medical care in Connecticut. We agree with the plaintiff. * * *

* * * [T]he time has come for the law in this state to abandon categorical allegiance to the doctrine of lex loci delicti in tort actions. Lex loci has lost its theoretical underpinnings. Its formerly broad base of support has suffered erosion. We need not decide today, however, whether to discard lex loci in all of its manifestations. It is sufficient for us to consider whether, in the circumstances of the present case, reason and justice require the relaxation of its stringent insistence on determining conflicts of laws solely by reference to the place where a tort occurred.

In deciding how to assess a replacement for lex loci, we recognize that the legal literature offers us various alternative approaches to the problems of choice of law. Three such approaches have gained widespread judicial acceptance: (1) the choice of law rules promulgated in the Restatement Second of Conflict of Laws; (2) the "governmental interest" approach developed by Professor Brainerd Currie; and (3) Professor Robert A. Leflar's theory of choice of law, in which the applicable law in multi-jurisdictional controversies is determined by reference to five "choice-influencing considerations." The Restatement (Second) approach, the product of more than a decade of research, incorporates some of the attributes of the latter two approaches, as well as others, in an attempt to "provide formulations that were true to the cases, were broad enough to permit further development in the law, and yet were able to give some guidance by pointing to what was thought would probably be the result reached in the majority of cases." W. Reese, "The Second Restatement of Conflict of Laws Revisited," 34 Mercer L. Rev. 501, 519 (1983). A majority of the courts that have abandoned lex loci have adopted the principles of the Restatement Second as representing the most comprehensive and equitably balanced approach to conflict of laws. It is therefore our conclusion that we too should incorporate the guidelines of the Restatement as the governing principles for those cases in which application of the doctrine of lex loci would produce an arbitrary, irrational result.

III. We turn now to an examination of the relevant provisions of the Restatement Second of Conflict of Laws in the context of the dispute presently before us. * * *

Applying the choice of law analysis of §§ 145 and 6 to the facts of this case involves a weighing of the relative significance of the various factors that § 6 lists. Of greatest importance for present purposes are the choices of policy emphasized in § 6 (2) (b), (c) and (e). We are not today concerned with a case that offends systemic policy concerns of another state or country, nor do the facts warrant an inference of justified expectations concerning the applicability of anything other than the law of the forum. Although the principles of certainty and ease of application must be taken into account, the Restatement cautions against attaching independent weight to these auxiliary factors, noting that they are ancillary to the goal of providing rational, fair choice of law rules. As comment i to § 6 states: "In a rapidly developing area, such as choice of law, it is often more important that good rules be developed than that predictability and uniformity of result should be assured through continued adherence to existing rules." See also Restatement (Second), Conflict of Laws § 6, comment j (policy in § 6 [2] [g] should "not be overemphasized, since it is obviously of greater importance that choice-of-law rules lead to desirable results").

For assistance in our evaluation of the policy choices set out in §§ 145(1) and 6 (2), we turn next to § 145(2) of the Restatement, which establishes black-letter rules of priority to facilitate the application of the principles of § 6 to tort cases. [cit.] Section 145(2) provides: "Contacts to be taken into account in applying the principles of § 6 to determine the law applicable to an issue include: (a) the place where the injury occurred, (b) the place where the conduct causing the injury occurred, (c) the domicil, residence, nationality, place of incorporation and place of business of the parties, and (d) the place where the relationship, if any, between the parties is centered. These contacts are to be evaluated according to their relative importance with respect to the particular issue."

In the circumstances of the present case, because the plaintiff was injured in Quebec and the tortious conduct occurred there, § 145(2) (a) and (b) weigh in favor of applying Quebec law. Because both parties are Connecticut domiciliaries and their relationship is centered here, § 145(2)(c) and (d) indicate that Connecticut law should be applied. To resolve this potential standoff, we need to recall that it is the significance, and not the number, of § 145(2) contacts that determines the outcome of the choice of law inquiry under the Restatement approach. As the concluding sentence of § 145(2) states, "[t]hese contacts are to be evaluated according to their relative importance with respect to the particular issue." [cit.]

In order to apply the § 6 guidelines to the circumstances of the present case, we must, therefore, turn our attention once more to the particular issue whose disparate resolution by two relevant jurisdictions gives rise to the conflict of laws. Specifically, we must analyze the respective policies and interests of Quebec, the place of injury, and Connecticut, the forum state, with respect to the issue of whether the plaintiff should be allowed to recover damages from the defendant in a private cause of action premised on the defendant's negligent operation of an automobile. In the process of that analysis, we must evaluate the relevance of each jurisdiction's § 145(2) contacts to this particular controversy.

We first consider the policies and interests of Quebec in this regard. Quebec, as the place of injury, has an obvious interest in applying its standards of conduct to govern the liability, both civil and criminal, of persons who use its highways. [cit.]

"This interest arises from the right and duty of the sovereign to protect those within its borders from injury to person or property * * * ." Comment, "Selection of Law Governing Measure of Damages for Wrongful Death," 61 Colum.L.Rev. 1497, 1510 (1961). If the issue at stake in the present controversy were whether the defendant's conduct was negligent, we might well conclude that Quebec's interest in applying its law was of paramount significance. [cit.]

In the present case, however, the relevant Quebec law expresses no interest in regulating the conduct of the defendant, but rather limits the liability exposure to which his conduct subjects him. Quebec's Automobile Insurance Act, Quebec Revised Statutes, chapter A-25, presumably embodies policies similar to that of our own no-fault automobile insurance act: assurance to automobile accident victims of access to expeditious and adequate financial compensation, and assurance to automobile owners of access to insurance at reasonable premiums. [cit.] Quebec, however, has chosen to implement this policy, in title II, § 4, with a provision which, like our workers' compensation act, [cit.] eschews investigation into the possible negligence of the defendant's conduct and limits the amount of damages the victim of the defendant's conduct may recover.[15] In *Reich v. Purcell*, 432 P.2d 727 (1967), Chief Justice Traynor, speaking with regard to statutory limitations on wrongful death damages, noted: "Limitations of damages ... have little or nothing to do with conduct. They are concerned not with how people should behave but with how survivors should be compensated. The state of the place of the wrong has little or no interest in such compensation when none of the parties reside there."

The policies behind Quebec's no-fault rule would not be substantially furthered by application of Quebec law in the circumstances of the present case. In this case, neither the victim nor the tortfeasor is a Quebec resident. There is no evidence on the record that the vehicle involved in the accident was insured or registered in Quebec. [cit.] Rather, the record indicates that the parties were merely "passing through" the province, and that the location of the accident was fortuitous. Clearly the goal of reducing insurance premiums in Quebec is not furthered by application of the Quebec no-fault act to an accident involving only nonresidents of Quebec, in an automobile that was not insured in the province. Quebec's interest in alleviating the administrative and judicial costs of automobile accident litigation is in no way implicated when, as in this case, a nonresident brings suit against another nonresident in a foreign jurisdiction. We note that a Quebec resident suing the defendant in Connecticut would not be subject to the Quebec act's lawsuit prohibition; under the Quebec act, such a plaintiff would be entitled to statutory compensation under Quebec law as well as any damages recoverable in a private action under Connecticut law. Quebec Revised Statutes, chapter A-25, title II, § 7.[16] Application of Quebec law in these circumstances would thus produce the same anomalous result that we

---

15. We note additionally that the Quebec act does not express a policy of immunizing tortfeasors from the consequences of their actions. * * *

16. Quebec Revised Statutes, chapter A-25, title II, § 7, provides in relevant part: "The victim of an accident that occurred outside Quebec who is entitled to the compensation provided for in this title may benefit by it while retaining his rights of action with regard to the excess under the law of the place where the accident occurred."

deplored in Simaitis v. Flood, 437 A.2d 828 (Conn.1980), since it would "bestow upon temporary visitors injured in Connecticut all the relief which [Connecticut law] affords, but deny that same relief to Connecticut residents" injured in Quebec. Id.[17]

The foregoing analysis leads us to conclude that Quebec's status as the place of injury is not a significant contact for purposes of our choice of law inquiry in this case. Accordingly, since Quebec has no other contacts with this litigation, we hold that Quebec has no interest in applying its no-fault act to bar the plaintiff's action.

In order to justify the application of Connecticut law to the issue at stake, however, we must consider whether Connecticut's contacts with the litigation give it a legitimate interest in applying its law to the controversy. We are persuaded that Connecticut does have the requisite significant contacts.[18]

Connecticut has a significant interest in this litigation because both the plaintiff and the defendant are, and were at the time of the accident, Connecticut domiciliaries. Consequently, to the extent that they might have anticipated being involved in an automobile accident, they could reasonably have expected to be subject to the provisions of Connecticut's no-fault act. More importantly, however, Connecticut has a strong interest in assuring that the plaintiff may avail herself of the full scope of remedies for tortious conduct that Connecticut law affords. [cit.] Connecticut's no-fault act serves similar purposes to Quebec's Automobile Insurance Act; [cit.] with one important exception: unlike the Quebec act, the Connecticut act embraces the policy of "providing the more seriously injured the opportunity to seek true redress" in a judicial forum. *Gentile v. Altermatt*, supra, 169 Conn. at 297 [(1975)]. To deny the plaintiff a cause of action in this case would frustrate this important purpose of the Connecticut no-fault statute. This is particularly true when, as in this case, the alleged consequences of the plaintiff's injury, including medical expenses and lost income, have been borne in Connecticut.

Our conclusion that we should look to the law of Connecticut rather than to the law of Quebec in this case should not be construed as a blanket endorsement of reliance on Connecticut law in all circumstances. We are persuaded that, in this case, justice and reason point to Connecticut as the jurisdiction whose laws bear the most significant relationship to the controversy at hand. We are reassured that courts in other jurisdictions, relying on the Restatement Second of Conflict of Laws, have equally concluded that they should disregard the law of a foreign jurisdiction that has at best a fortuitous and incidental relationship to the controversy to be adjudicated.

---

17. It is also significant for purposes of this analysis that Quebec provides only a limited right of recovery for nonresidents injured in automobile accidents within its territorial boundaries. Such nonresidents are entitled to compensation only to the extent that they are not responsible for the accident, "unless otherwise agreed between the Regie and the competent authorities of the place of residence of such victim." Quebec Revised Statutes, chapter A-25, title II, § 8.

18. Notwithstanding our conclusion that Connecticut is the only jurisdiction with a significant interest in applying its law to the present controversy, we decline to adopt the plaintiff's characterization of this case as a "false conflict." The plaintiff's interpretation of a false conflict, as one where the laws of two jurisdictions with contacts to the litigation differ, but only one has an interest in applying its law to the controversy, is commonly associated with the Currie governmental interest analysis approach to choice of law. [cit.] We note, however, that other commentators have declined to characterize such a situation as a false conflict, but rather have reserved that term to describe cases where application of the laws of two or more jurisdictions with contacts to the litigation reach identical results, thus eliminating any potential conflict of laws. [cit.]

[cit.] We can readily conceive of circumstances, however, in which the choice between the relevant jurisdictions would be much more problematic. For example, Quebec law would have been entitled to greater weight if the accident had involved a Quebec resident; see, e.g., *Dym v. Gordon*, 16 N.Y.2d 120, 125 (1965); or a unique configuration of Quebec roads; see, e.g., *Casey v. Manson Construction & Engineering Co.*, 247 Or. 274, 288 (1967); or if the defendant's negligent conduct, rather than the plaintiff's right to sue, had been at issue. The guiding principles of the Restatement command respect precisely because they encourage a searching case-by-case contextual inquiry into the significance of the interests that the law of competing jurisdictions may assert in particular controversies.

We therefore reverse the judgment of the Appellate Court upholding the trial court's granting of the motion to strike the plaintiff's complaint, and direct that this case be remanded to the trial court for further proceedings consistent with this opinion.

Notes and Questions

1. Compare the facts and the choice-of-law issue in *O'Connor* with those in *Babcock*. Any differences? Compare *O'Connor*'s choice-of-law approach with that of *Babcock*. Any differences? Did *O'Connor* endorse the distinction between issues of conduct regulation and issues of loss distribution? Did the *O'Connor* court's refusal to characterize the case as a false conflict affect the outcome?

2. A few years after *O'Connor* was decided, Quebec abandoned the *lex loci delicti* and adopted a statutory choice-of-law rule that calls for the application of the law of the parties' common domicile. See Quebec Civ. Code Art. 3126. Does the adoption of such a rule mean that now Quebec considers itself to be uninterested in applying its law to cases such as *O'Connor*? For an affirmative answer, see Miller v. White, 702 A.2d 392 (Vt.1997) (a case identical to *O'Connor* and reaching the same result), in which the court concluded that Quebec's new choice-of-law rule was "an indication of Quebec's weak interest in this type of action." Id. at 396. Although the *Miller* court did not use the term renvoi, is this not a renvoi-type syllogism? In any event, do you agree with the court's conclusion? Before you answer, keep in mind that at the time *O'Connor* was decided, Quebec still adhered to the *lex loci* rule. If Quebec was "uninterested" in *Miller*, was Quebec "interested" in *O'Connor*? Do the foreign state's choice-of-law rules indicate whether that state considers itself interested only when these rules are recent or "modern" but not when they are old or "traditional"? Should the forum pay less attention to the foreign state's choice-of-law rules when they belong to the latter rather than to the former category? Recall our discussion of renvoi after *ARTRA* and *Braxton*, supra 78 *et seq.* What should be the role of renvoi in policy-based choice-of-law approaches that resolve conflicts problems on the basis of state interests?

3. Who was the real defendant in *O'Connor*? Suppose that Mr. O'Connor's automobile insurance policy provided that the insurer was obligated to "discharge any obligations imposed on the insured by law for bodily injury resulting from his operation of the insured automobile." In such a case, should the word "law" be

confined to the law of Quebec? In Williams v. State Farm Mut. Auto. Ins. Co., 641 A.2d 783 (Conn.1994), an analogous case involving uninsured motorist coverage, the Connecticut Supreme Court answered this question in the affirmative. Is *Williams* reconcilable with *O'Connor*? Is the question of insurance coverage to be answered under the law governing the insurance contract (and, if so, which law is that) or under the law governing the tort action (and, if so, which law is that)? In State Farm Mut. Auto. Ins. Co. v. Gillette, 641 N.W.2d 662 (Wis.2002), the Wisconsin Supreme Court applied the pro-insured law of the insured's home state, Wisconsin, which was also the state in which he purchased the policy, rather than the law of the place of the accident, Manitoba.

4. Suppose that in *O'Connor* the law of Quebec, but not Connecticut, prohibited interspousal suits. Would the resulting conflict be identical to or different from the conflict involved in *Haumschild*, (supra 48)? Why?

5. **Babcock-*Pattern Cases Litigated in the Accident State.*** Suppose now that, in a conflict like the one described in Note 4, supra, the lawsuit is filed in the accident state. How should one resolve this conflict? Peters v. Peters, 634 P.2d 586 (Haw.1981) involved this pattern. This case arose out of a Hawaii traffic accident in which a New York domiciliary was injured while riding in a rented car driven by her husband. Hawaii, but not New York, had an interspousal immunity rule that barred the plaintiff's suit against him and ultimately his insurer. While announcing its general abandonment of the *lex loci delicti* rule, the Hawaii Supreme Court applied Hawaii law because the insurance policy issued on the rental car in Hawaii had been written in contemplation of Hawaii immunity law.

Nelson v. Hix, 522 N.E.2d 1214 (Ill.1988), *cert. denied*, 488 U.S. 925 (1988), which was decided under the Restatement (Second), reached the opposite conclusion. Mrs. Nelson, an Ontario domiciliary, was injured in a two-car collision in Illinois while riding in a car driven by her Ontario husband who had rented the car in Illinois. The driver of the other car was Mrs. Hix, an Illinois domiciliary. Mrs. Nelson sued her husband and Mrs. Hix for damages. The law of Illinois, but not Ontario, prohibited interspousal suits. The court applied Ontario law, basing its decision on § 169 of the Restatement (Second), which provides that intrafamily immunity issues are "usually" governed by "the local law of the state of the parties' domicile." The court stated:

[T]he domicile of the parties and the place where their marital relationship was centered is, in our opinion, more important to a resolution of the issue than where the accident and injury occurred. * * * [S]ection 169 of the Restatement (Second) recognizes that the "[s]tate of domicile is the one most concerned with the well-being of the spouses and protection of the marital relationships, and it is upon this that it bases its claim to primary interest in the outcome of the conflicts situation." [cit.] The State of domicile, moreover, "has the primary responsibility for establishing and regulating the incidents of the family relationship." *Emery v. Emery*, 289 P.2d 218, 223 (Cal.1955).

Illinois, on the other hand, has little interest in regulating the right of married foreign citizens to maintain actions in tort against each other. Because the Nelsons are not citizens of Illinois, this State has no governmental interest in the preservation of their marital relationship. Although Illinois possesses an interest in not having its courts used for collusive lawsuits, we believe that this interest is not furthered by barring interspousal tort suits by citizens of other States or countries.

Nelson, 522 N.E.2d at 1217-18. But what about the fact that--unlike *Babcock*, *O'Connor*, or *Haumschild*--the car involved in the *Nelson* accident was registered and insured in the accident state, Illinois, whose law prevented recovery against the driver and thus against his insurer? The court addressed this issue as follows:

Ontario's interest in regulating the incidents of the family relationships of its domiciliaries outweighs any interest Illinois may have in protecting the expectations of insurance carriers who have issued policies here. The Nelsons rented a car licensed and registered in Illinois, and purchased insurance covering the automobile for the rental period from an Illinois insurer. The insurance policy did not provide that claims under the policy were to be governed by the laws of Illinois. Automobiles are by their nature mobile, and insurers are on notice that they may be driven to States which prohibit interspousal tort suits by persons from jurisdictions that have abrogated that immunity.

Id. at 1218. What do you make of the last sentence? It seems to contemplate a *non*-Illinois (e.g. Ontario) car and insurance policy, which was driven *to* Illinois. However, the *Nelson* facts do not match, do they? Is not an Illinois insurer who insures an Illinois car in Illinois entitled to the application of the law of Illinois if the accident occurs there? Should the plaintiff always win, provided that the defendant is an insurance company?

Finally, what about the other defendant, Mrs. Hix? Does she stand to lose or to gain from the court's decision to apply Ontario law on the issue of interspousal immunity? Should this factor affect the court's decision on this issue?

Bryant v. Silverman
Supreme Court of Arizona, 1985.
146 Ariz. 41, 703 P.2d 1190.

GORDON, J., * * * This case arises out of a tragic airplane crash which took the lives of several victims. On December 31, 1981, Sun West Airlines Flight 104 departed from Albuquerque, New Mexico en route to Durango, Colorado. Upon reaching Durango, the plane crashed while attempting to land at the airport, killing the pilot and passengers Paul Bryant, Mary Peters and Joyce Branham. Joyce Branham's children, Stacy and Jimmy Sadler, Jr. survived the crash. The cause of the crash is disputed by plaintiffs and defendant.

At the time of the crash, Paul Bryant was domiciled in Arizona, Mary Peters in New Mexico, and Joyce Branham in Texas. Sun West Airlines (hereafter Sun West) was an Arizona corporation having its principal place of business in Phoenix and servicing cities in New Mexico, Colorado and Arizona. All three decedents were on their way to Colorado to enjoy ski holidays.

In February 1982, plaintiff Barbara Bryant filed a wrongful death action in Arizona for the death of her husband Paul Bryant against defendant Sun West.

Subsequently, similar actions were filed in Arizona for the deaths of Mary Peters, Joyce Branham and for the injuries to Stacy and Jimmy Sadler. All actions were consolidated.

After considering cross motions for summary judgment relating to the issues of compensatory and punitive damages, the trial judge found that Colorado had the most significant relationship to the occurrence and the parties on all compensatory and punitive damage issues, and therefore, held that Colorado law governed all damage issues. Under Colorado law, compensatory damages in wrongful death actions are limited to the net pecuniary loss suffered by the survivor (beneficiary). [cit.] Additionally, Colorado prohibits recovery of punitive damages in wrongful death actions. [cit.] All plaintiffs would prefer that Arizona law be applied to this case since Arizona places no limitation on compensatory or punitive damages. Accordingly, plaintiffs contend that Arizona law should govern the damage issues because plaintiff-Bryant, decedent-Paul Bryant, and defendant-Sun West were domiciled in Arizona at the time of the crash and because the misconduct occurred in Arizona. Sun West, on the other hand, argues that since Colorado was the place of injury and conduct and the place where the relationship between the parties arose, Colorado law should apply.

In determining which state's law to apply, this Court has adopted the rules embodied in the Restatement (Second) of Conflicts (1971) to analyze and solve conflicts problems arising in Arizona. [cit.] Restatement (Second) of Conflicts (1971) §§ 175 and 178 deal specifically with the choice of law principles in an action for wrongful death and to the damage issues in such an action. Restatement § 178 sets out the choice of law principles for wrongful death damages, and states:

> "§ 178. Damages. The law selected by application of the rule of §175 [wrongful death] determines the measure of damages in an action for wrongful death."

Comment b of this section notes that merely because the conduct and injury occur in one state does not *ipso facto* require application of that state's law to the issue of damages, but instead, the law of the state with the "dominant interest" or "greater interest" should govern:

> "b. *Rationale*. The choice-of-law principles stated in § 6 should be applied in determining the state whose local law will be applied to determine the measure of damages in a wrongful death action. In general, this should be the state which has the *dominant interest* in the determination of this issue. *The state of conduct and injury will not, by reason of these contacts alone, be the state which is primarily concerned with the measure of damages in a wrongful death action.* The local law of this state will, however, be applied unless some other state has a *greater interest* in the determination of this issue. In a situation where one state is the state of domicile of the defendant, the decedent and the beneficiaries, it would seem that, ordinarily at least, the wrongful death statute of this state should be applied to determine the measure of damages." (emphasis added)

Restatement § 178 points to § 175 for the principles in determining conflict issues in wrongful death cases:

"§ 175. Right of Action for Death. In an action for wrongful death, the local law of the state where the injury occurred determines the rights and liabilities of the parties unless, with respect to the particular issue, some other state has a *more significant relationship* under the principles stated in § 6 to the occurrence and the parties, in which event the local law of the other state will be applied." (emphasis added)

As in Restatement § 178, this section emphasizes that the state with the "most significant relationship" or "greater interest" should govern rather than the place of injury:

"d. *Rationale. The rule of this Section calls for application of the local law of the state where the injury occurred unless, with respect to the particular issue, some other state has a more significant relationship to the occurrence and the parties.* Whether there is such another state should be determined in the light of the choice-of-law principles stated in § 6. In large part, the answer to this question will depend upon whether some other state has a *greater interest* in the determination of the particular issue than the state where the injury occurred. The extent of the interest of each of the potentially interested states should be determined on the basis, among other things, of the purpose sought to be achieved by their relevant local law rules and of the particular issue involved (see § 145, Comments c-d)." (emphasis added)

Restatement § 175, comment d. According to Restatement §§ 175 and 178, determination of which state has the greater interest in damages is influenced largely by the factors set forth in Restatement §§ 6 and 145.

Restatement § 145 sets forth the general principles by which tort choice of law questions are to be decided:* * *

"These contacts are to be evaluated according to their relative importance with respect to the particular issue."

Restatement § 6 sets out the various policy considerations and other factors for making a choice of law selection: [cit.]

Our analysis starts with the four contacts specified in § 145(2), which will be taken into account in applying the principles enunciated in § 6 in ultimately determining whether Arizona or Colorado has the "most significant relationship" to the occurrence and the parties.[1] As to the first contact, the place where the injuries occurred is Colorado.

The location of the second contact, the place of the conduct causing the injury, is unclear. Both plaintiffs and defendant contest the cause of the crash. Plaintiffs' position is that the conduct occurred principally in Arizona because that is where Sun West negligently trained its pilots and adopted the policies relating to oxygen equipment in its fleet. Sun West argues that the cause of the crash was due to pilot error or mechanical failure which occurred exclusively in Colorado.

As to the third factor, plaintiff Bryant was domiciled in Arizona, as was her

---

1. Because our choice of law analysis could result in one state having the greater interest in compensatory damages and the other in punitive damages, we will apply the doctrine of depecage in resolving this case which allows us to apply different state laws to different issues. [cit.]

deceased husband, at the time of the crash. Sun West was incorporated and had its principal place of business in Arizona.[2]

Fourth, since the decedent, Bryant, purchased his ticket from Sun West in Durango, the contractual relationship between decedent and Sun West centered in Colorado.[3]

Thus, of the four contacts, two attach to Colorado, the place of injury and relationship between the parties, one attaches to Arizona, the domicile of the parties, and one is questionable, the place of conduct. The determination of which state has the most significant contacts, however, is primarily qualitative and not quantitative. [cit.] We must determine, therefore, the weight to be given each contact in light of the issues and facts of this case. See Restatement § 145(2) (providing that contacts are evaluated according to their relative importance to the particular issue).

Although Colorado is the state of injury, the state where the injury occurs does not have a strong interest in compensation if the injured plaintiff is a non-resident. [cit.] * * *[4]

As to punitive damages, in airplane crash cases the place of injury is much more fortuitous than the place defendant selects as his place of incorporation and principal place of business or the place of misconduct. Thus, the state where an injury occurs has less interest in deterrence and less ability to control behavior by deterrence or punishment than the state where the defendant airline is domiciled or the state where the misconduct occurred. *In re Air Crash Near Chicago*, 644 F.2d at 615 [(7th Cir.1981)], Cousins v. Instrument Flyers, Inc., 44 N.Y.2d 698 (1978). Thus, the place of injury carries little weight in our selection of the applicable state law on punitive damages.

The third factor, the domicile of plaintiff and defendant, is significant. Comment b of Restatement (Second) of Conflicts § 178 suggests that if the defendant, the decedent, and the beneficiaries are domiciled in one state, that state's law should govern the damage issues:

"b. * * * 'The state of conduct and injury will not, by reason of these contacts alone, be the state which is primarily concerned with the measure of damages in a wrongful death action. The local law of this state will, however, be applied unless some other state has a greater interest in the determination of this issue. *In a situation where one state is the state of domicil of the defendant, the decedent and the beneficiaries, it would seem that, ordinarily at least, the wrongful death statute of this state should be applied to determine the measure of damages.*'" (emphasis added)

---

2. Neither plaintiffs nor defendant argue that New Mexico or Texas wrongful death damage law should apply to this action, but instead all parties limited their arguments to Colorado and Arizona. Therefore, we will discuss all contacts in Arizona and Colorado and only those contacts of New Mexico or Texas when such contacts would favor application of Arizona or Colorado law. We need not decide whether in future cases different states' laws could be applied to different plaintiffs in the same case.

3. Joyce Branham purchased her ticket in Colorado and Mary Peters purchased her ticket in New Mexico.

4. The only interest of the state of injury would be in the compensation of those who rendered medical aid and other assistance to the injured parties. Where immediate death occurs, however, the state has no such interest. Griffith v. United Air Lines, supra, 203 A.2d at 807 [1964].

Many jurisdictions, including Arizona have determined that the state where plaintiff and defendant reside has a strong interest in making plaintiff whole and deterring wrongful conduct. [cit.] Since decedent Bryant, his beneficiaries, and defendant were all domiciled in Arizona at the time of the crash, Arizona has a strong interest in this case.

Finally, although the ticket purchase centered the relationship between the parties in Colorado, this contact is of relatively low importance to this case. Although the relationship between the parties is a contractual relationship, the terms of the contract are not in dispute but only give rise to the duty of care owed by the airline to the passenger on which this action is based. *See In re Air Crash Near Chicago*, 644 F.2d at 612 (place relationship occurred has low interest in either punishment or protection of nonresident defendants).

Thus, under the facts of this case the domicile contact carries great weight in our determination of which state's law to apply; less significant are the place of injury and the relationship.

After determining the distribution of the contacts and their relative weight, we must next determine the state of the applicable law in light of the choice of law principles stated in § 6 of the Restatement (Second) of Conflicts. As noted by Restatement § 175 comment d, "the answer to this question will depend upon whether some other state has a greater interest in the determination of the particular issue than the state where the injury occurred."

The harmonious relationship or commercial interaction between Arizona and Colorado would best be fostered by applying Arizona law. Application of Arizona damage law allowing unlimited compensatory and punitive damages would fully compensate the Arizona plaintiffs and would deter the wrongful conduct of Sun West or other Arizona based airlines in Arizona and other states' air space. Thus, any interest Colorado has in providing safe travel through its air space would be protected. Application of Colorado law, however, would shield Sun West from a high damage award and potentially leave the Arizona plaintiff not fully compensated. Additionally, Colorado law would not deter future misconduct in Colorado or Arizona.

Certainly, predictability and uniformity of result are of greatest importance when parties are likely to give advance thought to the legal consequences of their transactions, such as the effect and validity of contracts or wills, and not when negligence is at issue. [cit.]; Restatement (Second) of Conflicts § 6, comment c. Furthermore, since airplane accidents are not planned, these considerations are largely irrelevant. [cit.]

In resolving the factual issues on wrongful death damages, the jury is capable of applying Arizona or Colorado wrongful death damage principles with about equal ease. [cit.]

Protection of justified expectations also is of little importance in this case. Since airplane crash accidents are unanticipated negligent acts, it is not likely that either party acted with the consequences of his conduct in mind or the law to be applied should a dispute arise out of such negligent conduct. Additionally, Sun West did fly over New Mexico and other states which did not limit wrongful death damages, and therefore, should have expected that at some time it might be subject to the laws of those states and face large verdicts against it. Accordingly, Sun West could have protected itself. [cit.]

The three last considerations deal with policy: the basic policies underlying the particular field of law involved, here tort law, and the relevant policies of the forum state, Arizona, and other interested states, Colorado, New Mexico and Texas.

The basic policies underlying tort law are to provide compensation for the injured victims, and to deter intentional and deliberate tortious conduct by imposing punitive damages. Prosser & Keeton on Torts, § 2 (5th Ed.1984). Both Arizona and Colorado provide compensation for the injured victims, consistent with basic tort law. Only Arizona, however, allows punitive damages to deter similar future conduct. [cit.] Thus, basic tort law is better fostered by applying Arizona law.

In considering the relevant policies of Arizona and Colorado, the laws of both states differ significantly. Arizona has a strong policy interest in fully compensating injured plaintiffs to make them whole. Thus, Arizona allows unlimited recovery for actual damages, expenses for past and prospective medical care, past and prospective pain and suffering, lost earnings, and diminished earning capacity. [cit.] The policy of fully compensating an injured plaintiff is embodied in our Constitution, Art. 2, § 31, which reads: "No law shall be enacted in this state limiting the amount of damages to be recovered for causing the death or injury of any person." [cit.] Thus, Arizona has a strong interest in compensating plaintiff for her injuries because plaintiff is a domiciliary and also because compensation helps injured plaintiffs make their medical bill payments to Arizona medical providers, preventing them from becoming wards of the state. [cit.]

Colorado limits compensatory damages for wrongful death to plaintiff's net pecuniary loss. [cit.] This limitation prevents the jury from awarding speculative damages and more importantly, protects Colorado defendants from large verdicts. [cit.] As noted above, however, defendant Sun West Airlines is domiciled in Arizona with both its principal place of business and corporate offices there. Colorado's policy of limited liability is not fostered where defendant is not a resident of Colorado. Thus, Arizona's interest in compensation is stronger than Colorado's.

As to punitive damages, Arizona permits recovery of punitive damages in wrongful death actions. [cit.] The purpose of allowing punitive damages is to punish defendant for his conduct and deter defendant or others from engaging in similar conduct in the future. *Cassel v. Schacht*, [683 P.2d 294 (1984),] *supra*. Since Sun West is incorporated and has its principal place of business in Arizona, Arizona has a strong interest in assuring that one of its domiciliaries does not engage in gross, wanton, malicious or oppressive conduct.

On the other hand, Colorado does not permit punitive damages in a wrongful death action. [cit.] In interpreting the language of its wrongful death statute, Colorado courts determined that the general assembly had not authorized exemplary damages by the language employed in the statute. [cit.] The public policy behind such a denial is not clear. Perhaps it was to protect Colorado corporate defendants from excess liability. If so, since Sun West is domiciled in Arizona, Colorado has no interest in protecting an Arizona defendant. In any case, there does not appear to be a strong policy against punitive damages in Colorado because such damages are allowed in other tort actions. [cit.] Since this case involves an Arizona corporate defendant causing injury to an Arizona domiciliary, Arizona has the dominant interest in controlling Sun West's conduct.

Our last probe into public policy considerations concerns the policies of Texas and New Mexico relating to compensatory and punitive damages.

Texas, like Arizona, allows recovery for intangible personal losses. [cit.] Thus, the policies underlying wrongful death statutes relating to compensatory damages in Arizona and Texas do not differ.

The New Mexico wrongful death statute permits compensatory damages beyond pecuniary loss, [cit.], although not intangibles such as loss of society. * * * Thus New Mexico goes beyond Colorado pecuniary loss limitations and allows awards involving intangibles but not to the extent of Arizona. In order to foster the policy of New Mexico, Arizona law should be applied to avoid undercompensating the New Mexico plaintiff.

Both New Mexico and Texas permit recovery of punitive damages in wrongful death cases. [cit.] Thus, both of these states support use of Arizona law on punitive damages.

After considering the relevant factors and the interest of both states, we conclude that Arizona has the greatest interest in the determination of this case. Although the injury and relationship between the litigants centered in Colorado, the value of these contacts is minimal in this case. The domicile of the litigants, when considered with the policy behind both Colorado and Arizona damage laws, points to application of Arizona law. This determination best protects our citizens and those of New Mexico and Texas from wrongful conduct by another of our citizens, without affecting trade and travel between Arizona and Colorado.

The petitioners' prayer for relief is granted. The portion of the order of the respondent trial judge dated January 31, 1985, striking petitioners' claim for punitive damages for wrongful death and limiting petitioners' compensatory damages to net pecuniary loss is vacated, and the court is directed to grant the motion of petitioners for summary judgment that Arizona law applies to the action below. * * *

Notes and Questions

1. From a purely methodological perspective, *Bryant* is a good example of how one should apply the Restatement (Second). As noted earlier, the Restatement (Second) provides presumptive choice-of-law rules for specific tort issues and particular types of torts, and a general and residual section for all torts (§ 145). The *Bryant* court properly proceeds from the specific to the general. The court begins with the particular issue with regard to which the laws of the involved states differed--the amount of recoverable compensatory damages for wrongful death--and with the specific section the Restatement provides for such damages--§ 178. Because that section is not self-executing but refers to § 175 (applicable to wrongful death actions), the court properly follows this reference to § 175, which consists of a presumptive *lex loci* rule subject to the usual proviso that another state might have

a more significant relationship under the principles of § 6. Although § 175 refers only to § 6 (the general section for all conflicts), and not to § 145 (the general section for torts), the court correctly included in its analysis both the factual contacts of § 145 and the policy factors of § 6. The court also made proper use of the Restatement's official comments, which usually are helpful in guiding a court's application of the Restatement's rather vague sections.

However, the *Bryant* court seems to deviate from the Restatement's spirit when the court treats §§ 145 and 6 as non-communicative compartments and examines the § 145 contacts *in the abstract*, without correlating them either with the substantive law of the corresponding contact state or with the policies of § 6. Consider, for example, the court's statement that "the state where plaintiff and defendant reside has a strong interest in making plaintiff whole and deterring wrongful conduct." This statement is true when that state has a law that favors the plaintiff, but is this statement also true when that state has a law that bars, or significantly limits, the plaintiff's recovery? Similarly, the court's statement that "the state where the injury occurs does not have a strong interest in compensation if the injured plaintiff is a non-resident" may be generally true; however, depending on the defendant's contacts with that state, would that state not have the opposite interest in protecting the defendant, if its law, like Colorado's, favors the defendant by limiting recovery?

Incidentally, what do you think of the court's conclusion that the relationship between plaintiff Bryant and defendant Sun West was centered in Colorado, where plaintiff purchased the ticket? It is true that the purchase of the ticket created a contractual relationship with the airline, but is this the only relationship that § 6 contemplates? Could Bryant's survivors invoke another relationship, centered in Arizona, between Bryant, an Arizona domiciliary, and Sun West, an Arizona corporation? If so, what elements formed that relationship and how would it have affected the outcome of the case?

2. **Bryant** *and Compensatory damages*. The *Bryant* court recognized that one function of compensatory damages is to "help[] injured plaintiffs make their medical bill payments to * * * medical providers." The court concluded, however, that although Arizona had an interest in protecting its medical providers, Colorado did not have a corresponding interest because the victims, having been instantly killed, did not receive medical care in that state. Do you detect any inconsistency here?

The court also concluded that Colorado's *limitations* on compensatory damages were, inter alia, intended to protect "*Colorado* defendants from large verdicts" (emphasis added). But was the court correct in assuming that this protection should not be extended to Sun West because it was "not a resident of Colorado"? Is this an endorsement of Currie's "personal-law" principle? Sun West conducted business in Colorado by flying to and from that state regularly. Did Colorado, a ski resort state that depends on tourism, have an interest in protecting Sun West from large verdicts so as to ensure the continuation of its (and other airlines') flights to Colorado? For cases adopting such an argument, see In re Air Crash Disaster Near Chicago, 644 F.2d 594 (7th Cir.1981), *cert. denied* 454 U.S. 878 (applying pro-defendant law of state of intended landing and crash of airplane because that state had a "strong interest in having airlines fly in and out of the state, and . . . in protecting [them] by disallowing punitive damages." 644 F.2d at 615-16); Freeman v. World Airways, Inc., 596 F.Supp. 841 (D.Mass.1984) (applying pro-defendant law of state of intended landing and crash of airplane because that state "ha[d] a significant interest in regulating conduct (deterrence or encouragement) of planes arriving at [its airports] during the winter." Id. at 847).

Finally, if Colorado consciously has adopted a policy of protecting defendants such as Sun West rather than plaintiffs, would the application of Arizona law foster a "harmonious relationship or commercial interaction between Arizona and Colorado," as the court concluded?

3. **Bryan** *and Punitive Damages*. With regard to punitive damages, the Restatement (Second) provides no rule, presumptive or otherwise, thus leaving courts to their own devices. How do you evaluate the *Bryant* court's resolution of the punitive-damages conflict? Is the place of the injurious conduct an important factor in the choice of the law applicable to punitive damages? If so, where did the critical conduct occur in *Bryant*? Suppose that the conduct had occurred in Colorado, which did not allow punitive damages. Since the resulting injury also occurred in Colorado, would that state not have an interest in protecting from punitive damages a defendant whose activity had occurred within that state's territory and had caused damage there? For an affirmative answer, see the cases cited in Note 2, supra. If you have trouble accepting this answer in an airplane accident case, consider a products liability case in which the conduct (design, testing, and manufacture of the substandard product) as well as the resulting injury had occurred in Colorado. In such a case, would the fact that the defendant, or the plaintiff (or both) have their domicile outside Colorado negate Colorado's interest in protecting from punitive damages a defendant whose conduct had occurred within Colorado's borders? Should the victim's domicile be an independent factor in resolving punitive-damages conflicts? If the purpose of punitive damages is to punish the defendant and to deter potential defendants, rather than to compensate the victim who ex hypothesi is made whole through compensatory damages, why should the victim's domicile carry any weight at all? For a discussion of punitive damages conflicts, see infra Ch. 4.C.

4. How did the *Bryant* court handle the cases of the Texas and New Mexico plaintiffs? If you are not satisfied with the court's decision, keep in mind that neither of those plaintiffs pleaded the law of their respective domiciles, and *neither did the defendant*. Also, consider the alternatives. Which do you prefer: applying the same law to all passengers regardless of their respective domiciles, or applying a different law to each passenger depending on his or her respective domicile? Does the latter alternative raise any constitutional or fairness questions?

5. What do you think of the notion that when two parties are domiciled in different states whose law on the particular issue of loss distribution is substantially identical, those parties should be treated as if they were domiciled in the same state? The 1991 Louisiana codification was the first to adopt this notion. See La. Civ. Code art. 3544(1). For supporting rationale, see Symeonides, *Exegesis,* 723–25. Since then, the American Law Institute adopted this notion for mass tort conflicts. See infra Ch. 4, 314 *et seq.*

Milkovich v. Saari
Supreme Court of Minnesota, 1973.
295 Minn. 155, 203 N.W.2d 408.

TODD, J. * * * Plaintiff and both defendants are residents of Thunder Bay (formerly Port Arthur), Ontario, Canada. On November 8, 1968, they left Thunder Bay for Duluth, Minnesota, to shop and attend a play. The car belonged to defendant Erma Saari who drove the first part of the trip. At the United States Customs House at Pigeon River, Minnesota, defendant Judith Rudd took over the driving, and about 40 miles south of the border the car left the road and crashed into rock formations adjacent to the road, causing the injuries to plaintiff. Plaintiff was hospitalized at Duluth for approximately 1 1/2 months and thereafter returned to her home in Thunder Bay.

Defendant Saari's automobile was garaged, registered, and insured in the Province of Ontario, Canada. Ontario has a guest statute, and if the law of Ontario is to be applied to this case, plaintiff would have to establish gross negligence in order to recover. Minnesota does not have a guest statute. * * *

The choice-influencing considerations proposed by Professor Leflar * * * were adopted by our court in Schneider v. Nichols, [280 Minn. 139 (1968)] *supra*, indicating our preference for the better-law approach and our rejection of the guest statute concept of various jurisdictions. We have come to the conclusion in this case that plaintiff should be allowed to proceed with her action under our common-law rules of negligence and should not be bound by the guest statute requirements of the Province of Ontario.

* * * [T]he New York case of Kell v. Henderson, [263 N.Y S.2d 647 (1965)] *supra*, is on "all fours" with the facts of this case. Professor Leflar, * * * had occasion to comment on the effect of Kell v. Henderson, *supra*, in an article entitled, *Conflicts Law: More on Choice-Influencing Considerations*, 54 Calif. L. Rev. 1584. Professor Leflar set forth the fact situation of the Kell case. He then proceeded to analyze the decision in the light of these choice-influencing considerations. He pointed out that predictability was irrelevant since automobile accidents are seldom planned, and that, since the accident occurred in New York, that state was an appropriate jurisdiction in which to try the lawsuit. He further pointed out that neither international order or ease of judicial administration had much bearing on the case.

On the consideration of governmental interest, Professor Leflar found adequate support for the decision rendered by the New York court. In so doing, he rejected the concept of the practical interest of the state in the supervision and safety of its state highways since the rule in question, unlike rules of the road and definitions of negligence, does not bear upon vehicle operation as such. Instead, he pointed out that the factor to be considered is the relevant effect the New York rule has on the duty of host to guest and the danger of collusion between them to defraud the host's insurer. New York's interest in applying its own law rather than Ontario law on these issues, he found to be based primarily on its status as a justice-administering state. In that status, it is strongly concerned with seeing that persons who come into the

New York courts to litigate controversies with substantial New York connections have these cases determined according to rules consistent with New York concepts of justice, or at least not inconsistent with them. That will be as true for non-domiciliary litigants as for domiciliaries. This interest will not manifest itself clearly if the out-of-state rule does not run contrary to some strong socio-legal policy of the forum, but it will become a major consideration if there is such a strong opposing local policy.

Professor Leflar then pointed out that this consideration leads to preference for what is regarded as the better rule of law, that New York has such a preference, and that it is a vigorous one. He concluded that the combination of the last two items, governmental interest and better rule of law, called for the application of New York law. His statements and reasoning apply equally to the facts of this case and lead to the conclusion that Minnesota should apply its better rule of law and should allow plaintiff to proceed with her action.

Strong support for the better-rule-of-law concept appears in an article by Professor Albert A. Ehrenzweig, *"False Conflicts" and the "Better Rule": Threat and Promise in Multistate Tort Law*, 53 Va. L. Rev. 847, 853, in which he wrote:

"Express recognition of the forum's right and duty to apply its own better rule as such is an ancient tradition which apparently succumbed to the 19th century's internationalist conceptualism. We need only remember the priority given by early statutists to the *statuta favorabilia* of the forum against foreign *statuta odiosa*, or Master Aldricus' choice of the custom '*potior et utilior*,' or Byzantium's *philanthropoteron*. The widespread disregard of foreign Sunday laws, fellow-servant rules, and married women's incapacities, as well as statutes of frauds, and limitations on wrongful death damages, may serve as modern examples.

"Now, we shall, of course, not 'ask the judge simply to express a preference between two rules.' This would, indeed, 'abolish our centuries-old subject.' But we should face the 'fact of life' that judges, our best judges, often take advantage of the 'looseness in the joints of the [choice-of-law] apparatus,' or employ 'manipulative techniques such as characterization and renvoi,' and all-purpose tools such as the 'most significant relationship,' in order to substitute a better foreign rule for much 'that is archaic and foolish' in their own law. * * *

"Although the 'better-rule' principle is not generally capable of replacing conflicts rules, I see little justification within the limits set by settled law for the prevailing horror against the recognition of that principle as one of many determining the growth of conflicts law. The very growth of common-law rules is based on the judges' choice between competing principles, choices expressed in the process of overruling or distinguishing earlier judicial pronouncements." * * *

* * * We have already noted the relative unimportance of predictability of results to tort actions. Similarly, the simplification of the judicial task need not concern us to any great extent since we have no doubt our judicial system could in the appropriate case apply the guest statute rule of gross negligence as readily as our

common-law rule. Interstate and international relations are maintained without harm where, as here, the forum state has a substantial connection with the facts and issues involved. This requirement is amply met by the fact that the accident occurred in Minnesota, as well as by the fact that plaintiff was hospitalized for well over a month in the state.

The compelling factors in this case are the advancement of the forum's governmental interests and the application of the better law. While there may be more deterrent effect in our common-law rule of liability as opposed to the guest statute requirement of gross negligence, the main governmental interest involved is that of any "justice-administering state." Leflar, *Conflicts Law: More on Choice-Influencing Considerations*, 54 Calif. L. Rev. 1584, 1594. In that posture, we are concerned that our courts not be called upon to determine issues under rules which, however accepted they may be in other states, are inconsistent with our own concept of fairness and equity. We might also note that persons injured in automobile accidents occurring within our borders can reasonably be expected to require treatment in our medical facilities, both public and private. In the instant case, plaintiff incurred medical bills in a Duluth hospital which have already been paid, but we are loath to place weight on the individual case for fear it might offer even minor incentives to "hospital shop" or to create litigation-directed pressures on the payment of debts to medical facilities. Suffice it to say that we recognize that medical costs are likely to be incurred with a consequent governmental interest that injured persons not be denied recovery on the basis of doctrines foreign to Minnesota.

In our search for the better rule, we are firmly convinced of the superiority of the common-law rule of liability to that of the Ontario guest statute. We can find little reason for the strict limitation of a host's liability to his guest beyond the fear of collusive suits and the vague disapproval of a guest "biting the hand that feeds him." Neither rationale is persuasive. We are convinced the judicial system can uncover collusive suits without such overinclusive rules, and we do not find any discomfort in the prospect of a guest suing his host for injuries suffered through the host's simple negligence.

Accordingly, we hold that Minnesota law should be applied to this lawsuit. Affirmed.

PETERSON, J. (dissenting). * * * The "choice-influencing factor" in the majority opinion is simply that Minnesota law is "better law" because, unlike Ontario law, this state has no guest statute. Notwithstanding our undoubted preference for this forum's standard of liability, I am not persuaded that decision should turn on that factor alone. We may assume that these Canadian citizens have concurred in the rule of law of their own government as just, so the law of this American forum is not for them the "better" standard of justice. The litigation, indeed, was first initiated by plaintiff in the courts of Ontario and was later commenced in Minnesota as an act of forum shopping. * * *

Notes and Questions

1. *Milkovich* presents the converse pattern from that involved in *Babcock*. The issue was identical, except that in *Babcock* the host-driver and guest-passenger were domiciled in the recovery state, whereas in *Milkovich* they were domiciled in the non-recovery, guest-statute state. If *Babcock* unquestionably was a false conflict in which the parties' common domicile was the only interested state, *Milkovich* should also be a false conflict, should it not? Is it? Was the accident state as uninterested in *Milkovich* as in *Babcock*? If not, why not? Could the answer have something to do with the fact that Minnesota's law, unlike Ontario's, provided for recovery? Does this change the equation? Aside from its so-called interest "as a justice-administering state," what other Minnesota interests did the court invoke? If these interests are real, and since Ontario's interests are real, then *Milkovich* would not be a false conflict, would it? Would it be a true conflict or an apparent conflict? (See supra at 126).

2. What about Minnesota's so-called interest "as a justice-administering state"? According to *Milkovich*, that interest means that "our courts [should] not be called upon to determine issues under rules which * * * are inconsistent with our own concept of fairness and equity." But does not the very name of our subject, "conflict of laws," mean that the cases it encompasses involve conflicting concepts of justice and fairness? If each state were to adhere to its own concepts of justice and fairness, would this not mean a return to the medieval English practice according to which English courts never applied foreign law? See Ch. 1, supra.

The *Milkovich* court provides a more moderate description of the above "interest" when, in paraphrasing Professor Leflar's supporting discussion of an identical New York case, the court said that New York was:

> strongly concerned with seeing that persons who come into the New York courts to litigate controversies with substantial New York connections have these cases determined according to rules consistent with New York concepts of justice, or at least not inconsistent with them. That will be as true for non-domiciliary litigants as for domiciliaries.

Here there is at least one qualification, that the forum have "substantial * * * connections" with the controversy.[1] But notice, the reference is *not* to "the *most* substantial" connections. Does this mean that every time the forum's law is different from or "inconsistent" with foreign law, the forum has an interest in applying its law because the plaintiff chose to "come into" its courts? If this "interest" is allowed to control the choice-of-law question, would this not be an invitation to, and a glorification of, forum shopping? Would this mean the *abolition* of the entire choice-of-law question? Is there anything wrong with that?

Suppose that the insurer, who is the real defendant in guest-statute conflicts, sues

---

1. Another qualification following the quoted text is that the interest of the justice-administering state "will not manifest itself clearly if the out-of-state rule does not run contrary to some *strong socio-legal policy of the forum.*" (Emphasis added.) Is this simply a restatement of the *ordre public* doctrine? Remember *Owen v. Owen*, supra at 85? In *Milkovich*, was the application of the Ontario guest statute to a dispute between two Ontario citizens so repugnant to Minnesota's "strong socio-legal policy" as to justify the application of Minnesota law?

in Ontario for a declaratory judgment that the insurer is not obligated to provide coverage for Ms. Saari's liability *vis a vis* Ms. Milkovich. If Ontario were to follow *Milkovich*'s philosophy that, as a justice-administering state, Ontario "is strongly concerned with seeing that persons who come into [Ontario] courts to litigate controversies with substantial [Ontario] connections have these cases determined according to rules consistent with [Ontario] concepts of justice," would Ontario not have every reason to apply its own law? Should the private international law system encourage each state to resolve conflicts cases exclusively under its own notions of justice?

RESULT–ORIENTED APPROACHES

1. *Professor Leflar and the "Better–Law" Approach.* *Milkovich* relied heavily on the writings of Professor Robert A. Leflar. Leflar joined the conflicts revolution in the early 1960s and subscribed to the view that the first Restatement's rules should be replaced not by another set of rules, but rather by a set of flexible "choice-influencing considerations" that should guide the court's choice of the applicable law. In two successive law review articles (Leflar, *Choice-Influencing Considerations*; and Leflar, *More on Choice Influencing Considerations*) he finalized a non-hierarchical list of such considerations and provided thoughtful supporting rationale. The list comprises the following considerations:
   (a) Predictability of results;
   (b) Maintenance of interstate and international order;
   (c) Simplification of the judicial task;
   (d) Advancement of the forum's governmental interests; and
   (e) Application of the better rule of law.
Leflar argued that, through reference to these considerations, "courts can replace with statements of real reasons the mechanical rules and circuitously devised approaches which have appeared in the language of conflicts opinions, too often as cover-ups for the real reason that underlay the decisions." Leflar, *More on Choice Influencing Considerations*, 1585.

As the above list indicates, there is much more to Leflar's approach than the "better-law" consideration. As Leflar said, that criterion "is only one of five, more important in some types of cases than in others, almost controlling in some but irrelevant in others." Leflar, *American Conflicts* 300. At the same time, by not expressly assigning a residual role to this criterion, Leflar allowed it to become the decisive criterion in all the close cases, and in some not-so close cases as *Milkovich*. At least in the early years, this is precisely how courts employed this criterion, while paying lip service to the other four. If one adds the fact that, but for the better-law criterion, Leflar's list differs little from the lists proposed by other authors, or the list of §6 of the Restatement (Second), then it is understandable why Leflar's approach is deservedly known as "the better-law approach" and why one may criticize or praise it on that basis. Most of the criticism comes from academic circles.[1] Judges generally are more receptive and, as you see in *Milkovich*, some are enthusiastic supporters. For warm praise by Justice Todd, the author of the majority opinion in *Milkovich*, see Todd, *A Judge's View*.

Leflar's better-law approach is still followed in Minnesota and Wisconsin with regard to tort and contract conflicts, and in New Hampshire, Rhode Island, and Leflar's home state of Arkansas with regard to tort conflicts only. Thus, eight centuries after Magister Aldricus (see supra Ch. 1 at 7), the better-law approach has taken hold on American soil.

2. ***The Better-Law's Better Years.*** Is there a difference between the "better-law" criterion, on the one hand, and the interest of the forum "as a justice-administering state" in applying its own law, on the other? In theory, under the better-law criterion, a court may occasionally conclude that the other state's law is better than its own. Leflar insisted that this is possible: "Judges can appreciate as well as can anyone else the fact that their forum law in some areas is anachronistic." Leflar, *American Conflicts*, 107. See also Leflar, *More on Choice-Influencing Considerations*, 1588. (Incidentally, do you see any constitutional or other problems with a judge refusing to apply the *lex fori* on the ground that it is not "better" than the other state's law?) In contrast, a court adhering to the "justice-administering" concept almost always would believe itself to be bound to administer justice according to forum law.

In practice, courts tend to blend these two concepts. For example, in the five states that adopted Leflar's approach for tort conflicts, one finds only five supreme court cases that have applied foreign law. See Symeonides, *The Revolution Today*, §§ 73-76. Two of those cases were decided by the Supreme Court of Minnesota (see Bigelow v. Halloran, 313 N.W.2d 10 (Minn.1981); Jepson v. General Cas. Co. of Wisconsin, 513 N.W.2d 467 (Minn.1994)), and although in one of them (*Bigelow*) the court admitted that the other state's law was better than Minnesota's, this was a case in which the court could not avoid that law under any theory, traditional or modern. In the more than a dozen other cases involving tort conflicts, including the infamous *Allstate Ins. Co. v. Hague* (reproduced infra at 455), the same court applied the law of the forum, and in most of those cases the court's perception of the forum's law as being better was the decisive factor in the court's decision. In Minnesota's lower courts, this perception has led to extreme results. For example, two lower court cases held that a Minnesota pro-plaintiff rule was better than a pro-defendant foreign rule, even after the Minnesota legislature repealed the Minnesota rule and replaced it with a pro-defendant rule identical to the foreign rule. See Wille v. Farm Bureau Mut. Ins. Co. 432 N.W.2d 784 (Minn.App.1988); Meir v. Auto Owners Ins. Co., 1989 WL 14913 (Minn.App.1989). In Keeton v. Hustler Magazine, Inc., 549 A.2d 1187 (N.H.1988) (reproduced infra at 374), the New Hampshire Supreme Court took the same position. It held that New-Hampshire's six-year statute of limitation was better than the shorter statutes of other states, even after the New Hampshire

---

1. See, e.g., Cavers, *The Value of Principled Preferences*, 212–13, 214, 215; 1 Ehrenzweig, *PIL*, 97–98, 100–103; Scoles, Hay, Borchers & Symeonides, *Conflict of Laws*, 51-58. For praise by academic writers see a Symposium in 52 Ark. L. Rev. 1 (1999) (containing articles by Watkins, Cox, Felix, McDougal, Simson, Weintraub, and Whitten); Juenger, *Leflar's Contributions*, 413.

legislature had voted to shorten that statute.

Do these cases lend credibility to the accusation that the better-law approach encourages judicial subjectivism? Notice that in the above cases that applied forum law, that law favored a plaintiff with few contacts with the forum state, and disfavored a foreign corporation that was doing business in the forum state. Does this suggest that the better-law approach tends to favor plaintiffs? If it is true that this approach tends to favor the law of the forum and since, under American jurisdiction rules, plaintiffs usually have wide latitude in choosing the forum, then plaintiffs should fare better under the better-law approach, should they not?

Keep in mind, however, that the word "plaintiff" does not always mean the tort victim. Potential defendants such as insurers now have learned their forum-shopping lesson and have begun to strike first by filing actions for declaratory judgments in forums of their choice. See, e.g., the *ARTRA* case, supra Ch. 2; Kozyris & Symeonides, *Choice of Law in 1989*, 621-26. Does this practice turn pro-forum approaches on their head? In any event, in case you have formed the impression that Minnesota courts are adamantly pro-plaintiff, consider Lommen v. The City of East Grand Forks, 522 N.W.2d 148 (Minn.App.1994), which applied a Minnesota pro-defendant law to protect a Minnesota municipality whose police officer had crossed into North Dakota in hot pursuit of a suspect and had injured plaintiff, an unsuspecting resident of that state. Now consider which, if any, of the following charges is closer to the truth: the better-law approach is more likely than are other approaches to encourage: (a) favoritism toward forum *law*; (b) favoritism for *plaintiffs* as a class over defendants; (c) favoritism for *Minnesota* litigants; or (d) judicial subjectivism, which could allow any or all of (a)-(c).

3. ***Recent Trends in Better-Law States.*** In recent years, courts employing Leflar's approach have begun combining it with other approaches. See Symeonides, *The Revolution Today* §§ 77-79. As a result of this development, the better-law criterion now plays a less prominent role in choice-of-law decisions than it did previously. Indeed, in recent years, some courts have expressed misgivings on their ability to determine which law is better, or have tried to dispel the notion that better law and forum law are synonymous terms, while other courts have employed the better-law criterion only as a tie-breaker, or ignored it altogether. See id.

4. ***Professor Ehrenzweig and Forum Favoritism.*** While the better-law approach might be the indirect road to the application of the *lex fori*, Professor Albert A. Ehrenzweig, on whose writings *Milkovich* also relied, offers a more direct road to the *lex fori*. In keeping with the tradition inaugurated by Cook, Ehrenzweig postulates that the application of foreign law is the exception rather than the rule—an exception tolerated only in cases for which the forum's courts or legislature have established so-called "true" choice-of-law rules. 1 Ehrenzweig, *PIL* 75, 76, 89-90. In his opinion, such rules are very few and include, *inter alia*, the "rule of validation" for non-adhesion contracts, trusts and wills, and the *lex situs* rule for land cases. When no such "true" rules exist, the court is to apply the law of the forum, unless an examination of the policies underlying that law reveals that it is not intended for application to the case at hand. Even in such a case, the court should not examine the policies of the conflicting foreign rule but instead should dismiss the case without

prejudice. If dismissal is inappropriate, the court then should apply the *lex fori* as residual law, "as a matter of non-choice." Id. at 103-04. Thus, Ehrenzweig's favoritism for the *lex fori* is greater than is Currie's, since Ehrenzweig conceivably would apply the *lex fori* even in a false conflict in which the forum is not an interested state. Anticipating the dangers of forum shopping that his theory would generate, Ehrenzweig proposed transforming the negative doctrine of *forum non conveniens* into a positive test of *forum conveniens* that would abolish transient jurisdiction and would ensure that courts would not assume jurisdiction if the case does not have a sufficient nexus with the forum. Id. at 107-10. See also Ehrenzweig, *A Proper Law in a Proper Forum.*

5. *The "Best-Law" Approach.* While the better-law approach allows the court to choose the better law, that approach also limits the court to choosing between or among the laws of the states involved in the conflict. Professor Luther L. McDougal proposes that:

> [C]ourts should move one step further and apply the best rule of law to resolve choice of law cases, not simply the better rule of law. Application of the better rule of law implicitly assumes that a court is limited in its choice to one of two possibly applicable state laws. Courts are not so limited in their choice. Courts can, and should, in many cases construct and apply a law specifically created for the resolution of choice of law cases. Laws designed to resolve intrastate cases usually only reflect an accommodation of local state interests. The laws do not reflect an accommodation of the additional interests that are implicated in transstate cases. For this reason, state laws, even the better of the laws of the two states, will not result in the choice of law case being resolved in the most appropriate manner, that is by application of the best rule of law.

McDougal, *Best Rule of Law*, 483-84. Professor McDougal describes the best rule of law as the "one that best promotes net aggregate long-term common interests," id. at 484, and gives two examples of such rules:

> In the context of claims concerning the award of damages in transstate wrongful death actions * * * [t]he best rule of law applicable to claims concerning noneconomic losses is one of permitting complete recovery of all losses, pecuniary and nonpecuniary, and of all reasonable costs incurred in obtaining recovery, including reasonable attorneys' fees and litigation costs. The best rule of law applicable to claims concerning punitive damages is one of imposing punitive damages on individuals who engage in outrageous conduct and who are not adequately punished in the criminal process.

Id. at 533. What do you think of these proposals?

Professor Friedrich K. Juenger also advocated a type of best-law approach, although he preferred to call it the "substantive-law" approach so as to connect it to one of the oldest approaches--the approach of the Roman *Praetor peregrinus* (see supra Ch. 1) who, in resolving disputes between Roman and non-Roman citizens, constructed ad hoc substantive rules derived from the legal systems of Rome, Greece, and other Mediterranean countries. In a fascinating book called *Choice of Law and Multistate Justice*, Juenger traced the development and use of this approach from ancient Greece to Rome and through the middle ages to the twentieth century, and then explored the advantages of this approach over both the bilateral and the unilateral choice-of-law approaches.[2] In the end, however, Juenger retreats to a fall-back approach of constructing *from among the involved states* a rule of law that best accords with modern substantive-law trends and standards. For example, for products liability conflicts, Juenger proposed that from among the laws of the places of conduct, injury, acquisition of the product, and domicile of the parties, the court should choose "[a]s to each issue * * * that rule of decision which most closely accords with modern standards of products liability." Juenger, *Multistate Justice*, 197. What do you think of this proposal?

6. *Professor Weintraub and his Plaintiff–Favoring Rule*. Both the better-law and the best-law approaches let the court decide which law is better or best. An earlier proposal by Professor Russell J. Weintraub left little to the imagination. It provided that in tort cases that present either a true conflict or a no-interest scenario, the court should:

> Apply the Law That Will Favor the Plaintiff Unless One or Both of the Following Factors Is Present: a. That Law Is Anachronistic or Aberrational; b. the State With That Law Does Not Have Sufficient Contact With the Defendant or the Defendant's Actual or Intended Course of Conduct to Make Application of Its Law Reasonable.

R. Weintraub, *Commentary on the Conflict of Laws*, 360 (3d ed. 1986). In the 2001 edition of his *Commentary*, Weintraub conceded that the above proposed rule "was really an attempt at 'better law' analysis," R. Weintraub, *Commentary on the Conflict of Laws*, 356 (4th ed. 2001), which was necessary at a time when tort laws were so drastically different from state to state, with some states holding on to anachronistic anti-recovery rules. With so many states having since moved and continuing to move in the opposite direction, says Weintraub, "[t]imes have changed." Id.

Weintraub now proposes a new "consequences-based approach," see id. at 347 ff., which "chooses law with knowledge of the content of the laws of each of the [involved] states * * * [and] seeks to minimize the consequences that any such state is likely to experience if its law is not applied" Id. at 347. According to this approach, the court should (1) identify the policies underlying the conflicting laws of the involved states; (2) determine whether the non-application of a state's law would cause that state "to experience consequences that it is its policy to avoid," id. at 350; and (3) ensure that "application of the law of a state that will experience consequences * * * [is] fair to the parties in the light of their contacts with that state." Id. Regarding the better-law criterion, Weintraub emphatically states that it should only be used in non-false conflicts, and that "the better law should be selected by an objective determination that the disfavored law is anachronistic or aberra-

---

2. At least one judge, Jack B. Weinstein, of the US Eastern District of New York, has come very close to employing a "substantive-law approach" when he proposed the development of a "national consensus law of manufacturer's liability" for handling a complex product-liability class-action brought by the victims of agent orange. See In re Agent Orange Products Liability Litigation, 580 F.Supp. 690, 713 (E.D.N.Y.1984). Recently, however, Judge Weinstein seems to have moved in a different direction when he proposed the application of the law of the forum *qua* forum in a similar hypothetical case. See Weinstein, *Mass Tort Jurisdiction and Choice of Law*, 145.

tional." Id. at 417.

7. ***Letting the Plaintiff Choose***. Finally, rather than either letting the court choose the better or the best law, or telling the court which law is better or best, why not let the plaintiff choose? After all, does she not know best? Interestingly, not only does this concept have more proponents than the uninitiated might expect, but it has even been expressed in statutory form. For example, in products liability conflicts, the Swiss codification (art. 135(1), the Italian codification (art. 63), and the Quebec codification (art. 3128) let the plaintiff choose from among the laws of: (a) the tortfeasor's place of business or habitual residence; or (b) subject to a proviso, the place in which the product was acquired. The Hague Convention on the Law Applicable to Products Liability also allows plaintiffs to choose between the laws of the tortfeasor's principal place of business or the law of the place of injury, but only if certain contingencies are met. See Arts. 6 and 4-5. Similarly, Professor Cavers would let the plaintiff choose from among the laws of: (a) the place of manufacture; (b) the place of the plaintiff's habitual residence if that place coincides with either the place of injury or the place of the product's acquisition; or (c) the place of acquisition if that place is also the place of injury. Cavers, *Producer's Liability*, 728-29. Finally, Professor Weintraub carries this concept to its logical conclusion by also giving the defendant a choice. Under Weintraub's elaborate scheme, if certain contingencies are met, the defendant may choose the law of a state affiliated with the plaintiff, and if the defendant fails to exercise that option, then the plaintiff may choose either that same law or the law of a state affiliated with the defendant. See Weintraub, *Mass Tort Litigation*, 148.

What do you think of the notion of letting the litigants choose the applicable law? Interestingly, one of the opponents of this notion is no other than Professor Juenger. He charged that this notion:

> smacks of favoritism and implies an abdication of the judicial role. * * * To be sure, it is usually the victim who suffers from the fact that in many places legal progress has been slow in responding to the problem of how to deal with accidents that are inevitable in an industrialized society. Some tort rules, however, such as provisions for treble and punitive damages found in American law, overcompensate the plaintiff. Moreover, there could be honest differences of opinion about, for instance, the liability of middlemen for injuries caused by defective products. If the law of conflicts is charged with promoting sound substantive policies, courts rather than the parties must assume the task of "quality control."

Juenger, *Multistate Justice*, 197-98. Now what do you think?

8. ***Substantive Justice vs. Conflicts Justice***. Before you dismiss all result-selective approaches too quickly, keep in mind that a certain degree of result-selectivism has always been present in all efforts to resolve conflicts problems. For example, in Chapter 2 you witnessed courts manipulating the traditional theory in efforts to achieve what they considered to be the just result. More importantly, even the traditional system itself has long acquiesced to choice-of-law rules whose objective was to ensure a substantive result that is *a priori* considered to be "better." The same is true in codified conflicts systems in the rest of the world. Recent private

international law codifications are replete with result-oriented choice-of-law rules (*règles de conflit à coloration matérielle*) which, in one form or another, aim to accomplish a certain substantive result that the drafters considered *a priori* as desirable. More often than not, this result is one favored by the domestic law of not only the forum state, but also of most states that partake in the same legal tradition. This result may be one of the following: (1) favoring the formal or substantive validity of a juridical act, such as a testament, a marriage, or an ordinary contract; (2) favoring a certain status, such as the status of legitimacy or filiation, the status of a spouse, or even the dissolution of a status (divorce); or (3) favoring a particular party, such as a tort victim, a consumer, an employee, a maintenance obligee, or any other party whom the legal order considers weak or whose interests are considered worthy of protection. See Symeonides, *Private International Law*, 46-60. In the United States, as early as 1910, many states enacted statutes modeled after the Uniform Wills Act, which provide that a testament is to be treated as being valid as to form if it complies with the laws of any one of several states that have had some connection with the testator. See Chapter 4, infra at 420.

Are these statutes not premised on the notion that treating a testament as valid is "better" than treating the testament as invalid and then applying the intestacy rules? If yes, is this covert result-selectivism any less objectionable than the overt result-selectivism of the modern approaches described above? If yes, why? In any event, these latter approaches force us to return to a basic question asked in Chapter 2 (see supra at 25-26): Should conflicts law aspire to attain the same quality of justice as that to which domestic litigation aspires, or should conflicts law be content with a different type of justice, so-called conflicts justice? Is your opinion different now? Is this an "either/or" proposition? For a discussion of these questions, see Symeonides, *Material Justice*, 125.

b. An Interim Empirical Report on the Judicial Revolution

1. The Cases. Following the lead of the New York Court of Appeals in *Babcock*, 41 other state supreme courts have joined the revolution by abandoning the *lex loci delicti* rule.[1] These cases are depicted in the table below and are briefly discussed later. The last four columns of the table represent the four primary contacts that modern choice-of-law analysis considers pertinent in resolving tort conflicts. In addition to the place of injury, these contacts include the place of injurious conduct, and the domiciles of the tortfeasor and the injured person (hereinafter "victim"). The shaded cells represent the state whose law the court applied. The use of bold-faced type indicates a state with a pro-plaintiff law.

---

1. This count includes the District of Columbia and the Commonwealth of Puerto Rico.

Table 1. Departures from the *Lex Loci Delicti* Rule

		Contact States	Forum	Victim's domicile	State of injury	State of Conduct	Tortfeasor's Domicile
				Guest-Statute Cases			
1	*Babcock*	1963	NY	NY	ON	ON	NY
2	*Wilcox*	1965	WS	WS	NE	NE	WS
3	*Clark*	1966	NH	NH	VT	VT	NH
4	*Mellk*	1967	NJ	NJ	OH	OH	NJ
5	*Wessling*	1967	KY	KY	IN	IN	KY
6	*Woodward*	1968	RI	RI	MA	MA	RI
7	*Kennedy*	1969	MO	MO	IN	IN	MO
8	*Beaulieu*	1970	ME	ME	MA	MA	ME
9	*Rostek*	1973	CO	CO	SD	SD	CO
10	*Bishop*	1980	FL	FL	NC	NC	FL
				Interspousal-Immunity Cases			
11	*Armstrong*	1968	AK	AK	YU	YU	AK
12	*Schwartz*	1968	AZ	NY	AZ	AZ	NY
13	*Pevoski*	1976	MA	MA	NY	NY	MA
14	*Peters*	1981	HI	NY	HI	HI	NY
15	*Forsman*	1989	UT	CA	UT	UT	CA
				Intra-family Immunity Cases			
16	*Balts*	1966	MN	MN	WS	WS	MN
17	*Jagers*	1973	LA	LA	MS	MS	LA
				Worker's Compensation Immunity			
18	*Johnson v.P*	1985	ID	SAS	ID	ID	SAS
				Tort Action v. Administrative Remedy			
19	*O'Connor*	1986	CN	CN	Qu	Qu	CN
20	*Travelers*	1991	DE	DE	Qu	Qu	DE
				Loss of Consortium			
21	*Casey*	1967	OR	OR	OR/WA	WA	WA
22	*Motenko*	1996	NV	MA	MA/NV	NV	NV
				Compensatory Damages			
23	*Griffith*	1964	PA	PA	CO	?	ILL
24	*Fabricious*	1965	IA	IA	MN	MN	IA
25	*Fornaris*	1966	PR	PR	St.T	St.T	PR
26	*Reich*	1967	CA	OH/CA	MO	MO	CA
27	*Fox*	1971	OH	OH	ILL	ILL	OH
28	*Brickner*	1974	OK	OK	Mex	Mex	OK
29	*Johnson v.S*	1976	WA	KS	KS	WA	WA
30	*Gutierrez*	1979	TX	TX	Mex	Mex	TX
				Products Liability			
31	*Hubbard*	1987	IN	IN	ILL	IN	IN
32	*Phillips*	2000	MT	MT	KS	MI	MI
				Comparative Negligence			
33	*Mitchell*	1968	MS	MS	LA	LA	MS
34	*Issendorf*	1972	ND	ND	MN	MN	ND
35	*Wallis*	1977	AR	AR	MO	MO	PA
36	*Chambers*	1992	SD	SD	MO	MO	SD
37	*Hataway*	1992	TN	TN	AR	AR	TN

Other Issues

38	*Myers*	1967	DC	MD	MD	DC	DC
39	*Ingersoll*	1970	ILL	ILL	IA	ILL	ILL
40	*Sexton*	1982	MI	MI	VA	VA/MI	MI

Inconclusive Cases

41	*Crossley*	1977	NEB	NEB	CO	CO	CO
42	*Amiot*	1997	VT	ALB	Qu	VT	VT

2. General Observations. Of the 42 cases listed in the above table, the last two are inconclusive on the issues discussed here.[2] Thus, the following observations are based on the first 40 cases.

a. Forum and non-forum law. Thirty-six of the 40 cases applied the law of the forum state. Does this suggest that the abandonment of the *lex loci* rule has encouraged--or was motivated by--a "homeward trend"? Although subsequent cases tend to confirm this suggestion, only three of the 36 cases (*Griffith, Wallis,* and *Phillips*)[3] are vulnerable to this criticism in that the forum had only one contact--the victim's domicile. In the remaining 33 cases, the forum state was either the domicile of both parties or had three or two of the four pertinent contacts.

b. Pro-recovery law. Thirty-three of the 40 cases applied a law that favored the victim. Does this suggest that the abandonment of the *lex loci* rule has unleashed--or was motivated by--a pro-plaintiff bias? Although the first two decades of the revolution provided ammunition for such a criticism, the last two decades have produced more balanced cases.[4] In any event, one should note that, except for the three pro-forum cases noted above, in 30 of the 33 cases that applied a pro-plaintiff law the court had ample for so doing--that law was the law of the parties' common domicile and the conflicts were confined to loss-distribution issues.

c. Common-domicile cases. In 32 of the 40 cases, the tortfeasor and the victim were domiciled in the same state, and 31 of those cases applied the law of that state. The only case that applied another law (*Peters v. Peters*[5]) was distinguishable. In 28 of the 31 cases, the common domicile was in the forum state. In 25 of the 31 cases, the law of the common domicile favored the victim.

d. Split-domicile cases. In eight of the 40 cases, the parties were domiciled in different states, and five of those cases applied the law of the tortfeasor's domicile.

---

2. For the reasons, see Symeonides, *Territoriality and Personality,* § 4.2, from which this Note is adapted.

3. See Griffith v. United Air Lines, Inc., 203 A.2d 796 (Pa.1964) (applying Pennsylvania's pro-recovery law to an action arising from a Colorado airplane crash that killed a Pennsylvania domiciliary); Wallis v. Mrs. Smith's Pie Co., 550 S.W.2d 453 (Ark.1977) (case arising from a Missouri accident involving an Arkansas plaintiff and a Pennsylvania defendant; applying Missouri's rules of the road, but not Missouri's contributory-negligence rule; applying instead Arkansas's pro-plaintiff comparative-negligence rule); and Phillips v. General Motors Corp., 995 P.2d 1002 (Mont.2000) (applying Montana's pro-plaintiff compensatory and punitive damages law to a products liability action filed by the survivors of a Montana family who perished in an auto accident in Kansas while riding in a car manufactured by a Michigan defendant).

4. See Symeonides, *The Revolution Today* § 240.

5. *Peters* is described supra at 151. *Peters* is distinguishable because it involved a car rented and insured in the *locus* state.

In four of the latter cases,[6] that state was also the place of the tortfeasor's conduct and in three of those cases it had a pro-defendant law.[7] The remaining three of the split-domicile cases applied the pro-plaintiff law of the plaintiff's home state.[8]

3. Territoriality and Loss-Distribution Conflicts. All in all, of the 40 cases that abandoned the *lex loci* as a general rule: (a) 36 cases applied the law of a state that had a personal contact (domicile) with both or either parties, but not a territorial contact; (b) three cases applied the law of a state that had both a personal and a territorial contact; and (c) only one case (*Peters*) applied the law of a state that had only territorial but not personal contacts.

These numbers are not surprising since they are limited to cases that have *abandoned* the territorially-based *lex loci* rule. However, it is important to note the category of cases in which this abandonment occurred--the majority of them involve loss-distribution rules like the guest statute involved in *Babcock*, namely rules that, in the words of the New York Court of Appeals, "prohibit, assign, or limit liability after the tort occurs." Padula v. Lilarn Props. Corp. 644 N.E.2d 1001, 1002 (N.Y. 1994). The first 30 of the above 40 cases involved rules that "prohibit * * * liability" by immunizing the tortfeasor through a host-driver immunity,[9] interspousal immunity,[10] parent-child immunity,[11] worker's compensation immunity,[12] or rules that "limit * * * liability" by confining a tort victim to an administrative remedy,[13]

---

6. In the fifth case, Reich v. Purcell, 432 P.2d 727 (Cal.1967), the plaintiff was on his way to settle in California (the defendant's domicile) when the accident occurred.

7. The three cases are Casey v. Manson Constr. & Eng'g Co., 428 P.2d 898 (Or.1967); Motenko v. MGM Dist., Inc., 921 P.2d 933 (Nev.1996), and Johnson v. Spider Staging Corp., 555 P.2d 997 (Wash. 1976). In *Johnson*, which was a products liability case, the injury occurred in the victim's home state. In *Casey* and *Motenko*, the physical injury occurred in the tortfeasor's home state. However, because these cases involved actions for loss of consortium by the victim's spouse and child, respectively, one could argue that the injury had occurred in the plaintiff's home state. In the fourth case, Myers v. Gaither, 232 A.2d 577 (D.C.1967) the defendant's domicile, which was also the place of conduct, had a pro-plaintiff law.

8. These cases are *Griffith*, *Phillips*, and *Wallis*, described supra n. 3.

9. In addition to *Babcock*, these cases are Wilcox v. Wilcox, 133 N.W.2d 408 (Wis.1965) (Wisconsin parties, Nebraska accident and guest statute); Clark v. Clark, 222 A.2d 205 (N.H.1966) (New Hampshire parties, Vermont accident and guest statute); Mellk v. Sarahson, 229 A.2d 625 (N.J.1967) (New Jersey parties, Ohio accident and guest statute); Wessling v. Paris, 417 S.W.2d 259 (Ky.1967) (Kentucky parties, Indiana accident and guest statute); Woodward v. Stewart, 243 A.2d 917 (R.I.1968) (Rhode Island parties, Massachusetts accident and guest statute); Kennedy v. Dixon, 439 S.W.2d 173 (Mo.1969) (Missouri parties, Indiana accident and guest statute); Beaulieu v. Beaulieu, 265 A.2d 610 (Me.1970) (Maine parties, Massachusetts accident and guest statute); First Nat'l Bank v. Rostek, 514 P.2d 314 (Colo.1973) (Colorado parties, South Dakota accident and guest statute); and Bishop v. Florida Specialty Paint Co., 389 So.2d 999 (Fla.1980) (Florida parties, North Carolina airplane crash and airplane guest statute).

10. These cases are: Armstrong v. Armstrong, 441 P.2d 699 (Alaska 1968) (Alaska spouses, accident in Yukon territory which had immunity rule); Schwartz v. Schwartz, 447 P.2d 254 (Ariz.1968) (New York spouses, Arizona accident and immunity); Pevoski v. Pevoski, 358 N.E.2d 416 (Mass.1976) (Massachusetts spouses, New York accident and immunity); and Forsman v. Forsman, 779 P.2d 218 (Utah 1989) (California spouses, Utah accident and immunity). For Peters v. Peters, see supra n.5.

11. These cases are: Balts v. Balts, 142 N.W.2d 66 (Mn.1966) (Minnesota parent and child, Wisconsin accident and immunity); and Jagers v. Royal Indem. Co., 276 So. 2d 309 (La.1973) (Louisiana parent and child, Mississippi accident and immunity).

12. See Johnson v. Pischke, 700 P.2d 19 (Idaho 1985). In this case, which arose out of an Idaho accident involving Saskatchewan parties, the defendant qualified as the plaintiff's employer and thus was immune from a tort action under Saskatchewan, but not under Idaho law. The court applied Saskatchewan law.

13. See O'Connor v. O'Connor, 519 A.2d 13 (Conn.1986), supra 145; Travelers Indem. Co. v. Lake, 594 A.2d 38 (Del.1991) (applying Delaware's pro-plaintiff tort law to case arising from Quebec traffic accident involving Delaware parties. Quebec law limited recovery by providing an expedited administrative remedy in lieu of a tort action).

denying recovery for loss of consortium,[14] or limiting compensatory damages.[15] Of the remaining ten cases, two were products liability cases that involved both loss-distributing and conduct-regulating issues,[16] five cases involved the borderline issue of comparative negligence,[17] and three involved other issues that might also straddle the distinction between conduct-regulation and loss-distribution.[18]

Thus, it seems that loss-distribution conflicts have been the revolution's battle field. In this particular field, territoriality has lost significant ground, but as the perusal of the above cases indicates, this loss is confined to common-domicile cases (discussed below). As we shall see later, in other loss-distribution conflicts, territoriality continues to play a tie-breaking role, while in cases that involve conflicts between conduct-regulation rules territoriality remains virtually unchallenged

c. A RECAP ON COMMON-DOMICILE CASES

1. *The Cases.* As Table 1, supra, illustrates, the majority of cases that have abandoned the *lex loci* rule are loss-distribution conflicts in which the tortfeasor and the victim were domiciled in one state and the tort occurred in another state (hereafter "common-domicile" cases). Of the 42 cases in which a state abandoned the *lex loci* rule, 32 cases (or 76%) involved the common-domicile pattern and, except for *Peters*, 31 cases (or 97%) applied the loss-distribution rule of the parties' common domicile.

In the meantime, an additional 18 common-domicile cases have reached the

---

14. See Casey v. Manson Constr. & Eng'g Co., 428 P.2d 898 (Or.1967) (loss of consortium action by an Oregon plaintiff against a Washington defendant arising from Washington accident); Motenko v. MGM Dist., Inc., 921 P.2d 933 (Nev.1996) (loss of consortium action by a Massachusetts plaintiff against a Nevada defendant arising from a Nevada accident).

15. These cases are: Griffith v. United Air Lines, Inc., 203 A.2d 796 (Pa.1964) (wrongful death damages, Pennsylvania victim, Colorado airplane accident); Fabricious v. Horgen, 132 N.W.2d 410 (Iowa 1965) (Iowa parties, Minnesota accident; applying Minnesota law to negligence determination and Iowa law to eligibility for wrongful death action and measure of damages); Widow of Fornaris v. American Sur. Co., 93 P.R.R. 28 (P.R.1966) (Puerto Rico parties, accident in St. Thomas); Reich v. Purcell, 432 P.2d 727 (Cal.1967) (Missouri accident and limited damages, Colorado plaintiff, California defendant); Fox v. Morrison Motor Freight, 267 N.E.2d 405 (Oh.1971) (Ohio parties, Illinois traffic accident and limit on compensatory damages law); Brickner v. Gooden, 525 P.2d 632 (Okla.1974) (Oklahoma parties, accident in Mexico and limit on compensatory damages); Johnson v. Spider Staging Corp., 555 P.2d 997 (Wash.1976) (products liability action by a Kansas plaintiff against a Washington manufacturer for injury in Kansas caused by a scaffold manufactured in Washington; applying Washington pro-plaintiff compensatory damages law); Gutierrez v. Collins, 583 S.W.2d 312 (Tex.1979) (Texas parties, Mexico accident and limited compensatory damages).

16. See Hubbard Mfg. Co. v. Greeson, 515 N.E.2d 1071 (Ind.1987) (Illinois injury, Indiana parties and pro-manufacturer products liability law); Phillips v. General Motors Corp., 995 P.2d 1002 (Mont.2000) (described supra n. 3).

17. See Mitchell v. Craft, 211 So. 2d 509 (Miss. 1968) (comparative negligence, Mississippi parties, Louisiana accident); Issendorf v. Olson, 194 N.W.2d 750 (N.D. 1972) (Minnesota accident, North Dakota parties and contributory negligence rule); Chambers v. Dakotah Charter, Inc., 488 N.W.2d 63 (S.D. 1992) (Missouri accident, South Dakota parties and contributory negligence rule); Hataway v. McKinley, 830 S.W.2d 53 (Tenn. 1992) (Arkansas accident, Tennessee parties and contributory negligence rule); Wallis v. Mrs. Smith's Pie Co., 550 S.W.2d 453 (Ark. 1977) (described supra n.3).

18. See Myers v. Gaither, 232 A.2d 577 (D.C.1967) (accident in Maryland involving a D.C. defendant and a D.C. rule that imposed liability on a car owner for leaving keys in ignition of unattended car); Sexton v. Ryder Truck Rental, Inc., 320 N.W.2d 843 (Mich.1982) (vehicle owner's liability law, Michigan parties, Virginia accident). In Ingersoll v. Klein, 262 N.E.2d 593 (Ill.1970) all parties and the conduct were in Illinois but the injury allegedly occurred a few feet into the Iowa side of the Mississippi river when the defendant's car broke through the ice killing a passenger. The court refused to impose liability on the car owner under Iowa's car owner's statute and held that Illinois' wrongful death statute governed.

highest courts of the states that had previously abandoned the *lex loci* rule, and all but four of those cases also applied the law of the common domicile.[1] Thus, out of a total of 50 common-domicile loss-distribution conflicts that have reached state supreme courts in the post-*lex loci* era, 44 cases (or 88%) applied the law of the common domicile. As explained below, the six cases that applied another law are distinguishable, overruled, or discredited.

2. ***The Two Patterns.*** For purposes of choice-of-law analysis, common-domicile cases can be divided into two patterns, depending on the content of the laws of the involved states: (1) cases in which the law of the common domicile favors recovery more than the law of the state of conduct and injury (the *Babcock* pattern); and (2) cases like *Milkovich* in which the law of the common-domicile is less favorable to recovery than the law of the state of conduct and injury (converse *Babcock*).

a. The Babcock Pattern. Thirty-five of the 50 common-domicile cases involved the *Babcock* pattern, which presents the classic false conflict paradigm. All but two of the 35 cases applied the law of the common domicile. Of the two cases that did not apply the law of the common domicile, one was factually distinguishable, and the other has been overruled.[2] As you remember from chapter 2, even cases decided under the traditional theory, such as *Levy, Haumschild, Grant* and *Owen*, also reached the same result, albeit through manipulative techniques.

b. The Converse-Babcock Pattern. The remaining 15 of the 50 common-domicile cases involved the converse-*Babcock* pattern which, as seen in *Milkovich*, is not as clear a false conflict as *Babcock* was. Nevertheless, 11 of the 15 cases applied the law of the common domicile. Of the four cases that applied another law, the only one that is recent is factually distinguishable.[3] The remaining three cases are old examples of a court's pro-forum and pro-plaintiff biases displacing all other considerations. All three cases applied the pro-plaintiff law of the accident state, but in all three cases that state was also the forum. The fact that two of these cases, including *Milkovich*, were decided under the better-law approach,[4] while the third case was decided under the *lex fori* approach,[5] can explain the outcome better than any other factor. Of course, as seen in *Milkovich*, one could argue that in these cases the accident state is not as uninterested as Ontario was in *Babcock*, because the application of its pro-recovery would compensate persons injured within the territory and facilitate recovery of local medical costs. The question then is whether this interest is sufficiently strong to outweigh the interests of the common domicile. The

---

1. For citations and discussion, see Symeonides, *The Revolution Today*, §§ 129-33.

2. The distinguishable case was *Peters*, see supra n. 5. The second case Dym v. Gordon, 209 N.E.2d 792 (N.Y.1965), was also distinguishable because the parties had a less-than-transient relationship with the accident state and, additionally, the accident involved third parties. In any event, *Dym* must be deemed overruled by Tooker v. Lopez, 301 N.Y.S.2d 519 (N.Y.1969), and superseded by *Neumeier* rule 1. See infra 237.

3. See Martineau v. Guertin, 751 A.2d 776 (Vt.2000). In this case, the parties were domiciled in the same state but they resided in another state, and the accident occurred in a third state, the law of which was identical to the residence state. This factor tipped the scales in favor of the accident state.

4. The other case was Conklin v. Horner, 157 N.W.2d 579 (Wis.1968) (applying Wisconsin law and allowing an action by an Illinois guest-passenger against an Illinois host-driver and arising out of a Wisconsin accident. Illinois' guest statute barred the action).

5. See Arnett v. Thompson.433 S.W.2d 109 (Ky. 1968) (applying Kentucky law to allow an action between Ohio spouses that was barred by Ohio's interspousal immunity rule and guest statute).

majority of cases involving this pattern, including the more recent ones, answered this question in the negative and applied the law of the common domicile with little hesitation. For example, in Collins v. Trius, Inc., 663 A.2d 570 (Me.1995), the Maine court refused to apply Maine's pro-recovery law to the suits of Canadian passengers of a Canadian bus involved in an accident in Maine. The court noted that, "[a]lthough Maine ha[d] a significant interest in regulating conduct on its highways," id. at 573, the issue at stake--recovery for non-economic loss--was "primarily loss-allocating rather than conduct-regulating," id., and, as to such an issue, the parties's common domicile had the "superior" claim to apply it law.[6]

Thus, based on sheer numbers, one can safely conclude that, in loss-distribution conflicts of both the *Babcock* pattern and its converse, the majority of American courts that have abandoned the *lex loci* rule apply the law of the parties' common domicile, *regardless* of the particular choice-of-law methodology the court follows. As the New York Court of Appeals stated, in these cases, the state of the tort "has at best a minimal interest in determining the right of recovery or the extent of the remedy," (*Schultz v. Boy Scouts*, 491 N.Y.S.2d at 96, reproduced infra at 261) and proper analysis "favors the jurisdiction of common domicile because of its interest in enforcing the decisions of both parties to accept both the benefits and the burdens of identifying with that jurisdiction and to submit themselves to its authority." Id.

3. *A Common-Domicile Rule.* In the meantime, a similar development has occurred in other countries, either as a result of American influences or independently. Recent private international law codifications and international conventions have also accepted the premise that when both the tortfeasor and the victim are affiliated with the same country, either through domicile or nationality, the law of that country should govern their respective rights and obligations, even if the tort occurred in another country. This notion is implemented either through a common-domicile rule (as in the Swiss, Quebec, and Puerto Rico codifications, and the Hague Convention on Products Liability),[7] or through an exception from the *lex loci* rule. The exception is phrased either in common-domicile or common-habitual residence language (as in the German and Hungarian codifications, and a proposed European Union Regulation known as "Rome II"),[8] or in common-nationality language (as in the Italian, Polish, and Portuguese codifications).[9] All of these rules are phrased in bilateral terms that are not only forum-neutral, but party- and content-neutral as well. They authorize the application of the law of the common domicile, whether that law

---

6. The court based this conclusion on "the notion of a social contract, whereby a resident assents to casting her lot with others in accepting burdens as well as benefits of identification with a particular community, and ceding to its lawmaking agencies the authority to make judgments striking the balance between her private substantive interests and competing ones of other members of the community." Id.

7. See Swiss codif. Art. 133; Quebec Civ.Code, Art. 3126; Puerto Rican Draft Code, Art. 47(a); Hague Products Liability Convention, Art. 5.

8. See German codif. Art. 40(2); Hungarian codif., §32(3); European Union Regulation on the Law Applicable to Non-Contractual Obligations (2003) (hereafter "Rome II"), Art. 3(2).

9. See Italian codif., Art. 62; Polish codif., Art. 31(2); Portuguese Civ.Code, Art. 45. For an exception that displaces the *lex loci* when the parties have *either* a common nationality or a common habitual residence, see China's Model Draft Law of PIL, art. 114 (6th Draft 2002). Other codifications contain exceptions which, though not explicitly phrased in common-domicile language, are very likely to be employed in common-domicile situations. See, e.g., Austrian codif., §48(1) (if the parties have "a stronger connection to the law of one and the same state," that law displaces the law of the state of conduct.); English PIL Act of 1995 §12; Hague Traffic Accidents Convention of 1971, Art. 4.

favors the plaintiff (as in the *Babcock* pattern) or the defendant (as in the converse-*Babcock* pattern).

Do the American cases described above suggest that it is time for a similar common-domicile rule in the United States? Two states have answered this question in the affirmative, the first judicially, the second legislatively. In the 1973 case *Neumeier v. Kuhner*, which is reproduced infra 237, the New York Court of Appeals enunciated three choice-of-law rules for guest-statute conflicts (known as the *Neumeier* rules), which the same court later extended to other loss-distribution conflicts. The first of those rules calls for the application of the law of the parties' common-domicile, in both the *Babcock* pattern and its converse. In 1991, the State of Louisiana adopted a comprehensive conflicts codification that includes a similar but more flexible common-domicile rule for loss-distribution conflicts.[10]

4. ***Parties Domiciled in Different States that Have Identical Laws.*** Suppose that in *Babcock* the driver was domiciled in New Jersey, rather than New York, and that New Jersey's law was identical to New York's. Would this case not be as false a conflict as *Babcock* was, with Ontario being the uninterested state? If so, would there be any reason to apply Ontario law? For a negative answer to this question, see Article 3544(1) of the Louisiana codification, which extends the common-domicile rule to cases in which the tortfeasor and the victim are domiciled in different states that have "substantially identical" standard of loss distribution. What advantages, if any, do you see in this rule?

5. ***Pre-existing Relationship?*** In most of the American common-domicile cases, the tortfeasor and the victim had a pre-existing social or contractual relationship with each other, such as that of host-driver and guest passenger as in *Babcock*, husband and wife, or employer and employee. Should the existence of such a relationship be a prerequisite for the application of the common-domicile law? Suppose, for example, that the two co-domiciliaries did not know each other and were traveling in different cars when the accident occurred. Would such a case be different from *Babcock* as to justify a different result? Why, or why not?

Conversely, suppose that the tortfeasor and the victim are parties to a preexisting relationship, such as an employment contract, but they are not domiciled in the same state. Should such a case be governed by the law that governs that relationship regardless of other contacts or factors?[11] Why, or why not?

---

10. La. Civ. Code art. 3544(1) provides that the law of the common-domicile applies to "[i]ssues pertaining to loss distribution and financial protection * * * as between a person injured by an offense or quasi-offense and the person who caused the injury." However, unlike the *Neumeier* rule, the Louisiana rule is subject to escapes provided in articles 3547 ("exceptional cases") and 3548 ("corporate tortfeasors"), which authorize a judicial deviation from the common-domicile rule in appropriate cases. For a defense of these rules and exceptions by their drafter, see Symeonides, *Exegesis*, 715-25, 759-66.

11. For an affirmative answer to this question, see article 133(3) of the Swiss codification. For a similar but more flexible rule, see Rome II, Art. 3(3) (providing that the existence of such a relationship creates a presumption in favor of applying the law that governs that relationship, but only if the country of the otherwise applicable law--which could be either the *locus delicti* or the parties' common habitual residence-- does not have a "significant connection").

2. True Conflicts

a. CONTRACTS

Lilienthal v. Kaufman

Supreme Court of Oregon, 1964. 239 Or. 1, 395 P.2d 543.

DENECKE, J. This is an action to collect two promissory notes. The defense is that the defendant maker has previously been declared a spendthrift by an Oregon court and placed under a guardianship and that the guardian has declared the obligations void. The plaintiff's counter is that the notes were executed and delivered in California, that the law of California does not recognize the disability of a spendthrift, and that the Oregon court is bound to apply the law of the place of the making of the contract. The trial court rejected plaintiff's argument and held for the defendant.

This same defendant spendthrift was the prevailing party in our recent decision in Olshen v. Kaufman, 385 P.2d 161 (Or.1963). In that case the spendthrift and the plaintiff, an Oregon resident, had gone into a joint venture to purchase binoculars for resale. For this purpose plaintiff had advanced moneys to the spendthrift. The spendthrift had repaid plaintiff by his personal check for the amount advanced and for plaintiff's share of the profits of such venture. The check had not been paid because the spendthrift had had insufficient funds in his account. The action was for the unpaid balance of the check.

The evidence in that case showed that the plaintiff had been unaware that Kaufman was under a spendthrift guardianship. The guardian testified that he knew Kaufman was engaging in some business and had bank accounts and that he had admonished him to cease these practices; but he could not control the spendthrift.

The statute applicable in that case and in this one is ORS 126.335: "After the appointment of a guardian for the spendthrift, all contracts, except for necessaries * * * made by such spendthrift thereafter * * * are voidable." [cit.] We held in that case that the voiding of the contract by the guardian precluded recovery by the plaintiff * * *. Plaintiff does not seek to overturn the principle of that decision but contends it has no application because the law of California governs, and under California law the plaintiff's claims are valid.

The facts here are identical to those in Olshen v. Kaufman, supra, except for the California locale for portions of the transaction. The notes were for the repayment of advances to finance another joint venture to sell binoculars. The plaintiff was unaware that defendant had been declared a spendthrift and placed under guardianship. The guardian, upon demand for payment by the plaintiff, declared the notes void. The issue is solely one involving the principles of conflict of laws. * * *

Before entering the choice-of-law area of the general field of conflict of laws, we must determine whether the laws of the states having a connection with the controversy are in conflict. Defendant did not expressly concede that under the law of California the defendant's obligation would be enforceable, but his counsel did state that if this proceeding were in the courts of California, the plaintiff probably would recover. We agree.

At common law a spendthrift was not considered incapable of contracting. [cit.] Incapacity of a spendthrift to contract is a disability created by the legislature. California has no such legislation. In addition, the Civil Code of California provides that all persons are capable of contracting except minors, persons judicially determined to be of unsound mind, and persons deprived of civil rights. § 1556. Furthermore, § 1913 of the California Code of Civil Procedure provides: " * * * that the authority of a guardian * * * does not extend beyond the jurisdiction of the Government under which he was invested with his authority." * * *

Plaintiff contends that the substantive issue of whether or not an obligation is valid and binding is governed by the law of the place of making, California. This court has repeatedly stated that the law of the place of contract "must govern as to the validity, interpretation, and construction of the contract." [cit.]

This principle, that *lex loci contractus* must govern, however, has been under heavy attack for years. * * * As a result of this long and powerful assault, the principle is no longer a cornerstone of the law of conflicts. * * *

In this case California had more connection with the transaction than being merely the place where the contract was executed. The defendant went to San Francisco to ask the plaintiff, a California resident, for money for the defendant's venture. The money was loaned to defendant in San Francisco, and by the terms of the note, it was to be repaid to plaintiff in San Francisco.

On these facts, apart from *lex loci contractus*, other accepted principles of conflict of laws lead to the conclusion that the law of California should be applied. * * *

Thus far all signs have pointed to applying the law of California and holding the contract enforceable. There is, however, an obstacle to cross before this end can be logically reached. In Olshen v. Kaufman, supra, we decided that the law of Oregon, at least as applied to persons domiciled in Oregon contracting in Oregon for performance in Oregon, is that spendthrifts' contracts are voidable. Are the choice-of-law principles of conflict of laws so superior that they overcome this principle of Oregon law?

To answer this question we must determine, upon some basis, whether the interests of Oregon are so basic and important that we should not apply California law despite its several intimate connections with the transaction. The traditional method used by this court and most others is framed in the terminology of 'public policy.' The court decides whether or not the public policy of the forum is so strong that the law of the forum must prevail although another jurisdiction, with different laws, has more and closer contacts with the transaction. Included in 'public policy' we must consider the economic and social interests of Oregon. When these factors are included in a consideration of whether the law of the forum should be applied this traditional approach is very similar to that advocated by many legal scholars. This latter theory is 'that choice-of-law rules should rationally advance the policies or interests of the several states (or of the nations in the world community).' Hill Governmental Interest and the Conflict of Laws--A Reply to Professor Currie, 27 Chi.L.Rev. 463, 474 (1960); Currie, Selected Essays on the Conflict of Laws, 64–72

(1963). * * *

However, as previously stated, if we include in our search for the public policy of the forum a consideration of the various interests that the forum has in this litigation, we are guided by more definite criteria. In addition to the interests of the forum, we should consider the interests of the other jurisdictions which have some connection with the transaction.

Some of the interests of Oregon in this litigation are set forth in Olshen v. Kaufman, supra. The spendthrift's family which is to be protected by the establishment of the guardianship is presumably an Oregon family. The public authority which may be charged with the expense of supporting the spendthrift or his family, if he is permitted to go unrestrained upon his wasteful way, will probably be an Oregon public authority. These, obviously, are interests of some substance.

Oregon has other interests and policies regarding this matter which were not necessary to discuss in *Olshen*. As previously stated, Oregon, as well as all other states, has a strong policy favoring the validity and enforceability of contracts. This policy applies whether the contract is made and to be performed in Oregon or elsewhere.

The defendant's conduct,--borrowing money with the belief that the repayment of such loan could be avoided--is a species of fraud. Oregon and all other states have a strong policy of protecting innocent persons from fraud. 'The law * * * is intended as a protection to even the foolishly credulous, as against the machinations of the designedly wicked.' Johnson v. Cofer, 281 P.2d 981, 985 (Or.1955).

It is in Oregon's commercial interest to encourage citizens of other states to conduct business with Oregonians. If Oregonians acquire a reputation for not honoring their agreements, commercial intercourse with Oregonians will be discouraged. If there are Oregon laws, somewhat unique to Oregon, which permit an Oregonian to escape his otherwise binding obligations, persons may well avoid commercial dealings with Oregonians.

The substance of these commercial considerations, however, is deflated by the recollection that the Oregon Legislature has determined, despite the weight of these considerations, that a spendthrift's contracts are voidable.

California's most direct interest in this transaction is having its citizen creditor paid. As previously noted, California's policy is that any creditor, in California or otherwise, should be paid even though the debtor is a spendthrift. California probably has another, although more intangible, interest involved. It is presumably to every state's benefit to have the reputation of being a jurisdiction in which contracts can be made and performance be promised with the certain knowledge that such contracts will be enforced. Both of these interests, particularly the former, are also of substance.

We have, then, two jurisdictions, each with several close connections with the transaction, and each with a substantial interest, which will be served or thwarted, depending upon which law is applied. The interests of neither jurisdiction are clearly more important than those of the other. We are of the opinion that in such a case the public policy of Oregon should prevail and the law of Oregon should be applied; we should apply that choice-of-law rule which will "advance the policies or interests of"

Oregon. Hill, supra, 27 Chi.L.Rev. at 474.

Courts are instruments of state policy. The Oregon Legislature has adopted a policy to avoid possible hardship to an Oregon family of a spendthrift and to avoid possible expenditure of Oregon public funds which might occur if the spendthrift is required to pay his obligations. In litigation Oregon courts are the appropriate instrument to enforce this policy. The mechanical application of choice-of-law rules would be the only apparent reason for an Oregon court advancing the interests of California over the equally valid interests of Oregon. The present principles of conflict of laws are not favorable to such mechanical application.

We hold that the spendthrift law of Oregon is applicable and the plaintiff cannot recover.

Judgment affirmed.

O'CONNELL, J. (especially concurring). * * * In the *Olshen* case we had to choose between two competing policies; on one hand the policy of protecting the interest of persons dealing with spendthrifts which, broadly, may be described as the interest in the security of transactions, and on the other hand the policy of protecting the interests of the spendthrift, his family and the county. It was decided that the Oregon Legislature adopted the latter policy in preference to the former.

The case at bar involves the same choice even though the contract was made in California and it was to be performed there. The fact that California was the setting for the making and performance of the contract is of no significance except that it requires us to consider California's interest in protecting its own citizens. That interest is an interest in the security of commercial transactions and was before this court in the *Olshen* case. To distinguish the *Olshen* case it would be necessary to assume that although the legislature intended to protect the interest of the spendthrift, his family and the county when local creditors were harmed, the same protection was not intended where the transaction adversely affected foreign creditors. I see no basis for making that assumption. There is no reason to believe that our legislature intended to protect California creditors to a greater extent than our own.

GOODWIN, J. (dissenting). I am unable to agree with the conclusion of the majority. * * * In the case before us, I believe that the policy of both states, Oregon and California, in favor of enforcing contracts, has been lost sight of in favor of a questionable policy in Oregon which gives special privileges to the rare spendthrift for whom a guardian has been appointed. * * * I can see nothing * * * in Oregon's policy toward spendthrifts that warrants its extension to permit the taking of captives from other states down the road to insolvency.

I would enforce the contract.

Notes and Questions

1. **Brainerd Currie and True Conflicts.** *Lilienthal* met Currie's definition of a "true conflict" because both states involved in the case met his threshold of having an "interest" in applying their respective laws. Currie's prescription for such conflicts was to apply the law of the forum state, primarily because, in Currie's view, a judge is neither constitutionally empowered nor otherwise qualified to weigh conflicting

state interests. Such a weighing, Currie thought, was a "political function of a very high order * * * that should not be committed to courts in a democracy." Currie, *Selected Essays*, 182. See also id. at 278-79. Currie also spoke of the "embarrassment of [a court] having to nullify the interests of its own sovereign." Id. at 182. Yet, according to Currie's own analysis, in order to determine whether the conflict is a true one, the judge must identify and evaluate the interests of the involved states. Is such an evaluation so qualitatively different, less subjective or politically sensitive than is a weighing of interests? As Cavers put it, in Currie's analysis, "[w]eighing of interests after interpretation is condemned: weighing of interests in interpretation, condoned, not to say, encouraged." Cavers, *Contemporary Conflicts*, 148. Moreover, is Currie's portrayal of the judge's role consistent with your understanding of the basic tenets of the common-law tradition and the role judges actually enjoy in the American system of government? Do American judges refrain from evaluating and weighing conflicting social policies? As one observer put it, "[e]ver since conflicts law first developed, courts did precisely what Currie would forbid them to do; no judge has ever been impeached for inventing or applying a choice of law rule that sacrifices forum interests." Juenger, *Interstate Torts*, 206-7.

Currie's response to such observations was sharp and short: "I do not care whether courts undertake to weigh and balance conflicting interests or not," he said, but when they do, "such action can find its justification in politics, not in jurisprudence. * * * [L]et us not delude ourselves with any notion that we can control or predict the process by a juridical science of conflict of laws." Currie, *Selected Essays*, 600-01. See id. at 183, 274 for a more moderate response.

2. ***Currie's Forum Favoritism***. In summary, Currie thought that the *lex fori* should apply in every case in which the forum has an interest, even if that interest is not the stronger one. His analysis begins and ends with the *lex fori*. He begins with the basic presumption that the *lex fori* should be applied as a matter of course, and that only if good reason is shown should the judge consider applying another law. See Currie's summary, supra 116. Currie acknowledged such a reason only in one category of conflicts--a false conflict in which the forum is not interested. In all other cases he would apply the *lex fori*: (a) in a false conflict in which the forum is the interested state; (b) in a true conflict in which the forum is one of the interested states; (c) in the no-interest or unprovided-for case; and (d) even in a true conflict before a disinterested forum, if the court cannot dismiss on grounds of forum non conveniens. See id. In the words of one commentator, "Currie's analysis, which compels him to give to the forum's law such broad effects, would tend to fasten upon the international and the interstate communities * * * a legal order characterized by chaos and retaliation." von Mehren, *Book Review* 97 n. 2. What do you think?

Currie justified his forum favoritism with arguments that ranged from the practical to the philosophical. See, e.g., Currie, *Selected Essays*, 89, 93-94, 191, 197, 278-80, 323, 447, 489-90, 592, 627, 697. Toward the end of his life, he tried to mitigate his position by advocating a "restrained and enlightened interpretation" of the *lex fori*. See his summary supra at 116; Currie, *The Disinterested Third State*, 757. He did not, however, modify the basic premises of his theory, especially his view that courts are not the proper organs to weigh governmental interests.

3. ***True Conflicts before a Disinterested Forum***. Suppose that for some reason *Lilienthal* was litigated in Nevada and that Nevada was uninterested in the outcome. If the Nevada court were to follow interest analysis, how would the court resolve this true conflict between Oregon and California law? Currie thought that such cases are extremely rare. See Currie, *The Disinterested Third State*, 765, 773. He proposed that in such conflicts the court should decide the case "by a candid exercise of legislative discretion, resolving the conflict as it believes it would be resolved by a supreme legislative body." See his summary supra at 116. Why is it that with regard to such cases, those same courts that in Currie's view are unqualified to weigh governmental interests, now are capable of performing such a "supreme" task? Are they? Should they? Lest you mistake Currie for a better-law advocate, it should be noted that he specifically decried a better-law approach in any other type of true conflict. See Currie, *Selected Essays*, 104-06, 154 n. 82.

4. **Lilienthal *and State Interests***. Are you persuaded by the *Lilienthal* court's conclusion that, even from an interest-analysis perspective, that case was not sufficiently different from *Olshen v. Kaufman* as to justify a different result? For now, leave aside California's interests and compare Oregon's interests in *Olshen* with Oregon's interests in *Lilienthal*. Did these interests point in the same direction? Whether you agree or disagree with Oregon's spendthrift rule, that rule reflected the Oregon legislature's conscious decision to strike a balance between two competing social policies and to subordinate the general policies of "favoring the validity and enforceability of contracts" and "protecting innocent persons from fraud" to the specific policy of protecting the spendthrift's family. In a case like *Olshen*, which was confined exclusively within Oregon, an Oregon court would have no reason or basis to ignore this legislatively established balance and not to apply the spendthrift rule, would it? Was this true also of *Lilienthal*? Didn't the very fact that *Lilienthal* was not exclusively confined within Oregon produce a different balance between Oregon's general contract-favoring policies and its specific policy of protecting the families of spendthrifts, by adding to the strength of the former policies and detracting from the strength of the latter policy? (See supra 139-40 for the distinction between "domestic" and "multistate" interests.) The *Lilienthal* court came close to this conclusion when it recognized "Oregon's commercial interest to encourage citizens of other states to conduct business with Oregonians * * * [and to prevent] laws, somewhat unique to Oregon, [from] permit[ing] an Oregonian to escape his otherwise binding obligations." Should the court have taken the next step of concluding that this commercial interest--which was not present in *Olshen*--together with Oregon's other interest in "protecting innocent persons from fraud," should justify subordinating the spendthrift-protecting interest in *Lilienthal*? Another way of asking this question is: Did the spendthrift rule purport to cover out-of-state transactions?

5. **Lilienthal *and Party Expectations***. Compare the expectations of the two creditors, the Oregon creditor in *Olshen* and the California creditor in *Lilienthal*. Keep in mind that, although Currie downplayed this factor, the protection of justified party expectations is an important goal of conflicts law in particular and law in

general. In *Olshen*, the court applied Oregon's spendthrift rule to an Oregon creditor acting exclusively within his home state in a purely local transaction with another Oregon citizen. To the extent that creditor had any expectation about the applicable law, that expectation must have been that Oregon law would govern, for better or worse. Thus, the application of Oregon law in *Olshen* was not only fair (or at least not unfair) but also inevitable, was it not? Did *Lilienthal*, which involved a California creditor acting in his home state in a transaction that did not bear obvious multistate characteristics, warrant or at least permit a different result? For all we know, the California creditor might not have known that Mr. Kaufman was from another state, let alone a state with such a "unique" invalidating rule. Even if the creditor knew that Mr. Kaufman was from Oregon, should the creditor also have known about Oregon's law? Should every vendor in San Francisco's Fisherman's Wharf be required to investigate the whereabouts of every customer and to research the laws of all states or countries from which each customer comes? Was the concurring judge in *Lilienthal* correct in finding "no reason to believe that our legislature intended to protect California creditors to a greater extent than our own"? Was Oregon's *own* policy of "protecting innocent persons from fraud" stronger in *Lilienthal* than in *Olshen*?

6. Compare *Lilienthal* with *Milliken*, (supra at 30). Which of the two cases reached the better *result*? Why? Is it fair to say that the *Milliken* court reached a good result despite being bound by a mechanical choice-of-law rule, while the *Lilienthal* court reached a bad result despite the absence of a binding choice-of-law rule?

7. *Choice-of-Law Rules for Contractual Capacity*. In 1973, Oregon repealed its spendthrift rule. In 2002, Oregon enacted a choice-of-law codification for contracts, the pertinent part of which provides:

> ORS § 81.112. *Capacity to contract.* (1) A party has the capacity to enter into a contract if the party has that capacity under the law of the state in which the party resides or the law applicable to this issue under [other sections of this Act].

> (2) A party that lacks capacity to enter into a contract under the law of the state in which the party resides may assert that incapacity against a party that knew or should have known of the incapacity at the time the parties entered into the contract. * * *

You may assume that, under the codification's other provisions, California law would be applicable to the issue involved in *Lilienthal*. See Symeonides, *The Oregon Experience*, V.2. However, this would not be the end of the case, because the *Lilienthal* scenario would trigger consideration of subsection (2) of ORS § 81.112. Under the *Lilienthal* facts, would Mr. Kaufman have prevailed under subsection (2)? Suppose now that Mr. Kaufman was capable under Oregon law, but not under California law. Would subsection (2) be applicable in such a scenario. If yes, why? If not, why the difference? For discussion of these issues, see Symeonides, id. For a similar choice-of-law rule. See La.Civ.Code Art. 3537; Symeonides, *Six Celebrated Conflicts Cases*, 858-64 (discussing *Lilienthal* under that rule).

Similar rules exist outside the United States. Consider the differences between the following rules and explain how *Lilienthal* and *Milliken* would be decided under each rule: (1) Benelux Treaty Art. 2: "[A] person declared incapable by his law may not invoke his incapacity against one who, in a legal act, has in good faith and in conformity with the law of the place of the act considered him to be capable;" (2) Rome Convention Art. 11 (as well as German codif. Art. 12): "In a contract concluded between persons who are in the same country, a natural person who would have capacity under the law of that country may invoke his incapacity resulting from another law only if the other party to the contract was aware of this incapacity at the time of the conclusion of the contract or was not aware thereof as a result of negligence;" (3) Quebec Civ.Code Art. 3086: "A party to a juridical act who is incapable under the law of the country of his domicile may not invoke his incapacity if he was capable under the law of the country in which the other party was domiciled when the act was executed in that country, unless the other party was or should have been aware of the incapacity."

CURRIE'S SECOND THOUGHTS:
"RESTRAINT AND MODERATION" AND "APPARENT" CONFLICTS

Late in his short life, Currie responded to criticisms that his theory encouraged the selfish pursuit of state interests. He pointed to *Bernkrant* and *Ford Victoria* (reproduced below) both decided by his friend Justice Traynor, as examples of how a court faced with a potential true conflict can engage in a more restrained or enlightened interpretation of its law, thereby making it possible to resolve the conflict without having to apply the *lex fori*. Currie characterized these potential true conflicts as "apparent conflicts," which he defined as cases in which "each state would be constitutionally justified in asserting an interest, but on reflection the conflict is avoided by a moderate definition of the policy or interest of one state or the other," or as cases in which "reasonable men may disagree on whether a conflicting interest should be asserted." Currie, *The Disinterested Third State*, 763, 764. According to another definition, an apparent conflict is a conflict that appears to be true if all possible interests of the involved states in the abstract are considered, but which may well be false upon a closer investigation of the factual contacts and a more moderate interpretation of the policies involved. See Sedler, *Reformulation*, 187.

Currie admitted that "the three classes of cases [i.e., false, apparent, true] are a continuum with no clear internal boundaries," Currie, *Selected Essays*, 764, but he insisted that the process by which the judge determines whether the case should be placed in one or the other of these categories is qualitatively different than a weighing of state interests. See id. at 759.

People v. One 1953 Ford Victoria

Supreme Court of California, 1957,
48 Cal.2d 595, 311 P.2d 480.

TRAYNOR, J. In this proceeding to forfeit an automobile for an unlawful transportation of narcotics (Health & Saf. Code, §§ 11610-11629) the facts are undisputed.

On June 10, 1953, Willie Smith purchased the automobile from a dealer in Bexar County, Texas. Smith executed a note for the unpaid balance of the purchase price and gave the dealer a chattel mortgage on the automobile to secure payment. On the same day, the dealer assigned the note and mortgage to respondent, a Texas corporation engaged in the business of financing the sales of automobiles.

The mortgage prohibited the mortgagor from removing the automobile from Bexar County without the written consent of the mortgagee. In violation of this prohibition and without the knowledge of respondent, Smith brought the automobile to California.

On September 23, 1954, Smith used the automobile in California to transport marihuana, and the automobile was seized. [cit.] On March 1, 1955, the attorney general filed a notice of seizure and intended forfeiture. [cit.] Respondent answered, asserting its mortgage.

The hearing disclosed that Texas has no law providing for the forfeiture of automobiles used in the unlawful transportation of narcotics; that at the time respondent accepted the assignment of the note and mortgage it had no information that would place it on notice that the vehicle was to be used unlawfully; and that respondent made no investigation of Smith's moral responsibility, character, and reputation. [cit.]

The trial court concluded "[that] the validity and effect of the lien of ... [respondent] ... is governed by the laws of the State of Texas, which do not require an investigation of the moral responsibility, character and reputation of the purchaser," and entered judgment providing that the automobile be forfeited to the state of California subject to respondent's lien for the unpaid balance of the purchase price, $722.84. The People appeal from the part of the judgment recognizing respondent's lien.

The validity of respondent's mortgage is not in question. Admittedly the mortgage was valid in Texas, and it is valid here. [cit.] The People contend that despite the validity of the mortgage, respondent's interest in the automobile should be forfeited because respondent failed to investigate Smith's moral responsibility, character and reputation.

Section 11610 of the Health and Safety Code provides: "A vehicle used to unlawfully transport ... any narcotic ... shall be forfeited to the State." Section 11620 provides: "The claimant ... may prove his ... mortgage ... to be bona fide and that his ... interest was created after a reasonable investigation of the moral responsibility, character, and reputation of the purchaser, and without any knowledge that the vehicle was being, or was to be, used for the purpose charged...." Section 11622 provides: "In the event of such proof, the court shall order the vehicle released to the

... innocent ... mortgagee, ... it being the intention of this section to forfeit only the ... interest of the purchaser." The statute makes it clear that it does not contemplate the forfeiture of the interest of an innocent mortgagee. [cit.] To prove his innocence, however, a mortgagee whose interest arises out of a transaction in California must show not only that his mortgage is bona fide and that his interest was created without any knowledge that the vehicle was to be used unlawfully but also that he made the required "reasonable investigation." Respondent has proved that its mortgage is bona fide; that it was created in another state without any knowledge that the vehicle was to be used unlawfully or even that it was to be taken to California; and that the automobile was brought here in violation of an express contractual prohibition against removing the vehicle not only from Texas but from a specified county therein. The question is whether under these circumstances the "reasonable investigation" required of a California mortgagee to avoid forfeiture of his interest applies to respondent.

By requiring a "reasonable investigation" to avoid forfeiture of their interests in the event of prohibited use of automobiles, section 11620 in effect regulates the conduct of persons financing, and thereby facilitating, the sales thereof. [cit.] To avoid forfeiture such persons are required to investigate the moral responsibility, character, and reputation of prospective purchasers and mortgagors to diminish the possibility that automobiles will be placed in the hands of persons likely to use them to transport narcotics unlawfully. As applied to persons financing the sales of automobiles in California, a forfeiture for failure to make the required investigation is not unreasonable. Such persons may reasonably be expected to be familiar with California statutes regulating their activities and to make the "reasonable investigation" necessary to protect their interests from forfeiture. In the absence of a plain legislative direction to the contrary, however, the statute cannot reasonably be interpreted as requiring such investigation when the sales are financed in other states and the vehicles are taken to California, not only without the knowledge of those financing the sales, but in violation of express contractual prohibitions. [cit.] A person financing the sale of an automobile in Texas for use exclusively in that state will look to the laws of Texas for the determination of his rights and duties. He cannot reasonably be expected to familiarize himself with and comply in Texas with the statutes of the 48 or more jurisdictions into which the automobile could possibly be taken without his consent and in violation of express contractual prohibitions. Not only is section 11620 not made expressly applicable to an innocent mortgagee financing the sale of an automobile in another state for exclusive use there, but the statutory enumeration of relationships between the mortgagor and the state of California in the 1955 amendment to that section (Stats. 1955, ch. 1209, § 5), plainly indicates that in requiring a "reasonable investigation" to avoid forfeiture, the Legislature was preoccupied with California mortgagors and mortgagees.

It is contended that a holding that the "reasonable investigation" requirement is not applicable to respondent will subvert the enforcement of California's narcotics laws. We are not persuaded that such dire consequences will ensue. The state may still forfeit the interest of the wrongdoer. It has done so in this case. Moreover, the Legislature has made plain its purpose not to forfeit the interests of innocent mortgagees. It has not made plain that "reasonable investigation" of the purchaser is such an essential element of innocence that it must be made even by an out-of-state mortgagee although such mortgagee could not reasonably be expected to make such investigation.

The judgment is *affirmed.*

SCHAUER, J. (concurring) I concur in both the judgment and the reasoning upon which it is based, with the qualification that I do not join in any implication, if there be such, that California could constitutionally (by "a plain legislative direction," or otherwise) require as a condition of upholding contracts made in other states by residents of those states that the parties to such contracts comply with California's "reasonable investigation" statute.

Bernkrant v. Fowler

Supreme Court of California, 1961.
55 Cal.2d 588, 12 Cal.Rptr. 266, 360 P.2d 906.

TRAYNOR, J. * * * Some time before 1954 plaintiffs purchased the Granrud Garden Apartments in Las Vegas, Nevada. In 1954 the property was encumbered by [a] * * * a second deed of trust given to secure an installment note payable to Granrud at $200 per month plus interest. * * * In July 1954, there remained unpaid * * * approximately $24,000 on the note payable to Granrud. At that time Granrud wished to buy a trailer park and asked plaintiffs to refinance their obligations and pay a substantial part of their indebtedness to him. At a meeting in Las Vegas he stated that if plaintiffs would do so, he would provide by will that any debt that remained on the purchase price at the time of his death would be cancelled and forgiven. Plaintiffs then arranged for a new loan * * * [and] used the proceeds to pay * * * $13,114.20 of their indebtedness to Granrud. They executed a new note for the balance of $9,227 owing Granrud. * * *

Granrud died testate on March 4, 1956, a resident of Los Angeles County. His will, dated January 23, 1956, was admitted to probate, and defendant was appointed executrix of his estate. His will made no provision for cancelling the balance of $6,425 due on the note at the time of his death. Plaintiffs have continued to make regular payments of principal and interest to defendant under protest.

Plaintiffs brought this action to have the note cancelled and discharged and the property reconveyed to them and to recover the amounts paid defendant after Granrud's death. The trial court concluded that the action was barred by both the Nevada and the California statute of frauds * * *. [The Supreme Court concluded that the trial court had misread the Nevada statute and that the contract would be valid under Nevada law.]

We are therefore confronted with a contract that is valid under the law of Nevada but invalid under the California statute of frauds if that statute is applicable.

We have no doubt that California's interest in protecting estates being probated here from false claims based on alleged oral contracts to make wills is constitutionally sufficient to justify the Legislature's making our statute of frauds applicable to all such contracts sought to be enforced against such estates. [cit.] The Legislature, however, is ordinarily concerned with enacting laws to govern purely local transactions, and it has not spelled out the extent to which the statute of frauds is to apply to a contract having substantial contacts with another state. Accordingly, we must determine its scope in the light of applicable principles of the law of conflict of laws. (See People v. One 1953 Ford Victoria, [*supra*]).[cit.]

In the present case plaintiffs were residents of Nevada, the contract was made in Nevada, and plaintiffs performed it there. If Granrud was a resident of Nevada at the time the contract was made, the California statute of frauds, in the absence of a plain legislative direction to the contrary, could not reasonably be interpreted as applying to the contract even though Granrud subsequently moved to California and died here. [cit.] The basic policy of upholding the expectations of the parties by enforcing contracts valid under the only law apparently applicable would preclude an interpretation of our statute of frauds that would make it apply to and thus invalidate the contract because Granrud moved to California and died here. Such a case would be analogous to People v. One 1953 Ford Victoria, [supra]. * * * Another analogy is found in the holding that the statute of frauds did not apply to contracts to make wills entered into before the statute was enacted ([cit.]). Just as parties to local transactions cannot be expected to take cognizance of the law of other jurisdictions, they cannot be expected to anticipate a change in the local statute of frauds. Protection of rights growing out of valid contracts precludes interpreting the general language of the statute of frauds to destroy such rights whether the possible applicability of the statute arises from the movement of one or more of the parties across state lines or subsequent enactment of the statute. See Currie and Schreter, Unconstitutional Discrimination in the Conflict of Laws: Privileges and Immunities, 69 Yale L.J. 1323, 1334.

In the present case, however, there is no finding as to where Granrud was domiciled at the time the contract was made. Since he had a bank account in California at that time and died a resident here less than two years later it may be that he was domiciled here when the contract was made. Even if he was, the result should be the same. The contract was made in Nevada and performed by plaintiffs there, and it involved the refinancing of obligations arising from the sale of Nevada land and secured by interests therein. Nevada has a substantial interest in the contract and in protecting the rights of its residents who are parties thereto, and its policy is that the contract is valid and enforceable. California's policy is also to enforce lawful contracts. That policy, however, must be subordinated in the case of any contract that does not meet the requirements of an applicable statute of frauds. In determining whether the contract herein is subject to the California statute of frauds, we must consider both the policy to protect the reasonable expectations of the parties and the policy of the statute of frauds. [cit.] It is true that if Granrud was domiciled here at the time the contract was made, plaintiffs may have been alerted to the possibility that the California statute of frauds might apply. Since California, however, would have no interest in applying its own statute of frauds unless Granrud remained here until his death, plaintiffs were not bound to know that California's statute might ultimately be invoked against them. Unless they could rely on their own law, they would have to look to the laws of all of the jurisdictions to which Granrud might move regardless of where he was domiciled when the contract was made. We conclude, therefore, that the contract herein does not fall within our statute of frauds. [cit.] Since there is thus no conflict between the law of California and the law of Nevada, we can give effect to the common policy of both states to enforce lawful contracts and sustain Nevada's interest in protecting its residents and their reasonable expectations growing out of a transaction substantially related to that state without subordinating any legitimate interest of this state.

The judgment is *reversed*.

Notes and Questions

1. In both the *Ford Victoria* and *Bernkrant* cases, Justice Traynor asked the most pertinent question: Was the forum's substantive rule intended to be applied to the case at hand? Although this question may evoke memories of the Italian statutists and other European unilateralists (see Ch.1, supra), it is nevertheless an important question that should be asked not only by courts adhering to interest analysis, but also by any court that is not bound by preconceived or inchoate bilateral choice-of-law rules. Had the *Lilienthal* court asked this question, what do you think the answer would have been? To answer this question, Traynor resorts to the resources of statutory interpretation and tries to ascertain the rule's underlying intent with regard to out-of-state transactions. He well understands--and so should each student--that when, as is often the case, the legislature "has not spelled out the extent to which the [forum] statute * * * is to apply to a [case] having substantial contacts with another state * * *, we must determine its scope in the light of applicable principles of the law of conflict of laws." *Bernkrant*, supra. In some instances, one can surmise the legislative intent from the statute's language. In *Ford Victoria*, Traynor properly concluded that "the statutory enumeration of relationships between the mortgagor and the state of California in the 1955 amendment to [the California statute] * * * plainly indicates that in requiring a 'reasonable investigation' to avoid forfeiture, the Legislature was preoccupied with California mortgagors and mortgagees." More often than not, however, the statute's language is completely silent as to its intended territorial reach, as was the case in *Bernkrant* and *Lilienthal*. But, as Traynor observes in *Bernkrant*, mere silence does not imply a lack of intent. The intent is present, waiting to be discovered or re-constructed "in the light of applicable principles of the law of conflict of laws." *Bernkrant*, supra.

2. In delineating the intended territorial reach of California's forfeiture statute or its statute of frauds, Traynor adopted an enlightened and restrained view of the forum's interests, as Currie eventually suggested one should do. But to do so, Traynor had to go against or beyond some basic tenets of Currie's analysis and to consider factors that were not encompassed in Currie's calculus of interests. For example, Traynor implicitly rejected Currie's view that a state is interested in protecting its own citizens only and not out-of-staters similarly situated; he overcame Currie's reluctance to recognize interests other than those embodied in the particular statutes involved in the conflict and took cognizance of the forum's so-called "multistate interests" (see supra at 139-40); and, more importantly, he gave due

attention to the expectations of private parties involved in the conflict, especially parties acting outside the forum state. As noted earlier, Currie was unwilling to consider the expectations and interests of private parties except to the extent that those interests were subsumed under the interests of their respective states. See his statements quoted supra at 139–40. Compare those statements with, on the one hand, Traynor's treatment of the plaintiffs in *Bernkrant* and the Texas financier in *Ford Victoria*, and, on the other, with the treatment of the California creditor by the *Lilienthal* court.

b. TORTS

(1) SPLIT-DOMICILE INTRASTATE TORTS

Foster v. Leggett

Court of Appeals of Kentucky, 1972.
484 S.W.2d 827.

WALDEN, Special Commissioner. Appellant, plaintiff below, prosecutes this appeal from a summary judgment against her, in her capacity as personal representative, in an action to recover damages for the wrongful death of her decedent.

On September 9, 1967, appellant's decedent, while a guest passenger in an automobile owned and operated by appellee, was killed in a traffic accident north of Portsmouth, Ohio, * * * . Appellant administratrix filed suit in the Greenup County Circuit Court seeking to recover damages for the wrongful death of deceased and burial expenses, alleging both ordinary and gross negligence in the operation of the automobile by appellee. Appellee was before the court on personal service.

Appellee answered the suit, and, among other matters, pleaded section 4515.02 of the Ohio Revised Code, commonly known as the Guest Statute, which provides, in substance, that a nonpaying guest cannot recover damages for injury or death from the owner-operator of a motor vehicle, unless such injuries or death are caused by the wilful or wanton misconduct of such operator, owner, or person responsible for the operation of said motor vehicle.

Appellee's deposition revealed that * * * both he and decedent * * * were employed by the C & O Railroad and worked in the same office at Russell, in Greenup County, Kentucky. They had been so associated in this work for several years. The deceased, Mrs. Stringer, had lived all her life in Greenup County, Kentucky. Appellee * * * lived in Portsmouth, Ohio, across the Ohio River from Russell, Kentucky. Appellee made his home with his parents in Portsmouth, voted, paid taxes, licensed his automobile, and did his banking and other such activities as would indicate legal domicile in the State of Ohio. * * * Over the years, for convenience, appellee had often stayed at the Russell Y.M.C.A. For about one year prior to the accident appellee had kept a room rented at the "Y" by the week. He stayed in this room about two nights a week, on the average. Appellee and Mrs. Stringer had been dating for several months. The day before the fatal accident they * * * agreed that the next day they would go to Columbus, Ohio. * * * [where] they would have dinner, go to a show or the races, and return to Russell the night of the same day. Pursuant to this plan, appellee spent the night in his room at the "Y" and the next morning, drove his 1966 Dodge automobile, picked up decedent at her home and they proceeded on their journey to Columbus, Ohio. * * * A short distance north of Portsmouth, appellee * * * lost control of his automobile and crossed the median into the path or lane of a vehicle going south on the highway. Mrs. Stringer and the driver of this southbound vehicle were killed. * * *

The question to be determined is whether the law of Ohio or the law of Kentucky applies in this case. * * * In the case of Wessling v. Paris, Ky., 417 S.W.2d 259 (1967), we very substantially departed from the age-old and almost universal doctrine that liability for torts was governed by the law of the place where the tort occurred (lex loci delicti). * * *

When the court has jurisdiction of the parties its primary responsibility is to follow its own substantive law. The basic law is the law of the forum, which should not be displaced without valid reasons. We have not, therefore, tried to adopt a rule, or rules, for all cases of this kind which may come before us.

In the case at bar, contacts with Kentucky were numerous and significant. Decedent was a lifelong resident of Kentucky. While appellee was a resident of Ohio, he kept a rented room near his work in Kentucky, stayed in it on the average of two nights per week and all his employment and most of his social relationships were in Kentucky. The fatal journey began in Kentucky and was to have been concluded in Kentucky.

So we conclude that the reasons appellee here advances, that the accident occurred in the State of Ohio and that appellee was domiciled and had a residence in that state, are not sufficient in view of the contacts the State of Kentucky had with the parties to justify the displacement of the law of this forum with the law of the State of Ohio. We are now reaffirming our position taken in Wessling v. Paris, supra, that if there are significant contacts--not necessarily the most significant contacts-- with Kentucky, the Kentucky law should be applied.

The judgment is reversed and the case remanded for proceedings consistent with this opinion. * * *

REED, J. (dissenting). * * * In the case before us, the public policy of Ohio was to protect hosts from the claims of gratuitous guests except in instances of aggravated forms of negligence. The defendant was a resident of and domiciled in Ohio. The Ohio statute was meant to protect him. Surely it was meant to protect him while he drove on Ohio highways. Liability insurance afforded Ohio residents could well be negotiated and charged for on the basis of that state's law. The decision of the majority has extended a choice of law principle far beyond the general body of case law on which the Restatement principles are based and opens Kentucky as a forum which will instantly apply its own law upon any excuse whatever, regardless of policy considerations of sister states to the contrary. One would hope that the sister states do not afford residents and domiciliaries of Kentucky the same treatment in actions based upon conduct and injury in Kentucky. I, therefore, respectfully dissent and would affirm the judgment of the circuit court.

Notes and Questions

1. Although guest-statute conflicts have almost disappeared (only two state had such statutes in 2003), they are effective surrogates for exploring more complex loss-distribution conflicts. By now you have seen three permutations of a guest-statute conflict: *Babcock*, the classic false conflict; *Milkovich*, the not-so-false conflict; and now *Foster*, the true conflict. Although the *Foster* court did not rely on Currie and it focused on state contacts rather than on state interests, there is little doubt that it reached the very result Currie advocated. *Foster* followed what is known as the *lex fori* approach, which begins (and often ends) with a strong presumption in favor of the law of the forum. Thus, this approach is akin to Currie's, both ideologically and statistically.

2. Read again the part of *Foster* that enumerates the driver's contacts with Kentucky. Did those contacts outweigh his "legal domicile" in Ohio? In light of those contacts, would it be proper to conclude that *Foster* was not really a split-domicile case? Would such a conclusion render *Foster* less of a true conflict?

If *Foster* were a true split-domicile case, would the court's choice-of-law decision be acceptable to you? Why, or why not? For other cases involving the same pattern and issues as *Foster* but reaching the opposite choice-of-law decision, see infra 211 *et seq.*

3. *Michigan's* **Lex Fori** *Approach*. Cases such as *Foster* suggest that, whether or not inspired by Currie's or Ehrenzweig's teachings, forum-favoritism is intuitively appealing to some judges. In addition to Kentucky, at least two other states, Nevada and Michigan, follow a choice-of-law approach for tort conflicts that is grounded on a strong presumption in favor of the *lex fori*.

Michigan adopted the *lex fori* approach in 1982, in Sexton v. Ryder Truck Rental, Inc., 320 N.W.2d 843 (Mich.1982), and recently reiterated it in Sutherland v. Kennington Truck Service, Ltd., 562 N.W.2d 466 (Mich.1997). *Sutherland* arose out of a traffic accident in Michigan involving an Ohio plaintiff and an Ontario defendant. The plaintiff's action was timely under Michigan's three-year statute of limitation, but was barred by the two-year statutes of Ohio and Ontario. The court cited academic commentary according to which each of the modern approaches apply forum law "between fifty-five and seventy-seven percent of the time," id. at 469, and that "courts employing the new theories have a very strong preference for forum law that frequently causes them to manipulate the theories so that they end up applying forum law." Id. at 469-70. This preference, said the court, was "hardly surprising [because] the tendency toward forum law promotes judicial economy: judges and attorneys are experts in their state's law, but have to expend considerable time and resources to learn another state's law." Id. at 470. Turning "preference" into virtue, the court elevated this "tendency" into a choice-of-law method. According to this method, a Michigan court should apply Michigan law, unless a "rational reason" exists to do otherwise. Id. at 471. In determining whether such a rational reason exists, the court is to first examine whether the foreign state involved in the conflict has an interest in applying its law. If not, Michigan law applies. If yes, the court is to determine "if Michigan's interests mandate that Michigan law be applied, despite the foreign interests," id., in which case Michigan law again applies.

Applying this method, the court concluded that neither Ohio nor Ontario had an interest in applying their respective statutes of limitation. Thus, "the *lex fori* presumption [was] not overcome, and [the court] need not evaluate Michigan's interests." Id. at 473. The court based its conclusion that Ontario did not have an interest in applying its two-year statute (despite the fact that the statute favored the Ontario defendant) on the fact that, under Ontario's *lex loci delicti* rule, an Ontario court would have applied Michigan law. Id. at 472-73. Nevertheless, said the court, "we do not engage in renvoi because we decline to apply any of Ontario's law. We look at Ontario's choice of law rules merely to determine Ontario's interests." Id. at 473 n. 26. Do you agree that the *lex loci* rule (which the Michigan court had earlier discarded as being mechanical and oblivious to state interests) accurately reflected Ontario's interests in the sense this term is used in interest-analysis? Regardless of the answer, is it possible to conclude that Ontario was "uninterested" without using the *renvoi* syllogism? Is *renvoi* compatible with a *lex fori* approach?

4. ***Nevada's* Lex Fori *Approach.*** Nevada adopted the *lex fori* approach in Motenko v. MGM Dist., Inc., 921 P.2d 933 (Nev.1996). Under this approach, the *lex fori* governs, "unless another state has an *overwhelming* interest." Id. at 935 (emphasis added). However, the court defined this test in terms of contacts rather than interests, by stating that another state has an overwhelming interest if it has two or more of the following contacts: "(a) it is the place where the conduct giving rise to the injury occurred; (b) it is the place where the injury is suffered; (c) [it is the place where the parties have their common] domicile, residence, nationality, place of incorporation, or place of business * * *; (d) it is the place where the relationship, if any, between the parties is centered." Id. The court thought that this approach "meets the goal of a higher degree of certainty, predictability and uniformity of result[,] * * * allows a court to more frequently apply the law with which it is most familiar--its own law[, and] allows for some flexibility in order to avoid irrational and unjust results." Id. Are you convinced that this approach helps produce *interstate* "uniformity" of result? In any event, how would *Foster* be decided under this approach? Is this approach more or less forum-biased than the *Foster* approach?

In *Motenko*, the court held that Nevada law governed because the other involved state, Massachusetts, had less than two of the above contacts. *Motenko* was an action for loss of parental consortium brought by a Massachusetts domiciliary whose mother had been injured in defendant's Nevada hotel. Massachusetts, but not Nevada, allowed the action. The result was entirely reasonable and would have been reached under any other choice-of-law approach, traditional or modern: the victim's presence in Nevada was not fortuitous, the injury was caused by a defect in a Nevada *immovable*, the defendant was a Nevada corporation, and Nevada had a policy intended to protect that corporation. Thus the court enunciated an approach that went far beyond the needs of the particular case. This became evident in the next case to reach the same court, Northwest Pipe v. Eight Judicial Dist. Ct., 42 P.3d 244 (Nev. 2002).

Northwest Pipe arose out of a California traffic accident that caused the death of two Nevada domiciliaries and four California domiciliaries. Their survivors filed wrongful death actions in Nevada against the driver of the truck that caused the accident and his employer, both Oregon domiciliaries. The court rejected the defendants' argument that California law should govern, because they failed to rebut *Motenko*'s *lex fori* presumption. This was so because, in the court's opinion, California had only one of the non-forum contacts--the place of conduct. The court opined that the injury occurred in Nevada because this "was a wrongful death action in which the injury is to the survivors . . . [and] *almost* all the survivors are Nevada residents," id. at 245-46 (emphasis added), and, "although the deaths occurred in California, the injury to the survivors occurred in Nevada." Id. at 246.

Of course *not all* the survivors were Nevada residents. The survivors of the four California victims were California residents. For this reason, four of the court's seven members disagreed on this point, thus forming a majority for applying California law to the California plaintiffs' actions. Two members of the court dissented from the application of Nevada law to the Nevada victims as well. One of them observed that, under the court's approach, "it is unlikely that anything but Nevada law will ever apply." Id. at 248 (Agosti, J. dissenting). He stated that Nevada had "no relationship, significant or otherwise, to the occurrence of the accident," id., and that the application of Nevada law was "unreasonable" because "virtually every fact and circumstance giving rise to the causes of action, except the domicile of some of the plaintiffs, points to the application of California law." Id. Do you agree?

Cipolla v. Shaposka
Supreme Court of Pennsylvania, 1970.
439 Pa. 563, 267 A.2d 854.

COHEN, J. This is an appeal from a judgment entered against Michael Cipolla and his parents and natural guardians, appellants * * *. The record indicates that Michael Cipolla and John Shaposka, Jr., appellee, are former schoolmates at the Brown Technical School in Wilmington, Delaware. On January 24, 1966, after classes had ended for the day, appellee was driving Michael to appellants' home in Pennsylvania when the automobile in which they were riding became involved in a collision in Delaware in which Michael was injured. Shaposka is a Delaware resident as is his father in whose name the car was registered in Delaware.

The sole question involved in this appeal is whether the legal effect of the guest-host relationship should be determined by Delaware or Pennsylvania law. If Delaware law applies, appellants will be barred from recovering since Delaware's Guest Statute, Del.Code Ann. tit. 21, § 6101(a), prohibits a guest from recovering for his host's negligence. The statute does permit recovery for intentional or wilful or wanton misconduct, but appellants argue only that appellee was guilty of ordinary negligence. Pennsylvania has no guest statute, and if its law applies, appellants will be able to recover if they can prove appellee was negligent The court below concluded that Delaware law applied and granted appellee's motion for summary judgment.

Under our decisions in Kuchinic v. McCrory, 222 A.2d 897 (Pa.1966), McSwain v. McSwain, 215 A.2d 677 (Pa.1966), and Griffith v. United Air Lines,

Inc., 203 A.2d 796 (Pa.1964), we must determine whether Delaware or Pennsylvania has the greater interest in the application of its law to the question now before us. At the outset it might be noted that this case is much more difficult than either *Kuchinic* or *McSwain* for both of those cases presented a false conflict; that is, an analysis of the policies behind the competing laws indicated that in each case the application of one state's law (in *Kuchinic*, Georgia; in *McSwain*, Colorado) would not further those policies, Cavers, The Choice-of-Law Process, 29–30 (1965); *Kuchinic*, supra at 624 n.4. The fact that Cipolla is a resident of Pennsylvania which has adopted a plaintiff-protecting rule and Shaposka is a resident of Delaware which has adopted a defendant-protecting rule takes this case out of that category and requires us to undertake a deeper analysis than was necessary in those cases.

In determining which state has the greater interest in the application of its law, one method is to see what contacts each state has with the accident, the contacts being relevant only if they relate to the "policies and interests underlying the particular issue before the court." *Griffith*, supra at 21. When doing this it must be remembered that a mere counting of contacts is not what is involved. The weight of a particular state's contacts must be measured on a qualitative rather than quantitative scale. Tooker v. Lopez, 249 N.E.2d 394 (N.Y.1969).

As it is Pennsylvania's policy that its guests should be permitted to recover for injuries caused by their hosts' negligence and as appellants are Pennsylvania residents, Pennsylvania is a concerned jurisdiction and has a contact relevant to the issue before us. This is the only relevant contact with Pennsylvania, however. As it is Delaware's policy that its hosts should not be required to compensate their guests for their (the hosts') negligence and as appellee is a Delaware resident, Delaware is a concerned jurisdiction and has a contact relevant to the issue before us. The fact that the automobile involved in the accident is registered and housed in Delaware gives that state another contact for it appears that insurance rates will depend on the state in which the automobile is housed rather than the domicile of the owner or driver. Morris, Enterprise Liability and the Actuarial Process--The Insignificance of Foresight, 70 Yale L.J. 554, 574 (1961). Thus, it appears that Delaware's contacts are qualitatively greater than Pennsylvania's and that it has the greater interest in having its law applied to the issue before us.[2]

Also, it seems only fair to permit a defendant to rely on his home state's law when he is acting within that state.[3]

"Consider the response that would be accorded a proposal that was the opposite of this principle if it were advanced against a person living in the state of injury on behalf of a person coming there from a state having a higher standard of care or of financial protection. The proposal thus advanced would require the community the visitor entered to step up its standard of behavior for his greater safety or lift its financial protection to the level to which he was accustomed. Such a proposal would be rejected as unfair. By entering the state

---

2. In this analysis the fact that the accident occurred in Delaware is not a relevant contact because the Delaware statute does not set out a rule of the road.

3. See Cavers' Principle 2, supra at 146.

or nation, the visitor has exposed himself to the risk of the territory and should not subject persons living there to a financial hazard that their law had not created." Cavers, supra at 146-7.

Inhabitants of a state should not be put in jeopardy of liability exceeding that created by their state's law just because a visitor from a state offering higher protection decides to visit there. This is, of course, a highly territorial approach, but "departures from the territorial view of torts ought not to be lightly undertaken." Gordon v. Parker, 83 F. Supp. 40, 42 (D.Mass.1949). "To withdraw * * * actions and affairs from the reach of domestic law because the persons (or at least one of the persons) participating in them are not domestic to the state causes a wrench away from customary attitudes toward law that may lead the disadvantaged party to 'regard the distinction as involving a personal discrimination against him rather than as a step toward comity between states.'" Cavers, supra at 135. The very use of the term true conflict implies that there is no one correct answer, but as a general approach a territorial view seems preferable to a personal view.

These approaches to the solution of this true conflict lead to the conclusion that Delaware has a greater interest in the application of its law than does Pennsylvania.

Judgment affirmed.

BELL, J. Concurring. I believe the issues in this case should be determined and decided by lex loci delicti--see my dissenting Opinion in Griffith v. United Air Lines, [supra]. However, if this test be not applied, it is clear that the Majority Opinion is correct when it affirms the judgment, because Delaware's contacts were more important and both qualitatively and quantitatively greater than Pennsylvania's.

ROBERTS, J. Dissenting. I agree with the majority that the instant case presents us with a true conflict. I cannot agree, however, that the conflict is properly resolved by the application of Delaware law, and hence I must respectfully dissent.

* * * I do not believe * * * that Delaware passed its guest statute for the purpose of lowering the insurance rates of those who house their automobiles in Delaware. I reach this conclusion for several reasons. For one, even assuming that the barring of guest-host suits does result in lower costs to insurance companies, it is far from clear whether the benefits would inure to Delaware residents or merely aid insurance companies doing business in Delaware. Further, even if the savings were passed on to the consumer, the impact of this savings on insurance rates appears to me to be highly speculative. Professor Morris, in the article relied on by the majority, indicates that such guest claims are likely to have only a slight impact on insurance rates, particularly for a state which will not apply its guest statute in accidents which occur in common law jurisdictions. See Morris, [supra at] 575–76.

Of course, a statute could be passed for a particular purpose, even though it is poorly designed to effectuate that purpose. But I do not believe that is the case here, for neither the Legislature nor the courts of Delaware have ever mentioned low insurance rates as the purpose of the guest statute. In fact, the sole purpose of the Delaware guest statute, as set forth by its courts, "is to protect one who generously, without accruing benefit, has transported another in his motor vehicle." Engle v. Poland, 91 A. 2d 326 ([Del.Super.Ct.] 1952) * * *.

Since I do not believe that the Delaware guest statute was designed to lower insurance rates, I cannot agree that the domicile of the automobile is a relevant contact. Hence I cannot agree that, under *Griffith*, we must apply Delaware law because its contacts are "qualitatively greater" than Pennsylvania's.

The [majority's] second theory is based on the view that it is "only fair to permit a defendant to rely on his home state's law when he is acting within that state". I believe that this emphasis on the "territorial view of torts" is misplaced. As the majority notes, the guest statute is not conduct regulating, so the defendant was not in any sense relying on Delaware law when he was driving. Nor do I believe that the defendant's father was relying on Delaware law when he paid his premiums. It seems doubtful to me that the insured ever took into account the possibility that a Pennsylvania guest could not recover against him for a Delaware accident, but could for one in Pennsylvania or New Jersey. And if the majority means that the insurance company, here Allstate, relied on not being held liable when setting its rates, I agree with Professor Morris that "[t]he theory * * * is tautological. The rules of liability are to be dictated by insurance practices which are, in turn, dictated by the rules of liability. All that can be concluded from such a premise is that whatever is, should be." Morris, 70 Yale L.J. 554, 581–82 (1961) (footnote omitted).

* * * I believe that we are presented with a case where, on the basis of contacts, there is no predominantly concerned jurisdiction. Delaware seeks to protect the "generous host" from liability; Pennsylvania is concerned to see that a guest injured by his host's negligence is compensated for his injuries. In my view, each State has but one relevant contact with respect to host-guest liability—the domicile of the party who will benefit from their respective State's policy.

With the interests of both States evenly balanced, I believe that the appropriate method of resolving the conflict is to choose what has been termed "the better rule of law". * * *

In choosing the "better rule of law" I would examine the policies behind both rules to see which currently represents "the sounder view of the law". I would also refer to the decisions of other states, particularly when they make clear that the policy of one of the concerned jurisdictions is either "regressing" or "emerging". See A. Von Mehren & D. Trautman, The Law of Multistate Problems 377, 394 (1965). In this way the strength of the policies behind the differing rules of law can be assessed, and the rule with the "stronger policy" today can be chosen. See id. at 377; cf. Milliken v. Pratt, [Ch. 2] (concerning capacity of married women to make contracts).

To demonstrate which is the better rule of law in the instant case, I will examine the conflicts cases in the area of host-guest liability, the constructions which guest statute jurisdictions—including Delaware—give their statutes, and the views of courts and scholars on the policy underlying guest statutes. From this examination it will be seen that guest statutes such as Delaware's clearly represent "regressing" policies and that the common law rule represents the better rule of law.

In conflicts decisions involving guest statutes I have been unable to find a *single* case in the jurisdictions which have abandoned lex loci in which the guest statute, rather than the common law, has been chosen.* * *

In fact, Delaware itself construes its statute quite narrowly. [cit.] Nor will Delaware apply its guest statute to an accident which occurs in a common law jurisdiction. In Friday v. Smoot, 211 A. 2d 594 (Del.1965), Delaware applied New Jersey law allowing recovery for a host's negligence in an accident which occurred in New Jersey, but involved a Delaware guest and host. Although the rationale for this choice of law was the Court's refusal to abandon the rule of lex loci, the result of the decision is that Delaware itself limits the scope of its policy and the protection it will give to its resident-hosts. Clearly, if the accident involved in the instant case occurred at the end of the trip in Pennsylvania, rather than in the middle of the trip in Delaware, Delaware itself would apply Pennsylvania law and allow plaintiff to recover for the negligence of his host.

Not only do the results of the above cases show that guest statutes represent a regressing policy, weakened by numerous artificial exceptions, but the comments of courts and scholars on the matter well demonstrate that guest statutes do not represent the "better rule of law". Professor Pedrick has written:

> "At an early stage in automobile litigation and at a time when automobile insurance companies were concerned with limiting their function as far as possible a strange alliance between insurers and farm groups secured passage in a large number of states of the 'automobile guest statutes'. These statutes resulting from hitchhiker suits against uninsured or underinsured drivers and intra-family suits against insured defendants were aimed at relieving the driver (and his insurer) from liability save for the most horrendous performances at the wheel." * * *

Pedrick, "Taken for a Ride: The Automobile Guest and Assumption of Risk", 22 La. L. Rev. 90, 91-92 (1961) (footnotes omitted).

* * * After examining the views of the authorities around the country, judicial and academic, the construction that states place on their own guest statutes, and the construction which Delaware itself has adopted, I am led to the conclusion that allowing recovery by the guest for his host's negligence represents the better rule of law in the circumstances of the instant case. It must be remembered, however, that it is only because I believe that Delaware and Pennsylvania, on the basis of relevant contacts, are equally concerned that I feel free to choose either jurisdiction's law. I have in the end concluded that Pennsylvania's rule is the better rule of law, not out of "State chauvinism", but because I am firmly convinced that it represents "emerging" policy and the "sounder view of the law".

I dissent and would remand this case for trial.

Notes and Questions

1. *Cipolla* involved the identical pattern and issues as *Foster*, but reached the opposite result. Which of the two reached a better resolution of the conflict, and which offered better reasons?

2. Do you agree with *Cipolla*'s statement in footnote 2 that "the fact that the accident occurred in Delaware is not a relevant contact"? Is that statement consistent with the balance of the majority opinion following that footnote? If that statement is correct, then why were Delaware's contacts "qualitatively greater"?

3. Compare and contrast Justice Robert's dissenting opinion in *Cipolla* with the

majority opinion in *Milkovich*. Both opinions relied on the better-law notion and both favored the forum's law, but which one offers better reasons?

4. It has been reported that Mr. Shaposka was served with process in Pennsylvania while he was playing tennis with Mr. Cipolla. If this is true, does it lend credence to the argument that guest statutes can protect insurers from collusion between the host and the guest?

5. In your opinion, which of the two sides in *Cipolla* (Justice Roberts or Justice Cohen) had the better reasoning with regard to the impact of guest statutes on insurance rates? Professor Cavers, on whose writings the majority relied, spoke approvingly of the court's decision but he expressed reservations about the court's discussion of the insurance factor, the defendant's pre-accident expectations, and the car's Delaware registration. See Cavers, *Conflicts Justice*, 362 n. 8.

6. The *Cipolla* court's reliance on Professor Cavers' writings is indicative of his influence on the development of modern American conflicts law. More than thirty years after his pioneering *Critique* (supra 115), Cavers returned to the conflicts scene with his monumental book, *The Choice-of-Law Process*, in which he set forth his position with regard to the various conflicts approaches that had been proposed in the meantime. Although for the most part he remained sympathetic to some basic tenets of interest analysis, Cavers disassociated himself from Currie's "solution" of true conflicts and from Currie's insistence that conflicts should be resolved on an entirely ad hoc basis. The judicial applications of interest analysis convinced Cavers that Currie's rejection of all choice-of-law rules was bound to lead to an impasse. See Cavers, *Process*, 108-113, 122-123. Cavers saw the need to provide the judge with some affirmative directives that would be sufficiently specific as to facilitate a principled choice of law. Id. at 216-18. To that end, Cavers formulated seven "principles of preference," five for tort, described infra, and two for contract conflicts. Cavers conceded a "territorial bias" (id. at 134) in his torts principles, but "without apology." Id. at 139. Being among the first and most effective critics of the blind and mechanical territorialism of the traditional theory, Cavers was among the few who could credibly urge a return to a "principled" territorialism. When you read his torts principles infra, you should consider whether Cavers over-corrected Currie's heavy reliance on domicile.

Eger v. E.I. Du Pont DeNemours Co.
Supreme Court of New Jersey, 1988.
110 N.J. 133, 539 A.2d 1213.

HANDLER, J. Clifford Eger, a New Jersey resident, worked as a draftsman for Allstates Design and Development Co., Inc. (Allstates), a New Jersey corporation, from 1964 until 1983. During this time, E.I. du Pont DeNemours & Co. (Du Pont) hired Allstates as a subcontractor to provide various design, drafting, and model building services in connection with Du Pont's operation of the Savannah River Nuclear Plant, a South Carolina facility owned by the United States Department of Energy, which manufactures radioactive isotopes for defense and industrial uses.

On various occasions over the course of his nineteen-year employment with

Allstates, Eger was sent to the Savannah River facility to perform certain tasks in connection with his development of particular designs to suit engineering specifications provided by Du Pont. Plaintiffs allege that on one or more of his trips to the Savannah River facility, Eger was exposed to radioactivity that caused him to contract acute myeloblastic leukemia, a form of leukemia known to be caused by exposure to radiation and certain toxic chemicals.

Due to his illness, Eger left Allstates in July of 1983. Prior to his departure, in March of 1983, Eger filed a workers' compensation action in New Jersey against Allstates. Subsequently, in April of 1984, Eger and his wife, Mildred, brought a third-party tort action against Du Pont and Allstates, the hospital and doctors responsible for Du Pont's screening program, and various chemical companies. The plaintiffs have since dismissed without prejudice the common-law actions against Allstates and the chemical companies.

Du Pont moved for summary judgment, claiming that as the statutory employer of Eger under the South Carolina workers' compensation act, it was immune from common-law tort liability. The Law Division granted this motion * * * [and] the Appellate Division affirmed the trial court's ruling. We granted plaintiffs' petition for certification, [cit.] and now affirm the judgment of the Appellate Division. * * *

[T]he laws of New Jersey provide that the subcontractor is primarily liable for workers' compensation; the general contractor is only secondarily liable. Immunity from a third-party tort claim is conferred only on the subcontractor, who as the employer is obligated to provide workers' compensation coverage, while the general contractor remains exposed to tort liability. In contrast, South Carolina renders both the general contractor and the subcontractor directly responsible for providing workers' compensation coverage, and in return immunizes both from tort liability. Therefore, in this case, under New Jersey law, the Egers could bring a third-party action in tort against Du Pont and Du Pont could not claim immunity, while under South Carolina law Du Pont as a statutory employer responsible for workers' compensation coverage could claim absolute immunity from this tort action. * * *

III. We reach * * * [a decision] to honor the exclusive remedy provision of a foreign state's workers' compensation statute--on a balancing of the governmental interests involved. South Carolina has a genuine and legitimate interest in protecting the welfare of persons working within its borders, affixing responsibility for that protection, regulating the safety of the workplace, and allocating the financial costs resulting from employment accidents. To address these governmental concerns, South Carolina, as part of its comprehensive workers' compensation scheme, has required that a general contractor assume the burden of furnishing workers' compensation coverage for the employees of its subcontractors as if they were in fact employees of its own. This imposition of liability furthers South Carolina's interest in protecting the welfare of its workers by giving them the right to seek compensation benefits from either their immediate employer or the usually more fiscally responsible statutory employer, namely, the general contractor, [cit.] thus providing a safeguard against the insolvency of either potential source of benefits. [cit.]

Application of New Jersey law to allow a tort suit against a South Carolina general contractor such as Du Pont would undermine the foundation of that state's workers' compensation statute. Immunity from tort liability of a party obligated to provide compensation coverage is an essential element of the fundamental equation in every workers' compensation system * * * [T]he obligation to provide workers' compensation coverage and immunity from tort liability are linked in any integrated and comprehensive workers' compensation scheme. * * * [S]ubjecting a South Carolina general contractor to tort liability in addition to the expense of providing compensation coverage for all employment-related accidents would frustrate that state's interest in regulating the manner in which victims of industrial accidents are compensated.

The question remains whether New Jersey has any countervailing interest strong enough to warrant the imposition of tort liability under its law on a general contractor in situations where South Carolina has granted that general contractor immunity. Subjecting statutory employers such as Du Pont to tort claims by employees of subcontractors would have two possible consequences: it would allow plaintiffs to obtain additional damages beyond a workers' compensation award, and would permit the subcontractor to be reimbursed for any compensation benefits it has paid. New Jersey's interest in securing either of these consequences, however, is not strong enough to outweigh South Carolina's interest in immunizing general contractors required to provide workers' compensation coverage for subcontractors' employees from tort suits by those same employees. [cit.]

Turning first to the comparative importance of New Jersey's interest in encouraging added damage awards, the fact that plaintiffs in this case are protected by both Allstates' and Du Pont's compensation coverage and thus are assured of receiving compensation benefits plays a significant role in the weighing of governmental interests. * * * South Carolina has a great interest in having other states recognize the tort immunity conferred on general contractors, since this immunity is part of the *quid pro quo* that is fundamental to South Carolina's workers' compensation system. More importantly, New Jersey's interest in seeing that its injured residents receive compensation has not been neglected; it has been addressed through the workers' compensation system. * * * [A]n injured resident who is covered by workers' compensation is guaranteed payment of medical expenses and disability benefits for work-related accidents. His or her right to compensation does not depend on the inherently uncertain process of establishing tort liability. Therefore, workers' compensation, which was intended to prevent injured workers from becoming public charges by shifting to industry the expense of compensating work-related injuries, [cit.] reasonably satisfies the state's interest in providing a source of compensation for injured workers.[4] To the extent that a third party tort action would augment the employee's recovery, such a remedy is ancillary to the central goals of workers' compensation and is primarily for the benefit of the employee. [cit.] * * *

---

4. Moreover, to the extent that New Jersey's interest in providing adequate compensation to injured resident workers might be threatened by a foreign state's less generous compensation schedule, the injured employee retains the option of seeking compensation under the New Jersey statute. This practice, which allows the employee to seek the highest available amount of compensation, is consonant with the remedial purposes underlying compensation enactments * * *.

For the reasons expressed above, * * * the judgment of the Appellate Division is affirmed.

STEIN, J., dissenting. * * * In my view * * * South Carolina's interest in insulating a general contractor like Du Pont from tort liability is minimal. In comparison, New Jersey has a clear and compelling interest in providing redress, beyond the limited compensation made available through a workers' compensation award[.]* * * The injured worker lived in New Jersey, was employed by a New Jersey company, and thus understandably elected to prosecute his workers' compensation claim against his employer in New Jersey. No workers' compensation claim was filed in South Carolina. The record before us does not indicate the frequency with which the injured worker visited Du Pont's South Carolina plant, and there may be some question whether he could have maintained a workers' compensation action under South Carolina law. * * *

* * * [I]t is not at all apparent how the application of New Jersey law to allow this suit to be maintained against Du Pont would "undermine the foundation of that state's workers' compensation statute." Ante. Such a decision would simply reflect New Jersey's determination that the immunity accorded to a general contractor under South Carolina's workers' compensation law is far less significant to the operation of that statute than is the immunity accorded to the primary employer. The fact that South Carolina has provided in its workers' compensation statutes for an expansive immunity that includes parties other than the primary employer hardly compels the conclusion that that expansive immunity is fundamental to that state's workers' compensation system. The compensation systems of New Jersey and many other states apparently function adequately without according immunity to general contractors. * * *

On the other side of the equation is New Jersey's clear interest in providing adequate compensation to an injured domiciliary. Although the majority expresses the view that that interest has been addressed through the workers' compensation system, it is well recognized that the workers' compensation system does not always provide adequate redress for injuries sustained by a worker. * * *

This case does not present the question whether New Jersey should ignore the immunity granted by a sister state's workers' compensation statute to the primary employer who bears the ultimate liability for compensation benefits. A refusal to recognize that immunity might severely impair the fabric of a sister state's compensation scheme. But South Carolina's interest in according immunity to a general contractor whose workers' compensation liability is secondary under South Carolina law should not be accorded any such significance. Whatever weight that immunity may have under South Carolina's statutory scheme should yield to New Jersey's compelling interest in providing its workers an opportunity to recover adequate compensation for negligently inflicted injuries. * * *

Notes and Questions

1. *Eger* would also meet Currie's definition of a true conflict, but the *Eger* court defied Currie's proscription of weighing state interests. Is *Eger* a good example of

the proposition that courts are capable of competently weighing state interests? Was the court's weighing proper? Is there anything "undemocratic" or "embarrassing" (Currie, supra 182-83) in the court's conclusion that "New Jersey's interest * * * is not strong enough to outweigh South Carolina's interest"? Or does this conclusion result from the court heeding Currie's call for a restrained interpretation of the law of the forum? Is interest analysis capable of shedding its pro-forum, pro-recovery bias?

2. In Tucci v. Club Mediterranee, S.A., 107 Cal.Rptr.2d 401 (Cal.App.2001), which was decided under California's comparative impairment approach, the court applied the pro-defendant law of the Dominican Republic to an action of a California domiciliary who was injured while working in the defendant's club in the Dominican Republic. Under Dominican Republic law, the plaintiff would be confined to workers' compensation and Social Security benefits. Under California law, the plaintiff would be entitled to a tort action, because the employer had not procured workers' compensation insurance through a California carrier, as required by a California statute. The court noted that California had an interest in adequately providing for employees hired in California, and in assuring that employers who solicited California employees were adequately insured through credit-worthy carriers regulated by California. However, the court found that the Dominican Republic also had an interest in making sure that employers in that country "face limited and predictable financial liability * * * and in * * * predictably defining the duties and liabilities of employers doing business within its border, all with the goal of encouraging business investment and development there." Id. at 408-09. The court concluded that the law of the Dominican Republic should govern because that country's interests would be more impaired if its law was not applied.

3. Compare *Eger* with *Braxton* (supra Ch. 2 at 76). Which case made a better choice of law, and which case was better reasoned? Why?

4. Suppose that in *Eger* the laws of the two involved states were reversed. How would you resolve the resulting conflict and why? For a case involving this pattern, see Duhon v. Union Pacific Resources Co., 43 F.3d 1011 (5th Cir.1995).

5. Cleveland v. U.S. Printing Ink, Inc., 588 A.2d 194 (Conn.1991), involved a slightly different issue--whether a New Jersey employee who had received worker's compensation benefits from his New Jersey employer under the New Jersey statute should also recover additional benefits from the *same* employer under the more generous statute of Connecticut, the state of the injury. The plaintiff was a truck driver who spent 30-40% of his employment time driving through Connecticut to deliver defendant's products in the New England states. The court held that Connecticut's courts and agencies may apply its workers' compensation laws, if Connecticut is the place of: (1) the injury; (2) the employment contract; or (3) the employment relation. The court concluded that the application of Connecticut law in this case was justified in light of Connecticut's interest "in compensating injured employees to the fullest extent possible." Id. at 201. Three dissenters accused the majority of "abandon[ing] the most significant relationship criterion * * * and substitut[ing] a rule allowing a claimant to maximize his benefits to the extent permitted by any forum that may have jurisdiction." Id. at 203. The dissenters argued

that New Jersey had a more significant relationship to the employment relationship and a greater interest in "setting the appropriate level of compensation benefits to be paid by a New Jersey employer to a resident employee who spends most of his working time in that state." Id. They concluded by asking rhetorically: "Should Connecticut thus become a mecca for claimants from all corners of the world, provided there exists a sufficient jurisdictional basis for our courts to entertain the litigation?" Id. Was this a fair question? Why, or why not? Is *Cleveland* consistent with *Eger*? Why, or why not?

In Burse v. American International Airways, Inc., 808 A.2d 672 (Conn.2002), the employee was a pilot who was domiciled in Connecticut and was injured outside Connecticut while working for a Michigan-based airline. He argued that his employment contract had been made in Connecticut, because he received and accepted the employment offer through the telephone at his Connecticut home. The court found that the contract was formed at a later time while the pilot was in Michigan. The employee also argued that Connecticut was the place of his employment relationship because he resided there, received his pay checks there, and occasionally flew out of Connecticut. The court found that "Connecticut had, *at most*, a peripheral relationship to the employment." Id. at 679. The court also clarified that, for Connecticut law to apply under the *Cleveland* test, there must be "at a minimum, a showing of a *significant* relationship between Connecticut and either the employment contract or the employment relationship." Id. at 678

6. A Kentucky employee of a Kentucky corporation was killed in Louisiana as a result of an accident caused by a Kentucky co-employee. Under Kentucky worker's compensation law, the employer would be immune from a tort suit by the victim's survivors. Under Louisiana law, the employer would not be immune because the act that caused the employee's death would qualify as an "intentional act." How would you resolve the resulting conflict and why? For a case involving this pattern, see Rigdon v. Pittsburgh Tank & Tower Company, Inc., 682 So.2d 1303 (La.App.1996).

Biscoe v. Arlington County
United States Court of Appeals, District of Columbia Circuit, 1984.
738 F.2d 1352, 238 U.S.App.D.C. 206.

EDWARDS, J. This case involves the liability of Arlington County, Virginia, and one of its police officers [Michael Kyle], for serious injuries to an innocent bystander arising out of a negligent high-speed police pursuit of a suspected bank robber [Lyntellus Brooks] into the District of Columbia. As a result of the negligent pursuit, the plaintiff, Alvin Biscoe, had one of his legs severed and the other severely injured, ultimately requiring amputation. [The pursuit began in Virginia and continued into the District, where Officer Kyle apprehended and stopped Brooks' car but negligently failed to secure his arrest. Brooks reentered his car and, while being chased by Kyle, collided with the plaintiff's car. The jury found that Kyle was negligent, and that his employer, Arlington County, was liable on a theory of *respondeat superior* and that it was negligent in its training and supervision of Kyle. The awarded $4 million to Alvin Biscoe. Defendants appealed.]

* * * We have carefully reviewed each claim and have found none to merit reversal or remand. Accordingly, we affirm.

* * * [D]efendant Arlington County asserts that the District Court improperly declined to recognize the immunity from tort claims that the County retains *under Virginia law*. In support of this assertion, Arlington County argues that the United States Constitution's Full Faith and Credit Clause, U.S. Const. art. IV, § 1, compels application of Virginia immunity in this case, that principles of comity require that Virginia's immunity be recognized in the District, and that the District's choice of law rules require adoption of that aspect of Virginia law.

The first of these arguments may be readily dismissed on the basis of the Supreme Court's decision in *Nevada v. Hall*, 440 U.S. 410 (1979), which held that federal constitutional law does not prohibit one state's courts from entering a judgment against or asserting jurisdiction over another sovereign state. * * * [*Hall* is reproduced at 498, infra.]

We turn then to the County's second argument--that it is immune from suit in the District under principles of comity. *Nevada v. Hall* left open the possibility that a state might, as a matter of comity, recognize another state's immunity. The District of Columbia Court of Appeals, sitting *en banc,* has expressly declined to do so, however, and, as a court with diversity jurisdiction, we are bound to that determination. [cit.] * * * [Under District of Columbia precedents,] we simply have no reason to believe that the District of Columbia courts would give effect to Virginia's law out of deference or respect, when that law is contrary to the policies of the District. [cit.]

Finally, the County argues, proper application of the District's choice of law principles requires application of Virginia's rules on the immunity of its counties. * * *

The District of Columbia adopts the governmental interest analysis approach to resolve choice of law questions. * * * Where each state would have an interest in application of its own law to the facts, a true conflict exists and the law of the jurisdiction with the stronger interest will apply. *See, e.g., Mazza v. Mazza,* 475 F.2d 385, 392 (D.C.Cir.1973) (applying the law of the jurisdiction whose interest, on balance, was more significant).

There can be no doubt that this case presents a true conflict, and that the District Court properly resolved that conflict in favor of the law of the District. As a general matter, the immunity of Virginia's counties primarily reflects the state's concern for the financial integrity of its counties--a concern which, we have little doubt, can amply be met with the purchase of liability insurance. Immunity no doubt also reflects the state's concern that the prospect of liability will deter police officers from proper performance of their duties. These concerns generally might give Virginia a strong interest in its counties' continued immunity. However, that interest is considerably weakened when viewed in light of both the facts of this case and Virginia's official and governmental immunity scheme. First, Virginia's police officers are not immune from liability in this context, and their personal amenability to suit no doubt accomplishes at least some of the deterrence that it is feared would result were the County liable as well. [cit.] Second, under District law the County is liable only for negligent performance of nondiscretionary acts, which by definition leave to the Government actor little choice on procedure; the only actions deterred would be violations of a state's orders to its employees. Third, much as the prospect of liability might thwart discretionary decision-making, it may also deter misconduct, particularly in a nondiscretionary context. Fourth, the state of Virginia recently has waived its immunity from suit in tort in certain cases, although limiting the amount recoverable. *See* Virginia Tort Claims Act, Va.Code § 8.01-195.1 et seq. (1983 Supp.). This enactment, although not applicable to the counties, displays Virginia's awareness of the modern trend away from, and the absence of a need for sovereign immunity. [cit.] Thus, in the context we confront, the concern for deterrence is weak, if existent, and we are only left with Virginia's concern for the economic well-being of its counties. This concern, limited to the rare tort suit *arising out of acts outside Virginia,* simply is not an especially compelling one, particularly given the availability of liability insurance.

In contrast, the District's interest is plainly significant. Generally, a governmental entity's waiver of immunity signifies its dual interests in deterrence of potential tortfeasors and compensation of injured parties. Given the facts of this case, the former is strongly implicated, and the latter less so. First, as the site of most of the relevant conduct and all the injury, the District has a strong interest in deterring conduct of this kind. *See* Restatement (Second) of Conflict of Laws § 146 comment d (1971) (When conduct and injury occur in the same state, that state usually will be the state of dominant interest, since the two principal elements of the tort, conduct and injury, occurred within its territory. "The state where the defendant's conduct occurs has the dominant interest in regulating it and in determining whether it is tortious in character. Similarly, [it] will, usually at least, have the dominant interest in determining whether the interest affected is entitled to legal protection."). The defendants' acts "created the precise danger to District life and property" [cit.] that various District and Arlington County regulations sought to prevent, and liability would discourage such acts. Moreover, while a compensatory policy "has the greatest relevance to cases when the mishap occurs in the District and when District residents are plaintiffs," *Gaither v. Myers,* 404 F.2d 216, 223 (D.C.Cir.1968), this court has previously recognized the special and largely unique interest of the District in protecting persons who live in the surrounding suburbs and work in the District. As we have observed,

> [T]o confine the benefits of the ... rule to the territory ceded by the states of Maryland and Virginia to form the Nation's Capital would be to shun the present reality of the economically and socially integrated greater metropolitan area. It is commonplace that residents of Maryland are part of the Washington Metropolitan trading area, and that District residents and businesses have an interest in the well-being of these citizens of the Free State.

Id. at 223. In other words, when a plaintiff such as Dr. Biscoe, who is a Maryland resident working in the District, is injured in the District, District of Columbia courts have recognized a strong local interest in protecting that plaintiff. *See also* Restatement (Second) of Conflict of Laws § 146 comment e (1971) ("The local law of the state where the personal injury occurred is most likely to be applied when the injured person has a settled relationship to that state, either because he is domiciled or resides there or because he does business there.").

* * * [W]hen we look to Virginia choice of law rules to ascertain the interest of Virginia in application of its law to the facts of this case * * * [we find that] [u]nder Virginia law, the law of the site of the wrong applies. *McMillan v. McMillan,* 219 Va. 1127, 253 S.E.2d 662 (1979) (reaffirming Virginia's adherence to the rule of *lex loci delicti*--the law of the state where the tort occurs governs the substantive elements of the cause of action). Thus, to the extent that choice of law principles properly determine questions of immunity, Virginia would either apply the District's rules or have to fashion an exception based on its own policies. On balance, we conclude, the District's policies would be substantially more seriously thwarted by nonapplication of its law in this context than would those of Virginia, and we affirm the District Court's choice of law ruling. * * *

* * * For the foregoing reasons, we affirm the court's judgment. *So ordered.*

Notes and Questions

1. The District of Columbia, New Jersey, and California are the only jurisdictions that continue to follow interest analysis. As *Eger* and *Biscoe* demonstrate, the first two jurisdictions no longer heed Currie's proscription against weighing of state interests. As you will see from the next case, the same is true of California. Is this a positive development?

2. Most cases involving the same pattern as *Biscoe* have reached the same result, although some of them applied a different choice-of-law methodology. For documentation, see Symeonides, *The Revolution Today* §§ 142-45. One such case is Hall v. Nevada, 141 Cal.Rptr. 439 (Cal.App.1977), mentioned in *Biscoe*, which involved the additional issue of damages limitations. In *Hall*, an employee of the University of Nevada, an entity that enjoyed sovereign immunity under Nevada law, drove to California on official university business and caused an accident there, injuring a California domiciliary. The California court refused to recognize Nevada's immunity, or Nevada's $25,000 cap on damages. The court recognized Nevada's interest in protecting the financial well-being of Nevada entities, but found that interest to be much weaker than California's interest "in providing full protection to those who are injured on its highways through the negligence of both residents and nonresidents." Id. at 442. The court took special note of the fact that both "the [defendant's] activities and the [victim's] injuries took place in California," id., and concluded that "[b]y thus utilizing the public highways within our state to conduct its business, Nevada should fully expect to be held accountable under California laws." Id. The U.S. Supreme Court upheld the constitutionality of the California court's decision after noting, *inter alia*, California's "substantial" interest in "providing full protection to those who are injured on its highways." Nevada v. Hall, 440 U.S. 413, at 423 (1979), reproduced infra at 498.

3. The only case that reached the opposite result is Lommen v. The City of East

Grand Forks, 522 N.W.2d 148 (Minn.App.1994).[1] In this case, a Minnesota police officer began chasing a stolen car in Minnesota and continued into North Dakota where he collided with another car injuring its passenger, a North Dakota domiciliary. Under the law of Minnesota, but not North Dakota, both the officer and his employer, a Minnesota municipality, were immune from liability. Following Leflar's approach, the Minnesota court applied Minnesota law because the officer and his employer "had a substantial expectation of on-the-job tort immunity," id. at 150, (which apparently they can carry with them on a high-speed chase into other states), and because "Minnesota's ability to define the immunity of its officials should not vary according to the fortuitous facts of either the location of the accident or the citizenship of the injured party." Id. at 152. What about the expectations of the innocent North Dakota citizen who was maimed in North Dakota? Should her rights vary according to the fortuitous facts of the citizenship of the maimer or his employer?

4. *Biscoe* found that the District of Columbia was "the site of most of the relevant conduct." That conduct was Officer Kyle's negligent failure to secure the suspect's arrest after stopping him in the District and allowing him to leave his car engine running, as well as the subsequent high-speed chase in the District. Thus, to the extent that the plaintiff's action against the County was based on *respondeat superior*, one would conclude that the pertinent conduct had occurred in the District. However, the plaintiff had also argued and the jury agreed that the County was also negligent in its training and supervision of Officer Kyle, and this conduct apparently had occurred in Virginia. Should this factor make a difference in applying D.C. law to the action against the County? Why, or why not?

5. Dr. Biscoe, the plaintiff in *Biscoe*, was not a District of Columbia domiciliary. Even so, was the court not correct to treat him as if he were a D.C. domiciliary? Why, or why not?

6. The central issue in *Biscoe* was the County's immunity, which would qualify as a loss-distribution issue, despite having a bearing on conduct-regulation. District of Columbia v. Coleman, 667 A.2d 811 (D.C.App.1995), involved issues such as assumption of risk and contributory negligence that have a more direct bearing on conduct regulation. *Coleman* was a wrongful death action filed by the survivors of a Maryland domiciliary who was killed in Maryland by David Pigford, a District of Columbia police detective. Pigford was on an errand for his employer between two points in the District of Columbia when he drove through Maryland, where he encountered two men attacking another man. Responding to the victim's cries for help, Pigford intervened and in the process shot and killed one of the attackers, plaintiff's decedent.

Under Maryland law, Pigford and his employer could assert the defenses of contributory negligence and assumption of risk, either of which would bar plaintiff's

---

1. Harris v. City of Memphis, 119 F.Supp.2d 893 (E.D.Ark.2000), also applied the law of the immunity state, but did so out of comity rather than on the basis of choice-of-law principles. *Harris* applied Tennessee immunity law to an Arkansas plaintiff's action against a Tennessee city for failure to maintain adequate lighting on Arkansas side of bridge connecting Arkansas with Tennessee, which the city had contractually agreed to maintain.

recovery. Under D.C. law, those defenses would have been unavailable to a police officer who, like Pigford, had failed to follow certain statutes and ordinances prohibiting excessive force. The court reasoned that the policy behind D.C. law on this issue was "to promote the safety of citizens by deterring police use of excessive force," id. at 817, and that the major focus of this policy was on public safety "within the District itself, where the obligations and concerns of the District are paramount and where the police have the special authority to resort to use of force granted to law enforcement officers." Id. Since the conduct in question had occurred in Maryland,[2] the District did not have an interest in applying its law, and that law could not have "such extraterritorial effect as to bar the application by Maryland of its law." Id. at 820. On the other hand, said the court, "Maryland has the primary obligations and duties with respect to public safety in Maryland and the right to determine the circumstances under which liability shall attach for acts relating to public safety undertaken within its borders." Id. at 817-18. Maryland's decision to retain the defenses of contributory negligence and assumption of risk and to make them available to police officers such as Pigford, the court reasoned, were motivated by concerns about regulation of conduct and promotion of public safety. To the extent that these defenses are designed to make plaintiffs act more carefully, Maryland had an interest in applying these defenses since the plaintiff's decedent had acted in that state. See id. at 819. To the extent that these defenses were designed to affect the defendant's conduct by "encouraging 'good samaritans' to rescue victims without fear of liability," id. at 821, Maryland had an interest in applying these defenses since Pigford's attempt to rescue a victim had taken place in that state. Thus, under interest analysis, the court concluded, Maryland was the only interested jurisdiction and its law should apply. Do you agree with this conclusion?

(2) A RECAP ON SOME SPLIT-DOMICILE CONFLICTS

1. *Split-Domicile Cases*. Split-domicile cases may be grouped into many different categories, depending on where the conduct and the injury occurred and on the content of the involved states' laws. For a list of all the possibilities, see Symeonides, *The Revolution Today* § 127. In the most common cases that involve only two states and two parties, the conduct and the injury may occur in the home state of one of the parties (intrastate torts), or they may occur in different states (cross-border torts). When the conduct and the injury both occur in the home state of one of the parties and that state's law favors that party, the resulting conflict fits the definition of a true conflict under interest analysis. This Note discusses these conflicts.[1]

2. *The Foster/Cipolla Pattern.* In *Foster*, *Cipolla*, and *Eger*, the tortfeasor and the victim were domiciled in different states the laws of which favored their respective domiciliaries, and the conduct and injury both occurred in the tortfeasor's

---

2. See id. at 817. The court distinguished this case from *Zhou*, supra, in that "in *Zhou*, the negligent violation of the District statute (serving alcohol to an intoxicated person) occurred within the District." Id.

1. Cases in which that state's law favors the domiciliary of the other state are discussed infra at 242, and cross-border torts are discussed infra at 224.

home state. *Cipolla* and *Eger* applied the pro-defendant law of that state, while *Foster* applied the pro-plaintiff law of the victim's domicile (which was also the forum state).

A recent study of cases involving this pattern indicates that *Foster* is virtually alone in reaching this result. See Symeonides, *The Revolution Today* §§ 139-41.The study identified 24 cases involving this pattern[2] and, except for *Foster*, all of them resolved the conflict consistently with *Cipolla* and *Eger*. They resisted the temptation of applying the pro-plaintiff law of the plaintiff's home state--which in many of these cases was also the forum state--and instead applied the pro-defendant law of the defendant's home state, which was also the *locus delicti*. Some of these cases have been decided under the same "mixed" approach as *Cipolla*. However, more numerous are the cases decided under other approaches, such as the Restatement (Second), interest analysis, New York's *Neumeier* rules, and even the *lex-fori* and the better-law approaches. The following table depicts these cases, with shading indicating the state whose law the court applied.

Table 2. Foster/Cipolla Pattern Cases

Contact States	Forum	P's Dom	Injury	Conduct	D's Dom
Laws		**Pro-P**	Pro-D	Pro-D	Pro-D
1 *Foster*	KY	KY	OH	OH	OH
2 *Cipolla*	PA	PA	DE	DE	DE
3 *Eger*	NJ	NJ	SC	SC	SC
4 *Casey*	OR	OR	WA	WA	WA
5 *Tucci*	CA	CA	DomRep	DomRep	DomRep
6 *Bledsoe*	DC	DC	MD	MD	MD
7 *Shuder*	PA	PA	VA	VA	VA
8 *Blakesley*	PA	PA	TX	TX	TX
9 *Feldman*	NY	NY	Mex	Mex	Mex
10 *Barkanic*	NY	US	China	China	China
11 *Pascente*	NY	NY	CN	CN	CN
12 *Miller*	NY	CN	Quebec	Quebec	Quebec
13 *Reale*	NY	NY	PA	PA	PA
14 *Reed*	MN	MN	ND	ND	ND
15 *McBride*	DE	DE	MD	MD	MD
16 *Bowman*	OH	OH	ILL	ILL	ILL
17 *Benoit*	NH	MA	NH	NH	NH
18 *Evans*	PA	NJ	PA	PA	PA
19 *Amoroso*	NJ	PA	NJ	NJ	NJ
20 *Kranzler*	NY	NJ	NY	NY	NY
21 *Mascarella*	NY	PA	NY	NY	NY
22 *Motenko*	NV	MA	NV	NV	NV
23 *Ricci*	ME	RI	ME	ME	ME
24 *Marion*	FL	ILL	FL	FL	FL

2. All of these cases have been decided by courts that have abandoned the *lex loci* as a general rule. For citations and discussion see Symeonides, *The Revolution Today* 139-41. Some of these cases were decided by lower courts, including federal courts in diversity cases, and thus do not have precedential value. Nevertheless, these cases provide a representative picture of the practices of American courts in cases involving this pattern.

Casey v. Manson Constr. & Eng'g Co., 428 P.2d 898 (Or.1967), is representative of cases decided under the Restatement (Second). In *Casey*, a Washington defendant acting in Washington caused injury to an Oregon domiciliary. The victim's wife sued the defendant in Oregon for loss of consortium, a remedy that Oregon allowed but Washington did not. The Oregon court applied Washington law, reasoning that "Washington defendants should not be required to accommodate themselves to the law of the state of any traveler whom they might injure in Washington; [and] and that Washington's interest in the matter, which was protective of Washington defendants, was paramount to Oregon's interest in having its resident recover for her loss."[3]

Bledsoe v. Crowley, 849 F.2d 639 (D.C.Cir.1988) and *Tucci v. Club Mediterranee*, which was described supra at 205, are representative of cases decided under interest analysis. In *Bledsoe*, a medical malpractice case, a District of Columbia court refused to apply the District's pro-plaintiff law to the action of a D.C. domiciliary. Instead, the court applied the pro-defendant law of Maryland, where the medical services had been rendered, because that state was the "jurisdiction with the stronger interests." 849 F.2d at 641. A concurring judge would accord this result the status of an all-encompassing rule for medical malpractice conflicts. After pointing out that "patients are inherently on notice that journeying to new jurisdictions may expose them to [unfavorable] rules," id. at 647 (Williams, J., concurring), the judge concluded that "[t]he maxim 'When in Rome do as Romans do' bespeaks the common sense view that it is the traveler who must adjust." Id.

Thus, with the exception of *Foster*, all the other cases applied the law of the defendant's home state, which was also the place of both the conduct and the injury. In nine of the 24 cases, including *Foster*, that state was also the forum but, unlike *Foster*, these cases based the application of forum law on the forum's other contacts and interests rather than on the primacy of the *lex fori*. Except for *Foster*, none of the cases followed Currie's prescription that true conflicts be resolved through the application of forum law *as such*, none heeded his proscription of interest weighing, and none felt bound by his personal-law principle. In fact, 14 of the 24 cases applied the pro-defendant law of the non-forum state for the benefit of a non-forum defendant and at the expense of a forum plaintiff.

If one were to "restate" the results of the above cases in the form of a descriptive rule, this rule would provide as follows:

> *When the conduct and the injury occur in the tortfeasor's home state and that state's law favors the tortfeasor, that law governs* (even if the law of the victim's home state favors the victim)."

Is this a good rule? Why, or why not? In 1965, Professor Cavers proposed a similar rule (his Principle 2) providing as follows: "Where the liability laws of the state in which the defendant acted and caused an injury set a lower standard of * * * financial protection than do the laws of the home state of the person suffering the

---

3. This explanation is from Erwin v. Thomas, 506 P.2d 494, 497-98 (Or.1973), reproduced infra 233. See also *Casey*, 428 P.2d 898, 908 (Hollman, J. concurring) ("Washington citizens carrying on activities in Washington [should not] have to lift their financial protection to an unaccustomed level and one which would be dependent on the locality from which the injured party might come.")

injury, the laws of the state of conduct and injury should determine the standard of conduct or protection applicable to the case." Cavers, *Process* 146. As Cavers reasoned, "[i]nhabitants of [that state] should not be put in jeopardy of liabilities exceeding those [its] law creates simply because persons from states with higher standards of financial protection choose to visit there." Id. at 148-49. As *Bledsoe* stated, "it is the traveler who must adjust." Do you agree? The New York Court of Appeals adopted a similar rule, *Neumeier* Rule 2a, which is reproduced infra at 237, as did the Louisiana codification.[4]

3. ***The Biscoe Pattern.*** In *Biscoe*, the injury and "most of the relevant conduct" occurred in a jurisdiction that, although technically not the victim's domicile, was properly treated as such by the court. That jurisdiction had a law that favored the victim, while the defendants' home state had a law that favored the defendants. Thus, *Biscoe* involved the converse pattern from *Foster/Cipolla*. By parity of reasoning from cases like *Cipolla*, should not the *Biscoe*-pattern cases be governed by the law of the victim's home state? The case law supports an affirmative answer to this question.

The same study mentioned earlier has identified 12 cases involving this pattern. See Symeonides, *The Revolution Today* §§ 142-45. They are depicted in the following table.

Table 3. *Biscoe*-Pattern Cases

Contact States	Forum	P's Dom	Injury	Conduct	D's Dom
Laws		**Pro-P**	**Pro-P**	**Pro-P**	Pro-D
1 *Biscoe*	DC	DC	DC	DC	VA
2 *Hall*	CA	CA	CA	CA	NV
3 *Struebin*	IA	IA	IA	IA	ILL
4 *Laconis*	PA	PA	PA	PA	NJ
5 *Church*	MS	MS	MS	MS	AL
6 *Peterson*	COL	COL	COL	COL	TX
7 *Wendt*	MN	MN	MN	MN	IA
8 *Mianecki*	NV	NV	NV	NV	WS
9 *Skipper*	DC	DC	DC	DC	MD
10 *Pelican*	LA	LA	LA	LA	TX
11 *Lommen*	MN	ND	ND	ND	MN
12 *Harris*	ARK	ARK	ARK	ARK	TN

As the above table indicates, with the exception of the *Lommen* (discussed supra 210) and *Harris* cases, the latter of which is distinguishable (see id. n.1), it seems that American courts have accepted the proposition that, when a person is injured in

---

4. La.Civ.Code art. 3544(2)(a) provides that, "when both the injury and the conduct that caused it" occurred in the domicile of one party, the law of that state governs. For an identical rule, see Art. 47 of the Puerto Rico Draft Code. The Louisiana article makes explicit what is implicit in the *Neumeier* rule by requiring that both the conduct and the injury must occur in the tortfeasor's home state for that state's law to govern. Moreover, the article is confined to disputes between the tortfeasor and the victim and excludes, for example, disputes between joint tortfeasors, which are relegated to the flexible choice-of-law approach of Article 3542, the residual article. Finally, unlike the *Neumeier* rule, the Louisiana rule is subject to escapes. See La.Civ.Code Arts. 3547 ("exceptional cases") and 3548 ("corporate tortfeasors"). For the rationale for the Louisiana scheme by its drafter, see Symeonides, *Exegesis*, 715-66.

her home state by conduct in that state, she should be able to rely on the protection of that state's law, even if the tortfeasor is from another state whose law protects the tortfeasor. As Cavers explained, "the system of physical and financial protection [of the victim's domicile] would be impaired if a person who enters the territory of [that] state were not subject to its laws." Cavers, *Process*, 140. That state's domiciliaries "should not be put in jeopardy in [that state] simply because [an out-of-stater] * * * had come into [that state] from a state whose law provides a lower standard of financial protection." Id. at 142. The out-of-state defendant who is held to the higher standard of the state of injury "is not an apt subject for judicial solicitude. He cannot fairly claim to enjoy whatever benefits a state may offer those who enter its bounds and at the same time claim exemption from the burdens." Id. at 141. In other words, to quote *Bledsoe* again, "it is the traveler who must adjust."

Thus, if one were to compress the results of the cases into a descriptive rule, that rule would provide as follows:

> *When the conduct and injury occur in the victim's home state and that state's law favors the victim, that law applies* (even if the law of the tortfeasor's home state favors the tortfeasor).

Would this be a good prescriptive rule? Why, or why not? *Neumeier* Rule 2b, infra 237, produces the same results as the above stated rule, as does the Louisiana codification and Cavers's Principle 1.[5]

(3) SPLIT-DOMICILE CROSS-BORDER TORTS

Bernhard v. Harrah's Club

Supreme Court of California, 1976.
16 Cal.3d 313, 128 Cal.Rptr. 215, 546 P.2d 719,
cert. denied, 429 U.S. 859, 97 S.Ct. 159, 50 L.Ed.2d 136 (1976).

SULLIVAN, J. Plaintiff's complaint, containing only one count, alleged in substance the following: Defendant Harrah's Club, a Nevada corporation, owned and operated gambling establishments in the State of Nevada in which intoxicating liquors were sold, furnished to the public and given away for consumption on the premises. Defendant advertised for and solicited in California the business of California residents at such establishments knowing and expecting that many California residents would use the public highways in going to and from defendant's drinking and gambling establishments.

On July 24, 1971, Fern and Philip Myers, in response to defendant's advertisements and solicitations, drove from their California residence to defendant's gambling and drinking club in Nevada, where they stayed until the early morning hours of July 25, 1971. During their stay, the Myers were served numerous alcoholic

---

5. See La. Civ. Code Art 3542(2)(a), supra n. 4. Cavers's Principle 1 provides that "[w]here the liability laws of the state of injury set a higher standard of * * * financial protection against injury than do the laws of the state where the person causing the injury * * * had his home, the laws of the state of injury should determine the standard and the protection applicable to the case[.]" Cavers, *Process*, 139. The principle is subject to an escape for cases in which the parties had a pre-existing relationship. See id.

beverages by defendant's employees, progressively reaching a point of obvious intoxication rendering them incapable of safely driving a car. Nonetheless defendant continued to serve and furnish the Myers alcoholic beverages.

While still in this intoxicated state, the Myers drove their car back to California. Proceeding in a northeasterly direction on Highway 49, near Nevada City, California, the Myers' car, driven negligently by a still intoxicated Fern Myers, drifted across the center line into the lane of oncoming traffic and collided head-on with plaintiff Richard A. Bernhard, a resident of California, who was then driving his motorcycle along said highway. As a result of the collision plaintiff suffered severe injuries. Defendant's sale and furnishing of alcoholic beverages to the Myers, who were intoxicated to the point of being unable to drive safely, was negligent and was the proximate cause of the plaintiff's injuries in the ensuing automobile accident in California for which plaintiff prayed $100,000 in damages. * * *

We face a problem in the choice of law governing a tort action. As we have made clear on other occasions, we no longer adhere to the rule that the law of the place of the wrong is applicable in a California forum regardless of the issues before the court. [cit.] Rather we have adopted in its place a rule requiring an analysis of the respective interests of the states involved—the objective of which is "'to determine the law that most appropriately applies to the issue involved.'" [cit.]

The issue involved in the case at bench is the civil liability of defendant tavern keeper to plaintiff, a third person, for injuries allegedly caused by the former by selling and furnishing alcoholic beverages in Nevada to intoxicated patrons who subsequently injured plaintiff in California. Two states are involved: (1) California--the place of plaintiff's residence and domicile, the place where he was injured, and the forum; and (2) Nevada--the place of defendant's residence and the place of the wrong.

We observe at the start that the laws of the two states--California and Nevada--applicable to the issue involved are not identical. California imposes liability on tavern keepers in this state for conduct such as here alleged. * * * Nevada on the other hand refuses to impose such liability. In *Hamm v. Carson City Nugget, Inc.*, 450 P.2d 358, 359 (Nev.1969), the court held it would create neither common law liability nor liability based on the criminal statute banning sale of alcoholic beverages to a person who is drunk, because "if civil liability is to be imposed, it should be accomplished by legislative act after appropriate surveys, hearings, and investigations to ascertain the need for it and the expected consequences to follow." It is noteworthy that in *Hamm* the Nevada court in relying on the common law rule denying liability cited our [1955] decision in Cole v. Rush [cit.], later overruled by us in *Vesely* [v. Sager, 5 Cal.3d 153 (1971)] to the extent that it was inconsistent with that decision. [cit.]

Although California and Nevada, the two "involved states" [cit.], have different laws governing the issue presented in the case at bench, we encounter a problem in selecting the applicable rule of law only if both states have an interest in having their respective laws applied. "[Generally] speaking the forum will apply its own rule of decision unless a party litigant timely invokes the law of a foreign state. In such event he must demonstrate that the latter rule of decision will further the interest of the foreign state and therefore that it is an appropriate one for the forum to apply to the case before it. "[cit.]

Defendant contends that Nevada has a definite interest in having its rule of decision applied in this case in order to protect its resident tavern keepers like defendant from being subjected to a civil liability which Nevada has not imposed either by legislative enactment or decisional law. It is urged that in *Hamm v. Carson City Nugget, supra,* the Supreme Court of Nevada clearly delineated the policy underlying denial of civil liability of tavern keepers who sell to obviously intoxicated patrons: "Those opposed to extending liability point out that to hold otherwise would subject the tavern owner to ruinous exposure every time he poured a drink and would multiply litigation endlessly in a claim-conscious society. * * *" Accordingly defendant argues that the Nevada rule of decision is the appropriate one for the forum to apply.

Plaintiff on the other hand points out that California also has an interest in applying its own rule of decision to the case at bench. California imposes on tavern keepers civil liability to third parties injured by persons to whom the tavern keeper has sold alcoholic beverages when they are obviously intoxicated "for the purpose of protecting members of the general public from injuries to person and damage to property resulting from the excessive use of intoxicating liquor." (*Vesely v. Sager, supra,*) California, it is urged, has a special interest in affording this protection to all California residents injured in California.

Thus, since the case at bench involves a California resident (plaintiff) injured in this state by intoxicated drivers and a Nevada resident tavern keeper (defendant) which served alcoholic beverages to them in Nevada, it is clear that each state has an interest in the application of its respective law of liability and nonliability. It goes without saying that these interests conflict. Therefore, * * * for the first time since applying a governmental interest analysis as a choice of law doctrine * * *, we are confronted with a "true" conflicts case. We must therefore determine the appropriate rule of decision in a controversy where each of the states involved has a legitimate but conflicting interest in applying its own law in respect to the civil liability of tavern keepers.

* * * The father of the governmental interest approach, Professor Brainerd Currie, originally took the position that in a true conflicts situation the law of the forum should always be applied. [cit.] However, upon further reflection, Currie suggested that when under the governmental interest approach a preliminary analysis reveals an apparent conflict of interest upon the forum's assertion of its own rule of decision, the forum should reexamine its policy to determine if a more restrained interpretation of it is more appropriate. "[To] assert a conflict between the interests of the forum and the foreign state is a serious matter; the mere fact that a suggested broad conception of a local interest will create conflict with that of a foreign state is a sound reason why the conception should be reexamined, with a view to a more moderate and restrained interpretation both of the policy and of the circumstances in which it must be applied to effectuate the forum's legitimate purpose.... An analysis of this kind ... was brilliantly performed by Justice Traynor in *Bernkrant v. Fowler* [supra]." (Currie, *The Disinterested Third State* (1963) 28 Law & Contemp.

Prob., 754, 757; [cit.].) This process of reexamination requires identification of a "real interest as opposed to a hypothetical interest" on the part of the forum (Sedler, *Value of Principled Preferences*, 49 Texas L.Rev. 224) and can be approached under principles of "comparative impairment." (Baxter, *Choice of Law and the Federal System, supra*, 16 Stan.L.Rev. 1-22; Horowitz, *The Law of Choice of Law in California--A Restatement, supra*, 21 UCLA L.Rev. 719, 748-758.)

Once this preliminary analysis has identified a true conflict of the governmental interests involved as applied to the parties under the particular circumstances of the case, the "comparative impairment" approach to the resolution of such conflict seeks to determine which state's interest would be more impaired if its policy were subordinated to the policy of the other state. This analysis proceeds on the principle that true conflicts should be resolved by applying the law of the state whose interest would be the more impaired if its law were not applied. Exponents of this process of analysis emphasize that it is very different from a weighing process. The court does not "'weigh' the conflicting governmental interests in the sense of determining which conflicting law manifested the 'better' or the 'worthier' social policy on the specific issue. An attempted balancing of conflicting state policies in that sense ... is difficult to justify in the context of a federal system in which, within constitutional limits, states are empowered to mold their policies as they wish.... [The process] can accurately be described as ... accommodation of conflicting state policies, as a problem of allocating domains of law-making power in multi-state contexts-- limitations on the reach of state policies--s distinguished from evaluating the wisdom of those policies.... Emphasis is placed on the appropriate scope of conflicting state policies rather than on the 'quality' of those policies.... " (Horowitz, *The Law of Choice of Law in California--A Restatement, supra*, 21 UCLA L.Rev. 719, 753; see also Baxter, *Choice of Law and the Federal System, supra*, 16 Stan.L.Rev. 1, 18-19.) However, the true function of this methodology can probably be appreciated only casuistically in its application to an endless variety of choice of law problems. (See, e.g., the hypothetical situations set forth in *Baxter, op. cit.*, pp. 10-17.)

Although the concept and nomenclature of this methodology may have received fuller recognition at a later time, it is noteworthy that the core of its rationale was applied by Justice Traynor in his opinion for this court in *People v. One 1953 Ford Victoria* [supra]. * * * The crucial question confronting the court [in that case] was whether the "reasonable investigation" required by statute of a California mortgagee applied to the Texas mortgagee. Employing what was in substance a "comparative impairment" approach, the court answered the question in the negative. * * *

Mindful of the above principles governing our choice of law, we proceed to reexamine the California policy underlying the imposition of civil liability upon tavern keepers. At its broadest limits this policy would afford protection to all persons injured in California by intoxicated persons who have been sold or furnished alcoholic beverages while intoxicated regardless of where such beverages were sold or furnished. Such a broad policy would naturally embrace situations where the intoxicated actor had been provided with liquor by out-of-state tavern keepers. Although the State of Nevada does not impose such *civil* liability on its tavern keepers, nevertheless they are subject to *criminal* penalties under a statute making it unlawful to sell or give intoxicating liquor to any person who is drunk or known to be an habitual drunkard. [cit.]

We need not, and accordingly do not here determine the outer limits to which California's policy should be extended, for it appears clear to us that it must encompass defendant, who as alleged in the complaint, "[advertises] for and otherwise [solicits] in California the business of California residents at defendant Harrah's Club Nevada drinking and gambling establishments, knowing and expecting said California residents, in response to said advertising and solicitation, to use the public highways of the State of California in going and coming from defendant Harrah's Club Nevada drinking and gambling establishments." Defendant by the course of its chosen commercial practice has put itself at the heart of California's regulatory interest, namely to prevent tavern keepers from selling alcoholic beverages to obviously intoxicated persons who are likely to act in California in the intoxicated state. It seems clear that California cannot reasonably effectuate its policy if it does not extend its regulation to include out-of-state tavern keepers such as defendant who regularly and purposely sell intoxicating beverages to California residents in places and under conditions in which it is reasonably certain these residents will return to California and act therein while still in an intoxicated state. California's interest would be very significantly impaired if its policy were not applied to defendant.

Since the act of selling alcoholic beverages to obviously intoxicated persons is already proscribed in Nevada, the application of California's rule of civil liability would not impose an entirely new duty requiring the ability to distinguish between California residents and other patrons. Rather the imposition of such liability involves an increased economic exposure, which, at least for businesses which actively solicit extensive California patronage, is a foreseeable and coverable business expense. Moreover, Nevada's interest in protecting its tavern keepers from civil liability of a boundless and unrestricted nature will not be significantly impaired when as in the instant case liability is imposed only on those tavern keepers who actively solicit California business.

Therefore, upon reexamining the policy underlying California's rule of decision and giving such policy a more restrained interpretation for the purpose of this case pursuant to the principles of the law of choice of law discussed above, we conclude that California has an important and abiding interest in applying its rule of decision to the case at bench, that the policy of this state would be more significantly impaired if such rule were not applied and that the trial court erred in not applying California law. * * *

The judgment is reversed and the cause is remanded to the trial court with directions to overrule the demurrer and to allow defendant a reasonable time within which to answer.

Notes and Questions

1. Notice how smoothly the *Bernhard* court equated Currie's "apparent conflict" concept and his call for a "restrained interpretation of the law of the forum" (supra

186) with the court's earlier reasoning in *Bernkrant* (supra 189). Unlike *Bernkrant*, however, which subjected the *lex fori* to a restrained interpretation, *Bernhard* subjected the law of the *other* state to such an interpretation. Professor Kanowitz criticized *Bernhard* on this point as being inconsistent with Currie's theory. Kanowitz concedes that, although on one occasion Currie called for a "restrained interpretation of the policy or interest of the *one or the other*" state (see paragraph 4 of Currie's summary supra at 116) (emphasis added), most of Currie's other statements on this issue called for a restrained interpretation of the *lex fori* only. See Kanowitz, *Comparative Impairment*, 266-68.

Notice also how conveniently *Bernhard* fused *Bernkrant* and Currie's "apparent conflict" concept with Professor William F. Baxter's theory of comparative impairment. With *Bernhard*, comparative impairment has come to be viewed in California as an addendum to interest analysis, to be employed in cases of true conflicts.

2. ***Baxter's Comparative-Impairment Theory***. Professor Baxter agreed with Currie on two points: first, on the process of identifying and resolving false conflicts and, second, on the impropriety of weighing of governmental interests as a means of resolving true conflicts. Baxter, *Choice of Law*, 8, 5-6, 18-19. Echoing Currie, Baxter stated that "the weighing of interests involves super-value judgments that are incompatible with the judge's "non-political status." Id. at 5. Baxter did not, however, accept Currie's view that the application of the *lex fori* is the only possible solution for true conflicts. Baxter argued that a "normative resolution of real conflicts cases is possible" and that an examination of the basic premises underlying the federal system would reveal "normative principles which could and should serve as a foundation for choice-of-law rules." Id. at 8-9. To that end, Baxter proposed a formula known as "comparative impairment." See also Horowitz, *Toward a Federal Common Law*; Horowitz, *Choice of Law in California*.

Baxter distinguished between two types of governmental interests or objectives-- the "internal" and the "external." The internal objectives underlie each state's resolution of conflicting private interests in wholly domestic situations. The external objectives embody each state's goal "to make effective in all situations involving persons as to whom it has responsibility for legal ordering, the resolution of contending private interests the state has made for local purposes." Baxter, *Choice of Law*, 18. In a true conflict, ex hypothesi, this external objective conflicts with the corresponding external objective of a foreign state. Rather than automatically subordinating the external objective of the foreign state to that of the forum, as would Currie, Baxter would "subordinate * * * the external objective of the state whose internal objective will be least impaired in general scope and impact by subordination in cases like the one at hand." Id. In simpler words, Baxter would apply the law of that state whose interests would be most impaired if its law were not applied. Is this different from interest weighing? Is it fair to say that, rather than weighing state interests *as such*, comparative impairment weighs the *loss* that would result from subordinating the interest of one state to those of another? If so, does not the gravity of the loss depend on the strength and importance of the state interest at issue?

In any event, how is one to measure interest impairment? Baxter did not articulate specific criteria for this task, but he did illustrate the operation of his theory though several hypotheticals, of which the following is representative:

Suppose a State Y resident, while driving a truck on State X highways in violation of the X speed limit, causes injury to another resident of Y, and X but not Y attaches a per se negligence subrule to violations of its speed limits. Y lawmakers have a superior claim to control loss-distribution rights and duties between the Y residents involved. Although no X resident is involved, the fact that the proscribed conduct took place in X cannot be dismissed as irrelevant. The objective of the X lawmakers in passing the speed limit and one of their objectives in establishing the per se subrule was to create a condition of safety for the principal users of the state's highways, X residents. The application of X's per se rule in a case involving only Y residents is not totally unrelated to that objective: effectuation of the regulatory purpose of the per se rule depends on deterrence, which depends on expectation of the rule's application. * * * [Yet] X's per se rule ought not to be applied, because X's regulatory interest stands alone in opposition to Y's loss distribution interest. The suggestion is not that some rough parity in the number of instances allocated to each state is to be achieved; rather, it is that the X regulatory interest will not be impaired significantly if it is subordinated in the comparatively rare instances involving two nonresidents, who are residents of a state or states that reject the per se subrule. Conduct on X highways will not be affected by knowledge of Y residents that the X per se rule will not be applied to them if the person they injure happens to be a co-citizen. To the extent that the objective of the per se rule is loss-distribution rather than regulation, X has no legitimate interest in the rule's application because neither party is identified with X.

Baxter, *Choice of Law*, 12-13. Do you agree with Professor Baxter's proposed solution of the above hypothetical conflict?

3. Baxter also argued that in an ideal scheme, the resolution of conflicts of laws should be assigned to the federal courts rather than to state courts. In his words, since "the process of resolving conflicts cases is necessarily one of allocating spheres of legal control among states * * * [r]esponsibility for allocating spheres of legal control among member states of a federal system cannot sensibly be placed elsewhere than with the federal government." Id. at 22, 23. For, unlike federal courts, state courts are "active participants in the formulation and implementation of local policies," and thus cannot be impartial in "deciding when those policies will yield and when they will prevail over the competing policies of sister states. * * * Baseball's place as the favorite American pastime would not long survive if the responsibilities of the umpire were transferred to the first team member who managed to rule on a disputed event." Id.

4. Does *Bernhard* prove Baxter's point that state courts may be incapable of impartially refereeing interstate conflicts? Did the California court treat the interests of Nevada and California with equal attention or respect? First, the court failed to note that, almost three years before *Bernhard*, Nevada had repealed the statute imposing criminal sanctions on tavern owners selling liquor to intoxicated persons.

See 1973 Nev.Stats. 1062, ch. 604 § 8, S.B. 359 (eff. July 1, 1973). Second, the court did not pay sufficient attention to Nevada cases that had refused to impose civil liability on Nevada tavern owners vis a vis Nevada plaintiffs. See, e.g., Hamm v. Carson City Nugget, Inc., 450 P.2d 358 (Nev.1969). Were these cases not relevant in a case like *Bernhard*, which involved a non-Nevada plaintiff? Third, what about the court's conclusion that relatively few Nevada tavern keepers would be affected by its decision? Could one not argue that relatively few Californians would have been affected by a contrary decision applying Nevada law? Finally, what do you think of the following observation: "[H]ad the *Bernhard* case been brought in a Nevada court (and had that court adopted the comparative-impairment method), the ultimate result would have been diametrically opposed to the one reached by the California Supreme Court." Kanowitz, *Comparative Impairment*, 263. Even so, however, did *Bernhard* make a correct choice of law? Why, or why not?

5. Suppose that the Nevada defendant did not "actively solicit" California clientele. Would the California court still be justified in applying California law? Why, or why not?

Suppose that a few hundred miles separated the defendant's establishment from the Nevada/California border. Would the California court still be justified in applying California law? Why, or why not?

Suppose that in addition to repealing the above-mentioned criminal statute, Nevada enacted an "anti-dram shop act" expressly relieving tavern owners of civil liability for injury caused by their intoxicated patrons. In a case identical to *Bernhard*, would a California court be justified in applying California law? Why, or why not?

6. In Hoeller v. Riverside Resort Hotel, 820 P.2d 316 (Ariz.App.1991), which was decided under the Restatement (Second), the court applied Arizona's law which imposed civil liability on a Nevada casino owner under circumstances identical to those in *Bernhard*. An Arizona domiciliary who had become intoxicated in the Nevada casino drove back to Arizona and caused an accident there, injuring plaintiff, another Arizona domiciliary. The court compared Nevada's interest in "free[ing] tavern owners, and other alcohol purveyors such as casinos, from the cost and inconvenience of incurring either civil or criminal liability in the operation of their businesses," id. at 320, with Arizona's "strong interest in providing an opportunity for its residents to recover full compensation from persons and business that contribute to automobile accidents on Arizona highways * * * [and] in holding tortfeasors responsible for their actions' foreseeable effects in Arizona." Id. The court also took note of the high number of accidents caused by drunk drivers in the particular Arizona county and surmised that many of these drivers "were given free alcohol at casinos in Nevada." Id. at 318. The court also noted the casino's proximity to the Nevada/Arizona border and pointed out that the casino had gone to great lengths to attract Arizona clientele. Under these circumstances, the court reasoned, the casino should have known that "many of the patrons it seeks, many of those who sit at its tables and drink its [free] liquor, have come to the casino from Arizona and will return to Arizona * * * in an intoxicated condition and * * * may cause accidents that injure third persons in Arizona." Id. at 321.

Other dram shop act cases have reached the same result under similar circumstances. See Symeonides, *The Revolution Today*, § 179. One of these cases, Blamey v. Brown, 270 N.W.2d 884 (Minn.1978), *cert. denied,* 444 U.S. 1070 (1980), which was decided under Minnesota's better-law approach, was a closer case. The defendant, who operated a small tavern on the Wisconsin side of the Wisconsin/Minnesota border, did not advertise in Minnesota nor attempt to attract Minnesota customers. However, he occasionally sold liquor to Minnesota residents, as in the present case--he sold liquor to a Minnesota minor who drove back to Minnesota and caused an accident there injuring another Minnesota domiciliary. The court concluded that the bar's proximity to the border, and the defendant's knowledge that some of his customers were Minnesotans, allowed Minnesota courts to assume jurisdiction and to apply Minnesota's "better" law, which imposed liability on the bar owner.

7. *Louisiana's "Comparative Impairment."* The 1991 Louisiana Conflicts codification employs comparative-impairment *terminology.* Article 3515 of the Louisiana Civil Code, which is the codification's general and residual article, provides:

> Except as otherwise provided in this [codification], an issue in a case having contacts with other states is governed by the law of the state whose policies would be most seriously impaired if its law were not applied to that issue.

> That state is determined by evaluating the strength and pertinence of the relevant policies of all involved states in the light of: (1) the relationship of each state to the parties and the dispute; and (2) the policies and needs of the interstate and international systems, including the policies of upholding the justified expectations of parties and of minimizing the adverse consequences that might follow from subjecting a party to the law of more than one state.

The codification's drafter explained that the negative phrasing of the above article was intended to disassociate its approach

> from Brainerd Currie's 'governmental interest analysis' and other modern American approaches that seem to perceive the choice-of-law problem as a problem of interstate competition rather than as a problem of interstate co-operation in conflict avoidance. Instead, [the Louisiana codification] is based on the premise that the choice-of-law process should strive for ways to minimize the impairment of the interests of the involved states, rather than to maximize the interests of one state at the expense of the interests of the other states. This is accomplished by identifying the state which, in light of its relationship to the parties and the dispute and its policies rendered pertinent by that relationship, would bear the most serious legal, social, economic, and other consequences if its law were not applied to that issue.

Symeonides, *Exegesis*, 690. Another commentator characterized this as a "consequences-based approach." See Weintraub, *Commentary*, 355. The drafter acknowledged that this negative phraseology, coupled with the use of the word "impaired," was bound to evoke comparison with Baxter's comparative impairment approach. He warned, however, that:

> [t]he assumption that such a [terminological] resemblance entails an ideological

or philosophical affinity [between the two approaches] should not be taken for granted, but should be tested through a careful examination of the specifics. * * * [S]uch an examination will reveal * * * [that] the two approaches have much less in common than their acoustic resemblance might suggest. For example, the specific rules [of the Louisiana codification] deliberately steer away from the quantitative measurement of the impairment of state interests that is implicit, and sometimes even explicit, in Baxter's theory. Moreover, in designating the applicable law, these rules point to the law of a state other than the one to which Baxter would point. With regard to tort conflicts, one example would suffice to demonstrate this difference: In one of Baxter's famous hypotheticals [see supra Note 2], two motorists from state *Y* have a car accident in state *X* while driving in excess of the speed limit of the latter state. In this case, Professor Baxter would not apply the 'negligence-per-se' rule of state *X* because that state's regulatory interest embodied in the 'per se' rule will 'not be impaired significantly if it is subordinated in the *comparatively rare* instances involving two nonresidents.' Baxter, *Choice of Law*, 13 (emphasis added). In contrast, under [Louisiana's] Article 3543 * * *, the negligence per se rule will apply because it is a 'rule of the road' which operates territorially and because both the conduct and the resulting injury occurred in that state.
Symeonides, *Exegesis,* 691-92.[1]

(4) A Recap on Split-Domicile Cross-Border Torts

1. ***Cross-Border Torts***. *Bernhard* is similar to *Biscoe*, except that *Bernhard* involved a *cross-border* tort--although the injury occurred in the victim's home state, the critical conduct (the serving of the excessive liquor) had occurred in the defendant's home state. Other examples of cross-border torts are products liability cases, which are discussed in Chapter 4, as well as cases involving wrongful emissions, defamation, fraud, or other torts that can be committed from a distance. The most likely scenarios involving two states are those in which the conduct occurs in the tortfeasor's home state and the injury in the victim's home state. Depending on the content of each state's law, these cases can be divided into two patterns: (a) cases like *Bernhard* in which each state favors its own domiciliary; and (b) cases in which each state favors the domiciliary of the other state. This Note discusses cases of the *Bernhard* pattern.

2. ***Bernhard-Pattern Cases***. The fact that in these cases both the personal contacts (domiciles) and the territorial contacts (conduct and injury) are evenly split has a concomitant bearing on both state policies and party expectations, and creates more difficult conflicts than those present in intrastate torts like *Biscoe*. Nevertheless,

---

1. See also id. at 708: "Few people would dispute the fact that the speed limit of state *X* is a typical 'rule of the road' and that state *X* has an interest in applying this rule even to out-of-staters driving within that state. This interest is not diminished, if--in addition to, or *in lieu of*, criminal liability--state *X* chooses to impose on violators of its speed limit the civil sanction of 'negligence per se.' Not to apply the per se rule to an out-of-state motorist would impair state *X*'s ability to effectively ensure compliance with its speed limit. Professor Baxter recognizes this interest of state *X* but considers it less strong than the countervailing interest of state *Y* in controlling loss-distribution among its domiciliaries."

as a recent study demonstrates, American courts have generally shown little hesitation in applying the law of the victim's home state in *Bernhard* type cases. See Symeonides, *The Revolution Today* §§ 152-57. Many of these cases were products liability cases, while others involved other cross-border torts, including professional malpractice, fraud and deceptive practices. These cases applied the pro-plaintiff law of the plaintiff's home state and place of injury, rather than the pro-defendant law of the defendant's home state and place of manufacture. For citations, and discussion, see id. However, as in *Bernhard*, all of these cases involved circumstances that made it foreseeable that the defendant's conduct in his home state would have caused an injury in the victim's home state. For example, in all of the above products cases, the product was made available in the plaintiff's home state through ordinary commercial channels.

One representative non-products case is Kuehn v. Childrens Hospital, Los Angeles, 119 F.3d 1296 (7th Cir.1997), which was decided under Wisconsin's choice-influencing considerations. *Kuehn* was an action filed by the parents of a Wisconsin child who died in Wisconsin as a result of the negligence of a California hospital in improperly shipping to Wisconsin a package containing the child's bone marrow.[1] Under California law, the action did not survive the victim's death. Under Wisconsin law it did. The court applied Wisconsin law based in part on Wisconsin's interest "in obtaining for its residents the measure of relief that the state believes appropriate in tort cases." Id. at 1302. However, the court also explained why the California hospital should have foreseen the occurrence of the injury in Wisconsin, and thus the possibility of having to account under Wisconsin law--the hospital had shipped the package to Wisconsin based on a contractual arrangement with a Wisconsin hospital. Moreover, said the court, the only difference between California and Wisconsin law was "in the scope of liability for negligence, not in the standard of care. It [was] not as if California had required one method of packing and shipping bone marrow and Wisconsin another." Id.

In contrast, in Troxel v. A.I. duPont Institute, 636 A.2d 1179 (Pa.Super. 1994), *appeal denied* 647 A.2d 903 (Pa.1994), a medical malpractice case, the foreseeability element was somewhat tenuous, and this was probably one of the reasons the court reached the opposite result. Another reason may have been that, unlike *Kuehn* which involved the negligent shipping of a package, *Troxel* arose out of actual in-patient treatment and thus was a true medical malpractice action. In *Troxel*, a Delaware hospital treated a Pennsylvania patient after referral from a Pennsylvania doctor. The patient returned to Pennsylvania and, unaware that she was suffering from a contagious disease, communicated that disease to her pregnant friend, the plaintiff, whose in utero child died as a result of the disease. The plaintiff sued the hospital for failure to inform its patient of the contagious nature of her disease.

---

1. Pursuant to an agreement between the California hospital and a Wisconsin hospital, employees of the first hospital extracted bone marrow from the child and then shipped it to the Wisconsin hospital were it was to be reinserted into the child's bones. The marrow was improperly packaged and arrived in Wisconsin in unusable condition. This necessitated a second procedure which did not succeed in saving the child's life. This action was only for the negligence in improperly shipping the marrow and involved only a claim for the child's pre-death pain and suffering.

The Pennsylvania court recognized Pennsylvania's interest in protecting its citizens, but concluded that this interest was "superseded by Delaware's interest in regulating the delivery of health care services in Delaware," 636 A.2d at 1181, and in protecting defendants who acted in that state. The court said that, when acting in Delaware, defendant was "entitled to rely on the duties and protections provided by Delaware law." id. The court also stated that any rule that would allow patients to carry with them the protective law of their domicile "when [they] travel * * * to Delaware to obtain medical care * * * would be wholly unreasonable, for it would require hospitals and physicians to be aware of and be bound by the laws of all states from which patients came to them for treatment."[2]

This discussion of state interests simply confirms that these cases are veritable true conflicts, which in turn means that the two states' interests are equally strong and pertinent. One element that can tip the scales is the actor's ability reasonably to foresee where the act will manifest its direct consequences. In *Kuehn*, it was beyond question that the California hospital should have foreseen that the consequences of its negligence in sending a package to Wisconsin would have been felt in Wisconsin. Certainly, one could make the same argument in *Troxel*--the Delaware hospital doctors should have foreseen that, when they send an uncured and uniformed contagious patient back to her home in Pennsylvania, the consequences of that negligence would have been felt in Pennsylvania. The fact that the *Troxel* court did not accept this argument suggests that the court believed strongly that, from a systemic perspective, medical malpractice conflicts should be resolved invariably under the law of the place where the medical services are rendered, regardless of any other factors. As seen earlier, cases like *Bledsoe*, supra at 213, essentially have adopted this very concept.

However, is there not a difference between cases like *Bledsoe*, in which a patient chooses to go to an out-of-state hospital for treatment, and cases like *Troxel*, in which the victim has no relation with the hospital? Ms. Troxel never left her home state and was injured there. Did she not deserve to rely on the protective law of her own state? Stated another way, doesn't foreseeability have two sides--that of the tortfeasor, and that of the victim? When, as in *Bledsoe*, both sides can foresee the eventuality of the injury occurring in the victim's home state, the foreseeability criterion may be less critical in resolving the conflict. But when, as in *Troxel*, only the tortfeasor is in a position to foresee this eventuality and the victim cannot, shouldn't the scale tip against the tortfeasor?

3. *A Rule?* Subject to the above caveat regarding foreseeability, one can compress the results of the *Bernhard* pattern cases into the following descriptive rule:

> *When conduct originating in one state injures in another state a person domiciled in the latter state, the law of the latter state applies if it is more favorable to the injured person and if the occurrence of the injury in that state*

---

2. Id. In a subsequent decision, the court allowed the plaintiff's action to proceed against the Pennsylvania referring doctor. See Troxel v. A.I. duPont Institute, 675 A.2d 314 (Pa.Super.1996), *appeal denied* 685 A.2d 547 (Pa.1996).

was objectively foreseeable.

Is this a good rule? Why or why not? Professor Cavers, who also advocated the same result subject to the same proviso, offered the following rationale for it:

> Th[e] system of physical and financial protection [of the state of injury] would be impaired * * * if actions outside the state but having foreseeable effects within it were not also subject to its law. * * * [T]he fact that [the defendant] would be held to a lower standard of * * * damages back in the state where he had his home (or in the state where he acted) or, indeed, the fact that he enjoyed an immunity there, all would ordinarily seem matters of little consequence to the state of the injury. * * * If he has not entered the state but has caused harm within it by his act outside it, then, save perhaps where the physical or legal consequences of his action were not foreseeable, it is equally fair to hold him to the standards of the state into which he sent whatever harmful agent, animal, object or message caused the injury.

Cavers, *Process* 140, 141. What do you think of Cavers's rationale?

The Louisiana codification contains a rule like the one proposed above, and expressly subjects the application of the pro-recovery law of the victim's domicile to an objective foreseeability proviso.[3] Private international law codifications in the rest of the world have also adopted the same position (often presented under the rubric of *favor laesi*). For example Article 45(2) of the Portuguese Civil Code provides that "[i]f the law of the state of injury holds the actor liable but the law of the state where he acts does not, the law of the former state shall apply, provided the actor could foresee the occurrence of damage in that state as a consequence of his act or omission." See also Peruvian Civ.Code Art. 2097. However, some codifications fail to include an express foreseeability proviso. For example, Article 32(2) of the Hungarian codification authorizes the application of the law of the state of injury "[i]f it is preferable to the injured party" over the law of the conduct state, while the Italian and Venezuelan codifications do the reverse by applying the law of the injury state, unless the victim requests the application of the law of the conduct state. See Italian codif. Art. 62; Venezuelan codif. Art. 32(2). The German codification has a similar provision (Art. 40.1) but also provides escapes (Art. 41) that would enable courts to avoid harsh results. Finally, less problematic are the provisions of the Swiss and Quebec codifications, which include a foreseeability proviso, but do not condition the application of the law of the injury state on whether that law favors the victim or the tortfeasor.[4] Obviously, the foreseeability proviso is needed only when that law is unfavorable to the tortfeasor.

---

3. La. Civ. Code Art. 3544(2)(b) provides that "when the injury and the conduct that caused it occurred in different states, * * * the law of the state in which the injury occurred [applies], provided that (i) the injured person was domiciled in that state, (ii) the person who caused the injury should have foreseen its occurrence in that state, and (iii) the law of that state provided for a higher standard of financial protection for the injured person than did the law of the state in which the injurious conduct occurred."

4. See Swiss codif., Art. 133(2). See also id. Arts. 136-39 regarding antitrust, emissions, and injuries to rights of personality. For Quebec, see Quebec Civ.Code, Art. 3126. But see id. Art. 3129, which requires the application of Quebec law for injuries caused outside Quebec as a result of exposure to raw materials originating in Quebec.

Offshore Rental Co. v. Continental Oil Co.

Supreme Court of California, 1978.
22 Cal.3d 157, 148 Cal.Rptr. 867, 583 P.2d 721.

TOBRINER, J. This case presents a problem of conflict of laws. Plaintiff, a California corporation, sues for the loss of services of a "key" employee, whom defendant negligently injured on defendant's premises in Louisiana. The trial court, applying Louisiana law, concluded that plaintiff could not maintain a cause of action against defendant, and accordingly dismissed the complaint. Plaintiff appeals from the judgment, contending that under California law an employer has a cause of action for negligent injury to a key employee and that the trial court should therefore have applied California law. As we explain, we have concluded that the trial court correctly applied Louisiana law in this case, and thus we affirm the judgment.

Plaintiff Offshore Rental Company, a California corporation, maintains its principal place of business in California, but derives its revenues in large part from leasing oil drilling equipment in Louisiana's Gulf Coast area. Headquartered in New York, defendant Continental Oil Company, a Delaware corporation, does business in California, Louisiana, and other states.

In November 1967, plaintiff opened an office in Houston, Texas, for the purpose of establishing a base closer to the Gulf Coast. In June 1968 plaintiff's vice-president, Howard C. Kaylor, went from that office to Louisiana to confer with defendant's representatives. During the course of that trip defendant negligently caused injury to Kaylor on defendant's premises in Louisiana.

At the time of his injury, Kaylor was responsible for obtaining contracts for plaintiff's increased business in Louisiana. Although defendant compensated Kaylor for his injuries, plaintiff subsequently filed the underlying action in California to recover $5 million in damages occasioned by the loss of Kaylor's services. * * *

The matter presently before us involves two states: California, the forum, a place of business for defendant, as well as plaintiff's state of incorporation and principal place of business; and Louisiana, the locus of the business of both plaintiff and defendant out of which the injury arose, and the place of the injury.[2] * * * [T]he laws of Louisiana and California are not identical. In the leading case interpreting Louisiana law, *Bonfanti Industries, Inc. v. Teke, Inc.*, 224 So.2d 15 (La.App.1969) (affd. 226 So.2d 770 (La.1969)), a Louisiana corporation, relying on Louisiana Civil Code article 174, brought suit for the loss of services of one of its key officers occasioned by the Louisiana defendant's negligence. Although article 174 provides that "The master may bring an action against any man for beating or maiming his *servant*" (italics added), the Louisiana court held that the *corporate plaintiff* could state no cause of action in modern law for the loss of services of its officer. [cit.]

On the other hand, expressions in the California cases, although chiefly dicta, support the present plaintiff's assertion that California Civil Code section 49 grants a cause of action against a third party for loss caused by an injury to a key employee

---

2. Neither party has urged that the law of Delaware or Texas is applicable.

due to the negligence of the third party. Section 49 provides that "The rights of personal relations forbid: ... [para.] (c) Any injury to a servant which affects his ability to serve his master.... " Plaintiff contends that the master-servant relation protected by section 49 encompasses plaintiff's employment relationship with its injured vice-president, and thus that section 49 grants a cause of action against defendant for damages to plaintiff caused by defendant's negligence.

If we assume, for purposes of analysis, that section 49 does provide an employer with a cause of action for negligent injury to a key employee, the laws of California and Louisiana are directly in conflict. * * *

Turning first to Louisiana, we note that Louisiana's refusal to permit recovery for loss of a key employee's services is predicated on the view that allowing recovery would lead to "undesirable social and legal consequences." (*Bonfanti Industries, Inc. v. Teke, Inc., supra.*) We interpret this conclusion as indicating Louisiana's policy to protect negligent resident tortfeasors acting within Louisiana's borders from the financial hardships caused by the assessment of excessive legal liability or exaggerated claims resulting from the loss of services of a key employee. Clearly the present defendant is a member of the class which Louisiana law seeks to protect, since defendant is a Louisiana "resident" whose negligence on its own premises has caused the injury in question. Thus Louisiana's interest in the application of its law to the present case is evident: negation of plaintiff's cause of action serves Louisiana's policy of avoidance of extended financial hardship to the negligent defendant.

Nevertheless, we recognize as equally clear the fact that application of California law to the present case will further California's interest. California, through section 49, expresses an interest in protecting California employers from economic harm because of negligent injury to a key employee inflicted by a third party. Moreover, California's policy of protection extends beyond such an injury inflicted within California, since California's economy and tax revenues are affected regardless of the situs of physical injury. Thus, California is interested in applying its law in the present case to plaintiff Offshore, a California corporate employer that suffered injury in Louisiana by the loss of the services of its key employee.

Hence this case involves a true conflict between the law of Louisiana and the law of California. In *Bernhard v. Harrah's Club, supra,* we described the proper resolution of such a case. * * * [T]he resolution of true conflict cases may be described as "essentially a process of allocating respective spheres of lawmaking influence." (Baxter, *Choice of Law and the Federal System* (1963) 16 Stan.L.Rev. 1, 11-12.) The process of allocation demands several inquiries. First, while "[it] is not always possible to say fairly whether [the] policy [underlying a state's law] is one that was much more *strongly held* in the past than it is now, ... this ground of analysis should not be ignored." (Emphasis added.) (Von Mehren & Trautman, The Law of Multistate Problems (1965) p. 377.) * * * *"If one of the competing laws is archaic and isolated in the context of the laws of the federal union, it may not unreasonably have to yield to the more prevalent and progressive law, other factors of choice being roughly equal. A married woman's disability to make a contract,* imbedded in the law of one state, may be carried away by the current if contact is made with the main stream in another state. * * * " Freund, *Chief Justice Stone and* *the Conflicts of Laws*, (1946) 59 Harv. L. Rev. 1210, 1216.

Thus the current status of a statute is an important factor to be considered in a determination of comparative impairment: the policy underlying a jurisdiction's law may be deemed "attenuated and anachronistic and properly ... be limited to domestic occurrences in the event of [a multistate] clash of interests." (Freund, *Chief Justice Stone, supra*, 59 Harv.L.Rev. 1210, 1224.) Moreover, a particular statute may be an antique not only in comparison to the laws of the federal union, but also as compared with other laws of the state of its enactment. Such a statute may be infrequently enforced or interpreted even within its own jurisdiction, and, as an anachronism in that sense, should have a limited application in a conflicts case.

Another chief criterion in the comparative impairment analysis is the "maximum attainment of underlying purpose by all governmental entities. This necessitates identifying the focal point of concern of the contending lawmaking groups and ascertaining the *comparative pertinence* of that concern to the immediate case." (Italics added.) (Baxter, *Choice of Law, supra*, 16 Stan.L.Rev. 1, 12.) The policy underlying a statute may be less "comparatively pertinent" if the original object of the statute is no longer of pressing importance: a statute which was once intended to remedy a matter of grave public concern may since have fallen in significance to the periphery of the state's laws. As Professor Currie observed in another context, "If the truth were known, it would probably be that [those few states which have retained the archaic law of abatement have done so] simply because of the proverbial inertia of legal institutions, and that no real policy is involved." (Fn. omitted.) Selected Essays on The Conflict of Laws, (*supra*, p. 143.)

Moreover, the policy underlying a statute may also be less "comparatively pertinent" if the same policy may easily be satisfied by some means other than enforcement of the statute itself. Insurance, for example, may satisfy the underlying purpose of a statute originally intended to provide compensation to tort victims. The fact that parties may reasonably be expected to plan their transactions with insurance in mind may therefore constitute a relevant element in the resolution of a true conflict.

In sum, the comparative impairment approach to the resolution of true conflicts attempts to determine the relative commitment of the respective states to the laws involved. The approach incorporates several factors for consideration: the history and current status of the states' laws; the function and purpose of those laws.

Applying the comparative impairment analysis to the present case, we first probe the history and current status of the laws before us. The majority of common law states that have considered the matter do not sanction actions for harm to business employees, recognizing that even if injury to the master-servant relationship were at one time the basis for an action at common law, the radical change in the nature of that relationship since medieval times nullifies any right by a modern corporate employer to recover for negligent injury to his employees. With the decision in *Bonfanti Industries, Inc. v. Teke, Inc.*, *supra*, discarding the obsolete concept of recovery for loss of a servant's services, the Louisiana courts have thus joined the "main stream" of American jurisdictions: Louisiana law accords with the common law's consistent refusal generally to recognize a cause of action based on negligent, as opposed to intentional, conduct which interferes with the performance of a contract between third parties or renders its performance more expensive or burdensome. [cit.]

Indeed California has itself exhibited little concern in applying section 49 to the employer-employee relationship: despite the provisions of the antique statute, no California court has heretofore squarely held that California law provides an action for harm to business employees, and no California court has recently considered the issue at all. If, as we have assumed, section 49 does provide an action for harm to key corporate employees, in Professor Freund's words the section constitutes a law "archaic and isolated in the context of the laws of the federal union." We therefore conclude that the trial judge in the present case correctly applied Louisiana, rather than California, law, since California's interest in the application of its unusual and outmoded statute is comparatively less strong than Louisiana's corollary interest, so lately expressed, in its "prevalent and progressive" law.

An examination of the function and purpose of the respective laws before us provides additional support for our limitation of the reach of California law in the present case. The accident in question occurred within Louisiana's borders; although the law of the place of the wrong is not necessarily the applicable law for all tort actions [cit.], the situs of the injury remains a relevant consideration. At the heart of Louisiana's denial of liability lies the vital interest in promoting freedom of investment and enterprise *within Louisiana's borders*, among investors incorporated both in Louisiana and elsewhere. The imposition of liability on defendant, therefore, would strike at the essence of a compelling Louisiana law.

Furthermore, in connection with our search for the proper law to apply based on the "maximum attainment of underlying purpose by all governmental entities," we note the realistic fact that insurance is available to guard against the exigencies of the present case. As one commentator has remarked, "[The] fact that the potential [tort] victim does not usually calculate his risk and plan his insurance program accordingly, hardly detracts from the consideration that he can fairly be made to bear the consequences of not doing so." (Ehrenzweig, A Treatise on the Conflict of Laws (1962) pp. 575-576.) The present plaintiff, a business corporation, is a potential "victim" peculiarly able to calculate such risks and to plan accordingly. Plaintiff could have obtained protection against the occurrence of injury to its corporate vice-president by purchasing key employee insurance, certainly a reasonable and foreseeable business expense. By entering Louisiana, plaintiff "exposed [itself] to the risks of the territory," and should not expect to subject defendant to a financial hazard that Louisiana law had not created. (Cavers, The Choice-of-Law Process (1965) p. 147.)[12]

Although it is equally true that defendant is a business corporation able to calculate the risks of potential tort liability and to plan accordingly, because

---

12. We emphasize that plaintiff did not expose itself to any risk that Louisiana encourages negligent conduct by resident corporations. On the contrary, as a consequence of Louisiana's general policy against negligent behavior, defendant has already been obliged to compensate plaintiff's employee for his personal injuries.

defendant's operations in Louisiana presumably involved dealing with key employees of companies incorporated in diverse states defendant would most reasonably have anticipated a need for the protection of premises' liability insurance based on Louisiana law. Accordingly, under these circumstances, we conclude that the burden of obtaining insurance for the loss at issue here is most properly borne by the plaintiff corporation.

* * * Upon examination of the nature and purpose of the states' respective laws, * * * we have determined that the California statute has historically been of minimal importance in the fabric of California law, and that the Louisiana courts have recently interpreted their analogous Louisiana statute narrowly in light of that statute's obsolescence. We do not believe that California's interests in the application of its law to the present case are so compelling as to prevent an accommodation to the stronger, more current interest of Louisiana. We conclude therefore that Louisiana's interests would be the more impaired if its law were not applied, and consequently that Louisiana law governs the present case. Since the law of Louisiana provides no cause of action for the present plaintiff, we hold that the trial court correctly dismissed plaintiff's cause of action.

The judgment is affirmed.

Notes and Questions

1. Was the *Offshore* case a *real* true conflict? Why, or why not?

2. Was *Offshore* a straightforward application of comparative impairment as Baxter conceived it, or did the case go beyond or perhaps against that approach? For example, Baxter insisted that a court may weigh only the *effects* of the application or non-application of the competing rules. (See supra at 220). Did the *Offshore* court not engage in a comparative evaluation of the *rules themselves* and of their underlying policies?

The court relied, inter alia, on the writings of Professors von Mehren and Trautman, see infra Note 4, who had argued that in true conflicts one should consider the relative strength of the policies underlying the conflicting rules and the relative intensity of the interests of the involved states in applying those rules. Having concluded that California's rule was "archaic" or "anachronistic," the court then easily could find the rule to be "less 'comparatively pertinent'" and hence California's interests less "compelling" than Louisiana's. Had the *Lilienthal* court employed a similar analysis, what do you think the result might be?

Incidentally, does the use of the word "anachronistic" remind you of Weintraub's approach? See supra at 169. Professor Juenger has suggested that, in effect, *Offshore* followed a kind of better-law approach. See Juenger, *Leflar's Contribution*, 421-22. Do you agree?

3. What role did the insurance factor play in the resolution of the *Offshore* conflict? Do you agree with the court's handling of that factor? Why, or why not? Could one turn the insurance factor against the defendant?

4. ***von Mehren and Trautman's "Functional Analysis."*** In their 1965 casebook entitled *The Law of Multistate Problems*, Professors Arthur T. von Mehren

and Donald T. Trautman developed an approach to conflicts, which they call "functional analysis." See id. at 76, 102-105, 109-115, 178-210. The fact that the authors formulated this approach in the context of a casebook, coupled with the approach's subtlety and sophistication, impedes any attempt at summarization. It is fair to say, however, that the first four steps of functional analysis are methodologically, though not philosophically, similar to interest analysis and its identification of false conflicts and apparent conflicts. The major differences between the two methods appear in the handling of true conflicts. Unlike interest analysis, functional analysis openly advocates policy weighing, guided by specific criteria. The first criterion is the relevant strength of the policies of the involved states. In measuring the strength of the respective policies, the court is to consider the conviction with which a state adheres to a policy, the appropriateness of that state's rule to the effectuation of that policy, and the relative significance, to the states concerned, of the vindication of their policies. For example, all other factors being equal, the court should prefer an emerging rather than a regressing policy, or a policy underlying a specific rule rather than a policy underlying a general principle. The court also should engage in a comparative evaluation of the asserted policies, judging their strength and merits not only in comparison with the policies of other concerned states, but also in comparison with the policies of all states sharing the same legal and cultural tradition. For cases that cannot be resolved by a rational choice among the various domestic or multistate policies, the court may select a commonly-held multistate policy, or construct a new multistate rule, or, finally, apply the rule of the state that has the most effective control over the subject matter. Id. at 376-406.

For those cases that remain unresolved after all these steps, functional analysis proposes other guidelines, such as applying the rule that best promotes multistate activity or interferes least with the parties' intentions. Id. at 406-08. Only when all other routes have been explored and found to be ineffectual do von Mehren and Trautman admit that the forum appropriately may apply its own law, but on the condition that, all other factors being equal, the forum also is a concerned state. A neutral forum, in contrast, should not apply its own law, but it may apply the rule of a concerned state that approximates most closely the forum's rule. It is, however, desirable that such a forum exploit its impartial position and choose solutions that promote multistate activity and uniformity of decisions.

3. THE NO–INTEREST OR "UNPROVIDED–FOR" CASE

Erwin v. Thomas
Supreme Court of Oregon, 1973.
264 Or. 454, 506 P.2d 494.

HOLMAN, J. This is an action for damages for loss of consortium alleged to have been suffered when plaintiff's husband was injured in an accident. Plaintiff appealed from a judgment for defendant which was entered after a demurrer was sustained to plaintiff's complaint and plaintiff refused to plead further.

Defendant Thomas, while operating a truck in the state of Washington in the course of his employment for defendant Shepler, is alleged to have negligently injured plaintiff's husband. Defendant Thomas is an Oregon resident and his employer, defendant Shepler, is an Oregon corporation. Plaintiff and her injured husband are residents of Washington. Washington, by court decision, has followed the common law rule that no cause of action exists by a wife for loss of consortium. [cit.]. Oregon allows such an action, [cit.].

The issue is whether Oregon law or Washington law is applicable. It is with some trepidation that a court enters the maze of choice of law in tort cases. No two authorities agree. Until recently, this court was committed to the traditional, arbitrary, and much criticized rule that in tort cases the law of the place of the wrong, *lex loci delicti commissi*, governs. However, in the case of Casey v. Manson Constr. Co., 428 P.2d 898 (Or.1967), this court adopted the equally maligned and almost universally criticized "most significant relationship" approach of Restatement (Second) Conflict of Laws. * * *

Where, in the particular factual context, the interests and policies of one state are involved and those of the other are not (or, if they are, they are involved in only a minor way), reason would seem to dictate that the law of the state whose policies and interests are vitally involved should apply; or, if those of neither state are vitally involved, that the law of the forum should apply. It may well be that determining what interests or policies are behind the law of a particular state is far from an exact science and is something about which there can be legitimate disagreement; but, on the other hand, it is the kind of an exercise, for better or for worse, which courts do every day and, therefore, feel secure in doing. If such a claimed conflict can be so disposed of, whether it is called false or not, the disposition certainly seems preferable to wandering off into the jungle with a compass which everyone but its maker says is defective.

Let us examine the interests involved in the present case. Washington has decided that the rights of a married woman whose husband is injured are not sufficiently important to cause the negligent defendant who is responsible for the injury to pay the wife for her loss. It has weighed the matter in favor of protection of defendants. No Washington defendant is going to have to respond for damages in the present case, since the defendant is an Oregonian. Washington has little concern whether other states require non-Washingtonians to respond to such claims. Washington policy cannot be offended if the court of another state affords rights to a Washington woman which Washington does not afford, so long as a Washington defendant is not required to respond. The state of Washington appears to have no material or urgent policy or interest which would be offended by applying Oregon law.

On the other hand, what is Oregon's interest? Oregon, obviously, is protective of the rights of married women and believes that they should be allowed to recover for negligently inflicted loss of consortium. However, it is stretching the imagination more than a trifle to conceive that the Oregon Legislature was concerned about the rights of all the nonresident married women in the nation whose husbands would be injured outside of the state of Oregon. Even if Oregon were so concerned, it would offend no substantial Washington interest.

It is apparent, therefore, that neither state has a vital interest in the outcome of this litigation and there can be no conceivable material conflict of policies or interests if an Oregon court does what comes naturally and applies Oregon law. Professor Currie expresses it thusly:

" * * * The closest approximation to the renvoi problem that will be encountered under the suggested method is the case in which neither state has an interest in the application of its law and policy; in that event, the forum would apply its own law simply on the ground that that is the more convenient disposition * * *." B. Currie, Notes on Methods and Objectives in the Conflict of Laws, Selected Essays on the Conflict of Laws 184 (Footnote omitted) (1963).

An examination of the writings of those scholars who believe that an actual controversy exists in a situation similar to the present indicates, without an exception, they would reach the same result as we do, by either different or partially different reasoning.

The next question is whether our decision in Casey v. Manson Constr. Co., [supra], is incompatible with our disposition of the present case. In *Casey*, which adopted and applied Restatement (Second) Conflict of Laws, an actual conflict existed. An Oregon wife brought a loss of consortium action because of an injury to her husband, also an Oregon resident, which was negligently inflicted in Washington by a Washington resident. We there held that Washington defendants should not be required to accommodate themselves to the law of the state of residence of any traveler whom they might injure in Washington; that under the given circumstances, Washington's interest in the matter, which was protective of Washington defendants, was paramount to Oregon's interest in having its resident recover for her loss; and that Washington's relationship was the more significant and Washington law applied.

* * * We see no such conflict here. * * * We are little concerned whether we are presented with a false conflict or with an actual conflict capable of solution by resorting to our analysis of the interests and policies of the respective states. Where such policies and interests can be identified with a fair degree of assurance and there appears to be no substantial conflict, we do not believe it is necessary to have recourse in the "contacts" of Section 145(2) of Restatement (Second) Conflict of Laws.

The judgment of the trial court is reversed and the case is remanded for further proceedings.

BRYSON, J, dissenting. * * * Regardless of whether we follow the Restatement * * * or the law of the place of the wrong, I do not believe we can or should bestow Oregon statutory rights for women on women of the state of Washington.

Obviously the plaintiff could not bring this action in her state, Washington, but the majority opinion holds that by merely stepping over the state boundary into Oregon she is then bestowed with the right given wives who are residents of the state of Oregon, which includes the right of action for loss of consortium of her husband.

There is definitely a conflict in the policy of the states of Washington and Oregon regarding the right to bring an action for loss of consortium. I would affirm.

Notes and Questions

1. The no-interest case is the converse of a true conflict, and something between a true and a false conflict. It is a case in which a court following interest analysis concludes that none of the involved states is interested in having its law applied. This category of cases is known in conflicts literature as the "unprovided-for" case because interest analysis, the very methodology that articulated this category, did not provide a solution for it. The no-interest case is a theoretical construct that has meaning only in the context of methodologies like interest analysis that resolve conflicts cases on the basis of state interests. In this sense, Brainerd Currie is the discoverer if not the inventor of this category of conflicts cases. Yet, apparently because of his mistaken assumption that these cases would not arise frequently in practice, Currie had little to say about them. He simply offered some tentative suggestions that he ultimately rejected in favor of applying the law of the forum "since no good purpose will be served by putting the parties to the expense and the court to the trouble of ascertaining the foreign law." Currie, *Selected Essays*, 156, 152-56.

However, is it not true that, in order to conclude that the case is a no-interest case, the court first must ascertain the content of, and the policies underlying, the foreign state's law, so as to determine whether that state has or does not have an interest? Secondly, is it consistent with the basic premises of interest analysis to apply the law of a disinterested state? Does the no-interest case suggest that, sooner or later, a method that relies exclusively on state interests, especially "interests" as narrowly defined by Currie, will encounter an impasse? As one critic observed, "[h]aving defined the interests as domiciliary oriented, when you run out of domiciliaries to protect you run out of interests." Twerski, *Emperor's Clothes*, 108. By extension, might not one say that when you run out of interests, you run out of principled solutions?

2. Under Currie's personal-law principle, *Erwin* presented the no-interest paradigm in that each party was domiciled in a state whose law favored the domiciliary of the other state. The court followed Currie's prescriptions and, doing "what comes naturally," applied the law of the forum *qua* forum. However, *Erwin* is alone in following this particular prescription. Only two other cases involving this pattern have applied the forum's pro-plaintiff law, but both based that application on specific affirmative factors rather than on a gravitational tendency to do "what comes naturally." For example, in Labree v. Major, 306 A.2d 808 (R.I.1973), a case arising from a Massachusetts accident involving a Rhode Island defendant and a Massachusetts plaintiff, the court refused to apply Massachusetts' guest statute and applied Rhode Island's pro-plaintiff law based on a straight-forward plaintiff-always-wins philosophy. The court stated that, when the defendant is domiciled in a recovery state, "the plaintiff should recover no matter what the law of his residence or the place of the accident." Id. at 818. Similarly, in Farrell v. Davis Enterprises, Inc. 1996 WL 21128 (Pa.Super.1996), a case arising from a New Jersey accident involving a New Jersey plaintiff and Pennsylvania defendants, the court applied Pennsylvania's pro-plaintiff joint-and-several-liability rule, rather than New Jersey's pro-defendant

rule, because the court concluded that the Pennsylvania rule was in part designed to deter Pennsylvania tortfeasors.

3. Compare *Erwin* with *Casey v. Manson Constr. & Eng'g Co.* (discussed in *Erwin*, supra). Examine the two cases, first from the respective defendant's perspective. In *Casey*, the court applied Washington's pro-defendant law for the benefit of a Washington defendant who operated in Washington and injured an Oregon domiciliary. Why should the same court not extend the same benefit to the Oregon defendant in *Erwin*, who also operated in Washington and caused an injury there? From the respective plaintiff's perspective, in *Casey*, the court denied an Oregon plaintiff the benefit of Oregon's pro-plaintiff law. Why should the same court extend this benefit to a Washington plaintiff in *Erwin*?

4. One of Currie's followers, Professor Robert A. Sedler, argued that a solution to the no-interest case can be found if one focuses on the common policies of the involved states. Sedler noted that:

> usually the point as to which the laws of the involved states differ will involve a substantive rule that is an exception to the common policy reflected in what may be called the general law of both states. Since the state whose law represents an exception to that common policy has no interest in having its law applied * * * it is submitted that the common policy should come to the fore, and the exception should not be recognized.

Sedler, *Reformulation*, 235. In a case like *Neumeier v. Kuehner*, (reproduced below), the Ontario guest statute would be the exception to the general compensatory policy of both Ontario and New York. According to Sedler, since Ontario would not be interested in applying its guest statute because an Ontario host was not involved, "the common policy of both states in favor of recovery should prevail." Id. Would this idea work in *Erwin*? Which was the common policy of the two states and which was the exception?

Neumeier v. Kuehner

Court of Appeals of New York, 1972.
31 N.Y.2d 121, 335 N.Y.S.2d 64, 286 N.E.2d 454.

FULD, C.J. A domiciliary of Ontario, Canada, was killed when the automobile in which he was riding, owned and driven by a New York resident, collided with a train in Ontario. That jurisdiction has a guest statute, and the primary question posed by this appeal is whether in this action brought by the Ontario passenger's estate, Ontario law should be applied and the New York defendant permitted to rely on its guest statute as a defense.

The facts are quickly told. On May 7, 1969, Arthur Kuehner, the defendant's intestate, a resident of Buffalo, drove his automobile from that city to Fort Erie in the Province of Ontario, Canada, where he picked up Amie Neumeier, who lived in that town with his wife and their children. Their trip was to take them to Long Beach, also in Ontario, and back again to Neumeier's home in Fort Erie. However, at a railroad crossing in the Town of Sherkston--on the way to Long Beach--the auto was struck by a train of the defendant Canadian National Railway Company. Both

Kuehner and his guest-passenger were instantly killed.

Neumeier's wife and administratrix, a citizen of Canada and a domiciliary of Ontario, thereupon commenced this wrongful death action in New York against both Kuehner's estate and the Canadian National Railway Company. The defendant estate pleaded, as an affirmative defense, the Ontario guest statute and the defendant railway also interposed defenses in reliance upon it. In substance, the statute provides that the owner or driver of a motor vehicle is not liable for damages resulting from injury to, or the death of, a guest-passenger unless he was guilty of gross negligence. [cit.] It is worth noting, at this point, that, although our court originally considered that the sole purpose of the Ontario statute was to protect Ontario defendants and their insurers against collusive claims (see Babcock v. Jackson, [supra]), "Further research * * * has revealed the distinct possibility that one purpose, and perhaps the only purpose, of the statute was to protect owners and drivers against suits by ungrateful guests." (Reese, Choice of Law, 71 Col. L. Rev. 548, 558; see Trautman, Two Views on Kell v. Henderson: A Comment, 67 Col. L. Rev. 465, 469.)

The plaintiff, asserting that the Ontario statute "is not available * * * in the present action", moved * * * to dismiss the affirmative defenses pleaded. The court at Special Term, holding the guest statute applicable, denied the motions [cit.] but, on appeal, a closely divided Appellate Division reversed and directed dismissal of the defenses [cit.]. It was the court's belief that this result was dictated by Tooker v. Lopez (24 N.Y.2d 569 [1969]).

In reaching that conclusion, the Appellate Division misread our decision in the *Tooker* case--a not unnatural result in light of the variant views expressed in the three separate opinions written on behalf of the majority. It is important to bear in mind that in *Tooker*, the guest-passenger and the host-driver were both domiciled in New York, and our decision--that New York law was controlling--was based upon, and limited to, that fact situation. Indeed, two of the three judges who wrote for reversal--Judge Keating [cit.] and Judge Burke [cit.]--expressly noted that the determination then being made left open the question whether New York law would be applicable if the plaintiff passenger happened to be a domiciliary of the very jurisdiction which had a guest statute. Thus, Tooker v. Lopez did no more than hold that, when the passenger and driver are residents of the same jurisdiction and the car is there registered and insured, its law, and not the law of the place of accident, controls and determines the standard of care which the host owes to his guest.

What significantly and effectively differentiates the present case is the fact that, although the host was a domiciliary of New York, the guest, for whose death recovery is sought, was domiciled in Ontario, the place of accident and the very jurisdiction which had enacted the statute designed to protect the host from liability for ordinary negligence. It is clear that, although New York has a deep interest in protecting its own residents, injured in a foreign state, against unfair or anachronistic statutes of that state, it has no legitimate interest in ignoring the public policy of a foreign jurisdiction--such as Ontario--and in protecting the plaintiff guest domiciled and injured there from legislation obviously addressed, at the very least, to a resident riding in a vehicle traveling within its borders.

To distinguish *Tooker* on such a basis is not improperly discriminatory. It is quite true that, in applying the Ontario guest statute to the Ontario-domiciled passenger, we, in a sense, extend a right less generous than New York extends to a New York passenger in a New York vehicle with New York insurance. That, though, is not a consequence of invidious discrimination; it is, rather, the result of the existence of disparate rules of law in jurisdictions that have diverse and important connections with the litigants and the litigated issue.

The fact that insurance policies issued in this State on New York-based vehicles cover liability, regardless of the place of the accident (Vehicle and Traffic Law, § 311, subd. 4), certainly does not call for the application of internal New York law in this case. The compulsory insurance requirement is designed to cover a car-owner's liability, not *create* it; in other words, the applicable statute was not intended to impose liability where none would otherwise exist. This being so, we may not properly look to the New York insurance requirement to dictate a choice-of-law rule which would invariably impose liability. As Justice Moule wrote in the course of his dissenting opinion below ([cit.]), "The statute [cit.] does not purport to impose liability where none would otherwise exist. We must observe that Judge Keating's statement ([in] *Tooker*, [supra]) that the Legislature 'has evinced commendable concern not only for the residents of this State, but residents of other States who may be injured as a result of the activities of New York residents' was in the context, not of proving that New York had a governmental interest in overriding foreign rules of liability, but of demonstrating that it was immaterial in that case that the driver and passenger, while domiciliaries of New York, were attending college in Michigan. While New York may be a proper forum for actions involving its own domiciliaries, regardless of where the accident happened, it does not follow that we should apply New York law simply because some may think it is a better rule, where doing so does not advance any New York State interest, nor the interest of any New York State domiciliary."

When, in Babcock v. Jackson [supra], we rejected the mechanical place of injury rule in personal injury cases because it failed to take account of underlying policy considerations, we were willing to sacrifice the certainty provided by the old rule for the more just, fair and practical result that may best be achieved by giving controlling effect to the law of the jurisdiction which has the greatest concern with, or interest in, the specific issue raised in the litigation. (See, also, Tooker v. Lopez, [cit.] [concurring opn.], *supra*.) In consequence of the change effected--and this was to be anticipated--our decisions in multi-state highway accident cases, particularly in those involving guest-host controversies, have, it must be acknowledged, lacked consistency. This stemmed, in part, from the circumstance that it is frequently difficult to discover the purposes or policies underlying the relevant local law rules of the respective jurisdictions involved. It is even more difficult, assuming that these purposes or policies are found to conflict, to determine on some principled basis which should be given effect at the expense of the others.

The single all-encompassing rule which called, inexorably, for selection of the law of the place of injury was discarded, and wisely, because it was too broad to prove satisfactory in application. There is, however, no reason why choice-of-law rules, more narrow than those previously devised, should not be successfully developed, in order to assure a greater degree of predictability and uniformity, on the basis of our present knowledge and experience. (See, e.g., Cavers, The Choice of Law Process, 121-122; Reese, Choice of Law, 71 Col. L. Rev. 548, 555, 561-562; Reese, Choice of Law: Rules or Approach, 57 Corn. L. Rev. 315, 321 et seq.; Rosenberg, Comments on Reich v. Purcell, 15 UCLA L. Rev. 641, 642, 646-647.) "The time has come," I wrote in *Tooker*, "to endeavor to minimize what some have characterized as an ad hoc case-by-case approach by laying down guidelines, as well as we can, for the solution of guest-host conflicts problems." *Babcock* and its progeny enable us to formulate a set of basic principles that may be profitably utilized, for they have helped us uncover the underlying values and policies which are operative in this area of the law. To quote again from the concurring opinion in *Tooker*, "Now that these values and policies have been revealed, we may proceed to the next stage in the evolution of the law--the formulation of a few rules of general applicability, promising a fair level of predictability." Although it was recognized that no rule may be formulated to guarantee a satisfactory result in every case, the following principles were proposed as sound for situations involving guest statutes in conflicts settings:

"1. When the guest-passenger and the host-driver are domiciled in the same state, and the car is there registered, the law of that state should control and determine the standard of care which the host owes to his guest.

"2. [a] When the driver's conduct occurred in the state of his domicile and that state does not cast him in liability for that conduct, he should not be held liable by reason of the fact that liability would be imposed upon him under the tort law of the state of the victim's domicile. [b] Conversely, when the guest was injured in the state of his own domicile and its law permits recovery, the driver who has come into that state should not--in the absence of special circumstances--be permitted to interpose the law of his state as a defense.

"3. In other situations, when the passenger and the driver are domiciled in different states, the rule is necessarily less categorical. Normally, the applicable rule of decision will be that of the state where the accident occurred but not if it can be shown that displacing that normally applicable rule will advance the relevant substantive law purposes without impairing the smooth working of the multistate system or producing great uncertainty for litigants. (Cf. Restatement, 2d, Conflict of Laws, P.O.D., pt. II, §§ 146, 159 [later adopted and promulgated May 23, 1969].)"

The variant views expressed not only in *Tooker* but by Special Term and the divided Appellate Division in this litigation underscore and confirm the need for these rules. Since the passenger was domiciled in Ontario and the driver in New York, the present case is covered by the third stated principle. The law to be applied is that of the jurisdiction where the accident happened unless it appears that "displacing [the] normally applicable rule will advance the relevant substantive law purposes" of the jurisdictions involved. Certainly, ignoring Ontario's policy requiring proof of gross negligence in a case which involves an Ontario-domiciled guest at the expense of a New Yorker does not further the substantive law purposes of New York. In point of fact, application of New York law would result in the exposure of this State's domiciliaries to a greater liability than that imposed upon resident users of Ontario's highways. Conversely, the failure to apply Ontario's law would "impair"--to cull from the rule set out above--"the smooth working of the multi-state system [and] produce great uncertainty for litigants" by sanctioning forum shopping and thereby allowing a party to select a forum which could give him a larger recovery than the court of his own domicile. In short, the plaintiff has failed to show that this State's connection with the controversy was sufficient to justify displacing the rule of *lex loci delictus*.

Professor Willis Reese, the Reporter for the current Conflict of Laws Restatement, expressed approval of rules such as those suggested above; they are, he wrote, "the sort of rules at which the courts should aim" (Reese, Choice of Law, 71 Col. L. Rev. 548, 562; [cit.]). Indeed, in discussing the present case following the determination at Special Term that Ontario law should govern, he expressed the opinion that any other result would have been highly unreasonable ([cit.]): "So far as the New York law was concerned, Judge Keating had argued in Tooker v. Lopez that New York's motor vehicle compulsory insurance law revealed a 'commendable concern' not only for New York residents but also for non-residents injured by New Yorkers. On this basis, it could perhaps be argued that New York policy would be furthered by application of the New York rule imposing upon the driver the duty of exercising ordinary care for the protection of his guest. But could this argument really be made with a straight face in support of an Ontario guest picked up in Ontario and who enjoyed no similar protection under Ontario Law? Was the New York rule really intended to be manna for the entire world? One can well understand the relief with which the trial judge seized upon Judge Fuld's third rule and followed it by holding the Ontario statute applicable."

In each action, the Appellate Division's order should be reversed, that of Special Term reinstated, without costs, and the questions certified answered in the negative.

BREITEL, J. (concurring). I agree that there should be a reversal, but would place the reversal on quite narrow grounds. It is undesirable to lay down prematurely major premises based on shifting ideologies in the choice of law. * * * What the Babcock case taught and what modern day commentators largely agree is that *lex loci delictus* is unsoundly applied if it is done indiscriminately and without exception. It is still true, however, that the *lex loci delictus* is the normal rule, as indeed Chief Judge Fuld noted in the *Tooker* case, to be rejected only when it is evident that the situs of the accident is the least of the several factors or influences to which the accident may be attributed * * *. Certain it is that States are not concerned only with their own citizens or residents. They are concerned with events that occur within their territory, and are also concerned with the "stranger within the gates" (Juenger, op. cit., *supra*, at pp. 209-210).

In this case, none would have ever assumed that New York law should be applied just because one of the two defendants was a New York resident and his automobile was New York insured, except for the overbroad statements of Currie doctrine in the Tooker case, stemming from one particular school of academic thinking in the field of conflicts law [cit.].

Consequently, I agree that there should be a reversal and the defenses allowed to stand. The conclusion, however, rests simply on the proposition that plaintiff has failed by her allegations to establish that the relationship to this State was sufficient to displace the normal rule that the *lex loci delictus* should be applied, the accident being associated with Ontario, from inception to tragic termination, except for adventitious facts and where the lawsuit was brought.

BERGAN, J. (dissenting). * * * There is a difference of fundamental character between justifying a departure from *lex loci delictus* because the court will not, as a matter of policy, permit a New York owner of a car licensed and insured in New York to escape a liability that would be imposed on him here; and a departure based on the fact a New York resident makes the claim for injury. The first ground of departure is justifiable as sound policy; the second is justifiable only if one is willing to treat the rights of a stranger permitted to sue in New York differently from the way a resident is treated. Neither because of "interest" nor "contact" nor any other defensible ground is it proper to say in a court of law that the rights of one man whose suit is accepted shall be adjudged differently on the merits on the basis of where he happens to live. * * *

What the court is deciding today is that although it will prevent a New York car owner from asserting the defense of a protective foreign statute when a New York resident in whose rights it has an "interest" sues; it has no such "interest" when it accepts the suit in New York of a nonresident. This is an inadmissible distinction.

The order should be affirmed. * * *

Notes and Questions on Unprovided-For Cases

1. ***The Neumeier Pattern***. With *Neumeier* you have seen the last permutation of a guest-statute conflict, after having seen *Babcock* (false conflict), *Milkovich* (not-so-false), and *Foster/Cipolla* (true conflict). For those who subscribe to the assumptions of interest analysis, especially Currie's personal-law principle, *Neumeier* would be a no-interest or unprovided-for case that should be governed by the law of the forum as such. However, as *Neumeier* illustrates, not all courts subscribe to these assumptions. In fact, as noted earlier, only the *Erwin* court did.

Neumeier involved the same pattern as *Erwin*--in both cases, each party was domiciled in a state whose law favored the other party, and both the conduct and the injury occurred in the victim's home state. *Neumeier* applied the law of the victim's home state, while *Erwin* applied the law of the defendant's home state. A recent study has identified ten other cases involving the *Neumeier/Erwin* pattern. Five of those cases reached the same result as *Neumeier*, and five reached the same result as *Erwin*, though not for the same reasons. For citations and discussion, see Symeonides, *The Revolution Today*, §§ 147-48, 150.

2. Erny v. Estate of Merola, 792 A.2d 1208 (N.J.2002) is representative of the latter cases. As in *Neumeier* and *Erwin*, the plaintiff was domiciled in the accident state (New Jersey) that had a pro-defendant statute, and the two defendants were domiciled in a state (New York) that had a pro-plaintiff statute. The court managed to classify this as a false conflict in which New Jersey was uninterested and New York was interested in applying its law. The court found that the New Jersey statute

was designed to protect certain defendants and to reduce the costs of car insurance and, since neither defendant was domiciled in New Jersey nor drove a car insured there, New Jersey did not have an interest in applying the statute. In contrast, said the court, "New York placed more value in protecting the innocent victim * * * than reducing the cost of automobile insurance," id. at 1218, and this policy was "aimed at protecting innocent victims of New York vehicle registrants, whether injured or harmed in New York or elsewhere," id. at 1219, regardless of whether they were domiciled in or outside New York. Id. at 1220. In addition, said the court, the New York statute "encourages [New York] drivers to insure more adequately their vehicles and, inferentially, to drive with care." Id. Thus, that statute "expresses a weightier interest in both compensation and deterrence than does the New Jersey statute." Id. Consequently, the court concluded, application of the New York statute in this case, which "involv[ed] only New York defendants whose cars are registered and insured in New York [would] further that governmental interest," id., while application of the New Jersey statute "would not further New Jersey's interest in reducing liability insurance rates." Id. at 1220-21.

In concluding that New York had an interest in protecting non-New York victims injured outside New York, the New Jersey court relied on a 1970 federal district court case and conveniently overlooked *Neumeier*. Yet, the question remains: "Was the New York rule really intended to be manna for the entire world?" *Neumeier*, supra.

3. Miller v. Gay, 470 A.2d 1353 (Pa.Super.1984), is a guest-statute case identical to *Neumeier*. *Miller* arose out of a Delaware accident involving a Pennsylvania host-driver and a Delaware guest-passenger. Delaware, but not Pennsylvania, had a guest statute. The court applied the Delaware guest statute, barring the action, after concluding that neither state's relationship was more significant, and that reliance on state interests could not resolve the conflict. The court quoted *Cipolla*'s statement that defendants acting in their own state "should not be put in jeopardy of liability exceeding that created by their state's laws just because a visitor from a state offering higher protection decides to visit there." See supra 198. The *Miller* court turned this statement around as follows: "Analogously, we conclude that inhabitants of a state (here Delaware) should not be accorded rights not given by their home states, just because a visitor from a state offering higher protection decides to visit there." Id at 1356. Fair enough?

Nodak Mut. Ins. Co. v. American Family Mut. Ins. Co., 604 N.W.2d 91 (Min. 2000) and Boomsma v. Star Transp., Inc., 202 F. Supp.2d 869 (E.D.Wis.2002), illustrate that even cases decided in better-law states may end up applying the pro-defendant law of the accident state in *Neumeier*-type situations. *Nodak* involved an insurance subrogation dispute arising from a North Dakota accident between a North Dakota driver and a Minnesota driver. North Dakota law favored the Minnesota insurer, while Minnesota law favored the North Dakota insurer. Predictably, each insurer invoked the law of the other state. The North Dakota insurer argued that Minnesota law should govern because Minnesota had a "strong interest in not allowing its insurers to recover no-fault benefits from out-of-state insurers," 604 N.W.2d at 95, under another state's law so as to prevent those insurers from receiving "a windfall." Id. The court turned the argument around by pointing out that, if Minnesota law were applied then it would be the North Dakota insurer who would receive a windfall, because it would be able "to avoid paying * * * money that it might otherwise have to pay" under North Dakota law. Id. In the end, the court applied the law of North Dakota, in part because, in the absence of special circumstances, "the state where the accident occurred has the strongest governmental interest." Id. at 96.

In *Boomsma*, a Wisconsin federal court reached a similar result by applying Wisconsin's pro-defendant law, rather than Illinois' pro-plaintiff law, to a wrongful death action arising from a Wisconsin accident involving Wisconsin victims and an Illinois driver. The court acknowledged that Wisconsin's cap on wrongful death damages was not intended to protect foreign defendants, but concluded that Wisconsin law should govern because the plaintiffs failed to rebut the Second Restatement's *lex loci* presumption. After noting that "plaintiffs had no 'justified expectation' that Illinois law would apply to their claims," 202 F. Supp.2d at 879, the court observed: "[A]pplication of Illinois law * * * would endorse a kind of lottery system for Wisconsin plaintiffs who are injured in Wisconsin. The 'winners' of the lottery would be those injured by tortfeasors from other states that do not cap wrongful death damages. The 'losers' would be those injured by fellow Wisconsinites, against whom recovery is limited." Id.

In your opinion, which of the above *Neumeier*-pattern cases reached a better resolution of the choice-of-law question, and why?

4. ***The Converse-Neumeier Pattern (Hurtado)*** Suppose that in *Neumeier* the accident had occurred in New York, rather than Ontario. Since the law of each state would still favor the domiciliary of the other state, would not this case qualify as a no-interest case under interest analysis? The answer to this question depends on the policy that the court ascribes to the pro-plaintiff law of the accident state. If the court concludes that this law is motivated by a policy of deterring tortfeasors, then the accident state becomes interested in applying that law in order to deter conduct in that state. Thus, a potential no-interest case becomes a false conflict. Right or wrong, most courts have reached this conclusion in cases of this pattern. See Symeonides, *The Revolution Today* §§ 149-50.

One of these cases is Hurtado v. Superior Court, 522 P.2d 666 (Cal.1974). *Hurtado* was a wrongful death action filed by the survivors of a Mexico domiciliary who was killed in a California accident caused by the negligence of a California driver. Mexico, but not California, limited the amount of wrongful-death damages. The court concluded that Mexico did not have an interest in applying its pro-defendant limited-damages rule to non-Mexican defendants at the expense of Mexican plaintiffs. Based on the same premise, the court could have concluded that California also did not have an interest in applying its pro-plaintiff rule for the benefit of non-California plaintiffs at the expense of California defendants. However, the court found that the California rule was designed to deter negligent conduct in California. The court stated that California's "primary purpose" in creating a cause of action for wrongful death was not so much to compensate the victim as "to deter the kind of conduct within its borders which wrongfully takes life," id. at 671, and that the unlimited-damages aspect of the rule simply "strengthen[ed] the deterrent aspect of the civil sanction." Id. Thus, the court essentially reclassified the California rule as conduct-regulating. Hence, the court could not avoid the conclusion that California had an interest in applying the rule. As the court stated, "when the defendant is a resident of California and the tortious conduct * * * occurs here, California's deterrent policy of full compensation is clearly advanced by application of its own law." Id. at 671-72. Thus, what might have been a no-interest case, became a false conflict. The next case Kaiser-Georgetown Community Health Plan, Inc. v. Stutsman, 491 A.2d 502 (D.C.1985), infra 248, follows a similar analysis. You may reserve your opinion until you read that case.

A NOTE ON THE *NEUMEIER* RULES

The long-term importance of *Neumeier* lies in the three rules that the court enunciated for the resolution of guest-statute conflicts. The subsequent disappearance of guest statutes would have rendered these rules obsolete, but, as we shall see later, the same court expanded the scope of these rules to cover conflicts between rules of loss-distribution other than guest statutes. For this reason, and because New York has been the *avant-garde* of the conflicts revolution, the *Neumeier* rules continue to be important.

The following table illustrates the operation of these rules. In this table, the letters A, B, C, and D denote states. The abbreviation "Pro-D" indicates that the particular state has a pro-defendant loss-distribution rule, such as a guest statute, an immunity rule, or a limit on the amount of damages. The abbreviation "Pro-P" indicates that the state has a pro-plaintiff rule, such as the absence of guest statute, immunity rule, or other limits on recovery. The shading indicates the state whose law governs under the *Neumeier* rules, subject of course to the exceptions the rules provide. The first column indicates the applicable *Neumeier* rule, the second column indicates the various permutations of each rule, and the last column notes representative cases falling within each permutation.

TABLE 4. THE *NEUMEIER* RULES

Rule	Pattern	P's dom	*locus delicti*	D's dom	Case
1	a	A(Pro-P)	B(Pro-D)	A(Pro-P)	*Babcock*
1	b	B(Pro-D)	A(Pro-P)	B(Pro-D)	*Milkovich*
2	a	A(Pro-P)	B(Pro-D)	B(Pro-D)	*Foster/Cipolla*
2	b	A(Pro-P)	A(Pro-P)	B(Pro-D)	*Biscoe*

Rule	Pattern	P's dom	*locus delicti*	D's dom	Case
3	a	A(Pro-D)	A(Pro-D)	B(Pro-P)	*Neumeier*
3	b	A(Pro-D)	B(Pro-P)	B(Pro-P)	*Hurtado*
3	c	A(Pro-P)	B(Pro-D)	C(Pro-P)	
3	d	A(Pro-D)	B(Pro-P)	C(Pro-D)	
3	e	A(Pro-P)	B(Pro-D)	C(Pro-D)	
3	f	A(Pro-P)	B(Pro-P)	C(Pro-D)	
3	g	A(Pro-D)	B(Pro-D)	C(Pro-P)	
3	h	A(Pro-D)	B(Pro-P)	C(Pro-P)	

1. *Rule 1: Common-Domicile Cases. Neumeier* Rule 1 requires the application of the law of the parties' common domicile[1] in both the *Babcock* pattern and its converse (*Milkovich*), namely, regardless of whether the common-domicile law favors the victim or the tortfeasor. As noted supra at 176-78, this rule conforms with the results of the vast majority of cases involving these two patterns, as well as with rules adopted in other countries. Rule 1 does not allow any exceptions. As you remember from *Milkovich*, and as you will see in *Schultz*, infra 261, the rule encounters opposition in cases falling within the converse-*Babcock* pattern.

Notice that Rule 1 requires that the parties be domiciled in "the same state" for that state's law to apply. If the parties are domiciled in different states that have identical laws, as in patterns 3c and 3d, these cases would fall not within the scope of Rule 1 but rather within the scope of Rule 3, which calls for the application of the *lex loci*, subject to the escape Rule 3 provides. While it is likely that a court will avoid the *lex loci* by using the escape, would it not be preferable if Rule 1 directly authorized this result in these false conflicts? See supra 178.

2. *Rule 2: Split-Domicile True Conflicts.* Rule 2 deals with split-domicile cases that present the true conflict paradigm. The first sentence of Rule 2 (hereinafter **Rule 2a**) addresses situations of the *Foster/Cipolla* pattern (see supra 211-14), in which the conduct and injury occur in the tortfeasor's home state whose law protects him, while the victim is domiciled in a state whose law protects her. (See pattern 2a, supra.) Rule 2a unhesitantly directs the application of the law of the tortfeasor's domicile, without allowing any exceptions.

The second sentence of Rule 2 (hereinafter **Rule 2b**) addresses situations of the *Biscoe* pattern (supra 214-15), in which a person is injured in her home state whose law protects her, while the tortfeasor is domiciled in a state whose law protects him. (Pattern 2b.) Rule 2b provides that the law of the victim's domicile governs, but this time an escape is available since that law applies "in the absence of special circumstances."

When, as Rule 2 contemplates, *both* the conduct and the injury occur in the same state, Rule 2 produces results that are consistent with those reached by the

---

1. Rule 1 also requires that the car be registered in the state of the common domicile. Only one post-*Neumeier* case discussed this requirement and found it insignificant. See Gyory v. Radgowski, 369 N.Y.S.2d 583, 586–87 (Sup.Ct.1974). Obviously, this requirement is meaningless in conflicts not involving a traffic accident.

majority of cases in other states. See supra 211-15. However, the application of Rule 2 to *cross-border* conflicts encounters considerable difficulties. For example, in a case in which the plaintiff is injured in her home state whose law protects her, as a result of the defendant's conduct in his home state whose law protects him, both Rules 2a and 2b are applicable and they point in opposite directions. Similarly, if, in the same case, the conduct occurred in a third state, a conflict arises between Rule 2b and Rule 3. These problems are discussed later. See infra 268-70.

3. *Rule 3: All Other Cases.* Rule 3 is the residual rule, covering all situations falling outside the scope of Rules 1 and 2. As the above table illustrates, these "other situations" are quite numerous. In fact, they are even more numerous if one differentiates between the places of conduct and injury, or considers cases involving multiple plaintiffs or multiple defendants. According to the "less categorical" Rule 3, all of those cases are to be governed by the *lex loci delicti*, subject to the escape the rule provides.

Pattern 3a is the *Neumeier* pattern, in which the conduct and the injury occur at the victim's home state whose law protects the tortfeasor who is domiciled in another state. Pattern 3b is the converse pattern (*Hurtado*) in which the conduct and the injury occur in the tortfeasor's home state whose law protects the victim who is domiciled in another state. Both of these patterns present the no-interest paradigm, but Rule 3 calls for the application of the *lex loci*, rather than the *lex fori*. As noted earlier, this is consistent with the results reached by courts in other states. See supra 242-45.

Patterns 3c–3h describe some of the remaining permutations, which Rule 3 presumptively assigns to the *lex loci delicti*. In all of them, the parties are domiciled in different states and have an accident in a *third* state. Patterns 3c and 3d are functionally equivalent to the false conflicts present in patterns 1a (*Babcock*) and 1b (*Milkovich*), respectively. Similarly, patterns 3g and 3h are functionally analogous to the no-interest cases of Patterns 3a (*Neumeier*) and 3b (*Hurtado*), respectively. Finally, patterns 3e and 3f are analogous to the true conflicts of Patterns 2a (*Foster*) and 2b (*Biscoe*), respectively, except that a third state is now involved.

Pattern 3f was involved in Cook v. Goodhue, 842 F.Supp. 1509 (N.D.N.Y. 1994), which arose out of a New York traffic accident involving a Texas plaintiff and an Ontario defendant. The Ontario defendant invoked an Ontario rule that limited non-pecuniary damages to $240,000. Neither New York nor Texas imposed such a limitation. The court held that, under *Neumeier* Rule 3, New York law should govern unless the defendant satisfied the requirements for following the escape. Defendant argued that: (a) these circumstances are satisfied if displacing the *lex loci delicti* would promote the substantive policies of *either* of the other states involved in the conflict; and (b) since the application of Ontario's damages cap would promote Ontario's policy of protecting Ontario defendants, the requirements were satisfied in this case. "This is not so." said the court. "There is no 'either' in the rule. Otherwise, it would be very easy for a party to demonstrate that the application of a particular state's law will advance the purposes of that law. * * * Defendant must show that the purposes of *all* relevant substantive laws will be advanced by application of Canada's limit. This requirement includes the laws of New York and

Texas, as well as Canada." Id. at 1511 (emphasis added). Do you agree with this statement? Why?

4. Now step back and look at the shaded cells in the above table. Is it true that, subject to some escapes, the *Neumeier* rules require the application of the *lex loci* in all cases, except those in which both parties are domiciled in the same state? If so, did we need a revolution to reach this result?

Kaiser-Georgetown Comty. Health Plan, Inc. v. Stutsman
District of Columbia Court of Appeals, 1985, 491 A.2d 502.

MACK, J. This case presents a choice-of-law issue in the context of a medical malpractice action. Defendants, appellants here, are two District of Columbia corporations, Kaiser-Georgetown Community Health Plan, Inc. (Kaiser), a health maintenance organization (HMO), and Capital Area Permanente Medical Group, P.C. (Capital), a provider of health care that has contracted to provide health care services at medical facilities operated by Kaiser.

Plaintiff-appellee, Mary Stutsman, is a resident of Arlington County, Virginia, and is employed in the District. Mrs. Stutsman was enrolled as a Kaiser HMO subscriber and received health care from several physicians employed by Capital at Kaiser's Springfield, Virginia, medical facility. She brought this action in the Superior Court for malpractice arising out of the alleged negligence of Capital's employees. In the complaint, recovery is sought only as against Kaiser and Capital under a theory of respondeat superior. * * *

II. Appellants contend that the law of Virginia must be applied to this action because certain facts in this case--the plaintiff's residence in Virginia and her treatment there--demonstrate that Virginia has the most substantial contact with the events underlying the claim, and therefore the greater interest in the application of its law. They further argue that Virginia has a substantial public policy interest in limiting liability of providers of health care operating within that State. In this regard, the common law of malpractice has been modified in Virginia by the Virginia Medical Malpractice Act [cit.]. For acts of malpractice by "health care providers" occurring after April 1977 and prior to October 1983, the Act sets a $750,000 cap on liability [cit.]. Appellants maintain that they are "health care providers" within the meaning of the Act, that its liability-limiting provisions are therefore applicable to them, and that to apply District law (which does not limit liability) would frustrate the public policy of the State of Virginia expressed in the Malpractice Act. * * *

B. CHOICE OF LAW. Assuming, without deciding, that appellants are correct in their prediction that a Virginia court would decide to apply the Malpractice Act to protect both defendants in these circumstances, we nevertheless use our own choice-of-law principles to determine the law to be applied in an action filed in our courts, over which we indisputably have jurisdiction.

In this case we have before us "a set of facts giving rise to a lawsuit [that] justif[ies], in constitutional terms, application of the law of more than one jurisdiction." *Allstate Insurance Co. v. Hague*, 449 U.S. 302, 307 (1981) [Ch. 5] (plurality opinion). Appellants describe this case as involving "conduct occurring entirely within the Commonwealth of Virginia and asserted by one Virginia resident against two corporate residents of Virginia." [cit.] The case could just as easily be described as involving the vicarious liability of two District of Columbia corporations for medical malpractice upon a member of the District's workforce residing in the D.C. metropolitan area, whose relationship with the defendants grew out of her employment status within the District. *See Allstate*, 449 U.S. at 315 n.21.

Mrs. Stutsman's Virginia residence, contrary to appellants' assertion, does not mandate the application of Virginia law to this action, *see id.* at 315. At the time of the injury, Stutsman was employed within the District, and "[e]mployment status is not a sufficiently less important status than residence," when combined with other contacts, to prohibit our use of District of Columbia law and to require us to apply Virginia law here, *id.* at 317.

Similarly, we need not give controlling significance to the fact that the misdiagnosis of plaintiff's disease by employees of the defendants occurred in Virginia. A tort "need not occur within a particular jurisdiction for that jurisdiction to be connected to the occurrence. Numerous cases have applied the law of a jurisdiction other than the situs of the injury where there existed some other link between that jurisdiction and the occurrence." *Id.* at 314 & n.19 (citations omitted). Most jurisdictions have rejected the "wooden *lex loci delicti* doctrine," *id.* at 316 n.22, which in the past was the majority rule of decision governing choice-of-law in tort cases. [cit.] Where the location of the injury may be described as "fortuitous," the court is not bound by the law of the place of the tort. * * *

The relationship between the parties to the instant litigation can be described as centering around the District of Columbia, since the agreement to provide health care was a benefit of the plaintiff's District employment. The contract for health services between the parties does not specify that the plaintiff would be treated at Kaiser's Virginia clinic. Appellants do not take issue with plaintiff's assertion that she could have as easily requested treatment at the clinic closest to her workplace, in the District. In this sense, the happenstance of the alleged misdiagnosis in Virginia could be characterized as a "fortuity."

Further, there is nothing so "arbitrary [ ]or fundamentally unfair" amounting to a denial of due process in the adjudication of these defendants' negligence by the standards of the District, *see Allstate*, 449 U.S. at 313, 320 (Opinion of Brennan, J.); *id.* at 326 (Stevens, J., concurring). Both defendants are District of Columbia corporations, with primary places of business here. Neither can "claim unfamiliarity with the laws of [this] jurisdiction [or] surprise that the state courts might apply forum law to litigation in which [they are] involved." *Id.* at 317-18 (Opinion of Brennan, J.). There can be no "unfair surprise" to these defendants nor any "frustration of legitimate expectations" in our application of the District's law of negligence, for the defendants were aware that the plaintiff was both a resident of the metropolitan area[9] and a District employee. In addition, at the time the plaintiff

---

9. In this regard, we note with approval the remarks of the circuit court in *Gaither v. Myers*, 404 F.2d 216, 223 (1968): "It is true that [the District's] compensatory policy has the greatest relevance to cases when the mishap occurs in the District and when District residents are plaintiffs. However, to confine the benefits

(continued...)

became enrolled in the Kaiser plan, the defendants had no expectation that she would patronize only the Virginia clinic.

Although we are not bound to apply Virginia law here, we should choose to do so if, under our choice-of-law principles, we find that Virginia's interest in this litigation is substantial, and that application of District law would frustrate a clearly articulated public policy of that state.

In tort cases our decisions have used "governmental interests" analysis to determine whether we will apply our law to an action. [cit.] This approach requires us "to evaluate the governmental policies underlying the applicable laws and to determine which jurisdiction's policy would be most advanced by having its law applied to the facts of the case under review." *Williams*, 390 A.2d [4,] at 5-6 [D.C. 1978]. "When the policy of one state would be advanced by application of its law, and that of another state would not be advanced by application of its law, a false conflict appears and the law of the interested state prevails." Biscoe, 738 F.2d at 1360. A true conflict is presented when both states have an interest in applying their own laws to the underlying facts; in that event, the forum law will be applied unless the foreign state has a greater interest in the controversy. *Id.*;[10] [cit.]

An analysis of the competing interests of the District of Columbia and of Virginia in the application of their own laws and furtherance of their separate public policies in this litigation reveals no real conflict.

The District of Columbia has a substantial interest in this litigation. Both defendants are corporate citizens of the District of Columbia. The District has a significant interest, reflected in the fact that it imposes no cap on liability for malpractice, in holding its corporations liable for the full extent of the negligence attributable to them. See Allstate, 449 U.S. at 318 (Opinion of Brennan, J.).

In addition, the District has an interest in protecting a member of its work force who contracts for health services with a District of Columbia corporation within this forum and then is injured by the negligence of that corporation's agents. The plurality opinion in *Allstate* recognized a plaintiff's employment status within the forum state as "a very important contact" for choice of law purposes. 449 U.S. at 313. The importance of this contact derives from the fact that "[t]he State of employment has police power responsibilities towards the nonresident employee that are analogous, if somewhat less profound, than towards residents." *Id.* at 314. The work force of the forum state, wrote Justice Brennan, "is surely affected by the level of protection the State extends to it, either directly or indirectly. Vindication of the rights of [a plaintiff who is employed within the forum state], therefore, is an

---

9. (...continued)
of the [District's] rule to the territory ceded by the states of Maryland and Virginia to form the Nation's Capital would be to shun the present reality of the economically and socially integrated greater metropolitan area. It is a commonplace that residents of Maryland [and Virginia] are part of the Washington metropolitan trading area, and that District residents and businesses have an interest in the well-being of the[ ] citizens of [those] State[s]."

10. "The forum State's interest in the fair and efficient administration of justice" together with the "substantial savings [that] can accrue to the State's judicial system" when its judges are "able to apply law with which [t]he[y are] thoroughly familiar or can easily discover," tilt the balance in favor of applying the law of the forum state when the interests of both jurisdictions are equally weighty. See *Allstate*, 449 U.S. at 326 & n.14 (Stevens, J., concurring).

important state concern." *Id.* at 315.

Justice Powell, in his dissent in *Allstate*, agreed that forum employment "provides a significant contact for furtherance of some local policies," *id.* at 338–39, but argued that forum employment should be considered a sufficiently substantial contact to ground the use of local law by a court of the forum to decide the case only if the plaintiff's employment "form[s] a reasonable link between the litigation and a state policy," *id.* at 334. In other words, in the dissent's view, a state may use the plaintiff's employment within the forum as a basis for application of its own law only when there is "some connection between the facts giving rise to the litigation and the scope of the State's lawmaking jurisdiction." *Id.*

In *Allstate*, Minnesota had applied its law to an insurance dispute between a Wisconsin resident and a corporation doing business in Wisconsin and Minnesota; the dispute arose out of an accident between two Wisconsin residents. The *Allstate* plurality's decision upholding Minnesota's choice of law was based, *inter alia*, on the plaintiff's Minnesota employment. The dissent found no link between the plaintiff's forum employment and the litigation sufficient to uphold Minnesota's choice of law, for none of the issues involved in the litigation was "in any way affected or implicated by the [plaintiff's] employment status." *Id.* at 339 (Powell, J., dissenting).

In this case, in contrast, the relationship between the parties to the litigation grew out of the plaintiff's employment within the District. Even the dissent in *Allstate*, we believe, would uphold our choice of District law in this case, for the facts demonstrate the link required by Justice Powell between the plaintiff's employment here and the relationship between the parties that gave rise to the litigation.

We have found both significant contacts between the facts underlying this action and this forum, and a substantial interest by the District of Columbia in the application of its law to the case. We proceed to consider the corresponding interests of the State of Virginia.

Although Virginia undoubtedly has an interest in the welfare of its residents, the Malpractice Act, which appellants contend is the applicable Virginia law, cannot be said to further that interest in these circumstances. The above-described screening process that in most cases is a prerequisite to suit in malpractice cases, together with the cap on ultimate liability, were enacted into law by the State with the primary purpose of protecting Virginia health care providers from excessive liability. The statute may also have the effect of lowering malpractice premiums for health care providers operating in Virginia. Thus, Virginia residents may benefited incidentally by the Act in that the cost of medical malpractice insurance passed on to them through medical fees will be less than it would have been had the statute not been enacted. Nonetheless, the primary purpose of the Act is to protect Virginia health care providers from claimants who seek to recover damages in excess of the amount the Virginia legislature has deemed to be generally acceptable. Virginia undoubtedly has a general interest in the full compensation of its residents for injuries incurred by the negligence of another. Virginia has determined, however, that in the area of medical malpractice, its public policy interest in the limitation of liability of health care provider defendants may outweigh its interest in the full compensation of injured plaintiffs. Thus the Malpractice Act, which appellants argue would be applicable here if we were to decide the case under Virginia law, can in no sense be said to protect the interests of plaintiffs like Mrs. Stutsman.

Although the Malpractice Act applies to all "health care providers" (as the Act defines that term) that are licensed to provide health care in the State of Virginia, the State's interest in the application of its statute becomes attenuated when its intended beneficiaries are foreign corporations with principal places of business outside the State. This is so because the financial impact upon foreign defendants of a finding of liability in excess of the statutory cap will not fall most heavily within Virginia. *See Hitchcock [v. United States]*, 665 F.2d [354,] at 360 [1981].[12] Any financial impact that the State is likely to experience will derive not from the liability of these defendants but from the uncompensated injury of this plaintiff.

It is undoubtedly true that these defendants would be better served were we to apply Virginia's Malpractice Act here. Nevertheless, the interests of the State of Virginia and of these defendants are not identical. The above analysis reveals that the District has a substantial interest in this litigation, and that Virginia's interests would in fact be well-served, and its public policy not contravened, by the application of District law to the action. Accordingly, we affirm the trial court's decision that the District of Columbia's law of negligence is the most appropriate rule of decision in this case.

Notes and Questions

1. Under Currie's version of interest analysis, could *Stutsman* be characterized as a no-interest case? Virginia had a pro-defendant law but the defendants were foreign corporations, while the District of Columbia had a pro-plaintiff law, but the plaintiff was not domiciled there. How did the court conclude that this was "no real conflict" and that only the District was interested in applying its law?

2. What was the basis for the court's conclusion that the District had an interest in protecting the plaintiff? How did the court conclude that the District was interested in applying its unlimited recovery rule *against* the defendants? Is the court's statement that "[t]he District has a significant interest * * * in holding its corporations liable for the full extent of the negligence attributable to them" consistent with Currie's reading of governmental interests?

3. Is the District's unlimited-recovery rule designed to regulate conduct? If so, should the rule apply to conduct that occurs in another state and causes injury there? Compare with *District of Columbia v. Coleman*, supra 210-11.

4. Is the District's unlimited-recovery rule a loss-distribution rule? If so, why

---

12. The court in *Hitchcock* noted: "If a judgment were sustained against the corporation, the financial burden would surely fall on the business as a whole, headquartered out-of-state, rather than on the individual clinic. Virginia would thus not have the usual interest in having its law decide the financial responsibility of one of its residents. Washington, correspondingly, would have some interest in having its law applied to decide the liability of a business headquartered there, at least where, as here, the District has other substantial contacts with the litigation." 665 F.2d at 360. The *Hitchcock* analysis applies with equal force in this case.

was the District's interest greater than Virginia's? The defendants were domiciled in the District but operated in Virginia. The plaintiff was domiciled in Virginia but worked in the District. If the District's rule of unlimited recovery was a rule of loss distribution, so would be Virginia's rule of limited recovery. Why would Virginia not be interested in the application of its pro-defendant loss-distributing rule to protect a defendant who operated in that state? Could it be argued that, if this were a false conflict at all, it would be one in which *Virginia* was the interested state? Could it be that this was a true conflict in which the court, heeding Currie's call for "rational altruism," engaged in an "enlightened and restrained interpretation" of the law of the *other* state, and thus managed to construe that law away?

5. If *Stutsman* is a case in which the court exhibited "rational altruism," or plaintiff-favoritism, Stutsman v. Kaiser Found. Health Plan, 546 A.2d 367 (D.C.App. 1988) (hereafter *Stutsman II*), illustrates that such favoritism has its limits. *Stutsman II* was an action for loss of consortium filed by Donald Stutsman--the husband of Mary Stutsman, the plaintiff in *Stutsman I* who had died in the meantime. Loss of consortium actions were allowed by the law of the District of Columbia but not by the law of Virginia, which was the domicile of both plaintiffs. Thus the case was similar not only to *Erwin*, supra, but also to *Stutsman I*. Donald argued that, according to *Stutsman I*, the law of the District should apply "since Virginia has no interest in seeing its laws applied to deny recovery to its citizens for any injury perpetrated by District of Columbia corporations." Id. at 372. The district court agreed, but the Court of Appeals reversed. After distinguishing the two actions and emphasizing that "the tort of loss of consortium is a distinct cause of action for injury to the marriage itself," id. at 373, the Court of Appeals saw a "clear" and "obvious" interest on the part of Virginia

> in regulating the legal rights of married couples domiciled in Virginia. In pursuit of this interest, Virginia's legislature has eliminated the common law restrictions on a married woman's capacity to sue by giving a married woman the exclusive right to sue for damages for her personal injuries. [cit.] The purpose of this enactment was to enlarge the personal rights of married women and to grant them separate legal estates * * * [and] to grant the injured wife the sole right to seek damages for her personal injuries.

Id. at 374. Thus, the court concluded that, unlike *Stutsman I*, this was a "real conflict." The District "certainly has an interest in holding its corporations liable for negligent acts attributable to their agents," but "Virginia has the more significant interest." Id. This is so because:

> Virginia has enacted a statute tailored to the specific cause of action asserted here, and under Virginia choice of law principles a Virginia court would apply that state's own law if this case were before it. * * * Virginia has a clearly articulated policy of allowing only the wife to recover for her personal injuries. Under these circumstances we are unpersuaded that the District's interest in holding its corporations liable for their negligent acts outweighs Virginia's interest in establishing the legal rights of married couples residing in that state, particularly where the negligent conduct and the injury to the plaintiff all occurred in the state of the marital domicile. In addition, Virginia's choice of

law rules do not indicate a lesser interest in the application of its substantive law. Had this action been brought originally in Virginia, its courts would have applied Virginia law to Stutsman's loss of consortium claim because the conduct complained of occurred in Virginia. *Frye v. Commonwealth*, 345 S.E.2d 267, 272 (Va.1986); [cit.]. Furthermore, the application of Virginia law to Stutsman's loss of consortium action is consistent with the Stutsmans' reasonable expectations as to the standards by which their marital relations will be governed in the event of suit. * * * Virginia's clearly-expressed interest in regulating the legal rights of married couples domiciled within its borders would be seriously impaired by application of District law to this claim, [cit.], while the District has little recognizable interest in having its law govern the legal relationship of two persons married and living in Virginia. [cit.]

Id. at 374–76. The court distinguished this case from *Stutsman I* on the ground that Mary Stutsman, the plaintiff in *Stutsman I*, was a "'member of [D.C.'s] workforce'," id. at 374, and thus the District had an interest in protecting her. This interest was not present in *Stutsman II*, however, because "[t]he police power responsibilities upon which this interest is based * * * would not be served by permitting [Donald] Stutsman to maintain a suit for loss of consortium, since he is not a member of the District's work force." Id. Is this a valid distinction, or a sufficient reason for such a difference in result? Was Mary's action work-related?

6. Did you notice the use of *renvoi* reasoning in *Stutsman II*? Should that reasoning have been invoked in *Stutsman I*?

7. The *Stutsman II* court interpreted Virginia's rule denying husbands an action for loss of consortium as being an affirmative "policy of allowing *only* the wife to recover for her personal injuries" (emphasis added). The court also spoke repeatedly of Virginia's "obvious interest in regulating the legal rights of married couples domiciled in Virginia." Do you agree with the assumption underlying the first statement, namely, that the rule disallowing consortium actions was intended to regulate the rights of spouses *as between* themselves? Is this assumption consistent with the court's statement that the wife's personal injury action and the husband's loss of consortium action are two distinct actions? Is it not more realistic to assume that Virginia's rule was designed to protect *tortfeasors* from this *additional* exposure to liability? If so, was the court correct to conclude that Virginia's only interest consisted of "regulating the legal rights of married couples domiciled in Virginia"?

8. Compare *Erwin, Stutsman I*, and *Stutsman II*. The cases may not be reconcilable, but is it fair for critics, such as the author of these Notes, to criticize all three?

9. If the reasoning of *Stutsman I* and *II* cannot be reconciled, are the two cases *together* an example of Solomonian justice? Having accorded Mary Stutsman the benefit of the forum's generous personal-injury law, might the court have thought that it would be too much to do likewise with regard to Donald Stutsman's loss of consortium action? Nevertheless, did the Stutsman family not fare better financially than they would have fared had they sued in Virginia?

10. Read again footnote 9 of *Stutsman I*. Does "the present reality of the economically and socially integrated greater metropolitan area" that cuts across the

boundaries of three different jurisdictions mean that we may disregard such boundaries for choice-of-law purposes?

Ardoyno v. Kyzar
United States District Court, E.D. Louisiana, 1976.
426 F.Supp. 78.

RUBIN, J. Plaintiffs in this action are Louisiana domiciliaries, practicing law in Louisiana. A substantial portion of their business, as the facts of this case suggest, involves representation of Mississippi domiciliaries. In October, 1975, plaintiffs executed a contract in Louisiana to represent Mr. Fauver, a Mississippi domiciliary, in the courts of Louisiana. Mr. Kyzar, the defendant and also a Mississippi domiciliary, allegedly attempted to interfere with this contract through remarks made in Mississippi to Mr. Fauver. In addition to the action for interference with contractual relations, plaintiffs have alleged an action in slander based on the same remarks.

* * * The threshold issue in determining both these motions is whether the law of Louisiana or Mississippi is applicable. Mississippi law allows punitive damages for slander, [cit.], while Louisiana does not, [cit.]. Also, Louisiana does not recognize a cause of action for interference with a contract, [cit.], while Mississippi does. [cit.]
* * *

Because this Court is sitting in Louisiana, it is bound to follow the Louisiana approach to conflicts of law. *Klaxon* [infra Ch.6] * * * [U]nder [Louisiana's] *Jagers--Brinkley* approach, conflict analysis consists of two distinct steps. The first is to determine whether a false or true conflict exists. If a false conflict exists, as in *Jagers*, the law of the state that has the exclusive interest is applied. If the conflict is a true one, the court proceeds to the second stage and applies the principles of the Second Restatement to determine which of the competing interests ought to prevail. This analysis must be performed separately for every significant issue in the case, for, under interest analysis, "cases can be expected to arise with some frequency where different states have the greatest concern in the determination of different issues." Reese, Dépeçage: A Common Phenomenon in Choice of Law, 73 Columbia L.Rev. 58, 59 (1973).

I. INTERFERENCE WITH CONTRACTUAL RELATIONS. Application of Louisiana law is mandated by the *Brinkley* decision. *Brinkley and West, Inc. v. Foremost Insurance Co.*, 499 F.2d 928 (5th Cir.1974). *Brinkley* specifically held that Louisiana courts would not entertain a contractual interference action brought by a Louisiana resident against an outside predator, where that contract was made and performable within Louisiana. [cit.]

Plaintiffs' attempt to distinguish *Brinkley* is unpersuasive. They contend that, because the employer is a client and the employee is a lawyer, and because the outside predator (Mr. Kyzar) is not a competing employer, Louisiana's policy of ensuring the mobility of the labor force will not be served by applying Louisiana law.[5] This policy has been achieved by permitting anyone who believes that the employee who is restricted by his contract would be best served by employment elsewhere to induce that party to abandon his contract, while preserving the employer's contract action against the errant employee. If Louisiana were interested in allowing only competing employers to jeopardize an employment relation, or not interested in promoting fluidity in the employment of lawyers, presumably it would have provided an exception for such situations, as it has for instances of fraud or deception. It has not done so, and a federal court should not entertain a diversity case that a state court would likely dismiss.

Even if *Brinkley* were not dispositive, the case would simply present a false conflict. Louisiana, as noted, has an interest in labor mobility. It has the interest of every forum in applying its own law for purposes of ease of application, familiarity, and sound judicial administration. Louisiana courts are understandably reluctant to interpret the law of a sovereign sister state.

Mississippi, on the other hand, has no interest in having its law applied. Its interest in protecting employment contracts from interference is necessarily limited to contracts that will be performed in Mississippi or executed there. See *Brinkley*, supra. It is only with regard to such contracts that Mississippi can promote stability of contractual relations in Mississippi, or the commercial attractiveness of Mississippi as a place to contract.

The only situation in which Mississippi might pretend to an interest in a contract executed and to performed in another state, would be one where a Mississippian is a party to that contract and invokes the benefits of Mississippi law. Such is not the case here, as it is a Louisiana plaintiff who seeks the benefits of Mississippi law. Simply put, Mississippi is interested only in protecting Mississippi residents[8] and Mississippi contracts.

Because Mississippi has no interest in having its law apply, and Louisiana does have such an interest, Louisiana law ought to prevail. There is no need to resort to the provisions of the Second Restatement to resolve this conflict for no conflict exists.

II. THE ACTION FOR SLANDER. Unlike the claim for interference with contractual relations, this cause involves a true conflict. As in the interference action, Mississippi has no interest in extending the protection of its law to a Louisiana plaintiff. Mississippi has an interest only in protecting Mississippi domiciliaries. However, it does maintain an interest in preventing intentional torts committed, and causing injury, within its boundaries.[10]

---

5. According to the *Brinkley* court, "For conflicts purposes, the Louisiana rule suggests a strong domestic interest in protecting the labor force of the state from impediments to the job mobility that could conceivably occur if the original employer could threaten suit against the outside predator." 499 F.2d, at 934.

8. * * * A state's interest is always limited to its own domiciliaries or to acts that occur or have consequences within its borders. * * * Currie, Selected Essays in The Conflict of Laws, supra. at 85.

10. This is not a reversion to a vested rights approach, but an attempt to assay Mississippi's interests. Those interests will often correspond with the state's territorial limits. Mississippi has an interest in what speed limits are observed in its borders regardless of the domicile of the wrongdoer. A state has an interest in deterring torts that cause harm within its borders. While the court in *Jagers* concluded that Mississippi had no interest in applying its law on intra-family tort immunity to two Louisiana domiciliaries in a Mississippi accident, this is because intra-family tort immunity affects the relation of the family members.

(continued...)

The alleged interference with contract caused no injury in which Mississippi could properly be interested. The slander, however, gave rise to an injury within Mississippi, for, although the defamed party resided in Louisiana, his reputation suffered in Mississippi.[11] Mississippi has an interest in applying its punitive damage provisions to deter such slander.

Louisiana has an interest in avoiding speculative punitive damages in slander cases. If this interest is restricted to avoiding speculative damages against Louisiana domiciliaries, it would not be frustrated by applying Mississippi law in this case, and a false conflict would exist. We shall assume, however, that Louisiana's interest is in protecting the integrity of its judicial system, rather than domestic defendants, from what it might consider inherently speculative awards. Having discerned an interest of both Mississippi and Louisiana in having their law applied, we turn to the principles of the Second Restatement to resolve the conflict.

Section 149 of the Second Restatement explicitly provides: "In an action for defamation, the local law of the state where the publication occurs determines the rights and liabilities of the parties, except as stated in § 150 (on multistate defamation), unless, with respect to the particular issue, some other state has a more significant relationship under the principles stated in § 6 to the occurrence and the parties, in which event the local law of the other state will be applied."

Hence, unless the factors enumerated in Section 6 dictate otherwise, the Second Restatement would resolve the conflict in favor of the law of Mississippi.

With all due deference to the Fifth Circuit's admonition that several of the Section 6 factors are unhelpful in the tort area, *Brinkley*, supra, we find that in this case the factors enumerated do indeed aid in the determination.

Application of Mississippi law would serve to promote: the needs of the interstate and international system (factor a), for, in deferring to Mississippi law, Louisiana would promote mutual respect and harmonious relations amongst the sister states in their attempts to reconcile competing interests; the protection of justified expectations (factor d) that conduct in one's own state will be regulated by the law of that state;[16] the basic policies underlying the particular field of law (factor e), namely that First Amendment considerations are promoted by applying the law of the place of publication, thereby avoiding a complex of litigation under varying and unanticipated law; certainty, predictability and uniformity of result (factor f), for

---

10. (...continued)
Mississippi would maintain an interest in applying its traffic laws to the accident. Moreover, here the defamation was spoken by a Mississippian to a Mississippian their relation is a proper concern of Mississippi.

Thus, the place of the harm, while a primary determinant under the vested rights approach, remains functional as regards applying interest analysis to intentional torts. * * *

11. As noted, a substantial portion of plaintiff's business involved representation of Mississippians. Without engaging in the metaphysics that earmarked traditional analysis, plaintiff's reputation could be injured only where the alleged slander was heard, and that was in Mississippi.

16. According to Professor Couch, "... it would seem that greater interstate harmony, as well as accommodation of expectations, could be achieved by looking to the place where the events transpired." Couch, Louisiana Adopts Interest Analysis: Applause and Some Observations, 49 Tulane L.Rev. 1, 13 (1974). * * * "The fact of plaintiff's domicile in State A, when everything else occurs in State B, should not be enough to justify the application of the law of A, even by an A court. To put it another way, when a defendant acts entirely within his home state, and has no connection with plaintiff's home state, then the defendant should be subject to his own law, regardless of whether it favors him or not." *Couch*, supra, at 10.

the choice of Louisiana as a forum would not suffice to change the applicable substantive law; and of course the policies of interested states (factor c), namely the Mississippi policy of deterring slander.

Only ease of judicial administration (factor g), and the relevant policies of the forum (factor b), would be served by application of Louisiana law. Although courts ought not merely tally up how many of these factors favor each state, it is apparent that qualitatively as well as quantitatively, these factors favor application of Mississippi law, as presumptively provided for by Section 149.

Moreover, applying Mississippi law is "to subordinate, in the particular case, the external objective of the state whose internal objective will be least impaired." Baxter, Choice of Law and the Federal System, 16 Stan.L.Rev. 1, 18-19 (1963). [cit.] Louisiana has an obvious interest in protecting its domiciliaries from slander. It chose to subordinate that interest to its interest in avoiding speculative punitive damages. This subordinated interest, as well as Mississippi's external interest in deterring slander within its borders, will be attained by application of Mississippi law, while only the external interest of Louisiana in avoiding speculative damages will be frustrated.[19]

Additionally, regardless of any constitutional infirmities or questions of retroactivity, the Louisiana legislature has expressed its new intent that deterring slander through punitive damages is a more important interest.[20] It is the policy of the legislature, whether articulated over-broadly or belatedly, that the Court must discern and apply.[21] Hence, not only does Mississippi have the most significant relation to the cause of action for purposes of the Second Restatement §§ 6, 149, but the current policies of Louisiana and Mississippi regarding punitive damages for slander are best accommodated by application of Mississippi law.

Depecage, or the application of rules of different states to determine different issues in a case, has been well-accepted in conflict analysis. [cit.] Accordingly, Louisiana law ought to govern the interference action and Mississippi law should govern the slander action. * * *

Notes and Questions

1. What was the basis for the court's conclusion that, with regard to the action for interference with contractual relations, *Ardoyno* presented a false conflict? Notice that Louisiana's pro-defendant rule would benefit the Mississippi defendant, while Mississippi's pro-plaintiff rule would benefit the Louisiana plaintiff. If the court were to adopt Currie's personal-law principle, would not this be a no-interest case? Was

---

19. Mississippi has no subordinated interest in avoiding speculative damages since its judicial system is not involved.

20. La.Civ.Code, Art. 2315.1, enacted July 29, 1976, provides punitive damages in slander actions.

21. This decision is not based on the applicability of this new law; therefore, it is unnecessary for us to reach the issues of retroactivity and constitutionality. However, as a general rule, a court in assaying conflicting interests ought be concerned with those policies articulated by the legislature at the time of the judicial determination, not at the time of the relevant transaction. If the legislature has no current interest in promoting the policy, there is little purpose in the court giving weight to it. The court must of course be concerned with the legitimate expectations of the parties that the law applicable at the time they acted will remain controlling for purposes of later judicial determinations. See Currie, Selected Essays, supra, at 643.

the court correct to conclude that Louisiana was an interested state? What was the basis of Louisiana's interest?

2. What was the basis for the court's conclusion that, with regard to punitive damages, *Ardoyno* presented a true conflict? Notice that Louisiana's rule which, at the pertinent time, prohibited punitive damages would benefit the Mississippi defendant, while Mississippi's rule which allowed such damages would benefit the Louisiana plaintiff. Was the court correct to conclude in its preliminary analysis that, in principle, Louisiana had an interest in applying its rule prohibiting punitive damages? What do you make of the court's statement that this rule was designed to protect "the integrity of [Louisiana's] judicial system, rather than domestic defendants" by "avoiding speculative punitive damages in slander cases"? Is the process of assessing punitive damages any more speculative than, say, the process of assessing compensatory damages for a tort victim's pre-death mental pain and suffering or for the survivor's loss of companionship or affection? Be that as it may, was the court correct eventually to subordinate Louisiana's interest? What do you think of the statements contained in footnote 21? Compare these statements with the last two sentences of *Milliken v. Pratt*, supra Ch. 2.

A Note on Dépeçage

1. ***Dépeçage***. Notice that *Ardoyno* applied the laws of two different states in the two causes of action in the same case. *Stutsman I* and *II*, supra, applied the laws of two different states to two separate actions arising from the same facts but adjudicated separately. Both courts described this phenomenon as *dépeçage*. Technically, however, one should reserve the use of the term *dépeçage* for cases in which the court applies the laws of different states to different *substantive issues* in the same *cause of action*. Today, *dépeçage* is widely practiced by American courts and favored by the majority of academic commentators. It is neither a choice-of-law "*doctrine*" (*Bryant v. Silverman*, supra 152, n.1), nor a *goal* of the choice-of-law process. Rather, *dépeçage* is the result, often unintended, of the abandonment of the traditional theory's broad categories and the adoption of issue-by-issue analysis. See Notes after *Babcock*, supra 132. It is also a natural consequence, and an appropriate recognition, of the fact that the states involved in a case may be interested in different aspects of it or interested in varying degrees. As such, *dépeçage* is, *per se*, neither good nor bad.

In some cases, however, the application of the law of two different states to different issues in the same case may unintentionally defeat the policies of both states. In such cases, *dépeçage* is inappropriate and should be avoided. Brainerd Currie, whose analysis inevitably leads to *dépeçage*, warned against the dangers of its extreme use:

> True it is that choice of law must proceed on an issue-by-issue basis; but modern conflict-of-laws analysis can make no more serious mistake than to indulge in an unprincipled eclecticism, picking and choosing from among the available laws in order to reach a result that cannot be squared with the interests of any of the related states. Issue-by-issue analysis should not result in the

cumulation of negative policies to produce a result not contemplated by the law of either state. * * * It is one thing to fall between two stools; it is quite another to put together half a donkey and a half a camel, and then ride to victory on the synthetic hybrid.

Currie "J." in Cavers, *Process* 38, 39.

2. *Guarding Against Inappropriate* **Dépeçage**. The obvious and difficult question is how to distinguish appropriate *dépeçage* from inappropriate *dépeçage*. In this context it is worth recalling that the term *dépeçage* can be paraphrased in English as "picking and choosing." Generally speaking, this *picking and choosing is inappropriate when the rule of one state that is chosen is so closely interrelated to a rule of the same state that is not chosen that applying the one rule without the other would drastically upset the equilibrium established by the two rules and would distort and defeat the policies of that state.*

Suppose for instance that state *A*, a northern state, requires the use of snow tires for cars driven in that state during the winter months and the failure to use such tires is considered "negligence per se." State *B*, a southern state, does not require the use of snow tires. While driving in state *A* without snow tires, a state *B* domiciliary causes an accident resulting in the death of his passenger, also a state *B* domiciliary. In such a case, there is little argument that state *A* has a legitimate reason to insist on adherence to its snow-tire rule and on defining the consequences of non-compliance, and that state *B*'s no-snow-tire rule is simply irrelevant with regard to driving outside its borders. Suppose further that the two states differ in designating the beneficiaries of the victim's survival action, namely, that state *A* designates the victim's spouse as the exclusive beneficiary while state *B* includes as beneficiaries the victim's children. Here again, there is little argument that state *B* has the better claim to apply its law to this issue of loss distribution.

In this case, the resulting *dépeçage* is not inappropriate because the snow-tire rule of state *A* is not closely related, and perhaps not related at all, to the survival-action rule of the same state. The application of the former rule and the non-application of the latter would neither distort nor defeat the policies of that state, nor would such application disturb whatever equilibrium these two rules might establish between deterrence and compensation. The same would be true with regard to the application of state *B*'s survival-action rule without state *B*'s snow-tire rule.

In contrast, if, in the same hypothetical, the conduct-regulating rule and the loss-distributing rule of state *A* were closely interrelated and intended to be applied together as one "package," then to apply one rule without the other would overturn the equilibrium established by that package and would be inappropriate. For example, if state *A*'s snow-tire rule were coupled with a rule that reduced or increased by 10% the amount of damages that could be recovered from a defendant, depending on whether or not the defendant had used snow tires, then it would be inappropriate to apply the snow-tire rule without its intended companion rule regarding the amount of recoverable damages.

3. *Special substantive rules for multistate problems*. If *dépeçage*, that is, the application of the laws of different states to different substantive issues in the same cause of action, is often inappropriate, then what do you think of applying the laws

of different states to the *same* issue? Professor Arthur von Mehren was the first author in this country systematically to explore this idea. See von Mehren, *Special Substantive Rules*. He suggests that one can expediently resolve many true conflicts by compromising the conflicting policies of the involved states rather than by fully vindicating the policies of the one state and completely subordinating those of the other state. This compromise would take the form of a special substantive rule constructed ad hoc for the case at hand and derived from the laws of both or all states involved in the case. For example, one can resolve a true conflict between the strict-liability rule of one state and a no-liability rule of another state by constructing a special substantive rule that would allow the recovery of only half of plaintiff's actual damages, or of certain items only, such as medical expenses and loss of earnings. Id. at 367-69. Similarly, in a situation in which one state has a strict liability rule and a ceiling on recovery and the other state has a negligence rule and unlimited recovery, one can resolve the conflict through a special substantive rule that would allow the plaintiff to recover damages exceeding those imposed by the ceiling of the strict liability state if the plaintiff proves negligence, and below the ceiling if the plaintiff does not prove negligence. See id. at 369-70. For similar suggestions, see Twerski & Mayer, *Pragmatic Solution* (proposing, *inter alia*, that: a guest-statute conflict be resolved by allowing the suit but raising the standard of proof so that the guest-plaintiff can recover only if he proves ordinary negligence by "clear and convincing evidence." Id. at 793; a products liability conflict between a negligence and a strict liability rule be resolved by shifting the burden of proof to the defendant to show the absence of negligence. Id. at 799; a statute of frauds conflict be resolved by allowing the promisee to recover if she can prove the existence of the contract by clear and convincing evidence. Id. at 797).

What do you think of these solutions? They sound anomalous, do they not? But is this because "[w]e have become so accustomed by tradition and theory to ideas of conflict, choice and selection"? Trautman, *Federal Common Law*, 118. In contrast to the so-called "substantive law approach" (see supra Ch. 1 at 7), all the approaches we have studied thus far may differ as to how to resolve conflicts, but they all agree that the only way to do so is to choose and to apply the law of *one* of the states involved in the conflict, rather than to try to seek a common ground between or among such laws. Is it a good idea, in a discipline devoted to resolving conflicts, to reject *a priori* the notion of a compromise, of seeking a middle ground?

4. THE NEW YORK EXPERIENCE AFTER *NEUMEIER*

Schultz v. Boy Scouts of America
Court of Appeals of New York, 1985.
65 N.Y.2d 189, 491 N.Y.S.2d 90, 480 N.E.2d 679.

SIMONS, J. Plaintiffs, Richard E. and Margaret Schultz, instituted this action to recover damages for personal injuries they and their sons, Richard and Christopher, suffered because the boys were sexually abused by defendant Edmund Coakeley and for damages sustained as a result of Christopher's wrongful death after he committed suicide. Coakeley, a brother in the Franciscan order, was the boys' school teacher and leader of their scout troop. Plaintiffs allege that the sexual abuse occurred while Coakeley was acting in those capacities and the causes of action before us on this appeal charge defendants Boy Scouts of America, Inc., and the Brothers of the Poor of St. Francis, Inc. (sued as Franciscan Brothers of the Poor, Inc.), with negligently hiring and supervising him.

Plaintiffs are domiciled in New Jersey and some of the injuries were sustained there. Thus, a choice-of-law issue is presented because New Jersey recognizes the doctrine of charitable immunity and New York does not. Defendants contend New Jersey law governs this litigation and that its courts have already determined that plaintiffs' claims are barred in a separate action against the Roman Catholic Archdiocese of Newark (*see, Schultz v. Roman Catholic Archdiocese*, 472 A.2d 531 [N.J.1984]). Following the rationale of *Babcock v. Jackson* [supra] and similar cases, we hold that New Jersey law applies and that plaintiffs are precluded from relitigating its effect on the claims they assert. * * *

II. A. The choice-of-law question presented in the action against defendant Boy Scouts of America is whether New York should apply its law in an action involving codomiciliaries of New Jersey when tortious acts were committed in New York. This is the posture of the appeal although defendant is a Federally chartered corporation created exclusively for educational and charitable purposes pursuant to an act of Congress ([cit.]) that originally maintained its national headquarters in New Brunswick, New Jersey, but moved to Dallas, Texas, in 1979. New Jersey is considered defendant's domicile because its national headquarters was in that State [cit.]. Its change of domicile after the commission of the wrongs from New Jersey to Texas, which no longer recognizes the doctrine of charitable immunity [cit.], provides New York with no greater interest in this action than it would have without the change. Our decision recognizing a postaccident change in domicile in *Miller v. Miller* (237 N.E.2d 877 [N.Y.1968]) is distinguishable because in that case the defendant's domicile was changed to New York, which was the forum and also the plaintiff's domicile.

The question presented in the action against defendant Franciscan Brothers is what law should apply when the parties' different domiciles have conflicting charitable immunity rules. The Franciscan order is incorporated in Ohio and it is a domiciliary of that State. [cit.] At the time these causes of action arose Ohio, like New Jersey, recognized charitable immunity [cit.]. The Ohio rule denied immunity in actions based on negligent hiring and supervision, however [cit.], whereas New Jersey does not [cit.]. For this reason, no doubt, defendant Franciscan Brothers does not claim Ohio law governs and the choice is between the law of New York and the law of New Jersey.

As for the locus of the tort, both parties and the dissent implicitly assume it is New York because most of Coakeley's acts were committed here. Under traditional rules, the law of the place of the wrong governs all substantive issues in the action [cit.], but when the defendant's negligent conduct occurs in one jurisdiction and the plaintiff's injuries are suffered in another, the place of the wrong is considered to be the place where the last event necessary to make the actor liable occurred [cit.].

Thus, the locus in this case is determined by where the plaintiffs' injuries occurred.

The first and fourth causes of action, the wrongful death of Christopher and plaintiffs' own psychological and other injuries respectively, allege injuries inflicted in New Jersey. New York's only interests in these claims are as the forum State and as the jurisdiction where the tortious conduct underlying plaintiffs' claims against defendants, i.e., the negligent assignment and failure to dismiss Coakeley, occurred. Standing alone, these interests are insufficient to warrant application of New York law, at least when the relevant issue is a loss-distribution rule, like charitable immunity, rather than one regulating conduct [cit.]. The second and third causes of action seek damages for the psychological, emotional and physical injuries suffered by Christopher and Richard Schultz, injuries which occurred in both New York and New Jersey, because a fair reading of the complaint indicates that both boys suffered injuries when Coakeley molested them and also after they returned home. These two causes of action sufficiently implicate New York's interests to require a resolution of the choice-of-law problem in the case.

B. Historically, choice-of-law conflicts in tort actions have been resolved by applying the law of the place of the wrong. In *Babcock v Jackson* [supra], we departed from traditional doctrine, however, and refused to invariably apply the rule of *lex loci delicti* to determine the availability of relief for commission of a tort. * * *

Interest analysis became the relevant analytical approach to choice of law in tort actions in New York. "[The] law of the jurisdiction having the greatest interest in the litigation will be applied and * * * the [only] facts or contacts which obtain significance in defining State interests are those which relate to the purpose of the particular law in conflict" (*Miller v. Miller*, [cit.]). Under this formulation, the significant contacts are, almost exclusively, the parties' domiciles and the locus of the tort (*see*, *Tooker v. Lopez*, [cit.] [Fuld, Ch. J., concurring]; *Neumeier v. Kuehner*, [adopting the three governing rules proposed in *Tooker*, the first and third of which are pertinent to the facts of this appeal]).

Thus, under present rules, most of the nondomicile and nonlocus contacts relied on in *Babcock v. Jackson* (*supra*), such as where the guest-host relationship arose and where the journey was to begin and end, are no longer controlling in tort actions involving guest statutes (*see, Tooker v. Lopez,*). Both *Tooker* and *Neumeier* continued to place some importance on where the automobile involved was insured (*see, Babcock v. Jackson*), but this is not inconsistent with the present rule because usually a defendant host's automobile will be insured in the State of his domicile and also because it reflects a recognition that the insurer, rather than the individually named defendant, is often "the real party in interest" (*Miller v. Miller*). Insofar as issues of liability insurance might also be relevant in a case such as the one before us involving charitable immunity, the record provides no relevant information on the subject.

These decisions also establish that the relative interests of the domicile and locus jurisdictions in having their laws apply will depend on the particular tort issue in conflict in the case. Thus, when the conflicting rules involve the appropriate standards of conduct, rules of the road, for example, the law of the place of the tort "will usually have a predominant, if not exclusive, concern" (*Babcock v. Jackson*; *see*, Restatement [Second] of Conflicts of Law § 145 cmt. d, at 417-18) because the locus jurisdiction's interests in protecting the reasonable expectations of the parties who relied on it to govern their primary conduct and in the admonitory effect that applying its law will have on similar conduct in the future assume critical importance and outweigh any interests of the common-domicile jurisdiction (*see, Babcock v. Jackson*; Restatement [Second] of Conflict of Laws § 145 cmt. d, at 417-18; id. § 146 cmts d, e, at 431-33; *see also, Miller v. Miller*). Conversely, when the jurisdictions' conflicting rules relate to allocating losses that result from admittedly tortious conduct, as they do here, rules such as those limiting damages in wrongful death actions, vicarious liability rules, or immunities from suit, considerations of the State's admonitory interest and party reliance are less important. Under those circumstances, the locus jurisdiction has at best a minimal interest in determining the right of recovery or the extent of the remedy in an action by a foreign domiciliary for injuries resulting from the conduct of a codomiciliary that was tortious under the laws of both jurisdictions (*see, Tooker v. Lopez*; *Miller v. Miller*; *Babcock v. Jackson*). Analysis then favors the jurisdiction of common domicile because of its interest in enforcing the decisions of both parties to accept both the benefits and the burdens of identifying with that jurisdiction and to submit themselves to its authority.[2]

These considerations made the need for change in the *lex loci delicti* rule obvious in *Babcock*, but the validity of this interest analysis is more clearly demonstrated in the split domicile case of *Neumeier v. Kuehner* [*supra*]. In *Neumeier* we applied Ontario's guest statute in an action on behalf of an Ontario decedent against a New York defendant at least in part because the Ontario statute, which contained reciprocal benefits and burdens depending on one's status as either host or guest, was "obviously addressed" to Ontario domiciliaries such as plaintiff's decedent (*id.*). In *Babcock* New York had an important interest in protecting its own residents injured in a foreign State against unfair or anachronistic statutes of that State but it had no similar interest in *Neumeier* in protecting a guest domiciled in Ontario and injured there.

C. As to defendant Boy Scouts, this case is but a slight variation of our *Babcock* line of decisions and differs from them on only two grounds: (1) the issue involved is charitable immunity rather than a guest statute, and (2) it presents a fact pattern which one commentator has characterized as a "reverse" *Babcock* case because New York is the place of the tort rather than the jurisdiction of the parties' common domicile (*see*, Korn, *The Choice-of-Law Revolution: A Critique*, 83 Colum LRev 772, 789).

Although most of our major choice-of-law decisions after *Babcock* involved foreign guest statutes in actions for personal injuries, we have not so limited them, but have applied the *Babcock* reasoning to other tort issues as well ([such as] * * * damage limitation in wrongful death action[s]; * * * vicarious liability of automobile owner for negligence of driver; * * * survivor statute and wrongful death damages;

---

2. New York's rule holding charities liable for their tortious acts, or its rule of nonimmunity as the dissent characterizes it, is also a loss-allocating rule, just as New Jersey's charitable immunity statute is.

* * * statute authorizing direct action against liability insurer; * * * exclusivity of workers' compensation death benefits for industrial accident; * * * [and] * * * charitable immunity). Nor is there any logical basis for distinguishing guest statutes from other loss-distributing rules because they all share the characteristic of being postevent remedial rules designed to allocate the burden of losses resulting from tortious conduct in which the jurisdiction of the parties' common domicile has a paramount interest. There is even less reason for distinguishing *Babcock* here where the conflicting rules involve the defense of charitable immunity [cit.]. Both plaintiffs and defendant Boy Scouts in this case have chosen to identify themselves in the most concrete form possible, domicile, with a jurisdiction that has weighed the interests of charitable tortfeasors and their victims and decided to retain the defense of charitable immunity. Significantly, the New Jersey statute excepts from its protection actions by nonbeneficiaries of the charity who suffer injuries as a result of the negligence of its employees or agents (*see*, N.J.Stat.Ann. § 2A:53A-7). Plaintiffs and their sons, however, were beneficiaries of the Boy Scouts' charitable activities in New Jersey and should be bound by the benefits and burdens of that choice. Additionally, the State of New Jersey is intimately interested in seeing that the parties' associational interests are respected and its own loss-distributing rules are enforced so that the underlying policy, which is undoubtedly to encourage the growth of charitable work within its borders, is effectuated.

Thus, if this were a straight *Babcock* fact pattern, rather than the reverse, we would have no reason to depart from the first *Neumeier* rule and would apply the law of the parties' common domicile. Because this case presents the first case for our review in which New York is the forum-locus rather than the parties' common domicile, however, we consider the reasons most often advanced for applying the law of the forum-locus and those supporting application of the law of the common domicile.

The three reasons most often urged in support of applying the law of the forum-locus in cases such as this are: (1) to protect medical creditors who provided services to injured parties in the locus State, (2) to prevent injured tort victims from becoming public wards in the locus State and (3) the deterrent effect application of locus law has on future tort-feasors in the locus State [cit.]. The first two reasons share common weaknesses. First, in the abstract, neither reason necessarily requires application of the locus jurisdiction's law, but rather invariably mandates application of the law of the jurisdiction that would either allow recovery or allow the greater recovery [cit.]. They are subject to criticism, therefore, as being biased in favor of recovery. Second, on the facts of this case neither reason is relevant since the record contains no evidence that there are New York medical creditors or that plaintiffs are or will likely become wards of this State. Finally, although it is conceivable that application of New York's law in this case would have some deterrent effect on future tortious conduct in this State, New York's deterrent interest is considerably less because none of the parties is a resident and the rule in conflict is loss-allocating rather than conduct-regulating.

Conversely, there are persuasive reasons for consistently applying the law of the parties' common domicile. First, it significantly reduces forum-shopping opportunities, because the same law will be applied by the common-domicile and locus jurisdictions, the two most likely forums. Second, it rebuts charges that the forum-locus is biased in favor of its own laws and in favor of rules permitting recovery. Third, the concepts of mutuality and reciprocity support consistent application of the common-domicile law. In any given case, one person could be either plaintiff or defendant and one State could be either the parties' common domicile or the locus, and yet the applicable law would not change depending on their status. Finally, it produces a rule that is easy to apply and brings a modicum of predictability and certainty to an area of the law needing both.

As to defendant Franciscan Brothers, this action requires an application of the third of the rules set forth in *Neumeier* because the parties are domiciled in different jurisdictions with conflicting loss-distribution rules and the locus of the tort is New York, a separate jurisdiction. In that situation the law of the place of the tort will normally apply, unless displacing it "'will advance the relevant substantive law purposes without impairing the smooth working of the multi-state system or producing great uncertainty for litigants'" (*Neumeier v. Kuehner*). For the same reasons stated in our analysis of the action against defendant Boy Scouts, application of the law of New Jersey in plaintiffs' action against defendant Franciscan Brothers would further that State's interest in enforcing the decision of its domiciliaries to accept the burdens as well as the benefits of that State's loss-distribution tort rules and its interest in promoting the continuation and expansion of defendant's charitable activities in that State. Conversely, although application of New Jersey's law may not affirmatively advance the substantive law purposes of New York, it will not frustrate those interests because New York has no significant interest in applying its own law to this dispute. Finally, application of New Jersey law will enhance "the smooth working of the multi-state system" by actually reducing the incentive for forum shopping and it will provide certainty for the litigants whose only reasonable expectation surely would have been that the law of the jurisdiction where plaintiffs are domiciled and defendant sends its teachers would apply, not the law of New York where the parties had only isolated and infrequent contacts as a result of Coakeley's position as Boy Scout leader. Thus, we conclude that defendant Franciscan Brothers has met its burden of demonstrating that the law of New Jersey, rather than the law of New York, should govern plaintiffs' action against it.

III. * * * Accordingly, the order of the Appellate Division should be affirmed, with costs.

JASEN, J. (dissenting). I respectfully dissent. In my view, the majority overstates the significance of New Jersey's interests in having its law apply in this case and understates the interests of New York. * * * By casting the issue almost exclusively in terms of New Jersey's law of charitable immunity and the policy purposes represented thereby, the majority preordains its decision that the application of New Jersey law would best serve the interests deemed relevant. A more balanced approach, which recognizes that the conflict in this case involves not only New Jersey's law of charitable immunity but also New York's law of charitable nonimmunity, and which accords a proper analysis and fairer significance to the policies underlying the latter, would dictate a different result. Because New Jersey's interests in having its law of charitable immunity apply are rather attenuated in this case and, by sharp contrast, New York's interests as the "locus-forum" in applying its rule of charitable nonimmunity are overriding--especially in light of the heinous nature of the alleged tortious conduct involved and the repugnancy of immunizing those responsible from liability--it is my view that New York law should govern this case. A brief highlighting of those factors which I believe to be most pertinent illustrates what, in my view, the majority has either understated or overlooked.

New Jersey's interests, denominated by the majority as loss-distribution, are hardly pressing under the circumstances. While it is true that laws providing for charitable immunity typically are intended to serve the purpose of protecting and promoting the charities incorporated within a state's jurisdiction, that function is virtually irrelevant in this case. Presently, neither corporate defendant is a resident of New Jersey. * * *

Consequently, because the majority cannot in actuality rely upon New Jersey's interest in protecting resident charities--into which category neither corporate defendant now falls--the decision today is, in effect, predicated almost exclusively upon the plaintiffs' New Jersey domicile. What emerges from the majority's holding is an entirely untoward rule that nonresident plaintiffs are somehow less entitled to the protections of this State's law while they are within our borders. Besides smacking of arbitrary and injudicious discrimination against guests in this State and before our courts [cit.], such a position, without more, has severely limited, if any, validity in resolving conflicts questions. [cit.] This is especially so where, as here, the defendants' contacts with the foreign State are insignificant for the purposes of interest analysis while, at the same time, the parties' contacts with New York are so clear and direct, and the resulting interests of this State so strong.

There can be no question that this State has a paramount interest in preventing and protecting against injurious misconduct within its borders. This interest is particularly vital and compelling where, as here, the tortious misconduct involves sexual abuse and exploitation of children, regardless of the residency of the victims and the tortfeasors. [cit.] Despite the majority's denial, New York's law in question is intimately connected to this overriding interest.

As the majority stresses, a charitable immunity law such as New Jersey's typically serves a loss-distribution purpose reflecting a legislative paternalism toward resident charities. But that is obviously not true with regard to a rule, such as New York's, which denies charitable immunity. * * *

* * * New York has an interest in insuring that justice be done to nonresidents who have come to this State and suffered serious injuries herein. There is no cogent reason to deem that interest any weaker whether such guests are here for the purpose of conducting business or personal affairs, or, as in this case, have chosen to spend their vacation in New York. [cit.] Likewise, it cannot be denied that this State has a strong legitimate interest in deterring serious tortious misconduct, including the kind of reprehensible malfeasance that has victimized the nonresident infant plaintiffs in this case. Indeed, this deterrence function of tort law, whether it be in the form of imposing liability or denying immunity, is a substantial interest of the locus state which is almost universally acknowledged by both commentators and the courts to

be a prominent factor deserving significant consideration in the resolution of conflicts problems. * * * While the majority mentions New York's interest in deterrence, it dismisses that interest in short fashion by referring to the "rule in conflict" as being "loss-allocating rather than conduct-regulating." [cit.] Of course, there is not one but two rules at issue, and the majority's characterization is accurate only with regard to New Jersey's law granting immunity, not with regard to New York's rule denying the same. [cit.]

Moreover, New York's strong interest in deterring injurious misconduct, as well as in providing compensatory justice and protection to persons victimized by wrongdoing within this State, is reflected in the traditional principle of *lex loci* which, despite the majority's *sub silentio disavowal*, remains in this State "the general rule in tort cases to be displaced only in extraordinary circumstances". (*Cousins v. Instrument Flyers*, 376 N.E.2d 914 [1978]; *see also, Neumeier v. Kuehner*; *Tooker v. Lopez*). Indeed, despite the so-called "choice of law revolution" [cit.], *lex loci* is still acknowledged almost universally as a central factor in determining the state, or states, in which the significant interests lie. (*See,* Restatement [Second] of Conflict of Laws § 145[2][a], [b]; § 146.) This rule ought not to be applied mechanically or rigidly to reach absurd results. But, neither ought it to be disregarded indiscriminately, without giving due consideration to the nature or extent of the relationship which accrues between the tort in question and a particular jurisdiction because that jurisdiction is the locus state. (*See,* Reese, *The Second Restatement of Laws Revisited*, 34 Mercer L.Rev. 501, 513-15.) * * *

Notes and Questions

1. Before rebelling against the *Schultz* result, try, if you can, to block from your mind the "heinous nature of the alleged tortious conduct" and to think in terms of "conflicts justice." See supra, Chapter 2 at 26. *From a choice-of-law perspective,* was it appropriate for the court to apply New Jersey law to plaintiffs' actions against either defendant? If not, why not? If yes, why? Keep in mind that in a previous action arising from the same facts but filed against another defendant (the Roman Catholic Archdiocese of New Jersey), the New Jersey Supreme Court held that New Jersey's charitable immunity rule applied, barring the action. What, if any, bearing should that decision have on the New York court's decision in *Schultz*?

2. *Schultz v. Boy Scouts.* The *Schultz* court characterized Boy Scouts as plaintiffs' "codomiciliaries" because, "when tortious acts were committed," Boy Scouts had its national headquarters (i.e. domicile) in New Jersey. Thus, the case fell within the scope of *Neumeier* Rule 1. However, Rule 1 does not say that the critical time is the time of the tortious act, does it? Since the rule is designed for loss-allocation conflicts, should not the defendant's domicile at the time of this *loss-allocating decision* be at least as relevant as the defendant's domicile at the time of the act? For an analogous argument see footnote 21 in *Ardoyno*, supra. The *Schultz* court said that the fact that Boy Scouts had moved its domicile to Texas "provides New York with no greater interest * * * than it would have without the change." That is true, but does the change not detract from New Jersey's interest in protecting

Boy Scouts?

Unlike Rules 3 and 2b, *Neumeier* Rule 1 does not contain an escape clause. This can be problematic in cases of the converse-*Babcock* pattern, which (as *Milkovich* and now *Schultz* demonstrate) are not as clear false conflicts as *Babcock*. However, this is a problem only in the lower courts, not the Court of Appeals which, having enunciated these rules in the first place, retains the power to change them, within the confines of stare decisis. It is in this spirit that the court entertained the three standard arguments for not applying the law of the common domicile in cases of the converse-*Babcock* pattern. Are you convinced by the court's discussion and disposition of these arguments?

3. *Schultz v. Franciscans*. Both *Neumeier* and *Schultz v. Franciscans* fell within the scope of *Neumeier* Rule 3 which calls for the application of the *lex loci delicti*, subject to the escape the rule provides. *Neumeier* applied the rule, but *Schultz v. Franciscans* applied the escape. Is there an inconsistency between the two decisions on this issue? What do you think of the latter decision?

4. From a methodological perspective, the importance of *Schultz* lies in: (a) reaffirming the *Babcock* distinction between conduct-regulating and loss-distributing rules; and (b) expanding the scope of the *Neumeier* rules to encompass conflicts between loss-distribution rules other than guest statutes.

However, both of these developments carry their own technical difficulties. With regard to (a), *Schultz* itself illustrates the difficulties of applying this distinction. Although both sides agreed that New Jersey's immunity rule was loss distributing they disagreed on whether New York's no-immunity rule also fell in that category. We will revisit these difficulties later. With regard to (b), the problem is that the *Neumeier* rules do not differentiate between the place of the injurious conduct and the place of the resulting injury. This is because these rules were devised for guest-statute conflicts in which the driver's conduct and the resulting injury usually coincide in the same state. However, after *Schultz*'s extension, a differentiation between the place of conduct and the place of injury becomes necessary for all cross-border torts in which these two contacts do not coincide in the same state, or for cases like *Schultz* in which both the conduct and the injuries occurred in both states.

Rather than discussing the problem such cross-border torts might present to the application of the *Neumeier* rules, the *Schultz* court designated one of the two states, New York, as the "locus of the tort." This designation did not affect which of the *Neumeier* rules was applicable to the case.[1] However, in other cross-border torts decided under the *Neumeier* rules, the failure to differentiate between the places of conduct and injury may well affect the outcome, because, as noted earlier, such failure creates an internal conflict between the Rules 2a and 2b.

This conflict appears in split-domicile cross-border torts in which the victim is injured in her home state (whose law protects her) by the tortfeasor's conduct in his

---

1. It simply provided plaintiffs with a fighting chance to argue for the application of New York law. With regard to defendant Boy Scouts, designating New Jersey as the "locus" would have made the application of New Jersey law inevitable. With regard to defendant Franciscan Brothers, designating New Jersey as the locus of the tort would have led more directly to the application of New Jersey law under Rule 3, rather than under the escape from that rule, as had occurred in the actual case.

home state (whose law protects him). If the place of conduct is deemed to be the "locus of the tort," the case is covered by Rule 2a, which calls for the application of the law that protects the defendant. If the place of the injury is deemed to be the locus of the tort, the case is covered by Rule 2b, which, "in the absence of special circumstances," calls for the application of the law that protects the plaintiff. What are we to do then?

Similarly, if, in the same case, the conduct occurred in a third state, a conflict arises between Rule 2b and Rule 3. Again, if the locus of the tort is deemed to be in the state of injury and the victim's domicile, then Rule 2b applies and protects the victim. If the locus of the tort is deemed to be in the state of conduct, then Rule 2b becomes inapplicable. The case then falls within the residual Rule 3 (patterns 3e or 3f, supra) which, subject to the escape, calls for the application of the law of the locus of the tort. How should one resolve these internal conflicts?

5. One case that has attempted to answer these questions is Bankers Trust Co. v. Lee Keeling & Assocs., Inc., 20 F.3d 1092 (10th Cir.1994), which involved conduct in Oklahoma by an Oklahoma defendant, and injury in New York to a New York plaintiff. The court made two assumptions. The first was that the only way to resolve the internal conflict between the *Neumeier* rules was by "determin[ing] the place of the *injury*," id. at 1097 (emphasis added), in other words, that the "locus of the tort" as used in *Schultz* is synonymous with the place of the injury. Although several statements in *Schultz* may support this assumption, should these statements be taken literally? Didn't *Schultz* treat New York as the locus of the tort, although much of the injury occurred in New Jersey? *Bankers Trust's* second assumption was that, under *Schultz*, the place of the injury is at "'the place where the last event necessary to make the actor liable occurred.'" Id., quoting *Schultz*. While it is true that *Schultz* contains the phrase "the place of the wrong is considered to be the place where the last event necessary to make the actor liable occurred," that phrase is preceded by an important qualifier, is it not? See *Schultz*, supra. Was New York really the place of the last event in *Schultz*? Do you think that the New York Court of Appeals, the *avant-garde* of the conflicts revolution, would have returned so cavalierly to Beale without any discussion or warning?

Cooney v. Osgood Machinery, Inc.
Court of Appeals of New York, 1993.
81 N.Y.2d 66, 595 N.Y.S.2d 919, 612 N.E.2d 277.

KAYE, C.J. The issue on this appeal is whether a Missouri statute barring contribution claims against an employer--which conflicts with New York law permitting such claims--should be given effect in a third-party action pending here. Applying relevant choice of law principles, we conclude that the Missouri workers' compensation statute should be given effect, and therefore affirm the dismissal of the third-party complaint seeking contribution against a Missouri employer.

I. The facts relevant to this appeal are essentially undisputed. In 1957 or 1958, Kling Brothers, Inc. (succeeded in interest by third-party defendant Hill Acme Co.) manufactured a 16-foot wide "Pyramid Form Bending Roll," a machine to shape large pieces of metal. The device was sold in 1958 to a Buffalo company, American Standard Inc., through a New York sales agent, defendant Osgood Machinery, Inc., which assisted American in the setup and initial operation of the machine. American closed its Buffalo plant around 1961, and the history of the bending roll is obscured until 1969, when Crouse Company--which obtained the equipment in some unknown manner--sold the machine to Paul Mueller Co., a Missouri domiciliary.

Mueller installed the bending roll in its Springfield, Missouri plant and subsequently modified it by adding a foot switch. In October 1978, plaintiff Dennis J. Cooney, a Missouri resident working at the Missouri plant, was injured while cleaning the machine. The machine was running at the time--a piece of wood having been wedged in the foot switch--and Cooney was unable to reach the switch to stop the machine and avoid injury.

In Missouri, Cooney filed for and received workers' compensation benefits. Because under Missouri law an employer providing such benefits "shall be released from all other liability * * * whatsoever, whether to the employee or any other person" (Mo.Rev.Stat. § 287.120 [1]), he could not additionally sue his employer, Mueller, in tort. Cooney did, however, bring a products liability action against Osgood--the machine's initial sales agent--in Supreme Court, Erie County [New York]. (Missouri apparently would not have had personal jurisdiction over Osgood.)

Seeking contribution from parties it deems more culpable in the event it is found liable to Cooney, Osgood brought a third-party action against Mueller, American Standard, and Hill Acme. Mueller invoked the Missouri statute shielding employers from both direct claims by employees and contribution claims by others, and moved for summary judgment dismissing Osgood's third-party complaint. In light of the conflict between the Missouri statute and New York law permitting contribution claims against employers, Supreme Court undertook a choice of law analysis and concluded that New York law should apply. The Appellate Division unanimously reversed and dismissed the third-party complaint as well as all cross-claims against Mueller. We now affirm.

II. An inevitable consequence of a mobile society, where people and goods routinely cross state and national borders, is that disputes may implicate the interests of several jurisdictions having conflicting laws. Choice of law principles become relevant, however, only when a State can, consistent with the Full Faith and Credit and Due Process Clauses of the Constitution [cit.], choose between the conflicting laws. A State may lack sufficient nexus with a case so that choice of its law is arbitrary or fundamentally unfair (*Allstate Ins. Co. v. Hague*, 449 U.S. 302, 312-13) [Ch. 5]. Mueller argues that New York's connection with the case is so tenuous that a decision to apply New York contribution law would be unconstitutional. * * *

New York's contacts with the present case are, in the aggregate, sufficient to satisfy the constitutional threshold. Osgood has alleged that Mueller has a substantial presence in this State, and there is indication in the record that Mueller does business in New York. Additionally, Osgood, which seeks contribution under New York law, is a domiciliary of this State. Finally, Osgood's alleged tortious conduct with respect to the machine arose in New York, where the machine was ordered, operated for several years, and eventually shipped out of state.

We conclude, therefore, that this State has sufficient interest in the litigation so that if we chose to apply New York law on the contribution issue, that decision would not run afoul of the Federal Constitution. Accordingly, we turn to a choice of law analysis.

III. The traditional approach to choice of law problems arising in tort was simply to apply *lex loci delicti*, the law of the place of the tort, to all substantive issues in the case. * * * [I]n *Babcock* [*supra*] the Court adopted a more flexible approach intended to give "controlling effect to the law of the jurisdiction which, because of its relationship or contact with the occurrence or the parties, has the greatest concern with the specific issue raised in the litigation." (*Babcock*).

Of the various, sometimes competing, schools of thought on choice of law, the one that emerged as most satisfactory was "interest analysis," which sought to effect the law of the jurisdiction having the greatest interest in resolving the particular issue (*see, Schultz v. Boys Scouts of Am.*,) [*supra*]. An immediate distinction was drawn between laws that regulate primary conduct (such as standards of care) and those that allocate losses after the tort occurs (such as vicarious liability rules). If conflicting conduct-regulating laws are at issue, the law of the jurisdiction where the tort occurred will generally apply because that jurisdiction has the greatest interest in regulating behavior within its borders. But if competing "postevent remedial rules" are at stake other factors are taken into consideration, chiefly the parties' domiciles (*see, Schultz; Babcock*). [cit.]

In *Neumeier v. Kuehner* [supra], yet another guest statute case, the Court in seeking to return greater predictability and uniformity to the law, adopted a series of three rules that had been proposed by Chief Judge Fuld [cit.]. Although drafted in terms of guest statutes--drivers and passengers--these rules could, in appropriate cases, apply as well to other loss allocation conflicts (*see, Schultz* [supra] [applying first and third *Neumeier* rules to conflicting charitable immunity laws]).

The Neumeier Rules. Under the first *Neumeier* rule, when the driver-host and passenger-guest share a common domicile, that law should control. Indeed, when both parties are from the same jurisdiction, there is often little reason to apply another jurisdiction's loss allocation rules. The domiciliary jurisdiction, which has weighed the competing considerations underlying the loss allocation rule at issue, has the greater "interest in enforcing the decisions of both parties to accept both the benefits and the burdens of identifying with that jurisdiction and to submit themselves to its authority" (*Schultz*). Moreover, this rule reduces opportunities for forum shopping because the same law will apply whether the suit is brought in the locus jurisdiction or in the common domicile, the two most likely forums (*Schultz*).

The second *Neumeier* rule addresses "true" conflicts, where the parties are domiciled in different states and the local law favors the respective domiciliary. When plaintiff's State, for example, would allocate the loss to defendant but defendant's State would force plaintiff to bear the loss, a true conflict arises. The rule provides that when the driver's (defendant's) conduct occurred in the State of domicile and that State would not impose liability, the driver should not be exposed to liability under the law of the victim's domicile. Conversely, when the plaintiff-passenger is injured in the place of domicile and would be entitled to recover, the out-of-State driver should generally be unable to interpose the law of his or her domicile to defeat recovery [cit.]. In essence, then, the second *Neumeier* rule adopts a "place of injury" test for true conflict guest statute cases.

Finally, the third *Neumeier* rule, applicable to other split-domicile cases, provides that the usually governing law will be that of the place where the accident occurred, unless "displacing that normally applicable rule will advance the relevant substantive law purposes without impairing the smooth working of the multistate system or producing great uncertainty for litigants" [cit.]. This rule, too, generally uses the place of injury, or locus, as the determining factor.

Assuming that the interest of each state in enforcement of its law is roughly equal--a judgment that, insofar as guest statutes are concerned, is implicit in the second and third *Neumeier* rules--the situs of the tort is appropriate as a "tie breaker" because that is the only State with which both parties have purposefully associated themselves in a significant way (*see*, Korn, *The Choice-of-Law Revolution: A Critique*, 83 Colum.L.Rev 773, 801 [1983]). Moreover, locus is a neutral factor, rebutting an inference that the forum state is merely protecting its own domiciliary or favoring its own law (*see, Schultz*). Additionally, the place of injury was the traditional choice of law crucible. * * *

Contribution rules--as involved in the present case--are loss allocating, not conduct regulating. Had conduct-regulating been at issue here, our analysis would be greatly simplified, for the traditional rule of *lex loci delicti* almost invariably obtains. Similarly, if the parties shared the same domicile, we would generally apply that jurisdiction's loss distribution law. Instead, our analysis is necessarily more complicated, calling upon us to evaluate the relative interests of jurisdictions with conflicting laws and, if neither can be accommodated without substantially impairing the other, finding some other sound basis for resolving the impasse.

Interest Analysis. The general scheme of workers' compensation acts is that an employer regardless of culpability is required to make specified payments to an injured employee and in exchange, the law immunizes the employer from further liability. Immunity "is part of the *quid pro quo* in which the sacrifices and gains of employees and employers are to some extent put in balance, for, while the employer assumes a new liability without fault, [it] is relieved of the prospect of large damage verdicts" (2A Larsen, Workmen's Compensation Law § 65.11 [1993]). * * *

Missouri's decision to shield employers from contribution claims is thus a policy choice implicating significant state interests: "to deny a person the immunity granted ... by a worker's compensation statute of a given state would frustrate the efforts of that state to restrict the cost of industrial accidents and to afford a fair basis for predicting what these costs will be." (Restatement [Second] of Conflicts of Law § 184 comment *b*, at 547.) Indeed, as the Restatement concluded in a related context, for another State "to subject a person who has been held liable in worker's compensation to further unlimited liability in tort or wrongful death would frustrate the worker's compensation policy of the State in which the award was rendered." (Restatement [Second] of Conflicts of Law § 183, comment *c*, at 544.)

Arrayed against Missouri's interest in maintaining the integrity of its workers' compensation scheme is New York's interest in basic fairness to litigants. Under traditional joint and several liability rules, when more than one tortfeasor was responsible for plaintiff's injury, each was potentially liable for the entire judgment, irrespective of relative culpability. Indeed, plaintiff was not even required to sue all the wrongdoers, but could recover the entire judgment from the "deep pocket," who then had no recourse ([cit.]).

In *Dole v. Dow Chem. Co.* 282 N.E.2d 288 [1972], this Court mitigated the inequity by allowing a defendant that pays more than its fair share of a judgment, as apportioned by the factfinder in terms of relative fault, to recover the difference from a co-defendant. The Legislature, also recognizing the desirability of contribution, subsequently codified the *Dole* principles in CPLR Article 14 (L 1974, ch 742). Stated simply, the "goal of contribution, as announced in *Dole* and applied since, is fairness to tortfeasors who are jointly liable." (*Sommer* [supra]).

Manifestly, the interests of Missouri and New York are irreconcilable in this case. To the extent we allow contribution against Mueller, the policy underlying the Missouri workers' compensation scheme will be offended. Conversely, to the extent Osgood is required to pay more than its equitable share of a judgment, the policy underlying New York's contribution law is affronted. It is evident that one State's interest cannot be accommodated without sacrificing the other's, and thus an appropriate method for choosing between the two must be found.

This is a true conflict in the mold of *Neumeier*'s second rule, where the local law of each litigant's domicile favors that party, and the action is pending in one of those jurisdictions. Under that rule, the place of injury governs, which in this case means that contribution is barred. This holding is consistent with the result reached historically, and reflects application of a neutral factor that favors neither the forum's law nor its domiciliaries. Moreover, forum shopping by defendants--who might attempt to invoke CPLR 1403 and bring a separate action for contribution in New York if sued elsewhere ([cit.])--is eliminated.[2]

A primary reason that locus tips the balance, of course, is that ordinarily it is the place with which both parties have voluntarily associated themselves. In this case, there is some validity to Osgood's argument that it did nothing to affiliate itself with Missouri. Indeed, a decade after Osgood's last contact with the bending roll, the machine wound up in Missouri through no effort, or even knowledge, of Osgood. Moreover, the record establishes that Osgood was not in the business of distributing goods nationwide, but limited its activities to New York and parts of Pennsylvania, and thus Osgood may not have reasonably anticipated becoming embroiled in litigation with a Missouri employer.

For this reason, our decision to apply Missouri law rests as well on another factor that should, at times, play a role in choice of law: the protection of reasonable expectations (*see*, Restatement [Second] of Conflicts of Laws, § 6(2)(d); *Allstate Ins. Co. v. Hague*, 449 U.S. 302, 327 [Stevens, J., concurring]; *Schultz*, ["protecting the reasonable expectations of the parties" is one reason locus law is generally preferred

---

2. New York law permitting contribution against an employer is clearly a minority view. * * * A result that might impose New York law on the carefully structured workers' compensation schemes of other States—especially when the accident occurred there—is undesirable.

when there are conflicting conduct-regulating rules]).[3] In view of the unambiguous statutory language barring third-party liability and the Missouri Supreme Court's holding in *Ferriss* [cit.], Mueller could hardly have expected to be haled before a New York court to respond in damages for an accident to a Missouri employee at the Missouri plant. By contrast, in ordering its business affairs Osgood could have had no reasonable expectation that contribution would be available in a products liability action arising out of the sale of industrial equipment. Indeed, Osgood's activity in connection with the bending roll occurred in 1958, some 14 years before *Dole* was decided and the principles of full contribution were introduced into our law. Moreover, even under present law, contribution is not foolproof. A defendant, for example, may be unable to obtain jurisdiction over a joint tortfeasor; the joint tortfeasor may be insolvent or defunct (like Kling Bros. here); or defendant's own assets may be insufficient to pay its share of the judgment [cit.].

In sum, we conclude that Missouri law should apply because, although the interests of the respective jurisdictions are irreconcilable, the accident occurred in Missouri, and unavailability of contribution would more closely comport with the reasonable expectations of both parties in conducting their business affairs.

IV. Finally, we turn to Osgood's contention that New York's public policy precludes application of the Missouri statute in this case. Under the public policy exception, when otherwise applicable foreign law would "violate some fundamental principle of justice, some prevalent conception of good morals, some deep-rooted tradition of the common weal" (*Loucks v. Standard Oil Co.* [Ch.2]), the court may refuse to enforce it. * * *

Certainly, contribution is not a deeply rooted tradition of the common weal (*Loucks*), having been introduced into our law only relatively recently. Moreover, as noted, availability of contribution is not invariably guaranteed. And while Osgood claims that being forced to pay more than its equitable share of plaintiff's damages is unfair, "public policy is not measured by individual notions of expediency and fairness or by a showing that the foreign law is unreasonable or unwise" (*Schultz*). In the considered judgment of the Missouri legislature, employers providing workers compensation benefits are not amenable to claims for contribution. New York law is to the contrary. But as Judge Cardozo observed: "Our own scheme of legislation may be different. * * * That is not enough to show that public policy forbids us to enforce the foreign right. * * * We are not so provincial as to say that every solution of a problem is wrong because we deal with it otherwise at home." (*Loucks*). Osgood has not sustained its "heavy burden" of proving that the Missouri statute is offensive to our public policy (*Schultz*).

Accordingly, the order of the Appellate Division should be affirmed, with costs.

---

3. We have eschewed reliance on "the fictional expectation of the parties" based on mere contact with the locus of an accident (*Miller v. Miller*, 22 NY2d at 20), but reasonable, justifiable expectations are another matter.

Notes and Questions

1. *Cooney* begins with, and answers affirmatively, the question of whether it would be constitutionally permissible for New York to apply its law to Mueller. For now, you may assume that the court's answer was correct. When you study this matter in Chapter 5, infra, remember also to explore the converse question: Was it constitutionally permissible for New York to subject Osgood to Missouri law?

2. The court acknowledged that: "[Osgood] did nothing to affiliate itself with Missouri"; "the machine wound up in Missouri through no effort, or even knowledge, of Osgood"; "Osgood may not have reasonably anticipated becoming embroiled in litigation with a Missouri employer"; and "Missouri apparently would not have had personal jurisdiction over Osgood." Yet, the court subjected Osgood to Missouri law. Was the application of Missouri law consistent with the court's statements about the policy of protecting justified party expectations? From a different angle, do the above-quoted statements suggest that this case did not quite fit into the "mold" of the second *Neumeier* rule which, having being designed for guest-statute conflicts, contemplates only cases in which *both* parties associate themselves with the same state?

3. Although Mueller's contacts with New York were few, were they not more numerous than Osgood's contacts with Missouri? The court mentioned that Mueller did business in New York. Would it help to know whether Mueller had purchased the machine in New York? If Mueller had done so, and since Osgood had no involvement "or even knowledge" (*Cooney*) of that purchase, would the application of New York law be more unfair to Mueller than the application of Missouri law would be to Osgood? Did Osgood engage in conduct in New York that had foreseeable consequences in Missouri? Did Mueller engage in conduct in New York (buying the machine) and in Missouri (modifying the machine) that had foreseeable consequences in New York?

4. Notice that *Cooney* involved two distinct causes of action: (a) Cooney's products liability action against Osgood; and (b) Osgood's third-party action for contribution against Mueller (as well as American Standard and Hill Acme). Neither the Court of Appeals nor the lower courts discussed the question of which law would govern the first action. Would it be necessary or helpful to answer that question--if only tentatively--before answering the question of which law would govern the second action? Why or why not?

From a choice-of-law perspective, would it be appropriate to apply Missouri law to Cooney's products liability action? If yes (or, in any event, if Missouri law were applied to the first action), would it then be appropriate not to apply Missouri law to the second action? If not (or if New York law were applied to the first action), would it then be appropriate to apply Missouri law to the second action? In other words, is there a danger of an inappropriate *dépeçage* in this case? See also Augello v. 20166 Tenants Corp., 648 N.Y.S.2d 101 (N.Y.A.D. 1st Dept. 1996); Soo Line R.R. Co. v. Overton, 992 F.2d 640 (7th Cir.1993), *reh'g, en banc, denied*, (7th Cir.1993). Did the *Cooney* court recognize this danger?

5. The *Cooney* court stated that the conflict involved in that case was "in the

mold of *Neumeier*'s second rule, where the local law of each litigant's domicile favors that party * * * [and that] [u]nder that rule, the place of injury governs[.]" Is *Neumeier* Rule 2 really applicable to a case like *Cooney*, and, if so, is it capable of providing a solution? Keep in mind that the tort in *Cooney* was a cross-border tort *and* the particular issue was a contribution dispute between joint-tortfeasors, rather than a dispute between a tortfeasor (like the host-driver) and a victim (like the guest-passenger) in *Neumeier*. In light of these facts, how does one answer the following questions:

(a) Which party should be analogized to the injured guest-passenger under Rule 2b? Should it be Cooney (who actually was not a party to the third-party action), Osgood (who was the complaining plaintiff in the third-party action), or Mueller (who had paid worker's compensation for injury he sustained in his home state and whose law protected him)?

(b) Which party should be analogized to the defendant host-driver under Rule 2a? Should it be Osgood who was the defendant in the products liability action, but a plaintiff in the third-party action, and who acted in its home state whose law protected it; or should it be Mueller who was the actual defendant in the third-party action and who acted in his home state whose law favored him?

(c) Which injury is pertinent for purposes of the third-party action? Is it Cooney's personal injury (which occurred in Missouri), Mueller's financial injury (which also occurred in Missouri), or Osgood's financial injury (having to pay compensation to Cooney) which occurred in New York?

(d) Which conduct is pertinent for purposes of the third-party action? Was it Osgood's conduct in doing or not doing something with regard to the sale of the machine in New York, or was it Mueller's conduct in modifying the machine in Missouri? and

(e) In cases in which the conduct and injury occur in different states, is the place of conduct relevant for applying *Neumeier* Rule 2 or, for that matter, Rule 3?

Perhaps because it recognized the difficulty of these questions, the *Cooney* court eventually resorted to a full-fledged policy analysis for resolving the conflict. Nevertheless, are you persuaded that the *Neumeier* rules are capable of resolving conflicts arising from cross-border torts or conflicts involving disputes between joint tortfeasors?

6. In dollar terms, what does the *Cooney* holding mean for Osgood? Leaving aside the other two defendants (American Standard and Hill Acme), is Osgood stuck with paying 100% of Cooney's damages? Literally, this would be the result dictated by New York's joint and several liability rule and that state's refusal to adopt a comparative negligence rule. In a multistate case like *Cooney*, would it be appropriate to hold Osgood liable only for the percentage of Cooney's damages that is attributable to Osgood's fault? Professor Weintraub has proposed such a solution. See "Conference on Jurisdiction, Justice, and Choice of Law for the 21st Century: Case Four: Choice of Law Theory," 29 *N.E. L. Rev.* 669, 682-83 (1995). For a dissenting opinion, see Singer, id. at 692-701. Notice that adopting this solution would produce a result that is different than the result that either New York law or

Missouri law provide. For example, under New York's joint and several liability rule, a joint tortfeasor is liable for 100% of plaintiff's damages if the other tortfeasor is insolvent. The same is true under Missouri law, if the other tortfeasor is an employer who, like Mueller, is immunized by the worker's compensation statute. Why should Osgood be treated differently? Read again Professor von Mehren's proposals for "special substantive rules for multistate problems," supra at 261. Is this a case in which such a special substantive rule is warranted?

7. *Cooney* said that Osgood could not have expected its right of contribution to be foolproof because, *inter alia*, Osgood had sold the machine in 1958, some 14 years before New York recognized that right. In 1958, could Osgood have expected that it would be subject to strict liability for its involvement in that sale?

8. Despite all of the above questions, is *Cooney*'s resolution of the choice-of-law question a good one? Why, or why not?

9. The *Cooney* court described its analysis of the choice-of-law question as a process of "evaluat[ing] the relative interests of jurisdictions with conflicting laws and, if neither can be accommodated *without substantially impairing* the other, finding some other sound basis for resolving the impasse." (Emphasis added.) Was the court leaning towards a comparative impairment approach?

10. In footnote 2, the *Cooney* court stated that "New York law permitting contribution against an employer is clearly a minority view." Professors Juenger and Borchers have argued that this statement signifies a tilt for the better-law approach. See Juenger, *Babcock Revisited*, 741 n. 121; Borchers, *Conflicts Pragmatism*, 912 n. 205. Do you agree? In any event, three years after *Cooney*, New York amended the above law so as to make indemnification and contribution unavailable against the employer, except in cases of "grave injury" to the employee. See Omnibus Workers' Compensation Reform Act, L. 1996, ch. 635, § 90.

11. Was it necessary for the *Cooney* court, after concluding its laborious "interest analysis," also to consider Osgood's *ordre public* exception? To the extent that this exception involves a comparison of the policies of the foreign state with those of the forum state, is that comparison not an integral part of interest analysis itself? As Currie once said, in contrast to the traditional approach under which *ordre public* functions as a post-selection corrective, interest analysis "summon[s] public policy from the reserves and place[s] it in the front lines where it belongs," Currie, *Selected Essays* 88, and thus makes it an integral part of the selection process itself. If this is true, why should the party that objects to the application of forum law get two bites out of the apple? One may ask the same question with regard to cases that fall within *Neumeier* Rules 2b and 3, which contain built-in escapes. To the extent that these escapes are capable of directly repelling an obnoxious foreign law, do they not obviate the need for resorting to the traditional *ordre public* exception?

12. You should recall that under the traditional approach, the *ordre public* exception functioned as an exception to the application of foreign law, not of forum law. Although *Cooney* reaffirmed this point, a subsequent decision of the same court seems to subscribe to the notion that this exception may also be employed as a means of displacing the law *of the forum* when that law is applicable under the forum's choice-of-law analysis. In Zurich Ins. Co. v. Shearson Lehman Hutton, Inc.,

642 N.E.2d 1065 (N.Y.1994), the court concluded that New York's law was applicable to a dispute arising out of an insurance contract. Then, in an enigmatic *dictum*, the court stated: "Theoretically, in a proper case, a foreign State's sufficiently compelling public policy could preclude an application of New York law otherwise indicated by the grouping of contacts analysis, particularly where New York's policy is weak or uncertain." Id. at 1069. The court eventually concluded that this was not such a case, because New York's policy on the subject was strong and unambiguous. What do you think of this duplicative analysis?

13. Notice that the *Zurich* court described its choice-of-law analysis as "the grouping of contacts analysis." Indeed, one year before *Zurich*, the New York Court of Appeals decided *In re* Allstate Ins. Co. (Stolarz), 613 N.E.2d 936 (N.Y.1993), a case that also involved the interpretation of an insurance contract. The court made certain pronouncements that suggest at least a partial reversion to the "grouping of contacts" approach with regard to contract conflicts. After stating that interest analysis is the court's "preferred analytical tool in tort cases," id. at 938, because "in a typical tort case * * * strong governmental interests may underlie the choice of law issue," id. at 939, the court said:

> By contrast, contract cases often involve only the *private* economic interests of the parties, and analysis of the public policy underlying the conflicting contract laws may be inappropriate to resolution of the dispute. It may even be difficult to identify the competing 'policies' at stake, because the laws may differ only slightly, and evolve through the incremental process of common-law adjudication as a response to the facts presented. The 'center of gravity' or 'grouping of contacts' choice of law theory applied in contract cases (see, e.g., *Auten v. Auten* [supra]) enables the court to identify which law to apply without entering into the difficult, and sometimes inappropriate, policy thicket.

Id. The above statement, coupled with some other statements in *Stolarz*, suggests a dichotomy in the court's approach to contract conflicts: (a) interest analysis will be the "preferred approach" when "the policies underlying conflicting laws * * * are readily identifiable and reflect strong governmental interests;" and (b) center of gravity will be the preferred approach when the policies are not readily identifiable, when they do not reflect strong governmental interests, or when they "involve only the private economic interest of the parties." What do you think of this dichotomy?

5. CONDUCT-REGULATION CONFLICTS

Padula v. Lilarn Properties Corp.

Court of Appeals of New York, 1994.
84 N.Y.2d 519, 644 N.E.2d 1001, 620 N.Y.S.2d 310.

SMITH, J. Plaintiff is a resident of New York and defendant is a corporation incorporated under the laws of New York. Defendant owns property in Massachusetts, at which plaintiff was working, under a subcontracting agreement. Plaintiff sustained injuries when he fell from a scaffold while performing work on a construction project in Massachusetts. Plaintiff brought this action for damages, alleging violations of sections 200, 240(1) and 241(6) of the New York Labor Law and the rules and regulations thereunder. The issue here is the applicability of these sections of the Labor Law to this accident.

Defendant's motion for partial summary judgment dismissing plaintiff's causes of action * * * was granted by Supreme Court and affirmed by the Appellate Division * * *. This Court granted leave * * * to bring up for review the * * * Appellate Division order. [cit.]

We reject plaintiff's contention that New York law should apply here. New York's choice-of-law principles govern the outcome of this matter. In the context of tort law, New York utilizes interest analysis to determine which of two competing jurisdictions has the greater interest in having its law applied in the litigation. The greater interest is determined by an evaluation of the "'facts or contacts which * * * relate to the purpose of the particular law in conflict'" (*Schultz* [supra]). Two separate inquiries are thereby required to determine the greater interest: (1) what are the significant contacts and in which jurisdiction are they located; and, (2) whether the purpose of the law is to regulate conduct or allocate loss (*id.*).

As to the first inquiry concerning the significant contacts and the jurisdiction in which they are located, both the plaintiff employee and the defendant owner of the Massachusetts property are domiciliaries of New York State. The other relevant actors are not parties to this lawsuit. They include the plaintiff's employer (a subcontractor which is a New York domiciliary), the tenant of the property (a Massachusetts domiciliary who contracted with the general contractor), and the general contractor (a domiciliary of Vermont). The tort occurred in Massachusetts.

As to the second inquiry, a distinction must be made between a choice-of-law analysis involving standards of conduct and one involving the allocation of losses *(Schultz, supra).* In the former case the law of the place of the tort governs. As we stated in *Schultz*:

> "Thus, when the conflicting rules involve the appropriate standards of conduct, rules of the road, for example, the law of the place of the tort 'will usually have a predominant, if not exclusive, concern' * * * because the locus jurisdiction's interests in protecting the reasonable expectations of the parties who relied on it to govern their primary conduct and in the admonitory effect that applying its law will have on similar conduct in the future assume critical importance and outweigh any interests of the common-domicile jurisdiction." (*Schultz*, [supra]; *see also, Cooney v. Osgood Mach.*, [supra].)

Conduct-regulating rules have the prophylactic effect of governing conduct to prevent injuries from occurring. "If conflicting conduct-regulating laws are at issue, the law of the jurisdiction where the tort occurred will generally apply because that jurisdiction has the greatest interest in regulating behavior within its borders" (*Cooney, supra*).

Loss allocating rules, on the other hand, are those which prohibit, assign, or limit liability after the tort occurs, such as charitable immunity statutes (*e.g., Schultz, supra*), guest statutes (*e.g., Dym v. Gordon,* 16 N.Y.2d 120), wrongful death statutes (*e.g., Miller v. Miller,* 22 N.Y.2d 12), vicarious liability statutes (*e.g., Farber v.*

Smolack, 20 N.Y.2d 198), and contribution rules (*e.g., Cooney, supra*). Where the conflicting rules at issue are loss allocating and the parties to the lawsuit share a common domicile, the loss allocation rule of the common domicile will apply (*see, Cooney, supra* [setting forth the three *Neumeier* rules (cit.) which address the "common domicile" situation in rule No. 1]).

Thus, the fundamental question in this case, where the parties share a common domicile, is whether Labor Law §§ 240 and 241 are primarily conduct-regulating or loss-allocating. The relevant Labor Law provisions, sections 240 and 241, embody both conduct-regulating and loss-allocating functions requiring worksites be made safe (conduct-regulating) and failure to do so results in strict and vicarious liability of the owner of the property or the general contractor. We hold however, that sections 240 and 241 of the Labor Law are primarily conduct-regulating rules, requiring that adequate safety measures be instituted at the worksite and should not be applied to the resolution of this tort dispute arising in Massachusetts. Thus, Massachusetts law was properly applied.

Accordingly, the judgment of Supreme Court appealed from and the order of the Appellate Division brought up for review should be affirmed, with costs.

TITONE, J. (concurring). I vote to affirm in this case for the simple reason that the Labor Law, by its terms, is inapplicable to conduct occurring outside the State. My conclusion is based on Labor Law § 242, which provides that "the provisions of [article 10] and the rules issued thereunder shall be applicable * * * throughout the state." By its terms, the statute makes no provision for extraterritorial application of either article 10 or the Labor Commissioner's regulations. Moreover, under our State's rules of statutory construction, there is no basis for inferring extraterritorial effect in the face of legislative silence on the question (*see,* McKinney's Cons.Laws of N.Y., Book 1, Statutes § 149 ["all laws are co-extensive, and only co-extensive, with the political jurisdiction of the lawmaking power; and every statute in general terms is construed as having no extraterritorial effect"]).

In view of the foregoing, the choice-of-law "interest" analysis delineated in the writing is irrelevant * * *. Regardless of the nature or classification of the interests involved, Labor Law §§ 200, 240 and 241 can have no effect outside of New York in the absence of any indication of a legislative intent to extend the statute's reach in that manner.

Finally, even if New York's Legislature or its Commissioner did attempt to extend the reach of those provisions to out-of-State jobsites, I would have a serious question as to whether such efforts would be effective. As a matter of common sense, it would be unreasonable for New York's Labor Commissioner to establish safety rules for jobsites in Massachusetts. Indeed, the Appellate Division was right when it opined that "'[t]he New York Legislature is without authority to impose standards of conduct on contractors, owners and agents relating to a worksite located in a foreign jurisdiction.'" [cit.]

In sum, since there can be no liability under Labor Law §§ 200, 240 and 241 without a violation of the statutory and regulatory standard and since those standards are inapplicable in Massachusetts, there is no basis for invoking those provisions in this litigation, regardless of whether their purpose is to regulate conduct or allocate loss. Accordingly, I would eschew use of the choice-of-law *Schultz* analysis that the majority adopted in favor of a more direct approach based solely on the fact that plaintiff's causes of action depend on a regulatory scheme designed solely for use in New York. On that basis, I would affirm.

Notes and Questions

1. The statute involved in *Padula* imposed upon the owner of a building absolute liability for injury caused by a defective scaffold to a construction worker working on the building. Was the court correct not to apply this statute to a Massachusetts building? Why, or why not? What about the fact that *all* parties involved in the case (the building owner, the worker, and his employer) were New York domiciliaries? Why was *Neumeier* Rule 1 not applicable to this case?

2. In his concurring opinion, Justice Titone concluded that the New York statute, "by its terms, is inapplicable to conduct occurring outside the State" because the statute stated that it "shall be applicable * * * throughout the state." Is this the same as saying "throughout the state, *but not beyond*"?

What about the more general New York statute Titone quoted, which provides that "all laws are co-extensive, and only co-extensive, with the political jurisdiction of the lawmaking power; and every statute in general terms is construed as having no extraterritorial effect"? Did *Neumeier*, *Schultz*, and so many other New York cases that applied non-New York law violate this statute? Is there a difference on this issue between statutory law and judge-made?

3. Compare *Padula* with Justice Traynor's decisions in *Ford Victoria* and *Bernkrant*, supra 187, 189. All three cases framed the question as one of whether a statute of the forum state should determine the legal consequences of events or transactions that occurred outside that state. This way of framing the choice-of-law question echoes Cook and Currie's call for resorting to "the domestic method of ordinary statutory construction and interpretation," which is also characteristic of the "unilateral" choice-of-law approach developed earlier in Europe. See supra Ch. 1. Do these cases prove that, despite the appellation "unilateral"--which has particularly negative connotations in international relations today--this approach is capable of producing non-parochial solutions?

4. Like *Padula*, cases involving issues of worksite safety have *invariably* applied the law of the state in which the site is located--without regard to the parties' domiciles, and regardless of the choice-of-law methodology the court followed. The same is true of cases involving issues of premises liability, traffic safety, and other conduct-regulation issues. For documentation, see Symeonides, *The Revolution Today* § 169. As Judge Posner stated in Spinozzi v. ITT Sheraton Corp., 174 F.3d 842 (7th Cir.1999), a case involving safety standards in a foreign hotel, it would be both non-sensical and dangerous to impose on the hotel operator a duty to follow the safety standards in force in the home-states of the hotel guests. This would subject the operator "to a hundred different bodies of tort law," id. at 845, each imposing potentially inconsistent duties of care. "A resort might have a system of firewalls that under the law of some states or nations might be considered essential to safety and

in others might be considered a safety hazard." Id. Do you agree?

In Bauer v. Club Med Sales, Inc., 1996 WL 310076 (N.D.Cal.1996), a similar case involving a California vacationer and another American-owned hotel in Mexico, the court applied Mexican law because, although California had an interest in "protect[ing] its citizens traveling abroad," id. at *4., that interest should be subordinated to "Mexico's sovereignty interest in enforcing its own construction standards within its borders." Id. *Bauer* also involved an additional issue--the amount of damages for the victim's wrongful death. On this issue, the court took note of the parties' domicile, including defendant's status as an American corporation, and held that California's pro-recovery law should govern. Was this *dépeçage* appropriate?

THE DISTINCTION BETWEEN CONDUCT-REGULATING AND LOSS-DISTRIBUTING RULES

1. *Padula* illustrates the difficulties that New York courts have encountered in applying the *Babcock-Schultz* distinction between conduct-regulating and loss-distributing rules. Before *Padula* reached the New York Court of Appeals, six lower court cases had characterized the same scaffolding statute in *three* different ways. See Symeonides, *A View From the Trenches*, 17–18.

2. *The Status of the Distinction.* Despite these difficulties, the above distinction is not only well-entrenched in New York conflicts law, but has also been recognized elsewhere. "While not every state has decided the issue, there are no states that have rejected [it]."[1] As two recent studies have demonstrated, courts in many other states have adopted the same distinction, explicitly or implicitly.[2] In 1991, Louisiana codified this distinction, although it employed terminology intended to narrow down the category of conduct-regulating rules by referring to issues of "standards of conduct *and* safety." The codification distinguishes between these issues and "issues of loss-distribution or financial protection," and provides different choice-of-law rules for each category. For the former category, the codification discounts the parties' domicile and focuses on the places of conduct and injury.[3] For loss-distribution conflicts, the codification focuses on the parties' domicile, although it assigns a supporting role to the places of conduct and injury.[4]

In the meantime, a parallel, but not identical, distinction has emerged in Europe. For example, article 142(2) of the Swiss codification provides that, regardless of which law governs a tort case, "[r]ules of safety and conduct in force at the place of the act are [to be] taken into consideration." The Portuguese and Hungarian codifications contain similar provisions, as do the Hague conventions on traffic

---

1. Cross, *The Conduct-Regulating Exception*, 441.

2. See Cross, supra n.1 (providing "overwhelming evidence" id. at 437; Symeonides, *Revolution* §§ 105-112.

3. Article 3543 provides that the law of the conduct state governs, unless the injury occurred in another state that imposes a higher standard of conduct. In the latter case, the law of the state of injury governs, provided that the occurrence of the injury in that state was objectively foreseeable. For a similar provision, see Art. 46 of the Puerto Rico Draft Code.

4. See La. Civ. Code Art. 3544, described supra at 178 n.10 and 214 n.4 For a similar provision, see Art. 47 of the Puerto Rico Draft Code.

accidents and products liability, and a proposed European Union Regulation ("Rome II").[5]

3. *The Validity and Difficulties of the Distinction.* The above distinction corresponds to the two fundamental objectives of the law of torts--deterrence and compensation--with conduct-regulating rules serving the first objective, and loss-distributing rules serving the second objective. At the same time, this very distinction may imply that these two objectives are distinct enough to be separable; and this is a debatable proposition. For example, one author has argued that "compensation and deterrence * * * cannot be separated"[6] and that "*most* tort rules"[7] belong to both categories, because "*all* tort rules are loss-allocating * * * and most [of them] affect conduct."[8]

Indeed, like the *Padula* statute, many tort rules serve both conduct-regulating and loss-distributing objectives. *Schultz* provides another example--New York's *non-immunity* rule. The rule is loss-distributive to the extent it imposes financial responsibility on the actor and provides compensation for the victim. But the rule may also be conduct-regulating to the extent it affects the actor's conduct by providing an additional incentive to act more carefully. Dram shop acts like those involved in *Zhou* and *Bernhard* can also serve both conduct-regulating and loss-allocating objectives, namely: (1) providing additional incentives for tavern owners to act more carefully and not serve apparently intoxicated patrons; and (2) facilitating financial recovery for victims by making available to them an additional defendant, the tavern operator, and placing on the latter the economic loss of accidents caused by his drunk patrons. In contrast, a state's refusal to enact a dram shop act--or the enactment of an anti-dram shop act--may be motivated by loss-allocating rather than conduct-regulating considerations--shielding tavern operators or social hosts from financial responsibility, rather than encouraging them to act carelessly.

One can cite other examples of border-line or potentially dual-character rules, such as strict-liability rules, contributory-negligence rules, and "car-owner statutes," similar to those involved in *Levy,* supra Ch.2, which impose vicarious liability on car owners for injuries caused by a driver using the car with the owner's consent.

Admittedly, the above rules illustrate the practical difficulty of applying the above distinction in certain cases, but do they negate its validity? Does the existence of some, or many, dual-character rules mean that all tort rules are of dual character?

---

5. See Portuguese Civ.Code, Art. 45(3) (application of law of parties' common nationality or residence shall be "without prejudice to provisions of local laws that must be applied to all persons without differentiation"); Hungarian codif. §33.1 (regardless of the law applicable to the tort, "[t]he law of the place of the tortious conduct shall determine whether the tortious conduct was realized by the violation of traffic or other security regulations"); Hague Traffic Accidents Convention, Art. 9 ("account shall be taken of rules relating to the control and safety of traffic which were in force at the place and time of the accident."); Hague Products Liability Convention, Art. 9 ("consideration [is to be] given to the rules of conduct and safety prevailing in the State where the product was introduced into the market."); Rome II Regulation, Art. 13.

6. Perdue, *A Reexamination of the Distinction* 1252.

7. Id. (emphasis added).

8. Perdue, supra at id. (emphasis in original). See also id. ("All tort rules determine who will bear the loss and thus are all are loss-allocating. * * *. Loss allocation creates incentives for those who must bear the loss to behave differently than they would if they did not have to bear the loss.") For other writings questioning the validity of this distinction, see Weintraub, *Commentary,* 435; Hay & Ellis, *Rules and Approaches,* 369.

Even if this were true, doesn't *Padula* answer the question of how to handle these rules?

4. *A Rule's Primary Purpose and Function. Padula*'s criterion for distinguishing between conduct-regulating and loss-distributing rules is to examine the rule's *primary* purpose and function. Isn't this just another way of saying that one should look at the "policy" underlying the particular rule, which in turn is the essence of all policy-based choice-of-law approaches? This process may be difficult at times, but is it not preferable than either of the two extremes of American conflicts history: mechanical rules that lead inexorably to pre-ordained results, or completely rudderless approaches that lead to subjective ad hoc results? The process of determining whether a rule falls within the one or the other category may resemble the characterization process or the substance/procedure distinction under the traditional theory, but at least one author has argued that the similarity is only superficial. "The traditional theory sought to ascribe labels to rules without regard to their underlying purposes. In contrast, the process of distinguishing between conduct-regulating and loss-distributing rules seeks to ascertain the rule's purpose, and does so in a much more nuanced and focused manner. It asks the right questions and, more importantly, it is expected to provide reasons for the answers to which it arrives." Symeonides, *The Revolution Today* § 122. What do you think?

5. *Examples of Conduct-Regulating Rules*. Under *Padula*'s criterion, do you agree that the following qualify as examples of rules that are *primarily* conduct-regulating? (1) "Rules of the road." These rules are designed to ensure the safety of the public by defining permissible and impermissible conduct *and* by imposing sanctions on violators. This category is not as small as most commentators assume. It includes not only speed limits and traffic-light rules, but also rules that prescribe the civil sanctions for violating traffic rules, including presumptions and inferences attached to the violation. Consider, for example, a rule providing that a person involved in a collision while driving in excess of the speed limit, or while being intoxicated, is presumed to be negligent; or a rule providing that, in a rear-end vehicular collision, the driver of the rear car is presumed to be at fault; (2) Rules that prescribe safety standards for worksites, buildings, and other premises; (3) Rules that impose punitive damages; (4) Rules that define "alienation of affections" or "interference with marriage," or "interference with contract" as tortious conduct and grant an action against the actor.

6. *Examples of Loss-Distributing Rules*. Under *Padula*'s criterion, do you agree that the following qualify as examples of rules that are *primarily* loss-distributing: (1) guest statutes; (2) rules providing intrafamily or charitable immunity; (3) rules immunizing employers from a tort action if they are covered by worker's compensation; (4) rules imposing ceilings on the amount of damages or excluding certain types of damages, such as for pain and suffering; (5) rules defining the beneficiaries of wrongful death actions, survival actions, and loss of consortium actions; (6) rules providing that a tort action does not survive the tortfeasor's death; (7) rules dealing with contribution or indemnification among joint tortfeasors; (8) rules providing for no-fault automobile insurance; (9) statutes of repose, which protect manufactures from suits filed after a designated number of years from the

product's first use; (10) corporate-successor liability or non-liability rules; and (11) direct action statutes, namely statutes that allow the victim to directly sue the tortfeasor's insurer.

7. ***The Purpose and Utility of the Distinction.*** As Judge Weinstein observed: "Loss-allocation and conduct-regulation are not rigid categories. Rather, the distinction between them serves as a proxy for the ultimate question of which state has the greater interest in having its law applied to the litigation at hand." Hamilton v. Accu-Tek, 47 F.Supp. 330, 337 (E.D.N.Y.1999). Indeed, the distinction is not a taxonomical exercise to be conducted for its own sake. Rather, it is a starting point in the court's choice-of-law analysis. It directs the parties' and the court's attention to the right questions and defines the parameters of the choice-of-law debate. It stands for the simple proposition that, in conflicts between conduct-regulation rules, one should focus on the place or places of conduct and injury, whereas in conflicts between loss-distribution rules, one should also focus on the parties' contacts, if any, with other states.

On the other hand, if that is all the distinction serves, and given the practical difficulties of applying it in some cases, is the distinction worth having? Commentators, including two of this book's editors, differ widely on this point.[9] What is your opinion?

Gaither v. Myers

United States Court of Appeals District of Columbia Circuit, 1968.
404 F.2d 216, 131 U.S.App.D.C. 216.

LEVENTHAL, J. At about 11:25 p.m. on June 22, 1960, plaintiff Myers, a resident of Maryland, was driving on a Maryland road, about five miles from the District of Columbia line, when a speeding automobile * * * collided with the left rear portion of his car * * * and then * * * came to rest in a ditch on the right side of the road * * *. Minutes later the police arrived and upon investigation found that the carelessly driven car had been abandoned by its driver. The ownership of the abandoned auto was traced through its District of Columbia license tags to defendant Gaither. The trial court granted defendant's motion for a directed verdict. The D.C. Court of Appeals reversed and remanded for a new trial. We affirm * * *.

* * * We see no basis for upsetting the conclusion of the D.C. Court of Appeals that Gaither * * * was not driving his car--either personally or through an agent--at the time of the accident * * *.

* * * Plaintiff urges an alternative theory that defendant's liability may be premised on the alleged fact that Gaither unlawfully left his keys in his car. We agree that there is support in the evidence for this allegation and that such conduct provides an independent basis for liability.

Article XIV, § 98, of the District of Columbia Traffic and Motor Vehicle

---

9. For a negative answer, see Perdue, supra n.6, and the authors cited at n.8 supra. For an affirmative answer, see Cross, supra n.1; Reppy, *Codifying Interest Analysis*, 591; Symeonides, *The Revolution Today*, §§ 122-23.

Regulations provides:

> No person driving, or in charge of a motor vehicle shall permit it to stand unattended without first stopping the engine, locking the ignition, removing the key, and effectively setting the brake thereon and, when standing upon any grade, turning the front wheels to the curb or side of the highway.

* * * Under the law of the District of Columbia, if appellant's stolen car caused the damage in the District, instead of in Maryland, it is clear that, under the facts of our case, appellant's action would render him liable to the victim under a theory of negligence per se. Ross v. Hartman, 78 U.S.App.D.C. 217, 139 F.2d 14, (1943), cert. denied, 321 U.S. 790 (1944). In the Ross case the defendant left his keys in his truck after parking it in a public alley. A thief drove the truck away and within two hours ran down the plaintiff. In discussing the former District of Columbia regulation on locking the ignition, the court said:

> Since it is a safety measure, its violation was negligence. This negligence created the hazard and thereby brought about the harm which the ordinance was intended to prevent. It was therefore a legal or 'proximate' cause of the harm. * * * The fact that the intermeddler's conduct was itself a proximate cause of the harm, and was probably criminal, is immaterial.

139 F.2d 14, 15-16.

In the present case the collision occurred at a time and place not substantially removed from the time and place where the owner left the car in the street with the keys. As in the Ross case, this negligence caused the danger and damage that the ordinance intended to prevent, and the negligence is therefore the proximate cause of the mishap under the law of the District of Columbia. In other cases, where the mishap occurs substantially later and distant, the hiatus may tend to negative proximate cause. As stated in *Ross*, however, the mere fact that a thief stole the car is not, in and of itself, an independent and unforeseeable event that cuts off liability. We do not intimate what would be the result in such cases, but only decide the case at bar on its facts.

It is equally clear that under Maryland law, if the owner had left his keys in his car in Maryland, and the thief had negligently caused the accident in that state, the injured plaintiff could not recover from the owner. For although it is an offense in Maryland to leave one's keys in an unattended motor vehicle, the highest court of that state has ruled as a matter of law that the intervening conduct of a thief breaks the chain of proximate cause and insulates the offender from tort liability.

The question for decision is whether the District's tort rule concerning liability for violation of the traffic regulation applies where: the conduct prohibited by the regulation takes place in the District; and the immediate consequence of that violation (stealing of the car) occurs here; but the final sequence resulting in damage takes place in Maryland. To answer this question it is first necessary to ascertain the underlying policies and interests sought to be regulated and protected by the rules of the relevant jurisdictions and to determine whether on the facts of the case these differing state interests are in conflict.

We begin with the rule of the District, turning again to the 1943 landmark case of *Ross v. Hartman*, supra. There the court said:

The evident purpose of requiring motor vehicles to be locked is not to prevent theft for the sake of the owners or the police, but to promote the safety of the public in the streets. An unlocked motor vehicle * * * creates much more risk that meddling by children, thieves, or others will result in injuries to the public. * * * The rule we are adopting tends to make the streets safer by discouraging the hazardous conduct which the ordinance forbids. It puts the burden of the risk, as far as may be, upon those who create it.

The doctrine of *Ross v. Hartman* has been reaffirmed in intervening decisions of this court [cit.]. The strength of the District's policy of 'discouraging the hazardous conduct which the ordinance forbids' has not diminished during the intervening 25 years. On the contrary we have never had greater need for doctrines helping to deter injuries and crimes traceable in significant measure to keys left in unattended cars.

* * * [Recent] data distributed * * * [indicate] that in 1966 more than a million cars were stolen nationally and that about 24% of the stolen vehicles were involved in accidents. The theft problem is acute in the District of Columbia where, during 1967, there were over 13,000 auto thefts, an increase over 1966 of 30% as opposed to a national rise of 17%. The accident rate for stolen cars is estimated to be approximately 200 times the normal accident rate. And in the District of Columbia, 85% of the thieves do not possess operator's permits. A study has disclosed that of the total cars stolen, the key had been left in either the ignition or in the car in 42.3% of the cases.

Moreover, the authorities point out that auto theft is to a large extent a crime of opportunity, unusually inviting to young people, and is often the first major episode in a criminal career. The data reveal that 70% of the District of Columbia auto thefts are by offenders under the age of 21.

The District has a strong policy of deterrence of auto theft. That policy must be viewed in the light of the probabilities of consequential hazards. This perspective fosters our conclusion that there is a significant District of Columbia interest in the application of the District rule of liability to an actor who leaves his car keys accessible to a thief in the District, and sets in motion the sequence of events that enlarges the probability of, and in a significant number of instances contributes to, results of death, disability and destruction.

Aside from the purpose served by the tort rule of *Ross v. Hartman* in deterring highly hazardous motorist conduct, tort liability also has the purpose of shifting the loss from the injured victim and his creditors to the vehicle operator who, in turn, if he chooses, may procure insurance. It is true that this compensatory policy has the greatest relevance to cases when the mishap occurs in the District and when District residents are plaintiffs. However, to confine the benefits of the *Ross* rule to the territory ceded by the states of Maryland and Virginia to form the Nation's Capital would be to shun the present reality of the economically and socially integrated greater metropolitan area. It is a commonplace that residents of Maryland are part of the Washington metropolitan trading area, and that District residents and businesses have an interest in the well-being of these citizens of the Free State. We can not fairly impute to Congress, or its delegate, the parochial intention to restrict recovery based on violation of the District regulation to District residents, especially taking into account the national constituency of Congress, in the absence of an express disclaimer.

It is plain, in short, that a legitimate and indeed powerful policy and interest of the District of Columbia is involved in this case and is furthered by application of the rule of *Ross v. Hartman*.

Looking to the interests of Maryland, where the accident occurred and the plaintiff resides, its highest court has interpreted a nearly identical statute as being aimed at preventing theft, tampering with a car, or the starting of a car under its own momentum if the brakes should slip. While that court agrees that the statute creates a duty of safety to the public, this apparently is limited to the immediate vicinity of the parking place for the court says it does not extend 'to all the world, but must be a foreseeable duty to a class of which the plaintiff was a member.' [cit.] The court feels that the thief, an 'independent intervening cause', [cit.] and not the car owner, is the proximate cause of the accident. The Fourth Circuit, in explaining Maryland's law, said that the owner's negligence was too remote from the accident, where a thief intervenes, to find proximate cause.

Thus Maryland's interests are aimed at prevention of theft, tampering, accidental starting of a car, and possibly some very immediate injury. Maryland, however, also expresses an interest in protecting car owners from tort liability for injury caused by car thieves. Yet, that interest of Maryland in curtailing liability of a car owner, would not seem to extend to an owner like our defendant, who is not a citizen of Maryland but rather a resident of the District of Columbia. This seems especially true where it is a Maryland citizen who is being compensated for his injuries. It is obvious that the finding of such liability would in no way violate the other interest of Maryland in preventing theft or tampering with cars by requiring removal of keys from parked cars; if anything, it fosters that interest.

Thus, we are not concerned with any real 'conflict' between the interests of Maryland and the District in this case. The fact that two states have different rules where all the factors are oriented to one state does not necessarily mean that there is a 'conflict' in which one state demands and the other rejects the application of its rule to a situation where the pertinent factors arise in two or more states. Where there is no such conflict of interest in a multi-state situation, as this court and others have noted, there is a 'false conflicts' situation. In such a case application of the appropriate rule is simplified. We think the D.C. Court of Appeals was correct in its conclusion that appellant's liability turns on the District of Columbia's rule in *Ross v. Hartman*.

The cause is remanded for further proceedings consistent with this opinion. *So ordered.*

Notes and Questions

1. In interest analysis terminology, would you classify *Gaither* as a false conflict? Why, or why not?

2. Did the District of Columbia rule involved in *Gaither* fit *Padula*'s definition

of conduct-regulating rules as those that "have the prophylactic effect of governing conduct to prevent injuries from occurring"? Did the District have an interest in applying that rule, even though the injury occurred in Maryland and the victim (unlike *Zhou*, supra 136) was not a D.C. domiciliary? Why, or why not? Do you agree with the *Gaither* court that Maryland did not have an interest in applying its rule, even though the injury occurred there and the victim was a Maryland domiciliary? Why, or why not?

3. How relevant are the parties' domiciles in conduct-regulation conflicts? For example, if the defendant in *Gaither* was not a D.C. domiciliary, would D.C. have less of an interest in applying its rule? Conversely, if the plaintiff was a D.C. domiciliary, would D.C. have more of an interests in applying its rule? Even if the answer to both of these questions is affirmative, is it true that, as a general proposition, a state has an interest in enforcing its conduct-regulating rules even if neither the violator nor the victim is domiciled in that state? May a foreigner claim exemption from a state's traffic rules, or, if injured by conduct that violates these rules, may the state deny him the benefit of their protection?

4. Did the *Gaither* court give "extraterritorial effect" to D.C.'s ignition-key rule? Why, or why not?

5. ***Car-Owner Liability Statutes.*** Like *Gaither*, other cases involving cross-border torts in which the conduct violated the standards of the conduct state but not the standards of the state of injury have invariably applied the law of the conduct state. One group of cases involve car-owner liability statutes like the Connecticut statute involved in *Levy*, supra Ch.2, which impose vicarious liability on car owners for injuries caused by a driver using the car with the owner's consent (hereafter referred to as "car-owner statutes"). Unlike the D.C. statute involved in *Gaither* which seems to clearly fall in the conduct-regulation category, these statutes can be of a dual character. Some cases have characterized these statutes as loss-distributing, while others, including Connecticut cases, have characterized them as conduct-regulating. See Symeonides, *The Revolution Today* §§ 172, 175. The latter cases have applied the car-owner statute of the state in which the owner consented to the use of the car, even though the accident occurred in a state that did not have such a statute. For example, in Veasley v. CRST Int'l, Inc., 553 N.W.2d 896 (Iowa 1996), the court applied Iowa's car-owner statute to a case arising from an accident in Arizona, a state that did not have such a statute. The court found that one of the purposes of the Iowa statute was "to make vehicle owners responsible for the actions of others to whom they have entrusted their motor vehicle," id. at 899, and that to not apply this statute because the accident occurred in another state "would undermine the effectiveness of th[is] important statute." Id. Following the Restatement (Second), the court held that the Iowa statute should govern because, "based on the deterrence policy underlying [the statute,] * * * Iowa ha[d] a substantial connection regarding the responsibility of all persons or corporations with a local nexus that loan or lease motor vehicles to other entities." Id.

Similarly, in Burney v. PV Holding Corp., 553 N.W.2d 657 (Mich.App.1996), a Michigan court applied Michigan's car-owner statute to a case in which the driver rented the car in Michigan and caused an accident in Alabama, a state that did not have such a statute. The court found that Michigan had an interest in effectuating the purpose of its car-owner statute, which was "to place the risk of damage or injury on the person with ultimate control of the vehicle and thereby promote safety in transportation." Id. at 660. The court noted that this purpose "cannot be fully effectuated unless the owner's liability statutes are given uniform application to residents of this state traveling outside of Michigan as well as persons within our state," id., and that "[t]o enforce the[se] * * * statutes on the basis of where the accident occurred would undermine the[ir] effectiveness." Id.

6. **Dram Shop Acts.** If dram shop acts are conduct-regulating, then the *Zhou* case, supra 135, as well as Schmidt v. Driscoll Hotel, 82 N.W.2d 365 (Minn.1957), would also fit within this pattern. In both cases the tortious conduct, the serving of the liquor to an intoxicated patron, occurred in a state that had a dram shop act that imposed civil liability on tavern owners for this conduct, while the resulting injury occurred in a state that did not impose such liability. Both cases applied the dram shop act of the conduct state, after concluding that only that state had an interest in deterring this conduct, while the injury state did not have a countervailing interest. As the *Zhou* court put it, any interest the state of injury might have in protecting tavern owners from civil liability was "not implicated where the [tavern] is situated in [another state] and the unlawful conduct occurred therein." 534 A.2d at 1271. In both cases, the victim was also a domiciliary of the conduct state, and thus the application of that state's law could have also been based on that state's compensatory interests.

In Patton v. Carnrike, 510 F.Supp. 625 (N.D.N.Y.1981), the law of the state of the injury, Pennsylvania, allowed the defendant to assert the defense of improper parental supervision, which the law of the state of conduct, New York, did not allow. Two seventeen-year-old Pennsylvanians drove to New York and purchased beer from defendant's New York store in violation of the drinking-age provisions of New York's dram shop act. While drinking the beer on their return trip, the two youths were involved in a single-car accident in Pennsylvania that caused the death of one them. When his parents sued the New York liquor vendor under the New York act, the defendant asserted the defense of improper parental supervision under Pennsylvania law. The court refused to allow this defense because it would undermine "the efficacy of [New York's] Dram Shop Act." Id. at 629. The court reasoned that "New York ha[d] a compelling interest in maintaining the integrity of the Act's deterrent effect," id., and that the "goal of deterring unlawful sales [was] well served by preserving the vendor's complete liability irrespective of where the injury occurred," id., and irrespective of the "fortuity that the purchasers were residents of Pennsylvania." Id. at 630.

7. **Other Issues.** Pittman v. Maldania, Inc., 2001 WL 1221704 (Del.Super. 2001), is illustrative of cases involving other conduct-regulation issues. In this case, the defendant operated a water-ski rental office on the Delaware side of the Delaware/Maryland border. The state line runs exactly in front of the office door, so that one had to enter Delaware to rent the water skis, but use them in Maryland. The laws of both states prohibited renting to persons below sixteen, but (unlike Maryland) Delaware additionally required the showing of a valid driver's license.

Without asking the showing of such license, the defendant rented skis to two Pennsylvania vacationers, ages 14 and 15, who misrepresented their ages, and who later collided with each other while riding the skis in Maryland waters. One of them sued the defendant in Delaware and invoked Delaware law. The court held that Delaware law should govern, despite the presumption of Restatement (Second) § 146 in favor of the place of injury. The court found that: (1) this presumption was rebutted because the precise issue in this case was the defendant's conduct in renting the ski in Delaware to an underage person; (2) the Delaware statute reflected "a clear policy against renting jet skis to people who are unable to produce a valid driver's license"; (3) this policy was "part of a comprehensive statute on boating safety"; and (4) that such a "statute regulating conduct should be enforced throughout the state." The court also found that: (1) "Maryland ha[d] no conflicting policy;" (2) Delaware's law "[did] not interfere in any way with Maryland's regulation of water safety in its state"; and (3) the defendant, having acted in Delaware, could not complain about the application of Delaware law. Id. at *4.

7. Do you agree with the results of the above cases? Is it not true that, in all of these cases, the application of the conduct-regulating rule of the conduct-state promoted the policy of that state in policing conduct within its borders, without subordinating the policies of the law of the injury-state? Is it also not true that the effectiveness of the conduct-regulating rule of the conduct-state would be seriously impaired if exceptions to it were made for out-of-state injuries? Does the state of injury have a contrary interest in protecting conduct that occurred beyond its border but caused injury within? In other words, are these cases not classic false conflicts? Finally, is there anything unfair in subjecting a tortfeasor to the law of the state in which he acted, just because the resulting injury occurred in another state? In 1965, Professor Cavers proposed a principle that would produce the same result as the above cases. This principle provides that "[w]here the state in which a defendant acted has established special controls, including the sanction of civil liability, over conduct of the kind in which the defendant was engaged when he caused a foreseeable injury to the plaintiff in another state, the plaintiff * * * should be accorded the benefit of the special standards of conduct and of financial protection in the state of the defendant's conduct, even though the state of injury had imposed no such controls or sanctions." Cavers, *Process*, 159. Is this a good principle?

A RECAP ON CONDUCT-REGULATION CONFLICTS

1. *The Pertinent Contacts and Typical Patterns*. If one accepts the premise suggested in the pervious Note that the parties' domiciles are a less relevant contact in conduct-regulation conflicts[1] (than in loss-distribution conflicts), then the only contact left is the "locus of the tort." However--as you remember from *Carroll*, and as *Gaither* illustrates--the two constituent elements of a tort, the conduct and the injury, may occur in different states. Indeed, cross-border torts are more common

---

1. For reasons explained infra at 320, the defendant's domicile is a relevant factor in punitive-damages conflicts. These conflicts are discussed in chapter 4.

today than at the time of *Carroll*. When conduct in one state produces injury in another state, either state may qualify as the "locus of the tort." On can either recognize this fact and give due consideration to both contacts, or one can retreat to Beale's outmoded "last-event" notions and artificially designate one of those two places as the place of the tort.

Adopting the former option, as well as the premise that the parties' domiciles are not a significant *a priori* factor in conduct-regulation conflicts, one can classify these conflicts into the following four patterns:

(1) Cases like *Padula* in which the conduct and the injury occur in the same state (*Pattern 1*);

(2) Cases in which the conduct and the injury occur in different states, and in which:

(a) the two states prescribe the same standards of conduct (*Pattern 2*); or

(b) the two states prescribe different standards (designated with the adjectives "high" and "low"), and in which the particular conduct:

(i) as in *Gaither*, violates the ("higher") standards of the state of conduct, but not the ("lower") standards of the state of injury (*Pattern 3*); or

(ii) does not violate the ("lower") standards of the state of conduct, but does violate the ("higher") standards of the state of injury (*Pattern 4*).

TABLE 5. PATTERNS IN CONDUCT-REGULATION CONFLICTS

Pattern	Conduct	Injury
1. (*Padula*)	a	a
	A	**A**
2. (*Pardey*)	**A**	**B**
	a	b
3. (*Gaither*)	**A**	b
4. (*Bernhard*)	a	**B**

The above table depicts these patterns, with uppercase letters denoting a state with a high standard of conduct and lowercase letters denoting a state with a lower standard. The first column shows the names of a representative case from each pattern.

2. *Patterns 1-3.* In interest-analysis terminology, patterns 1-3 are three different variations of the false conflict paradigm. With regard to Patterns 1 and 3, the reasons for this conclusion should be obvious from *Padula* and *Gaither*, respectively, and the other cases falling within the same patterns. See Notes following these two cases.

Pattern 2 is but a slight variation of Pattern 1. The only difference is that in Pattern 2, the conduct and the injury occur in different states, which prescribe the same standard of conduct. In policy terms, these cases are virtually indistinguishable from Pattern 1 cases. Whether the court applies the law of the one or the other state, the outcome will be the same. Hence, applying the law of the conduct state is both sensible and non-controversial.

For example, in Pardey v. Boulevard Billiard Club, 518 A.2d 1349 (R.I.1986), both the conduct state (Rhode Island) and the injury state (Massachusetts) had dram shop acts imposing civil liability on a tavern owner whose intoxicated patrons caused injury to another person. A Massachusetts patron caused such injury in Massachusetts, after becoming intoxicated in defendant's Rhode Island tavern. The court noted Rhode Island's "substantial governmental interest," id. at 1352, in applying the Rhode Island act to violations occurring in that state, even when the resulting injury occurs in another state. The court also noted that "Massachusetts law is not offended by application of [the Rhode Island act] to this case since Massachusetts has its own dram shop law that regulates Massachusetts licensees. Application of Rhode Island law therefore effectuates, rather than frustrates, the policies of *both* states." Id. (emphasis added). Other dram shop act cases have recognized this elementary principle and have reached the same result under similar circumstances. See Symeonides, *The Revolution Today* §§ 171-73.

Another category of cases involves car-owner liability statutes which, as note supra, can be characterized as either loss-distributing or conduct- regulating. Accepting for now the latter characterization, when both the state in which the owner consented to the use of the car by another, and the state in which the driver caused the injury have such statutes, the court can apply the statute of either state without altering the outcome. In Elson v. Defren, 726 N.Y.S.2d 407 (N.Y.A.D. 2001), the two involved states, Idaho and New York, had similar car-owner liability statutes. The only difference was that the text of the New York statute limited it to cars operated in New York. The court found that, because of this territorial limitation, the New York statute was inapplicable, but this did not affect the outcome because, "under the law of both Idaho and New York, when a vehicle is involved in an accident within their respective borders, the owner of the vehicle is vicariously liable." Id at 412. Accordingly, said the court, "and without further inquiry, we apply Idaho law to effectuate the public policy reflected in the statutes of both jurisdictions." Id.

3. *Pattern 4: Conduct in State with Low Standard and Injury in State with High Standard.* Pattern 4 involves the most difficult cross-border torts. In this pattern the conduct in question does not violate the "lower" standards of the conduct-state, but violates the "higher" standards of the injury-state. In interest analysis terminology, these cases usually present the true conflict paradigm.

The argument for applying the higher standard of the state of injury is stronger in cases involving intentional torts than in negligence cases. Indeed, not many people would question the right of a state to punish conduct that is intended to produce, and does produce, detrimental effects within its territory, even when that conduct takes place outside the state. As Justice Holmes stated almost a century ago, "[a]cts done outside the jurisdiction, but intended to produce and producing detrimental effects within it, justify a state in punishing the cause of the harm." Strassheim v. Daily, 221 U.S. 280, 284 (1911). The U.S. Supreme Court has applied this "effects doctrine" in many cases, including Hartford Fire Ins. Co. v. California, 509 U.S. 764 (1993), which is reproduced infra Ch. 7. In *Hartford Fire*, the Court held that "the Sherman Act applies to foreign conduct that was meant to produce and did in fact produce some substantial effects in the United States." 509 U.S. at 795-96. The Court applied the Act to British insurance underwriters who, while in London, engaged in conduct designed to affect the California insurance market. Several lower-court cases have applied the Sherman Act in the same fashion, and one case, United States v. Nippon Paper Indus., 109 F.3d 1 (1st Cir. 1997), upheld under the Act a criminal prosecution of a Japanese defendant for conduct in Japan (price-fixing) that was intended to and did produce detrimental effects in the United States.

In cases involving negligent conduct, the argument for applying the higher standard of the state of injury may be less powerful psychologically, but it is still a fairly strong one, provided that the actor could have foreseen that his conduct in one state would produce injury in the other state. Suppose for example that a defendant operates a chemical plant near the state border and the plant emits substances or quantities that are permitted by that state but not by the neighboring state. If these substances cause injury in the latter state, would it not be reasonable to apply the law of the latter state? For an affirmative answer, see Professor Cavers's first "principle of preference." The principle provides that "[w]here the liability laws of the state of injury set a higher standard of conduct * * * than do the laws of the state where the person who caused the injury has acted * * * the laws of the place of injury shall determine the standard * * * applicable to the case." Cavers, *Process*, 139. See also id. at 141 (adding a foreseeability caveat).

Compare the above hypothetical case with *Bernhard v. Harrah's Club*, supra 215. Even if dram shop acts are loss-distributing rather than conduct-regulating, these two cases would present the same issues and dilemmas, would they not? If so, should a court not resolve them in the same way? As seen in the Note following *Bernhard*, this is precisely what courts have done.

4. *Summary and Rule for Conduct-Regulation Conflicts.* Now look back at the results reached by the cases reproduced or discussed in this section, from *Padula* to *Hartford Fire* and *Bernhard*. Does the following rule accurately describe these results?

> *Conflicts between conduct-regulating rules are governed by the law of the state of conduct, except when the injury foreseeably occurs in another state that imposes a higher standard of conduct, in which case the law of the latter state governs.*

In the United States, the Louisiana codification has adopted such a rule (La. Civ.Code art. 3543), and so has the Puerto Rico Draft Code (art. 46). A rule essentially producing the same result also appears in most codifications enacted in the last decades of the 20th century. For example, article 45(1)-(3) of the Portuguese Civil Code contains rules that are confined to conduct-regulation issues and are virtually identical to the above rule. Other codifications contain rules that, though not confined to conduct-regulation issues, resolve cross-border torts in the same way, with or without a foreseeability proviso. These rules are described supra at 227.

To a lesser or greater extent, all of the above rules favor plaintiffs, at least in true-conflicts. Is such a favoritism acceptable? Why, or why not? Which of the above rules provide safeguards for defendants? Are these safeguards adequate to make these rules fair?

Rules that impose punitive damages are *par excellence* conduct-regulating rules, which, however, have an additional punitive purpose that is not present in other conduct-regulating rules. Is the above italicized choice-of-law rule a good rule for resolving punitive-damages conflicts, or does it need additional safeguards to be fairer to defendants? For a discussion of these issues, see infra Ch. 4, 318 *et seq.*

6. A CONCLUDING NOTE ON TERRITORIALITY AND PERSONALITY[1]

From the beginning of its history, Private International Law approached the task of delineating the operation of state and national laws by posing questions such as the following: (1) do laws attach to a territory, or to the citizens or domiciliaries of that territory (territoriality versus personality)? (2) does a law operate only within the enacting state's territory, or beyond that territory as well (territoriality versus extraterritoriality)? and (3) does the application of a state's law within its territory necessarily exclude the application of the laws of other states?

These questions usually are compressed into two competing basic principles-- territoriality and personality of the laws--although it would be more accurate to speak of territoriality versus *non-territoriality*. Either way, the core question is when should the application of a state's law depend on territorial factors, and when should it depend on other, including personal, factors?

Through the centuries, various systems have provided different answers to the above question, with the pendulum swinging from territoriality to personality and vice versa, but without one principle completely dislodging the other. For example, in the days of the Roman Empire, the principle of personality was the dominant, but not exclusive, principle, whereas in the days of the Italian statutists, the two principles coexisted, with personality embodied in "personal" statutes and territoriality embodied in "real" statutes. With the emergence of modern nation-states and Jean Bodin's 16th century seminal works on territorial sovereignty, territoriality began to gain ground, a trend that Huber expressed in two of his famous axioms in the 17th century. See supra Ch. 1. In the United States Joseph Story gave his own strong endorsement to territoriality in the 19th century, and Joseph Beale elevated it to a commanding position in the 20th century. Beale believed that, "by its very nature law must apply to everything and must exclusively apply to everything within the boundary of its jurisdiction." 1 Beale, *Conflict of Laws* 46 (1935). Thus, under Beale's scheme, a state's law should govern all torts occurring, contracts made, and property located within its territory.

The American conflicts revolution studied in this chapter was a rebellion against many, if not all, aspects of Beale's system; but the revolution was also, if not primarily, a rebellion against the *lex loci delicti* rule and its underlying holistic assumption that all of torts law operates territorially. However, as *Babcock* framed it, the revolution's goal was not to banish the *lex loci* rule altogether, but rather to determine whether "the law of the place of the tort [should] *invariably* govern the availability of relief for the tort." *Babcock*, supra. This was far from being iconoclastic.

---

1. Adapted from Symeonides, *Territoriality and Personality.*

Following New York's lead in *Babcock*, 41 other jurisdictions have abandoned the *lex loci* rule as the inexorable rule for all tort conflicts. As this chapter illustrates, these jurisdictions now rely on multiple contacts, factors, and policies, all of which are antithetical to the single-mindedness of the *lex loci* rule. Most of the new factors, such as the parties' domicile and their pre-existing relationship, are non-territorial. This is true not only of the center-of-gravity and significant-contacts approaches, but also of the Restatement (Second), interest analysis, the better law, and other contemporary approaches. In terms of choice-of-law *methodology*, the above developments amounted to a true revolution. One of the effects of this revolution is that territoriality is no longer the exclusive operating principle in tort conflicts. In fact, at least in theory, this principle has all but disappeared.

However, if one were to focus on the actual *results* of the cases[2] decided under the new approaches since the *Babcock* days, then is it not true that territoriality is very much alive? For example, do you agree with the following:

(1) aside from loss-distribution conflicts of the common-domicile pattern, cases involving many other patterns have reached the same results as the *lex loci* rule would have produced: they applied the law of a state of injury, even if that state had additional contacts and even if the rationale for applying that law was partly based on those additional contacts or other factors; and

(2) in some other categories of cases, the courts applied the law of the place of conduct (rather than the place of injury) and thus produced a different result than the American version of the *lex loci* rule would produce. However, because the place of conduct is a territorial rather than a personal contact, these cases remain in the territorialist column, do they not?

What then is the actual position of territoriality in American tort conflicts today? The basic distinction *Babcock* enunciated between conduct-regulating and loss-distributing rules helps answer this question, and the following diagram attempts to depict the answer.

Issues	Loss Distribution			Conduct-Regulation	
Parties' Domiciles	Common domicile	Split-Domicile		Irrelevant	
Conduct & Injury	Irrelevant	Same state	Cross-Border	Same state	Cross-Border
Principle	**Personality**	**Person. vs. Territor.**		**Territoriality**	

The diagram suggests the following conclusions:

(1) Territoriality has lost significant ground to the personality principle in conflicts between loss-distribution rules. However, the ground lost is confined to one category of cases--cases in which both the tortfeasor and the victim are domiciled or have significant affiliations with the same state (common-

---

2. *Cf.* Weintraub, *Commentary*, 347 ("More important than what the commentators are up to as they deforest the land with the mountains of conflicts articles, is the results that the courts are reaching.")

domicile cases), and are involved in a tort that occurred in another state or states. In these cases, the courts have almost unanimously applied the law of the parties' common domicile. Thus, one can say that the principle of personality reigns supreme in loss-distribution conflicts of the common-domicile pattern.

(2) Conversely, territoriality continues to reign supreme in conflicts between conduct-regulating rules. In these conflicts, the courts disregard the parties' domiciles and focus on the two territorial contacts--the place of conduct and the place of injury. When both of these contacts are in the same state, the courts invariably apply the law of that state. When these contacts are in different states, the courts choose one of those states, as explained above. When they choose the law of the place of conduct, the result deviates from the *lex loci* rule as applied in the United States, but it is still a territorial result.

(3) This leaves the middle ground--loss-distribution conflicts of the split-domicile pattern. This is the arena in which territoriality and personality continue to challenge each other. (See the shaded cell.) Although the courts that have abandoned the *lex loci* rule consider both the personal and the territorial contacts, the majority of courts end up applying the law of the state that has the territorial contacts (even if that state also has a personal contact), rather than the state that has only a personal contact. In that sense, one can say that, at least for now, territoriality continues to carry the day in these middle conflicts.

In reviewing this chapter, do you agree with the above conclusions?

If one assumes that the goal of the American choice-of-law revolution was to banish territoriality from tort conflicts, one would have to conclude that the revolution has scored only a partial victory. However, as noted earlier, such an assumption would be incorrect. The revolution's goals were neither as deliberate nor as narrow. The chief goal was to free American choice-of-law from the shackles of a mechanical rule that inexorably required the application of the law of a state that had a single contact--which happened to be territorial--regardless of any other contacts or factors, and regardless of the issue involved in the conflict or the content of the conflicting laws. Judged in this light, the revolution has succeeded in demolishing not only this particular rule, but also the system that gave birth to it. Along the way, the revolution has brought about a new accommodation or equilibrium between territoriality and personality. Was the revolution worth it, and is this a good equilibrium?

IV. THE METHODOLOGICAL LANDSCAPE

Time now for "conflicts geography." After studying all of the above choice-of-law methodologies, one may be curious to know which of them are followed in the states of the United States. The table and maps reproduced below[1] may satisfy this curiosity, but they should be used with caution. In drawing the "methodological map" of American conflicts law, one cannot aspire to the precision expected in real cartography. Difficulties arise from a variety of sources, ranging from the occasional lack or dearth of authoritative precedent, to precedents that are either equivocal or exceedingly eclectic.

For example, for more than sixty years, the Supreme Court of New Hampshire has not had an opportunity to reconsider its last precedent to apply the *lex loci contractus* rule. In some states, the available supreme court precedents are equivocal, or even irreconcilable. For example, in contract conflicts, the precedents from Oklahoma and West Virginia are equivocal enough as to raise legitimate doubts on whether these states securely belong in the Restatement (Second) column. Similar doubts exist regarding Arkansas' classification as a significant-contacts state, because Arkansas precedents are virtually irreconcilable.

When methodological equivocation is intentional and appears in the same precedent, it can be described as eclecticism. This phenomenon, which appeared in the first years of the revolution, has become even more frequent in recent years. Whatever its intrinsic virtues, eclecticism is another obstacle to an accurate methodological classification. The column called "combined modern" that appears in Table 6, infra, reflects this eclecticism only to some extent--it includes only those states that overtly, knowingly, and repeatedly combine more than one modern methodology. If one were to include instances of unknowing, latent, or occasional eclecticism, that column would absorb most other columns. In this sense eclecticism may well be *the* dominant choice-of-law methodology in the United States today.

Additional limitations stem from the simplification that graphic technology dictates. For example, the maps below lump together the Restatement (Second) and "significant contacts" states, the interest-analysis and *lex-fori* states, and the states that follow a "combined modern" approach. Although the approaches grouped together are either ideologically or methodologically akin, they are not identical. In fact, even if one were to focus solely on the states following the Restatement (Second), the use of a single color for all of those states gives the misleading impression that they share the same degree of commitment to the Restatement. They do not. Some states use the Restatement solely as an escape from a traditional choice-of-law rule that co-exists with the Restatement. Some states use the Restatement as a camouflage for a "grouping of contacts" approach, while other states use it as a vehicle for restraining interest analysis. One can find

---

1. The Tables and maps are taken from Symeonides, *The Revolution Today* §§ 42, 58-103, to which the reader is referred for further discussion and documentation.

examples of such disparate treatment of the Restatement even in the same jurisdiction. Finally, some states prefer to use only the general, open-ended, and flexible sections of the Restatement (such as §§ 145, 187 and especially § 6) and avoid using the specific sections that contain mildly confining presumptive rules.

Even the use of the black color to indicate the states that follow the traditional approach may be misleading to the extent it suggests that these states are equally committed to that approach. They are not. For example, some of those states (e.g., Alabama, Georgia, Maryland, and Wyoming) have recently reaffirmed their commitment to the traditional approach, other states (e.g., South Carolina and Maryland for contracts) have made small steps in the direction of abandoning it, while other states (e.g. Rhode Island and Tennessee with regard to contract conflicts) appear ready to abandon it on the first available opportunity. Unfortunately, maps cannot show these gradations of commitment without using all the colors in the spectrum.

Be that as it may, with all the above caveats and qualifications, the following maps and table purport to show how the various states congregated in the various methodological camps in 2003.

Map 1. Torts

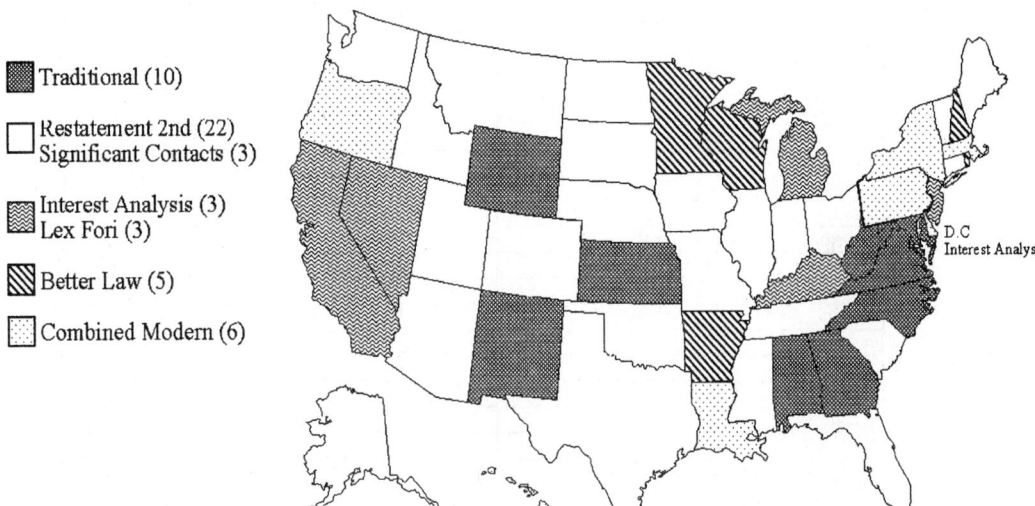

Traditional (10)

Restatement 2nd (22)
Significant Contacts (3)

Interest Analysis (3)
Lex Fori (3)

Better Law (5)

Combined Modern (6)

D.C
Interest Analysis

Map 2. Contracts

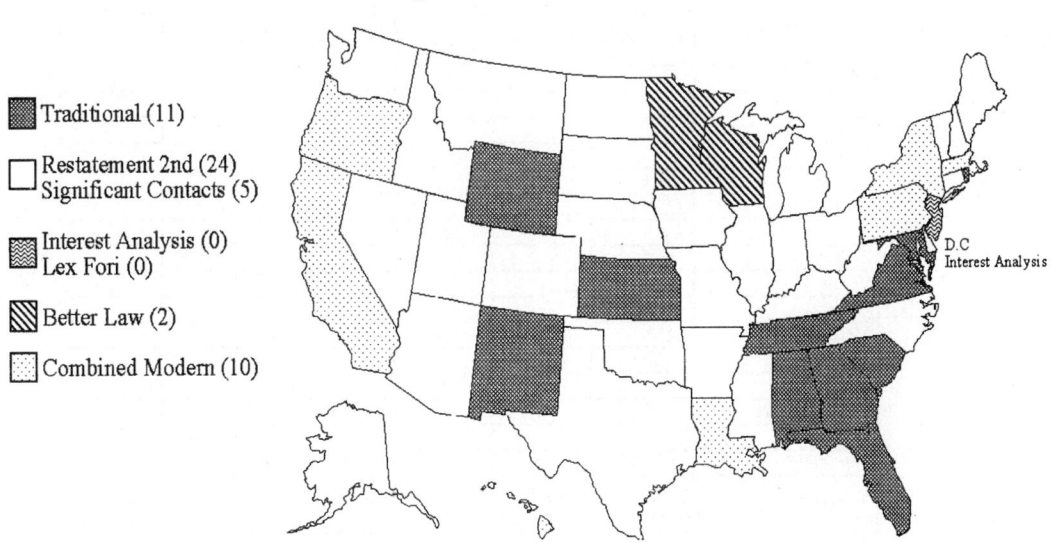

Traditional (11)

Restatement 2nd (24)
Significant Contacts (5)

Interest Analysis (0)
Lex Fori (0)

Better Law (2)

Combined Modern (10)

D.C
Interest Analysis

TABLE 6. ALPHABETICAL LIST OF STATES AND CHOICE-OF-LAW METHODOLOGIES

States	Traditional	Signif. contacts	Restate-ment 2d	Interest Analysis	Lex. Fori	Better Law	Combined Modern
Alabama	T+C						
Alaska			T+C				
Arizona			T+C				
Arkansas		C				T	
California				T			C
Colorado			T+C				
Connecticut			T+ C?				
Delaware			T+C				
District of Columbia				T			C
Florida	C		T				
Georgia	T+C						
Hawaii							T+C
Idaho			T+C				
Illinois			T+C				
Indiana		T+C					
Iowa			T+C				
Kansas	T+C						
Kentucky			C		T		
Louisiana							T+C
Maine			T+C				
Maryland	T+C						
Massachusetts							T+C
Michigan			C		T		
Minnesota						T+C	
Mississippi			T+C				
Missouri			T+C				
Montana			T+C				
Nebraska			T+C				
Nevada		C			T		
New Hampshire			C			T	
New Jersey				T			C
New Mexico	T+C						
New York							T+C
No. Carolina	T	C					
North Dakota		T					C
Ohio			T+C				
Oklahoma			T+C?				
Oregon							T+C
Pennsylvania							T+C
Puerto Rico		T+C					
Rhode Island	C					T	
So. Carolina	T+C						
So. Dakota			T+C				
Tennessee	C		T				
Texas			T+C				
Utah			T+C				
Vermont			T+C				
Virginia	T+C						
Washington			T+C				
West Virginia	T		C				
Wisconsin						T+C	
Wyoming	T+C						
TOTAL	52 Torts 52 Contr.	10 Torts 11 Contr.	3 Torts 5 Contr.	22 Torts 24 Contr.	3 Torts 0 Contr.	3 Torts 0 Contr.	5 Torts 2 Contr.	6 Torts 10 Contr.

T = Torts   C = Contracts

As the above table indicates, the Restatement (Second) group is the largest, while the interest-analysis group is the smallest. The interest-analysis column is completely blank in contract conflicts, and lists only three jurisdictions in tort conflicts. In light of the pivotal role that interest analysis played in the conflicts revolution, this development is nothing short of astonishing. Worse yet, a more literal classification might place even these three jurisdictions elsewhere, insofar as they engage in the very weighing of state interests that Currie proscribed. Thus, a more technical classification might move these states to different columns, leaving completely blank the interest-analysis column, four decades after Currie's death.

However, this should not suggest that Currie's influence has disappeared. First, an interest analysis traceable to Currie forms the core of most of the "combined modern" approaches followed in other states. Second, interest analysis is often heavily employed in states that generally follow the Restatement (Second), especially in cases in which the factual contacts are evenly divided between the involved jurisdictions. Thus, in the same manner that the high numerical following the Restatement (Second) tends to inflate its importance in deciding actual cases, the low numerical following of Currie's original approach tends to undervalue the importance of this approach in influencing judicial decisions.

The states listed under the "Combined-Modern" approach follow a combination of approaches other than the traditional one. In tort conflicts, California follows interest analysis with the addendum of Baxter's comparative impairment. However, in contract conflicts, at least those involving choice-of-law clauses, the California Supreme Court tends to rely heavily on the Restatement (Second) and to combine it with comparative impairment. New Jersey and the District of Columbia do likewise in contract conflicts, combining interest analysis with the Restatement (Second). Hawaii follows a combination of interest analysis, the Restatement (Second), and Leflar's choice-influencing considerations. North Dakota follows the same combination, but perhaps in different dosages, in contract conflicts. Massachusetts and Oregon follow a combination of interest analysis and the Restatement (Second). Pennsylvania does likewise, but in addition draws from Professor Cavers's principles of preference. Louisiana has its own comprehensive codification that draws from the general American conflicts experience, but also goes beyond that experience. Finally, New York is New York!

Chapter 4

CONFLICTS
ACROSS THE CURRICULUM

A. INTRODUCTION

The two previous chapters explore the basic questions of choice-of-law methodology and general theory through the medium of generic tort and contract conflicts. This chapter focuses on contemporary choice-of-law *practice* in other areas of the law, such as insurance, statutes of limitation, property, marital property, successions, status, and corporations.

Before doing so, this chapter examines some special issues of tort and contract conflicts in the context of: complex litigation, products liability, punitive damages, and contractual choice-of-law (party autonomy).

B. COMPLEX LITIGATION

In Re Air Crash Disaster at Sioux City, Iowa
United States District Court, N.D. Illinois, 1990.
734 F.Supp. 1425.

CONLON, J. In this consolidated multidistrict litigation arising from an air crash at Sioux City, Iowa, defendants United Airlines, Inc., McDonnell Douglas Corporation and General Electric Company (collectively "defendants") move the court to dismiss all punitive damages claims under Fed.R.Civ.P. 12(b)(6). In the alternative, defendants request an order determining the state law governing punitive damages in each of the eighteen cases before this court.

I. BACKGROUND. On July 19, 1989, United Airlines Flight 232 from Denver to Chicago crashed during an attempted emergency landing at Sioux City, Iowa, after the aircraft lost hydraulic power. Of the 296 people on board, 112 were killed in the tragic crash. The aircraft, owned and operated by United Airlines, was a DC-10 manufactured by McDonnell Douglas. General Electric manufactured the CF6–6 engines utilized on the aircraft.

Flight 232 passengers were from thirty states and two foreign countries. Ninety-three passengers were from Colorado. Eighteen cases were transferred to the Northern District of Illinois for pretrial purposes by order of the Judicial Panel on Multidistrict Litigation. The cases were transferred from district courts located in ten states.

United Airlines is a Delaware corporation with its principal place of business in Illinois. United maintained the aircraft in California. United's flight crew training center is located in Colorado. The aircraft's builder, McDonnell Douglas, is a Maryland corporation with its principal place of business in Missouri. McDonnell Douglas designed and manufactured the aircraft in California. The third defendant, General Electric, is a New York corporation with its principal place of business in New York. General Electric designed and manufactured the engines on Flight 232 in Ohio. * * *

IV. DETERMINATION OF STATE LAW APPLICABLE IN EACH CASE. * * * [D]efendants request the court to determine the law applicable to punitive damages in each case. A federal court ordinarily must apply the choice of law principles of the state in which it sits. *Klaxon Co. v. Stentor Electric Mfg. Co.*, 313 U.S. 487 (1941). When a case is transferred, the transferee court must apply the choice of law rules of the state where the transferor court sits. *Van Dusen v. Barrack*, 376 U.S. 612 (1964); *Air Crash Disaster Near Chicago*, 644 F.2d 594, 610 (7th Cir.), *cert. denied sub nom., Lin v. Am. Airlines*, 454 U.S. 878 (1981) ("Air Crash"). In this litigation, at least twelve cases originating in eight different states assert claims for punitive damages.

In *Air Crash*, the seventh circuit resolved the choice of law issues in consolidated multidistrict litigation regarding an air crash in Illinois. The court expressly adopted the concept of depecage, "the process of applying rules of different states on the basis of the precise issue involved." *Id.* at 611. Accordingly, this opinion resolves the choice of law question regarding only the issue of punitive damages.

* * * The applicable state law may not permit punitive damages in every case. Most states do not permit punitive damages in wrongful death actions. [cit.] States differ over whether to permit punitive damages in survival actions. Finally, although all relevant states permit punitive damages in personal injury actions, the applicable standards differ from state to state. * * * [A] plaintiff's domicile plays no role in determining which state law governs punitive damages. *Air Crash*, [cit.] The choice of law question depends entirely on activities conducted by defendants. These activities are common to all the consolidated cases. * * * Plaintiffs' * * * complaints contain allegations as to the situs of defendants' respective principal places of business. Plaintiffs have not suggested that any material issue of fact exists concerning where defendants' corporate nerve centers are located or where defendants' alleged wrongful conduct occurred. * * * [T]he locations where the conduct at issued occurred: Colorado (United Airlines), Ohio (General Electric), and California (McDonnell Douglas). * * *

A. Cases Transferred From California. Three cases were filed in federal courts located in California. California employs a "comparative impairment" analysis. Under this analysis, when a true conflict exists, a court should apply the law of the state whose interests would be more impaired if its law were not applied. *Bernhard v. Harrah's Club*, [supra Ch. 3].

Initially, the court must determine which states' interests to consider. In *Air*

Crash, the court applied California's comparative impairment test. [cit.] The court restricted the analysis to three states representing the principal place of business, the place of the alleged misconduct and the state in which the injury occurred.[10] The court noted that the domiciliary states of the plaintiffs or their representatives are not relevant to the question of punitive damages. [cit.]

After narrowing the analysis to the relevant states, the court must determine whether an apparent conflict exists between the punitive damages laws of those states. [cit.] If an apparent conflict exists, the court examines the applicable law to see if a "moderate and restrained interpretation" of the law reveals that only one state has a legitimate interest in the application of its policy. *Air Crash*, [cit.], citing *Bernhard*, [cit.]. When a restrained or moderate interpretation of state law fails to resolve the conflict, a "true" conflict exists.

True conflicts are resolved by applying the law of the state whose interest would be the more impaired if its law were not applied. *Id.*; [cit.]. The process is "'essentially a process of allocating respective spheres of lawmaking influence.'" [cit.] The court must consider (1) whether one state's punitive damages provision is more strongly held than that of other interested states, and (2) the "fit" between the purpose of each potentially applicable punitive damages provision and the circumstances of the case. *Air Crash.*

In this case, the injury occurred in Iowa. However, Iowa was not the place of departure or scheduled destination. Under any theory of liability, the fact that the accident occurred in Iowa was a mere fortuity. Consequently, Iowa's interest in the action does not merit further consideration under California choice of law principles. The analysis is limited to the principal place of business of each defendant and the place of the conduct at issue.

1. *United Airlines.* Under the comparative impairment test, the punitive damages laws of Illinois, California and Colorado must be considered regarding United Airlines. United has its principal place of business in Illinois. Both California and Colorado may have been the site of United's alleged wrongful conduct. The alleged wrongful conduct could relate to United's maintenance, testing and inspection of the aircraft in California. Punitive damages may be based upon the conduct of United's crew. United's flying personnel are principally trained in Colorado.

The punitive damages laws of these states substantially differ. California does not permit punitive damages in wrongful death actions. [cit.] California does permit punitive damages in survival actions and personal injury actions. [cit.] California requires clear and convincing evidence of oppression, fraud, or malice. [cit.] Under California law, "malice" is defined as conduct intended to cause injury to the plaintiff or despicable conduct carried on with a willful and conscious disregard of the rights and safety of others, and "oppression" means despicable conduct done in conscious disregard of the victim's rights. [cit.]

---

10. The court considered the interests of Illinois, the state in which the injury occurred, because "it is a state in which both the policies of protection of airline corporations and deterrence of misconduct are peculiarly important." *Air Crash*, 644 F.2d at 622.

Colorado does not permit punitive damages in wrongful death or survival actions. [cit.] In other actions, Colorado requires that conduct supporting punitive damages be proven "beyond a reasonable doubt." [cit.]. In addition, Colorado limits punitive damages awards for personal injury to the amount of actual damages unless the court determines that the defendant has continued the behavior in a willful and wanton manner. [cit.]

In general, Illinois does not permit punitive damages in wrongful death or survival actions. [cit.] Punitive damages are awarded in other actions "when torts are committed with fraud, actual malice, deliberate violence or oppression, or when the defendant acts willfully, or with such gross negligence as to indicate a wanton disregard of the rights of others." [cit.]

A true conflict exists in the availability of punitive damages under the laws of Colorado, California and Illinois. These laws reflect a balance reached by each state between deterrence of wrongful conduct and protection of defendants from excessive financial liability. *Air Crash*, [cit.]. Illinois, Colorado and California all have legitimate interests in controlling the activity of defendant United Airlines. Colorado and California's interests are limited to activity within their states. Illinois has an interest in activity performed in all three states. The appropriate method to resolve the conflict is to determine which state interest would be most impaired by failure to apply its law.

United Airlines argues that Illinois is not as committed to its punitive damages law as Colorado or California because Illinois common law rather than statutory authority defines the right to punitive damages. Common law authority is not necessarily inferior to statutory authority of another state. *See, id.* [*Air Crash*] (finding that California, Missouri, Illinois and New York all have strong commitments to their respective approaches to punitive damages). The state legislature may have purposefully acquiesced in the judicial resolution of the punitive damages standard. Defendants do not cite a case in which a state was found to lack a commitment to its punitive damages law. Consequently, the choice of law decision will be based upon the "fit" between the purpose of each state's punitive damages law and the circumstances of the case. *Id.* at 622 (citations omitted).

In general, plaintiffs raise two separate bases for punitive damages against United. First, plaintiffs contend that United recklessly maintained, tested or inspected the aircraft. United asserts that these alleged reckless acts could only occur in California. United contends that California has a direct deterrent interest in faulty maintenance performed in California and that California law should apply. The second basis for punitive damages is alleged reckless operation of the aircraft. United contends that allegations concerning the flight crew relate to the crew's training in Colorado. United asserts that Colorado law should govern punitive damages claims regarding the activity of the flight crew.

However, United is not engaged in the business of manufacturing planes or training flight crews. Although United may bring its aircraft to California for servicing and train its flight crews in Colorado, United's primary activity is to carry passengers. United's central hub and principal place of business are located in Illinois. Flight 232 was destined for Illinois. United argues that the locale of the wrongful conduct is closely associated with the conduct "because the likelihood of injury from the conduct is generally greater in that place." United Memorandum at 28. However, injury is unlikely to occur at the site of United's training or maintenance. It is likely to occur at United's primary place of business, where United flights frequently arrive and depart.[12]

Illinois is an appropriate forum to balance the deterrent function of punitive damages against the need to protect United Airlines from excessive financial liability. Illinois benefits from United's presence and Illinois risks the consequences of United's wrongful conduct. Illinois' interest in its law respecting punitive damages would be impaired more than either Colorado's or California's if its law were not applied. As United's principal place of business, Illinois law regarding punitive damages governs claims against United Airlines.

2. *McDonnell Douglas*. McDonnell Douglas designed and built the aircraft in California. Its principal place of business is Missouri. In *Air Crash*, McDonnell Douglas was a defendant. Under analogous circumstances, the seventh circuit wrestled with the question whether Missouri or California punitive damages policies would be more impaired if they were not applied. The court concluded that both states' policies would be equally impaired. The court decided that a California court would escape the quandary by applying Illinois law. *Air Crash*.

Subsequent decisions by California state courts indicate that in the event California shares an equal interest in application of its law with another state, a California court would apply California law. [cit.]. California courts have "repeatedly asserted that California has an important interest in regulating products manufactured in California." [cit.]. Since Missouri and California law would be equally impaired if not applied, California law governs claims for punitive damages against McDonnell Douglas.

3. *General Electric*. General Electric manufactured the engines on Flight 232 in Ohio. Its principal place of business is New York. As discussed above, Iowa was the fortuitous site of the crash, and Iowa has no real interest in imposing punitive damages against General Electric. Colorado has some interest in having its punitive damages law applied in this case because Denver has a busy airport from which Flight 232 departed. However, Ohio and New York have stronger interests than either Colorado or Iowa. Consequently, the comparative impairment analysis is limited to Ohio and New York.

A brief summary of the punitive damage laws of Ohio and New York reveals that a true conflict exists. Ohio prohibits punitive damage awards in wrongful death actions. [cit.] In order to award punitive damages in other actions, a jury must find clear and convincing evidence that a manufacturer "manifested a flagrant disregard of the safety of persons who might be harmed by the product in

---

12. The most recent data from the National Transportation Safety Board shows that 30.4% of all airline accidents in 1986 occurred during the taxi, takeoff and climb phase of operation, 43.4% occurred during the descent, approach and landing phase and only 17.4% occurred during the cruise phase. From 1981–1985, 55% of the fatal accidents occurred during the taxi, takeoff and climb phase, 25% occurred during descent, approach and landing, and 10% occurred during the cruise. United's motion, App. B. National Transportation Safety Board, Annual Review of Aircraft Accident Data--U.S. Air Carrier Operations Calendar Year 1986.

question." [cit.]

New York permits awards of punitive damages in wrongful death actions, [cit.], survival actions, [cit.], and ordinary personal injury actions. New York allows imposition of punitive damages for conduct that is "morally culpable, or is actuated by evil and reprehensible motives." [cit.].

General Electric argues that Ohio has expressed a stronger, more recent interest in the imposition of its punitive damages law. General Electric points out that Ohio law is codified and offers greater protection to a corporation than New York law. However, the fact that New York's punitive damage provision was not codified may imply that the state legislature agrees with the judicial resolution of the punitive damages standard. The fact that Ohio law affords greater protection to defendants than New York law indicates only that Ohio has struck a different balance between deterrence and protection than New York.

Ohio interests would be more impaired if its punitive damages policy were not applied. General Electric manufactures aircraft engines in Ohio and not in New York. General Electric's principal place of business is in New York because other holdings, including the National Broadcasting Company, Kidder, Peabody Group, Inc. and GE Turbine Operations, are located in New York. Since the alleged wrongful acts occurred in Ohio, and Ohio is the principal place of business of General Electric's aircraft engine manufacturing division, Ohio has a greater opportunity to balance interests of deterrence against protection of General Electric regarding airplane engine manufacturing. Ohio law governs the punitive damage claims against General Electric.

4. *Conclusion*. The three cases originally filed in California each assert claims for punitive damages based upon personal injuries. The punitive damage claims against United Airlines shall be governed by Illinois law. The claims against McDonnell Douglas shall be governed by California law. The claims against General Electric shall be governed by Ohio law.

B. Cases Transferred From Colorado, Iowa, New York, and Georgia and cases filed in Illinois. Six cases stating claims for punitive damages were filed in Colorado, Iowa, Illinois, New York and Georgia. Colorado, Iowa, Illinois and New York all apply the "most significant relationship" test described in § 145 *et seq.* of the Restatement (Second) of the Conflict of Laws ("the Restatement").[14] The Supreme Court of Georgia has never decided whether the Restatement should be applied in air crash cases, but Georgia would adopt the Restatement if the question were raised.[15] * * * The most significant relationship test must be applied independ

---

14. * * * The New York test is the functional equivalent of the Illinois (Restatement) test. *Air Crash*, 644 F.2d at 628–629.

15. Georgia's intermediate courts have applied the antiquated *lex loci delecti* [sic] rule. [cit.]. However, lower state court decisions are "not binding evidence of what the [state] Supreme Court would do in a similar case." *Green v. J.C. Penney Auto Ins. Co.*, 806 F.2d 759, 761 (7th Cir.1986). Citing the difficulty of applying the *lex loci* rule, * * * *Baltimore Football Club, Inc. v. Lockheed Corp.*, 525 F. Supp. 1206, 1208–1209 (N.D.Ga.1981) * * * relied on the seventh circuit's "most significant relationship" analysis in *Pittway v. Lockheed Aircraft Corp.*, 641 F.2d 524 (7th Cir.1981). The Georgia Supreme Court is not likely to apply the *lex loci* rule in air crash cases. *Cf.*, *Saloomey v. Jeppesen & Co.*, 707 F.2d 671, 674 (2d Cir.1983) (predicting that Connecticut Supreme Court would adopt the modern "most significant relationship" approach in the unique context of "a wrongful death action arising from an aviation accident,"

(continued...)

ently to each defendant.

1. *United Airlines.* The first issue is which states to consider. In this action, the states that must be considered are: Iowa, the place of the injury; Colorado and California, the places of the alleged misconduct; Illinois, the principal place of business of United Airlines; Delaware, the place of incorporation of United Airlines.[16] It is difficult to ascertain where the relationship between the parties is "centered." Since the relationship must have been centered in Colorado, California, Iowa or Illinois, the question need not be resolved. The interests of these states will be considered. The states of domicile of the plaintiffs are not relevant to the choice of punitive damage laws. *Air Crash.*

The interests of each state in application of its punitive damage laws must be considered. The purpose of punitive damages is punishment of the defendant and deterrence of future wrongdoing. These purposes are balanced against the danger of imposing excessive financial liability on the defendant.

As the site of the injury, Iowa has presumptively significant interests in the action. However, the eventual crash in Iowa was fortuitous. Iowa's interest or ability to deter United's conduct depended upon an unforeseen emergency landing in Sioux City. Illinois, Colorado and California each have a substantial connection to United's business activity, and a corresponding interest in balancing deterrence against protection of a defendant like United.

California has an interest in monitoring United's maintenance activity conducted in California. Colorado has an interest in regulating the training of United's flight crews in Colorado. United proposes that California law govern punitive damage claims arising from alleged faulty maintenance and Colorado law govern punitive damage claims arising from training the crew. However, it is unclear that corporate decisions resulting in allegedly wrongful acts by United would necessarily have occurred in either California or Colorado. Colorado and California derive substantial sales and income taxes, as well as other revenues, directly or indirectly from United's activities in their states.

United's principal place of business is Illinois. As discussed earlier, Illinois benefits from United's economic activity within the state, and Illinois suffers a substantial risk that wrongful behavior will result in an accident occurring on flights scheduled to arrive in or depart from Chicago. United may have committed wrongful acts relating to maintenance of the aircraft or training of its flight crew. Allegations concerning United's wrongful conduct may easily be recharacterized as permitting passengers to travel upon a faulty aircraft flown by an ill-trained crew. Illinois has the most significant relationship to United's passenger business. Consequently, Illinois is well placed to achieve a balance between deterrence of wrongful conduct and protection from excessive liability.

United argues that potential defendants would be encouraged to choose

---

15. (...continued)
notwithstanding that Connecticut previously applied *lex loci*).

16. Delaware's interest in this incident results from the formality of incorporation in Delaware. No activity related to the air crash occurred in Delaware. Consequently, Delaware's interest need not be discussed further.

their principal place of business to minimize punitive damage liability. However, defendants are just as likely to manipulate the location of their maintenance or training centers to minimize liability. The application of Illinois law achieves certainty, predictability and ease of application, as well as the purposes of punitive damages. Applying a single standard to the issue of punitive damages with respect to United's activities simplifies the issue. Accordingly, punitive damage claims in the consolidated cases subject to the Restatement are governed by Illinois law. As discussed earlier, Illinois does not permit punitive damage claims in survival actions or wrongful death actions.

2. *McDonnell Douglas*. The Restatement analysis regarding McDonnell Douglas is limited to California, site of the alleged wrongful conduct, Missouri, McDonnell Douglas' principal place of business, Maryland, its place of incorporation[17] and Iowa, the site of the injury. For the reasons stated above, Iowa law will not be applied. As between California and Missouri, in *Air Crash* the seventh circuit determined that these states had an equal interest in the application of their punitive damage laws and resolved the conflict by application of Illinois law, the site of the crash. Since no acceptable alternative to California or Missouri law exists in this case, a resolution to the conflict must be reached.

The Restatement § 145, comment c, provides: "if the primary purpose of the tort rule involved is to deter or punish misconduct, ... the state where the conduct took place may be the state of dominant interest and thus that of most significant relationship...." *See, Houston North Hosp. Prop. v. Telco Leasing, Inc.*, 688 F.2d 408, 409, n. 3b (5th Cir.1982). *See also*, Restatement § 145 comment e. At this early stage of the litigation, some doubt exists about the site of allegedly wrongful conduct. Conceivably, wrongful conduct resulting in the accident could have occurred in either state. However, the design and manufacture of the aircraft occurred in California. Since faulty design and manufacture are the basis for the punitive damage claims against McDonnell Douglas, California law appropriately governs these actions. California does not permit punitive damages in wrongful death actions but does permit punitive damages in survival actions.

3. *General Electric*. General Electric manufactured and designed the aircraft's engine in Ohio. New York is General Electric's principal place of business. General Electric's aircraft engine business takes place predominantly in Ohio. As discussed above, New York's relationship to General Electric's aircraft engine manufacturing business is objectively less than Ohio's interest. Accordingly, Ohio law governs punitive damage claims against General Electric. Ohio law permits punitive damages in survival actions but not in wrongful death actions.

C. *Cases Transferred From Pennsylvania and the District of Columbia*. Two cases asserting punitive damage claims were originally brought in Pennsylvania and the District of Columbia. Pennsylvania and the District of Columbia apply a combination of the governmental interest analysis and the most significant relationship test. In *Hercules[& Co. v. Shama Restaurant Corp.*, 566 A.2d 31, 40

---

17. Given the obviously greater interests of the other states, Maryland's interest as the formal place of incorporation need not be discussed.

(D.C.App.1989)], the District of Columbia Court of Appeals concurred with Judge Joyce Green in *In re Air Crash Disaster*, 559 F.Supp. 333, 342 (D.D.C.1983) that "the state with the 'most significant relationship' should also be the state whose policy is advanced by application of [its] law." *Hercules*, 566 A.2d at 41. In *Air Crash*, the seventh circuit observed that "the tests to be used, although containing significant differences, mandate an analytical inquiry which is basically the same." *Air Crash*, [cit.]. Since California's governmental interest analysis and the Restatement test produced the same result for each defendant, it is unnecessary to repeat the analysis with regard to the combined tests employed by Pennsylvania and the District of Columbia.

The choice of law rules of Pennsylvania and the District of Columbia would result in application of Illinois law to punitive damage claims against United, California law to claims against McDonnell Douglas and Ohio law to claims against General Electric.

V. CONCLUSIONS. Defendants' motions to bar punitive damage claims are denied. Plaintiffs' claims for punitive damages against United Airlines are governed by Illinois law. Plaintiffs' claims for punitive damages against McDonnell Douglas are governed by California law. Plaintiffs' punitive damage claims against General Electric are governed by Ohio law.

Plaintiffs may move to take expedited discovery as to any specifically identified disputed fact material to this court's choice of law analysis.

Notes and Questions

1. *Federal Courts and Multidistrict Litigation.* Under Klaxon Co. v. Stentor Elec. Mfg. Co., 313 U.S. 487 (1941) [infra, Ch. 6], a federal court sitting in diversity is bound to apply the choice-of-law rules of the state in which the court sits. Under Van Dusen v. Barrack, 376 U.S. 612 (1964) [infra, Ch. 6], when an action is transferred under 28 U.S.C. § 1404 from a federal court in one state to a federal court in another state, the transferee court is bound to apply the choice-of-law rules of the state of the transferor court. *Klaxon* and *Van Dusen* also apply when, as in *Sioux*, several actions are transferred and consolidated under 28 U.S.C. § 1407 (the multidistrict litigation statute). In Chapter 6, you will explore the history and rationale of *Klaxon* and *Van Dusen*. As you can see from *Sioux*, however, the combined effect of these two decisions imposes a heavy choice-of-law burden on the transferee court. In fact, compared to other consolidated cases, *Sioux* was a relatively easy case because: (a) although the accident from which it arose led to more than one hundred lawsuits by plaintiffs from thirty states and two foreign countries, this part of the case involved only 18 lawsuits that had been filed in only eight states; and (b) *Sioux* involved only the issue of punitive damages because defendants had offered not to contest liability for compensatory damages. Factor (a) reduced the court's *Van Dusen* burden. Factor (b) reduced the *Klaxon* burden by obviating the need to consider the law of the victims' domiciles (because the purpose of punitive damages is to punish or deter defendants rather than to compensate victims), thus freeing the court to focus on the states affiliated with the three defendants rather than

the states affiliated with the more numerous plaintiffs. (Can you imagine how much more difficult it would have been to decide the issue of compensatory damages?)

Even so, did the *Sioux* court not take a drastic methodological shortcut by lumping together the choice-of-law approaches of Pennsylvania and the District of Columbia, or by assuming that New York follows the Restatement (Second), or by "predicting" that Georgia, a *lex loci delicti* state, would also follow the Restatement (Second)? On what authority did the court rely for this prediction? As late as 2003, the Supreme Court of Georgia continued to adhere to the *lex loci* rule after having reaffirmed it in 1996. See Symeonides, *The Revolution Today* § 48.

Does the fact that able and conscientious judges find it necessary to take such liberties suggest either or both of the following: (a) that the *Van Dusen* burden is simply unbearable in consolidated multidistrict mass-disaster litigation; or (b) that courts do not believe that the different choice-of-law methodologies can or should affect the outcome of the case?

2. Notice how neat the *Sioux* results are:

	Contacts			Applicable Law		
Defendants	D's PPB	Conduct	Injury	Calif. cases	Rest.2d cases	Pa. & D.C. cases
United	Ill.	Cal. & Colo.	Iowa	Ill.	Ill.	Ill.
McDonnell	Mo.	Cal.	Iowa	Cal.	Cal.	Cal.
GE	N.Y.	Ohio	Iowa	Ohio	Ohio	Ohio

Are you impressed by the fact that the court managed to apply the law of the same state to each defendant under each of the three methodologies the court employed? Is there any inconsistency in the court's decision to apply the law of the defendant's principal place of business (rather than the law of the place of conduct) with regard to defendant United Airlines, and to apply the law of the place of conduct (rather than the defendant's principal place of business) with regard to defendant McDonnell Douglas? If not, why?

3. *Sioux* is not only easier than other single-event mass-disaster cases (which involve multiple individual claims that accrue at the same time), but also much easier than multiple-event disasters, such as the DES product liability cases, or the tobacco, asbestosis, or Agent Orange cases in which multiple claims latent for many years accrue at different times. Cases of this type have occupied federal courts for many years and have produced dozens of significant choice-of-law decisions, including one that promised or threatened to develop a "national consensus" substantive law for such cases. See *In re* Agent Orange Prods. Liab. Litig., 580 F.Supp. 690, 713 (E.D.N.Y.1984). While support for national substantive legislation for multistate products liability cases is not lacking, support for national choice-of-law legislation is more widespread and encompasses most of the judges who have had to decide cases similar to *Sioux*. See excerpts and discussion in Symeonides, *Commencing the National Debate*, 853–57.

4. ***The ALI's Complex Litigation Project.*** Heeding these appeals, the

American Law Institute approved the *Complex Litigation Project*[1] in 1993 and submitted it to Congress for enactment into law. The Project proposes the establishment of new mechanisms and standards for the intra-federal, state-to-federal, federal-to-state, and state-to-state transfer and consolidation of related geographically-dispersed actions, and provides a set of choice-of-law rules for mass-tort and mass-contract actions that are transferred to a federal court.

a. *Liability.* With regard to liability, § 6.01(d) of the Project provides four choice-of-law rules for resolving non-false conflicts. These rules, which apply in a successive order of elimination, require the application of the law of:

> [Rule 1] the state of conduct, if the injury is also in that state;
>
> [Rule 2] the state in which all plaintiffs and a defendant habitually reside or have their primary places of business, with regard to claims against that defendant;
>
> [Rule 3] the state in which all plaintiffs habitually reside or have their primary places of business,[2] if that state is also the place of injury; and
>
> [Rule 4] in all other cases, the state in which the injurious conduct occurred.

Do you think that Rule 1 is a sound rule when the issue in question is one of loss distribution rather than conduct regulation? Is Rule 2 a sound rule when the issue in question is one of conduct regulation rather than loss distribution? Is Rule 3 a good rule when the plaintiffs' state provides for a lower standard of recovery than either the defendant's state or the conduct state? Finally, if the *Sioux* court had to decide the defendants' liability under the above rules, would any of the first three rules be applicable in that case or, for that matter, in most airplane-disaster cases? If not, then Rule 4 would be applicable in the great majority of such cases, would it not? If so, is there not a danger that Rule 4 may provide a safe haven for manufacturers?[3]

b. *Compensatory Damages.* Section 6.05 of the Project provides that the same law that governs liability under § 6.01 also governs issues of "monetary relief," other than punitive damages. (§ 6.06 provides for punitive damages, see infra, 326.) The drafters recognize, however, that in some instances this objective may be undesirable, because "decisions regarding what damages are recoverable may reflect policy determinations involving how to allocate losses between parties, rather than the conduct-regulating policies that underlie the liability rules being applied." § 6.05 cmt. b. Thus, obliquely but expressly, the drafters recognize the distinction between

---

1. American Law Institute, *Complex Litigation: Statutory Recommendations and Analysis* (1994) [hereinafter "the Project"]. A symposium dedicated to the choice-of-law provisions of the Final Draft of this Project is published in 54 *La. L. Rev.* 833 (1994) and contains a preface by von Mehren, and articles by Trautman, Symeonides, Cooper, Juenger, Kalis, et al., Kozyris, Mullenix, Nafziger, Sedler, Seidelson, Shreve, and Wilkins.

2. Both Rule 2 and Rule 3 are supplemented by a sub-rule that provides that "[p]laintiffs shall be considered as sharing a common habitual residence or primary place of business if they are located in states whose laws are not in material conflict." § 6.01(d)(2) and (3).

3. Fortunately, all four rules are subject to escapes, the most prominent of which provides that, "[t]o avoid unfair surprise or arbitrary results," the transferee court may deviate from the above order of elimination, or it may "choose the applicable law on the basis of other factors that reflect the regulatory policies and legitimate interests of a particular state," other than the states that have the contacts mentioned in rules 1-4. § 6.01(e). For the history and scope of this and the other escapes, see Symeonides, *Commencing the National Debate* 859–60, 862–63, 866–67.

conduct-regulation and loss-distribution issues and subtly introduce issue-by-issue analysis and *dépeçage*. Subsection (b) of § 6.05 authorizes the court to sever issues of monetary relief, if it determines that these issues "involve policies different from those underlying the liability issues" and that the application of the law selected under § 6.01 to those issues "would ignore the interests of states whose policies regarding the measure of relief would be furthered by the application of their laws."

A Note on Choice of Law in Class Actions

1. Besides multidistrict litigation, class actions are another common way in which mass-tort cases are litigated. Most of them are multistate in that they arise from multistate events or involve plaintiffs from several states. In these actions, the choice-of-law inquiry "can make or break class certification."[1] Under Rule 23(b)(3) of the Federal Rules of Civil Procedure and equivalent provisions in state statutes, in order to obtain class certification, the movant must demonstrate, *inter alia*, that "questions of law *or* fact common to the members of the class predominate over any questions affecting only individual members." FRCP 23(b)(3) (emphasis added). Although this requirement is phrased in the disjunctive, courts have read it in the conjunctive and require commonality and predominance of questions of both fact *and* law. Moreover, regarding choice of law, courts have interpreted this provision as requiring the movant to demonstrate that the claims of all members of the class, or of an appropriate subclass, will be governed by the law of the same state.

Where do you think a class action plaintiff has a better chance to meet the above requirement: (a) in a state that follows the *lex loci delicti* rule, or (b) a state that follows one of the modern approaches? Why? Remember that the latter approaches proceed on an issue-by-issue basis and tend to focus heavily on the parties' domiciles when the case involves loss-distribution issues. Compare the cases described below.

2. In Spence v. Glock, 227 F.3d 308 (5th Cir.2000), a nationwide products-liability class action, the trial court granted class certification after accepting the plaintiffs' argument that the claims of all class plaintiffs would be governed by the law of Georgia, which was the place of the product's assembly and central distribution. However, the appellate court reversed after concluding that, under the Restatement (Second) followed in the forum state of Texas, Georgia was not the state of the "most significant relationship." To identify that state, said the court, "one must compare Georgia's contacts and the state policies those contacts implicate with those of the 50 other interested jurisdictions," id. at 312, such as the states in which the plaintiffs were domiciled or had bought the product.

3. In Philip Morris, Inc. v. Angeletti, 752 A.2d 200 (Md.2000), all plaintiffs were current domiciliaries of the forum state, Maryland, which followed the *lex-loci-delicti* rule. The plaintiffs claimed to have suffered injuries in Maryland as a result of smoking cigarettes manufactured by defendants. The lower court certified the

---

1. Cabraser, *Products Liability Class Actions*, 77. See also Phair, *Nationwide Class Actions*, 835; Ryan, *Uncertifiable?* 467.

class after finding that, under the *lex loci* rule, Maryland law would govern the claims of all class members. Maryland's highest court reversed. The court cited the first Restatement's "last event" rule which provides that, in cases of bodily harm caused by a "deleterious substance," the place of the tort is where the substance "takes effect upon the body." (See supra Ch.2, Notes after *Carroll*.) Under this rule, the court reasoned, the place of the tort was wherever "the harmful force [of nicotine] took effect upon the body," 752 A.2d at 231, and, since many of the plaintiffs had been smokers before they moved their domicile to Maryland, Maryland was not the place of the tort for all class claims. See id. 232-33.[2]

4. In *In re* Simon II Litigation, 211 F.R.D. 86 (E.D.N.Y.2002), a nationwide class action in which the plaintiffs claimed that the defendants tobacco companies had conspired to conceal the dangers of smoking, Judge Weinstein ruled that New York law would govern the punitive-damages claims of all plaintiffs.[3] He reasoned that in cross-border conduct-regulation conflicts, especially those in which the harm is caused through transitory goods, the place of causative misconduct should play an important role in the choice of the governing law. Weinstein concluded that, because substantial portions of defendants' alleged conspiracy were orchestrated in New York by defendants who had their principal place of business there, New York had "an obvious and substantial leading interest in ensuring that it does not become either a base or a haven for law breakers to wreak injury nationwide." Id. at 176. The fact that the home states of some of the plaintiffs denied or limited punitive damages "[did] not deny New York's authority to sensibly apply its own law to protect those it has a policy to safeguard [i.e. New Yorkers]," id., but also non-New Yorkers along with them, especially because, "without a centralized trial, [the plaintiffs] may be left without an effective remedy." Id. at 177.[4] At a more general level, Weinstein noted that, while the piecemeal adjudication of mass tort claims "generally denies efficiencies to plaintiffs, but automatically affords those litigation advantages to defendants, who are repeat litigators of the same issues," id. at 101, the aggregation of claims in a class action "restores balance in litigation power to ensure one of the primary goals of tort law: effective and administratively efficient deterrence and compensation." Id.

5. In the Matter of Bridgestone/Firestone Inc., 288 F.3d 1012 (7th Cir.2002) took exactly the opposite view of class actions. *Bridgestone/Firestone* was one of

---

2. For another case decertifying a class for failure to follow the last-act rule, see IBM Corp. v. Kemp, 536 S.E.2d 303 (Ga.App.2000) (holding that the last act, and thus the tort, occurred in the home states of each of the victims, and hence their claims would not be governed by the law of a single state.)

3. In an earlier phase of the same case (Simon v. Philip Morris Inc., 124 F.Supp.2d 46 (E.D.N.Y.2000), Weinstein ruled that (a) the defendants' liability should be determined under the law of New York, which was the location of the headquarters of the principal defendants and of much of the alleged conspiratorial activity; and (b) the plaintiffs' claims for compensatory damages would be divided into subclasses to be governed by the laws of other states. For a case reaching a similar result, see National Western Life Ins. Co. v. Rowe, 86 S.W.3d 285 (Tex.App.2002) (granting class certification in a nationwide insurance fraud class action after finding that the claims of class plaintiffs would be governed by the law of Texas, which was the place of the defendant's principal place of business and the place in which the defendant engaged in the conduct that injured the plaintiffs in other states).

4. But see Schein v. Stromboe, 102 S.W.3d 675 (Tex.2002) (decertifying a class in part because class members who live in states whose laws do not cap punitive damages "must suffer the limits imposed by Texas law," and class members whose states do not allow punitive damages "will get the benefit here that their own domicile does not confer." Id. at 695).

several product-liability cases involving disputes between the manufacturers of Bridgestone/Firestone tires and Ford Explorer cars, on the one hand, and domicilia ries of all 50 states who had used these tires or cars, on the other. The plaintiffs confined their class application to claims for economic losses caused by the defective tires or cars and excluded claims for personal injury or death. The district court certified the class after concluding that, under the significant-contacts approach of the forum state of Indiana, the plaintiffs' tort and contract claims would be governed by the laws of the state of each defendant's conduct (which also were the defendants' principal places of business)--Tennessee for Firestone, and Michigan for Ford.

The Seventh Circuit reversed. Writing for the court, Judge Easterbrook rejected the plaintiffs' characterization of their claims as contractual (breach of warranty and consumer fraud), and characterized as a "novelty" the district court's conclusion that "one state's law would apply to [tort] claims by consumers throughout the country." Id. at 1016. He posited that Indiana was "a *lex loci delicti* state [that] in all but exceptional cases applies the law of the place where harm occurred," id., and that the Indiana Supreme Court has not applied the law of the place of conduct, "not even once, [even though it] had plenty of opportunities."[5] Id. Since the plaintiffs' claims were for financial loss, "if any," said the judge, that loss was "suffered in the places where the vehicles and tires were purchased at excessive prices or resold at depressed prices. Those injuries occurred in all 50 states * * * [and thus] [t]he *lex loci delicti* principle points to the places of these injuries, not the defendants' corporate headquarters." Id. In turn, the need to apply the laws of so many states, which arguably varied considerably, rendered a single nationwide class unmanageable and thus noncertifiable. In closing, Judge Easterbrook offered a law and economics critique of class actions in general, which he characterized as being based on "the model of the central planner." Id. at 1020. He concluded that "only a decentralized process of multiple trials, involving different juries, and different standards of liability, in different jurisdictions will yield the information needed for accurate evaluation of mass tort claims." Id. at 1020 (internal citations omitted).[6]

In your opinion, which of the two judges, Weinstein or Easterbrook, reached a better resolution of the choice-of-law question, and why? Which judge's view of class actions do you find more persuasive and why?

---

5. For a slightly different reading of Indiana precedents, see Symeonides, *Choice of Law in 2002*, 30-34. Judge Easterbrook also stated that "neither Indiana *nor any other state* has applied a uniform place-of-the-defendant's-headquarters rule to products liability cases." 288 F.3d at 1016 (emphasis added). However, (as in *Simon II*, supra), the district court's holding regarding the application of Tennessee and Michigan law did not rest merely on the presence of the defendants' headquarters in those states but also, if not primarily, on the fact that the defendants' alleged misconduct also had occurred there. In reading the products liability section of this book, infra, see if you find other cases that applied the law of a state that had these two contacts.

6. For other nationwide consumer class actions following *Bridgestone/Firestone*, see, e.g., In re Propulsid Products Liability Litigation, 208 F.R.D. 133 (E.D.La.2002); In re Rezulin Products Liability Litigation, 210 F.R.D. 61 (S.D.N.Y.2002), Cartiglia v. Johnson & Johnson Co., 2002 WL 1009473 (N.J.Super.2002); Schein v. Stromboe, 102 S.W.3d 675 (Tex.2002). All four cases denied class certification after rejecting plaintiffs' argument of applying the law of the state of manufacture over the law of the states of injury.

C. PUNITIVE DAMAGES

1. ***Introduction.*** Punitive or exemplary damages are money damages assessed against a defendant in a civil action for misconduct that the legal system regards as heinous or egregious. The adjectives "punitive" and exemplary," often used interchangeably, express the two purposes of these damages--punishment and deterrence. Punishment or retribution is individual but backward looking, in that it focuses on the individual wrongdoer and his or her specific misconduct. The degree of punishment depends on both the egregiousness of the misconduct, and the wrongdoer's financial capacity to bear and internalize the punishment. Deterrence or prevention is more general and forward looking, in that it focuses not only on the individual wrongdoer, but on others who might consider engaging in similar misconduct in the future. Deterrence is achieved by attaching on the particular conduct a price tag that is much higher than the gains one might expect from engaging in that misconduct. Thus, punitive damages differ in important respects from compensatory damages, the purpose of which is to compensate the victim, and hence are proportional to the victim's harm or loss.[1]

2. ***Laws.*** As *Sioux* illustrates, states differ on the availability of punitive damages for specific actions, even though only one state, Nebraska, prohibits punitive damages *in all cases*. Since the 1980s, punitive damages have been the target of a movement known as "tort reform," which has had partial success in several states in limiting and/or making more difficult the recovery of punitive damages. The most common reforms have: (1) imposed caps on punitive damages awards (20 states); (2) raised the standard of proof for imposing punitive damages (19 states); (3) bifurcated the trial by separating punitive damages from other issues (16 states); (4) diverted a portion of the punitive damages award to a public fund (9 states); or (4) reformed jury instructions or assigned to judges rather than to jurors the assessment of punitive damages (2 states). See Symeonides, *Punitive-Damages Conflicts* § 1.1.

In the rest of the world, the vast majority of civil-law systems continue to reject punitive damages, not only in domestic cases but also in multistate cases. They routinely use the *ordre public* exception as the basis for refusing to award punitive damages under a foreign law or to recognize foreign judgments that award such damages. Some recent conflicts codifications contain blanket prohibitions against awarding punitive damages under any circumstances.[2] Article 24 of the proposed

---

1. The fact that punitive damages are awarded to a private plaintiff, in a civil trial, indicates their differences from criminal and civil fines, both of which inure to a public fund. Although a recent movement to direct a portion of punitive damages to a public fund tends to blur this distinction, that movement has had only limited success so far. At the same time, the fact that in a civil trial the defendant does not enjoy certain procedural protections of the criminal law (such as proof beyond a reasonable doubt, the right against self-incrimination, and the protection from double jeopardy and excessive fines) is one of the reasons for which punitive damages are controversial.

2. For example, articles 135(2) and 137(2) of the Swiss codification provide that, in products liability and obstruction to competition cases governed by foreign law, "no damages may be awarded in Switzerland other than those provided * * * under Swiss law." Similarly, article 40(3) of the German codification prohibits non-compensatory or "excessive" damages, while article 34 of the Hungarian codification provides somewhat cryptically that Hungarian courts "shall not * * * impose legal consequences not known to

(continued...)

European Union Regulation known as "Rome II" makes the prohibition of punitive damages under foreign law a matter of Union public policy binding on all the member countries.

3. *Pertinent Contacts*. As noted in chapter 3, the place of the injurious conduct and the place of the resulting injury are the most important contacts in conduct-regulation conflicts. Since punitive-damages rules obviously are conduct-regulating, these contacts are also important in punitive-damages conflicts. However, because punitive-damages rules have the additional purpose of punishing the tortfeasor, the tortfeasor's domicile (or principal place of business, or other similar affiliation) is also a relevant contact in these conflicts.

In interest-analysis terms, a state that has one or more of these contacts would normally have an interest in applying its law, whether or not it imposes punitive damages: (a) the state of the conduct has the right to regulate (police, deter, punish, *or* protect) conduct within its borders; (b) the state in which this conduct produces its effects--the injury--has a right to determine what sanctions are appropriate for such conduct; and (c) the state of the defendant's domicile has the right to determine whether the severe sanction of punitive damages should be imposed on one of its domiciliaries. If the law of that state provides for punitive damages, the application of that law serves its underlying purpose of punishing that tortfeasor and deterring him and others from engaging in similar conduct in the future. Conversely, when that law prohibits punitive damages, then its application would serve its underlying purpose of protecting that tortfeasor from excessive financial exposure.

This then leaves the domicile of the victim. If it is true that punitive damages are designed to punish and deter tortfeasors rather than to compensate victims who, *ex hypothesi*, are made whole through compensatory damages, then the victim's domicile *as such* is not a relevant contact, is it? Most American courts have answered this question in the affirmative, with few exceptions noted below.

4. *Possible Patterns*. Putting the three pertinent contacts and substantive laws in the mix produces eight typical patterns of potential or actual punitive-damages conflicts. Table 7, below, depicts these patterns. The last three columns represent the state or states that have these contacts. The previous two columns represent the forum state and the plaintiff's home state. These columns are left blank so as to underscore that the laws of these states *should* be irrelevant in resolving punitive-damages conflicts.

A recent study of punitive-damages conflicts indicates that American courts have awarded punitive damages in cases falling within each one of the eight patterns. However, the majority of cases that awarded punitive damages fall within patterns 1-4. In cases falling within patterns 5-8, for every case that awarded punitive damages, there is at least one other case that did not. For documentation and discussion, see Symeonides, *Punitive-Damages Conflicts* §§ 4.6-8.2.

---

2. (...continued)
Hungarian law." For a critique of these provisions, see Symeonides, *Punitive Damages Conflicts*, §§ 8.1-2.

Table 7. Patterns in Punitive Damages Conflicts

Pattern	Forum	Plaintiff	Injury	Conduct	Defendant
1.	---	---	Pun.	Pun.	Pun.
2.	---	---	No pun.	Pun.	Pun.
3.	---	---	Pun.	No. Pun.	Pun.
4.	---	---	Pun.	Pun.	No pun.
5.	---	---	No pun.	No pun.	Pun.
6.	---	---	No pun.	Pun.	No pun.
7.	---	---	Pun.	No pun.	No pun.
8.	---	---	No pun.	No pun	No pun.

5. ***Patterns 1-4: Solid Ground*** In cases involving ***Pattern 1***, a state that has all three pertinent contacts (or three states each of which have one pertinent contact) imposes punitive damages. For example, a defendant domiciled in a state that imposes punitive damages acts in that state and causes injury in that state to a domiciliary of another state. In such a case, if the victim's home state does not allow such damages, is there a good reason to deny such damages? Should the answer be different if the latter state is also the forum?

In patterns 2-4, a state with two relevant contacts (or two states, each of which have one relevant contact) imposes punitive damages, while a state with the third relevant contact does not. For example, in ***Pattern 2*** the tortfeasor is domiciled in a state that imposes punitive damages, and, while in that state, engages in conduct that causes injury in another state that does not impose such damages. In such a case, does the latter state have an interest in denying punitive damages? A case presenting this scenario is Jackson v. Travelers Ins. Co., 26 F.Supp.2d 1153 (S.D.Iowa 1998). The court held that Iowa's punitive-damages law applied to the insurer's bad faith practices in Iowa, even though the resulting injury to the Nebraska plaintiff had occurred in Nebraska, which did not allow such damages. The court found that Nebraska had no interest in protecting "all insurance companies nationwide regardless of whether they are Nebraska businesses," id. at 1162, nor "in preventing punitive damages awards from other states to Nebraska citizens." Id. at 1165. On the other hand, said the court, because Iowa "was the location of the *cause* of the injuries[,] * * * Iowa ha[d] a significant interest in using punitive damages to punish bad faith conduct that occurs in Iowa," id. (emphasis added), and the non-application of Iowa law "would wholly frustrate Iowa's interest in deterring outrageous conduct." Id. at 1164.

In ***Pattern 3***, a defendant domiciled in a state that imposes punitive damages engages in conduct in another state that does not impose such damages, and causes injury in a third state that imposes punitive damages. In re Air Crash Disaster at Washington D.C., 559 F.Supp. 333 (D.D.C.1983), involved this pattern. The defendant, a Florida-based airline, engaged in conduct in Virginia that caused its airplane to crash a few hundred yards into the District of Columbia. Both Florida and the D.C., but not Virginia, imposed punitive damages. The court applied D.C. law allowing punitive damages. Do you agree with this result? Why, or why not?

In *Pattern 4*, a tortfeasor domiciled in a state that does not impose punitive damages, engages in conduct in another state that imposes such damages and causes injury in the latter state or in another state that also imposes punitive damages. Is this a true conflict? Why, or why not? How should one resolve it?

All cases involving this pattern have allowed punitive damages under the law of the state of conduct and injury. For example, in Horowitz v. Schneider Nat. Inc., 708 F.Supp. 1573 (D.Wyo.1989), the court applied Wyoming's punitive-damages law to an action arising from a Wyoming traffic accident, even though none of the parties were Wyoming domiciliaries. Noting that the purpose of punitive damages "is not compensation of the victim * * * [but rather] deterrence through public condemnation," id. at 1577, the court concluded that Wyoming had a "paramount interest in the manner in which its highways are used and the care exercised by drivers." Id. Likewise, in Isley v. Capuchin Province, 878 F.Supp. 1021 (E.D.Mich. 1995), an action for sexual abuse arising out of events in Wisconsin and filed against an out-of-state religious order, a Michigan court applied Wisconsin law, which imposed punitive damages. The court concluded that Wisconsin had a "strong interest in protecting minors in Wisconsin from sexual abuse and in punishing those found guilty," id. at 1024, and that interest was much stronger than the interest of another state in protecting its defendants. Similarly, in Schoeberle v. United States, 2000 WL 1868130 (N.D.Ill.2000), the court held that the law of Iowa, which was the place of both the pertinent conduct and the injury, should govern the question of punitive damages, even though the plaintiffs and some of the defendants were domiciled in Wisconsin, which did not allow such damages for the action in question. The court concluded that "Wisconsin's interest in protecting its resident corporate defendant * * * from excessive liability [was] outweighed by Iowa's interest in applying its punitive damages law to conduct within its borders." Id. at *14. The court reasoned that, "[w]hen a balance between punishment and deterrence on the one hand and protection from excessive liability on the other must be struck, it is fitting that the state whose interests are more deeply affected should have its local law applied." Id. at *13. That state was Iowa, said the court, because, as the place of both the misconduct and the injury, "Iowa ha[d] an obvious interest * * * in punish[ing] those responsible for [the] misconduct * * * [and] in deterring such misconduct and occurrences in the future." Id.

6. *Patterns 5-7: Divided Ground.* Patterns 5-7 involve cases of cross-border torts that, by nature, present more difficult conflicts. In turn, this explains why courts are divided.

Pattern 5 is the converse of Pattern 4--the defendant's home state imposes punitive damages but the law of the state or states of conduct and injury prohibit them. Did *Sioux* or *Bryant v. Silberman* (supra Ch.3 at 152) involve this pattern? Under interest analysis, does Pattern 5 present a false conflict, a true conflict, or a no-interest case? Why? How should one resolve it? Although very few cases involved this scenario, most of them have denied punitive damages. See

Symeonides, *Punitive-Damages Conflicts*, §§ 6.2-6.3.

In *Pattern 6*, the state of conduct imposes punitive damages while the defendant's domicile and the place of injury are in a state, or states, that do not impose such damages. Did *Sioux* involve this pattern? Is this a true conflict? Why or why not? How should one resolve it? Cases involving this pattern have applied the law of any one of the three states.

For example, in Long v. Sears Roebuck & Co., 877 F.Supp. 8 (D.D.C. 1995), a products liability case, the court awarded punitive damages under the law of the state of wrongful conduct, which the court assumed to be the sale of a defective mower and a misrepresentation of its safety features. That conduct occurred in the District of Columbia, but injury occurred in Maryland while the Maryland buyer was using the mower. The court reasoned that (a) D.C. had an interest in deterring and punishing those defendants who engaged in reprehensible conduct in D.C. by selling unsafe products there and misrepresenting their safety features; and (b) Maryland did not have an interest in applying its non-punitive damages law to protect non-Maryland defendants.

In contrast, in Harlan Feeders v. Grand Laboratories, Inc., 881 F.Supp. 1400 (N.D.Iowa 1995), a product liability action arising from injury in Nebraska, the court applied Nebraska law, which prohibited punitive damages, rather than Iowa law, which allowed them. The product was manufactured in Iowa and sold to the Nebraska plaintiff in Nebraska. Noting that "Nebraska has made a policy choice that punitive damages are inappropriate," id. at 1410, the court equated that choice to a state "interest" and concluded that "that interest [was] not outweighed by Iowa's contrary interest in imposing punitive damages as a deterrent, at least not * * * where the plaintiff is a resident of Nebraska, not Iowa, where the alleged injury occurred in Nebraska, not Iowa, as a result of use of a product manufactured by a South Dakota, not an Iowa corporation, even when the corporation physically produced the product in Iowa." Id.

Finally, in In re Air Crash Disaster Near Chicago, 644 F.2d 594 (7th Cir. 1981), cert. denied 454 U.S. 878 (1981), a case similar to *Sioux* and arising out of an airplane crash in Illinois, the airline's home state (New York) did not allow punitive damages, but the state in which it maintained the aircraft (Oklahoma) allowed such damages. The court found a true conflict between the latter two states and broke the tie by applying the law of a third state, Illinois, which did not allow punitive damages. The court found that Illinois had a "strong interest in having airlines fly in and out of the state, and * * * in protecting [them] by disallowing punitive damages." 644 F.2d at 615-16. Similarly, in Freeman v. World Airways, Inc., 596 F.Supp. 841 (D.Mass. 1984), a case arising out of an airplane crash in Massachusetts, the court found that Massachusetts, which did not allow punitive damages, "ha[d] a significant interest in regulating conduct (deterrence or encouragement) of planes arriving at [its airports] during the winter." Id. at 847. The negligent conduct that caused the crash arguably occurred in other states that imposed punitive damages.

Compare the last two cases with *Bryant v. Silberman*, supra Ch. 2, and then with *Long* and *Harlan Feeders*, supra. From the choice-of-law perspective, which of these cases do you find more persuasive and why?

In *Pattern 7*, the state of the injury imposes punitive damages, but the state (or states) of the defendant's conduct and domicile prohibits such damages. In there much doubt that this is a true conflict? In any event, how should one resolve it? As in other cross-border torts, before imposing punitive damages under the law of the state of injury, should the court not require a showing that the occurrence of the injury in that state was objectively foreseeable? See supra, Ch. 3, 224-27. Moreover, in assessing punitive damages under the law of the state of injury, may the court punish the defendant (a) only for the conduct that caused injury in that state or (b) also for the conduct that caused injury in other states? The Supreme Court has answered the latter question in favor of (a). See BMW of North America, Inc. v. Gore, 517 U.S. 559 (1996), infra Ch. 5 (holding that although, in assessing the degree of reprehensibility of the defendant's conduct, Alabama may consider evidence of the defendant's non-Alabama conduct, nevertheless, in fixing the amount of punitive damages, Alabama may not punish the defendant for non-Alabama conduct that produced injuries outside Alabama).

Like other Supreme Court cases you will study in chapter 5, the *BMW* case simply delineates the constitutional limits of state choice-of-law decisions but does not impose a particular choice within those limits. In exercising their discretion within those limits, some cases have applied the law of the state of injury and others did not. One example from the former category is *In re* Air Crash Disaster at Washington D.C., 559 F.Supp. 333 (D.D.C.1983), a multiparty case like *Sioux* and arising from the crash of an Air Florida plane in the District of Columbia. In the products liability actions against Boeing--the company that manufactured the plane in its home state of Washington, which prohibited punitive damages--the court rejected Boeing's argument that Washington law should govern, by pointing out that, while Washington had chosen to protect manufacturers at the expense of victims, "the sovereignty of other states prevents [Washington] from placing on the scales the rights of those injured elsewhere." Id. at 359. The court then focused on the actions against the Florida-based airline, which was allegedly negligent in overseeing the de-icing of its plane before takeoff from the airport, which is located on the Virginia side of the Virginia-D.C. border. Virginia (unlike D.C.) prohibited punitive damages. The court found that, as between these two jurisdictions, D.C. had "the most significant relationship * * * [because] the injurious effects of the [Virginia] conduct were predominantly felt in the District." Id. at 356.

Another example is Kramer v. Showa Denko K.K., 929 F.Supp. 733 (S.D.N.Y.1996), a products liability case in which the court allowed punitive damages under the law of the state of injury, New York (which was also the victim's domicile). A Japanese defendant had manufactured the product in Japan, which did not allow punitive damages, but had marketed the product in New York and the victim bought it there. In contrast, Kelly v. Ford Motor Co., 933 F.Supp. 465 (E.D.Pa.1996), a similar products liability case, reached the opposite result. The court refused to apply the punitive damages law of the state of injury, Pennsylvania, which was also the victim's domicile and the place where he had acquired the product. Instead, the court applied the law of Michigan, the manufacturer's home state and place of manufacture, which prohibited punitive damages. The court acknowledged Pennsylvania's interests "in punishing defendants who injure its residents and * * * in deterring them and others from engaging in similar conduct which poses a risk to Pennsylvania's citizens." Id. at 470. However, the court also found that Michigan had "a very strong interest" in denying such damages, so as to ensure that "its domiciliary defendants are protected from excessive financial liability." Id. By insulating companies such as Ford, who conduct extensive business within its borders, said the court, "Michigan hopes to promote corporate migration into its economy * * * [which] will enhance the economic climate and well being of the state of Michigan by generating revenues." Id.

7. *Pattern 8: The Left Field.* Finally, in Pattern 8 the three pertinent contacts are in a state or states that do not impose punitive damages for the conduct in question. In such a case, is it appropriate to award punitive damages, if, for example, the victim's home state imposes such damages? Although most cases answer this question in the negative, one of the few cases that answered it in the affirmative is Phillips v. General Motors Corp., 995 P.2d 1002 (Mont.2000). *Phillips* awarded punitive damages to a Montana plaintiff under Montana law, even though Montana did not have any other pertinent contact and all other involved states prohibited or limited such damages. *Phillips* was a products liability action arising from a Kansas accident involving a truck that a Michigan defendant manufactured in Michigan. The court reasoned that, because "punitive damages serve to punish and deter conduct deemed wrongful--in this case, placing a defective product into the stream of commerce which subsequently injured a Montana resident," 995 P.2d at 1012, Montana had a strong interest in "deterring future sales of defective products in Montana and encouraging manufacturers to warn Montana residents about defects in their products as quickly and as thoroughly as possible." Id.

However, the sale of the truck took place not in Montana but in North Carolina, which did not impose punitive damages. The initial buyer was a North Carolina domiciliary who then sold the truck to another North Carolina domiciliary, the victim, who later moved his domicile to Montana. He was killed not in Montana, but in Kansas, which limited punitive damages. Was not Montana's interest in protecting its domiciliaries fully satisfied by applying Montana's compensatory damages law (which the court applied)? What about Michigan's interests in shielding from punitive damages Michigan defendants who manufacture products in Michigan?

Another group of cases falling within Pattern 8 are cases decided under the federal Antiterrorist and Effective Death Penalty Act of 1996 (28 U.S.C. § 1605(a)(7)) which imposes punitive damages for death or personal injury of U.S. citizens who are victims of attacks sponsored or aided by states designated as sponsors of terrorism. Here the only required nexus is the victim's citizenship--the conduct, the injury, and the defendant's domicile may all be, and usually are, in countries that do not allow punitive damages. One of the first cases decided under this Act was Flatow v. Islamic Republic of Iran, 999 F.Supp 1 (D.D.C. 1998), which arose out of the death of an American student killed in a suicide bomb attack in the Gaza Strip. The court held that the Act applied extraterritorially because Congress enacted it with the express purpose of "affect[ing] the conduct of terrorist states outside the United States, in order to promote the safety of United States citizens traveling overseas," id. at 15, and that this express purpose negated the usual presumption against extraterritoriality. Id. at 16. The court awarded $42 million in compensatory damages and $225 million in punitive damages. In Wagner v. Islamic Republic of Iran, 172 F.Supp.2d 128 (D.D.C.2001), the victim was a U.S. serviceman who was killed in the 1984 car-bombing of the U.S. embassy in Beirut, Lebanon. The court applied federal substantive law and awarded $300 million in punitive damages. Taking note of the September 11 attacks, the court said that "now, more than ever, * * * the acts of terrorists and their sponsors must be punished to the full extent to which civil damage awards might operate to suppress such activities in the future." Id. at 138.

From the choice-of-law perspective, which of the above cases, *Phillips* or *Flatow* and *Wagner* are more defensible and why?

8. *Rules for Punitive-Damages Conflicts*. The only statutory choice-of-law rule for punitive-damages conflicts, in the United States or elsewhere, is article 3546 of the Louisiana codification of 1991. This article is based upon the three contacts identified as pertinent in the above discussion: the defendant's domicile, the place of conduct, and the place of injury. It provides that *punitive damages may be awarded if all three or any two of these contacts are located in a state or states that allow such damages*. Thus, the article allows punitive damages in patterns 1-4, but not in patterns 5-8 of the above Table. Is this a sound rule, or is it too protective of defendants? For a defense by the rule's drafter see Symeonides, *Exegesis*, 735-59. In 1994, the ALI's Complex Litigation Project proposed a substantively identical but technically more comprehensive rule for mass tort cases. See Project § 6.06.

D. PRODUCTS LIABILITY

The law of products liability as a distinct body of law, at least partly independent from general tort and contract law from which it grew, is a relatively new phenomenon. Coincidentally, in the United States, its life parallels the life of the conflicts revolution--it was born in the 1960s, emancipated in the '70s, grew by leaps and bounds in the '80s when it also influenced the laws of other countries, and then began slowing down in the '90s.

For a variety of reasons, "Americans use their product liability law a lot while victims and courts elsewhere don't." Reimann, *Liability for Defective Products*, 54. Naturally, the higher the number of products liability lawsuits, the higher the likelihood that many of them will have multistate elements, thus producing conflicts of laws. This is particularly true in the United States, which is essentially a single market, yet artificially segregated by state boundaries into multiple diverse products-liability regimes. Thus, the American experience with products liability conflicts has been particularly rich, albeit inconclusive so far. This section attempts to provide a taste of this experience.

Gantes v. Kason Corporation
Supreme Court of New Jersey, 1996.
145 N.J. 478, 679 A.2d 106.

HANDLER, J., In this case, a young woman, working in a chicken processing plant in Georgia, was killed when struck in the head by a moving part of a machine. The machine had been manufactured [in New Jersey] more than thirteen years before the fatal accident by a New Jersey corporation with its principal place of business in Linden, New Jersey.

Representatives of the decedent, asserting that the machine was defective, brought this personal-injury action based on claims of survivorship and wrongful-death against the New Jersey manufacturer in the Law Division in Union County. The action was filed within New Jersey's two-year statute of limitations for personal-injury actions, but beyond Georgia's ten-year statute of repose applicable to products-liability claims against manufacturers. Because of the conflict between the two statutes, the case poses a fundamental choice-of-law issue over which statute applies and whether, depending on that choice, the action will be barred. * * *

II. * * * Because the action was brought in New Jersey, the issue must be determined in accordance with this State's choice-of-law rule. New Jersey's rule applies a flexible "governmental-interest" standard, which requires application of the law of the state with the greatest interest in resolving the particular issue that is raised in the underlying litigation. [cit.]

A. * * * The Georgia statute of repose bars the commencement of strict products-liability actions "after ten years from the date of the first sale for use or consumption of the personal property causing or otherwise bringing about the injury." [cit.] Ms. Gonzalez's accident occurred more than ten years after defendant made its "first sale for use" of the shaker machine, in November 1977. It is undisputed that this action is barred by Georgia's ten-year statute of repose applicable to products-liability actions.

New Jersey law provides that personal-injury actions, including those based on strict-products liability, are governed by a two-year statute of limitations. [cit.] It is clear that under New Jersey's statute of limitations, plaintiff's suit would not be barred because the complaint was filed less than two years after Ms. Gonzalez' accident.

B. The second prong of the governmental-interest analysis seeks to determine the interest that each state has in resolving the specific issue in dispute. That analysis requires the court to "identify the governmental policies underlying the law of each state and how those policies are affected by each state's contacts to the litigation and to the parties." [cit.] We look first to the policies that underlie the respective state statutes that are in conflict in this case.

In 1978, the Georgia legislature enacted its statute of repose, [cit.], as an amendment to its strict products-liability statute. [cit.] In Love v. Whirlpool Corporation, 449 S.E.2d 602 (Ga.1994), the Georgia Supreme Court explained that its legislature adopted the statute of repose to serve the dual purposes of stabilizing insurance underwriting and eliminating stale claims. * * *

New Jersey's statute of limitations applicable to personal-injury actions reflects well-articulated policy[, namely:] "(1) to stimulate litigants to pursue a right of action within a reasonable time so that the opposing party may have a fair opportunity to defend, thus preventing the litigation of stale claims, and (2) 'to penalize dilatoriness and serve as a measure of repose.'" [cit.] The purpose underlying any statute of limitations is "to 'stimulate to activity and punish negligence' and 'promote repose by giving security and stability to human affairs.'" [cit.]. In addition to encouraging the diligent and timely prosecution of claims, the statute of limitations is subject to the "discovery rule." [cit.] That dimension of the statute of limitations incorporates flexible, equitable considerations based on notions of fairness to the parties and the justice in allowing claims to be resolved on their merits. [cit.] We note, further, that New Jersey's statute of limitations applies to all personal-injury actions, including those based on strict products-liability. [cit.] New Jersey has no special rule, similar to Georgia's statute of repose, governing the accrual or limitation of products-liability actions.

Whether the policy that underlies the law of a state gives rise to a governmental interest calling for the application of that state's law depends on the nature of the contacts that the state has to the litigation and to the parties. * * *

In this case, * * * the machine causing the fatal injury was manufactured in, and placed into the stream of commerce from, this State. The question thus posed is whether, in the context of this litigation, those contacts give rise to a substantial governmental interest that would be served by applying New Jersey's statute of limitations and permitting this action to proceed.

The courts below acknowledged that, in this case, the only New Jersey interest implicated by its contacts with the parties is that derived from the status of the defendant as a domestic manufacturer. That interest is in deterring the manufacturing of unsafe products within its borders. However, both the trial court and Appellate Division majority determined that a deterrent interest is not significant enough to warrant the application of New Jersey's limitations law. [cit.]

This Court has recognized generally that a purpose of the tort laws is to encourage reasonable conduct, and, conversely, to discourage conduct that creates an unreasonable risk of injury to others. [cit.] * * * We note also that Georgia has recognized that "courts are concerned not only with compensation of the victims but with admonition of the wrongdoer" and that the "'prophylactic' fact of preventing future harm has been quite important in the field of torts." [cit.] * * *

The goal of deterrence, acknowledged generally to be part of tort law, is especially important in the field of products-liability law. * * * [T]his State's judiciary has been "in the vanguard of the development of a responsive and progressive products liability law" and "has led the country in its ideological commitment to the protection of consumers and concomitant consequence of inducing those who place products into the stream of commerce to act with social responsibility." [cit.] * * *

We conclude that this State has a strong interest in encouraging the manufacture and distribution of safe products for the public and, conversely, in deterring the manufacture and distribution of unsafe products within the state. That interest is furthered through the recognition of claims and the imposition of liability based on principles of strict products-liability law.

Both the Appellate Division majority and the trial court found that the interest in deterrence would be outweighed by the possibility of unduly discouraging manufacturing in New Jersey if products-liability actions were allowed in circumstances where they would be barred in the courts where the cause of action arose. [cit.] * * *

We disagree * * *. In light of this State's commitment to protection of the public against the manufacture and distribution of unsafe products and the strong governmental interest in deterrence against such practices, it does not seem "pointless" to apply this State's statute of limitations to resident manufacturers, even if the suit would be barred against foreign manufacturers. The difference in result is grounded in the distinctive policy concerns that each state has in making its domestic manufacturers amenable to suits. A governmental interest based on a policy of deterrence that seeks to discourage domestic manufacturers from the manufacture and distribution of unsafe products through the allowance of a products-liability action is not unnecessarily burdensome nor is it discriminatory or baseless.

It is significant that New Jersey's statute of limitations does not single out manufacturers or distributors of manufactured products as a class meriting special protection from personal-injury tort actions. New Jersey recently enacted a statute that provides and clarifies certain standards in products-liability actions, yet leaves intact many common-law principles that define that cause of action. [cit.] That statute does not prescribe a limitations period that is more lenient toward or protective of manufacturers than the general personal-injury limitations law applicable to other tortfeasors. It is also significant * * * that * * * [a]lthough our Legislature has enacted a statute of repose for certain causes of actions, [cit.], it has not enacted such a statute for personal-injury actions based on unsafe products.

The lower courts also concluded that application of New Jersey's statute of limitations would encourage forum shopping, which would increase litigation and needlessly burden the courts of this State. [cit.] However, this State's interest against forum shopping will not be compromised by the application of New Jersey's statute of limitations in the circumstances of this litigation. In essence, the policy against forum shopping is intended to ensure that New Jersey courts are not burdened with cases that have only "slender ties" to New Jersey. [cit.] In this case, plaintiff does not seek to use New Jersey's court system to litigate a dispute that has only a slight link to New Jersey and where the only plausible reason to select this State is because it is a hospitable forum. This action is materially connected to New Jersey by the fact that the allegedly defective product was manufactured in and then shipped from this State by the defendant-manufacturer.

We are satisfied, therefore, that New Jersey in this case has a cognizable and substantial interest in deterrence that would be furthered by the application of its statute of limitations, and that interest is not outweighed by countervailing concerns over creating unnecessary and discriminatory burdens on domestic manufacturers or by fears of forum shopping and increased litigation in the courts of this State.

C. The determination that New Jersey in this litigation has a cognizable and substantial interest does not end the inquiry into whether the choice of its statute of limitations law is appropriate to resolve the conflict over whether this action is time barred. New Jersey's interest in deterrence must be compared and weighed against any governmental interest that Georgia has in applying its statute of repose in light of Georgia's contacts with the litigation and the parties.

The Appellate Division upheld the conclusion of the trial court that Georgia has an important governmental interest derived from its statute of repose. In effect, the trial court characterized the Georgia statute of repose as expressing a broad policy to encourage manufacturing generally by barring products-liability actions after ten years from the date of sale of an alleged unsafe product; it rejected as "parochial" the notion that Georgia intended by its statute of repose to benefit only Georgia manufacturers. [cit.] However, Georgia's statute of repose was not enacted to create generally a favorable environment for manufacturing. Rather, the Georgia statute of repose was enacted as an effort to stabilize the Georgia insurance industry and to keep stale claims out of Georgia courts. [cit.] Thus, the question to be addressed is whether, in this case, those policy concerns give rise to a governmental interest that calls for the application of Georgia's statute of repose.

The answer is clear. Georgia has no contacts with the defendant manufacturer or with this lawsuit. Hence, its special policy concerns over the impact of "open-ended liability" on its insurance industry and stale claims on its courts do not, in the context of this litigation, give rise to a governmental interest that must be protected by applying its statute of repose to foreclose this suit in New Jersey. * * *

The lower courts were also persuaded by the fact that Georgia's substantive law would apply to the case, and that the Georgia statute at issue is one of repose, as opposed to a standard statute of limitations. * * * The lower courts reasoned that because the statute of repose was a substantive law * * *, it was entitled to more weight than a statute of limitations[.] * * *

That statutes of repose are generally considered substantive in nature does not compel its selection in this case, even though it is conceded that Georgia's substantive tort law will be applied. Whether Georgia's statute of repose must be applied as a constituent part of its substantive tort law depends not on its characterization as substantive law but on the issue-specific analysis that governs choice-of-law determinations and on whether the contacts that Georgia has with the parties and the litigation create a governmental interest that requires the application of its statute of repose to settle that issue. * * *

Here, although the plaintiffs are Georgia residents, that contact with the State of Georgia does not implicate the policies of its statute of repose, which is intended only to unburden Georgia courts and to shield Georgia manufacturers from claims based on product defects long after the product has been marketed or sold. Consequently, the application of Georgia's substantive law in these circumstances does not dictate the inclusion of its statute of repose. * * *

By contrast, New Jersey's policy in deterring tortious conduct of manufacturers is implicated by the defendant's material contacts with this State, and thus represents a substantial interest to be weighed against Georgia's interest in compensation of its resident plaintiffs. In the context of this litigation, Georgia's policy of fair compensation for injured domiciliaries is one that allows compensation, except if recovery is sought from a Georgia manufacturer because the defective product causing the accident was sold by that manufacturer more than ten years before the accident. The limitation on fair compensation expressed by that narrow exception is not raised in this case. Application of New Jersey law will not undermine Georgia's interest in compensating its injured residents because that interest is not actually implicated or compromised by allowing a products-liability action brought by Georgia residents to proceed against a non-Georgia manufacturer.

Finally, we note the trial court's conclusion that in their totality Georgia had more contacts than New Jersey and therefore was the "controlling state," whose law should be applied. [cit.] Although the contacts with each state must be compared and weighed, that analysis encompasses only those contacts that bear on the specific issue that is the focus of the legal conflict between the two states. * * *

Here, the narrow issue is whether the action will be deemed time-barred. Georgia's contacts with the litigation and the parties, though numerically greater, are not more significant or weighty than those of New Jersey in generating an interest that calls for the invocation of its laws to preclude a claim in New Jersey solely because of the passage of time. * * *

IV. The judgment of the Appellate Division is reversed, summary judgment is vacated, and the matter is remanded for a determination of the underlying disputed facts and the application of those facts to the choice-of-law question, consistent with this opinion.

GARIBALDI, J., dissenting. * * * The majority's opinion subjects New Jersey businesses to an increased risk of litigation that would be time-barred in the state where the injured person lives and where the accident occurred, increases forum shopping and further taxes an already overburdened court system, without offering any countervailing benefit to a New Jersey resident or business. For those reasons, I dissent.

* * * There are two major problems with the majority's reasoning. First, it substantially underestimates, misinterprets and misapplies Georgia's strong policy in having its statute of repose apply; and second, it focuses solely on New Jersey's interest in deterring the marketing of a defective product and ignores New Jersey's other substantial interests. * * *

The majority wrongly concludes that the Georgia Legislature's motives in enacting its ten-year statute of repose are limited solely to parochial concerns within the Georgia court system and the Georgia insurance market, and that those policies therefore are not implicated in the current case. * * *

First, the policy against stale claims is a general concern with respect to all lawsuits. Georgia's policy is certainly implicated if its residents, both individuals and corporations, have to go to other states to testify in cases that would be barred under its statute of repose. This case presents a perfect example of the inconveniences that will be imposed on Georgia residents when barred claims are allowed to be litigated in foreign states. Here the proofs, the witnesses, and medical records, as well as the scene of the accident, are in Georgia. Undoubtedly, to litigate this case, several Georgia residents will have to be witnesses and will have to come to New Jersey to testify. * * *

Similarly, allowing lawsuits in New Jersey about accidents that occur in Georgia might well increase insurance costs in that State * * * [because] when this case is tried, defendant may seek to join in this lawsuit those * * * companies, including [plaintiff's employer] which may be held liable to defendant for a portion of its losses. Such a result will undoubtedly increase the product liability insurance rates in Georgia and contribute to instability in that insurance market.

III. * * * Although the policy identified by the majority, deterring the manufacturing of unsafe products by suing the manufacturer is a laudable goal, its results are problematic. * * *

* * * [T]he majority subjects New Jersey manufacturers to an increased risk of litigation that would otherwise be time-barred in the state where the injured person lives and where the accident occurred. Such a result will have a chilling effect on new businesses coming into New Jersey. * * *

* * * The effect of the Court's decision is that every manufacturer located in New Jersey will remain potentially liable regardless of where the accident occurs. The majority's opinion also will open the door to forum shopping. With an already overburdened court system, our goal should be to lessen the strain on the court's limited resources, not to further deplete them.

I would affirm the judgment of the Appellate Division. * * *

Notes and Questions

1. **Gantes**. *Gantes* was chosen for this section because it is a much simpler case than the typical product liability conflict and thus it is a better pedagogical tool for illustrating the basic dilemmas encountered in such conflicts. The case revolves around a single issue, the pertinent contacts are grouped in two states only, and the underlying conflict is not as sharp as it might have been with a different configuration of contacts. Yet *Gantes* is noteworthy not only because of the court's thorough discussion of the involved policies, but also because of its refusal to take the easy way out. For example, if the *Gantes* court were to follow the traditional approach, the court could have characterized the forum's statute of limitation as being procedural and thus as being automatically applicable to all actions brought in the forum state. See supra Ch. 2. See, e.g., Baxter v. Sturm, Ruger & Co., Inc., 644 A.2d 1297 (Conn.1994). We shall return to this question later in this chapter. See infra Section G. However, the New Jersey Supreme Court had already rejected that approach in Heavner v. Uniroyal, Inc., 305 A.2d 412 (N.J.1973). Similarly, under interest analysis, the court could easily have characterized *Gantes* as an "unprovided for" case which, under Currie's prescriptions, would be subject "by default" to the *lex fori*. Instead, the court read the forum's interests in a non-protectionist way that led to the application of the forum's pro-plaintiff law for the benefit of a foreign plaintiff and at the expense of a forum defendant.

2. **The Pertinent Contacts**. What are the pertinent contacts in products liability conflicts? If we assume that all contacts that are relevant in other tort

conflicts are also relevant in products conflicts that are handled as tort conflicts,[1] these contacts will be: the conduct, the injury, and the victim's and the tortfeasor's domiciles or other similar affiliations. However, in many products conflicts, each of these contacts may present problems that usually are not present in generic tort conflicts.[2]

For example, where is the place of conduct in cases in which the product that caused the injury was designed in one state, tested in another, approved in another, and manufactured and assembled in yet another state?[3] Similarly, in certain categories of products, the injury may be peripatetic. Examples from recent experience include pharmaceuticals,[4] breast implants, or tobacco products used over long periods of time by their eventual victims while residing in several states. Regarding the domicile of the defendant, keep in mind that many products cases involve multiple defendants, from the manufacturer to the local dealer and several intermediaries. Even when the manufacturer is the only defendant, most manufacturers tend to be corporate entities whose connections to any single state are usually diffused or, as in *Sioux*, are unrelated to the particular products case. Finally, an additional contact that is relevant in products conflicts is the place where the product was sold. However, the relevance of this contact varies from case to case and from product to product. For example, in consumer products that are directly bought by the consumer and eventual victim, that contact is relevant but it should be irrelevant

---

1. Typically, cases involving defective products that have not caused physical injury to a person or to property other than the product itself are handled as contract conflicts. See, e.g., Rocky Mountain Helicopters, Inc. v. Bell Helicopter Textron, Inc., 24 F.3d 125 (10th Cir.1994) (negligence and breach of warranty action for damage to a helicopter caused by its defective design resolved under a contract analysis); R-Square Investments v. Teledyne Indus., Inc., 1997 WL 436245 (E.D.La.1997) (case involving a defective airplane engine that caused damage to the plane; employing contract analysis to claim for damage to the engine, and tort analysis to claim for damage to the plane and applying a different law to each claim); Boudreau v. Baughman, 368 S.E.2d 849 (N.C.1988) (breach of warranty case resolved under UCC § 1-105(1)); Premix-Marbletite Mfg. Corp. v. SKW Chemicals, Inc., 145 F.Supp.2d 1348 (S.D.Fla.2001) (applying Florida law under UCC § 1.105(1) to an action by Florida buyer against Georgia seller of defective product purchased and used in Florida, because Florida had an appropriate relation to the transactions at issue, being the place of negotiation, purchase, and delivery of the product and the buyer's domicile and injury).

2. For a comparative discussion of enacted and proposed choice-of-law rules for products conflicts, see Scoles, Hay, Borchers & Symeonides, *Conflict of Laws*, 848-55. For a comparison of the results that these rules would produce in the United States, see Symeonides, *The Revolution Today*, §§ 244-49. For a new proposed European Union rule, see *Rome II*, art. 4, discussed in Symeonides, *Tort Conflicts and Rome II*, §§ 7.1-2.

3. See, e.g., Dorman v. Emerson Elec. Co., 23 F.3d 1354 (8th Cir.1994), cert. denied, 115 S. Ct. 428 (1994) (involving a miter saw manufactured in Taiwan by a Taiwanese corporation under license from a Missouri corporation that had designed and tested that line of products in Missouri); Rutherford v. Goodyear Tire & Rubber Co., 943 F.Supp. 789 (W.D.Ky.1996), aff'd, 142 F.3d 436, (6th Cir.1998) (involving a car tire manufactured in Kansas by Goodyear, an Ohio corporation, purchased by Ford Motor Company, a Michigan corporation, and installed on a Ford car in Ford's Kentucky assembly plant).

4. See, e.g., Braune v. Abbott Laboratories, 895 F. Supp. 530 (E.D.N.Y.1995), involving a drug known as DES which was designed to prevent miscarriages, which doctors prescribed to pregnant women living in several states in the 1950s. The plaintiffs in *Braune* were among the daughters of those women, and had been exposed to DES during gestation in their mothers' wombs. As a result of that exposure, plaintiffs gradually developed various abnormalities including infertility, miscarriages, and cervical cancer, which became evident when the plaintiffs reached child-bearing age. Because, like their mothers, the plaintiffs had lived in several states, the question of where their injuries occurred was a particularly difficult one. Judge Weinstein concluded that the injuries occurred in the states in which they were diagnosed. What do you think of this conclusion? See also Millar-Mintz v. Abbott Laboratories, 645 N.E.2d 278 (Ill.App.1994) (applying Illinois's pro-plaintiff law to an action filed by a plaintiff whose mother had used DES in the 1940's while domiciled in Illinois. The plaintiff had lived in New York, California, and then in Illinois, where she was first advised of her infertility and its causal relation to her mother's use of DES).

in products like the airplane involved in *Sioux* which are purchased by someone other than the victim.

3. *Is the place of manufacture a significant contact?* When, as in *Gantes*,[5] the product was designed, tested, approved, and manufactured in the same state, the logistical difficulty of identifying the state of conduct is overcome, but does this mean that the place of manufacture is a pertinent or significant contact for choice-of-law purposes? Professor P. John Kozyris has argued to the contrary, because "the mere making of a product, however defective, does not create the risk of causing harm. * * * Production is only a preparatory act which does not rise to the level of the wrongful conduct. The tort does not commence until the product is placed in a position to cause harm; i.e. is distributed to a potential user." Kozyris, *Values and Methods*, 500. See also Rutherford v. Goodyear Tire & Rubber Co., 943 F.Supp. 789 (W.D.Ky.1996) ("Legal claims do not arise at the time or at the place of manufacture. They arise when an injury occurs. Thus, the place of injury, not the place of manufacture is the central focus of the cause of action." Id. at 793). Do you agree with these statements? Why or why not?

4. *The Gantes Pattern.* In the *Gantes* pattern of cases, the state with the manufacturer-affiliating contacts (place of manufacture and/or defendant's principal place of business) has a law that favors the victim, while the state with the victim-affiliating contacts (victim's domicile, place of injury, and often the place of the product's acquisition) has a law that favors the manufacturer. According to Currie, these are the unprovided-for cases in which neither state has an interest in applying its law, and which should be decided under the law of the forum *qua forum*.

A study of cases of this pattern decided in the years 1990 through 2002, indicates that more than half of them applied *non-forum* law, and that the cases that applied forum law, like *Gantes*, based that application on the forum's other contacts or interests. See Symeonides, *The Revolution Today* §§ 219–28. In fact, few of these cases accepted Currie's assumption that a state whose law disfavors the local litigant necessarily has no interest in applying it. For example, like *Gantes*, some cases applied the pro-plaintiff law of a defendant-affiliated state because of an affirmative policy of deterring the manufacture of substandard products. Similarly, some cases that applied the pro-defendant law of a plaintiff-affiliated state, did so either on the basis of a significant-contacts analysis that did not consider state interests, or by assuming that the pro-defendant law of the victim's state was not confined to local defendants but was intended to encompass foreign defendants as well. See id. However, the same study indicates that the cases that, like *Gantes*, applied the pro-plaintiff law of the state of manufacture are outnumbered by a ratio of 1:2 by the cases that applied the pro-defendant law of the state that had the plaintiff-affiliating contacts. See id. at § 219.

5. *Does the state of manufacture and/or the manufacturer's domicile really have an interest in holding its manufacturers to a higher standard? Gantes'*

---

5. Even in *Gantes*, "there was considerable evidence presented suggesting that the machine was in fact manufactured in New York," rather than New Jersey. *Gantes*, 679 A.2d at 118 (Garibaldi, J. dissenting). However, all other decisions regarding the manufacture of the product were apparently made in New Jersey.

main thesis is that the state of manufacture has an interest in holding its manufacturers to the high standard of its law, even when the victim is not a forum domiciliary and the injury occurs in another state that prescribes a lower standard. Other courts, including courts sitting in states with defendant-affiliating contacts, have taken the same position. For example, in McLennan v. American Eurocopter Corp., Inc., 245 F.3d 403 (5th Cir.2001), the court concluded that Texas had a strong interest in enforcing its strict product-liability law against manufacturers operating in that state, while noting that the application of that law did not impose an unexpected burden on a Texas-based manufacturer. In Mitchell v. Lone Star Ammunition, Inc., 913 F.2d 242 (5th Cir.1990), the court concluded that Texas had a "substantial interest" in applying it pro-plaintiff law "as an incentive to encourage safer design and to induce corporations to control more carefully the manufacturing processes." Id. at 250. In DeGrasse v. Sensenich Corp., 1989 WL 23775 (E.D.Pa.1989), the court concluded that applying Pennsylvania law, which favored an Arkansas plaintiff at the expense of a Pennsylvania manufacturer, was in line with Pennsylvania's interests because "Pennsylvania's policy involves the attainment of broader objectives than simply ensuring full recovery for its domiciliary plaintiffs * * * [such as] deterring the manufacture of defective products by, and assigning responsibility for such an activity to, Pennsylvania manufacturers." Id. at *4. Finally, in Lacey v. Cessna Aircraft Co., 932 F.2d 170 (3d Cir.1991), the court concluded that the application of Pennsylvania's strict liability law to a case involving a product that was manufactured in Pennsylvania and caused injury in British Columbia would "further Pennsylvania's interest in deterring the manufacture of defective products * * * but would not impair British Columbia's interest in fostering industry within its borders." Id. at 188.[6]

As altruistic as the *Gantes* thesis may be, is it sufficiently realistic? In addition to the arguments advanced by Justice Garibaldi, what other arguments would you make against this thesis? Professor Kozyris has argued that: (1) "[the assumption] that imposing the stricter standards of the state of production to the-out-of-state distribution and harm may indirectly improve the in-state component as well * * * is * * * questionable in its logic of prohibiting what should be lawful to deter what is unlawful," (2) that "[a] purported 'moral' concern of the state of production about local activities which endanger people worldwide * * * is [also] not persuasive;" and (3) "Preferring the law of the state of production over those of distribution, harm and personal connections of the parties would be inconsistent with considerations both of allocating sovereign authority and of fairness to the parties." Kozyris,

---

6. Even more numerous are the cases in which, without expressly articulating this policy, the courts allowed claims against a forum manufacturer that were barred by the statute of repose of the other, plaintiff-affiliated, state on the ground that the latter statute was not intended to protect forum manufacturers. For example, in Mahne v. Ford Motor Co., 900 F.2d 83 (6th. Cir. 1990), *cert. denied*, 498 U.S. 941 (1990), the court concluded that Florida's statute of repose was intended to protect Florida manufacturers, not Michigan manufacturers such as the ones involved in this case. The latter "cannot argue that applying Michigan law would defeat their expectations," said the court, and "[t]hus, there is simply no reason to extend the benefits of the Florida statute of repose to the Michigan defendants." *Mahne*, 900 F.2d at 88-89. See also Dabbs v. Silver Eagle Mfg. Co., 779 P.2d 1104 (Or.App.1989) review denied, 784 P.2d 1101 (Or.1989); Marchesani v. Pellerin-Milnor Corp., 269 F.3d 481 (5th Cir.2001); Davis v. Shiley, 75 Cal.Rptr.2d 826 (Cal.App. 1998). For discussion of these and additional cases, see Symeonides, *The Revolution Today* §§ 220-23.

Values and Methods, 501. What do you think?

Many courts have taken a similar view. For example, in Farrell v. Ford Motor Co., 501 N.W.2d 567 (Mich.App.1993), *appeal denied*, 519 N.W.2d 158 (Mich.1994), a product liability action arising out of a North Carolina accident and filed by a North Carolina domiciliary against Ford, a Michigan manufacturer, the court refused to apply Michigan's statute of limitation under which the action was timely because Michigan had "no interest in affording greater rights of tort recovery to a North Carolina resident than his own state affords him." 501 N.W.2d at 572. The court applied instead North Carolina's statute of repose which barred the action. The court based its decision on North Carolina's "economic interest to encourage manufacturers, such as Ford, to do business in North Carolina." Id. Although Ford did not have a manufacturing plant in that state, the court stated that Ford "gene rate[d] substantial commerce within the State of North Carolina," and thus that state had an "obvious and substantial interest in shielding Ford from open-ended products liability claims." Id.

Similarly, in Rutherford v. Goodyear Tire & Rubber Co., 943 F.Supp. 789 (W.D.Ky.1996), a product liability action arising from an Indiana injury caused by a product assembled in Kentucky, the court refused to apply Kentucky's statute of limitation under which the action was timely, and held the action barred under Indiana's statute of repose. The court reasoned that "Kentucky's product liability laws and its statute of limitations are designed primarily to protect its own citizens or those injured within its boundaries," id. at 792, and that Kentucky "has neither expressed nor implied a particular interest in regulating products assembled within its boundaries, except where those products cause injury in Kentucky or where they injure its citizens." Id.[7]

Which of the above lines of cases do you find more persuasive and why?

6. *Converse-Gantes Pattern*. Suppose that in *Gantes* the laws of the two states were reversed so that New Jersey, the state with the manufacturer-affiliating contacts, had a pro-manufacturer law and Georgia, the state with the victim-affiliating contacts, had a pro-victim law. Under Currie's analysis, this would be a true conflict which the court should decide under the law of the forum *qua* forum. In fact, in the same 12-year period covered by the above mentioned study: (a) only a slight majority (52%) of cases involving this pattern applied forum law; and (b) in more than half of these cases, the forum state had significant contacts other than being the forum (e.g., plaintiff's domicile, place of injury, and place of the product's acquisition), which would justify applying the law of that state even if it were not the forum. See Symeonides, *The Revolution Today*, §§ 204-18.

The majority of the true conflicts cases (66%) applied the pro-plaintiff law of a plaintiff-affiliated state. This would seem to support the prevalent assumption that American courts favor the plaintiff. Before accepting this assumption, however,

---

7.ʹ See also Vestal v. Shiley Inc., 1997 WL 910373 (C.D.Cal.1997) (noting California's interest in deterring California manufacturers from manufacturing defective products within its borders, but concluding that this interest was adequately served by applying California law to the many actions filed by California plaintiffs); Hall v. General Motors Corp., 582 N.W.2d 866 (Mich. App. 1998); Dorman v. Emerson Elec. Co., 23 F.3d 1354 (8th Cir.1994), *cert. denied*, 513 U.S. 964 (1994).

one should keep in mind that: (a) in more than half of these cases, the state whose law the court applied had either three or two plaintiff-affiliating contacts; and (b) more than twice as many *other* cases applied the laws of the states that had those same contacts, even when their respective laws did *not* favor the plaintiff. This may suggest that, at least subconsciously, courts rely more on contacts than on other choice-of-law factors.

7. *Forum Shopping*. Did the *Gantes* plaintiff engage in forum shopping? The answer depends on one's definition of forum shopping (since there is no commonly accepted definition). If one defines forum shopping as including all cases in which plaintiffs sue in states that have favorable substantive laws, then *Gantes* fits the definition as do 76% of the cases decided between 1990 and 2002. See Symeonides, *The Revolution Today* § 238. However, was there anything unfair in subjecting the *Gantes* defendant to litigation in its home state? What if the laws of the two states were reversed and (for that reason) the plaintiff had sued in Georgia? Would this qualify as forum shopping? Why, or why not?

On the other hand, if one defines forum shopping narrowly as to encompass only those cases in which a plaintiff unfairly exploits the jurisdictional rules to sue in a state that does not have relevant contacts other than the jurisdictional nexus with the defendant (e.g., doing business), then the percentage of forum-shopping drops down to single digits. See id. These cases are usually filed in states that have long statute of limitations (see Bonti v. Ford Motor Co., 898 F.Supp. 391 (S.D.Miss. 1995), *aff'd without op.*, 85 F.3d 625 (5th Cir.1996); Walls v. General Motors, 906 F.2d 143 (5th Cir.1990)), or in states like Minnesota which follow the better-law approach. (See Nesladek v. Ford Motor Co., 46 F.3d 734 (8th Cir.1995), *cert. denied*, 516 U.S. 814 (1995).) However, in none of these cases did the plaintiff's forum shopping pay off--all cases applied the pro-defendant law of a state other than the forum.

It seems that, unlike the *Gantes* plaintiff, most products liability plaintiffs tend to sue in their home state (which usually has additional contacts, such as the place of injury or the product's acquisition), even if that state has a pro-defendant law. For example, in more than half of the cases of the 1990-2002 period, the plaintiffs sued in their home states, even though in one third of those cases those states had *pro-defendant* laws. See Symeonides, supra at § 239. What do you think explains this trend?

8. *Plaintiff- or Forum- Favoritism.* By applying the forum's pro-plaintiff law, *Gantes* may lend credence to the prevailing assumption that modern approaches exhibit a bias in favor of: the *lex fori*; plaintiffs; or both. This assumption may have been accurate in the 1970s and 1980s, but the products-liability cases of the 1990-2003 period tend to negate it. The above mentioned study indicates that:

> (a) the cases that applied forum law barely rose above 50%. Even in true conflicts, this percentage was only 59%, and it drops to 44% in the more numerous no-interest cases;

> (b) slightly more than half of the cases applied a law that favored the *defendant*. Plaintiffs did enjoy a 2:1 advantage in true conflicts, but this advantage was swallowed up by an 1:2 disadvantage in the no-interest cases,

which were more numerous than true conflicts.
See Symeonides, supra at §§ 240, 242. Similarly, the cases do not support the assumption that courts tend to favor the local litigant--plaintiff or defendant. In fact, only 40% of the cases applied a law that favored the local litigant. See id. at § 241.

Do the above numbers suggest that Currie's influence over American conflicts law is rapidly diminishing?

E. PARTY AUTONOMY IN CONTRACTS

The principle of party autonomy, namely, that the parties to a multistate contract may, within certain limits, choose the law that would govern their contract, is almost as ancient as conflicts law itself. Indeed, it seems that party autonomy was recognized, albeit indirectly, by what may be regarded as the earliest known conflicts rule. A decree issued in Hellenistic Egypt in 120–118 B.C. provided that contracts written in the Egyptian language were subject to the jurisdiction of the Egyptian courts, which applied Egyptian law, whereas contracts written in Greek were subject to the jurisdiction of the Greek courts, which applied Greek law. Thus, by choosing the language of their contract, the parties could directly choose the forum and indirectly the applicable law. See Juenger, *Multistate Justice* 7-8. In the middle ages, the French commentator Dumoulin (1500-1566) resurrected and championed party autonomy, which has since been a gravamen of continental conflicts doctrine and practice. American transactional and judicial practice has also recognized this principle as early as 1825. See Wayman v. Southard, 23 U.S. (10 Wheat.) 1, 48 (1825); Pritchard v. Norton, 106 U.S. 124 (1882).

Erroneously assuming that party autonomy amounted to a license for private legislation, the drafters of the first Restatement decided to prohibit such a license. In turn, most courts, even those that followed the first Restatement, chose to ignore this prohibition. Recognizing this reality, § 187 of the Restatement (Second) formally sanctioned the principle of party autonomy, thus bringing American law in accord with most other western legal systems. This important section, which is followed by more American courts than any other provision of the Restatement (Second), including some courts that otherwise follow the traditional theory, provides as follows:

> (1) The law of the state chosen by the parties to govern their contractual rights and duties will be applied if the particular issue is one which the parties could have resolved by an explicit provision in their agreement directed to that issue.
>
> (2) The law of the state chosen by the parties to govern their contractual rights and duties will be applied even if the particular issue is one which the parties could not have resolved by an explicit provision in their agreement directed to that issue, unless either
>
> (a) the chosen state has no substantial relationship to the parties or the transaction and there is no other reasonable basis for the parties' choice, or
>
> (b) application of the law of the chosen state would be contrary to a fundamental policy of a state which has a materially greater interest than the

chosen state in the determination of the particular issue and which, under the rule of section 188, would be the state of the applicable law in the absence of an effective choice of law by the parties.

(3) In the absence of a contrary indication of intention, the reference is to the local law of the state of the chosen law.[1]

Whether or not party autonomy is the oldest choice-of-law principle, it is certainly the one most universally observed, indeed "perhaps the most widely accepted private international rule of our time." Weintraub, *Choice of Law for Contracts*, 271. It is also a principle that is widely honored in everyday transactional practice, both here and abroad. For example, about twenty percent of conflicts cases decided by intermediate courts and courts of last resort every year involve a choice-of-law clause. See Symeonides, *Choice of Law in 1995*, 221; *A View From the Trenches*, 54; *Choice of Law in 1993*, 642-43. Although this is a high percentage, it is probably even higher if one considers lower court cases that are not appealed or contracts that do not result in litigation. After all, one of the main advantages of choice-of-law clauses is their ability to avoid litigation. When litigation is unavoidable, choice-of-law clauses still are useful in reducing the court's burden of determining the applicable law.

DeSantis v. Wackenhut Corporation

Supreme Court of Texas, 1990.
793 S.W.2d 670, On Motion for Rehearing.

HECH, J., * * * I. A. Edward DeSantis * * * interviewed for a position with Wackenhut Corporation * * *, which was chartered and headquartered in Florida [and] was the third largest company in the nation specializing in furnishing security guards for businesses throughout the country. DeSantis met with Wackenhut's president, founder, and majority stockholder, George Wackenhut, at the company's offices in Florida, and the two agreed that DeSantis would immediately assume the position of Wackenhut's Houston area manager. * * *

At Wackenhut's request, DeSantis signed a noncompetition agreement at the inception of his employment. The agreement recites that it was "made and entered into" on August 13, 1981, in Florida, although DeSantis signed it in Texas. It also recites consideration "including but not limited to the Employee's employment by the Employer." In the agreement DeSantis covenanted that as long as he was employed by Wackenhut and for two years thereafter, he would not compete in any way with Wackenhut in a forty-county area in south Texas. DeSantis expressly acknowledged that Wackenhut's client list "is a valuable, special and unique asset of [Wackenhut's] business" and agreed never to disclose it to anyone. DeSantis also agreed never to divulge any confidential or proprietary information acquired through his employment with Wackenhut. Finally, DeSantis and Wackenhut agreed "that any questions concerning interpretation or enforcement of this contract shall be governed

---

1. Quoted with the permission of the copyright owner, The American Law Institute.

by Florida law."

DeSantis remained manager of Wackenhut's Houston office for nearly three years, until March 1984, when he resigned under threat of termination. * * * Following his resignation, DeSantis * * * formed a new company, Risk Deterrence, Inc. ("RDI"), to provide security consulting services and security guards to a limited clientele. The month following termination of his employment with Wackenhut, DeSantis sent out letters announcing his new ventures to twenty or thirty businesses, about half of which were Wackenhut clients. He added a postscript to letters to Wackenhut clients in which he disclaimed any intent to interfere with their existing contracts with Wackenhut. * * *

B. Wackenhut sued DeSantis and RDI in October 1984 to enjoin them from violating the noncompetition agreement, and to recover damages for breach of the agreement and for tortious interference with business relations. Wackenhut alleged that DeSantis and RDI were soliciting its clients' business using confidential client and pricing information which DeSantis obtained through his employment with Wackenhut. * * * DeSantis and RDI counterclaimed against Wackenhut, alleging that Wackenhut had fraudulently induced DeSantis to sign the noncompetition agreement, that the agreement violated state antitrust laws, and that enforcement of the agreement by temporary injunction was wrongful and tortiously interfered with DeSantis and RDI's contract and business relationships. * * *

II. We first consider what law is to be applied in determining whether the noncompetition agreement in this case is enforceable. Wackenhut contends that Florida law applies, as expressly agreed by the parties. DeSantis argues that Texas law applies, despite the parties' agreement.

A. This Court has not previously addressed what effect should be given to contractual choice of law provisions. We begin with what Chief Justice Marshall referred to as a principle of "universal law ... that, in every forum, a contract is governed by the law with a view to which it was made." Wayman v. Southard, 23 U.S. 1, 48 (1825). This principle derives from the most basic policy of contract law, which is the protection of the justified expectations of the parties. * * * The parties' understanding of their respective contractual rights and obligations depends in part upon the certainty with which they may predict how the law will interpret and enforce their agreement. Id.

When parties to a contract reside or expect to perform their respective obligations in multiple jurisdictions, they may be uncertain as to what jurisdiction's law will govern construction and enforcement of the contract. To avoid this uncertainty, they may express in their agreement their own choice that the law of a specified jurisdiction apply to their agreement. Judicial respect for their choice advances the policy of protecting their expectations. This conflict of laws concept has come to be referred to as party autonomy. * * * However, the parties' freedom to choose what jurisdiction's law will apply to their agreement cannot be unlimited. They cannot require that their contract be governed by the law of a jurisdiction which has no relation whatever to them or their agreement. And they cannot by agreement thwart or offend the public policy of the state the law of which ought otherwise to apply. So limited, party autonomy furthers the basic policy of contract law. With roots deep in two centuries of American jurisprudence, limited party autonomy has grown to be the modern rule in contracts conflict of laws. See Scoles, supra at 632-52; Weintraub, supra at 269-75; Restatement (Second) of Conflict of Laws ["the Restatement"] § 187 (1971).

The party autonomy rule has been recognized in this state. * * * We believe the rule is best formulated in section 187 of the Restatement and will therefore look to its provisions in our analysis of this case.

B. Section 187 states: * * * [see supra]

The issue before us—whether the noncompetition agreement in this case is enforceable—is not "one which the parties could have resolved by an explicit provision in their agreement." See Restatement (Second) of Conflict of Laws § 187 comment d (1971). We therefore apply section 187(2).

The parties in this case chose the law of Florida to govern their contract. Florida has a substantial relationship to the parties and the transaction because Wackenhut's corporate offices are there, and some of the negotiations between DeSantis and George Wackenhut occurred there. Thus, under section 187(2) Florida law should apply in this case unless it falls within the exception stated in section 187(2)(b). Whether that exception applies depends upon three determinations: first, whether there is a state the law of which would apply under section 188 of the Restatement absent an effective choice of law by the parties, or in other words, whether a state has a more significant relationship with the parties and their transaction than the state they chose; second, whether that state has a materially greater interest than the chosen state in deciding whether this noncompetition agreement should be enforced; and third, whether that state's fundamental policy would be contravened by the application of the law of the chosen state in this case. More particularly, we must determine: first, whether Texas has a more significant relationship to these parties and their transaction than Florida; second, whether Texas has a materially greater interest than Florida in deciding the enforceability of the noncompetition agreement in this case; and third, whether the application of Florida law in this case would be contrary to fundamental policy of Texas.

1. Section 188 of the Restatement provides that a contract is to be governed by the law of the state that "has the most significant relationship to the transaction and the parties," taking into account various contacts in light of the basic conflict of laws principles of section 6 of the Restatement. In this case, that state is Texas. Wackenhut hired DeSantis to manage its business in the Houston area. Although some of the negotiations between DeSantis and Wackenhut occurred in Florida, the noncompetition agreement was finally executed by DeSantis in Houston. The place of performance for both parties was Texas, where the subject matter of the contract was located. Wackenhut may also be considered to have performed its obligations in part in Florida, from where it supervised its various operations, including its Houston office. Still, the gist of the agreement in this case was the performance of personal services in Texas. As a rule, that factor alone is conclusive in determining

what state's law is to apply. See Restatement § 196 (1971).[4] In this case, the relationship of the transaction and parties to Texas was clearly more significant than their relationship to Florida.

2. Texas has a materially greater interest than does Florida in determining whether the noncompetition agreement in this case is enforceable. At stake here is whether a Texas resident can leave one Texas job to start a competing Texas business. Thus, Texas is directly interested in DeSantis as an employee in this state, in Wackenhut as a national employer doing business in this state, in RDI as a new competitive business being formed in the state, and in consumers of the services furnished in Texas by Wackenhut and RDI and performed by DeSantis. Texas also shares with Florida a general interest in protecting the justifiable expectations of entities doing business in several states. Florida's direct interest in the enforcement of the noncompetition agreement in this case is limited to protecting a national business headquartered in that state. Although it is always problematic for one state to balance its own interests fairly against those of another state, the circumstances of this case leave little doubt, if any, that Texas has a materially greater interest than Florida in deciding whether the noncompetition agreement in this case should be enforced.

3. Having concluded that Texas law would control the issue of enforceability of the noncompetition agreement in this case but for the parties' choice of Florida law, and that Texas' interest in deciding this issue in this case is materially greater than Florida's, we must finally determine under section 187(2)(b) of the Restatement whether application of Florida law to decide this issue would be contrary to fundamental policy of Texas. The Restatement offers little guidance in making this determination. Comment g states only that a "fundamental" policy is a "substantial" one, and that "[t]he forum will apply its own legal principles in determining whether a given policy is a fundamental one within the meaning of the present rule.... " Comment g to section 187 does suggest that application of the law of another state is not contrary to the fundamental policy of the forum merely because it leads to a different result than would obtain under the forum's law. We agree that the result in one case cannot determine whether the issue is a matter of fundamental state policy for purposes of resolving a conflict of laws. Moreover, the fact that the law of another state is materially different from the law of this state does not itself establish that application of the other state's law would offend the fundamental policy of Texas. In analyzing whether fundamental policy is offended under section 187(2)(b), the focus is on whether the law in question is a part of state policy so fundamental that the courts of the state will refuse to enforce an agreement contrary to that law, despite the parties' original intentions, and even though the agreement would be

---

4. Section 196 states: "*Contracts for the Rendition of Services*. The validity of a contract for the rendition of services and the rights created thereby are determined, in the absence of an effective choice of law by the parties, by the local law of the state where the contract requires that the services, or a major portion of the services, be rendered, unless, with respect to the particular issue, some other state has a more significant relationship under the principles stated in § 6 to the transaction and the parties, in which event the local law of the other state will be applied."

enforceable in another state connected with the transaction.[5]

Neither the Restatement nor the cases which have followed section 187 have undertaken a general definition of "fundamental policy", and we need not make the attempt in this case; for whatever its parameters, enforcement of noncompetition agreements falls well within them. This Court has held that "[a]n agreement not to compete is in restraint of trade and will not be enforced unless it is reasonable." * * * As a general rule, unreasonable restraints of trade, including unreasonable covenants not to compete, contravene public policy. * * * What noncompetition agreements are reasonable restraints upon employees in this state, therefore, is a matter of public policy. Moreover, that policy is fundamental in that it ensures a uniform rule for enforcement of noncompetition agreements in this state. See Restatement § 187 comment g (1971) ("a fundamental policy may be embodied in a statute which makes one or more kinds of contracts illegal or which is designed to protect a person against the oppressive use of superior bargaining power"). Absent such a policy, agreements involving residents of other states would be controlled by the law and policy of those states. An employee of one out-of-state employer might take a competing job and escape enforcement of a covenant not to compete because of the law of another state, while a neighbor suffered enforcement of an identical covenant because of the law of a third state. The resulting disruption of orderly employer-employee relations, as well as competition in the marketplace, would be unacceptable. Employers would be encouraged to attempt to invoke the most favorable state law available to govern their relationship with their employees in Texas or other states. These same considerations and others have led virtually every court that has addressed the question of whether enforcement of noncompetition agreements is a matter of fundamental or important state policy to answer affirmatively. Not many of these courts have considered the matter specifically in the context of section 187 of the Restatement, and yet, rather remarkably, many have nevertheless expressed similar conclusions.

We likewise conclude that the law governing enforcement of non-competition agreements is fundamental policy in Texas, and that to apply the law of another state to determine the enforceability of such an agreement in the circumstances of a case like this would be contrary to that policy. We therefore hold that the enforceability of the agreement in this case must be judged by Texas law, not Florida law.

III. We now consider whether the noncompetition agreement between DeSantis and Wackenhut is enforceable under Texas law. * * *

Having determined that Wackenhut has not shown that DeSantis' agreement not to compete is necessary to protect any legitimate business interest, or that the necessity of such protection outweighs the hardship of that agreement on DeSantis, we conclude that the agreement is unreasonable and therefore unenforceable. * * *

---

5. The trial court apparently concluded that this noncompetition agreement is enforceable under both Texas and Florida law. The court of appeals concluded that the agreement is enforceable under Florida law and did not consider whether it is enforceable under Texas law. DeSantis appears to concede that the agreement is enforceable under Florida law. Wackenhut strongly argues that the agreement is enforceable under Texas law.

Notes and Questions

1. **THE EXISTENCE OF AN AGREEMENT ON CHOICE OF LAW:** *Capacity, Consent, Formation, and Form.* A choice-of-law clause is itself an agreement that is usually contained in the contract that the clause purports to submit to the chosen law. Before one can properly speak of such an "agreement," however, one must first verify that it came into existence. Did the parties have the capacity to make such an agreement? Was their consent to it free of vices, such as duress, error, etc.? Was there a "meeting of the minds"? Was the agreement clothed in the requisite form? Suppose, for example, that Mrs. Pratt and Mr. Kaufman (the two parties in *Milliken* (Ch. 2) and *Lilienthal* (Ch. 3), respectively, whose capacity to contract was limited by the law of their home state) had "agreed" to the application of the law of the other state that did not limit their capacity. Would such an agreement automatically have vested these parties with the capacity they lacked? These questions do not arise often in practice, but when they do they raise a preliminary choice-of-law question: under which law should one answer these questions?

Of the three possible options, the Restatement (Second) employs two--it divides the above issues between the *lex fori* and the chosen law. To the former, the Restatement assigns issues of misrepresentation, duress, undue influence, or mistake. See id. § 187, cmt. b. To the latter, the Restatement assigns all other issues of formation and validity of the choice-of-law agreement, including capacity and form, by providing that they are "determined by the law chosen by the parties, *if they have made an effective choice.*" § 189 cmt. a, § 199 cmt. a, § 200 cmt. a. (See also Swiss codification art. 116(2) which provides that "the choice of law is governed by the chosen law.") Both options offer the advantage of practicality and judicial economy. In addition, if pressed, one can defend the *lex fori* option by arguing that, to the extent that a choice-of-law agreement displaces some of the forum's choice-of-law rules, the forum should be free to determine under its own substantive standards whether such an agreement exists before allowing such a displacement. But what about the option of applying the chosen law? Doesn't this entail some serious "bootstrapping"? Consider the *Milliken* and *Lilienthal* questions, supra. Does the policing mechanism of § 187(2)(b) resolve the bootstrapping problem?

Is it not more logical to assign these matters to the law that would have been applicable in the absence of a contractual choice of law (hereafter referred to as the *lex causae*)? This option is followed by, *inter alia*: the 1980 EEC Convention on Contractual Obligations (Rome Convention) (art. 3(4)), and the codifications of Germany (art. 27(4)), Louisiana (arts. 3537-3540); Oregon (§§ 81.110-81.115), and Puerto Rico (arts. 34-35). Although this option is logical, is it also practical, or does it undercut much of the efficiency and convenience that make choice-of-law clauses attractive to courts and litigants?

2. **ENFORCEABILITY OF A CHOICE-OF-LAW AGREEMENT:** *a. Preliminary Threshold: Connection with Chosen Law.* Assuming that an agreement as to the applicable law indeed exists, the next question is whether such agreement is enforceable in the particular case. *DeSantis* states that the parties "cannot require that their contract be governed by the law of a jurisdiction which has no relation whatever

to them or their agreement." If so, then, before examining the merits of the agreement, the court must be satisfied that the chosen jurisdiction has a certain geographical or other connection with the contract and the parties. Although some legal systems require satisfaction of this preliminary threshold (see, e.g., Spanish Civ. Code art. 10(5)), other systems bypass it altogether and police the agreement through other means.[1] The Restatement (Second), which *DeSantis* followed, adopts a middle road by distinguishing between: (a) issues that the parties "could have resolved by an explicit provision in their agreement" (§ 187(1)); and (b) issues that the parties could not have so resolved. This very important and sensible distinction is drawn from domestic contract law and parallels the ancient civil law distinction between "suppletive rules" (*jus dispositivum*) and "mandatory rules" (*jus cogens*).

With regard to issues of the first category, such as issues relating to "construction, to conditions precedent and subsequent, to sufficiency of performance and to excuse of nonperformance" (§ 187 cmt. c.), the Restatement does not require a connection with the state of the chosen law and imposes no other limitations on the parties' choice. See § 187(1). Why do you think this is so? Also, according to which law does one determine whether the particular issue is one of those that are within the parties' contractual power? See id. cmt. c. (*lex causae*); Armstrong Business Services, Inc. v. H & R Block, 96 S.W.3d 867, (Mo.App.2002) (*accord*). But see Swanson v. Image Bank, Inc. 43 P.3d 174 (Ariz.App.2002), *review granted* (applying law of forum *qua* forum).

With regard to the issues of the second category, the Restatement requires a showing of a "substantial relationship" (§ 187(2)(a)) with the state of the chosen law.[2] Even with regard to these issues, however, the absence of such a relationship can be cured by the presence of "[an]other reasonable basis for the parties' choice." Id. For example, the parties to a contract of maritime transportation between two countries with relatively undeveloped legal systems would have a reasonable basis to submit their contract to a well-known and mature law, such as English or American maritime law, even if the contract has no connection with England or the United States. See § 187 cmt. f.

b. Determining the Lex Limitatis. As *DeSantis* correctly states, the parties' freedom to choose the applicable law "cannot be unlimited." Indeed, although all legal systems recognize the principle of party autonomy, they also agree on the need for some limitations. Predictably, however, these limitations vary from one state to another. Thus, in a multistate contract that contains a choice-of-law clause, one of the important preliminary questions is which state's law will be used as the standard for determining whether such a clause will be enforced in the particular case. Of the possible options, one option that must be eliminated as circular is the chosen law.

---

1. See, e.g., UCC § 1-301(c) (with regard to non-consumer contracts); Rome Convention art. 3; Hague Sales Convention art. 7; Austrian codif. § 35; German codif. art. 27; La. Civ. Code art. 3540; Oregon codif. § 81.120. Section § 5-1401 of New York's General Obligations Law contains a unilateral rule that, with regard to certain contracts, invites the choice of New York law, "whether or not such contract * * * bears a reasonable relation to [New York]."

2. This requirement is rarely a problem because most parties tend to choose the law of a state with which at least one party is affiliated. But see Sentinel Industrial Contracting Corp. v. Kimmins Industrial Service Corp., 743 So.2d 954 (Miss.1999) (holding that choice of Texas law in a contract for the dismantlement of a Mississippi ammonia plant and its shipment and reassembly in Pakistan did not meet this requirement).

Thus, the answer must be sought between the *lex fori* and the *lex causae*. However, the available options are more than two, to wit: (1) the *lex fori* alone; (2) the *lex causae* alone; (3) the *lex causae* "and more"; (4) both the *lex fori* and the *lex causae*; and (5) either the *lex causae* or the *lex fori*.

The vast majority of systems, including the Restatement (Second) and UCC § 1-103(f), follow option (2).[3] However, the Restatement also seems to follow option (3) by providing in § 187(2)(b) that, in order to disregard the chosen law, the court must be satisfied not only that the law of another state would have been applicable in the absence of a contractual choice of law by the parties, but also that that state "has a materially greater interest than the chosen state in the determination of the particular issue." The Rome Convention adopts a similar standard by providing that the chosen law will be disregarded when "*all* the other elements relevant to the situation at the time of the choice are connected with one country only." Rome Convention, Art. 3(3). (See also the identical provision in Art. 27(3) of the German codification.) While a country that has "all" these elements most likely will be the state of the *lex causae*, the reverse is not true. Thus, a country that has significant connections may qualify as the state of the *lex causae* under the Convention but, unless that country has "all" the connections, its law may not be invoked to invalidate the parties' choice of another law.

c. What Threshold Should be Used to Invalidate the Parties' Choice?
After identifying the *lex limitatis*, the next question is how high a threshold to establish before invalidating the parties' choice of another law. If any difference between the *lex limitatis/causae* and the chosen law would defeat the parties's choice, then party autonomy would become a specious gift, would it not? As one court said, "[t]he result would be that parties would have the right to choose the application of another state's law only when that state's law is identical to [the *lex causae*]. Such an approach would be ridiculous." Cherokee Pump & Equipment, Inc. v. Aurora Pump, 38 F.3d 246, 252 (5th Cir.1994). Thus, there is a general consensus on the need for a higher threshold for multistate contracts than for fully domestic contracts. Predictably, however, the various systems differ in defining this threshold.

For example, the Restatement (Second) seems to set one of the highest thresholds when it provides in § 187(2)(b) that, before invalidating a choice-of-law clause, the court must be satisfied that: (a) the chosen law is "contrary to a *fundamental* policy" of the state of the *lex causae*; *and* (b) that that state has a "materially greater interest than the chosen state in the determination of the particular issue." The UCC eliminates the second hurdle--it invalidates the choice only if it violates a "fundamental" policy of a state "whose law would govern in the absence of agreement." UCC § 1-103(f). Other codifications take the same position. See, e.g., Louisiana codif. art. 3540, Oregon codif. § 81.125. In contrast, the Rome Convention

---

3. No system officially follows option (1), but, unlike the *DeSantis* court, some courts carelessly examine whether the chosen law contravenes the *lex fori* without explaining whether the *lex fori* also would have been the *lex causae*. Likewise, no system follows option (5), but the application of the traditional *ordre public* reservation may bring about the same result. Option (4) is followed by the Puerto Rican draft code which provides that the chosen law is not to be applied if it violates restrictions on party autonomy imposed by *both* the *lex fori* and the *lex causae*. For the rationale of this provision, see Symeonides, *The Puerto Rico Project*, 422-24.

seems to pose a low threshold when it provides in art. 3(3) that the chosen law may not "prejudice the application of rules * * * which cannot be derogated from by contract" ("mandatory rules"). However, as noted above, it is only "where *all* the other elements relevant to the situation * * * are connected with one country only" (id.) that the mandatory rules of that country may invalidate the parties' choice. Thus, ultimately the Rome Convention may be more liberal than the Restatement toward party autonomy. On the other hand, unlike the Restatement, the Convention exempts issues of contractual capacity and form from the scope of party autonomy and, through special provisions, protects consumers and employees from the consequences of an adverse choice of law. See Rome Convention arts. 5–6, discussed infra at 357. Similarly, the Swiss codification, which appears to be the most deferential to party autonomy (see arts. 116, 15), specifically prohibits choice-of-law clauses in consumer contracts and severely restricts them in employment contracts. (See arts. 120–21.) For similar protections for consumers, see UCC § 1-103(e); Oregon codif. § 81.115; Puerto Rico Draft Code, art. 41.

    d. "Fundamental" Policy. When is a policy "fundamental" in the sense of Restatement (Second) 187(2)(b)? The Restatement does not provide a definition but provides three examples of rules that do *not* embody such a policy (statutes of frauds, rules "tending to become obsolete," and "general rules of contract law, such as those concerned with the need for consideration," § 187 cmt. g), and examples of rules that embody such a policy (statutes that make certain contracts illegal, and statutes intended to protect one party from "the oppressive use of superior bargaining power," such as statutes protecting insureds against insurers. Id.) The Restatement also states that, to be fundamental in the sense of § 187(2)(b), a policy need not be as strong as the policy that justifies a refusal to apply foreign law under the traditional *ordre public* exception. See *Loucks*, supra Ch. 1.

    In Machado-Miller v. Mersereau & Shannon, LLP., 43 P.3d 1207 (Or.App. 2002), an Oregon court had to determine whether California's policy against non-compete agreements was fundamental under Restatement (Second) §187(2)(b) so as to defeat an Oregon choice-of-law clause in an Oregon employment contract. The court expressed serious misgivings about the facility and exactness of such a determination:

> To announce that a policy or a right is 'fundamental' is to announce a conclusion and not a premise, and the reasoning that leads to the conclusion is almost always obscure, hopelessly subjective, or expressed in verbal formulations that are of little help. * * * Further, whether a particular interest is deemed 'fundamental' under such indeterminate formulations depends on the level of generality at which the Court chooses to identify it. To the extent the interest is described at a high level of generality, it is likely to be 'fundamental,' and *vice versa*. Further, every piece of legislation, even the most apparently trivial, implements and therefore indicates the presence of some larger policy, which, in turn, serves an even larger one. A speed limit is not itself a fundamental policy statement, but its purpose is to promote highway safety, which is one way to protect the health, welfare and safety of citizens, which is, of course, one of the most fundamental of all

public policies.

43 P.3d at 1211. Eventually, the court concluded that California's policy was fundamental "in the dictionary sense [of] 'basic, underlying and primary,'" id. at 1212, because it was contained in statute phrased "at a high level of generality," id., and clearly stating a policy of prohibiting non-compete agreements in order to maximize competition and minimize restraints on trade. The statute provided that "every contract by which anyone is restrained from engaging in a lawful profession, trade, or business of any kind is to that extent void." California Business and Professional Code § 16600.

The court then turned to the question of whether California had a "materially greater interest" than Oregon in applying its law, a question the court described as requiring us the comparison of "incommensurables." The court acknowledged California's interests in not enforcing non-compete covenants in California, but "[o]n the other hand," said the court,

> Oregon's statute permitting noncompetition clauses * * * expresses a fundamental policy as well: protecting the rights of Oregon citizens to choose the terms of their own employment relations free from government interference. In providing a disincentive to leaving one employer for a higher bidder, Oregon's law promotes stable employment relations. It also protects Oregon employers from loss of employees in whose training they have invested considerable resources.

43 P.3d at 1212. After noting Oregon's contacts with the case, the court concluded: "We are therefore unable to say with any confidence that California's general or particular interests in the outcome of this case were *any* greater than Oregon's, and we can say with confidence that California's interests were not *materially* greater than Oregon's." Id. at 1213.

In the meantime, the 2001 Oregon codification adopted the "fundamental policy" criterion (but not the "materially greater interest" criterion) in scrutinizing choice-of-law clauses. The codification provides that a policy is fundamental "only if the policy reflects objectives or gives effect to essential public or societal institutions beyond the allocation of rights and obligations of parties to a contract at issue." O.R.S. §81.125(2). Is this formulation any less indeterminate than the Restatement's? Would it have helped the *Machado-Miller* or *DeSantis* courts? The codification also provides that the chosen law does not apply "to the extent that its application would: (a) Require a party to perform an act prohibited by the law of the state where the act is to be performed under the contract; [or] (b) Prohibit a party from performing an act required by the law of the state where it is to be performed under the contract[.]" § 81.125(1). Is this helpful? For the background of these provisions, see Symeonides, *The Oregon Experience*, VI.2.

A Note on Choice-of-Law Clauses and Non-Compete Agreements

In *DeSantis*, the employee was at all critical times a Texas domiciliary. Suppose though that, at the time of the contract that contained the Florida choice-of-law clause, the employee was a Florida domiciliary who was hired for work in

Florida and later moved to Texas after he resigned his Florida employment. In such a case, would Texas have either a "more significant relationship" or a "greater interest" than Florida?

Application Group, Inc. v. Hunter Group, Inc., 72 Cal.Rptr.2d 73 (Cal.App.1998) involved a similar scenario, with Maryland and California being the first and second employment states, respectively. The employee was a Maryland domiciliary who, after resigning her job with a Maryland employer, began working ("tele-commuting") for a competing California employer, apparently *without* physically moving her domicile to California. In the ensuing litigation in California, the court held that the non-compete clause contained in the Maryland contract was unenforceable in California. The court found that California met all three prongs for disregarding the Maryland choice-of-law clause under Restatement (Second) § 187(2), to wit: (1) California law would be applicable to this issue in the absence of the choice-of-law clause; (2) California had a materially greater interest in applying its law to this issue; and (3) enforcement of the non-compete clause would be contrary to a fundamental policy of California.

The court noted that, although Maryland had all the contacts relevant to the employment contract (which was not at issue), California had the contact that was most relevant with regard to the particular issue--the enforceability of the non-compete covenant in California. As to this issue, said the court, "the subject matter of the contract" was the employee's "subsequent employment which was, in this case, employment by a competitor who is 'located' in California." Id. at 87. Thus, to the extent that the covenant purported to restrict competition in California, California had the *most* pertinent contact which brought into play California's interest in protecting California employers and "business opportunities in California." Id. at 88.

The court concluded that California had a strong interest in protecting both the employee and the second (California) employer. With regard to the employee, California had "a strong interest in protecting the freedom of movement of persons whom California-based employers * * * wish to employ * * *, regardless of the person's state of residence." Id. at 85. With regard to the second employer, California had a "public policy which ensures that California employers will be able to compete effectively for the most talented, skilled employees in their industries, wherever they may reside," id., and thus California had an "interest in protecting its employers and their employees from anti-competitive conduct by out-of-state employers * * * who would interfere with or restrict these freedoms." Id.

What do you think of this decision? Consider the following comments of a California judge who dissented in a similar case in which the employee did move to California:

> Relocating to California is not a chance to walk away from valid contractual obligations, claiming California policy as a protective shield. We are not a political safe zone vis-à-vis our sister states, such that the mere act of setting foot on California soil somehow releases a person from the legal duties our sister states recognize.

Advanced Bionics Corp. v. Medtronic, Inc., 59 P.3d 231 (Cal.2002), Brown J., dissenting. See also id. (speaking of California's "political imperialism, absorbing every state into the California legal ethos.")

Faced with a similar situation, another court observed stoically that these are "[t]he aches and pains of federalism." Keener v. Convergy's Corp., 205 F.Supp.2d 1374, 1379 (S.D.Ga. 2002). In *Keener*, Ohio was the first employer's state and the employee's first domicile, while Georgia was the second employer's state and employee's new domicile. The Georgia federal court refused to enforce the Ohio choice-of-law clause and non-compete covenant because the latter was contrary to the free-competition policy embedded in Georgia's constitution. The court acknowledged that "[t]his may wind up encouraging non-Georgia employees to 'flee to Georgia' to shed their [non-compete covenants]." Id. at 1379. However, analogizing to "quickie divorces," the court said, "[t]he aches and pains of federalism * * * have long formed part of the American legal fabric." Id.[4]

Are these aches and pains really unavoidable? In any event, under these circumstances, would you advise the first employer to strike first by suing in the first employment state? Advanced Bionics Corp. v. Medtronic, Inc., 59 P.3d 231 (Cal. 2002), involved this scenario, with Minnesota and California being the first and second employment states, respectively. The first employer was a Minnesota corporation who hired a Minnesota domiciliary in that state for work to be performed there. The employment contract contained a Minnesota choice-of-law clause, as well as a non-compete covenant that was valid under Minnesota law. The employee quit his job with the Minnesota employer and was hired by Medtronic, a competing California employer, for work in California. The California employer filed in California an action seeking a declaration that the non-compete covenant was unenforceable in California. In the meantime, the Minnesota employer filed an action for an injunction in Minnesota enjoining the employee from violating the non-compete covenant. The lower courts in both states rendered conflicting judgments in favor of their respective employers (see Advanced Bionics Corp. v. Medtronic, Inc., 105 Cal.Rptr.2d 265 (Cal.App.2001); Medtronic, Inc. v. Advanced Bionics Corp., 630 N.W.2d 438 (Minn.App. 2001)), before the California Supreme Court set aside the California judgment. The court acknowledged that California had a "strong interest" in protecting the freedom of new California domiciliaries to seek employment in California, and that a California court "might reasonably conclude" that the Minnesota non-compete and choice-of-law clauses were "void in this state." 128 Cal. Rptr.2d at 179. However, the court specifically refused to base its decision regarding the propriety of an antisuit injunction on choice-of-law factors. Rather the court based its decision on sovereignty concerns and principles of judicial restraint and comity which required "that we exercise our power to enjoin parties in a foreign court sparingly." Id.

In light of the above, would you advise the first employer to include (in

---

4. On appeal the Eleventh Circuit Court of Appeals certified to the Georgia Supreme Court the question of whether Georgia would follow Restatement (Second) § 187(2) and whether in this case Georgia would have a materially greater interest to apply its law. See Keener v. Convergys Corp., 312 F.3d 1236 (11th Cir.2002). The latter court reaffirmed its refusal to adopt the Restatement as well as its refusal to enforce non-compete agreements. See Convergys Corp. v. Keener, 582 S.E.2d 84 (Ga.2003). The Eleventh Circuit affirmed the District Court opinion. See 2003 WL 21983010 (11th Cir.2003)

addition to a choice-of-law clause) a choice-of-forum clause conferring exclusive jurisdiction to the courts of the first employment state? Holeman v. National Business Institute, 94 S.W.3d 91 (Tex.App.2002), involved this scenario. A Georgia-based employer hired plaintiff for work in Texas and included in the contract a non-compete covenant, a Georgia choice-of-law clause, and a choice-of-forum clause mandating litigation in Georgia. After the employee began working for a competing Texas employer, the employee sued his former employer in Texas seeking a declaratory judgment that the covenant was unenforceable. Relying on the choice-of-forum clause, the trial court granted defendant's motion to dismiss, and the appellate court affirmed. The plaintiff argued, *inter alia*, that under *DeSantis*, a Texas court would not enforce the non-compete covenant and that the choice-of-forum clause was a sinister device to circumvent Texas law. The court rejected all of plaintiff's arguments, stating that enforcement of the choice-of-forum clause did not necessarily mean that a Georgia court would *not* apply Texas law and that, in any event, because of post-*DeSantis* legislative changes, it was unclear whether Texas would find the non-compete covenant unenforceable.

Nedlloyd Lines B.V. v. Superior Court

Supreme Court of California, 1992.
3 Cal.4th 459, 11 Cal.Rptr.2d 330, 834 P.2d 1148.

BAXTER, J. We granted review to consider the effect of a choice-of-law clause in a contract between commercial entities to finance and operate an international shipping business. In our order granting review, we limited our consideration to the question whether and to what extent the law of Hong Kong, chosen in the parties' agreement, should be applied in ruling on defendant's demurrer to plaintiff's complaint.

We conclude the choice-of-law clause, which requires that the contract be "governed by" the law of Hong Kong, a jurisdiction having a substantial connection with the parties, is fully enforceable and applicable to claims for breach of the implied covenant of good faith and fair dealing and for breach of fiduciary duties allegedly arising out of the contract. Our conclusion rests on the choice-of-law rules derived from California decisions and the Restatement Second of Conflict of Laws, which reflect strong policy considerations favoring the enforcement of freely negotiated choice-of-law clauses. Based on our conclusion, we will reverse the judgments of the Court of Appeal and remand for further proceedings.

* * * Plaintiff * * * Seawinds Limited (Seawinds) is a shipping company, * * * whose business consists of the operation of three container ships. Seawinds was incorporated in Hong Kong in late 1982 and has its principal place of business in Redwood City, California. Defendants and petitioners Nedlloyd Lines B.V., Royal Nedlloyd Group N.V., and KNSM Lines B.V. (collectively referred to as Nedlloyd) are interrelated shipping companies incorporated in the Netherlands with their principal place of business in Rotterdam.

In March 1983, Nedlloyd and other parties (including an Oregon corporation, a Hong Kong corporation, a British corporation, three individual residents of

California, and a resident of Singapore) entered into a contract with Seawinds to purchase shares of Seawinds' stock. The contract, which was entitled "Shareholders' Agreement in Respect of Seawinds Limited," stated that its purpose was "to establish [Seawinds] as a joint venture company to carry on a transportation operation." The agreement also provided that Seawinds would carry on the business of the transportation company and that the parties to the agreement would use "means reasonably available" to ensure the business was a success.

The shareholders' agreement between the parties contained the following choice-of-law and forum selection provision: "This agreement shall be governed by and construed in accordance with Hong Kong law and each party hereby irrevocably submits to the non-exclusive jurisdiction and service of process of the Hong Kong courts."

In January 1989, Seawinds sued Nedlloyd, alleging in essence that Nedlloyd breached express and implied obligations under the shareholders' agreement. * * * Seawinds' original and first amended complaint included causes of action for breach of contract, breach of the implied covenant of good faith and fair dealing (in both contract and tort), and breach of fiduciary duty. This matter comes before us after trial court rulings on demurrers to Seawinds' complaints.

Nedlloyd demurred to Seawinds' original complaint on the grounds that it failed to state causes of action for breach of the implied covenant of good faith and fair dealing (either in contract or in tort) and breach of fiduciary duty. In support of its demurrer, Nedlloyd contended the shareholders' agreement required the application of Hong Kong law to Seawinds' claims. In opposition to the demurrer, Seawinds argued that California law should be applied to its causes of action. * * *

I. THE PROPER TEST. * * * In determining the enforceability of arm's length contractual choice-of-law provisions, California courts shall apply the principles set forth in Restatement section 187, which reflects a strong policy favoring enforcement of such provisions.

* * * Briefly restated, the proper approach under Restatement section 187, subdivision (2) is for the court first to determine either: (1) whether the chosen state has a substantial relationship to the parties or their transaction, or (2) whether there is any other reasonable basis for the parties' choice of law. If neither of these tests is met, that is the end of the inquiry, and the court need not enforce the parties' choice of law.[5] If, however, either test is met, the court must next determine whether the chosen state's law is contrary to a fundamental policy of California.[6] If there is no such conflict, the court shall enforce the parties' choice of law. If, however, there is a fundamental conflict with California law, the court must then determine whether

---

5. As noted above, a different result might obtain under Restatement section 187, subdivision (1), which appears to allow the parties in some circumstances to specify the law of a state that has no relation to the parties or their transaction. * * *

6. To be more precise, we note that Restatement section 187, subdivision (2) refers not merely to the forum state--for example, California in the present case--but rather to the state " ... which, under the rule of § 188, would be the state of the applicable law in the absence of an effective choice of law by the parties." For example, there may be an occasional case in which California is the forum, and the parties have chosen the law of another state, but the law of yet a third state, rather than California's, would apply absent the parties' choice. In that situation, a California court will look to the fundamental policy of the third state in determining whether to enforce the parties' choice of law. The present case is not such a situation.

California has a "materially greater interest than the chosen state in the determination of the particular issue...." (Rest., § 187, subd. (2).) If California has a materially greater interest than the chosen state, the choice of law shall not be enforced, for the obvious reason that in such circumstance we will decline to enforce a law contrary to this state's fundamental policy.[7] We now apply the Restatement test to the facts of this case.

II. APPLICATION OF THE TEST IN THIS CASE. **A. Breach of contract**. * * * Hong Kong law, although not asserted as a bar to Seawinds' contract cause of action at the pleading stage, does govern all causes of action pleaded in the amended complaint, including the contract cause of action.

B. Implied covenant of good faith and fair dealing. 1. *Substantial relationship or reasonable basis*. As to the first required determination, Hong Kong-- "the chosen state"--clearly has a "substantial relationship to the parties." (Rest., § 187, subd.(2)(a).) The shareholders' agreement * * * shows that Seawinds is incorporated under the laws of Hong Kong and has a registered office there. The same is true of one of the shareholder parties to the agreement—Red Coconut Trading Co. The incorporation of these parties in Hong Kong provides the required "substantial relationship." (Id.,) com. f [substantial relationship present when "one of the parties is domiciled" in the chosen state]; Carlock v. Pillsbury Co. (D.Minn. 1989) 719 F.Supp. 791, 807 ["A party's incorporation in a state is a contact sufficient to allow the parties to choose that state's law to govern their contract."] * * *

Moreover, the presence of two Hong Kong corporations as parties also provides a "reasonable basis" for a contractual provision requiring application of Hong Kong law. "If one of the parties resides in the chosen state, the parties have a reasonable basis for their choice." (Consul Ltd. v. Solide Enterprises, Inc., supra, 802 F.2d 1143, 1147.) The reasonableness of choosing Hong Kong becomes manifest when the nature of the agreement before us is considered. A state of incorporation is certainly at least one government entity with a keen and intimate interest in internal corporate affairs, including the purchase and sale of its shares, as well as corporate management and operations. (See Corp.Code, § 102 [applying California's general corporation law to domestic corporations].)

2. *Existence of fundamental public policy*. We next consider whether application of the law chosen by the parties would be contrary to "a fundamental policy" of California. We perceive no fundamental policy of California requiring the application of California law to Seawinds' claims based on the implied covenant of

---

7. There may also be instances when the chosen state has a materially greater interest in the matter than does California, but enforcement of the law of the chosen state would lead to a result contrary to a fundamental policy of California. In some such cases, enforcement of the law of the chosen state may be appropriate despite California's policy to the contrary. (S.A. Empresa, etc. v. Boeing Co., supra, 641 F.2d 746, 749.) Careful consideration, however, of California's policy and the other state's interest would be required. No such question is present in this case, and we thus need not and do not decide how Restatement section 187 would apply in such circumstances.

good faith and fair dealing.[1] The covenant is not a government regulatory policy designed to restrict freedom of contract, but an implied promise inserted in an agreement to carry out the presumed intentions of contracting parties. * * * Seawinds directs us to no authority exalting the implied covenant of good faith and fair dealing over the express covenant of these parties that Hong Kong law shall govern their agreement. We have located none. Because Seawinds has identified no fundamental policy of our state at issue in its essentially contractual dispute with Nedlloyd, the second exception to the rule of section 187 of the Restatement does not apply.

    C. Fiduciary duty cause of action. 1. *Scope of the choice-of-law clause.* Seawinds contends that, whether or not the choice-of-law clause governs Seawinds' implied covenant claim, Seawinds' fiduciary duty claim is somehow independent of the shareholders' agreement and therefore outside the intended scope of the clause. Seawinds thus concludes California law must be applied to this claim. We disagree.

    When two sophisticated, commercial entities agree to a choice-of-law clause like the one in this case, the most reasonable interpretation of their actions is that they intended for the clause to apply to all causes of action arising from or related to their contract. Initially, such an interpretation is supported by the plain meaning of the language used by the parties. The choice-of-law clause in the shareholders' agreement provides: "This agreement shall be *governed by* and construed in accordance with Hong Kong law and each party hereby irrevocably submits to the non-exclusive jurisdiction and service of process of the Hong Kong courts." (Italics added.)[7]

    The phrase "governed by" is a broad one signifying a relationship of absolute direction, control, and restraint. Thus, the clause reflects the parties' clear contemplation that "the agreement" is to be completely and absolutely controlled by Hong Kong law. No exceptions are provided. In the context of this case, the agreement to be controlled by Hong Kong law is a shareholders' agreement that expressly provides for the purchase of shares in Seawinds by Nedlloyd and creates the relationship between shareholder and corporation that gives rise to Seawinds' cause of action. Nedlloyd's fiduciary duties, if any, arise from--and can exist only because of--the shareholders' agreement pursuant to which Seawinds' stock was purchased by Nedlloyd.

    In order to control completely the agreement of the parties, Hong Kong law must also govern the stock purchase portion of that agreement and the legal duties created by or emanating from the stock purchase, including any fiduciary duties. If Hong Kong law were not applied to these duties, it would effectively control only part of the agreement, not all of it. Such an interpretation would be inconsistent with

---

    1. [Editor's note. Under Hong Kong law, Seawinds had to demonstrate that "business efficacy," as Hong Kong courts understand that concept, requires that a good faith term be implied into the contract. Under California law, the contract is deemed to include an implied covenant of good faith and fair dealing.]

    7. * * * The agreement, of course, includes the choice-of-law clause itself. Thus the question of whether that clause is ambiguous as to its scope (i.e., whether it includes the fiduciary duty claim) is a question of contract interpretation that in the normal course should be determined pursuant to Hong Kong law. * * * The parties in this case, however, did not request judicial notice of Hong Kong law on this question of interpretation (Evid. Code, § 452, subd. (f)) or supply us with evidence of the relevant aspects of that law (Evid. Code, § 453, subd. (b)). The question therefore becomes one of California law. * * *

the unrestricted character of the choice-of-law clause.

Our conclusion in this regard comports with common sense and commercial reality. When a rational businessperson enters into an agreement establishing a transaction or relationship and provides that disputes arising from the agreement shall be governed by the law of an identified jurisdiction, the logical conclusion is that he or she intended that law to apply to all disputes arising out of the transaction or relationship. We seriously doubt that any rational business-person, attempting to provide by contract for an efficient and business-like resolution of possible future disputes, would intend that the laws of multiple jurisdictions would apply to a single controversy having its origin in a single, contract-based relationship. Nor do we believe such a person would reasonably desire a protracted litigation battle concerning only the threshold question of what law was to be applied to which asserted claims or issues. Indeed, the manifest purpose of a choice-of-law clause is precisely to avoid such a battle.

Seawinds' view of the problem--which would require extensive litigation of the parties' supposed intentions regarding the choice-of-law clause to the end that the laws of multiple states might be applied to their dispute--is more likely the product of postdispute litigation strategy, not predispute contractual intent. If commercially sophisticated parties (such as those now before us) truly intend the result advocated by Seawinds, they should, in fairness to one another and in the interest of economy in dispute resolution, negotiate and obtain the assent of their fellow parties to explicit contract language specifying what jurisdiction's law applies to what issues. * * *

For the reasons stated above, we hold a valid choice-of-law clause, which provides that a specified body of law "governs" the "agreement" between the parties, encompasses all causes of action arising from or related to that agreement, regardless of how they are characterized, including tortious breaches of duties emanating from the agreement or the legal relationships it creates.

2. *Enforceability of chosen law as to fiduciary duty claim.* Applying the test we have adopted (see pt. I, ante), we find no reason not to apply the parties' choice of law to Seawinds' cause of action for breach of fiduciary duty. As we have explained, Hong Kong, the chosen state, has a "substantial relationship to the parties" because two of those parties are incorporated there. Moreover, their incorporation in that state affords a "reasonable basis" for choosing Hong Kong law. (See pt. II.B.1., ante) Seawinds identifies no fundamental public policy of this state that would be offended by application of Hong Kong law to a claim by a Hong Kong corporation against its allegedly controlling shareholder. We are directed to no California statute or constitutional provision designed to preclude freedom of contract in this context. Indeed, even in the absence of a choice-of-law clause, Hong Kong's overriding interest in the internal affairs of corporations domiciled there would in most cases require application of its law. (See Rest., § 306 [obligations owed by majority shareholder to corporation determined by the law of the state of incorporation except in unusual circumstances not present here]; McDermott Inc. v. Lewis (Del.Supr.Ct.1987) 531 A.2d 206, 21-16 [corporate voting rights dispute governed by law of state of incorporation]; Matter of Reading Co. (3d Cir.1983) 711 F.2d 509, 517 [minority shareholder fiduciary duty claim governed by law of state

of incorporation].)

For strategic reasons related to its current dispute with Nedlloyd, Seawinds seeks to create a fiduciary relationship by disregarding the law Seawinds voluntarily agreed to accept as binding—the law of a state that also happens to be Seawinds' own corporate domicile. To allow Seawinds to use California law in this fashion would further no ascertainable fundamental policy of California; indeed, it would undermine California's policy of respecting the choices made by parties to voluntarily negotiated agreements. * * *

Lucas, C. J., Arabian, J., and George, J., concurred.

KENNARD, J., *Concurring and Dissenting*. * * * I agree with the majority that the parties' agreement, calling for the contract to be interpreted according to Hong Kong law, should be applied * * * in determining whether plaintiff * * * has stated a cause of action for breach of the implied covenant of good faith and fair dealing. I disagree, however, with the majority's conclusion that the choice-of-law clause * * * unambiguously extends to related noncontractual causes of action and therefore should be applied by the trial court in determining whether the plaintiff has stated a cause of action for breach of fiduciary duty. * * *

III. BREACH OF FIDUCIARY DUTY. *A. Existence of a Conflict*. The declaration of Nedlloyd's expert on Hong Kong law, William Catley, states: "Under Hong Kong law, a shareholder of a company owes no fiduciary duty to that company." Seawinds' expert on Hong Kong law, Geoffrey Miles, did not dispute this assertion in his declaration, although he had the opportunity to do so. Therefore, it is reasonable to conclude that if Hong Kong law governs Seawinds' cause of action for breach of fiduciary duty, to the extent the cause of action is premised on the "controlling shareholder" theory, it is barred.

California law, however, is to the contrary. * * * [T]his court held that majority or controlling shareholders owe a fiduciary duty to minority shareholders and to the corporation itself. * * *

Under California law, Seawinds is entitled to proceed on its breach of fiduciary duty cause of action against Nedlloyd in the latter's capacity as an alleged controlling shareholder. Under Hong Kong law, however, Seawinds is not entitled to proceed against Nedlloyd as a controlling shareholder as defined by Hong Kong law. Accordingly, a conflict of law exists.

B. Scope of the Choice-of-law Clause. * * * Unlike the forum-selection clause in *Smith*, it cannot be said of the choice-of-law clause in this case that it was clearly intended by the parties to encompass related noncontractual causes of action. Nor, however, can it be said that the choice-of-law clause here was plainly intended to exclude related noncontractual causes of action. Instead, the clause is ambiguous; it is not clear whether the parties intended it to govern related noncontractual causes of action. * * *

Accordingly, because the choice-of-law clause in this case does not unambiguously extend to noncontractual causes of action, it should not be applied by the trial court in determining whether the plaintiff has stated a cause of action for breach of fiduciary duty.

C. Defects of the Majority's Approach. * * * [U]nder the majority's approach, as I understand it, when two commercial entities agree to a choice-of-law clause in a contract, as a matter of law the clause applies to all conceivably related noncontractual causes of action, regardless of any ambiguous language in the clause or of the parties' actual intent regarding its coverage. The party resisting application of the choice-of-law clause will have no opportunity to show that it was intended to apply only to contractual causes of action. This rigid rule has, in my view, serious defects.

The majority ignores the most fundamental statutory command of contract law interpretation: "A contract must be so interpreted as to give effect to the mutual intention of the parties as it existed at the time of contracting, so far as the same is ascertainable and lawful." (Civ. Code, § 1636.) * * *

It is unrealistic to conclude that the choice-of-law clause in this case is not ambiguous. * * * Indeed, the ambiguity in the scope of this clause proceeds not so much from its language as from its context. Taken without reference to context, the clause is unambiguous, but not in the manner suggested by the majority. Because the clause refers only to "this Agreement," and not, like the similar clause at issue in Smith, to "matters arising under or growing out of this agreement. ..." (*Smith*, supra, 551 P.2d 1206 (italics in original)), it appears on its face not to apply to noncontractual causes of action. * * * [T]he goal of protecting contracting parties' reasonable expectations is not served by applying Hong Kong law to Seawinds' noncontractual cause of action for breach of fiduciary duty. Absent extrinsic evidence that the parties intended a broader application of their choice-of-law provision, the choice-of-law provision is most reasonably interpreted as applying only to contractual causes of action. Unlike the majority, therefore, I conclude that the trial court should not apply Hong Kong law to determine whether Seawinds has stated a cause of action for breach of fiduciary duty.

Notes and Questions

1. Unlike *DeSantis* which involved a contract between parties of relatively unequal bargaining power, *Nedlloyd* involved a contract between "sophisticated commercial entities" (*Nedlloyd*, supra) of relatively equal bargaining power. How much weight should one accord this factor in deciding whether to uphold a choice-of-law clause? Many systems specifically prohibit or restrict party autonomy in certain types of contracts in which the contracting parties tend to be in unequal bargaining positions. For example. the UCC differentiates consumer contracts from "business-to-business" transactions and provides that choice-of-law clauses in the former contracts "may not deprive the consumer of the protection of any rule [of the otherwise applicable law] which both is protective of consumers and may not be varied by agreement." UCC § 1-301(e)(2). Likewise, the Rome Convention provides that a choice-of-law clause "shall not have the result of depriving the consumer of the protection afforded to him by the mandatory rules of the law of the country in which he has his habitual residence," if that country has certain additional contacts

with the contract. See art. 5(2).[1] The same convention provides that in employment contracts a choice of law "shall not have the result of depriving the employee of the protection afforded to him by the mandatory rules of the law which would be applicable * * * in the absence of choice." Art. 6(1).[2]

Many states of the United States have also enacted statutes that restrict party autonomy in similar types of contracts. For example, an Iowa statute requires the application of Iowa law to franchises operated in Iowa, prohibits a contractual choice of another state's law, and provides that an Iowa choice-of-law clause does not alone render that statute applicable. See Ia.Stat. §§ 523H.2, 523H.14. Similar statutes are found in other states. See, e.g., Mn.Stat. § 80C.21 (franchises); Mn.Stat. § 325.064 (farm equipment dealerships). An Indiana statute requires the application of Indiana law to consumer credit transactions that have certain Indiana connections and prohibits a contractual choice of another state's law. See In.St. 24-4.5-1-201. Similar statutes are found in many other states. See, e.g., La.R.S. 9:3511, 9:3563, 51:1418. Even when they do not expressly prohibit choice-of-law clauses, these statutes typically prohibit an express or implied waiver of their provisions. Since a clause choosing another state's law is the functional equivalent of such a waiver, courts, especially those sitting in the enacting state, will disregard such a clause. Thus, before drafting a choice-of-law clause, one is well advised to research the statute books (not just the law reports) of all affected states.

2. **The Scope of the Choice-of-Law Clause**. *Nedlloyd* contains one of the better-reasoned discussions of the question of the scope of the choice-of-law clause. This question can arise even with regard to contractual issues[3] but, as in *Nedloyd*, the more common question is whether the clause encompasses non-contractual issues arising from the same contractual relationship that is the object of the clause. Examples of such issues from recent cases include quasi-contractual claims such as unjust enrichment, tort claims, unfair trade practices, statutes of limitation, attorney fees, and prejudgment interest. In *Nedlloyd*, all the justices who addressed this question assumed it to be simply one of contractual intent. Both sides assumed that the parties had the power to include non-contractual issues in their choice of law. The only disagreement was whether the phrasing of the clause was broad enough to include those issues. Yet, analytically, one should distinguish between contractual intent and contractual power, that is, between the intended scope and the permissible scope of the choice-of-law clause.

a. Intended Scope. Whether or not the parties intended to submit non-contractual issues to the law they chose is a relatively easy question of contractual interpretation that depends heavily (but not exclusively) on the phrasing of the

---

1. For similar provisions, see German codif. art. 29; Swiss codif. art. 120; Quebec Civ. Code art. 3117; Puerto Rico Draft Code art. 41.

2. For similar provisions, see Austrian codif. art. 44(3); German codif. art. 30; Quebec Civ. Code art. 3118; and Puerto Rico Draft Code art. 42.

3. See, e.g., Heating & Air Specialists, Inc. v. Jones, 180 F.3d 923 (8th Cir.1999) (holding that a clause providing that "the laws of the State of Texas shall govern [the contract's] interpretation," id. at 930, was confined to Texas' rules of contract construction and did not displace any other rules of the otherwise applicable Arkansas law). But see Kipin Industries v. Van Deilen Int'l, Inc., 182 F.3d 490 (6th Cir.1999) (concluding that to focus on the technical distinction between "interpret/construe" and "govern" would "yield an 'unwarranted,' 'strained and narrow construction of the [contract's] language.'" Id. at 494).

choice-of-law clause. The only difficulty is determining which state's law governs the interpretation. Since contractual interpretation very rarely involves issues of fundamental public policy, there is no need to interpret the clause according to the *lex causae*. Instead the choice is between the *lex fori* and the chosen law. The Restatement (Second) seems to point to the *lex fori*, while most European systems seem to lean toward the chosen law. Which option did the *Nedlloyd* court follow? See footnote 7 in *Nedlloyd*. Which option do you think is preferable and why?

b. Permissible Scope. A more difficult question is whether the parties have the power to select the law that will govern issues that are not purely contractual. One should not lightly assume an affirmative answer, because, after all, the principle of party autonomy has been born and nurtured exclusively in the area of contract law. Most civil law systems, for example, seem to subscribe to a negative answer.[4] Although this question has not been sufficiently explored in this country, *Nedlloyd* seems to represent an emerging trend. With few exceptions (see, e.g., Caton v. Leach Corp., 896 F.2d 939, 942-43 (5th Cir.1990)), many courts tend to assume that contracting parties have the power to submit to the chosen law not only the purely contractual disputes but also tort-like issues arising from the same contractual relationship, provided that the parties do so expressly. See Symeonides, *Choice of Law in 2002*, 67-68; *Choice of Law in 2001*, 38-40; *Choice of Law in 1999*, 160-61; *A View From the Trenches*, 63-65. Is this a good idea? Why, or why not? Consider the facts of Sutton v. Hollywood Video Entertainment Corp., 181 F.Supp.2d 504 (D.Md.2002).

Sutton was anything but a contract case, although the defendant tried to turn it into one. It was a tort action for malicious prosecution and false imprisonment filed against a Maryland video store owner who had the plaintiff arrested for allegedly stealing merchandise the previous night. Besides being innocent, the plaintiff was a customer/"member" of the defendant's video store, in that he had applied for and received a "membership" card allowing him to rent video discs. The membership agreement provided that "*any* dispute arising out of or *relating in anyway* to [plaintiff's] relationship with [defendant] shall be subject to final, non-appealable, binding arbitration. * * * Exclusive venue for any dispute resolution shall be in Portland, Oregon and Oregon law shall control for all purposes." Id. at 508 (emphasis added). Relying on the italicized language, the defendant moved to dismiss the action. Leaving aside questions of overreaching, if this were simply a question of contractual intent, should not the defendant prevail? He did not. Plaintiff's tort claims, said the court, "have nothing whatsoever to do with the video rental contracts." Id. at 511. "It is logically untenable" said the court, "that the membership agreements were meant to cover * * * accusations of theft. Taken to an extreme, Defendant's reading of the arbitration clause would require arbitration of claims such as a [defendant's] store ceiling falling in on customers, or a [defendant] store employee brutally attacking a customer * * * who has signed a membership

4. A preliminary draft of the European Union's Rome II Regulation would have allowed parties to agree on the law that would govern future torts between them, subject to some restrictions. However, the final text of Rome II allows such agreements only if they are "entered into after the dispute arose," Art. 10(1), and subjects them to further restrictions.

agreement." Id. at 512. Do you think that the defendant's argument deserved better treatment?

It may be worth noting, although it would not have affected the *Sutton* case, that the 2001 Oregon codification confines to contractual issues the parties' power to choose the applicable law. See Symeonides, *The Oregon Experience*, VI. In contrast, as noted earlier, most American courts continue to treat this as a question of contractual intent. At the same time, however, as *Sutton* illustrates, courts tend to scrutinize much more closely clauses that purport to encompass tort-like issues than do clauses confined to purely contractual issues.[5] The same is true for clauses that purport to encompass procedural-like questions.[6] Finally, courts are rather hostile toward choice-of-law clauses that purport to encompass statutes of limitation which traditionally are governed by the *lex fori*. See, Long v. Holland American Line Westours, Inc., 26 P.3d 430 (Alaska 2001); infra 390. What do you think might explain this hostility?

3. **Other Modalities of the Choice-of-law Clause.** *a. Mode of Expression.* Notice that Restatement (Second) § 187 does not require that the contractual choice of law be express. The comments permit an implied choice which one can infer "from the [contract's] provisions," but not a hypothetical choice. See §187 cmt. a. Compare with Rome Convention art. 3(1) ("The choice must be expressed or demonstrated with reasonable certainty by the terms of the contract *or the circumstances of the case*;" Hague Sales Convention art. 7(1) (same). See also Oregon codif. § 81.120 (providing that in standard-form contract drafted primarily by only one of the parties, the choice of law must be "express and conspicuous.")

b. Choice of More than One Law, or Choice for Part of the Contract. May the parties choose the law of more than one state to govern their contract? For example, in a contract to be performed in more than one state, may the parties subject questions of performance to the laws of the states of the respective performances? Recent conflicts codifications provide expressly for such a possibility, and, as a result of a recent revision, the Restatement (Second) does likewise. See § 187 cmt. i, as revised in 1988. Similarly, the parties may choose a law to govern only part of their contract. For similar provisions, see Rome Convention art. 3(1); Hague Sales Convention 7(1); German codif. art. 27(1); Oregon codif. § 81.120(1); Puerto Rico Draft Code art. 34; Louisiana Civ. Code art. 3540 cmt. (e). In such a case, the rest of the contract will be governed by the *lex causae*. Thus, this partial choice of

---

5. See, e.g, Inacom Corp. v. Sears, Roebuck & Co., 254 F.3d 683 (8th Cir.2001); Stagecoach Transp., Inc. v. Shadow, Inc., 741 N.E.2d 862 (Mass.App.2001); MBI Acquisition Partners, L.P. v. Chronicle Publishing Co., 2001 WL 148812 (W.D.Wis.2001); Twinlab Corp. v. Paulson, 724 N.Y.S.2d 496 (N.Y.A.D.2001); Florida Evergreen Foliage v. E.I. DuPont DeNemours & Co., 135 F.Supp.2d 1271 (S.D.Fla.2001); Krock v. Lipsay, 97 F.3d 640 (2d Cir.1996); Valley Juice Ltd., Inc. v. Evian Waters of France, Inc., 87 F.3d 604 (2d Cir.1996); Precision Screen Machines, Inc. v. Elexon, Inc., 1996 WL 495564 (N.D.Ill.1996); Shelley v. Trafalgar House Public Ltd. Co., 918 F.Supp. 515 (D.P.R.1996); Telemedia Partners Worldwide, Ltd. v. Hamelin Ltd., 1996 WL 41818 (S.D.N.Y.1996); Champlain Enterprises, Inc. v. United States, 945 F.Supp. 468 (N.D.N.Y.1996); Young v. W.S. Badcock Corp., 474 S.E.2d 87 (Ga.App.1996); Lyons v. Turner Const. Co., 551 N.E.2d 1062 (Ill.App.1990); Young v. Mobil Oil Corp., 735 P.2d 654 (Or.Ct.App.1987).

6. See, e.g. Maddox v. American Airlines, Inc., 298 F.3d 694 (8th Cir.2002) (prejudgment interest); North Bergen Rex Transport v. Trailer Leasing Co., 730 A.2d 843 (N.J.1999) (attorney fees); Weatherby Associates, Inc. v. Ballack, 783 So.2d 1138 (Fla.App.2001) (same).

law, as well as the choice of more than one law, may result in *dépeçage*. Is this "private" form of *dépeçage* any more objectionable than a *dépeçage* brought about by the court?

    c. Timing of the Choice. Although usually the parties' agreement on the applicable law is contained in the same contract that the agreement purports to regulate, recent codifications and international conventions expressly allow the parties to choose the applicable law at a later time, or to modify a choice they had made earlier, provided they do not prejudice the rights of third parties. See, e.g., Rome Convention art. 3(2); Hague Sales Convention art. 7(2); German codif. art. 27(2); Swiss codif. art. 116(3); Oregon codif. § 81.120(3); Puerto Rico Draft art. 34. How do you think this issue should be handled under the Restatement (Second)?

    d. Changes in the Chosen Law. What if the chosen law changes between the time it was chosen and the time of trial? An established English treatise addresses this issue by drawing a distinction between what it calls "choice" and "incorporation" of foreign law:

> If the parties explicitly or implicitly chose the proper law, they are normally regarded as having intended that that law should govern their relationship "as it exists from time to time." Thus, if during the existence of the contract [that] law * * * changes, * * * this will bind the parties. * * * On the other hand, where a foreign statute is incorporated into a contract as a contractual term, it remains part of the contract, although as a statute it may have been amended or repealed.

2 Dicey & Morris, The Conflict of Laws 1180 (11th ed. 1987). Do you agree with the first part of the above statement?

    e. Renvoi. Does the parties's choice of law include the conflicts law of the chosen state? Obviously, if the parties expressly included that law, there is no reason not to honor their choice, but what about the majority of cases in which the parties fail to address this issue expressly? In such cases, is it not logical to assume that parties who had the foresight to address the choice-of-law issue in advance in the hope of thereby preventing litigation also intended to avoid the complexities of *renvoi*? Most systems adopt this assumption and provide that, in the absence of an express contrary provision, a contractual choice of law is confined to the internal law of the chosen state. See Restatement (Second) § 187 cmt. h.

    4. ***The Choice of an Invalidating Law.*** What if the law chosen by the parties invalidates the contract, in whole or in part? When the chosen law invalidates *the whole* contract the Restatement (Second) provides that the choice should be disregarded because "it can be assumed that they did so by mistake." § 187 cmt. e. See also Quebec codif. art. 3112. Indeed, because the very principle of party autonomy is based on the desire to honor the intent of the parties, and because normally the parties are presumed to have intended to create a binding contract, there is good reason to treat the choice of an invalidating law as the result of an error that vitiates consent. However, there is authority to the contrary. For example, Foreman v. George Foreman Associates, Ltd., 517 F.2d 354, 356 (9th Cir.1975), invalidated a boxing contract under the chosen law of California. Cf. S.E.C. v. Elmas Trading Corp., 683 F.Supp. 743 (D.Nev.1987), *aff'd without op.*, 865 F.2d 265 (9th

Cir.1988). The expression "he who makes the bed ought to sleep in it" may capsulize the arguments for this solution which finds support in European literature. As one distinguished German author put it, "grounds for invalidity often protect one party, and he who chooses a law chooses its protection." Gerhard Kegel, Internationales Privatrecht 487 (7th ed. 1995). What do you think?

What about cases in which the chosen law invalidates *only a part* of the contract? Suppose, for example, that in *DeSantis* the parties had chosen the law of Texas (rather than Florida) which upheld the employment contract but not the non-compete covenant. The parties' expectations for a binding contract are satisfied, but should one party be allowed to "pick and choose" the favorable and discard the unfavorable provisions of the chosen law? The Restatement (Second) does not support this type of private eclecticism, and most cases have expressly rejected it. See, e.g., Boatland, Inc. v. Brunswick Corp., 558 F.2d 818 (6th Cir.1977) (invalidating under the chosen law a clause dealing with the termination of a dealership agreement); Hardy v. Monsanto Enviro-Chem Systems, Inc., 323 N.W.2d 270 (Mich.1982) (applying the chosen law to invalidate an indemnity clause); Stoot v. Fluor Drilling Services, Inc., 851 F.2d 1514 (5th Cir.1988) (accord); General Elec. Credit Corp. v. Beyerlein, 286 N.Y.S.2d 351 (Sup.Ct.1967), *aff'd*, 292 N.Y.S.2d 32 (A.D. 4th Dept. 1968) (applying the chosen law to invalidate a clause that cut off defenses against an assignee). See also authorities cited in Scoles, Hay, Borchers & Symeonides, *Conflicts of Laws* § 18.11. But see Kipin Indus. v. Van Deilen Int'l, Inc., 182 F.3d 490 (6th Cir.1999) (disregarding the chosen law "to the extent" it invalidated a part of the contract).

5. *Choice-of-Law Clauses and Class Actions.* Suppose that you advise a company that is about to begin selling products or services to customers throughout the United States. The company is concerned about the possibility of being sued in nationwide class actions by these customers and asks you to draft choice-of-law clauses to be inserted in its contracts with these customers so as to minimize the possibility of class certification. What should these clauses provide? See Washington Mutual Bank v. Superior Court, 15 P.3d 1071 (Cal. 2001) (nationwide class action by 25,000 mortgagors whose contracts with the defendant bank contained clauses calling for the application of the law of the states in which the mortgaged properties were situated); Forrest v. Verizon Communications, Inc., 805 A.2d 1007 (D.C. 2002) (contracts with internet users in several states contained Virginia choice-of-law clauses *and* choice-of-forum clauses designating Virginia as the exclusive forum; Virginia is one of only two states in the United States that lacks a class action procedure). For discussion of these and other cases, see Symeonides, *Choice of Law in 2002*, 38-40; *Choice of Law in 2001*, 83-87.

F. INSURANCE CONFLICTS

Insurance conflicts have earned their classification into a separate category, not only because of their sheer numbers, but also because they are rather sui generis in that they possess characteristics of both contract and tort. Even when the dispute is confined to the insurance contract and only involves the insured and the insurer, the resolution of the dispute is likely to have ramifications on third parties, such as those injured by the insured, and, to some extent, society at large. For example, when the disputed issue is whether the insurance contract is susceptible to a reading that would provide coverage for punitive damages (see infra 372), the issue appears to be merely one of contract interpretation, but its resolution also implicates certain tort policies, such as deterring the type of misconduct that evokes the imposition of punitive damages. Likewise, when, as in the case below, the dispute is whether the insurance contract obligates the insurer to pay for cleaning up environmental contamination caused by the insured, the resolution of that dispute affects not only the insurer and the insured, but also the environmental and economic well-being of the state in which the contaminated site is located. In one such case, the New Jersey Supreme Court observed:

> Choice of law with respect to interpreting insurance contracts develops a life of its own when considered in the context of hazardous waste sites. Because of the public's heightened sensitivity to environmental pollution in the last quarter century and because of the significant costs associated with these coverage disputes, a virtual avalanche of coverage litigation between carriers and their policyholders has ensued to determine who may be ultimately responsible for the payment of these costs. At the very core of these disputes, which have spawned hundreds of reported cases nationwide, is the interpretation to be accorded certain contractual language contained in comprehensive general liability (CGL) policies.

Pfizer, Inc. v. Employers Ins. of Wausau, 712 A.2d 634, 635 (N.J.1998) (internal quotations omitted).

Gilbert Spruance Co. v. Pennsylvania Mfrs. Ass'n Ins. Co.
Supreme Court of New Jersey, 1993.
134 N.J. 96, 629 A.2d 885.

CLIFFORD, J., We granted certification, [cit.], to address the sole question presented in the petition of defendant Pennsylvania Manufacturers' Insurance Company (PMA), namely, "whether a comprehensive general liability policy containing a pollution exclusion, issued by an out-of-state carrier and covering an out-of-state defendant's operations, should be construed pursuant to New Jersey law." In this case the waste alleged to be the source of the pollution was generated in Pennsylvania and deposited in New Jersey. The trial court balanced the factors set forth in *Restatement (Second) of Conflicts of Laws (Restatement)* section 6 (1971) (hereinafter section 6), and determined that Pennsylvania law should govern. The Appellate Division reversed, 603 A.2d 61 (N.J.Super.Ct.App.Div.1992), concluding that when waste predictably comes to rest in New Jersey, this state has the dominant significant relationship with the parties, the transaction, and the outcome of the controversy, and thus New Jersey law should govern. [cit.]

We agree with the Appellate Division's conclusion that when the parties to the insurance contract can reasonably foresee that a New Jersey waste site will receive the insured's waste products, New Jersey law should dictate the proper interpretation of the insuring agreement because this state had the dominant significant relationship. * * * We therefore affirm.

I. Plaintiff, The Gilbert Spruance Company (Spruance), is a Pennsylvania corporation that manufactures paint in Philadelphia. In the course of its operations during the 1970s and 1980s, Spruance consigned its waste to independent waste haulers, who transported the waste to dumps in New Jersey. Four of those dump sites * * * are the basis of multiple toxic-tort claims for personal injury and property damage against Spruance and are now the subject of public remediation-enforcement actions by the New Jersey Department of Environmental Protection (NJDEP) (now the Department of Environmental Protection and Energy).

From 1971 through 1988, Spruance purchased primary and excess Comprehensive General Liability (CGL) policies from PMA, a Pennsylvania corporation. The policies listed several locations of plant operations in various states, including Pennsylvania, Virginia, and North Carolina. PMA is licensed to sell property, liability, and workers' compensation insurance in numerous states, including Pennsylvania and New Jersey. The contracts at issue were negotiated and countersigned in Pennsylvania, and the premiums were paid there.

Each of the policies required PMA to provide a defense to Spruance for "suits" alleging liability for property damage or bodily injury that was insured under the policies in respect of occurrences or suits throughout the United States. From 1973 to 1988, the CGL policies issued by PMA to Spruance contained a standard pollution-exclusion clause, which provided that the insurance did not apply

> (f) to Bodily Injury or Property Damage Arising Out of the Discharge, Dispersal, Release or Escape of Smoke, Vapors, Soot, Fumes, Acids, Alkalis, Toxic Chemicals, Liquids or Gases, Waste Materials or Other Irritants, Contaminants or Pollutants Into or Upon Land, the Atmosphere or Any Watercourse or Body of Water; but This Exclusion Does Not Apply if Such Discharge, Release or Escape Is Sudden and Accidental * * *.

When Spruance submitted notice of the claims arising from the four New Jersey waste sites, PMA disclaimed coverage based on the pollution-exclusion clause.

Between 1988 and 1989 Spruance filed complaints against PMA * * * seeking a declaration of coverage. * * * In March 1989, Spruance filed a motion for summary judgment to establish PMA's duty to defend. Denying that motion, the trial court conducted a section 6 analysis and declared that the law of Pennsylvania rather than that of New Jersey applied to the interpretation of the pollution-exclusion clause. The court held that under Pennsylvania law, the pollution-exclusion clause supported PMA's disclaimer because the "discharge, dispersal release or escape" of the waste materials was not considered to be "sudden and accidental." [cit.] Under then-existing New Jersey law, however, "sudden and accidental" discharge could include the gradual release of pollutants. [cit.]. The trial court therefore granted PMA's motion for summary judgment.

On appeal to the Appellate Division, plaintiff contended that the trial court had erroneously decided the choice-of-law issue. Relying primarily on the reasoning in *Leksi, Inc. v. Federal Insurance Co.*, 736 F.Supp. 1331 (D.N.J.1990), and *Johnson Matthey, Inc. v. Pennsylvania Mfrs.' Ass'n Ins. Co.*, 593 A.2d 367

(N.J.Super.Ct.App.Div.1991), both of which were decided after the trial court had ruled in this case, the Appellate Division reversed and held that New Jersey law would apply to the interpretation of the "sudden and accidental" wording in the pollution-exclusion clause. [cit.]

The court recognized that the law of the principal location of the insured risk as understood by the parties, which *Restatement* section 193 makes controlling unless some other state has a more significant relationship to the parties and the transaction, does not govern when the insured operation or activity is predictably multi-state. [cit.] In that situation, section 6 factors should be used to identify the state with the most significant relationship. [cit.]

In its section 6 analysis the Appellate Division apparently placed significant, if not controlling, emphasis on New Jersey's interest in securing financial resources both to remediate New Jersey toxic-waste sites and to compensate victims of New Jersey pollution.[cit.] The court also found that the justified--i.e., objectively reasonable--expectations of the parties were protected because the parties could foresee that waste generated from a Philadelphia paint factory would come to rest in New Jersey and that generator responsibility would be measured by New Jersey law. * * * The court concluded that when out-of-state-generated waste predictably comes to rest in New Jersey and imposes legal liabilities here on the insured, New Jersey has the dominant and significant relationship with the parties, the transaction, and the outcome of the controversy. [cit.]

In adopting the site-specific-uniformity approach, the court rejected the uniform-contract-interpretation approach that another panel of the Appellate Division had advocated in *Westinghouse Electric Corp. v. Liberty Mut. Ins. Co.*, 559 A.2d 435 (N.J.Super.1989). The court pointed out that in *Johnson Matthey*, it had characterized nationwide uniformity of policy interpretation as "an illusory goal, not truly achievable or necessarily preferable." [cit.] The court concluded that "[s]ite-specific uniformity, on the other hand, is achievable, and represents a choice of the law of the jurisdiction that is most concerned with the outcome." [cit.] Moreover, the court noted, the failure to include a choice-of-law provision in the contracts "tends to show that uniform interpretation was not a conscious goal of the contracting parties." [cit.] * * *

II. Traditionally, the law of the place where the contract, including an insurance contract, was entered into determined the rights of the parties under the contract. [cit.] In *State Farm Mut. Auto. Ins. Co. v. Estate of Simmons*, 417 A.2d 488 (N.J.1980), we rejected the mechanical and inflexible *lex loci contractus* rule in resolving conflict-of-law issues in liability-insurance contracts. Instead, our courts have adopted a more flexible approach that focuses on the state that has the most significant connections with the parties and the transaction. [cit.] We held that because the law of the place of contract "generally comport[s] with the reasonable expectations of the parties concerning the principal situs of the insured risk," 417 A.2d 488, that forum's law should be applied "unless the dominant and significant relationship of another state to the parties and the underlying issue dictates that this basic rule should yield." *Ibid.* In making that determination, courts should rely on the factors and contacts set forth in *Restatement* sections 6 and 188. [cit.]

According to *Restatement* section 188, the general rule in contract actions is that the law of the state with the most significant relationship to the parties and the transaction under the principles stated in *Restatement* section 6 governs. [cit.] Section 188 lists several relevant "contacts," according to their relative importance, to be considered in the section 6 analysis, such as the domicile, residence, nationality, place of incorporation and place of business of the parties, and the places of contracting and performance. * * * Although *Restatement* section 188 provides the choice-of-law rule in respect of contracts in general, *Restatement* section 193 provides guidance in applying section 188's "relevant contacts" to the special case of casualty-insurance contracts, such as CGL policies: the court should apply the law of the state that "the parties understood was to be the principal location of the insured risk during the term of the policy, unless with respect to the particular issue, some other state has a more significant relationship under the principles stated in § 6 to the transaction and the parties * * *." Id. at 610. * * * Section 193 is based on the rationale that for a number of reasons

> the location of the risk is a matter of intense concern to the parties to the insurance contract. And it can often be assumed that the parties, to the extent that they thought about the matter at all, would expect that the local law of the state where the risk is to be principally located would be applied to determine many of the issues arising under the contract. Likewise, the state where the insured risk will be principally located during the term of the policy has a natural interest in the determination of issues arising under the insurance contract.

[*Restatement, supra*, § 193 comment c.] If the principal location of the insured risk is in a single state for a major portion of the insurance period, that location "is the most important contact to be considered in the choice of the applicable law, at least as to most issues." Id. § 193 comment b. However, the location of the risk has less significance when a movable risk is concerned or when "the policy covers a group of risks that are scattered throughout two or more states." *Ibid.*

Capitalizing on the flexible and interpretative nature of the "factors" set forth in *Restatement* section 6 and the "contacts" listed in *Restatement* section 188, as well as the rule of *Restatement* section 193 specifically pertaining to casualty--insurance contracts, our courts have created choice-of-law rules in the context of commercial insurance and pollution exclusion involving out-of-state waste generation, multi-state waste generation, and in-state waste generation with the waste ultimately coming to rest in New Jersey. The two main choice-of-law rules adopted by the Appellate Division are the uniform-contract-interpretation approach and the site-specific approach.

Under the uniform-contract-interpretation approach, the law of a single forum governs the interpretation of coverage under a casualty-insurance policy for multi-state claims arising from environmental damage in multiple jurisdictions. [cit.] Proponents of that approach contend that uniformity in contract interpretation deters forum shopping, [cit.] and advances both predictability, in that parties can more accurately forecast potential coverage, [cit.], and the expectations of purchasers of comprehensive nationwide coverage, who believe that they have bought "a single protection from liability irrespective of the particular state law under which that liability is determined so long as the risk, whether or not ultimately resulting in liability, is within the coverage." *Westinghouse, supra.*

The Appellate Division in *Westinghouse* adopted the uniform-contract-interpretation approach. * * * The *Westinghouse* court held that the plaintiff was "entitled to a single, consistent and final resolution of the choice of law question in a single comprehensive action which will bind it and all its insurers," id., and that "[t]his task is obviously manageable if the law of only one state is required to be restated," *id.* * * *

Appellate Division cases since *Westinghouse* have acknowledged the persuasive force of its view that an insurance clause regarding pollution coverage should have only one meaning no matter where the policy applies[.] * * * Nevertheless, those and other cases have rejected the uniform-contract-interpretation approach in favor of the site-specific rule. * * * The site-specific rule, as set forth in *Restatement* section 193, provides that a casualty-insurance policy should be interpreted under the substantive law of the state that the parties understood to be the principal location of the insured risk, unless another state has a more significant relationship to the parties, the transaction, and the outcome of the controversy under a *Restatement* section 6 analysis. *Restatement, supra,* § 193. When the waste-producing facility and the waste site are located in the same state, their common location makes the application of section 193 straightforward. [cit.]

In *Johnson Matthey,* * * * [t]he court rejected the uniform-contract-interpretation approach of the trial court and *Westinghouse,* reasoning that uniform interpretation of an insurance contract does not have "sufficient value to overcome the significant governmental interest of the various jurisdictions where the insured risks are located, or where the insured entity predictably is going to incur legal liabilities." Id. It was troubled by the likelihood of conflict and confusion "[i]f each nationwide insurer comes to court with its own nationwide policy interpretation derived from a different state of contracting * * *." Id. Moreover, the court recognized as elusive the goal of uniform contract-interpretation. * * * [T]he court applied the site-specific rule of *Restatement* section 193 and held that New Jersey law should govern because the location of the insured risk, i.e., the situs of Johnson Matthey's plant, was New Jersey. Ibid. Furthermore, the court found predictable that waste from a New Jersey plant would come to rest in New Jersey landfills. Ibid. In addition, the court reasoned that site-specific uniformity would provide certainty and consistency when the policy at issue covers multi-state risks because the parties can expect that policy-language interpretation will follow the law of the site of the risk. Id. 593 A.2d 367.

In conclusion, the court offered the following choice-of-law rule:

> We hold that a casualty insurance policy, wherever written, which is purchased to cover a New Jersey risk, alone or along with risks in other states, is subject to interpretation of its coverage and exclusion language according to New Jersey local law. Although this rule is peculiarly suitable to environmental litigation, in which large numbers of casualty insurance policies are involved, it is not limited to that setting. [Ibid.]

* * * The site-specific rule, as enunciated in *Johnson Matthey*, did not encompass the situation presented by this appeal, namely, an out-of-state facility that generates waste that predictably comes to rest in New Jersey, and a casualty-insurance policy that does not name or otherwise specifically identify a New Jersey risk.

When a principal location of risk, such as a manufacturing operation or activity, within the waste-site location is not identified by the contracting parties at the inception of the insurance policy, the "foreseeability" aspect of the site-specific rule has been extended to provide application of the law of the waste-site location. See *General Metalcraft, supra*, 796 F.Supp. at 802; *Leksi, supra*, 736 F.Supp. at 1336. In adopting such a rule in this case, the Appellate Division relied heavily on the federal district court decision in Leksi, *supra*, 736 F.Supp. 1331. * * * The *Leksi* court offered the following rule: "[I]n the absence of a choice of law provision, the state where the toxic waste comes to rest is the state whose law will apply, provided that it was reasonably foreseeable that the waste would come to rest there." Ibid. Objective foreseeability that the waste would ultimately be deposited in New Jersey was founded on the proximity of New Jersey to the waste-generation site and the fact that "there are as many or more landfills in New Jersey within close proximity to the *Leksi* plants than there are in Pennsylvania." Ibid.

III. Summarizing the foregoing discussion, we conclude that in determining the choice-of-law rule to govern casualty-insurance contracts, such as the CGL policies in this case, we look first to *Restatement* § 193. As stated previously, that section provides that the law of the state that "the parties understood was to be the principal location of the insured risk * * * [governs unless] some other state has a more significant relationship under the principles stated in § 6 to the transaction and the parties * * *." *Restatement, supra*, § 193. However, in certain cases when the "subject matter of the insurance is an operation or activity" and when "that operation or activity is predictably multistate, the significance of the principal location of the insured risk diminishes * * *." *Gilbert Spruance, supra*, 603 A.2d 61. In such situations, the governing law is that of the state with the dominant significant relationship according to the principles set forth in *Restatement* section 6. *Restatement* § 193; [cit.]

Remaining, however, is the knotty problem of how to determine where the insured "risk" is located. * * * In hazardous-waste cases, two potential principal locations of risk exist: the state of generation--here, Pennsylvania, or the state of disposal--here, New Jersey. See *A. Johnson & Co., supra*, 741 F.Supp. at 300. But see *Pittston, supra*, 795 F.Supp. at 692 (stating that principal location of insured risk was state within which waste-producing facility was situated). Comment b to *Restatement* section 193 provides that an insured risk "has its principal location, in the sense here used, in the state where it will be during at least the major portion of the insurance period." However, situations in which the insured risk cannot be located, at least principally, in a single state and in which the location of the risk has less significance include "where the policy covers a group of risks that are scattered throughout two or more states." *Ibid*.

We are thus presented with two options: we can arbitrarily choose either the state of generation, see *Johnson Matthey, supra,* or the state of disposal, see *A. Johnson & Co., supra,* 741 F.Supp. at 301, as the principal location of the insured risk, and assign section 193 significance to that state; or "because the risk at issue here was to some degree transient, a more extended analysis pursuant to § 6(2) is appropriate to determine whether, apart from or in addition to § 193 significance, [New Jersey] or [Pennsylvania] has a more significant relationship to the transaction and the parties." *A. Johnson & Co., supra,* 741 F.Supp. at 301. We choose the latter.

Substantially for the reasons expressed by Judge Brotman in *Leksi, supra,* a factually-analogous case in which waste generated in Pennsylvania came to rest in New Jersey, we agree with the Appellate Division that when applying the principles enunciated in *Restatement* section 6 to a case in which out-of-state generated waste foreseeably comes to rest in New Jersey, New Jersey has the dominant significant relationship. That section 6 analysis is based on factors specific to New Jersey, such as our "urgent concern for the health and safety of [our] citizens," *Johnson Matthey, supra,* as "demonstrated by the enactment of the Spill Compensation and Control Act, [cit.]; the Solid Waste Management Act, [cit.]; the Sanitary Landfill Facility Closure and Contingency Fund Act, [cit.]; the Environmental Cleanup Responsibility Act, [cit.]; and the Water Pollution Control Act, [cit.] * * *." Ibid.

We have no occasion to consider in this appeal the problem presented when waste generated in New Jersey predictably is disposed of in another state. In *Leksi* the court held without any qualification that "in the absence of a choice of law provision, the state where the toxic waste comes to rest is the state whose law will apply, provided that it was reasonably foreseeable that the waste would come to rest there." 736 F.Supp. at 1336. Specifically, we express no view on the proposition stated in *J. Josephson, Inc., supra,* that when another state is the foreseeable location of the waste-site, the court must engage in a section 6 analysis to determine if that state has the most significant relationship with the parties, the transaction, and the outcome of the controversy—an analysis that requires the court "to sift through and analyze, however laborious [the task], the competing and varied interests of the states involved * * *." 626 A.2d 81.

IV. As a final note, we distinguish *Westinghouse* as a case that involved multi-state sites while this case involves only one site in one state. [cit.] Nonetheless, in adopting the aforementioned choice-of-law rule, we necessarily reject the uniform-contract-interpretation approach substantially for the reasons stated by the Appellate Division, *supra,* [cit.], and by the court in *Johnson Matthey, supra*[.] * * *

V. The judgment of the Appellate Division is affirmed and the cause is remanded to the Law Division for further proceedings consistent with this opinion.
* * *

Notes and Questions

1. ***Environmental Pollution Insurance.*** *Spruance* is one of hundreds of cases decided during the late 1980s and 90s involving disputes between insurers and their insureds over liability for environmental contamination resulting from the insured's operations. Most of these disputes involve sites in, or other contacts with,

more than one state. *Spruance* contains a good, though not exhaustive, discussion of the two approaches courts have developed for cases of this type. The first approach, called "uniform-contract-interpretation" approach, focuses on the insurance contract and aspires to apply the law of a single state even when the contract covers multiple risks situated in different states. This approach usually leads to the application of the law of a state that is either the place of the making of the contract or has other significant connections with the contract and the parties. The second approach, called "site-specific approach," focuses on the place of the insured risk and is based on Restatement (Second) § 193. It abandons the goal of applying a single law to the whole contract and focuses instead on the interests of the state or states where the insured risks are located. The applicable law is usually the law of that state or states (the site-states), unless another state has a more significant relationship with regard to the particular issue.

What merits and demerits do you see in each of these approaches? Focusing on policies and consequences, which approach is more likely to produce a better result? Focusing on "ease of application" only, which approach is easier to apply? Keep in mind that many of the cases are far more complex than was *Spruance*. For example, Carrier Corp. v. Home Ins. Co., 648 A.2d 665 (Conn.Super. 1994), involved almost 400 policies issued in at least ten states by 19 insurance companies over a period of 30 years and covering 44 environmental sites located in several states. The court rejected the site-specific approach because, given "the large number of states in which relevant sites are found * * * '[this approach] would lead to inefficiency, jury confusion and the probability of inconsistent decisions in the same court with respect to the very same policy of insurance.'" Id. at 668. Notice that Restatement (Second) § 193, which is the basis for the site-specific approach, suggests that the court should treat each site as if it were insured by a separate policy and proceed accordingly. § 193 cmt. f. Does this suggestion resolve the problems the *Carrier* court identified? The *Carrier* court also disapproved of the uniform-contract-interpretation approach and agreed with plaintiff, who argued that "if this court were to apply exquisitely [sic] the place of contracting rule to each policy, '[t]his court would have to determine questions relating the same facts of a site with reference to the various laws governing each policy.'" *Carrier*, 648 A.2d at 668. So what is a court to do? "This court and the jury can handle the law of two states; but no more," said the court, id. at 669, and applied the laws of Massachusetts, where some of the policies had been issued, and New York, where some of the other policies had been issued and some of the risks were located. Is this decision unprincipled or simply realistic?

Does *Carrier* demonstrate that, despite good intentions and concerted efforts, approaches that may work in simple cases cannot work in complex "mega conflicts"? As another court observed, "a pointillistic approach to the factors stated in § 188 of the Restatement is not appropriate in this case which implicates nearly 500 insurance policies issued over a period of 35 years to seven corporations * * * by 41 insurers with actions being taken by the parties in an uncounted number of jurisdictions." Burlington Northern R.R. Co. v. Allianz Underwriters Ins. Co., 1994 WL 637011 at *6 (Del.Super.1994). Are these "mega conflicts" an apt subject for federal conflicts or substantive legislation? The American Law Institute thinks so. See Complex Litigation Project §§ 6.02, 6.03.

In the meantime, many states have enacted statutes that mandate the application of forum law to sites located in the forum state. See, e.g., Mich.Comp.Laws § 324.1804 ("The law to be applied * * *, including what constitutes 'pollution' is the law of this state, excluding choice of law rules."); Colo.Rev.Stat. §§ 13-1.5-104; Wis.Stat § 299.33(4). An Oregon statute provides that "Oregon law shall be applied in all cases where the contaminated property to which the action relates is located within the State of Oregon." Or.Rev.Stat. § 465.480(2)(a). However, the statute also provides that nothing in it "shall be interpreted to modify common law rules governing choice of law determinations for sites located outside the State of Oregon." Id. Thus, the statute preserves the possibility of applying Oregon law to non-Oregon sites as well!

2. Notice how narrowly the *Spruance* court phrased its holding as to confine it to "case[s] in which out-of-state generated waste foreseeably comes to rest in New Jersey" and to exclude the converse situation in which "waste generated in New Jersey predictably is disposed of in another state." Furthermore, the court implicitly confined its holding to situations in which, as in *Spruance*, New Jersey law provides for coverage and thus relieves New Jersey from having to foot the cleanup bill. Do these confines indicate a court that is appropriately cautious or a court that is determined to protect the forum's interests at any cost? Is this much different from the above Oregon statute?

In three post-*Spruance* cases decided on the same date, the New Jersey Supreme Court extended the site-specific approach to multisite-multistate cases. See Pfizer, Inc. v. Employers Ins. of Wausau, 712 A.2d 634 (N.J.1998); Unisys Corp. v. Ins. Co. of North America, 712 A.2d 649 (N.J.1998); HM Holdings, Inc. v. Aetna Cas. & Surety Co., 712 A.2d 645 (N.J.1998). After adopting the Restatement's notion of treating multistate risks insured under a single policy as if they were insured under separate policies, the court downplayed the logistical burden of applying the laws of multiple states by concluding that these laws can only fall into either one of two categories--pro-coverage or anti-coverage. However, the court subjected its endorsement of the site-specific approach to exceptions designed to protect New Jersey's interests. According to *Pfizer*, these interests are: "[1.] protection of the regulatory process in New Jersey, [2.] protection of New Jersey policyholders, [3.] protection of the victims of pollution, and [4.] protection of the New Jersey environment." *Pfizer*, 712 A.2d at 644. The *Pfizer* trilogy, in combination with *Spruance* and lower court cases that *Pfizer* cited with approval, suggest that: (a) when *any one* of the above New Jersey interests is implicated, New Jersey will likely apply its pro-coverage law, notwithstanding the contacts or interests of other states; and (b) when *none* of the above New Jersey interests are implicated, then New Jersey will apply the law of the site state, whether or not that law favors coverage, unless another state has a more significant relationship under Restatement (Second) § 6. For further discussion, see Symeonides, *Choice of Law in 1998*, 363-71.

3. *Insurability of Punitive Damages*. Another controversial issue in recent

litigation is whether an insurer should cover punitive damages assessed against the insured. As of 2003, 25 states allowed the insurability of punitive damages, nine states allowed it only in cases of vicarious liability, eight states prohibited it, and the remaining states had not taken a definitive stance. See J. Stein, *Personal Injury Damages*, § 4:37 (3d ed. 2003). In your opinion, what are the interests of a state that: (a) allows punitive damages in tort and allows insurance coverage of them? (b) prohibits punitive damages in tort and prohibits insurance coverage of them? (c) allows punitive damages in tort but prohibits insurance coverage of them? or (d) prohibits punitive damages in tort but allows insurance coverage of them? Should one characterize conflicts over punitive-damages coverage as contract or as tort conflicts? Regardless of the characterization, which types of policies should carry more weight in resolving such conflicts: (a) protecting the justified expectations of the insured and the insurer? or (b) deterring the type of misconduct that evokes punitive damages by not allowing the insured to pass on the pain of punitive damages to the insurer?

A common strategy in these cases is the use of declaratory judgment actions, either offensively or defensively. In many cases, the insurer brings such an action in one state and the insured in another, each of them racing to the most hospitable forum. Again, the basic choice-of-law options are: (a) to focus on the insurance contract; or (b) to focus on the place where the risk was located and materialized. Although the courts remain divided between these two options, it seems that the forum's own position on the issue of the insurability of punitive damages weighs heavily in choosing between these two options.[1]

4. *Insurance Statutes*. It is often said that the insurance industry is a highly regulated one. What is less well known is that statutory regulation extends deeply into the field of conflict of laws. In addition to the statutes mentioned earlier regarding environmental pollution, one can find several statutes that mandate the application of the law of the forum to insurance disputes that have certain contacts with the forum state. One of the most extreme statutes is a Nevada statute providing that it applies to: "1. *All* insurers authorized to transact insurance in this state; 2. *All* insurers having policyholders resident in this state; [and] 3. *All* insurers against whom a claim under an insurance contract may arise in this state." Nev.Rev.Stat. § 696B.020 (emphasis added). Similar statutes exist in other states. For example, a Texas statute provides that "[a]ny contract of insurance payable to any citizen or inhabitant of this State by any insurance company * * * doing business within this State shall be * * * governed by [the laws of this State] notwithstanding such * * * contract * * * may provide that the contract was executed and the premiums * * * should be payable without this State." Tex.Ins.Code Ann. § 21.42. A North Carolina statute provides that "[a]ll contracts of insurance on property, lives, or interests in

---

1. For representative cases, see Fluke Corp. v. Hartford Accident & Ind. Co., 34 P.3d 809 (Wash.2001); Hartford Accident & Ind. Co. v. American Red Ball Transit Co., Inc., 938 P.2d 1281 (Kan.1997); St. Paul Surplus Lines v. International Playtex, Inc., 777 P.2d 1259 (Kan. 1989), *cert. denied*, 493 U.S. 1036 (1990), *and later proceeding*, 1990 WL 35299 (Del.Super.1990); Zurich Ins. Co. v. Shearson Lehman Hutton, Inc., 642 N.E.2d 1065 (N.Y.1994); Meijer, Inc. v. General Star Indem. Co., 826 F.Supp. 241 (W.D.Mich.1993); United States Gypsum Co. v. Admiral Ins. Co., 643 N.E.2d 1226 (Ill.App.1994); Stonewall Surplus Lines Ins. Co. v. Johnson Controls, Inc., 17 Cal.Rptr.2d 713 (Cal.Ct.App.1993).

this State shall be deemed to be made therein, and all contracts of insurance the applications for which are taken within the State shall be deemed to be made within this State and are subject to the laws thereof." N.C.Gen.Stat. § 58-3-1.[2] Many of these statutes expressly prohibit the contractual choice of another state's law. For example, an Oregon statute provides that, for an insurance policy "delivered or issued for delivery in this state," any "condition, stipulation or agreement requiring such policy to be construed according to the laws of any other state or country * * * shall be invalid." Or.Rev.Stat. §§ 742.001, 742.018. See also Tex.Ins.Code Ann. § 21.42.

The above provisions are typical *unilateral* choice-of-law rules that delineate *a priori* the scope of application of the *lex fori* and essentially prevent a judicial choice-of-law analysis for all those cases that fall within their scope. Do these statutes: (a) disprove the assumption that legislatures are inactive in the conflicts field; or (b) support Currie's position regarding forum protectionism? In any event, attorneys would be well advised to search for such statutes before initiating litigation in a given state.

5. *Automobile Insurance Conflicts*. Automobile insurance conflicts are the most numerous among insurance conflicts. The majority of them involve the issue of uninsured or underinsured motorist (UM or UIM) coverage in actions brought by the insureds against their own insurers. The typical pattern is one in which a person who, in his or her home state purchased a policy insuring a car registered and garaged in that state, is involved in an accident in another state caused by an uninsured or underinsured motorist. A conflict results when the two states have different limits of or requirements for UM coverage, or take different positions on the validity of antistacking or setoff clauses contained in the policy. Like other insurance conflicts, these conflicts tend to depend heavily on local statutes, such as the ones described above. More common than the above are statutes that require the application of the law of the forum state if: (a) the insurance policy was delivered, or issued for delivery, in that state; or (b) the insured automobile is principally garaged there; or (c) the accident occurred there.

When the forum does not have such a statute, or when the court finds the statute inapplicable, the court resolves the conflict under the forum's judicial choice-of-law approach. Besides the few states that continue to follow the *lex loci contractus*, the majority of states follow approaches based on Restatement (Second) §§ 193 or 188 or other similar flexible approaches. Regardless of the approach, however, most recent cases exhibit a trend away from applying the law of the place of the accident *as such*, perhaps because most of them employ a contract choice-of-law analysis. Most recent cases apply the law of the state where the insured automobile is principally garaged, which usually is also the state in which the insured

---

2. See also Wis.Stat. § 632.09 ("Every insurance against loss or destruction of or damage to property in this state * * * is governed by the law of this state."; Min.Stat. § 60A.08(4) ("All contracts of insurance on property, lives, or interests in this state, shall be deemed to be made in this state."); Colo.Rev.Stat. § 10-4-711; Fla.Stat. § 627.727; Okla.Stat. tit.36§3636; La.Rev.Stat.§§ 22:611, 22:655 22:1406(D).

is domiciled and/or the policy has been delivered,[3] but one still finds cases that continue to apply the law of the accident state.[4]

G. STATUTES OF LIMITATION

Keeton v. Hustler Magazine, Inc.
Supreme Court of New Hampshire, 1988.
131 N.H. 6, 549 A.2d 1187.

JOHNSON, J., The United States Court of Appeals for the First Circuit * * * has certified to us the following questions of law arising out of a multi-state libel action: "1. Does New Hampshire follow an interstate single publication rule in libel cases? 2. If so, does New Hampshire permit a plaintiff to recover for distribution of a libel in jurisdictions whose own statutes of limitations would bar recovery, where neither party is a New Hampshire resident, where the only factual connection with New Hampshire is the distribution there of one percent or less of the total circulation of the material, and where the relevant statute of limitations has expired in every jurisdiction but New Hampshire?" For the reasons stated below, we answer that New Hampshire follows the single publication rule as formulated by the Restatement (Second) of Torts and that, in the circumstances described, we would apply our own statute of limitations to the plaintiff's entire libel action under that rule.

The facts of the underlying case, as represented by the parties, are briefly these. In October 1980, the plaintiff, Kathy Keeton, brought an action for libel against the defendants, Hustler Magazine, Inc., and its publisher Larry C. Flynt, in the United States District Court for the District of New Hampshire. The action was based on allegedly libelous material appearing in five issues of Hustler Magazine published between September 1975 and July 1976. Keeton had originally brought actions in Ohio in April 1977 for libel and invasion of privacy based on the May 1976 publication. However, the Ohio trial court dismissed the libel action in May 1978 finding that it was barred by Ohio's one-year statute of limitations. In September 1980, the Franklin County, Ohio, Court of Appeals affirmed the trial court's decision to dismiss Keeton's invasion of privacy claim on limitations grounds as well. By this date, the statute of limitations in every jurisdiction except New Hampshire (where the limitations period was then six years) barred Keeton's libel action. She instituted her New Hampshire suit within the month.

In response, Hustler and Flynt filed pre-trial motions to dismiss the New

---

3. For representative cases see State Farm Mut. Auto. Ins. Co. v. Gillette, 641 N.W.2d 662 (Wis.2002); Ohayon v. Safeco Ins. Co., 747 N.E.2d 206 (Ohio 2001); Cecere v. Aetna Ins. Co., 766 A.2d 696 (N.H.2001); Fortune Ins. Co. v. Owens, 526 S.E.2d 463 (N.C.2000); Ryals v. State Farm Mut. Ins. Co., 1 P.3d 803 (Idaho 2000) Great West Cas. Co. v. Hovaldt, 603 N.W.2d 198 (S.D.1999); U.S. Fidelity & Guar. Co. v. Preston, 26 S.W.3d 145 (Ky.2000); In re Allstate Ins. Co. (Stolarz), 613 N.E.2d 936 (N.Y.1993). For discussion of these and other cases, see Symeonides, *Choice of Law in 2002*, 70-73; *Choice of Law in 2001*, 46-56.

4. For cases applying the law of the state of the accident, see State Farm Mut. Auto. Ins. Co. v. Ballard, 54 P.3d 537 (N.M.2002); Nodak Mut. Ins. Co. v. American Family Mut. Ins. Co., 604 N.W.2d 91 (Mn.2000); Csulik v. Nationwide Mut. Ins. Co., 723 N.E.2d 90 (Ohio 2000); Williams v. State Farm Mut. Auto. Ins. Co., 641 A.2d 783 (Conn.1994).

Hampshire actions on grounds that included lack of personal jurisdiction, improper venue, and the statute of limitations. These motions resulted in a dismissal on personal jurisdiction grounds, which the United States Supreme Court eventually reversed. Keeton v. Hustler Magazine, Inc., 465 U.S. 770 (1984). On remand, the district court denied the defendants' renewed motions to dismiss on venue and limitations grounds, and the First Circuit refused to grant a writ of mandamus on these issues. Following a 1986 trial, in which the jury awarded Keeton two million dollars, the defendants again appealed on venue and limitations grounds to the First Circuit, which then agreed to consider the claims.

Keeton, the former associate publisher of Penthouse Magazine, is, and was at all times relevant to this action, a New York resident. Flynt and Hustler were Ohio residents at the time of the publications, but have been California residents since mid–1978. From the time of the libels through the present, Hustler has done business in New Hampshire, distributing between 10,000 and 15,000 copies of its magazine (or about one percent of its total circulation) throughout the State each month. The First Circuit determined that, in the context of a multi-state libel action under the single publication rule that would be barred in every State but New Hampshire, these circumstances presented complex legal questions with potential constitutional implications. Because that court found that New Hampshire had not yet addressed certain questions of State law relevant to this difficult and novel suit, this certification followed.

I. SINGLE PUBLICATION RULE. We first consider whether New Hampshire should follow the single publication rule in libel cases. Keeton urges us to adopt the rule, citing the benefits it affords plaintiffs, defendants, and the judicial system alike. The defendants do not argue to the contrary, but rather contend, for reasons addressed in part II, that we should not apply the New Hampshire statute of limitations to Keeton's suit for nationwide damages under the rule. * * *

The Restatement (Second) of Torts states the single publication rule as follows: "(3) Any one edition of a book or newspaper ... or similar aggregate communication is a single publication. (4) As to any single publication, (a) only one action for damages can be maintained; (b) all damages suffered in all jurisdictions can be recovered in the one action; and (c) a judgment for or against the plaintiff upon the merits of any action for damages bars any action for damages between the same parties in all jurisdictions." Restatement (Second) of Torts § 577A. * * * States adopting the rule generally hold, in addition, that the plaintiff's cause of action accrues for limitations purposes on the first date that the publisher releases the finished product for sale. [cit.]

We recognize the wisdom, in light of modern publishing practices, of adopting the single publication rule as described above. Without the rule, the burden that libel suits would place on parties and the courts might well be intolerable. We therefore join "[t]he great majority of States [that] now follow [the] rule" in libel actions. Keeton v. Hustler Magazine, Inc., 465 U.S. at 777 n. 8.

II. STATUTE OF LIMITATIONS. Because the statute of limitations has run on Keeton's libel claim in every State but New Hampshire, the second certified question essentially asks whether we would preserve that claim by applying our own statute to her entire action. We must therefore determine whether, consistent with New Hampshire choice of law rules and the United States Constitution, we may apply the New Hampshire statute of limitations to Keeton's suit for nationwide recovery under the single publication rule, where neither party is a New Hampshire resident and the defendants distributed approximately one percent of the libel in New Hampshire. We note, at the outset, that we have not been asked whether New Hampshire would apply its own substantive libel law to Keeton's claim and that we therefore do not address this issue. We add that we cannot now conceive of a case to which we would apply our own substantive law, but a foreign statute of limitations.

Flynt and Hustler argue that we should bar Keeton's claim entirely by refusing to apply our own statute of limitations to any part of her suit. To apply the New Hampshire statute, they say, would ill serve our interests in dismissing stale claims and discouraging forum shopping, and would violate the full faith and credit and due process requirements of the United States Constitution. They urge us to apply instead the statute of limitations either of New York (the plaintiff's domicile) or of Ohio or California (the defendants' previous and present domiciles), because each of these States has greater contacts with the claim as a whole than does New Hampshire. In the alternative, they argue that we should, and may, apply our own statute only to that portion of Keeton's damages attributable to distribution of the libel in New Hampshire. * * *

Keeton argues that there is no constitutional barrier to application of our statute to her entire suit and that this result is consistent with New Hampshire choice of law rules and the interests they are meant to serve. Moreover, she contends, the application of New Hampshire's statute is essential if the single publication rule is effectively to free courts, defendants, and plaintiffs from unnecessarily lengthy and complex litigation.

Neither our own choice of law rules nor the full faith and credit and due process requirements that the United States Supreme Court has enunciated typically require us to apply a statute of limitations other than our own. Both State and federal choice of law requirements traditionally apply only to the forum's choice among substantive rules. See Allstate Ins. Co. v. Hague, 449 U.S. 302 (1981) [Ch. 5]; Gordon v. Gordon, 387 A.2d 339 (N.H.1978). Like a number of other States, New Hampshire treats statutes of limitations as procedural. Id. at 360. * * *

Although constitutionality remained an open question at the time this case was argued, the United States Supreme Court's recent decision in Sun Oil Co. v. Wortman, 486 U.S. 717 (1988) [Ch. 5], appears to have disposed of this issue. * * * Because *Wortman* * * * appears to hold that we may constitutionally treat the statute of limitations as a procedural rule for choice of law purposes, we consider below only whether it is prudent to treat our statute of limitations as procedural, given the peculiarities of Keeton's suit.

A. New Hampshire Choice of Law Rules. When New Hampshire is the forum for a suit in which one or more other States also have an interest, we treat potential conflicts of law as follows: we first decide whether a relevant law is substantive or procedural; if it is substantive, we determine whether it actually conflicts with the laws of another interested State; if it is procedural, we generally apply our own law. *Gordon.* With two exceptions, our courts therefore apply New Hampshire statutes of limitations even when our statutory period differs from that of another interested State whose substantive law we have chosen to apply. We traditionally apply foreign statutes of limitations in such cases only when such statutes either "extinguish a right, or ... are an inherent part of a statutory scheme creating a right...." *Gordon* supra (citations omitted).

We choose among substantive laws by applying a balancing test composed of five choice-influencing considerations: "(1) the predictability of results; (2) the maintenance of reasonable orderliness and good relationships among the States in the federal system; (3) simplification of the judicial task; (4) advancement of the governmental interest of the forum; and (5) the court's preference for what it regards as the sounder rule of law." LaBounty v. American Ins. Co., 451 A.2d 161, 163 (N.H.1982); see Clark v. Clark, 222 A.2d 205, 208-09 (N.H.1966).

Like most States, New Hampshire recognizes the elimination of stale or fraudulent claims as the principal purpose of statutes of limitations. [cit.] Absent such statutes, a dilatory plaintiff might burden a defendant with suits of which he was not timely informed, [cit.] and clog court dockets, interfering with the "orderly administration of justice," [cit.] Statutes of limitations reflect the fact that it becomes more difficult and time-consuming both to defend against and to try claims as evidence disappears and memories fade with the passage of time. Such statutes thus represent the legislature's attempt to achieve a balance among State interests in protecting both forum courts and defendants generally against stale claims and in insuring a reasonable period during which plaintiffs may seek recovery on otherwise sound causes of action.

We agree that, given these purposes, statutes of limitations do differ from other procedural rules. We further believe, however, that the varied purposes that statutes of limitations are meant to serve justify the application of forum law, and thus the essential treatment of such statutes as procedural rules, in most instances, whether or not our choice of law principles advise application of New Hampshire substantive law.

It is, of course, the forum that is best able to decide when claims are so stale that they will burden its dockets, and only the forum has a significant interest in insuring that its dockets are not burdened by such claims. In addition, the forum has an interest in the defendant's protection from stale claims and the plaintiff's pursuit of recovery. We believe that, in any case in which either party is a New Hampshire resident or the cause of action arose in this State, the sum of our above stated forum interests in applying our own statute, in combination with the benefit of simplification afforded by regular application of our own rule, will tip the choice of law balance in favor of the application of our own limitations period to cases tried here. Thus, in such cases, our courts may typically apply the relevant New Hampshire statute without appeal to our choice-influencing considerations.

Keeton brought suit in New Hampshire to recover for injuries resulting from the defendants' distribution of libelous publications in New Hampshire as well as elsewhere. At the time of her suit, the New Hampshire legislature had determined that the proper balance among relevant interests of the forum, defendants, and plaintiffs supported a six-year statute of limitations for libel, and Keeton properly brought suit for libel within the appointed period. The legislature had not at the time of Keeton's suit (nor has it since) enacted a borrowing statute requiring the application of foreign statutes of limitations under any circumstances. Thus, unlike legislatures in many other States, it had taken no action indicating an absence of any interest on the part of New Hampshire in seeing its own statute of limitations applied to certain categories of suit. Furthermore, relevant foreign statutes do not express the kind of strong local policy concerns that we have traditionally recognized as warranting an exception to the rule that we will apply our own statute. The statutes of limitations in Ohio and California (the two States that might wish to protect domiciliaries) do not extinguish the right to sue for libel and are not "an inherent part of [some] statutory scheme creating [that] right." *Gordon*; see Cal.Civ.Proc.Code § 340 (Deering Supp.1988); Ohio Rev.Code Ann. § 2305.11 (Anderson Supp. 1987). The same is true of New York, the plaintiff's domicile. N.Y. Civ. Prac. L. & R. § 215 (Consol.1972).

Moreover, there is no indication, based on the peculiar facts of this case, that foreign interests in barring Keeton's claim outweigh forum interests in allowing it. In this regard we first note that foreign States have no reason to fear that application of our longer statute will, in fact, disadvantage the defendants. Because Flynt and Hustler distributed, in New Hampshire, significant numbers of the libelous publications that gave rise to the injuries for which Keeton sues, they had ample reason to anticipate that Keeton might bring suit against them here, to which we would apply our own law. Moreover, Flynt and Hustler do not even allege loss of evidence or other disadvantage resulting from the timing of Keeton's suit.

In comparing our own interest in entertaining Keeton's claims to foreign interests in barring those claims, we first note that where, as here, the forum's limitations period is longer than that of any State whose law is being considered, the forum's interest in protecting its dockets is not so strongly implicated as would be the case if a foreign statute were longer than our own. This is because an application of foreign law would not burden forum dockets. However, similar preferences expressed in foreign statutes are entirely irrelevant to the consideration of competing interests since the State expressing those preferences is not the forum.

Although our own interest in striking an appropriate balance between promoting protection for defendants and legitimate recovery for plaintiffs is less great than it would be if defendants or plaintiff were New Hampshire residents, it is nonetheless substantial. As noted above, this is because the defendants distributed, in this State, a significant number of libelous publications giving rise to the injuries for which Keeton sues. The interest that we invariably have in fair treatment of those who are defendants in cases tried here is only increased when the issues to be litigated involve activities those defendants pursued here. Similarly, our general interest in providing plaintiffs sufficient time to bring suit is enhanced when the injuries for which suit is brought were incurred in this State.

Like our own statute of limitations, relevant foreign statutes obviously express what foreign States take to be an appropriate balance among their interests regarding courts, defendants, and plaintiffs. However, it would be nearly impossible for us to discern the weight such States intend to accord these varied interests. We cannot be certain, for example, whether a State's shorter statute of limitations for libel expresses a great concern to protect dockets (which is irrelevant where the State is not the forum) or an enhanced concern to protect defendants from stale claims. So long as our own interests relevant to the choice among statutes of limitations are significant, our additional interest in simplifying the judicial function counsels that we apply our own statute of limitations rather than embark on the highly uncertain task of discerning precisely what weight a foreign legislature intended to accord the varied interests that statutes of limitations address.

We agree that the single publication rule complicates the analysis here by allowing the plaintiff to recover in any State where she was injured for injuries sustained nationwide. However, we must not allow this peculiarity to blind us to the fact that Keeton was injured in New Hampshire by the distribution of 10,000 to 15,000 copies of a libelous publication. The fact that she had never been in New Hampshire prior to trial does not mean that she suffered no injury here. Indeed, the trial court found her to be sufficiently well-known to be considered a "public figure" for purposes of her libel suit. Given both these facts and the ambiguity of the inquiry necessary to determine to what degree a State statute of limitations implicates each of the interests it addresses, it is not apparent to us why Keeton should be prevented from recovery anywhere because three States in which she arguably received greater injury, or which have some additional connection with the parties, have chosen to adopt shorter limitations periods.

In light of the above discussion, we believe that here, as in most cases, all relevant interests are best served by treating our statute of limitations as an essentially procedural rule and applying it to Keeton's action without further discussion. However, even if we were to treat the statute of limitations as a substantive rule, in light of the far-reaching consequences of applying our own statute to Keeton's entire claim, our choice-influencing considerations would only provide additional support for the choice of New Hampshire law. There is clearly a conflict among the laws of interested States. At the time of publication, the New Hampshire statute of limitations for libel was six years, while the statutory periods in New York, Ohio, and California (the foreign States most interested in this litigation) were one year. We therefore proceed to analyze the statute in light of our five choice-influencing considerations.

1. *Predictability of results.* Predictability of results, the first of our choice-influencing criteria, is usually implicated only in suits involving contractual or similar consensual transactions. [cit.] It emphasizes the importance of applying to the parties' bargain or other dealings the law on which they agreed to rely at the outset. There was, of course, no such agreement here. Furthermore, while it is true that a libel defendant can consider the law applicable to potential suits before making the decision to publish, he cannot, in making this decision, legitimately rely on the potential plaintiff's failure to bring timely suit. That action is entirely in the plaintiff's hands and beyond the defendant's control.

The predictability that results when courts apply the same law wherever suit is brought can also discourage forum shopping among plaintiffs. However, we do not believe that our decision to apply the New Hampshire statute of limitations in this case will significantly encourage unwanted forum shopping in later cases. First, we disagree with the Restatement authors that application of the New Hampshire statute in any way encourages what is typically understood as forum shopping. See Restatement (Second) of Conflict of Laws § 142 (1986 Revisions, Supplement; April 12, 1988, at 8). Forum shopping in the classic sense refers to a plaintiff's attempt to have a court apply the law that will win her the most favorable verdict, not to her attempt to find a forum whose statute of limitations will allow it to entertain her otherwise legitimate suit. See Black's Law Dictionary 590 (5th ed. 1979). In addition, our decision to apply our own statute of limitations does not determine what substantive law we would apply. Even the possibility that New Hampshire might apply its own libel law, which is comparatively unfavorable to plaintiffs, would discourage many multi-state libel plaintiffs from instituting suit here. Our first consideration thus provides no strong reason to prefer another statute of limitations to our own.

2. *Relationships among the States.* The second consideration, which counsels maintenance of reasonable orderliness among the States, requires only that "a court not apply the law of a State which does not have a substantial connection with the total facts and the particular issue being litigated." LaBounty, 451 A.2d at 164. Unlike cases in which the defendants merely did business in the forum, the injury for which Keeton sues occurred, at least in part, in this State. Moreover, distribution in New Hampshire was far from insubstantial. At the time of the libel, the defendants sold between 10,000 and 15,000 copies of Hustler Magazine in New Hampshire each month.

New Hampshire, of course, was not the sole place of the injury for which Keeton seeks recovery. However, it is implicit in the reasoning underlying the single publication rule that no one State is the sole place of injury in a multi-state libel action. It is the continuity of facts surrounding the production and distribution of many copies of a single publication that justifies courts in treating many separate actions for nationwide injuries as one. While New Hampshire was not the State of greatest distribution, it was connected with the basic facts necessary to prove the libel through distribution of a significant number of copies. In keeping with the assumptions underlying the single publication rule, New Hampshire's connection with the facts and issues to be litigated was substantial.

3. *Simplification.* We have already discussed the fact that simplification counsels us to avoid undertaking the difficult or impossible task of discerning the weights that foreign legislatures have attributed to the interests underlying particular statutes of limitations. We similarly determine that, while it might appear to simplify the judicial process to hold that we will regularly apply the statute of limitations of, for example, the plaintiff's domicile to multi-state libel actions, the result in fact would be just the opposite. To depart from our traditional rule by applying a foreign statute of limitations, when concerns other than simplification did not so dictate, would only complicate and confuse New Hampshire conflicts law for the future. We will not adhere blindly to a traditional rule whose application would be unwise or unfair in a particular case, but neither will we depart from a familiar and well-

founded rule, absent good reason to do so.

4. *Forum interests.* As noted in our discussion of the purposes underlying statutes of limitations and New Hampshire's substantial connection with the facts and issue to be litigated, our interest in applying our own statute to cases generally stems from our concern to insure the orderly administration of our courts and to protect the respective interests of defendants and plaintiffs. Given our inability reliably to discern the weights that other States accord their own interests relevant to the choice among statutes of limitations, we may conclude that there is, in essence, no conflicting foreign interest that outweighs this substantial forum interest.

5. *The sounder rule approach.* In addition to forum interests, our decision to apply the New Hampshire statute to Keeton's entire claim is based primarily on our view that this statute reflects the better rule of law. * * * [A] short statute of limitations may unduly prejudice plaintiffs * * * [A]n unusually short statute of limitations for libel is undesirable where a State applies the single publication rule. The better rule, in our view, is a longer statute. This view is consistent with New Hampshire's general preference for decisions on the merits, demonstrated by our comparatively long statutes of limitations for many causes of action, [cit.], and our liberal discovery rule for actions in tort, [cit.].

We recognize that the legislature's recent enactment of a three-year statute of limitations for libel actions might appear to suggest that the six-year statute was outmoded and should not apply to this case. [cit.]. However, we do not believe that the change warrants application of a foreign statute. Although the legislature has changed the limitations period, the change places New Hampshire in conformity with States having the longest statutes of limitations for libel. While the six-year statute was unusually long, the legislature's decision does not suggest that we should prefer to it a foreign limitations period so short that it may unduly burden plaintiffs.

We also note at this juncture that, contrary to the defendants' suggestion, it would be inconsistent with the goals of the single publication rule to apply our own statute to Keeton's New Hampshire injury alone. If recovery for damages sustained in each State depends, under the single publication rule, on whether or not its statute of limitations would bar the action, there appears to be no reason why each State's substantive libel law should not also apply to injuries occurring in that State. However, this would present courts and juries with the formidable if not impossible task of applying the law of each State to the injury there sustained. Such a result would significantly burden courts, plaintiffs, and defendants. The single publication rule treats what were formerly many actions and injuries as one in order to simplify suits and protect parties. In adopting and applying the rule, we will act consistently with these purposes by choosing a single statute of limitations applicable to a single cause of action. We take this to be the better approach to resolving conflicts of law in suits under the rule.

We therefore conclude not only that the combination of our forum interests and our interest in simplification counsel application of our statute in this as in most cases, but that a full-blown analysis based on our five choice-influencing considerations would provide ample further support for this conclusion. We emphasize that we would not anticipate requiring a choice-influencing analysis in any case in which this State was either the domicile of one of the parties or the place where the cause of action arose. Moreover, we make no decision regarding cases with which our connection is less substantial. Such cases must await our opportunity to consider the relevant issues based on a particular set of facts.

* * * We * * * answer both of the certified questions in the affirmative. *Remanded.*

SOUTER, J., dissenting: * * * The [majority's] holding is the product of two related rules. The first is that in litigation implicating the interests of more than one State and requiring choices of law to be made, procedural issues are to be resolved by the law of the forum State. Under the second, a statute of limitations is characterized as procedural, so that the statute of the forum State should customarily be applied.

I am aware of no objection to the first rule, and I raise no quarrel with it myself. * * *

The second rule, however, that the limitation of actions is a matter of procedure to be governed by the statute of the forum, is troublesome. Right on the face of it, a limitation statute is obviously distinguishable from such paradigm procedural examples as rules regulating service of process, the deposition of witnesses, or closing arguments of counsel. Whereas these latter rules prescribe how to prepare a case and conduct a trial once action has been brought, a statute of limitations determines whether an action can be maintained at all. And although the application of any procedural rule may have the potential to influence the outcome of a case, the application of a limitation statute can have a direct and dispositive effect, which garden-variety rules of procedure cannot claim for themselves. There is, then, nothing inherently persuasive in characterizing such a statute as merely procedural. * * *

The first group of authorities ranged against the majority's position are legislative enactments in some 35 States of so-called borrowing statutes, eliminating in differing degrees the assumption that the forum's limitation period ought generally to be applied. * * *

There is, second, the position taken by the overwhelming body of commentators, ranged against mechanical application of the forum's statute of limitations as merely procedural. * * * Third, there are the judicial rejections of the wooden procedural classification in favor of some variety of contemporary conflicts analysis, by courts less immune than today's majority to the criticism I have cited and quoted. * * * Fourth, there are the drafters of the Restatement, who are proposing to supersede the old view of limitations as procedural, see Restatement (Second) of Conflict of Laws § 142 (1971), with a provision calling for an ultimate appeal to interest and relationship analysis in resolving a conflict between limitation rules. See 1986 Revisions, Supp.: April 12, 1988, at 1. * * *

The majority, of course, claim to have done a *Clark* analysis, and to have reached the same result on the basis of "relevant choice-influencing considerations" that they previously reached on the basis of *Gordon.* It is, however, surprising to conclude as the majority do that New Hampshire, which received less than one percent of the libelous publications' circulation and experienced virtually no other contact with the parties, has an interest in either the parties, the events, or the litigation that justifies the application of its law as against the law of all other interested States. I respectfully submit that analysis following the *Clark* methodology will not support such a conclusion.

    * * * (1) The value of predictability is not to be confined to cases for the enforcement of consensually derived obligations. As Professor Leflar has explained, "[p]redictability of results includes the ideal that the decision in the litigation on a given set of facts should be the same regardless of where the litigation occurs, so that 'forum shopping' will benefit neither party." [cit.] Further argument is unnecessary to demonstrate the forum shopping represented by this case[.] * * *

    (2) The need for comity within the federal system behooves the forum to consider application of the relevant law of other jurisdictions whose substantial concerns with the problem at hand give them interests in the application of their respective laws. * * * Ohio and California may be taken together as the place of the defendants' business or residence, as a result of which those States gain interests in limiting the duration both of the defendants' financial exposure and of the jeopardy to free expression that a long limitation period visits on a publisher. [cit.] These States thus have a collective interest in the enforcement of their shorter, one-year limitation periods. [cit.] New York's interest derives from the plaintiff's residence there * * *. While it is true that New York may have no interest in limiting the plaintiff's opportunity to bring action elsewhere, its one-year statute also indicates that it lacks any interest in supporting the plaintiff's claim to benefit from the longer period that New Hampshire's statute would allow. By a parity of reasoning, the identity of New York's one-year period with the one-year periods common to Ohio and California means that among the three States there is no conflict of laws, and thus no occasion to view New York's interest as running counter to the interests of Ohio and California. There is therefore no reason here to question a conclusion * * * that the State of a publication's editorial office has the strongest interest in the application of its law, when the publication is sued for multistate libel. The need for comity, then, calls for consideration of this interest and the application of a one-year period.

    (3) On the third subject, the simplification of the judicial task, there is not much to be argued one way or another. While nothing could be easier than applying the forum's statute of limitations, no subject of foreign law could probably be ascertained with greater ease than a limitation period.

    (4) Concern for the advancement of the interests of New Hampshire as the forum State calls for an enquiry into three possible sources of State interest: the State's relationship to the parties, the effects of the publications in New Hampshire, and the very fact that the New Hampshire legislature saw fit to enact its statute of limitations as one element in the State's system of justice. * * * New Hampshire has no interest derived from a relationship with any of the parties, since they have had virtually no contacts with the State apart from this litigation in a federal court. * * * Although the State may still claim some interest in protecting the reputation of a non-resident, see Keeton v. Hustler Magazine, Inc., 465 U.S. at 777, there is no reason to believe that such an interest rises above the minimal level in this case. Nor

do the effects of the publications give rise to any significant State interest. The record before us contains no indication that any appreciable number of New Hampshire people had ever heard of the plaintiff at the time of the publications, let alone that they held her in any definite repute. Hence, any actual damage suffered because of the New Hampshire circulation was almost certainly smaller in proportion to the whole of her damages than even the percentage of Hustler's total circulation distributed in this State. * * * All that is left as a possible source of serious State interest in applying its own former limitation rule is, then, the State policy that was expressed in the rule itself. Statutes of limitations embody a dual policy against subjecting defendants to the trial of stale claims and against wasting the courts' time in their litigation. * * * [H]owever, * * * the policy underlying New Hampshire's six-year limitation period is a policy against litigating claims over six years old, not a policy calling affirmatively for the litigation of all claims under that age. Thus, there simply is no conflict as between the policies and interests of New Hampshire and those of the other three States. * * * New Hampshire has no genuine interest in the enforcement of its statute. * * * [T]he actual consequence that follows from the majority's view * * * is * * * nothing less than the revival of defamation actions that are dead under local law in every other jurisdiction of the United States. The revealing question, then, is not merely whether this State has an interest in applying its local rule, but whether it has an interest in encouraging defamation claims that are time-barred everywhere else to end up in New Hampshire for trial. The answer is no.

(5) Finally, considering a preference for the better rule forces us to make some judgment about the soundness of New Hampshire's old six-year statute. Only under New Hampshire law could this action have been brought, and in judging the wisdom of our former rule we may well ask whether they were all out of step but Jim. Actually, the New Hampshire legislature acknowledged as much in 1981 by shrinking the limitation period to three years, [cit.], which, if applicable, would have barred this action. * * * New Hampshire's six-year statute was anomalous, and the one-year periods of each of the other three arguably interested States expressed a patently better rule.

* * * I cannot, therefore, agree that the application of New Hampshire's statute of limitations is neither arbitrary nor unfair, as the majority insist, and I would answer the First Circuit's second question in the negative, for the reason that New Hampshire's limitation period may not properly be applied in this case. Given that answer, I have no occasion to comment on the constitutional analysis contained in the majority opinion.

THAYER, J., joins in the dissent.

Notes and Questions

1. *The Traditional Approach.* As you remember from studying the substance/procedure dichotomy (Ch. 2, supra), the traditional approach characterized issues of statutes of limitation as being procedural issues which, accordingly, were governed by the *lex fori*. The first Restatement provided as follows:

§ 603. If the action is barred by the statute of limitations of the forum, no action can be maintained though the action is not barred in the state where the cause of action arose.

§ 604. If the action is not barred by the statute of limitations of the forum, an action can be maintained, though the action is barred in the state where the cause of action arose.

To the extent it relied on this procedural characterization to justify applying the *lex fori*'s limitation period, *Keeton* is a typical application of the traditional approach. Notice that the *Keeton* court relied on this traditional characterization despite the fact that in all other respects the court has abandoned the traditional approach. This too is typical. Many states that have abandoned the traditional approach in tort and contract conflicts continue to adhere to that approach with regard to limitation conflicts. In fact, as of 2003, only 17 states have abandoned the traditional approach to limitations conflicts. See Symeonides, *Choice of Law in 1999*, 166 *et seq.*

Keeton, however, is atypical in two respects: (a) the first part of the majority opinion attempts to provide modern policy rationalizations for the procedural characterization of limitations. (What do you think of these rationalizations?); and (b) the second part of the opinion subjects the limitation issue to *a* choice-of-law analysis, the same analysis that New Hampshire courts employ with regard to other conflicts issues. Although this analysis produced the same result as the first part, the second part of the opinion is important from a methodological perspective in that it represents a transition from traditional to modern thinking, a transition that has been completed in some states but has not begun in others.

2. One of the arguments *Keeton* offered in support of the traditional approach was simplicity and ease of application. In essence, that approach exempts limitation issues from the scrutiny of the choice-of-law process and applies the *lex fori*'s limitation period, whether it is shorter or longer than that the foreign period. In which cases is the traditional approach more objectionable: (a) cases in which the forum's limitation period is shorter, or (b) cases such as *Keeton* in which the forum's limitation period is longer than that of the other state? Why?

The Uniform Statute of Limitations on Foreign Claims Act of 1957 took a more drastic position. It authorized the application of the limitation period of either the forum state or the state where the cause of action "arose," whichever period was shorter. If simplicity were the overriding goal, this Act would be ideal, would it not? If so, then why do you think that, in a thirty-year period, only three states adopted this Act (Okl., Pa., and W.Va.) before its drafters withdrew it in 1978?

3. Notice that the defendants in *Keeton* argued that, if the court were determined to apply New Hampshire's statute of limitation, the court should do so "only to that portion of Keeton's damages attributable to distribution of the libel in New Hampshire." Was this not a good argument? Should the court have accepted it? If the court were to accept this argument, would you disagree with the court's choice-of-law decision? Why, or why not?

4. Is the single-publication rule a rule of substantive law or a rule of conflicts law? Regardless of the answer, when it speaks of "nationwide recovery" is the rule intended to encompass recovery in states whose statutes of limitation have run?

5. In interpreting the pertinent jurisdictional rules of the European Union

(EU), the Court of Justice of the European Communities has held that the victim of a defamation may sue the publisher "either before the courts of the [EU] State where the publisher of the defamatory publication is established, which have jurisdiction to award damage for all the harm caused by the defamation, or before the courts of each [EU] State in which the publication was distributed and where the victim claims to have suffered injury to his reputation, which have jurisdiction to rule solely in respect of the harm caused in the [latter] State." *Fiona Shevill v. Press Alliance SA*, Case C 68/93, [1995] ECR I - 415, at § 33. Is this a sensible regime? Under this regime, New Hampshire could compensate Ms. Keeton only for the injuries she suffered in New Hampshire. On the other hand, if Ms. Keeton were to sue in the state of the publisher's "establishment," that state would have jurisdiction to compensate her for the injuries she suffered throughout the United States. However, under the choice-of-law regime currently prevailing in Europe, that state would apply on a distributive basis the substantive laws of each of the states in which Ms. Keeton suffered injuries, *including* the statutes of limitations of those states (because statutes of limitations are considered *substantive* in Europe). The proposed EU Regulation known as "Rome II," which will go into effect on January 1, 2005, preserves the plaintiff's option of suing in either the countries of injuries or the country of the publisher's establishment, and also retains the substantive characterization of limitations. With regard to choice of law, Rome II provides for the application of the law of the country in which both parties are domiciled and, in the absence of common domicile, the law of the country or countries of injury. However, the forum country may apply its own law if the law(s) of the other state(s) "would be contrary to the fundamental principles of the forum as regards freedom of expression and information." Rome II, Art. 6.

6. ***Traditional Exceptions to the Traditional Approach***. *a. Legislative Exceptions: Borrowing Statutes*. As *Keeton* graphically illustrates, the traditional approach is most deficient when the forum has a longer limitation period than the other involved states, because only then does this approach reward forum-shopping. This is why most criticisms against, and most efforts to improve, the traditional approach have concentrated on this category of cases. As early as the middle of the nineteenth century, state legislatures recognized the forum-shopping problem and began enacting "borrowing statutes" that authorize the borrowing of foreign limitation periods that are shorter than the forum's. By the middle of the twentieth century, 38 states had enacted a borrowing statute in one form or another.[1] Although these statutes vary in scope and detail,[2] all of them apply only when the forum's limitation period is *longer*, not shorter, than that of the other state. The state whose law is borrowed is typically the "state where the cause of action arose" and normally

---

1. In addition to New Hampshire, the jurisdictions that had *not* enacted such a statute are Ark., Conn., D.C., Ga., Md., Mi., N.J., N.M., N.D., S.C., S.D., and Vt. In recent years Ohio and Texas have repealed their borrowing statute.

2. For example, the statutes of 35 out of 38 states encompass all "actions" or "causes of action," without regard to whether these actions arise out of contracts, torts, etc., whereas Wisconsin's statute is confined to personal-injury actions and Virginia's and West Virginia's statutes are confined to actions "[u]pon a contract which was made and was to be performed in another state." Also many of these statutes exempt causes of action held by forum domiciliaries. See Flowers v. Carville, 310 F.3d 118 (9th Cir.2002)

is the state whose law would govern the merits of the action (hereinafter *lex causae*).

Borrowing statutes are potent weapons for curtailing forum shopping, particularly in states that have unusually long limitation periods. The lack of such a statute in New Hampshire deprived the *Keeton* court of such a weapon. The availability of such a weapon, however, does not always guarantee its use. This point is well illustrated by cases from Mississippi which, like New Hampshire, had a six-year limitation period for tort claims until the early 1990s, but which, unlike New Hampshire, has a borrowing statute. These cases exhibit great reluctance to apply this statute, even when it seems to fit a case in all respects. See, e.g., Shewbrooks v. A.C. & S., Inc., 529 So.2d 557 (Miss.1988); Williams v. Taylor Machinery, Inc., 529 So.2d 606 (Miss.1988). Moreover, many of the states that have abandoned the traditional approach in tort conflicts continue to apply their borrowing statutes in a mechanical fashion and are reluctant to find that the cause of action might have "arisen" or "accrued" in a state other than the state of injury. See Symeonides, *Choice of Law in 1999*, 168 *et seq.*. Even the New York Court of Appeals has not extended its *Babcock* approach to New York's borrowing statute. See Global Financial Corp. v. Triarc Corp., 715 N.E.2d 482 (N.Y.1999).

b. Judicial Exceptions. Courts following the *lex fori* rule for statutes of limitation have developed certain exceptions to that rule. One such exception authorizes the court to apply a foreign limitation period that is shorter than the forum's, if the foreign period is conceived or perceived as a limitation on the right itself, not merely the remedy, or, as *Keeton* said, when the foreign statutes "either extinguish a right, or * * * are an inherent part of a statutory scheme creating a right." The first Restatement recognized this exception in § 605 which provided that, "[i]f by law of the state which has created a right of action, it is made a condition of the right that it shall expire after a certain period of limitation has elapsed, no action begun after the period has elapsed can be maintained in any state." The common example is the wrongful death action which, not being recognized by the common law, was conferred by statute, ostensibly on the condition that it be brought within the time specified in the statute. See Gomez v. ITT Educational Serv., Inc. 71 S.W.3d 542 (Ark.2002). Another example is statutes of repose for products manufacturers like Georgia's statute in *Gantes*. These statutes extinguish the victim's action after the passage of a specified number of years from the time the product was marketed, and regardless of when the injury occurred. Courts usually characterize these statutes as substantive and thus employ the above exception whenever the foreign statute bars the action. See Baxter v. Sturm, Ruger & Co., Inc., 644 A.2d 1297 (Conn.1994); Cosme v. Whitin Mach. Works, Inc., 632 N.E.2d 832 (Mass. 1994); Tanges v. Heidelberg N. Am., Inc., 93 N.Y.2d 48 (1999).

7. Modern Approaches: a. The New Uniform Act. In 1982, the Commissioners on Uniform State Laws promulgated a new uniform act,[3] which, somewhat

---

3. See Uniform Conflict of Laws--Limitations Act, 12 U.L.A. 56 (1988). This Act has been adopted by Colorado, Montana, North Dakota, Oregon, and Washington. For an authoritative discussion of the Act by the Chairman of the Drafting Committee, see Leflar, *The New Conflicts--Limitations Act.* For representative cases, see Rice v. Dow Chem. Co., 875 P.2d 1213 (Wash.1994); Cropp v. Interstate Distr. Co., 880 P.2d 464
(continued...)

surprisingly, moved to the other end of the spectrum by adopting the premise that limitation periods are a substantive matter that should be governed by the *lex causae*.[4] Section 2 of the Uniform Act provides that: "if a claim is substantively based: (1) upon the law of one other state, the limitation period of that state applies; or (2) upon the law of more than one state, the limitation period of one of those states chosen by the law of conflict of laws of this State, applies." However, recognizing that often the forum has important interests in matters of limitation, this Act makes some concessions in favor of the *lex fori*. Section 4 of the Act authorizes resort to the *lex fori* if the limitation period of the *lex causae* "is substantially different from the limitation period of this State and has not afforded a fair opportunity to sue upon, or imposes an unfair burden in defending against, the claim."

The Act's approach may sound intuitively more logical than the traditional *lex fori* approach, but is it much better? Suppose for example that the forum's limitation period is shorter than the foreign period and is exclusively designed to serve purely procedural interests (e.g., relieving the courts from the burden of hearing stale claims). If the Section 4 exception is inapplicable, does the Act not deprive the forum of the ability to protect those interests?

b. The courts. Following the lead of the New Jersey Supreme Court in Heavner v. Uniroyal, Inc., 305 A.2d 412 (N.J.1973), some courts have abandoned the traditional approach to limitations issues and instead subjected these issues to the same choice-of-law analysis as other issues in the same case, and without any a priori reliance on the *lex fori*. These courts are still a minority, albeit a rapidly increasing one. The second part of the majority opinion in *Keeton* and Justice Souter's excellent dissenting opinion are representative of this trend. One of the differences between this approach and that of the Uniform Act is that, while the Act requires that the limitation issue and the other issues in the case must be governed by the *law of the same state*, the *Heavner* approach simply subjects these two categories of issues to the same choice-of-law *analysis*. Depending on the specifics of a case, this analysis may lead to the same or different laws for the two categories of issues.

c. The New Revision of the Restatement (Second). In 1988, responding to the above developments, the American Law Institute adopted a revised version of § 142 of the Restatement (Second), which provides as follows:

> (1) Whether an action will be maintained against the defense of the statute of limitations is determined under the principles stated in § 6. In the absence of exceptional circumstances which make such result unreasonable:
>
> (2) The forum will apply its own statute of limitations barring the action.

---

3. (...continued)
(Or.App.1994).

4. Although not directly influenced by the civil law, the new Act coincidentally reflects the civil-law approach which considers time limitations ("liberative prescription") as being merely a mode of extinction of an obligation and thus a substantive matter that is governed by the same law as that which governs the obligation (*lex causae*). See, e.g., Swiss codif., art. 148; German codif., art. 32; Quebec codif., art. 3131; Hungarian codif., § 30(4); Bustamante Code, art. 229; Peruvian Civ. Code, art. 2099; and Spanish Civ. Code, art. 10(10).

(3) The forum will apply its own statute of limitation permitting the action unless (a) maintenance of the action would serve no significant interest of the forum; and (b) the action would be barred under the statute of limitations of a state having a more significant relationship to the parties and the occurrence.[5]

Through its cross-reference to § 6, the first sentence of § 142 adopts an approach similar to *Heavner*--it instructs the court to choose the law applicable to limitations through the flexible principles of § 6, and without any a priori preference for either the *lex fori* or the *lex causae*. However, in the interest of judicial economy, the balance of § 142 supplements this approach with presumptive rules based on the *lex fori* approach. Notice that under § 142 the presumption in favor of the *lex fori* is much more difficult to rebut when the forum's limitation is shorter than when it is longer than the foreign period. Why do you think this is so? Has the Restatement (Second) found the golden mean? For critical discussion, see Weinberg, *The Limitations Debate*, 705-10. For representative cases, see New England Telephone & Telegraph Co. v. Gourdeau Construction Co., 647 N.E.2d 42 (Mass.1995); Federal Deposit Ins. Corp. v. Nordbrock, 102 F.3d 335 (8th Cir.1996). For similar approaches, see article 3549 of the Louisiana codification (discussed in Symeonides, *Two Surprises*, 530-48); article 8 of the Puerto Rico Draft Code (discussed in Symeonides, *Revising Puerto Rico's Conflicts Law*, 433-47).

Consider Ms. Keeton's action under each one of the above approaches, on the assumption that that approach is followed in New Hampshire, and determine if that action would have a better, worse, or the same fate. Do you think that the *Keeton* majority would have reached the same result regardless of the approach followed by the forum?

8. *Lessons Derived from Comparison*. The *Keeton* majority was correct to note "the varied purposes that statutes of limitations are meant to serve." Indeed, it is simplistic to think of statutes of limitation as being always procedural (as did the traditional common-law approach) or always substantive (as does the traditional civil-law approach). A rule of limitation may, and usually does, serve both substantive and procedural objectives or policies. For instance, a rule that subjects medical malpractice claims to a short limitation period serves substantive objectives by shielding doctors and their insurers from prolonged exposure to liability, but also serves procedural objectives by reducing the number of malpractice actions and thus helps to conserve judicial resources. Similarly, a rule that prohibits anticipatory waivers of the statute of limitation promotes substantive aims by protecting debtors from the coercive power creditors. At the same time, by preventing the lengthening of the limitation period beyond the time the *lex fori* considers appropriate, this rule serves procedural policies by protecting the courts from the burdens and dangers of adjudicating old claims. In contrast, a rule that prohibits the parties to certain insurance contracts from shortening a statutory limitation period subordinates the procedural policy of encouraging the early filing of actions to the preferred substantive policy of protecting insureds from the superior bargaining power of

---

5. Quoted with the permission of the copyright owner, The American Law Institute.

insurers.

Thus, the automatic application of the *lex fori* to all multistate cases (the traditional common-law approach) is as arbitrary as is the automatic application of the *lex causae* (the traditional civil-law approach). By exaggerating the procedural function of limitations and ignoring their substantive function, the first approach encourages forum shopping and ignores the legitimate interests of other states that may be more intimately related to the parties and their dispute. By overemphasizing the substantive function of limitations, the second approach deprives the forum *qua* forum of the ability to promote its own procedural interests. If these statements are accurate, then the search for appropriate solutions to limitations conflicts must eschew exclusive reliance on either the *lex fori* or the *lex causae* and should aim for a middle formula that should take into account the following policies:

> (a) the procedural and substantive policies embodied in the particular limitation rule of the *lex fori*;
>
> (b) the substantive policies embodied in the limitation rule of the *lex causae*;
>
> (c) the multistate policy of discouraging forum shopping; and
>
> (d) the federally-sanctioned policy of providing a forum for causes of action arising under that laws of sister-states.

Do you agree with the above? If so, what other policies or considerations would you include in the calculus?

9. ***Contractual Choice of Statutes of Limitation.*** When the parties to a contract insert in it a choice-of-law clause, does that clause encompass the statute of limitation of the chosen state?[6] Should the answer to the above question depend on whether: (a) the parties expressly included the limitation issue in their choice of the applicable law? (b) the chosen law's limitation period is longer or shorter than the forum's? (c) the forum state or the state whose law is chosen adheres to a procedural or substantive characterization of statutes of limitation? Should the answers to the above questions be different when the statute at issue is a statute of repose, rather than a statute of limitation?

H. PROPERTY

Autocephalous Greek-Orthodox Church of Cyprus v. Goldberg
United States District Court, S.D. Indiana, 1989.
717 F.Supp. 1374, *Aff'd.,* 917 F.2d 278 (7th Cir.1990).

NOLAND, J., SUMMARY OF DECISION. In this case the Court is asked to decide the right of possession as between the plaintiffs, the Autocephalous Greek-Orthodox Church of Cyprus ("Church of Cyprus") and the Republic of Cyprus, and

---

6. For representative cases, see Long v. Holland American Line Westours, Inc., 26 P.3d 430 (Alaska 2001); Nez v. Forney, 783 P.2d 471 (N.M.1989); Financial Bancorp, Inc. v. Pingree & Dahle, Inc., 880 P.2d 14 (Utah.Ct.App.1994); Hambrecht & Quist Venture Partners v. American Medical Int'l, Inc., 46 Cal.Rptr.2d 33 (Cal.App.1995); Manion v. Roadway Package System, Inc., 938 F.Supp. 512 (C.D.Ill.1996); In re Western United Nurseries, Inc. v. Estate of Adams, 191 B.R. 820 (Bankr.D.Ariz.1996); In re Fineberg, 202 B.R. 206 (Bankr.E.D.Pa.1996); Springfield Oil Services, Inc. v. Costello, 941 F.Supp. 45 (E.D.Pa. 1996).

the defendants, Peg Goldberg ("Goldberg") and Goldberg & Feldman Fine Arts, Inc., of four Byzantine mosaics created in the early sixth century. The mosaics, made of small chips of colored glass, were originally affixed to and for centuries remained in a church in Cyprus, a small island in the Mediterranean. In 1974, Turkish military forces invaded Cyprus and seized control of northern Cyprus, including the region where the church is located. At some point in the latter 1970s, during the Turkish military occupation of northern Cyprus, the mosaics were removed from their hallowed sanctuary. * * * [They were then smuggled into Germany where they were kept in hiding for several years until the defendant agreed to buy them following negotiations that took place in the Netherlands. The mosaics were then transported to the free trade zone of the Geneva airport in Switzerland where the defendant took delivery of them and shipped them immediately to Indiana, her home state.] The defendants * * * claim that * * * Goldberg should be awarded the mosaics because she purchased them in good faith and without information or reasonable notice that they were stolen. Having heard and reviewed all the evidence in the case, the Court concludes that possession of the mosaics must be awarded to the plaintiff, the Autocephalous Greek-Orthodox Church of Cyprus.

The Court concludes that because the place where the mosaics were purchased, Switzerland, has an insignificant relationship to this suit, and because Indiana has greater contacts and a more significant relationship to this suit, the substantive law of the state of Indiana should apply to this case. Under Indiana law, a thief obtains no title to or right to possession of stolen items. Therefore, a thief cannot pass any right of ownership of stolen items to subsequent purchasers. Because the mosaics were stolen from the rightful owner, the Church of Cyprus, Goldberg never obtained title to or right to possession of the mosaics. Under this analysis of Indiana law, it is unnecessary to consider whether Goldberg exercised good faith or due diligence in obtaining possession of the mosaics.

In the alternative, the Court considers the issues under Swiss law. Under Swiss law, in certain situations a thief may sell and pass good title to stolen items to a good faith purchaser. Whether one qualifies as a good faith purchaser is determined by evaluating certain factors. These factors are evaluated to determine whether the purchaser knew that the seller lacked title, or whether an honest and careful purchaser would have had doubts with respect to the seller's capacity to transfer property rights, and if so, then whether the purchaser reasonably inquired about the seller's ability to pass good title. Evaluating those factors under the facts of this case, the Court concludes that Goldberg is not a good faith purchaser under Swiss law. This is so because suspicious circumstances surrounded the sale of the mosaics which should have caused an honest and reasonably prudent purchaser in Goldberg's position to doubt whether the seller had the capacity to convey property rights, and because she failed to conduct a reasonable inquiry to resolve that doubt.

Therefore, principally under Indiana law and alternatively under Swiss law, Goldberg never obtained good title to or the right to possession of the mosaics. The Church of Cyprus, the original and rightful owner of the mosaics, has requested and made a proper showing for the return of the mosaics. The mosaics are unique. The paramount significance of their existence is as part of the religious, artistic, and cultural heritage of the Church and the Government of Cyprus, and as a part of the national unity of the Republic of Cyprus. Therefore, the Court orders that possession of the mosaics is awarded to the plaintiff, the Autocephalous Greek-Orthodox Church of Cyprus. * * *

IV. STATUTE OF LIMITATIONS. A federal district court sitting in diversity must follow state statutes of limitations. *Guaranty Trust Co. of New York v. York*, 326 U.S. 99 (1945). Moreover, a federal district court sitting in diversity must follow the choice-of-law rules of the state in which it sits. *Klaxon v. Elec. Mfg. Co.*, [infra Ch. 6]. Because in Indiana statutes of limitations are procedural in nature, Indiana choice-of-law rules state that the statute of limitations of the forum state, Indiana, will apply. [cit.] The Indiana code provides in relevant part:

> The following actions shall be commenced within six [6] years after the cause of action has accrued and not afterwards. ....
>
> Third. For injuries to property other than personal property, damages for any detention thereof, and for recovering possession of personal property.

* * * [T]he Court concludes that the Indiana statute of limitations providing specifically "for recovering possession of personal property" governs the issue of possession of the mosaics. Therefore, the plaintiffs' action is governed by a six-year statute of limitations.

Sometime between August 1976, when military force and threat of harm had forced church officials to leave the church involuntarily, and November 1979, the mosaics were removed from the Kanakaria Church. In November 1979 church and government officials first learned that the mosaics were missing from the Kanakaria Church. Goldberg acquired the mosaics in July 1988. The plaintiffs first learned that the mosaics were in Goldberg's possession in late 1988. The plaintiffs filed this action against Goldberg in March 1989. The defendants argue that the plaintiffs' cause of action first accrued in 1979 and that, because the complaint was not filed within six years thereof, plaintiffs' cause of action is barred. * * *

The Court holds that the plaintiffs' cause of action did not accrue in this case until the plaintiffs, using due diligence, knew or were on reasonable notice of the identity of the possessor of the mosaics. In this context a discovery rule should apply and prevent the statute from running until the plaintiffs knew or reasonably should have known who possessed the mosaics. * * *

V. CHOICE-OF-LAW. * * * *A. Indiana Law Analysis.* Indiana's traditional choice-of-law doctrine was *lex loci delicti commissi*, which dictated that the place where the wrong was committed governed which state's substantive law to apply. *Hubbard Mfg. Co., Inc. v. Greeson*, 515 N.E.2d 1071, 1073 (Ind.1987). This traditional rule has been modified, however. In *W.H. Barber Co. v. Hughes*, 63 N.E.2d 417 (Ind.1945), the traditional *lex loci* rule was modified in the area of contract law. "The modified rule allowed the state with the most significant contacts to apply its substantive law even if the breach occurred in another state." *Hubbard*, [cit.]. Similarly, in *Hubbard, supra*, the Indiana supreme court modified the traditional rule in the area of tort law, and adopted the "most significant contacts" analysis in torts as well as in contracts. [cit.] Today, *Hubbard* is the leading case to discuss Indiana's choice-of-law rules.[13]

In *Hubbard*, the Indiana supreme court adopted a two-step analysis to be used in determining choice of substantive law. The first step is to consider whether the place of the wrong "bears little connection" to the legal action. [cit.] If the contact is significant, then the Court must apply the substantive law of the state (or jurisdiction) where the wrong was committed. *Id.* The place where the wrong was committed in the present case is Switzerland; it was there that Goldberg took possession of and control over the mosaics. Switzerland "bears little connection" to the plaintiffs' cause of action. Neither the plaintiffs nor the defendants are citizens of Switzerland. None of the other individuals involved in the sale of the mosaics, namely, Dikman, Fitzgerald, van Rijn, or Faulk is a citizen of Switzerland. No Swiss citizen earned a profit on the sale of the mosaics, nor does any Swiss citizen own any interest in the mosaics.

Switzerland's lack of significant contacts is also highlighted by the fact that the mosaics never entered the Swiss stream of commerce. The mosaics were on Swiss soil no more than four days, during which time they remained in the free port area of the Geneva airport. The mosaics never passed through Swiss customs.

The defendants stress the fact that the money used to finance the purchase of the mosaics passed from Merchants Bank in Indianapolis to Goldberg, *via* a Swiss bank. However, the Swiss bank did not loan Goldberg money, nor does it have any security interest in the transaction. The Swiss bank merely served as a conduit to pass the funds from Merchants in Indianapolis to Goldberg. Defendants also dwell on the fact that the sale was consummated in Switzerland while both the buyer and seller were in that country. However, most of the negotiations for the sale occurred in The Netherlands, not Switzerland. Any contacts Switzerland may have had to the transaction at the heart of this suit were fortuitous and transitory. Switzerland has no significant interest in the application of its law to this suit. For the foregoing reasons, the Court concludes that Switzerland "bears little connection" to this suit; its contacts to this case are insignificant.

After a court has determined that the place where the wrong was committed bears little connection to the legal action, the second step in the *Hubbard* analysis is to apply additional factors to determine which state or jurisdiction has the more significant relationship or contacts. [cit.] Among the factors a court may consider are:

    (1) the place where the conduct causing the injury occurred;

    (2) the residence or place of business of the parties; and

    (3) the place where the relationship is centered.

[cit.] The Court concludes, after weighing these and other relevant factors, that

---

13. No Indiana case discusses choice-of-law rules in the context of a replevin action. However, *Hubbard* and *Barber* are significant in that they demonstrate the Indiana supreme court's modifications to Indiana's traditional *lex loci* rule. These modifications clearly indicate Indiana's shift to the most significant contacts analysis in choice-of-law determinations. [cit.] Therefore, this Court believes that the analysis set forth in *Hubbard* provides the proper analytical framework for the choice-of-law issue presented in a replevin case such as this.

    Further, the Court notes that conversion, a cause of action very similar to replevin, is a tort and therefore would fall under *Hubbard's* most significant contacts analysis for choice-of-law purposes. The fact that conversion would be analyzed under the most significant contacts approach is further support for this Court's decision to analyze this action for replevin under the most significant contacts approach as well.

Indiana has the most significant contacts to this suit. Therefore, Indiana law applies.

Indiana's contacts to this suit are more significant than those of any other jurisdiction. Defendant Peg Goldberg is a citizen of Indiana. Defendant Goldberg & Feldman Fine Arts, Inc. is an Indiana corporation with its principal place of business in Indiana. The purchase of the mosaics was effected largely through the efforts of an Indiana art dealer, Robert Fitzgerald. The purchase of the mosaics was financed by a loan obtained from an Indiana bank, Merchants; Merchants presently holds a security interest in the mosaics in the amount of $1,200,000. Several Indiana residents (Goldberg, Fitzgerald, Dr. Bick, Frenzel) and one Indiana corporation (Merchants) hold an interest in any profits realized on the resale of the mosaics. The original resale agreement among Goldberg, Fitzgerald, van Rijn, and Faulk stipulated that Indiana law would govern any disputes arising out of the agreement. This indicates Goldberg's belief that the laws of her home state, Indiana, were more significant to this transaction. Finally, the mosaics are presently in Indiana and have been in Indiana since they were transported from Geneva in July 1988. For these reasons, Indiana has a significant interest in the application of its law to this transaction. Therefore, the Court concludes that Indiana has the most significant contacts to this suit. Indiana law applies.

B. Swiss Law Analysis. The conclusion that Indiana substantive law applies in this case is bolstered by Swiss choice-of-law principles. As Professor Arthur von Mehren testified at trial:

> The choice of law rules of another system may assist in certain cases a forum in determining its ultimate choice of the applicable law * * * . [I]t may be of interest to the forum and of help to the forum in reaching a conclusion to consider what view would be taken by the courts of another legal order if the matter were before those courts.

Tr. 9 (von Mehren). This Court will now examine Swiss choice-of-law principles for whatever light they may shed on the issue of which jurisdiction's substantive law should be applied under the facts of this case. Swiss choice-of-law rules also dictate that Indiana substantive law should control.

As a general rule, Swiss law applies the so-called *lex situs* principle in determining choice-of-law in cases where the ownership of tangible, movable property is disputed. *Id.* at 10. Under the *lex situs* rule, a forum court must apply the substantive law of the place where the tangible, movable property was physically located at the time of its sale. *Id.* If this general rule applies in the present case, then Swiss law governs because the mosaics were physically present in Switzerland when the sale was consummated. However, the general rule does not apply in this case.

Swiss law recognizes an exception to the general *lex situs* rule. As Professor von Mehren explained, under Swiss choice-of-law rules,

> an exception is made for situations in which the goods though physically present, have only a fortuitous and transitory or casual connection with the legal order in question. This is often expressed as the exception for goods in transit.

Id. at 10, 11. If a transaction falls within this "in transit" exception, then the law of the situs does not apply; instead, the law of the place of destination applies. *Id.* at 11.

In the case *sub judice*, the place of destination is Indiana. Therefore, if the exception for property in transit applies, then Indiana substantive law governs.

The Court agrees with Professor von Mehren's opinion that the "in transit" exception applies in this case. Id. at 18. The mosaics were transported from Munich to Geneva. Upon their arrival in Geneva, the mosaics were placed in storage in the free port area of the Geneva airport; there they remained in storage for four days until being shipped to Indianapolis. The mosaics never passed through Swiss customs. The mosaics never entered the Swiss stream of commerce. Their presence in Switzerland was temporary, as was intended. Those involved with the transaction intended that if the sale were consummated, the mosaics were to be shipped to Indiana; if not, the mosaics were to be returned to Germany. For the foregoing reasons, the Court concludes that under Swiss law the "in transit" exception to the general *lex situs* rule would apply. Therefore, the law of the place of destination controls, which in this case is Indiana. Accordingly, Swiss choice-of-law rules would agree with this Court's earlier conclusion that Indiana substantive law controls under the facts of this case. * * *

Notes and Questions

1. ***Immovables***. As we have seen in Chapter 2, under the traditional theory, the law of the situs reigned supreme with regard to all issues pertaining to rights in immovable property. Neither the Restatement (Second) nor judicial practice during the conflicts revolution have done much to reduce the dominance of the *lex rei sitae*. For example, of the nine sections the Restatement (Second) devotes to immovables (§§ 223–232), two sections (§ 227, acquisition by adverse possession, and § 229, foreclosure of mortgage) call for the application of the "local law of the situs," while the remaining seven sections authorize the application of "the law that would be applied by the courts of the situs." The latter phrase is always accompanied by the adage: "These courts would usually apply their own local law in determining such questions." In Chapter 2, supra at 38–40, we examined the arguments for and against the situs rule. You may wish to review those arguments with the benefit of the knowledge you have acquired from Chapter 3.

2. ***Movables***. Despite its shortcomings, the situs rule has one undeniable advantage with regard to immovables: it is certain and predictable. The same is not true with regard to movables, which may move or be moved from one state to another. Thus, any choice-of-law rule that is based on situs as the exclusive connecting factor must confront the possibility that there may be more than one situs, a phenomenon that Europeans descriptively call *conflit mobile*. Rigid adherence to the law of the first situs would ignore the legitimate interest of the second situs in protecting persons who acquire rights in justifiable reliance upon the law of the second situs. Conversely, rigid adherence to the law of the second situs would lead to the divestiture of rights created while the thing was situated in the first situs. The conflict between the law of the two situses must be resolved in a way that takes into account the legitimate interests of each situs, without frustrating justified party expectations and without running afoul of the constitutionally sanctioned

principle that the mere movement of a thing from one state to another without more should not alter existing rights in that thing.

3. *The Restatement (Second)* restates the above-mentioned principle in § 247, which provides that "interests in a chattel are not affected by the mere removal of the chattel to another state." The same section provides, however, that "[s]uch interests * * * may be affected by dealings with the chattel in the other state." Id. Although it does not explain what exactly can affect such interests, the Restatement (Second) provides pointers that assist the search for answers. First, the Restatement draws the all-important distinction between the effect of a conveyance of an interest in a chattel: (a) as between the parties to the conveyance; and (b) vis a vis third parties, such as a person who has a pre-existing interest in that chattel. With regard to (a), the Restatement provides that the applicable law is the law of "the state which, with respect to the particular issue, has the most significant relationship to the parties, the chattel and the conveyance under the principles stated in § 6," and that, in identifying that state, "greater weight will usually be given to the location of the chattel * * * at the time of the conveyance than to any other contact." § 244. With regard to (b), the Restatement provides that the applicable law will "usually be * * * the law that would be applied by the courts of the state where the chattel was at the time of the conveyance * * * and that [t]hese courts would usually apply their own local law." § 245. For a recent case following the above provisions, see Lurie v. Blackwell, 51 P.3d 846 (Wyo. 2002) (holding that neither the chattel's removal from Missouri to Wyoming nor the owner's subsequent movement to Montana altered his rights in a chattel he acquired in Missouri as tenant by the entirety, even though neither Wyoming nor Montana recognized tenancies by the entirety). For security interests governed by the Uniform Commercial Code, see UCC §§ 9-301 through 9-307.

If the *Autocephalous* court[1] were to apply these sections of the Restatement (Second), would the outcome be the same or different? Why?

4. Art thievery and trade in stolen antiquities has been characterized as "the second international criminal activity after narcotics," and is estimated to net from one to ten billion dollars annually. Drum, *Haven for Stolen Art*, 9. See also Moore, *Antiquities Market*, 468 n. 12 and authorities cited therein. *Autocephalous* is one of several cases that have reached the American courts in recent years. For other such cases, see, e.g., Government of Peru v. Johnson, 720 F.Supp. 810 (C.D.Cal.1989), *aff'd without opinion* 933 F.2d 1013 (9th Cir.1991) (pre-Colombian artifacts); O'Keeffe v. Snyder, 416 A.2d 862 (N.J.1980) (O'Keeffe paintings); Mucha v. King, 792 F.2d 602 (7th. Cir.1986) (Mucha paintings); Kunstsammlungen Zu Weimar v. Elicofon, 678 F.2d 1150 (2d Cir.1982) (Dürer paintings); De Weerth v. Baldinger, 836 F.2d 103 (2d Cir.1987) *cert. denied*, 486 U.S. 1056 (1988) (Monet painting). Of the voluminous literature on this subject, the most exhaustive is Siehr, *International Art Trade*.

---

1. In the interest of full disclosure, it should be noted that author Symeonides, in addition to being a Cypriot, has served as consultant for plaintiffs and does not pretend to be unbiased.

5. Suppose that under the law of Cyprus, the mosaics, because of their ancient origin and religious and cultural significance, were classified as *rea extra commercium* (things out of commerce) and thus as insusceptible of being acquired by a private person, either through transfer or through adverse possession or acquisitive prescription. Suppose further that, after the thief of the mosaics had transported them to Germany, he did not keep them in hiding but instead possessed them "openly and publicly" for more than ten years. Finally, suppose that under German law a person, even the thief, who openly and publicly possesses a movable for more than ten years acquires ownership of it by acquisitive prescription. The Restatement (Second) provides that the acquisition of a chattel by adverse possession or prescription is governed by "the local law of the state where the chattel was at the time the transfer is claimed to have taken place." § 246. Here, of course, there was no "transfer" from one person to another, but the thief could claim that a transfer was effected by operation of German law at the moment he completed ten years in possession. If this argument were accepted, how would this conflict be resolved under § 246? How should a neutral court resolve this conflict under another policy-based approach, such as comparative impairment?

6. In *Autocephalous*, a transfer was attempted in Switzerland, the law of which--if interpreted most favorably to the transferee--could have vested title in the transferee had she been in good faith. If, unlike Ms. Goldberg, the transferee had been in good faith, how would a neutral court applying comparative impairment resolve the resulting conflict?

7. Moving now to Indiana, the *Autocephalous* court was correct to conclude that, in light of Switzerland's minimal, prefabricated, and transient contacts with the case, that country could not have a legitimate claim to apply its law. The court also concluded that, because Switzerland's contacts with the case were minimal, Indiana's relationship with the case was "the *most* significant." As between these two jurisdictions, the latter conclusion was correct. However, to the extent that the use of the superlative "most" may imply comparison with other involved jurisdictions, was this latter conclusion also correct with regard to Cyprus? Suppose, for example, that the law of Indiana conflicted with the law of Cyprus in that Indiana law protected the defendant while Cyprus law protected the plaintiffs. In such a case, would Indiana, where the mosaics had been secretively brought and kept for a few weeks, have had a more significant relationship than did Cyprus where the mosaics had been publicly and lawfully kept for over fourteen centuries? In answering this question, keep in mind that "no dealings with the chattel" (Restatement (Second) § 247) involving third parties had taken place within Indiana. The only attempted "deal" was in California where the defendant had offered to sell the mosaics to the Getty museum for the modest price of $28 million. The museum's curator politely refused the offer and notified the plaintiffs. The plaintiffs offered to buy back the mosaics but the defendant refused the offer.

8. *Why be more Roman than the Romans?* Does this saying partly describe the result in *Autocephalous*? If a Swiss court would not have applied Swiss law and in fact would have applied Indiana law, then why should an Indiana court do otherwise, especially when its own conflicts rules also pointed to Indiana law? To

the extent that the selection of the applicable law is based on the "wishes" of the other state to apply its law, aren't the choice-of-law rules of that state authentic statements of such wishes? Whether you call this notion *renvoi* or something else, it is a notion that is implicit in all modern policy-based analyses, including the one followed in *Autocephalous*.

9. The *Autocephalous* court applied Indiana property law and concluded that under that law the defendant could not have acquired ownership of the mosaics. However, the court also examined whether plaintiff's action to regain possession of the mosaics was barred by Indiana's statute of limitation. Characterizing statutes of limitation as procedural, the court concluded that the Indiana statute applied and that it did not bar the action. This issue, and especially the trial court's application of the discovery rule, was strongly contested on appeal, but the appellate court affirmed. See 917 F.2d 278 (7th Cir.1990).

Suppose, however, that the Indiana statute of limitation did bar the action. In such a case, the plaintiffs, despite their ownership, could not recover possession of the mosaics, and the defendant, despite her lack of ownership, would not be required to relinquish possession of them. Is there not something anomalous in such a result? If not, why? If yes, does the problem lie with Indiana's internal law, or is it a problem of conflicts law? Civil-law systems avoid this anomaly, both in their conflicts law and in their property law. As we have seen earlier, see supra 388 n.4, civil-law systems characterize issues of statutes of limitation as substantive and subject them to the same law as that which governs the merits of the action. Moreover, the property law of most civil-law systems adheres to the fundamental principle that ownership is never lost by the owner's non-use alone, although it may be lost as a result of adverse use by another person who meets the requirements of acquisitive prescription. Until such prescription accrues, however, the owner's action to recover possession of a thing he owns is not subject to any statute of limitation (called *liberative prescription*). In 1990, a New York court saw this problem in the same light and corrected lower courts and federal courts that had held otherwise. See Solomon R. Guggenheim Foundation v. Lubell, 550 N.Y.S.2d 618, 622 (Sup.Ct. 1990), *aff'd* 569 N.E.2d 426 (N.Y.1991) (involving a stolen Chagal *gouache*).

10. In 1991, the Institute of International Law proposed a rule providing that "[t]he transfer of ownership of works of art belonging to the cultural heritage of the country of origin shall be governed by the law of that country." See 81 *Revue critique*, 203 (1992). Do you think that such a rule is likely to be adopted in United States? Why, or why not? Does the following rule have a better chance?

> A person who is considered the owner of a thing under the law of the state in which the thing is situated at the time of the theft shall be entitled to the protection of that law even if the thing is later removed to another state whose law denies such protection, unless: (a) the other state has a materially greater connection to the case; *and* (b) the person knew or should have known of facts that would enable a diligent owner to take effective legal action against the possessor of the thing.

Symeonides, *On the Side of the Angels*, 752.

I. MARITAL PROPERTY

Hughes v. Hughes

Supreme Court of New Mexico, 1978.
91 N.M. 339, 573 P.2d 1194.

EASLEY, J. This suit for divorce and division of property was filed by plaintiff-appellant, Darthy Lindberg Hughes (Mrs. Hughes) against defendant-appellee-cross-appellant, James Lindberg Hughes (Col. Hughes). Mrs. Hughes appealed, claiming errors in the division of property by the trial judge.

We affirm in part and reverse in part.

The principal issue is particularly troublesome and is one of first impression in New Mexico. The resolution of the question may very materially affect the property rights of tens of thousands of New Mexico married people who were domiciled in and acquired money and property in non-community property jurisdictions, then sold the property, moved to New Mexico and invested their money in property in this state.[1]

The following are the essential facts necessary to frame the issue. The parties were first legally domiciled in Iowa, a "common-law" state where a wife has no vested interest in the wages of the husband or in property purchased with those wages. Money, accumulated solely from the wages of Col. Hughes while the parties were domiciled in Iowa, was later used to supply all the down payment on certain ranch property and more than one-half the down payment on some [115] apartments [situated in New Mexico and purchased after t]he parties became legal domiciliaries of New Mexico. The property doubled in value. This action was brought to obtain a divorce and divide the property.

The question: on divorce of a New Mexico couple, what are the wife's rights to share in the husband's separate property invested in this state but which was accumulated from his earnings during their marriage while domiciled in a non-community property state? * * *

CLAIMS OF THE PARTIES. Mrs. Hughes claims that at all times Col. Hughes represented to her and others that the ranch and apartments were to be jointly owned by them and that income therefrom would furnish the family additional support after Col. Hughes' retirement from the military service. She maintains that both the ranch and the 115 apartments are community property, or in the alternative, are the joint property of the parties and should be equally divided. She asserts that Col. Hughes is estopped to deny her one-half interest, or in the alternative, that he contracted with her for the ownership of a one-half interest.

She complains that Col. Hughes is relying on the Iowa law to establish his claim that all of the assets brought into New Mexico were his separate property, but that under the Iowa law, when a divorce is granted in that state, the courts equitably divide the husband's property with the wife, taking into consideration the wife's

---

1. 1970 Census figures show that 40% of the total population of New Mexico came from another state. [cit.]

contribution to the accumulation of the assets of the marriage.

Col. Hughes maintains that the ranch and the 115 apartments are his separate property by reason of having been purchased with separate property brought into this state from another jurisdiction. He contends that he never intended to vest a one-half interest in his property in New Mexico in his wife and that he took no actions and said nothing upon which she could base claims of estoppel or contract.

DECISION OF THE TRIAL COURT. The trial court decided that since all the money paid down on the ranch and more than half of that paid down on the 115 apartments was accumulated or borrowed while Col. Hughes was a resident of a common-law state, those properties were his sole and separate estate and that Mrs. Hughes would be allowed only the value of her one-half community property contribution to the subsequent annual payments. Under the trial court's decision the practical effect is that the appreciation in value of approximately $200,000.00 in the ranch and 115 apartments would be the property of Col. Hughes in which Mrs. Hughes would have no share.

CONFLICTS IN MARITAL–PROPERTY LAW. Migration of millions of people from the common-law marital-property states into the eight states, including New Mexico, that follow the civil law, or community property, system of marital property, has focused a great deal of attention on the conflicts between the two different legal systems. It seems inconceivable, to persons who have become accustomed to the concept of community ownership of all assets acquired during marriage, that a vast majority of the women in the United States do not have the advantage of those rights.

We disagree with the outmoded marital property systems of the non-community property states. We hold that the bare legal principle urged by Col. Hughes, that a wife has no interest in the wages, earnings, and profits of the husband or in the property accumulated by his efforts, can be characterized as a relic of the dark ages that should have equal place with the ancient cliche that "a woman's place is in the home, barefoot and pregnant." As will hereafter appear, even the common-law states have engrafted some exceptions onto the principle of the husband's sole ownership.

It comes as no surprise in this era of awakening of American womanhood that legislatures and courts in the common-law states are straining mightily to upgrade the marital-property rights of women.

The reasonableness of community ownership of marital property has been recognized by courts in non-community property states. It has been rightfully held that, viewed solely as a matter of economy, the labor, pain, and drudgery required of the mother in sustaining the home, giving birth to and rearing the children will often more than offset the contribution of the father to the family budget. * * *

Under community property law no distinction is made between husband and wife in respect to the right each has in the community property. The husband receives no higher or better title than does the wife. The plain public policy that this law expresses is that the wife shall have equal rights and equal dignity and shall be an equal benefactor in the matrimonial gain. "It is altogether fitting and proper that woman should be thus esteemed by the law in fixing her status if she is to be considered in fact as well as in theory an essential factor in the economy of the marital community." *La Tourette v. La Tourette*, 137 P. 426, 428 (Ariz.1914).

On the other hand, the non-community property states, including Iowa, where Col. Hughes was legally domiciled when he earned the money paid on the New Mexico property, hold to the principle that property accumulated by use of the husband's wages is his separate property. This conflicts with the community property concept of New Mexico. The first question that arises is whose law do we apply to determine the nature of the property in question?

This Court has followed what is overwhelmingly the general rule that funds or property, brought in from a non-community property state where the funds or property were there considered to be the separate property of an individual, will retain the same character when traceable into New Mexico property. [cit.] Therefore, it is clear from our decisions that where Col. Hughes brought money, accumulated from original earnings, into New Mexico it remained his separate property when it crossed the state line and was later invested here. We therefore resolve the conflict of laws in favor of applying the Iowa law to determine the character of the property traced to Col. Hughes' earnings.

The question then arises as to what law we apply to determine whether Mrs. Hughes has a legal or equitable right to have any portion of Col. Hughes' separate property awarded to her in this divorce action. It is at this juncture that we step into the quagmire.

Textwriters and other legal scholars have attempted for years to reconcile the morass of theories relating to community property and the conflicts-of-law. * * * There is surprisingly little law on the subject, and none in New Mexico, but the problem is evident in divorce cases as well as in the distribution of decedent's estates. Col. Hughes urges that when his money, classified as "separate" under Iowa law, was invested in New Mexico property, it remained "separate" and that therefore his wife has no interest, and, ipso facto, the husband takes all. Only a few courts in community property states have considered the issue, but they have held that separate property as defined in common-law jurisdictions is not the same creature as separate property under community property law. It is a case of comparing apples and oranges. *See, e. g., Rau v. Rau*, 432 P.2d 910 (Ariz.App.1967).

There are two distinct interpretations. Although wives in common-law states have no legal title to property purchased with the husband's earnings, the case law in those states has created many benefits, incidents, and immunities in favor of wives that attach themselves to such separate marital property. Therefore the wife, in many common-law states and certainly in Iowa, has inchoate equitable rights to her husband's separate property where she has made contributions to preserving and bettering that property, whereas in a typical community property state she has no such rights since she has community property rights instead. There is an obvious difference between property which first acquires its separate nature while the husband is domiciled in a community property state and his separate property that can be traced to property acquired in a common-law state where the wife has inchoate equitable rights in that property. * * *

[The court discusses *Rau v. Rau, supra,* and *Berle v. Berle*, 546 P.2d 407 (Idaho 1976), which had applied the law of the former domicile both for classifying and for distributing the property acquired in that state.]

Professor Marsh in his concise treatise, *Marital Property in Conflicts of Law* (1952), * * * points out that there is a great divergence in the laws of common-law states as well as the community property states regarding the meaning of various terms, including property terms, and the "characterization" given them under the laws of the various states. He calls attention to the complicated interplay of the laws regarding marital property with the laws of succession, taxes, divorces, dower, homestead, immunities, and other matters.

Marsh's theory is that where the law of the forum calls for looking at the law of another state, it is logical and reasonable to look at all of the law of the latter state and all dispositive rules, claims and legal relations. He favors applying the law of the selected jurisdiction as a whole, not merely part of such foreign law, prematurely chosen. * * *

It is to the credit of the California legislature that a more direct approach has been adopted to solve this conflicts problem. For a period of years extending from 1917 to 1961 the California legislature attempted to find a solution to the difference in marital-property laws. A legislative act created what is called "quasi-community property," which designates property acquired by a person domiciled outside California, which property would be separate property by the law of that domicile but which would have been community property if acquired while domiciled in California. Upon divorce, quasi-community property is to be divided in the same way as community property.

In *Addison v. Addison*, 399 P.2d 897 (Cal.1965) the supreme court held the above California statute constitutional.

We take into consideration the basic public policy of this state, the sociological impact of the rule we here establish and the purpose to be achieved by divorce and property settlement litigation. The state clearly has a vital interest in the community estate. It is obvious from our statutory framework concerning marital relationships, their creation, their dissolution and the manner in which the parties to the marriage may hold property, that the state deems itself to be an interested party. [cit.]

It follows that New Mexico courts should make a choice of laws that would achieve a fair division of marital property considering all of the circumstances and laws involved.

Although our statutes permit the invasion of a spouse's separate property under certain circumstances, § 22-7-6 B(1), N.M.S.A.1953 (Supp.1975), our legislature has not taken what appears to be a very desirable step as was done by the California lawmakers. Thus, it devolves upon this Court to make a choice of laws between those applicable in the State of New Mexico and those applicable in the State of Iowa to determine the extent to which Col. Hughes' separate property may be awarded to Mrs. Hughes. Although the property traceable to Col. Hughes' earnings was clearly his separate property, we hold that the characterization of this property as separate must be made under the applicable laws of the State of Iowa and therefore the property is subject to all the wife's incidents of ownership, claims, rights and legal relations provided in any and all of the laws of the State of Iowa that affect marital property.

Unjust results would obtain by applying the narrow interpretation of the term "separate" as it applies to property originally acquiring its separate character in New Mexico to the property involved in this case. We hold that such a misapplication is against the public policy of this state. It is unconscionable that Mrs. Hughes would, as a practical matter, be deprived of all interest in approximately $200,000.00 in property value, which was accumulated by the joint efforts of both parties, by a blind acceptance of a definition that considers only one of many applicable laws or factors. We must look to the whole law of Iowa bearing on marital property to determine the parties' rights in this property.

MARITAL PROPERTY UNDER IOWA LAW. Turning to the Iowa law, we find that state's supreme court frequently asserting that each case must be considered on its own fact situation. Although recognizing the legal principle that property accumulated from the husband's earnings is his separate property, the courts in divorce cases almost always award the wife a large part of the property acquired during coverture. In looking at a variety of these property division cases, we find that the amount of the husband's separate property that is given to the wife under circumstances fairly analogous to those in the instant case ranges from one-third to two-thirds of the property involved.

In *Schantz v. Schantz*, 163 N.W.2d 398 (Iowa 1968) the Iowa Supreme Court set forth guidelines to be used in awarding alimony and making a distribution of property on divorce. These included: the duration of the marriage; number of children, their ages and needs; net worth of property acquired with contributions of each party by labor or otherwise and net worth and present income of each party; conduct of the spouse; physical and mental health of each party; earning capacity of each party; training, education and life expectancy of each party; any sacrifice by either spouse in furthering or preserving the marriage; standards of living and the ability of one party balanced against the relative needs of the other; any other relevant factors which aid in reaching a fair and equitable determination as to respective rights. * * *

The trial court in our case found that the money in question that was paid as down payments on the ranch and the 115 apartments was borrowed or accumulated while the parties were domiciled in a common-law state. Based solely on these findings, the court concluded as a matter of law that Mrs. Hughes was not entitled to any share in these properties, except to receive the value of her share of the community funds used to pay for the same. We hold that the court entertained an erroneous belief as to the applicable law, having no guidance from New Mexico case law. The court obviously felt that the wife had absolutely no legal or equitable claim to a portion of this property.

We reverse the trial court on this issue and remand for that court to consider Mrs. Hughes' right to a share of these properties in light of this decision and the applicable Iowa case law. * * * *It is so ordered.*

Notes and Questions

1. **SUBSTANTIVE LAW:** *(a) Community–Property States.* As *Hughes* indicates, New Mexico is one of the eight states of the United States that adhere to the Spanish-based system of community property. The other seven states are Arizona, California, Idaho, Louisiana, Nevada, Texas, and Washington.[1] The rest of the states adhere to the common-law based separate-property system. In a community-property system, spouses who live under the regime of community property[2] co-own in a 50:50 ratio all property that is acquired by either of them during the marriage and is not classified as the separate property of the acquiring spouse. The definitions of community and separate property vary slightly from state to state but, generally, separate property encompasses property that a spouse owned before marriage and any property a spouse inherits or receives as gift during marriage. Whatever is not classified as separate property is (or is presumed to be), community property, and this includes the earnings of either spouse during marriage. The community-property regime terminates by a judgment of divorce or separation, or by the death of either spouse. When the regime terminates, the community property is subject to a 50:50 partition at the instance of either spouse or his or her heirs. Because most property is likely to be community property, the separate property of each spouse is in principle free of any claims in favor of the other. Thus, upon divorce, the separate property is not subject to partition, and, upon the death of the owning spouse, this property is not subject to inheritance rights in favor of the surviving spouse.

(b) Separate–Property States. Separate-property states begin with the premise that marriage does not affect the property acquisitions of either spouse. Thus, each spouse owns fully and exclusively property he or she acquired during the marriage. However, these states exhibit the same concern for protecting the non-acquiring spouse as do community-property states. While community-property states protect the non-earning spouse *during* the marriage by granting her or him a 50% present proprietary interest in all property classified as community property, separate property states protect the non-earning spouse through rights such as dower and equitable distribution that materialize *at the end* of the marriage. Thus, in cases of death of one spouse, the surviving spouse has a right to "take against the will" of the deceased spouse a certain portion (e.g., one-third or one-fourth) of all the property of the deceased, including, in some cases, property that would be classified as separate property in a community property state. In cases of divorce, courts following the "equitable distribution" doctrine described in *Hughes* may give to the non-owning spouse as much of the property of the owning spouse as is "fair and

---

1. Wisconsin also adheres to a form of community property, having adopted the Uniform Marital Property Act in 1983 which approximates the community-property system. See 9A U.L.A. 97 (1987). In the rest of the world, the legal systems of the French and Spanish legal families generally adhere to this system.

2. Despite contrary popular belief, not all spouses who live in a community-property state are subject to a community property regime. Rather, that regime (called "legal regime") applies only to the extent that the spouses have not validly agreed to displace it. Before marriage, prospective spouses are free to opt for a separate-property regime or, within certain limits, to modify the legal regime. During marriage, the spouses may also agree to modify or opt out of the legal regime in certain narrowly defined circumstances. One of those circumstances is when the spouses move to a community-property state.

equitable under the circumstances." This may in some cases reach or exceed 50% of the property and it may include property that would be classified as separate property in a community-property state. See Symeonides, *Migrant Spouses*, 12–14, 24–25.

2. **THE CONFLICTS PROBLEM.** Conflicts problems abound in this area of the law. Even when spouses are not as mobile as were the Hughes, spouses may live in a separate-property state and acquire immovable property in a community-property state, or *vice versa*. Which law should govern the respective interests of the spouses in such property? Civil-law systems focus on the spouses rather than on the property's location and generally assign these matters to the law that governs the marital relationship (usually the law of the matrimonial domicile) rather than the law of the situs of the property. Even these systems, however, encounter a difficult dilemma in cases like *Hughes* in which the spouses change their matrimonial domicile. In such cases, civil-law systems vacillate between the principle of immutability and the principle of mutability of the law governing the matrimonial regime. Thus, some systems take the position that the law governing the regime at the beginning of the marital relationship should remain applicable at the end of the relationship, regardless of any intervening change of domicile.[3] Other systems provide that the change of matrimonial domicile brings about a change in the law governing the matrimonial regime, a change that may be partial or total, prospective only or retrospective as well.[4] In all instances, these systems recognize the freedom of the spouses to agree on the law governing their property relations.[5] However, as is the case with other choice-of-law agreements, the spouses' agreement may not exceed the public policy limits of the otherwise governing law.

Common-law jurisdictions, including most American states that follow the community-property system, also recognize the spouses' freedom to agree on the governing law, subject to the same public policy limits. See, e.g., Restatement (Second) § 258(2). However, in contrast to civil-law systems, common-law systems focus *on the property* of the spouses, rather than on the spouses themselves. If the property in question is immovable, then the "whole law" of the situs state governs the respective rights of the spouses. See, e.g., Restatement (Second) §§ 233–34. If the property is movable, the applicable law is, in principle, the law of the state in which the acquiring spouse was domiciled *at the time of the acquisition*. See, id. § 258. The italicized phrase means that when the spouses change their domicile, movables they acquired in the new domicile will be governed by the law of the new domicile. Indeed, since the early 19th century, American conflicts law adopted the principle of *mutability* of the law governing the property relations of spouses. See Saul v. His Creditors, 5 Mart. (n.s.) 569 (La.1827). However, American conflicts law remains divided as to whether this mutability should be prospective only or

---

3. See, e.g., Peruvian Civ. Code, art. 2078; Argentine Draft, art. 24; Austrian codif. § 19; Greek Civ. Code, art. 15; Italian C.C., art. 19; Bustamante Code, art. 187.

4. See, e.g., Swiss codif. art. 55; German codif. art. 15; Hungarian codif. § 39; Spanish Civ. Code art. 9; and Hague Convention on the Law Applicable to Matrimonial Property Regimes, arts. 6–8 (1978).

5. See, e.g., Austrian codification, § 19; Italian Civ. Code, art. 19; German codification, art. 15(II); Swiss codification, arts. 52–53; Spanish Civ. Code, art. 9; Hague Convention on the Law Applicable to Matrimonial Property Regimes, art. 3.

retrospective as well, namely, whether movables the spouses acquired before the change of domicile should be governed by the law of the former or the new domicile. Before exploring this question, let us reiterate the obvious: the mere change of domicile does not *ipso facto* alter any existing property rights in assets previously acquired. See Restatement (Second) § 259. Rather, the question is whether the assets acquired in the former domicile should be subjected for certain purposes to the law of the new domicile, *when* a "critical" and pertinent event (e.g., the termination of the marriage by divorce or death) occurs after the change of domicile. The balance of this Note discusses the four approaches developed in the United States for answering this question.

3. **THE PROBLEM OF MOVING SPOUSES. a. FROM A SEPARATE–PROPERTY STATE TO A COMMUNITY–PROPERTY STATE.** Suppose that Henry and his wife Wilma lived most of their married lives in state X, a separate-property state. During that time, Henry acquired in his own name movable assets worth a total of $ 3 million, while Wilma stayed at home raising their children. Suppose that, under the law of state X: (a) in case divorce, Wilma would be entitled to 50% of Henry's $ 3 million under that state's equitable distribution doctrine; and that (b) in case of Henry's death before divorce, Wilma would be entitled to a statutory share of one-third of the $ 3 million. Suppose, however, that the "critical event," i.e., the divorce or Henry's death, occurs not while the spouses were domiciled in state X but rather six months after they moved their domicile to state Y, a community-property state. Wilma would then be before a state Y court, either in a divorce or a succession proceeding, asserting her rights or claims to the $ 3 million. Should the court determine these rights by applying the law of the former domicile, state X, or the law of the forum and present domicile, state Y.[6]

(1) The Traditional Approach. The first approach for answering this problem is the one the trial court applied in *Hughes*. It is referred to hereinafter as the "traditional approach." Under this approach, the court applies the law of the former domicile (state X) in determining the ownership of the property, i.e., in classifying it as community or separate, and then applies the law of the new domicile (state Y), the forum state, in distributing the property between the spouses. Since state X is a separate-property state, its law probably would not recognize the distinction between separate and community property. Consequently, all $3 million would be classified as Henry's separate property. Since state Y is a community-property state--and under its law the separate property of one spouse is, in principle, free of any claims in favor of the other--Wilma will receive *nothing* out of Henry's three million dollars. Is this bad? If yes, why? Does Wilma deserve any more sympathy than any other similarly situated "Wilma" who had lived all her life in state Y? If yes, why? Does this approach not distort the common policy of both the former and the new domicile? What is the common policy?

(2) The Pure Borrowed–Law Approach. The second approach is the one

---

6. Similar questions would arise if, with or without a change of domicile to state Y, Henry used the $3 million to buy an immovable in state Y. The questions then would be whether Wilma would be entitled to any rights in this immovable and whether this question should be answered under the law of state Y or state X.

employed by the Supreme Court of New Mexico in *Hughes*. Under this approach, the court applies the law of the former domicile (state X) both to classify and to distribute the property. This is the "pure borrowed-law approach" in that the forum borrows the law of the former domicile in its entirety. Under this approach, the court would award Wilma $1.5 million in a divorce proceeding and $1 million in a succession proceeding, that is, exactly the same amounts she would have received in a state X court. Do you see any problems with this approach?

(3) The Pure Quasi–Community Property Approach. The third approach is the pure "quasi-community approach." Under this approach, the court applies its own law (state Y) both to classify and to distribute the property. California was the first to develop this approach, and other community-property states like Texas have followed. California's version is more comprehensive in that, inter alia, it applies to both divorce cases and death cases. For divorce purposes, the California Family Code defines "quasi-community property" as including "all real or personal property, wherever situated, * * * acquired * * * by either spouse while domiciled elsewhere which would have been community property if the spouse who acquired the property had been domiciled in [California] at the time of its acquisition." Cal.Fam.Code § 4803.[7] Upon divorce or legal separation, the court is authorized to treat the quasi-community property as if it were community property and to divide it "equally" between the spouses. Cal.Fam.Code §§ 4800, 4800.5. For succession purposes, the California Probate Code defines "quasi-community property" as including "[a]ll personal property wherever situated, and all real property situated in [California] * * * acquired by a decedent while domiciled elsewhere that would have been the community property of the decedent and the surviving spouse if the decedent had been domiciled in [California] at the time of its acquisition." Cal.Prob.Code § 66. If the acquiring spouse dies while domiciled in California,[8] "one-half of the decedent's quasi-community property belongs to the surviving spouse and the other half belongs to the decedent." Cal.Prob.Code § 101.[9]

Thus, under the above provisions, if state Y were California, the amount that a California court would award Wilma would depend exclusively on how much of the $3 million would qualify as community property under California's internal law and hence as quasi-community property under the above provisions. If all of the $3 million would qualify as community property, then the court will award $1.5 million to Wilma, both in case of divorce and in case of Henry's death. If none of the $3 million would so qualify, then the court will award Wilma *nothing.* In between these two extremes lie several intermediate possibilities, but in most of them Wilma will receive less, or much less, than she would have received in state X. What do you

---

7. Section 5110 of the same Code provides that, unless expressly designated as separate property, "all real property situated in this state and all personal property wherever situated acquired during the marriage by a married person while domiciled in this state, * * * is community property."

8. If the decedent was domiciled outside California at the time of death, California's scheme of quasi-community property is in principle inapplicable. However, § 120 of the Probate Code provides that, with regard to California real property that is not classified as community property, the surviving spouse "has the same right to elect to take a portion of or interest in such property against the will of the decedent as though the property were located in the decedent's domicile at death."

9. The same 50:50 ratio applies to community property regardless of whether the decedent spouse was domiciled in California at the time of death. See id. § 100.

think of this approach?

(4) The "Fourth Approach." The 1991 Louisiana codification adopted a fourth approach that combines the quasi-community approach with the borrowed-law approach.[10] Under this approach, the state Y court begins with the forum's classification rules. If all the property qualifies as community under those rules, the court treats it as such under the forum's distribution rules and the case ends there.[11] Thus, in the above hypothetical, if all of the $3 million would be classified as community property under state Y's classification rules, the court would apply the distribution rules of state Y and would award Wilma $1.5 million. In this case this approach produces the same good or bad result as would the pure quasi-community approach.

The differences between these two approaches, however, become apparent in cases in which some or all of the $3 million does *not* qualify as quasi-community property under state Y law. Then, with regard to the part of the property that does not so qualify, the fourth approach authorizes the application of the distribution rules of state X.[12] For example, in a case in which none of the $3 million qualifies as community property under state Y law, the court will apply the distribution rules of state X and will award Wilma $1.5 million in a divorce proceeding and $1 million in a succession proceeding, respectively. Remember that in the identical case, Wilma would have received nothing under the pure quasi-community approach.

Professor William Reppy, one of the most knowledgeable experts in marital-property conflicts law, finds nothing wrong with giving Wilma nothing in such a case, because that is exactly how much she would have received had she been domiciled in state Y at all times. Reppy criticizes the fourth approach for giving Wilma more than other similarly situated wives who had lived all their lives in state Y. See Reppy, *Louisiana's Hybrid*, 4–6. What do you think? What should be the goal of the choice-of-law process in cases like Wilma's: (a) to treat her as if she were at all times a state X domiciliary? or (b) to treat her as if she were at all times a state Y domiciliary? For those who subscribe to the former goal, the pure borrowed-law approach of *Hughes* is perfect. For those who subscribe to the latter goal, the pure quasi-community approach is perfect. It treats Wilma exactly as long-time state Y domiciliaries. However, in so doing, this approach gives Wilma less than she would have received in her former domicile, both in divorce and in death cases.

What then of the fourth approach? It adopts the aspirational objectives of the borrowed-law approach but avoids most of its logistical difficulties. It also utilizes the practical advantages of the pure quasi-community approach (application of forum's classification rules) but also avoid its pitfalls (giving Wilma less than she would have received in her former domicile). In all divorce patterns, the fourth

---

10. See La.Civ.Code Art. 3526. For an explanation of the rationale and operation of this article and its differences from the pure quasi-community approach, see Symeonides, *Migrant Spouses*, 15–23.

11. See La.Civ.Code Art. 3526(1) ("Property that is classified as community property under the law of [the forum] shall be treated as community property under that law").

12. See La.Civ.Code Art. 3526(2) ("Property that is not classified as community property under the law of [the forum] shall be treated as the separate property of the acquiring spouse. However, the other spouse shall be entitled, in value only, to the same rights with regard to this property as would be granted by the law of the state in which the acquiring spouse was domiciled at the time of acquisition.").

approach succeeds in treating Wilma the same way as she would have been treated in her former domicile and thus corrects the problems encountered by the pure quasi-community approach in most of those patterns. However, in some death cases, the fourth approach "overcorrects" the problem and ends up giving Wilma not only more than she would have received under the internal law of state Y, but also more than she would have received under the internal law of state X. Thus, if the pure quasi-community approach is guilty of "under-protecting" Wilma in many divorce cases and many succession cases, the fourth approach is guilty of "over-protecting" Wilma in many succession cases. Which of these two phenomena do you think is the lesser evil and why? If over-protection of the non-owning spouse is bad--since it comes at the expense of Henry or his heirs--can it be avoided by private planning, such as by a matrimonial agreement, before or after the change of domicile, or by a carefully drafted will? If under-protection of the non-owning spouse is bad, can it be avoided? How?

B. FROM A COMMUNITY–PROPERTY STATE TO ANOTHER COMMU-NITY–PROPERTY STATE. Suppose that in the above hypothetical scenario both states X and Y are community-property states but differ in their classification of the $3 million. State X considers these funds as community property while state Y considers them as Henry's separate property. Under both the pure borrowed-law approach and the fourth approach, Wilma will receive $1.5 million. How much would Wilma receive under the pure quasi-community approach?

C. FROM A COMMUNITY–PROPERTY STATE TO A SEPARATE–PROPERTY STATE. Let us now reverse the facts of the original scenario, supra, so that state X, the former domicile, is a community-property state and state Y, the new domicile, is a separate-property state. Everything else remains the same, that is, the marriage is terminated six months after Henry and Wilma have moved to state Y, either because of a divorce or because of Henry's death. Consider now the following possibilities:

(1) Under the law of state X, the $3 million was classified as Henry's separate property and was free of any rights in favor of Wilma, but is subject to such rights under the internal law of state Y. Should the state Y court award Wilma any rights to the $ 3 million?

(2) Under the law of state X, the $3 million was classified as community property and thus was co-owned by Henry and Wilma when they moved to state Y. Suppose that under state Y law "*all*" of Henry's property is subject to rights in favor of Wilma. Should the court give Wilma any such rights to Henry's $1.5 million?

If the marriage terminates by Henry's death rather than by divorce and state Y is one of the thirteen states that have adopted the Uniform Disposition of Community Property Rights at Death Act of 1971,[13] the answers to the above questions are rather easy. This Act applies to "all personal property, wherever

---

13. These states are Alaska, Arkansas, Colorado, Connecticut, Florida, Hawaii, Kentucky, Michigan, Montana, New York, Oregon, Virginia and Wyoming. See 8A U.L.A (West Sup. 1995).

situated" that was acquired "as community property under the laws of another jurisdiction," and to "any real property situated in this state" that was acquired through funds that were classified "as community property under the laws of another jurisdiction." § 1. The Act provides that:

> Upon death of a married person, one-half of the property to which this Act applies is the property of the surviving spouse and is not subject to testamentary disposition by the decedent or distribution under the laws of succession of this State. One-half of that property is the property of the decedent and is subject to testamentary disposition or distribution under the laws of succession of this State * * * [and] is not subject to the surviving spouse's right to elect against the will.

§ 3. What would Wilma's rights be under the Act? Do you see any problems with the results the Act produces?

If the marriage terminates through divorce, rather than through Henry's death, how should a state Y court answer the above questions? For a case addressing similar questions, see *In re* Marriage of Whelchel, 476 N.W.2d 104 (Iowa.Ct.App. 1991)

D. IMMOVABLES. Suppose now that Henry and Wilma never left state X (the community-property state), and that state X classified the $3 million as community property. Henry used this amount to buy an immovable in his own name in state Y, a separate-property state. What are Wilma's rights to this immovable? A state X court would treat this immovable as if it were community property and protect Wilma accordingly. See, e.g., La. Civ. Code, art. 3525. Should a state Y court do likewise? What answer does the Uniform Act give to this question? The Act does not apply to divorce cases. How should one handle those cases? See Depas v. Mayo, 11 Mo. 314 (1848); Palmer v. Palmer, 654 So.2d 1 (Miss.1995) (both cases reached the same results as the Act).

What if Henry had sold or mortgaged the immovable in the meantime? Consider the following provisions of the Uniform Act.

> § 6. (a) If a surviving spouse has apparent title to property to which this Act applies, a purchaser for value or a lender taking a security interest in the property takes his interest in the property free of any rights of the personal representative or an heir or devisee of the decedent....
>
> (c) A purchaser for value or a lender need not inquire whether a vendor or borrower acted properly.
>
> (d) The proceeds of a sale or creation of a security interest shall be treated in the same manner as the property transferred to the purchaser for value or a lender.
>
> § 7. This Act does not affect rights of creditors with respect to property to which this Act applies.

J. SUCCESSIONS

Guidry v. Hardy

Court of Appeal of Louisiana, Third Circuit, 1971.
254 So.2d 675, *Writ Refused*, 260 La. 454, 256 So.2d 441 (1972).

HOOD, J. Plaintiff, Leroy A. Guidry, Jr., instituted this suit for judgment decreeing a document purporting to be the last will and testament of Leroy A. Guidry, Sr., to be null and void. The defendants are the decedent's widow, Ruth A. Guidry, and her son by a prior marriage, Doug A. Hardy (sometimes referred to as Doug A. Guidry). Judgment was rendered by the trial court decreeing the will to be invalid, * * *. Defendants appealed, and plaintiff has answered the appeal.

The questions presented are: (1) Should this proceeding be stayed pending final determination of a related suit in California? (2) Is the will valid as to form? * * * (4) Is the will invalid because of lack of testamentary capacity or undue influence? * * * (6) Is the will invalid, or should there be a reduction, on the ground that the bequests exceed the disposable portion of the testator's estate?

Leroy A. Guidry, Sr., died in California, the state of his domicile, on August 13, 1969. His closest surviving relatives are his widow, Ruth A. Guidry, and his only child, Leroy A. Guidry, Jr., the latter being the issue of a prior marriage.

The decedent was first married to Mrs. Frank H. Guidry. One child, [plaintiff] Leroy A. Guidry, Jr., was born of that union. The deceased and Frank H. Guidry were divorced by judgment rendered by a Nevada court on October 13, 1954. A few days after that divorce was granted the decedent married Ruth A. Guidry, one of the defendants in this suit, and he remained married to her until his death in 1969. No children were born of that union. Ruth A. Guidry had three children by a prior marriage, one of whom was Doug A. Hardy, the other defendant in this proceeding.

On May 22, 1968, the decedent, Leroy A. Guidry, Sr., executed a document which purported to be his last will and testament. He was living in California at that time, and the above mentioned document was executed in that state. In that document the testator purported to bequeath to his son, Leroy A. Guidry, Jr., only two items of movable property, a ship's clock and some movie film, both of which had only a nominal value, and he specifically stipulated that his heirs should receive no part of his estate except as therein provided. To his stepson, Doug A. Hardy, he bequeathed his hand tools. He then bequeathed all of the remainder of his estate, real and personal and wherever situated, to his widow, Ruth A. Guidry.

The estate left by the decedent includes movable and immovable property in California and several items of immovable property located in the state of Louisiana. There is evidence in the record tending to show that the Louisiana property belonging to this estate had a gross value of $257,416.65 at the time of the testator's death, and that the debts and taxes owed by it amount to approximately $60,000.00.

The will was presented for probate in California, and an opposition to the probate was filed by Leroy A. Guidry, Jr. The issues presented by that opposition were tried before a jury in the California court, and a verdict was rendered declaring the will to be invalid because of the "undue influence of Ruth A. Guidry." Judgment was rendered by the California trial court in accordance with that verdict, rejecting the prayer that the will be probated. An appeal was taken from that judgment, and on September 21, 1971, the Court of Appeal of the State of California, Second Appellate Division, Division One, affirmed the judgment of the trial court denying probate of the will.

The will has never been presented for probate in Louisiana. Nevertheless, this suit seeking a declaratory judgment decreeing the will to be invalid was filed on October 2, 1969. Plaintiff contends here that the will is invalid and unenforceable insofar as it affects Louisiana immovable property because: (1) The document lacked the formalities required by law for a valid testament; (2) the decedent lacked testamentary capacity; (3) the decedent's execution of the will was induced by Ruth Guidry's threat to commit him to an institution for the care of the mentally ill and by her false statements that his presumptive heirs no longer loved him; (4) the will and another document executed at about the same time constitute an agreement, in contravention of public policy, for the purpose of facilitating the dissolution of a marriage; and (5) the testator attempted to dispose of more than two-thirds of his property by gratuitous transactions during his life, and thus his donations infringed upon plaintiff's *legitime*.[1]

In this proceeding the trial court decreed the will to be invalid, basing that decision solely on the ground that the California court had decreed it to be invalid under the laws of that state, but he reserved to the parties the right to apply for a rehearing if the judgment of the California trial court should be modified or changed by a higher court. * * *

In this suit one of the grounds urged by plaintiff in attacking the validity of the purported will is that the testator did not have the capacity to make a will disposing of immovable property in Louisiana. The general rule is that issues relating to the capacity of the testator to make a will of immovable property will be resolved by applying the laws of the place where the property is situated, irrespective of the laws of the domicile of the testator or of the place where the will was executed. LSA–C.C. art. 10; LSA–C.C. art. 491; Selle v. Rapp, 220 S.W. 662 (Ark.1920); Hasling v. Martin, 38 So. 174 (La.1905); 16 Am.Jur.2d, Conflict of Laws, Sec. 59, Page 92; 15A C.J.S. Conflict of Laws § 16(5), Page 489; Restatement, Conflict of Laws, Sec. 249, Comment (a); LeFlar, American Conflicts Law, Sec. 196, Page 480 (1968).

* * * In the instant suit, insofar as property in Louisiana may be affected, the issue of whether the testator had the capacity to make a will on May 22, 1968, must be governed by the laws of Louisiana. It thus is immaterial what the ultimate decision of the California courts may be as to the capacity of Leroy A. Guidry, Sr., to make a will, and no useful purpose would be served by staying these proceedings.

---

1. [Editor's note: Under Louisiana law, the *legitime* or "forced share" is a percentage of the decedent's estate that the law reserves for qualified children of the deceased (called "forced heirs"). The size of this share depends on the number of children. In this case in which the deceased had one child, the share would be one third (today one fourth). The deceased could freely give the remaining two thirds ("disposable portion") to persons other than his son, but if he exceeded that portion, his bequests would be subject to reduction to the extent necessary to satisfy the son's *legitime*].

Our conclusion is that the trial court correctly denied defendants' motion to stay these proceedings until a final judgment is rendered in the California suit.

VALIDITY OF WILL AS TO FORM. The document purporting to be the will of Leroy A. Guidry, Sr., consists of two typed pages. The signature of the testator appears at the end of the second page. Following that signature is another page containing a subscription or declaration signed by two witnesses, J. William Phillips and Verna M. Phillips. The will, on its face, appears to have been executed according to a form which is prescribed by California law.

The will was not executed in a form prescribed by Louisiana law. Under the provisions of LSA–R.S. 9:2401, however, a will executed outside the state in a manner prescribed by the law of the place of its execution shall have the same force and effect in this state as if executed in the manner prescribed by the laws of this state, provided the will is in writing and subscribed by the testator. * * * We thus find the will has been executed in the manner prescribed by the law of the place of its execution, and that insofar as the form of the will is concerned it is entitled to the same force and effect as if executed in the manner prescribed by the laws of this state. * * *

TESTAMENTARY CAPACITY. Plaintiff contends that the will is invalid because the testator lacked testamentary capacity and because of "undue influence" on the part of the principal legatee, Mrs. Ruth Guidry.

The Louisiana Civil Code provides that a person, to make a donation inter vivos or mortis causa, must be of sound mind. LSA–C.C. art. 1475. Testamentary capacity is always presumed, and thus a presumption exists in favor of the validity of the will. [cit.]

The burden of proving lack of testamentary capacity at the time the will was executed is upon the party alleging it. [cit.] The degree of proof required to overcome the presumption of testamentary capacity is similar to that required in criminal cases to rebut and overcome the presumption of innocence which the law creates in favor of a person who is on trial for a crime. [cit.]

No inquiry is permitted into the motives which may have influenced a testator to make testamentary dispositions. "Undue influence," therefore, is not a ground for invalidating a will in Louisiana, as it is in California. [cit.] Evidence of force, duress or undue influence may be admitted in attacks upon the validity of wills, but that evidence should be considered only insofar as it tends to show lack of testamentary capacity. [cit.]

The trial judge observed in his reasons for judgment that "a jury in California ruled the will invalid on grounds of undue influence." On that ground he concluded, "like the California court did," that the will is invalid in Louisiana. We think the trial court erred in reaching that conclusion.

We have already determined that in this state a will cannot be annulled simply on a showing of "undue influence." To succeed here plaintiff must show lack of testamentary capacity on the part of the testator. An exceptionally heavy burden of proof rests on plaintiff to establish that circumstance. * * *

Our conclusion is that the testator, Leroy A. Guidry, Sr., understood the nature of the testamentary acts, that he was aware of the meaning of the will which he executed on May 22, 1968, and that he understood the effect of the provisions of that testament. We find that the testator was capable of executing the will at issue here, and that the trial judge erred in decreeing the will to be invalid because of "undue influence." * * *

INFRINGEMENT ON PLAINTIFF'S LEGITIME. Plaintiff contends alternatively that the will at issue here is without legal effect insofar as it relates to immovable property in this state, because of the fact that the testator disposed of more than two-thirds of his property * * * and that the Louisiana property belonging to his estate is not sufficient to satisfy his son's legitime. * * * [Louisiana] law provides that any disposal of property, whether inter vivos or mortis causa, which exceeds the disposable portion is not null, but only reducible to the quantum. LSA–C.C. art. 1502. * * * [W]e hold that plaintiff has failed to show that the will at issue here is unenforceable on the ground that the bequests infringe on plaintiff's legitime. Subject to the judgment rendered here, the question of whether there should be a reduction of the donations made by the testator must be determined by the trial court if and when the will is presented for probate and the estate is opened.

For the reasons herein set out, we reverse that part of the judgment appealed from which decrees that the document dated May 22, 1968, purporting to be a testament executed by Leroy A. Guidry, Sr., is without effect in the State of Louisiana; and judgment is hereby rendered declaring that document to be the valid will of the testator, Leroy A. Guidry, Sr., decreeing that the said Leroy A. Guidry, Sr., had testamentary capacity to execute that will, and declaring that such will is entitled to the same force and effect in the State of Louisiana as if executed in the manner prescribed by the laws of this state. * * * Affirmed in part, reversed in part, and rendered.

Estate of Renard

Surrogate's Court, N. Y. County, 1981.
108 Misc.2d 31, 437 N.Y.S.2d 860; Aff'd by 85 A.D.2d 501 447 N.Y.S.2d 573 (1st Dept. 1981).

MIDONICK, Surrogate. * * * This decedent was born a French citizen in 1899. For approximately 30 years, from 1941 to 1971, she was domiciled in New York. During that time, she became a United States citizen (in 1965). From 1941 until 1948 she was employed in the New York City law offices of Sullivan and Cromwell, where she was secretary to one of that firm's senior partners, William Nelson Cromwell. A lawyer-client relationship with the firm also arose in that period. On October 24, 1971 decedent returned to France, leaving the major portion of her assets here. She died on August 3, 1978, a French domiciliary. Her son, an adult, was then domiciled in California where he still resides. He is a citizen both of France and the United States.

After the decedent moved to France, Sullivan and Cromwell drafted a will for her which she executed in their Paris office, on June 20, 1972. This is the will the parties refer to as the "New York" will. It was admitted to probate in this court after the defeat of the son's motion opposing our jurisdiction. The executors are The Bank of New York and Arthur Dean, a Sullivan and Cromwell partner. This will designates New York law as controlling in the manner often recommended for wills of nonresidents disposing of assets located in this state:

> " * * * 'I hereby declare that I elect that this Will shall be admitted to original probate in the State of New York and shall be construed and regulated by the laws of the State of New York, and that the validity and effect thereof shall be determined by such laws.' * * * "

EPTL 3–5.1, subd. (h); [cit.]

The will purported to dispose of all of the decedent's assets. She left her Paris apartment to her "adopted son," the respondent here, subject to a life estate in her friend Yvonne Daumarie (who predeceased her). That friend was also given the contents of the apartment, but if she did not survive they too went to the son. After legacies of $6,000 to the son and $15,000 to others, the balance was divided equally between a French friend and a French charity. The charity has appeared in this proceeding to oppose the son's claim. The Attorney General has also appeared in opposition thereto. * * *

* * * The decedent's assets physically situated in New York at her death consisted of bank accounts and a brokerage account valued at approximately $320,000. The French property was the apartment and its contents, the value of which was variously estimated, in connection with the motion to dismiss the probate proceeding, at $75,000 by the executors and $150,000 by the son.

The issue presented is whether the son is entitled to claim his right of forced heirship under French law against the decedent's New York property. The law of France, in the tradition which the common law initially copied but rejected many centuries ago [cit.] severely circumscribes the free testamentary disposition of property. In the case of a deceased parent survived by one child, the child is entitled to one half of the parent's assets. The child's forced share interest extends to assets given away during the parent's lifetime. This share is apparently offset by lifetime gifts from the parent to the child. [cit.] The executors and the French charity concede that under French law an adopted son would have a one-half forced share. They cast the issue as being whether French law will be applied here. The parties have agreed that there is no need to prove French law at this stage of the proceeding.

(1) No constitutional mandate directs the resolution of this choice of law issue since there are adequate points of contact with both France and New York to render the application of the local law of either acceptable under the due process standards of reasonableness and fundamental fairness. *Allstate Ins. v. Hague*, 449 U.S. 302 (1981) [Ch. 5]. The New York contacts are, *inter alia*, decedent's 30 years' residence in this state, the physical location of her assets here, and her evident intention, as expressed in her will, to have New York law apply. The principle [sic] contact with France is, of course, that decedent died domiciled there. The traditional conflict of laws approach turns to the law of the domicile to determine succession to personal property. E.g., Restatement, Conflicts 2d, §§ 263, 265 (1971); Goodrich and Scoles, Handbook of the Conflict of Laws (4th ed. 1964) 323, 332–3.

Section 3–5.1 of the EPTL sets forth a series of choice of law rules relating to wills. Subdivision (h) is the relevant portion but the earlier provisions provide a background:

"(2) The intrinsic validity, effect, revocation or alteration of a testamentary disposition of personal property, and the manner in which such property devolves when not disposed of by will, are determined by the law of the jurisdiction in which the decedent was domiciled at death." (EPTL 3–5.1, subd. (b), par. (2))

The terms "intrinsic validity" and "effect" are defined as follows:

"'Intrinsic validity' relates to the rules of substantive law by which a jurisdiction determines the legality of a testamentary disposition, including the general capacity of the testator. (Subd. (a), par. (4))

'Effect' relates to the legal consequences attributed under the law of a jurisdiction to a valid testamentary disposition." (Subd. (a), par. (5))

Subdivision (h) then provides an exception to the general rule:

"Whenever a testator, not domiciled in this state at the time of death, provides in his will that he elects to have the disposition of his property situated in this state governed by the laws of this state, the intrinsic validity, including the testator's general capacity, effect, interpretation, revocation or alteration of any such disposition is determined by the local law of this state. * * * " (Emphasis added)

Clearly this decedent made the election contemplated in subdivision (h) to have the disposition of her property governed by New York law. The son contends that *Matter of Clark*, 236 N.E.2d 152 (N.Y.1968) constrains us to hold that this election does not permit a decedent to avoid the forced heirship of his or her domicile. *Clark* involved the language of a precursor statute, section 47 of the Decedent Estate Law (DEL), and a Virginia widow's right of election. * * * [After reviewing the legislative history of subdivision (h), the court concluded that the "[New York] Legislature intended subdivision (h) to permit a decedent, in a case like the one before the court, to avoid the application of the French law of forced heirship to her personalty by invoking New York law in her will," and that having been decided before the enactment of subdivision (h), the *Clark* case did not preclude this result. The court continued as follows:]

* * * [E]ven if subdivision (h) were not determinative here, the question is whether this decedent's intention to have New York law apply can be effectuated under the prevailing choice of law approach. Clearly, during the 30 years of the testatrix's New York residence, her son could not have had a forced heirship claim against her estate. This is not a case of the change of a matrimonial domicile involving a couple who moved their joint home to another jurisdiction; the decedent moved back to France but her son remained in California. Cf. *Matter of Crichton*, 228 N.E.2d 799 [N.Y. 1967]. New York has a long standing and substantial relationship with this decedent. When she moved to France, she retained her United States citizenship; she transferred her residence there but not the situs of her financial affairs.

France's contact with this estate is as the decedent's domicile at death. The traditional choice of law rule would presumably apply the law of the domicile but as the court pointed out in *Crichton* traditional conflict of laws rules often fail to take cognizance of the policies of other jurisdictions, and of the interests which those jurisdictions have in the application of their laws. *Matter of Crichton, supra*. Both *Crichton* and *Clark* make it clear that the Court of Appeals has moved away from mechanical choice of law rules to a balancing approach which requires the identification of the underlying policies in the conflicting laws of the relevant jurisdictions, and the examination of the contacts of those jurisdictions to see which has a superior connection with the occurrence and thus a superior interest in having its policy or law followed. *Neumeier v. Kuehner*, [Ch. 3]; [cit.]

The conflicting policies here are New York's interest in the freedom of testamentary disposition, under which a child's claim is protected only in very limited situations not relevant here, and France's policy of narrowly circumscribing testamentary freedom in favor of descendants. Nor does the law of California, where the son resides, support forced heirship by children. Of all United States of America jurisdictions, only Louisiana follows the forced heirship policies of the civil law. One day a uniform law, or state by state laws, may adopt a protective rule for infant children of decedents to continue support during infancy, rather than forced heirship, after the parent's death. [cit.] It has been suggested that the fundamental purpose of forced heirship systems is the protection of descendants residing in those jurisdictions. Yiannopoulos, Wills of Movables in American International Conflicts Law: A Critique of the Domiciliary "Rule", 46 Calif.L.Rev. 185 (1958). In any event, France's interest in having its policy implemented, if any, is attenuated here by the fact that the decedent's son was a resident of California when she died, and has remained such. Cf. *Neumeier v. Kuehner, supra; Matter of Crichton, supra.*

The factor of decedent's domicile at death need not be decisive. Apparently domicile came to be regarded as controlling because it was thought desirable to have a single law to provide unified results with regard to the distribution of a decedent's personalty wherever located. [cit.] It has been suggested that domicile is diminishing as a basis for locating true governmental interests. [cit.]

New York has abandoned the traditional choice of law rule with respect to tort actions, which looked to the law of the place where the tort occurred, in favor of the predominant interest approach. E.g., *Babcock v. Jackson*, [supra]; [cit.]. *Clark* and *Crichton* apply that same balancing approach rather than simply looking to the decedent's domicile. *Crichton* suggests that the predominant interest approach was applied in *Wyatt v. Fulrath* where New York law was applied to sustain a survivorship interest in a joint tenancy account against forced heirship claims based on the law of the domicile (211 N.E.2d 637 [N.Y. 1965]). Testators with assets in more than one country are usually advised to make separate wills for each country (ABA National Institute on International Estate Planning (1980) at p. 14), and of course, even the traditional rule which looked to the domicile for a uniform approach to succession accepted the hegemony of the local law of the situs of real property to determine its succession. Multiple administration is almost inevitable in multinational estates, further eroding the need for a uniform rule. See Conn.Gen.Stat. § 45–170 subd. (c) (eff. Oct. 1, 1980). Indeed, a respected commentator has suggested that the proclaimed rule which looked to the law of the domicile to govern testamentary succession to personalty was never supported by the cases in the area of international conflicts, particularly with respect to civil law forced heirship claims by the testator's descendants, where the testator's intention to have the law of the situs control was upheld by the courts. See *Matter of Prince*, 267 N.Y.S.2d 138 [(1964)]; *Yiannopoulos, supra* at p. 227. There is a significant distinction between enforcing a foreign domiciliary law regarding a spouse's elective share, which differs only in degree from our own law, since both recognize the spouse's claim, and enforcing a descendant's forced share which runs counter to our local policy. See *Yiannopoulos, supra* at p. 224; *Matter of Prince, supra*. Nor do the needs of the international system (Restatement, Conflicts 2d § 6, subd. (2), par. (a)) militate in favor of deference to the French law. France apparently applies its forced heirship law to personal property situated in that country, without regard to the fact that neither the testator nor the claiming child is domiciled there, so long as the child is a citizen of France. [cit.] In this court's view, the weight of the contacts with each jurisdiction must be considered. The French approach may reward a child's recent acquisition of French citizenship or residence with a windfall in the way of a forced share in the parent's estate. Our conflicts rules should not be extended to sanction such an approach, which might reward such changes made in contemplation of imminent death.

(3) It seems to this court that the domestic policy of testamentary freedom from forced heirship claims should prevail under the circumstances of this case, in the light of the decedent's long residence in New York and respondent's nonresidence in France. The son cites no case enforcing a descendant's forced share in these circumstances and the court does not believe that this case presents sufficient cause to apply French law. [cit.] Accordingly, the court holds that even if subdivision (h) were not controlling the paramount interest test for choice of law established in *Matter of Clark* sanctions the application of New York local law in this case. * * * Application granted.

Notes and Questions

1. From Chapter 2, supra 37-40 you should recall the first Restatement's approach to conflicts in the area of testate and intestate succession. The Restatement subjected virtually all issues of testate and intestate succession of immovables to the whole law of the situs and all issues of succession of movables to the whole law of the decedent's last domicile. From Chapter 3, supra 141-45, you should recall that the Restatement (Second) continues to adhere to this dichotomy or "scission" between immovables and movables and has done little to soften the rigidity of the first Restatement's rules. Indeed, this area of American conflicts law has remained largely unaffected by the conflicts revolution. As *Estate of Renard* demonstrates, however, this area of the law is not immune to statutory intervention or judicially-created exceptions, which may deviate from the solutions of the two Restatements.

2. **The "Scission" of the Estate.** Most common-law systems follow a sharp differentiation between immovables and movables, which can be traced to the feudal concept of tenurial ownership of land that prevailed during the period following the Norman conquest in England. In a society that essentially did not recognize the

individual ownership of land, it was only natural, if not inevitable, that the location of the land, and not the domicile of the tenant, would be the determinative factor. As one author put it, "[t]he feudal lords could not allow the descent of their land to be affected if one of their vassals should acquire a foreign domicile." Wolff, *PIL* 567. It was different, however, with regard to movables which, after all, were susceptible not only to full individual ownership but also to movement from one place to another. Their location at a given place at a given time was therefore much less important than was the owner's domicile. Although so much has changed since those formative years, the conflicts rules in this area of the law continue to give the impression that succession is still viewed more in terms of the sovereign's power over property than as a means of transmitting personal or familial wealth from one generation to the next.

Obviously, the above historical reasons for differentiating between movables and immovables have long disappeared. Are there any other valid reasons for continuing this differentiation today? Such a differentiation means, inter alia, that if a person dies domiciled in state X and owns immovables in states Y and Z, her succession will be governed by the law of three states: state X for all her movables, and states Y and Z for her immovables, respectively. (The New York statute discussed in *Estate of Renard* compounds this problem further by adding the possibility of a fourth state.) Is this a good idea? What problems does it create? Suppose that the laws of the three states differ in significant ways so that the decedent's will is valid in state X, partially valid (e.g., it simply violates an heir's forced share) in state Y, and totally void (e.g., lack of testamentary capacity) in state Z. What then? This regime of "scission" ensures uniform treatment of all immovables within a state regardless of who owns them but, as in *Guidry*, it treats non-uniformly the assets of a single estate. Which of the two uniformities is the more important?

3. ***The Principle of Unity of the Estate.*** In contrast to common-law systems, the majority of civil-law systems adhere to the principle of unity of the estate.[1] Under this principle the decedent's estate is treated as a single unit to be governed by a single law, regardless of whether it consists of movables or immovables and regardless of their respective location. The applicable law may be either the law of the last nationality (*lex patriae*) or the last domicile (*lex domicilii*) of the deceased, but it is always his or her personal law. Is this scheme better than the common-law scheme? It ensures the application of a single law, but does it also guarantee the application of the proper law? For example, do nationality, citizenship, or domicile always provide a meaningful connection? Can they be manipulated? The 1989 Hague Convention on the Law Applicable to the Estates of Deceased Persons, which adopts the principle of unity of the estate, attempts to address these questions. Article 3 provides:

1. Succession is governed by the law of the State in which the deceased at

---

1. Except for France and some members of the French legal family, most western European countries adhere to the principle of unity of the estate, with occasional exceptions for immovables situated within the enacting jurisdiction. With the exception of Argentina, Bolivia, Peru, and Uruguay, all Latin American countries follow the same principle. See Symeonides, *Exploring the "Dismal Swamp,"* 1035–36.

the time of his death was habitually resident, if he was then a national of that State.

2. Succession is also governed by the law of the State in which the deceased at the time of his death was habitually resident if he had been resident there for a period of no less than five years immediately preceding his death. However, in exceptional circumstances, if at the time of his death he was manifestly more closely connected with the State of which he was then a national, the law of that State applies.

3. In other cases succession is governed by the law of the State of which at the time of his death the deceased was a national, unless at that time the deceased was more closely connected with another State, in which case the law of the latter State applies.

What do you think of this scheme? Leaving aside the issue of Ms. Renard's selection of New York law, which state's law would be applicable in *Estate of Renard* under the Convention? Which state's law would be applicable in *Guidry*?

The United States participated actively in the drafting of the above Convention but, as with most other Hague conventions, the United States Senate has yet to ratify it. Would you urge your senator to vote in favor of ratification? Why, or why not?

4. *Testamentary Formalities*. One of the few issues that the *Guidry* court resolved correctly was to uphold the formal validity of the will despite its nonconformity with the formalities prescribed by Louisiana's internal law. The court's decision was based on a Louisiana statute modelled after the Uniform Wills Act of 1910 which was the first attempt to liberalize the law governing testamentary formalities. Today, most states have similar statutes that are modelled after the Uniform Probate Code.[2] These statutes, which supplement rather than replace the traditional common-law rule, contain so-called "rules of validation," namely, rules designed to validate the testament by alternative references to the laws of any of the states enumerated therein that would uphold the testament.[3] Under the Uniform Probate Code, these states are the state of making of the testament, or the state where, at the time of the making or at the time of death, the testator was domiciled, resided, or was a national. What policies support such validation rules? Do, or should, these policies extend to issues other than form?

5. *Testamentary Capacity, Undue Influence, and Vices of Consent*. Would you agree that the *Guidry* court missed the point completely when it upheld a testament that a California court had already declared invalid on grounds of undue influence? Although for technical reasons the California judgment was not binding

2. See Unif. Probate Code § 2–506, 8 U.L.A. 116 (1983). The Code has been adopted in Alaska, Arizona, Colorado, Florida, Hawaii, Idaho, Maine, Michigan, Minnesota, Montana, Nebraska, New Mexico, North Dakota, South Carolina, South Dakota, and Utah. 8 U.L.A. 1 (West Supp. 2003).

3. See Symeonides, *Exploring the "Dismal Swamp,"* 1043. A similar liberalizing trend can be seen in other countries. See id. at 1043–44. For example, the 1961 Hague Convention on the Conflicts of Laws Relating to the Form of Testamentary Dispositions, which is in force in 34 countries, provides that any of the following laws can be applied to validate a will as to form: place of making; nationality, domicile, or habitual residence of the testator at either the time of making or the time of death; and situs with regard to immovables.

on the Louisiana court under the Constitution's Full Faith and Credit clause, the choice-of-law question remains: why should the law of the situs *qua* situs govern issues such as testamentary capacity, undue influence, or vices of consent (duress, fraud, error, etc.), all of which pertain to the personal qualities, state of mind, or need for protection of the testator? The *Guidry* court based its decision on a "general rule" that the forum state never followed, although both Restatements did (see Restatement §§ 249 cmt. a, 306 cmt. b; Restatement (Second) §§ 239 cmts. a, c, 263 cmt. a.), namely that "issues relating to the capacity of the testator to make a will of immovable property will be resolved by applying the laws of the place where the property is situated, irrespective of the laws of the domicile of the testator or of the place where the will was executed." *Guidry*, supra. Besides the land "taboo," can you think of any good reason for having such a general rule? Can this rule survive a policy-based analysis of the type you studied in Chapter 3? Whatever the policies underlying Louisiana's rule that disallowed a showing of undue influence as a ground for invalidating a testament, were those policies relevant in a case like *Guidry* which, for all we know, had no other connection with Louisiana except for the location in that state of part of the decedent's estate? Conversely, whatever the policies underlying the California rule of undue influence, were those policies not relevant in a case involving a California testator and California heirs and legatees? Suppose for example that the California rule reflected any or all of the following policies: ensure that the decedent's testamentary volition was free, genuine, and unrestrained; discourage coercive conduct and to punish the perpetrator; indirectly protecting the testator's family by scrutinizing gifts to non-heirs. Under any of these possibilities, would California not have an interest in applying this rule? In sum, would you agree that the application of Louisiana law in *Guidry* defeated legitimate California interests without actually promoting any conceivable Louisiana interest? See Symeonides, *Exploring the "Dismal Swamp"*, 1068–70.

From a national perspective, does the above "general rule" not mean that if the testator owned movables and immovables in different states, there is a good chance that a court may treat him as capable of disposing some of his assets but not others? In the words of Ernst Rabel, "[t]hat eight pieces of land need eight different systems of liberty or restraint in testation is bad enough * * *; but that even the capacity to make a will * * * [is] independent in principle in every jurisdiction where an immovable is found transgresses the borders of tolerable tradition." Rabel, *Conflict of Laws*, 272. Do you agree? The Restatement (Second) opens the door for abandoning this tradition in some cases (see § 239 cmt. c.) but few states have done so. Interestingly, Louisiana is one of those states. The 1991 Louisiana codification provides that "[a] person is capable of making a testament if, at the time of making the testament, he possessed that capacity under the law of the state in which he was domiciled either at that time or at the time of death." La.Civ.Code art. 3529. See Symeonides, *Exploring the "Dismal Swamp"*, 1056-60. What do you think of this rule? Notice that: this rule applies regardless of whether the estate consists of immovables or movables and regardless of their respective situses; and that, with regard to movables, this rule differs from the prevailing American rule which requires the application of the whole law of "the state where the testator was domiciled *at the time of death*" (Restatement 2d § 263), whether or not it upholds the testament.

6. *Forced Shares and other Restraints of Disposition*. Both *Guidry* and *Renard* involved the issue of forced heirship. *Renard* correctly stated that "of all United States of America jurisdictions, only Louisiana follows the forced heirship policies of the civil law." This fact, however, does not render either of these two cases unique. It is a mistake, though a commonly-parroted one, to assume that none of the other states impose restrictions on a person's power to dispose of her property upon death. For example, in the previous section we have seen that many separate-property states provide for a type of forced share in favor of surviving spouses. Similarly, many common-law states have statutes that invalidate gifts to non-heirs made within a certain period before the donor's death. Finally, as *Guidry* illustrates, common-law states allow more challenges to a person's testament on grounds of undue influence or other similar grounds (and tend to take a much more liberal view of such challenges) than do civil-law states. Thus, in one form or another, directly or indirectly, most states impose certain restrictions on the testator's power of disposition for the benefit of his heirs. Since these restrictions differ from one state to the other, the choice-of-law question is which state's law should govern these restrictions. Again, the traditional and current American practice is to apply the whole law of the situs state with regard to immovables and the whole law of the decedent's last domicile with regard to movables. *Guidry* followed the first rule,[4] while *Renard* followed a statutory exception from the second rule.

Again, other than the situs "taboo," what justification is there for applying Louisiana law to this issue in *Guidry*? The two states involved in that case had struck a different balance between the competing policies of protecting the testator's freedom of disposition on the one hand, and protecting forced heirs on the other. Why should Louisiana's balance of protecting the heir prevail in a case in which neither that heir nor the testator were domiciled in Louisiana? Incidentally, the new Louisiana codification provides that, even with regard to Louisiana immovables, Louisiana's forced heirship law does *not* apply if the deceased was domiciled outside Louisiana at the time of death and left no forced heirs domiciled in that state at that time. La.Civ.Code art. 3533. Conversely, article 3534 provides that if the deceased died domiciled in Louisiana and left forced heirs domiciled there, the value of the decedent's foreign immovables shall be included in calculating his disposable portion and in satisfying the *legitime*. What do you think of these rules? How would the *Guidry* conflict be resolved under these rules? (For movables, the codification adopts the domicile rule (see art. 3532), and thus would resolve *Renard* under French law.)

In *Renard*, the plaintiff heir was not domiciled in France, whose law was designed to protect him. Although the testatrix was a French domiciliary (and had probably retained her French citizenship), she also had a thirty-year association with New York. To the extent that the court's decision is based on that association and the

---

4. *Guidry* did follow the situs rule. Although the court did not dispose of this issue in this declaratory judgment proceeding, the court relegated the matter to the trial court "if and when the will is presented for probate and the estate is opened" to be decided under Louisiana law.

heir's lack of association with France, the decision is acceptable, is it not? In fact this case may also be a good example of why even the domiciliary rule, which is much more likely to produce functionally sound results than is the situs rule, should be subject to exceptions in appropriate cases. However, *Renard* raises a host of different concerns to the extent it is based on either or both the testatrix's "election" of New York law or on the location of her money in that state.

7. ***The Testator's Choice of Law***. This brings us to the infamous subdivision (h) of § 3-5.1 of the New York's Estates Powers and Trusts Law (EPTL). This provision requires the application of New York even if, unlike Ms. Renard, the testator has never set foot in New York. All that is needed is for the testator to have sent her money to a New York bank and to "elect" New York law in her will. Notice that such an election would make New York law applicable to "the intrinsic validity, *including the testator's general capacity, effect*, interpretation, revocation or alteration" of any such testament. Is this party autonomy gone wild or what? What if, under the law of her domicile, the testator did not have capacity to "elect" New York law? Why is it that the "[New York] Legislature intended subdivision (h) to permit a decedent, in a case like the one before the court, to avoid the application of the French law of forced heirship"? *Renard*, supra. In one of the first cases involving a similar issue, the New York Court of Appeals spoke of "honor[ing the foreign citizens'] * * * intentional resort to the protection of our laws and their recognition of the general stability of our Government," Wyatt v. Fulrath, 211 N.E.2d 637, 639 (N.Y.1965),[5] while another court spoke of foreigners who deposit funds in American banks in order to "evade the currency laws in their native lands or to protect against the fallout from revolutions." Neto v. Thorner, 718 F.Supp. 1222, 1226 (S.D.N.Y. 1989). Does New York have a legitimate affirmative interest in enabling such foreigners to evade their countries' laws? Does New York have an interest in attracting bank deposits from citizens of other states or countries and thus preserving the "general stability" of its financial, if not its governmental, institutions? If yes, are there any countervailing interests or factors? Do the terms "needs of the interstate and international systems" (Restatement Second § 6) mean anything? Does subdivision (h) support the contention that the abandonment of the traditional dogma has unleashed previously dormant forces such as selfishness or protectionism? Even if this contention were true, would you prefer to go back to the old dogma?

In contrast to *Renard*, the testator in *In re* Estate of Rhoades, 607 N.Y.S.2d 893 (N.Y.Sup.Ct.1994), was able to disinherit his surviving spouse by *not* electing to have New York law govern his succession. The testator had died domiciled in Florida and his Florida testament bequeathed his interest in a New York immovable to his first wife. His second wife, also a Florida domiciliary, instituted proceedings in New York, asserting her right of election to "take against the will." Under Florida law, a surviving spouse's right to take against the will does not encompass immovables situated outside Florida. The court held that, under § 5–1.1(d)(7) of New

---

5. In *Wyatt*, two Spanish spouses had deposited funds in a New York joint bank account and had signed a routine bank form stipulating to the application of New York law. Treating this as an "election" of New York law, the court applied that law, which was contrary to Spanish marital property and succession law.

York's EPTL, this right "is not available to a spouse of a decedent who was not domiciled in [New York] at the time of death, unless such decedent elects * * * to have the disposition of his property situated in this state governed by the laws of this state," id. at 894, and that since the decedent had not made such an "election," the surviving spouse had no right to take against his will. The plaintiff argued that this was an "absurd result [in] that if a spouse wants to disinherit his/her spouse from receiving any property located in New York, he/she can move out of New York State, establish domicile in another state, and then execute a Will in the other state disinheriting a spouse." Id. The court responded: "This result, however unfortunate, is precisely what New York law allows. * * * [I]t must be assumed that the Legislature intended this result to occur." Id. Indeed, who said that the Legislature must be reasonable?[6]

Notice that subdivision (h) establishes a unilateral conflicts rule that applies only when a foreigner "elects" New York law, but not when a New Yorker elects a foreign law. In contrast, the Uniform Probate Code, which also allows the testator to choose the applicable law, phrases this principle in bilateral terms and subjects it to public policy limitations. Section 2–602 of the Code provides:

> The meaning and legal effect of a disposition in a will shall be determined by the local law of a particular state selected by the testator in his instrument unless the application of that law is contrary to the [forum's] provisions relating to the [surviving spouse's] elective share * * *, the provisions relating to exempt property and allowances * * *, or any other public policy of [the forum] State otherwise applicable to the disposition.[7]

Would any of these limitations be applicable in *Estate of Renard*?

The Hague Convention mentioned supra also accepts the principle that the testator "may designate the law of a particular State to govern the succession to the whole of his estate." Art. 5(1). However, such designation will be effective "only if at the time of the designation or of his death [the testator] was a national of that State or had his habitual residence there." Id.[8] Would the choice-of-law clause in Ms. Renard's testament be upheld under the Convention? What about the testator's choice of Maine law in *Estate of Wright* (supra, Ch. 2 at 69)?

---

6. For another case of disinherison by non-election, see Saunders v. Saunders, 796 So.2d 1253 (Fla.App.2001) *rev. denied* 819 So.2d 139 (Fla.2002). This case involved a Florida statute that provides that, "when a nonresident decedent * * * provides in her or his will that the testamentary disposition of * * * her or his real property in this state, shall be construed and regulated by the laws of this state, the validity and effect of the dispositions shall be determined by Florida law." F.S.A. § 731.106(2). The *Saunders* decedent, a Colorado domiciliary, did *not* provide in his will for the application of Florida law to his Florida realty. The Florida court held that Colorado law would govern the succession even with regard to the Florida realty, because the statute had displaced the common-law situs rule. Is this interpretation reasonable?

7. This section is in effect in Alaska, Arizona, Colorado, Hawaii, Idaho, Maine, Michigan, Minnesota, Montana, North Dakota, South Carolina, and Utah. 8 U.L.A. 1 (Supp. 2003). See also Mass.Gen.Laws Ann., Ch. 191 § 1A (1,2) (1994). Illinois has a unilateral rule like New York's. However, unlike the New York rule, the Illinois rule provides that the testator's choice of Illinois law is subject to judicial scrutiny, at least with regard to decedents domiciled in foreign countries. See Ill.Ann.Stat. Ch. 755, § 5/7–6 (1992).

8. Other foreign systems such as those of Switzerland, Italy, and Quebec, have recently accorded testators limited freedom to choose the applicable law, but have subjected that choice to both geographical and substantive limitations. See Symeonides, *Private International Law*, 56-57.

K. STATUS

Hermanson v. Hermanson
Supreme Court of Nevada, 1994.
110 Nev. 1400, 887 P.2d 1241.

PER CURIAM: Cindy Hermanson ("Cindy"), the biological mother of James Hermanson ("James"), appeals from a district court order finding that David Hermanson ("David") is the father of James. Cindy and David married [in California] when Cindy was six months pregnant with James in June, 1982. Cindy maintains that she informed David that she was pregnant with another man's child. David admits that Cindy never told him that he was the father of her unborn child.

James was born [in California] on October 12, 1982. The parties agree that things did not go well after James's birth. Cindy stated that for the three years following James's birth (1982–85), she moved in and out of David's residence, seeking temporary housing in battered women's shelters, and staying with various friends. Cindy sought protective orders and direct assistance in battered women's shelters on multiple occasions between 1982 and 1985.

In October, 1985, Cindy separated from David and relocated to Iowa with James. Between 1985 and 1988, Cindy raised James alone while attending nursing school. She applied for and received welfare. In May, 1990, Cindy completed nursing school in Iowa. In August, 1990, David and Cindy discussed a reconciliation. Cindy returned to Las Vegas with James in October, 1990. The reconciliation attempt lasted only thirty days.

Cindy filed for divorce in December, 1990. Cindy's divorce complaint asserted that there were no issue of the marriage, although David's name appeared on James's birth certificate. She also asserted that David knew, and had always known, that he was biologically unrelated to the child. David denied Cindy's assertions. * * *

In November, 1991, * * * the district court concluded that Cindy failed to rebut a conclusive presumption in the California Evidence Code that James was the issue of her marriage to David. * * * Cindy and David's divorce went to trial on April 1, 1993, on all matters other than paternity, and a decree was entered on August 25, 1993. It states that pursuant to the February 4, 1992 order, David is the father of James. The court awarded Cindy primary physical custody of James and it granted David joint legal custody of James and extensive visitation rights. Cindy filed a timely appeal.

On appeal, Cindy argues that the district court erred because it applied California law instead of Nevada law to determine James's paternity and because substantial evidence does not support a finding of equitable estoppel. We agree.

The district court applied California Evidence Code section 621 to determine the paternity of James Hermanson. California Evidence Code section 621, at the time the Hermansons lived in California, provided:[1]

> Notwithstanding any other provision of law, the issue of a wife cohabiting with her husband, who is not impotent, is *conclusively* presumed to be legitimate.

Cal. Evid. Code § 621 (West 1990) (emphasis added). The district court stated that there was no evidence on the record that David is either impotent or sterile. Because the parties were legally married and cohabiting at James's birth, the district court applied this conclusive presumption to find that David is the father of James.

This court has adopted the substantial relationship test to resolve conflict of law questions. *Sievers v. Diversified Mtg. Investors*, 603 P.2d 270 (Nev.1979). Under this test, the state whose law is applied must have a substantial relationship with the transaction; and the transaction must not violate a strong public policy of Nevada. *Id.* at 273.[2]

California's only relationship with this litigation is that James was born there and that David and Cindy resided there during the three years that they cohabited during their turbulent marriage. The parties have not resided in California for almost ten years. California has no substantial interest in having former California Evidence Code section 621 applied in this paternity action in the Nevada court system especially in light of the fact that the California Legislature has repealed California Evidence Code section 621.[3] Under California's current paternity statute, California Family Code section 7611, a paternity action may be brought "at any time." Thus, the prevailing public policy in California is that there is no statute of limitations for paternity actions.

Moreover, the district court's application of California Evidence Code section 621 violates a public policy of Nevada. Under NRS 126.081, a paternity action is "not barred until 3 years after the child reaches the age of majority." Nevada recognizes that minors have a right to have their paternity determined in a court of law. Therefore, Nevada affords them the opportunity to litigate their paternity for three years after the age of eighteen. In this case, James is presently twelve years old. He is a Nevada resident and should have the opportunity to have his paternity determined under Nevada law rather than precluded by a repealed California statute.

Choice of law analysis dictates that Nevada law applies to the determination of James's paternity. Because the district court applied California law, we conclude that the district court erred. * * *

Nevada's paternity statute, NRS 126.051, states, in pertinent part:

---

1. In *Michael H. v. Gerald D.*, 491 U.S. 110 (1989), the United States Supreme Court addressed the constitutionality of the conclusive presumption of paternity under California Evidence Code section 621. In a five-four decision containing five separate opinions, the Court held, after balancing the private interests of the parties with the interests of the state, that a conclusive presumption of paternity does not deny due process to a putative father. *Id.* at 130. However, several members of the court disagreed. *Michael H. v. Gerald D.*, 491 U.S. at 138–63 (Brennan, J., Marshall, J., Blackmun, J., and White, J., dissenting).

2. Some courts have applied the "origin of domicile" doctrine to determine that the law of the child's birthplace is the applicable law for paternity actions. [cit.] However, these cases reflect a traditional conflict of laws approach which Nevada has rejected by adopting the more modern substantial relationship test.

3. The California Legislature repealed California Evidence Code section 621—effective January 1, 1994. Thus, California's policy position on this conclusive presumption of paternity has changed. Under California's and Nevada's current paternity statutes, the presumption that a child born to a legally married couple is a child of the marriage is *rebuttable*.

1. A man is presumed to be the natural father of a child if: (a) He and the child's natural mother are or have been married to each other and the child is born during the marriage....

3. A presumption under this section may be rebutted in an appropriate action only by clear and convincing evidence.... The presumption is rebutted by a court decree establishing paternity of the child by another man.

NRS 126.051 provides for a *rebuttable* presumption of paternity and is the applicable statute in this matter. We reverse the district court's order finding that David is the father of James and remand this case to the district court for further proceedings consistent with this opinion.

Notes and Questions

1. *Hermanson* states that the Nevada Supreme Court "has adopted the substantial relationship test ... [u]nder [which] ... the state whose law is applied must have a substantial relationship with the transaction; and the transaction must not violate a strong public policy of Nevada." As authority for this statement, *Hermanson* cites Sievers v. Diversified Mtg. Investors, 603 P.2d 270 (Nev.1979), a *contract* case that applied the law of the state *chosen by the parties*, which state had a substantial relationship to the contract and the parties and whose law did not violate Nevada's public policy. Is *Sievers* really analogous to *Hermanson*? Two years after *Hermanson*, the same court adopted the *lex fori* approach for tort conflicts according to which the law of the forum governs "unless another state has an overwhelming interest." See Motenko v. MGM Dist., Inc., 921 P.2d 933 (Nev.1996), discussed *supra* 195 (Ch. 3). Should one assume that after *Motenko* status cases like *Hermanson* shall be decided under the *lex fori* approach? Regardless of the answer, does *Motenko* provide a more candid *a posteriori* rationale for *Hermanson*?

2. The "substantial relationship test" *Hermanson* used is acoustically similar, but not identical, to the "most significant relationship" formula of the Restatement (Second). Notice that *Hermanson* contains no reference to the Restatement. Had *Hermanson* relied on the Restatement, the pertinent provision would be § 287, which provides:

(1) Whether a child is legitimate is determined by the local law of the state which, with respect to the particular issue, has the most significant relationship to the child and the parent under the principles stated in § 6.

(2) The child will usually be held legitimate if this would be his status under the local law of the state where either (a) the parent was domiciled when the child's status of legitimacy is claimed to have been created or (b) the child was domiciled when the parent acknowledged the child as his own.

Which state's law would have been applicable in *Hermanson* under subsection 1 of § 287? Granting that Nevada had a "substantial relationship" with this case, did Nevada have the "most significant relationship * * * under the principles stated in § 6"? Which state's law would be applicable in *Hermanson* under subsection 2 of § 287?

The presumptive rule of subsection 2 is typical of many choice-of-law rules that are designed to produce a result that, from a substantive-law perspective, is considered preferable.[1] From that perspective, legitimacy was the preferred status because illegitimacy was not only a social stigma but also entailed denial of some important rights, such as inheritance or support. Rules like the California rule involved in *Hermanson* that imposed irrebuttable presumptions of paternity even in cases in which biological paternity was known not to exist, or that imposed very short time limits within which the presumed father could contest paternity, are examples of the substantive law's favor toward the status of legitimacy (*favor paternitatis*). However, because much of the legal discrimination against illegitimate children has been eliminated since the mid–1970s, the *raison d'etre* of such rules has been weakened considerably. *Hermanson* may well be a good example of conflicts law adjusting to changes in substantive law.

3. Smith v. Smith, 1994 WL 149445 (Minn.Ct.App.1994), presented the converse pattern from *Hermanson*--the law of the state of the child's birth and the mother's apparent domicile at the time (Oregon) did not impose a presumption of paternity, but the law of the mother's and child's present domicile (Minnesota) imposed such a presumption, which had become irrebuttable because of that state's statute of limitation. The Minnesota court applied Minnesota law because, inter alia:

> The purposes of the [Minnesota] Parentage Act are to impose a duty on a father to support his child, to ensure that the mother does not bear the full financial responsibility for a child, and to protect the public by preventing a child from becoming a public charge. [cit.] All of these purposes are served by applying the [Minnesota] presumption * * * that respondent is the biological father of [the child]. This furthers "the clear statutory purpose of promoting legitimacy." [cit.] The statute also reflects a governmental interest in preventing evidence of paternity from being concealed by requiring that the nonexistence of the father and child relationship presumed under [the Minnesota Act] be established early in a child's life.

Id. at *2. What do you learn from comparing *Smith* with *Hermanson*?

4. At least in a case involving the *Hermanson* pattern, are there not some dangers in *not* applying the law of the state where the child's mother was domiciled at the time of birth? One of the rationales of subsection 2 of § 287 of the Restatement (Second) is the desire to avoid "limping" relationships, namely, relationships recognized in one state but not in another. For example, once the status of legitimacy is invested in a person, that status should not be divested when that person or one or both of his parents move to another state. James Hermanson was born in California when both Cindy and David Hermanson had been domiciled there. James lived in California for three years and, as far as can be ascertained from the text of the opinion, he lived in Nevada for only two months (Oct. 1990–Dec. 1990) before his mother filed her divorce suit. The court speaks of Cindy "return[ing]" to Nevada, but it appears that any previous Nevada connections must have preceded James' birth

---

1. For foreign choice-of-law rules favoring filiation and legitimacy, see Symeonides, *Private International Law*, 52-54 (discussing rules from Austria, France, Germany, Holland, Italy, Japan, Peru, Portugal, Quebec, Switzerland, and Yugoslavia).

and perhaps the mother's marriage to David. Assuming for the moment that California had not repealed its irrebuttable presumption of paternity, are you concerned with the potential of forum shopping?

Suppose that California allowed an action to rebut the presumption but, like many other states, imposed a very short time limit within which to file such actions. Would this then turn this into a procedural question to be governed automatically by the *lex fori*? What if the laws of the two states were reversed?

5. What about the interest of the child in all of this? Citing NRS § 126.081, *Hermanson* speaks of the minors' "right to have their paternity determined in a court of law" and of Nevada's policy in "afford[ing] them the opportunity to litigate their paternity for three years after the age of eighteen." True enough. However, the court seems to ignore a companion provision, NRS § 126.101, which provides: "The child *must* be made a party to the action. If he is a minor, he must be represented by his general guardian or a guardian ad litem appointed by the court. The child's mother or father may not represent the child as guardian or otherwise." (Emphasis added.) California had a virtually identical provision. See Cal.Fam.Code § 7635 (West. Supp. 1997). Shouldn't James have been made a party to the *Hermanson* proceeding?

6. ***Other matters of status***. Whether James was David Hermanson's child is *par excellence* a question of personal status. In strict legal theory, the concept of status includes issues such as marriage, nationality or citizenship, capacity to be the subject of rights and duties (referred to in civil law systems as "personality"), and capacity to contract or to enter into other juridical acts. Foreign civil codes are replete with detailed rules for determining the law applicable to each of these matters. See, e.g., German codif., arts. 5–22; Swiss codif., arts. 33–85; Italian codif., arts. 20–24; Peruvian Civ. Code, arts. 2068–2087. In the United States, matters of citizenship are governed by federal law, while the two types of capacity are merged into one and both are relegated to the law that governs the contract or juridical act in question. Thus, at least under the traditional conflicts approach, the capacity of a person to be an heir or his capacity to make a testament are governed by the same law that governed the succession. Modern approaches allow for a separate treatment of each of these issues insofar as these approaches permit an issue-by-issue analysis.

7. ***Marriage.*** With regard to the status of a spouse, § 283 of the Restatement (Second) adopts a "most significant relationship" test, with a presumption that a marriage that was valid where contracted "will everywhere be recognized as valid unless it violates the strong public policy of another state which had the most significant relationship to the spouses and the marriage at the time of the marriage."[2] Until the 1960s, conflicts involving the validity of marriages were quite frequent because the substantive laws of the various states differed widely on the requirements for a valid marriage. Since then, those conflicts have gradually disappeared as the

---

2. For recent cases involving the converse scenario, see Donlann v. Maggurn, 55 P.3d 74 (Ariz.App. 2002), *rev. denied* 2/11/2003 (holding that a Mexican marriage that was formally invalid under Mexican law but valid under Arizona law was valid because, as the parties' pre- and post-marriage domicile, Arizona had the most significant relationship; Hudson Trail Outfitters v. District of Columbia Dept. of Employment Services, 801 A.2d 987 (D.C.2002) (similar scenario involving a Nicaraguan marriage, but holding the marriage invalid--thus wife did not lose her eligibility for worker's compensation benefits from the death of her previous husband).

laws of the various states began to converge. However, since the 1990s, marriage laws have begun diverging again. On the one hand, there is the push towards according same sex unions either the status of marriage or some of its incidents. For recent cases involving such unions, see Rosengarten v. Downes, 802 A.2d 170 (Conn.App.2002), *cert. granted*, 806 A.2d 1066 (Conn.2002) (refusing to dissolve a Vermont civil union); Burns v. Burns, 560 S.E.2d 47 (Ga.App.2002), *cert. denied* 7/15/2002 (holding that a Georgia woman who cohabited with a Vermont civil-union partner had violated a Georgia child-custody consent decree that prohibited the parents from cohabiting with non-relatives with whom they were "not legally married"). On the other hand, there is the new concept of "covenant marriage," which cannot be dissolved as easily as other marriages. See Spaht & Symeonides, *Covenant Marriage*, 1087-1120. Can the above Restatement provision adequately handle these new conflicts?

8. ***Divorce.*** Which state's law should govern the right to obtain a divorce? This is another question that, for the last three decades of the 20th century, had lost much of its relevance in the United States as state divorce laws gradually converged at the lowest common denominator. Even before this convergence, however, the question of which law governs divorce had been merged into the question of which state has jurisdiction to entertain a divorce action. As the Restatement (Second) proclaims in § 285, "[t]he local law of the domiciliary state in which the action is brought will be applied to determine the right to divorce." Once upon a time, the only state where such an action could be brought was the state of the *matrimonial* domicile. Under that regime, it was justifiably taken for granted that that state would apply its own divorce law. In Williams v. North Carolina, 317 U.S. 287 (1942), the U.S. Supreme Court held that the domicile of either spouse has jurisdiction to grant a divorce. The *Williams* court chose not to re-open the question of which law that state should apply in granting the divorce and, at least implicitly, allowed that state to apply its own law.[3] Thus, the state of the matrimonial domicile lost its control over the marital status of its domiciliaries. For two generations, this change has been accepted as both inevitable and beneficial. However, as the new covenant marriage legislation indicates, some states are attempting to reassert control over the marital status of their domiciliaries. Should the interstate system assist or ignore these attempts? See Spaht & Symeonides, supra, 1100-20.

9. ***Incidents of status and the "incidental" question.*** Suppose that the issue of James' status was not raised in a proceeding between Cindy and David Herman son, but rather:

> (a) in an action that Cindy filed as James' tutrix seeking to recover damages for the wrongful death of David Hermanson; or
>
> (b) in a succession proceeding in which Cindy and James are vying for

---

3. In other countries, the question of whether a court has jurisdiction to entertain a divorce action has remained separate from the question of which law that court will apply in granting the divorce. The latter law is usually "the law that governs the effects of the marriage," which is the law of a state with which *both* spouses are affiliated. In recent years, some countries allow the alternative application of the law of the forum state, but only if both spouses have a sufficient connection with that state. See Symeonides, *Private International Law*, 55-56 (discussing rules from Belgium, China, Germany, Holland, Hungary, Italy, Switzerland, and Yugoslavia).

inheritance rights in David Hermanson's estate; or

(c) in actions Cindy and David Hermanson filed against a tortfeasor, asking damages for the wrongful death of James.

Would Nevada's public policy be stronger or weaker in these actions than the court found it to be in *Hermanson*? How should one decide the status issue in each of these actions? Would it matter if Nevada law would (or would not) govern each of the main actions?

Suppose now that the validity of Cindy's marriage to David was questionable, and that the issue is raised in proceedings following David's death, as in cases (a) or (b) supra.

In all of the above actions, the question of whether James is David's child, or whether Cindy is David's spouse, is incidental or preliminary to the main issue of wrongful death or succession rights. Indeed, in the great majority of cases, issues of status arise in such an incidental fashion in wrongful death or succession proceedings. The Restatement (Second) draws a distinction between questions of "pure" status, such as the question involved in *Hermanson*, on the one hand, and the "incidents" or effects of such status on the other hand. One of the rationales or consequences of this distinction is to encourage a separate analysis of each category of questions and to allow more flexibility in determining the law governing the incidents of status. As noted earlier, the Restatement's rules on the status of marriage (§ 283) and legitimacy (§ 287) clearly tilt towards the validity of marriage (*favor matrimonii*) and legitimacy (*favor paternitatis*), and are based on the premise that a person's status should not change by the mere movement from one state to another. In contrast, the Restatement's rules on the incidents of these statuses (§§ 284, 288) do not contain such a tilt. They are based on the premise that, while the status itself should not be altered by movement from one state to another, the incidents of status may well be affected by such a movement. Sections 284 and 288 provide that, when a marriage is valid under the law applicable to it under § 293, or when the status of legitimacy has been accorded by the law applicable under § 287, the forum "usually" gives the same incidents to such a status as the forum's law provides. The word "usually" implies that the forum may choose not to accord certain of those incidents, or to accord certain incidents even when it does not fully recognize the status itself. For example, a state may prohibit the husband in a polygamous marriage from cohabiting with his wives within its territory but may allow such wives or their children to recover as "spouses" or "children," respectively, for the wrongful death of the husband. What do you think of this scheme?

L. CORPORATIONS

McDermott Inc. v. Lewis

Supreme Court of Delaware, 1987.
531 A.2d 206.

MOORE, J. We confront an important issue of first impression—whether a Delaware subsidiary of a Panamanian corporation may vote the shares it holds in its parent company under circumstances which are prohibited by Delaware law, but not the law of Panama. Necessarily, this involves questions of foreign law, and applicability of the internal affairs doctrine under Delaware law.

Plaintiffs, Harry Lewis and Nina Altman, filed these consolidated suits in the Court of Chancery in December, 1982 seeking to enjoin or rescind the 1982 Reorganization under which McDermott Incorporated, a Delaware corporation ("McDermott Delaware"), became a 92%-owned subsidiary of McDermott International, Inc., a Panamanian corporation ("International"). Lewis and Altman are stockholders of McDermott Delaware, which emerged from the Reorganization owning approximately 10% of International's common stock. Plaintiffs challenged this aspect of the Reorganization, and the Court of Chancery granted partial summary judgment in their favor, holding that McDermott Delaware could not vote its stock in International.

We conclude that the trial court erred in refusing to apply the law of Panama to the internal affairs of International. There was no nexus between International and the State of Delaware. Moreover, plaintiffs concede that the issues here do not involve the internal affairs of McDermott Delaware. Thus, we decline to follow *Norlin Corp. v. Rooney, Pace Inc.*, 744 F.2d 255 (2d Cir.1984), which prohibited a similar device involving a Panamanian subsidiary seeking to vote the shares it held in its Panamanian parent. Accordingly, we reverse. In so doing, we reaffirm the principle that the internal affairs doctrine is a major tenet of Delaware corporation law having important federal constitutional underpinnings.

I. International was incorporated in Panama on August 11, 1959, and is principally engaged in providing worldwide marine construction services to the oil and gas industry. Its executive offices are in New Orleans, Louisiana, and there are no operations in Delaware. International does not maintain offices in Delaware, hold meetings or conduct business here, have agents or employees in Delaware, or have any assets here.

McDermott Delaware and its subsidiaries operate throughout the United States in three principal industry segments: marine construction services, power generation systems and equipment, and engineered materials. McDermott Delaware's principal offices are in New Orleans.

Following the 1982 Reorganization, McDermott Delaware became a 92%-owned subsidiary of International. The public stockholders of International hold approximately 90% of the voting power of International, while McDermott Delaware holds about 10%.

The stated "principal purpose" of the reorganization, according to International's prospectus, was to enable the McDermott Group to retain, reinvest and redeploy earnings from operations outside the United States without subjecting such earnings to United States income tax. The prospectus also admitted that the 10% voting interest given to McDermott Delaware would be voted by International, "and such voting power could be used to oppose an attempt by a third party to acquire control of International if the management of International believes such use of the voting power would be in the best interests of the stockholders of International." An exchange offer, and thus the Reorganization, was supported by 89.59% of McDermott Delaware stockholders.

The applicable Panamanian law is set forth in the record by affidavits and opinion letters of Ricardo A. Durling, Esquire, and the deans of two Panamanian law schools, to support the claim that McDermott Delaware's retention of a 10% interest in International, and its right to vote those shares, is permitted by the laws of Panama. Significantly, the plaintiffs have not offered any contrary evidence. * * *

II. We note at the outset that if International were incorporated either in Delaware or Louisiana, its stock could not be voted by a majority-owned subsidiary. [cit.] No United States jurisdiction of which we are aware permits that practice.

Relying on *Norlin Corp. v. Rooney, Pace Inc.*, [supra], the Court of Chancery concluded that Panama in effect would refrain from applying its laws under the facts of this case. On that basis, the trial court then concluded that since both Delaware and Louisiana law prohibit a majority-owned subsidiary from voting its parent's stock, the device was improper. We consider this an erroneous application of both Delaware and Panamanian law.

Our analysis requires a two-step inquiry. First, we must determine if Panamanian law, in the factual context addressed by the Court of Chancery, permits International to vote its own shares through the device of McDermott Delaware's ownership. If it does not, then the inquiry ends. However, if Panamanian law permits the practice, we must consider the multifaceted issues inherent in the application of the internal affairs doctrine.

A. It is apparent that under limited circumstances the laws of Panama permit a subsidiary to vote the shares of its parent. Article 35 of Panamanian Cabinet Decree No. 247 of July 16, 1970, which is part of the General Corporation Law of Panama, restricts the exercise of voting rights on shares of certain Panamanian corporations, but Article 37 limits the scope of Article 35 to "corporations registered in the National Securities Commission [of Panama] and those whose shares are sold on the market ..." Opinion of Ricardo A. Durling, *supra*. Based on the facts before the Court of Chancery, it is undisputed that International was not required to register, nor had it registered, with the National Securities Commission. Further, International's shares were not "sold on the market," as that term is defined by the Attorney General of Panama. Reading Articles 35 and 37 together, it is apparent that Article 35's prohibition did not apply to International. * * *

Given the uncontroverted evidence of Panamanian law, establishing that a Panamanian corporation may place voting shares in a majority-owned subsidiary under the limited circumstances provided by Article 37, we turn to the fundamental issues presented by application of the internal affairs doctrine.

III. Internal corporate affairs involve those matters which are peculiar to the relationships among or between the corporation and its current officers, directors, and shareholders. *Edgar v. MITE Corp.*, 457 U.S. 624, 645 (1982). Restatement (Second) of Conflict of Laws § 313, Comment a (1971). It is essential to distinguish between acts which can be performed by both corporations and individuals, and those activities which are peculiar to the corporate entity.

Corporations and individuals alike enter into contracts, commit torts, and deal in personal and real property. Choice of law decisions relating to such corporate activities are usually determined after consideration of the facts of each transaction. *See* Reese and Kaufman, *The Law Governing Corporate Affairs: Choice of Law and the Impact of Full Faith and Credit*, 58 Colum.L.Rev. 1118, 1121 (1958) (hereinafter "Reese and Kaufman"). In such cases, the choice of law determination often turns on whether the corporation had sufficient contacts with the forum state, in relation to the act or transaction in question, to satisfy the constitutional requirements of due process. The internal affairs doctrine has no applicability in these situations. Rather, this doctrine governs the choice of law determinations involving matters *peculiar* to corporations, that is, those activities concerning the relationships *inter se* of the corporation, its directors, officers and shareholders.

The internal affairs doctrine requires that the law of the state of incorporation should determine issues relating to internal corporate affairs. [cit.] Under Delaware conflict of laws principles and the United States Constitution, there are appropriate circumstances which mandate application of this doctrine.

A. Delaware's well established conflict of laws principles require that the laws of the jurisdiction of incorporation—here the Republic of Panama—govern this dispute involving McDermott International's voting rights. [cit.]

The traditional conflicts rule developed by courts has been that internal corporate relationships are governed by the laws of the forum of incorporation. [cit.] As early as 1933, the Supreme Court of the United States noted:

> It has long been settled doctrine that a court—state or federal—sitting in one state will, as a general rule, decline to interfere with, or control by injunction or otherwise, the management of the internal affairs of a corporation organized under the laws of another state but will leave controversies as to such matters to the courts of the state of the domicile....

Rogers v. Guaranty Trust Co. of New York, 288 U.S. 123, 130 (1933) (citations omitted).

However, in *Western Air Lines, Inc. v. Sobieski*, 12 Cal.Rptr. 719 (Cal.App.1961), a California court upheld an order of the California Commissioner of Corporations directing a Delaware corporation having major contacts with California to follow the cumulative voting requirements imposed by California law. After the *Western Air* decision, commentators noted that the case signaled the alleged start of a "conflicts revolution." *See* Kozyris, *Corporate Wars and Choice of Law*, 1985 Duke L.J. 1 (hereinafter "Kozyris"); Kaplan, *Foreign Corporations and Local Corporate Policy*, 21 Vand.L.Rev. 433 (1968) (hereinafter "Kaplan"). The "new" conflicts theory weighs the interests and policies of the forum state in determining whether the law of the forum—lex fori—should be applied. *See*

Restatement (Second) of Conflict of Laws, §§ 302–06, 309 (1971). Thus, the *Western Air Lines* case "was to be the harbinger of a new conflicts approach in corporate law that would limit or perhaps discard the lex incorporationis." Kozyris, *supra* at 17.

A review of cases over the last twenty-six years, however, finds that in all but a few, the law of the state of incorporation was applied without any discussion. *Id.* at 17-18. In fact, twenty-six years after *Western Air* the following statement remains apt:

> The umbilical tie of the foreign corporation to the state of its charter is usually still religiously regarded as conclusive in determining the law to be applied in intracorporate disputes. The fundamental reexamination of the nature of conflict of laws over the past few years has virtually left foreign corporation matters remaining as a pocket of the past in a subject area which has otherwise been characterized by free inquiry, change and flux.

Kaplan, *supra* at 464.[10]

The policy underlying the internal affairs doctrine is an important one, and we decline to erode the principle:

> Under the prevailing conflicts practice, neither courts nor legislatures have maximized the imposition of local corporate policy on foreign corporations but have consistently applied the law of the state of incorporation to the entire gamut of internal corporate affairs. In many cases, this is a wise, practical, and equitable choice. It serves the vital need for a single, constant and equal law to avoid the fragmentation of continuing, interdependent internal relationships. The lex incorporationis, unlike the lex loci delicti, is not a rule based merely on the priori concept of territoriality and on the desirability of avoiding forum-shopping. It validates the autonomy of the parties in a subject where the underlying policy of the law is enabling. It facilitates planning and enhances predictability. In fields like torts, where the typical dispute involves two persons and a single or simple one-shot issue and where the common substantive policy is to spread the loss through compensation and insurance, the preference for forum law and the emphasis on the state interest in forum residents which are the common denominators of the new conflicts methodologies do not necessarily lead to unacceptable choices. By contrast, applying local internal affairs law to a foreign corporation just because it is amenable to process in the forum or because it has some local shareholders or some other local contact is apt to produce inequalities, intolerable confusion, and uncertainty, and intrude into the domain of other states that have a superior claim to regulate the same subject matter....

---

10. For an excellent discussion of the post-*Western Airlines* application of the internal affairs doctrine in the context of takeover litigation, see Kozyris, *supra* at 18–19. Since Professor Kozyris' article was published prior to the release of the *Norlin* opinion, the author did not have the opportunity to note that *Norlin* is the only known case which ignored the internal affairs doctrine in the context of corporate takeover litigation. Suffice it to say that in many leading cases the internal affairs doctrine was treated as axiomatic. [cit.]

Kozyris, *supra* at 98.

B. Given the significance of these considerations, application of the internal affairs doctrine is not merely a principle of conflicts law. It is also one of serious constitutional proportions—under due process, the commerce clause and the full faith and credit clause—so that the law of one state governs the relationships of a corporation to its stockholders, directors and officers in matters of internal corporate governance. The alternatives present almost intolerable consequences to the corporate enterprise and its managers. With the existence of multistate and multinational organizations, directors and officers have a significant right, under the fourteenth amendment's due process clause, to know what law will be applied to their actions. Stockholders also have a right to know by what standards of accountability they may hold those managing the corporation's business and affairs. That is particularly so here, given the significant fact that in the McDermott Group reorganization, and after full disclosure, 89.59% of the total outstanding common shares of McDermott Delaware were tendered in the exchange offer. Compare *Norlin.* Thus, by an overwhelming choice those stockholders received shares in International, and thereby selected the laws of Panama to govern inter se the corporate relations between themselves, International, its directors, officers and agents. Such issues have been the subject of litigation and scholarly discussions for decades. However, an attitude has developed in some quarters which exalts local interests over more fundamental doctrines. We approach such teachings with reservations.

Under the commerce clause *Pike v. Bruce Church, Inc.,* 397 U.S. 137, 142 (1970), determined that a state may regulate interstate commerce indirectly, but emphasized that the burden placed upon interstate commerce may not be excessive in relation to the local interests served by the regulation. In *Edgar v. MITE Corp.,* 457 U.S. 624 (1982), the Supreme Court ruled that under the commerce clause a state "has no interest in regulating the internal affairs of foreign corporations." *Id.* at 645–46. If that is so, then a court or state which attempts to displace the internal affairs doctrine carries a heavy burden to justify its actions.

The recent decision in *CTS Corp. v. Dynamics Corp. of America,* [481] U.S. [69], 107 S.Ct. 1637 (1987), (reversing 794 F.2d 250), seems to support this interpretation of *MITE*:

> This Court's recent Commerce Clause cases also have invalidated statutes that adversely may affect interstate commerce by subjecting activities to inconsistent regulations ... The Indiana Act poses no such problem. *So long as each State regulates voting rights only in the corporations it has created, each corporation will be subject to the law of only one state.* No principal [sic] of corporation law and practice is more firmly established than a State's authority to regulate domestic corporations, including the authority to define the voting rights of shareholders ... This beneficial free market system depends at its core upon the fact that *a corporation—except in the rarest situations—is organized under, and governed by, the law of a single jurisdiction, traditionally the corporate law of the state of its incorporation.*

CTS Corp., [481] U.S. at [88], 107 S.Ct. at 1649 (citations omitted) (emphases added). Thus, we conclude that application of the internal affairs doctrine is mandated by constitutional principles, except in "the rarest situations."[12]

In the early part of the twentieth century, the internal affairs doctrine was deemed to have constitutional support under the full faith and credit clause. [cit.] However, in 1935 the Supreme Court developed a balancing test to be used when evaluating whether full faith and credit was applicable. [cit.] A party bringing a full faith and credit claim thereafter bore the burden of establishing that conflicting interests of a foreign state were superior to those of the forum state. [cit.]

Order of United Commercial Travelers of America v. Wolfe, 331 U.S. 586 (1947) is the last Supreme Court decision which mandates application of the law of the state of organization to an entity's internal dealings under the full faith and credit clause. In *Wolfe*, the Supreme Court held that full faith and credit required that a dispute involving the internal affairs of a fraternal benefit society be governed by the laws of the state where the society was formed. *Id.* at 623–25. Although we recognize that there are lingering uncertainties concerning the vitality of *Wolfe*, we believe that full faith and credit commands application of the internal affairs doctrine except in the *rare* circumstance where national policy[15] is outweighed by a significant interest of the forum state in the corporation and its shareholders. Reese and Kaufman, *supra* at 1141.

Addressing the facts originally presented to the trial court and to us, we must conclude that due process and the commerce clause, in addition to principles of Delaware conflicts law, mandate reversal. Due process requires that directors, officers and shareholders be given adequate notice of the jurisdiction whose laws will ultimately govern the corporation's internal affairs. Under such circumstances, application of 8 Del.C. § 160(c) to International would unfairly and, in our opinion, unconstitutionally, subject those intimately involved with the management of the corporation to the laws of Delaware.

Moreover, application of Section 160(c) to International would violate the commerce clause. Delaware and Panama law clearly differ in their treatment of a subsidiary's voting rights under the facts originally presented here. For Delaware now to interfere in the internal affairs of a foreign corporation having no relationship whatever to this State clearly implies that International can be subjected to the differing laws of all fifty states on various matters respecting its internal affairs. Such a prohibitive burden has obvious commerce clause implications, and could not pass

---

12. *CTS Corp. v. Dynamics Corp. of America*, provides strong support for a conclusion that the commerce clause mandates that a state apply the internal affairs doctrine to disputes involving corporations organized under the laws of a sister state. *CTS Corp.* involved a challenge to Indiana's second generation corporate takeover statute. The Indiana statute applies only to Indiana corporations, and is thus distinguishable from the first generation of statutes struck down in *Edgar v. MITE Corp.*, which purported to govern the internal affairs of foreign corporations. In *MITE*, the Supreme Court held that Illinois violated the commerce clause by burdening interstate commerce when regulating the internal affairs of a foreign corporation. In *CTS Corp.*, the Court ruled that a state does not violate the commerce clause, notwithstanding heavy burdens imposed upon interstate commerce, if a state is merely regulating the internal affairs of its own corporations.

15. *See, e.g.*, Kozyris, *supra* at 34: "Elementary considerations of predictability, practicality, and equality call for both corporate governance and the common rights and obligations of shareholders to be subject to a single law. Full faith and credit gives primacy to the statute chosen by the parties with the consent of the state of incorporation."

constitutional muster. The substantial effect that would impose on interstate commerce triggers the *Pike v. Bruce Church, Inc.* balancing test. Since a state has no interest in regulating the internal affairs of a foreign corporation under *MITE*, Delaware has nothing left with which to counterbalance the burden that application of Section 160(c) on International would impose on interstate commerce. Given all the circumstances, the trial court's ruling cannot stand.[16]

IV. Plaintiffs protest the issuance of voting stock to McDermott Delaware on public policy grounds, relying on the following statement from *Norlin*:

> [The] statutes seek to safeguard minority shareholders from management attempts at self-perpetuation. If cross-ownership and cross-voting of stock between parents and subsidiaries were unregulated, officers and directors could easily entrench themselves by exchanging a sufficient number of shares to block any challenge to their autonomy....

744 F.2d at 262 (citation omitted).

In that regard, Delaware law prohibits cross-voting of stock by majority-owned subsidiaries of Delaware corporations. 8 Del.C. § 160(c). But here, we are called upon to apply the laws of Panama to a Panamanian corporation having no contacts with Delaware. We are not altering existing law governing Delaware corporations.

On the record before the Court of Chancery, we are not faced with some "Draconian" measure for the effectuation of a scheme designed solely to entrench existing management to the detriment of the corporation's shareholders. See *Unocal Corp. v. Mesa Petroleum Co.*, Del. Supr., 493 A.2d 946, 955 (1985). The facts here do not support an entrenchment claim. The size of the voting interest placed in McDermott Delaware, its stated principal purpose being for tax advantages, and the timing of the transaction, all sustain this conclusion. In short, there was no threat of any kind which implicated the policies discussed by us in *Unocal. Id.* at 954–59. If such issues should arise in a takeover context, they can be addressed in a proper way and at the proper time. [cit.]

In conclusion, the trial court erred as a matter of law in ignoring the uncontroverted Panamanian law, and in applying Delaware and/or Louisiana law to the internal affairs of International contrary to established Delaware law and important constitutional principles. Accordingly the judgment of the Court of Chancery is *Reversed*.

Notes and Questions

1. *McDermott* contains one of the strongest endorsements of the rule that the law of the state of incorporation (*lex incorporationis*) governs the internal affairs of corporations. How does the court define "internal affairs"? Naturally, "internal" affairs are juxtaposed to "external" affairs, that is, those arising from the corporation's relations with third parties. External affairs are not subject to special

---

16. However, we recognize that as a Panamanian corporation, McDermott International's rights here do not derive from the full faith and credit clause, which applies only to the laws of American states.

choice-of-law rules peculiar to corporations. As the Restatement (Second) states, "[t]he rights and liabilities of a corporation with respect to a third person that arise from a corporate act of a sort that can likewise be done by an individual are determined by the same choice-of-law principles as are applicable to non-corporate parties." § 301. What reasons does the *McDermott* court give for its endorsement of the *lex incorporationis* rule for the internal affairs of corporations? Are you surprised that Delaware so strongly favors this rule? Is it not true that, unlike this case, this rule would lead to the application of Delaware law in the majority of cases?

2. Suppose that the *McDermott* lawsuit had been filed in Louisiana, a state that had numerous significant connections with McDermott International. In such a case, should the artificial connection of incorporation in Panama prevail over Louisiana's factual and real connections with International? European systems avoid this problem by applying the law of the state where the corporation has its "real seat" (*siège réel*). Is this a better rule? Why or why not? American jurisdictions have tried to address this problem by refusing to apply the foreign *lex incorporationis* to so-called "pseudo-foreign" corporations. *Western Airlines v. Sobiesky*, which *McDermott* discusses, is a well-known example of such a refusal. Several states have enacted statutes that authorize the application of forum law to such corporations. For example, a California statute provides that California law applies "to the exclusion of" the law of the state of incorporation, to any foreign corporation that conducts more than 50% of its business in California and that has more than 50% of its shares owned by Californians. Cal. Corp. Code § 2115(a) and (b). Is the situation this statute contemplates one of those "rarest situations" referred to in *CTS Corp. v. Dynamics Corp. of America* (also discussed in *McDermott*), in which a deviation from the *lex incorporationis* will survive a constitutional challenge under the commerce and full faith and credit clauses of the federal constitution? If so, is this one of those "unusual case[s]" in which Restatement (Second) § 302 would authorize such a deviation?

Chapter 5

CONSTITUTIONAL LIMITS
ON CHOICE OF LAW

A. INTRODUCTION

In the prior chapters we explored the different approaches used to determine what law to apply. Although we considered policy arguments as to why one choice-of-law approach was better or fairer than another, we treated choice of law as entirely a matter of forum law—unconstrained by external controls.

If states were entirely independent, choice of law could be solely a matter of forum law, with the only external limitations being the difficulties of enforcement and the risk of retaliation by outsiders. States, of course, are not entirely independent. As part of the United States, they are constrained by federal law and the United States Constitution. As a result, there are a variety of things states cannot do, even within their own territory. For example, under Art. I, sec. 10, states cannot enter into treaties, coin money, or impair the obligation of contracts.

In this chapter we consider the constraints that the Constitution imposes on state choice of law. We shall focus in particular on the extent to which the Constitution prohibits states from regulating events occurring outside their borders or involving non-citizens.[1] New York can obviously set the speed limit for New York roads and define the standard of care owed to passengers in cars in New York. Can it also set the speed limit in Michigan or define the standard of care for drivers driving in Michigan? Does the Constitution limit New York's authority in these areas or does the Constitution eschew such limits, leaving them entirely to Congress and the practicalities of enforcement and fear of retaliation?

As you will see, the Supreme Court has concluded that the Constitution does indeed impose some limits on state choice of law. As Professor Laycock has explained, this is not surprising:

> Choice-of-law questions are about the allocation of authority among the several states. Allocation of authority is what constitutions do. The essential function of constitutions is to constitute the many units of government in our federal system

---

1. The scope of a state's authority to apply its own laws is sometimes called "legislative jurisdiction". The phrase is misleading because "legislative jurisdiction" includes common law as well as statutory rules. However the phrase is useful as a way to distinguish a state's regulatory or law-giving authority from its adjudicatory authority. As you will see, the Supreme Court has treated issues of legislative and adjudicatory authority as separate matters. We shall, therefore, initially examine them separately and then consider whether this distinction makes sense. See infra Ch. 8(E).

and define and limit the power of each. It would be an astonishing oversight if our fundamental law did not state general principles allocating authority among states and if those principles did not have implications for choice of law.[2] Laycock, *Equal Citizens*, 250. What may be surprising is how modest these constitutional constraints are. As you will see, the Supreme Court has allowed states wide latitude to apply their own laws in cases brought in their courts.

Constitutional limits on choice of law raise fundamental questions about the scope of state sovereignty in our federal system. Although many of these questions are explored in the context of relatively benign torts or contracts cases, they have implications for far more explosive matters. For example, could one state impose civil or criminal liability on its citizens who go to other states to take advantage of more liberal rules concerning the right to die, surrogate mother arrangements or abortion? See Kreimer, *The Law of Choice*, 451.

This chapter examines several constitutional provisions that may limit state choice of law. Collectively, these provisions raise concerns about fairness to individuals and about non-discrimination against other states and their citizens.

B. THE DUE PROCESS CLAUSE—A FIRST LOOK

Home Insurance Co. v. Dick
Supreme Court of the United States, 1930.
281 U.S. 397, 50 S.Ct. 338, 74 L.Ed. 926.

JUSTICE BRANDEIS delivered the opinion of the Court. Dick, a citizen of Texas, brought this action in a court of that State against Compañia General Anglo–Mexicana de Seguros S. A., a Mexican corporation, to recover on a policy of fire insurance for the total loss of a tug. Jurisdiction was asserted in rem through garnishment, by ancillary writs issued against The Home Insurance Company and Franklin Fire Insurance Company, which reinsured, by contracts with the Mexican corporation, parts of the risk which it had assumed. The garnishees are New York corporations. Upon them, service was effected by serving their local agents in Texas appointed pursuant to Texas statutes, which require the appointment of local agents by foreign corporations seeking permits to do business within the State.

The controversy here is wholly between Dick and the garnishees. The defendant has never been admitted to do business in Texas; has not done any business there; and has not authorized anyone to receive service of process or enter an appearance for it in this cause. * * *

[The garnishees'] * * * defense rests upon the following facts. This suit was not commenced till more than one year after the date of the loss. The policy provided: "It is understood and agreed that no judicial suit or demand shall be entered before any tribunal for the collection of any claim under this policy, unless such suits or demands are filed within one year counted as from the date on which such damage

---

2. This article originally appeared at 92 Colum.L.Rev. 249 (1992). Reprinted by permission.

occurs." This provision was in accord with the Mexican law to which the policy was expressly made subject. It was issued by the Mexican company in Mexico to one Bonner, of Tampico, Mexico, and was there duly assigned to Dick prior to the loss. It covered the vessel only in certain Mexican waters. The premium was paid in Mexico; and the loss was "payable in the City of Mexico in current funds of the United States of Mexico, or their equivalent elsewhere." At the time the policy was issued, when it was assigned to him, and until after the loss, Dick actually resided in Mexico, although his permanent residence was in Texas. The contracts of reinsurance were effected by correspondence between the Mexican company in Mexico and the New York companies in New York. Nothing thereunder was to be done, or was in fact done, in Texas.

In the trial court, the garnishees contended that since the insurance contract was made and was to be performed in Mexico, and the one year provision was valid by its laws, Dick's failure to sue within one year after accrual of the alleged cause of action was a complete defense to the suit on the policy; that this failure also relieved the garnishees of any obligation as reinsurers, the same defense being open to them, [cit.]; and that they, consequently, owed no debt to the Mexican company subject to garnishment. To this defense, Dick demurred, on the ground that Article 5545 of the Texas Revised Civil Statutes (1925) provides: "No person, firm, corporation, association or combination of whatsoever kind shall enter into any stipulation, contract, or agreement, by reason whereof the time in which to sue thereon is limited to a shorter period than two years. And no stipulation, contract, or agreement for any such shorter limitation in which to sue shall ever be valid in this State."

The trial court sustained Dick's contention and entered judgment against the garnishees. On appeal, both in the Court of Civil Appeals [cit.] and in the Supreme Court of the State [cit.], the garnishees asserted that, as construed and applied, the Texas statute violated the due process clause of the Fourteenth Amendment and the contract clause. Both courts treated the policy provision as equivalent to a foreign statute of limitation; held that Article 5545 related to the remedy available in Texas courts; concluded that it was validly applicable to the case at bar; and affirmed the judgment of the trial court. * * *

First. Dick contends that this Court lacks jurisdiction of the action, because the errors assigned involve only questions of local law and of conflict of laws. The argument is that while a provision requiring notice of loss within a fixed period, is substantive because it is a condition precedent to the existence of the cause of action, the provision for liability only in case suit is brought within the year is not substantive because it relates only to the remedy after accrual of the cause of action; that while the validity, interpretation and performance of the substantive provisions of a contract are determined by the law of the place where it is made and is to be performed, matters which relate only to the remedy are unquestionably governed by the lex fori; and that even if the Texas court erred in holding the statute applicable to this contract, the error is one of state law or of the interpretation of the contract, and is not reviewable here.

The contention is unsound. There is no dispute as to the meaning of the provision in the policy. It is that the insurer shall not be liable unless suit is brought within one year of the loss. Whether the provision be interpreted as making the commencement of a suit within the year a condition precedent to the existence of a cause of action, or as making failure to sue within the year a breach of a condition subsequent which extinguishes the cause of action, is not of legal significance here. Nor are we concerned with the question whether the provision is properly described as relating to remedy or to substance. However characterized, it is an express term in the contract of the parties by which the right of the insured and the correlative obligation of the insurer are defined. If effect is given to the clause, Dick cannot recover from the Mexican corporation and the garnishees cannot be compelled to pay. If, on the other hand, the statute is applied to the contract, it admittedly abrogates a contractual right and imposes liability, although the parties have agreed that there should be none.

The statute is not simply one of limitation. It does not merely fix the time in which the aid of the Texas courts may be invoked. Nor does it govern only the remedies available in the Texas courts. It deals with the powers and capacities of persons and corporations. It expressly prohibits the making of certain contracts. As construed, it also directs the disregard in Texas of contractual rights and obligations wherever created and assumed; and it commands the enforcement of obligations in excess of those contracted for. Therefore, the objection that, as applied to contracts made and to be performed outside of Texas, the statute violates the Federal Constitution, raises federal questions of substance; and the existence of the federal claim is not disproved by saying that the statute, or the one year provision in the policy, relates to the remedy and not to the substance.

That the federal questions were not raised in the trial court is immaterial. For, the Court of Civil Appeals and the Supreme Court of the State considered the questions as properly raised in the appellate proceedings and passed on them adversely to the federal claim. [cit.] The case is properly here on appeal. The motion to dismiss the appeal is overruled; and the petition for certiorari is, therefore, denied.

Second. The Texas statute as here construed and applied deprives the garnishees of property without due process of law. A State may, of course, prohibit and declare invalid the making of certain contracts within its borders. Ordinarily, it may prohibit performance within its borders, even of contracts validly made elsewhere, if they are required to be performed within the State and their performance would violate its laws. But, in the case at bar, nothing in any way relating to the policy sued on, or to the contracts of reinsurance, was ever done or required to be done in Texas. All acts relating to the making of the policy were done in Mexico. All in relation to the making of the contracts of re-insurance were done there or in New York. And, likewise, all things in regard to performance were to be done outside of Texas. Neither the Texas laws nor the Texas courts were invoked for any purpose, except by Dick in the bringing of this suit. The fact that Dick's permanent residence was in Texas is without significance. At all times here material, he was physically present and acting in Mexico. Texas was, therefore, without power to affect the terms of contracts so made. Its attempt to impose a greater obligation than that agreed upon and to seize property in payment of the imposed obligation violates the guaranty against deprivation of property without due process of law. Compañia General de

Tabacos v. Collector of Internal Revenue, 275 U.S. 87 [1927]; Aetna Life Ins. Co. v. Dunken, 266 U.S. 389 [1924]; New York Life Ins. Co. v. Dodge, 246 U.S. 357 [1918]. [cit.][5]

The cases relied upon, in which it was held that a State may lengthen its statute of limitations, are not in point. [cit.] In those cases, the parties had not stipulated a time limit for the enforcement of their obligations. It is true that a State may extend the time within which suit may be brought in its own courts, if, in doing so, it violates no agreement of the parties.[6] And, in the absence of a contractual provision, the local statute of limitation may be applied to a right created in another jurisdiction even where the remedy in the latter is barred. In such cases, the rights and obligations of the parties are not varied. When, however, the parties have expressly agreed upon a time limit on their obligation, a statute which invalidates the agreement and directs enforcement of the contract after the time has expired increases their obligation and imposes a burden not contracted for.

It is true also that a State is not bound to provide remedies and procedure to suit the wishes of individual litigants. It may prescribe the kind of remedies to be available in its courts and dictate the practice and procedure to be followed in pursuing those remedies. Contractual provisions relating to these matters, even if valid where made, are often disregarded by the court of the forum, pursuant to statute or otherwise. But the Texas statute deals neither with the kind of remedy available nor with the mode in which it is to be pursued. It purports to create rights and obligations. It may not validly affect contracts which are neither made nor are to be performed in Texas.

Third. Dick urges that Article 5545 of the Texas law is a declaration of its public policy; and that a State may properly refuse to recognize foreign rights which violate its declared policy. Doubtless, a State may prohibit the enjoyment by persons within its borders of rights acquired elsewhere which violate its laws or public policy; and, under some circumstances, it may refuse to aid in the enforcement of such rights. [cit.]; compare Fauntleroy v. Lum, 210 U.S. 230 [1908]. But the Mexican corporation never was in Texas; and neither it nor the garnishees invoked the aid of the Texas courts or the Texas laws. The Mexican corporation was not before the court. The garnishees were brought in by compulsory process. Neither has asked favors. They ask only to be let alone. We need not consider how far the State may go in imposing restrictions on the conduct of its own residents, and of foreign corporations which have received permission to do business within its borders; or how far it may go in refusing to lend the aid of its courts to the enforcement of rights acquired outside its borders. It may not abrogate the rights of parties beyond its borders having no relation to anything done or to be done within them.

---

5. The division of this Court in the *Tabacos* and *Dodge* cases was not on the principle here stated, but on the question of fact whether there were in those cases things done within the State of which the State could properly lay hold as the basis of the regulations there imposed. [cit.] In the absence of any such things, as in this case, the Court was agreed that a State is without power to impose either public or private obligations on contracts made outside of the State and not to be performed there. [cit.]

6. * * * There is a clear difference between the revival of a liability which is unenforceable only because a statute has barred the remedy regardless of the will of the parties, and the extension of a liability beyond the limit expressly agreed upon by the parties. [cit.]

Fourth. Finally, it is urged that the Federal Constitution does not require the States to recognize and protect rights derived from the laws of foreign countries—that as to them the full faith and credit clause has no application. [cit.] The claims here asserted are not based upon the full faith and credit clause. [cit.] They · rest upon the Fourteenth Amendment. Its protection extends to aliens. Moreover, the parties in interest here are American companies. The defense asserted is based on the provision of the policy and on their contracts of reinsurance. The courts of the State confused this defense with that based on the Mexican Code. They held that even if the effect of the foreign statute was to extinguish the right, Dick's removal to Texas prior to the bar of the foreign statute, removed the cause of action from Mexico and subjected it to the Texas statute of limitation. And they applied the same rule to the provision in the policy. Whether or not that is a sufficient answer to the defense based on the foreign law, we may not consider; for, no issue under the full faith and credit clause was raised. But in Texas, as elsewhere, the contract was subject to its own limitations. * * *

Reversed.

Notes and Questions

1. Notice how Texas obtained personal jurisdiction in *Dick*. The two American companies named as defendants reinsured risks insured by the Mexican company. Under the reinsurance contract, the American companies were required to reimburse the Mexican company if the insured-loss occurred. This was the "debt" that was attached in Texas. This debt owed to the Mexican company existed wherever the debtor was located. See Harris v. Balk, 198 U.S. 215 (1905). Because the American companies had offices in Texas, the debt was in Texas and the court could therefore attach the debt and use quasi-in-rem jurisdiction. Today, a state could not assert jurisdiction in this manner. See Rush v. Savchuk, 444 U.S. 320 (1980); Shaffer v. Heitner, 433 U.S. 186 (1977).

2. The Court notes that if the contract had been silent on the limitations period, Texas could have applied its own statute of limitations. This reflects a long-established principle that statutes of limitations are procedural, and that, for this reason, the forum can apply forum law on this matter. See generally Sun Oil Co. v. Wortman, 486 U.S. 717 (1988), infra. Why does the inclusion of a limitations period in the contract alter Texas' power to apply its own procedural rules? Is a state's power as a sovereign altered by private contracts to which the state is not a party?

3. Does the Due Process Clause allocate sovereignty among the states? Is that its purpose? Professor Ralph Whitten has argued that the use of due process to limit state choice of law is:

> founded upon the notion that the due process clause embodies a certain kind of territorial restraint on state lawmaking authority. Specifically, the test supposes that due process incorporates restrictions designed to regulate the status of the states as coequal sovereigns in the federal system. There is, however, no substantial evidence that the due process clause was understood in this way at the time it was ratified.

Whitten, *Due Process*, 904. Is *Dick* concerned with allocating sovereignty or does it have a different focus?

4. *Dick* might be viewed as constitutionalizing the vested rights approach to conflicts. Two other cases lend some support to this view. In New York Life Ins. Co. v. Dodge, 246 U.S. 357 (1918), Mr. Dodge purchased a life insurance policy from defendant's Missouri office. Later, he applied to defendant's New York office for a loan against the policy. When Dodge defaulted on a loan repayment, the insurance company treated the policy as having been forfeited and refused to pay proceeds following Dodge's death. New York law permitted the forfeiture, but Missouri law did not. The Supreme Court reversed Missouri's application of Missouri law to the contract, noting that the loan contract was "consummated" in New York.

In contrast, the Court allowed the application of Missouri law in the almost identical case of Mutual Life Ins. Co. v. Liebing, 259 U.S. 209 (1922). In *Liebing*, unlike *Dodge*, the original insurance contract included a promise to make a loan. Thus, the loan was covered by the original contract and governed by the law of the place where that contract had been made—in this case, Missouri.

On the other hand, *Dick* may not simply constitutionalize the rule of *lex loci contractus*. Justice Brandeis, the author of *Dick*, had dissented in *Dodge* on the ground that even though the contract was made in New York, the parties and transaction were sufficiently connected to Missouri to permit the application of its law. Brandeis found no such connecting factors in *Dick*. See *Dick*, supra n.5.

5. During the era of *Dodge* and *Dick*, the Supreme Court also invalidated other state economic and social legislation which the Court believed unreasonably interfered with liberty and property. See, e.g., Lochner v. New York, 198 U.S. 45 (1905) (law limiting the hours bakers could work unreasonably interfered with freedom of employers and employees to contract).

C. THE FULL FAITH AND CREDIT CLAUSE—A FIRST LOOK

Alaska Packers Assn. v. Industrial Accident Comm'n. of California

Supreme Court of the United States, 1935.
294 U.S. 532, 55 S.Ct. 518, 79 L.Ed. 1044.

JUSTICE STONE delivered the opinion of the Court. * * * On May 13, 1932, Palma, a non-resident alien, and appellant, doing business in California, executed at San Francisco a written contract of employment. Palma agreed to work for appellant in Alaska during the salmon canning season; the appellant agreed to transport him to Alaska and, at the end of the season, to return him to San Francisco where he was to be paid his stipulated wages, less advances. The contract recited that appellant had elected to be bound by the Alaska Workmen's Compensation Law and stipulated that the parties should be subject to and bound by the provisions of that statute. Section 58 of the California Workmen's Compensation Act was then in force, which provides:

"The commission shall have jurisdiction over all controversies arising out of injuries suffered without the territorial limits of this state in those cases where the injured employee is a resident of this state at the time of the injury and the contract of hire was made in this State, ..."

At that time the California Supreme Court had held * * * that this section was applicable to non-residents of California, since the privileges and immunities clause of the Federal Constitution prevented giving any effect to the requirement that the employee be a resident. The California Workmen's Compensation Act also provides, section 27(a): "No contract, rule or regulation shall exempt the employer from liability for the compensation fixed by this act, ..."

In August, 1932, after his return from Alaska to California, the employee applied for and later received an award by the California Commission in compensation for injuries received by him in the course of his employment in Alaska. * * *

In refusing to set aside the award of the state commission, the Supreme Court of California ruled, * * * that section 58 of the California Compensation Act was applicable to Palma, although a non-resident alien; that, as the contract of employment was entered into within the state, the stipulation that the Alaska Act should govern was invalid under section 27(a). It concluded that the Alaska statute afforded a remedy to the employee in Alaska and held that by setting up the defense of the Alaska statute in California the two statutes were brought into conflict, and that in the circumstances neither the due process clause nor the full faith and credit clause denied to the state the power to apply its own law, to the exclusion of the Alaska Act, in fixing and awarding compensation for the injury.

1. The question first to be considered is whether a state, which may constitutionally impose on employer and employee a system of compensation for injuries to the employee in the course of his employment within the state, [cit.] is precluded by the due process clause, in the special circumstances of this case, from imposing liability for injuries to the employee occurring in Alaska.

The California statute does not purport to have any extraterritorial effect, in the sense that it undertakes to impose a rule for foreign tribunals, nor did the judgment of the state supreme court give it any. The statute assumes only to provide a remedy to be granted by the California Commission for injuries, received in the course of employment entered into within the state, wherever they may occur. Compare Bradford Electric Light Co. v. Clapper, 286 U.S. 145, 153 [1932]. We assume that in Alaska the employee, had he chosen to do so, could have claimed the benefits of the Alaska statute, and that if any effect were there given to the California statute, it would be only by comity or by virtue of the full faith and credit clause. *Bradford Electric Light Co. v. Clapper.*

The due process clause denies to a state any power to restrict or control the obligation of contracts executed and to be performed without the state, as an attempt to exercise power over a subject matter not within its constitutional jurisdiction. [cit.]; *New York Life Ins. Co. v. Dodge*; *Home Insurance Co. v. Dick*; [cit.] Similarly, a state may not penalize or tax a contract entered into and to be performed outside the state, although one of the contracting parties is within the state. [cit.]

But where the contract is entered into within the state, even though it is to be performed elsewhere, its terms, its obligation and its sanctions are subject, in some measure, to the legislative control of the state. The fact that the contract is to be performed elsewhere does not of itself put these incidents beyond reach of the power which a state may constitutionally exercise. [cit.]

* * *

We cannot say that the statutory requirement of California, that the provisions for compensation shall extend to injuries without the state when the contract for employment was entered into within it, is given such an unreasonable application in the present case as to transcend constitutional limitations. The employee, an alien more than 2,000 miles from his home in Mexico, was, with fifty-three others, employed by petitioner in California. The contract called for their transportation to Alaska, some 3,000 miles distant, for seasonal employment of between two and three months, at the conclusion of which they were to be returned to California, and were there to receive their wages.

The meager facts disclosed by the record suggest a practice of employing workers in California for seasonal occupation in Alaska, under such conditions as to make it improbable that the employees injured in the course of their employment in Alaska would be able to apply for compensation there. It was necessary for them to return to California in order to receive their full wages. They would be accompanied by their fellow workers, who would normally be the witnesses required to establish the fact of the injury and its nature. The probability is slight that injured workmen, once returned to California, would be able to retrace their steps to Alaska, and there successfully prosecute their claims for compensation. Without a remedy in California, they would be remediless, and there was the danger that they might become public charges, both matters of grave public concern to the state.

California, therefore, had a legitimate public interest in controlling and regulating this employer-employee relationship in such fashion as to impose a liability upon the employer for an injury suffered by the employee, and in providing a remedy available to him in California. In the special circumstances disclosed, the state had as great an interest in affording adequate protection to this class of its population as to employees injured within the state. Indulging the presumption of constitutionality which attaches to every state statute, we cannot say that this one, as applied, lacks a rational basis or involved any arbitrary or unreasonable exercise of state power.

* * *

Petitioner, in relying on the Alaska statute as a defense in California, points out that it makes no distinction between residents and non-residents but gives a remedy to every employee injured in the course of his employment in Alaska, and invokes the rule, often followed in this Court, that suits to recover for personal injury are transitory, and that the jurisdiction creating the right may not, by restricting the venue, preclude recovery in any court outside the state having jurisdiction. [cit.] Tennessee Coal Iron & R. Co. v. George, 233 U.S. 354 [1914]. The Supreme Court of California, accepting this view, nevertheless refused to give effect to the Alaska statute because of its conflict with the California compensation act. Since each statute provides a different remedy, the court recognized that, by setting up the Alaska statute as a defense to the award of the Commission, the two statutes were brought into direct conflict. It resolved the conflict by holding that the courts of California were not bound by the full faith and credit clause to apply the Alaska statute instead of its own.

To the extent that California is required to give full faith and credit to the conflicting Alaska statute, it must be denied the right to apply in its own courts a statute of the state, lawfully enacted in pursuance of its domestic policy. We assume, as did the state court, that the remedy provided in the Alaska statute is one which could also be applied by the California courts, except for the conflict. We also assume, as the parties concede, that * * * the command of the full faith and credit clause is made applicable to territorial statutes with the same force and effect as that of the constitutional provision with respect to statutes of the states [cit.]. The subject of our inquiry is therefore whether the full faith and credit clause requires the state of California to give effect to the Alaska statute rather than its own.

It has often been recognized by this Court that there are some limitations upon the extent to which a state will be required by the full faith and credit clause to enforce even the judgment of another state, in contravention of its own statutes or policy. [cit.]

In the case of statutes, the extra-state effect of which Congress has not prescribed, where the policy of one state statute comes into conflict with that of another, the necessity of some accommodation of the conflicting interests of the two states is still more apparent. A rigid and literal enforcement of the full faith and credit clause, without regard to the statute of the forum, would lead to the absurd result that, wherever the conflict arises, the statute of each state must be enforced in the courts of the other, but cannot be in its own. Unless by force of that clause a greater effect is thus to be given to a state statute abroad than the clause permits it to have at home, it is unavoidable that this Court determine for itself the extent to which the statute of one state may qualify or deny rights asserted under the statute of another. [cit.]

The necessity is not any the less whether the statute and policy of the forum is set up as a defense to a suit brought under the foreign statute or the foreign statute is set up as a defense to a suit or proceedings under the local statute. In either case, the conflict is the same. In each, rights claimed under one statute prevail only by denying effect to the other. In both the conflict is to be resolved, not by giving automatic effect to the full faith and credit clause, compelling the courts of each state to subordinate its own statutes to those of the other, but by appraising the governmental interests of each jurisdiction, and turning the scale of decision according to their weight.

The enactment of the present statute of California was within state power and infringes no constitutional provision. Prima facie every state is entitled to enforce in its own courts its own statutes, lawfully enacted. One who challenges that right, because of the force given to a conflicting statute of another state by the full faith and credit clause, assumes the burden of showing, upon some rational basis, that of the conflicting interests involved those of the foreign state are superior to those of the forum. It follows that not every statute of another state will override a conflicting statute of the forum by virtue of the full faith and credit clause; that the statute of a state may sometimes override the conflicting statute of another, both at home and abroad; and, again, that the two conflicting statutes may each prevail over the other at home, although given no extraterritorial effect in the state of the other.

This was fully recognized by this Court in *Bradford Electric Light Co. v. Clapper*. There, upon an appraisal of the governmental interests of the two states, Vermont and New Hampshire, it was held that the Compensation Act of Vermont, where the status of employer and employee was established, should prevail over the conflicting statute of New Hampshire, where the injury occurred and the suit was brought. In reaching that conclusion, weight was given to the following circumstances: that liability under the Vermont Act was an incident of the status of employer and employee created within Vermont, and as such continued in New Hampshire where the injury occurred; that it was a substitute for a tort action, which was permitted by the statute of New Hampshire; that the Vermont statute expressly provided that it should extend to injuries occurring without the state and was interpreted to preclude recovery by proceedings brought in any other state; and that there was no adequate basis for saying that the compulsory recognition of the Vermont statute by the courts of New Hampshire would be obnoxious to the public policy of that state.

If, for the reasons given, the Vermont statute was held to override the New Hampshire statute in the courts of New Hampshire, it is hardly to be supposed that the Constitution would require it to be given any less effect in Vermont, even though the New Hampshire statute were set up as a defense to proceedings there. Similarly, in the present case, only if it appears that, in the conflict of interests which have found expression in the conflicting statutes, the interest of Alaska is superior to that of California, is there rational basis for denying to the courts of California the right to apply the laws of their own state. While in *Bradford Electric Light Co. v. Clapper*, it did not appear that the subordination of the New Hampshire statute to that of Vermont, by compulsion of the full faith and credit clause, would be obnoxious to the policy of New Hampshire, the Supreme Court of California has declared it to be contrary to the policy of the State to give effect to the provisions of the Alaska statute and that they conflict with its own statutes.

There are only two differences material for present purposes, between the facts of the *Clapper* case and those presented in this case: the employee here is not a resident of the place in which the employment was begun, and the employment was wholly to be performed in the jurisdiction in which the injury arose. Whether these differences, with a third—that the Vermont statute was intended to preclude resort to any other remedy even without the state—are, when taken with the differences between the New Hampshire and Alaska compensation laws, sufficient ground for withholding or denying any effect to the California statute in Alaska, we need not now inquire. But it is clear that they do not lessen the interest of California in enforcing its compensation act within the state, or give any added weight to the interest of Alaska in having its statute enforced in California. We need not repeat what we have already said of the peculiar concern of California in providing a remedy for those in the situation of the present employee. Its interest is sufficient to justify its legislation and is greater than that of Alaska, of which the employee was never a resident and to which he may never return. Nor should the fact that the employment was wholly to be performed in Alaska, although temporary in character, lead to any different result. It neither diminishes the interest of California in giving a remedy to the employee, who is a member of a class in the protection of which the state has an especial interest, nor does it enlarge the interest of Alaska whose temporary relationship with the employee has been severed.

The interest of Alaska is not shown to be superior to that of California. No persuasive reason is shown for denying to California the right to enforce its own laws in its own courts, and in the circumstances the full faith and credit clause does not require that the statutes of Alaska be given that effect.

Affirmed.

Notes and Questions

1. The phrase "public acts" has always been assumed to include statutes. See Laycock, *Equal Citizens*, 290. Professor Whitten has argued that this phrase does not include court-made law (i.e., common law), see Whitten, *Full Faith and Credit*, 56–60, though it is generally assumed today that the Full Faith and Credit Clause encompasses common law within the meaning of either "records," "judicial proceedings," or "public acts."

2. Suppose the employee in *Alaska Packers* had returned to Alaska and brought suit there. Would it have violated the Full Faith and Credit Clause for Alaska to apply Alaska law? *Clapper*, discussed in *Alaska Packers*, may suggest that application of Alaska law would violate the Full Faith and Credit Clause. In *Clapper* the Court explained: "The interest of New Hampshire [the state of injury] was only casual. Leon Clapper was not a resident there. He was not continuously employed there. So far as appears, he had no dependent there." 286 U.S. at 162. Moreover, in *Alaska Packers* the Court observed that California's interest "is greater than that of Alaska." If California has the greater interest, would not Alaska be required to apply California Law?

In Pacific Employers Insurance Co. v. Industrial Accident Comm'n, 306 U.S. 493 (1939), the Court held that California could apply its own workers' compensation act to a Massachusetts employer of a Massachusetts employee who was injured in California in the course of his employment. The Massachusetts statute provided that it was the exclusive remedy for injuries occurring both within and without the state, where the employment contract was entered into in Massachusetts. The Court explained:

> To the extent that California is required to give full faith and credit to the conflicting Massachusetts statute it must be denied the right to apply in its own courts its own statute, constitutionally enacted in pursuance of its policy to provide compensation for employees injured in their employment within the state. It must withhold the remedy given by its own statute to its residents by way of compensation for medical, hospital and nursing services rendered to the injured employee, and it must remit him to Massachusetts to secure the administrative remedy which that state has provided. We cannot say that the full

faith and credit clause goes so far.

While the purpose of that provision was to preserve rights acquired or confirmed under the public acts and judicial proceedings of one state by requiring recognition of their validity in other states, the very nature of the federal union of states, to which are reserved some of the attributes of sovereignty, precludes resort to the full faith and credit clause as the means for compelling a state to substitute the statutes of other states for its own statutes dealing with a subject matter concerning which it is competent to legislate. * * * And in cases like the present it would create an impasse which would often leave the employee remediless. Full faith and credit would deny to California the right to apply its own remedy, and its administrative machinery may well not be adapted to giving the remedy afforded by Massachusetts. Similarly, the full faith and credit demanded for the California Act would deny to Massachusetts the right to apply its own remedy, and its Department of Industrial Accidents may well be without statutory authority to afford the remedy provided by the California statute.

* * *

* * * Although Massachusetts has an interest in safeguarding the compensation of Massachusetts employees while temporarily abroad in the course of their employment, and may adopt that policy for itself, that could hardly be thought to support an application of the full faith and credit clause which would override the constitutional authority of another state to legislate for the bodily safety and economic protection of employees injured within it. Few matters could be deemed more appropriately the concern of the state in which the injury occurs or more completely within its power. * * *

Full faith and credit does not here enable one state to legislate for the other or to project its laws across state lines so as to preclude the other from prescribing for itself the legal consequences of acts within it.

Id. at 501–05. Notice that the Court does not focus on which state has the greater interest and instead stresses that both Massachusetts and California have legitimate interests.

But is simply being the situs of an injury always sufficient to give a state an interest? Carroll v. Lanza, 349 U.S. 408 (1955), suggests that this is sufficient. There the Missouri employee of a Missouri subcontractor was injured in Arkansas, but immediately returned to Missouri where he received all his medical treatment. After receiving compensation in Missouri under the Missouri Workers' Compensation Act, the employee brought suit in Arkansas against the general contractor. Such suits were barred by Missouri law, but permitted by the Arkansas law. In allowing Arkansas to apply its law, the Court explained:

The State where the tort occurs certainly has a concern in the problems following in the wake of the injury. The problems of medical care and of possible dependents are among these, as *Pacific Employers* emphasizes. [cit.] A State that legislates concerning them is exercising traditional powers of sovereignty. [cit.] Arkansas therefore has a legitimate interest in opening her courts to suits of this nature, even though in this case Carroll's injury may have cast no burden on her or on her institutions.

Id. at 413. One commentator has criticized *Carroll* arguing:

> *Carroll* is wrong. Its major arguable virtue is judicial economy since it
> simplifies the judicial task by not requiring interest analysis when the contact is
> the type that normally would be expected to give rise to a specific interest.
> *Carroll* also gives the states extremely wide latitude in the area of choice of law,
> and effectively permits them to follow Professor Beale and the first Restatement
> if they so desire. The costs, however, outweigh these "benefits."

Posnak, *A Very Well–Curried Leflar Approach*, 768.

3. Does *Alaska Packers* suggest a balancing approach to the Full Faith and
Credit Clause under which California can apply its laws only if its interests are equal
to or greater than other states? Assuming that weighing of interests is possible, would
not it be necessary for the Court to apply a *federal* standard for determining which
interest is greater? Does not this in essence imply a federal choice-of-law rule for
deciding true conflicts? Professor Laycock has argued that the Full Faith and Credit
Clause does indeed imply a federal choice-of-law standard. See Laycock, *Equal
Citizens*, 310.

Whatever the virtues of the balancing approach, as noted above, *Pacific
Employers* appears to reject that approach. Similarly, the Court has rejected a federal
choice of law standard. In Wells v. Simonds Abrasive Co., 345 U.S. 514, 516
(1953), the Court explained:

> The states are free to adopt such rules of conflict of laws as they choose,
> [cit.] subject to the Full Faith and Credit Clause and other constitutional
> restrictions. The Full Faith and Credit Clause does not compel a state to adopt
> any particular set of rules of conflict of laws; it merely sets certain minimum
> requirements which each state must observe when asked to apply the law of a
> sister state.

Compare the quote from *Wells* with Order of United Commercial Travelers v.
Wolfe, 331 U.S. 586 (1947). There, the defendant was a fraternal benefit society
incorporated in Ohio and licensed to do business in South Dakota. Under the
Society's constitution, which was valid in Ohio, beneficiaries were prohibited from
bringing suit against the society more than six months after the society disallowed
a claim. More than six months after denial of the claim, suit was brought in South
Dakota to recover death benefits on behalf of a South Dakota member. The Supreme
Court held that the Full Faith and Credit Clause prohibited South Dakota from
applying its law under which the six month limitation period was invalid.

The Court stated that "[t]he weight of public policy behind the general statute
of South Dakota, which seeks to avoid certain provisions in ordinary contracts, does
not equal that which makes necessary the recognition of the same terms of
membership for members of fraternal benefit societies wherever their beneficiaries
may be." Id. at 624. While this might be read as endorsing a return to a balancing of
interests approach, the case can also be read more narrowly. The Court noted that
allowing South Dakota to apply its law would create inequality among members of
the society. See id. at 610. Thus, the Court seemed to be balancing South Dakota's
interests not against Ohio's interests, but against the need for a uniform set of rules

to be applied to these entities. More recently, the Court has considered the need for a uniform set of laws to govern the internal affairs of corporations. See CTS Corp. v. Dynamics Corp. of America, 481 U.S. 69 (1987); Edgar v. MITE Corp., 457 U.S. 624 (1982). These more recent cases have focused on the Commerce Clause rather than the Full Faith and Credit Clause. See infra at 512.

D. A BIT OF BOTH—THE COURT'S CURRENT APPROACH

Allstate Insurance Co. v. Hague
Supreme Court of the United States, 1981.
449 U.S. 302, 101 S.Ct. 633, 66 L.Ed.2d 521.

JUSTICE BRENNAN announced the judgment of the Court and delivered an opinion, in which JUSTICE WHITE, JUSTICE MARSHALL, and JUSTICE BLACKMUN joined.

This Court granted certiorari to determine whether the Due Process Clause of the Fourteenth Amendment or the Full Faith and Credit Clause of Art. IV, § 1, of the United States Constitution bars the Minnesota Supreme Court's choice of substantive Minnesota law to govern the effect of a provision in an insurance policy issued to respondent's decedent. [cit.]

I. Respondent's late husband, Ralph Hague, died of injuries suffered when a motorcycle on which he was a passenger was struck from behind by an automobile. The accident occurred in Pierce County, Wis., which is immediately across the Minnesota border from Red Wing, Minn. The operators of both vehicles were Wisconsin residents, as was the decedent, who, at the time of the accident, resided with respondent in Hager City, Wis., which is one and one-half miles from Red Wing. Mr. Hague had been employed in Red Wing for the 15 years immediately preceding his death and had commuted daily from Wisconsin to his place of employment.

Neither the operator of the motorcycle nor the operator of the automobile carried valid insurance. However, the decedent held a policy issued by petitioner Allstate Insurance Co. covering three automobiles owned by him and containing an uninsured motorist clause insuring him against loss incurred from accidents with uninsured motorists. The uninsured motorist coverage was limited to $15,000 for each automobile.[3]

After the accident, but prior to the initiation of this lawsuit, respondent moved to Red Wing. Subsequently, she married a Minnesota resident and established residence with her new husband in Savage, Minn. At approximately the same time, a Minnesota Registrar of Probate appointed respondent personal representative of her deceased husband's estate. Following her appointment, she brought this action in Minnesota District Court seeking a declaration under Minnesota law that the $15,000 uninsured motorist coverage on each of her late husband's three automobiles could

---

3. Ralph Hague paid a separate premium for each automobile including an additional separate premium for each uninsured motorist coverage.

be "stacked" to provide total coverage of $45,000. Petitioner defended on the ground that whether the three uninsured motorist coverages could be stacked should be determined by Wisconsin law, since the insurance policy was delivered in Wisconsin, the accident occurred in Wisconsin, and all persons involved were Wisconsin residents at the time of the accident.

The Minnesota District Court disagreed. Interpreting Wisconsin law to disallow stacking, the court concluded that Minnesota's choice-of-law rules required the application of Minnesota law permitting stacking. The court refused to apply Wisconsin law as "inimical to the public policy of Minnesota" and granted summary judgment for respondent.

The Minnesota Supreme Court, sitting en banc, affirmed the District Court. The court, also interpreting Wisconsin law to prohibit stacking,[6] applied Minnesota law after analyzing the relevant Minnesota contacts and interests within the analytical framework developed by Professor Leflar.[7] [cit.] The state court, therefore, examined the conflict-of-laws issue in terms of (1) predictability of result, (2) maintenance of interstate order, (3) simplification of the judicial task, (4) advancement of the forum's governmental interests, and (5) application of the better rule of law. Although stating that the Minnesota contacts might not be, "in themselves, sufficient to mandate application of [Minnesota] law,"[8] [cit.] under the first four factors, the court concluded that the fifth factor—application of the better rule of law—favored selection of Minnesota law. The court emphasized that a majority of States allow stacking and that legal decisions allowing stacking "are fairly recent and well considered in light of current uses of automobiles." [cit.] In addition, the court found the Minnesota rule superior to Wisconsin's "because it requires the cost of accidents with uninsured motorists to be spread more broadly through insurance premiums than does the Wisconsin rule." [cit.] Finally, after rehearing en banc, the court buttressed its initial opinion by indicating "that contracts of insurance on motor vehicles are in a class by themselves" since an insurance company "knows the automobile is a movable item which will be driven from state to state." [cit.] From this premise the court concluded that application of Minnesota law was "not so arbitrary and unreasonable as to violate due process." [cit.]

II. It is not for this Court to say whether the choice-of-law analysis suggested by Professor Leflar is to be preferred or whether we would make the same choice-of-law decision if sitting as the Minnesota Supreme Court. Our sole function is to determine whether the Minnesota Supreme Court's choice of its own substantive law in this case exceeded federal constitutional limitations. Implicit in this inquiry is the recognition, long accepted by this Court, that a set of facts giving rise to a lawsuit, or a particular issue within a lawsuit, may justify, in constitutional terms, application

---

6. Respondent has suggested that this case presents a "false conflict." The court below rejected this contention and applied Minnesota law. Even though the Minnesota Supreme Court's choice of Minnesota law followed a discussion of whether this case presents a false conflict, the fact is that the court chose to apply Minnesota law. Thus, the only question before this Court is whether that choice was constitutional.

7. Minnesota had previously adopted the conceptual model developed by Professor Leflar in *Milkovich v. Saari* [supra, Ch. 3].

8. The court apparently was referring to sufficiency as a matter of choice of law and not as a matter of constitutional limitation on its choice-of-law decision.

of the law of more than one jurisdiction. See, e.g., *Watson v. Employers Liability Assurance Corp.*; [cit.]. See generally *Clay v. Sun Insurance Office, Ltd.* (hereinafter cited as *Clay II*). As a result, the forum State may have to select one law from among the laws of several jurisdictions having some contact with the controversy.

In deciding constitutional choice-of-law questions, whether under the Due Process Clause or the Full Faith and Credit Clause,[10] this Court has traditionally examined the contacts of the State, whose law was applied, with the parties and with the occurrence or transaction giving rise to the litigation. See *Clay II*. In order to ensure that the choice of law is neither arbitrary nor fundamentally unfair, see *Alaska Packers Assn. v. Industrial Accident Comm'n*, the Court has invalidated the choice of law of a State which has had no significant contact or significant aggregation of contacts, creating state interests, with the parties and the occurrence or transaction.[11]

Two instructive examples of such invalidation are *Home Ins. Co. v. Dick*, and John Hancock Mutual Life Ins. Co. v. Yates, 299 U.S. 178 (1936). In both cases, the selection of forum law rested exclusively on the presence of one nonsignificant forum contact.

Home Ins. Co. v. Dick involved interpretation of an insurance policy which had been issued in Mexico, by a Mexican insurer, to a Mexican citizen, covering a Mexican risk. The policy was subsequently assigned to Mr. Dick, who was domiciled in Mexico and "physically present and acting in Mexico," [cit.] although he remained a nominal, permanent resident of Texas. The policy restricted coverage to losses occurring in certain Mexican waters and, indeed, the loss occurred in those waters. Dick brought suit in Texas against a New York reinsurer. Neither the Mexican insurer nor the New York reinsurer had any connection to Texas. The Court held that application of Texas law to void the insurance contract's limita-

---

10. This Court has taken a similar approach in deciding choice-of-law cases under both the Due Process Clause and the Full Faith and Credit Clause. In each instance, the Court has examined the relevant contacts and resulting interests of the State whose law was applied. See, e. g., Nevada v. Hall, 440 U.S. 410, 424 (1979). Although at one time the Court required a more exacting standard under the Full Faith and Credit Clause than under the Due Process Clause for evaluating the constitutionality of choice-of-law decisions, see *Alaska Packers Assn. v. Industrial Accident Comm'n* (interest of State whose law was applied was no less than interest of State whose law was rejected), the Court has since abandoned the weighing-of-interests requirement. Carroll v. Lanza, 349 U.S. 408 (1955); see *Nevada v. Hall*, supra; Weintraub, *Due Process and Full Faith and Credit Limitations on a State's Choice of Law*, 44 Iowa L. Rev. 449 (1959). Different considerations are of course at issue when full faith and credit is to be accorded to acts, records, and proceedings outside the choice-of-law area, such as in the case of sister state-court judgments.

11. Prior to the advent of interest analysis in the state courts as the "dominant mode of analysis in modern choice of law theory," [cit.] the prevailing choice-of-law methodology focused on the jurisdiction where a particular event occurred. * * *

Hartford Accident & Indemnity Co. v. Delta & Pine Land Co., 292 U.S. 143 (1934), can, perhaps, best be explained as an example of that period. In that case, the Court struck down application by the Mississippi courts of Mississippi law which voided the limitations provision in a fidelity bond written in Tennessee between a Connecticut insurer and Delta, both of which were doing business in Tennessee and Mississippi. By its terms, the bond covered misapplication of funds "by any employee 'in any position, anywhere....'" [cit.] After Delta discovered defalcations by one of its Mississippi-based employees, a lawsuit was commenced in Mississippi.

That case, however, has scant relevance for today. It implied a choice-of-law analysis which, for all intents and purposes, gave an isolated event—the writing of the bond in Tennessee—controlling constitutional significance, even though there might have been contacts with another State (there Mississippi) which would make application of its law neither unfair nor unexpected. See Martin, *Personal Jurisdiction and Choice of Law*, 78 Mich. L. Rev. 872, 874, and n. 11 (1980).

tion-of-actions clause violated due process.[13]

The relationship of the forum State to the parties and the transaction was similarly attenuated in *John Hancock Mutual Life Ins. Co. v. Yates*. There, the insurer, a Massachusetts corporation, issued a contract of insurance on the life of a New York resident. The contract was applied for, issued, and delivered in New York where the insured and his spouse resided. After the insured died in New York, his spouse moved to Georgia and brought suit on the policy in Georgia. Under Georgia law, the jury was permitted to take into account oral modifications when deciding whether an insurance policy application contained material misrepresentations. Under New York law, however, such misrepresentations were to be evaluated solely on the basis of the written application. The Georgia court applied Georgia law. This Court reversed, finding application of Georgia law to be unconstitutional.

Dick and *Yates* stand for the proposition that if a State has only an insignificant contact with the parties and the occurrence or transaction, application of its law is unconstitutional. *Dick* concluded that nominal residence--standing alone--was inadequate; *Yates* held that a postoccurrence change of residence to the forum State--standing alone--was insufficient to justify application of forum law. Although instructive as extreme examples of selection of forum law, neither *Dick* nor *Yates* governs this case. For in contrast to those decisions, here the Minnesota contacts with the parties and the occurrence are obviously significant. Thus, this case is like *Alaska Packers*, Cardillo v. Liberty Mutual Ins. Co., 330 U.S. 469 (1947), and *Clay II*—cases where this Court sustained choice-of-law decisions based on the contacts of the State, whose law was applied, with the parties and occurrence.

In *Alaska Packers*, the Court upheld California's application of its Workmen's Compensation Act, where the most significant contact of the worker with California was his execution of an employment contract in California. The worker, a nonresident alien from Mexico, was hired in California for seasonal work in a salmon canning factory in Alaska. As part of the employment contract, the employer, who was doing business in California, agreed to transport the worker to Alaska and to return him to California when the work was completed. Even though the employee contracted to be bound by the Alaska Workmen's Compensation Law and was injured in Alaska, he sought an award under the California Workmen's Compensation Act. The Court held that the choice of California law was not "so arbitrary or unreasonable as to amount to a denial of due process," [cit.] because "[without] a remedy in California, [he] would be remediless," [cit.] and because of California's interest that the worker not become a public charge, [cit.].

In *Cardillo v. Liberty Mutual Ins. Co.*, supra, a District of Columbia resident, employed by a District of Columbia employer and assigned by the employer for the three years prior to his death to work in Virginia, was killed in an automobile crash in Virginia in the course of his daily commute home from work. The Court found the District's contacts with the parties and the occurrence sufficient to satisfy constitutional requirements, based on the employee's residence in the District, his

---

13. The Court noted that the result might have been different if there had been some connection to Texas upon "which the State could properly lay hold as the basis of the regulations there imposed." [cit.]

commute between home and the Virginia workplace, and his status as an employee of a company "engaged in electrical construction work in the District of Columbia and surrounding areas." [cit.]

Similarly, *Clay II* upheld the constitutionality of the application of forum law. There, a policy of insurance had issued in Illinois to an Illinois resident. Subsequently the insured moved to Florida and suffered a property loss in Florida. Relying explicitly on the nationwide coverage of the policy and the presence of the insurance company in Florida and implicitly on the plaintiff's Florida residence and the occurrence of the property loss in Florida, the Court sustained the Florida court's choice of Florida law.

The lesson from *Dick* and *Yates*, which found insufficient forum contacts to apply forum law, and from *Alaska Packers*, *Cardillo*, and *Clay II*, which found adequate contacts to sustain the choice of forum law, is that for a State's substantive law to be selected in a constitutionally permissible manner, that State must have a significant contact or significant aggregation of contacts, creating state interests, such that choice of its law is neither arbitrary nor fundamentally unfair. Application of this principle to the facts of this case persuades us that the Minnesota Supreme Court's choice of its own law did not offend the Federal Constitution.

III. Minnesota has three contacts with the parties and the occurrence giving rise to the litigation. In the aggregate, these contacts permit selection by the Minnesota Supreme Court of Minnesota law allowing the stacking of Mr. Hague's uninsured motorist coverages.

First, and for our purposes a very important contact, Mr. Hague was a member of Minnesota's work force, having been employed by a Red Wing, Minn., enterprise for the 15 years preceding his death. While employment status may implicate a state interest less substantial than does resident status, that interest is nevertheless important. The State of employment has police power responsibilities towards the nonresident employee that are analogous, if somewhat less profound, than towards residents. Thus, such employees use state services and amenities and may call upon state facilities in appropriate circumstances.

In addition, Mr. Hague commuted to work in Minnesota, a contact which was important in *Cardillo v. Liberty Mutual Ins. Co.*, (daily commute between residence in District of Columbia and workplace in Virginia), and was presumably covered by his uninsured motorist coverage during the commute. The State's interest in its commuting nonresident employees reflects a state concern for the safety and well-being of its work force and the concomitant effect on Minnesota employers.

That Mr. Hague was not killed while commuting to work or while in Minnesota does not dictate a different result. To hold that the Minnesota Supreme Court's choice of Minnesota law violated the Constitution for that reason would require too narrow a view of Minnesota's relationship with the parties and the occurrence giving rise to the litigation. An automobile accident need not occur within a particular jurisdiction for that jurisdiction to be connected to the occurrence. Similarly, the occurrence of a crash fatal to a Minnesota employee in another State is a Minnesota contact. If Mr. Hague had only been injured and missed work for a few weeks, the effect on the Minnesota employer would have been palpable and Minnesota's interest in having its employee made whole would be evident. Mr. Hague's death affects Minnesota's interest still more acutely, even though Mr. Hague will not return to the Minnesota work force. Minnesota's work force is surely affected by the level of protection the State extends to it, either directly or indirectly. Vindication of the rights of the estate of a Minnesota employee, therefore, is an important state concern.

Mr. Hague's residence in Wisconsin does not--as Allstate seems to argue--constitutionally mandate application of Wisconsin law to the exclusion of forum law. If, in the instant case, the accident had occurred in Minnesota between Mr. Hague and an uninsured Minnesota motorist, if the insurance contract had been executed in Minnesota covering a Minnesota registered company automobile which Mr. Hague was permitted to drive, and if a Wisconsin court sought to apply Wisconsin law, certainly Mr. Hague's residence in Wisconsin, his commute between Wisconsin and Minnesota, and the insurer's presence in Wisconsin should be adequate to apply Wisconsin's law.[22] [cit.] Employment status is not a sufficiently less important status than residence, [cit.] when combined with Mr. Hague's daily commute across state lines and the other Minnesota contacts present, to prohibit the choice-of-law result in this case on constitutional grounds.

Second, Allstate was at all times present and doing business in Minnesota. By virtue of its presence, Allstate can hardly claim unfamiliarity with the laws of the host jurisdiction and surprise that the state courts might apply forum law to litigation in which the company is involved. "Particularly since the company was licensed to do business in [the forum], it must have known it might be sued there, and that [the forum] courts would feel bound by [forum] law."[24] *Clay v. Sun Insurance Office Ltd.* (Black, J., dissenting). Moreover, Allstate's presence in Minnesota gave Minnesota an interest in regulating the company's insurance obligations insofar as they affected both a Minnesota resident and court-appointed representative—respondent—and a longstanding member of Minnesota's work force—Mr. Hague. [cit.]

Third, respondent became a Minnesota resident prior to institution of this

---

22. Of course Allstate could not be certain that Wisconsin law would necessarily govern any accident which occurred in Wisconsin, whether brought in the Wisconsin courts or elsewhere. Such an expectation would give controlling significance to the wooden lex loci delicti doctrine. While the place of the accident is a factor to be considered in choice-of-law analysis, to apply blindly the traditional, but now largely abandoned, doctrine, [cit.] would fail to distinguish between the relative importance of various legal issues involved in a lawsuit as well as the relationship of other jurisdictions to the parties and the occurrence or transaction. If, for example, Mr. Hague had been a Wisconsin resident and employee who was injured in Wisconsin and was then taken by ambulance to a hospital in Red Wing, Minn., where he languished for several weeks before dying, Minnesota's interest in ensuring that its medical creditors were paid would be obvious. Moreover, under such circumstances, the accident itself might be reasonably characterized as a bistate occurrence beginning in Wisconsin and ending in Minnesota. Thus, reliance by the insurer that Wisconsin law would necessarily govern any accident that occurred in Wisconsin, or that the law of another jurisdiction would necessarily govern any accident that did not occur in Wisconsin, would be unwarranted. [cit.]

If the law of a jurisdiction other than Wisconsin did govern, there was a substantial likelihood, with respect to uninsured motorist coverage, that stacking would be allowed. Stacking was the rule in most States at the time the policy was issued. * * *

24. There is no element of unfair surprise or frustration of legitimate expectations as a result of Minnesota's choice of its law. Because Allstate was doing business in Minnesota and was undoubtedly aware that Mr. Hague was a Minnesota employee, it had to have anticipated that Minnesota law might apply to an accident in which Mr. Hague was involved. [cit.] Indeed, Allstate specifically anticipated that Mr. Hague might suffer an accident either in Minnesota or elsewhere in the United States, outside of Wisconsin, since the policy it issued offered continental coverage. [cit.] At the same time, Allstate did not seek to control construction of the contract since the policy contained no choice-of-law clause dictating application of Wisconsin law. [cit.]

litigation. The stipulated facts reveal that she first settled in Red Wing, Minn., the town in which her late husband had worked. She subsequently moved to Savage, Minn., after marrying a Minnesota resident who operated an automobile service station in Bloomington, Minn. Her move to Savage occurred "almost concurrently," [cit.] with the initiation of the instant case. There is no suggestion that Mrs. Hague moved to Minnesota in anticipation of this litigation or for the purpose of finding a legal climate especially hospitable to her claim.[28] The stipulated facts, sparse as they are, negate any such inference. While *John Hancock Mutual Life Ins. Co. v. Yates*, held that a postoccurrence change of residence to the forum State was insufficient in and of itself to confer power on the forum State to choose its law, that case did not hold that such a change of residence was irrelevant. Here, of course, respondent's bona fide residence in Minnesota was not the sole contact Minnesota had with this litigation. And in connection with her residence in Minnesota, respondent was appointed personal representative of Mr. Hague's estate by the Registrar of Probate for the County of Goodhue, Minn. Respondent's residence and subsequent appointment in Minnesota as personal representative of her late husband's estate constitute a Minnesota contact which gives Minnesota an interest in respondent's recovery, an interest which the court below identified as full compensation for "resident accident victims" to keep them "off welfare rolls" and able "to meet financial obligations." [cit.]

In sum, Minnesota had a significant aggregation[29] of contacts with the parties and the occurrence, creating state interests, such that application of its law was neither arbitrary nor fundamentally unfair. Accordingly, the choice of Minnesota law by the Minnesota Supreme Court did not violate the Due Process Clause or the Full Faith and Credit Clause.

Affirmed.

JUSTICE STEWART took no part in the consideration or decision of this case.

JUSTICE STEVENS, concurring in the judgment. As I view this unusual case—in which neither precedent nor constitutional language provides sure guidance—two separate questions must be answered. First, does the Full Faith and Credit Clause *require* Minnesota, the forum State, to apply Wisconsin law? Second, does the Due Process Clause of the Fourteenth Amendment *prevent* Minnesota from applying its own law? The first inquiry implicates the federal interest in ensuring that Minnesota respect the sovereignty of the State of Wisconsin; the second implicates the litigants' interest in a fair adjudication of their rights.[3]

---

28. The dissent suggests that considering respondent's postoccurrence change of residence as one of the Minnesota contacts will encourage forum shopping. [cit.] This overlooks the fact that her change of residence was bona fide and not motivated by litigation considerations.

29. We express no view whether the first two contacts, either together or separately, would have sufficed to sustain the choice of Minnesota law made by the Minnesota Supreme Court.

3. The two questions presented by the choice-of-law issue arise only after it is assumed or established that the defendant's contacts with the forum State are sufficient to support personal jurisdiction. Although the choice-of-law concerns—respect for another sovereign and fairness to the litigants—are similar to the two functions performed by the jurisdictional inquiry, they are not identical. In World–Wide Volkswagen Corp. v. Woodson, 444 U.S. 286, 291–292 (1980) [Ch. 6], we stated:

The concept of minimum contacts, in turn, can be seen to perform two related, but distinguishable, functions. It protects the defendant against the burdens of litigating in a distant or inconvenient forum. And
(continued...)

I realize that both this Court's analysis of choice-of-law questions[4] and scholarly criticism of those decisions[5] have treated these two inquiries as though they were indistinguishable.[6] Nevertheless, I am persuaded that the two constitutional provisions protect different interests and that proper analysis requires separate consideration of each.

I. The Full Faith and Credit Clause is one of several provisions in the Federal Constitution designed to transform the several States from independent sovereignties into a single, unified Nation. [cit.] The Full Faith and Credit Clause implements this design by directing that a State, when acting as the forum for litigation having multistate aspects or implications, respect the legitimate interests of other States and avoid infringement upon their sovereignty. The Clause does not, however, rigidly require the forum State to apply foreign law whenever another State has a valid interest in the litigation. [cit.] On the contrary, in view of the fact that the forum State is also a sovereign in its own right, in appropriate cases it may attach paramount importance to its own legitimate interests. Accordingly, the fact that a choice-of-law decision may be unsound as a matter of conflicts law does not necessarily implicate the federal concerns embodied in the Full Faith and Credit Clause. Rather, in my opinion, the Clause should not invalidate a state court's choice of forum law unless that choice threatens the federal interest in national unity by unjustifiably infringing upon the legitimate interests of another State.

In this case, I think the Minnesota courts' decision to apply Minnesota law was plainly unsound as a matter of normal conflicts law. Both the execution of the insurance contract and the accident giving rise to the litigation took place in Wisconsin. Moreover, when both of those events occurred, the plaintiff, the decedent, and the operators of both vehicles were all residents of Wisconsin. Nevertheless, I do not believe that any threat to national unity or Wisconsin's sovereignty ensues from allowing the substantive question presented by this case to be determined by the law of another State.

---

3. (...continued)
it acts to ensure that the States, through their courts, do not reach out beyond the limits imposed on them by their status as coequal sovereigns in a federal system. [cit.]

While it has been suggested that this same minimum-contacts analysis be used to define the constitutional limitations on choice of law, see, e.g., Martin, *Personal Jurisdiction and Choice of Law*, 78 Mich. L. Rev. 872 (1980), the Court has made it clear over the years that the personal jurisdiction and choice-of-law inquiries are not the same. [cit.]

4. Although the Court has struck down a state court's choice of forum law on both due process, see, e.g., *Home Ins. Co. v. Dick*, and full faith and credit grounds, see, e.g., *John Hancock Mutual Life Ins. Co. v. Yates*, no clear analytical distinction between the two constitutional provisions has emerged. The Full Faith and Credit Clause, of course, was inapplicable in *Home Ins. Co.* because the law of a foreign nation, rather than of a sister State, was at issue; a similarly clear explanation for the Court's reliance upon the Full Faith and Credit Clause in *John Hancock Mutual Life Ins.* cannot be found. Indeed, *John Hancock Mutual Life Ins.* is probably best understood as a due process case. [cit.]

5. [cit.] The Court's frequent failure to distinguish between the two Clauses in the choice-of-law context may underlie the suggestions of various commentators that either the Full Faith and Credit Clause or the Due Process Clause be recognized as the single appropriate source for constitutional limitations on choice of law. Compare Martin, *Constitutional Limitations on Choice of Law*, 61 Cornell L. Rev. 185 (1976) (full faith and credit), with Reese, supra (due process); see also Kirgis, *The Roles of Due Process and Full Faith and Credit in Choice of Law*, 62 Cornell L. Rev. 94 (1976).

6. Even when the Court has explicitly considered both provisions in a single case, the requirements of the Due Process and Full Faith and Credit Clauses have been measured by essentially the same standard. *
* *

The question on the merits is one of interpreting the meaning of the insurance contract. Neither the contract itself, nor anything else in the record, reflects any express understanding of the parties with respect to what law would be applied or with respect to whether the separate uninsured motorist coverage for each of the decedent's three cars could be "stacked." Since the policy provided coverage for accidents that might occur in other States, it was obvious to the parties at the time of contracting that it might give rise to the application of the law of States other than Wisconsin. Therefore, while Wisconsin may have an interest in ensuring that contracts formed in Wisconsin in reliance upon Wisconsin law are interpreted in accordance with that law, that interest is not implicated in this case.

Petitioner has failed to establish that Minnesota's refusal to apply Wisconsin law poses any direct or indirect threat to Wisconsin's sovereignty.[13] In the absence of any such threat, I find it unnecessary to evaluate the forum State's interest in the litigation in order to reach the conclusion that the Full Faith and Credit Clause does not require the Minnesota courts to apply Wisconsin law to the question of contract interpretation presented in this case.

II. It may be assumed that a choice-of-law decision would violate the Due Process Clause if it were totally arbitrary or if it were fundamentally unfair to either litigant. I question whether a judge's decision to apply the law of his own State could ever be described as wholly irrational. For judges are presumably familiar with their own state law and may find it difficult and time consuming to discover and apply correctly the law of another State. The forum State's interest in the fair and efficient administration of justice is therefore sufficient, in my judgment, to attach a presumption of validity to a forum State's decision to apply its own law to a dispute over which it has jurisdiction.

The forum State's interest in the efficient operation of its judicial system is clearly not sufficient, however, to justify the application of a rule of law that is fundamentally unfair to one of the litigants. Arguably, a litigant could demonstrate such unfairness in a variety of ways. Concern about the fairness of the forum's choice of its own rule might arise if that rule favored residents over nonresidents, if it represented a dramatic departure from the rule that obtains in most American jurisdictions, or if the rule itself was unfair on its face or as applied.[15]

The application of an otherwise acceptable rule of law may result in unfairness to the litigants if, in engaging in the activity which is the subject of the litigation, they

---

13. It is clear that a litigant challenging the forum's application of its own law to a lawsuit properly brought in its courts bears the burden of establishing that this choice of law infringes upon interests protected by the Full Faith and Credit Clause. See *Alaska Packers Assn. v. Industrial Accident Comm'n.*

It is equally clear that a state court's decision to apply its own law cannot violate the Full Faith and Credit Clause where the application of forum law does not impinge at all upon the interests of other States. [cit.]

15. Discrimination against nonresidents would be constitutionally suspect even if the Due Process Clause were not a check upon a State's choice-of-law decisions. See Currie & Schreter, *Unconstitutional Discrimination in the Conflict of Laws: Equal Protection*, 28 U. Chi. L. Rev. 1 (1960); Currie & Schreter, *Unconstitutional Discrimination in the Conflict of Laws: Privileges and Immunities*, 69 Yale L. J. 1323 (1960); Note, *Unconstitutional Discrimination in Choice of Law*, 77 Colum. L. Rev. 272 (1977). Moreover, both discriminatory and substantively unfair rules of law may be detected and remedied without any special choice-of-law analysis; familiar constitutional principles are available to deal with both varieties of unfairness. [cit.]

could not reasonably have anticipated that their actions would later be judged by this rule of law. A choice-of-law decision that frustrates the justifiable expectations of the parties can be fundamentally unfair. This desire to prevent unfair surprise to a litigant has been the central concern in this Court's review of choice-of-law decisions under the Due Process Clause.[16]

Neither the "stacking" rule itself, nor Minnesota's application of that rule to these litigants, raises any serious question of fairness. As the plurality observes, "[s]tacking was the rule in most States at the time the policy was issued." [cit.] Moreover, the rule is consistent with the economics of a contractual relationship in which the policyholder paid three separate premiums for insurance coverage for three automobiles, including a separate premium for each uninsured motorist coverage. Nor am I persuaded that the decision of the Minnesota courts to apply the "stacking" rule in this case can be said to violate due process because that decision frustrates the reasonable expectations of the contracting parties.

Contracting parties can, of course, make their expectations explicit by providing in their contract either that the law of a particular jurisdiction shall govern questions of contract interpretation, or that a particular substantive rule, for instance "stacking," shall or shall not apply.[20] In the absence of such express provisions, the contract nonetheless may implicitly reveal the expectations of the parties. For example, if a liability insurance policy issued by a resident of a particular State provides coverage only with respect to accidents within that State, it is reasonable to infer that the contracting parties expected that their obligations under the policy would be governed by that State's law.

In this case, no express indication of the parties' expectations is available. The insurance policy provided coverage for accidents throughout the United States; thus, at the time of contracting, the parties certainly could have anticipated that the law of States other than Wisconsin would govern particular claims arising under the policy. By virtue of doing business in Minnesota, Allstate was aware that it could be sued in the Minnesota courts; Allstate also presumably was aware that Minnesota law, as well as the law of most States, permitted "stacking." Nothing in the record requires that a different inference be drawn. Therefore, the decision of the Minnesota courts to apply the law of the forum in this case does not frustrate the reasonable expectations of the contracting parties, and I can find no fundamental unfairness in

---

16. Upon careful analysis, most of the decisions of this Court that struck down on due process grounds a state court's choice of forum law can be explained as attempts to prevent a State with a minimal contact with the litigation from materially enlarging the contractual obligations of one of the parties where that party had no reason to anticipate the possibility of such enlargement. [cit.]

20. * * * In *Watson v. Employers Liability Assurance Corp.*, the insurance policy expressly provided that an injured party could not maintain a direct action against the insurer until after the insured's liability had been determined. The Court found that neither the Due Process Clause nor the Full Faith and Credit Clause prevented the Louisiana courts from applying forum law to permit a direct action against the insurer prior to determination of the insured's liability. As in *Clay*, the Court noted that the policy provided coverage for injuries anywhere in the United States. [cit.] An additional, although unarticulated, factor in Watson was the fact that the litigant urging that forum law be applied was not a party to the insurance contract. While contracting parties may be able to provide in advance that a particular rule of law will govern disputes between them, their expectations are clearly entitled to less weight when the rights of third-party litigants are at issue.

that decision requiring the attention of this Court.[23]

In terms of fundamental fairness, it seems to me that two factors relied upon by the plurality—the plaintiff's post-accident move to Minnesota and the decedent's Minnesota employment—are either irrelevant to or possibly even tend to undermine the plurality's conclusion. When the expectations of the parties at the time of contracting are the central due process concern, as they are in this case, an unanticipated postaccident occurrence is clearly irrelevant for due process purposes. The fact that the plaintiff became a resident of the forum State after the accident surely cannot justify a ruling in her favor that would not be made if the plaintiff were a nonresident. Similarly, while the fact that the decedent regularly drove into Minnesota might be relevant to the expectations of the contracting parties,[24] the fact that he did so because he was employed in Minnesota adds nothing to the due process analysis. The choice-of-law decision of the Minnesota courts is consistent with due process because it does not result in unfairness to either litigant, not because Minnesota now has an interest in the plaintiff as resident or formerly had an interest in the decedent as employee.

III. Although I regard the Minnesota courts' decision to apply forum law as unsound as a matter of conflicts law, and there is little in this record other than the presumption in favor of the forum's own law to support that decision, I concur in the plurality's judgment. It is not this Court's function to establish and impose upon state courts a federal choice-of-law rule, nor is it our function to ensure that state courts correctly apply whatever choice-of-law rules they have themselves adopted. Our authority may be exercised in the choice-of-law area only to prevent a violation of the Full Faith and Credit or the Due Process Clause. For the reasons stated above, I find no such violation in this case.

JUSTICE POWELL, with whom THE CHIEF JUSTICE and JUSTICE REHNQUIST join, dissenting. My disagreement with the plurality is narrow. I accept with few reservations Part II of the plurality opinion, which sets forth the basic principles that guide us in reviewing state choice-of-law decisions under the Constitution. The Court should invalidate a forum State's decision to apply its own law only when there are no significant contacts between the State and the litigation. This modest check on state power is mandated by the Due Process Clause of the Fourteenth

---

23. Comparison of this case with *Home Ins. Co. v. Dick*, confirms my conclusion that the application of Minnesota law in this case does not offend the Due Process Clause. In *Home Ins. Co.*, the contract expressly provided that a particular limitations period would govern claims arising under the insurance contract and that Mexican law was to be applied in interpreting the contract; in addition, the contract was limited in effect to certain Mexican waters. The parties could hardly have made their expectations with respect to the applicable law more plain. In this case, by way of contrast, nothing in the contract suggests that Wisconsin law should be applied or that Minnesota's "stacking" rule should not be applied. In this case, unlike *Home Ins. Co.*, the court's choice of forum law results in no unfair surprise to the insurer.

24. Even this factor may not be of substantial significance. At the time of contracting, the parties were aware that the insurance policy was effective throughout the United States and that the law of any State, including Minnesota, might be applicable to particular claims. The fact that the decedent regularly drove to Minnesota, for whatever purpose, is relevant only to the extent that it affected the parties' evaluation, at the time of contracting, of the likelihood that Minnesota law would actually be applied at some point in the future. However, because the applicability of Minnesota law was perceived as possible at the time of contracting, it does not seem especially significant for due process purposes that the parties may also have considered it likely that Minnesota law would be applied. This factor merely reinforces the expectation revealed by the policy's national coverage.

Amendment and the Full Faith and Credit Clause of Art. IV, § 1. I do not believe, however, that the plurality adequately analyzes the policies such review must serve. In consequence, it has found significant what appear to me to be trivial contacts between the forum State and the litigation.

I. At least since *Carroll v. Lanza*, the Court has recognized that both the Due Process and the Full Faith and Credit Clauses are satisfied if the forum has such significant contacts with the litigation that it has a legitimate state interest in applying its own law. The significance of asserted contacts must be evaluated in light of the constitutional policies that oversight by this Court should serve. Two enduring policies emerge from our cases.

First, the contacts between the forum State and the litigation should not be so "slight and casual" that it would be fundamentally unfair to a litigant for the forum to apply its own State's law. *Clay v. Sun Ins. Office, Ltd.* The touchstone here is the reasonable expectation of the parties. See Weintraub, *Due Process and Full Faith and Credit Limitations on a State's Choice of Law*, 44 Iowa L. Rev. 449, 445–457 (1959) (Weintraub). Thus, in *Clay*, the insurer sold a policy to Clay "'with knowledge that he could take his property anywhere in the world he saw fit without losing the protection of his insurance.'" [cit.] When the insured moved to Florida with the knowledge of the insurer, and a loss occurred in that State, this Court found no unfairness in Florida's applying its own rule of decision to permit recovery on the policy. The insurer "must have known it might be sued there." [cit.]

Second, the forum State must have a legitimate interest in the outcome of the litigation before it. *Pacific Employers Ins. Co. v. Industrial Accident Comm'n.* The Full Faith and Credit Clause addresses the accommodation of sovereign power among the various States. Under limited circumstances, it requires one State to give effect to the statutory law of another State. Nevada v. Hall, 440 U.S. 410, 423 (1979). To be sure, a forum State need not give effect to another State's law if that law is in "violation of its own legitimate public policy." Id. at 422. Nonetheless, for a forum State to further its legitimate public policy by applying its own law to a controversy, there must be some connection between the facts giving rise to the litigation and the scope of the State's lawmaking jurisdiction.

Both the Due Process and Full Faith and Credit Clauses ensure that the States do not "reach out beyond the limits imposed on them by their status as coequal sovereigns in a federal system." World–Wide Volkswagen Corp. v. Woodson, 444 U.S. 286, 292 (1980) (addressing Fourteenth Amendment limitation on state-court jurisdiction). As the Court stated in *Pacific Employers Ins. Co.*: "[T]he full faith and credit clause does not require one state to substitute for its own statute, *applicable to persons and events within it*, the conflicting statute of another state." [cit.] (emphasis added). The State has a legitimate interest in applying a rule of decision to the litigation only if the facts to which the rule will be applied have created effects within the State, toward which the State's public policy is directed. To assess the sufficiency of asserted contacts between the forum and the litigation, the court must determine if the contacts form a reasonable link between the litigation and a state policy. In short, examination of contacts addresses whether "the state has an interest in the application of its policy in this instance." Currie, *The Constitution and the*

Choice of Law: Governmental Interests and the Judicial Function, in B. Currie, Selected Essays on the Conflict of Laws 188, 189 (1963). If it does, the Constitution is satisfied.

John Hancock Mut. Life Ins. Co. v. Yates, illustrates this principle. A life insurance policy was executed in New York, on a New York insured with a New York beneficiary. The insured died in New York; his beneficiary moved to Georgia and sued to recover on the policy. The insurance company defended on the ground that the insured, in the application for the policy, had made materially false statements that rendered it void under New York law. This Court reversed the Georgia court's application of its contrary rule that all questions of the policy's validity must be determined by the jury. The Court found a violation of the Full Faith and Credit Clause, because "[in] respect to the accrual of the right asserted under the contract ... there was no occurrence, nothing done, to which the law of Georgia could apply." [cit.] In other words, the Court determined that Georgia had no legitimate interest in applying its own law to the legal issue of liability. Georgia's contacts with the contract of insurance were nonexistent. [cit.]

In summary, the significance of the contacts between a forum State and the litigation must be assessed in light of these two important constitutional policies.[3] A contact, or a pattern of contacts, satisfies the Constitution when it protects the litigants from being unfairly surprised if the forum State applies its own law, and when the application of the forum's law reasonably can be understood to further a legitimate public policy of the forum State.

II. Recognition of the complexity of the constitutional inquiry requires that this Court apply these principles with restraint. Applying these principles to the facts of this case, I do not believe, however, that Minnesota had sufficient contacts with the "persons and events" in this litigation to apply its rule permitting stacking. I would agree that no reasonable expectations of the parties were frustrated. The risk insured by petitioner was not geographically limited. See *Clay v. Sun Ins. Office, Ltd.* The close proximity of Hager City, Wis., to Minnesota, and the fact that Hague commuted daily to Red Wing, Minn., for many years should have led the insurer to realize that there was a reasonable probability that the risk would materialize in Minnesota. Under our precedents, it is plain that Minnesota could have applied its own law to an accident occurring within its borders. [cit.] The fact that the accident did not, in fact, occur in Minnesota is not controlling because the expectations of the litigants *before* the cause of action accrues provide the pertinent perspective. [cit.]

The more doubtful question in this case is whether application of Minnesota's substantive law reasonably furthers a legitimate state interest. The plurality attempts to give substance to the tenuous contacts between Minnesota and this litigation. Upon examination, however, these contacts are either trivial or irrelevant to the

---

3. The plurality today apparently recognizes that the significance of the contacts must be evaluated in light of the policies our review serves. It acknowledges that the sufficiency of the same contacts sometimes will differ in jurisdiction and choice-of-law questions. [cit.] The plurality, however, pursues the rationale for the requirement of sufficient contacts in choice-of-law cases no further than to observe that the forum's application of its own law must be "neither arbitrary nor fundamentally unfair." [cit.] But this general prohibition does not distinguish questions of choice of law from those of jurisdiction, or from much of the jurisprudence of the Fourteenth Amendment.

furthering of any public policy of Minnesota.

First, the postaccident residence of the plaintiff-beneficiary is constitutionally irrelevant to the choice-of-law question. *John Hancock Mut. Life Ins. Co. v. Yates.* The plurality today insists that *Yates* only held that a postoccurrence move to the forum State could not "in and of itself" confer power on the forum to apply its own law, but did not establish that such a change of residence was irrelevant. [cit.] What the *Yates* Court held, however, was that "there was no occurrence, *nothing* done, to which the law of Georgia could apply." [cit.] (emphasis added). Any possible ambiguity in the Court's view of the significance of a postoccurrence change of residence is dispelled by *Home Ins. Co. v. Dick*, cited by the Yates Court, where it was held squarely that Dick's postaccident move to the forum State was "without significance." [cit.]

This rule is sound. If a plaintiff could choose the substantive rules to be applied to an action by moving to a hospitable forum, the invitation to forum shopping would be irresistible. Moreover, it would permit the defendant's reasonable expectations at the time the cause of action accrues to be frustrated, because it would permit the choice-of-law question to turn on a postaccrual circumstance. Finally, postaccrual residence has nothing to do with facts to which the forum State proposes to apply its rule; it is unrelated to the substantive legal issues presented by the litigation.

Second, the plurality finds it significant that the insurer does business in the forum State. [cit.] The State does have a legitimate interest in regulating the practices of such an insurer. But this argument proves too much. The insurer here does business in all 50 States. The forum State has no interest in regulating that conduct of the insurer unrelated to property, persons, or contracts executed within the forum State. [cit.] The plurality recognizes this flaw and attempts to bolster the significance of the local presence of the insurer by combining it with the other factors deemed significant: the presence of the plaintiff and the fact that the deceased worked in the forum State. This merely restates the basic question in the case.

Third, the plurality emphasizes particularly that the insured worked in the forum State.[5] The fact that the insured was a nonresident employee in the forum State provides a significant contact for the furtherance of some local policies. [cit.] The insured's place of employment is not, however, significant in this case. Neither the nature of the insurance policy, the events related to the accident, nor the immediate question of stacking coverage is in any way affected or implicated by the insured's employment status. The plurality's opinion is understandably vague in explaining how trebling the benefits to be paid to the estate of a nonresident employee furthers any substantial state interest relating to employment. Minnesota does not wish its workers to die in automobile accidents, but permitting stacking will not further this

---

5. The plurality exacts double service from this fact, by finding a separate contact in that the insured commuted daily to his job. [cit.] This is merely a repetition of the facts that the insured lived in Wisconsin and worked in Minnesota. The State does have an interest in the safety of motorists who use its roads. This interest is not limited to employees, but extends to all nonresident motorists on its highways. This safety interest, however, cannot encompass, either in logic or in any practical sense, the determination whether a nonresident's estate can stack benefit coverage in a policy written in another State regarding an accident that occurred on another State's roads. * * *

interest. The substantive issue here is solely one of compensation, and whether the compensation provided by this policy is increased or not will have no relation to the State's employment policies or police power. [cit.]

Neither taken separately nor in the aggregate do the contacts asserted by the plurality today indicate that Minnesota's application of its substantive rule in this case will further any legitimate state interest. The plurality focuses only on physical contacts vel non, and in doing so pays scant attention to the more fundamental reasons why our precedents require reasonable policy-related contacts in choice-of-law cases. Therefore, I dissent.

Phillips Petroleum Co. v. Shutts

Supreme Court of the United States, 1985.
472 U.S. 797, 105 S.Ct. 2965, 86 L.Ed.2d 628.

JUSTICE REHNQUIST delivered the opinion of the Court. Petitioner is a Delaware corporation which has its principal place of business in Oklahoma. During the 1970's it produced or purchased natural gas from leased land located in 11 different States, and sold most of the gas in interstate commerce. Respondents are some 28,000 of the royalty owners possessing rights to the leases from which petitioner produced the gas; they reside in all 50 States, the District of Columbia, and several foreign countries. Respondents brought a class action against petitioner in the Kansas state court, seeking to recover interest on royalty payments which had been delayed by petitioner [pending the approval of price increases by the Federal Power Commission]. They recovered judgment in the trial court, and the Supreme Court of Kansas affirmed the judgment over petitioner's contentions that the Due Process Clause of the Fourteenth Amendment prevented Kansas from adjudicating the claims of all the respondents, and that the Due Process Clause and the Full Faith and Credit Clause of Article IV of the Constitution prohibited the application of Kansas law to all of the transactions between petitioner and respondents. 679 P. 2d 1159 (Kan.1984). We granted certiorari to consider these claims. [cit.] We reject petitioner's jurisdictional claim, but sustain its claim regarding the choice of law.

* * *

Respondents Irl Shutts, Robert Anderson, and Betty Anderson filed suit against petitioner in Kansas state court, seeking interest payments on their suspended royalties which petitioner had possessed pending the Commission's approval of the price increases. Shutts is a resident of Kansas, and the Andersons live in Oklahoma. Shutts and the Andersons own gas leases in Oklahoma and Texas. Over petitioner's objection the Kansas trial court granted respondents' motion to certify the suit as a class action under Kansas law. [cit.] The class as certified was comprised of 33,000 royalty owners who had royalties suspended by petitioner. The average claim of each royalty owner for interest on the suspended royalties was $100.

After the class was certified respondents provided each class member with notice through first-class mail. The notice described the action and informed each class member that he could appear in person or by counsel; otherwise each member would be represented by Shutts and the Andersons, the named plaintiffs. The notices also stated that class members would be included in the class and bound by the judgment unless they "opted out" of the lawsuit by executing and returning a "request for exclusion" that was included with the notice. The final class as certified contained 28,100 members; 3,400 had "opted out" of the class by returning the request for exclusion, and notice could not be delivered to another 1,500 members, who were also excluded. Less than 1,000 of the class members resided in Kansas. Only a minuscule amount, approximately one quarter of one percent, of the gas leases involved in the lawsuit were on Kansas land.

* * * The court found petitioner liable under Kansas law for interest on the suspended royalties to all class members. * * * No federal statutes touched on the liability for suspended royalties, and the court * * * held as a matter of Kansas equity law that the applicable interest rates for computation of interest on suspended royalties were the interest rates at which the gas company would have had to reimburse its customers had its interim price increase been rejected by the Commission. * * *

Petitioner raised two principal claims in its appeal to the Supreme Court of Kansas. It first asserted that the Kansas trial court did not possess personal jurisdiction over absent plaintiff class members as required by International Shoe Co. v. Washington, 326 U.S. 310 (1945), and similar cases. Related to this first claim was petitioner's contention that the "opt-out" notice to absent class members, which forced them to return the request for exclusion in order to avoid the suit, was insufficient to bind class members who were not residents of Kansas or who did not possess "minimum contacts" with Kansas. Second, petitioner claimed that Kansas courts could not apply Kansas law to every claim in the dispute. The trial court should have looked to the laws of each State where the leases were located to determine, on the basis of conflict of laws principles, whether interest on the suspended royalties was recoverable, and at what rate.

The Supreme Court of Kansas held that the entire cause of action was maintainable under the Kansas class-action statute, and the court rejected both of petitioner's claims. [cit.] First, it held that the absent class members were plaintiffs, not defendants, and thus the traditional minimum contacts test of *International Shoe* did not apply. The court held that nonresident class-action plaintiffs were only entitled to adequate notice, an opportunity to be heard, an opportunity to opt out of the case, and adequate representation by the named plaintiffs. If these procedural due process minima were met, according to the court, Kansas could assert jurisdiction over the plaintiff class and bind each class member with a judgment on his claim. The court surveyed the course of the litigation and concluded that all of these minima had been met.

The court also rejected petitioner's contention that Kansas law could not be applied to plaintiffs and royalty arrangements having no connection with Kansas. The court stated that generally the law of the forum controlled all claims unless "compelling reasons" existed to apply a different law. The court found no compelling reasons, and noted that "[the] plaintiff class members have indicated their desire to have this action determined under the laws of Kansas." * * *

[The Court held that Kansas did have personal jurisdiction over out-of-state plaintiffs. "We think that the procedure followed by Kansas, where a fully descriptive notice is sent first-class mail to each class member, with an explanation of the right to 'opt out,' satisfies due process."]

III. The Kansas courts applied Kansas contract and Kansas equity law to every claim in this case, notwithstanding that over 99% of the gas leases and some 97% of the plaintiffs in the case had no apparent connection to the State of Kansas except for this lawsuit. Petitioner protested that the Kansas courts should apply the laws of the States where the leases were located, or at least apply Texas and Oklahoma law because so many of the leases came from those States. The Kansas courts disregarded this contention and found petitioner liable for interest on the suspended royalties as a matter of Kansas law, and set the interest rates under Kansas equity principles.

Petitioner contends that total application of Kansas substantive law violated the constitutional limitations on choice of law mandated by the Due Process Clause of the Fourteenth Amendment and the Full Faith and Credit Clause of Article IV, § 1. We must first determine whether Kansas law conflicts in any material way with any other law which could apply. There can be no injury in applying Kansas law if it is not in conflict with that of any other jurisdiction connected to this suit.

[The Court discusses differences between the laws of Kansas and other states connected with the litigation.] * * *

The conflicts on the applicable interest rates, alone—which we do not think can be labeled "false conflicts" without a more thoroughgoing treatment than was accorded them by the Supreme Court of Kansas—certainly amounted to millions of dollars in liability. We think that the Supreme Court of Kansas erred in deciding on the basis that it did that the application of its laws to all claims would be constitutional.

Four Terms ago we addressed a similar situation in *Allstate Ins. Co. v. Hague.* In that case we were confronted with two conflicting rules of state insurance law. Minnesota permitted the "stacking" of separate uninsured motorist policies while Wisconsin did not. Although the decedent lived in Wisconsin, took out insurance policies and was killed there, he was employed in Minnesota, and after his death his widow moved to Minnesota for reasons unrelated to the litigation, and was appointed personal representative of his estate. She filed suit in Minnesota courts, which applied the Minnesota stacking rule.

The plurality in *Allstate* noted that a particular set of facts giving rise to litigation could justify, constitutionally, the application of more than one jurisdiction's laws. The plurality recognized, however, that the Due Process Clause and the Full Faith and Credit Clause provided modest restrictions on the application of forum law. * * *

The plurality in *Allstate* affirmed the application of Minnesota law because of the forum's significant contacts to the litigation which supported the State's interest in applying its law. [cit.] Kansas' contacts to this litigation, as explained by the Kansas Supreme Court, can be gleaned from the opinion below.

Petitioner owns property and conducts substantial business in the State, so Kansas certainly has an interest in regulating petitioner's conduct in Kansas. [cit.]

Moreover, oil and gas extraction is an important business to Kansas, and although only a few leases in issue are located in Kansas, hundreds of Kansas plaintiffs were affected by petitioner's suspension of royalties; thus the court held that the State has a real interest in protecting "the rights of these royalty owners both as individual residents of [Kansas] and as members of this particular class of plaintiffs." [cit.] The Kansas Supreme Court pointed out that Kansas courts are quite familiar with this type of lawsuit, and "[the] plaintiff class members have indicated their desire to have this action determined under the laws of Kansas." [cit.] Finally, the Kansas court buttressed its use of Kansas law by stating that this lawsuit was analogous to a suit against a "common fund" located in Kansas. [cit.]

We do not lightly discount this description of Kansas' contacts with this litigation and its interest in applying its law. There is, however, no "common fund" located in Kansas that would require or support the application of only Kansas law to all these claims. See, e. g., Hartford Life Ins. Co. v. Ibs, 237 U.S. 662 (1915). As the Kansas court noted, petitioner commingled the suspended royalties with its general corporate accounts. There is no specific identifiable res in Kansas, nor is there any limited amount which may be depleted before every plaintiff is compensated. Only by somehow aggregating all the separate claims in this case could a "common fund" in any sense be created, and the term becomes all but meaningless when used in such an expansive sense.

We also give little credence to the idea that Kansas law should apply to all claims because the plaintiffs, by failing to opt out, evinced their desire to be bound by Kansas law. Even if one could say that the plaintiffs "consented" to the application of Kansas law by not opting out, plaintiff's desire for forum law is rarely, if ever controlling. In most cases the plaintiff shows his obvious wish for forum law by filing there. "If a plaintiff could choose the substantive rules to be applied to an action ... the invitation to forum shopping would be irresistible." *Allstate* (opinion of Powell, J.). Even if a plaintiff evidences his desire for forum law by moving to the forum, we have generally accorded such a move little or no significance. *John Hancock Mut. Life Ins. Co. v. Yates*; *Home Ins. Co. v. Dick*. In *Allstate* the plaintiff's move to the forum was only relevant because it was unrelated and prior to the litigation. [cit.] Thus the plaintiffs' desire for Kansas law, manifested by their participation in this Kansas lawsuit, bears little relevance.

The Supreme Court of Kansas in its opinion in this case expressed the view that by reason of the fact that it was adjudicating a nationwide class action, it had much greater latitude in applying its own law to the transactions in question than might otherwise be the case:

> "The general rule is that the law of the forum applies unless it is expressly shown that a different law governs, and in case of doubt, the law of the forum is preferred.... Where a state court determines it has jurisdiction over a nationwide class action and procedural due process guarantees of notice and adequate representation are present, we believe the law of the forum should be applied unless compelling reasons exist for applying a different law.... Compelling reasons do not exist to require this court to look to other state laws to determine the rights of the parties involved in this lawsuit." [cit.]

We think that this is something of a "bootstrap" argument. The Kansas class-action statute, like those of most other jurisdictions, requires that there be "common issues of law or fact." But while a State may, for the reasons we have previously stated, assume jurisdiction over the claims of plaintiffs whose principal contacts are with other States, it may not use this assumption of jurisdiction as an added weight in the scale when considering the permissible constitutional limits on choice of substantive law. It may not take a transaction with little or no relationship to the forum and apply the law of the forum in order to satisfy the procedural requirement that there be a "common question of law." The issue of personal jurisdiction over plaintiffs in a class action is entirely distinct from the question of the constitutional limitations on choice of law; the latter calculus is not altered by the fact that it may be more difficult or more burdensome to comply with the constitutional limitations because of the large number of transactions which the State proposes to adjudicate and which have little connection with the forum.

Kansas must have a "significant contact or significant aggregation of contacts" to the claims asserted by each member of the plaintiff class, contacts "creating state interests," in order to ensure that the choice of Kansas law is not arbitrary or unfair. *Allstate*. Given Kansas' lack of "interest" in claims unrelated to that State, and the substantive conflict with jurisdictions such as Texas, we conclude that application of Kansas law to every claim in this case is sufficiently arbitrary and unfair as to exceed constitutional limits.

When considering fairness in this context, an important element is the expectation of the parties. See *Allstate*, (opinion of Powell, J.). There is no indication that when the leases involving land and royalty owners outside of Kansas were executed, the parties had any idea that Kansas law would control. Neither the Due Process Clause nor the Full Faith and Credit Clause requires Kansas "to substitute for its own [laws], applicable to persons and events within it, the conflicting statute of another state," *Pacific Employees Ins. Co. v. Industrial Accident Comm'n*, but Kansas "may not abrogate the rights of parties beyond its borders having no relation to anything done or to be done within them." *Home Ins. Co. v. Dick*.

Here the Supreme Court of Kansas took the view that in a nationwide class action where procedural due process guarantees of notice and adequate representation were met, "the law of the forum should be applied unless compelling reasons exist for applying a different law." [cit.] Whatever practical reasons may have commended this rule to the Supreme Court of Kansas, for the reasons already stated we do not believe that it is consistent with the decisions of this Court. We make no effort to determine for ourselves which law must apply to the various transactions involved in this lawsuit, and we reaffirm our observation in *Allstate* that in many situations a state court may be free to apply one of several choices of law. But the constitutional limitations laid down in cases such as *Allstate* and *Home Ins. Co. v. Dick*, must be respected even in a nationwide class action.

We therefore affirm the judgment of the Supreme Court of Kansas insofar as it upheld the jurisdiction of the Kansas courts over the plaintiff class members in this case, and reverse its judgment insofar as it held that Kansas law was applicable to all of the transactions which it sought to adjudicate. We remand the case to that court for further proceedings not inconsistent with this opinion.

It is so ordered.

JUSTICE POWELL took no part in the decision of this case.

JUSTICE STEVENS, concurring in part and dissenting in part. * * * As the Court recognizes, there "can be no [constitutional] injury in applying Kansas law if it is not in conflict with that of any other jurisdiction connected to this suit." [cit.] A fair reading of the Kansas Supreme Court's opinion in light of its earlier opinion in Shutts v. Phillips Petroleum Co., 567 P. 2d 1292 (Kan.1977) (hereinafter *Shutts I*), *cert. denied*, 434 U.S. 1068 (1978), reveals that the Kansas court has examined the laws of connected jurisdictions and has correctly concluded that there is no "direct" or "substantive" conflict between the law applied by Kansas and the laws of those other States. [cit.] Kansas has merely developed general common-law principles to accommodate the novel facts of this litigation—other state courts either agree with Kansas or have not yet addressed precisely similar claims. Consequently, I conclude that the Full Faith and Credit Clause of the Constitution did not require Kansas to apply the law of any other State, and the Fourteenth Amendment's Due Process Clause did not prevent Kansas from applying its own law in this case.

The Court errs today because it applies a loose definition of the sort of "conflict" of laws required to state a *constitutional* claim, allowing Phillips a tactical victory here merely on allegations of "putative" or "likely" conflicts. [cit.] The Court's choice-of-law analysis also treats the two relevant constitutional provisions as though they imposed the same constraints on the forum court. In my view, however, the potential impact of the Kansas choice on the interests of other sovereign States and the fairness of its decision to the litigants should be separately considered. See *Allstate Insurance Co. v. Hague* (Stevens, J., concurring in judgment). * * *

* * * [The Full Faith and Credit] Clause requires only that States accord "full faith and credit" to other States' laws—that is, acknowledge the validity and finality of such laws and attempt in good faith to apply them when necessary as they would be applied by home state courts. But as Justice Holmes explained, when there is "nothing to suggest that [one State's court] was not candidly construing [another State's law] to the best of its ability, ... even if it was wrong something more than an error of construction is necessary" to invoke the Constitution. [cit.]

Merely to state these general principles is to refute any argument that Kansas' decision below violated the Full Faith and Credit Clause. As the opinion in *Shutts I* indicates, the Kansas court made a careful survey of the relevant laws of Oklahoma and Texas, the only other States whose law is proffered as relevant to this litigation. But, as the Court acknowledges, [cit.] no other State's laws or judicial decisions were precisely on point, and, in the Kansas court's judgment, roughly analogous Texas and Oklahoma cases supported the results the Kansas court reached. The Kansas court expressly declared that, in a multistate action, a "court should also give careful consideration, as we have attempted to do, to any possible conflict of law problems." [cit.] While a common-law judge might disagree with the substantive legal determinations made by the Kansas court (although nothing in its opinion seems erroneous to me), that court's approach to the possible choices of law evinces precisely the "full faith and credit" that the Constitution requires.

It is imaginable that even a good-faith review of another State's law might still "unjustifiably [infringe] upon the legitimate interests of another State" so as to violate the Full Faith and Credit Clause. *Allstate* (Stevens, J., concurring in judgment). If, for example, a Texas oil company or a Texas royalty owner with an interest in a Texas lease were treated directly contrary to a stated policy of the State of Texas by a Kansas court through some honest blunder, the Constitution might bar such "parochial entrenchment" on Texas' interests. [cit.] But this case is so distant from such a situation that I need not pursue this theoretical possibility. * * *

III. It is nevertheless possible for a State's choice of law to violate the Constitution because it is so "totally arbitrary or ... fundamentally unfair" to a litigant that it violates the Due Process Clause. *Allstate* (Stevens, J., concurring in judgment). If the forum court has no connection to the lawsuit other than its jurisdiction over the parties, a decision to apply the forum State's law might so "[f]rustrate the justifiable expectations of the parties" as to be unconstitutional. [cit.]

Again, however, a constitutional claim of "unfair surprise" cannot be based merely upon an unexpected choice of a particular State's law—it must rest on a persuasive showing of an unexpected *result* arrived at by application of that law. Thus, absent any *conflict* of laws, in terms of the results they produce, the Due Process Clause simply has not been violated. This is because the underlying theory of a choice-of-law due process claim must be that parties plan their conduct and contractual relations based upon their legitimate expectations concerning the subsequent legal consequences of their actions. For example, they might base a decision on the belief that the law of a particular State will govern. But a change in that State's law in the interim between the execution and the performance of the contract would not violate the Due Process Clause. Nor would the Constitution be violated simply because a state court made an unanticipated ruling on a previously unanswered question of law—perhaps a choice-of-law question.

In this case it is perfectly clear that there has been no due process violation because this is a classic "false conflicts" case. Phillips has not demonstrated that any significant conflicts exist merely because Oklahoma and Texas state case law is *silent* concerning the equitable theories developed by the Kansas courts in this litigation, or even because the language of some Oklahoma and Texas statutes suggests that those States would "most likely" reach different results. * * *

The crux of my disagreement with the Court is over the standard applied to evaluate the sufficiency of allegations of choice-of-law conflicts necessary to support a constitutional claim. Rather than potential, "putative," or even "likely" conflicts, I would require demonstration of an *unambiguous* conflict with the *established* law of another State as an essential element of a constitutional choice-of-law claim. Arguments that a state court has merely applied general common-law principles in a novel manner, or reconciled arguably conflicting laws erroneously in the face of unprecedented factual circumstances should not suffice to make out a constitutional issue.

In this case, the Kansas Supreme Court's application of general principles of equity, its interpretation of the agreements, its reliance on the Commission's regulations, and its construction of general statutory terms contravened no established legal principles of other States and consequently cannot be characterized as either arbitrary or fundamentally unfair to Phillips. I therefore can find no due process violation in the Kansas court's decision. * * *

Notes and Questions

1. With the exception of Justice Stevens, the Court now accepts that the tests under the Full Faith and Credit and Due Process Clauses are the same. Are the purposes behind the two clauses the same? In *Allstate,* Justice Brennan observed that "at one time the Court required a more exacting standard under the Full Faith and Credit Clause than under the Due Process Clause." Was the test "more exacting" or did it have a different focus—with the Full Faith and Credit Clause concerned with the existence of state interests and the Due Process Clause concerned with expectations of and fairness to private parties?

2. In Watson v. Employers Liability Assurance Corp., 348 U.S. 66 (1954), Mrs. Watson was injured in Louisiana using a Toni Home Permanent manufactured by Gillette. She brought a direct action in Louisiana against Gillette's insurance company. The insurance policy was negotiated and issued in Massachusetts, delivered in Massachusetts and Illinois, and contained a provision, valid under both Massachusetts and Illinois law, prohibiting direct actions against the insurance company prior to an adjudication of the manufacturer's liability. In contrast, Louisiana law permitted direct action suits against insurers without first adjudicating the insured's liability.

The Supreme Court upheld Louisiana's application of its own law. The Court first distinguished *Dick*, noting that there "the subject matter of the contract related in no manner to anything that had been done or was to be done in Texas." Id. at 71. The Court concluded:

> Louisiana's direct action statute is not a mere intermeddling in affairs beyond her boundaries which are no concern of hers. Persons injured or killed in Louisiana are most likely to be Louisiana residents [and], even if not, Louisiana may have to care for them. Serious injuries may require treatment in Louisiana homes or hospitals by Louisiana doctors. The injured may be destitute. They may be compelled to call upon friends, relatives, or the public for help. Louisiana has manifested its natural interest in the injured by providing remedies for recovery of damages. It has a similar interest in policies of insurance which are designed to assure ultimate payment of such damages. Moreover Louisiana courts in most instances provide the most convenient forum for trial of these cases. But modern transportation and business methods have made it more difficult to serve process on wrongdoers who live or do business in other states. In this case efforts to serve the Gillette Company were answered by a motion to dismiss on the grounds that Gillette had no Louisiana agent on whom process could be served. * * * What has been said is enough to show Louisiana's legitimate interest in safeguarding the rights of persons injured there. In view of that interest, the direct action provisions here challenged do not

violate due process.

What we have said above goes far toward answering the Full Faith and Credit Clause contention. That clause does not automatically compel a state to subordinate its own contract laws to the laws of another state in which a contract happens to have been formally executed. Where, as here, a contract affects the people of several states, each may have interests that leave it free to enforce its own contract policies. [cit.] Of course Massachusetts also has some interest in the policy sued on in this case. The insurance contract was formally executed in that State and Gillette has an office there. But plainly these interests cannot outweigh the interest of Louisiana in taking care of those injured in Louisiana. Since this is true, the Full Faith and Credit Clause does not compel Louisiana to subordinate its direct action provisions to Massachusetts contract rules. [cit.] Id. at 72–73.

In Clay v. Sun Insurance Office, Ltd., 377 U.S. 179 (1964), a British company, licensed to do business in Illinois and Florida, issued to an Illinois citizen a "Personal Property Floater Policy (World Wide)." Several months after the policy was issued, the insured moved to Florida. Two years later, the insured property was damaged in Florida. The policy required that suit be brought within one-year. This limit was valid under Illinois law, but invalid under Florida law which allowed five years. The Supreme Court upheld the application of Florida law noting that the defendant knew that the insured and his property were in Florida and the defendant was licensed to do business in Florida. The Court concluded that "Florida has ample contacts with the present transaction and the parties to satisfy any conceivable requirement of full faith and credit or of due process." Are *Watson* and *Clay* consistent with *Dick*?

3. Compare *Hague* with *Clay* and *John Hancock Mutual Life Ins. Co. v. Yates* (discussed in *Allstate*). In all three cases the plaintiff moved after entering into the contract. In *Clay* the move was before the loss and in *Yates* and *Hague* it was after. Should the timing of the move matter for purposes of creating state interests? Should timing be relevant in evaluating unfair surprise? See *Allstate*, Brennan, J., n. 24.

4. Compare Minnesota's interests in *Hague* with Kansas' interests in *Shutts*. Were they really so different? In *Shutts*, Phillips Petroleum engaged in business in Kansas, some of the plaintiffs were from Kansas, and the oil and gas industry was very important to the state. If *Hague* is binding precedent, why were not these contacts, at least when aggregated, sufficient to permit Kansas to apply its laws?

5. Quoting from *Hague*, the Court in *Shutts* states that "for a State's substantive law to be selected in a constitutionally permissible manner, that State must have a significant contact or significant aggregation of contacts, creating state interests, such that choice of its law is neither arbitrary nor fundamentally unfair." 472 U.S. at 818. Professor Brilmayer has said of this test: "In a few brief words this test manages to combine the confusions and ambiguities of interest analysis and of the Second Restatement's 'most significant relationship' test with some sort of vague fairness requirement." Brilmayer, *Conflict of Laws*, 140. Do you agree?

6. Professor Posnak argues that the Court uses the language of interest analysis but does not correctly apply that approach. As to *Hague*, he observes that:

the plurality does not seem to realize that Currie used the word "interest" as a term of art and did not mean to connote care or concern. The plurality seems to be saying that if the forum has some contact with the controversy and this contact arguably generates any kind of care or concern about the outcome of the case, it is constitutionally sufficient to apply that state's law.

Posnak, *They Still Don't Get It*, 1178. He further explains that "policies are what the law was meant to accomplish in the domestic context. An 'interest' arises if it is reasonable to conclude that one of these policies would be advanced if that law were applied to the interstate set of facts in the case before the court." Id. at 1182.

How would the Court properly apply interest analysis as a constitutional test? In *Shutts*, for example, Kansas apparently believed that applying Kansas law would further Kansas' policies. If application of Kansas law is unconstitutional, is it because: (1) Kansas misunderstands its own goals? (2) Kansas was pursuing goals that are constitutionally invalid? or (3) Kansas' goals may be valid, but application of this law is not rationally related to the stated goals?

7. Was it constitutionally permissible for Oregon to apply Oregon law in *Lilienthal v. Kaufman*, supra at 179. Is *Lilienthal* distinguishable from *Dick*? See Hay, *Jurisdiction and Choice of Law*, 29. What about *Cooney v. Osgood Machinery, Inc.*, Ch. 3? Was it constitutional for New York to apply Missouri law in that case? See Silberman, *A Less than Complete "Contribution*," 1381 (arguing it is unconstitutional).

8. Consider the following case: Plaintiff was hired in Missouri to work in defendant's Missouri plant. After working there for 14 years, defendant promoted plaintiff and transferred him to North Carolina. Five years later, he was transferred and promoted again, this time to Wisconsin. Shortly after arriving in Wisconsin, a dispute arose and defendant fired plaintiff. Plaintiff returned to Missouri and sought a "service letter" from defendant in the form specified by Missouri law. When defendant refused, plaintiff brought suit in Missouri. Although defendant previously had a plant in Missouri and still distributed its products in Missouri, it no longer had any manufacturing facilities in that state. Is it constitutional for Missouri to apply the Missouri service letter statute to the defendant? In a case decided shortly after *Hague*, the Eighth Circuit held that the application of Missouri law was unconstitutional and the Supreme Court summarily affirmed. McCluney v. Jos. Schlitz Brewing Co., 649 F.2d 578 (8th Cir.1981), *aff'd*, 454 U.S. 1071 (1981). Is this case consistent with *Hague*?

9. In BMW of North America v. Gore, 517 U.S. 559 (1996), the plaintiff had purchased a new BMW automobile and later learned that the car had been repaired. He sued the distributor for compensatory and punitive damages and the jury returned a verdict in his favor, awarding $4,000 in compensatory damages and $4 million in punitive damages. The Alabama Supreme Court reduced the punitive damages award to $2 million on the grounds that in computing punitives, the jury had improperly multiplied the plaintiff's compensatory damages by the number of similar sales in other states. The Supreme Court held that even the reduced award of punitives was grossly excessive and violated due process. In its opinion, the Court observed: "Alabama does not have the power * * * to punish BMW for conduct that was lawful where it occurred and that had no impact on Alabama or its residents.

Nor may Alabama impose sanctions on BMW in order to deter conduct that is lawful in other jurisdictions." Id. at 572-573.

What about conduct in another state that was *unlawful* where committed? Can the forum impose punitive damages for this conduct? In State Farm Mutual Auto. Ins. Co. v. Campbell,123 S.Ct. 1513 (2003), the Supreme Court seemed to answer this question, at least in dicta: "A State cannot punish a defendant for conduct that may have been lawful where it occurred. . . . Nor, as a general rule, does a State have a legitimate concern in imposing punitive damages to punish a defendant for unlawful acts committed outside of the State's jurisdiction." Id. at 1522. See White v. Ford Motor Co., 312 F.3d 998 (9th Cir. 2002) (district court erred in failing to instruct jury that it could impose punitive damages only with respect to defendant's conduct in the forum state). Compare the Court's analysis in *BMW* and *State Farm* with *Bernhard v. Harrah's Club*, supra at 215. Is it permissible for California to impose damages on a Nevada bar for conduct in Nevada that causes an accident in California?

10. Can a state properly regulate the conduct of its citizens when they are in another state? For example, could a state which prohibits in-state gambling prohibit its citizens from gambling elsewhere? If Roe v. Wade, 410 U.S. 113 (1973) were overruled, could a state that outlawed abortions prohibit its citizens from getting an abortion in another state? See Brilmayer, *Interstate Preemption*; Kreimer, *The Law of Choice*; Rosen, *Extraterritoriality*. Compare these cases with *Babcock*, supra at 127, in which New York imposed liability on a New York citizen for conduct committed in Ontario, where Ontario would not have imposed liability.

11. How far can a state go in regulating the out-of-state conduct of firms doing business in the state? Consider the following cases:

Adventure Communications, Inc. v. Kentucky Registry of Election Fin., 191 F.3d 429 (4th Cir. 1999). The Fourth Circuit upheld a Kentucky statute imposing reporting requirements on broadcast media that sold advertising time to Kentucky gubernatorial candidates. Although the statute was applied to broadcasters located in West Virginia, the court concluded that "the Broadcasters' aggregate contacts with Kentucky, coupled with Kentucky's interest in enforcing its statutory requirements here, were sufficient to satisfy the demands of due process." Id. at 438.

Gerling Global Reinsurance Corp. of Am. v. Gallagher, 267 F.3d 1228 (11th Cir. 2001). A Florida statute required all insurance companies doing business in Florida to provide specified information concerning insurance policies issued by it or its corporate affiliates between 1920 and 1945 to Holocaust victims. The Eleventh Circuit held that the statute violated Due Process Clause limits on legislative jurisdiction noting that "we must look not only at whether the parties regulated by the Act have contacts with Florida, but also and more importantly here at whether the *subject* about which this Act seeks information has a sufficient nexus to Florida." Id. at 1238.

Gerling Global Reinsurance Corp. of Am. v. Low, 296 F.3d 832 (9th Cir. 2002), *rev'd on other grounds*, 123 S.Ct. 2374 (2003). The Ninth Circuit upheld the California Holocaust Victim Insurance Relief Act. The court distinguished *Gallagher* on the grounds that although the law required information about the transactions of foreign affiliates, the California law (unlike the Florida law) imposed the reporting obligation only on the company seeking to do business in California. If the California company was unwilling or unable to secure the necessary information from its foreign affiliate, it could disaffiliate itself from the foreign firm. As to the argument that the Act was intended to force foreign firms to pay Holocaust claims, the court observed that California had a legitimate interest in "protect[ing] its residents from insurance companies that have not paid valid insurance claims" and "informing California residents * * * about the character of the family of companies with whom they might contract for insurance." Id. at 842. The Supreme Court reversed on the grounds that the California law interfered with the President's ability to conduct foreign policy. See *American Insurance Ass'n v. Garamendi*, infra Ch.7. The Court did not discuss the broader question of the scope of the states' legislative jurisdiction.

Sun Oil Co. v. Wortman
Supreme Court of the United States, 1988.
486 U.S. 717, 108 S.Ct. 2117, 100 L.Ed.2d 743.

JUSTICE SCALIA delivered the opinion of the Court. Petitioner Sun Oil Company seeks reversal of a decision of the Supreme Court of Kansas that it is liable for interest on certain previously suspended gas royalties. Wortman v. Sun Oil Co., 241 Kan. 226, 755 P.2d 488 (1987) (*Wortman III*). The Kansas Supreme Court rejected petitioner's contentions that (1) the Full Faith and Credit Clause of the Constitution, Art. IV, § 1, and the Due Process Clause of the Fourteenth Amendment prohibited application of Kansas' statute of limitations so as to allow to proceed in Kansas courts a suit barred by the statute of limitations of the State whose substantive law governs the claim, and (2) those same Clauses of the Constitution mandated interpretations of other States' substantive laws concerning interest that were different from those arrived at by the Kansas courts. We granted certiorari. [cit.]

I. [In a remand following *Shutts*, the trial court applied the Kansas statute of limitations to all the claims. The court then held that as to the claims governed by Kansas substantive law, the applicable interest rate was that specified in Federal Power Commission (FPC) regulations. As to the claims governed by the laws of Texas, Oklahoma and Louisiana, the court held that, like Kansas, those states would apply the FPC rate rather than the lower rates specified in those states' statutes for contractual disputes.] * * *

II. This Court has long and repeatedly held that the Constitution does not bar application of the forum State's statute of limitations to claims that in their substance are and must be governed by the law of a different State. See, e. g., Wells v. Simonds Abrasive Co., 345 U.S. 514, 516–518 (1953); Townsend v. Jemison, 9 How. 407, 413-420 (1850); McElmoyle v. Cohen, 13 Pet. 312, 327–328 (1839). We granted certiorari to reexamine this issue. We conclude that our prior holdings are sound.

A. The Full Faith and Credit Clause provides:

"Full Faith and Credit shall be given in each State to the public Acts, Records, and judicial Proceedings of every other State. And the Congress may by general Laws prescribe the Manner in which such Acts, Records and Proceedings shall be proved, and the Effect thereof."

The Full Faith and Credit Clause does not compel "a state to substitute the statutes of other states for its own statutes dealing with a subject matter concerning which it is competent to legislate." *Pacific Employers Ins. Co. v. Industrial Accident Comm'n.* Since the procedural rules of its courts are surely matters on which a State is competent to legislate, it follows that a State may apply its own procedural rules to actions litigated in its courts. The issue here, then, can be characterized as whether a statute of limitations may be considered as a procedural matter for purposes of the Full Faith and Credit Clause.

Petitioner initially argues that *McElmoyle v. Cohen*, supra, was wrongly decided when handed down. The holding of *McElmoyle*, that a statute of limitations may be treated as procedural and thus may be governed by forum law even when the substance of the claim must be governed by another State's law, rested on two premises, one express and one implicit. The express premise was that this reflected the rule in international law at the time the Constitution was adopted. This is indisputably correct, see Le Roy v. Crowninshield, 15 F. Cas. 362, 365, 371 (No. 8,269) (Mass. 1820) (Story, J.) (collecting authorities), and is not challenged by petitioner. The implicit premise, which petitioner does challenge, was that this rule from international law could properly have been applied in the interstate context consistently with the Full Faith and Credit Clause.

The first sentence of the Full Faith and Credit Clause was not much discussed at either the Constitutional Convention or the state ratifying conventions. However, the most pertinent comment at the Constitutional Convention, made by James Wilson of Pennsylvania, displays an expectation that would be interpreted against the background of principles developed in international conflicts law. See 2 M. Farrand, The Records of the Federal Convention of 1787, p. 488 (rev. ed. 1966). Moreover, this expectation was practically inevitable, since there was no other developed body of conflicts law to which courts in our new Union could turn for guidance.

The reported state cases in the decades immediately following ratification of the Constitution show that courts looked without hesitation to international law for guidance in resolving the issue underlying this case: which State's law governs the statute of limitations. The state of international law on that subject being as we have described, these early decisions uniformly concluded that the forum's statute of limitations governed even when it was longer than the limitations period of the State whose substantive law governed the merits of the claim. [cit.] By 1820, the use of the forum statute of limitations in the interstate context was acknowledged to be "well settled." [cit.] Obviously, judges writing in the era when the Constitution was framed and ratified thought the use of the forum statute of limitations to be proper in the interstate context. Their implicit understanding that the Full Faith and Credit Clause did not preclude reliance on the international law rule carries great weight.

Moreover, this view of statutes of limitations as procedural for purposes of choice of law followed quite logically from the manner in which they were treated for domestic-law purposes. At the time the Constitution was adopted the rule was already well established that suit would lie upon a promise to repay a debt barred by the statute of limitations—on the theory, as expressed by many courts, that the debt constitutes consideration for the promise, since the bar of the statute does not extinguish the underlying right but merely causes the remedy to be withheld. [cit.] This is the same theory, of course, underlying the conflicts rule: the right subsists, and the forum may choose to allow its courts to provide a remedy, even though the jurisdiction where the right arose would not. See Graves v. Graves's Executor, [5 Ky. 207,] 208-209 [1810] ("The statute of limitations ... does not destroy the right but withholds the remedy. It would seem to follow, therefore, that the lex fori, and not the lex loci was to prevail with respect to the time when the action should be commenced").

The historical record shows conclusively, we think, that the society which adopted the Constitution did not regard statutes of limitations as substantive provisions, akin to the rules governing the validity and effect of contracts, but rather as procedural restrictions fashioned by each jurisdiction for its own courts. As Chancellor Kent explained in his landmark work, 2 J. Kent, Commentaries on American Law 462-463 (2d ed. 1832): "The period sufficient to constitute a bar to the litigation of sta[l]e demands, is a question of municipal policy and regulation, and one which belongs to the discretion of every government, consulting its own interest and convenience."

Unable to sustain the contention that under the original understanding of the Full Faith and Credit Clause statutes of limitations would have been considered substantive, petitioner argues that we should apply the modern understanding that they are so. It is now agreed, petitioner argues, that the primary function of a statute of limitations is to balance the competing substantive values of repose and vindication of the underlying right; and we should apply that understanding here, as we have applied it in the area of choice of law for purposes of federal diversity jurisdiction, where we have held that statutes of limitations are substantive, see Guaranty Trust Co. v. York, 326 U.S. 99 (1945).

To address the last point first: *Guaranty Trust* itself rejects the notion that there is an equivalence between what is substantive under the *Erie* doctrine and what is substantive for purposes of conflict of laws. [cit.] Except at the extremes, the terms "substance" and "procedure" precisely describe very little except a dichotomy, and what they mean in a particular context is largely determined by the purposes for which the dichotomy is drawn. In the context of our *Erie* jurisprudence, see Erie R. Co. v. Tompkins, 304 U.S. 64 (1938), that purpose is to establish (within the limits of applicable federal law, including the prescribed Rules of Federal Procedure) substantial uniformity of predictable outcome between cases tried in a federal court and cases tried in the courts of the State in which the federal court sits. See *Guaranty Trust*; Hanna v. Plumer, 380 U.S. 460, 467, 471-474 (1965). The purpose of the substance-procedure dichotomy in the context of the Full Faith and Credit Clause, by contrast, is not to establish uniformity but to delimit spheres of state legislative competence. How different the two purposes (and hence the appropriate meanings) are is suggested by this: It is never the case under *Erie* that either federal *or* state law—if the two differ—can properly be applied to a particular issue, cf. *Erie*; but since the legislative jurisdictions of the States overlap, it is frequently the case under the Full Faith and Credit Clause that a court can lawfully apply either the law of one State or the contrary law of another, see *Shutts III* ("[I]n many situations a state court may be free to apply one of several choices of law"). Today, for example, we do not hold that Kansas must apply its own statute of limitations to a claim governed in its substance by another State's law, but only that it may.

But to address petitioner's broader point of which the *Erie* argument is only a part—that we should update our notion of what is sufficiently "substantive" to require full faith and credit: We cannot imagine what would be the basis for such an updating. As we have just observed, the words "substantive" and "procedural" themselves (besides not appearing in the Full Faith and Credit Clause) do not have a precise content, even (indeed especially) as their usage has evolved. And if one consults the purpose of their usage in the full-faith-and-credit context, that purpose is quite simply to give both the forum State and other interested States the legislative jurisdiction to which they are entitled. If we abandon the currently applied, traditional notions of such entitlement we would embark upon the enterprise of constitutionalizing choice-of-law rules, with no compass to guide us beyond our own perceptions of what seems desirable. There is no more reason to consider recharacterizing statutes of limitation as substantive under the Full Faith and Credit Clause than there is to consider recharacterizing a host of other matters generally treated as procedural under conflicts law, and hence generally regarded as within the forum State's legislative jurisdiction. See, e. g., Restatement (Second) of Conflict of Laws § 131 (remedies available), § 133 (placement of burden of proof), § 134 (burden of production), § 135 (sufficiency of the evidence), § 139 (privileges) (1971).

In sum, long established and still subsisting choice-of-law practices that come to be thought, by modern scholars, unwise, do not thereby become unconstitutional. If current conditions render it desirable that forum States no longer treat a particular issue as procedural for conflict of laws purposes, those States can themselves adopt a rule to that effect, [cit.] or it can be proposed that Congress legislate to that effect under the second sentence of the Full Faith and Credit Clause, [cit.] It is not the function of this Court, however, to make departures from established choice-of-law precedent and practice constitutionally mandatory. We hold, therefore, that Kansas did not violate the Full Faith and Credit Clause when it applied its own statute of limitations.

B. Petitioner also makes a due process attack upon the Kansas court's application of its own statute of limitations.[3] Here again neither the tradition in place

---

3. Although petitioner takes up this issue after discussion of the full-faith-and-credit claim, and devotes much less argument to it, we may note that, logically, the full-faith-and-credit claim is entirely dependent upon it. It cannot possibly be a violation of the Full Faith and Credit Clause for a State to decline to apply another State's law in a case where that other State *itself* does not consider it applicable. Although in certain circumstances standard conflicts law considers a statute of limitations to bar the right and not just the remedy, see Restatement (Second) of Conflict of Laws § 143 (1971), petitioner concedes, [cit.] that (apart from the fact that Kansas does not so regard the out-of-state statutes of limitations at issue here) Texas, Oklahoma, and Louisiana view their own statutes as procedural for choice-of-law purposes, [cit.] A

(continued...)

when the constitutional provision was adopted nor subsequent practice supports the contention. At the time the Fourteenth Amendment was adopted, this Court had not only explicitly approved (under the Full Faith and Credit Clause) forum state application of its own statute of limitations, but the practice had gone essentially unchallenged. And it has gone essentially unchallenged since. "If a thing has been practiced for two hundred years by common consent, it will need a strong case for the Fourteenth Amendment to affect it." [cit.]

A State's interest in regulating the workload of its courts and determining when a claim is too stale to be adjudicated certainly suffices to give it legislative jurisdiction to control the remedies available in its courts by imposing statutes of limitations. Moreover, petitioner could in no way have been unfairly surprised by the application to it of a rule that is as old as the Republic. There is, in short, nothing in Kansas' action here that is "arbitrary or unfair," *Shutts III*, and the due process challenge is entirely without substance.

III. In *Shutts III*, we held that Kansas could not apply its own law to claims for interest by nonresidents concerning royalties from property located in other States. The Kansas Supreme Court has complied with that ruling, but petitioner claims that it has unconstitutionally distorted Texas, Oklahoma, and Louisiana law in its determination of that law made in *Shutts IV* and applied to this case in *Wortman III*.

To constitute a violation of the Full Faith and Credit Clause or the Due Process Clause, it is not enough that a state court misconstrue the law of another State. Rather, our cases make plain that the misconstruction must contradict law of the other State that is clearly established and that has been brought to the court's attention. [cit.] We cannot conclude that any of the interpretations at issue here runs afoul of this standard.

[The Court then discusses the law of Texas, Oklahoma, and Louisiana concerning interest.] * * *

For the reasons stated, the judgment of the Kansas Supreme Court is
Affirmed.

JUSTICE BRENNAN, with whom JUSTICE MARSHALL and JUSTICE BLACKMUN join, concurring in part and concurring in the judgment. I join Parts I and III of the Court's opinion. Although I also agree with the result the Court reaches in Part II, I reach that result through a somewhat different path of analysis.

For 150 years, this Court has consistently held that a forum State may apply its own statute of limitations period to out-of-state claims even though it is longer or shorter than the limitations period that would be applied by the State out of which the claim arose. See Wells v. Simonds Abrasive Co., 345 U.S. 514 (1953) (shorter); Townsend v. Jemison, 9 How. 407 (1850) (longer); McElmoyle v. Cohen, 13 Pet. 312 (1839) (shorter). The main question presented in this case is whether this line

---

3. (...continued)
full-faith-and-credit problem can therefore arise only if that disposition by those other States is invalid—that is, if they, as well as Kansas, are compelled to consider their statutes of limitations substantive. The nub of the present controversy, in other words, is the scope of constitutionally permissible legislative jurisdiction, and it matters little whether that is discussed in the context of the Full Faith and Credit Clause, as the litigants have principally done, or in the context of the Due Process Clause. Since we are largely traversing ground already covered, our discussion of the due process claim can be brief.

of authority has been undermined by more recent case law concerning the constitutionality of state choice-of-law rules. See *Phillips Petroleum Co. v. Shutts*; *Allstate Ins. Co. v. Hague*. I conclude that it has not.

I start, as did the Court in *Wells,* by emphasizing that "[t]he Full Faith and Credit Clause does not compel a state to adopt any particular set of rules of conflict of laws; it merely sets certain minimum requirements which each state must observe when asked to apply the law of a sister state." [cit.] The minimum requirements imposed by the Full Faith and Credit Clause[2] are that a forum State should not apply its law unless it has "'a significant contact or significant aggregation of contacts, creating state interests, such that choice of its law is neither arbitrary nor fundamentally unfair.'" *Phillips Petroleum*, quoting *Allstate* (plurality opinion of Brennan, J.) The constitutional issue in this case is somewhat more complicated than usual because the question is not the typical one of whether a State can constitutionally apply its substantive law where both it and another State have certain contacts with the litigants and the facts underlying the dispute. Rather the question here is whether a forum State can constitutionally apply its limitations period, which has mixed substantive and procedural aspects, where its contacts with the dispute stem only from its status as the forum.

Were statutes of limitations purely substantive, the issue would be an easy one, for where, as here, a forum State has no contacts with the underlying dispute, it has no substantive interests and cannot apply its own law on a purely substantive matter. Nor would the issue be difficult if statutes of limitations were purely procedural, for the contacts a State has with a dispute by virtue of being the forum always create state procedural interests that make application of the forum's law on purely procedural questions "neither arbitrary nor fundamentally unfair." *Phillips Petroleum*. Statutes of limitations, however, defy characterization as either purely procedural or purely substantive. The statute of limitations a State enacts represents a balance between, on the one hand, its substantive interest in vindicating substantive claims and, on the other hand, a combination of its procedural interest in freeing its courts from adjudicating stale claims and its substantive interest in giving individuals repose from ancient breaches of law. A State that has enacted a particular limitations period has simply determined that after that period the interest in vindicating claims becomes outweighed by the combination of the interests in repose and avoiding stale claims. One cannot neatly categorize this complicated temporal balance as either procedural or substantive.

Given the complex of interests underlying statutes of limitations, I conclude that the contact a State has with a claim simply by virtue of being the forum creates a sufficient procedural interest to make the application of its limitations period to wholly out-of-state claims consistent with the Full Faith and Credit Clause. This is clearest when the forum State's limitations period is shorter than that of the claim State. A forum State's procedural interest in avoiding the adjudication of stale claims

---

2. The minimum requirements imposed by the Due Process Clause are, in this context, the same as those imposed by the Full Faith and Credit Clause. See *Phillips Petroleum Co. v. Shutts*; *Allstate Ins. Co. v. Hague* (plurality opinion of Brennan, J.); id., at 332 (Powell, J., dissenting).

is equally applicable to in-state and out-of-state claims. That the State out of which the claim arose may have concluded that at that shorter period its substantive interests outweigh its procedural interest in avoiding stale claims would not make any difference; it would be "'neither arbitrary nor fundamentally unfair,'" *Phillips Petroleum*, for the forum State to conclude that its procedural interest is more weighty than that of the claim State and requires an earlier time bar, as long as the time bar applied in a nondiscriminatory manner to in-state and out-of-state claims alike.

The constitutional question is somewhat less clear where, as here, the forum State's limitations period is longer than that of the claim State. In this situation, the claim State's statute of limitations reflects its policy judgment that at the time the suit was filed the combination of the claim State's procedural interest in avoiding stale claims and its substantive interest in repose outweighs its substantive interest in vindicating the plaintiff's substantive rights. Assuming, for the moment, that each State has an equal substantive interest in the repose of defendants, then a forum State that has concluded that its procedural interest is less weighty than that of the claim State does not act unfairly or arbitrarily in applying its longer limitations period. The claim State does not, after all, have any substantive interest in *not* vindicating rights it has created. Nor will it do to argue that the forum State has no interest in vindicating the substantive rights of nonresidents: the forum State cannot discriminate against nonresidents, and if it has concluded that the substantive rights of its citizens outweigh its procedural interests at that period then it cannot be faulted for applying that determination evenhandedly.

If the different limitations periods also reflect differing assessments of the substantive interests in the repose of defendants, however, the issue is more complicated. It is, to begin with, not entirely clear whether the interest in the repose of defendants is an interest the State has as a forum or wholly as the creator of the claim at issue. Even if one assumes the latter, determining whether application of the forum State's longer limitations period would thwart the claim State's substantive interest in repose requires a complex assessment of the relative weights of both States' procedural and substantive interests. For example, a claim State may have a substantive interest in vindicating claims that, at a particular period, outweighs its substantive interest in repose standing alone but not the combination of its interests in repose and avoiding the adjudication of stale claims. Such a State would not have its substantive interest in repose thwarted by the claim's adjudication in a State that professed no procedural interest in avoiding stale claims, even if the forum State had less substantive interest in repose than the claim State, because the forum State would be according the claim State's substantive interests all the weight the claim State gives them. Such efforts to break down and weigh the procedural and substantive components and interests served by the various States' limitations periods would, however, involve a difficult, unwieldy and somewhat artificial inquiry that itself implicates the strong procedural interest any forum State has in having administrable choice-of-law rules.

In light of the forum State's procedural interests and the inherent ambiguity of any more refined inquiry in this context, there is some force to the conclusion that the forum State's contacts give it sufficient procedural interests to make it "'neither arbitrary nor fundamentally unfair,'" *Phillips Petroleum*, for the State to have a per se rule of applying its own limitations period to out-of-state claims—particularly where, as here, the States out of which the claims arise view their statutes of limitations as procedural. [cit.] The issue, after all, is not whether the decision to apply forum limitations law is wise as a matter of choice-of-law doctrine but whether the decision is within the range of constitutionally permissible choices, *Wells*, and we have already held that distinctions similar to those offered above "are too unsubstantial to form the basis for constitutional distinctions," id. (holding that it is constitutionally irrelevant whether the foreign limitations period is built into the statutory provision creating the out-of-state cause of action at issue). This conclusion may not be compelled, but the arguments to the contrary are at best arguable, and any merely arguable inconsistency with our current full-faith-and-credit jurisprudence surely does not merit deviating from 150 years of precedent holding that choosing the forum State's limitations period over that of the claim State is constitutionally permissible.

The Court's technique of avoiding close examination of the relevant interests by wrapping itself in the mantle of tradition is as troublesome as it is conclusory. It leads the Court to assert broadly (albeit in dicta) that States do not violate the Full Faith and Credit Clause by adjudicating out-of-state claims under the forum's own law on, inter alia, remedies, burdens of proof, and burdens of production. [cit.] The constitutionality of refusing to apply the law of the claim State on such issues was not briefed or argued before this Court, and whether, as the Court asserts without support, there are insufficient reasons for "recharacterizing" these issues (at least in part) as substantive is a question that itself presents multiple issues of enormous difficulty and importance which deserve more than the offhand treatment the Court gives them.

Even more troublesome is the Court's sweeping dictum that *any* choice-of-law practice that is "long established and still subsisting" is constitutional. [cit.] This statement on its face seems to encompass choice-of-law doctrines on purely substantive issues, and the blind reliance on tradition confuses and conflicts with the full-faith-and-credit test we articulated just three years ago in *Phillips Petroleum*. See also *Allstate*, n. 11 (plurality opinion of Brennan, J.) (stating that a 1934 case giving "controlling constitutional significance" to a traditional choice-of-law test "has scant relevance for today"). That certain choice-of-law practices have so far avoided constitutional scrutiny by this Court is in any event a poor reason for concluding their constitutional validity. Nor is it persuasive that the practice reflected the rule applied by States or in international law around the time of the adoption of the Constitution, [cit.] since "[t]he very purpose of the full faith and credit clause was to alter the status of the several states as independent foreign sovereignties," Milwaukee County v. M. E. White Co., 296 U.S. 268, 276–277 (1935), not to leave matters unchanged. The Court never offers a satisfactory explanation as to why tradition should enable States to engage in practices that, under our current test, are "arbitrary" or "fundamentally unfair." The broad range of choice-of-law practices that may, in one jurisdiction or another, be traditional are not before this Court and have not been surveyed by it, and we can only guess what practices today's opinion approves sight unseen. Nor am I much comforted by the fact that the Court opines on the constitutionality of traditional choice-of-law practices only to the extent they are "still subsisting," for few cases involve challenges to practices that no longer subsist. One wonders as well how future courts will determine which practices are traditional enough (or subsist strongly enough) to be constitutional, and about the utility of requiring courts to focus on such an uncertain and formalistic inquiry rather than on the fairness and arbitrariness of the choice-of-law rule at issue. Indeed, the disarray of the Court's test is amply demonstrated by the fact that two of the Justices necessary to form the Court leave open the issue of whether a forum State could constitutionally refuse to apply a shorter limitations period regarded as substantive by the foreign State, see post (O'Connor, J., joined by Rehnquist, C. J., concurring in part and dissenting in part), even though in many States the subsisting tradition of applying the forum's limitations period recognizes no exception for limitations periods considered substantive by the foreign State. See generally Restatement (Second) of Conflict of Laws § 143 and Reporter's Note (1971) (collecting cases).

In short, I fear the Court's rationale will cause considerable mischief with no corresponding benefit. This mischief is all the more unfortunate because it appears to stem from the misperception that this case cannot be resolved without conclusively labeling statutes of limitations as either "procedural" or "substantive." Having asked the wrong question (and an unanswerable one), it is no wonder the Court resorts to tradition rather than analysis to answer it. Because I believe a careful examination of the *Phillips Petroleum* test and the governmental interests created by the relevant contacts provides narrower and sounder grounds for affirming, I concur in the judgment.

JUSTICE O'CONNOR, with whom THE CHIEF JUSTICE joins, concurring in part and dissenting in part. The Court properly concludes that Kansas did not violate the Full Faith and Credit Clause or the Due Process Clause when it chose to apply its own statute of limitations in this case. Different issues might have arisen if Texas, Oklahoma, or Louisiana regarded its own shorter statute of limitations as substantive. Such issues, however, are not presented in this case, and they are appropriately left unresolved. Accordingly, I join Parts I and II of the Court's opinion.

In my view, however, the Supreme Court of Kansas violated the Full Faith and Credit Clause when it concluded that the three States in question would apply the interest rates set forth in the regulations of the Federal Power Commission (FPC). The Court correctly states that misconstruing those States' laws would not by itself have violated the Constitution, for the Full Faith and Credit Clause only required the Kansas court to adhere to law that was clearly established in those States and that had been brought to the Kansas court's attention. [cit.] Under the standard the Court articulates, however, the Clause was violated. Each of the three States has a statute setting an interest rate that is different from the FPC rate, and the Supreme Court of Kansas offered no valid reason whatsoever for ignoring those statutory rates. Neither has this Court suggested a colorable argument that could support the Kansas court's decision, and its affirmance of that decision effectively converts an important constitutional guarantee into a precatory admonition.

* * *

[The opinion discusses Texas, Oklahoma, and Louisiana law.]

Today's decision discards important parts of our decision in *Shutts III*, and of the Full Faith and Credit Clause. Faced with the constitutional obligation to apply the substantive law of another State, a court that does not like that law apparently need take only two steps in order to avoid applying it. First, invent a legal theory so novel or strange that the other State has never had an opportunity to reject it; then, on the basis of nothing but unsupported speculation, "predict" that the other State would adopt that theory if it had the chance. To call this giving full faith and credit to the law of another State ignores the language of the Constitution and leaves it without the capacity to fulfill its purpose. Rather than take such a step, I would remand this case to the Supreme Court of Kansas with instructions to give effect to the interest rates established by law in Texas, Oklahoma, and Louisiana. I therefore respectfully dissent.

Notes and Questions

1. In Wells v. Simonds Abrasive Co., 345 U.S. 514 (1953), the plaintiff was killed in Alabama and suit was brought in Pennsylvania under the Alabama wrongful death statute. The Court allowed Pennsylvania to apply its one-year limitations period rather than the two-year period that was contained in the Alabama wrongful death statute. The Court noted that Pennsylvania applied its one-year period to all wrongful death actions, regardless of where they arose and rejected the dissenters' argument that "it is Alabama law which giveth [the cause of action] and only Alabama law that taketh away." Id. at 527 (Jackson, J., dissenting). Is *Wells* distinguishable from *Wortman*? Consider Professor Posnak's analysis:

> If an otherwise interest-less forum chooses to apply its shorter statute of limitations so as to bar the claim, that would almost certainly advance a policy behind its statute of limitations (clear the docket of stale claims), thus giving such a state an "interest." But, in a case like *Wortman*, when the forum has the longer statute of limitations that would permit the claim to continue and when neither the plaintiff nor the claim is significantly affiliated with the forum, it is hard to imagine that any policy behind the forum's statute of limitations would be furthered by its application. The application of Kansas' statute of limitations did not contribute to anything Kansas had in mind when it passed its statute of limitations and it almost certainly frustrated the policy behind the shorter statute of limitations of the defendant's state. It was, therefore, irrational in Currie-terms, and it unduly denigrated the sovereignty of the defendant's state.

Posnak, *They Still Don't Get It*, 1181.

2. Justice Scalia suggests that the forum can apply its laws to matters that were traditionally deemed procedural. Which, if any, of the following would fall into that category: a requirement that the loser pay the winner's attorney's fees; the amount of damages available, see Kilberg v. Northeast Airlines, Inc., Ch. 2; the interest rate assessed against a defendant for wrongfully withholding funds?

3. Suppose that, shortly after *Sun Oil Co. v. Wortman*, the same plaintiffs as the

ones involved in that case filed against the same defendant a products liability action. The plaintiffs charged that Sun Oil Company had contaminated the plaintiffs' land in Texas, Oklahoma, and Louisiana by cleaning its wells with a detergent that turned out to be toxic. The detergent had been manufactured in Sun Oil's plant in a state other than Kansas. Suppose further that Texas, Oklahoma, and Louisiana have an identical statute of repose which bars the action after 10 years from the date the product was used, and regardless of when the injury was sustained or discovered. (You will recall from Ch. 4, supra at 387, that statutes of repose are considered substantive.) Under this statute, the plaintiffs' action would be untimely. Consider the following variations:

(a) Kansas, the forum state, does not have such a statute but instead has a statute of limitation which provides that a products liability action must be brought within two years from the date the injury is discovered. Under this statute, the plaintiffs' action would be timely. Would it be constitutional for Kansas to apply its statute of limitation? How do you think Justices Scalia, Brennan and O'Connor would analyze the situation?

(b) Same facts as in question (a), except that Kansas has a statute of repose which is similar to that of the other three states except that it provides for a 15 year period. Under this statute, the plaintiffs' action would be timely. Would it be constitutional for Kansas to apply this statute? Should the result or analysis be different than in (a)?

4. Consider the following situation. Some states have relatively long periods within which claimants can bring suit against their insurance companies. Your client, an insurance company, has expressed concern that after *Wortman* an aggrieved insured can seek out one of those "hospitable" states and assure application of that state's statute of limitation, even if that state has no contacts whatsoever with the contract in question. Your client wants to know whether its concern is well-founded and whether it can eliminate this problem by including a clause in its contracts specifying the period within which suit must be brought. What advice would you give?

5. Consider Part III of Justice Scalia's opinion in which he discusses the substantive content of state law. Given the Court's apparent willingness to indulge one state's misconstruction of another state's laws, does this suggest that the constitutional limits of choice of law are, as a practical matter, even more modest than the language of *Shutts* suggests?

E. A STATE'S OBLIGATION AND RIGHT TO PROVIDE A FORUM

Hughes v. Fetter

Supreme Court of the United States, 1951.
341 U.S. 609, 71 S.Ct. 980, 95 L.Ed. 1212.

JUSTICE BLACK delivered the opinion of the Court. Basing his complaint on the Illinois wrongful death statute, appellant administrator brought this action in the Wisconsin state court to recover damages for the death of Harold Hughes, who was fatally injured in an automobile accident in Illinois. The allegedly negligent driver and an insurance company were named as defendants. On their motion the trial court entered summary judgment "dismissing the complaint on the merits." It held that a Wisconsin statute, which creates a right of action only for deaths caused in that state, establishes a local public policy against Wisconsin's entertaining suits brought under the wrongful death acts of other states. The Wisconsin Supreme Court affirmed, notwithstanding the contention that the local statute so construed violated the Full Faith and Credit Clause of Art. IV, § 1 of the Constitution. * * *

We are called upon to decide the narrow question whether Wisconsin, over the objection raised, can close the doors of its courts to the cause of action created by the Illinois wrongful death act.[4] Prior decisions have established that the Illinois statute is a "public act" within the provision of Art. IV, § 1 that "Full Faith and Credit shall be given in each State to the public Acts ... of every other State." It is also settled that Wisconsin cannot escape this constitutional obligation to enforce the rights and duties validly created under the laws of other states by the simple device of removing jurisdiction from courts otherwise competent. We have recognized, however, that full faith and credit does not automatically compel a forum state to subordinate its own statutory policy to a conflicting public act of another state; rather, it is for this Court to choose in each case between the competing public policies involved. The clash of interests in cases of this type has usually been described as a conflict between the public policies of two or more states. The more basic conflict involved in the present appeal, however, is as follows: On the one hand is the strong unifying principle embodied in the Full Faith and Credit Clause looking toward maximum enforcement in each state of the obligations or rights created or recognized by the statutes of sister states; on the other hand is the policy of Wisconsin, as interpreted by its highest court, against permitting Wisconsin courts to entertain this wrongful death action.[10]

We hold that Wisconsin's policy must give way. That state has no real feeling of antagonism against wrongful death suits in general. To the contrary, a forum is regularly provided for cases of this nature, the exclusionary rule extending only so far as to bar actions for death not caused locally. The Wisconsin policy, moreover, cannot be considered as an application of the forum non conveniens doctrine, whatever effect that doctrine might be given if its use resulted in denying enforcement to public acts of other states. Even if we assume that Wisconsin could refuse, by reason of particular circumstances, to hear foreign controversies to which nonresidents were parties, the present case is not one lacking a close relationship with the state. For not only were appellant, the decedent and the individual defendant all residents of Wisconsin, but also appellant was appointed administrator and the

---

4. The parties concede, as they must, that if the same cause of action had previously been reduced to judgment, the Full Faith and Credit Clause would compel the courts of Wisconsin to entertain an action to enforce it. Kenney v. Supreme Lodge, 252 U.S. 411 [1920].

10. The present case is not one where Wisconsin, having entertained appellant's lawsuit, chose to apply its own instead of Illinois' statute to measure the substantive rights involved. This distinguishes the present case from those where we have said that "Prima facie every state is entitled to enforce in its own courts its own statutes, lawfully enacted." *Alaska Packers Assn. v. Commission*; see also, Williams v. North Carolina, 317 U.S. 287, 295–296 [1942].

corporate defendant was created under Wisconsin laws. We also think it relevant, although not crucial here, that Wisconsin may well be the only jurisdiction in which service could be had as an original matter on the insurance company defendant. And while in the present case jurisdiction over the individual defendant apparently could be had in Illinois by substituted service, in other cases Wisconsin's exclusionary statute might amount to a deprivation of all opportunity to enforce valid death claims created by another state.

Under these circumstances, we conclude that Wisconsin's statutory policy which excludes this Illinois cause of action is forbidden by the national policy of the Full Faith and Credit Clause. The judgment is reversed and the cause is remanded to the Supreme Court of Wisconsin for proceedings not inconsistent with this opinion.

Reversed and remanded.

JUSTICE FRANKFURTER, whom JUSTICE REED, JUSTICE JACKSON, and JUSTICE MINTON join, dissenting. * * * This Court should certainly not require that the forum deny its own law and follow the tort law of another State where there is a reasonable basis for the forum to close its courts to the foreign cause of action. The decision of Wisconsin to open its courts to actions for wrongful deaths within the State but close them to actions for deaths outside the State may not satisfy everyone's notion of wise policy. See *Loucks v. Standard Oil Co.*, [Ch.2]. But it is neither novel nor without reason. * * * Wisconsin may be willing to grant a right of action where witnesses will be available in Wisconsin and the courts are acquainted with a detailed local statute and cases construing it. It may not wish to subject residents to suit where out-of-state witnesses will be difficult to bring before the court, and where the court will be faced with the alternative of applying a complex foreign statute—perhaps inconsistent with that of Wisconsin on important issues—or fitting the statute to the Wisconsin pattern. The legislature may well feel that it is better to allow the courts of the State where the accident occurred to construe and apply its own statute, and that the exceptional case where the defendant cannot be served in the State where the accident occurred does not warrant a general statute allowing suit in the Wisconsin courts. The various wrongful death statutes are inconsistent on such issues as beneficiaries, the party who may bring suit, limitations on liability, comparative negligence, and the measure of damages. [cit.] The measure of damages and the relation of wrongful death actions to actions for injury surviving death have raised extremely complicated problems, even for a court applying the familiar statute of its own State. [cit.] These diversities reasonably suggest application by local judges versed in them. [cit.]

No claim is made that Wisconsin has discriminated against the citizens of other States and thus violated Art. IV, § 2 of the Constitution. [cit.] Nor is a claim made that the lack of a forum in Wisconsin deprives the plaintiff of due process. [cit.] Nor is it argued that Wisconsin is flouting a federal statute. [cit.] The only question before us is how far the Full Faith and Credit Clause undercuts the purpose of the Constitution, made explicit by the Tenth Amendment, to leave the conduct of domestic affairs to the States. Few interests are of more dominant local concern than matters governing the administration of law. This vital interest of the States should not be sacrificed in the interest of a merely literal reading of the Full Faith and Credit

Clause.

* * *

Finally, it may be noted that there is no conflict here in the policies underlying the statute of Wisconsin and that of Illinois. The Illinois wrongful death statute has a proviso that "no action shall be brought or prosecuted in this State to recover damages for a death occurring outside of this State where a right of action for such death exists under the laws of the place where such death occurred and service of process in such suit may be had upon the defendant in such place." [cit.] The opinion of the Court concedes that "jurisdiction over the individual defendant apparently could be had in Illinois by substituted service." [cit.] Thus, in the converse of the case at bar—if Hughes had been killed in Wisconsin and suit had been brought in Illinois—the Illinois courts would apparently have dismissed the suit. There is no need to be "more Roman than the Romans."

Notes and Questions

1. Would it have been constitutional for Wisconsin to have applied its own substantive law and dismissed the suit for failure to state a claim? What about dismissal on grounds of forum non conveniens? How would dismissal on these bases be any different from the actual case? Does it make sense to make the constitutionality of the dismissal turn on the state's justification? See Martin, *Constitutional Limitations*, at 219–20; Kirgis, *The Roles of Due Process and Full Faith and Credit*, at 118.

2. In Broderick v. Rosner, 294 U.S. 629 (1935), New York law provided that bank shareholders of New York banks were liable for the debts of the bank. The New York Superintendent of Banks brought suit in New Jersey against New Jersey shareholders of a New York bank. New Jersey law required that in any such suit, all shareholders must be joined. Because of personal jurisdiction, all shareholders could not be joined, and New Jersey dismissed the suit. The Supreme Court reversed, explaining:

> The power of a State to determine the limits of the jurisdiction of its courts and the character of the controversies which shall be heard therein is subject to the limitations imposed by the Federal Constitution. [cit.] A "State cannot escape its constitutional obligations [under the full faith and credit clause] by the simple device of denying jurisdiction in such cases to courts otherwise competent." [cit.] * * * But the room left for the play of conflicting policies is a narrow one. One State need not enforce the penal laws of another. [cit.] A State may adopt such system of courts and form of remedy as it sees fit. It may in appropriate cases apply the doctrine of forum non conveniens. [cit.] But it may not, under the guise of merely affecting the remedy, deny the enforcement of claims otherwise within the protection of the full faith and credit clause, when its courts have general jurisdiction of the subject matter and the parties.

Id. at 642–43.

3. Compare *Hughes* with *Wells v. Simonds Abrasive Co.*, supra. In *Wells*, the Court allowed Pennsylvania to apply its one year statute of limitation to an Alabama

claim that would not have been time barred in Alabama. Is the door-closing in *Wells* distinguishable from *Hughes*?

4. In *Hughes*, the Court observed that Wisconsin had no feeling of antagonism toward wrongful death actions. If it did have such a feeling, would that be a valid basis for refusing to enforce the cause of action? Does it violate the Full Faith and Credit Clause for a forum to refuse to enforce a cause of action on grounds of public policy? Is not dismissal on these grounds inconsistent with the "strong unifying principle embodied in the Full Faith and Credit Clause"? Professor Kramer has argued that the Full Faith and Credit clause should be read to prohibit states from rejecting a sister state's laws because of disagreement with the underlying policy choice. "The central object of the Clause was, in fact, to eliminate a state's prideful unwillingness to recognize other states' laws or judgments on the ground that these are inferior or unacceptable." Kramer, *Same-Sex Marriage*, at 1986. Do you agree?

Disagreement with the underlying policy is not a valid basis for a state to refuse to enforce a federal cause of action. See, e.g., Howlett v. Rose, 496 U.S. 356 (1990); Mondou v. New York, N.H. & H.R. Co., 223 U.S. 1 (1912). Similarly, states are required to enforce federal penal statutes. See Testa v. Katt, 330 U.S. 386 (1947). States are permitted to apply "neutral procedural rules to federal claims," *Howlett*, 496 U.S. at 372. However, states are required to treat federal law "as if it emanated from its own legislature," id. at 371, because, "the Constitution and laws passed pursuant to it are as much laws in the States as laws passed by the state legislature." Id. at 367.

5. It is common for long-arm statutes to differentiate between tortious acts committed within the state and those committed outside the state. See, e.g., O.C.G.A.. § 9–10–91 (2002). In the latter case, the statute may require systematic contacts with the state. Of course, the Constitution may require greater contacts in the case of an out-of-state tort, but can a state require more than the constitutional minimum for out-of-state torts? Is not that discriminating between in-state and out-of-state causes of action?

Tennessee Coal, Iron & R.R. Co. v. George
Supreme Court of the United States, 1914.
233 U.S. 354, 34 S.Ct. 587, 58 L.Ed. 997.

JUSTICE LAMAR delivered the opinion of the court. Wiley George, the defendant in error, was an engineer employed by the Tennessee Coal, Iron and Railroad Company at its steel plant in Jefferson County, Alabama. While he was under a locomotive repairing the brakes, a defective throttle allowed steam to leak into the cylinder causing the engine to move forward automatically in consequence of which he was seriously injured. He brought suit by attachment, in the City Court of Atlanta, Georgia, founding his action on § 3910 of the Alabama Code of 1907, which makes the master liable to the employee when the injury is "caused by reason of any defect in the condition of the ways, works, machinery or plant connected with or used in the business of the master or employer."

The defendant filed a plea in abatement in which it was set out that § 6115 of that Code also provided that "all actions under said section 3910 must be brought in a court of competent jurisdiction within the State of Alabama and not elsewhere." The defendant thereupon prayed that the action be abated because "to continue said case on said statutory cause of action given by the statutes of Alabama and restricted by said statutes to the courts of Alabama, ... would be a denial so far as the rights of this defendant are concerned, of full faith and credit to said public acts of the State of Alabama in the State of Georgia, contrary to the provisions of Art. 4, § 1 of the Constitution of the United States." A demurrer to the plea in abatement was sustained and the judgment for the plaintiff thereafter entered was affirmed by the Court of Appeals. The case was then brought to this court.

The record raises the single question as to whether the full faith and credit clause of the Constitution prohibited the courts of Georgia from enforcing a cause of action given by the Alabama Code, to the servant against the master, for injuries occasioned by defective machinery, when another section of the same Code provided that suits to enforce such liability "must be brought in a court of competent jurisdiction within the State of Alabama *and not elsewhere.*"

There are many cases where right and remedy are so united that the right cannot be enforced except in the manner and before the tribunal designated by the act. For the rule is well settled that "where the provision for the liability is coupled with a provision for a special remedy, that remedy, and that alone, must be employed." [cit.]

But that rule has no application to a case arising under the Alabama Code relating to suits for injuries caused by defective machinery. For, whether the statute be treated as prohibiting certain defenses, as removing common law restrictions or as imposing upon the master a new and larger liability, it is in either event evident that the place of bringing the suit is not part of the cause of action,—the right and the remedy are not so inseparably united as to make the right dependent upon its being enforced in a particular tribunal. The cause of action is transitory and like any other transitory action can be enforced "in any court of competent jurisdiction within the State of Alabama...." But the owner of the defective machinery causing the injury may have removed from the State and it would be a deprivation of a fixed right if the plaintiff could not sue the defendant in Alabama because he had left the State nor sue him where the defendant or his property could be found because the statute did not permit a suit elsewhere than in Alabama. The injured plaintiff may likewise have moved from Alabama and for that, or other, reason may have found it to his interest to bring suit by attachment or in personam in a State other than where the injury was inflicted.

The courts of the sister State trying the case would be bound to give full faith and credit to all those substantial provisions of the statute which inhered in the cause of action or which name conditions on which the right to sue depend. But venue is no part of the right; and a State cannot create a transitory cause of action and at the same time destroy the right to sue on that transitory cause of action in any court having jurisdiction. That jurisdiction is to be determined by the law of the court's creation and cannot be defeated by the extraterritorial operation of a statute of another State, even though it created the right of action.

The case here is controlled by the decision of this court in Atchison & T. & S.

F. Ry. v. Sowers, 213 U.S. 55, 59, 70 [1909], where the New Mexico statute, giving a right of action for personal injuries and providing that suits should be brought after certain form of notice in a particular district, was preceded by the recital that "it has become customary for persons claiming damages for personal injuries received in this Territory to institute and maintain suits for the recovery thereof in other States and Territories to the increased cost and annoyance and manifest injury and oppression of the business interests of this Territory and in derogation of the dignity of the courts thereof." Despite this statement of the public policy of the Territory, the judgment obtained by the plaintiff in Texas was affirmed by this court * * *.

It is claimed, however, that the decision in the *Sowers Case* is not in point because the plaintiff was there seeking to enforce a common law liability, while here he is asserting a new and statutory cause of action. But that distinction marks no difference between the two cases because in New Mexico, common law liability is statutory liability—the adopting statute (Compiled Laws, § 1823), providing that "the common law as recognized in the United States of America shall be the rule of practice and decision."

The decision in the *Sowers Case*, however, was not put upon the fact that the suit was based on a common law liability. The court there announced the general rule that a transitory cause of action can be maintained in another State even though the statute creating the cause of action provides that the action must be brought in local domestic courts.

In the present case the Georgia court gave full faith and credit to the Alabama act and its judgment is
    Affirmed.

Notes and Questions

1. In Crider v. Zurich Ins. Co., 380 U.S. 39 (1965), the Court held that Alabama could grant relief under the Georgia Workers' Compensation Act even though Georgia law gave exclusive enforcement authority to an administrative board in Georgia. The suit involved a claim brought against a Georgia defendant by an Alabama plaintiff for injuries suffered in Alabama. The Court stressed Alabama's significant interest under these circumstances. In *George*, what connection did Georgia have to the underlying transaction? Was it sufficiently connected that it could have applied its own substantive law? Does a forum need a connection in order to ignore portions of an interested state's localizing provision?

2. In *Crider*, an Alabama court was allowed to award compensation under the Georgia Workers' Compensation Act, even though the courts of Georgia had no such authority. Are not there legitimate reasons for which a state would want all the cases brought before one administrative agency? Notice that while all *courts* may be largely fungible, administrative agencies are frequently used because of their unique expertise.

3. The Court in *George* says that "a State cannot create a transitory cause of action and at the same time destroy the right to sue on the transitory cause of action in any court having jurisdiction." What in the Constitution prohibits this?

4. In *George* and *Crider* the Court permitted the forum to ignore the localizing provision of another state's statute. *Must* a state disregard such a provision? Does the *George* Court hold that the Alabama localizing provision is unconstitutional? After *Hughes* would it be constitutional for one state to dismiss a suit in deference to another state's localizing provision? Does it matter what the justification for the localizing provision is? In other words, must a localizing provision be justified on grounds other than hostility to or distrust of other state's courts?

5. The Uniform Child Custody Jurisdiction Act and the Uniform Child Custody Jurisdiction and Enforcement Act, discussed in Chapter 8, designates a "home state." Under these Acts, all other states are expected to decline jurisdiction so that one state will have responsibility for custody orders and modifications. Is this inconsistent with *Tennessee Coal*?

6. In *George*, could Alabama enjoin the parties from litigating in Georgia? In Cole v. Cunningham, 133 U.S. 107 (1890), the Supreme Court held that it did not violate the Full Faith and Credit Clause for a state in which an insolvency proceeding was pending to enjoin a creditor from bringing suit in other states to collect the debtor's assets. Relying on *Cole*, states do sometimes enjoin litigation in other states. See *Injunction by State Court Against Action in Court of Another State*, 6 A.L.R. 2d 896. Are these injunctions consistent with the holding in *George*?

State courts cannot enjoin a litigant from filing or prosecuting an action in federal court. See General Atomic Co. v. Felter, 434 U.S. 12 (1977); Donovan v. Dallas, 377 U.S. 408 (1964). The Anti–Injunction Act, 28 U.S.C. § 2283, prohibits federal courts from enjoining or staying a state court proceeding except where expressly authorized by statute or "where necessary in aid of its jurisdiction, or to protect or effectuate its judgments."

7. Congress has the power to grant the federal courts exclusive jurisdiction over certain areas. The Court has explained:

[I]t is manifest that the judicial power of the United States is in some cases unavoidably exclusive of all State authority, and that in all others it may be made so at the election of Congress. We agree fully with this conclusion. The legislation of Congress has proceeded upon this supposition. The Judiciary Act of 1789, in its distribution of jurisdiction to the several Federal courts, recognizes and is framed upon the theory that in all cases to which the judicial power of the United States extends, Congress may rightfully vest exclusive jurisdiction in the Federal courts. * * *

[The federal courts' jurisdiction of admiralty and maritime cases] has been made exclusive by Congress, and that is sufficient, even if we should admit that in the absence of its legislation the State courts might have taken cognizance of these causes. But there are many weighty reasons why it was so declared. "The admiralty jurisdiction," says Mr. Justice Story, "naturally connects itself, on the one hand, with our diplomatic relations and the duties to foreign nations and their subjects; and, on the other hand, with the great interests of navigation and commerce, foreign and domestic. There is, then, a peculiar wisdom in giving to the national government a jurisdiction of this sort which cannot be yielded, except for the general good, and which multiplies the securities for the public peace abroad, and gives to commerce and navigation the most encouraging support at home."

The Moses Taylor, 71 U.S. (4 Wall.) 411, 429-31 (1867). The Court has never questioned whether Congress has an adequate basis for conferring exclusive jurisdiction on the federal courts. Compare exclusive federal jurisdiction with *George*. Why cannot a state confine causes of action it created to its own courts when the federal government can?

Nevada v. Hall

Supreme Court of the United States, 1979.
440 U.S. 410, 99 S.Ct. 1182, 59 L.Ed.2d 416.

JUSTICE STEVENS delivered the opinion of the Court. In this tort action arising out of an automobile collision in California, a California court has entered a judgment against the State of Nevada that Nevada's own courts could not have entered. We granted certiorari to decide whether federal law prohibits the California courts from entering such a judgment or, indeed, from asserting any jurisdiction over another sovereign State.

The respondents are California residents. They suffered severe injuries in an automobile collision on a California highway on May 13, 1968. The driver of the other vehicle, an employee of the University of Nevada, was killed in the collision. It is conceded that he was driving a car owned by the State, that he was engaged in official business, and that the University is an instrumentality of the State itself.

Respondents filed this suit for damages in the Superior Court for the city of San Francisco, naming the administrator of the driver's estate, the University, and the State of Nevada as defendants. Process was served on the State and the University pursuant to the provisions of the California Vehicle Code authorizing service of process on nonresident motorists. The trial court granted a motion to quash service on the State, but its order was reversed on appeal. The California Supreme Court held, as a matter of California law, that the State of Nevada was amendable to suit in California courts and remanded the case for trial. [cit.] * * *

On remand, Nevada filed a pretrial motion to limit the amount of damages that might be recovered. A Nevada statute places a limit of $25,000 on any award in a tort action against the State pursuant to its statutory waiver of sovereign immunity. Nevada argued that the Full Faith and Credit Clause of the United States Constitution required the California courts to enforce that statute. Nevada's motion was denied, and the case went to trial.

The jury concluded that the Nevada driver was negligent and awarded damages of $1,150,000. The Superior Court entered judgment on the verdict and the Court of Appeal affirmed. After the California Supreme Court denied review, the State of Nevada and its University successfully sought a writ of certiorari. [cit.]

Despite its importance, the question whether a State may claim immunity from suit in the courts of another State has never been addressed by this Court. The question is not expressly answered by any provision of the Constitution; Nevada argues that it is implicitly answered by reference to the common understanding that no sovereign is amenable to suit without its consent—an understanding prevalent when the Constitution was framed and repeatedly reflected in this Court's opinions. In order to determine whether that understanding is embodied in the Constitution, as Nevada claims, it is necessary to consider (1) the source and scope of the traditional doctrine of sovereign immunity; (2) the impact of the doctrine on the framing of the Constitution; (3) the Full Faith and Credit Clause; and (4) other aspects of the Constitution that qualify the sovereignty of the several States.

I. The doctrine of sovereign immunity is an amalgam of two quite different concepts, one applicable to suits in the sovereign's own courts and the other to suits in the courts of another sovereign.

The immunity of a truly independent sovereign from suit in its own courts has been enjoyed as a matter of absolute right for centuries. Only the sovereign's own consent could qualify the absolute character of that immunity.

The doctrine, as it developed at common law, had its origins in the feudal system. Describing those origins, Pollock and Maitland noted that no lord could be sued by a vassal in his own court, but each petty lord was subject to suit in the courts of a higher lord. Since the King was at the apex of the feudal pyramid, there was no higher court in which he could be sued. The King's immunity rested primarily on the structure of the feudal system and secondarily on a fiction that the King could do no wrong.

We must, of course, reject the fiction. It was rejected by the colonists when they declared their independence from the Crown, and the record in this case discloses an actual wrong committed by Nevada. But the notion that immunity from suit is an attribute of sovereignty is reflected in our cases.

Mr. Chief Justice Jay described sovereignty as the "right to govern"; that kind of right would necessarily encompass the right to determine what suits may be brought in the sovereign's own courts. Thus, Mr. Justice Holmes explained sovereign immunity as based "on the logical and practical ground that there can be no legal right as against the authority that makes the law on which the right depends."

This explanation adequately supports the conclusion that no sovereign may be sued in its own courts without its consent, but it affords no support for a claim of immunity in another sovereign's courts. Such a claim necessarily implicates the power and authority of a second sovereign; its source must be found either in an agreement, express or implied, between the two sovereigns, or in the voluntary decision of the second to respect the dignity of the first as a matter of comity.

This point was plainly stated by Mr. Chief Justice Marshall in The Schooner Exchange v. McFaddon, 7 Cranch 116 [1812], which held that an American court could not assert jurisdiction over a vessel in which Napoleon, the reigning Emperor of France, claimed a sovereign right. In that case, the Chief Justice observed:

"The jurisdiction of courts is a branch of that which is possessed by the nation as an independent sovereign power.

"The jurisdiction of the nation within its own territory is necessarily exclusive and absolute. It is susceptible of no limitation not imposed by itself. Any restriction upon it, deriving validity from an external source, would imply a diminution of its sovereignty to the extent of the restriction, and an investment of that sovereignty to the same extent in that power which could impose such restriction.

"All exceptions, therefore, to the full and complete power of a nation within its own territories, must be traced up to the consent of the nation itself. They can flow from no other legitimate source." Id. at 136.

After noting that the source of any immunity for the French vessel must be found in American law, the Chief Justice interpreted that law as recognizing the common usage among nations in which every sovereign was understood to have waived its exclusive territorial jurisdiction over visiting sovereigns, or their representatives, in certain classes of cases.

The opinion in *The Schooner Exchange* makes clear that if California and Nevada were independent and completely sovereign nations, Nevada's claim of immunity from suit in California's courts would be answered by reference to the law of California. It is fair to infer that if the immunity defense Nevada asserts today had been raised in 1812 when *The Schooner Exchange* was decided, or earlier when the Constitution was being framed, the defense would have been sustained by the California courts. By rejecting the defense in this very case, however, the California courts have told us that whatever California law may have been in the past, it no longer extends immunity to Nevada as a matter of comity.

Nevada quite rightly does not ask us to review the California courts' interpretation of California law. Rather, it argues that California is not free, as a sovereign, to apply its own law, but is bound instead by a federal rule of law implicit in the Constitution that requires all of the States to adhere to the sovereign-immunity doctrine as it prevailed when the Constitution was adopted. Unless such a federal rule exists, we of course have no power to disturb the judgment of the California courts.

II. Unquestionably the doctrine of sovereign immunity was a matter of importance in the early days of independence. Many of the States were heavily indebted as a result of the Revolutionary War. They were vitally interested in the question whether the creation of a new federal sovereign, with courts of its own, would automatically subject them, like lower English lords, to suits in the courts of the "higher" sovereign.

But the question whether one State might be subject to suit in the courts of another State was apparently not a matter of concern when the new Constitution was being drafted and ratified. Regardless of whether the Framers were correct in assuming, as presumably they did, that prevailing notions of comity would provide adequate protection against the unlikely prospect of an attempt by the courts of one State to assert jurisdiction over another, the need for constitutional protection against that contingency was not discussed.

The debate about the suability of the States focused on the scope of the judicial power of the United States authorized by Art. III. In The Federalist, Hamilton took the position that this authorization did not extend to suits brought by an individual against a nonconsenting State. The contrary position was also advocated and actually prevailed in this Court's decision in Chisholm v. Georgia, 2 Dall. 419 [1793].

The *Chisholm* decision led to the prompt adoption of the Eleventh Amendment. That Amendment places explicit limits on the powers of federal courts to entertain suits against a State.[19]

The language used by the Court in cases construing these limits, like the language used during the debates on ratification of the Constitution, emphasized the widespread acceptance of the view that a sovereign State is never amenable to suit without its consent. But all of these cases, and all of the relevant debate, concerned questions of federal-court jurisdiction and the extent to which the States, by ratifying the Constitution and creating federal courts, had authorized suits against themselves in those courts. These decisions do not answer the question whether the Constitution places any limit on the exercise of one's State's power to authorize its courts to assert jurisdiction over another State. Nor does anything in Art. III authorizing the judicial power of the United States, or in the Eleventh Amendment limitation on that power, provide any basis, explicit or implicit, for this Court to impose limits on the powers of California exercised in this case. A mandate for federal-court enforcement of interstate comity must find its basis elsewhere in the Constitution.

III. Nevada claims that the Full Faith and Credit Clause of the Constitution requires California to respect the limitations on Nevada's statutory waiver of its immunity from suit. That waiver only gives Nevada's consent to suits in its own courts. Moreover, even if the waiver is treated as a consent to be sued in California, California must honor the condition attached to that consent and limit respondents' recovery to $25,000, the maximum allowable in an action in Nevada's courts.

The Full Faith and Credit Clause does require each State to give effect to official acts of other States. A judgment entered in one State must be respected in another provided that the first State had jurisdiction over the parties and the subject matter. Moreover, in certain limited situations, the courts of one State must apply the statutory law of another State. Thus, in *Bradford Electric Light Co. v. Clapper*, the Court held that a federal court sitting in New Hampshire was required by the Constitution to apply Vermont law in an action between a Vermont employee and a Vermont employer arising out of a contract made in Vermont. But this Court's decision in *Pacific Employers Insurance Co. v. Industrial Accident Comm'n*, clearly establishes that the Full Faith and Credit Clause does not require a State to apply another State's law in violation of its own legitimate public policy.[22]

* * *

* * * The interest of California afforded such respect in the *Pacific Employers*

---

19. The Eleventh Amendment provides: "The Judicial power of the United States shall not be construed to extend to any suit in law or equity, commenced or prosecuted against one of the United States by Citizens of another State, or by Citizens or Subjects of any Foreign State."

Even as so limited, however, the Eleventh Amendment has not accorded the States absolute sovereign immunity in federal-court actions. The States are subject to suit by both their sister States and the United States. See, e. g., North Dakota v. Minnesota, 263 U.S. 365, 372 [1923]; United States v. Mississippi, 380 U.S. 128, 140–141 [1965]. Further, prospective injunctive and declaratory relief is available against States in suits in federal court in which state officials are the nominal defendants. See Ex parte Young, 209 U.S. 123 [1908]; Edelman v. Jordan, 415 U.S. 651 [1974]. See generally Baker, *Federalism and the Eleventh Amendment*, 48 U. Colo. L. Rev. 139 (1977).

22. See also *Alaska Packers Assn. v. Industrial Accident Comm'n*; Bonaparte v. Tax Court, 104 U.S. 592 [1881] (holding that a law exempting certain bonds of the enacting State from taxation did not apply extraterritorially by virtue of the Full Faith and Credit Clause).

Insurance case was in providing for "the bodily safety and economic protection of employees injured within it." [cit.] In this case, California's interest is the closely related and equally substantial one of providing "full protection to those who are injured on its highways through the negligence of both residents and nonresidents." [cit.] To effectuate this interest, California has provided by statute for jurisdiction in its courts over residents and nonresidents alike to allow those injured on its highways through the negligence of others to secure full compensation for their injuries in the California courts.

In further implementation of that policy, California has unequivocally waived its own immunity from liability for the torts committed by its own agents and authorized full recovery even against the sovereign. As the California courts have found, to require California either to surrender jurisdiction or to limit respondents' recovery to the $25,000 maximum of the Nevada statute would be obnoxious to its statutorily based policies of jurisdiction over nonresident motorists and full recovery. The Full Faith and Credit Clause does not require this result.[24]

IV. Even apart from the Full Faith and Credit Clause, Nevada argues that the Constitution implicitly establishes a Union in which the States are not free to treat each other as unfriendly sovereigns, but must respect the sovereignty of one another. While sovereign nations are free to levy discriminatory taxes on the goods of other nations or to bar their entry altogether, the States of the Union are not. Nor are the States free to deny extradition of a fugitive when a proper demand is made by the executive of another State. And the citizens in each State are entitled to all privileges and immunities of citizens in the several States.

Each of these provisions places a specific limitation on the sovereignty of the several States. Collectively they demonstrate that ours is not a union of 50 wholly independent sovereigns. But these provisions do not imply that any one State's immunity from suit in the courts of another State is anything other than a matter of comity. Indeed, in view of the Tenth Amendment's reminder that powers not delegated to the Federal Government nor prohibited to the States are reserved to the States or to the people, the existence of express limitations on state sovereignty may equally imply that caution should be exercised before concluding that unstated limitations on state power were intended by the Framers.

In the past, this Court has presumed that the States intended to adopt policies of broad comity toward one another. But this presumption reflected an understanding of state policy, rather than a constitutional command. As this Court stated in Bank of Augusta v. Earle, 13 Pet. 519, 590 [1839]:

> "The intimate union of these states, as members of the same great political family; the deep and vital interests which bind them so closely together; should lead us, in the absence of proof to the contrary, to presume a greater degree of comity, and friendship, and kindness towards one another, than we should be

---

24. California's exercise of jurisdiction in this case poses no substantial threat to our constitutional system of cooperative federalism. Suits involving traffic accidents occurring outside of Nevada could hardly interfere with Nevada's capacity to fulfill its own sovereign responsibilities. We have no occasion, in this case, to consider whether different state policies, either of California or of Nevada, might require a different analysis or a different result.

authorized to presume between foreign nations. And when (as without doubt must occasionally happen) the interest or policy of any state requires it to restrict the rule, it has but to declare its will, and the legal presumption is at once at an end."

In this case, California has "declared its will"; it has adopted as its policy full compensation in its courts for injuries on its highways resulting from the negligence of others, whether those others be residents or nonresidents, agents of the State, or private citizens. Nothing in the Federal Constitution authorizes or obligates this Court to frustrate that policy out of enforced respect for the sovereignty of Nevada.[29]

In this Nation each sovereign governs only with the consent of the governed. The people of Nevada have consented to a system in which their State is subject only to limited liability in tort. But the people of California, who have had no voice in Nevada's decision, have adopted a different system. Each of these decisions is equally entitled to our respect.

It may be wise policy, as a matter of harmonious interstate relations, for States to accord each other immunity or to respect any established limits on liability. They are free to do so. But if a federal court were to hold, by inference from the structure of our Constitution and nothing else, that California is not free in this case to enforce its policy of full compensation, that holding would constitute the real intrusion on the sovereignty of the States—and the power of the people—in our Union.

The judgment of the California Court of Appeal is

Affirmed.

JUSTICE BLACKMUN, with whom THE CHIEF JUSTICE and JUSTICE REHNQUIST join, dissenting. * * * There is no limit to the breadth of the Court's rationale, which goes beyond the approach taken by the California Court of Appeal in this case. That court theorized that Nevada was not "sovereign" for purposes of this case because sovereignty ended at the California–Nevada line. * * *

That reasoning finds no place in this Court's opinion. Rather, the Court assumes that Nevada is "sovereign," but then concludes that the sovereign-immunity doctrine has no *constitutional* source. Thus, it says, California can abolish the doctrine at will. By this reasoning, Nevada's amenability to suit in California is not conditioned on its agent's having committed a tortious act in California. Since the Court finds no constitutional source for the sovereign-immunity doctrine, California, so far as the Federal Constitution is concerned, is able and free to treat Nevada, and any other State, just as it would treat any other litigant. The Court's theory means that State A constitutionally can be sued by an individual in the courts of State B on any cause of action, provided only that the plaintiff in State B obtains jurisdiction over State A consistently with the Due Process Clause.

The Court, by its footnote 24, purports to confine its holding to traffic-accident torts committed outside the defendant State, and perhaps even to traffic "policies." Such facts, however, play absolutely no part in the reasoning by which the Court

---

29. Cf. Georgia v. Chattanooga, 264 U.S. 472, 480 [1929] ("Land acquired by one State in another State is held subject to the laws of the latter and to all the incidents of private ownership. The proprietary right of the owning State does not restrict or modify the power of eminent domain of the State wherein the land is situated").

reaches its conclusion. * * *

The Court's expansive logic and broad holding—that so far as the Constitution is concerned, State A can be sued in State B on the same terms any other litigant can be sued—will place severe strains on our system of cooperative federalism. States in all likelihood will retaliate against one another for respectively abolishing the "sovereign immunity" doctrine. States' legal officers will be required to defend suits in all other States. States probably will decide to modify their tax-collection and revenue systems in order to avoid the collection of judgments. In this very case, for example, Nevada evidently maintains cash balances in California banks to facilitate the collection of sales taxes from California corporations doing business in Nevada. [cit.] Under the Court's decision, Nevada will have strong incentive to withdraw those balances and place them in Nevada banks so as to insulate itself from California judgments. If respondents were forced to seek satisfaction of their judgment in Nevada, that State, of course, might endeavor to refuse to enforce that judgment, or enforce it only on Nevada's terms. The Court's decision, thus, may force radical changes in the way States do business with one another, and it imposes, as well, financial and administrative burdens on the States themselves.

I must agree with the Court that if the judgment of the California Court of Appeal is to be reversed, a constitutional source for Nevada's sovereign immunity must be found. I would find that source not in an express provision of the Constitution but in a guarantee that is implied as an essential component of federalism. * * *

JUSTICE REHNQUIST, with whom THE CHIEF JUSTICE joins, dissenting. Like my Brother Blackmun, I cannot agree with the majority that there is no constitutional source for the sovereign immunity asserted in this case by the State of Nevada. I think the Court's decision today works a fundamental readjustment of interstate relationships which is impossible to reconcile not only with an "assumption" this and other courts have entertained for almost 200 years, but also with express holdings of this Court and the logic of the constitutional plan itself.

* * *

I am also concerned about the practical implications of this decision. The federal system as expressed in the Constitution—with the exception of representation in the House—is built on notions of state parity. No system is truly federal otherwise. This decision cannot help but induce some "Balkanization" in state relationships as States try to isolate assets from foreign judgments and generally reduce their contacts with other jurisdictions. That will work to the detriment of smaller States—like Nevada—who are more dependent on the facilities of a dominant neighbor—in this case, California.

The problem of enforcement of a judgment against a State creates a host of additional difficulties. Assuming Nevada has no sizeable assets in California, can the plaintiff obtain enforcement of California's judgment in Nevada courts? Can Nevada refuse to give the California judgment "full faith and credit" because it is against state policy? Can Nevada challenge the seizure of its assets by California in this Court? If not, are the States relegated to the choice between the gamesmanship and tests of strength that characterize international disputes, on the one hand, and the midnight seizure of assets associated with private debt collection on the other?

I think the Framers and our predecessors on this Court expressed the appropriate limits on the doctrine of state sovereign immunity. Since the California judgment under review transgresses those limits, I respectfully dissent.

Notes and Questions

1. If California retained sovereign immunity for itself, would it have been constitutional for California to (1) apply Nevada law allowing claims up to $25,000, or (2) deny Nevada sovereign immunity and apply the rules of tort liability applicable to private parties? See Peterson v. State of Texas, 635 P.2d 241 (Colo.App.1981) (Colorado rejected sovereign immunity claim of Texas although Colorado law granted immunity to Colorado entities under similar circumstances).

2. Suppose California law waives immunity but provides that California shall be liable only for gross negligence. In *Nevada v. Hall,* could California apply a simple negligence standard to Nevada's conduct? Cf. *Biscoe v. Arlington County,* supra Ch. 3 at 206 (Virginia emergency vehicle causes accident in D.C.; held: defendant not protected by a D.C. law which provides that D.C. emergency vehicles liable only for gross negligence).

3. Although *Nevada v. Hall* allows states to hear claims against sister states, some states grant immunity as a matter of comity. See, e.g., University of Iowa Press v. Urrea, 440 S.E.2d 203 (Ga.1993); Schoeberlein v. Purdue University, 544 N.E.2d 283 (Ill. 989) (collecting and discussing numerous cases from other states).

4. Suppose Hall had been a citizen of Arizona who was hit while vacationing in California. If Hall sued Nevada in Arizona, could Nevada have objected that Arizona lacked personal jurisdiction? Does the Fourteenth Amendment protect *states* from due process violations? See Simmons v. State of Montana, 670 P.2d 1372 (Mont.1983) (applying Fourteenth Amendment cases and finding no personal jurisdiction over State of Oregon; no discussion of whether that Amendment applies to state defendants); Underwood v. University of Kentucky, 390 So.2d 433 (Fla.App.1980) (no personal jurisdiction over State of Kentucky; analysis based on state long arm statute). Cf. South Carolina v. Katzenbach, 383 U.S. 301, 323–24 (1966) (a state is not "person" protected by the Fifth Amendment). If suit in Arizona were not dismissed for lack of personal jurisdiction, could Arizona apply Arizona law of sovereign immunity? If states are not protected by the Fourteenth Amendment, on what basis could Nevada object? Is sovereign immunity comparable to standing and therefore a procedural matter as to which the forum can apply its own law? See see Restatement (Second) § 125; *Wortman,* supra.

5. How can Mr. Hall enforce his judgment? If there are California citizens who owe taxes to Nevada, can California garnish those taxes? See Struebin v. Illinois, 421 N.W.2d 874 (Iowa), *cert. denied,* 488 U.S. 851 (1988) (allowing garnishment). Cf. Foreign Sovereign Immunities Act, 28 U.S.C. § 1610(a) & (b) (imposing limits on the types of property owned by foreign states against which enforcement may be sought). Can he enforce the judgment in any other state? See Ch. 10.

6. Nevada was sufficiently outraged by *Nevada v. Hall* that its state legislature

sought a constitutional amendment that would have made states immune from suit in all other states except where they waived immunity. Nevada Assembly Joint Resolution, No. 29 (1979).

7. In Franchise Tax Bd. of California v. Hyatt, 123 S.Ct. 1683 (2003), the shoe was on the other foot. There, a Nevada citizen brought suit in Nevada state court against a California state tax agency alleging that in its efforts to collect back taxes from Hyatt, the agency had committed various torts including invasion of privacy, abuse of process, and fraud. California law provides complete immunity for state agencies carrying out their official duties. Nevada law also confers immunity but not for intentional torts. California argued that Nevada was required under the Full Faith and Credit Clause to apply California law and relied specifically on note 24 of Nevada v. Hall. The Supreme Court rejected this argument noting that "[t]here is no principled distinction between Nevada's interests in tort claims arising out of its university employee's automobile accident, at issue in *Hall*, and California's interests in the tort claims here arising out of its tax collection agency's residency audit." Id. at 1690. With respect to the full faith and credit argument, the Court reviewed Bradford Electric, Alaska Packers and Pacific Employers and noted that "we abandoned the balancing-of-interests approach to conflict of laws under the Full Faith and Credit Clause." Id. at 1688. The Court concluded: "In short, we heed the lessons learned as a result of *Bradford Elec. Light Co.*, and its progeny. Without a rudder to steer us, we decline to embark on the constitutional course of balancing coordinate States' competing sovereign interests to resolve conflicts of laws under the Full Faith and Credit Clause." Id. at 1690. See also Mianecki v. Second Judicial Dist. Court, 658 P.2d 422 (Nev.1983), *cert. denied*, 464 U.S. 806 (1983) (Nevada allowed a tort suit against Wisconsin in the Nevada courts and rejected Wisconsin's argument that it should decline jurisdiction as a matter of comity).

8. The Supreme Court has created federal common law rules applicable to disputes between states concerning interstate waters and pollution. See Illinois v. City of Milwaukee, 406 U.S. 91, 103 (1972); Hinderlider v. La Plata River & Cherry Creek Ditch Co., 304 U.S. 92, 110 (1938). Should the Court have created a federal common law rule concerning interstate immunity? See Rogers, *Sovereign Immunity*, 470. Consider the following: Suppose that the Nevada driver had damaged property belonging to the State of California and California brought suit against Nevada. Under Art. III and 28 U.S.C. § 1251, the Supreme Court would have original jurisdiction. What law would the Supreme Court apply? Presumably the Court would apply a federal choice of law rule. Should the choice of law issue in *Nevada v. Hall* be treated differently than choice of law in the hypothetical California v. Nevada case? Federal common law is discussed in Ch. 6(D).

9. It has long been held that states may criminally prosecute federal officers for violations of state law, although the officers have the right to remove the action to federal court if they wish. See 28 U.S.C. § 1442. It has even been held that a state court-martial has jurisdiction to prosecute a militiaman for violating *federal* law. See Houston v. Moore, 18 U.S. (5 Wheat.) 1 (1820).

Somewhat less clear is the scope of a state court's authority to enjoin federal officials or issue writs of mandamus or habeas corpus against federal officials. The

Supreme Court has held that state courts have no authority to issue writs of mandamus, see McClung v. Silliman, 19 U.S. (6 Wheat.) 598 (1821) or habeas corpus, see Tarble's Case, 80 U.S. (13 Wall.) 397 (1871), against federal officials. In *Tarble's Case*, the Court explained that "no State can authorize one of its judges or courts to exercise judicial power, by *habeas corpus* or otherwise, within the jurisdiction of another and independent government." Id. at 405. Despite the sweeping language of *Tarble's Case*, some commentators have argued that there is no constitutional limit on such state authority. Compare Arnold, *The Power of State Courts*, 1389 (states have this constitutional authority unless Congress statutorily removes jurisdiction), with Redish & Woods, *Congressional Power*, 89 (state courts lack constitutional power).

Compare the state-federal context with the state-state context. Does a state court in California have authority to enjoin a Nevada official? Is there anything in the Constitution that takes away such authority? Cf. *Nevada v. Hall*. In the international context, the act of state doctrine limits the authority of one country judicially to question the official acts of another country. See Ch. 7. Should a similar doctrine exist in the interstate context? Would it matter whether the Nevada official were ordered to comply with California law or Nevada law? Consider the following argument: Although *Nevada v. Hall* implies that the California courts can require Nevada officials to comply with California law, it would be far more intrusive and indeed inconsistent with sovereignty for California to order Nevada or a Nevada official to comply with Nevada law. The reason is that it is entirely up to Nevada to decide how to allocate functions among the branches of its government. Thus, even if Nevada statutory law appears to impose certain requirements on its officials, Nevada may also give its executive officers authority to abrogate those requirements. In short, cases challenging a Nevada officer's application of a Nevada law necessarily present issues relating to the distribution of law-making and law declaring power among the branches of the Nevada government. Neither the federal government, nor another state has the authority to dictate to a sovereign state what its law must be in these areas.

F. PRIVILEGES AND IMMUNITIES, EQUAL PROTECTION AND THE COMMERCE CLAUSE AS LIMITS ON CHOICE OF LAW

The Full Faith and Credit Clause, which we have already examined, addresses intersovereign relations—it requires states to treat other states as equals. The Full Faith and Credit Clause thus helps bind the states together into one nation. However, the Constitution recognizes that our national unity is threatened not only by states disrespecting other states, but also by states treating unfairly citizens or businesses from other states. Such unfair treatment might manifest itself either in overt discrimination against out-of-state citizens or businesses, or through rules that unduly burden interstate commerce or travel.

Several provisions in the Constitution address the problems of discrimination against out-of-staters and undue burdens on interstate activity. Those provisions include the Privileges and Immunities Clause of Article IV, the Commerce Clause in Article I, and the Equal Protection Clause of the Fourteenth Amendment. This section will briefly examine these constitutional provisions and consider what implications they might have for choice-of-law.

1. DISCRIMINATION

a. An Overview of Doctrine. The Privileges and Immunities Clause and the Equal Protection Clause are explicitly directed at the problem of discrimination. In addition, the Court has held that the Commerce Clause has an anti-discrimination component as well. The Privileges and Immunities Clause explicitly prohibits discrimination based on citizenship. It requires that states grant to citizens of other states all the "Privileges and Immunities" it grants to its own citizens. The Equal Protection Clause prohibits other types of discrimination, and the Commerce Clause has been held to prohibit discrimination against interstate or out-of-state business activity.

Applying the Privileges and Immunities Clause, the Court struck down the following: a New Hampshire law that limited admission to the bar to New Hampshire residents, Supreme Court of New Hampshire v. Piper, 470 U.S. 274 (1985); the "Alaska Hire" Act which gave employment preference to Alaska residents over nonresidents for jobs arising out of oil and gas leases, Hicklin v. Orbeck, 437 U.S. 518 (1978); a South Carolina law which required a license fee of $25 for shrimp boats owned by residents and $2500 for such boats owned by nonresidents, Toomer v. Witsell, 334 U.S. 385 (1948); and a Georgia statute permitting only residents to secure abortions, Doe v. Bolton, 410 U.S. 179 (1973).

The Court has imposed several important limitations on the scope of the Privileges and Immunities Clause. First, the clause does not prohibit discrimination in all matters, but protects only "those privileges and immunities which are, in their nature, fundamental; which belong, of right, to the citizens of all free governments; and which have, at all times, been enjoyed by the citizens of the several states which compose this Union." Corfield v. Coryell, 6 F. Cas. 546, 551 (E.D.Pa.1823) (No. 3,230). The Court has explained that the Clause:

> was intended to "fuse into one Nation a collection of independent, sovereign States." [cit.] Recognizing this purpose, we have held that it is "[only] with respect to those 'privileges' and 'immunities' bearing on the vitality of the Nation as a single entity" that a State must accord residents and nonresidents equal treatment. [cit.]

Piper, 470 U.S. at 279. The Court has held that access to the state's courts, the right to own private property and the right to engage in private employment or commercial activity are protected by the clause, but that recreational activity, such as sport hunting, is not protected. See Baldwin v. Fish & Game Comm'n of Montana, 436 U.S. 371, 388 (1978).

Second, even as to fundamental rights, the clause does not prohibit all differences in the treatment afforded residents and nonresidents. As the Court explained in *Piper*:

The Clause does not preclude discrimination against nonresidents where (i) there is a substantial reason for the difference in treatment; and (ii) the discrimination practiced against nonresidents bears a substantial relationship to the State's objective.

470 U.S. at 284.

Finally, the Privileges and Immunities Clause does not apply to corporations. See Hemphill v. Orloff, 277 U.S. 537, 548–50 (1928); Blake v. McClung, 172 U.S. 239. 432 (1898). However, discrimination between local and out-of-state corporations may violate the Equal Protection Clause or the Commerce Clause. See Metropolitan Life Ins. Co. v. Ward, 470 U.S. 869 (1985) (discriminatory taxation struck down under Equal Protection Clause); Bendix Autolite Corp. v. Midwesco Enterprises, Inc., 486 U.S. 888 (1988) (discriminatory statute of limitations struck down under Commerce Clause). Indeed, the Court has held that discrimination against interstate commerce is "virtually per se invalid." Brown–Forman Distillers Corp. v. New York State Liquor Auth., 476 U.S. 573, 579 (1986).

b. Implications for Choice of Law. The prohibition on discrimination may have implications for choice of law. Currie, in his famous essay on *Milliken v. Pratt*, offers the following question and answer: "[T]he legislature decides in favor of protecting married women. *What* married women? Why, those with whose welfare Massachusetts is concerned, of course—i.e., Massachusetts married women." Currie, *Married Women's Contracts*, 234. But does not Currie's answer suggest that Massachusetts is engaged in exactly the kind of discrimination against out-of-staters that the Supreme Court has prohibited? Some commentators believe so. Professor Laycock has argued that "[i]f legislatures acted generally on Currie's view that they owe nothing to the citizens of sister states, the Union would be destroyed." Laycock, *Equal Citizens*, 275. Indeed, Currie took the discrimination attack very seriously, and co-authored two essays addressing the issue. See Currie & Schreter, *Privileges and Immunities*, 1323; Currie & Schreter, *Equal Protection*, 1.

Consider the following hypothetical: A New York driver vacations with two friends in Michigan, one from New York, one from Michigan. The driver has an accident in Michigan and is sued by the two passengers in New York. Michigan has a guest statute but New York does not. New York applies New York law to the New York passenger and allows a recovery. However, as to the Michigan passenger, the New York court applies Michigan law and denies recovery. Has not New York treated the Michigan passenger differently solely on the basis of his citizenship? Does this implicate a "fundamental right" protected by the Privileges and Immunities Clause? Is it constitutional?

Even assuming a fundamental right is involved, one response is that the different treatment is permissible because New York applied Michigan law to the Michigan citizen. If Michigan citizens do not like Michigan law, they have adequate redress—they can go to the Michigan legislature. Moreover, the Privileges and Immunities Clause only prohibits discrimination where there is no substantial reason for it. If the reason New York treats the Michigan passenger differently than the New York passenger is out of comity and deference to the laws of Michigan, is not that an adequate justification?

Some commentators believe not. Dean Ely has argued that the Court's decision in *Austin v. New Hampshire*, 420 U.S. 656 (1975), precludes this argument. There, the Supreme Court struck down under the Privileges and Immunities Clause a New Hampshire income tax which applied to New Hampshire derived income of non-residents but exempted similar income of residents. The tax was capped at the amount that would have been owed to the nonresident's home state if earned there, and was not imposed at all if the home state did not credit the nonresident for the amount paid to New Hampshire. Thus, New Hampshire essentially applied to nonresidents their home state's tax rates. Nonetheless, the Court struck down the tax. See Ely, *The State's Interest*, 186–87.

Professor Kramer has offered a different objection applicable in an "unprovided-for case." His argument is illustrated by *Erwin v. Thomas*, Ch. 3. There, the plaintiff brought a claim for loss of consortium in Oregon court based on an accident that happened in Washington. The plaintiff was from Washington, which did not recognize loss of consortium; the defendant was from Oregon which did recognize such claims. Professor Kramer argues:

> Washington's failure to allow such recovery does not reflect an affirmative policy to disable plaintiff-wives from recovering for loss of consortium. Washington is simply less generous to wives than Oregon. As a result, Oregon cannot defend withholding the benefit of its law in terms of deference to the interests of the plaintiff's home state. Oregon's only justification is indifference to nonresidents, and that justification is insufficient under the privileges and immunities clause.

Kramer, *The Myth of the "Unprovided For" Case*, 1073.

If a state cannot apply different law solely on the basis of the citizenship of the parties, can it do so solely on the basis of where events occurred? Differentiating on this basis would not violate the Privileges and Immunities Clause but might it be an irrational distinction that violates the Equal Protection Clause? Is it rational for Alabama to deny recovery in *Carroll*, Ch. 2, if it would have granted recovery in an otherwise identical case in which the injury occurred a few miles earlier? Currie suggested that some traditionally based conflicts rules violate the Equal Protection Clause. Currie & Schreter, *Equal Protection*, 49–50.

If choice of law based on citizenship and choice of law based on territorial connection are both unconstitutional, what is left? As between the two approaches, is there reason to think one approach is more favored under the Constitution? Professor Gergen has observed: "Arguments that the interest-based or territorial approach unfairly treats people unequally usually derive entirely from the author's views on the merit of a territorial or a personal order. The debate is really over two different forms of inequality, each of which is arbitrary in its own way." Gergen, *Equality and the Conflict of Laws*, 894. Professor Laycock has responded:

> [T]he Privileges and Immunities Clause expressly forbids discrimination on the basis of citizenship. Nothing in the Constitution expressly forbids discrimination on the basis that the disputes arose in territory subject to the laws of different states. The opposite is true: * * * territorial discrimination is inherent in the

decision to preserve the states as quasi-sovereign territorial entities.[1]
Laycock, *Equal Citizens*, 278. Do you think there are applications of interest analysis that are unconstitutional?

2. UNDUE BURDENS ON INTERSTATE COMMERCE

In addition to prohibiting discrimination against nonresidents, the Court has also struck down state rules that, though neutral in application, nonetheless unreasonably burden interstate commerce. The Court has summarized the law in this area as follows:

> Where the statute regulates even-handedly to effectuate a legitimate local public interest, and its effects on interstate commerce are only incidental, it will be upheld unless the burden imposed on such commerce is clearly excessive in relation to the putative local benefits. [cit.] If a legitimate local purpose is found, then the question becomes one of degree. And the extent of the burden that will be tolerated will of course depend on the nature of the local interest involved, and on whether it could be promoted as well with a lesser impact on interstate activities.

Pike v. Bruce Church, Inc., 397 U.S. 137, 142 (1970).

Applying this principle, the Court in Bibb v. Navajo Freight Lines, Inc., 359 U.S. 520 (1959), struck down an Illinois law requiring trucks in that state to use curved mudflaps. Straight mudflaps were legal in forty-five states, curved mudflaps were illegal in Arkansas and not required in any other state. The Court found that the case was "one of those cases—few in number—where local safety measures that are nondiscriminatory place an unconstitutional burden on interstate commerce." Id. at 529. See Kassel v. Consolidated Freightways Corp., 450 U.S. 662 (1981) (striking down Iowa law which prohibited the use of 65 foot double-trailer trucks). Because of the burden that inconsistent regulations placed on interstate commerce, Illinois was not permitted to apply its law. Could this principle limit choice of law?

The Court has also found states' "extraterritorial" application of their laws to interfere with interstate commerce. In evaluating a challenge on this basis, the Court has made clear that the Commerce Clause imposes different limitations than does the Due Process Clause. See Bendix Autolite Corp. v. Midwesco Enterprises, Inc., 486 U.S. 888, 894 (1988). In Quill Corp. v. North Dakota, 504 U.S. 298 (1992), the Court struck down on Commerce Clause grounds a state tax on out-of-state mail order businesses with no physical presence in the state. The Court explained:

> Despite the similarity in phrasing, the nexus requirements of the Due Process and Commerce Clauses are not identical. The two standards are animated by different constitutional concerns and policies.
>
> Due process centrally concerns the fundamental fairness of governmental activity. Thus, at the most general level, the due process nexus analysis requires that we ask whether an individual's connections with a State are substantial enough to legitimate the State's exercise of power over him. We have, therefore,

---

1. This article originally appeared at 92 Colum.L.Rev. 249 (1992). Reprinted by permission.

often identified "notice" or "fair warning" as the analytic touchstone of due process nexus analysis. In contrast, the Commerce Clause, and its nexus requirement, are informed not so much by concerns about fairness for the individual defendant as by structural concerns about the effects of state regulation on the national economy.

Id. at 312.

In Brown-Forman Distillers Corp. v. New York State Liquor Authority, 476 U.S. 573 (1986), the Court struck down a law requiring all sellers of liquor to wholesalers in New York to file a price schedule and affirm that they would not sell anywhere in the country at a price lower than the lowest price posted in New York. The net effect was to make it illegal for a distiller to reduce its price in other states during the period that the posted New York price was in effect. The Court found that the law "regulates out-of-state transactions in violation of the Commerce Clause. * * * While New York may regulate the sale of liquor within its borders, and may seek low prices for its residents, it may not 'project its legislation into [other States] by regulating the price to be paid' for liquor in those States." Id. at 582-83. Compare *Brown-Forman* with *Lilienthal v. Kaufman*, supra at 179. Was not Oregon regulating commercial transactions in California when it refused to enforce the contract made in California? Does *Lilienthal* violate the Commerce Clause? Consider also *People v. One 1953 Ford Victoria*, supra at 187. Would it have violated the Commerce Clause if California had applied its laws in that case?

In CTS Corp. v. Dynamics Corp. of America, 481 U.S. 69 (1987), the Court upheld an Indiana anti-takeover statute imposing shareholder voter requirements that made it more difficult to acquire an Indiana corporation. The law applied only to Indiana corporations but was challenged under the Commerce Clause on the theory that it affected non-Indiana stockholders who might wish to sell their stock to a non-Indiana tender offeror. In upholding the law, the Court explained that "this Act applies only to corporations incorporated in Indiana. We reject the contention that Indiana has no interest in providing for the shareholders of its corporations the voting autonomy granted by the Act." Id. at 93. The Court distinguished Edgar v. MITE Corp., 457 U.S. 624 (1982), which had struck down an Illinois anti-takeover law that applied to non-Illinois corporations. One implication of *CTS* and *MITE* seems to be that the state of incorporation can regulate a corporation's internal affairs, but no other state can. Does this suggest that with respect to choice-of-law in corporate governance, the Commerce Clause requires a particular choice of law rule (i.e., law of the place of incorporation)? Are there other areas as to which the Commerce Clause might require a particular choice of law rule? See Horowitz, *The Commerce Clause*, 806.

As states have increasingly begun to regulate Internet transactions, some courts have invalidated such regulations on Commerce Clause grounds. See, e.g., American Civil Liberties Union v. Johnson, 194 F.3d 1149 (10th Cir.1999); American Libraries Ass'n v. Pataki, 969 F. Supp. 160 (S.D.N.Y.1997); Goldsmith & Sykes, *Dormant Commerce Clause*. See Chapter 13 for discussion of some of the unique challenges presented by the Internet and cyberspace.

Chapter 6

CHOICE OF LAW IN FEDERAL COURT

A. INTRODUCTION

In conflicts jurisprudence, the choice-of-law question centers on which state's law the forum should apply. When litigation occurs in federal court or involves federal law, the forum confronts a further choice—the possibility of applying federal law. This chapter explores that question.

B. *ERIE* AND ITS PROGENY (STATE LAW IN FEDERAL COURT)

1. ***The Rules of Decision Act.*** In determining what law applies in federal court, an important starting point is the Rules of Decision Act, 28 U.S.C. § 1652. That Act provides:

> The laws of the several states, except where the Constitution or treaties of the United States or Acts of Congress otherwise require or provide, shall be regarded as rules of decision in civil actions in the courts of the United States, in cases where they apply.

Under the Rules of Decision Act, as under the Supremacy Clause, if there is preemptive federal law on point, it applies. But does the Rules of Decision Act mean that state law controls on absolutely all matters not covered by a federal statute, treaty or the Constitution? The Act could be interpreted that way, but the Court has never done so.

2. ***Swift v. Tyson.*** In Swift v. Tyson, 41 U.S. (16 Pet.) 1 (1842), the Supreme Court narrowly construed the Rules of Decision Act phrase "laws of the several states." The Court held that the Act requires federal courts to apply state statutes and state common law rules only on matters of "local law," e.g., involving rights or title to real estate and immovable property. According to *Swift*, if there was no state statute on point and the matter involved an area of "general" rather than "local" law, the Rules of Decision Act did not apply and the federal courts were free to develop their own federal common law rules.

3. ***Erie.*** All this changed with the landmark decision in Erie Railroad Co. v. Tompkins, 304 U.S. 64 (1938). Tompkins sued the Erie company after being hit by a train while on a railroad right of way. Although the accident occurred in Pennsylvania, the suit was filed in federal court in the defendant's home state of New York, with federal jurisdiction based on diversity. The tort issue was what standard

of care the railroad owed to persons walking without permission on the right of way. The railroad argued that although there was no state statute on point this was a matter of local law and, under Pennsylvania law, Tompkins was a trespasser to whom the railroad was liable only for willful or wanton conduct. Tompkins argued in response that the railroad's duty should be determined by the federal courts as a matter of general law. Neither party challenged the basic frame work established by *Swift v. Tyson*. Nonetheless, in an opinion by Justice Brandeis, the Court overruled *Swift*.[1]

The Court offered several reasons. The Court first cited the historical evidence presented by Charles Warren that the phrase "laws of the several states" was intended merely as a shorthand expression that encompassed both state statutory law and its unwritten common law. Id.. at 73. The Court next observed that states had not moved to adopt the general (federal) common law, and that the lack of uniformity between the law applied in state and federal courts produced "mischievous results." Id. at 74. The Court explained:

> Diversity of citizenship jurisdiction was conferred in order to prevent apprehended discrimination in state courts against those not citizens of the State. *Swift v. Tyson* introduced grave discrimination by non-citizens against citizens. It made rights enjoyed under the unwritten "general law" vary according to whether enforcement was sought in the state or in the federal court; and the privilege of selecting the court in which the right should be determined was conferred upon the non-citizen. Thus, the doctrine rendered impossible equal protection of the law. In attempting to promote uniformity of law throughout the United States, the doctrine had prevented uniformity in the administration of the law of the State.

Id. at 74–75.

The Court's third and least understood reason was "the unconstitutionality of the course pursued [as a result of *Swift*]." Id. at 77–78. The Court explained:

> The fallacy underlying the rule declared in *Swift v. Tyson* is made clear by Mr. Justice Holmes. The doctrine rests upon the assumption that there is "a transcendental body of law outside of any particular State but obligatory within it unless and until changed by statute," that federal courts have the power to use their judgment as to what the rules of common law are; and that in the federal courts "the parties are entitled to an independent judgment on matters of general law":
>
> > "but law in the sense in which courts speak of it today does not exist without some definite authority behind it. The common law so far as it is enforced in a State, whether called common law or not, is not the common law generally but the law of that State existing by the authority of that State without regard to what it may have been in England or anywhere else...."

---

1. Notwithstanding the demise of *Swift*, at least one state incorporates into its choice of law rules a distinction between statutory and common law rules. Georgia will apply other states' statutes and interpretations of those statutes. However, where purely common law rules are involved, Georgia applies *Georgia* common law. See Frank Briscoe Co. v. Georgia Sprinkler Co., 713 F.2d 1500, 1503 (11th Cir.1983); White v. Borders, 123 S.E.2d 170 (Ga. App.1961); Rees, *Choice of Law in Georgia*, 789.

"the authority and only authority is the State, and if that be so, the voice adopted by the State as its own [whether it be of its Legislature or of its Supreme Court] should utter the last word."

Thus the doctrine of *Swift v. Tyson* is, as Mr. Justice Holmes said, "an unconstitutional assumption of powers by courts of the United States which no lapse of time or respectable array of opinion should make us hesitate to correct." In disapproving that doctrine we do not hold unconstitutional § 34 of the Federal Judiciary Act of 1789 or any other Act of Congress. We merely declare that in applying the doctrine this Court and the lower courts have invaded rights which in our opinion are reserved by the Constitution to the several States.

Id. at 79–80.

The constitutional basis of *Erie* has been a matter of great scholarly debate. See, e.g., Ely, *The Irrepressible Myth of Erie*, 693; Hill, *The Erie Doctrine*, 427; Merrill, *The Common Law Powers*, 1; Mishkin, *Last Words on Erie*, 1682. For example, there is no question that Congress could specify the standard of care owed to trespassers on the right of way of an interstate railroad. If Congress could have regulated this area, why is it unconstitutional for the federal courts to specify a common law rule? Some have responded that the federal courts' judicial authority is not necessarily as broad as Congress' legislative authority and that *Erie* can thus be understood as a separation of powers case. See Merrill, *The Common Law Powers*, 13–24.

Why shouldn't the grant of diversity jurisdiction be understood to include a grant of common law law-making authority to the federal courts? The Supreme Court has held that the grant of admiralty jurisdiction in Art. III, § 2, implicitly grants federal courts federal common law authority. The Court has explained:

It certainly could not have been intended to place the rules and limits of maritime law under the disposal and regulation of the several States, as that would have defeated the uniformity and consistency at which the Constitution aimed on all subjects of a commercial character affecting the intercourse of the States with each other or with foreign states.

Southern Pac. Co. v. Jensen, 244 U.S. 205, 215 (1917). Could not a similar argument be made that the grant of diversity jurisdiction carries with it law making-authority? Notwithstanding these arguments, the *Erie* Court appears to have rejected them. See Ely, supra, 87 Harv. L. Rev. at 713.

Whatever the foundations of *Erie*, it is now clear that federal courts are to apply state law on matters such as the applicable standard of care. But neither *Erie*, nor the cases applying it, require federal courts to apply state law on absolutely all matters. As Justice Reed observed in his concurrence in *Erie*, "no one doubts federal power over procedure." Id. at 92. In the years since *Erie* the Court has struggled with where to draw the line between matters of "procedure" and matters of "substance." In a series of cases, the Court attempted to delineate what matters constituted "procedure" as to which federal courts could apply federal law.

4. ***Guaranty, Byrd, and Hanna.*** In Guaranty Trust Co. v. York, 326 U.S. 99 (1945), the Court held that a federal court sitting in diversity must apply the state

statute of limitations. The Court reasoned that:

> In essence, the intent of that decision was to insure that, in all cases where a federal court is exercising jurisdiction solely because of the diversity of citizenship of the parties, the outcome of the litigation in the federal court should be substantially the same, so far as legal rules determine the outcome of a litigation, as it would be if tried in a State court.

Id. at 109. The Court later applied this "outcome test" to several other cases. See Ragan v. Merchants Transfer & Warehouse Co., 337 U.S. 530 (1949) (state law determines when an action is "commenced" for purposes of statute of limitations despite Fed. R. Civ. P. 3 which provides that "an action is commenced by filing a complaint"); Woods v. Interstate Realty Co., 337 U.S. 535 (1949) (applying a state "door closing statute" that barred suits by out-of-state corporations that had failed to properly register in the state); Cohen v. Beneficial Indus. Loan Corp., 337 U.S. 541 (1949) (applying state requirement that plaintiff in shareholders derivative suit post bond).

Several years later, in Byrd v. Blue Ridge Rural Elec. Coop., Inc., 356 U.S. 525 (1958), the Court appeared to adopt a different approach. The case involved a claim under the South Carolina workers compensation act. Under South Carolina law, the question of whether a worker was an "employee" for purposes of the statute was determined by the judge, not a jury. Nonetheless, the Court held that in federal court, this issue was to be decided by the jury. The Court did not rest its analysis on the Seventh Amendment. Instead, the Court used a balancing test in which the Court considered (1) whether the state rule was "bound up with" state-created rights and obligations, (2) the federal interest in applying a federal rule; and (3) the effect on outcome.

Professor Allan Stein has argued that *Byrd* essentially used interest analysis. He explains:

> The *Byrd* Court employed a technique which would be recognized today as "interest analysis." It determined that the only policy driving the state preference for a judicial determination of the statutory employee question was administrative convenience * * * Accordingly, no state policy would be implicated by a federal departure from state practice. In conflicts terminology, there was a "false conflict."

Stein, *Erie and Court Access*, 1954–55. Is interest analysis an appropriate approach for resolving state-federal conflicts? What should the federal court do when there is a true conflict?

Nearly two decades later, in Hanna v. Plumer, 380 U.S. 460 (1965), the Court seemed to signal a return to an outcome test. The Court explained that where there is no Federal Rule of Civil Procedure or other preemptive federal law on point, the court should focus on "the twin aims of the *Erie* rule: discouragement of forum-shopping and avoidance of inequitable administration of the laws." Thus, if the failure to apply a state rule in federal court would be viewed by litigants as so significant that they would choose their forum on that basis, then the federal court should apply the state rule.

Hanna did not explain the relationship between the balancing test of *Byrd* and the modified outcome test of *Hanna*. Some commentators have argued that *Hanna* overruled *Byrd*. As Professor Martin Redish explained:

> * * * *Hanna* represented a significant shift in approach for deciding Rules of Decision Act cases—one away from the system-oriented analysis employed in *Byrd* toward a return to a litigant-oriented view of *Erie* and the statute. The goal of *Erie*, implied the *Hanna* Court, was not to maintain a balance within the federal system but rather to protect citizens from the dangers of forum shopping and the inequitable administration of the law.

Redish, *Federal Jurisdiction*, 225. He has also argued that the *Hanna* test should be discarded in favor of a balancing test, such as that used in *Byrd*. Do you agree?

5. Gasperini. In the years following *Hanna*, the Supreme Court largely ignored *Byrd*. However, in Gasperini v. Center for Humanities, Inc., 518 U.S. 415 (1996), *Byrd* has once again returned to some prominence. The suit involved a diversity case in federal court in New York. The Supreme Court held that in reviewing whether to grant a new trial on grounds that the jury verdict was excessive, the federal district court should apply the standard specified by New York law rather than a federal standard. In reaching this conclusion, the Court cited *Hanna* and *Guaranty Trust* and concluded that application of a federal standard would result in substantial variations between state and federal awards in violation of the "twin aims of *Erie*."

The Court then went on to consider the standard to be used by courts of appeals in reviewing district court decisions concerning new trials on grounds of the verdict's excessiveness. The Court held that federal courts of appeals were not required to apply the standard of review dictated by New York law. In reaching this conclusion the Court focused on *Byrd*. According to the Court, *Byrd* held that "the *Guaranty Trust* 'outcome determination' test was an insufficient guide in cases presenting countervailing federal interest." Id. at 432. In *Gasperini* the Court found a sufficient countervailing federal interest based on "practical reasons combine[d] with Seventh Amendment constraints." Id. at 438.

Gasperini highlights that the approach of *Byrd* has not been abandoned, but it remains unclear when the Court will invoke *Hanna* and when it will invoke *Byrd*. Professor Erwin Chemerinsky has argued that *Hanna* and *Byrd* can be combined into the following test. First one inquires whether application of a federal standard would violate the "twin aims of *Erie*." If not, then the federal standard applies. If so, one then inquires whether despite the effect on outcome, there is an overriding federal interest which justifies applying the federal standard applies. Chemerinsky, *Federal Jurisdiction*, 301–02. What do you think of this approach?

6. *The Federal Rules of Civil Procedure*. *Hanna* also clarified the proper analysis when there is a Federal Rule of Civil Procedure on point. The Federal Rules of Civil Procedure were promulgated by the Supreme Court, pursuant to a federal statute, the Rules Enabling Act. The Act explicitly provides that it shall preempt any conflicting law: "All laws in conflict with [the Federal Rules of Civil Procedure] shall be of no further force or effect." 28 U.S.C. § 2072(b). Thus, where there is a valid Federal Rule of Civil Procedure on point, it applies, just as any preemptive federal legislation would apply. In *Gasperini*, the Court reiterated this point, explaining: "It is settled that if the Rule in point is consonant with the Rules

Enabling Act [cit.] and the Constitution, the Federal Rule applies regardless of contrary state law." 518 U.S. at 427 n.7.

To be valid, a Federal Rule must first be within Congress' constitutional authority. *Hanna* suggests that Congress derives its authority to specify rules of procedure for the federal courts from its power to create the federal court system. According to the Court, this authority extends to anything "rationally capable of classification" as procedure.

How broad is this power? Is it coextensive with *state* power to specify the rules of procedure? See *Sun Oil Co. v. Wortman*, Ch. 5. In *Wortman*, Justice Scalia holds that a state forum can apply its own statute of limitations and suggests that the forum can also apply its own rules concerning remedies, burden of proof, burden of production, sufficiency of the evidence, and privileges. Does Congress' power to specify the rules of procedure for federal courts extend to the items on Justice Scalia's list?

While Congress could enact directly rules of procedure for the federal courts, the Rules Enabling Act delegates to the Supreme Court authority to promulgate such rules. Obviously, Congress cannot delegate more authority than it has, so rules promulgated by the Supreme Court must be within Congress' authority. In addition, the rules must be within the Scope of the Rules Enabling Act, which provides:

> (a) The Supreme Court shall have the power to prescribe general rules of practice and procedure and rules of evidence for cases in the United States district courts (including proceedings before magistrates thereof) and courts of appeals.
>
> (b) Such rules shall not abridge, enlarge or modify any substantive right. All laws in conflict with such rules shall be of no further force or effect after such rules have taken effect.

28 U.S.C. § 2072. Subpart (b) appears to impose an important restriction on the power granted by (a). However, the Supreme Court has interpreted (b) as simply restating rather than restricting (a). According to the Court, the test for validity is whether a Rule "really regulates procedure." Sibbach v. Wilson & Co., 312 U.S. 1, 14 (1941). If the Rule really does regulate procedure then, according to the Court, it cannot possibly alter or amend substantive rights.

The Supreme Court has never struck down a Federal Rule of Civil Procedure. This is not surprising given the process by which the Rules are promulgated. As the Court has explained:

> The Federal Rules of Civil Procedure are not enacted by Congress, but "Congress participates in the rulemaking process." [cit.] Additionally, the Rules do not go into effect until Congress has had at least seven months to look them over. [cit.] A challenge to [a Rule] can therefore succeed "only if the Advisory Committee, this Court, and Congress erred in their prima facie judgment that the Rule ... transgresses neither the terms of the Enabling Act nor constitutional restrictions." [cit.]

Business Guides, Inc. v. Chromatic Communications Enterprises, Inc., 498 U.S. 533, 552 (1991).

Where a Federal Rule of Civil Procedure is arguably involved, the real battle ground is not whether the Rule is valid, but whether it is on point. This question involves determining the Rule's intended scope. Subpart (b) of the Rules Enabling Act seems to have its biggest impact here: where a broad interpretation of a Rule may impinge on substantive rights, the Court will likely interpret the Rule narrowly. For example, Rule 3 of the Federal Rules provides that "a civil action is commenced by filing a complaint." In Walker v. Armco Steel Corp., 446 U.S. 740 (1980), the Supreme Court held that this Rule does not address the question of when an action is commenced for purposes of a statute of limitations. Therefore, a federal court should apply a state law provision that the statute of limitations continues to run until the time of service and is not tolled by the filing of the complaint. In Semtek Int'l Inc. v. Lockheed Martin Corp., 531 U.S. 497 (2001), infra Chapter 11(B), the Court offered a similarly narrow interpretation of Rule 41(b) when it concluded that this Rule does not specify the preclusive effect of an involuntary dismissal.

The Court does not always construe Federal Rules as narrowly as possible. For example, Rule 38 of the Federal Rules of Appellate Procedure provides: "If a court of appeals shall determine that an appeal is frivolous, it may award just damages and single or double costs to the appellee." In contrast, Alabama state law provides for a mandatory award of 10% of the judgment against any appellee who obtains a stay of judgment and loses on appeal. In Burlington Northern R.R. Co. v. Woods, 480 U.S. 1 (1987), the Supreme Court held that Rule 38 mandates an exercise of discretion and that the Rule therefore displaces the mandatory state rule.

It is difficult to generalize about how properly to interpret any Rule. One treatise optimistically observes: "perceived collisions between a Rule and state substantive law often are simply the product of careless thinking about the Rule and difficulties tend to dissipate upon a careful reading of the relevant passage and a little reflection." 19 Wright, Miller & Cooper, *Federal Practice and Procedure*, at 310.

C. *ERIE* AND CHOICE OF LAW

The accident at issue in *Erie* occurred in Pennsylvania and the litigation occurred in federal court in New York. The Supreme Court did not address the question of *which* state law the federal court should apply and on remand, the federal court applied Pennsylvania state law. It was not until Klaxon Co. v. Stentor Elec. Mfg. Co., 313 U.S. 487 (1941), that the Supreme Court squarely addressed the choice-of-law question.

Klaxon Co. v. Stentor Electric Manufacturing Co., Inc.
Supreme Court of the United States, 1941.
313 U.S. 487, 61 S.Ct. 1020, 85 L.Ed. 1477.

JUSTICE REED delivered the opinion of the Court. The principal question in this case is whether in diversity cases the federal courts must follow conflict of laws rules prevailing in the states in which they sit. * * *

In 1918, respondent, a New York corporation, transferred its entire business to petitioner, a Delaware corporation. Petitioner contracted to use its best efforts to further the manufacture and sale of certain patented devices covered by the agreement, and respondent was to have a share of petitioner's profits. The agreement was executed in New York, the assets were transferred there, and petitioner began performance there although later it moved its operations to other states. Respondent was voluntarily dissolved under New York law in 1919. Ten years later it instituted this action in the United States District Court for the District of Delaware, alleging that petitioner had failed to perform its agreement to use its best efforts. Jurisdiction rested on diversity of citizenship. In 1939 respondent recovered a jury verdict of $100,000, upon which judgment was entered. Respondent then moved to correct the judgment by adding interest at the rate of six percent from June 1, 1929, the date the action had been brought. The basis of the motion was the provision in § 480 of the New York Civil Practice Act directing that in contract actions interest be added to the principal sum "whether theretofore liquidated or unliquidated." The District Court granted the motion, taking the view that the rights of the parties were governed by New York law and that under New York law the addition of such interest was mandatory. [cit.] The Circuit Court of Appeals affirmed, [cit.], and we granted certiorari, limited to the question whether § 480 of the New York Civil Practice Act is applicable to an action in the federal court in Delaware. [cit.]

The Circuit Court of Appeals was of the view that under New York law the right to interest before verdict under § 480 went to the substance of the obligation, and that proper construction of the contract in suit fixed New York as the place of performance. It then concluded that § 480 was applicable to the case because "it is clear by what we think is undoubtedly the better view of the law that the rules for ascertaining the measure of damages are not a matter of procedure at all, but are matters of substance which should be settled by reference to the law of the appropriate state according to the type of case being tried in the forum. The measure of damages for breach of a contract is determined by the law of the place of performance; Restatement, Conflict of Laws § 413." The court referred also to § 418 of the Restatement, which makes interest part of the damages to be determined by the law of the place of performance. Application of the New York statute apparently followed from the court's independent determination of the "better view" without regard to Delaware law, for no Delaware decision or statute was cited or discussed.

We are of opinion that the prohibition declared in *Erie R. Co. v. Tompkins*, against such independent determinations by the federal courts, extends to the field of conflict of laws. The conflict of laws rules to be applied by the federal court in Delaware must conform to those prevailing in Delaware's state courts. Otherwise, the accident of diversity of citizenship would constantly disturb equal administration of justice in coordinate state and federal courts sitting side by side. See *Erie R. Co. v. Tompkins*. Any other ruling would do violence to the principle of uniformity within a state, upon which the *Tompkins* decision is based. Whatever lack of uniformity this may produce between federal courts in different states is attributable to our federal system, which leaves to a state, within the limits permitted by the Constitution, the right to pursue local policies diverging from those of its neighbors. It is not for the federal courts to thwart such local policies by enforcing an independent "general law" of conflict of laws. Subject only to review by this Court on any federal question that may arise, Delaware is free to determine whether a given matter is to be governed by the law of the forum or some other law. [cit.] This Court's views are not the decisive factor in determining the applicable conflicts rule. [cit.] And the proper function of the Delaware federal court is to ascertain what the state law is, not what it ought to be.

* * *

Respondent makes the further argument that the judgment must be affirmed because, under the full faith and credit clause of the Constitution, the state courts of Delaware would be obliged to give effect to the New York statute. The argument rests mainly on the decision of this Court in *John Hancock Mutual Life Ins. Co. v. Yates*, where a New York statute was held such an integral part of a contract of insurance, the Georgia was compelled to sustain the contract under the full faith and credit clause. Here, however, § 480 of the New York Civil Practice Act is in no way related to the validity of the contract in suit, but merely to an incidental item of damages, interest, with respect to which courts at the forum have commonly been free to apply their own or some other law as they see fit. Nothing in the Constitution ensures unlimited extraterritorial recognition of all statutes or of any statute under all circumstances. *Pacific Employers Insurance Co. v. Industrial Accident Comm'n.* The Full faith and credit clause does not go so far as to compel Delaware to apply § 480 if such application would interfere with its local policy.

Accordingly, the judgment is reversed and the case remanded to the Circuit Court of Appeals for decision in conformity with the law of Delaware.

Reversed.

Notes and Questions

1. In the debates on the ratification of the Constitution, one of the described benefits of diversity jurisdiction was that it would provide a means by which non-citizens could avoid unfair laws of the forum. See Baxter, *Choice of Law*, 37–39. If diversity jurisdiction does not protect against unfair laws, what purpose does it serve? Professor Baxter has argued that *Erie* and *Klaxon* have reduced the diversity clause to a "trivial function"? Id. at 34. Do you agree?

2. Is *Klaxon* constitutionally mandated? A number of commentators have argued that it is not. Professor Baxter has argued that the Full Faith and Credit Clause might provide a basis for federal courts to develop federal choice-of-law rules. See Baxter, *Choice of Law*, 23. Others have suggested that federal law-making authority can be derived from general principles of federalism. "[T]he ordering of the relations among the States of the Union is a uniquely *federal* function. The reach of state laws * * * should no more be left to the unilateral determination by individual states than is the determination of their physical boundaries." Scoles, Hay, Borchers & Symeonides, *Conflict of Laws*, 177-78. Do you agree?

3. Is *Klaxon* mandated by the Rules of Decision Act? Historian Wilfred Ritz has argued that "the laws of the several states" as it was used in the 1789 version of the Rules of Decision Act "does not mean that the national courts are to apply the law of a particular state, such as the law of the state where the trial at common law is held. If this meaning had been intended, the word used almost certainly would

have been 'respective' and not 'several'." Ritz, *History of the Judiciary Act*, 140. Indeed, Professor Ritz concluded that the Rules of Decision Act, as originally enacted, "is a direction to the national courts to apply American law, as distinguished from English law." Id. at 148. *Swift v. Tyson* was overruled in part because of the historical analysis provided by Charles Warren. Should *Erie* or *Klaxon* be reconsidered in light of new historical data?

4. In Griffin v. McCoach, 313 U.S. 498 (1941), the Supreme Court applied *Klaxon* to a case brought in federal court pursuant to the Federal Interpleader Act, 28 U.S.C. § 1335. That Act provides for nationwide service of process and this allows the federal action to include parties who could not have been joined in a state court suit because of lack of personal jurisdiction. Does it make sense for a federal court to apply the choice-of-law rules of the state in which it sits when the action in question could not have been brought in that state?

5. In Day & Zimmermann, Inc. v. Challoner, 423 U.S. 3 (1975), the Supreme Court reaffirmed the holding of *Klaxon*. The plaintiffs in that case were soldiers who were injured or killed in Cambodia by prematurely exploding ammunition. Suit was brought under state tort law in federal court in Texas. The court of appeals refused to apply the Texas "place of the injury" choice-of-law rule, on the grounds that "as a matter of federal choice of law, *we could not apply the law of a jurisdiction that had no interest in the case*, no policy at stake." 512 F.2d 77, 80 (5th Cir.1975). (Do you agree that Cambodia was a disinterested state?) The Supreme Court reversed, per curiam, holding that the federal court was required to apply the Texas place of the wrong choice-of-law rule which looked to the place of the injury. Should the choice-of-law rules which govern liability towards United States soldiers acting while on duty be governed by state law? You should reconsider this question after reading Part D of this chapter, infra.

6. In *Day & Zimmermann*, the court of appeals suggested that Texas would not have applied its traditional rule to the facts of this particular case. 512 F.2d at 84-85. Sometimes lawyers conclude that a federal court attempting to predict the choice-of-law rule of a state will be more reluctant than state courts would be to innovate with respect to choice-of-law doctrine. As a result, litigants who want to persuade a court to abandon the *lex loci* or otherwise modify existing choice-of-law doctrine may prefer state court to federal court. See Weintraub, *Commentary*, at 594-96. Lee Kreindler, the lawyer who represented the plaintiff in *Kilberg v. Northeast Airlines, Inc.*, Ch. 2 at 60, reported that he went to great lengths to ensure that at least one of the defendants in the case was non-diverse from the plaintiff so that the case would not be removable to federal court. Is forum shopping to avoid federal court any less troubling than forum shopping to get into federal court?

7. The *Klaxon* rule led Judge Friendly to observe, "Our principle task * * * is to determine what the New York courts would think the California courts would think on an issue about which neither has thought." Nolan v. Transocean Air Lines, 276 F.2d 280, 281 (2d Cir.1960).

8. In *Klaxon*, suppose Delaware would apply its own rule concerning interest because it considered this a matter of procedure. Under these circumstances should a federal court in Delaware apply Delaware law? Instead of applying Delaware law

on the interest issue, couldn't the federal court accept Delaware's characterization of the issue as procedural and therefore apply forum, i.e., federal, law? See Boyd Rosene & Assocs., Inc. v. Kansas Mun. Gas Agency, 174 F.3d 1115 (10th Cir. 1999); Yohannon v. Keene Corp., 924 F.2d 1255, 1263-65 (3d Cir.1991); Sampson v. Channell, 110 F.2d 754 (1st Cir.), *cert. denied*, 310 U.S. 650 (1940).

9. Does Congress have constitutional authority to enact a federal choice-of-law statute applicable in federal court? Could it also enact a choice-of-law statute applicable in state court? Would either of these be a good idea? See Gottesman, *Draining the Dismal Swamp*, 1. You should reconsider this question after reading the next case.

Note on Transfer Within the Federal System

Several provisions of federal law permit cases to be transferred from one federal district court to another. Section 1404 provides:

> For the convenience of parties and witnesses, in the interest of justice, a district court may transfer any civil action to any other district or division where it might have been brought.

28 U.S.C. § 1404(a). A § 1404 transfer is permitted even where jurisdiction and venue are proper in the original forum. The transfer may be sought by either party or the judge sua sponte. Where suit is filed originally in a district that lacks personal jurisdiction or in which venue is improper, the suit may be dismissed or transferred pursuant to § 1406. See Goldlawr, Inc. v. Heiman, 369 U.S. 463 (1962).

When a case is transferred under § 1404, what law should the transferee court apply--the law of the state in which it sits or the law of the state of the transferor court? In Van Dusen v. Barrack, 376 U.S. 612 (1964), the Supreme Court held that when a defendant seeks a § 1404(a) transfer, that transfer is simply a change of courtroom and should not change the law that is applied. The Court was concerned that if a change of venue brought with it a change of law, then § 1404(a) would be used "by defendants to defeat the advantages accruing to plaintiffs who have chosen a forum which, although it was inconvenient, was proper venue." Id. at 634. Therefore, the Court held that the district court to which the case is transferred should apply whatever law the transferring court would have applied.

In Ferens v. John Deere Co., 494 U.S. 516 (1990), the Supreme Court went even further and held that even where the *plaintiff* requests the § 1404 transfer, the transferee court (the receiving court) should apply the law that the transferor (the original court) would have applied. The facts of *Ferens* are quite striking. The plaintiff was injured in a tractor accident in Pennsylvania. After the two-year Pennsylvania limitations period had expired, the plaintiff brought suit against John Deere in federal court in Mississippi.[2] At that time, Mississippi had a six-year statute

---

2. Subsequent to *Ferens*, Mississippi shortened its general limitations period to three years. See Miss. Code Ann. § 15-1-49 (1995). Mississippi also has a "borrowing statute" which provides:

> When a cause of action has accrued outside of this state, and by the laws of the place outside this state where such cause of action accrued, an action thereon cannot be maintained by reason of lapse of time, then no action thereon shall be maintained in this state; provided, however, that
>
> (continued...)

of limitations which it considered "procedural" and applicable to any claim filed in Mississippi. Thus, under *Klaxon*, a federal court in Mississippi would likewise be required to apply the Mississippi statute of limitations. The plaintiff did not, however, actually litigate in Mississippi federal court. Instead, shortly after filing his complaint, the plaintiff moved for a § 1404 transfer to Pennsylvania, which was granted. The Supreme Court held that the federal court in Pennsylvania should apply the Mississippi statute of limitations because a transfer under § 1404 "does not change the law applicable to a diversity case," 494 U.S. at 523, and this should remain true regardless of who initiates the transfer.

Justice Kennedy, writing for the majority, argued that "[a]pplying the transferee law * * * would undermine the *Erie* rule in a serious way. It would mean that initiating a transfer under § 1404(a) changes the state law applicable to a diversity case." Id. at 526. Justice Scalia, writing for the dissenters, replied that "[t]he plaintiffs were seeking to achieve exactly what *Klaxon* was designed to prevent: the use of a Pennsylvania federal court instead of a Pennsylvania state court in order to obtain application of a different substantive law." Id. at 535.

Justice Scalia argued that where a case is transferred at the request of the plaintiff or by the judge sua sponte, the law of the transferee court should apply. But doesn't this approach create another set of *Erie* problems? Under Justice Scalia's approach, Ferens would face a different potential result in Mississippi state court than Mississippi federal court. If the case were removed to federal court, the federal judge could transfer the case and thereby change the law that would be applied. What about a rule that the law changes only if the transfer is at the request of the plaintiff. Would this be an improvement over Justice Scalia's suggestion or would it simply mean that in the next case like *Ferens*, the plaintiff would not actually move for a transfer but instead point out to the judge how inconvenient the location was and hope the judge would transfer sua sponte?

Are there any other solutions to the *Ferens* dilemma? What about a federal choice-of-law rule. Justice Kennedy observed:

> [O]ne might contend that, because no per se rule requiring a court to apply either the transferor law or the transferee law will seem appropriate in all circumstances, we should develop more sophisticated federal choice-of-law rules for diversity actions involving transfers. [cit.] To a large extent, however, state conflicts-of-law rules already ensure that appropriate laws will apply to diversity cases. Federal law, as a general matter, does not interfere with these rules. See *Sun Oil*. In addition, even if more elaborate federal choice-of-law rules would not run afoul of *Klaxon* and *Erie*, we believe that applying the law of the transferor forum effects the appropriate balance between fairness and simplicity. Cf. R. Leflar, American Conflicts Law § 143, p. 293 (3d ed. 1977)

2. (...continued)

> where such a cause of action has accrued in favor of a resident of this state, this state's law on the period of limitation shall apply.

Id. at § 15-1-65. Notice that this statute treats residents and non-residents differently. Does this discrimination violate the Privileges and Immunities Clause? In Canadian N. Ry. v. Eggen, 252 U.S. 553 (1920), the Supreme Court held that such statutes are permissible provided that non-residents have a reasonable amount of time within which to bring suit.

(arguing against a federal common law of conflicts).

Id. at 532. Is the real problem in *Ferens* created not by *Van Dusen*, but by *Sun Oil Co. v. Wortman*, Ch. 5, which permits Mississippi to apply its statute of limitations to a claim that is totally unconnected to Mississippi? See Martin, *Statutes of Limitations*, 414-15.

Although the Supreme Court has not addressed the question, there is general agreement that *Van Dusen* does not apply to § 1406 transfers or other cases in which personal jurisdiction or venue were improper in the transferor court. See 15 Wright, Miller & Cooper, *Federal Practice*, 365–36. Why should this be so?

Where related litigation is pending in multiple federal districts, 28 U.S.C. § 1407 allows all the cases to be transferred to one district for pretrial proceedings. This consolidation does not alter the law to be applied—the court must still apply the law that would have been applied in the original forum. The results can be extraordinarily complex. For example, in In re Paris Air Crash of March 3, 1974, 399 F.Supp. 732 (C.D.Cal.1975), 203 actions stemming from the crash of a Turkish airplane near Paris were consolidated. The district court lamented:

> The law on "choice of law" in the various states and in the federal courts is a veritable jungle, which, if the law can be found out, leads not to a "rule of action" but a reign of chaos dominated in each case by the judge's "informed guess" as to what some *other* state than the one in which he sits *would* hold *its* law to be. * * * Most of the cases are involved with such a "guess" as to the law of one other state or perhaps as many as three. Here * * * this Court would have to "guess" what the courts in 24 foreign and 12 domestic jurisdictions would hold on the facts in this case, including their "choice-of-law" rules, and who knows what laws of what country or state that would lead to.

Id. at 739–40 (emphasis in original).

Judge Weinstein confronted a similar dilemma in the Agent Orange litigation. There, Viet Nam War veterans alleged they suffered injury as a result of exposure in Viet Nam to defendants' herbicides. Suits from around the country were consolidated and included plaintiffs from nearly every state as well as several foreign countries. The Second Circuit had earlier ruled that the case was not controlled by federal common law. See In re "Agent Orange" Product Liability Litigation, 635 F.2d 987, 993 (2d. Cir.1980), *cert. denied*, 454 U.S. 1128 (1981). Facing massive choice-of-law problems, Judge Weinstein concluded that in this situation, all states would in fact apply the same substantive law—they would all apply "national-consensus law" and they would all agree on the content of "national-consensus law." In re "Agent Orange" Product Liability Litigation, 580 F.Supp. 690, 710-13 (E.D.N.Y.1984).

Review the discussion of the ALI Complex Litigation Project, supra at 314-16. Some might argue that any statute, even a less than perfect one, would be better than the current mess. Do you agree?

Stewart Organization, Inc. v. Ricoh Corp.

Supreme Court of the United States, 1988.
487 U.S. 22, 108 S.Ct. 2239, 101 L.Ed.2d 22.

JUSTICE MARSHALL delivered the opinion of the Court. This case presents the issue whether a federal court sitting in diversity should apply state or federal law in adjudicating a motion to transfer a case to a venue provided in a contractual forum-selection clause.

I. The dispute underlying this case grew out of a dealership agreement that obligated petitioner company, an Alabama corporation, to market copier products of respondent, a nationwide manufacturer with its principal place of business in New Jersey. The agreement contained a forum-selection clause providing that any dispute arising out of the contract could be brought only in a court located in Manhattan.[1] Business relations between the parties soured under circumstances that are not relevant here. In September 1984, petitioner brought a complaint in the United States District Court for the Northern District of Alabama. The core of the complaint was an allegation that respondent had breached the dealership agreement, but petitioner also included claims for breach of warranty, fraud, and antitrust violations.

Relying on the contractual forum-selection clause, respondent moved the District Court either to transfer the case to the Southern District of New York under 28 U.S.C. § 1404(a) or to dismiss the case for improper venue under 28 U.S.C. § 1406. The District Court denied the motion. [cit.] It reasoned that the transfer motion was controlled by Alabama law and that Alabama looks unfavorably upon contractual forum-selection clauses. The court certified its ruling for interlocutory appeal, see 28 U.S.C. § 1292(b) (1982 ed., Supp. IV), and the Court of Appeals for the Eleventh Circuit accepted jurisdiction.

On appeal, a divided panel of the Eleventh Circuit reversed the District Court. [The case was then heard en banc.] * * * The en banc court, citing Congress' enactment or approval of several rules to govern venue determinations in diversity actions, first determined that "[v]enue is a matter of federal procedure." [cit.] The Court of Appeals then applied the standards articulated in the admiralty case of The Bremen v. Zapata Off–Shore Co., 407 U.S. 1 (1972), to conclude that "the choice of forum clause in this contract is in all respects enforceable generally as a matter of federal law.... " [cit.] We now affirm under somewhat different reasoning.

II. Both the panel opinion and the opinion of the full Court of Appeals referred to the difficulties that often attend "the sticky question of which law, state or federal, will govern various aspects of the decisions of federal courts sitting in diversity." 779 F.2d, at 645. A district court's decision whether to apply a federal statute such as § 1404(a) in a diversity action, however, involves a considerably less intricate analysis than that which governs the "relatively unguided *Erie* choice." Hanna v. Plumer, 380

---

1. Specifically, the forum-selection clause read: "Dealer and Ricoh agree that any appropriate state or federal district court located in the Borough of Manhattan, New York City, New York, shall have exclusive jurisdiction over any case or controversy arising under or in connection with this Agreement and shall be a proper forum in which to adjudicate such case or controversy." [cit.]

U.S. 460, 471 (1965). Our cases indicate that when the federal law sought to be applied is a congressional statute, the first and chief question for the district court's determination is whether the statute is "sufficiently broad to control the issue before the Court." Walker v. Armco Steel Corp., 446 U.S. 740, 749-50 (1980); Burlington Northern R. Co. v. Woods, 480 U.S. 1, 4-5 (1987). This question involves a straightforward exercise in statutory interpretation to determine if the statute covers the point in dispute. [cit.][4]

If the district court determines that a federal statute covers the point in dispute, it proceeds to inquire whether the statute represents a valid exercise of Congress' authority under the Constitution. [cit.] If Congress intended to reach the issue before the District Court, and if it enacted its intention into law in a manner that abides with the Constitution, that is the end of the matter. * * *[6]

III. Applying the above analysis to this case persuades us that federal law, specifically 28 U.S.C. § 1404(a), governs the parties' venue dispute.

A. At the outset we underscore a methodological difference in our approach to the question from that taken by the Court of Appeals. * * * [W]e disagree with the court's articulation of the relevant inquiry as "whether the forum selection clause in this case is unenforceable under the standards set forth in *The Bremen*." [cit.] Rather, the first question for consideration should have been whether § 1404(a) itself controls respondent's request to give effect to the parties' contractual choice of venue and transfer this case to a Manhattan court. For the reasons that follow, we hold that it does.

B. Section 1404(a) provides: "For the convenience of parties and witnesses, in the interest of justice, a district court may transfer any civil action to any other district or division where it might have been brought." Under the analysis outlined above, we first consider whether this provision is sufficiently broad to control the issue before the court. That issue is whether to transfer the case to a court in Manhattan in accordance with the forum-selection clause. We believe that the statute, fairly construed, does cover the point in dispute.

Section 1404(a) is intended to place discretion in the district court to adjudicate motions for transfer according to an "individualized, case-by-case consideration of convenience and fairness." *Van Dusen v. Barrack*. A motion to transfer under § 1404(a) thus calls on the district court to weigh in the balance a number of case-specific factors. The presence of a forum-selection clause such as the parties entered into in this case will be a significant factor that figures centrally in the

---

4. Our cases at times have referred to the question at this stage of the analysis as an inquiry into whether there is a "direct collision" between state and federal law. See, e.g., *Walker v. Armco Steel Corp.*; *Hanna v. Plumer*. Logic indicates, however, and a careful reading of the relevant passages confirms, that this language is not meant to mandate that federal law and state law be perfectly coextensive and equally applicable to the issue at hand; rather, the "direct collision" language, at least where the applicability of a federal statute is at issue, expresses the requirement that the federal statute be sufficiently broad to cover the point in dispute. See *Hanna v. Plumer*. It would make no sense for the supremacy of federal law to wane precisely because there is no state law directly on point.

6. If no federal statute or Rule covers the point in dispute, the district court then proceeds to evaluate whether application of federal judge-made law would deserve the so-called "twin aims of the *Erie* rule: discouragement of forum-shopping and avoidance of inequitable administration of the laws." *Hanna v. Plumer*. If application of federal judge-made law would disserve these two policies, the district court should apply state law. [cit.]

district court's calculus. In its resolution of the § 1404(a) motion in this case, for example, the District Court will be called on to address such issues as the convenience of a Manhattan forum given the parties' expressed preference for that venue, and the fairness of transfer in light of the forum-selection clause and the parties' relative bargaining power. The flexible and individualized analysis Congress prescribed in § 1404(a) thus encompasses consideration of the parties' private expression of their venue preferences.

Section 1404(a) may not be the only potential source of guidance for the District Court to consult in weighing the parties' private designation of a suitable forum. The premise of the dispute between the parties is that Alabama law may refuse to enforce forum-selection clauses providing for out-of-state venues as a matter of state public policy.[9] If that is so, the District Court will have either to integrate the factor of the forum-selection clause into its weighing of considerations as prescribed by Congress, or else to apply, as it did in this case, Alabama's categorical policy disfavoring forum-selection clauses. Our cases make clear that, as between these two choices in a single "field of operation," [cit.], the instructions of Congress are supreme. [cit.]

It is true that § 1404(a) and Alabama's putative policy regarding forum-selection clauses are not perfectly coextensive. Section 1404(a) directs a district court to take account of factors other than those that bear solely on the parties' private ordering of their affairs. The district court also must weigh in the balance the convenience of the witnesses and those public-interest factors of systemic integrity and fairness that, in addition to private concerns, come under the heading of "the interest of justice." It is conceivable in a particular case, for example, that because of these factors a district court acting under § 1404(a) would refuse to transfer a case notwithstanding the counterweight of a forum-selection clause, whereas the coordinate state rule might dictate the opposite result.[10] [cit.] But this potential conflict in fact frames an additional argument for the supremacy of federal law. Congress has directed that multiple considerations govern transfer within the federal court system, and a state policy focusing on a single concern or a subset of the factors identified in § 1404(a) would defeat that command. Its application would impoverish the flexible and multifaceted analysis that Congress intended to govern motions to transfer within the federal system. The forum-selection clause, which represents the parties' agreement as to the most proper forum, should receive neither dispositive consideration (as respondent might have it) nor no consideration (as Alabama law might have it), but rather the consideration for which Congress

---

9. In its application of the standards set forth in *The Bremen* to this case, the Court of Appeals concluded that the Alabama policy against the enforcement of forum-selection clauses is intended to apply only to protect the jurisdiction of the state courts of Alabama and therefore would not come into play in this case, in which case this dispute might be much ado about nothing. [cit.] Our determination that § 1404(a) governs the parties' dispute notwithstanding any contrary Alabama policy makes it unnecessary to address the contours of state law. See n.4, supra.

10. The dissent does not dispute this point, but rather argues that if the forum-selection clause would be *unenforceable* under state law, then the clause cannot be accorded any weight by a federal court. [cit.] Not the least of the problems with the dissent's analysis is that it makes the applicability of a federal statute depend on the content of state law. [cit.] If a State cannot pre-empt a district court's consideration of a forum-selection clause by holding that the clause is automatically enforceable, it makes no sense for it to be able to do so by holding the clause automatically void.

provided in § 1404(a). Cf. Norwood v. Kirkpatrick, 349 U.S. 29, 32 (1955) (§ 1404(a) accords broad discretion to district court, and plaintiff's choice of forum is only one relevant factor for its consideration). This is thus not a case in which state and federal rules "can exist side by side ... each controlling its own intended sphere of coverage without conflict." *Walker v. Armco Steel Corp.*

Because § 1404(a) controls the issue before the District Court, it must be applied if it represents a valid exercise of Congress' authority under the Constitution. The constitutional authority of Congress to enact § 1404(a) is not subject to serious question. As the Court made plain in *Hanna*, "the constitutional provision for a federal court system ... carries with it congressional power to make rules governing the practice and pleading in those courts, which in turn includes a power to regulate matters which, though falling within the uncertain area between substance and procedure, are rationally capable of classification as either." [cit.] Section 1404(a) is doubtless capable of classification as a procedural rule, and indeed, we have so classified it in holding that a transfer pursuant to § 1404(a) does not carry with it a change in the applicable law. See *Van Dusen v. Barrack.* It therefore falls comfortably within Congress' powers under Article III as augmented by the Necessary and Proper Clause. [cit.]

We hold that federal law, specifically 28 U.S.C. § 1404(a), governs the District Court's decision whether to give effect to the parties' forum-selection clause and transfer this case to a court in Manhattan. We therefore affirm the Eleventh Circuit order reversing the District Court's application of Alabama law. The case is remanded so that the District Court may determine in the first instance the appropriate effect under federal law of the parties' forum-selection clause on respondent's § 1404(a) motion.

It is so ordered.

JUSTICE KENNEDY, with whom Justice O'Connor joins, concurring. I concur in full. I write separately only to observe that enforcement of valid forum-selection clauses, bargained for by the parties, protects their legitimate expectations and furthers vital interests of the justice system. Although our opinion in *The Bremen v. Zapata Off-Shore Co.*, involved a Federal District Court sitting in admiralty, its reasoning applies with much force to federal courts sitting in diversity. The justifications we noted in *The Bremen* to counter the historical disfavor forum-selection clauses had received in American courts should be understood to guide the District Court's analysis under § 1404(a).

The federal judicial system has a strong interest in the correct resolution of these questions, not only to spare litigants unnecessary costs but also to relieve courts of time-consuming pretrial motions. Courts should announce and encourage rules that support private parties who negotiate such clauses. Though state policies should be weighed in the balance, the authority and prerogative of the federal courts to determine the issue, as Congress has directed by § 1404(a), should be exercised so that a valid forum-selection clause is given controlling weight in all but the most exceptional cases. See *The Bremen.*

JUSTICE SCALIA, dissenting. I agree with the opinion of the Court that the initial question before us is whether the validity between the parties of a contractual forum-selection clause falls within the scope of 28 U.S.C. § 1404(a). [cit.] I cannot agree, however, that the answer to that question is yes. Nor do I believe that the federal courts can, consistent with the twin-aims test of *Erie R. Co. v. Tompkins*, fashion a judge-made rule to govern this issue of contract validity.

I. When a litigant asserts that state law conflicts with a federal procedural statute or formal Rule of Procedure, a court's first task is to determine whether the disputed point in question in fact falls within the scope of the federal statute or Rule. In this case, the Court must determine whether the scope of § 1404(a) is sufficiently broad to cause a direct collision with state law or implicitly to control the issue before the Court, i.e., validity between the parties of the forum-selection clause, thereby leaving no room for the operation of state law. [cit.] I conclude that it is not.

Although the language of § 1404(a) provides no clear answer, in my view it does provide direction. The provision vests the district courts with authority to transfer a civil action to another district "[f]or the convenience of parties and witnesses, in the interest of justice." This language looks to the present and the future. * * * In holding that the validity between the parties of a forum-selection clause falls within the scope of § 1404(a), the Court inevitably imports, in my view without adequate textual foundation, a new *retrospective* element into the court's deliberations, requiring examination of what the facts were concerning, among other things, the bargaining power of the parties and the presence or absence of overreaching at the time the contract was made. [cit.]

The Court largely attempts to avoid acknowledging the novel scope it gives to § 1404(a) by casting the issue as how much *weight* a district court should give a forum-selection clause as against other factors when it makes its determination under § 1404(a). I agree that if the weight-among-factors issue were before us, it would be governed by § 1404(a). That is because, while the parties may decide who between them should bear any inconvenience, only a court can decide how much weight should be given under § 1404(a) to the factor of the parties' convenience as against other relevant factors such as the convenience of witnesses. But the Court's description of the issue begs the question: what law governs whether the forum-selection clause is a *valid* or *invalid* allocation of any inconvenience between the parties. If it is invalid, i.e., should be voided, between the parties, it cannot be entitled to any weight in the § 1404(a) determination. Since under Alabama law the forum-selection clause should be voided, [cit.], in this case the question of what weight should be given the forum-selection clause can be reached only if as a preliminary matter federal law controls the issue of the validity of the clause between the parties.[1]

---

1. Contrary to the opinion of the Court, there is nothing unusual about having "the applicability of a federal statute depend on the content of state law." [cit.] We have recognized that precisely this is required when the application of the federal statute depends, as here, on resolution of an underlying issue that is fundamentally one of state law. [cit.] Nor is the approach I believe is required undermined by the fact that there would still be some situations where the state-law rule on the validity of a forum-selection clause would not be dispositive of the issue of transfer between federal courts. When state law would hold a forum-selection clause invalid the federal court could nonetheless order transfer to another federal court under § 1404(a), but it could do so only if such transfer was warranted without regard to the forum-selection clause. This is not at all remarkable since whether to transfer a case from one federal district court to another

(continued...)

Second, § 1404(a) was enacted against the background that issues of contract, including a contract's validity, are nearly always governed by state law. It is simply contrary to the practice of our system that such an issue should be wrenched from state control in absence of a clear conflict with federal law or explicit statutory provision. * * * Section 1404(a) is simply a venue provision that nowhere mentions contracts or agreements, much less that the validity of certain contracts or agreements will be matters of federal law. It is difficult to believe that state contract law was meant to be pre-empted by this provision that we have said "should be regarded as a federal judicial housekeeping measure," *Van Dusen v. Barrack*, that we have said did not change "the relevant factors" which federal courts used to consider under the doctrine of forum non conveniens, [cit.], and that we have held can be applied retroactively because it is procedural [cit.]. It seems to me the generality of its language—"[f]or the convenience of parties and witnesses, in the interest of justice"—is plainly insufficient to work the great change in law asserted here.

Third, it has been common ground in this Court since *Erie*, that when a federal procedural statute or Rule of Procedure is not on point, substantial uniformity of predictable outcome between federal and state courts in adjudicating claims should be striven for. See also *Klaxon Co. v. Stentor Electric Mfg. Co.* This rests upon a perception of the constitutional and congressional plan underlying the creation of diversity and pendent jurisdiction in the lower federal courts, which should quite obviously be carried forward into our interpretation of ambiguous statutes relating to the exercise of that jurisdiction. We should assume, in other words, when it is fair to do so, that Congress is just as concerned as we have been to avoid significant differences between state and federal courts in adjudicating claims. [cit.] Thus, in deciding whether a federal procedural statute or Rule of Procedure encompasses a particular issue, a broad reading that would create significant disuniformity between state and federal courts should be avoided if the text permits. [cit.] As I have shown, the interpretation given § 1404(a) by the Court today is neither the plain nor the more natural meaning; at best, § 1404(a) is ambiguous. I would therefore construe it to avoid the significant encouragement to forum shopping that will inevitably be provided by the interpretation the Court adopts today.

* * *

Notes and Questions

1. Forum selection clauses are analyzed differently than choice-of-law clauses. The traditional view is that forum selection clauses are unenforceable because private parties cannot oust the court of jurisdiction. See Restatement of Conflict of

---

1. (...continued)
for reasons other than the contractual agreement of the parties is plainly made a matter of federal law by § 1404(a). When, on the other hand, state law would hold a forum-selection clause valid, I agree with Justice Kennedy's concurrence that under § 1404(a) such a valid forum-selection clause is to be "given controlling weight in all but the most exceptional cases." [cit.] And even in those exceptional cases where a forum-selection clause is valid under state law but transfer is unwarranted because of some factor other than the convenience of the parties, the district court should give effect to state contract law by dismissing the suit.

Laws § 332 (1934). A few states continue too treat forum selection clauses as unenforceable. See Freer, *Erie's Mid-Life Crisis*, 1096, n.31. The more modern approach, followed by the majority of states and embodied in The Bremen v. Zapata Off-Shore Co., 407 U.S. 1 (1972), and the Restatement (Second) § 80, upholds forum selection clauses so long as they are not the result of overreaching or similar unfairness. See Annotation, *Validity of Contractual Provision Limiting Place or Court in Which Action May Be Brought*, 31 A.L.R. 4th 404 (1984). In 1997, Alabama adopted the majority approach. See Professional Ins. Corp. v. Sutherland, 700 So.2d 347 (Ala., 1997).

2. Justice Kennedy, in his concurrence, suggests there is a federal policy in favor of enforcing forum selection clauses. What is the source of this federal policy? Is this federal policy equally applicable to cases in state court?

3. Suppose a case was originally filed in Alabama state court which dismissed the case on the basis of the forum selection clause. The case is then filed in federal court in Alabama. Should the federal court dismiss the case? Transfer the case? If it transfers the case, would Alabama choice-of-law rules apply in the subsequent litigation? Professor Freer has argued that where the transfer is from a state that would have dismissed the suit, it should be a § 1406 transfer which would mean that the transferred case would not take Alabama choice-of-law rules with it. Freer, *Erie's Mid-Life Crisis*, 1128-29. What do you think of this view? See Jackson v. West Telemarketing Corp. Outbound, 245 F.3d 518, 523 (5th Cir.), *cert. denied*, 534 U.S. 972 (2001) (transfer on the basis of forum selection clause was a § 1406 transfer).

4. Suppose one party to the contract contends that the forum selection clause is invalid because it was a later amendment to the contract, made without consideration. In deciding whether to transfer the case, what weight, if any, should a federal court give to the clause?

5. In a non-transfer situation (such as when the chosen forum is in a foreign country), what law governs the validity of a choice-of-forum clause? *The Bremen*, set forth a federal standard, but *Bremen* was an admiralty decision. In diversity cases, the lower courts have split on whether state or federal law controls. Compare Alexander Proudfoot Co. World Headquarters v. Thayer, 877 F.2d 912 (11th Cir.1989) (applying state law) with Manetti-Farrow, Inc. v. Gucci Am., Inc., 858 F.2d 509, 512 (9th Cir.1988) (applying federal law). See Borchers, *Forum Selection*, 68–81; *Conference on Jurisdiction, Justice, and Choice of Law for the Twenty-First Century: Case One: Choice of Forum Clauses*, 29 N.E. L. Rev. 517 (1995); Note, *Forum Selection Clauses: Problems of Enforcement in Diversity Cases and State Courts*, 35 Colum. J. Transnat'l L. 663 (1997). Cf. Allied-Bruce Terminix Co., Inc. v. Dobson, 513 U.S. 265 (1995) (Scalia, J. dissenting) ("A strong argument can be made that such forum-selection [i.e., arbitration] clauses concern procedure rather than substance."). See also Amermed Corp. v. Disetronic Holding AG, 6 F.Supp. 2d 1371, 1373 (N.D. Ga. 1998) (noting that federal courts are split on this issue and that "[s]cholars are similarly adrift").

6. The federal courts have developed a common law doctrine of forum non conveniens. See Piper Aircraft Co. v. Reyno, 454 U.S. 235 (1981); Gulf Oil Corp. v. Gilbert, 330 U.S. 501 (1947). Under this doctrine, where the federal court

concludes that the more appropriate forum is another county, the court may dismiss the suit. Most states have a similar doctrine, although a few states have significantly limited the availability of forum non conveniens dismissals. See Weintraub, *Forum Non Conveniens*, 334 n.101, 343-51.

Where state law differs from the federal approach to forum non conveniens, is a federal court required to follow state law? The Supreme Court specifically left open this question in Piper Aircraft, 454 U.S. at 248 n.13. More recently, in American Dredging Co. v. Miller, 510 U.S. 443 (1994), the Court appears to have answered the question—at least in dicta. The issue in *American Dredging* was whether in a suit in state court under the Jones Act (a federal maritime statute), the state court was required to apply the federal doctrine of forum non conveniens. The Court held that the state was not so required. In a footnote, the Court wrote:

> It is because forum non conveniens is not a substantive right of the parties, but a procedural rule of the forum, that the dissent is wrong to say our decision will cause federal-court forum non conveniens determinations in admiralty cases to be driven, henceforth, by state law—i.e., that the federal court in a State with the Louisiana rule may as well accept jurisdiction, since otherwise the state court will. [cit.] That is no more true of forum non conveniens than it is to venue. Under both doctrines, the object of the dismissal is achieved whether or not the party can then repair to a state court in the same location. Federal courts will continue to invoke forum non-conveniens to decline jurisdiction in appropriate cases, whether or not the State in which they sit chooses to burden its judiciary with litigation better handled elsewhere.

Id. at 454 n.4. Do you agree with the Court's analysis? See Stein, *Erie and Court Access*, 1935. The courts of appeal that have addressed this issue have generally concluded that federal law applies. See Monegro v. Rosa, 211 F.3d 509, 511 (9th Cir. 2000), *cert. denied*, 531 U.S. 1112 (2001), and cases cited therein.

7. On remand of *Ricoh* from the Supreme Court, the district court in Alabama held that a transfer to New York would be too burdensome for the Alabama party. Stewart Org., Inc. v. Ricoh Corp., 696 F.Supp. 583 (N.D.Ala.1988). The Eleventh Circuit granted a writ of mandamus to compel the transfer. In re Ricoh Corp., 870 F.2d 570 (11th Cir.1989).

D. FEDERAL COMMON LAW

The same day that the Court decided *Erie* and held that there was no federal general common law, the Court decided Hinderlider v. La Plata River & Cherry Creek Ditch Co., 304 U.S. 92 (1938), and held that "whether the water of an interstate stream must be apportioned between the two states is a question of 'federal common law' upon which neither the statutes nor the decisions of either state can be conclusive." Thus, although there is no *general* federal common law, the federal courts do have the power to create federal common law in certain limited areas of "uniquely federal interests." Texas Indus., Inc. v. Radcliff Materials, Inc., 451 U.S. 630, 640 (1981). For a discussion of the relationship between *Erie* and federal common law, see Merrill, *The Common Law Powers*, 1.

As in *Hinderlider*, the Court has routinely fashioned federal common law to resolve disputes between states concerning boundaries or interstate waterways. For example, in Kansas v. Colorado, 206 U.S. 46 (1907), Kansas brought suit against Colorado seeking to restrain it from diverting water from the Arkansas River to irrigate land in Colorado. The Supreme Court took jurisdiction of the case and applied federal common law to adjudicate the dispute, explaining:

> [W]henever * * * the action of one State reaches through the agency of natural laws into the territory of another State, the question of the extent and the limitations of the rights of the two States becomes a matter of justiciable dispute between them, and this court is called upon to settle that dispute in such a way as will recognize the equal rights of both and at the same time establish justice between them. In other words, through these successive disputes and decisions this court is practically building up what may not improperly be called interstate common law.

Id. at 97-98.

Federal common law cases that have relied on this rationale have all included states as parties. However, couldn't interstate concerns be implicated in a private suit? For example, the dispute in *Kansas v. Colorado* might have come to the Court as private litigation between a downstream Kansas landowner and an upstream Colorado landowner. Each might rely on the law of her respective state. Wouldn't a uniform federal common law of choice of law help to "recognize the equal rights of both [states] and at the same time establish justice between them"? See id. Indeed, couldn't the argument be made that all choice of law should be a matter of federal law? See Horowitz, *Federal Common Law of Choice of Law*, 1191.

Even if federal common law for interstate disputes is confined to cases in which states are parties, should *Nevada v. Hall*, supra at 498, have been controlled by federal common law? See Rogers, *Sovereign Immunity*, 449.

The Court has also held that the rights and obligations of the United States under its contracts are controlled by federal common law. See United States v. Kimbell Foods, Inc., 440 U.S. 715 (1979); Clearfield Trust Co. v. United States, 318 U.S. 363 (1943). In most of these cases, the United States was itself a party. However, in Boyle v. United Techs. Corp., 487 U.S. 500 (1988), the Court held that federal common law controlled the availability of a "military contractor's defense," even in a purely private tort suit. There, the family of a pilot killed in a military helicopter brought suit against the helicopter's manufacturer. The Supreme Court held that the manufacturer was shielded from liability by a federal common law defense.

Another area in which the court has applied federal common law is where the United State's relations with foreign countries are implicated and there is a need for uniformity. In Banco Nacional de Cuba v. Sabbatino, 376 U.S. 398 (1964), an American broker purchased sugar from a subsidiary of a Cuban corporation. While the sugar was aboard ship in Cuba, the Cuban government nationalized the property of the Cuban corporation. The issue before the Court was who had title to the sugar, and this turned on whether the nationalization was recognized. The Supreme Court held that the question of the legal effect in the United States of the expropriation was a matter of federal law. "[T]he competence and function of the Judiciary and the National Executive in ordering our relationships with other members of the international community must be treated exclusively as an aspect of federal law." Id. at 425. The Court held that federal common law recognized the "act of state" doctrine and that hence Cuba had title to the sugar. See infra at 573-75.

Are there other international cases involving choice of law or jurisdiction that should be governed by federal common law? For example, in *Asahi*, infra at 620, the Court specifically referred the "the Federal Governments's interest in its foreign relations policies" and unique burdens on aliens as reasons for restraint in exercising jurisdiction. Might not the same also be true with respect to choice of law? Should all choice-of-law cases with international elements be governed by federal common law? See Chapter 7 (C) infra.

Most recently, in Semtek Int'l Inc. v. Lockheed Martine Corp., 531 U.S. 497 (2001). The Court held that the preclusive effect of federal judgments, including federal diversity judgments, are governed by federal common law. *Semtek* and its implications are explored more fully in Chapter 11(B).

Once the court has decided that federal common law applies, it must determine the content of that law. In federal common law as well as federal statutory law, the Court sometimes "borrows" state law to fill the gaps. For example, in De Sylva v. Ballentine, 351 U.S. 570 (1956), the issue was whether federal copyright law entitled an illegitimate child to the statutory right of "children" to renew the copyright of their deceased parents. Although the Court could have developed on federal definition of "children," the Court instead held that the statute applied to any child who under state law would be an heir to the copyright holder.

The Court used a similar approach in Kamen v. Kemper Fin. Servs., Inc., 500 U.S. 90 (1991). Before commencing a shareholders' derivative action under Fed. R. Civ. P. 23.1, a shareholder must certify that she sought redress from the corporate directors. The question before Court was the scope of this "demand" requirement in a shareholder's derivative suit based on the Federal Investment Company Act. The Court applied the law of the place of incorporation, explaining:

> It is clear that the contours of the demand requirement in a derivative action founded on the ICA are governed by *federal* law. Because the ICA is a federal statute, any common law rule necessary to effectuate a private cause of action under that statute is necessarily federal in character. [cit.]

It does not follow, however, that the content of such a rule must be wholly the product of a federal court's own devising. Our cases indicate that a court should endeavor to fill the interstices of federal remedial schemes with uniform federal rules only when the scheme in question evidences a distinct need for nationwide legal standards, see e.g., *Clearfield Trust Co. v. United States*, or when express provisions in analogous statutory schemes embody congressional policy choices readily applicable to the matter at hand, see e.g., *Boyle*; [cite] Otherwise, we have indicated that federal courts should "incorporat[e] [state law] as the federal rule of decision," unless "application of [the particular] state law [in question] would frustrate specific objectives of the federal programs." United States v. Kimbell Foods, Inc., 440 U.S. 715 (1979). The presumption that state law should be incorporated into federal common law is particularly strong in areas in which private parties have entered legal relationships with the expectation that their rights and obligations would be governed by state-law standards.

500 U.S. at 97-98.

Of course, where federal law incorporates state law, the court must determine *which* state law. The Federal Tort Claims Act imposes tort liability on the United States based on "the law of the place where the act or omission occurred." Does this language refer to the whole law or the internal law of the place of the tort? In Richards v. United States, 369 U.S. 1, 11 (1962), the Court concluded that the statute referred to whole law.

Under the Supremacy Clause, states are required to apply federal law, including federal common law, even in matters litigated in state court. Thus, if a case similar to *Boyle* were brought in state court, the state would be required to apply the "government contractor defense" set forth in *Boyle*. But how far does this obligation extend? Must the state court use the same procedures as would be applied in federal court? The Court has held that the state must follow those procedures that are "part and parcel of the remedy afforded," Dice v. Akron, Canton & Youngstown R.R. Co., 342 U.S. 359, 363 (1952). Applying this test, the Court has held that under the Federal Employers' Liability Act, there is a right to a jury on the issue of the validity of a release, see id., and, under the same Act, the defendant has the burden of proving contributory negligence, see Central Vermont Ry. Co. v. White, 238 U.S. 507 (1915).

Similarly in Brown v. Western Ry. of Alabama, 338 U.S. 294 (1949), a state court dismissed an FELA action on the grounds that the complaint was inadequate. The state relied on a state rule that required pleading allegations be construed "most strongly against the pleader." The Supreme Court reversed, explaining that "[s]trict local rules of pleading cannot be used to impose unnecessary burdens upon rights of recovery authorized by federal laws." 338 U.S. at 298.

Compare the results in these cases with *Sun Oil Co. v. Wortman*, supra at 480. Do states have greater authority to apply their own procedural rules to causes of action created by other states than to causes of action created by the federal government? Should these situations be treated differently?

Chapter 7

CHOICE OF LAW
IN THE INTERNATIONAL ARENA

A. INTRODUCTION

Although the previous chapters contain several cases, including *Babcock, O'Connor, Milkovich,* and *Neumeier,* involving conflicts between state law and the laws of foreign countries, the focus of those chapters has been on interstate conflicts. It is now time to turn to international conflicts.

Is it safe to say that, at least in the four aforementioned cases, the foreign dimension of the conflict did not have a bearing on either the outcome or the choice-of-law methodology utilized? If yes, was this a coincidence? Was it because in all four cases the foreign country involved was neighboring and friendly Canada, or was it because Canada was not too concerned with the rights of guest-passengers or motorists in general? Are the differences between interstate and international conflicts such as to require or justify a different approach for each category? What is the attitude and practice of American courts towards international conflicts?

These are some of the questions we explore in this chapter. First we examine conflicts between federal law and foreign law, and then conflicts between state law and foreign law.

B. CONFLICTS BETWEEN FEDERAL LAW AND FOREIGN LAW

Lauritzen v. Larsen
Supreme Court of the United States, 1953.
345 U.S. 571, 73 S.Ct. 921, 97 L.Ed. 1254.

Mr. Justice JACKSON delivered the opinion of the Court. The key issue in this case is whether statutes of the United States should be applied to this claim of maritime tort. Larsen, a Danish seaman, while temporarily in New York joined the crew of the Randa, a ship of Danish flag and registry, owned by petitioner, a Danish citizen. Larsen signed ship's articles, written in Danish, providing that the rights of crew members would be governed by Danish law and by the employer's contract with the Danish Seamen's Union, of which Larsen was a member. He was negligently injured aboard the Randa in the course of employment, while in Havana harbor.

Respondent brought suit under the Jones Act[1] on the law side of the District Court for the Southern District of New York and demanded a jury. Petitioner contended that Danish law was applicable and that, under it, respondent had received all of the compensation to which he was entitled. * * * [T]he court ruled that American rather than Danish law applied, and the jury rendered a verdict of $4,267.50. The Court of Appeals, Second Circuit, affirmed. * * * We granted certiorari. * * *

* * * The shipowner, supported here by the Danish Government, asserts that the Danish law supplies the full measure of his obligation and that maritime usage and international law as accepted by the United States exclude the application of our incompatible statute. [Danish law was generally more favorable to the shipowner than United States law, under the circumstances of this case.]

* * * [In arguing for the application of the Jones Act, respondent] relies upon the literal catholicity of its terminology. If read literally, Congress has conferred an American right of action which requires nothing more than that plaintiff be "any seaman who shall suffer personal injury in the course of his employment." It makes no explicit requirement that either the seaman, the employment or the injury have the slightest connection with the United States. Unless some relationship of one or more of these to our national interest is implied, Congress has extended our law and opened our courts to all alien seafaring men injured anywhere in the world in service of watercraft of every foreign nation—a hand on a Chinese junk, never outside Chinese waters, would not be beyond its literal wording.

But Congress in 1920 wrote these all-comprehending words, not on a clean slate, but as a postscript to a long series of enactments governing shipping. All were enacted with regard to a seasoned body of maritime law developed by the experience of American courts long accustomed to dealing with admiralty problems in reconciling our own with foreign interests and in accommodating the reach of our own laws to those of other maritime nations.

The shipping laws of the United States, set forth in Title 46 of the United States Code, 46 U.S.C.A., comprise a patchwork of separate enactments, some tracing far back in our history and many designed for particular emergencies. While some have been specific in application to foreign shipping and others in being confined to American shipping, many give no evidence that Congress addressed itself to their foreign application and are in general terms which leave their application to be judicially determined from context and circumstance. By usage as old as the Nation, such statutes have been construed to apply only to areas and transactions in which American law would be considered operative under prevalent doctrines of international law. * * *

---

1. "Any seaman who shall suffer personal injury in the course of his employment may, at his election, maintain an action for damages at law, with the right of trial by jury, and in such action all statutes of the United States modifying or extending the common-law right or remedy in cases of personal injury to railway employees shall apply * * *." 46 U.S.C. § 688, 46 U.S.C.A. § 688.

This doctrine of construction is in accord with the long-heeded admonition of Mr. Chief Justice Marshall that "an Act of Congress ought never to be construed to violate the law of nations if any other possible construction remains...." The Charming Betsy, 2 Cranch 64, 118 [1804.] * * * This is not, as sometimes is implied, any impairment of our own sovereignty, or limitation of the power of Congress. * * * On the contrary, we are simply dealing with a problem of statutory construction rather commonplace in a federal system by which courts often have to decide whether "any" or "every" reaches to the limits of the enacting authority's usual scope or is to be applied to foreign events or transactions. * * *

Congress could not have been unaware of the necessity of construction imposed upon courts by such generality of language and was well warned that in the absence of more definite directions than are contained in the Jones Act it would be applied by the courts to foreign events, foreign ships and foreign seamen only in accordance with the usual doctrine and practices of maritime law.

Respondent places great stress upon the assertion that petitioner's commerce and contacts with the ports of the United States are frequent and regular, as the basis for applying our statutes to incidents aboard his ships. But the virtue and utility of sea-borne commerce lies in its frequent and important contacts with more than one country. If, to serve some immediate interest, the courts of each were to exploit every such contact to the limit of its power, it is not difficult to see that a multiplicity of conflicting and overlapping burdens would blight international carriage by sea. * * *

* * * Maritime law, like our municipal law, has attempted to avoid or resolve conflicts between competing laws by ascertaining and valuing points of contact between the transaction and the states or governments whose competing laws are involved. The criteria, in general, appear to be arrived at from weighing of the significance of one or more connecting factors between the shipping transaction regulated and the national interest served by the assertion of authority. * * * [I]n dealing with international commerce we cannot be unmindful of the necessity for mutual forbearance if retaliations are to be avoided; nor should we forget that any contact which we hold sufficient to warrant application of our law to a foreign transaction will logically be as strong a warrant for a foreign country to apply its law to an American transaction.

In the case before us, two foreign nations can claim some connecting factor with this tort—Denmark, because, among other reasons, the ship and the seaman were Danish nationals; Cuba, because the tortious conduct occurred and caused injury in Cuban waters. The United States may also claim contacts because the seaman had been hired in and was returned to the United States, which also is the state of the forum. We therefore review the several factors which, alone or in combination, are generally conceded to influence choice of law to govern a tort claim, particularly a maritime tort claim, and the weight and significance accorded them.

1. *Place of the Wrongful Act.*—The solution most commonly accepted as to torts in our municipal and in international law is to apply the law of the place where the acts giving rise to the liability occurred, the *lex loci delicti commissi*. This rule of locality, often applied to maritime torts, would indicate application of the law of

Cuba, in whose domain the actionable wrong took place. The test of location of the wrongful act or omission, however sufficient for torts ashore, is of limited application to shipboard torts, because of the varieties of legal authority over waters she may navigate. * * * [T]he territorial standard is so unfitted to an enterprise conducted under many territorial rules * * * that it usually is modified by the more constant law of the flag. * * * The locality test, for what it is worth, affords no support for the application of American law in this case and probably refers us to Danish in preference to Cuban law, though this point we need not decide, for neither party urges Cuban law as controlling.

2. *Law of the Flag.*—Perhaps the most venerable and universal rule of maritime law relevant to our problem is that which gives cardinal importance to the law of the flag. * * * This Court has said that the law of the flag supersedes the territorial principle, even for purposes of criminal jurisdiction of personnel of a merchant ship, because it "is deemed to be a part of the territory of that sovereignty (whose flag it flies), and not to lose that character when in navigable waters within the territorial limits of another sovereignty." * * * Some authorities reject, as a rather mischievous fiction, the doctrine that a ship is constructively a floating part of the flagstate, but apply the law of the flag on the pragmatic basis that there must be some law on shipboard, that it cannot change at every change of waters, and no experience shows a better rule than that of the state that owns her. * * * These considerations are of such weight in favor of Danish and against American law in this case that it must prevail unless some heavy counterweight appears.

3. *Allegiance or Domicile of the Injured.*—* * * [E]ach nation has a legitimate interest that its nationals and permanent inhabitants be not maimed or disabled from self-support. In some later American cases, courts have been prompted to apply the Jones Act by the fact that the wrongful act or omission alleged caused injury to an American citizen or domiciliary. * * * Admittedly, respondent is neither citizen nor resident of the United States. * * * His presence in New York was transitory and created no such national interest in, or duty toward, him as to justify intervention of the law of one state on the shipboard of another.

4. *Allegiance of the Defendant Shipowner.*—* * * [I]n recent years a practice has grown, particularly among American shipowners, to avoid stringent shipping laws by seeking foreign registration eagerly offered by some countries. Confronted with such operations, our courts on occasion have pressed beyond the formalities of more or less nominal foreign registration to enforce against American shipowners the obligations which our law places upon them. But here again the utmost liberality in disregard of formality does not support the application of American law in this case, for it appears beyond doubt that this owner is a Dane by nationality and domicile.

5. *Place of Contract.*—Place of contract, which was New York, is the factor on which respondent chiefly relies to invoke American law. It is one which often has significance in choice of law in a contract action. But a Jones Act suit is for tort, * * * [and] this action does not seek to recover anything due under the contract or damages for its breach.

The place of contracting in this instance, as is usual to such contracts, was fortuitous. A seaman takes his employment, like his fun, where he finds it; a ship takes on crew in any port where it needs them. The practical effect of making the *lex loci contractus* govern all tort claims during the service would be to subject a ship to a multitude of systems of law, to put some of the crew in a more advantageous position than others, and not unlikely in the long run to diminish hirings in ports of countries that take best care of their seamen.

But if contract law is nonetheless to be considered, we face the fact that this contract was explicit that the Danish law and the contract with the Danish union were to control. * * *

We do not think the place of contract is a substantial influence in the choice between competing laws to govern a maritime tort.

6. *Inaccessibility of Foreign Forum.*—It is argued, and particularly stressed by an amicus brief, that justice requires adjudication under American law to save seamen expense and loss of time in returning to a foreign forum. This might be a persuasive argument for exercising a discretionary jurisdiction to adjudge a controversy; but it is not persuasive as to the law by which it shall be judged. * * * Confining ourselves to the case in hand, we do not find this seaman disadvantaged in obtaining his remedy under Danish law from being in New York instead of Denmark. * * *

7. *The Law of the Forum.*—It is urged that, since an American forum has perfected its jurisdiction over the parties and defendant does more or less frequent and regular business within the forum state, it should apply its own law to the controversy between them. * * * We have held it a denial of due process of law when a state of the Union attempts to draw into control of its law otherwise foreign controversies, on slight connections, because it is a forum state. [cit.]; *Home Insurance Co. v. Dick*, [supra 442]. The purpose of a conflict-of-laws doctrine is to assure that a case will be treated in the same way under the appropriate law regardless of the fortuitous circumstances which often determine the forum. * * *

This review of the connecting factors which either maritime law or our municipal law of conflicts regards as significant in determining the law applicable to a claim of actionable wrong shows an overwhelming preponderance in favor of Danish law. The parties are both Danish subjects, the events took place on a Danish ship, not within our territorial waters. Against these considerations is only the fact that the defendant was served here with process and that the plaintiff signed on in New York, where the defendant was engaged in our foreign commerce. The latter event is offset by provision of his contract that the law of Denmark should govern. * * * [W]e can find no justification for interpreting the Jones Act to intervene between foreigners and their own law because of acts on a foreign ship not in our waters.

In apparent recognition of the weakness of the legal argument, a candid and brash appeal is made by respondent and by amicus briefs to extend the law to this situation as a means of benefiting seamen and enhancing the costs of foreign ship operation for the competitive advantage of our own. We are not sure that the interest of this foreign seaman, who is able to prove negligence, is the interest of all seamen or that his interest is that of the United States. Nor do we stop to inquire which law does whom the greater or the lesser good. The argument is misaddressed. It would be within the proprieties if addressed to Congress. Counsel familiar with the traditional attitude of this Court in maritime matters could not have intended it for us.

The judgment below is reversed and the cause remanded to District Court for proceedings consistent herewith.

Reversed and remanded.

Mr. Justice BLACK agrees with the Court of Appeals and would affirm its judgment. * * *

Hartford Fire Insurance Co. v. California
Supreme Court of the United States, 1993.
509 U.S. 764, 113 S.Ct. 2891, 125 L.Ed.2d 612.

JUSTICE SOUTER. * * * The Sherman Act makes every contract, combination, or conspiracy in unreasonable restraint of interstate or foreign commerce illegal. 26 Stat. 209, as amended, 15 U.S.C. § 1. These consolidated cases present questions about the application of that Act to the insurance industry, both here and abroad. The plaintiffs (respondents here) allege that both domestic and foreign defendants (petitioners here) violated the Sherman Act by engaging in various conspiracies to affect the American insurance market. * * * [A] group of foreign defendants argues that the principle of international comity requires the District Court to refrain from exercising jurisdiction over certain claims against it. We hold that * * * the principle of international comity does not preclude District Court jurisdiction over the foreign conduct alleged.

I. The two petitions before us stem from consolidated litigation comprising the complaints of 19 States and many private plaintiffs alleging that the defendants, members of the insurance industry, conspired in violation of § 1 of the Sherman Act to restrict the terms of coverage of commercial general liability (CGL) insurance available in the United States. Because the cases come to us on motions to dismiss, we take the allegations of the complaints as true.

A. According to the complaints, the object of the conspiracies was to force certain primary insurers (insurers who sell insurance directly to consumers) to change the terms of their standard CGL insurance policies to conform with the policies the defendant insurers wanted to sell. * * * [The complaints alleged a violation of § 1 of the Sherman Act by certain London reinsurers who conspired to: (a) coerce primary insurers in the United States to offer CGL coverage on a claims-made basis, thereby making "occurrence CGL coverage ... unavailable in the State of California for many risks;" (b) limit coverage of pollution risks in North America, thereby rendering "pollution liability coverage ... almost entirely unavailable for the vast majority of casualty insurance purchasers in the State of California;" and (c) limit coverage of seepage, pollution, and property contamination risks in North America, "thereby eliminating such coverage in the State of California."]

C. * * * After the actions had been consolidated for litigation in the Northern

District of California * * * [t]he District Court * * * dismissed the three claims that named only certain London-based defendants, invoking international comity and applying the Ninth Circuit's decision in Timberlane Lumber Co. v. Bank of America, N.T. & S.A., 549 F.2d 597 (1976).

The Court of Appeals reversed. * * * [A]s to the three claims brought solely against foreign defendants, the court applied its Timberlane analysis, but concluded that the principle of international comity was no bar to exercising Sherman Act jurisdiction.

We granted certiorari * * * to address the application of the Sherman Act to the foreign conduct at issue. [cit.]. We now affirm[.] * * *

III. * * * At the outset, we note that the District Court undoubtedly had jurisdiction of these Sherman Act claims, as the London reinsurers apparently concede. See Tr. of Oral Arg. 37 ("Our position is not that the Sherman Act does not apply in the sense that a minimal basis for the exercise of jurisdiction doesn't exist here. Our position is that there are certain circumstances, and that this is one of them, in which the interests of another State are sufficient that the exercise of that jurisdiction should be restrained").[21] Although the proposition was perhaps not always free from doubt, see American Banana Co. v. United Fruit Co., 213 U.S. 347 (1909), it is well established by now that the Sherman Act applies to foreign conduct that was meant to produce and did in fact produce some substantial effect in the United States. [cit.][22] Such is the conduct alleged here: that the London reinsurers engaged in unlawful conspiracies to affect the market for insurance in the United States and that their conduct in fact produced substantial effect.[23] See 938 F.2d, at 933.

According to the London reinsurers, the District Court should have declined to exercise such jurisdiction under the principle of international comity.[24] The Court of Appeals agreed that courts should look to that principle in deciding whether to

---

21. One of the London reinsurers * * * argues that the Sherman Act does not apply to its conduct in attending a single meeting at which it allegedly agreed to exclude all pollution coverage from its reinsurance contracts. * * * [Nevertheless] the allegations, which we are bound to credit, remain that it participated in conduct that was intended to and did in fact produce a substantial effect on the American insurance market.

22. Justice Scalia believes that what is at issue in this litigation is prescriptive, as opposed to subject-matter, jurisdiction. Post, at 2918. The parties do not question prescriptive jurisdiction, however, and for good reason: it is well established that Congress has exercised such jurisdiction under the Sherman Act. See G. Born & D. Westin, International Civil Litigation in United States Courts 542, n. 5 (2d ed. 1992) (Sherman Act is a "prime exampl[e] of the simultaneous exercise of prescriptive jurisdiction and grant of subject matter jurisdiction").

23. Under § 402 of the Foreign Trade Antitrust Improvements Act of 1982 (FTAIA), 96 Stat. 1246, 15 U.S.C. § 6a, the Sherman Act does not apply to conduct involving foreign trade or commerce, other than import trade or import commerce, unless "such conduct has a direct, substantial, and reasonably foreseeable effect" on domestic or import commerce. § 6a(1)(A). The FTAIA was intended to exempt from the Sherman Act export transactions that did not injure the United States economy, [cit.], and it is unclear how it might apply to the conduct alleged here. Also unclear is whether the Act's "direct, substantial, and reasonably foreseeable effect" standard amends existing law or merely codifies it. [cit.]. We need not address these questions here. Assuming that the FTAIA's standard affects this litigation, and assuming further that that standard differs from the prior law, the conduct alleged plainly meets its requirements.

24. Justice Scalia contends that comity concerns figure into the prior analysis whether jurisdiction exists under the Sherman Act. [cit.]. This contention is inconsistent with the general understanding that the Sherman Act covers foreign conduct producing a substantial intended effect in the United States, and that concerns of comity come into play, if at all, only after a court has determined that the acts complained of are subject to Sherman Act jurisdiction. * * * In any event, the parties conceded jurisdiction at oral argument, see supra, at 2908–2909, and we see no need to address this contention here.

exercise jurisdiction under the Sherman Act. Id., at 932. This availed the London reinsurers nothing, however. To be sure, the Court of Appeals believed that "application of [American] antitrust laws to the London reinsurance market 'would lead to significant conflict with English law and policy,'" and that "[s]uch a conflict, unless outweighed by other factors, would by itself be reason to decline exercise of jurisdiction." Id., at 933 (citation omitted). But other factors, in the court's view, including the London reinsurers' express purpose to affect United States commerce and the substantial nature of the effect produced, outweighed the supposed conflict and required the exercise of jurisdiction in this litigation. Id., at 934.

When it enacted the [Foreign Trade Antitrust Improvements Act] FTAIA, 96 Stat. 1246, 15 U.S.C. § 6a, Congress expressed no view on the question whether a court with Sherman Act jurisdiction should ever decline to exercise such jurisdiction on grounds of international comity. See H.R.Rep. No. 97–686, p. 13 (1982) ("If a court determines that the requirements for subject matter jurisdiction are met, [the FTAIA] would have no effect on the court['s] ability to employ notions of comity ... or otherwise to take account of the international character of the transaction") (citing Timberlane). We need not decide that question here, however, for even assuming that in a proper case a court may decline to exercise Sherman Act jurisdiction over foreign conduct (or, as Justice Scalia would put it, may conclude by the employment of comity analysis in the first instance that there is no jurisdiction), international comity would not counsel against exercising jurisdiction in the circumstances alleged here.

The only substantial question in this litigation is whether "there is in fact a true conflict between domestic and foreign law." Societe Nationale Industrielle Aerospatiale v. United States Dist. Court for Southern Dist. of Iowa, 482 U.S. 522, 555, (1987) (Blackmun, J., concurring in part and dissenting in part). The London reinsurers contend that applying the Act to their conduct would conflict significantly with British law, and the British Government, appearing before us as amicus curiae, concurs. [cit.] They assert that Parliament has established a comprehensive regulatory regime over the London reinsurance market and that the conduct alleged here was perfectly consistent with British law and policy. But this is not to state a conflict. "[T]he fact that conduct is lawful in the state in which it took place will not, of itself, bar application of the United States antitrust laws," even where the foreign state has a strong policy to permit or encourage such conduct. Restatement (Third) Foreign Relations Law § 415, Comment j; [cit.]. No conflict exists, for these purposes, "where a person subject to regulation by two states can comply with the laws of both." Restatement (Third) Foreign Relations Law § 403, Comment e. Since the London reinsurers do not argue that British law requires them to act in some fashion prohibited by the law of the United States, [cit.], or claim that their compliance with the laws of both countries is otherwise impossible, we see no conflict with British law. See Restatement (Third) Foreign Relations Law § 403, Comment e, § 415, Comment j. We have no need in this litigation to address other considerations that might inform a decision to refrain from the exercise of jurisdiction on grounds of international comity.

IV. The judgment of the Court of Appeals is affirmed * * * and the cases are remanded for further proceedings consistent with this opinion. It is so ordered.

JUSTICE SCALIA. * * * I dissent from the Court's ruling concerning the extraterritorial application of the Sherman Act. * * *

The Petitioners * * *, various British corporations and other British subjects, argue that certain of the claims against them constitute an inappropriate extraterritorial application of the Sherman Act. It is important to distinguish two distinct questions raised by this petition: whether the District Court had jurisdiction, and whether the Sherman Act reaches the extraterritorial conduct alleged here. On the first question, I believe that the District Court had subject-matter jurisdiction over the Sherman Act claims against all the defendants (personal jurisdiction is not contested). Respondents asserted nonfrivolous claims under the Sherman Act, and 28 U.S.C. § 1331 vests district courts with subject-matter jurisdiction over cases "arising under" federal statutes. As precedents such as *Lauritzen v. Larsen*, [supra], make clear, that is sufficient to establish the District Court's jurisdiction over these claims. * * *

The second question--the extraterritorial reach of the Sherman Act--has nothing to do with the jurisdiction of the courts. It is a question of substantive law turning on whether, in enacting the Sherman Act, Congress asserted regulatory power over the challenged conduct. See EEOC v. Arabian American Oil Co., 499 U.S. 244 (1991) (Aramco) ("It is our task to determine whether Congress intended the protections of Title VII to apply to United States citizens employed by American employers outside of the United States"). If a plaintiff fails to prevail on this issue, the court does not dismiss the claim for want of subject-matter jurisdiction—want of power to adjudicate; rather, it decides the claim, ruling on the merits that the plaintiff has failed to state a cause of action under the relevant statute. * * *

There is, however, a type of "jurisdiction" relevant to determining the extraterritorial reach of a statute; it is known as "legislative jurisdiction," Aramco, supra, 499 U.S., at 253; Restatement (First) Conflict of Laws § 60 (1934), or "jurisdiction to prescribe," 1 Restatement (Third) of Foreign Relations Law of the United States 235 (1987) (hereinafter Restatement (Third)). This refers to "the authority of a state to make its law applicable to persons or activities," and is quite a separate matter from "jurisdiction to adjudicate," see id., at 231. There is no doubt, of course, that Congress possesses legislative jurisdiction over the acts alleged in this complaint: Congress has broad power under Article I, § 8, cl. 3, "[t]o regulate Commerce with foreign Nations," and this Court has repeatedly upheld its power to make laws applicable to persons or activities beyond our territorial boundaries where United States interests are affected. [cit.] But the question in this litigation is whether, and to what extent, Congress has exercised that undoubted legislative jurisdiction in enacting the Sherman Act.

Two canons of statutory construction are relevant in this inquiry. The first is the "longstanding principle of American law 'that legislation of Congress, unless a contrary intent appears, is meant to apply only within the territorial jurisdiction of the United States.'" Aramco, supra. Applying that canon in Aramco, we held that the version of Title VII of the Civil Rights Act of 1964 then in force, [cit.], did not extend outside the territory of the United States even though the statute contained broad provisions extending its prohibitions to, for example, "'any activity, business, or industry in commerce.'" [Aramco], 499 U.S., at 249. We held such "boilerplate language" to be an insufficient indication to override the presumption against extraterritoriality. Id., at 251. The Sherman Act contains similar "boilerplate language," and if the question were not governed by precedent, it would be worth considering whether that presumption controls the outcome here. We have, however, found the presumption to be overcome with respect to our antitrust laws; it is now well established that the Sherman Act applies extraterritorially. [cit.]

But if the presumption against extraterritoriality has been overcome or is otherwise inapplicable, a second canon of statutory construction becomes relevant: "[A]n act of congress ought never to be construed to violate the law of nations if any other possible construction remains." Murray v. Schooner Charming Betsy, 2 Cranch 64, 118 (1804) (Marshall, C.J.). This canon is "wholly independent" of the presumption against extraterritoriality. Aramco, 499 U.S., at 264. It is relevant to determining the substantive reach of a statute because "the law of nations," or customary international law, includes limitations on a nation's exercise of its jurisdiction to prescribe. See Restatement (Third) §§ 401–16. Though it clearly has constitutional authority to do so, Congress is generally presumed not to have exceeded those customary international-law limits on jurisdiction to prescribe.

Consistent with that presumption, this and other courts have frequently recognized that, even where the presumption against extraterritoriality does not apply, statutes should not be interpreted to regulate foreign persons or conduct if that regulation would conflict with principles of international law. * * * [T]he principle was expressed in United States v. Aluminum Co. of America, 148 F.2d 416 (C.A.2 1945), the decision that established the extraterritorial reach of the Sherman Act. In his opinion for the court, Judge Learned Hand cautioned "we are not to read general words, such as those in [the Sherman] Act, without regard to the limitations customarily observed by nations upon the exercise of their powers; limitations which generally correspond to those fixed by the 'Conflict of Laws.'" Id., at 443.

More recent lower court precedent has also tempered the extraterritorial application of the Sherman Act with considerations of "international comity." [cit.] The "comity" they refer to is not the comity of courts, whereby judges decline to exercise jurisdiction over matters more appropriately adjudged elsewhere, but rather what might be termed "prescriptive comity": the respect sovereign nations afford each other by limiting the reach of their laws. That comity is exercised by legislatures when they enact laws, and courts assume it has been exercised when they come to interpreting the scope of laws their legislatures have enacted. It is a traditional component of choice-of-law theory. See J. Story, Commentaries on the Conflict of Laws § 38 (1834) (distinguishing between the "comity of the courts" and the "comity of nations," and defining the latter as "the true foundation and extent of the obligation of the laws of one nation within the territories of another"). Comity in this sense includes the choice-of-law principles that, "in the absence of contrary congressional direction," are assumed to be incorporated into our substantive laws having extraterritorial reach. Romero, supra; see also Lauritzen, supra; Hilton v. Guyot, 159 U.S. 113, 162–166 (1895). Considering comity in this way is just part of determining whether the Sherman Act prohibits the conduct at issue.

In sum, the practice of using international law to limit the extraterritorial reach of statutes is firmly established in our jurisprudence. In proceeding to apply that practice to the present cases, I shall rely on the Restatement (Third) for the relevant principles of international law. Its standards appear fairly supported in the decisions of this Court construing international choice-of-law principles (Lauritzen, Romero, and McCulloch) and in the decisions of other federal courts, especially Timberlane. Whether the Restatement precisely reflects international law in every detail matters little here, as I believe this litigation would be resolved the same way under virtually any conceivable test that takes account of foreign regulatory interests.

Under the Restatement, a nation having some "basis" for jurisdiction to prescribe law should nonetheless refrain from exercising that jurisdiction "with respect to a person or activity having connections with another state when the exercise of such jurisdiction is unreasonable." Restatement (Third) § 403(1). The "reasonableness" inquiry turns on a number of factors including, but not limited to: "the extent to which the activity takes place within the territory [of the regulating state]," id., § 403(2)(a); "the connections, such as nationality, residence, or economic activity, between the regulating state and the person principally responsible for the activity to be regulated," id., § 403(2)(b); "the character of the activity to be regulated, the importance of regulation to the regulating state, the extent to which other states regulate such activities, and the degree to which the desirability of such regulation is generally accepted," id., § 403(2)(c); "the extent to which another state may have an interest in regulating the activity," id., § 403(2)(g); and "the likelihood of conflict with regulation by another state," id., § 403(2)(h). Rarely would these factors point more clearly against application of United States law. The activity relevant to the counts at issue here took place primarily in the United Kingdom, and the defendants in these counts are British corporations and British subjects having their principal place of business or residence outside the United States. Great Britain has established a comprehensive regulatory scheme governing the London reinsurance markets, and clearly has a heavy "interest in regulating the activity," id., § 403(2)(g). [cit.] Finally, § 2(b) of the McCarran-Ferguson Act allows state regulatory statutes to override the Sherman Act in the insurance field, subject only to the narrow "boycott" exception set forth in § 3(b)—suggesting that "the importance of regulation to the [United States]," Restatement (Third) § 403(2)(c), is slight. Considering these factors, I think it unimaginable that an assertion of legislative jurisdiction by the United States would be considered reasonable, and therefore it is inappropriate to assume, in the absence of statutory indication to the contrary, that Congress has made such an assertion.

It is evident from what I have said that the Court's comity analysis, which proceeds as though the issue is whether the courts should "decline to exercise ... jurisdiction," [cit.], rather than whether the Sherman Act covers this conduct, is simply misdirected. I do not at all agree, moreover, with the Court's conclusion that the issue of the substantive scope of the Sherman Act is not in the cases. [cit.]. To be sure, the parties did not make a clear distinction between adjudicative jurisdiction and the scope of the statute. Parties often do not, as we have observed (and have declined to punish with procedural default) before. [cit.] It is not realistic, and also not helpful, to pretend that the only really relevant issue in this litigation is not before us. In any event, if one erroneously chooses, as the Court does, to make adjudicative jurisdiction (or, more precisely, abstention) the vehicle for taking account of the needs of prescriptive comity, the Court still gets it wrong. It concludes that no "true conflict" counseling nonapplication of United States law (or rather, as it thinks, United States judicial jurisdiction) exists unless compliance with United States law would constitute a *violation* of another country's law. [cit.]. That breathtakingly broad proposition, which contradicts the many cases discussed earlier, will bring the Sherman Act and other laws into sharp and unnecessary conflict with the legitimate interests of other countries—particularly our closest trading partners.

In the sense in which the term "conflic[t]" was used in Lauritzen, and is generally understood in the field of conflicts of laws, there is clearly a conflict in this litigation. The petitioners here, like the defendant in Lauritzen, were not compelled by any foreign law to take their allegedly wrongful actions, but that no more precludes a conflict-of-laws analysis here than it did there. [cit.]. Where applicable foreign and domestic law provide different substantive rules of decision to govern the parties' dispute, a conflict-of-laws analysis is necessary. See generally R. Weintraub, Commentary on Conflict of Laws 2-3 (1980); Restatement (First) of Conflict of Laws § 1, Comment c and Illustrations (1934).

Literally the *only* support that the Court adduces for its position is § 403 of the Restatement (Third)—or more precisely Comment e to that provision, which states:

> "Subsection (3) [which says that a State should defer to another state if that State's interest is clearly greater] applies only when one state requires what another prohibits, or where compliance with the regulations of two states exercising jurisdiction consistently with this section is otherwise impossible. It does not apply where a person subject to regulation by two states can comply with the laws of both...."

The Court has completely misinterpreted this provision. Subsection (3) of § 403 (requiring one State to defer to another in the limited circumstances just described) comes into play only after subsection (1) of § 403 has been complied with—i.e., after it has been determined that the exercise of jurisdiction by *both* of the two States is not "unreasonable." That prior question is answered by applying the factors (inter alia) set forth in subsection (2) of § 403, that is, precisely the factors that I have discussed in text and that the Court rejects.

* * *

I would reverse the judgment of the Court of Appeals on this issue, and remand to the District Court with instructions to dismiss for failure to state a claim on the three counts at issue * * *.

Notes and Questions

1. ***"Prescriptive" or Legislative Jurisdiction to Regulate Cases With Foreign Elements***. *Hartford Fire* is one of the Supreme Court's most recent decisions on the extraterritorial reach of federal statutes. Both the majority and the dissenting opinions

agree that Congress has the constitutional authority ("legislative" or "prescriptive" jurisdiction, which is contrasted to "adjudicatory" or "judicial" jurisdiction) to regulate conduct occurring outside the United States. The two sides simply disagree on whether the conduct involved in this case falls within the intended reach of the congressional exercise of that authority. Indeed, from the United States' perspective, there is no doubt that Congress has the constitutional power to regulate, or define the legal significance of, events occurring outside the United States. For example, a perusal of Section 8 of Article I of the Constitution reveals several grants of such power, e.g., to "define and punish Piracies and Felonies committed on the high Seas, and Offenses against the Law of Nations," to "regulate Commerce with foreign Nations," to provide for copyright and patent protection, and to "make all Laws which shall be necessary and proper for carrying into Execution * * * all other Powers vested * * * in the Government of the United States." As *Lauritzen* and *Hartford Fire* indicate, Congress has made extensive use of this power.

2. *Constitutional Limitations on the Extraterritorial Reach of Federal Statutes.* In Chapter 5 we studied the limits that the United States Constitution imposes on the power of the states of the United States to regulate cases with foreign elements. Does the Constitution impose similar limitations on the power of Congress to do likewise? The Full Faith and Credit clause is clearly inapplicable to international conflicts and does not bind the federal government, but what about other constitutional clauses, such as the Due Process clause of the Fifth Amendment? If *Home Insurance Co. v. Dick*, supra at 442, had involved a conflict between Mexican and federal (rather than Texan) law would the outcome have been different? Should it? The Supreme Court has not directly answered this question, but in *Lauritzen* the Court intimated that the judicial application of American law to international conflicts is subject to the restraints of the Due Process clause. (Cf. United States v. Curtiss-Wright Export Corp., 299 U.S. 304 (1936), referring to the President's power to sign executive agreements: "like every other governmental power, must be exercised in subordination to the applicable provisions of the Constitution.") Also, in deciding cases involving criminal statutes, lower courts have assumed that the exercise of congressional power is subject to Due Process limitations, but so far they have not held such exercise to have exceeded those limitations. See, e.g., United States v. Greer, 956 F.Supp. 531, 535 (D.Vt.1997) and authorities cited therein. ("Although it is clear that Congress has the power to enact statutes that exceed the limits of international law, it may not exceed the limits of the due process clause."); United States v. Davis, 905 F.2d 245, 248-49 (9th Cir.1990), *cert. denied*, 498 U.S. 1047 (1991) ("In order to apply extraterritorially a federal criminal statute to a defendant consistently with due process, there must be sufficient nexus between the defendant and the United States so that such application would not be unreasonable or fundamentally unfair."); United States v. Juda, 46 F.3d 961 (9th Cir.1995), *cert. denied sub nom.* Paris v. United States, 514 U.S. 1090, and *cert. denied* 515 U.S. 1169 (1995).

In any event, in most cases in which a party urges the court to apply a federal statute to foreign events, the question is not whether the statute *can* apply to such events but rather whether it should be so applied. In turn, this question depends on congressional intent as evidence by the statute's language and other factors.

3. *Statutes that are Expressly Applicable to Extraterritorial Events.* When a federal statute contains language that clearly makes it applicable to foreign conduct, the prevailing view is that the court must apply it to such conduct even if the application would violate international law. Judge Learned Hand articulated this view in United States v. Aluminum Company of America (*Alcoa*), 148 F.2d 416 (2d Cir.1945):

> We are concerned only with whether Congress chose to attach liability to the conduct outside the United States of persons not in allegiance to it. That being so, the only question open is whether Congress intended to impose the liability, and whether our own Constitution permitted it to do so: as a court of the United States, we cannot look beyond our law.

Id. at 443. Does the last sentence remind you of Brainerd Currie's views? Are these views more defensible in international conflicts than in interstate conflicts?

Congress has enacted several statutes, especially in recent years, that expressly apply to extraterritorial events. The following are some examples.

(a) The Alien Tort Claims Act (ATCA), originally enacted in 1879, confers on federal district courts "original jurisdiction of any civil action by an alien for a tort only, committed in violation of the law of nations or a treaty of the United States." 28 U.S.C. §1350. The ATCA does not expressly confer a cause of action but the courts have interpreted it as creating an independent private cause of action for violations of "well-established, universally recognized, and obligatory" norms of international law. Neither the plaintiff nor the events on which the action is based need have any connection with the United States. As for the defendant, all that is needed is in personam jurisdiction, but tag jurisdiction suffices. See Kadic v, Karadzic, 70 F.3d 232 (2d Cir.1995), *cert. denied*, 116 S.Ct. 2524 (1996) (human rights violations in Bosnia). For other representative cases, see Filartiga v. Pena-Irala, 630 F.2d 876 (2d Cir.1980) (death by torture in Paraguay); In re Estate of Marcos Human Rights Litigation, 978 F.2d 493 (2d Cir.1991), and Hilao v. Estate of Marcos, 103 F.3d 787 (9th Cir.1996) (human rights violations in the Philippines).

(b) The Torture Victim Protection Act (TVPA), which was enacted in 1992 as a statutory note to the ATCA, provides that "an individual who, under actual or apparent authority, or color of law, of any foreign nation (1) subjects an individual to torture * * * or * * * to extrajudicial killing" shall be liable for damages. 28 U.S.C. § 1350 Note. The TVPA expressly confers a substantive cause of action, but does not itself confer federal jurisdiction. For this reason, plaintiffs often invoke both the ATCA and the TVPA. The courts have held that, once jurisdiction is established under the ATCA, the court also has jurisdiction to hear the plaintiff's TVPA claims. Again, neither the plaintiff nor the events on which the action is based need have any connection with the United States. In fact, the Act contemplates foreign plaintiffs, foreign events, and defendants acting under color of *foreign* law, thus excluding defendants who (whether foreign on American) have acted under color of *United States law*. For representative cases, see Alvarez-Machain v. United States, 331 F.3d 604 (9th Cir. 2003) (kidnapping in Mexico); Kadic v. Karadzic, supra; Mehinovic v. Vuckovic, 198 F.Supp.2d 1322 (N.D.Ga.2002) (human rights violations in

Bosnia).

Neither the ATCA nor the TVPA indicate which substantive law determines the availability and amount of damages. Federal courts have applied four different substantive laws, with or without a choice-of-law analysis, to wit: (a) international law; (b) the law of the foreign country in which the underlying events occurred; (c) the law of the American forum state; or (d) federal common law. The courts have awarded both compensatory and punitive damages.

(c) The Federal Anti-Terrorist Act of 1991 (ATA) provides that any United States national injured "by reason of an act of international terrorism may sue therefor in any appropriate district court of the United States and shall recover threefold the damages he or she sustains and the cost of the suit including attorney's fees." 18 U.S.C. § 2333(a). For representative cases applying this Act, see Estates of Ungar v. The Palestinian Authority, 153 F.Supp.2d 76 (D.R.I. 2001).

(d) The Antiterrorist and Effective Death Penalty Act of 1996 (AEDPA) was enacted as an amendment to the Federal Sovereign Immunities Act (FSIA) (28 U.S.C. § 1601 *et seq.*) See 28 U.S.C. § 1605(a)(7). The AEDPA lifts the sovereign immunity of foreign states designated by the U.S. State Department as sponsors of terrorism (Cuba, Iran, Iraq, North Korea, Sudan, and Syria) and provides a cause of action to U.S. citizens killed or injured by acts of terrorism sponsored or aided by these states. For representative cases applying this Act, see Wagner v. Islamic Republic of Iran, 172 F.Supp.2d 128 (D.D.C.2001); Flatow v. Islamic Republic of Iran, 999 F.Supp 1 (D.D.C.1998).

4. *Statutes that are Silent on their Extraterritorial Reach: Statutory Construction*. Like the statutes involved in *Lauritzen* and *Hartford Fire*, most federal statutes are either silent on the question of their extraterritorial reach or contain "boilerplate language" whose "literal catholicity," if taken at face value, would make them applicable to any and all extraterritorial events. In such cases, it is the courts' task to define the extraterritorial reach of these statutes. In discharging this task, *Lauritzen* begins with the premise that the process of delineating the extraterritorial reach of federal statutes is the familiar process of "statutory construction[, a] * * * commonplace in a federal system by which courts often have to decide whether 'any' or 'every' reaches to the limits of the enacting authority's usual scope or is to be applied to foreign events or transactions." Incidentally, does this remind you of the method Cook and Currie proposed (see supra 114, 126, 137-38) and Justice Traynor employed in *People v. One Ford Victoria*, and *Bernkrant v. Fowler (*supra 187, 189)? Do both the majority and the dissenting opinions in *Hartford Fire* subscribe to the above premise, apart from their disagreements on other points? According to Justice Scalia, this interpretative process encompasses two "canons of construction." Did the majority opinions in *Hartford Fire* and *Lauritzen* employ both of those canons?

5. *The Presumption Against Extraterritoriality*. One of the first major cases involving the extraterritorial reach of a federal statute was The Apollon, 22 U.S. (9 Wheat.) 362 (1824), decided by none other than Justice Story, the intellectual father of American conflicts law. Influenced by Huber's views on territorial sovereignty (see supra Ch. 1), Story wrote that "[t]he laws of no nation can justly extend beyond

its own territory, except so far as regards its own citizens." Id. at 370. Relying on this principle and on the "law of nations," Story articulated the following presumption: "[H]owever general and comprehensive the phrases used in our municipal laws may be, they must always be restricted in construction, to places and persons, upon whom the legislature have authority and jurisdiction." Id.

This presumption against extraterritoriality was rigidly applied throughout the 19th century and Justice Holmes reaffirmed it in even stronger terms in American Banana Co. v. United Fruit Co., 213 U.S. 347 (1909), which refused to apply the Sherman Act to an American company's conduct in Costa Rica. Reflecting the choice-of-law philosophy of the time, Holmes said that "[t]he general and almost universal rule is that the character of an act as lawful or unlawful must be determined wholly by the law of the country where the act is done." Id. at 356. Although acknowledging that "[t]his principle was carried to an extreme in *Milliken v. Pratt*" (supra at 30), Holmes concluded that, for a state "to lay hold of the actor, to treat him according to its own notions rather than those of the place where he did the acts, not only would be unjust, but would be an interference with the authority of another sovereign, contrary to the comity of nations." Id.

The presumption against extraterritoriality was applied at least through the first two decades of the 20th century, but was gradually eroded by the so-called "effects doctrine," which is discussed below. Incidentally, did *Lauritzen* employ this presumption? In 1991, the Supreme Court resurrected the presumption in EEOC v. Arabian American Oil Co., 499 U.S. 244 (1991) (*Aramco*). *Aramco* held that Title VII of the Civil Rights Act of 1964 did not apply to allegedly discriminatory employment practices of an American employer against an American employee in Saudi Arabia, because "legislation of Congress, unless a contrary intent appears, is meant to apply only within the territorial jurisdiction of the United States." 499 U.S at 248. *Aramco* was legislatively overruled by the Civil Rights Act of 1991. See 105 Stat. 1077, § 2000e(f). Thereafter, the Court reiterated the presumption against extraterritoriality in two cases decided three months before *Hartford Fire*. See Smith v. United States, 507 U.S. 197 (1993); Sale v. Haitian Centers Council, Inc., 509 U.S. 155 (1993).

The majority opinion in *Hartford Fire* does not contain any reference to *Aramco, Smith,* or *Sale*. Does this mean that the Court has abandoned the presumption against extraterritoriality? If not, should the Court do so? Why, or why not? Is the presumption consistent with contemporary American choice-of-law doctrine and practice as reflected in Chapter 3? Does the presumption square with congressional or presidential pronouncements in the foreign policy field, especially after "September 11," or should this not be a relevant factor?

6. *"International Comity."* Since 1804, American courts have professed adherence to Justice Marshall's pronouncement that "an act of congress ought never to be construed to violate the law of nations if any other possible construction remains." Murray v. Schooner Charming Betsy, 6 U.S. (2 Cranch) 64, 118 (1804). Both *Lauritzen* and Justice Scalia's dissenting opinion in *Hartford Fire* expressly rely on this "canon" of statutory construction. According to Scalia, this canon is "wholly independent" of the presumption against extraterritoriality because it applies

even "if the presumption against extraterritoriality has been overcome or is otherwise inapplicable." What exactly is the source and binding force of this canon? Justice Marshall spoke of the "law of nations," *Lauritzen* spoke of the "prevalent doctrines of international law," Learned Hand spoke of "limitations customarily observed by nations * * * [that] generally correspond to those fixed by the 'Conflict of Laws'," and Justice Scalia spoke of "international comity." Are these concepts synonymous? Is any of them equivalent to the admonition of Restatement (Second) § 6 to consider "the needs of the interstate and *international* systems"? In any event, has the above "canon" survived *Hartford Fire*? The majority opinion contains three grudging statements concerning the role of international comity. Identify those statements and determine their meaning.

Incidentally, while it is debatable whether the language of the Sherman Act itself makes the Act applicable extraterritorially, the language of the Foreign Trade Antitrust Improvements Act of 1982 (FTAIA) (quoted in *Hartford Fire* at n. 23) is much clearer in authorizing the application of the Sherman Act to this case, is it not? If so, can the Supreme Court refuse to apply the Sherman Act on grounds of "international comity"? Even if the FTAIA were unclear on this issue, the fact remains that numerous Supreme Court precedents cited by both opinions in *Hartford Fire* have sanctioned the extraterritorial application of the Sherman Act. In light of those precedents, would it be appropriate to refuse to apply the Sherman Act on grounds of comity, *without* overruling or distinguishing those precedents? Did Justice Scalia distinguish these precedents?

7. ***The "Effects Doctrine."*** After the first two decades of the 20th century and especially after World War II, the presumption against extraterritoriality gradually eroded when courts began to focus on the effects of the conduct at issue rather than on the place of conduct. The leading case on what is now known as the "effects doctrine" is United States v. Aluminum Company of America (*Alcoa*), 148 F.2d 416 (2d Cir.1945), decided by Judge Learned Hand. Historically, however, one of the first articulations of this doctrine was Justice Holmes' statement in Strassheim v. Daily, 221 U.S. 280 (1911), that "[a]cts done outside the jurisdiction, but intended to produce and producing detrimental effects within it, justify a state in punishing the cause of harm." Id. at 284. The Restatement (Second) Foreign Relations Law § 18 (1965) and Restatement (Third) Foreign Relations Law § 402 (1971), both endorse this doctrine, as does Justice Souter's statement in *Hartford Fire* that "the Sherman Act applies to foreign conduct that was meant to produce and did in fact produce some substantial effect in the United States." What are the pros and cons of this doctrine? Is it consistent with contemporary American choice-of-law doctrine in interstate conflicts? For example, is *Bernhard v. Harrah's (*supra at 215) an application of the effects doctrine?

Notice that, as articulated in *Strassheim* and applied in *Hartford Fire*, the effects doctrine presupposes concurrence of two elements: (a) the foreign conduct must have been intended to produce effects in the United States; *and* (b) must have produced such effects in the United States. Does the presence of either one of these elements without the other suffice to sustain the assertion of United States prescriptive jurisdiction? Suppose for example that, in *Hartford Fire*, the London reinsurers: (a) did not intend to target the American insurance market but did in fact affect it adversely; or (b) they did conspire to affect that market but, for some reason, they were unsuccessful. What then? Can there be an effect without effect?

With regard to (a), suppose that a factory located just north of the U.S.-Canadian border negligently emits polluting substances that exceed the quantities permitted by U.S. environmental laws and the effect of this pollution are felt in the United States. May, and should, an American court apply these laws in such a case? See Fettig, *Transboundary Water Pollution*, 117 (advocating criminal prosecution of Mexican polluters under California law).

With regard to (b), note that, under U.S. antitrust law, horizontal price fixing is a per se offense in the sense that a mere agreement to fix prices constitutes the offense even if no effects are shown. See United States v. Cocony-Vacuum Oil Co., 310 US 150, 224. n.59 (1940). Under *Hartford Fire*, may an American court apply this law to a foreign agreement to fix prices in the United States, even if the agreement did not in fact affect prices in the United States? For a case upholding a criminal prosecution of a Japanese defendant for a price-fixing agreement in Japan that was intended to have affect in the United States, see United States v. Nippon Paper Industries, 109 F.3d 1 (1st Cir.1997). However, the prosecution claimed that the agreement did produce such effects in the United States, although it failed to carry its burden of proof upon remand. See United States v. Nippon Paper Industries, 62 F.Supp.2d 173 (D.Mass.1999).

Nippon Paper is the only reported case of criminal prosecution of foreign defendants for foreign conduct violating the Sherman Act. However, since *Hartford Fire*, the Antitrust Division of the U.S. Department of Justice has increased its use of criminal sanctions against foreign companies acting abroad as well as the severity of the sanctions, especially fines. In 1997 and 1998, 90% of the fines the Division collected were imposed on foreign companies, and in 1999, a year in which the Division collected more fines than in the entire history of the Sherman Act, almost all of the fines were assessed against foreign companies acting abroad. In addition, following plea agreements and consent judgments, several foreign executives now serve prison time in the United States for similar conduct. See Ellis, *Extraterritorial Criminal Enforcement of U.S. Antitrust Laws*, 478-79.

The Webb-Pomerene Act of 1918 (15 U.S.C. §§ 61-65) and the Export Trading Act of 1982 (15 U.S.C. §§ 4001-4003, 4011-4021) exempt from the scope of the Sherman Act American companies that enter into price-fixing agreements as long as the agreements are limited to exports and they are filed with the U.S. authorities. Is it appropriate to punish foreign companies for price fixing with regard to imports and to immunize American companies for price fixing with regard to exports? An Australian official has called this "U.S. legislative and judicial imperialism." See Ellis, supra at 479.

German antitrust law provides that it is applicable to "all restraints on competition that have effect within the [German] territory * * * even if they are caused outside of this territory." Gesetz gegen Wettbewerbsbeschränkungen [GWB] § 98(2). In the European Union, Article 81 (formerly 85) of the Treaty of Rome prohibits practices that "have as their object or effect the prevention, restriction, or distortion of competition within the [European Union]." The European Court of Justice upheld the European Commission's imposition of sanctions against foreign companies for foreign anti-competitive conduct that had effects within the Union, but the Court based its decision on the fact that this conduct was "implemented" within the Union through agents of, or parties contracting with, the defendants. See The Wood Pulp Case, [1988] E.C.R. 5193 (1988). Thus, the Court stopped short of adopting the "effects doctrine," although the European Court of First Instance later expressly relied on this doctrine. See Gencor Ltd. v. Commission, [1999] E.C.R. II-753, P90 (1999).

8. *Methodology*. In *Hartford Fire*, Justice Scalia called for a "conflict-of-laws analysis" for determining whether to apply the Sherman Act to foreign conduct. Does this call imply that the *Hartford Fire* majority did not use a conflict-of-laws analysis or that it used an analysis that did not meet with Scalia's approval? Did the majority simply use a "unilateral" rather than a "bilateral" approach? (See supra 9, 11.)

Did *Lauritzen* use a grouping-of-contacts methodology? Notice that *Lauritzen* also spoke of "reconciling our own with foreign interests and * * * accommodating the reach of our own laws to those of other maritime nations." Is this different from an interest analysis tempered by enlightened self-restraint or comparative impairment analysis? From a methodological perspective, what is the difference between the approaches the Court employed in *Lauritzen* and *Hartford Fire*, respectively?

9. *Foreign "Governmental" Interests*. Notice that in both *Lauritzen* and *Hartford Fire* the governments of Denmark and the United Kingdom, respectively, submitted amicus curiae briefs arguing against the application of American law. This is a frequent phenomenon in international conflicts cases that reach the Supreme Court. For pertinent documentation, see Symeonides, *Maritime Conflicts*, 225, 227-28, 246-47. Besides illustrating that "governmental" interests *are* implicated in conflicts disputes involving private parties, does this phenomenon also point to a significant difference between interstate and international conflicts? Should courts be more or less solicitous of the interests of foreign countries than of sister states?

Admittedly, in *Hartford Fire*, the United Kingdom had a great interest in having British law apply, or at least in ensuring that the Sherman Act did not apply. By the same token, California's interest in the application of the Sherman Act was at least as strong, was it not? If yes, then what did the Court mean when it said that there was "no conflict with British law" or when it did not see a "true conflict"? Did the Court use the quoted terms in the same sense as Justice Scalia (or as we have used them in Chapter 3)? The Court stated that since it was not "impossible" for defendants to comply with the laws of both countries, there was no conflict. Is this not too high a threshold for ever applying foreign law? Why, or why not? (One commentator concluded that the Court confused conflict with compulsion. Lowenfeld, *Reflections on the Insurance Antitrust Case*, 42). On the other hand, did Justice Scalia overstate his case when he thought it "unimaginable that an assertion of legislative jurisdiction by the United States would be considered reasonable"?

10. *American "Governmental" Interests*. In interest analysis terminology, how would you classify the conflict in *Lauritzen*? Why? The *Lauritzen* court spoke of

"the national interest served by the assertion of [legislative] authority." Did the United States have an interest in applying the Jones Act in that case? Assisted by two Seamen's Unions, the plaintiff argued that the application of the Jones Act and the resulting imposition of the Act's higher compensation standards on foreign shipowners would promote the interest of the United States in making American shipping competitive with foreign shipping. Predictably, the defendant shipowner and the three foreign governments that filed amicus briefs vehemently disputed this argument. The Court rejected it, saying, *inter alia*, that it should be addressed to Congress. Undoubtedly, the plaintiff's argument was self serving, but was it as far fetched as it sounds? Before you answer, consider the following information.

In 1915, five years before enacting the Jones Act, Congress enacted the Seamen's Act, which, *inter alia*, applies to wages claims of *foreign* seamen serving on *foreign* vessels. See Ch. 153 § 4, 38 Stat. 1165 (1915) (codified as amended at 46 U.S.C. § 597 (1976), repealed in 1983 by Pub. L. 98–99, § 4(b), 97 Stat. 600-604). The stated congressional policy behind this over-expansive reach of American legislative jurisdiction was "to equalize on foreign vessels the burdens placed by American law * * * upon the American merchant marine, by making such foreign vessels * * * subject to regulations affecting American vessels." Brief for the United States as amicus curiae at 4, Strathearn S.S. Co. v. Dillon, 252 U.S. 348 (1920). The United States forcefully advocated this policy in its amicus brief and the Court adopted it in *Strathearn*, a case involving a British seaman and vessel. The Court rejected the argument that the Act should be confined to American seamen, because "such limited construction would have a tendency to prevent the employment of American seamen, and to promote the engagement of those who were not entitled to sue for * * * wages under the provisions of the law." Id. at 355. The Court agreed that "the purpose of Congress [was] to place American and foreign seamen on an equality of right * * * with equal opportunity to resort to the courts of the United States for the enforcement of the act." Id.

Without agreeing with either the wisdom or the effectiveness of this policy, is it not plausible to argue that if Congress thought that the application of the Seamen's Act to foreign seamen's *wage* claims would enhance the operating costs of foreign shipping to the competitive advantage of American shipping, then the application of the Jones Act and the resulting imposition of its much heavier compensation standards on foreign shipping would be a much more efficacious way of attaining the same end? True enough, the Jones Act, unlike the Seaman's Act, did not contain language that expressly made it applicable to foreign shipping. However, as *Lauritzen* said, "Congress in 1920 wrote these all comprehending words [of the Jones Act] not on a clean slate, but as a postscript to a long series of enactments governing shipping," the most recent of which was the 1915 Seamen's Act. Absent a showing of a dramatic change in congressional sentiments, why should one assume that Congress switched from the nationalistic mindset of the Seamen's Act to the internationalist mindset ascribed to the Jones Act by *Lauritzen*? Be that as it may, should not one applaud *Lauritzen* for refusing to apply the Jones Act in that particular case? Why, or why not?

11. **Maritime Conflicts.** In Romero v. International Terminal Operating Co., 358

U.S. 354 (1959), the Court encountered a case that was identical to *Lauritzen*, except that the seaman's injury had occurred while the foreign-flag ship was in American waters. The Court dismissed the argument that the American locus of the injury called for a different result than in *Lauritzen*. The Court reasoned that the plaintiff's recovery "should not depend on the wholly fortuitous circumstances of the place of injury," id. at 384, and that to subject ships to shifting standard of compensation "as the vessel passes the boundaries of territorial waters would be not only an onerous but also an unduly speculative burden, disruptive of international commerce and without basis in the expressed policies of this country." Id. Hellenic Lines Ltd. v. Rhoditis, 398 U.S. 306 (1970), was identical to *Romero*, except that the shipowner, though a foreign national, was also a long-term permanent resident of the United States and had managed his shipping operations out of his offices in New York and New Orleans. Thus, he had an American "base of operations," and this factor--which *Rhoditis* added to the seven *Lauritzen* factors--made the difference and justified the application of American law. The Court noted that the *Lauritzen* test was "not a mechanical one," id. at 308, and that the significance of the eight factors "must be considered in light of the national interest served by the assertion of Jones Act jurisdiction." Id. at 309. Justice Harlan complained that courts tend to be "mesmerized by contacts * * * notwithstanding the purported eschewal of a mechanical application of the *Lauritzen* test." Id. at 318 (Harlan J., dissenting). Half a century after *Lauritzen*, Harlan's statement continues to accurately describe the decisions of most lower courts in maritime conflicts. Although the *Lauritzen* test was a significant improvement over the traditional approach, the test was and is prone to mechanical application in the lower courts. The Court has yet to revisit the matter and thus has not had the opportunity to take account of the progress that American conflicts law has made in the interim. For an attempt to modernize the *Lauritzen* test, see Neely v. Club Med Management Services, Inc., 63 F.3d 166 (3d Cir.1995); Symeonides, *Maritime Conflicts*, 242-64.

C. CONSTITUTIONAL LIMITATIONS ON STATE ACTION IN THE INTERNATIONAL ARENA

American Insurance Ass'n v. Garamendi
Supreme Court of the United States, 2003.
___ U.S. ____, 123 S.Ct. 2374.

JUSTICE SOUTER delivered the opinion of the Court. California's Holocaust Victim Insurance Relief Act of 1999 (HVIRA or Act), Cal. Ins.Code Ann. §§ 13800-13807 (West Cum.Supp.2003), requires any insurer doing business in that State to disclose information about all policies sold in Europe between 1920 and 1945 by the company itself or any one "related" to it. The issue here is whether HVIRA interferes with the National Government's conduct of foreign relations. We hold that it does, with the consequence that the state statute is preempted.

I. A. The Nazi Government of Germany engaged not only in genocide and enslavement but theft of Jewish assets, including the value of insurance policies, and in particular policies of life insurance, a form of savings held by many Jews in Europe before the Second World War. Early on in the Nazi era, loss of livelihood forced Jews to cash in life insurance policies prematurely, only to have the government seize the proceeds of the repurchase, and many who tried to emigrate from Germany were forced to liquidate insurance policies to pay the steep "flight taxes" and other levies imposed by the Third Reich to keep Jewish assets from leaving the country. [cit.] Before long, the Reich began simply seizing the remaining policies outright. In 1941, the 11th Decree of the Reich Citizenship Law declared the confiscation of assets (including insurance policies) of Jews deported to the concentration camps, and two years later the 13th Decree did the same with respect to property of the dead, each decree requiring banks and insurance companies to identify Jewish accounts and transmit the funds to the Reich treasury. After the war, even a policy that had escaped confiscation was likely to be dishonored, whether because insurers denied its existence or claimed it had lapsed from unpaid premiums during the persecution, or because the government would not provide heirs with documentation of the policyholder's death. [cit.] Responsibility as between the government and insurance companies is disputed, but at the end of the day, the fact is that the value or proceeds of many insurance policies issued to Jews before and during the war were paid to the Reich or never paid at all.

These confiscations and frustrations of claims fell within the subject of reparations, which became a principal object of Allied diplomacy soon after the war. * * * The effect of the [post-WW II] Agreements was curtailed, however, and attention to reparations intentionally deferred, when the western allies moved to end their occupation and reestablish a sovereign Germany as a buffer against Soviet expansion. * * * In the meantime, the western allies placed the obligation to provide restitution to victims of Nazi persecution on the new West German Government. * * * West Germany enacted its own restitution laws in 1953 and 1956, [cit.], and signed agreements with 16 countries for the compensation of their nationals, including the Luxembourg Agreement with Israel, [cit.]. Despite a payout of more than 100 billion deutsch marks as of 2000, [cit.], these measures left out many claimants and certain types of claims, and when the agreement reunifying East and West Germany, [cit.], was read by the German courts as lifting the [1953] London Debt Agreement's moratorium on Holocaust claims by foreign nationals, class-action lawsuits for restitution poured into United States courts against companies doing business in Germany during the Nazi era. [cit.]

These suits generated much protest by the defendant companies and their governments, to the point that the Government of the United States took action to try to resolve "the last great compensation related negotiation arising out of World War II." [cit.] From the beginning, the Government's position, represented principally by Under Secretary of State (later Deputy Treasury Secretary) Stuart Eizenstat, stressed mediated settlement "as an alternative to endless litigation" promising little relief to aging Holocaust survivors. SER 953 (press conference by Secretary of State Albright). Ensuing negotiations at the national level produced the German Foundation Agreement, signed by President Clinton and German Chancellor Schroder in July 2000, in which Germany agreed to enact legislation establishing a foundation funded with 10 billion deutsch marks contributed equally by the German Government and German companies, to be used to compensate all those "who suffered at the hands of German companies during the National Socialist era." Agreement Concerning the Foundation "Remembrance, Responsibility and the Future," 39 Int'l Legal Materials 1298 (2000).

The willingness of the Germans to create a voluntary compensation fund was conditioned on some expectation of security from lawsuits in United States courts, and after extended dickering President Clinton put his weight behind two specific measures toward that end. SER 937 (letter from President Clinton to Chancellor Schroder committing to a "mechanism to provide the legal peace desired by the German government and German companies"); [cit.]. First, the Government agreed that whenever a German company was sued on a Holocaust-era claim in an American court, the Government of the United States would submit a statement that "it would be in the foreign policy interests of the United States for the Foundation to be the exclusive forum and remedy for the resolution of all asserted claims against German companies arising from their involvement in the National Socialist era and World War II." 39 Int'l Legal Materials, at 1303. Though unwilling to guarantee that its foreign policy interests would "in themselves provide an independent legal basis for dismissal," that being an issue for the courts, the Government agreed to tell courts "that U.S. policy interests favor dismissal on any valid legal ground." *Id.,* at 1304. On top of that undertaking, the Government promised to use its "best efforts, in a manner it considers appropriate," to get state and local governments to respect the foundation as the exclusive mechanism. *Id.,* at 1300.

As for insurance claims specifically, both countries agreed that the German Foundation would work with the International Commission on Holocaust Era Insurance Claims (ICHEIC), a voluntary organization formed in 1998 by several European insurance companies, the State of Israel, Jewish and Holocaust survivor associations, and the National Association of Insurance Commissioners, the organization of American state insurance commissioners. The job of the ICHEIC, chaired by former Secretary of State Eagleburger, includes negotiation with European insurers to provide information about unpaid insurance policies issued to Holocaust victims and settlement of claims brought under them. It has thus set up procedures for handling demands against participating insurers, including "a reasonable review ... of the participating companies' files" for production of unpaid policies, "an investigatory process to determine the current status" of insurance policies for which claims are filed, and a "claims and valuation process to settle and pay individual claims," employing "relaxed standards of proof." SER 1236-1237.

In the pact with the United States, Germany stipulated that "insurance claims that come within the scope of the current claims handling procedures adopted by the [ICHEIC] and are made against German insurance companies shall be processed by the companies and the German Insurance Association on the basis of such procedures and on the basis of additional claims handling procedures that may be agreed among the Foundation, ICHEIC, and the German Insurance Association." 39 Int'l Legal Materials, at 1299. And in a supplemental agreement formalized in October 2002, the German Foundation agreed to set aside 200 million deutsch marks, to be used for insurance claims approved by the ICHEIC and a portion of the ICHEIC's operating expenses, with another 100 million in reserve if the initial fund should run out. [cit.] The foundation also bound itself to contribute 350 million deutsch marks to a "humanitarian fund" administered by the ICHEIC, and it agreed to work with the German Insurance Association and the German insurers who had joined the ICHEIC, "with a view to publishing as comprehensive a list as possible of holders of insurance policies issued by German companies who may have been Holocaust victims," [cit.]. Those efforts, which control release of information in ways that respect German privacy laws limiting publication of business records, have resulted in the recent release of the names of over 360,000 Holocaust victims owning life insurance policies issued by German insurers. [cit.]

The German Foundation pact has served as a model for similar agreements with Austria and France, and the United States Government continues to pursue comparable agreements with other countries. [cit.]

B. While these international efforts were underway, California's Department of Insurance began its own enquiry into the issue of unpaid claims under Nazi-era insurance policies, prompting state legislation designed to force payment by defaulting insurers. In 1998, the state legislature made it an unfair business practice for any insurer operating in the State to "fai[l] to pay any valid claim from Holocaust survivors." Cal. Ins.Code Ann. § 790.15(a) (West Cum.Supp.2003). The legislature placed "an affirmative duty" on the Department of Insurance "to play an independent role in representing the interests of Holocaust survivors," including an obligation to "gather, review, and analyze the archives of insurers ... to provide for research and investigation" into unpaid insurance claims. §§ 12967(a)(1), (2).

State legislative efforts culminated the next year with passage of Assembly Bill No. 600, 1999 Cal. Stats. ch. 827, the first section of which amended the State's Code of Civil Procedure to allow state residents to sue in state court on insurance claims based on acts perpetrated in the Holocaust and extended the governing statute of limitations to December 31, 2010. Cal.Civ.Proc.Code Ann. § 354.5 (West Cum.Supp.2003). The section of the bill codified as HVIRA, at issue here, requires "[a]ny insurer currently doing business in the state" to disclose the details of "life, property, liability, health, annuities, dowry, educational, or casualty insurance policies" issued "to persons in Europe, which were in effect between 1920 and 1945." Cal. Ins.Code Ann. § 13804(a) (West Cum.Supp.2003). The duty is to make disclosure not only about policies the particular insurer sold, but also about those sold by any "related company," *ibid.*, including "any parent, subsidiary, reinsurer, successor in interest, managing general agent, or affiliate company of the insurer," § 13802(b), whether or not the companies were related during the time when the policies subject to disclosure were sold, § 13804(a). Nor is the obligation restricted to policies sold to "Holocaust victims" as defined in the Act, § 13802(a); it covers policies sold to anyone during that time, § 13804(a). The insurer must report the current status of each policy, the city of origin, domicile, or address of each policyholder, and the names of the beneficiaries, § 13804(a), all of which is to be put in a central registry open to the public, § 13803. The mandatory penalty for default is suspension of the company's license to do business in the State, § 13806, and there are misdemeanor criminal sanctions for falsehood in certain required representations about whether and to whom the proceeds of each policy have been distributed, § 13804(b).

HVIRA was meant to enhance enforcement of both the unfair business practice provision and the provision for suit on the policies in question by "ensur[ing] that any involvement [that licensed California insurers] or their related companies may have had with insurance policies of Holocaust victims are *[sic]* disclosed to the state." § 13801(e); see *ibid.* (HVIRA is designed to "ensure the rapid resolution" of unpaid insurance claims, "eliminating the further victimization of these policyholders and their families"); [cit.] (HVIRA was proposed to "ensure that Holocaust victims or their heirs can take direct action on their own behalf with regard to insurance policies and claims"). While the legislature acknowledged that "[t]he international Jewish community is in active negotiations with responsible insurance companies through the [ICHEIC] to resolve all outstanding insurance claims issues," it still thought the Act "necessary to protect the claims and interests of California residents, as well as to encourage the development of a resolution to these issues through the international process or through direct action by the State of California, as necessary." § 13801(f).

After HVIRA was enacted, administrative subpoenas were issued against several subsidiaries of European insurance companies participating in the ICHEIC. [cit.] Immediately, in November 1999, Deputy Secretary Eizenstat wrote to the insurance commissioner of California that although HVIRA "reflects a genuine commitment to justice for Holocaust victims and their families, it has the unfortunate effect of damaging the one effective means now at hand to process quickly and completely unpaid insurance claims from the Holocaust period, the [ICHEIC]." SER 975. The Deputy Secretary said that "actions by California, pursuant to this law, have already threatened to damage the cooperative spirit which the [ICHEIC] requires to resolve the important issue for Holocaust survivors," and he also noted that ICHEIC Chairman Eagleburger had expressed his opposition to "sanctions and other pressures brought by California on companies with whom he is obtaining real cooperation." *Id.,* at 976. The same day, Deputy Secretary Eizenstat also wrote to California's Governor making the same points, and stressing that HVIRA would possibly derail the German Foundation Agreement: "Clearly, for this deal to work ... German industry and the German government need to be assured that they will get 'legal peace,' not just from class-action lawsuits, but from the kind of legislation represented by the California Victim Insurance Relief Act." *Id.,* at 970. These expressions of the National Government's concern proved to be of no consequence, for the state commissioner announced at an investigatory hearing in December 1999 that he would enforce HVIRA to its fullest, requiring the affected insurers to make the disclosures, leave the State voluntarily, or lose their licenses. ER 1097.

II. After this ultimatum, the petitioners here, several American and European insurance companies and the American Insurance Association (a national trade association), filed suit for injunctive relief against respondent insurance commissioner of California, challenging the constitutionality of HVIRA. The District Court issued a preliminary injunction against enforcing the Act, reflecting its probability judgment that "HVIRA is unconstitutional based on a violation of the federal foreign affairs power and a violation of the Commerce Clause." App. to Pet. for Cert. 110a. On appeal, the Ninth Circuit rejected these grounds for questioning the Act but left the preliminary injunction in place until the District Court could consider whether plaintiffs were likely to succeed on their due process claim. *Gerling Global Reinsurance Corp. of America v. Low,* 240 F.3d 739, 754 (2001).

On remand, the District Court addressed two points. Although it held the Act to be within the State's "legislative jurisdiction," as it applied only to insurers licensed to do business in the State, the District Court granted summary judgment to the petitioners on the ground of a procedural due process violation in "mandating license suspension for non-performance of what may be impossible tasks without allowing for a meaningful hearing." *Gerling Global Reinsurance Corp. of America v. Low,* 186 F.Supp.2d 1099, 1108, 1113 (E.D.Cal.2001). In a second appeal, the same panel of the Ninth Circuit reversed again. While it agreed that the Act was not beyond the State's legislative authority, the Court of Appeals rejected the conclusion that procedural due process required an opportunity for insurers to raise an impossibility excuse for noncompliance with the law, 296 F.3d 832, 845-848 (2002), and it reaffirmed its prior ruling that the Act violated neither the foreign affairs nor the foreign commerce powers, *id.,* at 849. Given the importance of the issue, we granted certiorari, 537 U.S. 1100 (2003), and now reverse.

III. The principal argument for preemption made by petitioners and the United States as *amicus curiae* is that HVIRA interferes with foreign policy of the Executive Branch, as expressed principally in the executive agreements with Germany, Austria, and France. The major premises of the argument, at least, are beyond dispute. There is, of course, no question that at some point an exercise of state power that touches on foreign relations must yield to the National Government's policy, given the "concern for uniformity in this country's dealings with foreign nations" that animated the Constitution's allocation of the foreign relations power to the National Government in the first place. *Banco Nacional de Cuba v. Sabbatino,* 376 U.S. 398, 427, n. 25 (1964); see *Crosby v. National Foreign Trade Council,* 530 U.S. 363, 381-382, n. 16 (2000) ("'[T]he peace of the WHOLE ought not to be left at the disposal of a part'" (quoting The Federalist No. 80, pp. 535-536 (J. Cooke ed.1961) (A.Hamilton))); The Federalist No. 44, p. 299 (J. Madison) (emphasizing "the advantage of uniformity in all points which relate to foreign powers"); The Federalist No. 42, p. 279 (J. Madison) ("If we are to be one nation in any respect, it clearly ought to be in respect to other nations"); see also *First Nat. City Bank v. Banco Nacional de Cuba,* 406 U.S. 759, 769 (1972) (plurality opinion) (act of state doctrine was "fashioned because of fear that adjudication would interfere with the conduct of foreign relations"); *Japan Line, Ltd. v. County of Los Angeles,* 441 U.S. 434, 449 (1979) (negative Foreign Commerce Clause protects the National Government's ability to speak with "one voice" in regulating commerce with foreign countries (internal quotation marks omitted)).

Nor is there any question generally that there is executive authority to decide what that policy should be. Although the source of the President's power to act in foreign affairs does not enjoy any textual detail, the historical gloss on the "executive

Power" vested in Article II of the Constitution has recognized the President's "vast share of responsibility for the conduct of our foreign relations." *Youngstown Sheet & Tube Co. v. Sawyer,* 343 U.S. 579, 610-611 (1952) (Frankfurter, J., concurring). While Congress holds express authority to regulate public and private dealings with other nations in its war and foreign commerce powers, in foreign affairs the President has a degree of independent authority to act. See, *e.g., Chicago & Southern Air Lines, Inc. v. Waterman S.S. Corp.,* 333 U.S. 103, 109 (1948) ("The President ... possesses in his own right certain powers conferred by the Constitution on him as Commander-in-Chief and as the Nation's organ in foreign affairs"); *Youngstown, supra,* at 635-636, n. 2 (Jackson, J., concurring in judgment and opinion of Court) (the President can "act in external affairs without congressional authority" (citing *United States v. Curtiss-Wright Export Corp.,* 299 U.S. 304 (1936))); *First Nat. City Bank v. Banco Nacional de Cuba, supra,* at 767 (the President has "the lead role ... in foreign policy" (citing *Sabbatino, supra*)); *Sale v. Haitian Centers Council, Inc.,* 509 U.S. 155, 188 (1993) (the President has "unique responsibility" for the conduct of "foreign and military affairs").

At a more specific level, our cases have recognized that the President has authority to make "executive agreements" with other countries, requiring no ratification by the Senate or approval by Congress, this power having been exercised since the early years of the Republic. See *Dames & Moore v. Regan,* 453 U.S. 654, 679, 682-683 (1981); *United States v. Pink,* 315 U.S. 203, 223, 230 (1942); *United States v. Belmont,* 301 U.S. 324, 330-331 (1937); see also L. Henkin, Foreign Affairs and the United States Constitution 219, 496, n. 163 (2d ed.1996) ("Presidents from Washington to Clinton have made many thousands of agreements ... on matters running the gamut of U.S. foreign relations"). * * * Given the fact that the practice goes back over 200 years to the first Presidential administration, and has received congressional acquiescence throughout its history, the conclusion "[t]hat the President's control of foreign relations includes the settlement of claims is indisputable." *Pink, supra,* at 240 (Frankfurter, J., concurring); see 315 U.S., at 223-225 (opinion of the Court); *Belmont, supra,* at 330- 331; *Dames & Moore, supra,* at 682.

* * * Generally, * * * valid executive agreements are fit to preempt state law, just as treaties are, and if the agreements here had expressly preempted laws like HVIRA, the issue would be straightforward. See *Belmont, supra,* at 327, 331; *Pink, supra,* at 223, 230-231. But petitioners and the United States as *amicus curiae* both have to acknowledge that the agreements include no preemption clause, and so leave their claim of preemption to rest on asserted interference with the foreign policy those agreements embody. Reliance is placed on our decision in *Zschernig v. Miller,* 389 U.S. 429 (1968).

Zschernig dealt with an Oregon probate statute prohibiting inheritance by a nonresident alien, absent showings that the foreign heir would take the property "without confiscation" by his home country and that American citizens would enjoy reciprocal rights of inheritance there. Two decades earlier, *Clark v. Allen,* 331 U.S. 503 (1947), had held that a similar California reciprocity law "did not on its face intrude on the federal domain," *Zschernig, supra,* at 432, but by the time Zschernig (an East German resident) brought his challenge, it was clear that the Oregon law in practice had invited "minute inquiries concerning the actual administration of foreign law," 389 U.S., at 435, and so was providing occasions for state judges to disparage certain foreign regimes, employing the language of the anti-Communism prevalent here at the height of the Cold War, [cit.]. Although the Solicitor General, speaking for the State Department, denied that the state statute "unduly interfere[d] with the United States' conduct of foreign relations," *id.,* at 434, the Court was not deterred from exercising its own judgment to invalidate the law as an "intrusion by the State into the field of foreign affairs which the Constitution entrusts to the President and the Congress," *id.,* at 432.

The *Zschernig* majority relied on statements in a number of previous cases open to the reading that state action with more than incidental effect on foreign affairs is preempted, even absent any affirmative federal activity in the subject area of the state law, and hence without any showing of conflict. * * *

Justice Harlan, joined substantially by Justice White, disagreed with the *Zschernig* majority on this point, arguing that its implication of preemption of the entire field of foreign affairs was at odds with some other cases suggesting that in the absence of positive federal action "the States may legislate in areas of their traditional competence even though their statutes may have an incidental effect on foreign relations." 389 U.S., at 459 (opinion concurring in result)[.] * * * He would, however, have found preemption in a case of "conflicting federal policy," see *id.,* at 458-459, and on this point the majority and Justices Harlan and White basically agreed: state laws "must give way if they impair the effective exercise of the Nation's foreign policy," *id.,* at 440 (opinion of the Court). * * *

It is a fair question whether respect for the executive foreign relations power requires a categorical choice between the contrasting theories of field and conflict preemption evident in the *Zschernig* opinions, but the question requires no answer here. For even on Justice Harlan's view, the likelihood that state legislation will produce something more than incidental effect in conflict with express foreign policy of the National Government would require preemption of the state law. And since on his view it is legislation within "areas of ... traditional competence" that gives a State any claim to prevail, 389 U.S., at 459, it would be reasonable to consider the strength of the state interest, judged by standards of traditional practice, when deciding how serious a conflict must be shown before declaring the state law preempted. [cit.] Judged by these standards, we think petitioners and the Government have demonstrated a sufficiently clear conflict to require finding preemption here.

IV. A. To begin with, resolving Holocaust-era insurance claims that may be held by residents of this country is a matter well within the Executive's responsibility for foreign affairs. Since claims remaining in the aftermath of hostilities may be "sources of friction" acting as an "impediment to resumption of friendly relations" between the countries involved, *Pink, supra,* at 225, there is a "longstanding practice" of the national Executive to settle them in discharging its responsibility to maintain the Nation's relationships with other countries, *Dames & Moore,* 453 U.S., at 679. The issue of restitution for Nazi crimes has in fact been addressed in Executive Branch diplomacy and formalized in treaties and executive agreements over the last half century, and although resolution of private claims was postponed by the Cold War, securing private interests is an express object of diplomacy today, just as it was addressed in agreements soon after the Second World War. Vindicating victims injured by acts and omissions of enemy corporations in wartime is thus within the traditional subject matter of foreign policy in which national, not state, interests are overriding, and which the National Government has addressed.

The exercise of the federal executive authority means that state law must give way where, as here, there is evidence of clear conflict between the policies adopted by the two. The foregoing account of negotiations toward the three settlement agreements is enough to illustrate that the consistent Presidential foreign policy has been to encourage European governments and companies to volunteer settlement funds in preference to litigation or coercive sanctions. [cit.] As for insurance claims in particular, the national position, expressed unmistakably in the executive agreements signed by the President with Germany and Austria, has been to encourage European insurers to work with the ICHEIC to develop acceptable claim procedures, including procedures governing disclosure of policy information. See German Foundation Agreement, 39 Int'l Legal Materials, at 1299, 1303 (declaring the German Foundation to be the "exclusive forum" for demands against German companies and agreeing to have insurance claims resolved under procedures developed through negotiation with the ICHEIC); [cit.] This position, of which the agreements are exemplars, has also been consistently supported in the high levels of the Executive Branch, as mentioned already, [cit.]. The approach taken serves to resolve the several competing matters of national concern apparent in the German Foundation Agreement: the national interest in maintaining amicable relationships with current European allies; survivors' interests in a "fair and prompt" but nonadversarial resolution of their claims so as to "bring some measure of justice ... in their lifetimes"; and the companies' interest in securing "legal peace" when they settle claims in this fashion. 39 Int'l Legal Materials, at 1304. As a way for dealing with insurance claims, moreover, the voluntary scheme protects the companies' ability to abide by their own countries' domestic privacy laws limiting disclosure of policy information. See Brief for Federal Republic of Germany as *Amicus Curiae* 12-13.[13]

California has taken a different tack of providing regulatory sanctions to compel disclosure and payment, supplemented by a new cause of action for Holocaust survivors if the other sanctions should fail. The situation created by the California legislation calls to mind the impact of the Massachusetts Burma law on the effective exercise of the President's power, as recounted in the statutory preemption case, *Crosby v. National Foreign Trade Council,* 530 U.S. 363 (2000). HVIRA's economic compulsion to make public disclosure, of far more information about far

---

13. The dissent would discount the executive agreements as evidence of the Government's foreign policy governing disclosure, saying they "do not refer to state disclosure laws specifically, or even to information disclosure generally." [cit.] (opinion of GINSBURG, J.). But this assertion gives short shrift to the agreements' express endorsement of the ICHEIC's voluntary mechanism, which encompasses production of policy information, not just actual payment of unpaid claims. The dissent would also dismiss the other Executive Branch expressions of the Government's policy, insisting on nothing short of a formal statement by the President himself. But there is no suggestion that these high-level executive officials were not faithfully representing the President's chosen policy, and there is no apparent reason for adopting the dissent's "nondelegation" rule to apply within the Executive Branch.

more policies than ICHEIC rules require, employs "a different, state system of economic pressure," and in doing so undercuts the President's diplomatic discretion and the choice he has made exercising it. *Id.,* at 376. Whereas the President's authority to provide for settling claims in winding up international hostilities requires flexibility in wielding "the coercive power of the national economy" as a tool of diplomacy, *id.,* at 377, HVIRA denies this, by making exclusion from a large sector of the American insurance market the automatic sanction for noncompliance with the State's own policies on disclosure. "Quite simply, if the [California] law is enforceable the President has less to offer and less economic and diplomatic leverage as a consequence." *Ibid.* (citing *Dames & Moore,* 453 U.S., at 673). The law thus "compromise[s] the very capacity of the President to speak for the Nation with one voice in dealing with other governments" to resolve claims against European companies arising out of World War II. 530 U.S., at 381.

Crosby's facts are replicated again in the way HVIRA threatens to frustrate the operation of the particular mechanism the President has chosen. The letters from Deputy Secretary Eizenstat to California officials show well enough how the portent of further litigation and sanctions has in fact placed the Government at a disadvantage in obtaining practical results from persuading "foreign governments and foreign companies to participate voluntarily in organizations such as ICHEIC." Brief for United States as *Amicus Curiae* 15; * * *. In addition to thwarting the Government's policy of repose for companies that pay through the ICHEIC, California's indiscriminate disclosure provisions place a handicap on the ICHEIC's effectiveness (and raise a further irritant to the European allies) by undercutting European privacy protections. See ER 1182, 3131 (opinions of the German Government that public disclosure of all European insurance policies "is not permissible" under German privacy law); Brief for United States as *Amicus Curiae* 18 (noting protests from the German and Swiss Governments). It is true, of course, as it is probably true of all elements of HVIRA, that the disclosure requirement's object of obtaining compensation for Holocaust victims is a goal espoused by the National Government as well. But "[t]he fact of a common end hardly neutralizes conflicting means," *Crosby, supra,* at 379, and here HVIRA is an obstacle to the success of the National Government's chosen "calibration of force" in dealing with the Europeans using a voluntary approach, 530 U.S., at 380.

B. The express federal policy and the clear conflict raised by the state statute are alone enough to require state law to yield. If any doubt about the clarity of the conflict remained, however, it would have to be resolved in the National Government's favor, given the weakness of the State's interest, against the backdrop of traditional state legislative subject matter, in regulating disclosure of European Holocaust-era insurance policies in the manner of HVIRA.

The commissioner would justify HVIRA's ambitious disclosure requirement as protecting "legitimate consumer protection interests" in knowing which insurers have failed to pay insurance claims. Brief for Respondent 1, 42-44. But, quite unlike a generally applicable "blue sky" law, HVIRA effectively singles out only policies issued by European companies, in Europe, to European residents, at least 55 years ago. Cal. Ins.Code Ann. § 13804(a) (West Cum.Supp.2003); see also § 790.15(a) (mandating license suspension only for "fail[ure] to pay any valid claim from Holocaust survivors"). Limiting the public disclosure requirement to these policies raises great doubt that the purpose of the California law is an evaluation of corporate reliability in contemporary insuring in the State.

Indeed, there is no serious doubt that the state interest actually underlying HVIRA is concern for the several thousand Holocaust survivors said to be living in the State. § 13801(d) (legislative finding that roughly 5,600 documented Holocaust survivors reside in California). But this fact does not displace general standards for evaluating a State's claim to apply its forum law to a particular controversy or transaction, under which the State's claim is not a strong one. "Even if a plaintiff evidences his desire for forum law by moving to the forum, we have generally accorded such a move little or no significance." *Phillips Petroleum Co. v. Shutts,* 472 U.S. 797, 820 (1985); see *Allstate Ins. Co. v. Hague,* 449 U.S. 302, 311 (1981) ("[A] postoccurrence change of residence to the forum State--standing alone--[i]s insufficient to justify application of forum law").

But should the general standard not be displaced, and the State's interest recognized as a powerful one, by virtue of the fact that California seeks to vindicate the claims of Holocaust survivors? The answer lies in recalling that the very same objective dignifies the interest of the National Government in devising its chosen mechanism for voluntary settlements, there being about 100,000 survivors in the country, only a small fraction of them in California. [cit.] As against the responsibility of the United States of America, the humanity underlying the state statute could not give the State the benefit of any doubt in resolving the conflict with national policy.

C. The basic fact is that California seeks to use an iron fist where the President has consistently chosen kid gloves. We have heard powerful arguments that the iron fist would work better, and it may be that if the matter of compensation were considered in isolation from all other issues involving the European allies, the iron fist would be the preferable policy. But our thoughts on the efficacy of the one approach versus the other are beside the point, since our business is not to judge the wisdom of the National Government's policy; dissatisfaction should be addressed to the President or, perhaps, Congress. The question relevant to preemption in this case is conflict, and the evidence here is "more than sufficient to demonstrate that the state Act stands in the way of [the President's] diplomatic objectives." *Crosby, supra,* at 386.

* * *

VI. The judgment of the Court of Appeals for the Ninth Circuit is reversed. *So ordered.*

Justice GINSBURG, with whom Justice STEVENS, Justice SCALIA, and Justice THOMAS join, dissenting. * * *

III. A. The President's primacy in foreign affairs, I agree with the Court, empowers him to conclude executive agreements with other countries. Our cases do not catalog the subject matter meet for executive agreement, but we have repeatedly acknowledged the President's authority to make such agreements to settle international claims. And in settling such claims, we have recognized, an executive agreement may preempt otherwise permissible state laws or litigation. The executive agreements to which we have accorded preemptive effect, however, warrant closer inspection than the Court today endeavors. * * *

* * * The Court states that if the executive "agreements here had expressly preempted laws like HVIRA, the issue would be straightforward." One can safely demur to that statement, for, as the Court acknowledges, no executive agreement before us expressly preempts the HVIRA. Indeed, no agreement so much as mentions the HVIRA's sole concern: public disclosure.

B. Despite the absence of express preemption, the Court holds that the HVIRA interferes with foreign policy objectives implicit in the executive agreements. I would not venture down that path.

The Court's analysis draws substantially on *Zschernig v. Miller*, 389 U.S. 429 (1968). * * * We have not relied on *Zschernig* since it was decided, and I would not resurrect that decision here. The notion of "dormant foreign affairs preemption" with which *Zschernig* is associated resonates most audibly when a state action "reflect[s] a state policy critical of foreign governments and involve[s] 'sitting in judgment' on them." L. Henkin, Foreign Affairs and the United States Constitution 164 (2d ed.1996); * * *. The HVIRA entails no such state action or policy. It takes no position on any contemporary foreign government and requires no assessment of any existing foreign regime. It is directed solely at private insurers doing business in California, and it requires them solely to disclose information in their or their affiliates' possession or control. I would not extend *Zschernig* into this dissimilar domain.

Neither would I stretch *Belmont, Pink*, or *Dames & Moore* to support implied preemption by executive agreement. In each of those cases, the Court gave effect to the express terms of an executive agreement. In *Dames & Moore,* for example, the Court addressed an agreement explicitly extinguishing certain suits in domestic courts. 453 U.S., at 665; [cit.]. Here, however, none of the executive agreements extinguish any underlying claim for relief. [cit.] The United States has agreed to file precatory statements advising courts that dismissing Holocaust-era claims accords with American foreign policy, but the German Foundation Agreement confirms that such statements have no legally binding effect. [cit.] It remains uncertain, therefore, whether even *litigation* on Holocaust-era insurance claims must be abated in deference to the German Foundation Agreement or the parallel agreements with Austria and France. Indeed, ambiguity on this point appears to have been the studied aim of the American negotiating team. See Eizenstat, Imperfect Justice, at 272-273 [2003] (describing the "double negative" that satisfied German negotiators and preserved the flexibility sought by Justice Department litigators).

If it is uncertain whether insurance *litigation* may continue given the executive agreements on which the Court relies, it should be abundantly clear that those agreements leave *disclosure* laws like the HVIRA untouched. * * * [T]he Court invalidates a state disclosure law on grounds of conflict with foreign policy "embod[ied]" in certain executive agreements, although those agreements do not refer to state disclosure laws specifically, or even to information disclosure generally. It therefore is surely an exaggeration to assert that the "HVIRA threatens to frustrate the operation of the particular mechanism the President has chosen" to resolve Holocaust-era claims. If that were so, one might expect to find some reference to laws like the HVIRA in the later-in-time executive agreements. There is none.

To fill the agreements' silences, the Court points to statements by individual members of the Executive Branch. [cit.] But we have never premised foreign affairs preemption on statements of that order. Cf. *Barclays Bank PLC v. Franchise Tax Bd. of Cal.,* 512 U.S. 298 (1994) ("Executive Branch actions--press releases, letters, and *amicus* briefs" that "express federal policy but lack the force of law" cannot render a state law unconstitutional under the Foreign Commerce Clause.). We should not do so here lest we place the considerable power of foreign affairs preemption in the hands of individual sub-Cabinet members of the Executive Branch. Executive officials of any rank may of course be expected "faithfully [to] represen[t] the President's policy," but no authoritative text accords such officials the power to invalidate state law simply by conveying the Executive's views on matters of federal policy. The displacement of state law by preemption properly requires a considerably more formal and binding federal instrument.

Sustaining the HVIRA would not compromise the President's ability to speak with one voice for the Nation. To the contrary, by declining to invalidate the HVIRA in this case, we would reserve foreign affairs preemption for circumstances where the President, acting under statutory or constitutional authority, has spoken clearly to the issue at hand. "[T]he Framers did not make the judiciary the overseer of our government." *Dames & Moore,* 453 U.S., at 660 (quoting *Youngstown Sheet & Tube Co. v. Sawyer,* 343 U.S. 579, 594 (1952) (Frankfurter, J., concurring)). And judges should not be the expositors of the Nation's foreign policy, which is the role they play by acting when the President himself has not taken a clear stand. As I see it, courts step out of their proper role when they rely on no legislative or even executive text, but only on inference and implication, to preempt state laws on foreign affairs grounds.

In sum, assuming, *arguendo,* that an executive agreement or similarly formal foreign policy statement targeting disclosure could override the HVIRA, there is no such declaration here. Accordingly, I would leave California's enactment in place, and affirm the judgment of the Court of Appeals.

Notes and Questions

1. *Zschernig: Preemption in Extremis.* "There is, of course, no question that at some point an exercise of state power that touches on foreign relations must yield to the National Government's policy, given the 'concern for uniformity in this country's dealings with foreign nations' that animated the Constitution's allocation of the foreign relations power to the National Government in the first place." So said the Court in *Garamendi.* Indeed, there is no question on the main point, but the problem is, "of course," that the Constitution does not fully answer the question of exactly when a state law must yield to the federal government's *policy.* The Constitution designates the President as Commander in Chief (Art. II, § 2), places within his executive power the conduct of diplomacy, including the power to

negotiate treaties (Art. II, § 2), and gives Congress power "to regulate Commerce with foreign Nations" as well as a panoply of financial and war powers to support the conduct of foreign policy (Const. Art I, § 8). However, the Constitution expressly prohibits states from engaging only in the most direct foreign policy activities: "enter[ing] into any Treaty, Alliance, or Confederation * * * Agreement or Compact with * * * another Power or engag[ing] in War[.]" (Art. I, § 10). Moreover, the supremacy clause (Art. VI) provides that state law must yield to the Constitution, federal laws, and treaties, but says nothing about federal *policies*, at least policies not embodied in laws, treaties or, as per the Court's jurisprudence, presidential executive agreements.

Even so, in *Zschernig v. Miller*, the Supreme Court held that an Oregon statute was preempted by the nation's foreign policy, even though (a) the statute was on a subject (inheritance) that the Tenth Amendment reserves to the legislative competence of states; (b) the federal policy was not expressed in any particular document; and (c) the federal government had formally stated that the statute did not interfere with the conduct of foreign affairs. In a concurring opinion, Justice Stewart opined that it should be immaterial whether the federal government had articulated a position on the subject.

> We deal here with the basic allocation of power between the States and the Nation. Resolution of so fundamental a constitutional issue cannot vary from day to day with the shifting winds at the State Department. Today, we are told, Oregon's statute does not conflict with the national interest. Tomorrow it may. But, however that may be, the fact remains that the conduct of our foreign affairs is entrusted under the Constitution to the National Government, not to the probate courts of the several States.

Zschernig, 389 U.S. at 443 (Stewart J., concurring).

In an opinion concurring in the result, Justice Harlan criticized the majority for striking down the statute not because of what it provided but rather because it "afford[ed] state court judges an opportunity to criticize in dictum the policies of foreign governments, and that these dicta may adversely affect our foreign relations." 389 U.S. at 461. He found this reason to be untenable "because logically it would apply to many other types of litigation which come before the state courts." Id. After all, said Harlan, "judges have been known to utter dicta critical of foreign governmental policies even in purely domestic cases, so that the mere possibility of offensive utterances can hardly be the test." Id. He then offered three examples of situations in which judges "inquire into the administration of foreign law": (a) before recognizing a foreign-country judgment, judges inquire on whether the judgment "was rendered under a system which does not provide impartial tribunals or procedures compatible with the requirements of due process of law" (see infra Ch. 12); (b) in ascertaining the content of foreign law, judges inquire as to how that law is actually administered by the foreign authorities ("law in action" as opposed the "law in the books"); and (c) courts may refuse to apply the law of a foreign country that is shown to be "uncivilized." Id. at 461–62. See also *Walton*, supra 105 (Ch. 2). One can add more examples, such as when, under the *ordre public* exception, a court examines the argument that the foreign law or judgment is "repugnant," "obnoxious" or "shocking" to the forum's sense of justice and fairness (see supra 87 (Ch. 2) and infra 846 (Ch. 12)), or when, in a forum non conveniens analysis, the court inquires into the true availability of an alternative forum in another country. Did Justice Harlan make a good case that inquiring into the actual administration of foreign law is a widespread practice in American conflicts law? If yes, did *Zschernig* outlaw this practice because of the possibility that such practice may have a bearing on the conduct of foreign affairs?

Be that as it may, *Zschernig* represents the Court's most assertive position on the whole question of foreign-affairs preemption of state law. For an incisive contemporaneous critique, see Linde, *A New Foreign-Relations Restraint*, 594-607. Short of repudiating *Zschernig*, the Court could not avoid the result it reached in *Garamendi*, since in the latter case, the foreign policy was embodied in an executive agreement, albeit one that did not by its language preempt state law.

2. ***Garamendi***. What is the status of *Zschernig* after *Garamendi*? What is the test for determining "[the] point [at which] an exercise of state power that touches on foreign relations must yield to the National Government's policy," when, in other words, the state law crosses the forbidden line? The fact that the pertinent foreign policy was embodied in a presidential executive agreement made the preemption question easier in *Garamendi* than in *Zschernig* and narrowed the disagreements between the two sides. Did Justice Ginsburg concede that an executive agreement that expressly purports to preempt state law automatically prevails over state law? If it is true that federal *policy* preempts state law, why should it matter where or how that policy is expressed? Does a statement by the President (e.g., in his State of the Union address) or by the Secretary of State suffice? Compare United States v. Pink, 315 U.S. 203, 230-31 ("state law must yield when it is inconsistent with, or impairs * * * the superior Federal policy *evidenced by a treaty or international compact or agreement*." (Emphasis added.) In *Garamendi*, the California statute was enacted before the President signed the executive agreements. Should not this be a relevant factor? Finally, if the agreement contains preemptive language, does the agreement prevail over any state law that deals with the same subject, even if the two do not conflict? Conversely, if as in *Garamendi* the agreement does not contain preemptive language, then does the majority opinion require a showing that the state law conflicts with the agreement before declaring the state law invalid?

3. An eminent student of the law of foreign affairs, Professor Harold Maier, notes that "[t]he principle of federalism echoes a fundamental principle of democracy: that governmental decisions made at the local level are more likely to reflect the will of the people most directly affected by them," and that "decisions in cases involving possible state intrusion into foreign affairs must continue to strike an appropriate balance between preservation of the values of local self-government and the need for national uniformity in matters of international affairs." Maier, *Preemption of State Law*, 837. In seeking this balance, says Maier, courts should consider the following questions:

(1) Does the limited constituency of the state provide an appropriate political context in which to make the policy judgment required to reach a decision?

(2) Is the pertinent information that must be weighed to determine the wisdom of the policy decision available to the state decision maker(s)?

(3) Will any possible adverse effects of the decision fall upon the entire nation or be localized within the state making the decision?

Id. at 838. If the answer to any one of these questions points away from the state, the state law is preempted, otherwise it should be upheld, provided it otherwise lies within the state's Tenth Amendment competence. Id. at 839. Is this a sound formula? Why, or why not? Did *Garamendi* engage in a similar balancing act?

4. The communist regimes that succeeded the Nazis in the countries of Eastern Europe continued the "theft of Jewish assets, including the value of insurance policies" that *Garamendi* described with regard to Germany. Many of the victims' descendants who live in the United States have filed lawsuits in the United States against the insurance companies involved. See, e.g., In re Assicurazioni Generali S.p.A. Holocaust Insurance Litigation, 228 F.Supp.2d 348 (S.D.N.Y.2002). The President has not signed executive agreements with those countries. To the extend that these lawsuits rely on statutes like California's HVIRA, does *Garamendi* foreclose the outcome of these lawsuits? To the extent that these lawsuits depend on common law or statutes other than HVIRA-type statutes, does *Garamendi* foreclose the outcome of these lawsuits? Note that the reason *Zschernig* invalidated the Oregon statute was not that the statute itself interfered with the conduct of foreign affairs (the Court had earlier upheld a similar California statute). Rather it was because it provided courts with the opportunity to criticize the communist regimes of Eastern Europe, and that criticism had the potential of interfering with the conduct of foreign affairs. Does the same logic apply to these new lawsuits against former communist and now friendly nations, or has *Garamendi* repudiated that logic?

5. *Due Process Limitations*. At least seven other states (Arizona, Florida, Maryland, Minnesota, New York, Texas, and Washington) have enacted statutes similar to California's HVIRA. Are these statutes vulnerable to a Due Process challenge of the type mounted in, e.g., *Allstate Ins. v. Hague* (supra Ch.5)? In *Garamendi*, the Ninth Circuit answered this question in the negative (see Gerling Global Reinsurance Corp. of America v. Low, 296 F.3d 832 (9th Cir.2002)), but the Eleventh Circuit answered it in the affirmative in an action filed by the same insurance companies. See Gerling Global Reinsurance Corp. of America v. Gallagher, 267 F.3d 1228 (11th Cir.2001). Florida had argued that, since these companies did business in Florida, they had sufficient contacts with Florida to permit regulation by Florida. The court rejected the argument, pointing out that what is needed is not only sufficient contacts with the affected party, but also sufficient contacts with the *subject* of the state's regulation. In this case, the subject was the foreign practices of foreign insurers (the plaintiffs' German affiliates) who had no connection with Florida. Thus, the court concluded, "[t]he reporting provisions violate Due Process to that extent, *regardless* of whether there are minimum contacts between the State of Florida and these particular plaintiffs, the (nominally) regulated parties." Id. at 1238 (emphasis in original).

The Ninth Circuit distinguished *Gallagher* on the ground that (a) the Florida statute obligated directly both Florida *and foreign* insurers to provide information, whereas the California statute in *Garamendi/Low* required information from the California insurers only; and (b) the Florida statute imposed substantive obligations on the insurers, whereas the California statute did not *itself*[14] impose such obligations but was merely a "reporting statute." *Low*, 296 F.3d at 839. As such, the California statute passed constitutional muster, the court reasoned, because: (1) it did not directly regulate foreign companies, and thus it was not necessary to show the existence of minimum contacts with those companies; and (2) it did not purport to regulate the substance of foreign transactions, and thus it was not necessary to show the existence of "significant contacts" under *Allstate Ins. Co. v. Hague*, supra Ch. 5.

If the Supreme Court were to decide the Due Process issue, do you think that the Court would uphold the Ninth Circuit or the Eleventh Circuit decision? Would it be possible to uphold both decisions?

6. As noted earlier, a self-executing federal treaty preempts state law. Moreover, the Court has held that the federal government's treaty power may extend into matters that the Tenth Amendment reserves to the law-making competence of states. See Missouri v. Holland, 252 U.S. 416 (1920). For example, in Hauenstein v. Lynham, 100 U.S. (10 Otto) 483 (1879), the Court upheld against a Tenth Amendment challenge the 1850 Swiss–U.S. treaty on inheritance that was involved in *Estate of Wright (*supra 69). To the extent that the states can be said to have an indirect voice--through the Senate's advice and consent--in the treaty making process this result is palatable, is it not? Does the Tenth Amendment limit the preemptive effect of executive agreements in which there was no congressional participation?

7. *The Act of State Doctrine* is a judicially-created doctrine derived from federal powers over foreign affairs. It provides that American courts, state or federal, "will generally refrain from examining the validity of a taking by a foreign state of property within its own territory, or from sitting in judgment on other acts of a governmental character done by a foreign state within its own territory and applicable there." Restatement (Third) of Foreign Relations Law, § 443 (1987). The Supreme Court enunciated this doctrine in Underhill v. Hernandez, 168 U.S. 250 (1897), which affirmed a dismissal of a suit for damages brought by a U.S. citizen against a former Venezuelan military commander who was responsible for the plaintiff's wrongful detention during a coup in Venezuela. Relying mostly on notions of international comity, the Court declared:

> Every sovereign State is bound to respect the independence of every other sovereign State, and the courts of one country will not sit in judgment on the acts of the government of another done within its own territory. Redress of grievances by reason of such acts must be obtained through the means open to be availed of by sovereign powers as between themselves.

Id. at 252. Building on *Underhill* and intervening cases, the Supreme Court in Banco Nacional de Cuba v. Sabbatino, 376 U.S. 398 (1964), explained the act of state

---

14. Together with HVIRA, California added new provisions to its Civil Procedure and Insurance codes, which: (a) allowed Californians to sue on Holocaust-era policies; (a) extended the statute of limitations to 2011; and authorizes suspending the license of any insurer who fails to pay on valid Holocaust-era policies. However, in earlier litigation, the court held that the insurers who were plaintiffs in *Low* lacked standing to challenge these provisions.

doctrine in terms of domestic separation-of-powers principles. *Sabbatino* arose out of a suit by a state-owned Cuban bank seeking payment for sugar it had sold to a U.S. broker. The broker refused payment, and instead paid the proceeds to a U.S. receiver, on the ground that the bank's title to the sugar was invalid, having been derived from the Cuban government's 1960 expropriations of U.S. owned properties, which expropriations, the broker argued, were illegal under international law. The district court agreed with this argument, but the Supreme Court reversed. The Court declared that "the Judicial Branch will not examine the validity of a taking of property within its own territory by a foreign sovereign government, extant and recognized by this country at the time of suit, * * * even if the complaint alleges that the taking violates customary international law." Id. at 428. The Court also explained that the act of state doctrine is a matter of federal common law because the problems surrounding the doctrine are "intrinsically federal." Id. at 427. Thus, the doctrine is binding on state courts ("the rules of international law should not be left to divergent and perhaps parochial state interpretations," id. at 425), as well as on federal courts, even in diversity cases. Is *Zschernig* an application of the act of state doctrine?

This doctrine has been described as a "limitation on the exercise of * * * adjudicatory jurisdiction, * * * [as] a mechanism of judicial abstention to allow the judiciary prudentially to avoid litigating a foreign sovereign's public conduct committed within its territory * * * [and thus] avoid being enmeshed in matters of foreign affairs which could risk embarrassment to the executive." Oliver et al., *The International Legal System*, 624. However, the doctrine has also been described as "a special rule of conflict of laws" that functions in a way that displaces the *ordre public* reservation. Restatement (Third) § 443, Reporter's Note 1. As the Reporter of the Restatement (Third) opines:

> The normal rule of choice of law in most act of state cases would point to application of the law of the state where the act took place; that rule may be disregarded in certain instances where the law thus chosen would violate the strong public policy of the forum, e.g., a policy against expropriation without compensation. [cit.] The act of state doctrine requires a court to disregard that public policy and to give effect to the foreign law.

Id. W.S. Kirkpatrick & Co. v. Environmental Tectonics Corp., 493 U.S. 400 (1990), which is the Supreme Court's latest pronouncement on the doctrine, seems to lend support to the above view. Although the Court held the doctrine inapplicable because this case did not require passing judgment on the validity of the acts of a foreign government, the Court thought it necessary to explain that "the act of state is not some vague doctrine of abstention but [rather] a '*principle of decision* binding on federal and state courts alike.'" Id. at 406 (quoting from *Sabbatino*, emphasis in original). After reiterating the obligation of American courts to decide cases properly presented to them, the Court said:

> The act of state doctrine does not establish an exception [from the above obligation] for cases and controversies that may embarrass foreign governments, but merely requires that, in the process of deciding, the acts of foreign sovereigns taken within their own jurisdiction shall be deemed valid.

Id. at 408. The precise scope of this "principle of decision" is defined by a series of

Supreme Court decisions, as well as unreviewed lower court decisions, that suggest that this principle may not be as broad as the above formulation implies. For example, although the Supreme Court has not produced a majority opinion defining the exceptions to the act of state doctrine, it has been assumed that the doctrine does not apply to "commercial acts" of foreign states, or to cases in which the executive branch informs the court that adjudication of the case will not impede the conduct of foreign affairs. For an in-depth exposition of the scope of, and exceptions to, the act of state doctrine, see Born, *International Civil Litigation*, 685–752; Oliver et al., *The International Legal System*, 623–71.

8. ***The Doctrine of Foreign Sovereign Compulsion*** provides that American law will not be applied to forbid conduct that is compelled by the law of the place of the conduct, or to require conduct that is prohibited by the law of the place of conduct. See Restatement (Third), § 441; Interamerican Refining Corp. v. Texaco Maracaibo, Inc., 307 F.Supp. 1291 (D.Del.1970). Would the defendants in *Hartford Fire* qualify for the protection of this doctrine? Notice that the defendants argued that their conduct in London was simply "lawful" under British law, not that it was "compelled" by that law. Thus, as Justice Souter retorted, it was not "impossible" for them to comply with both British and American law.

Is the doctrine of Foreign Sovereign Compulsion: (a) an international limitation on national legislative jurisdiction; (b) a self-imposed national limitation with constitutional underpinnings motivated by respect for foreign sovereignty and international comity; or (c) a flexible choice-of-law rule motivated by concerns of fairness to private parties? Returning to *Hartford Fire*, suppose that the defendant's conduct had been compelled by British law, but, as in the actual case, that conduct was intended to and did produce direct and substantial effects in the United States. (If this scenario is not realistic, assume that the conduct took place in a country engaging in "commercial warfare" with the United States.) Should the Sovereign Compulsion Doctrine apply in such a case? Is government-sponsored commercial warfare less objectionable or dangerous than private commercial warfare?

9. ***The Foreign Commerce Clause***. "The Congress shall have Power To * * * regulate Commerce with foreign Nations, and among the several States," says Section 8 of Article I of the Constitution. Is this power different, broader or narrower, with regard to foreign commerce than with regard to interstate commerce? Does the above-quoted clause restrict the power of states to affect foreign commerce more than their power to affect interstate commerce? The Supreme Court has answered this question in the affirmative. See, e.g., Japan Line Ltd. v. County of Los Angeles, 441 U.S. 434, 445-50 (1979); Container Corporation of America v. Franchise Tax Board, 463 U.S. 159 (1983). What do you think accounts for this difference?

10. ***State Courts and Foreign Relations***. In Patrickson v. Dole Food Co., Inc., 251 F.3d 795 (9th Cir.2001), workers from Costa Rica, Ecuador, Guatemala, and Panama filed a class action against Dole and other major food and chemical companies claiming that they suffered injuries from being exposed to toxic pesticides used or manufactured by the defendants. This is one of many similar actions filed by foreign agricultural workers, with uneven success. In some of these cases the

plaintiffs obtained large awards, while in other cases the defendants obtained forum non conveniens dismissals. See, e.g., Delgado v. Shell Oil Co., 231 F.3d 165 (5th Cir.2000), *cert. denied*, 532 U.S. 972 (2001); Sibaja v. Dow Chem. Co., 757 F.2d 1215 (11th Cir.1985); Lowry & Frank, *Exporting Banned Pesticides*, 140.

    Patrickson was initially filed in state court in Hawaii and, because Dole is a Hawaii corporation, the action could not be removed to federal court on diversity grounds. Dole sought removal on federal-question jurisdiction grounds, arguing that the case implicated "the 'uniquely federal' interest in foreign relations, and so it must be heard in a federal forum," *Patrickson*, 251 F.3d at 801, because, by granting relief, American courts would "damage the banana industry--one of the most important sectors of [foreign] countries' economies." Id. at 800. The Second, Fifth, and Eleventh Circuits have accepted this argument in similar cases. See Republic of Philippines v. Marcos, 806 F.2d 344 (2d Cir.1986); Torres v. Southern Peru Copper Corp., 114 F.3d 540 (5th Cir.1997); Pacheco de Perez v. AT & T Co., 139 F.3d 1368 (11th Cir.1998). However, the *Patrickson* court concluded that the other circuits had misinterpreted *Banco Nacional de Cuba v. Sabbatino*, supra, which held that cases involving foreign relations should be governed by a uniform federal common law but did not hold that those cases must be decided only in the federal courts. *Patrickson* reasoned that state courts are as competent to apply federal law as the federal courts. If state courts are wrong, the Supreme Court can correct them, thus ensuring nationwide uniformity with regard to foreign relations. *Patrickson*, 251 F.3d at 802. Although Congress could grant to federal courts exclusive jurisdiction over all matters pertaining to foreign relations, it has chosen not to do so. The court reasoned that, given the congressional silence, there was no reason to judicially assert federal-question jurisdiction over a case "simply because a foreign government has expressed a special interest in its outcome," id. at 803, or because its interests may be affected, however indirectly, by the outcome. After all, said the court,

> [t]hat the case is litigated in federal court, rather than in state court, will not reduce the impact of the decision on the foreign government. Federal judges, like state judges, cannot dismiss a case because a foreign government finds it irksome, nor can they tailor their rulings to accommodate a non-party. Federal judges, like state judges, are bound to decide cases before them according to the rule of law.

Id. The Supreme Court affirmed *Patrickson* with regard to other issues raised by Dole's co-defendants, the manufacturers of the pesticides. See Dole Food Co. v. Patrickson, ___ U.S. ___, 123 S.Ct. 1655 (2003). However, Dole did not seek review of the issues discussed above, and thus the Court did not address them.

    10. *Federal Law for State/Foreign Law Conflicts?* Does Congress have the constitutional power to enact a comprehensive choice-of-law statute binding the states on how to resolve state/foreign law conflicts? Does Congress have such power with regard to interstate conflicts? If the answers to the first question is "no" and to the second question "yes," is this paradoxical? Why, or why not? If the answer to the first question is "yes," then on which constitutional clause would Congress' power rest?

D. CONFLICTS BETWEEN STATE LAW AND FOREIGN LAW

D'Agostino v. Johnson & Johnson, Inc.
Supreme Court of New Jersey, 1993.
133 N.J. 516, 628 A.2d 305.

[Plaintiff, a United States citizen domiciled in Switzerland, was hired in that country by Cilag, a Swiss subsidiary of defendant Johnson & Johnson (J & J), a New Jersey corporation engaged in the manufacture of pharmaceuticals. The contract was an at-will employment contract and contained a choice of Swiss law. Among plaintiff's duties was the registration with the Swiss authorities of new pharmaceuticals produced by Cilag for J & J. Such registration was one prerequisite for eventually obtaining FDA permission for the sale of these products in the United States. During the Swiss registration process, plaintiff was instructed by his Cilag supervisor, a Swiss citizen, to pay certain sums described as "consulting fees" to a member of the Swiss regulatory agency, the "College of Experts." Perceiving the payment to be a bribe, plaintiff refused to do so and was fired. He filed a wrongful termination suit in New Jersey against J & J, alleging that its executive officers in New Jersey had "orchestrated" both the payment of the bribe and his retaliatory firing for refusing to pay it. If proven, this conduct would be in direct violation of the Federal Corrupt Practices Act (FCPA), which had been "incorporated" into New Jersey law by New Jersey precedents. Such violation would have rendered the plaintiff's discharge unlawful under New Jersey law. Under Swiss law, the alleged bribes would be considered "consulting fees" and the plaintiff's discharge would be lawful. The trial court applied New Jersey law and granted partial judgment for plaintiff. The Appellate Division reversed, applying Swiss law.]

O'HERN, J. * * * In this appeal we must consider the question * * * whether Swiss or domestic law governs the claims asserted in the New Jersey forum against a New Jersey corporation and its officers. We hold that because the underlying controversy 1) involves an alleged violation in New Jersey of the Foreign Corrupt Practices Act, 15 U.S.C.A. §§ 78dd-1 to-2 (hereinafter FCPA), which sets forth a domestic policy against bribery of a foreign regulatory official; 2) involves the participation of a United States citizen who might have been exposed to criminal prosecution had the conduct violated the FCPA and was an alleged violation of a New Jersey corporation's internal policy against such overseas commercial bribery; and 3) because violation of the governmental policies could have an indirect effect on the domestic market for pharmaceutical products and the health and welfare of this forum's citizens, New Jersey's interests in resolving this dispute under its laws outweigh the Swiss interest in the at-will employment relationship that would not seek to deter such conduct through its civil law. * * *

III. The determinative law is "that of the state with the greatest interest in governing the *particular issue*" and that the "*qualitative*, not the quantitative, nature of a state's contacts ultimately determines whether its law should apply." *Veazey* [v. Doremus, 103 N.J. 244,] at 248, 510 A.2d 1187 (1986), (emphasis added). In their

Appellate Division brief, defendants pose the issue this way: "There is a single fact that is dispositive of this appeal and that fact is undisputed: the employment relationship at issue was a Swiss employment relationship. New Jersey has no cognizable interest in regulating Swiss employment relationships." Of course that is true. New Jersey has no interest in regulating Swiss employment relationships. But this case is not about regulating just Swiss employment relationships. It is as much about regulating the conduct of parent companies in New Jersey that engage in corrupt practices through a subsidiary's employees. For the "particular issue" here is the tort liability of a domestic corporation for ordering and directing the discharge of a subsidiary's employee for the refusal to participate in corrupt practices. That issue is not encapsulated within a Swiss employment doctrine but embraces as well the conduct here of a New Jersey parent company that has assertedly engaged in conduct that would violate a clear mandate of public policy. Defendants and the Appellate Division agreed that New Jersey has virtually no interest in this dispute because the terms of the *Pierce* [v. Ortho Pharmaceutical Corp., 84 N.J. 58, 417 A.2d 505 (1980)] doctrine [which prohibits such retaliatory discharges] do not extend to a foreign resident employed in another country. But the *Pierce* doctrine is policy neutral. It draws its life only from the underlying state policy and applies only when the underlying state policy applies. The question is: does the FCPA constitute a state policy and does the FCPA have an intended extraterritorial effect?

A. We will consider first whether a clear mandate of public policy relates to a domestic company's overseas activities, and then examine New Jersey's contacts with that mandate, if it exists, in the circumstances of this case.

In New Jersey, in the absence of a contract, an employee may be fired for any reason, be it good cause, no cause, or even morally-wrong cause, but not when the discharge is contrary to a clear mandate of public policy. [cit.]; see also the Conscientious Employee Protection Act, N.J.S.A. 34:19–1 to–8 (protecting employee from retaliatory discharge, including when employee refuses to participate in activity that violates law, regulation, or rule; is criminal; or is against clear mandate of public policy concerning public health, safety, welfare, or environment).
* * *

1. Federal law and policy can constitute New Jersey's clear mandate of public policy. [The court explains how the FCPA has been incorporated into New Jersey law by New Jersey precedents.] * * *

2. Our analysis is not finished. The mere existence of a policy does not mean that it will be invoked. * * * That requires a weighing of the competing interests. *
* *

The FCPA makes unlawful the giving of a gift to a foreign official in order to influence a decision of a foreign government. 15 U.S.C.A. §§ 78dd-1,-2.

The FCPA was intended to stop bribery of foreign officials and political parties by domestic corporations. Bribery abroad was considered a "severe" United States foreign policy problem; it embarrasses friendly governments, causes a decline of foreign esteem for the United States and casts suspicion on the activities of our enterprises, giving credence to our foreign opponents. H.R.Rep. No. 640, 95th Cong., 1st Sess. 5 (1977). The FCPA thus represents a legislative judgment that our foreign relations will be bettered by a strict anti-bribery statute. [Clayco Petroleum Corp. v. Occidental Petroleum Corp., 712 F.2d 404, 408 (9th Cir.1983) (footnote omitted), cert. denied, 464 U.S. 1040 (1984).]

The FCPA expresses a strong public interest against the bribing of foreign officials by domestic companies. * * * Congress, through the FCPA, has expressed a need to protect the public against the bribing of foreign officials by domestic companies. That federal policy represents a clear mandate of state policy, especially when a violation of the federal policy has an impact on the health and welfare of the forum state. The record contains evidence that members of the College of Experts participated in institutional review boards analyzing clinical results for drugs Cilag was attempting to register in Switzerland. Those boards were necessary not for registration in Switzerland but for the Swiss documents to be used in the United States for the registration of the drug by the Food and Drug Administration. New Jersey is a worldwide leader in the pharmaceutical markets. The effect of commercial bribery abroad has a potential effect on New Jersey and the health and welfare of its citizens.

On the other side of our balancing analysis is the interest of comity that is implicated by the extraterritorial application of the FCPA in a wrongful-discharge case. The FCPA expressly applies extraterritorially to United States citizens working for foreign subsidiaries of domestic companies. 15 U.S.C.A. § 78dd–2(a)(2)(B) (subjecting United States citizen working overseas to five-years imprisonment for violating FCPA). "[A]pplication of United States law to *United States nationals* abroad ordinarily raises considerably less serious questions of international comity than does the application of United States law to *foreign nationals* abroad." EEOC v. Arabian Am. Oil Co., 499 U.S. 244, 274 (1991) (Marshall, J., dissenting). In EEOC the Court explained that because Congress did not intend the protections of Title VII to apply to United States citizens employed by American employers in foreign countries, overseas practices of subsidiaries were not subject to the law.

However, Congress has since legislatively overruled the Supreme Court. 42 U.S.C.A. § 2000e-1(c); [cit.]. Unlike its original intent in Title VII, Congress explicitly intends that the FCPA apply to conduct of American companies and employees in foreign countries. * * * We also note that the Conscientious Employee Protection Act, N.J.S.A. 34:19-1 to-8, has codified much of the common-law retaliatory-discharge claim and includes an activity that is a violation of law or a crime. We do not suggest that the "whistle blower" act itself has an extraterritorial effect; rather it reflects our common-law employment law, which will apply extraterritorially only when the underlying clear mandate of public policy is intended to have an extraterritorial effect.

Not only can federal policy constitute state policy, it can also apply extraterritorially when Congress intends that the policy have overseas applications. The FCPA is intended to govern United States citizens abroad, and applying the policies of the FCPA to D'Agostino's claim is an intended and permissible extraterritorial effect. In declining to assert jurisdiction over foreign subsidiaries the FCPA focuses liability on the parent and the United States national acting as its overseas operative. * * * One court recently summarized the FCPA Conference

Report as stating "that American parent corporations would remain indirectly liable for violations of the FCPA by a subsidiary" and "that United States individuals (citizens, nationals or residents) could be liable if acting in relation to the affairs of a foreign subsidiary of an issuer or domestic concern." Dooley v. United Technologies Corp., 803 F.Supp. 428, 439 (D.D.C.1992). Not only could D'Agostino be liable under the FCPA, but more likely J & J could be held liable as a parent of a subsidiary whose agent bribed a foreign official.

* * * The FCPA's policy of preventing the bribery of foreign officials by domestic companies, combined with the alleged reason for the bribe—to influence the registration of drugs in Switzerland and the United States—suggests a strong public interest in this case. Any opposing interest involving extraterritoriality does not outweigh this forum's interests in preventing bribery, which could have a negative impact on public health and safety in New Jersey. Having determined that the mandate of public policy is beneficial to the public, we must consider New Jersey's and Switzerland's "contacts" with the potential tort liability of a domestic corporation for ordering and directing the discharge of a foreign subsidiary's employee for the refusal to participate in corrupt practices.

B. * * * We recognize that Switzerland has an interest in governing the employment relationships between a Swiss company and a Swiss resident. Switzerland does have an undoubted interest in preventing bribery, although that interest is not a policy effectuated through such Swiss employment law; rather, it is a policy underlying Swiss criminal law. And Switzerland does have a strong interest in maintaining a uniform approach to employee/employer relations (as with any state), especially when one considers its small size, location, tradition of neutrality, and openness to trade, foreign business, and foreign employees. Thus, Switzerland has an interest in having its law apply to an employment relationship involving a Swiss resident and a Swiss company. [cit.] But it does not have an interest in condoning corporate bribery orchestrated beyond its boundaries.

This is not a case (allegedly) in which an obscure overseas operative of J & J was involved in commercial bribery unknown to the home office. At oral argument counsel for J & J had to concede, in the procedural posture of the case, that we must decide the choice-of-law question as if what plaintiff called the "driving engine" and scheme to bribe and fire were "headquarters generated" and that the bribes were intended and expected to affect the regulatory process. * * *

In addition, D'Agostino was hired through the efforts of an employment agency chosen by J & J and was interviewed by the J & J organization in Germany, not in Switzerland. D'Agostino thought he was entering into a long-term career with J & J that would eventually involve a United States-based position with the company. Both D'Agostino's hiring and termination announcements were issued by J & J's international subsidiary in New Jersey and distributed to J & J's managers and Executive Committee in New Jersey. Plaintiff's firing followed shortly after a meeting at J & J's corporate headquarters in New Jersey at which the unsuccessful registration of a drug was discussed.

Those alleged facts and inferences reveal J & J's extensive supervisory role and involvement in Cilag and D'Agostino's employment situation. As noted, the thesis of plaintiff's case is that J & J orchestrated in New Jersey the bribing of a foreign official, allegedly in violation of the FCPA and potentially subjecting a United States citizen to criminal prosecution, and plaintiff's subsequent dismissal for failing to pay the bribe. If proven, the extensive New Jersey contacts and the qualitative nature of the underlying controversy lead us to conclude that New Jersey law should govern this dispute.

C. * * * Switzerland has a strong interest in at-will employment * * *. However, New Jersey has a qualitatively different interest in protecting employees against wrongful discharges ordered by New Jersey corporations. * * * Allowing New Jersey law to apply provides the fairness and certainty for the parties * * *. J & J, as a New Jersey company, is well aware of the FCPA and its dictates. In fact, it has its own Policy Statement against the use of corporate funds for unlawful purposes, including bribes or payoffs.

Incorporating the FCPA as a clear mandate of New Jersey policy does not undermine any valid expectation of J & J. Hence, we are not exporting New Jersey employment law so much as applying New Jersey domestic policy, drawn from federal sources, to a domestic company. * * * New Jersey law does not regulate conduct outside the state. Rather, New Jersey law regulates conduct in New Jersey, such as J & J's alleged orchestration of the bribing of a foreign official and firing of plaintiff. To use an extreme example, we would not doubt that New Jersey law could interdict a criminal conspiracy, orchestrated in New Jersey, to harm interests elsewhere. See N.J.S.A. 2C:1–3(a)(3) (stating that conduct outside New Jersey can constitute conspiracy as long as one act in furtherance of conspiracy occurs in New Jersey). * * *

As we have stated, the question is not whether the *Pierce* policy is exportable (or follows a New Jerseyan everywhere), but whether a New Jersey policy has an intended and permissible extraterritorial effect. See discussion, supra. In many (if not most) instances the forum policies are not intended to have extraterritorial effect. For example, we might consider the hypothetical case of a researcher forbidden by federal law to conduct fetal research in the United States who, as an employee of a foreign subsidiary of a New Jersey company, is ordered to do fetal research in Canada. The employee would not have a retaliatory-discharge claim based on the forum law because, unlike the FCPA, such a law would not seek to regulate conduct outside of the United States. A parent company in New Jersey that requires a Canadian employee of a subsidiary to do such research would not thereby violate a clear mandate of public policy. The issue is always the policymaker's intent to affect extraterritorial events. * * *

V. * * * In considering all of the other factors and the quality of New Jersey's interest in the underlying controversy as well as this State's contacts with the controversy, we believe that as between Switzerland and this forum New Jersey has the greatest interest. In particular, we do not see how a domestic corporation could have any "justified expectations," Restatement, supra, § 6, that it was free to put at jeopardy overseas employees who refuse to participate in commercial bribery. In making such a ruling, we do not export New Jersey employment law to the overseas subsidiaries of domestic corporations. We incorporate a domestic policy intended to affect, at most here, conduct in New Jersey that has a forbidden extraterritorial effect. The allegations in this case present a distinct New Jersey involvement both in the hiring and firing of D'Agostino. * * *

The premise of plaintiff's case is that the J & J officials ordered and directed the plan to dismiss him; his case cannot hereafter be converted into one of respondeat superior or vicarious liability for the unplanned acts of Swiss managers. If the facts are as J & J asserts, the discharge will implicate only Swiss interests, and the case will be dismissed under applicable principles of Swiss law. If the facts are as plaintiff asserts, that the payments that he refused to make were intended to influence Swiss regulatory officials, an asserted violation of the FCPA, and if J & J ordered D'Agostino's discharge and employment quarantine for refusal to go along with the arrangement and its coverup, the case implicates important New Jersey interests that are qualitatively greater than the Swiss interest in employment relationships and therefore calls for the application of domestic law. We repeat, however, what we said at the outset of the opinion: these are but D'Agostino's allegations that remain to be proven.

The judgment of the Appellate Division is reversed and the matter remanded for further proceedings consistent with this opinion.

For reversal and remandment—Chief Justice Wilentz and Justices Clifford, Handler, O'Hern, Dreier, Long and Stein—7.

Notes and Questions

1. Did *D'Agostino* present the converse fact pattern from that involved in *Hartford Fire*, supra? Where did the defendant's critical conduct occur in *D'Agostino*, and where did it produce its effects? If, as the court repeatedly stated, the critical conduct occurred in New Jersey, then why was the court so concerned about the "extraterritorial application" of New Jersey law? What is extraterritorial about applying forum law to conduct that occurs within the forum state? If the conduct's effects occur outside the forum state, is the application of forum law to such a case considered extraterritorial application? Where did the effects occur in *D'Agostino*?

Notice that D'Agostino sued J & J for its own conduct rather than for the conduct of its Swiss subsidiary. Would the answer to the above questions be different if the plaintiff's suit was based on "respondeat superior or vicarious liability for the unplanned acts of Swiss managers"? *D'Agostino*, supra. Why, or why not?

2. Since New Jersey law incorporated the FCPA and since "[t]he FCPA expressly applies extraterritorially to United States citizens working for foreign subsidiaries of domestic companies," what was all the fuss about in *D'Agostino*? What was "the particular issue" at stake in that case? Was it the application of the FCPA as such, or was it the application of New Jersey *employment* law which attached certain consequences to the firing of an employee for refusing to violate the FCPA?

Did the *D'Agostino* court feel bound by any "presumption against extraterritoriality"? If not, why do you think this is so? Is it because the state law in question was non-statutory? Are common-law rules exempted from this presumption? Or are state laws in general, as opposed to federal laws, immune from this presumption? If the New Jersey court felt less bound by a presumption against extraterritoriality, could it be because New Jersey has abandoned the territorially-based choice-of-law theory and has replaced it with the almost anti-territorial interest analysis?

3. In addition to having adopted the FCPA, New Jersey had enacted its own "whistle blower" act, the Conscientious Employee Protection Act (CEPA), which protects employees from retaliatory discharge for refusing to violate applicable law. Although CEPA was enacted after D'Agostino's discharge and thus was inapplicable to that case, the *D'Agostino* court expressed doubts as to whether that Act could be applied extraterritorially. In Mehlman v. Mobil Oil Corporation, 676 A.2d 1143 (N.J.Super.1996), the defendant Mobil invoked those doubts to prevent the application of CEPA in a suit by one of its employees whom Mobil fired for commenting in Japan that the gasoline sold by one of Mobil's Japanese subsidiaries contained excessive quantities of benzene. The court distinguished *D'Agostino*, stating that, unlike that case which involved the firing of a Swiss domiciliary working in Switzerland, the plaintiff in *Mehlman* "was not a Japanese employee working in Japan; he was a New Jersey citizen employed in New Jersey by a domestic company. As New Jersey law unquestionably applies here, CEPA has not been given extraterritorial application." 676 A.2d at 1159. Again, does this mean that *D'Agostino* applied New Jersey law extraterritorially?

The defendant in *Mehlman* also argued that the application of CEPA would effectively "'mandate limiting benzene levels' in Japanese gasoline in a way that burdens a multinational corporation in the conduct of foreign commerce," id., and that such application "unavoidably interferes with our nation's foreign policy," id. at 1161 (citing *Zschernig*). This was an imaginative argument, was it not? What would be your response?

4. *D'Agostino* employed governmental interest analysis, a choice-of-law methodology that is vulnerable to the criticism of forum favoritism and protectionism of forum litigants (see supra 139-41). Does *D'Agostino* provide sufficient refutation of such a criticism? Remember that even Brainerd Currie acknowledged the potential for discrimination inherent in his analysis but thought that the Equal Protection and Privileges and Immunities clauses of the Constitution would control undue protectionism, while the Due Process and Full Faith and Credit Clauses would control excessive forum favoritism. (See supra 141.) Does the fact that two of these clauses do not apply to international conflicts increase the potential for protectionism and forum favoritism in these conflicts? If not, why? If yes, then what, if anything, is wrong with a little protectionism or forum favoritism in international conflicts? Can the handling of these conflicts interfere with the conduct of foreign affairs? See *Zschernig*, supra.

Is Professor Leflar's "better-law approach," supra Ch. 3, more likely to lead to the selection of forum law in international than in interstate conflicts? In denying the apparent de facto pro-forum tilt of this approach, Professor Leflar said that "[j]udges can appreciate as well as can anyone else the fact that their forum law in some areas is anachronistic." Leflar et al., *American Conflicts* 107. Are judges less likely to do so in international conflicts?

5. Interest analysis, like all other policy-based choice-of-law methodologies, relies heavily on identifying the policies and interests reflected in the competing substantive laws. In studying interstate conflicts, we have seen that ascertaining the policies embodied in the laws of sister states is not an easy enterprise. Is it not significantly more difficult to ascertain, and understand, the policies embodied in the laws of foreign countries, especially those that do not adhere to the common-law tradition? Did the *D'Agostino* court have any difficulty in ascertaining the content of Swiss law? If not, might this lack of difficulty have anything to do with the fact that the party that relied on foreign law happened to be a wealthy corporation with ample means at its disposal? Compare those means with those available to the injured plaintiff in *Walton v. Arabian American Oil Co.* (supra 105). In any event, if ascertaining the policies embodied in non-forum law is more difficult in international conflicts than in interstate conflicts, would this render all policy-based analyses unsuitable for international conflicts? Should we return to jurisdiction-selecting rules for such conflicts?

6. Although the *D'Agostino* court treated the interests of Switzerland with respect, is it likely that, in identifying the policies and interests of foreign countries, other courts may make unflattering comments about those policies and interests? If so, is this likelihood any greater in international conflicts than in interstate conflicts, at least when the country involved is less friendly to the United States than Switzerland? If courts make unflattering comments or ignore legitimate foreign interests, do they cross *Zschernig*'s forbidden line?

One can ask the same question with regard to cases applying the traditional theory. As you remember from chapter 2, the *ordre public* exception allows a court to refuse to apply a foreign law that is found to be "obnoxious" or "shocking" to the forum's sense of justice and fairness. Is this exception more likely to be employed in international than in interstate conflicts? When a court employs this exception in international conflicts, does it risk crossing *Zschernig* forbidden line?

Along similar lines, consider Weidner Communications, Inc. v. H.R.H. Prince Bandar Al Faisal, 859 F.2d 1302 (7th Cir.1988), which involved the enforceability of a choice-of-forum clause conferring exclusive jurisdiction to the courts of the defendant's country. The plaintiff, an American businessman, had signed the clause in that country, during a meeting in defendant's palace and under conditions the plaintiff perceived as coercive. The plaintiff testified that, immediately before that meeting:

> I had been taken by a servant of [defendant] Prince Bandar's to the town square * * * where punishment was publicly inflicted upon criminals. Numerous statements were made to me by Prince Bandar's servant about the power possessed by Prince Bandar * * * to imprison or otherwise punish people, including foreigners, at their whim,.... A meeting was then held at which Prince Bandar attempted to [have me sign the agreement containing the above clause] * * * and went into an apparent rage at my refusal to do so. I considered Prince Bandar's actions, taken together with the references made to punishment or imprisonment, to pose a threat to my personal safety and well being and,

therefore, left Prince Bandar's home, returned to the United States and have not since returned to [that country].

859 F.2d at 1303, n.2. The court must have given some credence to these allegations (which the defendant did not address, see id.), because the court eventually held the choice-of-forum clause unenforceable, partly because of these allegations. The court referred to the "alleged attempt to physically intimidate [plaintiff]" and stated that:

> [t]his intimidation * * * [contributed to] a transactional environment clearly demonstrating "undue influence or overweening bargaining power" of the type that may affect the enforceability of the clause * * *. At the very least it cannot be fairly said that the [clause] was "freely negotiated" between persons possessing equal bargaining power.

Id. at 1309. This is quite a diplomatic (under)statement, is it not? Does it not prove that American judges are as adept in avoiding unflattering remarks about foreign citizens or conditions in foreign countries as American diplomats are?

* * *

7. Finally, look back through this and the previous chapters and compare the choice-of-law approaches American courts employ in the following categories of conflicts cases: (a) conflicts between state law and foreign-country law; (b) conflicts between federal law and foreign-country law; and (c) conflicts between the laws of states of the United States. Do these approaches differ, and if so, to what extent?

Part II

JURISDICTION

Chapter 8

PERSONAL JURISDICTION
IN INTERSTATE CASES

Earlier, we examined the constitutional limits on state law-making authority. In this chapter we examine constitutional limits on judicial authority. One could imagine a system in which the scope of judicial and legislative authority was co-extensive. Under such an approach, if a state had authority to adjudicate, it also could apply its own laws. Conversely, if a state were sufficiently connected to a dispute that its laws could be applied, then it would follow that the state could adjudicate the dispute.

However, in the United States, and in the world generally, adjudicatory authority is not coextensive with legislative authority. The United States Supreme Court has repeatedly stressed that judicial jurisdiction and choice of law are distinct inquiries. Moreover, the tests articulated by the Supreme Court seem to constrain state judicial authority more than state legislative jurisdiction. This has prompted one professor to quip: "To believe that a defendant's contacts with the forum state should be stronger under the due process clause for jurisdictional purposes than for choice of law is to believe that an accused is more concerned with where he will be hanged than whether." Silberman, *The End of an Era*, 88. As we explore the constitutional limits on state adjudicatory authority, you should bear in mind several issues that we will examine throughout the chapter: In what respect, if any, is the exercise of judicial authority different than the exercise of legislative authority? Should there be different tests for the exercise of judicial and legislative authority? Are limits on state judicial authority necessary to preserve state sovereignty, individual liberty, or both?

A. INTRODUCTION AND HISTORY

1. Theoretical Foundations of Jurisdiction.[1] Personal jurisdiction can be viewed as a specific application of a core question in political philosophy--when can a government legitimately exercise authority? The feudal systems of medieval Europe saw governmental authority as resting on a complex of rights and duties existing between lord and tenant. Tenants owed loyalty and services to their lord; in return, he protected them and rendered them justice. The existence and legitimacy of governmental authority flowed from this personal bond. As the modern State

---

1. This section is largely drawn from von Mehren, *Adjudicatory Authority*, 31-56.

emerged, other explanations of, and justifications for, governmental authority largely replaced the relational theory. One view, associated with such figures as Bodin, Hobbes, and Austin, emphasized the reality of power and its hierarchical organization; power became in a sense its own justification. Another perspective, found in the works of Locke and Bentham among many others, views society and government in more instrumental and utilitarian terms.

To the central question of political philosophy--"Why should one obey the state and respect its institutions?"--the Hobbesian answered that authority--effective power--was indispensable to ordered civil society. For Lockeans, on the other hand, consent--real or implied--rather than brute necessity and efficacy was the source of authority.

Both philosophies are instrumental in the sense that each sees society as existing to secure certain goals. Yet both interpose between an instrumental evaluation of law and legal institutions a dogmatic proposition. For thinkers in the Hobbesian tradition, the necessity and reality of governmental power dominates discourse. Thus John Austin (1790-1850) felt "the grip of a certain idea, the idea that law is simply the impressing of the will of the stronger upon the weaker. Austin's chief virtue was that he systematically developed, defended, and refined this idea, stripping it of excess philosophical baggage."[2] If Hobbesian dogma puts too great store on power, Lockeans overemphasize consent; in real life, governments act in the absence of anything resembling consent on the part of at least some of those affected and in resolving disputes apply rules and principles to which the individual can hardly be taken to have agreed.

As already remarked, instrumental themes, implicit in the dogmatic propositions advanced by Hobbes and Locke, have become a fundamental concern of contemporary political philosophy. Instrumentalism takes many forms; perhaps the most pervasive and influential is utilitarianism, associated with the name of Jeremy Bentham (1748-1832). For the utilitarian, the answer to the question when one should obey the State is "just as far as obedience will contribute more to the general happiness than disobedience." For utilitarian instrumentalism, "the state is not a super-entity with purposes and a will of its own, but a human contrivance to enable men to realize so many of their desires as possible."[3] Contemporary theorists often disagree profoundly with Bentham's hedonic calculus--the sum of pleasures and pains of individuals--but accept the proposition that, in many ways, an instrumental view of political authority and of governmental activity comes closer to the mark than Hobbes's power or Locke's consent metaphor.

In the case of multisystem or multistate controversies, the situation is different in at least two crucial respects. Firstly, controversies that are, in the light of a given general theory, indubitably within one legal order's adjudicatory authority may well be connected in a way significant for the exercise of adjudicatory authority to other legal orders as well. These connections may--or may not--be of the same nature as those that relate the controversy to the first legal order. For example, where both

---

2. H. Morris, John Austin, in The Encyclopedia of Philosophy I (ed. P. Edwards) 209, at 210 (1967).

3. D. Monro, Jeremy Bentham, in id. 280, at 284.

parties are nationals of one State their dispute may be over real property situated in another State. A relational theory can unhesitatingly assign adjudicatory authority to the first State; a power theory, to the second. Moreover, where the legal orders concerned accept the same general theory, that theory may justify the exercise of adjudicatory authority by more than one of them. A power theory, for example, justifies jurisdiction as well in the state in which all the parties live as in the state where the real property, whose ownership is in dispute, is located. Likewise, an instrumental theory may well recognize in more than one legal order a plausible claim to exercise adjudicatory authority over a given dispute.

The rationales for asserting adjudicatory authority that inform relational and power theories obviously leave out of account considerations that could well significantly affect a legal order's jurisdictional practices. Specifically, civilized societies may have an inherent obligation to dispense justice even as to persons with whom they are not directly connected. Should a State have adjudicatory authority to enforce its criminal laws that punish universal crimes such as "piracy, slave trade, attacks on or hijacking of aircraft, genocide, war crimes, and perhaps certain acts of terrorism." *Restatement (Third)* §§ 404, 423. Exercises of adjudicatory authority so justified typically concern alleged criminal offenses; however, some argue that, in principle, adjudicatory authority exists in these matters over claims sounding in tort or restitution. In these situations, do our common humanity and shared civilized values permit--or perhaps even require--national legal orders to act as surrogates for an--as yet unrealized--international legal order?

Whether and when it is appropriate for nations to claim adjudicatory authority in these matters on such bases is today a much discussed issue. Those who resist special jurisdictional rules for war-crimes and violations of human-rights cases argue that endless opportunities for forum shopping will be offered and courts will often be seised for political purposes. On the other hand, the proposition that an inherent right and duty exists to defend human rights which justifies every legal order-- regardless of its lack of specific concerns in the matter--is attractive to many. In 1993, Belgium enacted legislation giving its courts universal jurisdiction over anyone who commits a violation of the 1949 Geneva Conventions and Additional Protocols. However, its exercise of jurisdiction over people and events with no connection to Belgium was very controversial and in 2003 it amended its law to apply only if the victim or suspect was a Belgian citizen or long-term resident at the time of the alleged crime.

2. The Historical Antecedents of Contemporary Jurisdiction Doctrine. In D'Arcy v. Ketchum, 52 U.S. (11 How.) 165 (1850), the Supreme Court held that Louisiana was not required to give full faith and credit to a New York judgment rendered against a Louisiana resident who had neither been personally served in New York nor otherwise brought within the jurisdiction of the New York courts. Although *D'Arcy* did not require enforcement of the judgment, it did not prohibit enforcement either. That step came a few years later in the landmark case of Pennoyer v. Neff, 95 U.S. (5 Otto) 714 (1877). Building on *D'Arcy*, the Court held that a state could validly exercise jurisdiction under only two conditions: either the plaintiff attached the defendant's property in the state at the outset of the case giving the court in rem or quasi-in-rem jurisdiction, or the plaintiff served process on the defendant within the state giving the court in personam jurisdiction. According to the Court, these requirements flowed from "two well-established principles of public law respecting the jurisdiction of an independent State over persons and property.* * * One of these principles is, that every State possesses exclusive jurisdiction and sovereignty over persons and property within its territory. * * * The other principle of public law referred to follows from the one mentioned; that is, that no State can exercise direct jurisdiction and authority over persons or property without its territory." Id. at 722.

In addition, the Court held that the Fourteenth Amendment's Due Process Clause prohibits states from entering or enforcing a judgment inconsistent with those criteria. Thus, where there was neither property in the state nor in-state service, other states were not only free to ignore the judgment, they were required to ignore it.

While *Pennoyer v. Neff* offered a straight-forward territorial formula for determining whether a state obtained jurisdiction, the approach was ill-suited to an increasingly mobile society. For example, under traditional doctrine, a corporation was thought to exist only as a creature of the state law that created it, and, thus, it was thought not to exist outside of the borders of that state. Under this view, a corporation could be sued only in its state of incorporation. See, e.g., Peckham v. North Parish in Haverhill, 33 Mass. 274, 286 (1834). Early 20th century industrialization brought with it a significant increase in multistate corporate activities. In response, the Court developed the doctrine that a corporation which conducted sufficient activity in a state was "present" within that state and therefore amenable to service there.

Increased mobility put similar pressure on the jurisdictional doctrine for individuals. One solution was to subject an individual to suit in her domicile, regardless of whether she is physically served there. Thus, in Milliken v. Meyer, 311 U.S. 457 at 462-64 (1940), the Court explained:

> Domicile in the state is alone sufficient to bring an absent defendant within the reach of the state's jurisdiction * * *. As in case of the authority of the United States over its absent citizens [cit.], the authority of a state over one of its citizens is not terminated by the mere fact of his absence from the state. The state which accords him privileges and affords protection to him and his property by virtue of his domicile may also exact reciprocal duties. * * * One such incident of domicile is amenability to suit within the state even during sojourns without the state, where the state has provided and employed a reasonable method for apprising such an absent party of the proceedings against him.

Another approach held that a defendant who engaged in certain activities "consented" to jurisdiction. For example, a Massachusetts statute provided that a non-resident who operated a motor vehicle in the state was deemed to have appointed the Massachusetts registrar of motor vehicles as his agent for service of process. In Hess v. Pawloski, 274 U.S. 352 (1927), the Supreme Court upheld this statute, asserting on the one hand that mere transaction of business in a state does not imply consent, but on the other hand that a state may require a person driving a vehicle in the state to appoint a state official as his agent for service of process. What does "consent" mean in this context? Suppose that before driving into Massachusetts, the defendant had written the state explaining that he was coming to the state but that he would not consent to the appointment of a state official as his agent. Would this disclaimer be effective?

3. The Modern Era.[4] The consent and presence rationales were attempts to reconcile modern realities with *Pennoyer's* constraints. In the landmark case of International Shoe Co. v. Washington, 326 U.S. 310 (1945), the Supreme Court articulated a new conceptual approach. The State of Washington sued International Shoe in Washington seeking to collect unemployment taxes on commissions the company had paid to its Washington salesmen. The company was a Missouri corporation with its headquarters in Missouri. It had no office in Washington and was not licensed to do business there. Its Washington salesmen displayed samples in Washington and transmitted orders to the company headquarters. Washington State served notice on one of the salesmen in Washington and sent a copy to the corporate headquarters in Missouri. The lower court and the parties focused their arguments on whether the company's activities in Washington were sufficient to constitute presence. The Court rejected this approach, explaining:

> [N]ow that the *capias ad respondendum* has given way to personal service of summons or other form of notice, due process requires only that in order to subject a defendant to a judgment in personam, if he be not present within the territory of the forum, he have certain minimum contacts with it such that the maintenance of the suit does not offend "traditional notions of fair play and substantial justice." [cit.]
>
> * * * To say that the corporation is so far "present" there as to satisfy due process requirements, for purposes of taxation or maintenance of suits against it in the courts of the state, is to beg the question to be decided. For the terms "present" or "presence" are used merely to symbolize those activities of the corporation's agent within the state which courts will deem to be sufficient to satisfy the demands of due process. * * *
>
> It is evident that the criteria by which we mark the boundary line between those activities which justify the subjection of a corporation to suit, and those which do not, cannot be simply mechanical or quantitative. The test is not merely, as has sometimes been suggested, whether the activity, which the corporation has seen fit to procure through its agents in another state, is a little more or a little less. [cit.] Whether due process is satisfied must depend rather upon the quality and nature of the activity in relation to the fair and orderly administration of the laws which it was the purpose of the due process clause to insure. That clause does not contemplate that a state may make binding a judgment in personam against an individual or corporate defendant with which the state has no contacts, ties, or relations. [cit.]
>
> But to the extent that a corporation exercises the privilege of conducting

---

4. For a comprehensive discussion of the development of American jurisdiction law and comparisons with European developments, see von Mehren, *Adjudicatory Authority* 68-301.

activities within a state, it enjoys the benefits and protection of the laws of that state. The exercise of that privilege may give rise to obligations, and, so far as those obligations arise out of or are connected with the activities within the state, a procedure which requires the corporation to respond to a suit brought to enforce them can, in most instances, hardly be said to be undue. [cit.]

Id. at 316-19. The more open-ended "minimum contacts" analysis set forth in *International Shoe* has largely replaced the more formalistic approach of *Pennoyer*. The new approach still leaves many questions unanswered--some theoretical, some practical. These questions are explored below.

International Shoe provides an interesting illumination of the relationship between jurisdiction and choice of law. The real issue for the litigants was whether Washington was permitted to tax the defendant. The defendant's general counsel viewed the case "primarily as tax case," not as a personal jurisdiction case. Cameron & Johnson, *Death of a Salesman?*, 798-99.

If the court had found no jurisdiction, then the defendant would have escaped liability because no other state would have enforced Washington's tax laws. (Remember the tax exception, supra at 96 *et seq*.) The Court could have found personal jurisdiction but denied Washington the power to tax. Nonetheless, the Court treated the jurisdiction and taxation questions as being intertwined, explaining at the end of the opinion:

> Appellant having rendered itself amenable to suit upon obligations arising out the activities of its salesmen in Washington, the state may maintain the present suit in personam to collect the tax laid upon the exercise of the privilege of employing appellant's salesmen within the state. For Washington has made one of those activities, which taken together establish appellant's "presence" there for purposes of suit, the taxable event by which the state brings appellant within reach of its taxing power. The state thus has constitutional power to lay the tax and to subject appellant to suit to recover it. The activities which establish its "presence" subject it alike to taxation by the state and to suit to recover the tax.

326 U.S. 310 at 321.

Should the fact that a court has jurisdiction always mean that it can apply its law? Conversely, should lack of jurisdiction mean that that state's laws cannot be applied? Throughout the remainder of this chapter, you should consider these and other questions concerning the relationship between jurisdiction and choice of law.

B. THE UNDERLYING THEORY OF PERSONAL JURISDICTION

1. Jurisdiction as a Protection of State Sovereignty

World-Wide Volkswagen Corp. v. Woodson
Supreme Court of the United States, 1980.
444 U.S. 286, 100 S.Ct. 559, 62 L.Ed.2d 490.

JUSTICE WHITE delivered the opinion of the Court. The issue before us is whether, consistently with the Due Process Clause of the Fourteenth Amendment, an Oklahoma court may exercise in personam jurisdiction over a nonresident automobile retailer and its wholesale distributor in a products-liability action, when the defendants' only connection with Oklahoma is the fact that an automobile sold in New York to New York residents became involved in an accident in Oklahoma.

I. Respondents Harry and Kay Robinson purchased a new Audi automobile from petitioner Seaway Volkswagen, Inc. (Seaway), in Massena, N. Y., in 1976. The following year the Robinson family, who resided in New York, left that State for a new home in Arizona. As they passed through the State of Oklahoma, another car struck their Audi in the rear, causing a fire which severely burned Kay Robinson and her two children.[1]

The Robinsons subsequently brought a products-liability action in the District Court for Creek County, Okla., claiming that their injuries resulted from defective design and placement of the Audi's gas tank and fuel system. They joined as defendants the automobile's manufacturer, Audi NSU Auto Union Aktiengesellschaft (Audi); its importer, Volkswagen of America, Inc. (Volkswagen); its regional distributor, petitioner World-Wide Volkswagen Corp. (World-Wide); and its retail dealer, petitioner Seaway. Seaway and World-Wide entered special appearances,[3] claiming that Oklahoma's exercise of jurisdiction over them would offend the limitations on the State's jurisdiction imposed by the Due Process Clause of the Fourteenth Amendment.

The facts presented to the District Court showed that World-Wide is incorporated and has its business office in New York. It distributes vehicles, parts, and accessories, under contract with Volkswagen, to retail dealers in New York, New Jersey, and Connecticut. Seaway, one of these retail dealers, is incorporated and has its place of business in New York. Insofar as the record reveals, Seaway and World-Wide are fully independent corporations whose relations with each other and with Volkswagen and Audi are contractual only. Respondents adduced no evidence that either World–Wide or Seaway does any business in Oklahoma, ships or sells any products to or in that State, has an agent to receive process there, or purchases advertisements in any media calculated to reach Oklahoma. In fact, as respondents' counsel conceded at oral argument, [cit.], there was no showing that any automobile sold by World–Wide or Seaway has ever entered Oklahoma with the single exception of the vehicle involved in the present case.

Despite the apparent paucity of contacts between petitioners and Oklahoma, * * * [Oklahoma] rejected their constitutional claim and * * * [found that it had] in personam jurisdiction over them.

* * *

II. The Due Process Clause of the Fourteenth Amendment limits the power of a state court to render a valid personal judgment against a nonresident defendant. Kulko v. California Superior Court, 436 U.S. 84, 91 (1978). A judgment rendered

---

1. The driver of the other automobile does not figure in the present litigation.

3. Volkswagen also entered a special appearance in the District Court, but unlike World–Wide and Seaway did not seek review in the Supreme Court of Oklahoma and is not a petitioner here. Both Volkswagen and Audi remain as defendants in the litigation pending before the District Court in Oklahoma.

in violation of due process is void in the rendering State and is not entitled to full faith and credit elsewhere. *Pennoyer v. Neff.* Due process requires that the defendant be given adequate notice of the suit, Mullane v. Central Hanover Trust Co., 339 U.S. 306, 313–314 (1950), and be subject to the personal jurisdiction of the court, *International Shoe Co. v. Washington.* In the present case, it is not contended that notice was inadequate; the only question is whether these particular petitioners were subject to the jurisdiction of the Oklahoma courts.

As has long been settled, and as we reaffirm today, a state court may exercise personal jurisdiction over a nonresident defendant only so long as there exist "minimum contacts" between the defendant and the forum State. *International Shoe.* The concept of minimum contacts, in turn, can be seen to perform two related, but distinguishable, functions. It protects the defendant against the burdens of litigating in a distant or inconvenient forum. And it acts to ensure that the States, through their courts, do not reach out beyond the limits imposed on them by their status as coequal sovereigns in a federal system.

The protection against inconvenient litigation is typically described in terms of "reasonableness" or "fairness." We have said that the defendant's contacts with the forum State must be such that maintenance of the suit "does not offend 'traditional notions of fair play and substantial justice.'" *International Shoe,* quoting Milliken v. Meyer, 311 U.S. 457, 463 (1940). The relationship between the defendant and the forum must be such that it is "reasonable ... to require the corporation to defend the particular suit which is brought there." [cit.] Implicit in this emphasis on reasonableness is the understanding that the burden on the defendant, while always a primary concern, will in an appropriate case be considered in light of other relevant factors, including the forum State's interest in adjudicating the dispute, see *McGee v. International Life Ins. Co.*; the plaintiff's interest in obtaining convenient and effective relief, see *Kulko v. California Superior Court,* at least when that interest is not adequately protected by the plaintiff's power to choose the forum, cf. Shaffer v. Heitner, 433 U.S. 186, 211, n.37 (1977); the interstate judicial system's interest in obtaining the most efficient resolution of controversies; and the shared interest of the several States in furthering fundamental substantive social policies, see *Kulko v. California Superior Court.*

The limits imposed on state jurisdiction by the Due Process Clause, in its role as a guarantor against inconvenient litigation, have been substantially relaxed over the years. As we noted in *McGee,* this trend is largely attributable to a fundamental transformation in the American economy:

"Today many commercial transactions touch two or more States and may involve parties separated by the full continent. With this increasing nationalization of commerce has come a great increase in the amount of business conducted by mail across state lines. At the same time modern transportation and communication have made it much less burdensome for a party sued to defend himself in a State where he engages in economic activity."

The historical developments noted in *McGee,* of course, have only accelerated in the generation since that case was decided.

Nevertheless, we have never accepted the proposition that state lines are irrelevant for jurisdictional purposes, nor could we, and remain faithful to the principles of interstate federalism embodied in the Constitution. The economic interdependence of the States was foreseen and desired by the Framers. In the Commerce Clause, they provided that the Nation was to be a common market, a "free trade unit" in which the States are debarred from acting as separable economic entities. [cit.] But the Framers also intended that the States retain many essential attributes of sovereignty, including, in particular, the sovereign power to try causes in their courts. The sovereignty of each State, in turn, implied a limitation on the sovereignty of all of its sister States--a limitation express or implicit in both the original scheme of the Constitution and the Fourteenth Amendment.

Hence, even while abandoning the shibboleth "[t]he authority of every tribunal is necessarily restricted by the territorial limits of the State in which it is established," *Pennoyer v. Neff*, we emphasized that the reasonableness of asserting jurisdiction over the defendant must be assessed "in the context of our federal system of government," *International Shoe*, and stressed that the Due Process Clause ensures not only fairness, but also the "orderly administration of the laws," id. As we noted in *Hanson v. Denckla*:

> "As technological progress has increased the flow of commerce between the States, the need for jurisdiction over nonresidents has undergone a similar increase. At the same time, progress in communications and transportation has made the defense of a suit in a foreign tribunal less burdensome. In response to these changes, the requirements for personal jurisdiction over nonresidents have evolved from the rigid rule of *Pennoyer v. Neff*, to the flexible standard of *International Shoe*. But it is a mistake to assume that this trend heralds the eventual demise of all restrictions on the personal jurisdiction of state courts.*
> * * Those restrictions are more than a guarantee of immunity from inconvenient or distant litigation. They are a consequence of territorial limitations on the power of the respective States."

Thus, the Due Process Clause "does not contemplate that a state may make binding a judgment in personam against an individual or corporate defendant with which the state has no contacts, ties, or relations.""*International Shoe*.

Even if the defendant would suffer minimal or no inconvenience from being forced to litigate before the tribunals of another State; even if the forum State has a strong interest in applying its law to the controversy; even if the forum State is the most convenient location for litigation, the Due Process Clause, acting as an instrument of interstate federalism, may sometimes act to divest the State of its power to render a valid judgment. *Hanson v. Denckla*.

III. Applying these principles to the case at hand, we find in the record before us a total absence of those affiliating circumstances that are a necessary predicate to any exercise of state-court jurisdiction. Petitioners carry on no activity whatsoever in Oklahoma. They close no sales and perform no services there. They avail themselves of none of the privileges and benefits of Oklahoma law. They solicit no business there either through salespersons or through advertising reasonably calculated to reach the State. Nor does the record show that they regularly sell cars at wholesale or retail to Oklahoma customers or residents or that they indirectly, through others, serve or seek to serve the Oklahoma market. In short, respondents seek to base jurisdiction on one, isolated occurrence and whatever inferences can be drawn therefrom: the fortuitous circumstance that a single Audi automobile, sold in New York to New York residents, happened to suffer an accident while passing through Oklahoma.

It is argued, however, that because an automobile is mobile by its very design and purpose it was "foreseeable" that the Robinsons' Audi would cause injury in Oklahoma. Yet "foreseeability" alone has never been a sufficient benchmark for personal jurisdiction under the Due Process Clause. In *Hanson v. Denckla*, it was no doubt foreseeable that the settlor of a Delaware trust would subsequently move to Florida and seek to exercise a power of appointment there; yet we held that Florida courts could not constitutionally exercise jurisdiction over a Delaware trustee that had no other contacts with the forum State. In *Kulko v. California Superior Court*, it was surely "foreseeable" that a divorced wife would move to California from New York, the domicile of the marriage, and that a minor daughter would live with the mother. Yet we held that California could not exercise jurisdiction in a child-support action over the former husband who had remained in New York.

If foreseeability were the criterion, a local California tire retailer could be forced to defend in Pennsylvania when a blowout occurs there, see Erlanger Mills, Inc. v. Cohoes Fibre Mills, Inc., 239 F.2d 502, 507 (4th Cir.1956); a Wisconsin seller of a defective automobile jack could be haled before a distant court for damage caused in New Jersey, Reilly v. Phil Tolkan Pontiac, Inc., 372 F.Supp. 1205 (D.N.J.1974); or a Florida soft-drink concessionaire could be summoned to Alaska to account for injuries happening there, see Uppgren v. Executive Aviation Services, Inc., 304 F.Supp. 165, 170–171 (D.Minn.1969). Every seller of chattels would in effect appoint the chattel his agent for service of process. His amenability to suit would travel with the chattel.* * *[11]

This is not to say, of course, that foreseeability is wholly irrelevant. But the foreseeability that is critical to due process analysis is not the mere likelihood that a product will find its way into the forum State. Rather, it is that the defendant's conduct and connection with the forum State are such that he should reasonably anticipate being haled into court there. See *Kulko v. California Superior Court*; [cit.]. The Due Process Clause, by ensuring the "orderly administration of the laws," *International Shoe*, gives a degree of predictability to the legal system that allows potential defendants to structure their primary conduct with some minimum assurance as to where that conduct will and will not render them liable to suit.

When a corporation "purposefully avails itself of the privilege of conducting activities within the forum State," *Hanson v. Denckla*, it has clear notice that it is

---

11. Respondents' counsel, at oral argument, [cit.] sought to limit the reach of the foreseeability standard by suggesting that there is something unique about automobiles. It is true that automobiles are uniquely mobile, [cit.] that they did play a crucial role in the expansion of personal jurisdiction through the fiction of implied consent, e.g., *Hess v. Pawloski*, and that some of the cases have treated the automobile as a "dangerous instrumentality." But today, under the regime of *International Shoe*, we see no difference for jurisdictional purposes between an automobile and any other chattel. The "dangerous instrumentality" concept apparently was never used to support personal jurisdiction; and to the extent it has relevance today it bears not on jurisdiction but on the possible desirability of imposing substantive principles of tort law such as strict liability.

subject to suit there, and can act to alleviate the risk of burdensome litigation by procuring insurance, passing the expected costs on to customers, or, if the risks are too great, severing its connection with the State. Hence if the sale of a product of a manufacturer or distributor such as Audi or Volkswagen is not simply an isolated occurrence, but arises from the efforts of the manufacturer or distributor to serve, directly or indirectly, the market for its product in other States, it is not unreasonable to subject it to suit in one of those States if its allegedly defective merchandise has there been the source of injury to its owner or to others. The forum State does not exceed its powers under the Due Process Clause if it asserts personal jurisdiction over a corporation that delivers its products into the stream of commerce with the expectation that they will be purchased by consumers in the forum State. Cf.* Gray v. American Radiator & Standard Sanitary Corp., 176 N.E.2d 761 (Ill.1961).

But there is no such or similar basis for Oklahoma jurisdiction over World–Wide or Seaway in this case. Seaway's sales are made in Massena, N.Y. World–Wide's market, although substantially larger, is limited to dealers in New York, New Jersey, and Connecticut. There is no evidence of record that any automobiles distributed by World-Wide are sold to retail customers outside this tristate area. It is foreseeable that the purchasers of automobiles sold by World-Wide and Seaway may take them to Oklahoma. But the mere "unilateral activity of those who claim some relationship with a nonresident defendant cannot satisfy the requirement of contact with the forum State." *Hanson v. Denckla.*

In a variant on the previous argument, it is contended that jurisdiction can be supported by the fact that petitioners earn substantial revenue from goods used in Oklahoma. The Oklahoma Supreme Court so found, [cit.], drawing the inference that because one automobile sold by petitioners had been used in Oklahoma, others might have been used there also. While this inference seems less than compelling on the facts of the instant case, we need not question the court's factual findings in order to reject its reasoning.

This argument seems to make the point that the purchase of automobiles in New York, from which the petitioners earn substantial revenue, would not occur *but for* the fact that the automobiles are capable of use in distant States like Oklahoma. Respondents observe that the very purpose of an automobile is to travel, and that travel of automobiles sold by petitioners is facilitated by an extensive chain of Volkswagen service centers throughout the country, including some in Oklahoma.[12] However, financial benefits accruing to the defendant from a collateral relation to the forum State will not support jurisdiction if they do not stem from a constitutionally cognizable contact with that State. See *Kulko v. California Superior Court.* In our view, whatever marginal revenues petitioners may receive by virtue of the fact that their products are capable of use in Oklahoma is far too attenuated a contact to justify that State's exercise of in personam jurisdiction over them.

---

*[Editor's footnote: *The Bluebook* (15 ed. 1991) explains "cf." as follows: "Cited authority supports a proposition different from the main proposition but sufficiently lends analogous support.... The citation's relevance will usually be clear to the reader only if it is explained. Parenthetical explanations ... are therefore strongly recommended."]

12. As we have noted, petitioners earn no direct revenues from these service centers. [cit.]

Because we find that petitioners have no "contacts, ties, or relations" with the State of Oklahoma, *International Shoe*, the judgment of the Supreme Court of Oklahoma is
Reversed.

JUSTICE BRENNAN, dissenting. * * * The Court's opinions focus tightly on the existence of contacts between the forum and the defendant. In so doing, they accord too little weight to the strength of the forum State's interest in the case and fail to explore whether there would be any actual inconvenience to the defendant. * * *

Surely *International Shoe* contemplated that the significance of the contacts necessary to support jurisdiction would diminish if some other consideration helped establish that jurisdiction would be fair and reasonable. The interests of the State and other parties in proceeding with the case in a particular forum are such considerations. *McGee v. International Life Ins. Co.*, for instance, accorded great importance to a State's "manifest interest in providing effective means of redress" for its citizens. [cit.]

* * *

In [this case], the interest of the forum State and its connection to the litigation is strong. The automobile accident underlying the litigation occurred in Oklahoma. The plaintiffs were hospitalized in Oklahoma when they brought suit. Essential witnesses and evidence were in Oklahoma. [cit.] The State has a legitimate interest in enforcing its laws designed to keep its highway system safe, and the trial can proceed at least as efficiently in Oklahoma as anywhere else.

The petitioners are not unconnected with the forum. Although both sell automobiles within limited sales territories, each sold the automobile which in fact was driven to Oklahoma where it was involved in an accident. It may be true, as the Court suggests, that each sincerely intended to limit its commercial impact to the limited territory, and that each intended to accept the benefits and protection of the laws only of those States within the territory. But obviously these were unrealistic hopes that cannot be treated as an automatic constitutional shield.

An automobile simply is not a stationary item or one designed to be used in one place. An automobile is *intended* to be moved around. Someone in the business of selling large numbers of automobiles can hardly plead ignorance of their mobility or pretend that the automobiles stay put after they are sold. It is not merely that a dealer in automobiles foresees that they will move. [cit.] The dealer actually intends that the purchasers will use the automobiles to travel to distant States where the dealer does not directly "do business." The sale of an automobile does *purposefully* inject the vehicle into the stream of interstate commerce so that it can travel to distant States. [cit.]

This case is similar to Ohio v. Wyandotte Chemicals Corp., 401 U.S. 493 (1971). There we indicated, in the course of denying leave to file an original--jurisdiction case, that corporations having no direct contact with Ohio could constitutionally be brought to trial in Ohio because they dumped pollutants into streams outside Ohio's limits which ultimately, through the action of the water, reached Lake Erie and affected Ohio. No corporate acts, only their consequences, occurred in Ohio. The stream of commerce is just as natural a force as a stream of water, and it was equally predictable that the cars petitioners released would reach distant States.[10]

The Court accepts that a State may exercise jurisdiction over a distributor which "serves" that State "indirectly" by "deliver[ing] its products into the stream of commerce with the expectation that they will be purchased by consumers in the forum State." [cit.] It is difficult to see why the Constitution should distinguish between a case involving goods which reach a distant State through a chain of distribution and a case involving goods which reach the same State because a consumer, using them as the dealer knew the customer would, took them there.[11] In each case the seller purposefully injects the goods into the stream of commerce and those goods predictably are used in the forum State.[12]

Furthermore, an automobile seller derives substantial benefits from States other than its own. A large part of the value of automobiles is the extensive, nationwide network of highways. Significant portions of that network have been constructed by and are maintained by the individual States, including Oklahoma. The States, through their highway programs, contribute in a very direct and important way to the value of petitioners' businesses. Additionally, a network of other related dealerships with their service departments operates throughout the country under the protection of the laws of the various States, including Oklahoma, and enhances the value of petitioners' businesses by facilitating their customers' traveling.

Thus, the Court errs in its conclusion, [cit.], that "petitioners have *no* 'contacts, ties, or relations'" with Oklahoma. There obviously are contacts, and, given Oklahoma's connection to the litigation, the contacts are sufficiently significant to make it fair and reasonable for the petitioners to submit to Oklahoma's jurisdiction.

* * *

It may be that affirmance of the judgment[ ] * * * would approach the outer limits of *International Shoe's* jurisdictional principle. But that principle, with its almost exclusive focus on the rights of defendants, may be outdated. * * *

As the Court acknowledges, [cit.] both the nationalization of commerce and the ease of transportation and communication have accelerated in the generation since 1957. The model of society on which the *International Shoe* Court based its opinion is no longer accurate. Business people, no matter how local their businesses, cannot assume that goods remain in the business' locality. Customers and goods can be anywhere else in the country usually in a matter of hours and always in a matter of a very few days.

In answering the question whether or not it is fair and reasonable to allow a particular forum to hold a trial binding on a particular defendant, the interests of the

---

10. One might argue that it was more predictable that the pollutants would reach Ohio than that one of petitioners' cars would reach Oklahoma. The Court's analysis, however, excludes jurisdiction in a contiguous State such as Pennsylvania as surely as in more distant States such as Oklahoma.

11. For example, I cannot understand the constitutional distinction between selling an item in New Jersey and selling an item in New York expecting it to be used in New Jersey.

12. The manufacturer in the case cited by the Court, Gray v. American Radiator & Standard Sanitary Corp., 176 N.E.2d 761 (Ill.1961), had no more control over which States its goods would reach than did the petitioners in this case.

forum State and other parties loom large in today's world and surely are entitled to as much weight as are the interests of the defendant. The "orderly administration of the laws" provides a firm basis for according some protection to the interests of plaintiffs and States as well as of defendants. Certainly, I cannot see how a defendant's right to due process is violated if the defendant suffers no inconvenience. [cit.]

The conclusion I draw is that constitutional concepts of fairness no longer require the extreme concern for defendants that was once necessary. Rather, as I wrote in dissent from *Shaffer v. Heitner* (emphasis added), minimum contacts must exist "among the *parties*, the contested transaction, and the forum State."[15] The contacts between any two of these should not be determinative. * * *

The Court's opinion * * * suggests that the defendant ought to be subject to a State's jurisdiction only if he has contacts with the State "such that he should reasonably anticipate being haled into court there."[18] [cit.] There is nothing unreasonable or unfair, however, about recognizing commercial reality. Given the tremendous mobility of goods and people, and the inability of businessmen to control where goods are taken by customers (or retailers), I do not think that the defendant should be in complete control of the geographical stretch of his amenability to suit. Jurisdiction is no longer premised on the notion that nonresident defendants have somehow impliedly consented to suit. People should understand that they are held responsible for the consequences of their actions and that in our society most actions have consequences affecting many States. When an action in fact causes injury in another State, the actor should be prepared to answer for it there unless defending in that State would be unfair for some reason other than that a state boundary must be crossed.

In effect the Court is allowing defendants to assert the sovereign rights of their home States. The expressed fear is that otherwise all limits on personal jurisdiction would disappear. But the argument's premise is wrong. I would not abolish limits on jurisdiction or strip state boundaries of all significance [cit.]; I would still require the plaintiff to demonstrate sufficient contacts among the parties, the forum, and the litigation to make the forum a reasonable State in which to hold the trial.

I would also, however, strip the defendant of an unjustified veto power over certain very appropriate fora—a power the defendant justifiably enjoyed long ago when communication and travel over long distances were slow and unpredictable and when notions of state sovereignty were impractical and exaggerated. But I repeat that that is not today's world. If a plaintiff can show that his chosen forum State has a sufficient interest in the litigation (or sufficient contacts with the defendant), then the defendant who cannot show some real injury to a constitutionally protected interest [cit.] should have no constitutional excuse not to appear.

---

15. In some cases, the inquiry will resemble the inquiry commonly undertaken in determining which State's law to apply. That it is fair to apply a State's law to a nonresident defendant is clearly relevant in determining whether it is fair to subject the defendant to jurisdiction in that State. [cit.]

18. The Court suggests that this is the critical foreseeability rather than the likelihood that the product will go to the forum State. But the reasoning begs the question. A defendant cannot know if his action will subject him to jurisdiction in another State until we have declared what the law of jurisdiction is.

* * *

[The dissenting opinion of Justices Marshall and Blackmun omitted.]

Notes and Questions

1. *World-Wide Volkswagen* highlights several important points about personal jurisdiction doctrine in the United States. First, the Court views personal jurisdiction as bound up with concerns about sovereignty. This understanding of personal jurisdiction is evident in *Pennoyer* which relied on principles of "public law respecting the jurisdiction of an independent State." The *World-Wide Volkswagen* Court explains, quoting from *Hanson v. Denkla,* that the limitations on personal jurisdiction are "a consequence of territorial limitations on the power of states." The Court further explains that "the Due Process Clause, acting as an instrument of interstate federalism, may sometimes act to divest the state of its power to render a valid judgment." In what sense is the Due Process Clause "an instrument of interstate federalism"? Does the Fourteenth Amendment protect sates from other states? See generally Whitten, *Constitutional Limitations on State-Court Jurisdiction.* As discussed in the next section, the Court subsequently reformulated the sovereignty concern into an individual liberty interest, but even reformulated, the Court has retained the underlying premise that personal jurisdiction reflects a view about the scope of state sovereignty. This view is consistent with the treatment of personal jurisdiction is the international arena. Personal jurisdiction, or jurisdiction to adjudicate as it is sometimes called, is increasingly viewed as falling within the domain of customary international law and international agreement. See *Restatement (Third)*, Chapter 2, introductory note.

A second concern that the Court identifies is one about convenience or burden to the defendant. The Court in *World-Wide Volkswagen* does not offer much discussion of this concern because having found insufficient contacts, it id not have to address the reasonableness element. This issue is addressed in more detail in later cases. See, e.g., *Burger King Corp. v. Rudzewicz*, infra at 610; *Asahi Metal Indus. Co. v. Superior Court of Calif.*, infra at 620. Some commentators have argued that convenience or reasonableness should be the sole criteria for personal jurisdiction. See, e.g., Redish, *Due Process, Federalism, and Personal Jurisdiction*, at 1135.

2. The Court makes clear that effects within the forum are not alone sufficient for a state to exercise jurisdiction. Indeed, foreseeability of events in the forum is also not sufficient. The defendant must have purposeful contacts with the forum. Is this requirement a necessary corollary of territorial based sovereignty? Other countries assert jurisdiction on the basis of effects. For example, within the European Union, the plaintiff in a tort case may bring suit where tortious injury occurs. See Brussels II, Art. 5(3). Similarly, § 421(j) of the Restatement (Third) of the Law of Foreign Relations provides that jurisdiction is proper where a defendant carried on activities outside the forum that had "a substantial, direct, and foreseeable effect within the state."

3. What constitutes purposeful availment? Consider the following cases. (The contours of purposeful availment are explored further in connection with *Asahi*

Metal Indus. Co. v. Superior Court of Calif, infra at 620.)

(a) A pedestrian is hit in Minnesota by a drunk driver. The pedestrian sues the Wisconsin bar where the driver became intoxicated. Can the pedestrian bring suit in Minnesota? Does it matter whether the bar knew that many patrons (or this patron in particular) were from Minnesota? See West American Ins. Co. v. Westin, Inc., 337 N.W.2d 676 (Minn.1983) (dismissing suit for lack of jurisdiction).

(b) Suppose Jones, in New York, receive an unsolicited phone call from a reporter in Philadelphia. Jones makes defamatory remarks about Smith that are published in the Philadelphia paper. Can Smith sue Jones in Pennsylvania? Compare Dion v. Kiev, 566 F.Supp. 1387 (E.D.Pa.1983) (upholding jurisdiction), with Ticketmaster-New York v. Alioto, 26 F.3d 201 (1st Cir.1994) (finding no jurisdiction).

4. The Court's analysis in *World-Wide Volkswagen* focuses entirely on the defendant. In the actual case, the Robinsons were badly burned and spent many months in the burn ward of an Oklahoma hospital. Should the Court have considered the burden on them if they must go to New York to pursue their claim? Jurisdiction within the European Union does take into account the relative position of the parties, at least as to certain categories of cases. For example, consumers are permitted to sue in the place of their domicile, and an employer can sue an employee only in the employees domicile. See Brussels II, Arts. 15, 20, supra at 602.

5. Justice Brennan, in his dissent, relied on McGee v. International Life Insurance Co., 355 U.S. 220 (1957). There, a California citizen purchased a life insurance policy from an Arizona insurance company. After a Texas insurance company took over the Arizona firm, the Texas company mailed a reinsurance certificate to the California insured. The insured in turn sent his premiums from California. The insured died in California, and a dispute arose concerning the policy. The beneficiaries sued the Texas insurance company in California state court. Although there was no evidence that the defendant had ever solicited or done any insurance business in California apart from this particular policy, the Supreme Court found that there was jurisdiction. The Court explained:

> Turning to this case we think it apparent that the Due Process Clause did not preclude the California court from entering a judgment binding on respondent. It is sufficient for purposes of due process that the suit was based on a contract which had substantial connection with that State. [cit.] The contract was delivered in California, the premiums were mailed from there and the insured was a resident of that State when he died. It cannot be denied that California has a manifest interest in providing effective means of redress for its residents when their insurers refuse to pay claims. These residents would be at a severe disadvantage if they were forced to follow the insurance company to a distant State in order to hold it legally accountable. When claims were small or moderate individual claimants frequently could not afford the cost of bringing an action in a foreign forum—thus in effect making the company judgment proof. Often the crucial witnesses—as here on the company's defense of suicide—will be found in the insured's locality. Of course there may be inconvenience to the insurer if it is held amendable to suit in California where

it had this contract but certainly nothing which amounts to a denial of due process. [cit.] There is no contention that respondent did not have adequate notice of the suit or sufficient time to prepare its defenses and appear.

Id. at 223-24. According to the majority in *World-Wide Volkswagen*, what role does state interest play in determining whether there is personal jurisdiction?

6. Consider the relationship between personal jurisdiction and choice of law. In *World-Wide Volkswagen*, would Oklahoma have a sufficient interest that it could apply its laws? See, e.g., *Watson v. Employers Liability Assurance Corp.*, supra at 476. Does the Court allow states less autonomy with respect to personal jurisdiction than with respect to choice of law? Are the sovereignty or fairness factors different with respect to jurisdiction than choice of law? Given that there are limits on choice of law, is there any need for limits on personal jurisdiction?

7. Suppose that Audi had a wholly-owned subsidiary doing business in Oklahoma. Would the contacts of the subsidiary be sufficient to subject the parent to jurisdiction? Since the conduct of a corporation is ordinarily not attributed to its shareholders for liability purposes, courts do not automatically attribute corporate conduct to its shareholders for purposes of personal jurisdiction. See Cannon Mfg. Co. v. Cudahy Packing Co., 267 U.S. 333 (1925); Restatement (Second) § 52, cmt.b.

On the other hand, consistent with principles of purposeful availment, when a parent corporation in one state acts through its subsidiary in order to conduct business in a second state, it may be appropriate to treat the parent as have contacts with that second state. For example, a subsidiary may function as the parent's agent. As one court noted, "if a parent uses a subsidiary to do what it otherwise would have done itself, it has purposefully availed itself of the privilege of doing business in the forum." Gallagher v. Mazda Motor of America, Inc., 781 F. Supp. 1079, 1085 (E.D. Pa. 1992). See, e.g., Boryk v. deHavilland Aircraft Co., 341 F.2d 666, 668 (2d Cir.1965); Larball Publishing v. CBS, Inc., 664 F.Supp. 704, 707 (S.D.N.Y.1987); Frummer v. Hilton Hotels Int'l, 227 N.E.2d 851 (N.Y.), *cert. denied*, 389 U.S. 923 (1967). Similarly, a parent corporation may so dominate its subsidiary that it would be unjust to continue to consider them as distinct entities. The subsidiary in essence functions as the "alter ego" of the parent. A non-exhaustive list of factors that courts look to include: using the subsidiary merely as a marketing conduit, completely controlling not only the day to day and long term operations of the subsidiary, inadequate funding of the subsidiary, sharing common stock, directors, and business departments, and forming the sole source of business for the subsidiary. See generally Doe v. Unocal Corp., 248 F.3d 915, 926 (9th Cir. 2001); Gundle Lining Constr. Corp. v. Adams County Asphalt, 85 F.3d 201, 208 (5th Cir. 1996). See generally Althouse, *Conspiracy Theory*, 234; Born, *International Civil Litigation*, 151-70; Brilmayer & Paisley, *Personal Jurisdiction and Substantive Legal Relations*, 1; Note, *Jurisdiction over a Parent Corporation*, 327.

8. The plaintiffs' substantive allegation was that the car was defectively designed and manufactured. Therefore, if liability existed, it would in all likelihood fall ultimately on Audi and Volkswagen, not on the New York dealer and wholesaler who were challenging jurisdiction. Why did the parties litigate all the way to the Supreme Court over the presence of parties who were unlikely to be liable? In the

actual litigation, the answer to this question has nothing to do with abstract questions of liberty or federalism. Instead, the personal jurisdiction issue was part of a strategic battle over whether the case would be litigated in state court or federal court. The plaintiff had filed suit in state court in an Oklahoma county in which the juries had a reputation for being very pro-plaintiff. Both sides believed that a federal jury, drawn from a wider geographic area, was likely to be much less generous. Therefore, the defendants wanted to remove the case to federal court, and the plaintiffs wanted it to remain in state court. The Robinsons were on their way to Arizona, but because they never arrived at their intended new home they were still domiciliaries of New York. Seaway and World-Wide were both citizens of New York and thus if they remained in the suit, they would make the parties non-diverse and the case non-removable. Seaway and World-Wide were largely indifferent as to whether they remained in the suit. As a result, Audi and Volkswagen financed the personal jurisdiction litigation for Seaway and World-Wide. See Adams, *The Rest of the Story*, 1122.

2. Jurisdiction as a Protection of Individual Liberty

Three years after *World-Wide Volkswagen*, in an opinion again written by Justice White, the Court de-emphasized sovereignty as the focus of personal jurisdiction. "The personal jurisdiction requirement recognizes and protects an individual liberty interest. It represents a restriction on judicial power not as a matter of sovereignty, but as a matter of individual liberty. * * * The restriction on state sovereign power described in *World-Wide Volkswagen Corp.*, however, must be seen as ultimately a function of the individual liberty interest preserved by the Due Process Clause." Insurance Corp. of Ireland v. Compagnie des Bauxites de Guinee, 456 U.S. 694, 702-03 & n.10 (1982).

What liberty interest is it that personal jurisdiction protects? Freedom from a biased forum? Is there any reason to believe that Oklahoma would have been more biased against Seaway than Washington would have been against International Shoe? Does personal jurisdiction protect freedom from an inconvenient forum? Is the inconvenience in *World-Wide Volkswagen* and *International Shoe* significantly different?

Although the justification for restricting personal jurisdiction has now shifted from sovereignty to individual liberty, the test has not changed. The Court continues to require, as it said in *World-Wide Volkswagen*, that the defendant have "purposefully avail[ed] itself of the privilege of conducting activities within the forum state." How is the requirement of purposefulness related to the defendant's liberty?

Professor Margaret Stewart has justified the purposefulness requirement as follows:

> By choosing to act within the forum, however, the defendant does choose to affiliate himself to some degree with a sovereign entity. Absent that choice, he may assert a right to remain unconnected with the entity, and to be treated by that entity as unconnected to it—a right which is waived by his purposeful conduct. Case law recognition of this right is implicit in the oft-repeated refrain

that a state lacks the authority to assert jurisdiction over a defendant who has no contacts, ties, or relationship with the state. The state's lack of authority simply reflects the defendant's right to be free from certain assertions of such authority-- his right to be, and to be treated as, unconnected.

The source of this right of "unconnectedness" rests on two premises, each inherent in the United States structure of government. One is the continuing constitutional relevance of state lines, which mark off one sovereign from another and which, therefore, still define the entity with which a party may choose to remain unconnected. An expansive understanding of federal regulatory authority, unrestricted as a practical matter by any constitutionally compelled recognition of areas of activity left solely to state control, has substantially reduced the importance of these lines in other contexts. That understanding does not reduce their importance in the jurisdictional context, however. The ability of each state to create and control its own judiciary, one inherent attribute of sovereignty, was perhaps the attribute least affected by the adoption of the Constitution; the independence of those judiciaries has not been radically altered in the intervening two hundred years. Whether continued recognition of their independence and source of authority in state sovereignty is either wise or necessary in today's age of rapid transportation, multi-state activities and increasing national control is not the issue. That recognition is mandated by history and can be refused only if the concept of a nation of states is abrogated by constitutional amendment.

The second premise underlying an individual's right to remain unconnected with, and to be treated as unconnected to, a sovereign is equally basic to our governmental structure. That the legitimacy of all governmental authority derives from the "consent" of those governed is a political truism, even though the most minimal reflection reveals that only rarely, if ever, does everyone subject to any exercise of that authority agree with the exercise. "Consent" in this sense cannot imply the right to refuse to accept regulation or regulated consequences; there is no freedom to "opt out." Rather, consent is derived from the right to participate in the decision-making process, so that the authority which is exercised over those governed is exercised by them. Those not within the polity, those without the right to participate in the creation and control of its authority, those who are "unconnected," cannot be subject to its authority, whether regulatory or judicial.[1]

Stewart, *A New Litany of Personal Jurisdiction*, 18–19; see also Epstein, *Consent, Not Power*. If personal jurisdiction is a doctrine fundamentally based on consent, does that tell us anything about how the doctrine should be applied? In determining jurisdiction, should it matter what the defendant actually expected or thought about jurisdiction? Can one "consent" without knowing it? How should we determine the scope of a defendant's consent? In *International Shoe*, by purposefully employing workers in Washington, the company consented to be sued in Washington for

---

1. Margaret G. Stewart, *A New Litany of Personal Jurisdiction*, 60 U.Colo.L.Rev. 5 (1989). Reprinted with permission of the University of Colorado Law Review.

unemployment taxes. Did this purposeful conduct also constitute consent to be sued in Washington by workers injured at a Missouri factory?

If you accept a consent theory of personal jurisdiction, does it follow that the Constitution limits states' adjudicative authority? Consider the following argument: There is no reason to struggle to interpret the Fourteenth Amendment to cover the problem of personal jurisdiction. Though the drafters of the Constitution may well have been concerned about states exercising sovereign authority over those who lacked the requisite connection with the state, they provided a straightforward solution in the grant of diversity jurisdiction. In most situations where a state might attempt to assert authority inappropriately over a non-citizen, diversity of citizenship will exist. To the extent Congress is concerned about such problems, it may allow defendants to remove the case and litigate before the defendant's own sovereign, i.e., the United States. Do you agree? See Perdue, *Personal Jurisdiction and the Beetle in the Box*, 549.

Professor Lea Brilmayer has offered a somewhat different explanation for the purposefulness component of personal jurisdiction. She explains:

> The reason for limiting jurisdiction to cases where the defendant had some control over the eventual location of the product is to prevent the forum from always shifting the costs to persons to whom its sovereignty does not extend, namely, the out-of-state consumers who have no contact with the forum. If the defendant deliberately sent a product into the State, he has a choice to stop marketing there if the costs of doing business exceed the value to him of that market. And the State is unlikely to impose upon him jurisdictional burdens exceeding the actual cost of his activities there, because the State does not want to discourage his activities in the State unless the benefits of the activities are less than the burdens. But if jurisdiction can be asserted even where the defendant had no control, these checks cannot be assumed to be adequate. Since the defendant cannot structure his conduct in a way that makes him immune to suit there, the State is not adequately restrained by the possibility that the defendant will withdraw from its markets. And it cannot be inferred that taking advantage of activity in the forum was sufficiently profitable, even given the added jurisdictional costs, that the defendant may fairly be presumed to have agreed to take his chances.

Brilmayer, *How Contacts Count*, 95–96. Why cannot states distribute losses onto out-of-staters? After all, in the context of choice of law, the Supreme Court has recognized that when the forum has a legitimate interest in a controversy, it has no obligation to defer to the interests of another state. See Nevada v. Hall, 440 U.S. 410, 421-24 (1979); Pacific Employers Ins. Co. v. Industrial Accident Comm'n, 306 U.S. 493, 502-03 (1939); Alaska Packers Assn v. Industrial Accident Comm'n, 294 U.S. 532, 547 (1935).

Is economic efficiency enhanced by making plaintiffs travel to defendants' states rather than the other way around? Consider the following argument: If the car dealer in *World-Wide Volkswagen* could be sued anywhere that the car blew up, then the seller would have to either curtail sales or raise the price in order to cover the costs of potential distant litigation. But does not this argument look at only half the transaction? If the car buyer knows that she must return to New York to litigate, no matter where she is when her dispute arises, will she not value the car less and thus curtail her purchases?

3. Personal Jurisdiction in Federal Court

The personal jurisdiction authority of states is limited by the Fourteenth Amendment and by each state's own statutory limits. In federal court, the analysis is somewhat different. First, it is the Fifth Amendment, not the Fourteenth Amendment that imposes due process restrictions on the federal government. Second, the federal courts must determine what if any non-constitutional limits to impose. These non-constitutional limits are, for the most part, addressed either by federal legislation or by Rule 4 of the Federal Rules of Civil Procedure.

In a few areas, Congress has legislatively provided for nationwide service of process. See, e.g., 15 U.S.C. § 22 (antitrust claims); 15 U.S.C. §§ 77v(a), 78aa (securities claims); 18 U.S.C. § 1965 (RICO); 28 U.S.C. § 1695 (derivative suits); 28 U.S.C. § 2361 (interpleader). Where nationwide service of process exists, a defendant may be sued in any judicial district, regardless of where she is served with process. But are there any constitutional limitations on nationwide service? Can a defendant be required to litigate in a federal district court located in a state with which the defendant has no connections?

Although the Supreme Court has not directly addressed the issue, most lower courts have held that all the Fifth Amendment requires is contacts with the "sovereign," i.e., the United States. Thus, it is constitutional for a citizen of Florida to be sued in federal court in Texas, since the defendant's contacts with Florida obviously are contacts with the United States. See Federal Trade Commission v. Jim Walter Corp., 651 F.2d 251 (5th Cir.1981). Accord Busch v. Buchman, Buchman & O'Brien, 11 F.3d 1255 (5th Cir.1994); Go-Video, Inc. v. Akai Electric Co., 885 F.2d 1406 (9th Cir.1989); Fitzsimmons v. Barton, 589 F.2d 330 (7th Cir.1979); Mariash v. Morrill, 496 F.2d 1138 (2d Cir.1974); Travis v. Anthes Imperial Ltd., 473 F.2d 515 (8th Cir.1973). In contrast, a minority of courts have held that even where sufficient national contacts exist, basic fairness considerations embodied in the Due Process Clause limit where within the United States litigation may be brought. See Republic of Panama v. BCCI Holdings (Luxembourg), 119 F.3d 935 (11th Cir.1997) Horne v. Adolph Coors Co., 684 F.2d 255 (3d Cir.1982); Duckworth v. Medical Electro-Therapeutics, Inc., 768 F.Supp. 822 (S.D.Ga.1991); Oxford First Corp. v. PNC Liquidating Corp., 372 F.Supp. 191 (E.D.Pa.1974). See generally Born, *International Civil Litigation*, 174–82.

For most cases in federal court, Congress has not provided nationwide service of process. Under Rule 4(k)(1)(A) of the Federal Rules of Civil Procedure, if a defendant is subject to personal jurisdiction in a state, then she is also subject to personal jurisdiction in the federal district or districts located in that state. There are situations in which although there is no state court jurisdiction, federal court jurisdiction would be appropriate. Two such situations are: (1) the defendant has sufficient contacts with the state to meet the requirements of the Fourteenth

Amendment, but the state long-arm statute does not extend to the full extent allowed by the Fourteenth Amendment, or (2) the defendant lacks sufficient contacts with the state to meet the requirements of the Fourteenth Amendment, but has sufficient contacts with the United States to meet the requirements of the Fifth Amendment. Rule 4(k)(2) addresses these situations, at least in some cases. That Rule provides:

> If the exercise of jurisdiction is consistent with the Constitution and laws of the United States, serving a summons or filing a waiver of service is also effective, with respect to claims arising under federal law, to establish personal jurisdiction over the person of any defendant who is not subject to the jurisdiction of the courts of general jurisdiction of any state.

One of the complications for a plaintiff seeking to use Rule 4(k)(2) is that the Rule is only available if there is no state that would have jurisdiction. How does the plaintiff meet this burden? Obviously, it would be quite burdensome if the plaintiff were required to list all 50 states and explain as to each why there is no jurisdiction. The Seventh Circuit has offered an ingenious solution to this problem. The court explained:

> A defendant who wants to preclude use of Rule 4(k)(2) has only to name some other state in which the suit could proceed. Naming a more appropriate state would amount to a consent to personal jurisdiction there. *** If, however, the defendant contends that he cannot be sued in the forum state and refuses to identify any other where suit is possible, then the federal court is entitled to use Rule 4(k)(2).

IST Int'l, Inc. v. Borden Ladner Gervais LLP, 256 F.3d 548, 552 (7th Cir. 2001).

Although Rule 4(k)(2) is limited in scope, it can be quite useful. Consider for example Graduate Management Admissions Council v. Raju, 2003 U.S.Dist. LEXIS 979 (E.D.Va.). There the plaintiff brought federal copyright, trademark, cyberpiracy and unfair competition claims against an Indian citizen who ran a web site that offered material to prepare for the Graduate Management Admission Test. Suit was brought in federal court in Virginia but the court found that the defendant had insufficient contacts with Virginia to satisfy the Fourteenth Amendment. However, the court upheld personal jurisdiction relying on Rule 4(k)(2). The court found that the defendant had "targeted the United States market" and had sufficient contacts with the United States as a whole to satisfy Rule 4(k)(2). The court listed a number of aspects of the web site which supported the conclusion that the site was targeted at the U.S.: the price for items was in U.S. dollars, there was a toll free number for U.S. citizens, and testimonials on the site featured U.S. citizens.

C. PERSONAL JURISDICTION IN PRACTICE

In this section we explore in greater detail the circumstances in which the courts have and have not found personal jurisdiction. As you read these cases, consider whether the doctrine implements the purposes behind the limitations on judicial jurisdiction. You should also consider some more pragmatic questions: Why did the plaintiff choose the particular forum and why did the defendant contest jurisdiction? Was the forum particularly convenient or inconvenient for one side? What other fora were available? To what extent were the plaintiff's and defendant's forum preferences influenced by choice of law considerations?

1. Purposeful Contacts and Reasonableness

Whatever its theoretical justification, the Supreme Court has held that absent consent or waiver, a state has personal jurisdiction only if the defendant has "purposefully availed" herself of the benefits of that state. Physically going to a state constitutes a clear case of purposeful availment. Therefore, if a driver drives into a state, hits a pedestrian, and drives out, the pedestrian may sue him in the state where the accident occurred.

Although intentional physical presence suffices to establish a purposeful connection with the state, physical presence is not necessary. For example, in Calder v. Jones, 465 U.S. 783 (1984), the Court upheld jurisdiction in California against the editor and writer of an allegedly defamatory article about a California resident. The article was published in the *National Enquirer* and distributed in California, and the *National Enquirer* did not contest jurisdiction. However, the writer and editor did their work on the article in Florida and neither traveled to California in connection with the article. Notwithstanding their lack of physical connection with California, the Court upheld jurisdiction over the writer and editor, explaining:

> The allegedly libelous story concerned the California activities of a California resident. It impugned the professionalism of an entertainer whose television career was centered in California. The article was drawn from California sources, and the brunt of the harm, in terms both of respondent's emotional distress and the injury to her professional reputation, was suffered in California. In sum, California is the focal point both of the story and of the harm suffered. Jurisdiction over petitioners is therefore proper in California based on the "effects" of their Florida conduct in California.

Id. at 788-89.

Burger King Corp. v. Rudzewicz

Supreme Court of the United States, 1985.
471 U.S. 462, 105 S.Ct. 2174, 85 L.Ed.2d 528.

JUSTICE BRENNAN delivered the opinion of the Court. The State of Florida's long-arm statute extends jurisdiction to "[a]ny person, whether or not a citizen or resident of this state," who, *inter alia*, "[b]reach[es] a contract in this state by failing to perform acts required by the contract to be performed in this state," so long as the cause of action arises from the alleged contractual breach. Fla. Stat. § 48.193 (1)(g) (Supp. 1984). The United States District Court for the Southern District of Florida, sitting in diversity, relied on this provision in exercising personal jurisdiction over a Michigan resident who allegedly had breached a franchise agreement with a Florida corporation by failing to make required payments in Florida. The question presented is whether this exercise of long-arm jurisdiction offended "traditional conception[s] of fair play and substantial justice" embodied in the Due Process

Clause of the Fourteenth Amendment. *International Shoe.*

I. A. Burger King Corporation is a Florida corporation whose principal offices are in Miami. It is one of the world's largest restaurant organizations, with over 3,000 outlets in the 50 States, the Commonwealth of Puerto Rico, and 8 foreign nations. Burger King conducts approximately 80% of its business through a franchise operation that the company styles the "Burger King System"–"a comprehensive restaurant format and operating system for the sale of uniform and quality food products." [cit.] Burger King licenses its franchisees to use its trademarks and service marks for a period of 20 years and leases standardized restaurant facilities to them for the same term. In addition, franchisees acquire a variety of proprietary information concerning the "standards, specifications, procedures and methods for operating a Burger King Restaurant." [cit.] They also receive market research and advertising assistance; ongoing training in restaurant management; and accounting, cost-control, and inventory-control guidance. By permitting franchisees to tap into Burger King's established national reputation and to benefit from proven procedures for dispensing standardized fare, this system enables them to go into the restaurant business with significantly lowered barriers to entry.

In exchange for these benefits, franchisees pay Burger King an initial $40,000 franchise fee and commit themselves to payment of monthly royalties, advertising and sales promotion fees, and rent computed in part from monthly gross sales. Franchisees also agree to submit to the national organization's exacting regulation of virtually every conceivable aspect of their operations. Burger King imposes these standards and undertakes its rigid regulation out of conviction that "[u]niformity of service, appearance, and quality of product is essential to the preservation of the Burger King image and the benefits accruing therefrom to both Franchisee and Franchisor." [cit.]

Burger King oversees its franchise system through a two-tiered administrative structure. The governing contracts provide that the franchise relationship is established in Miami and governed by Florida law, and call for payment of all required fees and forwarding of all relevant notices to the Miami headquarters. The Miami headquarters sets policy and works directly with its franchisees in attempting to resolve major problems. [cit.] Day-to-day monitoring of franchisees, however, is conducted through a network of 10 district offices which in turn report to the Miami headquarters.

The instant litigation grows out of Burger King's termination of one of its franchisees, and is aptly described by the franchisee as "a divorce proceeding among commercial partners." [cit.] The appellee John Rudzewicz, a Michigan citizen and resident, is the senior partner in a Detroit accounting firm. In 1978, he was approached by Brian MacShara, the son of a business acquaintance, who suggested that they jointly apply to Burger King for a franchise in the Detroit area. MacShara proposed to serve as the manager of the restaurant if Rudzewicz would put up the investment capital; in exchange, the two would evenly share the profits. Believing that MacShara's idea offered attractive investment and tax-deferral opportunities, Rudzewicz agreed to the venture. [cit.]

Rudzewicz and MacShara jointly applied for a franchise to Burger King's

Birmingham, Michigan, district office in the autumn of 1978. Their application was forwarded to Burger King's Miami headquarters, which entered into a preliminary agreement with them in February 1979. During the ensuing four months it was agreed that Rudzewicz and MacShara would assume operation of an existing facility in Drayton Plains, Michigan. MacShara attended the prescribed management courses in Miami during this period, [cit.] and the franchisees purchased $165,000 worth of restaurant equipment from Burger King's Davmor Industries division in Miami. Even before the final agreements were signed, however, the parties began to disagree over site-development fees, building design, computation of monthly rent, and whether the franchisees would be able to assign their liabilities to a corporation they had formed. During these disputes Rudzewicz and MacShara negotiated both with the Birmingham district office and with the Miami headquarters.[7] With some misgivings, Rudzewicz and MacShara finally obtained limited concessions from the Miami headquarters, signed the final agreements, and commenced operations in June 1979. By signing the final agreements, Rudzewicz obligated himself personally to payments exceeding $1 million over the 20-year franchise relationship.

The Drayton Plains facility apparently enjoyed steady business during the summer of 1979, but patronage declined after a recession began later that year. Rudzewicz and MacShara soon fell far behind in their monthly payments to Miami. Headquarters sent notices of default, and an extended period of negotiations began among the franchisees, the Birmingham district office, and the Miami headquarters. After several Burger King officials in Miami had engaged in prolonged but ultimately unsuccessful negotiations with the franchisees by mail and by telephone, headquarters terminated the franchise and ordered Rudzewicz and MacShara to vacate the premises. They refused and continued to occupy and operate the facility as a Burger King restaurant.

B. Burger King commenced the instant action in the United States District Court for the Southern District of Florida in May 1981, invoking that court's diversity jurisdiction pursuant to 28 U.S.C. § 1332(a) and its original jurisdiction over federal trademark disputes pursuant to § 1338(a). Burger King alleged that Rudzewicz and MacShara had breached their franchise obligations "within [the jurisdiction of] this district court" by failing to make the required payments "at plaintiff's place of business in Miami, Dade County, Florida," [cit.], and also charged that they were tortiously infringing its trademarks and service marks through their continued, unauthorized operation as a Burger King restaurant [cit.]. Burger King sought damages, injunctive relief, and costs and attorney's fees. Rudzewicz and MacShara entered special appearances and argued, inter alia, that because they were Michigan residents and because Burger King's claim did not "arise" within the Southern District of Florida, the District Court lacked personal jurisdiction over them. The District Court denied their motions after a hearing, holding that, pursuant to Florida's long-arm statute, "a non-resident Burger King franchisee is subject to the

---

7. Although Rudzewicz and MacShara dealt with the Birmingham district office on a regular basis, they communicated directly with the Miami headquarters in forming the contracts; moreover, they learned that the district office had "very little" decision making authority and accordingly turned directly to headquarters in seeking to resolve their disputes. [cit.]

personal jurisdiction of this Court in actions arising out of its franchise agreements." [cit.] Rudzewicz and MacShara then filed an answer and a counterclaim seeking damages for alleged violations by Burger King of Michigan's Franchise Investment Law, Mich. Comp. Laws § 445.1501 et seq. (1979).

After a 3–day bench trial, the court again concluded that it had "jurisdiction over the subject matter and the parties to this cause." [cit.] [On the merits, the court entered judgment against Rudzewicz and MacShara. Rudzewicz appealed and the court of appeals. A divided panel of that Circuit reversed the judgment, concluding that the District Court could not properly exercise personal jurisdiction over Rudzewicz.] * * *

II. A. The Due Process Clause protects an individual's liberty interest in not being subject to the binding judgments of a forum with which he has established no meaningful "contacts, ties, or relations." *International Shoe.* By requiring that individuals have "fair warning that a particular activity may subject [them] to the jurisdiction of a foreign sovereign," *Shaffer v. Heitner,* (Stevens, J., concurring in judgment), the Due Process Clause "gives a degree of predictability to the legal system that allows potential defendants to structure their primary conduct with some minimum assurance as to where that conduct will and will not render them liable to suit," *World-Wide Volkswagen Corp.*

* * *

We have noted several reasons why a forum legitimately may exercise personal jurisdiction over a nonresident who "purposefully directs" his activities toward forum residents. A State generally has a "manifest interest" in providing its residents with a convenient forum for redressing injuries inflicted by out-of-state actors. Id. at 223; see also *Keeton v. Hustler Magazine, Inc.* Moreover, where individuals "purposefully derive benefit" from their interstate activities, *Kulko v. California Superior Court,* it may well be unfair to allow them to escape having to account in other States for consequences that arise proximately from such activities; the Due Process Clause may not readily be wielded as a territorial shield to avoid interstate obligations that have been voluntarily assumed. And because "modern transportation and communications have made it much less burdensome for a party sued to defend himself in a State where he engages in economic activity," it usually will not be unfair to subject him to the burdens of litigating in another forum for disputes relating to such activity. *McGee v. International Life Insurance Co.*

Notwithstanding these considerations, the constitutional touchstone remains whether the defendant purposefully established "minimum contacts" in the forum State. *International Shoe.* Although it has been argued that foreseeability of causing *injury* in another State should be sufficient to establish such contacts there when policy considerations so require, the Court has consistently held that this kind of foreseeability is not a "sufficient benchmark" for exercising personal jurisdiction. *World-Wide Volkswagen.* Instead, "the foreseeability that is critical to due process analysis ... is that the defendant's conduct and connection with the forum State are such that he should reasonably anticipate being haled into court there." * * *

This "purposeful availment" requirement ensures that a defendant will not be haled into a jurisdiction solely as a result of "random," "fortuitous," or "attenuated" contacts, [cit.], or of the "unilateral activity of another party or a third person." [cit.] Jurisdiction is proper, however, where the contacts proximately result from actions by the defendant *himself* that create a "substantial connection" with the forum State. [cit.] Thus where the defendant "deliberately" has engaged in significant activities within a State, [cit.] or has created "continuing obligations" between himself and residents of the forum, [cit.], he manifestly has availed himself of the privilege of conducting business there, and because his activities are shielded by "the benefits and protections" of the forum's laws it is presumptively not unreasonable to require him to submit to the burdens of litigation in that forum as well.

Jurisdiction in these circumstances may not be avoided merely because the defendant did not *physically* enter the forum State. Although territorial presence frequently will enhance a potential defendant's affiliation with a State and reinforce the reasonable foreseeability of suit there, it is an inescapable fact of modern commercial life that a substantial amount of business is transacted solely by mail and wire communications across state lines, thus obviating the need for physical presence within a State in which business is conducted. So long as a commercial actor's efforts are "purposefully directed" toward residents of another State, we have consistently rejected the notion that an absence of physical contacts can defeat personal jurisdiction there. *Keeton v. Hustler Magazine, Inc.*; see also *Calder v. Jones*; *McGee v. International Life Insurance Co.*; [cit.].

Once it has been decided that a defendant purposefully established minimum contacts within the forum State, these contacts may be considered in light of other factors to determine whether the assertion of personal jurisdiction would comport with "fair play and substantial justice." *International Shoe*. Thus courts in "appropriate case[s]" may evaluate "the burden on the defendant," "the forum State's interest in adjudicating the dispute," "the plaintiff's interest in obtaining convenient and effective relief," "the interstate judicial system's interest in obtaining the most efficient resolution of controversies," and the "shared interest of the several States in furthering fundamental substantive social policies." *World-Wide Volkswagen*. These considerations sometimes serve to establish the reasonableness of jurisdiction upon a lesser showing of minimum contacts than would otherwise be required. See, e.g., *Keeton v. Hustler Magazine, Inc.*; *Calder v. Jones*; *McGee v. International Life Insurance Co*. On the other hand, where a defendant who purposefully has directed his activities at forum residents seeks to defeat jurisdiction, he must present a compelling case that the presence of some other considerations would render jurisdiction unreasonable. Most such considerations usually may be accommodated through means short of finding jurisdiction unconstitutional. For example, the potential clash of the forum's law with the "fundamental substantive social policies" of another State may be accommodated through application of the forum's choice-of-law rules. Similarly, a defendant claiming substantial inconvenience may seek a change of venue. Nevertheless, minimum requirements inherent in the concept of "fair play and substantial justice" may defeat the reasonableness of jurisdiction even if the defendant has purposefully engaged in forum activities. *World-Wide Volkswagen*; see also Restatement (Second) of Conflict of Laws §§ 36–37 (1971). As we previously have noted, jurisdictional rules may not be employed in such a way as to make litigation "so gravely difficult and inconvenient" that a party unfairly is at a "severe disadvantage" in comparison to his opponent. The Bremen v. Zapata Off-Shore Co., 407 U.S. 1, 18 (1972) (re forum-selection provisions); *McGee v. International Life Insurance Co.*

B. (1). Applying these principles to the case at hand, we believe there is substantial record evidence supporting the District Court's conclusion that the assertion of personal jurisdiction over Rudzewicz in Florida for the alleged breach of his franchise agreement did not offend due process. At the outset, we note a continued division among lower courts respecting whether and to what extent a contract can constitute a "contact" for purposes of due process analysis. If the question is whether an individual's contract with an out-of-state party *alone* can automatically establish sufficient minimum contacts in the other party's home forum, we believe the answer clearly is that it cannot. The Court long ago rejected the notion that personal jurisdiction might turn on "mechanical" tests, [cit.] or on "conceptualistic ... theories of the place of contracting or of performance," [cit.]. Instead, we have emphasized the need for a "highly realistic" approach that recognizes that a "contract" is "ordinarily but an intermediate step serving to tie up prior business negotiations with future consequences which themselves are the real object of the business transaction." [cit.] It is these factors—prior negotiations and contemplated future consequences, along with the terms of the contract and the parties' actual course of dealing—that must be evaluated in determining whether the defendant purposefully established minimum contacts within the forum.

In this case, no physical ties to Florida can be attributed to Rudzewicz other than MacShara's brief training course in Miami.[22] Rudzewicz did not maintain offices in Florida and, for all that appears from the record, has never even visited there. Yet this franchise dispute grew directly out of "a contract which had a *substantial connection with that State.*" *McGee v. International Life Insurance Co.* (emphasis added). Eschewing the option of operating an independent local enterprise, Rudzewicz deliberately "reach[ed] out beyond" Michigan and negotiated with a Florida corporation for the purchase of a long-term franchise and the manifold benefits that would derive from affiliation with a nationwide organization.[cit.] Upon approval, he entered into a carefully structured 20–year relationship that envisioned continuing and wide-reaching contacts with Burger King in Florida. In light of Rudzewicz' voluntary acceptance of the long-term and exacting regulation of his business from Burger King's Miami headquarters, the "quality and nature" of his relationship to the company in Florida can in no sense be viewed as "random,"

---

22. The Eleventh Circuit held that MacShara's presence in Florida was irrelevant to the question of Rudzewicz' minimum contacts with that forum, reasoning that "Rudzewicz and MacShara never formed a partnership" and "signed the agreements in their individual capacities." [cit.] The two did jointly form a corporation through which they were seeking to conduct the franchise, however. [cit.] They were required to decide which one of them would travel to Florida to satisfy the training requirements so that they could commence business, and Rudzewicz participated in the decision that MacShara would go there. We have previously noted that when commercial activities are "carried on in behalf of" an out-of-state party those activities may sometimes be ascribed to the party, *International Shoe*, at least where he is a "primary participan[t]" in the enterprise and has acted purposefully in directing those activities, *Calder v. Jones*. Because MacShara's matriculation at Burger King University is not pivotal to the disposition of this case, we need not resolve the permissible bounds of such attribution.

"fortuitous," or "attenuated." *Hanson v. Denckla*; *Keeton v. Hustler Magazine, Inc.*; *World-Wide Volkswagen*. Rudzewicz' refusal to make the contractually required payments in Miami, and his continued use of Burger King's trademarks and confidential business information after his termination, caused foreseeable injuries to the corporation in Florida. For these reasons it was, at the very least, presumptively reasonable for Rudzewicz to be called to account there for such injuries.

The Court of Appeals concluded, however, that in light of the supervision emanating from Burger King's district office in Birmingham, Rudzewicz reasonably believed that "the Michigan office was for all intents and purposes the embodiment of Burger King" and that he therefore had no "reason to anticipate a Burger King suit outside of Michigan." [cit.] This reasoning overlooks substantial record evidence indicating that Rudzewicz most certainly knew that he was affiliating himself with an enterprise based primarily in Florida. The contract documents themselves emphasize that Burger King's operations are conducted and supervised from the Miami headquarters, that all relevant notices and payments must be sent there, and that the agreements were made in and enforced from Miami.[cit.] Moreover, the parties' actual course of dealing repeatedly confirmed that decisionmaking authority was vested in the Miami headquarters and that the district office served largely as an intermediate link between the headquarters and the franchisees. When problems arose over building design, site-development fees, rent computation, and the defaulted payments, Rudzewicz and MacShara learned that the Michigan office was powerless to resolve their disputes and could only channel their communications to Miami. Throughout these disputes, the Miami headquarters and the Michigan franchisees carried on a continuous course of direct communications by mail and by telephone, and it was the Miami headquarters that made the key negotiating decisions out of which the instant litigation arose. [cit.]

Moreover, we believe the Court of Appeals gave insufficient weight to provisions in the various franchise documents providing that all disputes would be governed by Florida law. The franchise agreement, for example, stated:

"This Agreement shall become valid when executed and accepted by BKC at Miami, Florida; it shall be deemed made and entered into in the State of Florida and shall be governed and construed under and in accordance with the laws of the State of Florida. The choice of law designation does not require that all suits concerning this Agreement be filed in Florida." [cit.]

[cit.] The Court of Appeals reasoned that choice-of-law provisions are irrelevant to the question of personal jurisdiction, relying on *Hanson v. Denckla* for the proposition that "the center of gravity for choice-of-law purposes does not necessarily confer the sovereign prerogative to assert jurisdiction." [cit.] This reasoning misperceives the import of the quoted proposition. The Court in *Hanson* and subsequent cases has emphasized that choice-of-law *analysis*—which focuses on all elements of a transaction, and not simply on the defendant's conduct—is distinct from minimum-contacts jurisdictional analysis—which focuses at the threshold solely on the defendant's purposeful connection to the forum. Nothing in our cases, however, suggests that a choice-of-law *provision* should be ignored in considering whether a defendant has "purposefully invoked the benefits and protections of a State's laws" for jurisdictional purposes. Although such a provision standing alone would be insufficient to confer jurisdiction, we believe that, when combined with the 20-year interdependent relationship Rudzewicz established with Burger King's Miami headquarters, it reinforced his deliberate affiliation with the forum State and the reasonable foreseeability of possible litigation there. As Judge Johnson argued in his dissent below, Rudzewicz "purposefully availed himself of the benefits and protections of Florida's laws" by entering into contracts expressly providing that those laws would govern franchise disputes. [cit.][24]

(2). Nor has Rudzewicz pointed to other factors that can be said persuasively to outweigh the considerations discussed above and to establish the *unconstitutionality* of Florida's assertion of jurisdiction. We cannot conclude that Florida had no "legitimate interest in holding [Rudzewicz] answerable on a claim related to" the contacts he had established in that State. *Keeton v. Hustler Magazine*, Inc.; see also *McGee v. International Life Insurance Co.* (noting that State frequently will have a "manifest interest in providing effective means of redress for its residents").[25] Moreover, although Rudzewicz has argued at some length that Michigan's Franchise Investment Law [cit.] governs many aspects of this franchise relationship, he has not demonstrated how Michigan's acknowledged interest might possibly render jurisdiction in Florida *unconstitutional*.[26] Finally, the Court of Appeals' assertion that the Florida litigation "severely impaired [Rudzewicz'] ability to call Michigan witnesses who might be essential to his defense and counterclaim," [cit.] is wholly without support in the record. And even to the extent that it is inconvenient for a party who has minimum contacts with a forum to litigate there, such considerations most frequently can be accommodated through a change of venue. [cit.] Although the Court has suggested that inconvenience may at some point become so substantial as to achieve *constitutional* magnitude,[cit.], this is not such a case.

The Court of Appeals also concluded, however, that the parties' dealings involved "a characteristic disparity of bargaining power" and "elements of surprise," and that Rudzewicz "lacked fair notice" of the potential for litigation in Florida

---

24. In addition, the franchise agreement's disclaimer that the "choice of law designation does not *require* that all suits concerning this Agreement be filed in Florida," [cit.] reasonably should have suggested to Rudzewicz that by negative implication such suits *could* be filed there.

The lease also provided for binding arbitration in Miami of certain condemnation disputes, [cit.] and Rudzewicz conceded the validity of this provision at oral argument, [cit.]. Although it does not govern the instant dispute, this provision also should have made it apparent to the franchisees that they were dealing directly with the Miami headquarters and that the Birmingham district office was *not* "for all intents and purposes the embodiment of Burger King." [cit.]

25. Complaining that "when Burger King is the plaintiff, you won't 'have it your way' because it sues all franchisees in Miami," [cit.] Rudzewicz contends that Florida's interest in providing a convenient forum is negligible given the company's size and ability to conduct litigation anywhere in the country. We disagree. Absent compelling considerations, cf. *McGee v. International Life Insurance Co.*, a defendant who has purposefully derived commercial benefit from his affiliations in a forum may not defeat jurisdiction there simply because of his adversary's greater net wealth.

26. Rudzewicz has failed to show how the District Court's exercise of jurisdiction in this case might have been at all inconsistent with Michigan's interests. To the contrary, the court found that Burger King had fully complied with Michigan law [cit.], and there is nothing in Michigan's franchise Act suggesting that Michigan would attempt to assert exclusive jurisdiction to resolve franchise disputes affecting its residents. In any event, minimum-contacts analysis presupposes that two or more States may be interested in the outcome of a dispute, and the process of resolving potentially conflicting "fundamental substantive social policies," *World-Wide Volkswagen*, can usually be accommodated through choice-of-law rules rather than through outright preclusion of jurisdiction in one forum. [cit.]

because the contractual provisions suggesting to the contrary were merely "boilerplate declarations in a lengthy printed contract. [cit.]" Rudzewicz presented many of these arguments to the District Court, contending that Burger King was guilty of misrepresentation, fraud, and duress; that it gave insufficient notice in its dealings with him; and that the contract was one of adhesion. [cit.] After a 3-day bench trial, the District Court found that Burger King had made no misrepresentations, that Rudzewicz and MacShara "were and are experienced and sophisticated businessmen," and that "at no time" did they "ac[t] under economic duress or disadvantage imposed by" Burger King. [cit.] Federal Rule of Civil Procedure 52(a) requires that "[f]indings of fact shall not be set aside unless clearly erroneous," and neither Rudzewicz nor the Court of Appeals has pointed to record evidence that would support a "definite and firm conviction" that the District Court's findings are mistaken. [cit.] To the contrary, Rudzewicz was represented by counsel throughout these complex transactions and, as Judge Johnson observed in dissent below, was himself an experienced accountant "who for five months conducted negotiations with Burger King over the terms of the franchise and lease agreements, and who obligated himself personally to contracts requiring over time payments that exceeded $1 million." [cit.] Rudzewicz was able to secure a modest reduction in rent and other concessions from Miami headquarters[cit.]; moreover, to the extent that Burger King's terms were inflexible, Rudzewicz presumably decided that the advantages of affiliating with a national organization provided sufficient commercial benefits to offset the detriments.

III. Notwithstanding these considerations, the Court of Appeals apparently believed that it was necessary to reject jurisdiction in this case as a prophylactic measure, reasoning that an affirmance of the District Court's judgment would result in the exercise of jurisdiction over "out-of-state consumers to collect payments due on modest personal purchases" and would "sow the seeds of default judgments against franchisees owing smaller debts." [cit.] We share the Court of Appeals' broader concerns and therefore reject any talismanic jurisdictional formulas; "the facts of each case must [always] be weighed" in determining whether personal jurisdiction would comport with "fair play and substantial justice." [cit.][29] The "quality and nature" of an interstate transaction may sometimes be so "random," "fortuitous," or "attenuated" that it cannot fairly be said that the potential defendant "should reasonably anticipate being haled into court" in another jurisdiction. [cit.] We also have emphasized that jurisdiction may not be grounded on a contract whose terms have been obtained through "fraud, undue influence, or overweening bargaining power" and whose application would render litigation "so gravely difficult and inconvenient that [a party] will for all practical purposes be deprived of his day in court." The Bremen v. Zapata Off-Shore Co., 407 U.S. at 12, 18. Cf. Fuentes v. Shevin, 407 U.S. 67, 94-96 (1972); National Equipment Rental, Ltd. v. Szukhent, 375 U.S. 311, 329 (1964) (Black, J., dissenting) (jurisdictional rules may

---

29. This approach does, of course, preclude clear-cut jurisdictional rules. But any inquiry into "fair play and substantial justic"" necessarily requires determinations "in which few answers will be written 'in black and white. The greys are dominant and even among them the shades are innumerable.'" *Kulko v. California Superior Court.*

not be employed against small consumers so as to "crippl[e] their defense"). Just as the Due Process Clause allows flexibility in ensuring that commercial actors are not effectively "judgment proof" for the consequences of obligations they voluntarily assume in other States, [cit.] so too does it prevent rules that would unfairly enable them to obtain default judgments against unwitting customers. [cit.]

For the reasons set forth above, however, these dangers are not present in the instant case. Because Rudzewicz established a substantial and continuing relationship with Burger King's Miami headquarters, received fair notice from the contract documents and the course of dealing that he might be subject to suit in Florida, and has failed to demonstrate how jurisdiction in that forum would otherwise be fundamentally unfair, we conclude that the District Court's exercise of jurisdiction pursuant to Fla. Stat. § 48.193(1)(g) (Supp. 1984) did not offend due process. The judgment of the Court of Appeals is accordingly reversed, and the case is remanded for further proceedings consistent with this opinion.

It is so ordered.

JUSTICE POWELL took no part in the consideration or decision of this case.

[Dissent of Justice Stevens omitted.]

Notes and Questions

1. What weight should the court give to a choice of law clause? If the contract had specified New York law, would that subject the defendants to jurisdiction in New York? The contract did not include a consent to jurisdiction clause. Professor Russell Weintraub has suggested that this omission may have been intentional because the Michigan Franchise Investment Act had been interpreted to prohibit consent to jurisdiction clauses. Weintraub, *Commentary*, 139. By giving weight to the choice of law clause, is Justice Brennan allowing franchisors to circumvent the Michigan prohibition?

2. Compare Brennan's opinion in *Burger King* with his choice of law opinion in *Allstate Ins. Co. v. Hague*, supra at 455. How does his constitutional test for judicial jurisdiction differ from his test for legislative authority?

3. Consider the discussion of reasonableness in Part II A of the opinion. Some have suggested that this is where Justice Brennan finally "has it his way." Justice Brennan explains that if the defendant has purposeful minimum contacts, the next step is to determine whether jurisdiction "would comport with 'fair play and substantial justice.'" Although he suggests that "minimum contacts" and "reasonableness" are two prongs of the personal jurisdiction inquiry, he also suggests that these prongs are not wholly separate, so that if jurisdiction is really reasonable, lesser contacts would suffice. Under this approach, would *World-Wide Volkswagen* have come out differently?

4. An Arizona buyer makes a long-term contract with a Missouri seller of containers. The buyer frequently calls and faxes the Missouri seller with orders. The containers were shipped from a factory in North Carolina to the buyer in Arizona. Can the buyer be sued in Missouri for breach of contract? See CPC-Rexcell, Inc. v. La Corona Foods, Inc., 912 F.2d 241 (8th Cir.1990).

5. Compare *Burger King* with *Lilienthal v. Kaufman*, supra at 179. If the spendthrift had sued the California seller in Oregon seeking to rescind the contract, would the seller have been subject to jurisdiction in Oregon?

Asahi Metal Industry Co. v. Superior Court of California
Supreme Court of the United States, 1987.
480 U.S. 102, 107 S.Ct. 1026, 94 L.Ed.2d 92.

JUSTICE O'CONNOR announced the judgment of the Court and delivered the unanimous opinion of the Court with respect to Part I, the opinion of the Court with respect to Part II–B, in which The Chief Justice, Justice Brennan, Justice White, Justice Marshall, Justice Blackmun, Justice Powell, and Justice Stevens join, and an opinion with respect to Parts II–A and III, in which The Chief Justice, Justice Powell, and Justice Scalia join.

This case presents the question whether the mere awareness on the part of a foreign defendant that the components it manufactured, sold, and delivered outside the United States would reach the forum State in the stream of commerce constitutes "minimum contacts" between the defendant and the forum State such that the exercise of jurisdiction "does not offend 'traditional notions of fair play and substantial justice.'" [cit.]

I. On September 23, 1978, on Interstate Highway 80 in Solano County, California, Gary Zurcher lost control of his Honda motorcycle and collided with a tractor. Zurcher was severely injured, and his passenger and wife, Ruth Ann Moreno, was killed. In September 1979, Zurcher filed a product liability action in the Superior Court of the State of California in and for the County of Solano. Zurcher alleged that the 1978 accident was caused by a sudden loss of air and an explosion in the rear tire of the motorcycle, and alleged that the motorcycle tire, tube, and sealant were defective. Zurcher's complaint named, inter alia, Cheng Shin Rubber Industrial Co., Ltd. (Cheng Shin), the Taiwanese manufacturer of the tube. Cheng Shin in turn filed a cross-complaint seeking indemnification from its codefendants and from petitioner, Asahi Metal Industry Co., Ltd. (Asahi), the manufacturer of the tube's valve assembly. Zurcher's claims against Cheng Shin and the other defendants were eventually settled and dismissed, leaving only Cheng Shin's indemnity action against Asahi.

California's long-arm statute authorizes the exercise of jurisdiction "on any basis not inconsistent with the Constitution of this state or of the United States." [cit.] Asahi moved to quash Cheng Shin's service of summons, arguing the State could not exert jurisdiction over it consistent with the Due Process Clause of the Fourteenth Amendment.

In relation to the motion, the following information was submitted by Asahi and Cheng Shin. Asahi is a Japanese corporation. It manufactures tire valve assemblies in Japan and sells the assemblies to Cheng Shin, and to several other tire manufacturers, for use as components in finished tire tubes. Asahi's sales to Cheng Shin took place in Taiwan. The shipments from Asahi to Cheng Shin were sent from Japan to Taiwan. Cheng Shin bought and incorporated into its tire tubes 150,000 Asahi valve assemblies in 1978; 500,000 in 1979; 500,000 in 1980; 100,000 in 1981; and 100,000 in 1982. Sales to Cheng Shin accounted for 1.24 percent of Asahi's income in 1981 and 0.44 percent in 1982. Cheng Shin alleged that approximately 20 percent of its sales in the United States are in California. Cheng Shin purchases valve assemblies from other suppliers as well, and sells finished tubes throughout the world.

In 1983 an attorney for Cheng Shin conducted an informal examination of the valve stems of the tire tubes sold in one cycle store in Solano County. The attorney declared that of the approximately 115 tire tubes in the store, 97 were purportedly manufactured in Japan or Taiwan, and of those 97, 21 valve stems were marked with the circled letter "A", apparently Asahi's trademark. Of the 21 Asahi valve stems, 12 were incorporated into Cheng Shin tire tubes. The store contained 41 other Cheng Shin tubes that incorporated the valve assemblies of other manufacturers. [cit.] An affidavit of a manager of Cheng Shin whose duties included the purchasing of component parts stated: "'In discussions with Asahi regarding the purchase of valve stem assemblies the fact that my Company sells tubes throughout the world and specifically the United States has been discussed. I am informed and believe that Asahi was fully aware that valve stem assemblies sold to my Company and to others would end up throughout the United States and in California.'" [cit.] An affidavit of the president of Asahi, on the other hand, declared that Asahi "'has never contemplated that its limited sales of tire valves to Cheng Shin in Taiwan would subject it to lawsuits in California.'" [cit.] The record does not include any contract between Cheng Shin and Asahi. [cit.]

* * *

[The California Supreme Court held that California had personal jurisdiction over Asahi.]

II. A. The Due Process Clause of the Fourteenth Amendment limits the power of a state court to exert personal jurisdiction over a nonresident defendant."[T]he constitutional touchstone" of the determination whether an exercise of personal jurisdiction comports with due process "remains whether the defendant purposefully established 'minimum contacts' in the forum State." *Burger King Corp. v. Rudzewicz.* Most recently we have reaffirmed the oft-quoted reasoning of *Hanson v. Denckla*, that minimum contacts must have a basis in "some act by which the defendant purposefully avails itself of the privilege of conducting activities within the forum State, thus invoking the benefits and protections of its laws." *Burger King.* "Jurisdiction is proper ... where the contacts proximately result from actions by the defendant *himself* that create a 'substantial connection' with the forum State." [cit.]

Applying the principle that minimum contacts must be based on an act of the defendant, the Court in *World-Wide Volkswagen Corp.* rejected the assertion that a *consumer's* unilateral act of bringing the defendant's product into the forum State was a sufficient constitutional basis for personal jurisdiction over the defendant. * * *

* * * Since *World-Wide Volkswagen*, lower courts have been confronted with cases in which the defendant acted by placing a product in the stream of commerce, and the stream eventually swept defendant's product into the forum State, but the

defendant did nothing else to purposefully avail itself of the market in the forum State. Some courts have understood the Due Process Clause, as interpreted in *World-Wide Volkswagen*, to allow an exercise of personal jurisdiction to be based on no more than the defendant's act of placing the product in the stream of commerce. Other courts have understood the Due Process Clause and the above-quoted language in *World-Wide Volkswagen* to require the action of the defendant to be more purposefully directed at the forum State than the mere act of placing a product in the stream of commerce.

* * *

We now find this latter position to be consonant with the requirements of due process. The "substantial connection," [cit.], between the defendant and the forum State necessary for a finding of minimum contacts must come about by *an action of the defendant purposefully directed toward the forum State*. [cit.] The placement of a product into the stream of commerce, without more, is not an act of the defendant purposefully directed toward the forum State. Additional conduct of the defendant may indicate an intent or purpose to serve the market in the forum State, for example, designing the product for the market in the forum State, advertising in the forum State, establishing channels for providing regular advice to customers in the forum State, or marketing the product through a distributor who has agreed to serve as the sales agent in the forum State. But a defendant's awareness that the stream of commerce may or will sweep the product into the forum State does not convert the mere act of placing the product into the stream into an act purposefully directed toward the forum State.

Assuming, arguendo, that respondents have established Asahi's awareness that some of the valves sold to Cheng Shin would be incorporated into tire tubes sold in California, respondents have not demonstrated any action by Asahi to purposefully avail itself of the California market. Asahi does not do business in California. It has no office, agents, employees, or property in California. It does not advertise or otherwise solicit business in California. It did not create, control, or employ the distribution system that brought its valves to California. [cit.] There is no evidence that Asahi designed its product in anticipation of sales in California. [cit.] On the basis of these facts, the exertion of personal jurisdiction over Asahi by the Superior Court of California* exceeds the limits of due process.

B. The strictures of the Due Process Clause forbid a state court from exercising personal jurisdiction over Asahi under circumstances that would offend "'traditional notions of fair play and substantial justice.'" [cit.]

We have previously explained that the determination of the reasonableness of the exercise of jurisdiction in each case will depend on an evaluation of several factors. A court must consider the burden on the defendant, the interests of the forum State, and the plaintiff's interest in obtaining relief. It must also weigh in its determination "the interstate judicial system's interest in obtaining the most efficient

---

*We have no occasion here to determine whether Congress could, consistent with the Due Process Clause of the Fifth Amendment, authorize federal court personal jurisdiction over alien defendants based on the aggregate of *national* contacts, rather than on the contacts between the defendant and the State in which the federal court sits. [cit.]

resolution of controversies; and the shared interest of the several States in furthering fundamental substantive social policies." *World-Wide Volkswagen.*

A consideration of these factors in the present case clearly reveals the unreasonableness of the assertion of jurisdiction over Asahi, even apart from the question of the placement of goods in the stream of commerce.

Certainly the burden on the defendant in this case is severe. Asahi has been commanded by the Supreme Court of California not only to traverse the distance between Asahi's headquarters in Japan and the Superior Court of California in and for the County of Solano, but also to submit its dispute with Cheng Shin to a foreign nation's judicial system. The unique burdens placed upon one who must defend oneself in a foreign legal system should have significant weight in assessing the reasonableness of stretching the long arm of personal jurisdiction over national borders.

When minimum contacts have been established, often the interests of the plaintiff and the forum in the exercise of jurisdiction will justify even the serious burdens placed on the alien defendant. In the present case, however, the interests of the plaintiff and the forum in California's assertion of jurisdiction over Asahi are slight. All that remains is a claim for indemnification asserted by Cheng Shin, a Taiwanese corporation, against Asahi. The transaction on which the indemnification claim is based took place in Taiwan; Asahi's components were shipped from Japan to Taiwan. Cheng Shin has not demonstrated that it is more convenient for it to litigate its indemnification claim against Asahi in California rather than in Taiwan or Japan.

Because the plaintiff is not a California resident, California's legitimate interests in the dispute have considerably diminished. The Supreme Court of California argued that the State had an interest in "protecting its consumers by ensuring that foreign manufacturers comply with the state's safety standards." [cit.] The State Supreme Court's definition of California's interest, however, was overly broad. The dispute between Cheng Shin and Asahi is primarily about indemnification rather than safety standards. Moreover, it is not at all clear at this point that California law should govern the question whether a Japanese corporation should indemnify a Taiwanese corporation on the basis of a sale made in Taiwan and a shipment of goods from Japan to Taiwan. [cit.] The possibility of being haled into a California court as a result of an accident involving Asahi's components undoubtedly creates an additional deterrent to the manufacture of unsafe components; however, similar pressures will be placed on Asahi by the purchasers of its components as long as those who use Asahi components in their final products, and sell those products in California, are subject to the application of California tort law.

World-Wide Volkswagen also admonished courts to take into consideration the interests of the "several States," in addition to the forum State, in the efficient judicial resolution of the dispute and the advancement of substantive policies. In the present case, this advice calls for a court to consider the procedural and substantive policies of other *nations* whose interests are affected by the assertion of jurisdiction by the California court. The procedural and substantive interests of other nations in a state court's assertion of jurisdiction over an alien defendant will differ from case to case. In every case, however, those interests, as well as the Federal Government's interest in its foreign relations policies, will be best served by a careful inquiry into the reasonableness of the assertion of jurisdiction in the particular case, and an unwillingness to find the serious burdens on an alien defendant outweighed by minimal interests on the part of the plaintiff or the forum State. "Great care and reserve should be exercised when extending our notions of personal jurisdiction into the international field." United States v. First National City Bank, 379 U.S. 378, 404 (1965) (Harlan, J., dissenting). [cit.]

Considering the international context, the heavy burden on the alien defendant, and the slight interests of the plaintiff and the forum State, the exercise of personal jurisdiction by a California court over Asahi in this instance would be unreasonable and unfair.

III. Because the facts of this case do not establish minimum contacts such that the exercise of personal jurisdiction is consistent with fair play and substantial justice, the judgment of the Supreme Court of California is reversed, and the case is remanded for further proceedings not inconsistent with this opinion.

It is so ordered.

JUSTICE BRENNAN, with whom Justice White, Justice Marshall, and Justice Blackmun join, concurring in part and concurring in the judgment.

I do not agree with the interpretation in Part II–A of the stream-of-commerce theory, nor with the conclusion that Asahi did not "purposely avail itself of the California market." [cit.] I do agree, however, with the Court's conclusion in Part II–B that the exercise of personal jurisdiction over Asahi in this case would not comport with "fair play and substantial justice," [cit.] This is one of those rare cases in which "minimum requirements inherent in the concept of 'fair play and substantial justice' ... defeat the reasonableness of jurisdiction even [though] the defendant has purposefully engaged in forum activities." *Burger King Corp.* I therefore join Parts I and II–B of the Court's opinion, and write separately to explain my disagreement with Part II–A.

* * * The stream of commerce refers not to unpredictable currents or eddies, but to the regular and anticipated flow of products from manufacture to distribution to retail sale. As long as a participant in this process is aware that the final product is being marketed in the forum State, the possibility of a lawsuit there cannot come as a surprise. Nor will the litigation present a burden for which there is no corresponding benefit. A defendant who has placed goods in the stream of commerce benefits economically from the retail sale of the final product in the forum State, and indirectly benefits from the State's laws that regulate and facilitate commercial activity. These benefits accrue regardless of whether that participant directly conducts business in the forum State, or engages in additional conduct directed toward that State. Accordingly, most courts and commentators have found that jurisdiction premised on the placement of a product into the stream of commerce is consistent with the Due Process Clause, and have not required a showing of additional conduct.

The endorsement in Part II–A of what appears to be the minority view among

Federal Courts of Appeals represents a marked retreat from the analysis in *World-Wide Volkswagen.* * * *

* * * The Court [in that case] concluded its illustration by referring to *Gray v. American Radiator & Standard Sanitary Corp.* a well-known stream-of-commerce case in which the Illinois Supreme Court applied the theory to assert jurisdiction over a component-parts manufacturer that sold no components directly in Illinois, but did sell them to a manufacturer who incorporated them into a final product that was sold in Illinois. [cit.]

The Court in *World-Wide Volkswagen* thus took great care to distinguish "between a case involving goods which reach a distant State through a chain of distribution and a case involving goods which reach the same State because a consumer ... took them there." [cit.] The California Supreme Court took note of this distinction, and correctly concluded that our holding in *World-Wide Volkswagen* preserved the stream-of-commerce theory. [cit.]

In this case, the facts found by the California Supreme Court support its finding of minimum contacts. The court found that "[a]lthough Asahi did not design or control the system of distribution that carried its valve assemblies into California, Asahi was aware of the distribution system's operation, and it knew that it would benefit economically from the sale in California of products incorporating its components." [cit.] Accordingly, I cannot join the determination in Part II–A that Asahi's regular and extensive sales of component parts to a manufacturer it knew was making regular sales of the final product in California is insufficient to establish minimum contacts with California.

JUSTICE STEVENS, with whom Justice White and Justice Blackmun join, concurring in part and concurring in the judgment.

The judgment of the Supreme Court of California should be reversed for the reasons stated in Part II–B of the Court's opinion. While I join Parts I and II–B, I do not join Part II–A for two reasons. First, it is not necessary to the Court's decision. * * * [T]his case fits within the rule that "minimum requirements inherent in the concept of 'fair play and substantial justice' may defeat the reasonableness of jurisdiction even if the defendant has purposefully engaged in forum activities." *Burger King.* Accordingly, I see no reason in this case for the plurality to articulate "purposeful direction" or any other test as the nexus between an act of a defendant and the forum State that is necessary to establish minimum contacts.

Second, even assuming that the test ought to be formulated here, Part II–A misapplies it to the facts of this case. The plurality seems to assume that an unwavering line can be drawn between "mere awareness" that a component will find its way into the forum State and "purposeful availment" of the forum's market. [cit.] Over the course of its dealings with Cheng Shin, Asahi has arguably engaged in a higher quantum of conduct than "[t]he placement of a product into the stream of commerce, without more...." [cit.] Whether or not this conduct rises to the level of purposeful availment requires a constitutional determination that is affected by the volume, the value, and the hazardous character of the components. In most circumstances I would be inclined to conclude that a regular course of dealing that results in deliveries of over 100,000 units annually over a period of several years would constitute "purposeful availment" even though the item delivered to the forum State was a standard product marketed throughout the world.

Notes and Questions

1. *World-Wide Volkswagen* seemed to separate the concerns of contacts and reasonableness, while *Burger King* seemed to move these two inquiries closer together. Has *Asahi* split them apart again?

2. On the issue of whether the defendant has sufficient contacts, no opinion commands a majority. How do the approaches of Justices O'onnor, Brennan and Stevens differ? Which approach do you find the most persuasive? Consider Vandelune v. 4B Elevator Components Unlimited, 148 F.3d 943 (8th Cir.), *cert. denied*, 525 U.S. 1018 (1998). There, Synatel, a British corporation sold a component part (an "M700") for grain elevators to Braine, another British company. Braine marketed this part through B4, a United States affiliate located in Illinois. Synatel sold a total of 19 M700s to B4, 81 of which B4 resold into Iowa. Following a grain elevator accident in Iowa, the Eighth Circuit upheld jurisdiction over Synatel in Iowa. The court stressed that Synatel designed its product for United States markets, particularly the grain elevator market and noted that Synatel employees had attended meetings at B4's facilities in Peoria, Illinois, "about eighty miles from the Iowa border." The court explained that "when a foreign manufacturer 'pours its products' into a regional distributor with the expectation that the distributor will penetrate a discrete, multi-State trade area, the manufacturer has 'purposefully reaped the benefits' of the laws of each State in that trade area for due process purposes." Id. at 948. Is this holding consistent with Justice O'Connor's opinion?

3. A manufacturer sells its products to a distributor, which in turn sells the product in the forum. If a consumer is injured in the forum can she sue the manufacturer in the forum? If not, does this mean manufacturers can insulate themselves from jurisdiction by dealing through a distributor? Should manufacturers dealing through distributors be treated differently than manufacturers of component parts? See Lesnick v. Hollingsworth & Vose Co., 35 F.3d 939 (4th Cir.1994), *cert. denied*, 513 U.S. 1151 (1995); Falkirk Mining Co. v. Japan Steel Works, 906 F.2d 369 (8th Cir.1990); Dehmlow v. Austin Fireworks, 963 F.2d 941 (7th Cir.1992); Cox v. Hozelock, Ltd., 411 S.E.2d 640 (N.C. App.), *cert. denied*, 506 U.S. 824 (1992).

4. Compare *Asahi* with *Cooney v. Osgood Machinery*, supra at 270. Under the opinions of Justices O'Connor, Brennan or Stevens would Osgood have been subject to personal jurisdiction in Missouri?

5. After *Asahi*, lower courts have split on the question of how to evaluate stream of commerce cases. Some courts, applying the dicta of *World-Wide Volkswagen* as they did prior to *Asahi*, have used an approach that resembles Justice Brennan's *Asahi* opinion. See Ruston Gas Turbines, Inc. v. Donaldson Co., 9 F.3d 415 (5th Cir. 1993); Dehmlow v. Austin Fireworks, 963 F.2d 941, 947 (7th Cir.1992); Irving v. Owens-Corning Fiberglas Corp., 864 F.2d 383, 386 (5th Cir.), *cert. denied*, 493 U.S.

823 (1989). Other courts have adopted an approach more closely resembling Justice O'Connor's *Asahi* opinion. See Madara v. Hall, 916 F.2d 1510 (11ᵗʰ Cir. 1990); Lesnick v. Hollingsworth & Vose Co., 35 F.3d 939, 945-946 (4th Cir.1994); *cert. denied*, 513 U.S. 1151 (1995); Boit v. Gar-Tec Products, Inc., 967 F.2d 671, 682-83 (1st Cir.1992); Falkirk Mining Co. v. Japan Steel Works, Ltd., 906 F.2d 369, 375–76 (8th Cir.1990). Still others have attempted to apply both tests. See Pennzoil Prods. Co. v. Colelli & Assoc., 149 F.3d 197 (3ʳᵈ Cir. 1998). Finally, at least one court has explicitly adopted the approach articulated by Justice Stevens in *Asahi*. See Abuan v. General Electric Co., 735 F.Supp. 1479, 1485-86 (D.Guam, 1990), *aff'd on other grounds*, 3 F.3d 329 (9th Cir.), *cert. denied*, 510 U.S. 1116 (1994).

6. Compare the opinion in *Asahi* with the approach of the Canadian Supreme Court:

> [W]here a foreign defendant carelessly manufactures a product in a foreign jurisdiction which enters into the normal channels of trade and he knows or ought to know both that as a result of his carelessness a consumer may well be injured and it is reasonably foreseeable that the product would be used or consumed where the plaintiff used or consumed it, then the forum in which the plaintiff suffered damage is entitled to exercise judicial jurisdiction over that foreign defendant. This rule recognizes the important interest a State has in injuries suffered by persons within its territory. It recognizes that the purpose of negligence as a tort is to protect against carelessly inflicted injury and thus that the predominating element is damage suffered. *By tendering his products in the market place directly or through normal distributive channels, a manufacturer ought to assume the burden of defending those products wherever they cause harm as long as the forum into which the manufacturer is taken is one that he reasonably ought to have had in his contemplation when he so tendered his goods.*

De Savoye v. Morguard Investments Ltd., 76 D.L.R. 4th 256, 276, 24 A.C.W.S. 3d 478 (1990). What do you think of the Canadian approach?

2. General Jurisdiction

Helicopteros Nacionales de Colombia, S.A. v. Hall
Supreme Court of the United States, 1984.
466 U.S. 408, 104 S.Ct. 1868, 80 L.Ed.2d 404.

JUSTICE BLACKMUN delivered the opinion of the Court. We granted certiorari in this case [cit.], to decide whether the Supreme Court of Texas correctly ruled that the contacts of a foreign corporation with the State of Texas were sufficient to allow a Texas state court to assert jurisdiction over the corporation in a cause of action not arising out of or related to the corporation's activities within the State.

I. Petitioner Helicopteros Nacionales de Colombia, S. A. (Helicol), is a Colombian corporation with its principal place of business in the city of Bogota in that country. It is engaged in the business of providing helicopter transportation for oil and construction companies in South America. On January 26, 1976, a helicopter owned by Helicol crashed in Peru. Four United States citizens were among those who lost their lives in the accident. Respondents are the survivors and representatives of the four decedents.

At the time of the crash, respondents' decedents were employed by Consorcio, a Peruvian consortium, and were working on a pipeline in Peru. Consorcio is the alter ego of a joint venture named Williams–Sedco–Horn (WSH). The venture had its headquarters in Houston, Tex. Consorcio had been formed to enable the venturers to enter into a contract with Petro Peru, the Peruvian state-owned oil company. Consorcio was to construct a pipeline for Petro Peru running from the interior of Peru westward to the Pacific Ocean. Peruvian law forbade construction of the pipeline by any non-Peruvian entity.

Consorcio/WSH needed helicopters to move personnel, materials, and equipment into and out of the construction area. In 1974, upon request of Consorcio/WSH, the chief executive officer of Helicol, Francisco Restrepo, flew to the United States and conferred in Houston with representatives of the three joint venturers. At that meeting, there was a discussion of prices, availability, working conditions, fuel, supplies, and housing. Restrepo represented that Helicol could have the first helicopter on the job in 15 days. The Consorcio/WSH representatives decided to accept the contract proposed by Restrepo. Helicol began performing before the agreement was formally signed in Peru on November 11, 1974. The contract was written in Spanish on official government stationery and provided that the residence of all the parties would be Lima, Peru. It further stated that controversies arising out of the contract would be submitted to the jurisdiction of Peruvian courts. In addition, it provided that Consorcio/WSH would make payments to Helicol's account with the Bank of America in New York City. [cit.]

Aside from the negotiation session in Houston between Restrepo and the representatives of Consorcio/WSH, Helicol had other contacts with Texas. During the years 1970-1977, it purchased helicopters (approximately 80% of its fleet), spare parts, and accessories for more than $4 million from Bell Helicopter Company in Fort Worth. In that period, Helicol sent prospective pilots to Fort Worth for training and to ferry the aircraft to South America. It also sent management and maintenance personnel to visit Bell Helicopter in Fort Worth during the same period in order to receive "plant familiarization" and for technical consultation. Helicol received into its New York City and Panama City, Fla., bank accounts over $5 million in payments from Consorcio/WSH drawn upon First City National Bank of Houston.

Beyond the foregoing, there have been no other business contacts between Helicol and the State of Texas. Helicol never has been authorized to do business in Texas and never has had an agent for the service of process within the State. It never has performed helicopter operations in Texas or sold any product that reached Texas, never solicited business in Texas, never signed any contract in Texas, never had any employee based there, and never recruited an employee in Texas. In addition, Helicol never has owned real or personal property in Texas and never has maintained an office or establishment there. Helicol has maintained no records in Texas and has no shareholders in that State. None of the respondents or their decedents were domiciled in Texas, [cit.][5] but all of the decedents were hired in Houston by Consorcio/WSH to work on the Petro Peru pipeline project.

Respondents instituted wrongful-death actions in the District Court of Harris County, Tex., against Consorcio/WSH, Bell Helicopter Company, and Helicol. Helicol filed special appearances and moved to dismiss the actions for lack of in personam jurisdiction over it. The motion was denied. After a consolidated jury trial, judgment was entered against Helicol on a jury verdict of $1,141,200 in favor of respondents. [cit.]

* * * In ruling that the Texas courts had in personam jurisdiction, the Texas Supreme Court first held that the State's long-arm statute reaches as far as the Due Process Clause of the Fourteenth Amendment permits. [cit.] Thus, the only question remaining for the court to decide was whether it was consistent with the Due Process Clause for Texas courts to assert in personam jurisdiction over Helicol. [cit.]

II. The Due Process Clause of the Fourteenth Amendment operates to limit the power of a State to assert in personam jurisdiction over a nonresident defendant. *Pennoyer v. Neff.* Due process requirements are satisfied when in personam jurisdiction is asserted over a nonresident corporate defendant that has "certain minimum contacts with [the forum] such that the maintenance of the suit does not offend 'traditional notions of fair play and substantial justice.'" *International Shoe Co. v. Washington.* When a controversy is related to or "arises out of" a defendant's contacts with the forum, the Court has said that a "relationship among the defendant, the forum, and the litigation" is the essential foundation of in *personam* jurisdiction. *Shaffer v. Heitner.*

Even when the cause of action does not arise out of or relate to the foreign corporation's activities in the forum State,[6] due process is not offended by a State's subjecting the corporation to its in personam jurisdiction when there are sufficient contacts between the State and the foreign corporation. Perkins v. Benguet Consolidated Mining Co., 342 U.S. 437 (1952); see *Keeton v. Hustler Magazine, Inc.* In *Perkins*, the Court addressed a situation in which state courts had asserted general jurisdiction over a defendant foreign corporation. During the Japanese occupation of the Philippine Islands, the president and general manager of a Philippine mining corporation maintained an office in Ohio from which he conducted activities on behalf of the company. He kept company files and held directors' meetings in the office, carried on correspondence relating to the business, distributed salary checks drawn on two active Ohio bank accounts, engaged an Ohio bank to act as transfer agent, and supervised policies dealing with the rehabilitation of the corporation's properties in the Philippines. In short, the foreign corporation,

---

5. Respondents' lack of residential or other contacts with Texas of itself does not defeat otherwise proper jurisdiction. *Keeton v. Hustler Magazine, Inc.*; *Calder v. Jones.* We mention respondents' lack of contacts merely to show that nothing in the nature of the relationship between respondents and Helicol could possibly enhance Helicol's contacts with Texas. The harm suffered by respondents did not occur in Texas. Nor is it alleged that any negligence on the part of Helicol took place in Texas.

6. When a State exercises personal jurisdiction over a defendant in a suit not arising out of or related to the defendant's contacts with the forum, the State has been said to be exercising "general jurisdiction" over the defendant. See Brilmayer, *How Contacts Count: Due Process Limitations on State Court Jurisdiction*, 1980 S. Ct. Rev. 77, 80–81; Von Mehren & Trautman, 79 Harv. L. Rev. at 1136–1144; *Calder v. Jones.*

through its president, "ha[d] been carrying on in Ohio a continuous and systematic, but limited, part of its general business," and the exercise of general jurisdiction over the Philippine corporation by an Ohio court was "reasonable and just." [cit.]

All parties to the present case concede that respondents' claims against Helicol did not "arise out of," and are not related to, Helicol's activities within Texas.[7] We thus must explore the nature of Helicol's contacts with the State of Texas to determine whether they constitute the kind of continuous and systematic general business contacts the Court found to exist in *Perkins*. We hold that they do not.

It is undisputed that Helicol does not have a place of business in Texas and never has been licensed to do business in the State. Basically, Helicol's contacts with Texas consisted of sending its chief executive officer to Houston for a contract-negotiation session; accepting into its New York bank account checks drawn on a Houston bank; purchasing helicopters, equipment, and training services from Bell Helicopter for substantial sums; and sending personnel to Bell's facilities in Fort Worth for training.

The one trip to Houston by Helicol's chief executive officer for the purpose of negotiating the transportation-services contract with Consorcio/WSH cannot be described or regarded as a contact of a "continuous and systematic" nature, as *Perkins* described it,[cit.], and thus cannot support an assertion of in personam jurisdiction over Helicol by a Texas court. Similarly, Helicol's acceptance from Consorcio/WSH of checks drawn on a Texas bank is of negligible significance for purposes of determining whether Helicol had sufficient contacts in Texas. There is no indication that Helicol ever requested that the checks be drawn on a Texas bank or that there was any negotiation between Helicol and Consorcio/WSH with respect to the location or identity of the bank on which checks would be drawn. Common sense and everyday experience suggest that, absent unusual circumstances, the bank on which a check is drawn is generally of little consequence to the payee and is a matter left to the discretion of the drawer. Such unilateral activity of another party or a third person is not an appropriate consideration when determining whether a defendant has sufficient contacts with a forum State to justify an assertion of jurisdiction. [cit.]

The Texas Supreme Court focused on the purchases and the related training trips in finding contacts sufficient to support an assertion of jurisdiction. We do not agree

---

7. [cit.] Because the parties have not argued any relationship between the cause of action and Helicol's contacts with the State of Texas, we, contrary to the dissent's implication, [cit.] assert no "view" with respect to that issue.

The dissent suggests that we have erred in drawing no distinction between controversies that "relate to" a defendant's contacts with a forum and those that "arise out of" such contacts. [cit.] This criticism is somewhat puzzling, for the dissent goes on to urge that, for purposes of determining the constitutional validity of an assertion of specific jurisdiction, there really should be no distinction between the two. [cit.]

We do not address the validity or consequences of such a distinction because the issue has not been presented in this case. Respondents have made no argument that their cause of action either arose out of or is related to Helicol's contacts with the State of Texas. Absent any briefing on the issue, we decline to reach the questions (1) whether the terms "arising out of" and "related to" describe different connections between a cause of action and a defendant's contacts with a forum, and (2) what sort of tie between a cause of action and a defendant's contacts with a forum is necessary to a determination that either connection exists. Nor do we reach the question whether, if the two types of relationship differ, a forum's exercise of personal jurisdiction in a situation where the cause of action "relates to," but does not "arise out of," the defendant's contacts with the forum should be analyzed as an assertion of specific jurisdiction.

with that assessment, for the Court's opinion in Rosenberg Bros. & Co. v. Curtis Brown Co., 260 U.S. 516 (1923) (Brandeis, J., for a unanimous tribunal), makes clear that purchases and related trips, standing alone, are not a sufficient basis for a State's assertion of jurisdiction.

The defendant in *Rosenberg* was a small retailer in Tulsa, Okla., who dealt in men's clothing and furnishings. It never had applied for a license to do business in New York, nor had it at any time authorized suit to be brought against it there. It never had an established place of business in New York and never regularly carried on business in that State. Its only connection with New York was that it purchased from New York wholesalers a large portion of the merchandise sold in its Tulsa store. The purchases sometimes were made by correspondence and sometimes through visits to New York by an officer of the defendant. The Court concluded: "Visits on such business, even if occurring at regular intervals, would not warrant the inference that the corporation was present within the jurisdiction of [New York]." [cit.]

This Court in *International Shoe* acknowledged and did not repudiate its holding in *Rosenberg*. [cit.] In accordance with *Rosenberg*, we hold that mere purchases, even if occurring at regular intervals, are not enough to warrant a State's assertion of in personam jurisdiction over a nonresident corporation in a cause of action not related to those purchase transactions.[12] Nor can we conclude that the fact that Helicol sent personnel into Texas for training in connection with the purchase of helicopters and equipment in that State in any way enhanced the nature of Helicol's contacts with Texas. The training was a part of the package of goods and services purchased by Helicol from Bell Helicopter. The brief presence of Helicol employees in Texas for the purpose of attending the training sessions is no more a significant contact than were the trips to New York made by the buyer for the retail store in *Rosenberg*. [cit.]

III. We hold that Helicol's contacts with the State of Texas were insufficient to satisfy the requirements of the Due Process Clause of the Fourteenth Amendment.[13] Accordingly, we reverse the judgment of the Supreme Court of Texas.

It is so ordered.

JUSTICE BRENNAN, dissenting. [Justice Brennan first disagrees with the majority's conclusion that there are insufficient contacts for general jurisdiction.] *

---

12. This Court in *International Shoe* cited *Rosenberg* for the proposition that "the commission of some single or occasional acts of the corporate agent in a state sufficient to impose an obligation or liability on the corporation has not been thought to confer upon the state authority to enforce it." [cit.] Arguably, therefore, *Rosenberg* also stands for the proposition that mere purchases are not a sufficient basis for either general or specific jurisdiction. Because the case before us is one in which there has been an assertion of general jurisdiction over a foreign defendant, we need not decide the continuing validity of *Rosenberg* with respect to an assertion of specific jurisdiction, i.e., where the cause of action arises out of or relates to the purchases by the defendant in the forum State.

13. As an alternative to traditional minimum-contacts analysis, respondents suggest that the Court hold that the State of Texas had personal jurisdiction over Helicol under a doctrine of "jurisdiction by necessity." See *Shaffer v. Heitner*. We conclude, however, that respondents failed to carry their burden of showing that all three defendants could not be sued together in a single forum. It is not clear from the record, for example, whether suit could have been brought against all three defendants in either Colombia or Peru. We decline to consider adoption of a doctrine of jurisdiction by necessity—a potentially far-reaching modification of existing law—in the absence of a more complete record.

* *

II. The Court also fails to distinguish the legal principles that controlled our prior decisions in *Perkins* and *Rosenberg*. In particular, the contacts between petitioner Helicol and the State of Texas, unlike the contacts between the defendant and the forum in each of those cases, are significantly related to the cause of action alleged in the original suit filed by the respondents. Accordingly, in my view, it is both fair and reasonable for the Texas courts to assert specific jurisdiction over Helicol in this case.

By asserting that the present case does not implicate the specific jurisdiction of the Texas courts, [cit.] the Court necessarily removes its decision from the reality of the actual facts presented for our consideration.[3] Moreover, the Court refuses to consider any distinction between contacts that are "related to" the underlying cause of action and contacts that "give rise" to the underlying cause of action. In my view, however, there is a substantial difference between these two standards for asserting specific jurisdiction. Thus, although I agree that the respondents' cause of action did not formally "arise out of" specific activities initiated by Helicol in the State of Texas, I believe that the wrongful-death claim filed by the respondents is significantly related to the undisputed contacts between Helicol and the forum. On that basis, I would conclude that the Due Process Clause allows the Texas courts to assert specific jurisdiction over this particular action.

The wrongful-death actions filed by the respondents were premised on a fatal helicopter crash that occurred in Peru. Helicol was joined as a defendant in the lawsuits because it provided transportation services, including the particular helicopter and pilot involved in the crash, to the joint venture that employed the decedents. Specifically, the respondent Hall claimed in her original complaint that "Helicol is ... legally responsible for its own negligence through its pilot employee." [cit.] Viewed in light of these allegations, the contacts between Helicol and the State of Texas are directly and significantly related to the underlying claim filed by the respondents. The negotiations that took place in Texas led to the contract in which Helicol agreed to provide the precise transportation services that were being used at the time of the crash. Moreover, the helicopter involved in the crash was purchased by Helicol in Texas, and the pilot whose negligence was alleged to have caused the crash was actually trained in Texas. [cit.] This is simply not a case, therefore, in which a state court has asserted jurisdiction over a nonresident defendant on the basis of wholly unrelated contacts with the forum. Rather, the contacts between Helicol and the forum are directly related to the negligence that was alleged in the respondent Hall's original complaint.[4] Because Helicol should have expected to be amenable to suit in the Texas courts for claims directly related to these contacts, it

---

3. Nor do I agree with the Court that the respondents have conceded that their claims are not related to Helicol's activities within the State of Texas. Although parts of their written and oral arguments before the Court proceed on the assumption that no such relationship exists, other portions suggest just the opposite.
* * *

4. The jury specifically found that "the pilot failed to keep the helicopter under proper control," that "the helicopter was flown into a treetop fog condition, whereby the vision of the pilot was impaired," that "such flying was negligence," and that "such negligence ... was a proximate cause of the crash." [cit.] On the basis of these findings, Helicol was ordered to pay over $1 million in damages to the respondents.

is fair and reasonable to allow the assertion of jurisdiction in this case.

Despite this substantial relationship between the contacts and the cause of action, the Court declines to consider whether the courts of Texas may assert specific jurisdiction over this suit. Apparently, this simply reflects a narrow interpretation of the question presented for review. [cit.] It is nonetheless possible that the Court's opinion may be read to imply that the specific jurisdiction of the Texas courts is inapplicable because the cause of action did not formally "arise out of" the contacts between Helicol and the forum. In my view, however, such a rule would place unjustifiable limits on the bases under which Texas may assert its jurisdictional power.

Limiting the specific jurisdiction of a forum to cases in which the cause of action formally arose out of the defendant's contacts with the State would subject constitutional standards under the Due Process Clause to the vagaries of the substantive law or pleading requirements of each State. For example, the complaint filed against Helicol in this case alleged negligence based on pilot error. Even though the pilot was trained in Texas, the Court assumes that the Texas courts may not assert jurisdiction over the suit because the cause of action "did not 'arise out of,' and [is] not related to," that training. [cit.] If, however, the applicable substantive law required that negligent training of the pilot was a necessary element of a cause of action for pilot error, or if the respondents had simply added an allegation of negligence in the training provided for the Helicol pilot, then presumably the Court would concede that the specific jurisdiction of the Texas courts was applicable.

Our interpretation of the Due Process Clause has never been so dependent upon the applicable substantive law or the State's formal pleading requirements. At least since *International Shoe Co. v. Washington* the principal focus when determining whether a forum may constitutionally assert jurisdiction over a nonresident defendant has been on fairness and reasonableness to the defendant. To this extent, a court's specific jurisdiction should be applicable whenever the cause of action arises out of *or* relates to the contacts between the defendant and the forum. It is eminently fair and reasonable, in my view, to subject a defendant to suit in a forum with which it has significant contacts directly related to the underlying cause of action. Because Helicol's contacts with the State of Texas meet this standard, I would affirm the judgment of the Supreme Court of Texas.

Notes and Questions

1. How extensive must a defendant's contacts be to establish general jurisdiction? In *Helicopteros* the defendant purchased $4 million of helicopters over seven years. Why was that not "systematic and continuous"? Compare *Helicopteros* with *Perkins*. Why were the defendant's contacts sufficient in *Perkins*? Lower courts vary widely on what are sufficient contacts for general jurisdiction. Compare Nichols v. G.D. Searle & Co., 991 F.2d 1195 (4th Cir.1993) (17 to 21 employees in forum and annual sales in forum of $9 to $13 million not sufficient for general jurisdiction); Hughes v. A.H. Robins Co., 490 A.2d 1140 (D.C. 1985) (regularly sending sales representatives, advertising, and maintaining an office to monitor congressional

legislation not sufficient for general jurisdiction), with Denn v. Southern Peru Copper Corp., 508 P.2d 340 (Ariz. App. 1973) (systematic recruiting of employees through advertising and use of an independent contractor as a recruiter sufficient for general jurisdiction); Bankhead Enterprises, Inc. v. Norfolk & W. Ry. Co., 642 F.2d 802 (5th Cir.1981) (defendant leased office and employee sales agents and clerical staff; sufficient for general jurisdiction); Bryant v. Finnish Nat'l Airline, 208 N.E.2d 439 (N.Y. 1965) (one and a half room office with several employees sufficient for general jurisdiction).

2. Professor von Mehren who along with Professor Trautman first set forth the categories of general and specific jurisdiction, has explained the distinction as follows:

> The appropriateness of claims of general jurisdiction * * * [is] assessed *ex ante* without regard to the specific controversy before the court. [It] must satisfy a "group norm" requirement; the appropriateness of the jurisdictional claim made must be demonstrated for the generality of the situations in which this class of adjudicatory authority is claimed. * * * Claims of specific jurisdiction and of universal jurisdiction, on the other hand, rest directly on the proposition that, *in light of the circumstances of the particular case*, litigational justice permits--or, when universal jurisdiction is claimed, requires--the exercise of adjudicatory authority. The appropriateness assessment is *ex post* and controversy specific.

von Mehren, *Adjudicatory Authority*, 64. See infra at 690, 694. Thus, tag jurisdiction or jurisdiction based on domicile or state of incorporation all meet the criteria for general jurisdiction. In *Helicopteros* does the Court apply a "group norm" or does it instead consider "the circumstances of the particular case"?

3. Why have general jurisdiction at all? Commentators have offered different explanations. Professor Mary Twitchell argues that general jurisdiction serves one essential function, that is, "providing one forum where a defendant may always be sued." In keeping with this function, she would limit general jurisdiction to the defendant's "home base." Twitchell, *The Myth of General Jurisdiction*, 667.

Professor Lea Brilmayer sees a more expansive role for general jurisdiction. She argues that general jurisdiction derives from sovereign authority of a state to regulate the activities of its members or other "insiders." She explains:

> The two bases of jurisdiction [general and specific] * * * constitute alternative aspects of a State's sovereignty, namely, self-governance and territoriality. Systematic unrelated activity, such as domicile, incorporation, or doing business, suggests that the person or corporate entity is enough of an "insider" that he may safely be relegated to the State's political processes. * * * These two bases are independent threshold tests, so that a greater quantum of unrelated activity does not compensate for attenuated related contacts.[1]

Brilmayer, *How Contacts Count*, 87-88. What level of activity would make an entity an "insider?" Should the court focus on the entity's in-state business activities or its political activities? For an excellent discussion of general jurisdiction, see Borchers,

---

1. ©1981 by the University of Chicago. Reprinted by permission.

General Jurisdiction; Juenger, *General Jurisdiction*, Twitchell, *Doing-Business Jurisdiction.*

Professor William Richman offers a different perspective. He argues that general and specific jurisdiction are simply two extremes on a continuum for assessing fairness.

> As the quantity and quality of the defendant's forum contacts increase, a weaker connection between the plaintiff's claim and those contacts is permissible; as the quantity and quality of the defendant's forum contacts decrease, a stronger connection between the plaintiff's claim and those contacts is required. The concepts of general jurisdiction and specific jurisdiction are simply the two opposite ends of this sliding scale.

Richman, *A Sliding Scale*, 1345. Interestingly, Professor Twitchell argues that "most cases finding general jurisdiction will involve a dispute that is at least tenuously related to the defendant's forum contacts." Twitchell, *Doing-Business Jurisdiction*, at 190.

4. How does general jurisdiction apply to natural persons? In Milliken v. Meyer, 311 U.S. 457 (1940), the Court upheld jurisdiction over an absent defendant in his place of domicile. If a person is domiciled in one state and resides in a different state, would she be subject to suit in both states? Should an individual be subject to general jurisdiction based on business contacts? See ABKCO Indus., Inc. v. Lennon, 377 N.Y.S.2d 362 (N.Y.Sup.Ct.1975) (general jurisdiction over Ringo Starr upheld in New York based on his New York recording and composing activities). Justice Scalia has expressed some uncertainty on this question. See Burnham v. Superior Court, 495 U.S. 604, 610 n.1 (1990), infra at 648.

5. How closely must the contacts be related to the cause of action for a case to be deemed a specific jurisdiction case? Is it sufficient that the contacts "relate to" the cause of action or must the cause of action "arise out of" the contacts? Consider the situation of Audi in *World-Wide Volkswagen*. Audi presumably sold cars to Oklahoma but not the car that blew up. Is this connection enough for specific jurisdiction? Professor Twitchell has argued it should be:

> [I]t is the fact that this accident occurred within the forum, coupled with the similarity between the manufacturer's conduct in the forum and the conduct underlying the plaintiff's cause of action, that makes exercising jurisdiction over this claim particularly reasonable. Having sold and serviced identical cars in the state, the manufacturer will have foreseen such suits and insured against them. Furthermore, the forum has a very strong interest in regulating the manufacturer's conduct in this suit, not just because this particular automobile malfunctioned there, but because state residents are buying many similar cars and operating them on the forum's highways. The fact that the car was not actually sold within the state is, in this context, fortuitous. A court need not decide whether it is fair to hold the manufacturer subject to jurisdiction on all causes of action in the forum in order to decide that it is fair in this particular case. Specific jurisdiction, in which the nature of the cause of action is taken into account when considering fairness, not general jurisdiction, is the key to proper jurisdictional analysis under these circumstances.

Twitchell, *The Myth of General Jurisdiction*, 661–62. Professor Brilmayer, in contrast, has argued for a narrower approach, explaining:

> A contact is related to the controversy if it is the geographical qualification of a fact relevant to the merits. A forum occurrence which would ordinarily be alleged as part of a comparable domestic complaint is a related contact. In contrast, an occurrence in the forum State of no relevance to a totally domestic cause of action is an unrelated contact, a purely jurisdictional allegation with no substantive purpose. If a fact is irrelevant in a purely domestic dispute, it does not suddenly become related to the controversy simply because there are multistate elements.[1]

Brilmayer, *How Contacts Count*, 82–83. With whom do you agree? Lower courts have disagreed on how closely the cause of actions must relate to the contacts. Compare Third Nat'l Bank v. WEDGE Group, Inc., 882 F.2d 1087, 1091 (6th Cir.1989), *cert. denied*, 493 U.S. 1058 (1990) (sufficient that cause of action "relates to" contacts), with Marino v. Hyatt Corp., 793 F.2d 427 (1st Cir.1986) (cause of action must arise from the contacts).

6. Look back at the Supreme Court cases on the constitutional limits on choice of law and see if you can determine the basis for personal jurisdiction. Although most of the cases do not state the basis for jurisdiction, it appears likely that in at least *Clay*, *Hague*, *Shutts* and *Wortman*, the forum relied on general jurisdiction, either through general business contacts or the presence of an in-state agent for service of process. Should general jurisdiction be eliminated or limited to only the defendant's one "home base" as a way of curtailing forum shopping for choice of law reasons?

7. Some other countries consider general "doing business" jurisdiction to be unreasonable. The Draft Hague Convention on Jurisdiction and Foreign Judgments in Civil and Commercial Matters would have prohibited jurisdiction on the basis of "the carrying on of commercial or other activities by the defendant in that State, except where the dispute is directly related to those activities." The possibility of eliminating such jurisdiction was one of the bases of U.S. concern about the Draft Convention. See Juenger, *General Jurisdiction*, 164-65. See infra 706 et seq. Many countries reject this form of jurisdiction. Japan, for example, allows jurisdiction where the defendant has a place of business. Weintraub, *Commentary*, 176.

3. Jurisdiction Based on Property

In *Pennoyer v. Neff* the Supreme Court recognized that mere presence of property within the forum was sufficient to establish jurisdiction, provided the property was attached at the commencement of litigation. The Court applied this principle in Harris v. Balk, 198 U.S. 215 (1905). Harris owed Balk money and Balk owed Epstein money. Harris and Balk were from North Carolina and Epstein from Maryland. When Harris traveled to Maryland, Epstein sued Balk by serving Harris and hence "attaching" Harris and thereby attaching Harris' debt to Balk. The Court

---

1. ©1981 by the University of Chicago. Reprinted by permission.

reasoned that Harris' indebtedness to Balk was Balk's property and the property was located wherever the debtor, Harris, was located. The Court upheld jurisdiction in Maryland finding that Balk's Maryland property had been properly attached at the outset of litigation.

Shaffer v. Heitner

Supreme Court of the United States, 1977.
433 U.S. 186, 97 S.Ct. 2569, 53 L.Ed.2d 683.

JUSTICE MARSHALL delivered the opinion of the Court. The controversy in this case concerns the constitutionality of a Delaware statute that allows a court of that State to take jurisdiction of a lawsuit by sequestering any property of the defendant that happens to be located in Delaware. Appellants contend that the sequestration statute as applied in this case violates the Due Process Clause of the Fourteenth Amendment both because it permits the state courts to exercise jurisdiction despite the absence of sufficient contacts among the defendants, the litigation, and the State of Delaware and because it authorizes the deprivation of defendants' property without providing adequate procedural safeguards. We find it necessary to consider only the first of these contentions.

I. Appellee Heitner, a nonresident of Delaware, is the owner of one share of stock in the Greyhound Corp., a business incorporated under the laws of Delaware with its principal place of business in Phoenix, Ariz. On May 22, 1974, he filed a shareholder's derivative suit in the Court of Chancery for New Castle County, Del., in which he named as defendants Greyhound, its wholly owned subsidiary Greyhound Lines, Inc., and 28 present or former officers or directors of one or both of the corporations. In essence, Heitner alleged that the individual defendants had violated their duties to Greyhound by causing it and its subsidiary to engage in actions that resulted in the corporations being held liable for substantial damages in a private antitrust suit and a large fine in a criminal contempt action. The activities which led to these penalties took place in Oregon.

Simultaneously with his complaint, Heitner filed a motion for an order of sequestration of the Delaware property of the individual defendants pursuant to Del. Code Ann., Tit. 10, § 366 (1975). This motion was accompanied by a supporting affidavit of counsel which stated that the individual defendants were nonresidents of Delaware. * * * The requested sequestration order was signed the day the motion was filed. Pursuant to that order, the sequestrator "seized" approximately 82,000 shares of Greyhound common stock belonging to 19 of the defendants, and options belonging to another 2 defendants. These seizures were accomplished by placing "stop transfer" orders or their equivalents on the books of the Greyhound Corp. So far as the record shows, none of the certificates representing the seized property was physically present in Delaware. The stock was considered to be in Delaware, and so subject to seizure, by virtue of Del. Code Ann., Tit. 8, § 169 (1975), which makes Delaware the situs of ownership of all stock in Delaware corporations.

All 28 defendants were notified of the initiation of the suit by certified mail directed to their last known addresses and by publication in a New Castle County newspaper. The 21 defendants whose property was seized (hereafter referred to as appellants) responded by entering a special appearance for the purpose of moving to quash service of process and to vacate the sequestration order. They contended that the ex parte sequestration procedure did not accord them due process of law and that the property seized was not capable of attachment in Delaware. In addition, appellants asserted that under the rule of *International Shoe Co. v. Washington* they did not have sufficient contacts with Delaware to sustain the jurisdiction of that State's courts.

The Court of Chancery rejected these arguments in a letter opinion which emphasized the purpose of the Delaware sequestration procedure:

"The primary purpose of 'sequestration' as authorized by 10 Del. C. § 366 is not to secure possession of property pending a trial between resident debtors and creditors on the issue of who has the right to retain it. On the contrary, as here employed, 'sequestration' is a process used to compel the personal appearance of a nonresident defendant to answer and defend a suit brought against him in a court of equity. [cit.] * * * If the defendant enters a general appearance, the sequestered property is routinely released * * *." [cit.]

* * *

II. The Delaware courts rejected appellants' jurisdictional challenge by noting that this suit was brought as a quasi in rem proceeding. Since quasi in rem jurisdiction is traditionally based on attachment or seizure of property present in the jurisdiction, not on contacts between the defendant and the State, the courts considered appellants' claimed lack of contacts with Delaware to be unimportant. This categorical analysis assumes the continued soundness of the conceptual structure founded on the century-old case of *Pennoyer v. Neff*.

[The Court reviews the cases from *Pennoyer* to *International Shoe*. The Court concludes that "the relationship among the defendant, the forum, and the litigation, rather than the mutually exclusive sovereignty of the States on which the rules of *Pennoyer* rest, became the central concern of the inquiry in to personal jurisdiction."] * * *

No equally dramatic change has occurred in the law governing jurisdiction in rem. There have, however, been intimations that the collapse of the in personam wing of *Pennoyer* has not left that decision unweakened as a foundation for in rem jurisdiction. Well-reasoned lower court opinions have questioned the proposition that the presence of property in a State gives that State jurisdiction to adjudicate rights to the property regardless of the relationship of the underlying dispute and the property owner to the forum. [cit.] The overwhelming majority of commentators have also rejected *Pennoyer'* premise that a proceeding "against" property is not a proceeding against the owners of that property. Accordingly, they urge that the "traditional notions of fair play and substantial justice" that govern a State's power to adjudicate in personam should also govern its power to adjudicate personal rights to property located in the State. [cit.]

Although this Court has not addressed this argument directly, we have held that property cannot be subjected to a court's judgment unless reasonable and appropriate efforts have been made to give the property owners actual notice of the action. [cit.];

Walker v. City of Hutchinson, 352 U.S. 112 (1956); Mullane v. Central Hanover Bank & Trust Co., 339 U.S. 306 (1950). This conclusion recognizes, contrary to *Pennoyer*, that an adverse judgment in rem directly affects the property owner by divesting him of his rights in the property before the court. [cit.] Moreover, in *Mullane* we held that Fourteenth Amendment rights cannot depend on the classification of an action as in rem or in personam, since that is

> "a classification for which the standards are so elusive and confused generally and which, being primarily for state courts to define, may and do vary from state to state." [cit.]

It is clear, therefore, that the law of state-court jurisdiction no longer stands securely on the foundation established in *Pennoyer*. We think that the time is ripe to consider whether the standard of fairness and substantial justice set forth in *International Shoe* should be held to govern actions in rem as well as in personam.

III. The case for applying to jurisdiction in rem the same test of "fair play and substantial justice" as governs assertions of jurisdiction in personam is simple and straightforward. It is premised on recognition that "[t]he phrase, 'judicial jurisdiction over a thing,' is a customary elliptical way of referring to jurisdiction over the interests of persons in a thing." Restatement (Second) of Conflict of Laws § 56, Introductory Note (1971) (hereafter Restatement). This recognition leads to the conclusion that in order to justify an exercise of jurisdiction in rem, the basis for jurisdiction must be sufficient to justify exercising "jurisdiction over the interests of persons in a thing."[23] The standard for determining whether an exercise of jurisdiction over the interests of persons is consistent with the Due Process Clause is the minimum-contacts standard elucidated in *International Shoe*.

This argument, of course, does not ignore the fact that the presence of property in a State may bear on the existence of jurisdiction by providing contacts among the forum State, the defendant, and the litigation. For example, when claims to the property itself are the source of the underlying controversy between the plaintiff and the defendant, it would be unusual for the State where the property is located not to have jurisdiction. In such cases, the defendant's claim to property located in the State would normally indicate that he expected to benefit from the State's protection of his interest. The State's strong interests in assuring the marketability of property within its borders and in providing a procedure for peaceful resolution of disputes about the possession of that property would also support jurisdiction, as would the likelihood that important records and witnesses will be found in the State.[28] The presence of property may also favor jurisdiction in cases, such as suits for injury suffered on the land of an absentee owner, where the defendant's ownership of the property is conceded but the cause of action is otherwise related to rights and duties growing out of that ownership.

It appears, therefore, that jurisdiction over many types of actions which now are

---

23. It is true that the potential liability of a defendant in an in rem action is limited by the value of the property, but that limitation does not affect the argument. The fairness of subjecting a defendant to state-court jurisdiction does not depend on the size of the claim being litigated. Cf. *Fuentes v. Shevin.* [cit.]

28. We do not suggest that these illustrations include all the factors that may affect the decision, nor that the factors we mentioned are necessarily decisive.

or might be brought in rem would not be affected by a holding that any assertion of state-court jurisdiction must satisfy the *International Shoe* standard.[30] For the type of quasi in rem action typified by *Harris v. Balk* and the present case, however, accepting the proposed analysis would result in significant change. These are cases where the property which now serves as the basis for state-court jurisdiction is completely unrelated to the plaintiff's cause of action. Thus, although the presence of the defendant's property in a State might suggest the existence of other ties among the defendant, the State, and the litigation, the presence of the property alone would not support the State's jurisdiction. If those other ties did not exist, cases over which the State is now thought to have jurisdiction could not be brought in that forum.

Since acceptance of the *International Shoe* test would most affect this class of cases, we examine the arguments against adopting that standard as they relate to this category of litigation. Before doing so, however, we note that this type of case also presents the clearest illustration of the argument in favor of assessing assertions of jurisdiction by a single standard. For in cases such as *Harris* and this one, the only role played by the property is to provide the basis for bringing the defendant into court. Indeed, the express purpose of the Delaware sequestration procedure is to compel the defendant to enter a personal appearance. In such cases, if a direct assertion of personal jurisdiction over the defendant would violate the Constitution, it would seem that an indirect assertion of that jurisdiction should be equally impermissible.

The primary rationale for treating the presence of property as a sufficient basis for jurisdiction to adjudicate claims over which the State would not have jurisdiction if *International Shoe* applied is that a wrongdoer "should not be able to avoid payment of his obligations by the expedient of removing his assets to a place where he is not subject to an in personam suit." [cit.] This justification, however, does not explain why jurisdiction should be recognized without regard to whether the property is present in the State because of an effort to avoid the owner's obligations. Nor does it support jurisdiction to adjudicate the underlying claim. At most, it suggests that a State in which property is located should have jurisdiction to attach that property, by use of proper procedures, as security for a judgment being sought in a forum where the litigation can be maintained consistently with *International Shoe*. [cit.] Moreover, we know of nothing to justify the assumption that a debtor can avoid paying his obligations by removing his property to a State in which his creditor cannot obtain personal jurisdiction over him. The Full Faith and Credit Clause, after all, makes the valid in personam judgment of one State enforceable in all other States.[36]

It might also be suggested that allowing in rem jurisdiction avoids the uncertainty

---

30. [cit.] We do not suggest that jurisdictional doctrines other than those discussed in text, such as the particularized rules governing adjudications of status, are inconsistent with the standard of fairness. [cit.]

36. Once it has been determined by a court of competent jurisdiction that the defendant is a debtor of the plaintiff, there would seem to be no unfairness in allowing an action to realize on that debt in a State where the defendant has property, whether or not that State would have jurisdiction to determine the existence of the debt as an original matter. [cit.]

inherent in the *International Shoe* standard and assures a plaintiff of a forum.[37] We believe, however, that the fairness standard of *International Shoe* can be easily applied in the vast majority of cases. Moreover, when the existence of jurisdiction in a particular forum under *International Shoe* is unclear, the cost of simplifying the litigation by avoiding the jurisdictional question may be the sacrifice of "fair play and substantial justice." That cost is too high.

We are left, then, to consider the significance of the long history of jurisdiction based solely on the presence of property in a State. Although the theory that territorial power is both essential to and sufficient for jurisdiction has been undermined, we have never held that the presence of property in a State does not automatically confer jurisdiction over the owner's interest in that property. This history must be considered as supporting the proposition that jurisdiction based solely on the presence of property satisfies the demands of due process, [cit.] but it is not decisive."[T]raditional notions of fair play and substantial justice" can be as readily offended by the perpetuation of ancient forms that are no longer justified as by the adoption of new procedures that are inconsistent with the basic values of our constitutional heritage. [cit.] The fiction that an assertion of jurisdiction over property is anything but an assertion of jurisdiction over the owner of the property supports an ancient form without substantial modern justification. Its continued acceptance would serve only to allow state-court jurisdiction that is fundamentally unfair to the defendant.

We therefore conclude that all assertions of state-court jurisdiction must be evaluated according to the standards set forth in *International Shoe* and its progeny.[39]

IV. The Delaware courts based their assertion of jurisdiction in this case solely on the statutory presence of appellants' property in Delaware. Yet that property is not the subject matter of this litigation, nor is the underlying cause of action related to the property. Appellants' holdings in Greyhound do not, therefore, provide contacts with Delaware sufficient to support the jurisdiction of that State's courts over appellants. If it exists, that jurisdiction must have some other foundation.

Appellee Heitner did not allege and does not now claim that appellants have ever set foot in Delaware. Nor does he identify any act related to his cause of action as having taken place in Delaware. Nevertheless, he contends that appellants' positions as directors and officers of a corporation chartered in Delaware provide sufficient "contacts, ties, or relations," *International Shoe*, with that State to give its courts jurisdiction over appellants in this stockholder's derivative action. This argument is based primarily on what Heitner asserts to be the strong interest of Delaware in supervising the management of a Delaware corporation. That interest is said to derive from the role of Delaware law in establishing the corporation and defining the obligations owed to it by its officers and directors. In order to protect this interest,

---

37. This case does not raise, and we therefore do not consider, the question whether the presence of a defendant's property in a State is sufficient basis for jurisdiction when no other forum is available to the plaintiff.

39. It would not be fruitful for us to re-examine the facts of cases decided on the rationales of *Pennoyer* and *Harris* to determine whether jurisdiction might have been sustained under the standard we adopt today. To the extent that prior decisions are inconsistent with this standard, they are overruled.

appellee concludes, Delaware's courts must have jurisdiction over corporate fiduciaries such as appellants.

This argument is undercut by the failure of the Delaware Legislature to assert the state interest appellee finds so compelling. Delaware law bases jurisdiction, not on appellants' status as corporate fiduciaries, but rather on the presence of their property in the State. Although the sequestration procedure used here may be most frequently used in derivative suits against officers and directors, [cit.] the authorizing statute evinces no specific concern with such actions. Sequestration can be used in any suit against a nonresident, [cit.] and reaches corporate fiduciaries only if they happen to own interests in a Delaware corporation, or other property in the State. But as Heitner' failure to secure jurisdiction over seven of the defendants named in his complaint demonstrates, there is no necessary relationship between holding a position as a corporate fiduciary and owning stock or other interests in the corporation. If Delaware perceived its interest in securing jurisdiction over corporate fiduciaries to be as great as Heitner suggests, we would expect it to have enacted a statute more clearly designed to protect that interest.

Moreover, even if Heitner's assessment of the importance of Delaware's interest is accepted, his argument fails to demonstrate that Delaware is a fair forum for this litigation. The interest appellee has identified may support the application of Delaware law to resolve any controversy over appellants' actions in their capacities as officers and directors.[44] But we have rejected the argument that if a State's law can properly be applied to a dispute, its courts necessarily have jurisdiction over the parties to that dispute.

"[The State] does not acquire ... jurisdiction by being the 'center of gravity' of the controversy, or the most convenient location for litigation. The issue is personal jurisdiction, not choice of law. It is resolved in this case by considering the acts of the [appellants]." *Hanson v. Denckla.*

Appellee suggests that by accepting positions as officers or directors of a Delaware corporation, appellants performed the acts required by *Hanson v. Denckla.* He notes that Delaware law provides substantial benefits to corporate officers and directors, and that these benefits were at least in part the incentive for appellants to assume their positions. It is, he says, "only fair and just" to require appellants, in return for these benefits, to respond in the State of Delaware when they are accused of misusing their power. [cit.]

But like Heitner's first argument, this line of reasoning establishes only that it is appropriate for Delaware law to govern the obligations of appellants to Greyhound and its stockholders. It does not demonstrate that appellants have "purposefully avail[ed themselves] of the privilege of conducting activities within the forum State," *Hanson v. Denckla,* in a way that would justify bringing them before a Delaware tribunal. Appellants have simply had nothing to do with the State of Delaware. Moreover, appellants had no reason to expect to be haled before a Delaware court.

---

44. In general, the law of the State of incorporation is held to govern the liabilities of officers or directors to the corporation and its stockholders. [cit.] The rationale for the general rule appears to be based more on the need for a uniform and certain standard to govern the internal affairs of a corporation than on the perceived interest of the State of incorporation. [cit.]

Delaware, unlike some States, has not enacted a statute that treats acceptance of a directorship as consent to jurisdiction in the State. And "[i]t strains reason ... to suggest that anyone buying securities in a corporation formed in Delaware 'impliedly consents' to subject himself to Delaware's ... jurisdiction on any cause of action." [cit.] Appellants, who were not required to acquire interests in Greyhound in order to hold their positions, did not by acquiring those interests surrender their right to be brought to judgment only in States with which they had "minimum contacts."

The Due Process Clause "does not contemplate that a state may make binding a judgment ... against an individual or corporate defendant with which the state has no contacts, ties, or relations." *International Shoe*. Delaware's assertion of jurisdiction over appellants in this case is inconsistent with that constitutional limitation on state power. The judgment of the Delaware Supreme Court must, therefore, be reversed.

It is so ordered.

JUSTICE REHNQUIST took no part in the consideration or decision of this case.

JUSTICE POWELL, concurring. I agree that the principles of *International Shoe*, should be extended to govern assertions of in rem as well as in personam jurisdiction in a state court. I also agree that neither the statutory presence of appellants' stock in Delaware nor their positions as directors and officers of a Delaware corporation can provide sufficient contacts to support the Delaware courts' assertion of jurisdiction in this case.

I would explicitly reserve judgment, however, on whether the ownership of some forms of property whose situs is indisputably and permanently located within a State may, without more, provide the contacts necessary to subject a defendant to jurisdiction within the State to the extent of the value of the property. In the case of real property, in particular, preservation of the common-law concept of quasi in rem jurisdiction arguably would avoid the uncertainty of the general *International Shoe* standard without significant cost to "'traditional notions of fair play and substantial justice.'" [cit.]

Subject to the foregoing reservation, I join the opinion of the Court.

JUSTICE STEVENS, concurring in the judgment. The Due Process Clause affords protection against "judgments without notice." *International Shoe* (opinion of Black, J.). Throughout our history the acceptable exercise of in rem and quasi in rem jurisdiction has included a procedure giving reasonable assurance that actual notice of the particular claim will be conveyed to the defendant. Thus, publication, notice by registered mail, or extraterritorial personal service has been an essential ingredient of any procedure that serves as a substitute for personal service within the jurisdiction.

The requirement of fair notice also, I believe, includes fair warning that a particular activity may subject a person to the jurisdiction of a foreign sovereign. If I visit another State, or acquire real estate or open a bank account in it, I knowingly assume some risk that the State will exercise its power over my property or my person while there. My contact with the State, though minimal, gives rise to predictable risks.

Perhaps the same consequences should flow from the purchase of stock of a corporation organized under the laws of a foreign nation, because to some limited extent one's property and affairs then become subject to the laws of the nation of domicile of the corporation. As a matter of international law, that suggestion might be acceptable because a foreign investment is sufficiently unusual to make it appropriate to require the investor to study the ramifications of his decision. But a purchase of securities in the domestic market is an entirely different matter.

One who purchases shares of stock on the open market can hardly be expected to know that he has thereby become subject to suit in a forum remote from his residence and unrelated to the transaction. * * *

How the Court's opinion may be applied in other contexts is not entirely clear to me. I agree with Mr. Justice Powell that it should not be read to invalidate quasi in rem jurisdiction where real estate is involved. I would also not read it as invalidating other long-accepted methods of acquiring jurisdiction over persons with adequate notice of both the particular controversy and the fact that their local activities might subject them to suit. My uncertainty as to the reach of the opinion, and my fear that it purports to decide a great deal more than is necessary to dispose of this case, persuade me merely to concur in the judgment.

JUSTICE BRENNAN, concurring in part and dissenting in part. I join Parts I–III of the Court's opinion. I fully agree that the minimum-contacts analysis developed in *International Shoe*, represents a far more sensible construct for the exercise of state-court jurisdiction than the patchwork of legal and factual fictions that has been generated from the decision in *Pennoyer v. Neff*. It is precisely because the inquiry into minimum contacts is now of such overriding importance, however, that I must respectfully dissent from Part IV of the Court's opinion.

[Justice Brennan argues that it was inappropriate for the Court to consider whether Delaware's assertion of jurisdiction met the "minimum contacts" test. He says of the Court's discussion of this point that "a purer example of an advisory opinion is not to be found."] * * *

Nonetheless, because the Court rules on the minimum-contacts question, I feel impelled to express my view. While evidence derived through discovery might satisfy me that minimum contacts are lacking in a given case, I am convinced that as a general rule a state forum has jurisdiction to adjudicate a shareholder derivative action centering on the conduct and policies of the directors and officers of a corporation chartered by that State. Unlike the Court, I therefore would not foreclose Delaware from asserting jurisdiction over appellants were it persuaded to do so on the basis of minimum contacts.

* * *

In this instance, Delaware can point to at least three interrelated public policies that are furthered by its assertion of jurisdiction. First, the State has a substantial interest in providing restitution for its local corporations that allegedly have been victimized by fiduciary misconduct, even if the managerial decisions occurred outside the State. * * * Second, state courts have legitimately read their jurisdiction expansively when a cause of action centers in an area in which the forum State possesses a manifest regulatory interest. E.g., *McGee v. International Life Ins. Co.*, (insurance regulation); Travelers Health Assn. v. Virginia, 339 U.S. 643 (1950) (blue sky laws). * * * Finally, a State like Delaware has a recognized interest in affording a convenient forum for supervising and overseeing the affairs of an entity that is purely the creation of that State's law. * * *

To be sure, the Court is not blind to these considerations. It notes that the State's interests "may support the application of Delaware law to resolve any controversy over appellants' actions in their capacities as officers and directors." [cit.] But this, the Court argues, pertains to choice of law, not jurisdiction. I recognize that the jurisdictional and choice-of-law inquiries are not identical. *Hanson v. Denckla.* But I would not compartmentalize thinking in this area quite so rigidly as it seems to me the Court does today, for both inquiries "are often closely related and to a substantial degree depend upon similar considerations." Id. (Black, J., dissenting). In either case an important linchpin is the extent of contacts between the controversy, the parties, and the forum State. While constitutional limitations on the choice of law are by no means settled, [cit.], important considerations certainly include the expectancies of the parties and the fairness of governing the defendants' acts and behavior by rules of conduct created by a given jurisdiction. [cit.] These same factors bear upon the propriety of a State's exercising jurisdiction over a legal dispute. At the minimum, the decision that it is fair to bind a defendant by a State's laws and rules should prove to be highly relevant to the fairness of permitting that same State to accept jurisdiction for adjudicating the controversy.

Furthermore, I believe that practical considerations argue in favor of seeking to bridge the distance between the choice-of-law and jurisdictional inquiries. Even when a court would apply the law of a different forum, as a general rule it will feel less knowledgeable and comfortable in interpretation, and less interested in fostering the policies of that foreign jurisdiction, than would the courts established by the State that provides the applicable law. See, e.g., Gulf Oil Co. v. Gilbert, 330 U.S. 501 (1947); [cit.]. Obviously, such choice-of-law problems cannot entirely be avoided in a diverse legal system such as our own. Nonetheless, when a suitor seeks to lodge a suit in a State with a substantial interest in seeing its own law applied to the transaction in question, we could wisely act to minimize conflicts, confusion, and uncertainty by adopting a liberal view of jurisdiction, unless considerations of fairness or efficiency strongly point in the opposite direction.

* * *

Notes and Questions

1. A number of other countries allow "assets" jurisdiction under which a court acquires in personam jurisdiction allowing judgments of any size based on the presence of property. As one commentator explained: "a Russian may leave his galoshes in a hotel in Berlin and may be sued in Berlin for a debt of 100,000 Mark because of the 'presence of assets within the jurisdiction'" Nadelmann, *Jurisdictionally Improper Fora*, at 329. See Born, *Reflections on Judicial Jurisdiction*, at 14. In

addition, as *Shaffer* notes, jurisdiction by attachment or quasi-in-rem jurisdiction (in which jurisdiction is limited to the value of the property attached) has long been recognized as a basis for jurisdiction in this country. How can a traditionally accepted mechanism of jurisdiction violate "traditional notions of fair play and substantial justice?"

2. Does the Court hold that a defendant can be subject to jurisdiction by attachment only if she would be subject to in personam jurisdiction? Some commentators have interpreted *Shaffer* this way, see Shreve & Raven–Hanson, *Understanding Civil Procedure*, 63; see also Leflar, McDougal & Felix, *American Conflicts*, 135, and some language in the opinion seems to support this conclusion. The Court asserts that where the property is unrelated to the claim and serves solely as a basis to bring the defendant into court, "if a direct assertion of personal jurisdiction over the defendant would violate the Constitution, it would seem that an indirect assertion of that jurisdiction should be equally impermissible." 433 U.S. at 209. The Court also notes that although in an in rem action the potential liability of the defendant is limited to the value of the property, "[t]he fairness of subjecting a defendant to state-court jurisdiction does not depend on the size of the claim being litigated." Id. at 207 n.23. The Court concludes that "all assertions of state-court jurisdiction must be evaluated according to the standards set forth in *International Shoe* and its progeny." Id. 212.

In contrast, Professor Weintraub has argued that although all assertions of jurisdiction must be evaluated under the *International Shoe* standard, that "is not the same as saying that those standards must provide the same answer no matter what the form of jurisdiction asserted. In cases that would fall close to the due process line if full personal jurisdiction were asserted, the less drastic remedy of allowing the plaintiff to reach the defendant's assets in the state may be reasonable." Weintraub, *Commentary*, 206. Which interpretation of *Shaffer* do you think is correct? Several courts have upheld jurisdiction based on the attachment of a bank account in the forum on the theory that maintenance of the account was a purposeful contact. See, e.g., Banco Ambrosiano v. Artoc Bank & Trust, 464 N.E.2d 432 (N.Y. 1982); Cameco Indus. Inc. v. Mayatrac, S.A., 789 F.Supp. 200 (D.Md.1992) Are these cases consistent with the majority opinion in *Shaffer*? See Mushlin, *The New Quasi in Rem Jurisdiction*.

3. As discussed infra at 662-63, divorce was traditionally treated as an in rem proceeding. However, in footnote 30 of *Shaffer*, the Court excludes "adjudications of status," i.e. divorce, from its analysis. Why should divorce jurisdiction be treated differently from other in rem proceedings?

4. Consider Part IV of the majority opinion in *Shaffer*. Why is not becoming the director of a Delaware corporation a sufficient contact for those directors to be sued in personam in Delaware for breaches of their obligations as directors? Is *Shaffer* consistent with *Burger King*?

5. If there is no personal jurisdiction over the directors in Delaware, where would jurisdiction be proper? Would it be proper in Arizona, the place of Grey-hound's headquarters? If so, could Arizona constitutionally apply its law concerning fiduciary obligations of corporate officers? Compare *Shaffer* with Edgar v. MITE

Corp., 457 U.S. 624 (1982), CTS Corp. v. Dynamics Corporation of America, 481 U.S. 69 (1987), discussed supra at 512.

6. At common law, courts distinguished between "local" and "transitory" causes of action. Local actions included suits that directly affected title to or possession of land. Other types of suits concerning land, such as trespass or breach of contract to convey, were sometimes also included in this category. A local claim could only be brought where the property in question was located. In contrast, a transitory action could be brought anywhere there was personal jurisdiction. While states vary on where to draw the line between local and transitory actions, nearly all recognize the distinction. As a result, certain types of suits involving land, such as suits for possession or to quiet title, must be brought where the land is located. The Supreme Court has held that a state court decree purporting to transfer directly land in another state is not subject to enforcement under the Full Faith and Credit Clause. See Ch. 10.

7. The Internet may be bringing renewed interest to in rem jurisdiction. The 1999 Anticybersquatting Consumer Protection Act, 15 U.S.C. § 1125(d)(2)(A), provides that if an Internet domain name violates the rights of a registered trademark and the trademark owner is not able to obtain in personam jurisdiction over the offending domain name owner, the trademark owner may bring an in rem action against the domain name. For purposes of such an action, the "situs" of the domain name is deemed to be the place where the domain name "registrar, registry, or other domain name authority" is located. In Caesars World, Inc. v. Caesars-Palace.com, 112 F. Supp.2d 502 (E.D. Va. 2000), the court upheld the constitutionality of the statute. The court held that even if there were insufficient contacts constitutionally to support in personam jurisdiction, the exercise under the statute of in rem jurisdiction was constitutional. The court concluded that "under *Shaffer*, there must be minimum contacts to support personal jurisdiction only in those in rem proceedings where the underlying cause of action is unrelated to the property which is located in the forum state. Here the property, that is, the domain name, is not only related to the cause of action but is its entire subject matter." Id. at 504. The court also rejected the argument that a domain name registration is not a proper kind of thing to serve as a res: "There is no prohibition on a legislative body making something property. Even if a domain name is no more than data, Congress can make data property and assign its place of registration as its situs." Id. In contrast, other courts have held that after *Shaffer*, minimum contacts are required for in rem jurisdiction. See Fleetboston Financial Corp. v. Fleetbostonfinancial.com, 138 F. Supp.2d 121 (D. Mass. 2001). See generally Struve & Wagner, *Realspace Sovereign in Cyberspace*; Lee, *In Rem Jurisdiction in Cyberspace*.

4. Transient Jurisdiction

Burnham v. Superior Court of California

Supreme Court of the United States, 1990.
495 U.S. 604, 110 S.Ct. 2105, 109 L.Ed.2d 631.

JUSTICE SCALIA announced the judgment of the Court and delivered an opinion in which The Chief Justice and Justice Kennedy join, and in which Justice White joins with respect to Parts I, II–A, II–B, and II–C.

The question presented is whether the Due Process Clause of the Fourteenth Amendment denies California courts jurisdiction over a nonresident, who was personally served with process while temporarily in that State, in a suit unrelated to his activities in the State.

I. Petitioner Dennis Burnham married Francie Burnham in 1976 in West Virginia. In 1977 the couple moved to New Jersey, where their two children were born. In July 1987 the Burnhams decided to separate. They agreed that Mrs. Burnham, who intended to move to California, would take custody of the children. Shortly before Mrs. Burnham departed for California that same month, she and petitioner agreed that she would file for divorce on grounds of "irreconcilable differences."

In October 1987, petitioner filed for divorce in New Jersey state court on grounds of "desertion." * * * Mrs. Burnham, after unsuccessfully demanding that petitioner adhere to their prior agreement to submit to an "irreconcilable differences" divorce, brought suit for divorce in California state court in early January 1988.

In late January, petitioner visited southern California on business, after which he went north to visit his children in the San Francisco Bay area, where his wife resided. He took the older child to San Francisco for the weekend. Upon returning the child to Mrs. Burnham's home on January 24, 1988, petitioner was served with a California court summons and a copy of Mrs. Burnham's divorce petition. He then returned to New Jersey.

Later that year, petitioner made a special appearance in the California Superior Court, moving to quash the service of process on the ground that the court lacked personal jurisdiction over him because his only contacts with California were a few short visits to the State for the purposes of conducting business and visiting his children. * * * [The California courts upheld personal jurisdiction on the ground that the defendant was served with process in the state.]

II. A. * * * To determine whether the assertion of personal jurisdiction is consistent with due process, we have long relied on the principles traditionally followed by American courts in marking out the territorial limits of each State's authority. That criterion was first announced in *Pennoyer v. Neff.* * * * In what has become the classic expression of the criterion, we said in *International Shoe Co. v. Washington*, that a state court's assertion of personal jurisdiction satisfies the Due Process Clause if it does not violate "'traditional notions of fair play and substantial justice.'" [cit.] Since *International Shoe*, we have only been called upon to decide whether these "traditional notions" permit States to exercise jurisdiction over absent defendants in a manner that deviates from the rules of jurisdiction applied in the 19th century. We have held such deviations permissible, but only with respect to suits arising out of the absent defendant's contacts with the State.[1] See, e.g., *Helicopteros Nacionales de Colombia v. Hall.* The question we must decide today is whether due process requires a similar connection between the litigation and the defendant's contacts with the State in cases where the defendant is physically present in the State at the time process is served upon him.

B. Among the most firmly established principles of personal jurisdiction in American tradition is that the courts of a State have jurisdiction over nonresidents who are physically present in the State. The view developed early that each State had the power to hale before its courts any individual who could be found within its borders, and that once having acquired jurisdiction over such a person by properly serving him with process, the State could retain jurisdiction to enter judgment against him, no matter how fleeting his visit. [cit.] That view had antecedents in English common-law practice, which sometimes allowed "transitory" actions, arising out of events outside the country, to be maintained against seemingly nonresident defendants who were present in England. [cit.] Justice Story believed the principle, which he traced to Roman origins, to be firmly grounded in English tradition: "[B]y the common law[,] personal actions, being transitory, may be brought in any place, where the party defendant may be found," for "every nation may ... rightfully exercise jurisdiction over all persons within its domains." J. Story, Commentaries on the Conflict of Laws §§ 554, 543 (1846). [cit.]

Recent scholarship has suggested that English tradition was not as clear as Story thought, [cit.]. Accurate or not, however, judging by the evidence of contemporaneous or near-contemporaneous decisions, one must conclude that Story's understanding was shared by American courts at the crucial time for present purposes: 1868, when the Fourteenth Amendment was adopted. * * *

Decisions in the courts of many States in the 19th and early 20th centuries held that personal service upon a physically present defendant sufficed to confer jurisdiction, without regard to whether the defendant was only briefly in the State or whether the cause of action was related to his activities there. [Citations to 13 state cases.] Although research has not revealed a case deciding the issue in every State's courts, that appears to be because the issue was so well settled that it went unlitigated. [cit.] Opinions from the courts of other States announced the rule in dictum. [Citations to eight state cases.] Most States, moreover, had statutes or common-law rules that exempted from service of process individuals who were

---

1. We have said that"[e]ven when the cause of action does not arise out of or relate to the foreign corporation's activities in the forum State, due process is not offended by a State's subjecting the corporation to its in personam jurisdiction when there are sufficient contacts between the State and the foreign corporation." *Helicopteros Nacionales de Colombia v. Hall.*

Our only holding supporting that statement, however, involved "regular service of summons upon [the corporation's] president while he was in [the forum State] acting in that capacity." See *Perkins v. Benguet Consolidated Mining Co.* It may be that whatever special rule exists permitting "continuous and systematic" contacts, [cit.] to support jurisdiction with respect to matters unrelated to activity in the forum applies *only* to corporations, which have never fitted comfortably in a jurisdictional regime based primarily upon "de facto power over the defendant's person." *International Shoe.* We express no views on these matters–and, for simplicity's sake, omit reference to this aspect of "contacts"-based jurisdiction in our discussion.

brought into the forum by force or fraud, [cit.] or who were there as a party or witness in unrelated judicial proceedings [cit.]. These exceptions obviously rested upon the premise that service of process conferred jurisdiction. [cit.] Particularly striking is the fact that, as far as we have been able to determine, *not one* American case from the period (or, for that matter, not one American case until 1978) held, or even suggested, that in-state personal service on an individual was insufficient to confer personal jurisdiction. Commentators were also seemingly unanimous on the rule. [cit.]

This American jurisdictional practice is, moreover, not merely old; it is continuing. It remains the practice of, not only a substantial number of the States, but as far as we are aware all the States and the Federal Government—if one disregards (as one must for this purpose) the few opinions since 1978 that have erroneously said, on grounds similar to those that petitioner presses here, that this Court's due process decisions render the practice unconstitutional. See Nehemiah v. Athletics Congress of U.S.A., 765 F.2d 42, 46-47 (3d Cir.1985); Schreiber v. Allis-Chalmers Corp., 448 F.Supp. 1079, 1088–91 (D.C.Kan.1978), rev'd on other grounds, 611 F.2d 790 (10th Cir.1979); Harold M. Pitman Co. v. Typecraft Software Ltd., 626 F.Supp. 305, 310-14 (N.D.Ill.1986); [cit.]. We do not know of a single state or federal statute, or a single judicial decision resting upon state law, that has abandoned in-state service as a basis of jurisdiction. Many recent cases reaffirm it. [cit.]

C. Despite this formidable body of precedent, petitioner contends, in reliance on our decisions applying the *International Shoe* standard, that in the absence of "continuous and systematic" contacts with the forum, a nonresident defendant can be subjected to judgment only as to matters that arise out of or relate to his contacts with the forum. This argument rests on a thorough misunderstanding of our cases.

* * * Our opinion in *International Shoe* made explicit the underlying basis of [earlier] * * * decisions: Due process does not necessarily *require* the States to adhere to the unbending territorial limits on jurisdiction set forth in *Pennoyer*. The validity of assertion of jurisdiction over a nonconsenting defendant who is not present in the forum depends upon whether "the quality and nature of [his] activity" in relation to the forum, [cit.] renders such jurisdiction consistent with "'traditional notions of fair play and substantial justice.'" [cit.] Subsequent cases have derived from the *International Shoe* standard the general rule that a State may dispense with in-forum personal service on nonresident defendants in suits arising out of their activities in the State. * * *

Nothing in *International Shoe* or the cases that have followed it, however, offers support for the very different proposition petitioner seeks to establish today: that a defendant's presence in the forum is not only unnecessary to validate novel, nontraditional assertions of jurisdiction, but is itself no longer sufficient to establish jurisdiction. That proposition is unfaithful to both elementary logic and the foundations of our due process jurisprudence. The distinction between what is needed to support novel procedures and what is needed to sustain traditional ones is fundamental * * *. The short of the matter is that jurisdiction based on physical presence alone constitutes due process because it is one of the continuing traditions of our legal system that define the due process standard of "traditional notions of fair play and substantial justice." That standard was developed by *analogy* to "physical presence," and it would be perverse to say it could now be turned against that touchstone of jurisdiction.

D. Petitioner's strongest argument, though we ultimately reject it, relies upon our decision in *Shaffer v. Heitner*. * * *

It goes too far to say, as petitioner contends, that *Shaffer* compels the conclusion that a State lacks jurisdiction over an individual unless the litigation arises out of his activities in the State. *Shaffer*, like *International Shoe*, involved jurisdiction over an *absent defendant*, and it stands for nothing more than the proposition that when the "minimum contact" that is a substitute for physical presence consists of property ownership it must, like other minimum contacts, be related to the litigation. Petitioner wrenches out of its context our statement in *Shaffer* that "all assertions of state-court jurisdiction must be evaluated according to the standards set forth in *International Shoe* and its progeny." [cit.] When read together with the two sentences that preceded it, the meaning of this statement becomes clear. * * * *Shaffer* was saying, * * * not that all bases for the assertion of *in personam* jurisdiction (including, presumably, in-state service) must be treated alike and subjected to the "minimum contacts" analysis of *International Shoe*; but rather that *quasi in rem* jurisdiction, that fictional "ancient form," and in personam jurisdiction, are really one and the same and must be treated alike—leading to the conclusion that *quasi in rem* jurisdiction, i.e., that form of *in personam* jurisdiction based upon a "property ownership" contact and by definition unaccompanied by personal, in-state service, must satisfy the litigation-relatedness requirement of *International Shoe*. The logic of *Shaffer's* holding-which places all suits against absent nonresidents on the same constitutional footing, regardless of whether a separate Latin label is attached to one particular basis of contact—does not compel the conclusion that physically present defendants must be treated identically to absent ones. As we have demonstrated at length, our tradition has treated the two classes of defendants quite differently, and it is unreasonable to read *Shaffer* as casually obliterating that distinction. *International Shoe* confined its "minimum contacts" requirement to situations in which the defendant "be not present within the territory of the forum," [cit.] and nothing in *Shaffer* expands that requirement beyond that.

It is fair to say, however, that while our holding today does not contradict *Shaffer*, our basic approach to the due process question is different. We have conducted no independent inquiry into the desirability or fairness of the prevailing in-state service rule, leaving that judgment to the legislatures that are free to amend it; for our purposes, its validation is its pedigree, as the phrase *"traditional notions of fair play and substantial justice"* makes clear. *Shaffer* did conduct such an independent inquiry, asserting that "'traditional notions of fair play and substantial justice' can be as readily offended by the perpetuation of ancient forms that are no longer justified as by the adoption of new procedures that are inconsistent with the basic values of our constitutional heritage" [cit.] Perhaps that assertion can be sustained when the "perpetuation of ancient forms" is engaged in by only a very small minority of the States.[4] Where, however, as in the present case, a jurisdictional principle is both firmly approved by tradition and still favored, it is impossible to imagine what standard we could appeal to for the judgment that it is "no longer justified." While in no way receding from or casting doubt upon the holding of *Shaffer* or any other case, we reaffirm today our time-honored approach. [cit.] For new procedures, hitherto unknown, the Due Process clause requires analysis to determine whether "traditional notions of fair play and substantial justice" have been offended. [cit.] But a doctrine of personal jurisdiction that dates back to the adoption of the Fourteenth Amendment and is still generally observed unquestionably meets that standard.

III. A few words in response to Justice Brennan's opinion concurring in the judgment: It insists that we apply "contemporary notions of due process" to determine the constitutionality of California's assertion of jurisdiction. [cit.] But our analysis today comports with that prescription, at least if we give it the only sense allowed by our precedents. The "contemporary notions of due process" applicable to personal jurisdiction are the enduring "*traditional* notions of fair play and substantial justice" established as the test by *International Shoe.* By its very language, that test is satisfied if a state court adheres to jurisdictional rules that are generally applied and have always been applied in the United States.

But the concurrence's proposed standard of "contemporary notions of due process" requires more: It measures state-court jurisdiction not only against traditional doctrines in this country, including current state-court practice, but also against each Justice's subjective assessment of what is fair and just. Authority for that seductive standard is not to be found in any of our personal jurisdiction cases. It is, indeed, an outright break with the test of "traditional notions of fair play and substantial justice," which would have to be reformulated "*our* notions of fair play and substantial justice."

The subjectivity, and hence inadequacy, of this approach becomes apparent when the concurrence tries to explain *why* the assertion of jurisdiction in the present case meets its standard of continuing-American-tradition-*plus*-innate-fairness. Justice Brennan lists the "benefits" Mr. Burnham derived from the State of California—the fact that, during the few days he was there, "[h]is health and safety [were] guaranteed by the State's police, fire, and emergency medical services; he [was] free to travel on the State's roads and waterways; he likely enjoy[ed] the fruits of the State's economy." [cit.] Three days' worth of these benefits strike us as powerfully inadequate to establish, as an abstract matter, that it is "fair" for California to decree the ownership of all Mr. Burnham's worldly goods acquired during the 10 years of his marriage, and the custody over his children. We daresay a contractual exchange swapping those benefits for that power would not survive the "unconscionability" provision of the Uniform Commercial Code. Even less persuasive are the other "fairness" factors alluded to by Justice Brennan. It would create "an asymmetry," we

---

4. *Shaffer* may have involved a unique state procedure in one respect: Justice Stevens noted that Delaware was the only State that treated the place of incorporation as the situs of corporate stock when both owner and custodian were elsewhere. [cit.]

are told, if Burnham were *permitted* (as he is) to appear in California courts as a plaintiff, but were not *compelled* to appear in California courts as defendant; and travel being as easy as it is nowadays, and modern procedural devices being so convenient, it is no great hardship to appear in California courts. [cit.] The problem with these assertions is that they justify the exercise of jurisdiction over *everyone, whether or not* he ever comes to California. The only "fairness" elements setting Mr. Burnham apart from the rest of the world are the three days' "benefits" referred to above—and even those, do not set him apart from many other people who have enjoyed three days in the Golden State (savoring the fruits of its economy, the availability of its roads and police services) but who were fortunate enough not to be served with process while they were there and thus are not (simply by reason of that savoring) subject to the general jurisdiction of California's courts. [cit.] In other words, even if one agreed with Justice Brennan's conception of an equitable bargain, the "benefits" we have been discussing would explain why it is "fair" to assert general jurisdiction over Burnham-returned-to-New-Jersey-after-service only at the expense of proving that it is also "fair" to assert general jurisdiction over Burnham-returned-to-New-Jersey-*without*-service--which we *know* does not conform with "contemporary notions of due process."

There is, we must acknowledge, one factor mentioned by Justice Brennan that *both* relates distinctively to the assertion of jurisdiction on the basis of personal in-state service *and* is fully persuasive—namely, the fact that a defendant voluntarily present in a particular State has a "reasonable expectatio[n]" that he is subject to suit there.[cit.] By formulating it as a "reasonable expectation" Justice Brennan makes that seem like a "fairness" factor; but in reality, of course, it is just tradition masquerading as "fairness." The only reason for charging Mr. Burnham with the reasonable expectation of being subject to suit is that the States of the Union assert adjudicatory jurisdiction over the person, and have always asserted adjudicatory jurisdiction over the person, by serving him with process during his temporary physical presence in their territory. That continuing tradition, which anyone entering California should have known about, renders it "fair" for Mr. Burnham, who voluntarily entered California, to be sued there for divorce--at least "fair" in the limited sense that he has no one but himself to blame. Justice Brennan's long journey is a circular one, leaving him, at the end of the day, in complete reliance upon the very factor he sought to avoid: The existence of a continuing tradition is not enough, fairness also must be considered; fairness exists here because there is a continuing tradition.

While Justice Brennan's concurrence is unwilling to confess that the Justices of this Court can possibly be bound by a continuing American tradition that a particular procedure is fair, neither is it willing to embrace the logical consequences of that refusal--or even to be clear about what consequences (logical or otherwise) it does embrace. Justice Brennan says that "[f]or these reasons [i.e., because of the reasonableness factors enumerated above], as a rule the exercise of personal jurisdiction over a defendant based on his voluntary presence in the forum will satisfy the requirements of due process." [cit.] The use of the word "rule" conveys the reassuring feeling that he is establishing a principle of law one can rely upon--but of course he is not. Since Justice Brennan's only criterion of constitutionality is "fairness," the phrase "as a rule" represents nothing more than his estimation that, *usually*, all the elements of "fairness" he discusses in the present case will exist. But what if they do not? Suppose, for example, that a defendant in Mr. Burnham's situation enjoys not three days' worth of California's "benefits," but 15 minutes' worth. Or suppose we remove one of those "benefits"--"enjoy[ment of] the fruits of the State's economy"--by positing that Mr. Burnham had not come to California on business, but only to visit his children. Or suppose that Mr. Burnham were demonstrably so impecunious as to be unable to take advantage of the modern means of transportation and communication that Justice Brennan finds so relevant. Or suppose, finally, that the California courts lacked the "variety of procedural devices," [cit.] that Justice Brennan says can reduce the burden upon out-of-state litigants. One may also make additional suppositions, relating not to the absence of the factors that Justice Brennan discusses, but to the presence of additional factors bearing upon the ultimate criterion of "fairness." What if, for example, Mr. Burnham were visiting a sick child? Or a dying child? [cit.] Since, so far as one can tell, Justice Brennan's approval of applying the in-state service rule in the present case rests on the presence of *all* the factors he lists, and on the absence of any others, every different case will present a different litigable issue. Thus, despite the fact that he manages to work the word "rule" into his formulation, Justice Brennan's approach does not establish a rule of law at all, but only a "totality of the circumstances" test, guaranteeing what traditional territorial rules of jurisdiction were designed precisely to avoid: uncertainty and litigation over the preliminary issue of the forum's competence. It may be that those evils, necessarily accompanying a freestanding "reasonableness" inquiry, must be accepted at the margins, when we evaluate nontraditional forms of jurisdiction newly adopted by the States, see, e.g., *Asahi Metal Industry Co. v. Superior Court of California*. But that is no reason for injecting them into the core of our American practice, exposing to such a "reasonableness" inquiry the ground of jurisdiction that has hitherto been considered the very *baseline* of reasonableness, physical presence.

The difference between us and Justice Brennan has nothing to do with whether "further progress [is] to be made" in the "evolution of our legal system." [cit.] It has to do with whether changes are to be adopted as progressive by the American people or decreed as progressive by the Justices of this Court. Nothing we say today prevents individual States from limiting or entirely abandoning the in-state-service basis of jurisdiction. And nothing prevents an overwhelming majority of them from doing so, with the consequence that the "traditional notions of fairness" that this Court applies may change. But the States have overwhelmingly declined to adopt such limitation or abandonment, evidently not considering it to be progress.[5] The

---

5. I find quite unacceptable as a basis for this Court's decisions Justice Brennan's view that "the *raison d'être* of various constitutional doctrines designed to protect out-of-staters, such as the Art. IV Privileges and Immunities Clause and the Commerce Clause," [cit.] entitles this Court to brand as "unfair," and hence unconstitutional, the refusal of all 50 States "to limit or abandon bases of jurisdiction that have become obsolete," [cit.]. "Due process" (which is the constitutional text at issue here) does not mean that process which shifting majorities of this Court feel to be "due"; but that process which American society--

(continued...)

question is whether, armed with no authority other than individual Justices' perceptions of fairness that conflict with both past and current practice, this Court can compel the States to make such a change on the ground that "due process" requires it. We hold that it cannot.

* * *

Because the Due Process Clause does not prohibit the California courts from exercising jurisdiction over petitioner based on the fact of in-state service of process, the judgment is

Affirmed.

JUSTICE WHITE, concurring in part and concurring in the judgment. I join Parts, I, II–A, II–B, and II–C of Justice Scalia's opinion and concur in the judgment of affirmance. The rule allowing jurisdiction to be obtained over a nonresident by personal service in the forum State, without more, has been and is so widely accepted throughout this country that I could not possibly strike it down, either on its face or as applied in this case, on the ground that it denies due process of law guaranteed by the Fourteenth Amendment. Although the Court has the authority under the Amendment to examine even traditionally accepted procedures and declare them invalid, e.g., *Shaffer v. Heitner*, there has been no showing here or elsewhere that as a general proposition the rule is so arbitrary and lacking in common sense in so many instances that it should be held violative of due process in every case. Furthermore, until such a showing is made, which would be difficult indeed, claims in individual cases that the rule would operate unfairly as applied to the particular nonresident involved need not be entertained. At least this would be the case where presence in the forum State is intentional, which would almost always be the fact. Otherwise, there would be endless, fact-specific litigation in the trial and appellate courts, including this one. Here, personal service in California, without more, is enough, and I agree that the judgment should be affirmed.

JUSTICE BRENNAN, with whom Justice Marshall, Justice Blackmun, and Justice O'Connor join, concurring in the judgment.

I agree with Justice Scalia that the Due Process Clause of the Fourteenth Amendment generally permits a state court to exercise jurisdiction over a defendant if he is served with process while voluntarily present in the forum State. I do not perceive the need, however, to decide that a jurisdictional rule that "'has been immemorially the actual law of the land,'" [cit.] automatically comports with due process simply by virtue of its "pedigree." Although I agree that history is an important factor in establishing whether a jurisdictional rule satisfies due process requirements, I cannot agree that it is the *only* factor such that all traditional rules of jurisdiction are, ipso facto, forever constitutional. Unlike Justice Scalia, I would

---

(...continued)

self-interested American society, which expresses its judgments in the laws of self-interested States–has traditionally considered "due." The notion that the Constitution, through some penumbra emanating from the Privileges and Immunities Clause and the Commerce Clause, establishes this Court as a Platonic check upon the society's greedy adherence to its traditions can only be described as imperious.

undertake an "independent inquiry into the ... fairness of the prevailing in-state service rule." [cit.] I therefore concur only in the judgment.

I. I believe that the approach adopted by Justice Scalia's opinion today--reliance solely on historical pedigree--is foreclosed by our decisions in *International Shoe* and *Shaffer v. Heitner*. In *International Shoe*, we held that a state court's assertion of personal jurisdiction does not violate the Due Process Clause if it is consistent with "'traditional notions of fair play and substantial justice.'" [cit.] In *Shaffer*, we stated that "*all* assertions of state-court jurisdiction must be evaluated according to the standards set forth in *International Shoe* and its progeny." [cit.] The critical insight of *Shaffer* is that all rules of jurisdiction, even ancient ones, must satisfy contemporary notions of due process. * * *

While our holding in *Shaffer* may have been limited to quasi in rem jurisdiction, our mode of analysis was not. Indeed, that we were willing in *Shaffer* to examine anew the appropriateness of the quasi in rem rule—until that time dutifully accepted by American courts for at least a century—demonstrates that we did not believe that the "pedigree" of a jurisdictional practice was dispositive in deciding whether it was consistent with due process. We later characterized *Shaffer* as "abandon[ing] the outworn rule of *Harris v. Balk*, that the interest of a creditor in a debt could be extinguished or otherwise affected by any State having transitory jurisdiction over the debtor." *World-Wide Volkswagen Corp. v. Woodson*; [cit.]. If we could discard an "ancient form without substantial modern justification" in *Shaffer*, we can do so again. Lower courts, commentators, and the American Law Institute all have interpreted *International Shoe* and *Shaffer* to mean that *every* assertion of state-court jurisdiction, even one pursuant to a "traditional" rule such as transient jurisdiction, must comport with contemporary notions of due process. Notwithstanding the nimble gymnastics of Justice Scalia's opinion today, it is not faithful to our decision in *Shaffer*.

II. Tradition, though alone not dispositive, is of course *relevant* to the question whether the rule of transient jurisdiction is consistent with due process.[7] Tradition is salient not in the sense that practices of the past are automatically reasonable today; indeed, under such a standard, the legitimacy of transient jurisdiction would be called into question because the rule's historical "pedigree" is a matter of intense debate. The rule was a stranger to the common law[8] and was rather weakly implanted in American jurisprudence "at the crucial time for present purposes: 1868, when the Fourteenth Amendment was adopted." [cit.] For much of the 19th century, American courts did not uniformly recognize the concept of transient jurisdiction, and it

---

7. I do not propose that the "contemporary notions of due process" to be applied are no more than "each Justice's subjective assessment of what is fair and just." [cit.] Rather, the inquiry is guided by our decisions beginning with *International Shoe Co.* and the specific factors that we have developed to ascertain whether a jurisdictional rule comports with "traditional notions of fair play and substantial justice." See, e.g., *Asahi Metal Industry Co. v. Superior Court of California*, (noting "several factors," including "the burden on the defendant, the interests of the forum State, and the plaintiff's interest in obtaining relief"). This analysis may not be "mechanical or quantitative," [cit.], but neither is it "freestanding," [cit.], or dependent on personal whim. Our experience with this approach demonstrates that it is well within our competence to employ.

8. As Justice Scalia's opinion acknowledges, American courts in the 19th century erected the theory of transient jurisdiction largely upon Justice Story's historical interpretation of Roman and continental sources. Justice Scalia's opinion conceded that the rule's tradition "was not as clear as Story thought," [cit.] in fact, it now appears that as a historical matter Story was almost surely wrong. * * *

appears that the transient rule did not receive wide currency until well after our decision in *Pennoyer v. Neff.*

Rather, I find the historical background relevant because, however murky the jurisprudential origins of transient jurisdiction, the fact that American courts have announced the rule for perhaps a century (first in dicta, more recently in holdings) provides a defendant voluntarily present in a particular State *today* "clear notice that [he] is subject to suit" in the forum. [cit.] Regardless of whether Justice Story's account of the rule's genesis is mythical, our common understanding *now*, fortified by a century of judicial practice, is that jurisdiction is often a function of geography. The transient rule is consistent with reasonable expectations and is entitled to a strong presumption that it comports with due process. "If I visit another State, ... I knowingly assume some risk that the State will exercise its power over my property or my person while there. My contact with the State, though minimal, gives rise to predictable risks." *Shaffer v. Heitner* (Stevens, J., concurring in judgment); [cit.]. Thus, proposed revisions to the Restatement (Second) of Conflict of Laws § 28, (1986), provide that "[a] state has power to exercise judicial jurisdiction over an individual who is present within its territory unless the individual's relationship to the state is so attenuated as to make the exercise of such jurisdiction unreasonable."[11]

By visiting the forum State, a transient defendant actually "avail[s]" himself, [cit.], of significant benefits provided by the State. His health and safety are guaranteed by the State's police, fire, and emergency medical services; he is free to travel on the State's roads and waterways; he likely enjoys the fruits of the State's economy as well. Moreover, the Privileges and Immunities Clause of Article IV prevents a state government from discriminating against a transient defendant by denying him the protections of its law or the right of access to its courts. [cit.] Subject only to the doctrine of forum non conveniens, an out-of-state plaintiff may use state courts in all circumstances in which those courts would be available to state citizens. Without transient jurisdiction, an asymmetry would arise: A transient would have the full benefit of the power of the forum State's courts as a plaintiff while retaining immunity from their authority as a defendant. [cit.]

The potential burdens on a transient defendant are slight. "'[M]odern transportation and communications have made it much less burdensome for a party sued to defend himself'" in a State outside his place of residence. *Burger King.* That the defendant has already journeyed at least once before to the forum—as evidenced by the fact that he was served with process there—is an indication that suit in the forum likely would not be prohibitively inconvenient. Finally, any burdens that do arise can be ameliorated by a variety of procedural devices.[13] For these reasons, as a rule the

---

11. As the Restatement suggests, there may be cases in which a defendant's involuntary or unknowing presence in a State does not support the exercise of personal jurisdiction over him. The facts of the instant case do not require us to determine the outer limits of the transient jurisdiction rule.

13. For example, in the federal system, a transient defendant can avoid protracted litigation of a spurious suit through a motion to dismiss for failure to state a claim or through a motion for summary judgment. Fed. Rules Civ. Proc. 12(b)(6) and 56. He can use relatively inexpensive methods of discovery, such as oral deposition by telephone (Rule 30(b)(7)), deposition upon written questions (Rule 31), interrogatories (Rule 33), and requests for admission (Rule 36), while enjoying protection from harassment (Rule 26(c)), and possibly obtaining costs and attorney's fees for some of the work involved (Rules 37(a)(4), (b)-(d)).

(continued...)

exercise of personal jurisdiction over a defendant based on his voluntary presence in the forum will satisfy the requirements of due process. [cit.]

In this case, it is undisputed that petitioner was served with process while voluntarily and knowingly in the State of California. I therefore concur in the judgment.

JUSTICE STEVENS, concurring in the judgment. As I explained in my separate writing, I did not join the Court's opinion in *Shaffer v. Heitner*, because I was concerned by its unnecessarily broad reach. [cit.] The same concern prevents me from joining either Justice Scalia's or Justice Brennan's opinion in this case. For me, it is sufficient to note that the historical evidence and consensus identified by Justice Scalia, the considerations of fairness identified by Justice Brennan, and the common sense displayed by Justice White, all combine to demonstrate that this is, indeed, a very easy case.[1] Accordingly, I agree that the judgment should be affirmed.

Notes and Questions

1. Although the Court unanimously upholds jurisdiction, no opinion commands a majority. Which opinion do you find most persuasive?

2. Suppose Mr. Burnham had been extradited to California and served with process there while in police custody. Could California constitutionally assert jurisdiction?

3. In the criminal area, the defendant's presence is considered both necessary and sufficient for jurisdiction, and jurisdiction is valid regardless of how the defendant was brought into the state. See United States v. Alvarez-Machain, 504 U.S. 655 (1992); Frisbie v. Collins, 342 U.S. 519 (1952); Ker v. Illinois, 119 U.S. 436 (1886).

4. Does transient jurisdiction violate the Commerce Clause? Does not the possibility of being subject to general jurisdiction wherever one travels burden and discourage interstate travel? See Bendix Autolite Corp. v. Midwesco Enterprises, Inc., 486 U.S. 888 (1988). Cf. Quill Corp. v. North Dakota, 504 U.S. 298, 312 (1992) (state could assert jurisdiction over an out-of-state mail-order, but taxing that business violated the Commerce Clause; "[d]espite the similarity in phrasing, the nexus requirements of the Due Process and Commerce Clauses are not identical").

5. In *Kulko* the Court was concerned that allowing jurisdiction would discourage a custodial parent from agreeing to a change in custody. Does not the result in *Burnham* discourage non-custodial parents from visiting their children?

6. The underlying law suit in *Burnham* was a divorce action. The traditional rule, left undisturbed by *Shaffer*, is that divorce is an action in rem and does not require in personam jurisdiction. However, in personam jurisdiction is required for the court to issue a property settlement order or to award child support or alimony. Is it

---

(...continued)

Moreover, a change of venue may be possible. 28 U.S.C. § 1404. In state court, many of the same procedural protections are available, as is the doctrine of forum non conveniens, under which the suit may be dismissed. [cit.]

1. Perhaps the adage about hard cases making bad law should be revised to cover easy cases.

sensible to have different jurisdictional rules for the status and property components of divorce? Jurisdiction in family law cases is explored later in this chapter.

7. How does Justice Scalia reconcile the result of *Shaffer* with his historical approach? Professor Weintraub argues that under Scalia's reading of *Shaffer*, "state courts can go back to using quasi in rem jurisdiction so long as they do not purport to affect interests in property that has no reasonable connection with the forum." Weintraub, *Rejecting Transient Jurisdiction*, 622. Do you agree?

8. Compare Justice Scalia's opinion in *Burnham* with his opinion in *Sun Oil Co. v. Wortman*, supra at 480. Do you find his historical approach any more or less appropriate for choice of law than for jurisdiction?

9. Does not transient jurisdiction, like expansive general jurisdiction, increase the plaintiff's choice of law options by increasing her choices of fora? Should the Court have considered this in formulating the jurisdiction rule?

10. Does in-state service on a corporate agent subject the corporation to general jurisdiction? In James-Dickinson Farm Mortgage Co. v. Harry, 273 U.S. 119, 122 (1927), the Supreme Court held: "Jurisdiction over a corporation of one State cannot be acquired in another State or district in which it has no place of business and is not found, merely by serving process upon an executive officer temporarily therein, even if he is there on business of the company." Does it make sense to treat transient corporate agents differently from transient individuals? Under Justice Scalia's approach in *Burnham*, does it matter whether the different treatment makes sense?

11. States require that out-of-state corporations seeking to do business within the state must register to do business and must appoint an in-state agent for service of process. A number of courts have held that the appointment of such an agent operates as "consent" to general jurisdiction. See, e.g., Sondergard v. Miles, Inc., 985 F.2d 1389 (8th Cir.), *cert. denied*, 510 U.S. 814 (1993); Knowlton v. Allied Van Lines, Inc. 900 F.2d 1196 (8th Cir.1990). Indeed, the Supreme Court in *Bendix* seemed to assume that appointment of a registered agent had this effect. See 486 U.S. at 892. Other courts have held to the contrary. For example, in Wenche Siemer v. Learjet Acquisition Corp., 966 F.2d 179, 183 (5th Cir.1992), *cert. denied*, 506 U.S. 1080 (1993), the court explained:

> To assert, as plaintiffs do, that mere service on a corporate agent automatically confers *general jurisdiction* displays a fundamental misconception of corporate jurisdictional principles. This concept is directly contrary to the historical rationale of *International Shoe* and subsequent Supreme Court decisions. See *International Shoe*; *Perkins v. Benguet Consolidated Mining Co.*; [cit.]. In *Perkins*, the Supreme Court upheld general jurisdiction over a Philippine corporation that had been served in Ohio by serving its president while he was conducting the corporation's business in the state, but only after a thorough "minimum contacts" and fairness analysis. [cit.] The Court refused to find jurisdiction based solely upon service on the president, and went on to state that the fact that a corporation's activities caused it to have a registered agent in the forum state was "helpful but not a conclusive test" in the jurisdictional equation. * * * A registered agent, from any conceivable perspective, hardly amounts to "the general business presence" of a corporation so as to sustain an

assertion of general jurisdiction. [cit.]

Not only does the mere act of registering an agent not create Learjet's general business presence in Texas, it also does not act as consent to be hauled into Texas courts on any dispute with any party anywhere concerning any matter. The Texas Business Corporation Act provides that service on a registered foreign corporation may be affected by serving its president, any vice president, or the registered agent of the corporation. [cit.]. No Texas state court decision has held that this provision acts as a consent to jurisdiction over a corporation in a case such as ours--that is where plaintiffs are non-residents and the defendant is not conducting substantial activity within the state. Learjet does not contest the "potential" jurisdiction of Texas courts. They do assert and we agree that the appointment of an agent for process has not been a waiver of its right to due process protection.

Is *Wenche Siemer* consistent with *Burnham*? Does it violate the Commerce Clause for a state to require an out-of-state business to consent to general jurisdiction as a condition of doing business in the state? See Lewis, *An Unconstitutional Condition Perpetuated*; Note, *Registration Statutes, Personal Jurisdiction, and the Problem of Predictability*, 103 Colum. L. Rev. 1163 (200).

12. Jurisdiction based solely on the transient presence of the defendant is rejected by most countries of western Europe. See Brussels II, Annex 1; Hay, *Transient Jurisdiction*, 600. Some commentators have argued that such jurisdiction violates international law. See Restatement (Third) § 421 cmt. e & reporter's notes at 310–11; Weintraub, *Rejecting Transient Jurisdiction*, 615–16.

5. Consent as a Means to Grant or Oust a Court of Jurisdiction

The constitutional limitation on personal jurisdiction is an individual right that can be waived either expressly or impliedly. For example, parties to a contract may expressly consent to jurisdiction in a specified forum. Such clauses are sufficient to confer jurisdiction where neither party was coerced and the parties understood the clause' significance. See D.H. Overmyer Co., Inc. v. Frick Co., 405 U.S. 174 (1972); National Equip. Rental Ltd. v. Szukhent, 375 U.S. 311 (1964).

A defendant may also waive her personal jurisdiction rights by appearing in an action and failing to raise a timely objection to the court's jurisdiction, see Fed. R. Civ. Pro. 12 (h)(1), or by failing to comply with court orders such as discovery orders. For example, in Insurance Corp. of Ireland, Ltd. v. Compagnie des Bauxites de Guinee, 456 U.S. 694 (1982), the defendant appeared and moved to dismiss for lack of personal jurisdiction. The district court allowed discovery on the question of the defendant's contacts with the forum. When the defendant refused to comply with court's discovery orders, the court imposed as a sanction under Rule 37(b) a finding that the jurisdictional facts were established. The Supreme Court upheld the sanction explaining:

> The expression of legal rights is often subject to certain procedural rules: The failure to follow those rules may well result in a curtailment of the rights. Thus, the failure to enter a timely objection to personal jurisdiction constitutes,

under Rule 12(h)(1), a waiver of the objection. A sanction under Rule 37(b)(2)(A) consisting of a finding of personal jurisdiction has precisely the same effect.

Id. at 705.

In addition to consenting to jurisdiction, parties to a transaction sometimes agree to a forum-selection clause in which they designate one forum as the *exclusive* situs for litigation. Older cases refused to honor such agreements on the grounds that it would violate public policy to permit private parties to "oust" the court of jurisdiction. The modern trend is to enforce these forum selection clauses.

The landmark case is The Bremen v. Zapata Off-Shore Co., 407 U.S. 1 (1972). The suit grew out of a contract between Unterweser, a German corporation, and Zapata, a Texas-based American corporation, to tow Zapata's drilling rig from Louisiana to Italy. The contract provided that "[a]ny dispute arising must be treated before the London Court of Justice." Id. at 2. In the course of the towage, the drill rig was damaged, and Zapata then sued Unterweser in federal court in Florida. The district court refused to dismiss the action, but the Supreme Court reversed, holding that forum-selection clauses "are prima facie valid and should be enforced unless enforcement is shown by the resisting party to be 'unreasonable' under the circumstances." Id. at 10. The Court rejected the "ouster" argument, calling it a vestigal legal fiction." Id. at 12. The Court found that "[t]here are compelling reasons why a freely negotiated private international agreement, unaffected by fraud, undue influence, or overweening bargaining power, such as that involved here, should be given full effect," and stressed that the "elimination of * * * uncertainties by agreeing in advance on a forum acceptable to both parties is an indispensable element in international trade, commerce, and contracting." Id at 12-13. The Court concluded that "in the light of present-day commercial realities and expanding international trade we conclude that the forum clause should control absent a strong showing that it should be set aside." Id. at 15. See infra at 686-87.

Zapata involved a fully negotiated contract between international corporations, but forum-selection clauses have been enforced in other contexts as well. In Carnival Cruise Lines, Inc., v. Shute, 499 U.S. 585 (1991), the plaintiff was injured on a cruise ship off the west coast of Mexico. She sued the Florida-based cruise line, filing in federal court in her home state of Washington where she had purchased the ticket. The district court dismissed for lack of personal jurisdiction. The Supreme Court affirmed the dismissal, but on the basis of the forum-selection clause printed on the back of the cruise ticket. That clause stated that "all disputes and matters whatsoever arising under, in connection with or incident to this Contract shall be litigated, if at all, in and before a Court located in the State of Florida, U.S.A., to the exclusion of the Courts of any other state or country." Id. at 587-88.

In upholding the provision, the Court noted that such provisions serve useful functions:

First, a cruise line has a special interest in limiting the fora in which it potentially could be subject to suit. Because a cruise ship typically carries passengers from many locales, it is not unlikely that a mishap on a cruise could subject the cruise line to litigation in several different fora. [cit.] Additionally, a clause establishing ex ante the forum for dispute resolution has the salutary effect of dispelling any confusion about where suits arising from the contract must be brought and defended, sparing litigants the time and expense of pretrial motions to determine the correct forum and conserving judicial resources that otherwise would be devoted to deciding those motions. [cit.] Finally, it stands to reason that passengers who purchase tickets containing a forum clause like that at issue in this case benefit in the form of reduced fares reflecting the savings that the cruise line enjoys by limiting the fora in which it may be sued.

Id. at 593-94. The Court did not hold that such clauses are automatically enforceable. "It bears emphasis that forum-selection clauses contained in form passage contracts are subject to judicial scrutiny for fundamental fairness." Id. at 595. But the Court concluded that this provision was not unfair:

Any suggestion of such a bad-faith motive is belied by two facts: Petitioner has its principal place of business in Florida, and many of its cruises depart from and return to Florida ports. Similarly, there is no evidence that petitioner obtained respondents' accession to the forum clause by fraud or overreaching. Finally, respondents have conceded that they were given notice of the forum provision and, therefore, presumably retained the option of rejecting the contract with impunity.

Id. at 595.

Zapata and *Shute* were both admiralty cases, but several states have explicitly relied on *Zapata* as the basis for enforcing forum-selection clauses in other contexts. See Societe Jean Nicolas et Fils v. Mousseux, 597 P.2d 541 (Ariz.1979); Smith, Valentino & Smith, Inc. v. Superior Court, 551 P.2d 1206 (Cal.1976)(en banc). The Restatement (Second) § 80 expressly favors enforcement of such clauses. What law governs the validity of a forum-selection clause? The most common approach is to apply the law of the forum, but where a forum-selection clause is combined with a choice of law clause (as it frequently is), the forum could apply the designated law to determine the validity of the forum-selection clause. See Borchers, *Forum Selection*, 81. Which approach is the most sensible? What if under the designated law the forum-selection clause is invalid?

6. Jurisdiction in Family Law Cases

Divorce and the attendant issues of property division, alimony and child custody raise some unique jurisdictional issues. Traditionally, divorce was treated as an in rem proceeding in which the court had to have jurisdiction over "the marriage," but not in personam jurisdiction over the spouses. The marriage was thought to be "located" in the state of the matrimonial domicile and, hence, that was the state with jurisdiction to grant a divorce. See Haddock v. Haddock, 201 U.S. 562, 576-77 (1906). More recently, the Court has held that any state that is the domicile of *either* spouse has jurisdiction to grant a divorce. See Williams v. North Carolina, 317 U.S. 287 (1942). It is not necessary that both spouses be domiciled in the state—indeed, so long as one spouse is domiciled in the forum, that court can validly grant a divorce even if the other spouse has no connection or contacts with that forum.

While it is clear that domicile is a sufficient basis for divorce jurisdiction, it is less clear whether domicile is always necessary.[1] The Uniform Marriage and Divorce Act, 9A U.L.A. § 302 (a)(1), permits divorce jurisdiction for armed services personnel who have resided in the state for 90 days. Similarly, the Restatement (Second) grants a non-domicile state divorce jurisdiction "if either spouse has such a relationship to the state as would make it reasonable for the state to dissolve the marriage." Restatement (Second) § 72. See Garfield, *The Transitory Divorce Action*, 501.

Jurisdiction to grant a divorce does not carry with it jurisdiction to award alimony or other property settlements. The Court has held that these property and monetary offshoots of divorce require in personam jurisdiction as set forth in *International Shoe* and its progeny. See Kulko v. Superior Court, 436 U.S. 84 (1978); Estin v. Estin, 334 U.S. 541 (1948).

With respect to child custody, the jurisdictional prerequisites are less clear. One Supreme Court case, May v. Anderson, 345 U.S. 528 (1953), appears to require in personam jurisdiction over the absent parent. In that case, the father secured an ex parte divorce in his domicile of Wisconsin. The Wisconsin divorce court also awarded the father custody. He then sought enforcement of the custody decree in Ohio, where the mother and children lived, and the Ohio state court enforced the Wisconsin decree. The Supreme Court, writing without a majority opinion, reversed. Some have interpreted *May* narrowly as holding only that the Full Faith and Credit Clause did not require enforcement of the decree, rather than that the Due Process Clause prohibited enforcement. See, e.g., In re Marriage of Hudson, 434 N.E.2d 107, 118 (Ind.App.1982), *cert. denied*, 459 U.S. 1202 (1983). Relying on footnote 30 in *Shaffer*, some commentators have concluded that custody concerns a matter of "status" and hence in personam jurisdiction is not required. See Bodenheimer & Neeley-Kvarme, *Jurisdiction Over Child Custody*, 229.

All states have now adopted the Uniform Child Custody Jurisdiction Act or the new Uniform Child Custody Jurisdiction Enforcement Act, which base custody jurisdiction on the home state of the child rather than on personal jurisdiction over the parents. See also Parental Kidnapping Prevention Act, 28 U.S.C. § 1738A. Courts and commentators have split on whether, for custody determinations, the Due Process Clause requires in personam jurisdiction over the parents, although the majority view appears to be that it is not required. Compare Goldfarb v. Goldfarb, 268 S.E.2d 648 (Ga.1980); Pratt v. Pratt, 431 A.2d 405 (R.I.1981); McAtee v. McAtee, 323 S.E.2d 611, 616–17 (W.Va.1984); Restatement (Second) § 79 (in personam jurisdiction not required), with Ex parte Dean, 447 So.2d 733 (Ala.1984); Coombs, *Interstate Child Custody*, 735–62; Sherman, *Child Custody Jurisdiction*,

---

1. One interesting Third Circuit case held that it was a violation of due process for the Virgin Islands to grant a divorce where neither spouse was domiciled in the Virgin Islands even where both spouses consented to the court's jurisdiction. Alton v. Alton, 207 F.2d 667 (3d Cir.1953), vacated as moot, 347 U.S. 610 (1954). The court stressed that "adherence to the domiciliary requirement is necessary if our states are really to have control over the domestic relations of their citizens." Id. at 676. Is the purpose of the due process clause to allocate authority among states, see *World-Wide Volkswagen*, or to protect individual's rights? See Insurance Corp. of Ireland v. Compagnie des Bauxites de Guinee, 456 U.S. 694, 702–03 n.10 (1982) If it is the latter, whose rights would be harmed if the Virgin Islands granted the divorce?

713.

Child custody proceedings involving Indian children raise some unique jurisdictional problems. The Indian Child Welfare Act, 25 U.S.C. §§ 1901–1963, grants to Indian tribes exclusive jurisdiction over certain child custody proceedings involving Indian children who resides within the reservation of the tribe. However, the Act explicitly excludes custody determination in connection with a divorce proceeding. See Atwood, *Fighting over Indian Children: The Uses and Abuses of Jurisdictional Ambiguity*, 1051. Conflicts problems involving Indian tribes are explored further in Chapter 13.

D. PERSONAL JURISDICTION AND THE INTERNET

Cybersell, Inc. v. Cybersell, Inc.
United States Court of Appeals for the Ninth Circuit, 1997
130 F.3d 414

We are asked to hold that the allegedly infringing use of a service mark in a home page on the World Wide Web suffices for personal jurisdiction in the state where the holder of the mark has its principal place of business. Cybersell, Inc., an Arizona corporation that advertises for commercial services over the Internet, claims that Cybersell, Inc., a Florida corporation that offers web page construction services over the Internet, infringed its federally registered mark and should be amenable to suit in Arizona because cyberspace is without borders and a web site which advertises a product or service is necessarily intended for use on a world wide basis. The district court disagreed, and so do we. Instead, applying our normal "minimum contacts" analysis, we conclude that it would not comport with "traditional notions of fair play and substantial justice," [cit.], for Arizona to exercise personal jurisdiction over an allegedly infringing Florida web site advertiser who has no contacts with Arizona other than maintaining a home page that is accessible to Arizonans, and everyone else, over the Internet. We therefore affirm.

I. Cybersell, Inc. is an Arizona corporation, which we will refer to as Cybersell AZ. It was incorporated in May 1994 to provide Internet and web advertising and marketing services, including consulting. The principals of Cybersell AZ are Laurence Canter and Martha Siegel, known among web users for first "spamming" the Internet. Mainstream print media carried the story of Canter and Siegel and their various efforts to commercialize the web.

On August 8, 1994, Cybersell AZ filed an application to register the name "Cybersell" as a service mark. The application was approved and the grant was published on October 30, 1995. Cybersell AZ operated a web site using the mark from August 1994 through February 1995. The site was then taken down for reconstruction.

Meanwhile, in the summer of 1995, Matt Certo and his father, Dr. Samuel C. Certo, both Florida residents, formed Cybersell, Inc., a Florida corporation (Cybersell FL), with its principal place of business in Orlando. Matt was a business school student at Rollins College, where his father was a professor; Matt was particularly interested in the Internet, and their company was to provide business consulting services for strategic management and marketing on the web. At the time the Certos chose the name "Cybersell" for their venture, Cybersell AZ had no home page on the web nor had the PTO granted their application for the service mark

As part of their marketing effort, the Certos created a web page at http://www.cybsell.com/cybsell/index.htm. The home page has a logo at the top with "CyberSell" over a depiction of the planet earth, with the caption underneath "Professional Services for the World Wide Web" and a local (area code 407) phone number. It proclaims in large letters "Welcome to CyberSell!" A hypertext link allows the browser to introduce himself, and invites a company not on the web – but interested in getting on the web – to "Email us to find out how!"

Canter found the Cybersell FL web page and sent an e-mail on November 27, 1995 notifying Dr. Certo that "Cybersell" is a service mark of Cybersell AZ. Trying to disassociate themselves from the Canters, the Certos changed the name of Cybersell FL to WebHorizons, Inc. on December 27 (later it was changed again to WebSolvers, Inc.) and by January 4, 1996, they had replaced the CyberSell logo at the top of their web page with WebHorizons, Inc. The WebHorizons page still said "Welcome to CyberSell!"

Cybersell AZ filed the complaint in this action January 9, 1996 in the District of Arizona, alleging trademark infringement, unfair competition, fraud, and RICO violations. On the same day Cybersell FL filed suit for declaratory relief with regard to use of the name "Cybersell" in the United States District Court for the Middle District of Florida, but that action was transferred to the District of Arizona and consolidated with the Cybersell AZ action. Cybersell FL moved to dismiss for lack of personal jurisdiction. The district court denied Cybersell AZ's request for a preliminary injunction, then granted Cybersell FL's motion to dismiss for lack of personal jurisdiction. Cybersell AZ timely appealed.

II. [The court found that the requirements of the Arizona long arm statute were met.] * * * A court may assert either specific or general jurisdiction over a defendant. [cit.] Cybersell AZ concedes that general jurisdiction over Cybersell FL doesn't exist in Arizona, so the only issue in this case is whether specific jurisdiction is available. * * *

A. Since the jurisdictional facts are not in dispute, we turn to the first requirement, which is the most critical. As the Supreme Court emphasized in *Hanson v. Denckla*, "it is essential in each case that there be some act by which the defendant purposefully avails itself of the privilege of conducting activities within the forum State, thus invoking the benefits and protections of its laws." [cit.] * * *

We have not yet considered when personal jurisdiction may be exercised in the context of cyberspace, but the Second and Sixth Circuits have had occasion to decide whether personal jurisdiction was properly exercised over defendants involved in transmissions over the Internet, see CompuServe, Inc. v. Patterson, 89 F.3d 1257 (6th Cir. 1996); Bensusan Restaurant Corp. v. King, 937 F. Supp. 295 (S.D.N.Y. 1996), aff'd, 126 F.3d 25 (2d Cir. 1997), as have a number of district courts. Because this is a matter of first impression for us, we have looked to all of these cases for guidance. Not surprisingly, they reflect a broad spectrum of Internet use on the one hand, and contacts with the forum on the other. As *CompuServe* and *Bensusan* seem to represent opposite ends of the spectrum, we start with them.

CompuServe is a computer information service headquartered in Columbus, Ohio, that contracts with individual subscribers to provide access to computing and information services via the Internet. It also operates as an electronic conduit to provide computer software products to its subscribers. Computer software generated and distributed in this way is often referred to as "shareware." Patterson is a Texas resident who subscribed to CompuServe and placed items of "shareware" on the CompuServe system pursuant to a "Shareware Registration Agreement" with CompuServe which provided, among other things, that it was "to be governed by and construed in accordance with" Ohio law. During the course of this relationship, Patterson electronically transmitted thirty-two master software files to CompuServe, which CompuServe stored and displayed to its subscribers. Sales were made in Ohio and elsewhere, and funds were transmitted through CompuServe in Ohio to Patterson in Texas. In effect, Patterson used CompuServe as a distribution center to market his software. When Patterson threatened litigation over allegedly infringing CompuServe software, CompuServe filed suit in Ohio seeking a declaratory judgment of noninfringement. The court found that Patterson's relationship with CompuServe as a software provider and marketer was a crucial indicator that Patterson had knowingly reached out to CompuServe's Ohio home and benefitted from CompuServe's handling of his software and fees. Because Patterson had chosen to transmit his product from Texas to CompuServe's system in Ohio, and that system provided access to his software to others to whom he advertised and sold his product, the court concluded that Patterson purposefully availed himself of the privilege of doing business in Ohio.

By contrast, the defendant in *Bensusan* owned a small jazz club known as "The Blue Note" in Columbia, Missouri. He created a general access web page that contained information about the club in Missouri as well as a calendar of events and ticketing information. Tickets were not available through the web site, however. To order tickets, web browsers had to use the names and addresses of ticket outlets in Columbia or a telephone number for charge-by-phone ticket orders, which were available for pick-up on the night of the show at the Blue Note box office in Columbia. Bensusan was a New York corporation that owned "The Blue Note," a popular jazz club in the heart of Greenwich Village. Bensusan owned the rights to the "The Blue Note" mark. Bensusan sued King for trademark infringement in New York. The district court distinguished King' passive web page, which just posted information, from the defendant's use of the Internet in *CompuServe* by observing that whereas the Texas Internet user specifically targeted Ohio by subscribing to the service, entering into an agreement to sell his software over the Internet, advertising through the service, and sending his software to the service in Ohio,

> King has done nothing to purposefully avail himself of the benefits of New York. King, like numerous others, simply created a Web site and permitted anyone who could find it to access it. Creating a site, like placing a product into the stream of commerce, may be felt nationwide-or even worldwide-but, without more, it is not an act purposefully directed toward the forum state.

Bensusan, 937 F. Supp. at 301 (citing the plurality opinion in Asahi Metal Indus. Co. v. Superior Court, 480 U.S. 102, 112 (1992)). Given these facts, the court reasoned that the argument that the defendant "should have foreseen that users could access the site in New York and be confused as to the relationship of the two Blue Note clubs is insufficient to satisfy due process." 937 F. Supp. at 301.

"Interactive" web sites present somewhat different issues. Unlike passive sites such as the defendant's in *Bensusan,* users can exchange information with the host computer when the site is interactive. Courts that have addressed interactive sites have looked to the "level of interactivity and commercial nature of the exchange of information that occurs on the Web site" to determine if sufficient contacts exist to warrant the exercise of jurisdiction. See, e.g., Zippo Mfg. Co. v. Zippo Dot Com, Inc., 952 F. Supp. 1119, 1124 (W.D. Pa. 1997) (finding purposeful availment based on Dot Com's interactive web site and contracts with 3000 individuals and seven Internet access providers in Pennsylvania allowing them to download the electronic messages that form the basis of the suit); Maritz, Inc. v. Cybergold, Inc., 947 F. Supp. 1328, 1332-33 (E.D. Mo.) (browsers were encouraged to add their address to a mailing list that basically subscribed the user to the service), reconsideration denied, 947 F. Supp. 1338 (1996).

Cybersell AZ points to several district court decisions which it contends have held that the mere advertisement or solicitation for sale of goods and services on the Internet gives rise to specific jurisdiction in the plaintiff's forum. However, so far as we are aware, no court has ever held that an Internet advertisement alone is sufficient to subject the advertiser to jurisdiction in the plaintiff's home state. [cit.] Rather, in each, there has been "something more" to indicate that the defendant purposefully (albeit electronically) directed his activity in a substantial way to the forum state.

Inset Systems, Inc. v. Instruction Set, Inc., 937 F. Supp. 161 (D. Conn. 1996), is the case most favorable to Cybersell AZ's position. Inset developed and marketed computer software throughout the world; Instruction Set, Inc. (ISI) provided computer technology and support. Inset owned the federal trademark "INSET"; but ISI obtained "INSET.COM" as its Internet domain address for advertising its goods and services. ISI also used the telephone number "800-US-INSET." Inset learned of ISI's domain address when it tried to get the same address, and filed suit for trademark infringement in Connecticut. The court reasoned that ISI had purposefully availed itself of doing business in Connecticut because it directed its advertising activities via the Internet and its toll-free number toward the state of Connecticut (and all states); Internet sites and toll-free numbers are designed to communicate with people and their businesses in every state; an Internet advertisement could reach as many as 10,000 Internet users within Connecticut alone; and once posted on the Internet, an advertisement is continuously available to any Internet user.

Cybersell AZ further points to the court's statement in EDIAS Software International, L.L.C. v. BASIS International Ltd., 947 F. Supp. 413 (D. Ariz. 1996), that a defendant "should not be permitted to take advantage of modern technology through an Internet Web page and forum and simultaneously escape traditional notions of jurisdiction." Id. at 420. In that case, EDIAS (an Arizona company) alleged that BASIS (a New Mexico company) sent advertising and defamatory statements over the Internet through e-mail, its web page, and forums. However, the court did not rest its minimum contacts analysis on use of the Internet alone; in addition to the Internet, BASIS had a contract with EDIAS, it made sales to EDIAS and other Arizona customers, and its employees had visited Arizona during the course of the business relationship with EDIAS.

Some courts have also given weight to the number of "hits" received by a web page from residents in the forum state, and to other evidence that Internet activity was directed at, or bore fruit in, the forum state. [cit.] In sum, the common thread, well stated by the district court in *Zippo,* is that "the likelihood that personal jurisdiction can be constitutionally exercised is directly proportionate to the nature and quality of commercial activity that an entity conducts over the Internet." *Zippo,* 952 F. Supp. at 1124.

B. Here, Cybersell FL has conducted no commercial activity over the Internet in Arizona. All that it did was post an essentially passive home page on the web, using the name "CyberSell," which Cybersell AZ was in the process of registering as a federal service mark. While there is no question that anyone, anywhere could access that home page and thereby learn about the services offered, we cannot see how from that fact alone it can be inferred that Cybersell FL deliberately directed its merchandising efforts toward Arizona residents.

Cybersell FL did nothing to encourage people in Arizona to access its site, and there is no evidence that any part of its business (let alone a continuous part of its business) was sought or achieved in Arizona. To the contrary, it appears to be an operation where business was primarily generated by the personal contacts of one of its founders. While those contacts are not entirely local, they aren't in Arizona either. No Arizonan except for Cybersell AZ "hit" Cybersell FL's web site. There is no evidence that any Arizona resident signed up for Cybersell FL's web construction services. It entered into no contracts in Arizona, made no sales in Arizona, received no telephone calls from Arizona, earned no income from Arizona, and sent no messages over the Internet to Arizona. The only message it received over the Internet from Arizona was from Cybersell AZ. Cybersell FL did not have an "800" number, let alone a toll-free number that also used the "Cybersell" name. The interactivity of its web page is limited to receiving the browser's name and address and an indication of interest -- signing up for the service is not an option, nor did anyone from Arizona do so. No money changed hands on the Internet from (or through) Arizona. In short, Cybersell FL has done no act and has consummated no transaction, nor has it performed any act by which it purposefully availed itself of the privilege of conducting activities, in Arizona, thereby invoking the benefits and protections of Arizona law.

We therefore hold that Cybersell FL's contacts are insufficient to establish "purposeful availment." Cybersell AZ has thus failed to satisfy the first prong of our three-part test for specific jurisdiction. We decline to go further solely on the footing that Cybersell AZ has alleged trademark infringement over the Internet by Cybersell FL's use of the registered name "Cybersell" on an essentially passive web page advertisement. Otherwise, every complaint arising out of alleged trademark infringement on the Internet would automatically result in personal jurisdiction wherever the plaintiff's principal place of business is located. That would not comport with traditional notions of what qualifies as purposeful activity invoking the benefits and protections of the forum state. See Peterson v. Kennedy, 771 F.2d 1244, 1262 (9th Cir. 1985) (series of phone calls and letters to California physician regarding plaintiff's injuries insufficient to satisfy first prong of test).

III. Cybersell AZ also invokes the "effects" test employed in Calder v. Jones, 465 U.S. 783 (1984), and Core-Vent Corp. v. Nobel Industries, 11 F.3d 1482 (9th Cir. 1993), with respect to intentional torts directed to the plaintiff, causing injury where the plaintiff lives. However, we don't see this as a *Calder* case. Because Shirley Jones was who she was (a famous entertainer who lived and worked in California) and was libeled by a story in the National Enquirer, which was published in Florida but had a nationwide circulation with a large audience in California, the Court could easily hold that California was the "focal point both of the story and of the harm suffered" and so jurisdiction in California based on the "effects" of the defendants' Florida conduct was proper. *Calder,* 465 U.S. at 789. There is nothing comparable about Cybersell FL's web page. Nor does the "effects" test apply with the same force to Cybersell AZ as it would to an individual, because a corporation "does not suffer harm in a particular geographic location in the same sense that an individual does." *Core-Vent,* 11 F.3d at 1486. Cybersell FL's web page simply was not aimed intentionally at Arizona knowing that harm was likely to be caused there to Cybersell AZ.

IV. We conclude that the essentially passive nature of Cybersell FL's activity in posting a home page on the World Wide Web that allegedly used the service mark of Cybersell AZ does not qualify as purposeful activity invoking the benefits and protections of Arizona. As it engaged in no commercial activity and had no other contacts via the Internet or otherwise in Arizona, Cybersell FL lacks sufficient minimum contacts with Arizona for personal jurisdiction to be asserted over it there. Accordingly, its motion to dismiss for lack of personal jurisdiction was properly granted.

Affirmed.

Notes and Questions

1. In *Cybersell*, the court adopts a test, first articulated in the *Zippo* case, which considers whether a web site is active, passive or somewhere in between. The court concludes that the website in question falls into the middle category. What factors should the court consider in evaluating these situations? The number of "hits" from or transactions with forum residents? See People Solutions, Inc. v. People Solutions, Inc., 2000 U.S. Dist. LEXIS 10444 (N.D. Tex. 2000); Maritz Inc. v. Cybergold Inc., 947 F. Supp. 1328 (E.D. Mo.. 1996). The amount of information that the web site provides? See Stomp, Inc. v. NeatO, LLC, 61 F. Supp. 2d 1074 (C.D. Cal. 1999); Rainy Day Books, Inc. v. Rainy Day Books & Cafe, L.L.C., 186 F. Supp. 2d 1158 (D. Ka. 2002). The *Zippo* test has been endorsed by a number of courts. See, e.g., ALS Scan, Inc. v. Digital Serv. Consultants, Inc., 293 F.3d 707, 714-715 (4th Cir. 2002); Mink v. AAAA Development LLC, 190 F.3d 333, 336 (5th Cir. 1999).

Increasingly, however, the test has been criticized as it has become more apparent that most sites fall in the middle category. Moreover, some commentators have argued that for both economic and technological reasons the distinction between passive and active sites may be becoming less meaningful. See Geist, *Toward Greater Certainty*, at 1379-80.

2. The Seventh Circuit has stated that "there can be no serious doubt after *Calder* that the state in which the victim of a tort suffers the injury may entertain a suit against the accused tortfeasor." Janmark Inc. v. Reidy, 132 F.3d 1200, 1202 (7th Cir. 1997). A number of other courts and commentators do indeed have doubts that the place of the injury always has jurisdiction. See,.e.g, Young v. New Haven Advocate, 315 F.3d 256, 262-263 (4th Cir. 2002), *cert. denied*, 123 S.Ct. 2092 (2003); Pavlovich v. Superior Court, 58 P.3d 2, 8-9 (Cal. 2002); Redish, *New Wine and Old Bottles*, at 596-600. Nonetheless, if the Seventh Circuit approach were applied in the internet context would that mean that someone who posts material on the web is potentially subject to jurisdiction everywhere the material can be accessed? Should this be the rule? Although this would expand jurisdiction, would not that expansion be consistent with the breadth of harm that can potentially be inflicted? See id. at 606 ("An individual or entity may so easily and quickly reach the entire world with its messages that it is simply not helpful to inquire whether, in taking such action, that individual or entity has consciously and carefully made the decision either to affiliate with the forum state or seek to acquire its benefits.").

3. In *Cybersell* the court stressed that no one in Arizona had accessed the Florida site. What if people in other states had accessed the site and as a result, the Arizona company had lost money. Given that the Florida company knew of the existence of the Arizona company could not it have predicted the harm in Arizona? Should that be enough for jurisdiction? Compare the following cases:

Bancroft & Masters, Inc.v. Augusta Nat'l, Inc., 223 F.3d 1082 (9th Cir. 2000). Augusta National, Inc. (AGI) holds a registered trademark for the mark "Masters" and operates a website under the domain name "masters.org." Bancroft & Masters (B&M) is a California computer company that in 1997 registered the domain name "masters.com." In 1997, ANI sent a letter to NSI, the United States registrar of domain names, located in Virginia. Under NSI procedures, once the complaint letter was received, B&M had to either stop using the domain name or obtain a declaratory judgment establishing its rights to the name. B&M brought a declaratory judgment action against ANI in California. The court upheld jurisdiction over ANI explaining: "ANI acted intentionally when it sent its letter to NSI. The letter was expressly aimed at California because it individually targeted B&M, a California corporation doing business almost exclusively in California. Finally, the effects of the letter were primarily felt, as ANI knew they would be, in California." Id. at 1088.

Young v. New Haven Advocate, 315 F.3d 256 (4th Cir. 2002), *cert. denied*, 123 S.Ct. 2092 (2003). Faced with overcrowding in its prisons, Connecticut began to house some of its prisoners in Virginia's correctional facilities. After a New Haven newspaper did a series of articles on the allegedly harsh conditions at the Virginia prison, the Virginia warden of the prison brought a defamation action in Virginia against the newspaper. The articles in question were posted on the newspaper's web site and thus were available in Virginia. The court of appeals held that although the stories in question were about a Virginia warden of a Virginia prison, the web site was "decidedly local." It therefore held that here was no jurisdiction over the newspaper in Virginia.

4. Other countries have allowed jurisdiction on the basis of where the effects were felt rather than requiring purposefulness or targeting by the defendant. In one case, a French court ordered U.S based Yahoo! to install filters to prevent French residents from accessing sites on Yahoo that offered Nazi memorabilia for sale. See County Court of Paris, Interim Court Order, League Against Racism & Antisemitism – LICRA v. Yahoo! Inc., No. RG 00/05308 (Nov. 20, 2000). Australia has likewise upheld jurisdiction in its courts based solely on an injury to reputation suffered by an Australian plaintiff in Australia from material posted in the U.S. on a web site by a U.S. company. See Dow Jones & Co., Inc. v. Gutnick, [2002] HCA 56 (10 December 2002) (High Court of Australia).

5. There has been an outpouring of articles on jurisdiction and the Internet. A few of these sources are: American Bar Association, *Global Cyberspace Jurisdiction*; Geist, *Toward Greater Certainty*; Perrit, *Jurisdiction in Cyberspace*; Redish, *New Wine and Old Bottles*; Stein, *Jurisdiction in Cyberspace*.

E. THE RELATIONSHIP BETWEEN LIMITS ON JUDICIAL AND LEGISLATIVE JURISDICTION—A RECAP

The constitutional restrictions on choice of law limit a state's law-making power while personal jurisdiction restrictions limit judicial jurisdiction. The tests applied to limit legislative and judicial jurisdiction are different and sometimes yield different conclusions. In *Shutts*, for example, Kansas had judicial jurisdiction but was not permitted to apply its law. In contrast, in *Cooney*, the New York Court of Appeals applied Missouri law to a party over whom Missouri could not have asserted jurisdiction. Does it make sense to differentiate between these two, to apply different tests and to hold that a state's law-making power and judicial power are not coextensive?

Some have argued that it is not sensible to differentiate between legislative and adjudicative jurisdiction because once a court has jurisdiction, it in fact applies local law:

> To think and speak about a court in one jurisdiction choosing to "apply" the rules of law of another jurisdiction seriously mis-characterizes the judicial decision-making process. Once it is conceded that a forum has judicial jurisdiction, that forum unavoidably controls or determines the results in that case between the parties before it. Even if the forum court decides to "apply" a foreign state's rules of law, the forum does not apply that law as an agent of the foreign state or as a surrogate for the foreign state's courts. Rather, it makes its own "law" when it decides the case, using only for guidance the local law policies that the foreign state's courts would apply if the case were being decided as a wholly domestic case in the foreign state.

Maier & McCoy, *A Unifying Theory*, 252. See Cox, *There Is No Law But Forum*

Law, 1. Do you agree that a forum purporting to apply some other state's law is in fact applying forum law? If you do agree, what are the implications of this for judicial jurisdiction? Should we retain the current test for judicial jurisdiction and dispense with the remaining modest constitutional limits on choice of law or vice versa? In the alternative, should we combine the tests and hold that judicial jurisdiction exists only where both minimum contacts and the test for choice of law are met? Or should we start over and attempt to reformulate one test that encompasses both judicial jurisdiction and choice of law?

Others have argued that it is appropriate to retain separate tests for judicial jurisdiction and choice of law because the two tests are addressed to different relationships.

> The jurisdictional inquiry addresses the permissibility of requiring the defendant to litigate in the forum. The focus is on the defendant's "individual liberty interests." * * *

> Choice of law also involves the defendant's "liberty interest:" whether to be free from, or subject to liability. But it also involves competing state interests in determining the applicable law, the forum law or another. This is a federalism concern of a kind that jurisdiction is not. It derives not so much from the Due Process Clause as it does from the Full Faith and Credit Clause * * *.

Hay, *Jurisdiction and Choice of Law*, 34. Do you agree that different concerns underlie the limitations on judicial and legislative jurisdiction?

At a pragmatic level, choice of law and judicial jurisdiction are surely interrelated. One reason a plaintiff may choose a particular forum is because of its choice of law rules. By limiting jurisdiction, we limit the plaintiff's choices among fora and hence limit to some extent choice of law.

While some complain that it is illogical for the judicial jurisdiction test to be more demanding than the choice of law test, one can argue that it is *because* of the limits on judicial jurisdiction that more significant choice of law restrictions are unnecessary. If jurisdiction is doing the heavy lifting for choice of law, should this role for jurisdiction be explicitly acknowledged and taken into account in structuring an appropriate test for jurisdiction? See Perdue, *Personal Jurisdiction and the Beetle in the Box*, 570–73.

Regardless of the scope of constitutional authority, there may be pragmatic reasons for continuing to separate the questions of jurisdiction and choice of law. As Professor von Mehren has argued:

> Linking adjudicatory authority and choice of law in either way is highly problematic in the contemporary world. Making jurisdiction turn on the applicability of forum law--the applicability of forum law on the claim of jurisdiction--merges choice of law and adjudicatory authority, with potentially great costs to both. In particular, automatic application of the forum's internal-law rules in controversies where general jurisdiction is taken on the basis of the defendant's domicile or habitual residence or upon service upon him within the jurisdiction, would produce randomly unacceptable results. * * *

> Making authority to adjudicate in the international sense turn on the applicability to the underlying controversy of domestic rules and principles

would also present severe administrative problems. Especially in systems that approach choice of law through rule--rather than jurisdiction--selecting methods, the applicability *vel non* of the forum's domestic law often would not be established until the controversy had been fully presented to the court. Were the local law then held inapplicable, time and effort spent would have been wasted. Arbitrary choice-of-law solutions would be encouraged for, once litigation had progressed to this point, the temptation would be great to apply local law and dispose of the controversy on the merits. * * *

[On the other hand, it is not the case] that the legal system never links the assertion of adjudicatory authority with the application of the forum's domestic law. Whether--and to what extent--such linkage occurs varies with the subject matter and the legal order in question. Two areas in which linkage occurs with some frequency are divorce and compensation of workers for injuries suffered in the course of employment. In other areas of law, a court may exceptionally encounter a situation where the choice-of-law process cannot function effectively; in such cases it may likewise be appropriate to relax the separateness principle.

von Mehren, *Adjudicatory Authority*, 36-39.

Chapter 9

JURISDICTION
IN INTERNATIONAL CASES

A. INTRODUCTION

Many issues and difficulties presented by entirely domestic litigation, on the one hand, and transnational litigation, on the other, are similar. In various respects, however, the latter encounter difficulties and issues that are not faced by the former. An important basic difference between the two types of litigation is that local lawyers are typically less at ease where foreign rules and practices regulate, at least in part, such matters as service of process, pretrial preparation (discovery, for example), issues of privilege, prescription, choice-of-law rules, and applicable substantive-law rules and principles. In transnational litigation barriers--rooted in culture, history, language, and sociology--to full understanding of the controversy that has arisen are more frequent and more difficult to overcome than in domestic litigation. Moreover, at the end of the day, the concerned legal orders may differ as to what constitutes substantive justice.

In this section we discuss various consequences for issues of adjudicatory authority that flow from the transnational character of litigation. Theory and practice in these matters are today far more complex and sophisticated than was true only half a century ago. Due in large measure to the increasing globalization of economic activity, the emergence of new technology, in particular the Internet, and the evolution of the Europe of the Coal and Steel Community into the European Union, that in 2003 had twenty-five Member States, today adjudicatory authority in the international sense has, in many contexts, far greater economic, political, and sociological importance than was the case even only twenty-five years ago. Indeed, it has been increasingly difficult for a State, acting alone, as well as for States acting in concert through international agreements, to deal with these problems.

The chapter first discusses service of process and notice requirements and then forum-selection agreements. It next considers the scope of adjudicatory authority in transnational litigation, looking first at litigation in U.S. courts and then turns to approaches in other countries. Finally, it considers the role of international conventions.

B. NOTICE REQUIREMENTS (SERVICE OF PROCESS) AND FORUM SELECTION CLAUSES FOR TRANSNATIONAL CONTROVERSIES

1. Notice Requirements; Service of Process

In order to obtain an adjudication on the merits of one's claim against another person, two requirements must be satisfied: The legal order's adjudicatory authority must be established and reasonable, and appropriate efforts undertaken to apprise absent parties of the proceedings. These requirements are satisfied by a single event where the legal order's claim of adjudicatory authority rests on service of process within its territory on the defendant. At one full swoop, service establishes the forum's adjudicatory authority and apprises the defendant of the proceedings.

When the claim of adjudicatory authority rests on a basis other than service of process, adjudicatory authority and giving notice become separable requirements. The Supreme Court of the United States in Milliken v. Meyer, 311 U.S. 457, 462-64 (1940), made clear that:

> Domicile in the state is alone sufficient to bring an absent defendant within the reach of the state's jurisdiction * * *. As in case of the authority of the United States over its absent citizens [cit.], the authority of a state over one of its citizens is not terminated by the mere fact of his absence from the state. The state which accords him privileges and affords protection to him and his property by virtue of his domicile may also exact reciprocal duties. * * * *One such incident of domicile is amenability to suit within the state even during sojourns without the state, where the state has provided and employed a reasonable method for apprising such an absent party of the proceedings against him.*

(Emphasis supplied). As the Court made clear in Mullane v. Central Hanover Bank & Trust Co., 339 U.S. 306, 314 (1950), what is needed to satisfy the service requirement is simply "notice reasonably calculated, under all the circumstances, to apprise interested parties of the pendency of the action and afford them an opportunity to present their objections."

Where the *notice* function of service is in question, two policy issues arise: (1) Do the forms of notice-giving recognized by the adjudicating legal order provide "a reasonable method for apprising * * * an absent party of the proceedings against him" and (2) in the interest of predictability and administrability, should only one or a few forms of notice be accepted as capable of satisfying the notice requirement. Absent constitutional-law constraints, obligations under customary international law, or requirements of conventions, the legal order seised of the controversy decides under its law these questions; conversely, if recognition or enforcement abroad of the resulting judgment is sought, the legal order addressed regulates them under its law.

Volkswagenwerk Aktiengesellschaft v. Schlunk

Supreme Court of the United States, 1988.
486 U.S. 694, 108 S.Ct. 2104, 100 L.Ed.2d 722.

JUSTICE O'CONNOR delivered the opinion of the Court. This case involves an attempt to serve process on a foreign corporation by serving its domestic subsidiary which, under state law, is the foreign corporation's involuntary agent for service of process. We must decide whether such service is compatible with the Convention on Service Abroad of Judicial and Extrajudicial Documents in Civil and Commercial Matters, Nov. 15, 1965 (Hague Service Convention), [1969] 20 U. S. T. 361, T. I. A. S. No. 6638.

I. The parents of respondent Herwig Schlunk were killed in an automobile accident in 1983. Schlunk filed a wrongful death action on their behalf in the Circuit Court of Cook County, Illinois. Schlunk alleged that Volkswagen of America, Inc. (VWoA), had designed and sold the automobile that his parents were driving, and that defects in the automobile caused or contributed to their deaths. * * * Schlunk successfully served his complaint on VWoA, and VWoA filed an answer denying that it had designed or assembled the automobile in question. Schlunk then amended the complaint to add as a defendant Volkswagen Aktiengesellschaft (VWAG), which is the petitioner here. VWAG, a corporation established under the laws of the Federal Republic of Germany, has its place of business in that country. VWoA is a wholly owned subsidiary of VWAG. Schlunk attempted to serve his amended complaint on VWAG by serving VWoA as VWAG's agent.

VWAG filed a special and limited appearance for the purpose of quashing service. VWAG asserted that it could be served only in accordance with the Hague Service Convention, and that Schlunk had not complied with the Convention's requirements. The Circuit Court denied VWAG's motion. It first observed that VWoA is registered to do business in Illinois and has a registered agent for receipt of process in Illinois. The court then reasoned that VWoA and VWAG are so closely related that VWoA is VWAG's agent for service of process as a matter of law, notwithstanding VWAG's failure or refusal to appoint VWoA formally as an agent. The court relied on the facts that VWoA is a wholly owned subsidiary of VWAG, that a majority of the members of the board of directors of VWoA are members of the board of VWAG, and that VWoA is by contract the exclusive importer and distributor of VWAG products sold in the United States. The court concluded that, because service was accomplished within the United States, the Hague Service Convention did not apply.

* * *

II. The Hague Service Convention is a multilateral treaty that was formulated in 1964 by the Tenth Session of the Hague Conference of Private International Law. The Convention revised parts of the Hague Conventions on Civil Procedure of 1905 and 1954. The revision was intended to provide a simpler way to serve process abroad, to assure that defendants sued in foreign jurisdictions would receive actual and timely notice of suit, and to facilitate proof of service abroad. [cit.] Representatives of all 23 countries that were members of the Conference approved the

Convention without reservation. Thirty-two countries, including the United States and the Federal Republic of Germany, have ratified or acceded to the Convention. [cit.]

The primary innovation of the Convention is that it requires each state to establish a central authority to receive requests for service of documents from other countries. Once a central authority receives a request in the proper form, it must serve the documents by a method prescribed by the internal law of the receiving state or by a method designated by the requester and compatible with that law. Art. 5. The central authority must then provide a certificate of service that conforms to a specified model. Art. 6. A state also may consent to methods of service within its boundaries other than a request to its central authority. Arts. 8–11, 19. The remaining provisions of the Convention that are relevant here limit the circumstances in which a default judgment may be entered against a defendant who had to be served abroad and did not appear, and provide some means for relief from such a judgment. Arts. 15, 16.

Article 1 defines the scope of the Convention, which is the subject of controversy in this case. It says: "The present Convention shall apply in all cases, in civil or commercial matters, where there is occasion to transmit a judicial or extrajudicial document for service abroad." 20 U. S. T. at 362. * * * This language is mandatory * * *. By virtue of the Supremacy Clause, U.S. Const., Art. VI, the Convention pre-empts inconsistent methods of service prescribed by state law in all cases to which it applies. Schlunk does not purport to have served his complaint on VWAG in accordance with the Convention. Therefore, if service of process in this case falls within Article 1 of the Convention, the trial court should have granted VWAG's motion to quash.

* * *

The Convention does not specify the circumstances in which there is "occasion to transmit" a complaint "for service abroad." But at least the term "service of process" has a well-established technical meaning. Service of process refers to a formal delivery of documents that is legally sufficient to charge the defendant with notice of a pending action. [cit.] The legal sufficiency of a formal delivery of documents must be measured against some standard. The Convention does not prescribe a standard, so we almost necessarily must refer to the internal law of the forum state. If the internal law of the forum state defines the applicable method of serving process as requiring the transmittal of documents abroad, then the Hague Service Convention applies.

The negotiating history supports our view that Article 1 refers to service of process in the technical sense. The committee that prepared the preliminary draft deliberately used a form of the term "notification" (formal notice), instead of the more neutral term "remise" (delivery), when it drafted Article 1. [cit.] Then, in the course of the debates, the negotiators made the language even more exact. The preliminary draft of Article 1 said that the present Convention shall apply in all cases in which there are grounds *to transmit or to give formal notice of* a judicial or extrajudicial document in a civil or commercial matter to a person staying abroad. [cit.] To be more precise, the delegates decided to add a form of the juridical term "signification" (service), which has a narrower meaning than "notification" in some countries, such as France, and the identical meaning in others, such as the United States. [cit.] The delegates also criticized the language of the preliminary draft because it suggested that the Convention could apply to transmissions abroad that do not culminate in service. [cit.] The final text of Article 1, eliminates this possibility and applies only to documents transmitted for service abroad. The final report confirms that the Convention does not use more general terms, such as delivery or transmission, to define its scope because it applies only when there is both transmission of a document from the requesting state to the receiving state, and service upon the person for whom it is intended. [cit.]

* * *

VWAG protests that it is inconsistent with the purpose of the Convention to interpret it as applying only when the internal law of the forum requires service abroad. One of the two stated objectives of the Convention is "to create appropriate means to ensure that judicial and extrajudicial documents to be served abroad shall be brought to the notice of the addressee in sufficient time." [cit.] The Convention cannot assure adequate notice, VWAG argues, if the forum's internal law determines whether it applies. VWAG warns that countries could circumvent the Convention by defining methods of service of process that do not require transmission of documents abroad. Indeed, VWAG contends that one such method of service already exists and that it troubled the Conference: *notification au parquet.*

Notification au parquet permits service of process on a foreign defendant by the deposit of documents with a designated local official. Although the official generally is supposed to transmit the documents abroad to the defendant, the statute of limitations begins to run from the time that the official receives the documents, and there allegedly is no sanction for failure to transmit them. [cit.] At the time of the 10th Conference, France, the Netherlands, Greece, Belgium, and Italy utilized some type of *notification au parquet.* [cit.]

There is no question but that the Conference wanted to eliminate *notification au parquet.* [cit.] It included in the Convention two provisions that address the problem. Article 15 says that a judgment may not be entered unless a foreign defendant received adequate and timely notice of the lawsuit. Article 16 provides means whereby a defendant who did not receive such notice may seek relief from a judgment that has become final. [cit.] Like Article 1, however, Articles 15 and 16 apply only when documents must be transmitted abroad for the purpose of service. [cit.] VWAG argues that, if this determination is made according to the internal law of the forum state, the Convention will fail to eliminate variants of notification au parquet that do not expressly require transmittal of documents to foreign defendants. Yet such methods of service of process are the least likely to provide a defendant with actual notice.

The parties make conflicting representations about whether foreign laws authorizing *notification au parquet* command the transmittal of documents for service abroad within the meaning of the Convention. The final report is itself somewhat equivocal. It says that, although the strict language of Article 1 might raise a question as to whether the Convention regulates *notification au parquet,* the understanding of the drafting Commission, based on the debates, is that the Convention would apply. [cit.] Although this statement might affect our decision as to whether the Convention applies to *notification au parquet*, an issue we do not resolve today, there is no comparable evidence in the negotiating history that the Convention was meant to apply to substituted service on a subsidiary like VWoA, which clearly does not require service abroad under the forum's internal law. Hence neither the language of the Convention nor the negotiating history contradicts our interpretation of the Convention, according to which the internal law of the forum is presumed to determine whether there is occasion for service abroad.

Nor are we persuaded that the general purposes of the Convention require a different conclusion. One important objective of the Convention is to provide means to facilitate service of process abroad. Thus the first stated purpose of the Convention is "to create" appropriate means for service abroad, and the second stated purpose is "to improve the organization of mutual judicial assistance for that purpose by simplifying and expediting the procedure." [cit.] By requiring each state to establish a central authority to assist in the service of process, the Convention implements this enabling function. Nothing in our decision today interferes with this requirement.

VWAG correctly maintains that the Convention also aims to ensure that there will be adequate notice in cases in which there is occasion to serve process abroad. Thus compliance with the Convention is mandatory in all cases to which it applies [cit.] and Articles 15 and 16 provide an indirect sanction against those who ignore it. [cit.]. Our interpretation of the Convention does not necessarily advance this particular objective, inasmuch as it makes recourse to the Convention's means of service dependent on the forum's internal law. But we do not think that this country, or any other country, will draft its internal laws deliberately so as to circumvent the Convention in cases in which it would be appropriate to transmit judicial documents for service abroad. For example, there has been no question in this country of excepting foreign nationals from the protection of our Due Process Clause. Under that Clause, foreign nationals are assured of either personal service, which typically will require service abroad and trigger the Convention, or substituted service that provides "notice reasonably calculated, under all the circumstances, to apprise interested parties of the pendency of the action and afford them an opportunity to present their objections." Mullane v. Central Hanover Bank & Trust Co., 339 U.S. 306, 314 (1950).[1]

---

1. The concurrence believes that our interpretation does not adequately guarantee timely notice, which it denominates the "primary" purpose of the Convention, albeit without authority. [cit.] The concurrence instead proposes to impute a substantive standard to the words, "service abroad." [cit.] Evidently, a method of service would not be deemed to be "service abroad" within the meaning of Article 1 unless it provides notice to the recipient "in due time." [cit.] This due process notion cannot be squared with the plain meaning of the words, "service abroad." The contours of the concurrence's substantive standard are not defined, and we note that it would create some uncertainty even on the facts of this case. If the substantive standard tracks the Due Process Clause of the Fourteenth Amendment, it is not self-evident that substituted service on a subsidiary is sufficient with respect to the parent. In the only cases in which it has considered the question, this Court held that the activities of a subsidiary are not necessarily enough to render a parent subject to a court's jurisdiction, for service of process or otherwise. Cannon Mfg. Co. v. Cudahy Packing Co., 267 U.S. 333, 336–337 (1925); Consolidated Textile Corp. v. Gregory, 289 U.S. 85, 88 (1933); [cit.] Although the particular relationship between VWAG and VWoA might have made substituted service valid
(continued...)

Furthermore, nothing that we say today prevents compliance with the Convention even when the internal law of the forum does not so require. The Convention provides simple and certain means by which to serve process on a foreign national. Those who eschew its procedures risk discovering that the forum's internal law required transmittal of documents for service abroad, and that the Convention therefore provided the exclusive means of valid service. In addition, parties that comply with the Convention ultimately may find it easier to enforce their judgments abroad. [cit.] For these reasons, we anticipate that parties may resort to the Convention voluntarily, even in cases that fall outside the scope of its mandatory application.

III. In this case, the Illinois long-arm statute authorized Schlunk to serve VWAG by substituted service on VWoA, without sending documents to Germany. [cit.] VWAG has not petitioned for review of the Illinois Appellate Court's holding that service was proper as a matter of Illinois law. VWAG contends, however, that service on VWAG was not complete until VWoA transmitted the complaint to VWAG in Germany. According to VWAG, this transmission constituted service abroad under the Hague Service Convention.

VWAG explains that, as a practical matter, VWoA was certain to transmit the complaint to Germany to notify VWAG of the litigation. Indeed, as a legal matter, the Due Process Clause requires every method of service to provide "notice reasonably calculated, under all the circumstances, to apprise interested parties of the pendency of the action and afford them an opportunity to present their objections." *Mullane v. Central Hanover Bank & Trust Co.*, supra at 314. VWAG argues that, because of this notice requirement, every case involving service on a foreign national will present an "occasion to transmit a judicial ... document for service abroad" within the meaning of Article 1. [cit.] VWAG emphasizes that in this case, the Appellate Court upheld service only after determining that "the relationship between VWAG and VWoA is so close that it is certain that VWAG 'was fully apprised of the pendency of the action' by delivery of the summons to VWoA." [cit.]

We reject this argument. Where service on a domestic agent is valid and complete under both state law and the Due Process Clause, our inquiry ends and the Convention has no further implications. Whatever internal, private communications take place between the agent and a foreign principal are beyond the concerns of this case. The only transmittal to which the Convention applies is a transmittal abroad that is required as a necessary part of service. And, contrary to VWAG's assertion, the Due Process Clause does not require an official transmittal of documents abroad every time there is service on a foreign national. Applying this analysis, we conclude that this case does not present an occasion to transmit a judicial document for service abroad within the meaning of Article 1. Therefore the Hague Service Convention does not apply, and service was proper. The judgment of the Appellate Court is

---

1. (...continued)
in this case, a question that we do not decide, the factbound character of the necessary inquiry makes us doubt whether the standard suggested by the concurrence would in fact be "remarkably easy" to apply [cit.]

Affirmed.

[Concurrence of Justice Brennan omitted].

Notes and Questions

1. The Hague Service Convention of 1965 and the Inter-American Convention on Letters Rogatory of 1975, together with the Additional Protocol to the Inter-American Convention on Letters Rogatory of 1979, provide machinery to accomplish tasks that had traditionally required the use of letters rogatory sent through diplomatic channels from one State to another requesting judicial assistance. An important innovation is the establishment in the States parties to one or both Conventions of a Central Authority to facilitate the service of certain documents transmitted to it by the Central Authority of a requesting State party. The efficiency of the Central Authorities varies; some have been unreliable. Until very recently, the U.S. Central Authority, which has functioned well, was in the Department of Justice. In 2003, considerations of costs and efficiency caused the Department of Justice to privatize the U.S. Central Authority.

2. What purpose or purposes justify service of process requirements? Would service pursuant to the Service Convention standing alone establish the adjudicatory authority of Illinois in the *Schlunk* case? Or is something more required? If so, what? Does the refusal of a State to serve a defendant preclude, in principle, the forum State from asserting adjudicatory authority in the matter?

In a recent decision, the German Constitutional Court preliminarily enjoined a German court from serving process under the Hague Service Convention for a U.S. class action. See Bundesverfassungsgericht, 25 July 2003 (2 BvR 1198/03). The class action for $ 17 billion in damages was brought by various U.S. music copyright owners against media conglomerate Bertelsmann AG for alleged copyright violations through the latter's participation in Napster, the now bankrupt computer-based music file exchange system. The Court indicated that service in such a case might violate fairness standards guaranteed by the German Constitution if the class action is brought frivolously in order to exercise pressure on the defendant. The Court took the position that in the case of such violation, Article 13 of the Convention (ordre public) would dispense Germany from its obligations under the Convention. The Court indicated that denying the injunction and having defendant Bertelsmann attack the enforcement in Germany later on was insufficient to protect defendant's constitutional rights because it would subject defendant to enforcement in the United States. What do you think about this argument?

3. What is the functional justification for a service of process requirement? Can these purposes be served efficiently by procedures that do not utilize the Central Authority system? Whose law determines whether a particular procedure is acceptable to a State considering whether it can properly assert adjudicatory authority in the international sense? Whose law determines whether a judgment that does not observe Article 10 of the Hague Service Convention is entitled to recognition in a State party to the Service Convention?

4. In the United States, process can generally be served by private citizens,

see Fed. R. Civ. Pro. 4(c)(2), and a number of states accept service by mail. Article 10 of the Hague Service Convention provides that, where "the State of destination does not object, the * * * Convention shall not interfere with (a) the freedom to send judicial documents by postal channels, directly to persons abroad." A number of States have declared their objection to service by mail. For example, the German government has argued that

> German sovereignty is violated in cases where foreign judicial documents are served directly by mail within the Federal Republic of Germany. By such direct service, an act of sovereignty is conducted without any control by German authorities on the territory of the Federal Republic of Germany.

Diplomatic Note dated September 27, 1979 from the Embassy of the Federal Republic of Germany to the U.S. Department of State, quoted in Born, *International Civil Litigation*, 777.

States that have objected under Article 10 are, as a matter of international law, relieved of their obligation to recognize and enforce such judgments rendered by courts of States party to the Service Convention. The question remains whether, where the State of destination has objected to service by mail, the rendering State is under an international obligation to deny enforcement of the judgments of its *own* courts. Of course, if in the particular proceeding the notice given the defendant did not satisfy the forum's due process (or natural justice) standards, the judgment will be denied recognition and enforcement by the rendering State. If, however, the notice given meets due process standards should not the judgment be enforceable at home unless the Hague Service Convention clearly provides otherwise? The objection to service by mail is based on the view that service of process is a sovereign act and, as such, must be an act of the local sovereign. If the United States treats service of process in the *Schlunk* context as an issue solely of adequate notice, so long as the notice given to the defendants is constitutionally adequate, is the adjudicatory authority of the Illinois courts affected? Is there any reason of policy why failure to observe Article 10 procedures should affect the judgment's enforcement at home?

5. Justice Brennan, in his concurrence in *Schlunk*, rejected the majority's conclusion that domestic law determined whether service abroad was required. He argued:

> Under the Court's analysis, * * * a forum nation could prescribe direct mail service to any foreigner and deem service effective upon deposit in the mailbox, or could arbitrarily designate a domestic agent for any foreign defendant and deem service complete upon receipt domestically by the agent even though there is little likelihood that service would ever reach the defendant.

486 U.S. at 710–11. He nonetheless concurred in the result on the ground that the Hague Service Convention does not prohibit the type of service that was at issue in the case. Is Brennan saying that a form of notification that had "little likelihood" of "ever reach[ing] the defendant" would be acceptable under Illinois law? Under the Constitution of the United States?

6. Under the majority's interpretation, the applicability of the Convention

depends on when, as a matter of domestic law, service is complete. State laws may vary on this point. Consider the following analysis of New York Law:

[T]he Hague Convention does not come into play if service is made upon the defendant, or upon defendant's agent, within the United States. In that regard, one must distinguish between B.C.L. § 306 and B.C.L. § 307.

Section 306 provides that one may serve New York Corporations, and foreign corporations *licensed* to do business in New York, by delivering two copies of the process to the Secretary of State as agent for the corporation. "Service of process on such corporation shall be complete when the secretary of state is so served." The Secretary of State then sends one of the copies to the corporation. "The jurisdictional act is the delivery of the two copies to the Secretary. The latter's failure to forward one to the corporation does not void the service." *A fortiori*, if the Secretary transmits the process to the foreign corporation abroad in some manner that violates the Convention, personal jurisdiction over the defendant would still exist. (Needless to say, the Secretary should comply with the Convention even if his failure to do so will have no direct impact upon the litigants.)

Under B.C.L. § 307 one may serve *unlicensed* foreign corporations that are subject to jurisdiction in New York under article 3 of the C.P.L.R. by delivering one copy of the process to the Secretary of State as agent for the corporation and then personally delivery, or mailing, notice of that service, with a copy of the process, to the corporation. Failure to deliver or send a copy of the process to the foreign corporation is a fatal jurisdictional defect.

New York State Bar Assoc., *Service of Process Abroad: A Nuts and Bolts Guide.* 122 F.R.D. 63, 73–74 (1989). Do you agree with the conclusion that the Convention does not "come into play" when service is effected under § 306? Should the New York Secretary of State comply with the Convention when acting pursuant to § 306?

7. How burdensome is it to serve process pursuant to the Hague Convention? Are there practical reasons to comply with the Convention even when compliance might not be required? The *Schlunk* Court offers the pragmatic reminder that "parties that comply with the Convention ultimately may find it easier to enforce their judgments abroad."

2. Forum Selection Agreements

Subject to constraints flowing from internationally applicable principles and obligations, each legal order is free to open its courts for the adjudication of controversies. Various considerations of theory and practice, explain a legal order's willingness to entertain transnational controversies.

Parties that can choose the forum to be seised among those potentially available enjoy a considerable advantage. The availability *vel non* of pretrial discovery, direct and cross-examination, and jury trial as well as the ability to control choice-of-law rules and principles that forum selection allows give a significant advantage to the party who selects the forum. An effective forum selection agreement enables, as the case may be, one party alone or both parties in concert to determine the legal order whose courts will adjudicate a given matter.

Forum selection clauses that are truly international may well deserve different treatment, so far as the acceptability of forum selection clauses is concerned, than would be accorded were domestic agreements and litigations in question. The Supreme Court made this point in Scherk v. Alberto-Culver Co. Inc. 417 U.S. 506, 515 (1974), when it upheld an arbitration agreement in an international case and distinguished an earlier case that had involved an entirely domestic situation.

> [In the earlier case, the] parties, the negotiations, and the subject matter of the contract were all situated in this country, and no credible claim could have been entertained that any international conflict-of-laws problems would arise. In [the case at hand], by contrast, in the absence of the arbitration provision considerable uncertainty existed at the time of the agreement, and still exists, concerning the law applicable to the resolution of disputes arising out of the contract.

> Such uncertainty will almost inevitably exist with respect to any contract touching two or more countries, each with its own substantive laws and conflict-of-laws rules. A contractual provision specifying in advance the forum in which disputes shall be litigated and the law to be applied is, therefore, an almost indispensable precondition to achievement of the orderliness and predictability essential to any international business transaction. Furthermore, such a provision obviates the danger that a dispute under the agreement might be submitted to a forum hostile to the interests of one of the parties or unfamiliar with the problem area involved.

> A parochial refusal by the courts of one country to enforce an international arbitration agreement would not only frustrate these purposes, but would invite unseemly and mutually destructive jockeying by the parties to secure tactical litigation advantages. In the present case, for example, it is not inconceivable that if Scherk had anticipated that Alberto-Culver would be able in this country to enjoin resort to arbitration he might have sought an order in France or some other country enjoining Alberto-Culver from proceeding with its litigation in the United States. Whatever recognition the courts of this country might ultimately have granted to the order of the foreign court, the dicey atmosphere of such a legal no-man's-land would surely damage the fabric of international commerce and trade, and imperil the willingness and ability of businessmen to enter into international commercial agreements.

Historically, American courts, federal and state alike, generally declined to enforce forum selection clauses. They were seen as "contrary to public policy," or as an attempt to oust the jurisdiction of the courts not selected. In 1958, the Fifth Circuit Court of Appeals in Carbon Black Export, Inc. v. The Monrosa, 254 F.2d 297, at 300-01 (en banc), *cert. dismissed*, 359 U.S. 180 (1959), denied enforcement to a forum selection clause on the ground that "agreements in advance of a controversy whose object is to oust the jurisdiction of the courts are contrary to public policy and will not be enforced."

In The Bremen v. Zapata Off-Shore Co., 407 U.S. 1 (1972), the Supreme

Court held that, in federal district courts sitting in admiralty, forum selection clauses are "prima facie valid and should be enforced unless enforcement is shown by the resisting party to be unreasonable under the circumstances." Id. at 10. Chief Justice Burger's opinion for the court in *The Bremen* reflects a very different assessment of the opportunities and the risks presented by forum selection clauses than was advanced in *Carbon Black*. The Chief Justice reasoned as follows:

> Not surprisingly, foreign businessmen prefer, as do we, to have disputes resolved in their own courts, but if that choice is not available, then in a neutral forum with expertise in the subject matter. Plainly, the courts of England meet the standards of neutrality and long experience in admiralty litigation. The choice of that forum was made in an arm's-length negotiation by experienced and sophisticated businessmen, and absent some compelling and countervailing reason it should be honored by the parties and enforced by the courts.
>
> The argument that such clauses are improper because they tend to "oust" a court of jurisdiction is hardly more than a vestigial legal fiction. It appears to rest at core on historical judicial resistance to any attempt to reduce the power and business of a particular court and has little place in an era when all courts are overloaded and when businesses once essentially local now operate in world markets. It reflects something of a provincial attitude regarding the fairness of other tribunals. No one seriously contends in this case that the forum-selection clause "ousted" the District Court of jurisdiction over Zapata's action. The threshold question is whether that court should have exercised its jurisdiction to do more than give effect to the legitimate expectations of the parties, manifested in their freely negotiated agreement, by specifically enforcing the forum clause.
>
> There are compelling reasons why a freely negotiated private international agreement, unaffected by fraud, undue influence, or overweening bargaining power, such as that involved here, should be given full effect. In this case, for example, we are concerned with a far from routine transaction between companies of two different nations contemplating the tow of an extremely costly piece of equipment from Louisiana across the Gulf of Mexico and the Atlantic Ocean, through the Mediterranean Sea to its final destination in the Adriatic Sea. In the course of its voyage, it was to traverse the waters of many jurisdictions. The *Chaparral* could have been damaged at any point along the route, and there were countless possible ports of refuge. That the accident occurred in the Gulf of Mexico and the barge was towed to Tampa in an emergency were mere fortuities. It cannot be doubted for a moment that the parties sought to provide for a neutral forum for the resolution of any disputes arising during the tow. Manifestly much uncertainty and possibly great inconvenience to both parties could arise if a suit could be maintained in any jurisdiction in which an accident might occur or if jurisdiction were left to any place where the Bremen or Unterweser might happen to be found. The elimination of all such uncertainties by agreeing in advance on a forum acceptable to both parties is an indispensable element in international trade,

commerce, and contracting. There is strong evidence that the forum clause was a vital part of the agreement, and it would be unrealistic to think that the parties did not conduct their negotiations, including fixing the monetary terms, with the consequences of the forum clause figuring prominently in their calculations. Under these circumstances, as Justice Karminski reasoned in sustaining jurisdiction over Zapata in the High Court of Justice, "the force of an agreement for litigation in this country, freely entered into between two competent parties, seems to me to be very powerful."

Thus, in the light of present-day commercial realities and expanding international trade we conclude that the forum clause should control absent a strong showing that it should be set aside. Although their opinions are not altogether explicit, it seems reasonably clear that the District Court and the Court of Appeals placed the burden on Unterweser to show that London would be a more convenient forum than Tampa, although the contract expressly resolved that issue. The correct approach would have been to enforce the forum clause specifically unless Zapata could clearly show that enforcement would be unreasonable and unjust, or that the clause was invalid for such reasons as fraud or overreaching. Accordingly, the case must be remanded for reconsideration.

Id. at 11-15.

Notes and Questions

1. In the U.S. some state courts still either do not enforce forum selection clauses, or have ambiguous case law on the point. The traditional justification for non-enforcement is that private parties cannot by their agreement oust a court of jurisdiction: "How can two individuals by private agreement limit or otherwise alter the 'jurisdiction' of the great courts of state or nation!" 6A Arthur Corbin, Corbin on Contracts § 1431, at 381-82 (1962). Courts also express a desire to protect local citizens' rights of access to justice, see Insurance Co. v. Morse, 87 U.S. (20 Wall.) 445, 451, (1874), as well as concern about possible fraud or overreaching in the formation of the contract. In addition, forum selection clauses may make it more difficult for litigants to vindicate rights that are perceived to be of public significance. Are these reasons for non-enforcement less compelling in international causes? Conversely, are the reasons for enforcement more compelling in international cases?

2. In Carnival Cruise Lines, Inc. v. Shute, 499 U.S. 585 (1991), see supra at 661, the Court upheld a forum selection clause contained in a vacation cruise ticket. The plaintiff from Washington State had been injured on a ship while in international waters off the coast of Mexico. The Court held that the clause was not unreasonable and the plaintiff failed to satisfy the "heavy burden of proof" required "to set aside the clause on grounds of inconvenience." Id. at 595. The ticket specified Florida as the selected forum.

Notwithstanding *Carnival Cruise Lines*, some courts have refused to enforce forum selection clauses on the ground that the clauses were unreasonable, see Corna v. American Hawaii Cruises, Inc., 794 F.Supp. 1005 (D.Ha.1992); Pearcy Marine

v. Seacor Marine, 847 F.Supp. 57 (S.D.Tex.1993), unduly burdensome, see Effron v. Sun Line Cruises, 857 F.Supp. 1079 (S.D.N.Y.1994), or the result of fraud or coercion, see Farmland Indus. Inc. v. Frazier-Parrott Commodities, Inc., 806 F.2d 848 (8th Cir.1986); M.G.J. Indus. Inc. v. Greyhound Finance Corp., 826 F.Supp. 430 (M.D.Fla.1993).

3. In federal cases, where jurisdiction does not rest on diversity of citizenship, the courts apply the principles of *The Bremen* and *Carnival Cruise* favoring enforcement of exclusive forum selection clauses. See Scoles, Hay, Borchers & Symeonides, *Conflict of Laws*, § 11.3. In diversity cases, however, federal courts are generally required to apply the "substantive" law, including conflict of laws principles, that the court of the state in which the federal court is sitting would apply. This requirement does not create problems when the relevant state law respecting forum selection clauses accords, as it usually does, with the federal pro-enforcement view. On the other hand, where, as is exceptionally the case, the state law in question still adheres to the "ouster" doctrine, a federal court in a diversity case may face a difficult choice if the forum selection clause points to the law of another state or a foreign nation. In such cases federal courts

> are approximately equally divided between applying state [law which would deny effect to the clause] and federal law [which would give effect to it]. Application of federal law has, of course, the advantage of reducing the incentive for interstate forum shopping, * * * [while] application of state law preserves uniformity of outcome as between a federal court and its home state's courts.

Id. at 475.

4. In both *The Bremen* and *Scherk*, the U.S. Supreme Court stressed the international aspect of the controversy as a reason for enforcing the clauses. In deciding whether to enforce a forum selection clause in an international case, should a U.S. court consider whether the home courts of the foreign parties would enforce such an agreement against their nationals? Are there other aspects of contract law that should be applied differently when the contract involves foreign parties? If so, should all cases involving international transactions be governed by federal common law rather than by the varying laws of the 50 states? See, e.g., Appell v. George Philip & Son, Ltd., 760 F.Supp. 167, 168 (D.Nev.1991); Taylor v. Titan Midwest Constr. Corp., 474 F.Supp. 145, 147 (N.D.Tex.1979); Maier, *The Three Faces of Zapata*, 387.

6. Arbitration clauses are "a specialized kind of forum selection clauses." Arbitration is now widely used in international matters in order to secure competent, expeditious, and neutral adjudications that might not be available in national courts. Where national law accepts the institution of arbitration, it recognizes a private dispute-resolution process that not only establishes the territorial situs--the seat--of the suit but allows the parties, directly or indirectly, to determine as well the procedures to be followed by the private tribunal and the rules and principles of substantive law that the adjudicating arbitrators are to apply.

The United Nations Convention on the Recognition and Enforcement of Foreign Arbitral Awards (usually referred to as the New York Convention of 1958) is today in force in 133 States. Nonetheless, many aspects of the arbitral process in international matters are still regulated by national law. These laws have become more and more user friendly as States have sought to make their respecting national laws attractive and thus bring international arbitration to their commercial and legal centers. Among the competing centers are Brussels, Cairo, Geneva, Hong Kong, London, New York, Paris, Singapore, and Zurich.

7. Professor Stephen Burbank has commented in unfavorable terms on the Supreme Court's approach to choice-of-forum clauses in *Carnival Cruise Lines* as well as the Court's interpretation of the Federal Arbitration Act that drastically reduced the power of states to protect consumers and employees against overreaching arbitration clauses:

> The Supreme Court's approach to choice of court clauses in *Carnival Cruise Lines* [cit.] is redolent with a notion of freedom of contract that, however much one might like to confine it to an age when there was no indoor plumping, evidently reflects an enduring strain of American thought bound up with belief in individual freedom and responsibility and a fear of paternalistic government. The Court's approach to the interpretation of the Federal Arbitration Act, in turn, deprives the states of the United States of the power to protect those thought to be vulnerable to overreaching unless they are willing to change their entire law of contracts in order to address particular problems arising out of contracts to arbitrate.[1]

Burbank, *Paths to a Via Media*, ___

If you would ask Professor Burbank whether the difficulties encountered in the effort to accomplish a Hague Jurisdiction and Recognition Convention were ultimately rooted not in juridical differences but rather in sociological differences, such as a "belief in individual freedom and responsibility," what would you expect him to say? Are sociological differences more important today than they have been a half century ago?

8. Choice of forum clauses, including agreements to arbitrate, can be used in conjunction with a choice of law clause to avoid the substantive law of a State whose law would otherwise govern the matter. Should this be a basis for invalidating either (or both) clauses? In Mitsubishi Motors Corp. v. Soler Chrysler–Plymouth, Inc., 473 U.S. 614, 637 n.19 (1985), the U.S. Supreme Court enforced the parties' agreement to arbitrate but observed in dicta that "in the event the choice-of-forum and choice-of-law clauses operated in tandem as a prospective waiver of a party's right to pursue statutory remedies for antitrust violations, we would have little hesitation in condemning the agreement as against public policy."

9. Some jurists think that a well drawn choice of court convention would be very successful. For them, "[g]lobal practice under the New York Arbitration Convention offers proof that a very basic choice of forum rule, accompanied by a corresponding rule on recognition and enforcement of the resulting award, can achieve dramatic success in the global community." Brand, *Forum Selection*, 86. In

---

1. For a discussion of the Supreme Court's interpretation of the FAA, see von Mehren, *Adjudicatory Authority*, 291-301.

a circular letter of April 23, 2003 to the Member States of the Hague Conference on Private International Law, the Secretary-General of the Conference provided the draft text of a convention on choice of court agreements that had been elaborated by an informal working group. After evaluating the responses of the Conference's Member States, it appears that "there is sufficient support for the reference of the draft to a Special Commission." Accordingly, the Secretary-General convened a Commission that met in December 2003 and began consideration of the proposal.

C. ADJUDICATORY AUTHORITY IN INTERNATIONAL CASES: AMERICAN THEORY AND PRACTICE

Helicopteros Nacionales de Colombia v. Hall
Supreme Court of the United States, 1984.
466 U.S. 408, 104 S.Ct. 1868, 80 L.Ed.2d 404.

Please read the opinion reproduced at 627, supra.

Asahi Metal Industry Co. v. Superior Court of California
Supreme Court of the United States, 1987.
480 U.S. 102, 107 S.Ct. 1026, 94 L.Ed.2d 92.

Please read the opinion reproduced at 620, supra.

Notes and Questions

1. Do you think the results in *Helicopteros* or *Asahi* would have been different if the defendants had been U.S. corporations? Should the results have been different?

2. Professor von Mehren has argued that in allocating litigational burdens, weight should be given to the parties' comparative ability to bear those burdens and that this assessment should be made in terms

> of the *class* of plaintiffs or defendants to which the parties belong. Considerations of administrability, planning, predictability, and objectivity require this approach to jurisdictional rules generally. * * * Thus, in deciding whether jurisdiction should be claimed, it is relevant that the plaintiff is a consumer or an insured but not that he is a pauper or a millionaire. Jurisdictional rules based on the relative ability principle could, however, give weight to the individualized situation of the plaintiff or the defendant in deciding whether to refuse to exercise jurisdiction under the doctrine of forum non conveniens.

> Many important claims of specific jurisdiction made by legal orders that approach jurisdiction in terms of fairness can be explained as resting, at least in large measure, on the defendant class's relatively greater ability, as compared with that of the related plaintiff class, to bear the litigational burdens of litigating in the other party's forum. It is interesting, therefore, to explore how jurisdictional standards designed to give significant weight to the

parties' relative litigational abilities might be developed and to consider the form that such standards might take. The basic proposition is that a class of plaintiffs whose ability to bear the burden of litigation is clearly significantly less than that of the related class of defendants should receive special treatment for jurisdictional purposes. Further analysis of the characteristics of classes of plaintiffs and defendants that affect their respective abilities to bear litigational burdens is thus needed.

For reasons of administrability, planning, predictability, and objectivity, a relative ability analysis should be structured in terms of the localized or multistate character of the activities of the class of parties normally related to the type of controversy in question. The premise is that a party's economic and psychological ability to litigate in the other party's forum, as well as his expectations with respect to the possibility that he may have to do so, decrease as a direct function of the degree to which his normal activities are localized and have only local effects. Accordingly, for jurisdictional purposes the following situations can be distinguished: (1) multistate plaintiff, localized defendant; (2) both parties localized; (3) both parties multistate; (4) localized plaintiff, multistate defendant. These situations proceed from the one in which a jurisdictional preference for the defendant is most plausible to the situation in which the preference is least plausible.

von Mehren, *Adjudicatory Jurisdiction*, 313-14. Should--and does--the Court in *Helicopteros* and *Asahi*, respectively, take into account the parties' comparative ability to bear the litigational burdens entailed in litigating the matter in the American courts?

3. The *Helicopteros* Court rejected the plaintiff's argument that this was an appropriate case of "jurisdiction by necessity." See *Helicopteros, supra* at 631 n.13. Should necessity ever be a basis for a U.S. court to take jurisdiction? What should constitute "necessity"? Should it be sufficient for jurisdiction that any likely award in the foreign court would be a tiny percentage of any likely award from a U.S. court? See Born, *International Civil Litigation*, 111 n.1.

4. In its amicus brief in *Helicopteros*, the United States argued:

The United States Trade Representative has informed us that while many American export transactions do not require the seller to provide training to the personnel of the buyer, the purchase-training agreement between Helicol and Bell Helicopter in the instant case is typical in certain sectors of the economy. The Trade Representative has advised us that the provision of training by the seller is especially important in the export of high technology, turnkey projects such as nuclear power plants; in such transactions, the seller, as part of the sale transaction, customarily provides training for local personnel involved in the maintenance, overhaul and operation of the plant. The training often takes place at the manufacturer's facilities (i.e., in the United States) because of the specialized and complex nature of the training equipment and procedures. The Trade Representative has advised Congress that services of this nature "are critical to exports of high technology and capital goods."

* * *

Thus, to the extent that the decision below relies on Helicol's purchase of its helicopter fleet in Texas, coupled with the presence of Helicol employees in Texas to receive training on the operation and maintenance of the helicopters, it has a significant potential for discouraging foreign firms from purchasing American products. This would thwart positive efforts of Congress and the Executive Branch to make American firms and products more competitive internationally.

Should the court take such considerations into account?

5. The *Asahi* Court refers to "the Federal interest in its foreign relations policies." Is this one of the interests protected by the Fourteenth Amendment? Why is it a basis for invalidating jurisdiction? Will the United States' foreign policy interests be enhanced by prohibiting jurisdiction in cases such as this? If you were negotiating a trade treaty with the Japanese on behalf of the United States, would *Asahi* increase or decrease your negotiating position?

6. The *Asahi* Court expresses great concern about subjecting foreigners to jurisdiction in American courts. Should personal jurisdiction be approached differently in the international context? Should a similar concern about protecting foreigners apply in the choice of law arena? Should *Watson v. Employers Liability Assurance Corp.,* supra at 476, *Clay v. Sun Ins. Office, Ltd.,* supra at 477, or *Allstate Ins. Co. v. Hague,* supra at 455, have been decided differently if the defendants in those cases had been foreign corporations?

7. The Japanese courts would apparently have exercised jurisdiction over a U.S. manufacturer whose product caused injury in Japan, and likewise over a third-party defendant in a comparable situation to that in *Asahi*. See Silberman, *Judicial Jurisdiction*, 402. Should the Court have considered this? See Weintraub, *Asahi*, 64-66. The Belgian Judicial Code § 636 provides that in certain cases "a foreigner may refuse the jurisdiction of the Belgian courts, if the same right exists for a Belgian in the country of the foreigner." Is this a sensible approach?

D. ADJUDICATORY AUTHORITY IN INTERNATIONAL CASES: THEORIES AND PRACTICE ABROAD

1. THE FOUR BASIC CATEGORIES OF ADJUDICATORY AUTHORITY

a. The Insularity of Traditional Terminologies. The terms utilized in contemporary discussions of adjudicatory jurisdiction vary considerably from one legal order to another. French jurists distinguish ordinary (*ordinaires*) and supplementary (*supplementaires*)[1] bases of adjudicatory authority (*compétence*). Anglo-Americans have long spoken of jurisdiction over "persons" and over "things": jurisdiction *in personam, in rem,* and *quasi in rem*. German law recognizes *allgemeiner Gerichtsstand* (general jurisdiction) and *besonderer Gerichtsstand*

---

1. The latter term is applied to jurisdiction based on the plaintiff's or the defendant's French nationality.

(special jurisdiction).[2]

Each of these vocabularies reflects contingent historical and systemic considerations and implies different conceptual frameworks. The French usage reflects the declining importance in contemporary thinking and decisional law of jurisdiction based on the plaintiff's--or the defendant's--nationality. Having once enjoyed pride of place in French practice, these two bases are now seen as "supplementing" various so-called ordinary jurisdictional bases.

The traditional common-law terminology tells us more about adjudicatory authority. Two distinctions are taken: one--between persons and things--relates to the objects over which, in a formal sense, adjudicatory authority is exercised; the other respects the judgment's scope, does it seek to bind the whole world or only the parties and their privies?

The expressions used in the German literature--general and special jurisdiction--adopt a third perspective. For German jurists a general jurisdictional basis is one that establishes, in principle, adjudicatory authority irrespective of the type of claim or controversy involved; a special basis is one available either only for certain types of claims or only where the claim or the controversy out of which the litigation arose has a significant connection with the forum. The sole characteristic common to all special jurisdictions in the German sense is that none constitutes a basis of general jurisdiction as defined by § 12 of the German Code of Civil Procedure (ZPO): "The court, where a person has his *allgemeinen Gerichtsstand*, is competent (*zuständig*) for all actions (*Klagen*) brought against him, except where an exclusive *Gerichtsstand* is provided for the action." German law recognizes only two important bases of general jurisdiction: jurisdiction over a natural person at his permanent residence (*Wohnsitz*); ZPO § 13, jurisdiction over a juristic person at its seat (*Sitz*). ZPO § 17. Despite quite different characteristics *inter se*, all other important jurisdictional bases can be denominated "special" in the sense of not being a general basis as defined by § 12.

ZPO § 23 establishes adjudicatory authority for "pecuniary (*vermögensrechtliche)* claims" "against a person who has no domestic *Wohnsitz*" at the place where "his property (*Vermögen*) is." The claim to be litigated can result from a contractual, delictual, or other obligation and no linkage is required between the claim and the assets that form the basis for jurisdiction. Section 23 jurisdiction is "special" because it is limited to actions for "pecuniary claims." ZPO § 29 provides a special jurisdiction whose characteristics are very different: Adjudicatory authority over "controversies arising out of a contractual relationship or over its existence (*Bestehen*)" lies with the courts of the place "where the disputed duty (*Verpflichtung*) was to be performed."

None of these nomenclatures is satisfactory for comparative and theoretical work. The French terminology has very little explanatory power and rests on developments particular to French law. Common-law usages have greater explanatory potential but are closely tied to historical developments and to a specific

---

2. *Gerichtsstand* comprehends both venue and jurisdiction to adjudicate in the international sense. For purposes of the present discussion only the second sense of the word is relevant.

jurisdictional theory, that of power. Furthermore, the dichotomy on which the terminology rests is fatally flawed; it fails to recognize that adjudication always involves a determination of the rights and duties of persons; things never have rights or duties but are the subjects and objects of rights and duties. A final difficulty is that the terminology tends to obscure the policy considerations that are relevant in evaluating the appropriateness of exercising adjudicatory authority. For example, so-called jurisdiction "quasi in rem" suggests that a close relationship at the level of policy exists with jurisdiction "in rem." This relationship may be considered strong by systems that accept the power theory but is weak in those based on other rationales. For systems that basically reject the power theory, markedly different reasons must justify exercise of so-called *in rem* and *quasi in rem* jurisdiction.

The German concepts of general and special jurisdiction are also unsatisfactory for comparative purposes. The special-jurisdiction category is too broad and lumps together jurisdictional bases that lack a significant common denominator. For example, §§ 23 and 29's theoretical bases are very different yet both are categorized as special jurisdictions.

b. A Terminology for Comparative and Theoretical Purposes: General Jurisdiction, Category-Specific Jurisdiction, Specific Jurisdiction, and Universal Jurisdiction. In the early 1960's Professors Donald Trautman and Arthur von Mehren proposed a doctrinally neutral terminology[3] designed not only for the discussion of jurisdictional bases used in the United States but for comparative analysis as well. They took a basic distinction between *general* and *specific* jurisdiction. The former exists where a person is considered to be connected either directly--through, for example, physical presence, the doing of business, incorporation, habitual residence, or domicile--or indirectly--in particular, through the ownership of local property--with a legal order in such a way as to justify, subject to relatively limited exceptions, its courts' power to adjudicate essentially any kind of controversy involving that person regardless whether the matters in issue derive from, or are related to, the circumstances relied upon to establish adjudicatory authority. *Specific* jurisdiction exists, on the other hand, where adjudicatory authority extends *only* to controversies deriving from, or closely related to, the very circumstances that are relied upon to establish the forum's jurisdiction.

These two types of adjudicatory authority can be either *unlimited* or *limited*. *Unlimited* jurisdiction exists where a judgment runs in principle against the judgment debtor's global assets, existing or future; jurisdiction is *limited* where judgment may not be given in an amount that exceeds the value of the debtor's specific funds or assets located--at the time the action is entertained--on the forum's territory that ground the court's jurisdiction. In the contemporary world, a widely accepted basis for unlimited general jurisdiction is the defendant's domicile or habitual residence. The jurisdiction is *general*--the matters to be litigated need not have any special

3. This now widely used terminology, first employed by the Supreme Court of the United States in Helicopteros Nacionales de Columbia, S.A.v. Hall, 466 U.S. 408 (1984), and the analysis on which it rests were advanced in von Mehren & Trautman, *Multistate Problems*, 653-656; see also von Mehren & Trautman, *Jurisdiction to Adjudicate*. 1121-1179, espec. 1135-1137, 1164-1166; von Mehren, *Adjudicatory Jurisdiction*, 282-290.

connection or affiliation with the forum's community--and *unlimited*--judgment is given for the full value of the claim regardless of the value of the judgment debtor's assets present on the forum's territory. Traditional common law *quasi in rem* jurisdiction, on the other hand, is a *limited general* jurisdiction: *General* because the presence in the jurisdiction of assets belonging to the true defendant establishes the forum's adjudicatory jurisdiction over any claim that can give rise to a money judgment, including claims having no connection with the asset or the fact of its presence in the forum; *limited* because the judgment given cannot exceed the value of the defendant's assets on which the forum's adjudicatory authority rests.

Analysis of claims of adjudicatory authority in terms of general and specific jurisdiction leaves out of account two further classes of adjudicatory authority. In his 1996 General Course at the Hague Academy of International Law, Professor von Mehren introduced the concept of category-specific jurisdiction. These claims of adjudicatory authority are general in the sense that, unlike specific jurisdiction, the particular claims to be litigated need not be linked to the forum but, unlike general jurisdiction, the adjudicatory authority claimed extends only to controversies of a particular juridical character, for example, contractual or tortious (delictual) claims.

To complete the proposed scheme of bases on which adjudicatory authority in the international sense can be asserted a fourth basis--universal jurisdiction--should be added. Such claims of adjudicatory authority are grounded on an inherent duty resting, in rare and extreme situations, upon all civilized societies to dispense justice even though none of the grounds that establish general, category-specific, or specific jurisdiction are present. As the Belgium example suggests, see supra at 692, the claims of universal jurisdiction are likely to be problematic and exceedingly rare in practice.

2. AN OVERVIEW OF ADJUDICATORY AUTHORITY IN OTHER COUNTRIES

In most countries adjudicatory authority is a creature of statutory, not constitutional law. In many civil law countries, the traditional foundational jurisdictional principle is that defendants can be sued at their domicile or, as in France,[4] in the country of their nationality. See de Vries & Lowenfeld, *Jurisdiction in Personal Actions*, 306. The basic rule of domicile or nationality is supplemented by alternative jurisdictional bases in particular categories of claims such as torts, contract or property, and special rules of domicile covering corporate branch offices. See Weser, *Bases of Judicial Jurisdiction*, 323. For example, in contracts cases, German law provides jurisdiction at the place where the disputed performance was to be made, see German Code of Civil Procedure (ZPO) § 29. In torts cases, German law permits suit in the place where the act was committed, which includes not only

---

4. Article 15 of the Civil Code of France provides: "A Frenchman may be called before a French court for obligations contracted by him in a foreign country, even towards an alien." Article 15 jurisdiction exists regardless of whether the French defendant has a domicile or residence in France. Moreover, this provision has traditionally been considered exclusive. As a result, absent a treaty, France will not, in principle, enforce a foreign judgment against a French defendant unless the defendant clearly waived his right to a French court.

where the conduct occurred but also where the harmful effects resulted. See German ZPO § 32; BGH 15 Nov. 1993, BGHZ 124, 237, at 245.

Among the bases of general jurisdiction recognized by some legal orders for asserting adjudicatory authority but not accepted in American theory and practice are:

(1) Nationality of the Plaintiff. Article 14 of the Civil Code of France provides that"[a]n alien, even one not residing in France, may be summoned before the French courts for the fulfillment of obligations contracted by him in France with a French person; he may be brought before the French courts for obligations contracted by him in a foreign country toward French people." Article 14 jurisdiction has been severely criticized even in France. No treaty on recognition of foreign judgments concluded by France with another country provides for recognition of a French judgment based on Article 14. Nonetheless, the French courts have consistently refused to exploit possibilities for limiting the Article's scope. For example, Article 14 is applicable to any French national regardless of whether he is domiciled in France, and is not limited to consensual arrangements such as contract. For the history of Article 14, see von Mehren & Trautman, *Multistate Problems,* 668-670.

(2) Unlimited Jurisdiction based on the local presence of property: Section 23 of the German ZPO provides:

> For complaints asserting pecuniary claims against a person who has no domicile within the country, the court of the district within which this person has property, or within which is found the object claimed by the complaint, has jurisdiction. Where the property is in the nature of a debt owed the defendant, the debtor's domicile is considered the place where the property is located, and when the claim is secured, the place where the security is located is also so considered.

Section 23 is available to foreign as well as German plaintiffs. Neither this section nor the decisions applying it distinguish between tangible and intangible assets. Nor is the judgment resulting from an assertion of § 23 jurisdiction in any way limited to the value of the assets on which jurisdiction is based. A proposal to limit § 23 was made and rejected in the Reichstag committee that considered the provision. See P. v. M., 4 R.G.Z. 408, 410-11 (2d Civ. Sen., Apr. 29, 1881). The committee explained:

> Usually, of course, the plaintiff will not utilize this basis for jurisdiction when he cannot expect any satisfaction out of the property that the defendant has in the district. But a plaintiff is not precluded from using this basis for jurisdiction in cases in which such satisfaction cannot be expected. And in some situations this makes considerable sense. The creditor who is inconvenienced by his debtor's lack of domicile, may seek, for the time being, only a judgment which he can, at some later opportunity use at once in pursuing his rights.

The German approach to jurisdiction based on local assets was adopted by Austria and Japan. See Nadelmann, *Jurisdictionally Improper Fora,* 330. Reportedly, in a paternity suit in Austria, the court secured jurisdiction over French skier

Jean-Claude Killy by seizing a pair of his underwear left in a hotel in Austria. See Siegel, *In Vagrant Verse*, 62–63.

(3) Retaliatory Jurisdiction. In response to exorbitant jurisdictional provisions, some countries adopted retaliatory jurisdictional provisions. For example, prior to 1995, under Article 4(4) of the Italian Code of Civil Procedure, an Italian court had jurisdiction over a suit involving a foreign defendant if a court in the foreigner's home state would have had jurisdiction in an identical case against an Italian citizen. Article 4 was repealed by Article 73 of the Law of 31 May 1995.

(4) England's Rule 6.20. In England, the primary bases for jurisdiction are service within the forum and submission. See J.G. Collier, *Conflict of Laws* 72 (3rd ed. 2001). In other cases, the plaintiff may seek permission from the court to serve process outside of England. (Service of the writ confers jurisdiction.) Such permission is governed by Civil Procedure Rule 6.20, which is set out below. It replaced Order 11 of the Supreme Court Rules in 2000. The case law establishes that the decision to grant permission is a matter of discretion which in close cases should be exercised in the defendant's favor. The court will consider factors that American courts would address under the label of *forum non conveniens,* such as convenience and the availability of alternative fora. See id. at 75. Rule 6.20 provides:

* * * [A] claim form may be served out of the jurisdiction with the permission of the court if –

General Grounds. (1) a claim is made for a remedy against a person domiciled within the jurisdiction. (2) a claim is made for an injunction ordering the defendant to do or refrain from doing an act within the jurisdiction. (3) a claim is made against someone on whom the claim form has been or will be served and – (a) there is between the claimant and that person a real issue which it is reasonable for the court to try; and (b) the claimant wishes to serve the claim form on another person who is a necessary or proper party to that claim. (3A) a claim is a [* * * counter] claim and the person to be served is a necessary or proper party to the claim against the [* * * counter] claimant.

Claims for interim remedies. (4) a claim is made for an interim remedy * * *.

Claims in relation to contracts. (5) a claim is made in respect of a contract where the contract – (a) was made within the jurisdiction; (b) was made by or through an agent trading or residing within the jurisdiction; (c) is governed by English law; or (d) contains a term to the effect that the court shall have jurisdiction to determine any claim in respect of the contract. (6) a claim is made in respect of a breach of contract committed within the jurisdiction. (7) a claim is made for a declaration that no contract exists where, if the contract was found to exist, it would comply with the conditions set out in paragraph (5).

Claims in tort. (8) a claim is made in tort where – (a) damage was sustained within the jurisdiction; or (b) the damage sustained resulted from an act committed within the jurisdiction.

Enforcement. (9) a claim is made to enforce any judgment or arbitral award.

Claims about property within the jurisdiction. (10) the whole subject matter of a claim relates to property located within the jurisdiction.

Claims about trusts etc. (11) a claim is made for any remedy which might be obtained in proceedings to execute the trusts of a written instrument where – (a) the trusts ought to be executed according to English law; and (b) the person on whom the claim form is to be served is a trustee of the trusts. (12) a claim is made for any remedy which might be obtained in proceedings for the administration of the estate of a person who died domiciled within the jurisdiction. (13) a claim is made in probate proceedings which includes a claim for the rectification of a will. (14) a claim is made for a remedy against the defendant as constructive trustee where the defendant's alleged liability arises out of acts committed within the jurisdiction. (15) a claim is made for restitution where the defendant's alleged liability arises out of acts committed within the jurisdiction.

* * *

Admiralty claims. (17A) a claim is– (a) in the nature of salvage and any part of the services took place within the jurisdiction; or (b) to enforce a claim under section 153, 154 or 175 of the Merchant Shipping Act 1995(a).

* * *

3. GERMAN THEORIES OF ADJUDICATORY AUTHORITY

Doctrinal and theoretical considerations have played a much less important role for jurisdictional theory and practice in Germany than in the United States. Several considerations explain this difference: Germany achieved political unity in 1871; with respect to adjudicatory authority, the Reich was--nd the Bundesrepublik remains--a centralized rather than a federal state. In 1877, the adjudicatory authority of German courts was regulated by national legislation which basically applied the same rules to venue and to jurisdiction to adjudicate in the international sense. As would be expected, so long as this linkage was accepted the resulting claims of adjudicatory authority were reasonable; moreover, for the most part, the rules adopted could be satisfactorily explained as well in terms of power as of fairness. In this formative period, German economic and social life was relatively localized; so far as adjudicatory authority was concerned, jurists were not under pressure to provide theoretical explanations and justifications and courts were comfortable in their role as expounders and appliers of the relevant statutory provisions.

Constitutional and Statutory Framework. The Constitution of the Reich gave the federal government broad powers in various fields, including civil procedure, the organization of courts, bankruptcy, criminal law, and criminal procedure.[1] In 1877, the Code of Civil Procedure (*Zivilprozeßordnung*) was enacted. The ZPO contains

---

1. Under the Constitution of 1871, the federal power extended to commercial law, bills of exchange, and obligations. In 1873, the Constitution was amended to extend the federal power over the entire field of private law.

the basic provisions on which still today rest German thinking and practice respecting jurisdiction to adjudicate in the international sense. Although the Code has undergone significant changes in some areas, these changes have not affected appreciably jurisdiction to adjudicate.[2] By and large, the Code treats venue and jurisdiction together and in the same way. This unitary approach was so self evident for the drafters that neither through explicit statement nor terminology[3] does the ZPO make clear to the uninitiated that provisions such as § 12 apply, at one and the same time, to venue (*örtliche Zuständigkeit*) and to adjudicatory authority in the international sense (*internationale Zuständigkeit*). ZPO § 12 reads as follows:

> *Concept of allgemeiner Gerichtsstand* (*general jurisdiction*). The court, where a person is subject to general jurisdiction, is competent for all actions brought against him except where an exclusive jurisdiction is provided for the action.

ZPO § 13 continues: "The general jurisdiction of a person is determined by his *Wohnsitz* (dwelling place)." As a purely textual matter, §§ 12 and 13 could be read as applicable to venue alone, or to international jurisdiction alone, or to both. The same ambiguity is displayed by the great majority of the jurisdictional provisions that came into force in 1877.

A general theory of adjudicatory jurisdiction can be teased out of Book I, title 2 of the ZPO; however, the Code's drafters made no effort to provide such a theory and were undisturbed by the dissonant note introduced by § 23, see supra (unlimited general jurisdiction based on presence of property, whose value can be insignificant, in the state). Nor is a general theory advanced by the Code as to why venue and jurisdictional rules should, for the most part, be the same. In the Germany of the 1870's, international jurisdiction problems were no doubt neither numerous nor pressing. In all events, the dominant concerns of German jurists at the end of the century were an ongoing effort to establish legal unity while refining and adapting to contemporary circumstances a continental European legal science whose origins trace back to Irnerius's lectures at Bologna at the close of the eleventh century.

With the promulgation of the German Civil Code (BGB) in 1900, the basic institutional, procedural, and substantive elements of the new unified law were in place, but the effort to understand, explicate, and refine the BGB and the other codes had just begun. From World War I to the early 1950's a variety of circumstances hampered the work of jurists: wars, inflation, political turmoil, the rise of the Third Reich in the 1930's, the outbreak of World War II, and the defeat and the Occupation that followed explain in the large part why general theoretical discussion of international adjudicatory authority remained exceedingly sparse. A further contributing reason, of course not specific to Germany, is that until after World War II international economic and social intercourse was far less pervasive, varied, and intense than it has now become.

By the late 1960's the German scene was ready for comprehensive theoretical

---

2. However, the Brussels Convention and Regulation, see infra at 704, has changed German law on this and related matters in many important respects so far as relations within the European Union are concerned.

3. The ZPO uses the term *allgemeiner Gerichtsstand*, which is not specific to either venue or adjudicatory jurisdiction.

discussions of adjudicatory jurisdiction. The reshaping of American jurisdictional theory and practice stemming from the *International Shoe* decision in 1945, was by then well known in Europe. In 1968, moreover, negotiations among members of the European Economic Community on a Convention on Jurisdiction and Enforcement of Foreign Judgments in Civil and Commercial Matters were completed.[4] Further-more, after four years of work,[5] the Hague Conference on Private International Law approved in 1966 a Convention on the Recognition and Enforcement of Foreign Judgments in Civil and Commercial Matters.[6] Preparation of these two Conventions not only stimulated interest in jurisdictional theory and practice, but deepened knowledge and understanding of many legal systems' views respecting these matters.

Not until 1969, did a major German doctrinal work on jurisdiction to adjudicate appear -- Andreas Heldrich's *Internationale Zuständigkeit und anwendbares Recht* (1969). This treatise signaled the renewed German interest in adjudicatory authority in international litigation and recognition and enforcement of foreign judgments. For a discussion of the practice that began in 1969, see von Mehren, *Adjudicatory Authority*, 142-178.

Both American and German thinking and practice respecting adjudicatory authority in the international sense are far more probing and sophisticated today than when the 20th century began. American and German jurists explore many of the same themes; the solutions they propose are often quite different. German jurists typically have greater faith in, and place more emphasis on, jurisdictional requirements--couched in relatively objective terms--which are not unduly difficult to administer and yield reasonably predictable results. Their American counterparts are more willing to work with open-ended propositions that take into account the circumstances of particular cases.

The greater variety and complexity of the American jurisdictional scene, as compared with the German, is due in part to the fact that jurisdictional law in the United States has traditionally been largely the province of the individual states of the Union. The federal control exercised over state claims of adjudicatory authority is still today for the most part limited to judicial curbs, imposed on constitutional grounds, over exorbitant state claims of adjudicatory authority; federal legislation does not establish the jurisdictional bases on which state courts can claim adjudicatory authority. Each state can go its own way, so far as jurisdiction is concerned, subject to a vacillating fact-specific control exercised by the Supreme Court of the United States under the Due Process Clause of the Fourteenth Amendment.

In Germany, on the other hand, since 1871 the central government has regulated through legislation the bases on which adjudicatory jurisdiction in the

---

4. Sept. 28, 1968, 1262 U.N.T.S. 153. Negotiation on the Brussels Convention began in 1959. The Convention entered into force in 1973 for the original Contracting States (Belgium, France, Federal Republic of Germany, Italy, Luxembourg, and The Netherlands)

5. See Conférence de La Haye de droit internationale privé, Actes et documents de la session extraordinaire 13 au 26 avril 1966: Éxécution des jugements (1969).

6. February 1, 1971, 1144 U.N.T.S. 249. Having been signed by Cyprus, The Netherlands, and Portugal, the convention has technically entered into force. However, it is not in effect because the aforesaid States have not concluded the required bilateral agreements, nor are they likely to do so.

international sense may be exercised. Due in part to the relatively unsophisticated nature of German thinking respecting jurisdiction at the time these rules were first enacted, they were largely derived from provisions respecting venue, a far less complex matter than adjudicatory authority in the international sense. For both historical and institutional reasons, until relatively recently court-administered due-process standards could not play an important role in German jurisdictional theory and practice. Only after World War II was the Federal Constitutional Court given authority to set aside legislation or other forms of governmental action on the ground that a constitutional requirement of natural justice or due process was violated. The legislature, not a high court applying constitutional standards, determined the jurisdictional bases that courts could invoke.

Differences in the historical and institutional circumstances that these two legal orders faced explain to a considerable extent why their juristic theories and practices today differ significantly. In the course of the 20th Century, as American and German jurists gave increasing weight to teleological considerations, both came to see jurisdiction as a more complex problem than their predecessors had realized. To some extent, moreover, the constitutional differences narrowed as the German Constitutional Court began to subject governmental action to constitutional standards derived from the Basic Law of 1949.

Notes and Questions

1. In the Commission charged in 1949 with the preparation of a possible revision of the French Civil Code which never materialized, the following discussion of Articles 14 and 15 occurred:

PRESIDENT [DE LA MORANDIÈRE]: In my youth the writers were rather hostile to the maintenance of this rule. It is true that euphoria ruled in international relations. Do these articles really have great practical importance? Are they often and deliberately used by French nationals? I ask the judges.

MR. ANCEL: I do not believe that these articles are very often applied; however, the rule is a traditional one. Under present conditions its maintenance can easily be understood. In a world better ordered than our own, one in which international relations were normal, such a rule would seem archaic.

PRESIDENT: I believe that this was the thought of the Sub–Commission which retained this rule without enthusiasm, regretting that the present state of international organization did not permit its abandonment.

[1949–1950] Travaux de la Commission de Reforme du Code Civil 730 (1951), translated in Nadelmann & von Mehren, *Remarks on the Proposed Codification,* 415. What aspects of world conditions might Judge Ancel had have in mind?

2. The Belgian system--the European system standing closest to the French in its traditions, rules, and institutions–repealed Article 14 and at the same time provided for general adjudicatory jurisdiction on the basis of property located in the country. Did this change represent an improvement?

3. How would cases such as *World-Wide Volkswagen, Burger King, Asahi*

and *Burnham*, supra Ch. 8, be decided under England's Rule 6.20?

4. Do you think England's Rule 6.20 adequately protects the rights of defendants and plaintiffs? Does Rule 6.20 unduly interfere with the sovereignty of other nations?

5. Would it be a good idea if Congress were to enact legislation which would regulate adjudicatory authority in international litigation in the United States? Would such a statute be constitutional? Should the United States support efforts to fashion a broadly acceptable convention regulating jurisdiction in international cases? See the effort by the International Jurisdiction and Judgment Project of the American Law Institute (ALI)[1]; von Mehren, *A New Approach*, 271 ff.; Lowenfeld, *Reaction to the von Mehren Report*, 289 ff.; von Mehren, *International Control of Civil Procedure*, 13 ff.; Adler, *If We Build it, Will They Come?* 79 ff.; van Boeschoten, *A European View*, 47 ff.

E. REGULATION OF ADJUDICATORY AUTHORITY BY INTERNATIONAL CONVENTIONS

In the course of the 20th century, cross-border activity in most, if not all, areas of social, intellectual, and commercial activity increased significantly in both volume and intensity. Our lives as individuals, as members of groups and associations economic, political, and social in nature, as citizens of nations, and as members of the human race have become increasingly "delocalized." In many respects, we lead far more globalized lives than our forefathers did when the 19th century ended.

These changes in our world's infrastructure and conditions of living have profoundly affected almost every aspect of our existence. The problems created and the forces released have many consequences, some profound--others trivial, some conflicting--others harmonious or convergent. These developments have led to international efforts to regulate various aspects of the rules and practices of private international law including those that address jurisdiction to adjudicate and recognition and enforcement of foreign judgments.

In its nature, private international law is concerned with contexts in which two or more legal orders have a significant stake. Efforts to provide mechanisms for handling controversies respecting such matters began in ancient times and have continued ever since. Interest in establishing through multilateral international instruments, various rules and practices of private international law grew in the last half of the 19th century. One consequence was the creation in 1893 of the Hague Conference on Private International Law. Efforts to "conventionalize" areas of private international law continued throughout the 20th century; its closing decades saw the entrance into force of the United Nations Convention on the Recognition and Enforcement of Foreign Arbitral Awards of 1958, the European Union's Brussels Convention on jurisdiction and the enforcement of judgments in civil and commercial matters of 1968, and the Lugano Convention of 1988. In the century's last decade, the Hague Conference began work on a world-wide convention on

---

1. For the present stage of this project see the ALI website at <http://www.ali.org/>.

jurisdiction and the recognition and enforcement of foreign judgments.

Traditionally, treaties dealing with jurisdiction and enforcement matters were single; they regulated recognition and enforcement-- indirect jurisdiction-- but not direct jurisdiction--adjudicatory authority. Double conventions--treaties that address both jurisdiction to adjudicate and recognition and enforcement of foreign judgments--do not appear until the second half of the 20th century. The pioneering multilateral double convention was the United Nations Convention on the Recognition and Enforcement of Foreign Arbitral Awards of 1958 which, despite its title, regulates not only recognition, but also jurisdiction to adjudicate.

1. The Brussels Convention and Regulation

In 1968, the first double convention to deal broadly with both jurisdiction and recognition appeared, the Brussels Convention on jurisdiction and the enforcement of judgments in civil and commercial matters.[1] As a full-fledged double convention must, Brussels required that certain bases of jurisdiction be made available, prohibits the use of all other jurisdictional bases, and mandates that all judgments rendered on convention-required bases be, subject to certain prescribed defenses, recognized and enforced in all States party to the convention.

The Brussels Convention had initiated a new epoch in the effort to achieve international agreement on issues of adjudicatory authority and enforcement of foreign judgments. Unlike most previous conventions in this area, Brussels was not a universal but a regional convention. It achieved a degree of agreement respecting these matters far greater than that of any previous international instrument. In this the drafters were greatly assisted by the circumstance that the legal cultures of the six original Member States--Belgium, France, The Federal Republic of Germany, Italy, Luxembourg, and The Netherlands--had, in many respects, already been harmonized by historical forces. The high degree of harmonization that the drafters of Brussels sought to--and did--achieve, would doubtless have been far more elusive had the United Kingdom, representing the common-law tradition, been at the negotiating table in Brussels.

Due ultimately to the gathering economic and political momentum of the movement towards a European federation, the Brussels mold, set in 1968, proved to be unbreakable. States that had crafted a regional convention to advance an emerging economic and political union, had little need or incentive to strike meaningful compromises with States that, after 1973, aspired to join that union. The club offered admission only on a take-it-or-leave-it basis.

Reflecting the increasing economic and political integration of Europe, the

---

1. Some federal systems, in particular the United States, have long provided functional approximations of double conventions. Technically, the American system specifies prohibited, but not required, bases; states may, but are not constitutionally required to, invoke jurisdiction if the claim of adjudicatory authority is constitutionally permissible. In American practice, constitutionally permitted bases can be seen as equivalent to required bases in the sense that, generally speaking, every state takes jurisdiction where the Constitution permits. States are, of course, required by the full faith and credit clause of the federal constitution to recognize and enforce sister-state judgments rendered on a constitutionally acceptable basis of adjudicatory authority.

Brussels Convention was, for most purposes, replaced in 2002 by the Brussels Regulation (known as "Brussels II"). The latter's text follows closely that of the Convention as it stood at the close of the 20th Century.

THE BRUSSELS REGULATION

Council Regulation (EC) No 44/2001 of 22 December 2000 on jurisdiction and the recognition and enforcement of judgments in civil and commercial matters

* * *

CHAPTER II. JURISDICTION
Section 1. General provisions

Article 2. 1. Subject to this Regulation, persons domiciled in a Member State shall, whatever their nationality, be sued in the courts of that Member State.

2. Persons who are not nationals of the Member State in which they are domiciled shall be governed by the rules of jurisdiction applicable to nationals of that State.

Article 3. 1. Persons domiciled in a Member State may be sued in the courts of another Member State only by virtue of the rules set out in Sections 2 to 7 of this Chapter.

2. In particular the rules of national jurisdiction [* * *] shall not be applicable as against them[:

- in France: Articles 14 and 15 of the civil code (Code civil),

* * *

- in the United Kingdom: the rules which enable jurisdiction to be founded on:

　(a) the document instituting the proceedings having been served on the defendant during his temporary presence in the United Kingdom; or

　(b) the presence within the United Kingdom of property belonging to the defendant; or

　(c) the seizure by the plaintiff of property situated in the United Kingdom.[2]]

Article 4. 1. If the defendant is not domiciled in a Member State, the jurisdiction of the courts of each Member State shall, subject to Articles 22 and 23, be determined by the law of that Member State.

2. As against such a defendant, any person domiciled in a Member State may, whatever his nationality, avail himself in that State of the rules of jurisdiction there in force, and in particular those specified in Annex I, in the same way as the nationals of that State.

Section 2. Special jurisdiction

Article 5. A person domiciled in a Member State may, in another Member State, be sued:

1. (a) in matters relating to a contract, in the courts for the place of performance of the obligation in question;

　(b) for the purpose of this provision and unless otherwise agreed, the place

---

2.　The national laws reproduced here in brackets are contained in Annex I of the Convention.

of performance of the obligation in question shall be:

- in the case of the sale of goods, the place in a Member State where, under the contract, the goods were delivered or should have been delivered,

- in the case of the provision of services, the place in a Member State where, under the contract, the services were provided or should have been provided,

(c) if subparagraph (b) does not apply then subparagraph (a) applies;

2. in matters relating to maintenance, in the courts for the place where the maintenance creditor is domiciled or habitually resident or, if the matter is ancillary to proceedings concerning the status of a person, in the court which, according to its own law, has jurisdiction to entertain those proceedings, unless that jurisdiction is based solely on the nationality of one of the parties;

3. in matters relating to tort, delict or quasi-delict, in the courts for the place where the harmful event occurred or may occur;

4. as regards a civil claim for damages or restitution which is based on an act giving rise to criminal proceedings, in the court seised of those proceedings, to the extent that that court has jurisdiction under its own law to entertain civil proceedings;

5. as regards a dispute arising out of the operations of a branch, agency or other establishment, in the courts for the place in which the branch, agency or other establishment is situated;

6. as settlor, trustee or beneficiary of a trust created by the operation of a statute, or by a written instrument, or created orally and evidenced in writing, in the courts of the Member State in which the trust is domiciled;

7. as regards a dispute concerning the payment of remuneration claimed in respect of the salvage of a cargo or freight, in the court under the authority of which the cargo or freight in question: (a) has been arrested to secure such payment, or (b) could have been so arrested, but bail or other security has been given; provided that this provision shall apply only if it is claimed that the defendant has an interest in the cargo or freight or had such an interest at the time of salvage.

Article 6. A person domiciled in a Member State may also be sued:

1. where he is one of a number of defendants, in the courts for the place where any one of them is domiciled, provided the claims are so closely connected that it is expedient to hear and determine them together to avoid the risk of irreconcilable judgments resulting from separate proceedings;

2. as a third party in an action on a warranty or guarantee or in any other third party proceedings, in the court seised of the original proceedings, unless these were instituted solely with the object of removing him from the jurisdiction of the court which would be competent in his case;

3. on a counter-claim arising from the same contract or facts on which the original claim was based, in the court in which the original claim is pending;

4. in matters relating to a contract, if the action may be combined with an action against the same defendant in matters relating to rights in rem in immovable property, in the court of the Member State in which the property is situated.

* * *

Section 4 Jurisdiction over consumer contracts

Article 15. 1. In matters relating to a contract concluded by a person, the consumer, for a purpose which can be regarded as being outside his trade or profession, jurisdiction shall be determined by this Section, without prejudice to Article 4 and point 5 of Article 5, if: (a) it is a contract for the sale of goods on instalment credit terms; or (b) it is a contract for a loan repayable by instalments, or for any other form of credit, made to finance the sale of goods; or (c) in all other cases, the contract has been concluded with a person who pursues commercial or professional activities in the Member State of the consumer's domicile or, by any means, directs such activities to that Member State or to several States including that Member State, and the contract falls within the scope of such activities.

2. Where a consumer enters into a contract with a party who is not domiciled in the Member State but has a branch, agency or other establishment in one of the Member States, that party shall, in disputes arising out of the operations of the branch, agency or establishment, be deemed to be domiciled in that State.

3. This Section shall not apply to a contract of transport other than a contract which, for an inclusive price, provides for a combination of travel and accommodation.

Article 16. 1. A consumer may bring proceedings against the other party to a contract either in the courts of the Member State in which that party is domiciled or in the courts for the place where the consumer is domiciled.

2. Proceedings may be brought against a consumer by the other party to the contract only in the courts of the Member State in which the consumer is domiciled.

3. This Article shall not affect the right to bring a counter-claim in the court in which, in accordance with this Section, the original claim is pending.

Article 17. The provisions of this Section may be departed from only by an agreement:

1. which is entered into after the dispute has arisen; or

2. which allows the consumer to bring proceedings in courts other than those indicated in this Section; or

3. which is entered into by the consumer and the other party to the contract, both of whom are at the time of conclusion of the contract domiciled or habitually resident in the same Member State, and which confers jurisdiction on the courts of that Member State, provided that such an agreement is not contrary to the law of that Member State.

2. The Unsuccessful Effort to Produce a Hague Convention on International Jurisdiction and Foreign Judgments

In October 1996, the Hague Conference began an effort to draft an international convention on jurisdiction, recognition and enforcement of foreign judgements in civil and commercial matters.[3] By June 2001, after five years of work, it became apparent that the effort had reached an impasse, and that the Member States were unable to reach agreement on a number of major areas, including: the Internet and e-commerce; activity-based jurisdiction; consumer and employment contracts; and patents, trademarks, copyrights and other intellectual property rights.

What does the failure to reach agreement on the Convention suggest about future such efforts? Professor von Mehren has argued:

> In the first half of the twentieth century, international instruments dealing with private international law, including jurisdiction and recognition and enforcement of judgments, were either bilateral or universal in character. Harmonization on a bilateral basis was, by and large, compatible with efforts to achieve harmonization on a worldwide basis. The former prepared the ground for--and supplemented--the latter.
>
> The second half of the century witnessed the rise of a third type of international instrument, one multilateral in nature but regional rather than universal in scope. In 1968, the Brussels Convention changed fundamentally the role of international instruments in the area of jurisdiction and enforcement of foreign judgments by harmonizing the law respecting these matters on a regional basis. To the bilateral and the universal approaches to harmonization, a regional approach was thus added. The regional and universal approaches have, at least so far, proved to be incompatible where harmonization of the general law of jurisdiction to adjudicate and recognition and enforcement of foreign judgments is concerned. Put another way, once a regional harmonization of these matters is in place, the incentive for the parties to the regional instrument to harmonize the same area of law on a universal basis is greatly reduced.
>
> If this analysis is correct, universal instruments cannot hope to harmonize effectively the general areas of private international law once effective regional harmonizations, dealing broadly with the subject matter, are in place. The most that can then be accomplished is to provide a general convention to fill the space not yet occupied by existing regional harmonizations. Such a general harmonization will, however, find it difficult to attract support.

von Mehren, *Adjudicatory Authority*, 423-24.

Nonetheless, there are certainly areas as to which universal conventions offer significant advantages over regional ones. Child abduction and adoption are two such areas and these are addressed by two Hague Conventions – the Convention of October 1980 on the Civil Aspects of International Child Abduction and that of 22 May 1993 on Protection of Children and Co-Operation in Respect of Intercountry Adoption. It remains to be seen what the Hague Conference can accomplish in other areas.

---

3. Final Act of the Eighteenth Session, Part B, No. 1., 35 I.L.M. 1391, at 1405 (1996). For an account of another member of the U.S. Delegation of the negotiations, see Brand, *In Search of a Global Convention*, 11-32.

Notes and Questions

1. In a recent symposium held in Barcelona, Professor Willibald Posh has argued that sociological differences are at the root of the failure of the Hague Conference on Private International Law to agree on a convention addressing jurisdiction to adjudicate and recognition of judgments. See Posh, *Resolving Business Disputes.* What differences might he have in mind? Do you agree with him?

Professor Stephen Burbank, a participant in the same symposium, described one "important . . . legal difference that has obvious legal impact":

> In many developed countries in the western world the State directly affords, or provides administrative or other mechanisms that afford, assistance to those who have been injured to a greater degree than in the United States, where as a result litigation picks up the slack. The same is true of mechanisms to vindicate important regulatory interests. These differences reflect in the fundamental differences in attitudes towards the proper role of the State and of private initiatives in ordering social life, with predictable effects on general attitudes towards not only litigation but also the status quo and how, if at all, it should be altered.
>
> From this perspective, however regrettable the contingent fee, the American Rule on cost-shifting, and the institution of the jury trial in civil cases may appear to a European, they are logical incidents of a system that distrusts government, that leans heavily on private litigation to compensate for injury and to enforce important social norms, but that does not provide legal aid that is worthy of the name.[5] And from this perspective it is not only the self-interest of entrepreneurial American plaintiff's lawyers that prompts resistance to attempts to reduce the availability of litigation forums in the United States when an American alleges injury for which a foreign enterprise may be legally responsible and/or where the activities of that foreign enterprise are alleged to trigger an American regulatory interest. Forced to pursue vindication thousand of miles from home, and without alternative (that is, non-litigation) means of vindication, our putative American plaintiff might lose not only favorable substantive law but that which experience suggests may be more important in many cases, to wit, that ability to secure representation and to develop evidence necessary to establish liability (discovery).

Burbank, *Paths to a Via Media*, __. For discussion of differences regarding American and European attitudes towards punitive damages, see Symeonides, *Punitive Damages Conflicts*,§§1.2, 2.5, 8.2. See also Behr, *Punitive Damages in American and German Law*.

2. In light of the above differences are you confident that a successful universal convention regulating jurisdiction to adjudicate and recognition and enforcement of the resulting judgments can be produced by the Hague Conference within the next two decades? In the longer run? How do you see the future?

---

5. Any doubt on that score as to the contingency fee should forever have been banished when our friends in England, who for more than a century derided contingency fee litigation "litigation on spec," adopted its genteel cousin, the conditional fee, as a result of inability any longer adequately to fund legal aid. See Burbank, The Roles of Litigation, 80 Wash.U.L.Q. 705, 710-11 (2002)

Part III

RECOGNITION OF JUDGMENTS

Chapter 10

RECOGNITION OF
SISTER-STATE JUDGMENTS

If a judgment is to be effective, at some point we must treat it as final and enforceable. Accordingly, all states have rules of res judicata, or preclusion, which delineate the extent to which a prior judgment must be enforced or treated as preclusive in subsequent litigation. While states are free to adopt their own rules for intrastate recognition of judgments, federal law--primarily the Full Faith and Credit Clause and the Full Faith and Credit Statute, now codified at 28 U.S.C. § 1738-- controls interstate recognition of judgments.

This chapter focuses on interstate enforceability of judgments. However, we begin by briefly reviewing intrastate res judicata which has underlying policies similar to those in the interstate arena.

A. AN OVERVIEW OF RES JUDICATA RULES

A simple case illustrates the basic rules of res judicata.[1] Suppose that Mrs. Rush hits a pothole while riding her motorcycle. She is injured and the motorcycle is damaged. Mrs. Rush sues the city seeking reimbursement for the damage to the motorcycle, alleging that the city negligently failed to maintain the roads. Her complaint mentions nothing about personal injury. Her suit is successful, and she is awarded $100. Could she bring a second suit alleging the damage to her motorcycle was greater than $100? Could the city resist an enforcement proceeding, alleging that the award was too high or that it has a wonderful defense that it neglected to raise? In every jurisdiction, the answer to both these questions is no. The doctrine of *claim preclusion*, sometimes called *res judicata*, would treat the judgment as a conclusive adjudication of both the question of liability and the amount of damages. The prior litigation adjudicated Mrs. Rush's claim for damage to her motorcycle, and future litigation concerning the same claim is prohibited.

Suppose that Mrs. Rush files a second law suit, but this case seeks money for her personal injury. Personal injury was never raised in the first case and therefore was not actually adjudicated. Could the plaintiff bring this second suit? Most states

---

1. These facts are based on the case of Rush v. City of Maple Heights, 167 Ohio St. 221, 147 N.E.2d 599 (Ohio), *cert. denied*, 358 U.S. 814 (1958).

would prohibit the second suit, again relying on claim preclusion. The first litigation is deemed to have adjudicated the entire claim, even those aspects of the claim that were never actually litigated. States differ in how broadly they construe "claim" for preclusion purposes. The trend in this country is to define "the claim" as including "all rights of the plaintiff to remedies against the defendant with respect to all or any part of the transaction, or series of connected transactions, out of which the action arose." Restatement (Second) of Judgments § 24(1) (1982). Despite growing acceptance of the Restatement approach, some states retain narrower and more formal approaches which focus on whether the same legal "rights" or legal "wrongs" are involved in the second suit. A state that uses one of these narrower approaches might allow a subsequent suit for personal injury.[2]

A judgment must meet three criteria before it can have preclusive effect. First, the judgment must be *valid*. A judgment that violates due process, such as one entered without personal jurisdiction or without proper notice, is not valid and will not be given preclusive effect. See id. § 1. Second, the judgment must be *final*. An interlocutory or interim order will not have preclusive effect. However, a judgment may be considered final even if an appeal is pending. Finally, the judgment must be "*on the merits.*" This commonly used phrase is somewhat misleading. It means that claim preclusion does not bar a second suit on the same claim where the first judgment is a dismissal for lack of jurisdiction, improper venue, or improper joinder, or where the plaintiff is granted a dismissal "without prejudice." See id. § 20. However, the court need not have actually reached "the merits." A dismissal for failure to prosecute or as a sanction for discovery abuse and a default judgment are all judgments that would be given preclusive effect. See 18A Wright, Miller & Cooper, *Federal Practice* § 4435.

In addition to claim preclusion, many states, as well as the federal courts, have compulsory counterclaim rules.[3] A defendant who fails to raise a compulsory counterclaim is precluded from suing on that counterclaim in subsequent litigation. See Restatement (Second) of Judgments § 22.

Returning to our motorcycle hypothetical, suppose that Mr. Rush was a passenger on the motorcycle and he brings suit against the city for his injuries. The first question is whether his claim is precluded by virtue of his wife's prior suit. It would not be precluded. First, all states would agree that Mr. Rush's claim is a different claim from Mrs. Rush's claim. See id. § 34(3). Even the broad Restatement definition of claim includes only the rights of "*the* plaintiff to remedies against *the* defendant" (emphasis added). Second, Mr. Rush was not a party to the prior litigation and due process prevents giving preclusive effect to judgments in a manner that would deny a person who was not a party (or otherwise fully and fairly represented) his or her day in court. See Richards v. Jefferson County, 517 U.S. 793 (1996).

Even though Mr. Rush's case involves a different claim than that in Mrs. Rush's

---

2. Likewise in many foreign jurisdictions, a subsequent claim for personal injury would not be precluded.

3. Under Fed. R. Civ.P. 13(a), a compulsory counterclaim arises out of the same transaction or series of connected transactions, out of which the action arose.

suit, there may be a number of issues that are common to both suits. For example, whether the city negligently failed to maintain the road may be central to both cases. When an issue has been fully litigated and decided, the principle of *issue preclusion* may apply and prevent relitigation of that issue. The basic principle of issue preclusion is that once an issue has been fully litigated and decided, that determination should be given effect in other litigation raising the same issue. The primary motivation for issue preclusion, sometimes called *collateral estoppel*, is efficiency. Once an issue has been decided, it is a waste of time and court resources to present and evaluate the same evidence again. (Notice that issue preclusion can only arise if the second suit involves a different claim; otherwise, claim preclusion would prevent the second suit). See Restatement (Second) of Judgments § 27.

The availability of issue preclusion also depends on the parties involved. As has been noted above, a person ordinarily cannot be bound by litigation to which he or she was not a party. Therefore, if Mrs. Rush had lost her case, a finding of no liability on the part of the city could not be used against Mr. Rush because he was not a party to her case. But if Mrs. Rush won her suit, could the liability finding be used against the city in the second suit by Mr. Rush? The city had its day in court in the first suit; thus, we do not have a due process problem. Nonetheless, the traditional approach would not allow Mr. Rush to take advantage of the city's prior loss to Mrs. Rush because of a lack of "mutuality." Under this traditional approach, a litigant could use issue preclusion only if that litigant was himself bound by the prior adjudication. The basic concern is one of fairness. Mr. Rush, because he was not a party to the first case, could simply wait and see the result of that case. If the city won, Mr. Rush would not be bound, but if the city lost, Mr. Rush could take advantage of the ruling. Thus, the risks posed to Mr. Rush and to the city would not be reciprocal, and many courts found unfair this lack of mutual risk. The requirement of mutuality has been abandoned in many states as well as in federal court, but some states retain the traditional doctrine.

In Parklane Hosiery Co. v. Shore, 439 U.S. 322 (1979), the Supreme Court abandoned the requirement of mutuality in federal courts. In a prior case, Parklane Hosiery had been sued in federal court by the S.E.C. for alleged violations of federal securities laws. The Court found that Parklane's proxy statement was false and misleading and awarded the S.E.C. injunctive relief. Parklane was then sued by a shareholder seeking damages for the same securities violations about which the S.E.C. had sued. The Supreme Court declined to apply a categorical rule and instead held that in cases such as this of non-mutual offensive issue preclusion, trial courts have discretion to determine whether to apply issue preclusion. "The general rule should be that in cases where a plaintiff could easily have joined in the earlier action or where * * * the application of offensive estoppel would be unfair to a defendant, a trial judge should not allow the use of offensive collateral estoppel." Id. at 331. Under the facts of *Parklane*, the Court held that preclusion was appropriate. Subsequent to *Parklane*, the Court added another exception. In United States v. Mendoza, 464 U.S. 154 (1984), the Court held that a plaintiff could not use non-mutual preclusion against the government because allowing its use "would substantially thwart the development of important questions of law by freezing the first final decision rendered on a particular legal issue." 464 U.S. at 160.

In addition to the mutuality problem, courts recognize some exceptions to the general rule of issue preclusion. See Restatement (Second) of Judgments § 28. For example, most courts will not give effect to a prior determination when there were significant differences in the procedures available or in the incentives to litigate vigorously. Thus, a determination made in small claims court in which there was only a small amount at stake would probably not be given preclusive effect in a second suit in which hundreds of thousands of dollars are at stake.

The rules of preclusion put a priority on finality, repose, and the efficient resolution of disputes. These values must sometimes be balanced against the conflicting values of assuring correct and just results. As Judge Learned Hand observed, the rules of preclusion "must be treated as a compromise between two conflicting interests: the convenience of avoiding a multiplicity of suits and the adequacy of the remedies afforded for conceded wrongs." Lyons v. Westinghouse Elec. Corp., 222 F.2d 184, 189 (2d Cir.1955). Each jurisdiction must make its own judgment as to how best to strike that balance in intrastate enforcement of judgments. When we move to *inter*state enforcement of judgments, we confront a classic issue in conflict of laws—to what extent may an enforcing state strike a different balance than did the rendering state? It is to this problem that we now turn.

B. FULL FAITH AND CREDIT TO INTERSTATE JUDGMENTS

In Chapter 5, we examined the impact of the Full Faith and Credit Clause and its implementing legislation, 28 U.S.C. § 1738, on choice of law. Here we examine their impact on interstate enforcement of judgments.

1. The Basic Policies

Fauntleroy v. Lum
Supreme Court of the United States, 1908.
210 U.S. 230, 28 S.Ct. 641, 52 L.Ed. 1039.

JUSTICE HOLMES delivered the opinion of the Court. This is an action upon a Missouri judgment brought in a court of Mississippi. The declaration set forth the record of the judgment. The defendant pleaded that the original cause of action arose in Mississippi out of a gambling transaction in cotton futures; that he declined to pay the loss; that the controversy was submitted to arbitration [in Mississippi], the question as to the illegality of the transaction, however, not being included in the submission; that an award was rendered against the defendant; that thereafter, finding the defendant temporarily in Missouri, the plaintiff brought suit there upon the award; that the trial court refused to allow the defendant to show the nature of the transaction and that by the laws of Mississippi the same was illegal and void, but directed a verdict if the jury should find that the submission and award were made, and remained unpaid; and that a verdict was rendered and the judgment in suit entered upon the same. [The plaintiff argued that under the Full Faith and Credit

Clause, Mississippi was required to enforce the judgment. The Mississippi Supreme Court rejected this argument and refused to enforce the judgment.] * * *

The main argument urged by the defendant to sustain the judgment below is addressed to the jurisdiction of the Mississippi courts.

The laws of Mississippi make dealing in futures a misdemeanor, and provide that contracts of that sort, made without intent to deliver the commodity or to pay the price, "shall not be enforced by any court." [cit.] The defendant contends that this language deprives the Mississippi courts of jurisdiction, and that the case is like Anglo-American Provision Co. v. Davis Provision Co., 191 U.S. 373 [1903]. There the New York statutes refused to provide a court into which a foreign corporation could come, except upon causes of action arising within the State, etc., and it was held that the State of New York was under no constitutional obligation to give jurisdiction to its Supreme Court against its will. One question is whether that decision is in point.

No doubt it sometimes may be difficult to decide whether certain words in a statute are directed to jurisdiction or to merits, but the distinction between the two is plain. One goes to the power, the other only to the duty of the Court. Under the common law it is the duty of a court of general jurisdiction not to enter a judgment upon a parol promise made without consideration; but it has power to do it, and, if it does, the judgment is unimpeachable, unless reversed. Yet a statute could be framed that would make the power, that is, the jurisdiction of the Court dependent upon whether there was a consideration or not. Whether a given statute is intended simply to establish a rule of substantive law, and thus to define the duty of the Court, or is meant to limit its power, is a question of construction and common sense. When it affects a court of general jurisdiction and deals with a matter upon which that court must pass, we naturally are slow to read ambiguous words, as meaning to leave the judgment open to dispute, or as intended to do more than to fix the rule by which the court should decide.

The case quoted concerned a statute plainly dealing with the authority and jurisdiction of the New York court. The statute now before us seems to us only to lay down a rule of decision. The Mississippi court in which this action was brought is a court of general jurisdiction and would have to decide upon the validity of the bar, if the suit upon the award or upon the original cause of action had been brought there. The words "shall not be enforced by any court" are simply another, possibly less emphatic, way of saying that an action shall not be brought to enforce such contracts. As suggested by the counsel for the plaintiff in error, no one would say that the words of the Mississippi statute of frauds, "An action shall not be brought whereby to charge a defendant," [cit.] go to the jurisdiction of the Court. Of course it could be argued that logically they had that scope, but common sense would revolt. * * * We regard this question as open under the decisions below, and we have expressed our opinion upon it independent of the effect of the judgment, although it might be that, even if jurisdiction of the original cause of action was withdrawn, it remained with regard to a suit upon a judgment based upon an award, whether the judgment or award was conclusive or not. But it might be held that the law as to jurisdiction on one case followed the law in the other, and therefore we proceed at once to the further question, whether the illegality of the original cause of action in Mississippi can be relied upon there as a ground for denying a recovery upon a judgment of another State.

The doctrine laid down by Chief Justice Marshall was "that the judgment of a state court should have the same credit, validity, and effect in every other court in the United States, which it had in the State where it was pronounced, and that whatever pleas would be good to a suit thereon in such State, and none others, could be pleaded in any other court of the United States." Hampton v. McConnel, 3 Wheat. 234 [1818]. There is no doubt that this quotation was supposed to be an accurate statement of the law as late as Christmas v. Russell, 72 U.S. (5 Wall.) 290 [1866], where an attempt of Mississippi, by statute, to go behind judgments recovered in other States was declared void, and it was held that such judgments could not be impeached even for fraud.

* * *

We assume that the statement of Chief Justice Marshall is correct. It is confirmed by the [Full Faith and Credit Act], providing that the said records and judicial proceedings "shall have such faith and credit given to them in every court within the United States, as they have by law or usage in the courts of the State from whence the said records are or shall be taken." [cit.] Whether the award would or would not have been conclusive, and whether the ruling of the Missouri court upon that matter was right or wrong, there can be no question that the judgment was conclusive in Missouri on the validity of the cause of action. [cit.] A judgment is conclusive as to all the *media concludendi* [cit.]; and it needs no authority to show that it cannot be impeached either in or out of the State by showing that it was based upon a mistake of law. Of course a want of jurisdiction over either the person or the subject-matter might be shown. [cit.] But as the jurisdiction of the Missouri court is not open to dispute the judgment cannot be impeached in Mississippi even if it went upon a misapprehension of the Mississippi law. [cit.]

We feel no apprehensions that painful or humiliating consequences will follow upon our decision. No court would give judgment for a plaintiff unless it believed that the facts were a cause of action by the law determining their effect. Mistakes will be rare. In this case the Missouri court no doubt supposed that the award was binding by the law of Mississippi. If it was mistaken it made a natural mistake. The validity of its judgment, even in Mississippi, is, as we believe, the result of the Constitution as it always has been understood, and is not a matter to arouse the susceptibilities of the States, all of which are equally concerned in the question and equally on both sides.

Judgment reversed.

JUSTICE WHITE, with whom concurred Justice Harlan, Justice McKenna and Justice Day, dissenting. * * *

* * * This court now reverses on the ground that the due faith and credit clause obliged the courts of Mississippi, in consequence of the action of the Missouri court, to give efficacy to transactions in Mississippi which were criminal, and which were against the public policy of that State. Although not wishing in the slightest degree

to weaken the operation of the due faith and credit clause as interpreted and applied from the beginning, it to me seems that this ruling so enlarges that clause as to cause it to obliterate all state lines, since the effect will be to endow each State with authority to overthrow the public policy and criminal statutes of the others, thereby depriving all of their lawful authority. Moreover, the ruling now made, in my opinion, is contrary to the conceptions which caused the due faith and credit clause to be placed in the Constitution, and substantially overrules the previous decisions of this court interpreting that clause. My purpose is to briefly state the reasons which lead me to these conclusions.

The foundation upon which our system of government rests is the possession by the States of the right, except as restricted by the Constitution, to exert their police powers as they may deem best for the happiness and welfare of those subject to their authority. * * * The due faith and credit clause it is now decided means that residents of a State may within such State do acts which are violative of public policy, and yet that a judgment may be rendered in another State giving effect to such transactions, which judgment it becomes the duty of the State whose laws have been set at defiance to enforce. It must follow, if one State by the mere form of a judgment has this power, that no State has in effect the authority to make police regulations, or, what is tantamount to the same thing, is without power to enforce them. * * *

When the Constitution was adopted the principles of comity by which the decrees of the courts of one State were entitled to be enforced in another were generally known, but the enforcement of those principles by the several States had no absolute sanction, since they rested but in comity. Now it cannot be denied that under the rules of comity recognized at the time of the adoption of the Constitution, and which at this time universally prevail, no sovereignty was or is under the slightest moral obligation to give effect of a judgment of a court of another sovereignty, when to do so would compel the State in which the judgment was sought to be executed to enforce an illegal and prohibited contract, when both the contract and all the acts done in connection with its performance had taken place in the latter State. This seems to me conclusive of this case, since both in treatises of authoritative writers (Story, Conflict of Law § 609), and by repeated adjudications of this court it has been settled that the purpose of the due faith and credit clause was not to confer any new power, but simply to make obligatory that duty which, when the Constitution was adopted rested, as has been said, in comity alone. * * *

No special reference has been made by me to the arbitration, because that is assumed by me to be negligible. If the cause of action was open for inquiry for the purpose of deciding whether the Missouri court had jurisdiction to render a judgment entitled to be enforced in another State, the arbitration is of no consequence. The violation of law in Mississippi could not be cured by seeking to arbitrate in that State in order to fix the sum of the fruits of the illegal acts. The ancient maxims that something cannot be made out of nothing, and that which is void for reasons of public policy cannot be made valid by confirmation or acquiescence, seem to my mind decisive.

I therefore dissent.

Yarborough v. Yarborough

Supreme Court of the United States, 1933.
290 U.S. 202, 54 S.Ct. 181, 78 L.Ed. 269.

JUSTICE BRANDEIS delivered the opinion of the Court. On August 10, 1930, Sadie Yarborough, then sixteen years of age, was living with her maternal grandfather, R. D. Blowers, at Spartanburg, South Carolina. Suing by him as guardian ad litem, she brought this action in a court of that State to require her father, W.A. Yarborough, a resident of Atlanta, Georgia, to make provision for her education and maintenance. She alleged "that she is now ready for college and is without funds and, unless the defendant makes provision for her, will be denied the necessities of life and an education, and will be dependent upon the charity of others."[1] Jurisdiction was obtained by attachment of defendant's property. Later he was served personally within South Carolina.

In bar of the action, W. A. Yarborough set up, among other defenses, a judgment entered in 1929 by the Superior Court of Fulton County, Georgia, in a suit for divorce brought by him against Sadie's mother. He alleged that by the judgment the amount thereafter to be paid by him for Sadie's education and maintenance had been determined; that the sum so fixed had been paid; and that the judgment had been fully satisfied by him. He claimed that in Georgia the judgment was conclusive of the matter here in controversy; that having been satisfied, it relieved him, under the Georgia law, of all obligation to provide for the education and maintenance of their minor child; and that the full faith and credit clause of the Federal Constitution (Art. IV, § 1) required the South Carolina court to give to that judgment the same effect in this proceeding which it has, and would have, in Georgia. The trial court denied the claim; ordered W. A. Yarborough to pay to the grandfather, as trustee, fifty dollars monthly for Sadie's education and support; and to pay $300 as fees of her counsel. It directed that the property held under the attachment be transferred to R. D. Blowers, trustee, as security for the performance of the order. The judgment was affirmed by the Supreme Court of South Carolina. * * *

[In the prior divorce proceeding, Mrs. Yarborough had requested permanent alimony for the support of herself and Sadie and for Sadie's education. The court awarded alimony and ordered that $1,750 be put in trust for Sadie for her support, education and other needs. The court decree stated that the amounts awarded were "in full settlement of temporary and permanent alimony ... and in full settlement of all other demands of every nature whatsoever between the parties." Sadie was personally present during these proceedings, but she was not made a party and no guardian ad litem was appointed. Mr. Yarborough complied fully with the alimony and support orders.]

By the law of Georgia, it is the duty of the father to provide for the maintenance and education of his child until maturity. Wilful abandonment of a minor child,

---

1. There was no suggestion that plaintiff would be destitute or become a public charge. Indeed, her grandfather testified that he was able and willing to provide $125 a month for her education and maintenance (the amount sought by plaintiff), if her father was unable to do so.

leaving it in a dependent condition, is a misdemeanor. The mere loss of custody by the father does not relieve him of his obligation to provide for maintenance and education, even where the custody passes to the mother pursuant to a decree of divorce. If the father fails to make such provision, any person (including a divorced wife) who furnishes necessaries of life to his minor child, may recover from him therefor, unless precluded by the terms of the decree in the divorce suit or otherwise. In case of total divorce, the court is authorized to make, by its decree, final or permanent provision for the maintenance and education of children during minority, and thus fix the extent of the father's obligation. But even if the decree for total divorce fails to include a provision for the support of minor children, they cannot maintain in their own names, or by guardian ad litem, or by next friend, an independent suit for an allowance for education and maintenance.

First. It was contended below in the trial court, and there held, that the provision of the decree of the Georgia court directing the payment to [a] * * * trustee of $1,750 to be "expended by him in his discretion for the benefit of the minor child, including her education, support, maintenance, medical attention and other necessary items of expenditure" was not intended to relieve the father from all further liability to support Sadie. This contention appears to have been abandoned. It is clear that Mrs. Yarborough, her husband and the court intended that this provision should absolve Sadie's father from further obligation to support her. That the term "permanent alimony" as used in the decree of the Georgia court, means a final provision for the minor child is shown by both the legislation of the State and the decisions of its highest court. The refusal of the South Carolina court to give the judgment effect as against Sadie is now sought to be justified on other grounds.

* * *

Third. It is contended that the Georgia decree is not binding upon Sadie, because she was not a formal party to the suit, was not served with process and no guardian ad litem was appointed for her therein. In Georgia, as elsewhere, a property right of a minor can ordinarily be affected by legal proceedings only if these requirements are complied with. But the obligation imposed by the Georgia law upon the father to support his minor child does not vest in the child a property right. This is shown by the fact, among other things, that the minor cannot maintain in his own name, or by guardian ad litem or by next friend, a suit against his father to enforce the obligation. The provision which the Georgia law makes of permanent alimony for the child during minority is a legal incident of the divorce proceeding. As that suit embraces within its scope the disposition and care of minor children, jurisdiction over the parents confers *eo ipso* jurisdiction over the minor's custody and support. Hence, by the Georgia law, a consent (or other) decree in a divorce suit, fixing permanent alimony for a minor child is binding upon it, although the child was not served with process, was not made a formal party to the suit, and no guardian ad litem was appointed therein.

Fourth. It is contended that the order for permanent alimony is not binding upon Sadie because she was not a resident of Georgia at the time it was entered. Being a minor, Sadie's domicile was Georgia, that of her father; and her domicile continued to be in Georgia until entry of the judgment in question. She was not capable by her own act of changing her domicile. * * * The character and extent of the father's obligation, and the status of the minor, are determined ordinarily not by the place of the minor's residence but by the law of the father's domicile. Moreover, this is not a case where the scope of the jurisdiction acquired by the Georgia court rests upon the effectiveness of service by publication upon a nonresident. Mrs. Yarborough filed a cross-bill, as well as an answer; and in the cross-bill prayed "that provision for permanent alimony be made for the" support and education of Sadie. Thus the court acquired complete jurisdiction of the marriage status and, as an incident, power to finally determine the extent of her father's obligation to support his minor child.

Fifth. The fact that Sadie has become a resident of South Carolina does not impair the finality of the judgment. South Carolina thereby acquired the jurisdiction to determine her status and the incidents of that status. Upon residents of that State it could impose duties for her benefit. Doubtless, it might have imposed upon her grandfather who was resident there a duty to support Sadie. But the mere fact of Sadie's residence in South Carolina does not give that State the power to impose such a duty upon the father who is not a resident and who long has been domiciled in Georgia. He has fulfilled the duty which he owes her by the law of his domicile and the judgment of its court. Upon that judgment he is entitled to rely. It was settled by Sistare v. Sistare, 218 U.S. 1 (1910), that the full faith and credit clause applies to an unalterable decree of alimony for a divorced wife. The clause applies, likewise, to an unalterable decree of alimony for a minor child. We need not consider whether South Carolina would have power to require the father, if he were domiciled there, to make further provision for the support, maintenance, or education of his daughter.

Reversed.

JUSTICE STONE, dissenting. I think the judgment should be affirmed.

The divorce decree of the Georgia court purported to adjudicate finally, both for the present and for the future, the right of a minor child of the marriage to support and maintenance, by directing her father to make a lump sum payment for that purpose. More than two years later, after the minor had become a domiciled resident of South Carolina, and after the sum paid had been exhausted, a court of that State, on the basis of her need as then shown, has rendered a judgment directing further payments for her support out of property of the father in South Carolina, in addition to that already commanded by the Georgia judgment.

For present purposes we may take it that the Georgia decree, as the statutes and decisions of the State declare, is unalterable and, as pronounced, is effective to govern the rights of the parties in Georgia. But there is nothing in the decree itself, or in the history of the proceedings which led to it, to suggest that it was rendered with any purpose or intent to regulate or control the relationship of parent and child, or the duties which flow from it, in places outside the State of Georgia where they might later come to reside. It would hardly be thought that Georgia, by judgment of its courts more than by its statutes, would attempt to regulate the relationship of parents and child domiciled outside of the State at the very time the decree was rendered; and, in the face of constitutional doubts that arise here, it is far from clear that its decree is to be interpreted as attempting to do more than to regulate that relationship while the infant continued to be domiciled within the State. But if we are to read the decree as though it contained a clause, in terms, restricting the power of any other state, in which the minor might come to reside, to make provision for her support, then, in the absence of some law of Congress requiring it, I am not persuaded that the full faith and credit clause gives sanction to such control by one state of the internal affairs of another.

Congress has said that the public records and the judicial proceedings of each state are to be given such faith and credit in other states as is accorded to them in the state "from which they are taken." [cit.] But this broad language has never been applied without limitations. See McElmoyle v. Cohen, 38 U.S. (13 Pet.) 312 [1839]. Between the prohibition of the due process clause, acting upon the courts of the state from which such proceedings may be taken, and the mandate of the full faith and credit clause, acting upon the state to which they may be taken, there is an area which federal authority has not occupied. As this Court has often recognized, there are many judgments which need not be given the same force and effect abroad which they have at home, and there are some, though valid in the state where rendered, to which the full faith and credit clause gives no force elsewhere. In the assertion of rights, defined by a judgment of one state, within the territory of another, there is often an inescapable conflict of interest of the two states, and there comes a point beyond which the imposition of the will of one state beyond its own borders involves a forbidden infringement of some legitimate domestic interest of the other. That point may vary with the circumstances of the case; and in the absence of provisions more specific than the general terms of the congressional enactment this Court must determine for itself the extent to which one state may qualify or deny rights claimed under proceedings or records of other states.

* * *

The question presented here is whether the support and maintenance of a minor child, domiciled in South Carolina, is so peculiarly a subject of domestic concern that Georgia law can not impair South Carolina's authority. The subject matter of the judgment in each state is the duty which government may impose on a parent to support a minor child. The maintenance and support of children domiciled within a state, like their education and custody, is a subject in which government itself is deemed to have a peculiar interest and concern. Their tender years, their inability to provide for themselves, the importance to the state that its future citizens should be clothed, nourished and suitably educated, are considerations which lead all civilized countries to assume some control over the maintenance of minors. The states very generally make some provision from their own resources for the maintenance and support of orphans or destitute children, but in order that children may not become public charges the duty of maintenance is one imposed primarily upon the parents, according to the needs of the child and their ability to meet those needs. This is usually accomplished by suit brought directly by some public officer, by the child by guardian or next friend, or by the mother, against the father for maintenance and support. The measure of the duty is the needs of the child and the ability of the parent to meet those needs at the very time when performance of the duty is invoked. Hence, it is no answer in such a suit that at some earlier time provision was made for the child, which is no longer available or suitable because of his greater needs, or because of the increased financial ability of the parent to provide for them, or that the child may be maintained from other sources.

In view of the universality of these principles it comes as a surprise that any state, merely because it has made some provision for the support of a child, should, either by statute or judicial decree, so tie its own hands as to foreclose all future inquiry into the duty of maintenance however affected by changed conditions.[17]

Even though the Constitution does not deny to Georgia the power to indulge in such a policy for itself, it by no means follows that it gives to Georgia the privilege of prescribing that policy for other states in which the child comes to live. * * *

* * * Here the Georgia decree did not end the relationship of parent and child, as a decree of divorce may end the marriage relationship. Had the infant continued to reside in Georgia, and had she sought in the courts of South Carolina to compel the application of property of her father, found there, to her further maintenance and support, full faith and credit to the Georgia decree applied to its own domiciled resident might have required the denial of any relief. [cit.] But when she became a domiciled resident of South Carolina, a new interest came into being,—the interest of the State of South Carolina as a measure of self-preservation to secure the adequate protection and maintenance of helpless members of its own community and its prospective citizens. That interest was distinct from any which Georgia could conclusively regulate or control by its judgment, even though rendered while the child was domiciled in Georgia. The present decision extends the operation of the full faith and credit clause beyond its proper function of affording protection to the domestic interests of Georgia and makes it an instrument for encroachment by Georgia upon the domestic concerns of South Carolina.

Notes and Questions

1. In the choice-of-law context, the Supreme Court has held that the Full Faith and Credit Clause does not require a state with a legitimate interest to defer to the interests of other states. See, e.g., Allstate Ins. Co. v. Hague, 449 U.S. 302 (1981); Nevada v. Hall, 440 U.S. 410, 421-24 (1979); Pacific Employers Ins. Co. v. Indus. Accident Comm'n, 306 U.S. 493, 502-03 (1939). Is there any reason to apply the Full Faith and Credit Clause differently with respect to laws than with respect to judgments?

2. The Court in *Yarborough* declined to decide whether South Carolina could impose further support obligations on the father if he were domiciled there. What difference would it make where the father was domiciled? Does the Full Faith and Credit Clause allow states to ignore judgments entered against one of their domiciliaries? If the father moved to South Carolina, could that state impose a new obligation on him? Could it do so while at the same time fully respecting the Georgia judgment? See Reese & Johnson, *Full Faith and Credit to Judgments*, 174.

3. The support decree in *Yarborough* was not modifiable. Today, child-support

---

17. Georgia seems to be the only state to do so. * * *

decrees are modifiable in all fifty states, including Georgia. If a judgment is not final or is subject to modification, then, as the Supreme Court has observed,: "'the forum has at least as much leeway to disregard the judgment, to qualify it, or to depart from it as does the state where it was rendered.'" Kovacs v. Brewer, 356 U.S. 604, 607 (1958) (quoting New York ex rel. Halvey v. Halvey, 330 U.S. 610, 615 (1947)). In Sistare v. Sistare, 218 U.S. 1 (1909), the Supreme Court held that a modifiable decree for alimony is entitled to full faith and credit as to past due installments, if the right to the past installments was "absolute and vested." However, the Court also held that if the past installments were subject retroactively to modification, then the decree was not final and not subject to full faith and credit. Although the Constitution des not require enforcement of modifiable decrees, the Full Faith and Credit for Child Support Orders Act, 28 U.S.C. § 1738B, does require enforcement of such orders provided they satisfy the requirements of the Act. Moreover, the Act limits the circumstances under which a second state can modify a sister state's decree.

4. In *Fauntleroy*, the Missouri court refused to apply Mississippi law, under which the transaction was illegal. In so doing did not Missouri violate its obligation to give full faith and credit to the laws of another state? Why should a judgment that violates the Full Faith and Credit Clause be enforceable under that clause? If you represented the litigant who lost in Missouri, what would you have done?

5. In *Fauntleroy*, the Court concluded that the Mississippi law did not deny jurisdiction to the Mississippi courts. Would the result have been different if Mississippi did remove jurisdiction from its courts to enforce such judgments? In Kenney v. Supreme Lodge, 252 U.S. 411, 415 (1920), the Supreme Court rejected this strategy, explaining that "a State cannot escape its constitutional obligations by the simple device of denying jurisdiction in such cases to courts otherwise competent."

6. The underlying contract in *Fauntleroy* was one that Mississippi considered not only unenforceable, but criminal. Should a state be required to enforce all judgments of sister states, regardless of how offensive the judgment is to the enforcing state? In the notorious *Dred Scott* case, 60 U.S. (19 How.) 393 (1857), Dred Scott, a slave, had spent several years with his master in the free state of Illinois and the free territory of Minnesota. Upon returning to Missouri, Scott brought suit in Missouri state court claiming that, as a result of his residence in Illinois and Minnesota, he was now free. The Missouri Supreme Court rejected the argument, holding that Missouri was entitled to disregard the emancipation policies of its sister states. If prior to suing in Missouri, Scott had secured a judgment from an Illinois court declaring him to be free, would Missouri have been obligated to enforce the judgment? Suppose instead that following the Missouri decision, Scott had sued for his freedom in a free state. Would that state have been required to enforce the Missouri judgment?

7. Section 117 of the Restatement (Second) provides:

A valid judgment rendered in one State of the United States will be recognized and enforced in a sister State even though the strong public policy of the latter State would have precluded recovery in its courts on the original claim.

Section 103 of the same Restatement suggests that there is an exception to § 117.

Section 103 provides:

A judgment rendered in one State of the United States need not be recognized or enforced in a sister State if such recognition or enforcement is not required by the national policy of full faith and credit because it would involve an improper interference with important interests of the sister State.

The comment to § 103 states that application of this principle "will be extremely rare." The comment goes on to give three examples of its application: injunctions against suits in another state, child custody orders, and the principle that an enforcing state is permitted to apply its own statute of limitations concerning enforcement actions. Do these examples support the general rule articulated in § 103? See Scoles, Hay, Borchers & Symeonides, *Conflict of Laws* § 24.21. Professor Ehrenzweig has described § 103 as a "startling proposition" supported by "no authority whatsoever." Ehrenzweig, *The Second Conflicts Restatement*, 1240. In light of § 117, what "important interests" could a state invoke to refuse to enforce a judgment under § 103?

8. For the first several decades of our nation's history, it was unclear whether "full faith and credit" required that a judgment be enforced, or merely that it be admitted as prima facie evidence of the debt. In Mills v. Duryee, 11 U.S. (7 Cranch) 481 (1813), the Supreme Court settled the issue and held that judgments from other states must be given conclusive effect. It is not entirely clear, however, whether this holding was an interpretation of the Constitution or of the Full Faith and Credit Statute, now codified at 28 U.S.C. § 1738. See Nadelmann, *Full Faith and Credit to Judgments*, 66–70.

9. Even after *Mills*, neither the Full Faith and Credit Clause nor the Statute has been interpreted to require direct execution of a sister-state judgment. Instead, both these provisions contemplate that a judgment creditor will file a new and separate action on the debt in the enforcing state. In the Constitutional Convention, James Madison suggested that direct execution of sister state judgments be required, but his suggestion was rejected. See Ross, *Full Faith and Credit*, 148.

10. The cumbersome procedure of filing a new lawsuit has been mitigated by wide adoption of the Uniform Enforcement of Foreign Judgments Act, 13 U.L.A. 149 (1985). Under that Act, the holder of a properly authenticated judgment from one jurisdiction may file the judgment in another jurisdiction with the clerk of court. Once filed, the clerk sends notice of the filing to the judgment debtor and the judgment is then treated as a local judgment. Similarly, a federal judgment can be registered in any other federal court and then enforced. 28 U.S.C. § 1963.

11. Within the European Union, enforcement of judgements is governed by a European Community Council regulation. Under that regulation, "a judgment shall not be recognized" "if such recognition is manifestly contrary to public policy in the Member State in which recognition is sought." Brussels II, Art. 34(1).

Thomas v. Washington Gas Light Co.

Supreme Court of the United States, 1980.
448 U.S. 261, 100 S.Ct. 2647, 65 L.Ed.2d 757.

JUSTICE STEVENS announced the judgment of the Court and delivered an opinion, in which Justice Brennan, Justice Stewart, and Justice Blackmun joined.

Petitioner received an award of disability benefits under the Virginia Workmen's Compensation Act. The question presented is whether the obligation of the District of Columbia to give full faith and credit to that award bars a supplemental award under the District's Workmen's Compensation Act.

Petitioner is a resident of the District of Columbia and was hired in the District of Columbia. During the year that he was employed by respondent, he worked primarily in the District but also worked in Virginia and Maryland. He sustained a back injury while at work in Arlington, Va., on January 22, 1971. Two weeks later he entered into an "Industrial Commission of Virginia Memorandum of Agreement as to Payment of Compensation" providing for benefits of $62 per week. Several weeks later the Virginia Industrial Commission approved the agreement and issued its award directing that payments continue "during incapacity," subject to various contingencies and changes set forth in the Virginia statute. [cit.]

In 1974, petitioner notified the Department of Labor of his intention to seek compensation under the District of Columbia Act. Respondent opposed the claim primarily on the ground that since, as a matter of Virginia law, the Virginia award excluded any other recovery "at common law or otherwise" on account of the injury in Virginia,[4] the District of Columbia's obligation to give that award full faith and credit precluded a second, supplemental award in the District.

The Administrative Law Judge agreed with respondent that the Virginia award must be given res judicata effect in the District to the extent that it was res judicata in Virginia. He held, however, that the Virginia award, by its terms, did not preclude a further award of compensation in Virginia. Moreover, he construed the statutory prohibition against additional recovery "at common law or otherwise" as merely covering "common law and other remedies under Virginia law." After the taking of medical evidence, petitioner was awarded permanent total disability benefits payable from the date of his injury with a credit for the amounts previously paid under the Virginia award. [cit.]

The Benefits Review Board upheld the award. [cit.] Its order, however, was reversed by the United States Court of Appeals for the Fourth Circuit, * * * which squarely held that a "second and separate proceeding in another jurisdiction upon the same injury after a prior recovery in another State [is] precluded by the Full Faith and Credit Clause." We granted certiorari [cit.], and now reverse.

---

4. Virginia Code § 65.1–40 (1980) provides:
   "Employee's rights under Act exclude all others.—The rights and remedies herein granted to an employee when he and his employer have accepted the provisions of this Act respectively to pay and accept compensation on account of personal injury or death by accident shall exclude all other rights and remedies of such employee, his personal representative, parents, dependents or next of kin, at common law or otherwise, on account of such injury, loss of service or death."

I. Respondent contends that the District of Columbia was without power to award petitioner additional compensation because of the Full Faith and Credit Clause of the Constitution or, more precisely, because of the federal statute implementing that Clause.[10] An analysis of this contention must begin with two decisions from the 1940's that are almost directly on point: Magnolia Petroleum Co. v. Hunt, 320 U.S. 430 [1943] and Industrial Comm'n of Wisconsin v. McCartin, 330 U.S. 622 [1947].

In *Magnolia*, a case relied on heavily both by respondent and the Court of Appeals, the employer hired a Louisiana worker in Louisiana. The employee was later injured during the course of his employment in Texas. A tenuous majority held that Louisiana was not permitted to award the injured worker supplementary compensation under the Louisiana Act after he had already obtained a recovery from the Texas Industrial Accident Board:

> "Respondent was free to pursue his remedy in either state but, having chosen to seek it in Texas, where the award was res judicata, the full faith and credit clause precludes him from again seeking a remedy in Louisiana upon the same grounds." [cit.]

Little more than three years later, the Court severely curtailed the impact of *Magnolia*. In *McCartin*, the employer and the worker both resided in Illinois and entered into an employment contract there for work to be performed in Wisconsin. The employee was injured in the course of that employment. He initially filed a claim with the Industrial Commission of Wisconsin. Prior to this Court's decision in *Magnolia*, the Wisconsin Commission informed him that under Wisconsin law, he could proceed under the Illinois Workmen's Compensation Act, and then claim compensation under the Wisconsin Act, with credit to be given for any payments made under the Illinois Act. Thereafter, the employer and the employee executed a contract for payment of a specific sum in full settlement of the employee's right under Illinois law. The contract expressly provided, however, that it would "'not affect any rights that applicant may have under the Workmen's Compensation Act of the State of Wisconsin.'" [cit.] The employee then obtained a supplemental award from the Wisconsin Industrial Commission; but the Wisconsin state courts vacated it under felt compulsion of the intervening decision in *Magnolia*.

This Court reversed, holding without dissent that *Magnolia* was not controlling. Although the Court could have relied exclusively on the contract provision reserving the employee's rights under Wisconsin law to distinguish the case from *Magnolia*, Mr. Justice Murphy's opinion provided a significantly different ground for the Court's holding when it said:

> "[T]he reservation spells out what we believe to be implicit in [the Illinois Workmen's Compensation] Act—namely, that an ... award of the type here involved does not foreclose an additional award under the laws of another state. And in the setting of this case, that fact is of decisive significance." [cit.]

Earlier in the opinion, the Court had stated that "[o]nly some unmistakable

---

10. The statute places on courts in the District of Columbia the same obligation to respect state judgments as is imposed on the courts of the several States. [cit.]

language by a state legislature or judiciary would warrant our accepting ... a construction" that a workmen's compensation statute "is designed to preclude any recovery by proceedings brought in another state." [cit.] The Illinois statute, which the Court held not to contain the "unmistakable language" required to preclude a supplemental award in Wisconsin, broadly provided:

> "'No common law or statutory right to recover damages for injury or death sustained by any employee while engaged in the line of his duty as such employee, other than the compensation herein provided, shall be available to any employee who is covered by the provisions of this act, ...'" [cit.]

The Virginia Workmen's Compensation Act's exclusive-remedy provision, see n.4, supra, is not exactly the same as Illinois'; but it contains no "unmistakable language" directed at precluding a supplemental compensation award in another State that was not also in the Illinois Act. Consequently, *McCartin* by its terms, rather than the earlier *Magnolia* decision, is controlling as between the two precedents. Nevertheless, the fact that we find ourselves comparing the language of two state statutes, neither of which has been construed by the highest court of either State, in an attempt to resolve an issue arising under the Full Faith and Credit Clause makes us pause to inquire whether there is a fundamental flaw in our analysis of this federal question.

II. We cannot fail to observe that, in the Court's haste to retreat from *Magnolia*, it fashioned a rule that clashes with normally accepted full faith and credit principles. It has long been the law that "the judgment of a state court should have the same credit, validity, and effect, in every other court in the United States, which it had in the state where it was pronounced." [cit.] This rule, if not compelled by the Full Faith and Credit Clause itself, [cit.], is surely required by 28 U.S.C. § 1738, which provides that the "Acts, records and judicial proceedings ... [of any State] shall have the same full faith and credit in every court within the United States ... as they have by law or usage in the courts of [the] State ... from which they are taken." [cit.] Thus, in effect, by virtue of the full faith and credit obligations of the several States, a State is permitted to determine the extraterritorial effect of its judgments; but it may only do so indirectly, by prescribing the effect of its judgments within the State.

The *McCartin* rule, however, focusing as it does on the extraterritorial intent of the rendering State, is fundamentally different. It authorizes a State, by drafting or construing its legislation in "unmistakable language," directly to determine the extraterritorial effect of its workmen's compensation awards. An authorization to a state legislature of this character is inconsistent with the rule established in Pacific Employers Ins. Co. v. Industrial Accident Comm'n, 306 U.S. 493, 502 (1939):

> "This Court must determine for itself how far the full faith and credit clause compels the qualification or denial of rights asserted under the laws of one state, that of the forum, by the statute of another state."

It follows inescapably that the *McCartin* "unmistakable language" rule represents an unwarranted delegation to the States of this Court's responsibility for the final arbitration of full faith and credit questions.[15] The Full Faith and Credit Clause "is one of the provisions incorporated into the Constitution by its framers for the purpose of transforming an aggregation of independent, sovereign States into a nation." [cit.] To vest the power of determining the extraterritorial effect of a State's own laws and judgments in the State itself risks the very kind of parochial entrenchment on the interests of other States that it was the purpose of the Full Faith and Credit Clause and other provisions of Art. IV of the Constitution to prevent. [cit.]

Thus, a re-examination of *McCartin's* "unmistakable language" test reinforces our tentative conclusion that it does not provide an acceptable basis on which to distinguish *Magnolia*. But if we reject that test, we must decide whether to overrule either *Magnolia* or *McCartin*. In making this kind of decision, we must take into account both the practical values served by the doctrine of stare decisis and the principles that inform the Full Faith and Credit Clause.

III. The doctrine of stare decisis imposes a severe burden on the litigant who asks us to disavow one of our precedents. For that doctrine not only plays an important role in orderly adjudication; it also serves the broader societal interests in evenhanded, consistent, and predictable application of legal rules. When rights have been created or modified in reliance on established rules of law, the arguments against their change have special force.[18]

It is therefore appropriate to begin the inquiry by considering whether a rule that permits, or a rule that forecloses, successive workmen's compensation awards is more consistent with settled practice. The answer to this question is pellucidly clear.

It should first be noted that *Magnolia*, by only the slimmest majority [cit.] effected a dramatic change in the law that had previously prevailed throughout the United States. See Mr. Justice Black's dissent in *Magnolia*. [cit.] Of greater importance is the fact that as a practical matter the "unmistakable language" rule of construction announced in *McCartin* left only the narrowest area in which *Magnolia* could have any further precedential value. For the exclusivity language in the Illinois Act construed in *McCartin* was typical of most state workmen's compensation laws. Consequently, it was immediately recognized that *Magnolia* no longer had any significant practical impact. Moreover, since a state legislature seldom focuses on

---

15. See [cit.]; Reese & Johnson, The Scope of Full Faith and Credit to Judgments, 49 Colum. L. Rev. 153, 161–162 (1949) * * *: "Full faith and credit is a national policy, not a state policy. Its purpose is not merely to demand respect from one state for another, but rather to give us the benefits of a unified nation by altering the status of otherwise 'independent, sovereign states.' Hence it is for federal law, not state law, to prescribe the measure of credit which one state shall give to another's judgment. In this regard, it is interesting to note that in dealing with full faith and credit to statutes the Supreme Court in recent years has accorded no weight to language which purported to give a particular statute extraterritorial effect. There is every reason why a similar attitude should be taken with respect to judgments.["]

18. The doctrine of stare decisis has a more limited application when the precedent rests on constitutional grounds, because "correction through legislative action is practically impossible." [cit.]

The full faith and credit area presents special problems, because the Constitution expressly delegates to Congress the authority "by general Laws [to] prescribe the Manner in which [the States'] Acts, Records and Proceedings shall be proved, *and the Effect thereof.*" (Emphasis added.) Yet it is quite clear that Congress' power in this area is not exclusive, for this Court has given effect to the Clause beyond that required by implementing legislation. * * *

* * * [W]hile Congress clearly has the power to increase the measure of faith and credit that a State must accord to the laws or judgments of another State, there is at least some question whether Congress may cut back on the measure of faith and credit required by a decision of this Court. [cit.]

the extraterritorial effect of its enactments, and since a state court has even less occasion to consider whether an award under its State's law is intended to preclude a supplemental award under another State's Workmen's Compensation Act, the probability that any State would thereafter announce a new rule against supplemental awards in other States was extremely remote. As a matter of fact, subsequent cases in the state courts have overwhelmingly followed *McCartin* and permitted successive state workmen's compensation awards. Thus, all that really remained of *Magnolia* after *McCartin* was a largely theoretical difference between what the Court described as "unmistakable language" and the broad language of the exclusive-remedy provision in the Illinois Workmen's Compensation Act involved in *McCartin*.

This history indicates that the principal values underlying the doctrine of stare decisis would not be served either by attempting to revive *Magnolia* or by attempting to preserve the uneasy coexistence of *Magnolia* and *McCartin*. The latter attempt could only breed uncertainty and unpredictability, since the application of the "unmistakable language" rule of *McCartin* necessarily depends on a determination by one state tribunal of the effect to be given to statutory language enacted by the legislature of a different State. And the former would represent a rather dramatic change that surely would not promote stability in the law. Moreover, since *Magnolia* has been so rarely followed, there appears to be little danger that there has been any significant reliance on its rule. We conclude that a fresh examination of the full faith and credit issue is therefore entirely appropriate.

IV. Three different state interests are affected by the potential conflict between Virginia and the District of Columbia. Virginia has a valid interest in placing a limit on the potential liability of companies that transact business within its borders. Both jurisdictions have a valid interest in the welfare of the injured employee—Virginia because the injury occurred within that State, and the District because the injured party was employed and resided there. And finally, Virginia has an interest in having the integrity of its formal determinations of contested issues respected by other sovereigns.

The conflict between the first two interests was resolved in Alaska Packers Assn. v. Industrial Accident Comm'n, 294 U.S. 532 [1935], and a series of later cases. In *Alaska Packers*, California, the State where the employment contract was made, was allowed to apply its own workmen's compensation statute despite the statute of Alaska, the place where the injury occurred, which was said to afford the exclusive remedy for injuries occurring there. [cit.] The Court held that the conflict between the statutes of two States ought not to be resolved "by giving automatic effect to the full faith and credit clause, compelling the courts of each state to subordinate its own statutes to those of the other, but by appraising the governmental interests of each jurisdiction, and turning the scale of decision according to their weight." [cit.]

The converse situation was presented in *Pacific Employers Ins. Co. v. Industrial Accident Comm'n*. In that case the injury occurred in California, and the objection to California's jurisdiction was based on a statute of Massachusetts, the State where the employee resided and where the employment contract had been made. The Massachusetts statute provided that the remedy afforded was exclusive of the worker's "'right of action at common law or under the law of any other jurisdiction."' [cit.] Again, however, California was permitted to provide the employee with an award under the California statute.

The principle that the Full Faith and Credit Clause does not require a State to subordinate its own compensation policies to those of another State has been consistently applied in more recent cases. Carroll v. Lanza, 349 U.S. 408 [1955]; Crider v. Zurich Ins. Co., 380 U.S. 39 [1965]; Nevada v. Hall, 440 U.S. 410 [1979]. Indeed, in the *Nevada* case the Court not only rejected the contention that California was required to respect a statutory limitation on the defendant's liability, but did so in a case in which the defendant was the sovereign State itself asserting, alternatively, an immunity from any liability in the courts of California.

It is thus perfectly clear that petitioner could have sought a compensation award in the first instance either in Virginia, the State in which the injury occurred, *Carroll v. Lanza*; *Pacific Employers*; or in the District of Columbia, where petitioner resided, his employer was principally located, and the employment relation was formed, [cit.]; *Alaska Packers*. And as those cases underscore, compensation could have been sought under either compensation scheme even if one statute or the other purported to confer an exclusive remedy on petitioner. Thus, for all practical purposes, respondent and its insurer would have had to measure their potential liability exposure by the more generous of the two workmen's compensation schemes in any event. It follows that a State's interest in limiting the potential liability of businesses within the State is not of controlling importance.

It is also manifest that the interest in providing adequate compensation to the injured worker would be fully served by the allowance of successive awards. In this respect the two jurisdictions share a common interest and there is no danger of significant conflict.

The ultimate issue, therefore, is whether Virginia's interest in the integrity of its tribunal's determinations forecloses a second proceeding to obtain a supplemental award in the District of Columbia. We return to the Court's prior resolution of this question in *Magnolia*.

The majority opinion in *Magnolia* took the position that the case called for a straightforward application of full faith and credit law: the worker's injury gave rise to a cause of action; relief was granted by the Texas Industrial Accident Board; that award precluded any further relief in Texas; and further relief was therefore precluded elsewhere as well. The majority relied heavily on Chicago, R.I. & P.R. Co. v. Schendel, 270 U.S. 611 [1926], for the propositions that a workmen's compensation award stands on the same footing as a court judgment, and that a compensation award under one State's law is a bar to a second award under another State's law. [cit.]

But *Schendel* did not compel the result in *Magnolia*. [cit.] In *Schendel*, the Court held that an Iowa state compensation award, which was grounded in a contested factual finding that the deceased railroad employee was engaged in intrastate commerce, precluded a subsequent claim under the Federal Employers' Liability Act (FELA) brought in the Minnesota state courts, which would have required a finding that the employee was engaged in interstate commerce. *Schendel* therefore involved the unexceptionable full faith and credit principle that resolutions of factual matters underlying a judgment must be given the same res judicata effect in the forum State as they have in the rendering State. See *Durfee v. Duke*, 375 U.S. 106 [1963]; *Sherrer v. Sherrer*, 334 U.S. 343 [1948]. The Minnesota courts could not have granted relief under the FELA and also respected the factual finding made in Iowa.

In contrast, neither *Magnolia* nor this case concerns a second State's contrary resolution of a factual matter determined in the first State's proceedings. Unlike the situation in *Schendel*, which involved two mutually exclusive remedies, compensation could be obtained under either Virginia's or the District's workmen's compensation statutes on the basis of the same set of facts. A supplemental award gives full effect to the facts determined by the first award and also allows full credit for payments pursuant to the earlier award. There is neither inconsistency nor double recovery.

We are also persuaded that *Magnolia's* reliance on *Schendel* for the proposition that workmen's compensation awards stand on the same footing as court judgments was unwarranted. To be sure, as was held in *Schendel*, the factfindings of state administrative tribunals are entitled to the same res judicata effect in the second State as findings by a court. But the critical differences between a court of general jurisdiction and an administrative agency with limited statutory authority forecloses the conclusion that constitutional rules applicable to court judgments are necessarily applicable to workmen's compensation awards.

A final judgment entered by a court of general jurisdiction normally establishes not only the measure of the plaintiff's rights but also the limits of the defendant's liability. A traditional application of res judicata principles enables either party to claim the benefit of the judgment insofar as it resolved issues the court had jurisdiction to decide. Although a Virginia court is free to recognize the perhaps paramount interests of another State by choosing to apply that State's law in a particular case, the Industrial Commission of Virginia does not have that power. Its jurisdiction is limited to questions arising under the Virginia Workmen's Compensation Act. [cit.] Typically, a workmen's compensation tribunal may only apply its own State's law. In this case, the Virginia Commission could and did establish the full measure of petitioner's rights under Virginia law, but it neither could nor purported to determine his rights under the law of the District of Columbia. Full faith and credit must be given to the determination that the Virginia Commission had the authority to make; but by a parity of reasoning, full faith and credit need not be given to determinations that it had no power to make. Since it was not requested, and had no authority, to pass on petitioner's rights under District of Columbia law, there can be no constitutional objection to a fresh adjudication of those rights.

It is true, of course, that after Virginia entered its award, that State had an interest in preserving the integrity of what it had done. And it is squarely within the purpose of the Full Faith and Credit Clause, as explained in *Pacific Employers*, "to preserve rights acquired or confirmed under the public acts" of Virginia by requiring other States to recognize their validity. [cit.] Thus, Virginia had an interest in having respondent pay petitioner the amounts specified in its award. Allowing a supplementary recovery in the District does not conflict with that interest.

As we have already noted, Virginia also has a separate interest in placing a ceiling on the potential liability of companies that transact business within the State. But past cases have established that that interest is not strong enough to prevent other States with overlapping jurisdiction over particular injuries from giving effect to their more generous compensation policies when the employee selects the most favorable forum in the first instance. Thus, the only situations in which the *Magnolia* rule would tend to serve that interest are those in which an injured workman has either been constrained by circumstances to seek relief in the less generous forum or has simply made an ill-advised choice of his first forum.

But in neither of those cases is there any reason to give extra weight to the first State's interest in placing a ceiling on the employer's liability than it otherwise would have had. For neither the first nor the second State has any overriding interest in requiring an injured employee to proceed with special caution when first asserting his claim. Compensation proceedings are often initiated informally, without the advice of counsel, and without special attention to the choice of the most appropriate forum. Often the worker is still hospitalized when benefits are sought as was true in this case. And indeed, it is not always the injured worker who institutes the claim. [cit.] This informality is consistent with the interests of both States. A rule forbidding supplemental recoveries under more favorable workmen's compensation schemes would require a far more formal and careful choice on the part of the injured worker than may be possible or desirable when immediate commencement of benefits may be essential.

Thus, whether or not the worker has sought an award from the less generous jurisdiction in the first instance, the vindication of that State's interest in placing a ceiling on employers' liability would inevitably impinge upon the substantial interests of the second jurisdiction in the welfare and subsistence of disabled workers--interests that a court of general jurisdiction might consider, but which must be ignored by the Virginia Industrial Commission. The reasons why the statutory policy of exclusivity of the other jurisdictions involved in *Alaska Packers* and *Pacific Employers*, could not defeat California's implementation of its own compensation policies therefore continue to apply even after the entry of a workmen's compensation award.

Of course, it is for each State to formulate its own policy whether to grant supplemental awards according to its perception of its own interests. We simply conclude that the substantial interests of the second State in these circumstances should not be overridden by another State through an unnecessarily aggressive application of the Full Faith and Credit Clause, as was implicitly recognized at the time of *McCartin*.

We therefore would hold that a State has no legitimate interest within the context of our federal system in preventing another State from granting a supplemental compensation award when that second State would have had the power to apply its workmen's compensation law in the first instance. The Full Faith and Credit Clause should not be construed to preclude successive workmen's compensation awards. Accordingly, *Magnolia Petroleum Co. v. Hunt* should be overruled.

The judgment of the Court of Appeals is reversed, and the case is remanded. *So ordered.*

JUSTICE WHITE, with whom The Chief Justice and Justice Powell join, concurring in the judgment. I agree that the judgment of the Court of Appeals should be reversed, but I am unable to join in the reasoning by which the plurality reaches that result. Although the plurality argues strenuously that the rule of today's decision is limited to awards by state workmen's compensation boards, it seems to me that the underlying rationale goes much further. If the employer had exercised its statutory right of appeal to the Supreme Court of Virginia and that Court upheld the award, I presume that the plurality's rationale would nevertheless permit a subsequent award in the District of Columbia. Otherwise, employers interested in cutting off the possibility of a subsequent award in another jurisdiction need only seek judicial review of the award in the first forum. But if such a judicial decision is not preclusive in the second forum, then it appears that the plurality's rationale is not limited in its effect to judgments of administrative tribunals.

The plurality contends that unlike courts of general jurisdiction, workmen's compensation tribunals generally have no power to apply the law of another State and thus cannot determine the rights of the parties thereunder. [cit.] Yet I see no reason why a judgment should not be entitled to full res judicata effect under the Full Faith and Credit Clause merely because the rendering tribunal was obligated to apply the law of the forum—provided, of course, as was certainly the case here, that the forum could constitutionally apply its law. The plurality's analysis seems to grant state legislatures the power to delimit the scope of a cause of action for federal full faith and credit purposes merely by enacting choice-of-law rules binding on the State's workmen's compensation tribunals. The plurality criticizes the *McCartin* case for vesting in the State the power to determine the extraterritorial effect of its own laws and judgments, [cit.]; yet it seems that its opinion is subject to the same objection. In any event, I am not convinced that Virginia, by instructing its Industrial Commission to apply Virginia law, could be said to have intended that the cause of action which merges in the Virginia judgment would not include claims under the laws of other States which arise out of precisely the same operative facts.

As a matter of logic, the plurality's analysis would seemingly apply to many everyday tort actions. I see no difference for full faith and credit purposes between a statute which lays down a forum-favoring choice-of-law rule and a common-law doctrine stating the same principle. Hence when a court, having power in the abstract to apply the law of another State, determines by application of the forum's choice-of-law rules to apply the substantive law of the forum, I would think that under the plurality's analysis the judgment would not determine rights arising under the law of some other State. Suppose, for example, that in a wrongful-death action the court enters judgment on liability against the defendant, and determines to apply the law of the forum which sets a limit on the recovery allowed. The plurality's analysis would seem to permit the plaintiff to obtain a subsequent judgment in a second forum for damages exceeding the first forum's liability limit.

The plurality does say that factual determinations by a workmen's compensation board will be entitled to collateral-estoppel effect in a second forum. [cit.] While this rule does, to an extent, circumscribe the broadest possible implications of the plurality's reasoning, there would remain many cases, such as the wrongful-death example discussed above, in which the second forum could provide additional recovery as a matter of substantive law while remaining true to the first forum's factual determinations. Moreover, the dispositive issues in tort actions are frequently mixed questions of law and fact as to which the second forum might apply its own rule of decision without obvious violation of the principles articulated by four Members of the Court. Actions by the defendant which satisfy the relevant standard of care in the first forum might nevertheless be considered "negligent" under the law of the second forum.

Hence the plurality's rationale would portend a wide-ranging reassessment of the principles of full faith and credit in many areas. Such a reassessment is not necessarily undesirable if the results are likely to be healthy for the judicial system and consistent with the underlying purposes of the Full Faith and Credit Clause. But at least without the benefit of briefs and arguments directed to the issue, I cannot conclude that the rule advocated by the plurality would have such a beneficial impact.

One purpose of the Full Faith and Credit Clause is to bring an end to litigation. As the Court noted in Riley v. New York Trust Co., 315 U.S. 343, 348-49 (1942):

> "Were it not for this full faith and credit provision, so far as the Constitution controls the matter, adversaries could wage again their legal battles whenever they met in other jurisdictions. Each state could control its own courts but itself could not project the effect of its decisions beyond its own boundaries."

The plurality's opinion is at odds with this principle of finality. Plaintiffs dissatisfied with a judgment would have every incentive to seek additional recovery elsewhere, so long as the first forum applied its own law and there was a colorable argument that as a matter of law the second forum would permit a greater recovery. It seems to me grossly unfair that the plaintiff, having the initial choice of the forum, should be given the additional advantage of a second adjudication should his choice prove disappointing. Defendants, on the other hand, would no longer be assured that the judgment of the first forum is conclusive as to their obligations, and would face the prospect of burdensome and multiple litigation based on the same operative facts. Such litigation would also impose added strain on an already overworked judicial system.

Perhaps the major purpose of the Full Faith and Credit Clause is to act as a nationally unifying force. [cit.] The plurality's rationale would substantially undercut that function. When a former judgment is set up as a defense under the Full Faith and Credit Clause, the court would be obliged to balance the various state interests involved. But the State of the second forum is not a neutral party to this balance. There seems to be a substantial danger--not presented by the firmer rule of res judicata--that the court in evaluating a full faith and credit defense would give controlling weight to its own parochial interests in concluding that the judgment of the first forum is not res judicata in the subsequent suit.

I would not overrule either *Magnolia* or *McCartin*. To my mind, Mr. Chief Justice Stone's opinion in *Magnolia* states the sounder doctrine; as noted, I do not see any overriding differences between workmen's compensation awards and court judgments that justify different treatment for the two. However, *McCartin* has been on the books for over 30 years and has been widely interpreted by state and federal courts as substantially limiting *Magnolia*. Unlike the plurality's opinion, *McCartin* is not subject to the objection that its principles are applicable outside the workmen's compensation area. Although I find *McCartin* to rest on questionable foundations, I am not now prepared to overrule it. And I agree with the plurality that *McCartin*, rather than *Magnolia*, is controlling as between the two precedents since the Virginia Workmen's Compensation Act lacks the "unmistakable language" which *McCartin* requires if a workmen's compensation award is to preclude a subsequent award in another State. I therefore concur in the judgment.

JUSTICE REHNQUIST, with whom Justice Marshall joins, dissenting. This is clearly a case where the whole is less than the sum of its parts. In choosing between two admittedly inconsistent precedents, Magnolia Petroleum Co. v. Hunt, and *Industrial Comm'n of Wisconsin v. McCartin*, six of us agree that the latter decision, *McCartin*, is analytically indefensible. [cit.] The remaining three Members of the Court concede that it "rest[s] on questionable foundations." [cit.] Nevertheless, when the smoke clears, it is *Magnolia* rather than *McCartin* that the plurality suggests should be overruled. [cit.] Because I believe that *Magnolia* was correctly decided, and because I fear that the rule proposed by the plurality is both ill-considered and ill-defined, I dissent.

* * *

One might suppose that, having destroyed *McCartin's ratio decidendi*, the plurality would return to the eminently defensible position adopted in *Magnolia*. But such is not the case. The plurality instead raises the banner of "stare decisis" and sets out in search of a new rationale to support the result reached in *McCartin*, significantly failing to even attempt to do the same thing for *Magnolia*.

If such post hoc rationalization seems a bit odd, the theory ultimately chosen by the plurality is even odder. It would seem that, contrary to the assumption of this Court for at least the past 40 years, a judgment awarding workmen's compensation benefits is no longer entitled to full faith and credit unless, and only to the extent that, such a judgment resolves a disputed issue of fact. I believe that the plurality's justification for such a theory, which apparently first surfaced in a cluster of articles written in the wake of *Magnolia*, does not withstand close scrutiny.

The plurality identifies three different "state interests" at stake in the present case: Virginia's interest in placing a limit on the potential liability of companies doing business in that State, Virginia's interest in the "integrity of its formal determinations of contested issues," and a shared interest of Virginia and the District of Columbia in the welfare of the injured employee. [cit.] The plurality then undertakes to balance these interests and concludes that none of Virginia's concerns outweighs the concern of the District of Columbia for the welfare of petitioner.

Whenever this Court, or any court, attempts to balance competing interests it risks undervaluing or even overlooking important concerns. I believe that the plurality's analysis incorporates both errors. First, it asserts that Virginia's interest in limiting the liability of businesses operating within its borders can never outweigh the District of Columbia's interest in protecting its residents. In support of this proposition it cites *Alaska Packers* and *Pacific Employers*. Both of those cases, however, involved the degree of faith and credit to be afforded *statutes* of one State by the courts of another State. The present case involves an enforceable *judgment* entered by Virginia after adjudicatory proceedings. In *Magnolia* Mr. Chief Justice Stone, who authored *both Alaska Packers* and *Pacific Employers*, distinguished those two decisions for precisely this reason, chastising the lower court in that case for overlooking "the distinction, long recognized and applied by this Court, ... between the faith and credit required to be given to judgments and that to which local common and statutory law is entitled under the Constitution and laws of the United States."[cit.] This distinction, which has also been overlooked by the plurality here, makes perfect sense, since Virginia surely has a stronger interest in limiting an employer's liability to a fixed amount when that employer has already been haled before a Virginia tribunal and adjudged liable than when the employer simply claims the benefit of a Virginia statute in a proceeding brought in another State.

In a similar vein, the plurality completely ignores any interest that Virginia might assert in the finality of its adjudications. While workmen's compensation awards may be "nonfinal" in the sense that they are subject to continuing supervision and modification, Virginia nevertheless has a cognizable interest in requiring persons who avail themselves of its statutory remedy to eschew other alternative remedies that might be available to them. Otherwise, as apparently is the result here, Virginia's efforts and expense on an applicant's behalf are wasted when that applicant obtains a duplicative remedy in another State.

At base, the plurality's balancing analysis is incorrect because it recognizes no significant difference between the events that transpired in this case and those that *would* have transpired had petitioner initially sought his remedy in the District of Columbia. But there are differences. The Commonwealth of Virginia has expended its resources, at petitioner's behest, to provide petitioner with a remedy for his injury and a resolution of his "dispute" with his employer. That employer similarly has expended its resources, again at petitioner's behest, in complying with the judgment entered by Virginia. These efforts, and the corresponding interests in seeing that those efforts are not wasted, lie at the very heart of the divergent constitutional treatment of judgments and statutes. [cit.] In this case, of course, Virginia and respondent employer expended very few resources in the administrative process. But that observation lends no assistance to the plurality, which would flatly hold that Virginia has absolutely no power to guarantee that a workmen's compensation award will be treated as a final judgment by other States.

In further support of its novel rule, the plurality attempts to distinguish the judgment entered in this case from one entered by a "court of general jurisdiction." [cit.] Specifically, the plurality points out that the Industrial Commission of Virginia, unlike a state court of general jurisdiction, was limited by statute to consideration of Virginia law. According to the plurality, because the Commission "was not requested, and had no authority, to pass on petitioner's rights under District of Columbia law, there can be no constitutional objection to a fresh adjudication of those rights." [cit.]

This argument might have some force if petitioner had somehow had Virginia law thrust upon him against his will. In this case, however, petitioner was free to choose the applicable law simply by choosing the forum in which he filed his initial claim. Unless the District of Columbia has an interest in forcing its residents to accept its law regardless of their wishes, I fail to see how the Virginia Commission's inability to look to District of Columbia law impinged upon that latter jurisdiction's interests. I thus fail to see why petitioner's election, as consummated in his Virginia award, should not be given the same full faith and credit as would be afforded a judgment entered by a court of general jurisdiction.

I suspect that my Brethren's insistence on ratifying *McCartin's* result despite condemnation of its rationale is grounded in no small part upon their concern that injured workers are often coerced or maneuvered into filing their claims in jurisdictions amenable to their employers. There is, however, absolutely no evidence of such overreaching in the present case. Indeed, had there been "fraud, imposition, [or] mistake" in the filing of petitioner's claim, he would have been permitted, upon timely motion, to vacate the award. See Harris v. Diamond Construction Co., 36 S.E.2d 573, 577 (Va.1946). In this regard, the award received by petitioner is treated no differently than any other judicial award, nor should it be.

There are, of course, exceptional judgments that this Court has indicated are not entitled to full faith and credit. See, e.g., Huntington v. Attril[l], 146 U.S. 657 (1892) (penal judgments); Fall v. Eastin, 215 U.S. 1 (1909) (judgment purporting to convey property in another State). Such exceptions, however, have been "few and far between...." Williams v. North Carolina, 317 U.S. 287, 295 (1942). Furthermore, as this Court noted in *Magnolia*, there would appear to be no precedent for an exception in the case of a money judgment rendered in a civil suit. See 320 U.S., at 438. In this regard, there is no dispute that the award authorized by the Industrial Commission of Virginia here is, at least as a matter of Virginia law, equivalent to such a money judgment. [cit.]

I fear that the plurality, in its zeal to remedy a perceived imbalance in bargaining power, would badly distort an important constitutional tenet. Its "interest analysis," once removed from the statutory choice-of-law context considered by the Court in *Alaska Packers* and *Pacific Employers*, knows no metes or bounds. Given the modern proliferation of quasi-judicial methods for resolving disputes and of various tribunals of limited jurisdiction, such a rule could only lead to confusion. I find such uncertainty unacceptable, and prefer the rule originally announced in *Magnolia*, a rule whose analytical validity is, even yet, unchallenged.

The Full Faith and Credit Clause did not allot to this Court the task of "balancing" interests where the "public Acts, Records, and judicial Proceedings" of a State were involved. It simply directed that they be given the "Full Faith and Credit" that the Court today denies to those of Virginia. I would affirm the judgment of the court below.

Notes and Questions

1. According to Justice Stevens, the *McCartin* rule risks "parochial entrenchment

on the interests of other States." How so? Would it be "parochial" for a state to demand extraterritorial enforcement of its workers' compensation awards? Why is this any more "parochial" than the result in *Fauntleroy v. Lum*? Does it undermine of the Full Faith and Credit Clause when the state which issues a workers compensation award provides that other states are free to supplement the award?

2. Compare Justice Stevens' opinion in *Thomas* with Justice Stone's dissent in *Yarborough*. Was not South Carolina's interest in *Yarborough* at least as great as D.C.'s in *Thomas*? What about *Fauntleroy v. Lum*? There the rendering forum, Missouri, appeared to have no interest other than having been the forum, and Mississippi appears to have had a significant interest. Can *Thomas* and *Fauntleroy* be reconciled?

3. Justice Stevens suggests that one reason to treat workers' compensation awards differently than court judgments is that the Virginia workers' compensation tribunal is required to apply Virginia law. Suppose in *Yarborough* Georgia had a choice of law statute requiring Georgia courts always to apply Georgia law. Would the Georgia court judgment no longer be entitled to full faith and credit? Can *Thomas* and *Yarborough* be reconciled?

4. Justice Stevens would give preclusive effect to the "factfindings" of administrative tribunals. Would this category include determinations such as: "The plaintiff was an 'employee' for purposes of workers compensation." "The injury was work-related." "The plaintiff is completely disabled." "The plaintiff broke her leg and missed 10 weeks of work?"

5. Would the result in *Thomas* have been different if the Virginia award had been appealed and upheld by a Virginia court? What if the Virginia award had explicitly prohibited a further award by D.C.? See United Airlines, Inc. v. Kozel, 536 S.E. 2d 473 (Va. App. 2000).

6. Consider the following variation on *Thomas*: The injured worker brings a tort suit in a Virginia court. The defendant moves to dismiss on grounds that workers' compensation is the exclusive remedy. The court refuses to dismiss, finding that the worker does not meet the Virginia statutory definition of "employee." At trial, the court finds the worker was contributorily negligent and enters judgment for the defendant. Could the worker then bring a workers' compensation claim in D.C.?

7. After *Thomas*, has *McCartin* been overruled? Six Justices agreed that it should be overruled. Notice, however, there is no majority opinion in *Thomas*. In Marks v. United States, 430 U.S. 188, 193 (1977), the Supreme Court explained: "When a fragmented Court decides a case and no single rationale explaining the result enjoys the assent of five Justices, 'the holding of the Court may be viewed as that position taken by those Members who concurred in the judgment on the narrowest grounds.'" Does this mean that Justice White's opinion is the holding of the Court and that *McCartin* is still good law? A number of courts have so held. See Kindle v. Cudd Pressure Control, Inc., 792 F.2d 507, 513 (5th Cir.1986), *cert. denied*, 479 U.S. 1030 (1987); Gulf Interstate Geophysical/Gulf Interstate Piping v. Indus. Comm'n, 555 N.E.2d 989, 992 (Ill.App.1990); LeBlanc v. United Engineers & Constructors, Inc., 584 A.2d 675, 678 (Me.1991); R & T Constr. Co. v. Judge, 594 A.2d 99, 103 (Md.1991).

8. Subsequent to *Thomas*, the Supreme Court held that the Full Faith and Credit *Statute* (§ 1738) does not apply to administrative adjudications, see University of Tenn. v. Elliott, 478 U.S. 788, 794 (1986), or arbitration, see McDonald v. City of West Branch, 466 U.S. 284, 287-88 (1984). The rationale for this conclusion is that § 1738 refers to "[t]he Acts of the legislature" and "[t]he records and judicial proceedings of any *court*" (emphasis added) and that unreviewed administrative determinations and arbitration awards are not "court" or "judicial" proceedings. Does this interpretation of § 1738 require a rethinking of the workers' compensation cases? Notice that § 1738 uses "court" in two places: in addition to the use of the word noted above, the statute requires full faith and credit "in every other *court* within the United States" (emphasis added). Does this second use of "court" mean that an administrative tribunal does not have to give full faith and credit to a prior judgment? Even if the Full Faith and Credit *Statute* does not apply to workers' compensation cases, the Full Faith and Credit *Clause* itself might apply. However, some have argued that the clause is not as demanding as the statute. Professor Whitten asserts:

> [T]he Full Faith and Credit Clause does not directly require the states to *enforce or apply* the statutes, records, or judgments of other states. It merely commands that the states admit the public acts, records, and judicial proceedings of other states as conclusive evidence of their existence and contents, delegating exclusively to Congress the more significant task of establishing conflict-of-laws rules to determine when one state must give effect to the laws of another.

Whitten, *Full Faith and Credit*, 55. Does this explain the result in *Thomas*?

9. In *Nevada v. Hall*, supra at 498, the Court upheld a California tort judgment against the State of Nevada for over $1 million. Nevada law limited suits against the state to $25,000. If Mr. Hall sought to enforce his judgment in Nevada, would Nevada be required to give the judgment full faith and credit? See Kent Count v. Shepherd, 713 A.2d 290, 303-304 (Del. 1998) ("State of Maryland's suggestion that the judgments which will be entered against it * * * by the Delaware Superior Court are unenforceable in the courts of Maryland, appears to be completely contrary to the history, purpose, and well-established interpretation of the Full Faith and Credit Clause, including the most recent pronouncement by the United States Supreme Court in *Baker* earlier this year").

Suppose Nevada secured a declaratory judgment from a Nevada court against Hall (perhaps through transient jurisdiction) stating that Nevada's liability is limited to $25,000. In a subsequent tort suit brought by Hall in California, would California be required to give full faith and credit to the declaratory judgment and limit the damages to $25,000?

10. For an excellent discussion of *Thomas*, see Sterk, *Full Faith and Credit*, 1329.

2. Requirements for Recognition

Durfee v. Duke

Supreme Court of the United States, 1963.
375 U.S. 106, 84 S.Ct. 242, 11 L.Ed.2d 186.

JUSTICE STEWART delivered the opinion of the Court. * * * In 1956 the petitioners brought an action against the respondent in a Nebraska court to quiet title to certain bottom land situated on the Missouri River. The main channel of that river forms the boundary between the States of Nebraska and Missouri. The Nebraska court had jurisdiction over the subject matter of the controversy only if the land in question was in Nebraska. Whether the land was Nebraska land depended entirely upon a factual question—whether a shift in the river's course had been caused by avulsion or accretion. The respondent appeared in the Nebraska court and through counsel fully litigated the issues, explicitly contesting the court's jurisdiction over the subject matter of the controversy.[4] After a hearing the court found the issues in favor of the petitioners and ordered that title to the land be quieted in them. The respondent appealed, and the Supreme Court of Nebraska affirmed the judgment after a trial de novo on the record made in the lower court. The State Supreme Court specifically found that the rule of avulsion was applicable, that the land in question was in Nebraska, that the Nebraska courts therefore had jurisdiction of the subject matter of the litigation, and that title to the land was in the petitioners. [cit.] The respondent did not petition this Court for a writ of certiorari to review that judgment.

Two months later the respondent filed a suit against the petitioners in a Missouri court to quiet title to the same land. Her complaint alleged that the land was in Missouri. The suit was removed to a Federal District Court by reason of diversity of citizenship. The District Court after hearing evidence expressed the view that the land was in Missouri, but held that all the issues had been adjudicated and determined in the Nebraska litigation, and that the judgment of the Nebraska Supreme Court was res judicata and "is now binding upon this court." The Court of Appeals reversed, holding that the District Court was not required to give full faith and credit to the Nebraska judgment, and that normal res judicata principles were not applicable because the controversy involved land and a court in Missouri was therefore free to retry the question of the Nebraska court's jurisdiction over the subject matter. [cit.] We granted certiorari to consider a question important to the administration of justice in our federal system. [cit.] For the reasons that follow, we reverse the judgment before us.

The constitutional command of full faith and credit, as implemented by Congress, requires that "judicial proceedings ... shall have the same full faith and credit in every court within the United States ... as they have by law or usage in the courts of such State ... from which they are taken." Full faith and credit thus

---

4. This is, therefore, not a case in which a party, although afforded an opportunity to contest subject-matter jurisdiction, did not litigate the issue. Cf. Chicot County Drainage Dist. v. Baxter State Bank, 308 U.S. 371 [1940].

generally requires every State to give to a judgment at least the res judicata effect which the judgment would be accorded in the State which rendered it. * * *

It is not questioned that the Nebraska courts would give full res judicata effect to the Nebraska judgment quieting title in the petitioners. It is the respondent's position, however, that whatever effect the Nebraska courts might give to the Nebraska judgment, the federal court in Missouri was free independently to determine whether the Nebraska court in fact had jurisdiction over the subject matter, i.e., whether the land in question was actually in Nebraska.

In support of this position the respondent relies upon the many decisions of this Court which have held that a judgment of a court in one State is conclusive upon the merits in a court in another State only if the court in the first State had power to pass on the merits—had jurisdiction, that is, to render the judgment. As Mr. Justice Bradley stated the doctrine in the leading case of Thompson v. Whitman, 18 Wall. 457 [1873], "we think it clear that the jurisdiction of the court by which a judgment is rendered in any State may be questioned in a collateral proceeding in another State, notwithstanding the provision of the fourth article of the Constitution and the law of 1790, and notwithstanding the averments contained in the record of the judgment itself." [cit.] The principle has been restated and applied in a variety of contexts.

However, while it is established that a court in one State, when asked to give effect to the judgment of a court in another State, may constitutionally inquire into the foreign court's jurisdiction to render that judgment, the modern decisions of this Court have carefully delineated the permissible scope of such an inquiry. From these decisions there emerges the general rule that a judgment is entitled to full faith and credit--even as to questions of jurisdiction--when the second court's inquiry discloses that those questions have been fully and fairly litigated and finally decided in the court which rendered the original judgment.

With respect to questions of jurisdiction over the person,[8] this principle was unambiguously established in Baldwin v. Iowa State Traveling Men's Assn., 283 U.S. 522 [1931]. There it was held that a federal court in Iowa must give binding effect to the judgment of a federal court in Missouri despite the claim that the original court did not have jurisdiction over the defendant's person, once it was shown to the court in Iowa that that question had been fully litigated in the Missouri forum. "Public policy," said the Court, "dictates that there be an end of litigation; that those who have contested an issue shall be bound by the result of the contest, and that matters once tried shall be considered forever settled as between the parties. We see no reason why this doctrine should not apply in every case where one voluntarily appears, presents his case and is fully heard, and why he should not, in the absence of fraud, be thereafter concluded by the judgment of the tribunal to which he has submitted his cause." 283 U.S. at 525–26.

Following the *Baldwin* case, this Court soon made clear in a series of decisions

---

8. It is not disputed in the present case that the Nebraska courts had jurisdiction over the respondent's person. She entered a general appearance in the trial court, and initiated the appeal to the Nebraska Supreme Court.

that the general rule is no different when the claim is made that the original forum did not have jurisdiction over the subject matter. [cit.] In each of these cases the claim was made that a court, when asked to enforce the judgment of another forum, was free to retry the question of that forum's jurisdiction over the subject matter. In each case this Court held that since the question of subject-matter jurisdiction had been fully litigated in the original forum, the issue could not be retried in a subsequent action between the parties.

[In Davis v. Davis, 305 U.S. 32 (1938)] it was held that the courts of the District of Columbia were required to give full faith and credit to a decree of absolute divorce rendered in Virginia, despite the claim that the Virginia court had lacked jurisdiction because the plaintiff in the Virginia proceedings had not been domiciled in that State. In the course of the opinion the Court stated:

> "As to petitioner's domicil for divorce and his standing to invoke jurisdiction of the Virginia court, its finding that he was a bona fide resident of that State for the required time is binding upon respondent in the courts of the District. She may not say that he was not entitled to sue for divorce in the state court, for she appeared there and by plea put in issue his allegation as to domicil, introduced evidence to show it false, took exceptions to the commissioner's report, and sought to have the court sustain them and uphold her plea. Plainly, the determination of the decree upon that point is effective for all purposes in this litigation." 305 U.S. at 40.

This doctrine of jurisdictional finality was applied even more unequivocally in Treinies v. Sunshine Mining Co., [308 U.S. 66 (1939)], involving title to personal property, and in Sherrer v. Sherrer, [334 U.S. 343 (1948)], involving, like *Davis*, recognition of a foreign divorce decree. In *Treinies*, the rule was succinctly stated: "One trial of an issue is enough. 'The principles of res judicata apply to questions of jurisdiction as well as to other issues,' as well to jurisdiction of the subject matter as of the parties." [cit.]

The reasons for such a rule are apparent. In the words of the Court's opinion in Stoll v. Gottlieb, [305 U.S. 165 (1938)], "We see no reason why a court, in the absence of an allegation of fraud in obtaining the judgment, should examine again the question whether the court making the earlier determination on an actual contest over jurisdiction between the parties, did have jurisdiction of the subject matter of the litigation.... Courts to determine the rights of parties are an integral part of our system of government. It is just as important that there should be a place to end as that there should be a place to begin litigation. After a party has his day in court, with opportunity to present his evidence and his view of the law, a collateral attack upon the decision as to jurisdiction there rendered merely retries the issue previously determined. There is no reason to expect that the second decision will be more satisfactory than the first." 305 U.S. at 172.

To be sure, the general rule of finality of jurisdictional determinations is not without exceptions. Doctrines of federal pre-emption or sovereign immunity may in some contexts be controlling. Kalb v. Feuerstein, 308 U.S. 433 [1940]; [cit.].[12] But no such overriding considerations are present here. While this Court has not before had occasion to consider the applicability of the rule of *Davis*, *Stoll*, *Treinies*, and *Sherrer* to a case involving real property, we can discern no reason why the rule should not be fully applicable.

It is argued that an exception to this rule of jurisdictional finality should be made with respect to cases involving real property because of this Court's emphatic expressions of the doctrine that courts of one State are completely without jurisdiction directly to affect title to land in other States. This argument is wide of the mark. Courts of one State are equally without jurisdiction to dissolve the marriages of those domiciled in other States. But the location of land, like the domicile of a party to a divorce action, is a matter "to be resolved by judicial determination." [cit.] The question remains whether, once the matter has been fully litigated and judicially determined, it can be retried in another State in litigation between the same parties. Upon the reason and authority of the cases we have discussed, it is clear that the answer must be in the negative.

It is to be emphasized that all that was ultimately determined in the Nebraska litigation was title to the land in question as between the parties to the litigation there. Nothing there decided, and nothing that could be decided in litigation between the same parties or their privies in Missouri, could bind either Missouri or Nebraska with respect to any controversy they might have, now or in the future, as to the location of the boundary between them, or as to their respective sovereignty over the land in question. [cit.] Either State may at any time protect its interest by initiating independent judicial proceedings here. [cit.]

For the reasons stated, we hold in this case that the federal court in Missouri had the power and, upon proper averments, the duty to inquire into the subject matter jurisdiction of the Nebraska courts to render the decree quieting title to the land in the petitioners. We further hold that when that inquiry disclosed, as it did, that the jurisdictional issues had been fully and fairly litigated by the parties and finally determined in the Nebraska courts, the federal court in Missouri was correct in ruling that further inquiry was precluded. Accordingly the judgment of the Court of Appeals is reversed, and that of the District Court is affirmed.

It is so ordered.

JUSTICE BLACK, concurring. Petitioners and respondent dispute the ownership

---

12. It is to be noted, however, that in neither of these cases had the jurisdictional issues actually been litigated in the first forum.

The Restatement of Conflict of Laws recognizes the possibility of such exceptions:

"Where a court has jurisdiction over the parties and determines that it has jurisdiction over the subject matter, the parties cannot collaterally attack the judgment on the ground that the court did not have jurisdiction over the subject matter, unless the policy underlying the doctrine of res judicata is outweighed by the policy against permitting the court to act beyond its jurisdiction. Among the factors appropriate to be considered in determining that collateral attack should be permitted are that

"(a) the lack of jurisdiction over the subject matter was clear;

"(b) the determination as to jurisdiction depended upon a question of law rather than of fact;

"(c) the court was one of limited and not of general jurisdiction;

"(d) the question of jurisdiction was not actually litigated;

"(e) the policy against the court's acting beyond its jurisdiction is strong."

Restatement, Conflict of Laws, § 451 (2) (Supp. 1948). See Restatement, Judgments, § 10 (1942).

of a tract of land adjacent to the Missouri River, which is the boundary between Nebraska and Missouri. Resolution of this question turns on whether the land is in Nebraska or Missouri. Neither State, of course, has power to make a determination binding on the other as to which State the land is in. U.S. Const., Art. III, § 2; 28 U.S.C. § 1251(a). However, in a private action brought by these Nebraska petitioners, the Nebraska Supreme Court has held that the disputed tract is in Nebraska. In the present suit, brought by this Missouri respondent in Missouri, the United States Court of Appeals has refused to be bound by the Nebraska court's judgment. I concur in today's reversal of the Court of Appeals' judgment, but with the understanding that we are not deciding the question whether the respondent would continue to be bound by the Nebraska judgment should it later be authoritatively decided, either in an original proceeding between the States in this Court or by a compact between the two States under Art. I, § 10, that the disputed tract is in Missouri.

Notes and Questions

1. In Pennoyer v. Neff, 95 U.S. (5 Otto) 714, 729 (1877), Justice Field stated:

In the earlier cases, it was supposed that the act [§ 1738] gave to all judgments the same effect in other States which they had by law in the State where rendered. But this view was afterwards qualified so as to make the act applicable only when the court rendering the judgment had jurisdiction of the parties and of the subject-matter, and not to preclude an inquiry into the jurisdiction of the court in which the judgment was rendered, or the right of the State itself to exercise authority over the person or the subject matter.

This traditional view that an enforcing court could always inquire into the subject matter jurisdiction of the rendering state was based on the premise that a judgment by a court that lacked authority was void and thus could be disregarded. What is wrong with the traditional view? Why should anyone have to respect the judgment of a court that lacks subject matter jurisdiction? Is there any difference between the judgment of a court that lacks subject matter jurisdiction and the judgment of an impostor judge?

2. *Durfee* illustrates the so-called "Bootstrap Principle." See Dobbs, *The Bootstrap Principle*, 1241. This principle is based on the premise that courts have jurisdiction to decide their own jurisdiction and that a decision by a court that it has jurisdiction is no different than any other decision a court might make. A decision concerning jurisdiction may be wrong, but like other errors, the proper route for correcting errors is to appeal. What is the source of a court's jurisdiction to decide jurisdiction?

As to personal jurisdiction, a court's jurisdiction to decide jurisdiction is conferred by the defendant when she raises the issue. As Professor Dobbs argues, "when a defendant appears in litigation against him and moves to dismiss for want of jurisdiction of his person, he is surely conceding the court's jurisdiction to determine the issue he has raised." Id. at 1007. Because subject matter jurisdiction is not conferred by the parties, jurisdiction to decide subject matter jurisdiction must have a different source. As to subject matter jurisdiction, jurisdiction to decide jurisdiction must derive from the legislative body or constitution that creates the court. Professor Dobbs argues that we should ordinarily assume that in creating a court, the legislature authorizes that court to determine its jurisdiction. He explains the reason for the assumption as follows:

> [U]nder settled rules, if a court has jurisdiction to dismiss for want of jurisdiction, it has jurisdiction to retain the case. It may be error to dismiss or retain the case, but in either event it has jurisdiction to decide the issue. Of course, the legislature might change this rule by fiat. It might say that courts have jurisdiction to decide correctly and no other jurisdiction. But unless a legislature says this specifically, there is no reason to assume that it intended such a rule, because such a rule would not be consonant with a court's power to dismiss for want of jurisdiction.

Id. at 1011-12. Should the bootstrap principle be applied when the validity of a judgment is challenged in another state's courts?

3. Under the bootstrap principle, should we assume there are any limitations to a court's jurisdiction to decide jurisdiction? Suppose a small claims court or a justice of the peace grants a divorce? Or a probate court declares a city zoning ordinance unconstitutional? See State ex rel. City of Mayfield Heights v. Bartunek, 231 N.E.2d 326 (Ohio App.1967). Should these judgments be immune from collateral attack in *another* state?

4. The Restatement (Second) of Judgments § 12 recognizes the principle of jurisdiction to decide jurisdiction, but suggests the following limitations on that principle:

> When a court has rendered a judgment in a contested action, the judgment precludes the parties from litigating the question of the court's subject matter jurisdiction in subsequent litigation except if:
>
> > (1) The subject matter of the action was so plainly beyond the court's jurisdiction that its entertaining the action was a manifest abuse of authority; or
> >
> > (2) Allowing the judgment to stand would substantially infringe the authority of another tribunal or agency of government; or
> >
> > (3) The judgment was rendered by a court lacking capability to make an adequately informed determination of a question concerning its own jurisdiction and as a matter of procedural fairness the party seeking to avoid the judgment should have opportunity belatedly to attack the court's subject matter jurisdiction.[1]

5. One situation in which the bootstrap principle does not apply is where Congress has mandated that it shall not apply. In Kalb v. Feuerstein, 308 U.S. 433 (1940), a judgment of foreclosure was entered against a debtor in a state court while the debtor had a petition for bankruptcy pending in federal bankruptcy court. The Supreme Court held that under the Bankruptcy Act, filing a bankruptcy petition ousted state courts of jurisdiction. The Court further held that Congress intended to

---

1. Quoted with the permission of the copyright owner, The American Law Institute.

permit collateral attacks on the jurisdiction of state court judgments entered during bankruptcy.

6. In other contexts, the Supreme Court has been reluctant to assume that Congress meant to eliminate the usual preclusion rules. For example, although the Court has recognized that passage of the Reconstruction Era civil rights laws, e.g., 42 U.S.C. § 1983, was at least partially motivated by concerns over the adequacy of state courts as protectors of federal rights, the Court has nonetheless rejected the argument that § 1983 limits the preclusive effect of prior state adjudication involving those federal rights. See Migra v. Warren City Sch. Dist. Bd. of Educ., 465 U.S. 75 (1984); Allen v. McCurry, 449 U.S. 90 (1980). The Court has also held that even though § 1738 does not require enforcement of administrative determinations, federal courts hearing § 1983 actions should nonetheless give the same preclusive effect to prior fact finding by a state agency as that state's courts would give the finding. See University of Tenn. v. Elliott, 478 U.S. 788 (1986). These cases are discusses further in Chapter 11.

7. In both *Durfee* and *Baldwin v. Iowa State Men's Traveling Ass'n.* (discussed in *Durfee*), there was a full adjudication of the issue of jurisdiction in the rendering state. But suppose the issue is not raised in the first case, then what? With respect to personal jurisdiction, the defendant's failure to raise the issue is treated as a waiver. By not objecting to personal jurisdiction, the defendant *confers* jurisdiction by consent. What about subject matter jurisdiction, which may not be conferred by consent? In Des Moines Navigation & R.R. Co. v. Iowa Homestead Co., 123 U.S. 552 (1887), the Supreme Court held that a state court must give effect to a prior federal judgment, even though the record in the original federal case affirmatively demonstrated that the parties were not diverse and the issue of jurisdiction had not been raised by the parties or mentioned by the court. Likewise, in Chicot County Drainage Dist. v. Baxter State Bank, 308 U.S. 371 (1940), the Supreme Court prohibited a collateral attack on grounds of lack of subject matter jurisdiction. In that case, a district court sitting in a bankruptcy proceeding had ordered the cancellation of certain bonds and the issuance of different bonds in their place. Subsequent to this decree, in an unrelated case, another court had declared unconstitutional the legislation pursuant to which the district court had acted. Holders of the original bonds brought suit to enforce them and argued that the cancellation of those bonds was void. The Court rejected this argument, observing that federal courts have authority to determine their own jurisdiction and that "[t]heir determinations of such questions, while open to direct review, may not be assailed collaterally." Id. at 376. According to the Court, this principle applied to the case, even though the issue of jurisdiction had not been actually litigated in the first case. Is this carrying the bootstrap principle too far?

8. What about default judgments? Defendants are permitted to collaterally attack default judgments on grounds of lack of personal jurisdiction. See Pennoyer v. Neff, 95 U.S. (5 Otto) 714,(1877). Should they also be permitted to attack default judgments on subject matter jurisdiction grounds? The Restatement (Second) of Judgments permits a defendant to collaterally attack a default judgment on this basis, see id. at § 65, except where "[g]ranting the relief would impair another person's

substantial interest of reliance on the judgment." Id. at § 66(2). However, there are few modern decisions that have sustained a collateral attack on a default judgment where the sole issue is lack of subject matter jurisdiction. See id. at § 12, cmt. f; Moore, *Collateral Attack on Subject Matter Jurisdiction*, 551–553; 18A Wright, Miller & Cooper, *Federal Practice*, § 4428 at 15-16.

9. Absent an applicable constitutional provision, such as the Due Process Clause or federal preemption as in *Kalb*, it is the rendering state's law that determines whether a collateral attack on subject matter jurisdictional grounds is permitted. See Restatement (Second) § 97. If the rendering state would permit a collateral attack for lack of jurisdiction, other states can collaterally attack on this basis as well. See id. § 105.

10. A dismissal in one court for lack of jurisdiction, does not bar a subsequent suit in a court that does have jurisdiction. See Restatement 2d of Judgments § 20(1)(a). Suppose the first court dismisses on grounds that the limitations period has run, does such a dismissal bar a subsequent suit in a court that would apply a longer limitations period? The traditional answer is that the second suit is not barred unless the limitations period is integral to the cause of action so that when the period runs, the cause of action is extinguished. See Reinke v. Boden, 45 F.3d 166, 169–70 (7th Cir.), *cert. denied*, 516 U.S. 817 (1995); Warner v. Buffalo Drydock Co., 67 F.2d 540, 541 (2d Cir.1933), *cert. denied*, 291 U.S. 678 (1934); Lee v. Swain Bldg. Materials Co., 529 So.2d 188, 190-191 (Miss. 1988); Restatement (Second) § 110, cmt. b; Restatement of Judgments § 19, cmt,. f, Reporter's Notes. But see Steve D. Thompson Trucking, Inc. v. Dorsey Trailers, Inc., 870 F.2d 1044, 1046 (5th Cir.1989) ("[a]llowing plaintiffs who fail to comply with applicable statutes of limitations to move to the next state over would have undesirable effect of encouraging forum shopping and rewarding dilatory conduct"); Sautter v. Interstate Power Co., 567 N.W. 2d 755 (Minn. Ct. App. 1997) (Full Faith and Credit Clause required court to give preclusive effect to prior statute of limitations dismissal from another state).

Baker v. General Motors Corp.

Supreme Court of the United States, 1998.

522 U.S. 222, 118 S.Ct. 657, 138 L.Ed.2d 580

JUSTICE GINSBURG delivered the opinion of the Court. This case concerns the authority of one State's court to order that a witness' testimony shall not be heard in any court of the United States. In settlement of claims and counterclaims precipitated by the discharge of Ronald Elwell, a former General Motors Corporation (GM) engineering analyst, GM paid Elwell an undisclosed sum of money, and the parties agreed to a permanent injunction. As stipulated by GM and Elwell and entered by a Michigan County Court, the injunction prohibited Elwell from "testifying, without the prior written consent of [GM], . . . as . . . a witness of any kind . . . in any litigation already filed, or to be filed in the future, involving [GM] as an owner, seller, manufacturer and/or designer . . . ." GM separately agreed, however, that if Elwell were ordered to testify by a court or other tribunal, such testimony would not be actionable as a violation of the Michigan court's injunction or the GM-Elwell agreement.

After entry of the stipulated injunction in Michigan, Elwell was subpoenaed to testify in a product liability action commenced in Missouri by plaintiffs who were not involved in the Michigan case. The question presented is whether the national full faith and credit command bars Elwell's testimony in the Missouri case. We hold that Elwell may testify in the Missouri action without offense to the full faith and credit requirement.

I. Two lawsuits, initiated by different parties in different states, gave rise to the full faith and credit issue before us. One suit involved a severed employment relationship, the other, a wrongful-death complaint. We describe each controversy in turn.

A. *The Suit Between Elwell and General Motors.* [Ronald Elwell was a GM employee. In 1991, he sued GM in Michigan state court alleging wrongful discharge. Elwell claimed that GM had retaliated after he testified in a Georgia tort suit and stated that the GM pickup truck fuel system was inferior to competing products.] * * * GM counterclaimed, contending that Elwell had breached his fiduciary duty to GM by disclosing privileged and confidential information and misappropriating documents. In response to GM's motion for a preliminary injunction, and after a hearing, the Michigan trial court, on November 22, 1991, enjoined Elwell from

> "consulting or discussing with or disclosing to any person any of General Motors Corporation's trade secrets[,] confidential information or matters of attorney-client work product relating in any manner to the subject matter of any products liability litigation whether already filed or [to be] filed in the future which Ronald Elwell received, had knowledge of, or was entrusted with during his employments with General Motors Corporation." [cit.]

In August 1992, GM and Elwell entered into a settlement under which Elwell received an undisclosed sum of money. The parties also stipulated to the entry of a permanent injunction and jointly filed with the Michigan court both the stipulation and the agreed-upon injunction. The proposed permanent injunction contained two proscriptions. The first substantially repeated the terms of the preliminary injunction; the second comprehensively enjoined Elwell from

> "testifying, without the prior written consent of General Motors Corporation, either upon deposition or at trial, as an expert witness, or as a witness of any kind, and from consulting with attorneys or their agents in any litigation already filed, or to be filed in the future, involving General Motors Corporation as an owner, seller, manufacturer and/or designer of the product(s) in issue." [cit.]

To this encompassing bar, the consent injunction made an exception: "[This provision] shall not operate to *interfere with the jurisdiction of the Court in . . . Georgia* [where the litigation involving the fuel tank was still pending]." [cit.] No other noninterference provision appears in the stipulated decree. On August 26, 1992, with no further hearing, the Michigan court entered the injunction precisely as tendered by the parties.

Although the stipulated injunction contained an exception only for the Georgia action then pending, Elwell and GM included in their separate settlement agreement a more general limitation. If a court or other tribunal ordered Elwell to testify, his testimony would "in no way" support a GM action for violation of the injunction or the settlement agreement: "'It is agreed that [Elwell's] appearance and testimony, if any, at hearings on Motions to quash subpoena or at deposition or trial or other official proceeding, if the Court or other tribunal so orders, will in no way form a basis for an action in violation of the Permanent Injunction or this Agreement.'" [cit.]

In the six years since the Elwell-GM settlement, Elwell has testified against GM both in Georgia (pursuant to the exception contained in the injunction) and in several other jurisdictions in which Elwell has been subpoenaed to testify.

B. *The Suit Between the Bakers and General Motors.* [In September 1991, the Bakers brought a wrongful death action against GM in federal court in Missouri. The suit grew out of an auto accident in which the plaintiffs' mother was killed.] * * *

The Bakers sought both to depose Elwell and to call him as a witness at trial. GM objected to Elwell's appearance as a deponent or trial witness on the ground that the Michigan injunction barred his testimony. In response, the Bakers urged that the Michigan injunction did not override a Missouri subpoena for Elwell's testimony. The Bakers further noted that, under the Elwell-GM settlement agreement, Elwell could testify if a court so ordered, and such testimony would not be actionable as a violation of the Michigan injunction.

After *in camera* review of the Michigan injunction and the settlement agreement, the Federal District Court in Missouri allowed the Bakers to depose Elwell and to call him as a witness at trial. * * *

At trial, Elwell testified in support of the Bakers' claim that the alleged defect in the fuel pump system contributed to the postcollision fire. In addition, he identified and described a 1973 internal GM memorandum bearing on the risk of fuel-fed engine fires. Following trial, the jury awarded the Bakers $11.3 million in damages, and the District Court entered judgment on the jury's verdict.

The United States Court of Appeals for the Eighth Circuit reversed the District Court's judgment, ruling, *inter alia*, that Elwell's testimony should not have been admitted. [cit.] Assuming, *arguendo*, the existence of a public policy exception to the full faith and credit command, the Court of Appeals concluded that the District Court erroneously relied on Missouri's policy favoring disclosure of relevant, nonprivileged information, [cit.] for Missouri has an "equally strong public policy in favor of full faith and credit" [cit.]. * * *

II. A. * * * The animating purpose of the full faith and credit command, as this Court explained in Milwaukee County v. M. E. White Co., 296 U.S. 268 (1935), "was to alter the status of the several states as independent foreign sovereignties, each free to ignore obligations created under the laws or by the judicial proceedings of the others, and to make them integral parts of a single nation throughout which a remedy upon a just obligation might be demanded as of right, irrespective of the state of its origin." [cit.] See also Estin v.Estin, 334 U.S. 541, 546 (1948) (the Full Faith and Credit Clause "substituted a command for the earlier principles of comity and this basically altered the status of the States as independent sovereigns").

Our precedent differentiates the credit owed to laws (legislative measures and common law) and to judgments. "In numerous cases this Court has held that credit must be given to the judgment of another state although the forum would not be required to entertain the suit on which the judgment was founded." *Milwaukee County*, 296 U.S. at 277. The Full Faith and Credit Clause does not compel "a state to substitute the statutes of other states for its own statutes dealing with a subject matter concerning which it is competent to legislate." Pacific Employers Ins. Co. v. Industrial Accident Comm'n, 306 U.S. 493, 501 (1939); see Phillips Petroleum Co. v. Shutts, 472 U.S. 797, 818-819 (1985). Regarding judgments, however, the full faith and credit obligation is exacting. A final judgment in one State, if rendered by a court with adjudicatory authority over the subject matter and persons governed by the judgment, qualifies for recognition throughout the land. For claim and issue preclusion (res judicata) purposes, in other words, the judgment of the rendering State gains nationwide force. [cit.]

A court may be guided by the forum State's "public policy" in determining the *law* applicable to a controversy. See Nevada v. Hall, 440 U.S. 410, 421-424 (1979). But our decisions support no roving "public policy exception" to the full faith and credit due *judgments*. See *Estin*, 334 U.S. at 546 (Full Faith and Credit Clause "ordered submission . . . even to hostile policies reflected in the judgment of another State, because the practical operation of the federal system, which the Constitution designed, demanded it."); Fauntleroy v. Lum, 210 U.S. 230, 237 (1908) (judgment of Missouri court entitled to full faith and credit in Mississippi even if Missouri judgment rested on a misapprehension of Mississippi law). In assuming the existence of a ubiquitous "public policy exception" permitting one State to resist recognition of another State's judgment, the District Court in the Bakers' wrongful-death action, [cit.] misread our precedent. "The full faith and credit clause is one of the provisions incorporated into the Constitution by its framers for the purpose of transforming an aggregation of independent, sovereign States into a nation." [cit.] We are "aware of [no] considerations of local policy or law which could rightly be deemed to impair the force and effect which the full faith and credit clause and the Act of Congress require to be given to [a money] judgment outside the state of its rendition." Magnolia Petroleum Co. v. Hunt, 320 U.S. 430, 438 (1943).

The Court has never placed equity decrees outside the full faith and credit domain. Equity decrees for the payment of money have long been considered equivalent to judgments at law entitled to nationwide recognition. See, e.g., Barber v. Barber, 323 U.S. 77 (1944) (unconditional adjudication of petitioner's right to recover a sum of money is entitled to full faith and credit); see also A. Ehrenzweig, Conflict of Laws § 51, p. 182 (rev. ed. 1962) (describing as "indefensible" the old doctrine that an equity decree, because it does not "merge" the claim into the judgment, does not qualify for recognition). We see no reason why the preclusive effects of an adjudication on parties and those "in privity" with them, *i.e.*, claim preclusion and issue preclusion (res judicata and collateral estoppel), should differ depending solely upon the type of relief sought in a civil action. Cf. *Barber*, 323 U.S. at 87 (Jackson, J., concurring) (Full Faith and Credit Clause and its implementing statute speak not of "judgments" but of "'judicial proceedings' without limitation");

Fed. Rule Civ. Proc. 2 (providing for "one form of action to be known as 'civil action,'" in lieu of discretely labeled actions at law and suits in equity).

Full faith and credit, however, does not mean that States must adopt the practices of other States regarding the time, manner, and mechanisms for enforcing judgments. Enforcement measures do not travel with the sister state judgment as preclusive effects do; such measures remain subject to the even-handed control of forum law. See McElmoyle ex rel. Bailey v. Cohen, 13 Peters 312, 325 (1839) (judgment may be enforced only as "laws [of enforcing forum] may permit"); see also Restatement (Second) of Conflict of Laws § 99 (1969) ("The local law of the forum determines the methods by which a judgment of another state is enforced.").

Orders commanding action or inaction have been denied enforcement in a sister State when they purported to accomplish an official act within the exclusive province of that other State or interfered with litigation over which the ordering State had no authority. Thus, a sister State's decree concerning land ownership in another State has been held ineffective *to transfer title*, see Fall v. Eastin, 215 U.S. 1 (1909), although such a decree may indeed preclusively adjudicate the rights and obligations running between the *parties* to the foreign litigation, see, e.g., Robertson v. Howard, 229 U.S. 254, 261 (1913) ("It may not be doubted that a court of equity in one State in a proper case could compel a defendant before it to convey property situated in another State."). And antisuit injunctions regarding litigation elsewhere, even if compatible with due process as a direction constraining parties to the decree, see Cole v. Cunningham, 133 U.S. 107 (1890), in fact have not controlled the second court's actions regarding litigation in that court. See, e.g., James v. Grand Trunk Western R. Co., 14 Ill. 2d 356, 372, 152 N.E.2d 858, 867 (1958); see also E. Scoles & P. Hay, Conflict of Laws § 24.21, p. 981 (2d ed. 1992) (observing that antisuit injunction "does not address, and thus has no preclusive effect on, the merits of the litigation [in the second forum]").[9] Sanctions for violations of an injunction, in any event, are generally administered by the court that issued the injunction. [cit.]

B. With these background principles in view, we turn to the dimensions of the order GM relies upon to stop Elwell's testimony. Specifically, we take up the question: What matters did the Michigan injunction legitimately conclude?

As earlier recounted, [cit.] the parties before the Michigan County Court, Elwell and GM, submitted an agreed-upon injunction, which the presiding judge signed. While no issue was joined, expressly litigated, and determined in the Michigan

---

9. This Court has held it impermissible for a state court to enjoin a party from proceeding in a federal court, see Donovan v. Dallas, 377 U.S. 408 (1964), but has not yet ruled on the credit due to a state court injunction barring a party from maintaining litigation in another State, see Ginsburg, Judgments in Search of Full Faith and Credit: The Last-in-Time Rule for Conflicting Judgments, 82 Harv. L. Rev. 798, 823 (1969); see also Reese, Full Faith and Credit to Foreign Equity Decrees, 42 Iowa L. Rev. 183, 198 (1957) (urging that, although this Court "has not yet had occasion to determine [the issue], ... full faith and credit does not require dismissal of an action whose prosecution has been enjoined," for to hold otherwise "would mean in effect that the courts of one state can control what goes on in the courts of another"). State courts that have dealt with the question have, in the main, regarded antisuit injunctions as outside the full faith and credit ambit. See id., at 823, and n. 99; see also id., at 828-829 ("The current state of the law, permitting [an antisuit] injunction to issue but not compelling any deference outside the rendering state, may be the most reasonable compromise between . . . extreme alternatives," i.e., "[a] general rule of respect for antisuit injunctions running between state courts," or "a general rule denying the states authority to issue injunctions directed at proceedings in other states").

proceeding,[11] that order is *claim* preclusive between Elwell and GM. Elwell's claim for wrongful discharge and his related contract and tort claims have "merged in the judgment," and he cannot sue again to recover more. [cit.] Similarly, GM cannot sue Elwell elsewhere on the counterclaim GM asserted in Michigan. [cit.]

Michigan's judgment, however, cannot reach beyond the Elwell-GM controversy to control proceedings against GM brought in other States, by other parties, asserting claims the merits of which Michigan has not considered. Michigan has no power over those parties, and no basis for commanding them to become intervenors in the Elwell-GM dispute. See Martin v. Wilks, 490 U.S. 755, 761-763 (1989). Most essentially, Michigan lacks authority to control courts elsewhere by precluding them, in actions brought by strangers to the Michigan litigation, from determining for themselves what witnesses are competent to testify and what evidence is relevant and admissible in their search for the truth. See Restatement (Second) of Conflict of Laws, §§ 137-139 (1969 and rev. 1988) (forum's own law governs witness competence and grounds for excluding evidence); [cit.].

As the District Court recognized, Michigan's decree could operate against Elwell to preclude him from *volunteering* his testimony. [cit.] But a Michigan court cannot, by entering the injunction to which Elwell and GM stipulated, dictate to a court in another jurisdiction that evidence relevant in the Bakers' case-- a controversy to which Michigan is foreign--shall be inadmissible. This conclusion creates no general exception to the full faith and credit command, and surely does not permit a State to refuse to honor a sister state judgment based on the forum's choice of law or policy preferences. Rather, we simply recognize that, just as the mechanisms for enforcing a judgment do not travel with the judgment itself for purposes of Full Faith and Credit, see McElmoyle ex rel. Bailey v. Cohen, 13 Peters 312 (1839); see also Restatement (Second) of Conflict of Laws § 99, and just as one State's judgment cannot automatically transfer title to land in another State, see Fall v. Eastin, 215 U.S. 1 (1909), similarly the Michigan decree cannot determine evidentiary issues in a lawsuit brought by parties who were not subject to the jurisdiction of the Michigan court. [cit.][12]

The language of the consent decree is informative in this regard. Excluding the then-pending Georgia action from the ban on testimony by Elwell without GM's

---

11. In no event, we have observed, can issue preclusion be invoked against one who did not participate in the prior adjudication. See Blonder-Tongue Laboratories Inc., v. University of Ill. Foundation, 402 U.S. 313, 329 (1971); Hansberry v. Lee, 311 U.S. 32, 40 (1940). Thus, Justice Kennedy emphasizes the obvious in noting that the Michigan judgment has no preclusive effect on the Bakers, for they were not parties to the Michigan litigation. [cit.] Such an observation misses the thrust of GM's argument. GM readily acknowledges "the commonplace rule that a person may not be bound by a judgment *in personam* in a case to which he was not made a party." [cit.] But, GM adds, the Michigan decree does not bind the Bakers; it binds *Elwell* only. Most forcibly, GM insists that the Bakers cannot object to the binding effect GM seeks for the Michigan judgment because the Bakers have no constitutionally protected interest in obtaining the testimony of a particular witness. [cit.] Given this argument, it is clear that issue preclusion principles, standing alone, cannot resolve the controversy GM presents.

12. Justice Kennedy inexplicably reads into our decision a sweeping exception to full faith and credit based solely on "the integrity of Missouri's judicial processes." [cit.] The Michigan judgment is not entitled to full faith and credit, we have endeavored to make plain, because it impermissibly interferes with Missouri's control of litigation *brought by parties who were not before the Michigan court*. Thus, Justice Kennedy's hypothetical, [cit.] misses the mark. If the Bakers had been parties to the Michigan proceedings and had actually litigated the privileged character of Elwell's testimony, the Bakers would of course be precluded from relitigating that issue in Missouri. [cit.]

permission, the decree provides that it "shall not operate to *interfere with the jurisdiction* of the Court in . . . Georgia." [cit.] But if the Michigan order, extended to the Georgia case, would have "interfer[ed] with the jurisdiction" of the Georgia court, Michigan's ban would, in the same way, "interfere with the jurisdiction" of courts in other States in cases similar to the one pending in Georgia.

In line with its recognition of the interference potential of the consent decree, GM provided in the settlement agreement that, if another court ordered Elwell to testify, his testimony would "in no way" render him vulnerable to suit in Michigan for violation of the injunction or agreement. [cit.] The Eighth Circuit regarded this settlement agreement provision as merely a concession by GM that "some courts might fail to extend full faith and credit to the [Michigan] injunction." [cit.] As we have explained, however, Michigan's power does not reach into a Missouri courtroom to displace the forum's own determination whether to admit or exclude evidence relevant in the Bakers' wrongful-death case before it. In that light, we see no altruism in GM's agreement not to institute contempt or breach-of-contract proceedings against Elwell in Michigan for giving subpoenaed testimony elsewhere. Rather, we find it telling that GM ruled out resort to the court that entered the injunction, for injunctions are ordinarily enforced by the enjoining court, not by a surrogate tribunal. [cit.]

In sum, Michigan has no authority to shield a witness from another jurisdiction's subpoena power in a case involving persons and causes outside Michigan's governance. Recognition, under full faith and credit, is owed to dispositions Michigan has authority to order. But a Michigan decree cannot command obedience elsewhere on a matter the Michigan court lacks authority to resolve. See *Thomas* v. *Washington Gas Light Co.*, ("Full faith and credit must be given to [a] determination that [a State's tribunal] had the authority to make; but by a parity of reasoning, full faith and credit need not be given to determinations that it had no power to make.").

* * *

JUSTICE SCALIA, concurring in the judgment. I agree with the Court that enforcement measures do not travel with sister-state judgments as preclusive effects do. [cit.] It has long been established that "the judgment of a state Court cannot be enforced out of the state by an execution issued within it." McElmoyle ex rel. Bailey v. Cohen, 13 Peters 312, 325 (1839). To recite that principle is to decide this case.

General Motors asked a District Court in Missouri to *enforce* a Michigan injunction. The Missouri court was no more obliged to enforce the Michigan injunction by preventing Elwell from presenting his testimony than it was obliged to enforce it by holding Elwell in contempt. The Full Faith and Credit Clause "'did not make the judgments of other States domestic judgments to all intents and purposes, but only gave a general validity, faith, and credit to them, *as evidence*. No execution can issue upon such judgments without a new suit in the tribunals of other States.'" Thompson v. Whitman, 85 U.S. 457 (1874) (emphasis added) (quoting J. Story, Conflict of Laws § 609). A judgment or decree of one State, to be sure, may be grounds for an action (or a defense to one) in another. But the Clause and its implementing statute

"establish a rule of evidence, rather than of jurisdiction. While they make the record of a judgment, rendered after due notice in one State, conclusive evidence in the courts of another State, or of the United States, of the matter adjudged, they do not affect the jurisdiction, either of the court in which the judgment is rendered, or of the court in which it is offered in evidence. Judgments recovered in one State of the Union, when proved in the courts of another government, whether state or national, within the United States, differ from judgments recovered in a foreign country in no other respect than in not being reexaminable on their merits, nor impeachable for fraud in obtaining them, if rendered by a court having jurisdiction of the cause and of the parties." Wisconsin v. Pelican Ins. Co., 127 U.S. 265, 291-292 (1888) (citation omitted).

The judgment that General Motors obtained in Michigan "'does not carry with it, into another State, the efficacy of a judgment upon property or persons, to be enforced by execution. To give it the force of a judgment in another State, it must be made a judgment there; and can only be executed in the latter as its laws may permit.'" Lynde v. Lynde, 181 U.S. 183, 187 (1901) (quoting *McElmoyle*). [cit.]

Because neither the Full Faith and Credit Clause nor its implementing statute requires Missouri to execute the injunction issued by the courts of Michigan, I concur in the judgment.

JUSTICE KENNEDY, with whom JUSTICES O'CONNOR and THOMAS join, concurring in the judgment. I concur in the judgment. In my view the case is controlled by well-settled full faith and credit principles which render the majority's extended analysis unnecessary and, with all due respect, problematic in some degree. This separate opinion explains my approach.

I. The majority, of course, is correct to hold that when a judgment is presented to the courts of a second State it may not be denied enforcement based upon some disagreement with the laws of the State of rendition. Full faith and credit forbids the second State from questioning a judgment on these grounds. There can be little doubt of this proposition. We have often recognized the second State's obligation to give effect to another State's judgments even when the law underlying those judgments contravenes the public policy of the second State. [cit.]

My concern is that the majority, having stated the principle, proceeds to disregard it by announcing two broad exceptions. First, the majority would allow courts outside the issuing State to decline to enforce those judgments "purport[ing] to accomplish an official act within the exclusive province of [a sister] State." [cit.] Second, the basic rule of full faith and credit is said not to cover injunctions "interfer[ing] with litigation over which the ordering State had no authority." [cit.] The exceptions the majority recognizes are neither consistent with its rejection of a public policy exception to full faith and credit nor in accord with established rules implementing the Full Faith and Credit Clause. As employed to resolve this case, furthermore, the exceptions to full faith and credit have a potential for disrupting judgments, and this ought to give us considerable pause.

Our decisions have been careful not to foreclose all effect for the types of injunctions the majority would place outside the ambit of full faith and credit. These authorities seem to be disregarded by today's holding. For example, the majority chooses to discuss the extent to which courts may compel the conveyance of property in other jurisdictions. That subject has proven to be quite difficult. Some of our cases uphold actions by state courts affecting land outside their territorial reach. [cit.] Nor have we undertaken before today to announce an exception which denies full faith and credit based on the principle that the prior judgment interferes with litigation pending in another jurisdiction. [cit.] As a general matter, there is disagreement among the state courts as to their duty to recognize decrees enjoining proceedings in other courts. [cit.]

Subjects which are at once so fundamental and so delicate as these ought to be addressed only in a case necessarily requiring their discussion, and even then with caution lest we announce rules which will not be sound in later application. [cit.] We might be required to hold, if some future case raises the issue, that an otherwise valid judgment cannot intrude upon essential processes of courts outside the issuing State in certain narrow circumstances, but we need not announce or define that principle here. Even if some qualification of full faith and credit were required where the judicial processes of a second State are sought to be controlled in their procedural and institutional aspects, the Court's discussion does not provide sufficient guidance on how this exception should be construed in light of our precedents. The majority's broad review of these matters does not articulate the rationale underlying its conclusions. In the absence of more elaboration, it is unclear what it is about the particular injunction here that renders it undeserving of full faith and credit. The Court's reliance upon unidentified principles to justify omitting certain types of injunctions from the doctrine's application leaves its decision in uneasy tension with its own rejection of a broad public policy exception to full faith and credit.

The following example illustrates the uncertainty surrounding the majority's approach. Suppose the Bakers had anticipated the need for Elwell's testimony in Missouri and had appeared in a Michigan court to litigate the privileged character of the testimony it sought to elicit. Assume further the law on privilege were the same in both jurisdictions. If Elwell, GM, and the Bakers were before the Michigan court and Michigan law gave its own injunction preclusive effect, the Bakers could not relitigate the point, if general principles of issue preclusion control. Perhaps the argument can be made, as the majority appears to say, that the integrity of Missouri's judicial processes demands a rule allowing relitigation of the issue; but, for the reasons given below, we need not confront this interesting question. * * *

II. In the case before us, of course, the Bakers were neither parties to the earlier litigation nor subject to the jurisdiction of the Michigan courts. The majority pays scant attention to this circumstance, which becomes critical. The beginning point of full faith and credit analysis requires a determination of the effect the judgment has in the courts of the issuing State. In our most recent full faith and credit cases, we have said that determining the force and effect of a judgment should be the first step in our analysis. [cit.] A conclusion that the issuing State would not give the prior judgment preclusive effect ends the inquiry, making it unnecessary to determine the existence of any exceptions to full faith and credit. [cit.] We cannot decline to inquire into these state-law questions when the inquiry will obviate new extensions or exceptions to full faith and credit. [cit.]

If we honor the undoubted principle that courts need give a prior judgment no more force or effect that the issuing State gives it, the case before us is resolved. Here the Court of Appeals and both parties in their arguments before our Court seemed to embrace the assumption that Michigan would apply the full force of its judgment to the Bakers. Michigan law does not appear to support the assumption.

The simple fact is that the Bakers were not parties to the Michigan proceedings, and nothing indicates Michigan would make the novel assertion that its earlier injunction binds the Bakers or any other party not then before it or subject to its jurisdiction. For collateral estoppel to apply under Michigan law, "'the same parties must have had a full opportunity to litigate the issue, and there must be mutuality of estoppel.'" [cit.] * * * Since the Bakers were not parties to the Michigan proceedings and had no opportunity to litigate any of the issues presented, it appears that Michigan law would not treat them as bound by the judgment. The majority cites no authority to the contrary.

It makes no difference that the judgment in question is an injunction. The Michigan Supreme Court has twice rejected arguments that injunctions have preclusive effect in later litigation, relying in no small part on the fact that the persons against whom preclusion is asserted were not parties to the earlier litigation. [cit.]

The opinion of the Court of Appeals suggests the Michigan court which issued the injunction intended to bind third parties in litigation in other States. [cit.] The question, however, is not what a trial court intended in a particular case but the preclusive effect its judgment has under the controlling legal principles of its own State. Full faith and credit measures the effect of a judgment by all the laws of the rendering State, including authoritative rulings of that State's highest court on questions of issue preclusion and jurisdiction over third parties. [cit.]

The fact that other Michigan trial courts refused to reconsider the injunction but instead required litigants to return to the trial court which issued it in the first place sheds little light on the substance of issue preclusion law in Michigan. In construing state law, we must determine how the highest court of the State would decide an issue. [cit.]

In this case, moreover, those Michigan trial courts which declined to modify the injunction did not appear to base their rulings on preclusion law. They relied instead on Michigan Court Rule 2.613(B), which directs parties wishing to modify an injunction to present their arguments to the court which entered it. [cit.] Rule 2.613(B) is a procedural rule based on comity concerns, not a preclusion rule. It reflects Michigan's determination that, within the State of Michigan itself, respect for the issuing court and judicial resources are best preserved by allowing the issuing court to determine whether the injunction should apply to further proceedings. As a procedural rule, it is not binding on courts of another State by virtue of full faith and credit. [cit.] The Bakers have never appeared in a Michigan court, and full faith and credit cannot be used to force them to subject themselves to Michigan's jurisdiction. [cit.]

Under Michigan law, the burden of persuasion rests on the party raising preclusion as a defense. [cit.] In light of these doctrines and the absence of contrary authority, one cannot conclude that GM has carried its burden of showing that Michigan courts would bind the Bakers to the terms of the earlier injunction prohibiting Elwell from testifying. The result should come as no surprise. It is most unlikely that Michigan would give a judgment preclusive effect against a person who was not a party to the proceeding in which it was entered or who was not otherwise subject to the jurisdiction of the issuing court. [cit.]

Although inconsistent on this point, GM disavows its desire to issue preclude the Bakers, claiming "the only party being 'bound' to the injunction is Elwell." [cit.] This is difficult to accept because in assessing the preclusive reach of a judgment we look to its practical effect. [cit.] Despite its disclaimer, GM seeks to alter the course of the suit between it and the Bakers by preventing the Bakers from litigating the admissibility of Elwell's testimony. Furthermore, even were we to accept GM's argument that the Bakers are essentially irrelevant to this dispute, GM's argument is flawed on its own terms. Elwell, in the present litigation, does not seek to relitigate anything; he is a witness, not a party.

In all events, determining as a threshold matter the extent to which Michigan law gives preclusive effect to the injunction eliminates the need to decide whether full faith and credit applies to equitable decrees as a general matter or the extent to which the general rules of full faith and credit are subject to exceptions. Michigan law would not seek to bind the Bakers to the injunction and that suffices to resolve the case. For these reasons, I concur in the judgment.

Notes and Comments

1. After *Baker* is there any public policy exception to the full faith and credit due to judgments?

2. Some older commentary and cases suggest that equity decrees are not entitled to full faith and credit, see, e.g., Restatement § 449(1), apparently because, long ago, equity decrees were not considered to have preclusive effect even where rendered. See Willard Barbour, Note, The Extra-Territorial Effect of the Equitable Decree, 17 *Mich. L. Rev.* 527, 539-41 (1919). In *Baker*, the Court rejects the argument that equity decrees are outside the scope of the Full Faith and Credit Clause, although the Court does not require *all* equity decrees be enforced. As the Court explains, "a Michigan decree cannot command obedience elsewhere on a matter the Michigan court lacks authority to resolve." Of course this statement begs the question of what matters Michigan lacks authority to decide. Suppose that GM secured an injunction in Michigan enjoining Elwell from breaching in Missouri a non-competition agreement? Would Missouri be required to enforce that injunction? See Price, *The Equity Conflict*, 835-837.

3. Compare *Baker* with Matsushita Elec. Indus. Co. v. Epstein, 516 U.S. 367 (1996). There, shareholders of Matsushita filed a class action in state court based on state law claims. The class action was settled and the state court entered judgment based on the settlement. One of the provisions of the settlement incorporated into the judgment was a provision that all the class members waived any claims they might have based on federal securities claims—claims over which the federal courts have

exclusive jurisdiction. In Matsushita was the state court purporting to resolve matters as to which it lacked authority? Is the difference between *Baker* and *Matsushita* that in *Baker* the state court was exceeding a territorial conception of authority? See Maltz, *The Place of Baker* (arguing that Baker reflects "territorial notions of sovereignty and power").

4. Justice Ginsburg relies on Fall v. Eastin, 215 U.S. 1 (1909). There a Washington court had granted the parties a divorce, issued a decree granting the wife certain lands in Nebraska and ordered the husband to transfer title to the wife. When the husband refused to comply with the order, a Washington commissioner executed a deed to the Nebraska land. After the husband deeded the land to his sister, the wife brought a quiet title action in Nebraska. The Supreme Court affirmed a judgment in favor of the husband holding the Washington court could not directly affect title to the land. The Court acknowledged that an equity court having in personam jurisdiction "has the power to require a defendant 'to do or to refrain from doing anything beyond the limits of its territorial jurisdiction which it might have required to be done or omitted within the limits of such territory.'" However, the Court stressed that where the land is located in another state, the decree itself cannot convey actual title to that land. In *Baker*, did the Michigan decree "purport[] to accomplish an official act within the exclusive province of" another state?

5. Justice Ginsburg states that "antisuit injunctions regarding litigation elsewhere *** have not controlled the second court's action regarding litigation in that court." Notice that she does not cite any Supreme Court authority for this proposition. Indeed, the Supreme Court has never directly ruled on the enforceability of antisuit injunctions. Consider the situation in James v. Grand Trunk Western R.R. Co., 152 N.E.2d 858 (Ill.), *cert. denied*, 358 U.S. 915 (1958). The plaintiff brought suit in Illinois under the Michigan Wrongful Death Act. After the complaint was filed in Illinois, the defendant obtained an injunction from a Michigan court which ordered plaintiff not to proceed with the Illinois suit. The Illinois court then issued a counter-injunction enjoining the defendant from enforcing the Michigan injunction action. The Illinois court explained: "[T]his court need not, and will not, countenance having its right to try cases, of which it has proper jurisdiction, determined by the courts of other States, through their injunctive process." Id. at 867. Should the Illinois court be required to give full faith and credit to the Michigan injunction? Is the impingement on Illinois any more significant than the impingement on Mississippi in *Fauntleroy v. Lum*? See Ginsburg, *The Last-in-Time Rule*, 823-30.

6. How important is it that the Bakers were not parties to the Michigan case? Suppose they had brought their suit against GM in Michigan. Would it violate due process for Michigan to enforce the Elway decree in the Baker's suit? If recognition would violate due process then the Full Faith and Credit discussion is irrelevant. If it would not violate due process then why would it matter whether they were parties? See Price, *The Equity Conflict*, 775-776.

7. Enforcement procedures. The Court notes that full faith and credit "does not mean that States must adopt the practices of other States regarding the time, manner, and mechanisms for enforcing judgments." Thus in McElmoyle v. Cohen, 38 U.S. (13 Pet.) 312 (1839), the Court held that an enforcing state may apply its statute of

limitations for judgments and refuse to enforce a judgment that was still enforceable in the rendering state. The Court explained that the judgment is conclusive as to "the merits," but that statutes of limitations concern "remedy" "and consequently * * * the *lex fori* must prevail." Id. at 327. Similarly, in Watkins v. Conway, 385 U.S. 188 (1966), the Court upheld at Georgia statute which allowed a shorter time for enforcing foreign judgments than for enforcing Georgia judgments. The Court reasoned that the Georgia statute did not inappropriately disadvantage sister state judgments because the Georgia time limit ran not from the date of the original judgment but from the date of the latest revival of the judgment.

On the other hand, one state's ability to apply its own rules concerning enforcement may be affected by subsequent actions by other states. In Union Nat'l Bank v. Lamb, 337 U.S. 38 (1949), Missouri had rendered a judgment and under Missouri law, no judgment can be revived after ten years from its rendition. Eighteen years after the original Missouri judgment, the judgment creditor "revived" the Missouri judgment in a Colorado proceeding. He then sought enforcement in Missouri. Missouri refused to enforce the judgment on the grounds that the Colorado action should not be treated as a new judgment. It then applied its statute of limitations for enforcement and since the original judgment was more than ten years old, it refused to enforce the judgment. The Supreme Court reversed, holding that it was Colorado law not Missouri law which should be used to determine the effect of the Colorado court's action.

8. In 2000, a Florida jury awarded a $145 billion punitive damage award against R.J. Reynolds. Under Florida law, R.J. Reynolds could stay execution of the judgment pending an appeal, but only by posting a bond equal to $120% of the judgment, an amount that exceeded the company's net worth. Most of the company's assets and operations were located in Georgia, Kentucky, North Carolina, and Virginia, and in response to the Florida judgment, these states enacted legislation under which a judgment debtor could stay execution pending appeal by posting a much smaller bond. Some legal experts opined that these state statutes were unconstitutional. Do you agree? Professor Finch has argued that although the finality of a judgment and its res judicata effect are determined by the law of the rendering state, the amount of a security bond is a matter of procedure that is governed by the enforcing court's procedural law. See Finch, *Punitive Damages.*

9. Can the enforcing state take away the "jurisdiction" of its courts to enforce certain types of judgments? You will recall that in *Fauntleroy*, the Supreme Court rejected Mississippi's argument that its courts lacked "jurisdiction" to enforce gambling contracts. The Court rejected a similar argument in Kenney v. Supreme Lodge, 252 U.S. 411 (1920). There the Illinois Supreme Court had refused to enforce an Alabama wrongful death judgment, relying on an Illinois statute that prohibited suits for deaths occurring out of state. The Supreme Court reversed, stating:

> [T]he fact that here the original cause of action could not have been maintained in Illinois is not an answer to a suit upon the judgment. * * * [I]t is plain that a State cannot escape its constitutional obligations by the simple device of denying jurisdiction in such cases to courts otherwise competent.

Id. at 415.

3. *Whose Rules of Preclusion*

Although all states have preclusion rules that limit relitigation of claims and issues, there are some significant variations in the scope of these doctrines. For example, some states define "claim" more narrowly than others and hence would allow a second suit on a somewhat different claim that arises out of the same transaction as the first suit. Moreover, states differ as to what, if any, claims qualify as compulsory counterclaims and therefore are barred in subsequent litigation. Finally, some states have abandoned the requirement of mutuality as a prerequisite for issue preclusion, while others retain that requirement. These variations sometimes make it necessary to determine which state's preclusion laws apply.

Generally, the enforcing state must apply the preclusion rules of the rendering state or at least give as much effect to the judgment as the rendering state would. See *Durfee v. Duke*, supra (enforcing state required to give "at least the res judicata effect which the judgment would be accorded in the State which rendered it"). Thus, if a claim or issue would have been precluded in the rendering state, full faith and credit requires that all other states preclude it as well.

A somewhat different situation is presented when the rendering state would not preclude future litigation, but the enforcing state would like to give preclusive effect. Some courts have concluded that in this situation, the enforcing state may apply its own preclusion rules. See, e.g., Finley v. Kesling, 433 N.E.2d 1112 (Ill.App.1982); Hart v. American Airlines, 304 N.Y.S.2d 810 (N.Y.Sup.Ct.1969). These courts have reasoned that it does not offend the principles of full faith and credit for one state to give *more* deference than the rendering state would. Do you agree? Was the Full Faith and Credit Clause intended to assure "respect" for judgments or to assure uniformity in enforcement?

Regardless of what the Full Faith and Credit *Clause* means, the Full Faith and Credit *Statute* seems to be more specific. It provides that a judicial proceeding "shall have the *same* full faith and credit in every court" as it would have in the rendering court. 28 U.S.C. § 1738 (emphasis added). The Supreme Court has never addressed the question of whether this statute prohibits a *state* from giving greater effect to a judgment than would the rendering sister state. The Court has concluded, however, that this statute prohibits a *federal* court from giving greater effect than would the rendering state court. In Marrese v. American Acad. of Orthopaedic Surgeons, 470 U.S. 373, 380, 384 (1985), infra at 796, the Court held that § 1738 requires federal courts "to refer to the preclusion law of the State in which judgment was rendered" and rejected "the view that § 1738 allows a federal court to give a state court judgment greater preclusive effect than the state courts themselves would give to it." Do you agree with the Court's interpretation of the statute? Are any other interpretations possible? See Caust-Ellenbogen, *Interstate Preclusion*, 593 (1990); Shreve, *Preclusion and Federal Choice of Law*, 1209. Can the statute fairly be interpreted to prohibit *federal courts* from granting greater preclusive effect while at the same time allowing *state courts* to give greater effect?

Notwithstanding *Durfee* and *Marrese*, it has been argued that certain aspects of preclusion doctrine are simply not covered by the requirements of full faith and credit.

"Faith and credit" can be limited to the rules that ensure effective stability and enforcement. It is even possible to argue that some preclusion rules are really not attributes of the judgment, or "judicial proceeding," at all. Instead, they are matters of local procedural law that other courts are free to reject in the sweeping freedom that exists in choosing domestic over foreign law outside the realm of judgments.

18B Wright, Miller & Cooper, *Federal Practice* § 4467 at 37. See Carrington, *Collateral Estoppel*, 381. How should one distinguish those aspects of preclusion doctrine that are attributes of the judgment and those that are mere matters of procedure? Should one do a type of interest analysis and evaluate the purposes underlying the particular preclusion rule? See, e.g., Williams v. Ocean Trans. Lines, Inc., 425 F.2d 1183, 1188-89 (3d Cir.1970) ("If the policy behind the collateral estoppel rule is the same as that of the full faith and credit clause [and statute]," then apply the law of the rendering state, but "[i]f the rule is based on a policy of preserving courts from the onerous burden of relitigating issues fully and fairly disposed of once," then apply law of the enforcing forum); Erichson, *Interjurisdictional Preclusion*; Shreve, *Preclusion and Federal Choice of Law*, 1255-57.

If one agrees that in some cases the enforcing state need not follow the rendering state's preclusion rules, one then must decide when those cases occur. Advocates of a more flexible approach disagree about when to use preclusion rules. Consider the following:

(1) Scope of the claim: rendering state law would allow a second suit related but not identical to the first suit; enforcing state law would not. Compare Carrington, *Collateral estoppel* at 386-87 (enforcing state can apply its preclusion law), with Shreve, *Preclusion and Federal Choice of Law*, at 1261 (enforcing state cannot apply its preclusion law), with 18B Wright, Miller & Cooper, *Federal Practice*, at 47-48 (enforcing state can apply its preclusion law, but the preclusive effect the enforcing state gives the judgment does not prevent further litigation back in the rendering state).

(2) Compulsory counterclaims: rendering state requires compulsory counterclaims to be raised; enforcing state does not. Compare Carrington, *Collateral Estoppel*, at 390-91 (enforcing state can hear the counterclaim that rendering state would bar), with 18B Wright, Miller & Cooper, *Federal Practice*, at 44 (enforcing state cannot hear the counterclaim).

(3) Mutuality: rendering state requires mutuality and therefore would not give preclusive effect in a second case with different parties; enforcing state does not require mutuality. Compare Carrington, supra, at 388-89 (enforcing state can give preclusive effect when rendering state would not), and Shreve, supra, at 1258 (same), with 18B Wright, Miller & Cooper, *Federal Practice*, at 49-50 (enforcing state cannot give preclusive effect when rendering state would not). How would you decide these cases? Is a clear rule, such as always applying the

law of the rendering state, preferable to a more flexible and uncertain approach, such as considering sister state interests?

4. Penal and Tax Judgments

In Huntington v. Attrill, 146 U.S. 657 (1892), a New York court applied New York law and held corporate directors personally liable for certain corporate debts because the directors had falsely sworn that the corporation was fully capitalized. Maryland refused to enforce the judgment, stating "it is well settled that no state will enforce penalties imposed by the laws of another State." The Supreme Court reversed, but did so on the ground that the New York law was not penal. The Court observed:

> The question whether a statute of one State which in some aspects may be called penal, is a penal law in the international sense, so that it cannot be enforced in the courts of another State, depends upon the question whether its purpose is to punish an offence against the public justice of the State, or to afford a private remedy to a person injured by the wrongful act.

Id. at 673-74. The Court further explained: "Penal laws, strictly and properly, are those imposing punishment for an offence committed against the State, and which by the English and American constitutions, the executive of the State has the power to pardon." Id. at 667. Historically, Anglo-American courts also did not enforce either penal or tax judgments of other states. The Restatement of Foreign Relations offers the following justifications: "The rule appears to reflect a reluctance of courts to subject foreign public law to judicial scrutiny * * *, combined with reluctance to enforce law that may conflict with the public policy of the forum state." Restatement (Third) of Foreign Relations § 483, Reporters' Note 2 (1987). How persuasive do you find these reasons?

If "penal" judgments are exempt from full faith and credit, how broad is this exemption? Would it include treble damage awards or punitive damages? In Holbein v. Rigot, 245 So.2d 57 (Fla.1971), the Florida Supreme Court enforced a Texas award of punitive damages in a suit alleging fraudulent misrepresentations. The court explained:

> [O]ur holding is that plaintiffs' Texas suit insofar as it sought to recover punitive damages was based on common law liability arising from fraud to redress a private wrong inflicted on plaintiffs and did not purport to redress a public wrong predicated on a statute that is penal in the international sense which may not be enforced in the courts of other states. [cit.] Here the defendant is punished for the purpose of reparation to those aggrieved by his offense.

Id. at 61. See Miller v. Kingsley, 230 N.W.2d 472 (Neb.1975) (Nebraska court enforced a judgment for punitive damages even though such damages were prohibited in Nebraska); Restatement (Third) of Foreign Relations § 483 cmt. b ("Some [foreign] states consider judgments penal for purposes of non-recognition if multiple, punitive, or exemplary damages are awarded * * *. In the United States, such judgments are not considered penal for this purpose.") See generally Finch, *Punitive Damage Awards*, at 528-561; Leflar, *Penal and Governmental Claims*, 193.

In Milwaukee County v. M.E. White Co., 296 U.S. 268 (1935), the Supreme Court held that once a tax liability has been reduced to a judgment, it is entitled to full faith and credit. In reaching this conclusion, the Court assumed without deciding that one state is not required to enforce the revenue *laws* of another state. However, the Court held that once a *judgment* has been entered based on revenue laws, the judgment must be enforced. The Court explained:

> In a suit upon a money judgment for a civil cause of action the validity of the claim upon which it was founded is not open to inquiry, whatever its genesis. * * *
>
> In numerous cases this Court has held that credit must be given to the judgment of another state although the forum would not be required to entertain the suit on which the judgment was founded; that considerations of policy of the forum which would defeat a suit upon the original cause of action are not involved in a suit upon the judgment and are insufficient to defeat it.

Id. at 275-77. Although the Court expressly left open the question whether a judgment "created by the penal law, in the international sense" was entitled to full faith and credit, the Court upheld enforcement of a 2% delinquency "penalty." Id. at 279. The Court noted that "the record does not disclose that the nominal penalty arose under a penal law or is of such a nature as to preclude suit to recover it outside the state of Wisconsin." Id. at 280. If a monetary penalty payable to the government for violation of a revenue law is not "penal," can any civil remedy be considered "penal?" Given the court's rationale, is there any basis for treating punitive judgments differently from other judgments?

5. *Inconsistent Judgments*

When an enforcing court is confronted with two prior and inconsistent judgments, to which judgment should it give full faith and credit? In Treinies v. Sunshine Mining Co., 308 U.S. 66 (1939), the Supreme Court held that the judgment later in time should be enforced. There, a Washington probate court had determined that certain stock should go to the decedent's husband. The decedent's daughter then brought suit in Idaho seeking the stock. The Idaho court held that the Washington court lacked jurisdiction and that therefore it need not give the Washington judgment full faith and credit. The Idaho court awarded the stock to the daughter. The husband then returned to Washington and brought a quiet title action. The corporation whose stock was at issue then filed an interpleader action in federal court. The federal district court enjoined the Washington quiet title action but had to determine whether to give effect to the Washington probate judgment or the later Idaho judgment. The Supreme Court held that it was the later Idaho judgment that should be enforced. The Court explained:

> The Court of Appeals correctly determined that the issue of jurisdiction *vel non* of the Washington court could not be relitigated in this interpleader. As the Idaho District Court was a court of general jurisdiction, its conclusions are unassailable collaterally except for fraud or lack of jurisdiction. The holding by the Idaho court of no jurisdiction in Washington necessarily determined the

question raised here as to the Idaho jurisdiction against Miss Treinies' contention. She is bound by that judgment.

Id. at 78.

Does the last-in-time rule make sense? Does not it encourage a litigant to escape an unfavorable ruling by relitigating in a second state? What recourse does a litigant have when a court of another state wrongly ignores a prior judgment? Suppose the husband in *Treinies* had sought certiorari on the Idaho decree but the Supreme Court had denied certiorari. Should the Idaho judgment still be entitled to full faith and credit? See Ginsburg, *The Last-in-Time Rule*, 798.

In *Treinies*, would Washington have been required to enforce the Idaho judgment, even though Idaho ignored a prior Washington decree? Some courts have held that it would not, reasoning that full faith and credit does not require a state to favor a sister state judgment over its own. See e.g., Porter v. Porter, 416 P.2d 564 (Ariz.1966), *cert. denied*, 386 U.S. 957 (1967); Colby v. Colby, 369 P.2d 1019 (Nev.), *cert. denied*, 371 U.S. 888 (1962). The Restatement (Second) of Judgments § 15, cmt. e, quoting Restatement (Second) § 114, cmt. b, notes:

> Although the later judgment is ordinarily held conclusive even though it erroneously denied res judicata effect to the earlier judgment, the rule may be different if the error consisted of a denial of full faith and credit to the judgment of a sister state and the losing party was denied review in the Supreme Court of the United States. "In such a situation, it might be thought inappropriate to require that conclusive effect be given under full faith and credit to the later inconsistent judgment."[1]

Do you agree that forum 1 should be able to ignore the forum 2 judgment even though all other courts must enforce the forum 2 judgment?

C. SPECIAL RECOGNITION PROBLEMS OF FAMILY LAW

1. Recognition of Divorce Judgments

For much of our history, most states' laws severely limited the availability of divorce. The result was that a few states, such as Nevada, became "divorce mills," offering no-fault divorces as one of the enticements to visit the state. This in turn presented courts with the full faith and credit issue of when one state must recognize a divorce granted by another state.

---

1. Quoted with the permission of the copyright owner, The American Law Institute.

Williams v. North Carolina [II]
Supreme Court of the United States, 1945.
325 U.S. 226, 65 S.Ct. 1092, 89 L.Ed. 1577.

JUSTICE FRANKFURTER delivered the opinion of the Court. This case is here to review judgments of the Supreme Court of North Carolina, affirming convictions for bigamous cohabitation, assailed on the ground that full faith and credit, as required by the Constitution of the United States, was not accorded divorces decreed by one of the courts of Nevada. Williams v. North Carolina, 317 U.S. 287 [1942] [*Williams I*], decided an earlier aspect of the controversy. It was there held that a divorce granted by Nevada, on a finding that one spouse was domiciled in Nevada, must be respected in North Carolina, where Nevada's finding of domicil was not questioned though the other spouse had neither appeared nor been served with process in Nevada and though recognition of such a divorce offended the policy of North Carolina. The record then before us did not present the question whether North Carolina had the power "to refuse full faith and credit to Nevada divorce decrees because, contrary to the findings of the Nevada court, North Carolina finds that no bona fide domicil was acquired in Nevada." *Williams I*. This is the precise issue which has emerged after retrial of the cause following our reversal. Its obvious importance brought the case here. [cit.]

* * *

* * * [T]he [Full Faith and Credit] Clause does not make a sister-State judgment a judgment in another State. The proposal to do so was rejected by the Philadelphia Convention. 2 Farrand, The Records of the Federal Convention of 1787, 447, 448. "To give it the force of a judgment in another state, it must be made a judgment there." McElmoyle v. Cohen, 13 Pet. 312, 325 [1839]. It can be made a judgment there only if the court purporting to render the original judgment had power to render such a judgment. A judgment in one States is conclusive upon the merits in every other State, but only if the court of the first State had power to pass on the merits—had jurisdiction, that is, to render the judgment.

"It is too late now to deny the right collaterally to impeach a decree of divorce made in another state, by proof that the court had no jurisdiction, even when the record purports to show jurisdiction ..." It was "too late" more than forty years ago. German Savings & Loan Society v. Dormitzer, 192 U.S. 125, 128 [1904].

Under our system of law, judicial power to grant a divorce--jurisdiction, strictly speaking--is founded on domicil. Bell v. Bell, 181 U.S. 175 [1901]; Andrews v. Andrews, 188 U.S. 14 [1903]. The framers of the Constitution were familiar with this jurisdictional prerequisite, and since 1789 neither this Court nor any other court in the English-speaking world has questioned it. Domicil implies a nexus between person and place of such permanence as to control the creation of legal relations and responsibilities of the utmost significance. The domicil of one spouse within a State gives power to that State, we have held, to dissolve a marriage wheresoever contracted. In view of *Williams I*, the jurisdictional requirement of domicil is freed from confusing refinements about "matrimonial domicil," [cit.], and the like. Divorce, like marriage, is of concern not merely to the immediate parties. It affects personal rights of the deepest significance. It also touches basic interests of society. Since divorce, like marriage, creates a new status, every consideration of policy makes it desirable that the effect should be the same wherever the question arises.

It is one thing to reopen an issue that has been settled after appropriate opportunity to present their contentions has been afforded to all who had an interest in its adjudication. This applies also to jurisdictional questions. After a contest these cannot be relitigated as between the parties. [cit.] But those not parties to a litigation ought not to be foreclosed by the interested actions of others; especially not a State which is concerned with the vindication of its own social policy and has no means, certainly no effective means, to protect that interest against the selfish action of those outside its borders. The State of domiciliary origin should not be bound by an unfounded, even if not collusive, recital in the record of a court of another State. As to the truth or existence of a fact, like that of domicil, upon which depends the power to exert judicial authority, a State not a party to the exertion of such judicial authority in another State but seriously affected by it has a right, when asserting its own unquestioned authority, to ascertain the truth or existence of that crucial fact.[6]

These considerations of policy are equally applicable whether power was assumed by the court of the first State or claimed after inquiry. This may lead, no doubt, to conflicting determinations of what judicial power is founded upon. Such conflict is inherent in the practical application of the concept of domicil in the context of our federal system.[7] [cit.] What was said in Worcester County Trust Co. v. Riley, [302 U.S. 292 (1937)] is pertinent here. "Neither the Fourteenth Amendment nor the full faith and credit clause requires uniformity in the decisions of the courts of different states as to the place of domicil, where the exertion of state power is dependent upon domicil within its boundaries." [cit.] If a finding by the court of one State that domicil in another State has been abandoned were conclusive upon the old domiciliary State, the policy of each State in matters of most intimate concern could be subverted by the policy of every other State. This Court has long ago denied the existence of such destructive power. The issue has a far reach. For domicil is the foundation of probate jurisdiction precisely as it is that of divorce. The ruling in Tilt v. Kelsey, 207 U.S. 43 [1907] regarding the probate of a will, is equally applicable to a sister-State divorce decree: "the full faith and credit due to the proceedings of the New Jersey court do not require that the courts of New York shall be bound by its adjudication on the question of domicil. On the contrary, it is open to the courts of any state, in the trial of a collateral issue, to determine, upon the evidence produced, the true domicil of the deceased." [cit.]

Although it is now settled that a suit for divorce is not an ordinary adversary proceeding, it does not promote analysis, as was recently pointed out, to label divorce proceedings as actions in rem. *Williams I.* But insofar as a divorce decree partakes of some of the characteristics of a decree in rem, it is misleading to say that

---

6. We have not here a situation where a State disregards the adjudication of another State on the issue of domicil squarely litigated in a truly adversary proceeding.

7. Since an appeal to the Full Faith and Credit Clause raises questions arising under the Constitution of the United States, the proper criteria for ascertaining domicil, should these be in dispute, become matters for federal determination. [cit.]

all the world is party to a proceeding in rem. [cit.] All the world is not party to a divorce proceeding. What is true is that all the world need not be present before a court granting the decree and yet it must be respected by the other forty-seven States provided—and it is a big proviso—the conditions for the exercise of power by the divorce-decreeing court are validly established whenever that judgment is elsewhere called into question. In short, the decree of divorce is a conclusive adjudication of everything except the jurisdictional facts upon which it is founded, and domicil is a jurisdictional fact. To permit the necessary finding of domicil by one State to foreclose all States in the protection of their social institutions would be intolerable.

But to endow each State with controlling authority to nullify the power of a sister State to grant a divorce based upon a finding that one spouse had acquired a new domicil within the divorcing State would, in the proper functioning of our federal system, be equally indefensible. No State court can assume comprehensive attention to the various and potentially conflicting interests that several States may have in the institutional aspects of marriage. The necessary accommodation between the right of one State to safeguard its interest in the family relation of its own people and the power of another State to grant divorces can be left to neither State.

The problem is to reconcile the reciprocal respect to be accorded by the members of the Union to their adjudications with due regard for another most important aspect of our federalism whereby "the domestic relations of husband and wife ... were matters reserved to the States," [cit.], and do not belong to the United States. In re Burrus, 136 U.S. 586, 593, 594 [1890]. The rights that belong to all the States and the obligations which membership in the Union imposes upon all, are made effective because this Court is open to consider claims, such as this case presents, that the courts of one State have not given the full faith and credit to the judgment of a sister State that is required by Art. IV, § 1 of the Constitution.

But the discharge of this duty does not make of this Court a court of probate and divorce. Neither a rational system of law nor hard practicality calls for our independent determination, in reviewing the judgment of a State court, of that rather elusive relation between person and place which establishes domicil. "It is not for us to retry the facts," as was held in a case in which, like the present, the jurisdiction underlying a sister-State judgment was dependent on domicil. [cit.] The challenged judgment must, however, satisfy our scrutiny that the reciprocal duty of respect owed by the States to one another's adjudications has been fairly discharged, and has not been evaded under the guise of finding an absence of domicil and therefore a want of power in the court rendering the judgment.

What is immediately before us is the judgment of the Supreme Court of North Carolina. We have authority to upset it only if there is want of foundation for the conclusion that that Court reached. The conclusion it reached turns on its finding that the spouses who obtained the Nevada decrees were not domiciled there. The fact that the Nevada court found that they were domiciled there is entitled to respect, and more. The burden of undermining the verity which the Nevada decrees import rests heavily upon the assailant. But simply because the Nevada court found that it had power to award a divorce decree cannot, we have seen, foreclose reexamination by another State. Otherwise, as was pointed out long ago, a court's record would establish its power and the power would be proved by the record. Such circular reasoning would give one State a control over all the other States which the Full Faith and Credit Clause certainly did not confer. [cit.] If this Court finds that proper weight was accorded to the claims of power by the court of one State in rendering a judgment the validity of which is pleaded in defense in another State, that the burden of overcoming such respect by disproof of the substratum of fact--here domicil--on which such power alone can rest was properly charged against the party challenging the legitimacy of the judgment, that such issue of fact was left for fair determination by appropriate procedure, and that a finding adverse to the necessary foundation for any valid sister-State judgment was amply supported in evidence, we can not upset the judgment before us. And we cannot do so even if we also found in the record of the court of original judgment warrant for its finding that it had jurisdiction. If it is a matter turning on local law, great deference is owed by the courts of one State to what a court of another State has done. [cit.] But when we are dealing as here with an historic notion common to all English-speaking courts, that of domicil, we should not find a want of deference to a sister State on the part of a court of another State which finds an absence of domicil where such a conclusion is warranted by the record.

When this case was first here, North Carolina did not challenge the finding of the Nevada court that petitioners had acquired domicils in Nevada. * * * Upon retrial, however, the existence of domicil in Nevada became the decisive issue. The judgments of conviction now under review bring before us a record which may be fairly summarized by saying that the petitioners left North Carolina for the purpose of getting divorces from their respective spouses in Nevada and as soon as each had done so and married one another they left Nevada and returned to North Carolina to live there together as man and wife. Against the charge of bigamous cohabitation under § 14-183 of the North Carolina General Statutes, petitioners stood on their Nevada divorces and offered exemplified copies of the Nevada proceedings. The trial judge charged that the State had the burden of proving beyond a reasonable doubt that (1) each petitioner was lawfully married to one person; (2) thereafter each petitioner contracted a second marriage with another person outside North Carolina; (3) the spouses of petitioners were living at the time of this second marriage; (4) petitioners cohabited with one another in North Carolina after the second marriage. The burden, it was charged, then devolved upon petitioners "to satisfy the trial jury, not beyond a reasonable doubt nor by the greater weight of the evidence, but simply to satisfy" the jury from all the evidence, that petitioners were domiciled in Nevada at the time they obtained their divorces. The court further charged that "the recitation" of bona fide domicil in the Nevada decree was "prima facie evidence" sufficient to warrant a finding of domicil in Nevada but not compelling "such an inference." If the jury found, as they were told, that petitioners had domicils in North Carolina and went to Nevada "simply and solely for the purpose of obtaining" divorces, intending to return to North Carolina on obtaining them, they never lost their North Carolina domicils nor acquired new domicils in Nevada. Domicil, the jury was instructed, was that place where a person "has voluntarily fixed his abode ... not for a mere special or temporary purpose, but with a present intention of making it his home, either permanently or for an indefinite or unlimited length of time."

The scales of justice must not be unfairly weighted by a State when full faith and credit is claimed for a sister-State judgment. But North Carolina has not so dealt with the Nevada decrees. She has not raised unfair barriers to their recognition. North Carolina did not fail in appreciation or application of federal standards of full faith and credit. Appropriate weight was given to the finding of domicil in the Nevada decrees, and that finding was allowed to be overturned only by relevant standards of proof. There is nothing to suggest that the issue was not fairly submitted to the jury and that it was not fairly assessed on cogent evidence.

* * * It would be highly unreasonable to assert that a jury could not reasonably find that the evidence demonstrated that petitioners went to Nevada solely for the purpose of obtaining a divorce and intended all along to return to North Carolina. Such an intention, the trial court properly charged, would preclude acquisition of domicils in Nevada. See Williamson v. Osenton, 232 U.S. 619 [1914]. And so we can not say that North Carolina was not entitled to draw the inference that petitioners never abandoned their domicils in North Carolina, particularly since we could not conscientiously prefer, were it our business to do so, the contrary finding of the Nevada court.

If a State cannot foreclose, on review here, all the other States by its finding that one spouse is domiciled within its bounds, persons may, no doubt, place themselves in situations that create unhappy consequences for them. This is merely one of those untoward results inevitable in a federal system in which regulation of domestic relations has been left with the States and not given to the national authority. But the occasional disregard by any one State of the reciprocal obligations of the forty-eight States to respect the constitutional power of each to deal with domestic relations of those domiciled within its borders is hardly an argument for allowing one State to deprive the other forty-seven States of their constitutional rights. Relevant statistics happily do not justify lurid forebodings that parents without number will disregard the fate of their offspring by being unmindful of the status of dignity to which they are entitled. But, in any event, to the extent that some one State may, for considerations of its own, improperly intrude into domestic relations subject to the authority of the other States, it suffices to suggest that any such indifference by a State to the bond of the Union should be discouraged not encouraged.

In seeking a decree of divorce outside the State in which he has theretofore maintained his marriage, a person is necessarily involved in the legal situation created by our federal system whereby one State can grant a divorce of validity in other States only if the applicant has a bona fide domicil in the State of the court purporting to dissolve a prior legal marriage. The petitioners therefore assumed the risk that this Court would find that North Carolina justifiably concluded that they had not been domiciled in Nevada. Since the divorces which they sought and received in Nevada had no legal validity in North Carolina and their North Carolina spouses were still alive, they subjected themselves to prosecution for bigamous cohabitation under North Carolina law. The legitimate finding of the North Carolina Supreme Court that the petitioners were not in truth domiciled in Nevada was not a contingency against which the petitioners were protected by anything in the Constitution of the United States. A man's fate often depends, as for instance in the enforcement of the Sherman Law, on far greater risks that he will estimate "rightly, that is, as the jury subsequently estimates it, some matter of degree. If his judgment is wrong, not only may he incur a fine or a short imprisonment, as here; he may incur the penalty of death." * * * Mistaken notions about one's legal rights are not sufficient to bar prosecution for crime.

We conclude that North Carolina was not required to yield her State policy because a Nevada court found that petitioners were domiciled in Nevada when it granted them decrees of divorce. North Carolina was entitled to find, as she did, that they did not acquire domicils in Nevada and that the Nevada court was therefore without power to liberate the petitioners from amenability to the laws of North Carolina governing domestic relations. And, as was said in connection with another aspect of the Full Faith and Credit Clause, our conclusion "is not a matter to arouse the susceptibilities of the states, all of which are equally concerned in the question and equally on both sides." *Fauntleroy v. Lum.*

As for the suggestion that *Williams I*, foreclosed the Supreme Court of North Carolina from ordering a second trial upon the issue of domicil, it suffices to refer to our opinion in the earlier case.

   Affirmed.

JUSTICE MURPHY, concurring. * * * The State of Nevada has unquestioned authority, consistent with procedural due process, to grant divorces on whatever basis it sees fit to all who meet its statutory requirements. It is entitled, moreover, to give to its divorce decrees absolute and binding finality within the confines of its borders.

But if Nevada's divorce decrees are to be accorded full faith and credit in the courts of her sister states it is essential that Nevada have proper jurisdiction over the divorce proceedings. This means that at least one of the parties to each ex parte proceeding must have a bona fide domicil within Nevada for whatever length of time Nevada may prescribe.

* * *

By being domiciled and living in North Carolina, petitioners secured all the benefits and advantages of its government and participated in its social and economic life. As long as petitioners and their respective spouses lived there and retained that domicil, North Carolina had the exclusive right to regulate the dissolution of their marriage relationships. However harsh and unjust North Carolina's divorce laws may be thought to be, petitioners were bound to obey them while retaining residential and domiciliary ties in that state.

* * *

JUSTICE RUTLEDGE, dissenting. Once again the ghost of "unitary domicil" returns on its perpetual round, in the guise of "jurisdictional fact," to upset judgments, marriages, divorces, undermine the relations founded upon them, and make this Court the unwilling and uncertain arbiter between the concededly valid laws and decrees of sister states. * * *

Nevada's judgment has not been voided. It could not be, if the same test applies to sustain it as upholds the North Carolina conviction. It stands, with the marriages founded upon it, unimpeached. For all that has been determined or could be, unless another change is in the making, petitioners are lawful husband and wife in Nevada. *Williams I*; *Williams v. North Carolina II*, ante. They may be such everywhere outside North Carolina. Lawfully wedded also, in North Carolina, are the divorced spouse of one and his wife, taken for all we know in reliance upon the Nevada decree. That is, unless another jury shall find they too are bigamists for their reliance. No such jury has been impanelled. But were one called, it could pronounce the Nevada decree valid upon the identical evidence from which the jury in this case drew the contrary conclusion. That jury or it and another, if petitioners had been tried separately, could have found one guilty, the other innocent, upon that evidence unvaried by a hair. And, by the Court's test, we could do nothing but sustain the contradictory findings in all these cases.

I do not believe the Constitution has thus confided to the caprice of juries the faith and credit due the laws and judgments of sister states. Nor has it thus made that question a local matter for the states themselves to decide. Were all judgments given the same infirmity, the full faith and credit clause would be only a dead constitutional letter.

* * *

I. What, exactly are the effects of the decision? The Court is careful not to say that Nevada's judgment is not valid in Nevada. To repeat, the Court could not so declare it, unless a different test applies to sustain that judgment than supports North Carolina's. Presumably the same standard applies to both; and each state accordingly is free to follow its own policy, wherever the evidence, whether the same or different, permits conflicting inferences of domicil, as it always does when the question becomes important.

This must be true unless, contrary to the disclaimer, this Court itself is "to retry the facts." The Court no more could say that the Nevada evidence permitted no conclusion of domicil there than it now can say the North Carolina evidence would not allow a finding either way. This apparently is conceded. The proof was not identical. But it was not so one-sided in either case that only one conclusion was compelled. The evidence in Nevada was neither that strong nor that weak. Seldom, if ever, is it so.

The necessary conclusion follows that the Nevada decree was valid and remains valid within her borders. So the marriage is good in Nevada, but void in North Carolina, just as it was before "the jurisdictional requirement of domicil [was] freed from confusing refinements about 'matrimonial domicil,' [cit.] and the like." [cit.]

* * *

It is always a serious matter for us to say that one state is bound to give effect to another's decision, founded in its different policy. That mandate I would not join in any case if not compelled by the only authority binding both the states and ourselves. Conceivably it might have been held that the full faith and credit clause has no application to the matters of marriage and divorce. But the Constitution has not left open that choice. And such has not been the course of decision. The clause applies, but from today it would seem only to compel "respect" or something less than faith and credit, whenever a jury concludes "not unreasonably," by ultimate inference from the always conflicting circumstantial evidence, that it should not apply. Wherever that situation exists, the finding that there was no "bona fide" domiciliary intent comes in every practical effect to this and nothing more.

Permitting the denial is justified, it is said, because we must have regard also for North Carolina's laws, policies and judgments. And so we must. But thus to state the question is to beg the controlling issue. By every test remaining effective, and not disputed, Nevada had power to alter the petitioner's marital status. She made the alteration. If it is valid, neither North Carolina nor we are free to qualify it by saying it shall not be effective there, while it is effective in Nevada, and stands without impeachment for ineffectiveness there.

Just that denial is what the terms of the Constitution and the Act of Congress implementing them forbid. It is exactly for the situation where state policies differ that the clause and the legislation were intended. Without such differences, the need for constitutional limitation was hardly one of magnitude. The apparent exceptions for fraud and want of jurisdiction were never intended to enable the states to disregard the provision and each other's policies, crystallized in judgment, when every requisite for jurisdiction has been satisfied and no showing of fraud has been presented. They have a different purpose, one consistent with the constitutional mandate, not destructive of its effect. That purpose is to make sure that the state's policy has been applied in the judgment, not to permit discrediting it or the judgment when the one validly crystallizes the other. Such an exception, grafted upon the clause, but nullifies it. It does so totally when the weight and quality of the difference in policies has no bearing on the issue.

* * *

JUSTICE BLACK, dissenting. * * * The petitioners were married in Nevada. North Carolina has sentenced them to prison for living together as husband and wife in North Carolina. This Court today affirms those sentences without a determination that the Nevada marriage was invalid under that State's laws This holding can be supported, if at all, only on one of two grounds: (1) North Carolina has extra-territorial power to regulate marriages within Nevada's territorial boundaries, or (2) North Carolina can punish people who live together in that state as husband and wife even though they have been validly married in Nevada. A holding based on either of these two grounds encroaches upon the general principle recognized by this Court that a marriage validly consummated under one state's laws is valid in every other state. If the Court is today abandoning that principle, it takes away from the states a large part of their hitherto plenary control over the institution of marriage. A further consequence is to subject people to criminal prosecutions for adultery and bigamy merely because they exercise their constitutional right to pass from a state in which they were validly married into another state which refuses to recognize their marriage. Such a consequence runs counter to the basic guarantees of our federal union. [cit.] It is true that persons validly married under the laws of one state have been convicted of crime for living together in other states.[6] But those state convictions were not approved by this Court. And never before today has this Court decided a case upon the assumption that men and women validly married under the laws of one state could be sent to jail by another state for conduct which involved nothing more than living together as husband and wife.

* * *

Notes and Questions

1. The facts of Williams are that Mr. Williams, a store owner from a small North Carolina town, eloped to Nevada with Mrs. Hendrix, the wife of the store's clerk. After their brief sojourn in Nevada, the couple returned to a nearby town and set up housekeeping. By the time of the second trial, the original Mrs. Williams had died, and Mr. Hendrix had himself remarried. For more about of the circumstances surrounding *Williams I* and *II*, see Powell, *And Repent at Leisure*, 930.

2. Although the Court in *Williams II* focuses on whether Nevada had "jurisdiction," should the real issue have been choice of law? See Alton v. Alton, 207 F.2d 667, 685 (3d Cir.1953) (Hastie, J., dissenting), *vacated as moot*, 347 U.S. 610 (1954). If Nevada were to apply North Carolina divorce law, would the plaintiffs have any incentive to file for divorce in Nevada? If Nevada had applied North Carolina law, would its judgment have been subject to collateral attack? Many other countries separate jurisdiction and choice of law in divorce cases, see Spaht & Symeonides, *Covenant Marriage*, at 1107-08.

3. The Court states that "[u]nder our system of law, judicial power to grant a divorce is found on domicile." Whose law of domicile applies? Nevada, North Carolina, or federal law? Footnote 7 in the majority Justice Frankfurter's opinion suggests that it is governed by federal law. But if there is a federal standard for domicile, must Nevada recognize North Carolina's determination that this standard was not met? Notice that Justice Murphy asserts that Nevada is entitled "to give its divorce decree absolute and binding finality within the confines of it s borders." Likewise Justice Rutledge states that "petitioners are lawfully married in Nevada."

In Colby v. Colby, 369 P.2d 1019 (Nev.1962), *cert. denied*, 371 U.S. 888 (1962), the wife had obtained a Nevada divorce and the husband a divorce *a mensa et thoro* (separation from bed and board) in Maryland. In the Maryland proceeding, the wife had pleaded the prior Nevada divorce., but the Maryland court declared the Nevada divorce to be void. When the husband sought to set vacate the Nevada divorce, the Nevada court refused, explaining that the husband "does not here ask us to merely accord full faith and credit to the Maryland decree. Instead, we are asked to give it greater credit and respect than the prior decree of our own state lawfully entered. Full faith and credit does not require, nor does it contemplate, such action from us." Id. at 1023.

---

6. This question has arisen most frequently in the application of state law making it a criminal offense for persons of different races to live together as husband and wife. See e.g., State v. Bell, 7 Baxt. (Tenn.) 9 [1872]. That case has been explained as a holding that "Without denying the validity of a marriage in another State, the privileges flowing from marriage may be subject to the local law." *Yarborough v. Yarborough.* [cit.]

4. In *Williams II*, the Court allowed North Carolina to attack collaterally the Nevada divorce. Likewise, the Court has held that the absent spouse in an ex parte divorce can collaterally attack. See Esenwein v. Commonwealth, 325 U.S. 279 (1945). However, the Court later held that in the case of a bilateral divorce (where both parties appeared), neither the parties nor non-parties such as children can collaterally attack the decree. See Sherrer v. Sherrer, 334 U.S. 343 (1948), Johnson v. Muelberger, 340 U.S. 581 (1951). After *Sherrer* and *Johnson*, can a state collaterally attack a bilateral divorce through a bigamy prosecution? Would North Carolina's interest in *Williams II* have been any less if both spouses had shown up at the Nevada proceeding? Compare von Mehren & Trautman, *Recognition of Foreign Adjudications*, 1632 (state can collaterally attack bilateral divorce) with A. Ehrenzweig, *Conflict of Laws* 248 (1959) (contra). If some form of collateral attack is permitted, should a court in the first instance take this into account in deciding whether to take jurisdicition? For a discussion of the relationship between jurisdiction and enforcement, see von Mehren, *Adjudicatory Authority*, 52-56.

5. The Restatement (Second) cites *Williams II* as support for § 103 which provides that full faith and credit does not require enforcement of a sister state judgment where to do so "would involve an improper interference with important interests of the sister State." Is this a proper reading of *Williams II*?

6. You will notice that the focus in *Williams II* is on whether North Carolina must recognize the Nevada *divorce*, not whether it must recognize the subsequent Nevada *marriage*. Marriage, unlike divorce, is not a judicial judgment and is treated as an issue of choice of law rather than recognition of a judgment. As a matter of choice of law, states typically apply the law of the state of celebration, so that if a marriage is valid where entered into it would be valid everywhere. See Restatement (Second) § 283(2). However, states also apply a public policy exception and marriages that violate a strong public policy of a second state will not be recognized by that state. See Scoles, Hay, Borchers & Symeonides, *Conflict of Laws*, 557-65. In *Williams II*, North Carolina had a sufficient interest that it could constitutionally apply its law of marriage. Thus, the only constitutional question was whether it was required to recognize the divorce.

Questions about the obligation to recognize particular marriages has garnered new attention as some states consider permitting same-sex marriages. In response to this issue, Congress enacted the "Defense of Marriage Act," 28 U.S.C. § 1738C, which provides:

> No State, territory, or possession of the United States, or Indian tribe, shall be required to give effect to any public act, record, or judicial proceeding of any other State, territory, possession, or tribe respecting a relationship between persons of the same sex that is treated as a marriage under the laws of such other State, territory, possession, or tribe, or a right or claim arising from such relationship.

How, if at all, does this statute change the situation that would otherwise exist? Suppose, for example, that one state authorized same-sex marriage. Would other states be required under the Full Faith and Credit Clause to recognize the marriage? Would other states be required to recognize the marriage if that state granted a declaratory judgment to a same sex couple declaring the couple's marriage valid? If the Full Faith and Credit Clause does require recognition of the marriage or the declaratory judgment, can Congress by statute eliminate that obligation? See Thomas v. Washington Gas Light Co., 448 U.S. 261, 273 n.18 (1980). See generally Borchers, *Interjurisdictional Recognition*; Kramer, *Same-Sex Marriage*; Cox, *Same-Sex Marriage and Choice of Law*; Hovermill, *Conflict of Laws and Morals*; Henson, *Same-Sex Marriages.*

Assuming § 1738C is constitutional, how broad is it? Suppose a gay couple is married in a state that permits such marriages. One spouse is killed in an accident and the other sues for wrongful death under a statute that allows such suits only by spouses. If the surviving spouse secures a judgment, can other states refuse to enforce that judgment under § 1738C? Suppose a probate court holds that the surviving spouse is entitled to the decedent's estate under intestate succession. Must other states respect that judgment?

7. During the 18th and 19th centuries, divorces in many states were granted by private bills passed by state legislatures. See generally Richard Chused, Private Acts in Public Places: A Social History of Divorce in the Formative Era of American Family Law (1994). If the divorce at issue in *Williams II* had been granted by the legislature, would the result have been different? Should a legislative divorce be analyzed under the doctrine applicable to judgments, discussed in this chapter, or under the doctrine applicable to laws, discussed in Chapter 5?

2. Recognition of Child Custody and Support Judgments

With the liberalization of divorce laws across the country, issues concerning recognition of sister state divorces have largely disappeared. Far more significant are problems concerning enforcement of child support and custody decrees.

A state has jurisdiction to grant a divorce if one spouse is domiciled in the forum. See supra at 662-63. It is not necessary that the other spouse have any connection with the state. By contrast, a suit for child support is treated like any other suit for money and the court has jurisdiction only if the defendant has purposeful contacts with the forum. See Kulko v. Superior Court, 436 U.S. 84 (1978). Almost all support orders are modifiable and as a result these orders were traditionally considered not final and therefore not subject to the requirements of the Full Faith and Credit Clause. See Restatement (Second) § 109. This changed in 1994 with the enactment of Full Faith and Credit for Child Support Orders Act, 28 U.S.C. § 1738B, which requires states to enforce child support decrees that meet the requirements of that Act. The Act also prohibits other states from modifying support decrees unless neither the child nor any "contestant," i.e., parent, is a resident of the state that issued the original decree. Thus, if one parent moves away from the state of the original decree but the other parent or the child remains, the parent who moved will not be able to get the decree modified in her new home but will have to seek modification in the original state's courts.

Child custody decrees present some unique and difficult problems. As discussed earlier, in custody it is not clear whether due process requires that the defendant have purposeful contacts with the forum. Notwithstanding May v. Anderson, 345 U.S. 528 (1953), the plurality opinion of which can be read to require this, many states have held that the presence of the child is sufficient. The Uniform Child Custody Jurisdiction Act, ("UCCJA"), 9 U.L.A. 115 (1968), the Uniform Child Custody Jurisdiction and Enforcement Act, ("UCCJEA"), 9 U.L.A. 649 (1999), and the Parental Kidnapping Protection Act, ("PKPA"), 28 U.S.C. § 1738A, discussed below, require only that the state rendering the decree be the "home State" of the child. Compare 28 U.S.C. § 1738B(C)(1)(B) (requiring that in suit for child support, the forum not only be "home state" but also have "personal jurisdiction" over the defendant).

With respect to recognition and enforcement of custody decrees, it is clear that a second state can make any modification that the rendering state could have made. Virtually all custody decrees are modifiable once there has been a determination that circumstances have changed since the initial custody award. This option created great incentives for a non-custodial parent unhappy about a custody order to snatch his or her own child, take the child to another state that the parent thought would be more sympathetic, and seek modification of the custody order there. In response to this problem, all the states enacted in some form UCCJA. The UCCJA attempted to limit the number of states where a custody order could be modified by prescribing the criteria for jurisdiction and for enforcing and modifying of decrees. The UCCJA did not, however, completely eliminate incentives for parents to snatch their children in search of a more hospitable forum because some of the provisions were quite flexible and gave a state ample room "to indulge a parochial preference for its own initial jurisdiction." Coombs, *Interstate Child Custody*, 724.

In 1980, in an attempt to further reduce incentives to engage in interstate forum shopping in child custody disputes, Congress acting pursuant to its power under the Full Faith and Credit Clause enacted the PKPA. The Act requires states to enforce child custody decrees that are consistent with the jurisdictional criteria specified in the Act. The most significant basis for jurisdiction under the PKPA is "home state" jurisdiction. The home state is the state in which the child lived for the preceding six months. If a child is removed from a home state by a parent and the other parent remains there then that state continues to be a "home state" for six months. Once a child custody decree has been entered, another state may not modify that decree unless the second state has jurisdiction and the first state no longer has jurisdiction (or has declined to exercise it). This forces parties who would like a modification to return to the state that issued the decree rather than snatching the child and heading for a more hospitable state.

There were some unfortunate inconsistencies between the UCCJA and the PKPA. For example, the UCCJA permitted jurisdiction "in the best interests of the child." In contrast, the PKPA permits "best interest" jurisdiction *only* if no other state would have home state jurisdiction. As a result of this and other problems, a new uniform act, the UCCJEA, was promulgated in 1997. As of 2003, the UCCJEA has been adopted in 33 states. See generally Coombs, *Rerun of Seize-and-Run*; Levy & McCarthy, *Critique*.

The interplay between state law and the PKPA is illustrated by Curtis v. Curtis,

789 P.2d 717 (Utah.Ct.App.1990). Lauralee and William Curtis were granted a divorce by Utah. The court awarded custody of the couple's four younger children to Lauralee and of the three older children to William. Ten weeks later, Lauralee consented to the children's visiting William over a long weekend. Without Lauralee's knowledge, William took the children to Mississippi where he allegedly learned that the children had been abused while in Lauralee's custody. Several days later, William filed a complaint in Mississippi state court seeking modification of the Utah decree to award him custody. The Mississippi court entered an order granting custody to William. Lauralee then filed suit in Utah, requesting that William be held in contempt of court for failing to return the children to Utah. In ruling on Lauralee's request, must Utah give full faith and credit to the Mississippi order?

To answer this question, you must first determine whether Mississippi's modification of Utah's decree was permissible under § 1738A(f). Subsection (f) requires that the modifying court have jurisdiction and that the original court no longer have jurisdiction or have declined jurisdiction. In *Curtis*, the Utah Court of Appeals concluded that the requirrements of (f) had not been met. The court noted that the Mississippi court had confused personal jurisdiction with the requirements of the PKPA and mistakenly concluded that because Lauralee had appeared in the Mississippi action and litigated custody, the Mississippi court had authority to modify the original Utah decree.

The Mississippi Supreme Court later agreed with the Utah Court of Appeals' decision in Curtis v. Curtis, 574 So.2d 24 (Miss.1990). The Mississippi court explained:

> This case is of a genre that tests the law's capacity to regulate human behavior. Interstate parental kidnappings following family breakups have been a scourge upon society. A decade ago the federal government and then this (and every other) state enacted comprehensive laws designed to end interstate jurisdictional wars wherein the courts of the several states had treated kidnapped children like cross-country ping pong balls.

> This case presents a classic case of the parental and judicial behavior the statutes were designed to and do proscribe. A valid Utah decree granted custody of four children to their mother. Ten weeks later, the father took advantage of his weekend visitation and wrongfully brought the children to Mississippi and enlisted the aid of this state's courts to give him custody. The children have since been caught in the middle of a tug of war.

> We hold the Utah courts never lost jurisdiction of the matter of the permanent custody of the children. With this we adjudge the legal issues tendered. In doing this almost three years after the fact, we have no illusion that we have ability to put Humpty Dumpty back together again. We hope from this fall all may know of our seriousness of purpose that the law's injunction be respected.

Id. at 25. The Mississippi court also noted an interesting point glossed over by the Utah Court of Appeals. After William had wrongfully removed the children to Mississippi and after the Mississippi court had awarded William open-ended temporary custody, despite finding that it lacked jurisdiction to modify the Utah custody decree, "Lauralee secured the services of Jerry Cobb, a Viet Nam veteran and self-styled 'mercenary,' and they came to Mississippi and (re)kidnapped the children and returned them to Utah." Id. at 27. It was after this kidnapping that the Mississippi court modified the Utah custody decree, finding that it had homestate jurisdiction. As this incident suggests, sometimes the bad legal analysis in custody cases may be influenced by the bad behavior of the parties.

In *Curtis*, both Utah and Mississippi agreed that Utah was the proper forum to resolve the custody dispute. However, states do not always agree and conflicting custody orders are sometimes entered. What happens then? In Thompson v. Thompson, 484 U.S. 174 (1988), the Supreme Court rejected the argument that the PKPA provides an implied cause of action in federal court to determine which of two conflicting state custody decisions is valid. The Court explained:

> At the time Congress passed the PKPA, custody orders held a peculiar status under the full faith and credit doctrine, which requires each State to give effect to the judicial proceedings of other States, see U.S. Const., Art. IV, § 1; 28 U.S.C. § 1738. The anomaly traces to the fact that custody orders characteristically are subject to modification as required by the best interests of the child. As a consequence, some courts doubted whether custody orders were sufficiently "final" to trigger full faith and credit requirements [cit.], and this Court had declined expressly to settle the question. [cit.] Even if custody orders were subject to full faith and credit requirements, the Full Faith and Credit Clause obliges States only to accord the same force to judgments as would be accorded by the courts of the State in which the judgment was entered. Because courts entering custody orders generally retain the power to modify them, courts in other States were no less entitled to change the terms of custody according to their own views of the child's best interest. [cit.] For these reasons, a parent who lost a custody battle in one State had an incentive to kidnap the child and move to another State to relitigate the issue. This circumstance contributed to widespread jurisdictional deadlocks like this one, and more importantly, to a national epidemic of parental kidnapping. At the time the PKPA was enacted, sponsors of the Act estimated that between 25,000 and 100,000 children were kidnapped by parents who had been unable to obtain custody in a legal forum. [cit.]
>
> A number of States joined in an effort to avoid these jurisdictional conflicts by adopting the Uniform Child Custody Jurisdiction Act (UCCJA), 9 U.L.A. §§ 1–28 (1979). The UCCJA prescribed uniform standards for deciding which State could make a custody determination and obligated enacting States to enforce the determination made by the State with proper jurisdiction. The project foundered, however, because a number of States refused to enact the UCCJA while others enacted it with modifications. In the absence of uniform national standards for allocating and enforcing custody determinations, noncustodial parents still had reason to snatch their children and petition the courts of any of a number of haven States for sole custody.
>
> The context of the PKPA therefore suggests that the principal problem Congress was seeking to remedy was the inapplicability of full faith and credit

requirements to custody determinations.

Id. at 180-81. If parents cannot go to federal district court to resolve conflicting custody orders, what can they do? Note, *Interstate Child Custody*, 1329.

Chapter 11

FEDERAL-STATE
RECOGNITION OF JUDGMENTS

A. INTRODUCTION

Chapter 10 addressed state enforcement of the judgments of other states. The problems of interjurisdictional enforcement and preclusion become more complex when we introduce federal courts. The area has been described by one commentator as "an exquisitely difficult subject." Burbank, *Interjurisdictional Preclusion*, 829. The additional complexity stems primarily from two doctrines that are inapplicable in the interstate context--federal supremacy and *Erie*. The interaction of these two doctrines with principles of preclusion and full faith and credit produces some unique problems.

This chapter will first examine state and federal recognition of federal judgments. It will then examine the special problems of federal court recognition of state judgments concerning or affecting matters of federal law.

B. RECOGNITION OF FEDERAL JUDGMENTS BY STATE AND FEDERAL COURTS

1. Source of the Obligation to Enforce Federal Judgments

Neither the Full Faith and Credit Clause nor the Full Faith and Credit Statute, § 1738, mentions recognition of *federal* judgments. Nonetheless, states are required to recognize and enforce federal judgments. Federal jurisdiction would have little value if the rights established in federal litigation were subject to complete relitigation in state courts or other federal courts. As the Supreme Court explained in Deposit Bank of Frankfort v. Board of Councilmen, 191 U.S. 499, 517 (1903):

> [I]t is equally well settled that a right claimed under the Federal Constitution, finally adjudicated in the Federal courts, can never be taken away or impaired by state decisions. The same reasoning which permits to the States the right of final adjudication upon purely state questions requires no less respect for the final decisions of the Federal courts of questions of national authority and jurisdiction.

Although the Supreme Court has been emphatic about states' obligation to enforce federal judgments, it has been less clear about the source of this obligation. What possible sources are there? See 18B Wright, Miller & Cooper, *Federal Practice* § 4468.

2. What Law Determines the Preclusive Effect of a Federal Judgment

Semtek International Inc. v. Lockheed Martin Corp.

Supreme Court of the United States, 2001.
531 U.S. 497, 121 S. Ct. 1021, 149 L. Ed. 2d 32 (2001).

JUSTICE SCALIA delivered the opinion of the Court. This case presents the question whether the claim-preclusive effect of a federal judgment dismissing a diversity action on statute-of-limitations grounds is determined by the law of the State in which the federal court sits.

I. Petitioner filed a complaint against respondent in California state court, alleging inducement of breach of contract and various business torts. Respondent removed the case to the United States District Court for the Central District of California on the basis of diversity of citizenship, [cit.] and successfully moved to dismiss petitioner's claims as barred by California's 2-year statute of limitations. In its order of dismissal, the District Court, adopting language suggested by respondent, dismissed petitioner's claims "in [their] entirety on the merits and with prejudice." [cit.] Without contesting the District Court's designation of its dismissal as "on the merits," petitioner appealed to the Court of Appeals for the Ninth Circuit, which affirmed the District Court's order. [cit.] Petitioner also brought suit against respondent in the State Circuit Court for Baltimore City, Maryland, alleging the same causes of action, which were not time barred under Maryland's 3-year statute of limitations. Respondent sought injunctive relief against this action from the California federal court under the All Writs Act, 28 U.S.C. § 1651, and removed the action to the United States District Court for the District of Maryland on federal-question grounds (diversity grounds were not available because Lockheed "is a Maryland citizen," [cit.]. The California federal court denied the relief requested, and the Maryland federal court remanded the case to state court because the federal question arose only by way of defense, [cit.]. Following a hearing, the Maryland state court granted respondent's motion to dismiss on the ground of res judicata. Petitioner then returned to the California federal court and the Ninth Circuit, unsuccessfully moving both courts to amend the former's earlier order so as to indicate that the dismissal was not "on the merits." Petitioner also appealed the Maryland trial court's order of dismissal to the Maryland Court of Special Appeals. The Court of Special Appeals affirmed, holding that, regardless of whether California would have accorded claim-preclusive effect to a statute-of-limitations dismissal by one of its own courts, the dismissal by the California federal court barred the complaint filed in Maryland, since the res judicata effect of federal diversity judgments is prescribed by federal law, under which the earlier dismissal was on the merits and claim preclusive. [cit.] After the Maryland Court of Appeals declined to review the case, we granted certiorari. [cit.]

II. Petitioner contends that the outcome of this case is controlled by Dupasseur v. Rochereau, 21 Wall. 130, 135 (1875), which held that the res judicata effect of a federal diversity judgment "is such as would belong to judgments of the State courts rendered under similar circumstances," and may not be accorded any "higher sanctity or effect." Since, petitioner argues, the dismissal of an action on statute-of-limitations grounds by a California state court would not be claim preclusive, it follows that the similar dismissal of this diversity action by the California federal court cannot be claim preclusive. While we agree that this would be the result demanded by *Dupasseur*, the case is not dispositive because it was decided under the Conformity Act of 1872, which required federal courts to apply the procedural law of the forum State in nonequity cases. That arguably affected the outcome of the case. See *Dupasseur, supra,* at 135. See also Restatement (Second) of Judgments § 87, Comment *a,* p. 315 (1980) (hereinafter Restatement) ("Since procedural law largely determines the matters that may be adjudicated in an action, state law had to be considered in ascertaining the effect of a federal judgment").

Respondent, for its part, contends that the outcome of this case is controlled by Federal Rule of Civil Procedure 41(b), which provides as follows:

"Involuntary Dismissal: Effect Thereof. For failure of the plaintiff to prosecute or to comply with these rules or any order of court, a defendant may move for dismissal of an action or of any claim against the defendant. Unless the court in its order for dismissal otherwise specifies, a dismissal under this subdivision and any dismissal not provided for in this rule, other than a dismissal for lack of jurisdiction, for improper venue, or for failure to join a party under Rule 19, operates as an adjudication upon the merits."

Since the dismissal here did not "otherwise specif[y]" (indeed, it specifically stated that it *was* "on the merits"), and did not pertain to the excepted subjects of jurisdiction, venue, or joinder, it follows, respondent contends, that the dismissal "is entitled to claim preclusive effect." [cit.]

Implicit in this reasoning is the unstated minor premise that all judgments denominated "on the merits" are entitled to claim-preclusive effect. That premise is not necessarily valid. The original connotation of an "on the merits" adjudication is one that actually "pass[es] directly on the substance of [a particular] claim" before the court. Restatement § 19, Comment *a,* at 161. That connotation remains common to every jurisdiction of which we are aware. See ibid. ("The prototyp[ical] [judgment on the merits is] one in which the merits of [a party's] claim are in fact adjudicated [for or] against the [party] after trial of the substantive issues"). And it is, we think, the meaning intended in those many statements to the effect that a judgment "on the merits" triggers the doctrine of res judicata or claim preclusion. See, e.g., Parklane Hosiery Co. v. Shore, 439 U.S. 322, 326, n.5 (1979) ("Under the doctrine of res judicata, a judgment on the merits in a prior suit bars a second suit involving the same parties or their privies based on the same cause of action"); Goddard v. Security Title Ins. & Guarantee Co., 92 P.2d 804, 806 (Cal. 1939) ("[A] final judgment, rendered upon the merits by a court having jurisdiction of the cause . . . is a complete bar to a new suit between [the parties or their privies] on the same cause of action" (internal quotation marks and citations omitted)).

But over the years the meaning of the term "judgment on the merits" "has gradually undergone change," [cit.] and it has come to be applied to some judgments (such as the one involved here) that do *not* pass upon the substantive merits of a claim and hence do *not* (in many jurisdictions) entail claim-preclusive effect. [cit.]

That is why the Restatement of Judgments has abandoned the use of the term -- "because of its possibly misleading connotations," Restatement § 19, Comment *a,* at 161.

In short, it is no longer true that a judgment "on the merits" is necessarily a judgment entitled to claim-preclusive effect; and there are a number of reasons for believing that the phrase "adjudication upon the merits" does not bear that meaning in Rule 41(b). To begin with, Rule 41(b) sets forth nothing more than a default rule for determining the import of a dismissal (a dismissal is "upon the merits," with the three stated exceptions, unless the court "otherwise specifies"). This would be a highly peculiar context in which to announce a federally prescribed rule on the complex question of claim preclusion, saying in effect, "All federal dismissals (with three specified exceptions) preclude suit elsewhere, unless the court otherwise specifies."

And even apart from the purely default character of Rule 41(b), it would be peculiar to find a rule governing the effect that must be accorded federal judgments by other courts ensconced in rules governing the internal procedures of the rendering court itself. Indeed, such a rule would arguably violate the jurisdictional limitation of the Rules Enabling Act: that the Rules "shall not abridge, enlarge or modify any substantive right," 28 U.S.C. § 2072(b). [cit.] In the present case, for example, if California law left petitioner free to sue on this claim in Maryland even after the California statute of limitations had expired, the federal court's extinguishment of that right (through Rule 41(b)'s mandated claim-preclusive effect of its judgment) would seem to violate this limitation.

Moreover, as so interpreted, the Rule would in many cases violate the federalism principle of *Erie R. Co. v. Tompkins,* by engendering "'substantial' variations [in outcomes] between state and federal litigation" which would "[l]ikely . . . influence the choice of a forum," Hanna v. Plumer, 380 U.S. 460, 467-468 (1965). See also Guaranty Trust Co. v. York, 326 U.S. 99, 108-110 (1945). Cf. Walker v. Armco Steel Corp., 446 U.S. 740, 748-753 (1980). With regard to the claim-preclusion issue involved in the present case, for example, the traditional rule is that expiration of the applicable statute of limitations merely bars the remedy and does not extinguish the substantive right, so that dismissal on that ground does not have claim-preclusive effect in other jurisdictions with longer, unexpired limitation periods. See Restatement (Second) of Conflict of Laws § § 142(2), 143 (1969); Restatement of Judgments § 49, Comment *a* (1942). Out-of-state defendants sued on stale claims in California and in other States adhering to this traditional rule would systematically remove state-law suits brought against them to federal court -- where, unless otherwise specified, a statute-of-limitations dismissal would bar suit everywhere.[1]

Finally, if Rule 41(b) did mean what respondent suggests, we would surely have relied upon it in our cases recognizing the claim-preclusive effect of federal

---

1. Rule 41(b), interpreted as a preclusion-establishing rule, would not have the two effects described in the preceding paragraphs -- arguable violation of the Rules Enabling Act and incompatibility with *Erie R. Co. v. Tompkins* -- if the court's failure to specify an other-than-on-the-merits dismissal were subject to reversal on appeal whenever it would alter the rule of claim preclusion applied by the State in which the federal court sits. No one suggests that this is the rule, and we are aware of no case that applies it.

judgments in federal-question cases. Yet for over half a century since the promulgation of Rule 41(b), we have not once done so. [cit.]

We think the key to a more reasonable interpretation of the meaning of "operates as an adjudication upon the merits" in Rule 41(b) is to be found in Rule 41(a), which, in discussing the effect of voluntary dismissal by the plaintiff, makes clear that an "adjudication upon the merits" is the opposite of a "dismissal without prejudice":

"Unless otherwise stated in the notice of dismissal or stipulation, the dismissal is without prejudice, except that a notice of dismissal operates as an adjudication upon the merits when filed by a plaintiff who has once dismissed in any court of the United States or of any state an action based on or including the same claim."

[cit.] The primary meaning of "dismissal without prejudice," we think, is dismissal without barring the plaintiff from returning later, to the same court, with the same underlying claim. That will also ordinarily (though not always) have the consequence of not barring the claim from *other* courts, but its primary meaning relates to the dismissing court itself. Thus, Black's Law Dictionary (7th ed. 1999) defines "dismissed without prejudice" as "removed from the court's docket in such a way that the plaintiff may refile the same suit on the same claim,"id., at 482, and defines "dismissal without prejudice" as "[a] dismissal that does not bar the plaintiff from refiling the lawsuit within the applicable limitations period," ibid.

We think, then, that the effect of the "adjudication upon the merits" default provision of Rule 41(b) -- and, presumably, of the explicit order in the present case that used the language of that default provision -- is simply that, unlike a dismissal "without prejudice," the dismissal in the present case barred refiling of the same claim in the United States District Court for the Central District of California. That is undoubtedly a necessary condition, but it is not a sufficient one, for claim-preclusive effect in other courts.[2]

III. Having concluded that the claim-preclusive effect, in Maryland, of this California federal diversity judgment is dictated neither by *Dupasseur* v. *Rochereau*, as petitioner contends, nor by Rule 41(b), as respondent contends, we turn to consideration of what determines the issue. Neither the Full Faith and Credit Clause, U.S. Const., Art. IV, § 1, nor the full faith and credit statute, 28 U.S.C. § 1738, addresses the question. By their terms they govern the effects to be given only to state-court judgments (and, in the case of the statute, to judgments by courts of territories and possessions). And no other federal textual provision, neither of the Constitution nor of any statute, addresses the claim-preclusive effect of a judgment in a federal diversity action.

It is also true, however, that no federal textual provision addresses the claim-

---

2. We do not decide whether, in a diversity case, a federal court's "dismissal upon the merits" (in the sense we have described), under circumstances where a state court would decree only a "dismissal without prejudice," abridges a "substantive right" and thus exceeds the authorization of the Rules Enabling Act. We think the situation will present itself more rarely than would the arguable violation of the Act that would ensue from interpreting Rule 41(b) as a rule of claim preclusion; and if it is a violation, can be more easily dealt with on direct appeal.

preclusive effect of a federal-court judgment in a federal-question case, yet we have long held that States cannot give those judgments merely whatever effect they would give their own judgments, but must accord them the effect that this Court prescribes. [cit.] The reasoning of that line of cases suggests, moreover, that even when States are allowed to give federal judgments (notably, judgments in diversity cases) no more than the effect accorded to state judgments, that disposition is by direction of *this* Court, which has the last word on the claim-preclusive effect of *all* federal judgments:

> "It is true that for some purposes and within certain limits it is only required that the judgments of the courts of the United States shall be given the same force and effect as are given the judgments of the courts of the States wherein they are rendered; but it is equally true that whether a Federal judgment has been given due force and effect in the state court is a Federal question reviewable by this court, which will determine for itself whether such judgment has been given due weight or otherwise. . . .

> "When is the state court obliged to give to Federal judgments only the force and effect it gives to state court judgments within its own jurisdiction? Such cases are distinctly pointed out in the opinion of Mr. Justice Bradley in *Dupasseur* v. *Rochereau* [which stated that the case was a diversity case, applying state law under state procedure]." [cit.]

In other words, in *Dupasseur* the State was allowed (indeed, required) to give a federal diversity judgment no more effect than it would accord one of its own judgments only because reference to state law was *the federal rule that this Court deemed appropriate*. In short, federal common law governs the claim-preclusive effect of a dismissal by a federal court sitting in diversity. [cit.]

It is left to us, then, to determine the appropriate federal rule. And despite the sea change that has occurred in the background law since *Dupasseur* was decided-- not only repeal of the Conformity Act but also the watershed decision of this Court in *Erie*--we think the result decreed by *Dupasseur* continues to be correct for diversity cases. Since state, rather than federal, substantive law is at issue there is no need for a uniform federal rule. And indeed, nationwide uniformity in the substance of the matter is better served by having the same claim-preclusive rule (the state rule) apply whether the dismissal has been ordered by a state or a federal court. This is, it seems to us, a classic case for adopting, as the federally prescribed rule of decision, the law that would be applied by state courts in the State in which the federal diversity court sits. See Gasperini v. Center for Humanities, Inc., 518 U.S. 415, 429-431 (1996); Walker v. Armco Steel Corp., 446 U.S. at 752-753; Bernhardt v. Polygraphic Co. of America, 350 U.S. 198, 202-205 (1956); Palmer v. Hoffman, 318 U.S. 109, 117 (1943); Klaxon Co. v. Stentor Elec. Mfg. Co., 313 U.S. 487, 496 (1941); Cities Service Oil Co. v. Dunlap, 308 U.S. 208, 212 (1939). As we have alluded to above, any other rule would produce the sort of "forum-shopping . . . and . . . inequitable administration of the laws" that *Erie* seeks to avoid, *Hanna,* since filing in, or removing to, federal court would be encouraged by the divergent effects that the litigants would anticipate from likely grounds of dismissal. [cit.]

This federal reference to state law will not obtain, of course, in situations in which the state law is incompatible with federal interests. If, for example, state law did not accord claim-preclusive effect to dismissals for willful violation of discovery orders, federal courts' interest in the integrity of their own processes might justify a contrary federal rule. No such conflict with potential federal interests exists in the present case. Dismissal of this state cause of action was decreed by the California federal court only because the California statute of limitations so required; and there is no conceivable federal interest in giving that time bar more effect in other courts than the California courts themselves would impose.

* * *

Because the claim-preclusive effect of the California federal court's dismissal "upon the merits" of petitioner's action on statute-of-limitations grounds is governed by a federal rule that in turn incorporates California's law of claim preclusion (the content of which we do not pass upon today), the Maryland Court of Special Appeals erred in holding that the dismissal necessarily precluded the bringing of this action in the Maryland courts. The judgment is reversed, and the case remanded for further proceedings not inconsistent with this opinion.

It is so ordered.

Notes and Questions

1. The Court holds that the preclusive effect of a federal judgment is governed by federal common law. It then incorporates state law as the content of the federal common law rule. How is this approach different from a traditional Erie analysis?

2. Should state law govern all preclusive aspects of a federal diversity judgment? Suppose state law narrowly defines the scope of a claim and would allow separate suits for personal injuries and property damage arising from the same suit, should this state rule apply to a federal judgment in that state? What about matters of issue preclusion such as the mutuality requirement? See Matosantos Commercial Corp. v. Applebee's Int'l, 245 F.3d 1203, 1208 (10th Cir. 2001); 18B Wright, Miller & Cooper, *Federal Practice & Procedure* § 4472.

3. The Court reads Rule 41 narrowly. Are you persuaded by the Court's interpretation of the Rule? Should other Federal Rules of Civil Procedure be similarly interpreted? Consider, for example, Rule 13(a) which provides that "[a] pleading shall state as a counterclaim" any claim which the pleader has against the opposing party that arises out of the same transaction or occurrence. If a defendant fails to plead a compulsory counterclaim, is the defendant barred from bringing that claim in this same court? In any court? If the Rule is interpreted to bar suit in any court would this go beyond the scope of the Rules Enabling Act?

4. The traditional rule is that a dismissal on grounds of a statute of limitations does not bar a subsequent suit in another forum with a longer limitations period. See supra at 746. As a result, the holding in *Semtek* produces an anomaly. Suppose the first dismissal had been from a California state court. A Maryland court would be free to apply its long limitations period and entertain the claim. However, if the first dismissal were from a California federal court, then, after *Semtek*, the Maryland court would be required to apply California law. Do you think this anomaly is one

that the Court meant to endorse? See Burbank, *Semtek,* at 1051-52.

C. RECOGNITION OF STATE JUDGMENTS BY FEDERAL COURTS

Although the Full Faith and Credit Clause does not require federal courts to recognize state judgments, § 1738 does. This requirement raises some unique problems where the state court judgment concerns matters of federal substantive law.

Kremer v. Chemical Construction Corp.
Supreme Court of the United States, 1982.
456 U.S. 461, 102 S.Ct. 1883, 72 L.Ed.2d 262.

JUSTICE WHITE delivered the opinion of the Court. As one of its first acts, Congress directed that all United States courts afford the same full faith and credit to state court judgments that would apply in the State's own courts. Act of May 26, 1790, ch. 11, 1 Stat. 122, 28 U.S.C. § 1738. More recently, Congress implemented the national policy against employment discrimination by creating an array of substantive protections and remedies which generally allows federal courts to determine the merits of a discrimination claim. Title VII of the Civil Rights Act of 1964, 78 Stat. 253, as amended, 42 U.S.C. § 2000e et seq. (1976 ed. and Supp. IV). The principal question presented by this case is whether Congress intended Title VII to supersede the principles of comity and repose embodied in § 1738. Specifically, we decide whether a federal court in a Title VII case should give preclusive effect to a decision of a state court upholding a state administrative agency's rejection of an employment discrimination claim as meritless when the state court's decision would be res judicata in the State's own courts.

I. Petitioner Rubin Kremer emigrated from Poland in 1970 and was hired in 1973 by respondent Chemical Construction Corp. (Chemico) as an engineer. Two years later he was laid off, along with a number of other employees. Some of these employees were later rehired, but Kremer was not although he made several applications. In May 1976, Kremer filed a discrimination charge with the Equal Employment Opportunity Commission (EEOC), asserting that his discharge and failure to be rehired were due to his national origin and Jewish faith. Because the EEOC may not consider a claim until a state agency having jurisdiction over employment discrimination complaints has had at least 60 days to resolve the matter, § 706(c), 42 U.S.C. § 2000e–5(c), the Commission referred Kremer's charge to the New York State Division of Human Rights (NYHRD), the agency charged with enforcing the New York law prohibiting employment discrimination. [cit.]

After investigating Kremer's complaint,[3] the NYHRD concluded that there was no probable cause to believe that Chemico had engaged in the discriminatory practices complained of. The NYHRD explicitly based its determination on the findings that Kremer was not rehired because one employee who was rehired had

---

3. Kremer's complaint filed with the NYHRD alleged discrimination on the basis of age and religion, and did not contain a separate claim concerning national origin.

greater seniority, that another employee who was rehired filled a lesser position than that previously held by Kremer, and that neither Kremer's creed nor age was a factor considered in Chemico's failure to rehire him. The NYHRD's determination was upheld by its Appeal Board as "not arbitrary, capricious or an abuse of discretion." Kremer again brought his complaint to the attention of the EEOC and also filed, on December 6, 1977, a petition with the Appellate Division of the New York Supreme Court to set aside the adverse administrative determination. On February 27, 1978, five justices of the Appellate Division unanimously affirmed the Appeal Board's order. Kremer could have sought, but did not seek, review by the New York Court of Appeals.

Subsequently, a District Director of the EEOC ruled that there was no reasonable cause to believe that the charge of discrimination was true and issued a right-to-sue notice. The District Director refused a request for reconsideration, noting that he had reviewed the case files and considered the EEOC's disposition as "appropriate and correct in all respects."

Kremer then brought this Title VII action in District Court, claiming discrimination on the basis of national origin and religion.[4] Chemico argued from the outset that Kremer's Title VII action was barred by the doctrine of res judicata. The District Court initially denied Chemico's motion to dismiss. [cit.] The court noted that the Court of Appeals for the Second Circuit had recently found such state determinations res judicata in an action under 42 U.S.C. § 1981, Mitchell v. National Broadcasting Co., 553 F.2d 265 (1977), but distinguished Title VII cases because of the statutory grant of de novo federal review. Several months later the Second Circuit extended the *Mitchell* rule to Title VII cases. Sinicropi v. Nassau County, 601 F.2d 60 (per curiam), *cert. denied*, 444 U.S. 983 (1979). The District Court then dismissed the complaint on grounds of res judicata. [cit.] The Court of Appeals refused to depart from the *Sinicropi* precedent and rejected petitioner's claim that *Sinicropi* should not be applied retroactively. [cit.]

A motion for rehearing en banc was denied, and petitioner filed for a writ of certiorari. We issued the writ [cit.] to resolve this important issue of federal employment discrimination law over which the Courts of Appeals are divided. We now affirm.

II. Section 1738 requires federal courts to give the same preclusive effect to state court judgments that those judgments would be given in the courts of the State from which the judgments emerged.[6] Here the Appellate Division of the New York

---

4. No further mention was made of age discrimination, which is not covered by Title VII. Nor has petitioner argued at any point that his national origin claim was in any sense distinct from his claim of religious discrimination. Of course, if Kremer desired to make such a claim, he was obligated to first bring it before the NYHRD. [cit.] Moreover, "[a] party cannot escape the requirements of full faith and credit and res judicata by asserting its own failure to raise matters clearly within the scope of a prior proceeding." [cit.]

6. * * * [T]his Court has consistently emphasized the importance of the related doctrines of res judicata and collateral estoppel in fulfilling the purpose for which civil courts had been established, the conclusive resolution of disputes within their jurisdiction. Under res judicata, a final judgment on the merits of an action precludes the parties or their privies from relitigating issues that were or could have been raised in that action. [cit.] Under collateral estoppel, once a court decides an issue of fact or law necessary to its judgment, that decision precludes relitigation of the same issue on a different cause of action between the same parties. [cit.] Thus, invocation of res judicata and collateral estoppel "relieve[s] parties of the cost and

(continued...)

Supreme Court has issued a judgment affirming the decision of the NYHRD Appeals Board that the discharge and failure to rehire Kremer were not the product of the discrimination that he had alleged. There is no question that this judicial determination precludes Kremer from bringing "any other action, civil or criminal, based upon the same grievance" in the New York courts. [cit.] By its terms, therefore, § 1738 would appear to preclude Kremer from relitigating the same question in federal court.

Kremer offers two principal reasons why § 1738 does not bar this action. First, he suggests that in Title VII cases Congress intended that federal courts be relieved of their usual obligation to grant finality to state court decisions. Second, he urges that the New York administrative and judicial proceedings in this case were so deficient that they are not entitled to preclusive effect in federal courts and, in any event, the rejection of a state employment discrimination claim cannot by definition bar a Title VII action. We consider this latter contention in Part III.

A. Allen v. McCurry, 449 U.S. 90, 99 (1980), made clear that an exception to § 1738 will not be recognized unless a later statute contains an express or implied partial repeal. There is no claim here that Title VII expressly repealed § 1738; if there has been a partial repeal, it must be implied. "It is, of course, a cardinal principle of statutory construction that repeals by implication are not favored," [cit.] and whenever possible, statutes should be read consistently. There are, however,

> "'two well-settled categories of repeals by implication--(1) where provisions in the two acts are in irreconcilable conflict, the later act to the extent of the conflict constitutes an implied repeal of the earlier one; and (2) if the later act covers the whole subject of the earlier one and is clearly intended as a substitute, it will operate similarly as a repeal of the earlier act. But, in either case, the intention of the legislature to repeal must be clear and manifest....'" [cit.]

The relationship of Title VII to § 1738 does not fall within either of these categories. * * *

No provision of Title VII requires claimants to pursue in state court an unfavorable state administrative action, nor does the Act specify the weight a federal court should afford a final judgment by a state court if such a remedy is sought. While we have interpreted the "civil action" authorized to follow consideration by federal and state administrative *agencies* to be a "trial de novo," [cit.] neither the statute nor our decisions indicate that the final judgment of a state *court* is subject to redetermination at such a trial. Similarly, the congressional directive that the EEOC should give "substantial weight" to findings made in state proceedings [cit.] indicates only the minimum level of deference the EEOC must afford all state determinations; it does not bar affording the greater preclusive effect which may be

---

6. (...continued)
vexation of multiple lawsuits, conserve[s] judicial resources, and, by preventing inconsistent decisions, encourage[s] reliance on adjudication." [cit.] When a state court has adjudicated a claim or issue, these doctrines also serve to "promote the comity between state and federal courts that has been recognized as a bulwark of the federal system." [cit.]

required by § 1738 if judicial action is involved.[7] To suggest otherwise, to say that either the opportunity to bring a "civil action" or the "substantial weight" requirement implicitly repeals § 1738, is to prove far too much. For if that is so, even a full trial on the merits in state court would not bar a trial de novo in federal court and would not be entitled to more than "substantial weight" before the EEOC. The state courts would be placed on a one-way street; the finality of their decisions would depend on which side prevailed in a given case.

Since an implied repeal must ordinarily be evident from the language or operation of a statute, the lack of such manifest incompatibility between Title VII and § 1738 is enough to answer our inquiry. No different conclusion is suggested by the legislative history of Title VII. * * *

It is sufficiently clear that Congress, both in 1964 and 1972, though wary of assuming the adequacy of state employment discrimination remedies, did not intend to supplant such laws. We conclude that neither the statutory language nor the congressional debates suffice to repeal § 1738's longstanding directive to federal courts.

B. Our finding that Title VII did not create an exception to § 1738 is strongly suggested if not compelled by our recent decision in *Allen v. McCurry* that preclusion rules apply in 42 U.S.C. § 1983 actions and may bar federal courts from freshly deciding constitutional claims previously litigated in state courts. Indeed, there is more in § 1983 to suggest an implied appeal of § 1738 than we have found in Title VII. In *Allen*, we noted that "one strong motive" behind the enactment of § 1983 was the "grave congressional concern that the state courts had been deficient in protecting federal rights." [cit.] Nevertheless, we concluded that "much clearer support than this would be required to hold that § 1738 and the traditional rules of preclusion are not applicable to § 1983 suits." [cit.]

Because Congress must "clearly manifest" its intent to depart from § 1738, our prior decisions construing Title VII in situations where § 1738 is inapplicable are not dispositive. They establish only that *initial resort* to state administrative remedies does not deprive an individual of a right to a federal trial de novo on a Title VII claim. In McDonnell Douglas Corp. v. Green, 411 U.S. 792 (1973), and Chandler v. Roudebush, 425 U.S. 840 (1976), we held that the "civil action" in federal court following an EEOC decision was intended to be a trial de novo. This holding, clearly supported by the legislative history, is not a holding that a prior state court judgment can be disregarded.

* * *

Finally, the comity and federalism interests embodied in § 1738 are not compromised by the application of res judicata and collateral estoppel in Title VII cases. Petitioner maintains that the decision of the Court of Appeals will deter

---

7. EEOC review of discrimination charges previously rejected by state agencies would be pointless if the federal courts were bound by such agency decisions. [cit.] Nor is it plausible to suggest that Congress intended federal courts to be bound further by state administrative decisions than by decisions of the EEOC. Since it is settled that decisions by the EEOC do not preclude a trial *de novo* in federal court, it is clear that unreviewed administrative determinations by state agencies also should not preclude such review even if such a decision were to be afforded preclusive effect in a State's own courts. [cit.]

claimants from seeking state court review of their claims ultimately leading to a deterioration in the quality of the state administrative process. On the contrary, stripping state court judgments of finality would be far more destructive to the quality of adjudication by lessening the incentive for full participation by the parties and for searching review by state officials. Depriving state judgments of finality not only would violate basic tenets of comity and federalism, [cit.] but also would reduce the incentive for States to work towards effective and meaningful antidiscrimination systems.

III. The petitioner nevertheless contends that the judgment should not bar his Title VII action because the New York courts did not resolve the issue that the District Court must hear under Title VII--whether Kremer had suffered discriminatory treatment--and because the procedures provided were inadequate. Neither contention is persuasive. Although the claims presented to the NYHRD and subsequently reviewed by the Appellate Division were necessarily based on New York law, the alleged discriminatory acts are prohibited by both federal and state laws. The elements of a successful employment discrimination claim are virtually identical; petitioner could not succeed on a Title VII claim consistently with the judgment of the NYHRD that there is no reason to believe he was terminated or not rehired because of age or religion. The Appellate Division's affirmance of the NYHRD's dismissal necessarily decided that petitioner's claim under New York law was meritless, and thus it also decided that a Title VII claim arising from the same events would be equally meritless.[21]

The more serious contention is that even though administrative proceedings and judicial review are legally sufficient to be given preclusive effect in New York, they should be deemed so fundamentally flawed as to be denied recognition under § 1738. We have previously recognized that the judicially created doctrine of collateral estoppel does not apply when the party against whom the earlier decision is asserted did not have a "full and fair opportunity" to litigate the claim or issue. [cit.] "Redetermination of issues is warranted if there is reason to doubt the quality, extensiveness, or fairness of procedures followed in prior litigation." [cit.]

Our previous decisions have not specified the source or defined the content of the requirement that the first adjudication offer a full and fair opportunity to litigate. But for present purposes, where we are bound by the statutory directive of § 1738, state proceedings need do no more than satisfy the minimum procedural requirements of the Fourteenth Amendment's Due Process Clause in order to qualify for the full faith and credit guaranteed by federal law. It has long been established that § 1738 does not allow federal courts to employ their own rules of res judicata in determining the effect of state judgments. Rather, it goes beyond the common law and commands a federal court to accept the rules chosen by the State from which the judgment is taken. As we recently noted in *Allen v. McCurry*, supra, "though the federal courts may look to the common law or to the policies supporting res judicata

---

21. * * * It is well established that judicial affirmance of an administrative determination is entitled to preclusive effect. [cit.] There is no requirement that judicial review must proceed de novo if it is to be preclusive. Furthermore, as we have explained, Congress did not draft the de novo requirement in order to deny preclusive effect to state decisions. [cit.]

and collateral estoppel in assessing the preclusive effect of decisions of other federal courts, Congress has specifically required all federal courts to give preclusive effect to state-court judgments whenever the courts of the State from which the judgments emerged would do so." [cit.]

The State must, however, satisfy the applicable requirements of the Due Process Clause. A State may not grant preclusive effect in its own courts to a constitutionally infirm judgment, and other state and federal courts are not required to accord full faith and credit to such a judgment. Section 1738 does not suggest otherwise; other state and federal courts would still be providing a state court judgment with the "same" preclusive effect as the courts of the State from which the judgment emerged. In such a case, there could be no constitutionally recognizable preclusion at all.[24]

We have little doubt that Kremer received all the process that was constitutionally required in rejecting his claim that he had been discriminatorily discharged contrary to the statute. * * *

IV. In our system of jurisprudence the usual rule is that merits of a legal claim once decided in a court of competent jurisdiction are not subject to redetermination in another forum. Such a fundamental departure from traditional rules of preclusion, enacted into federal law, can be justified only if plainly stated by Congress.[27] Because there is no "affirmative showing" of a "clear and manifest" legislative purpose in Title VII to deny res judicata or collateral estoppel effect to a state court judgment affirming that a claim of employment discrimination is unproved, and because the procedures provided in New York for the determination of such claims offer a full and fair opportunity to litigate the merits, the judgment of the Court of Appeals is

Affirmed.

JUSTICE BLACKMUN, with whom JUSTICE BRENNAN and JUSTICE MARSHALL join, dissenting.

* * *

The Court purports to give preclusive effect to the New York court's decision. But the Appellate Division made no finding one way or the other concerning the *merits* of petitioner's discrimination claim. The NYHRD, not the New York court, dismissed petitioner's complaint for lack of probable cause. In affirming, the court merely found that the *agency's* decision was not arbitrary or capricious. Thus, although it claims to grant a state *court* decision preclusive effect, in fact the Court bars petitioner's suit based on the state *agency's* decision of no probable cause. The Court thereby disregards the express provisions of Title VII, for, as the Court acknowledges, Congress has decided that an adverse state agency decision will not

---

24. The Court's decisions enforcing the Full Faith and Credit Clause of the Constitution, Art. IV, § 1, also suggest that what a full and fair opportunity to litigate entails is the procedural requirements of due process. [cit.] Section 1738 was enacted to implement the Full Faith and Credit Clause, [cit.] and specifically to insure that federal courts, not included within the constitutional provision, would be bound by state judgments. [cit.] It is therefore reasonable that § 1738 be subject to no more restriction than the Full Faith and Credit Clause.

27. One example is the authorization for federal courts to reexamine state findings upon a request for a writ of habeas corpus. 28 U.S.C. § 2254.

prevent a complainant's subsequent Title VII suit.

Finally, if the Court is in fact giving preclusive effect only to the state *court* decision, the Court misapplies 28 U.S.C. § 1738 by barring petitioner's suit. The state reviewing court never considered the merits of petitioner's discrimination claim, the subject matter of a Title VII suit in federal court. It is a basic principle of preclusion doctrine, [cit.] that a decision in one judicial proceeding cannot bar a subsequent suit raising issues that were not relevant to the first decision. "If the legal matters determined in the earlier case differ from those raised in the second case, collateral estoppel has no bearing on the situation." [cit.] Here, the state court decided only whether the state agency decision was arbitrary or capricious. Since the discrimination claim, not the validity of the state agency's decision, is the issue before the federal court, under § 1738 the state court's decision by itself cannot preclude a federal Title VII suit.

Thus, the Court is doing one of two things: either it is granting preclusive effect to the state agency's decision, a course that it concedes would violate Title VII, or it is misapplying § 1738 by giving preclusive effect to a state court decision that did not address the issue before the federal court. Instead of making one of these two mistakes, the Court should accept the fact that the New York state court judicial review is simply the end of the state administrative process, the state "proceedings." The Court searches in vain for a partial repeal of § 1738 in Title VII because it is blind to the fact that judicial review is a part--indeed, a distinctly secondary part--of the administration of discrimination claims filed before the NYHRD.

* * *

Perhaps the most disturbing aspect of the Court's decision is its tendency to cut back upon * * * critical policies underlying Title VII.

* * * Congress intended that state antidiscrimination procedures be an integral part of the Nation's battle against discrimination. For that reason, Congress did not pre-empt state antidiscrimination agencies [cit.] and instead gave state and local authorities an initial opportunity to resolve discrimination complaints. [cit.]

The Court's decision is directly contrary to this congressional intent. The lesson of the Court's ruling is: *An unsuccessful state discrimination complainant should not seek state judicial review.* If a discrimination complainant pursues state judicial review and loses--a likely result given the deferential standard of review in state court--he forfeits his right to seek redress in a federal court. If, however, he simply bypasses the state courts, he can proceed to the EEOC and ultimately to federal court. Instead of a deferential review of an agency record, he will receive in federal court a de novo hearing accompanied by procedural aids such as broad discovery rules and the ability to subpoena witnesses. Thus, paradoxically, the Court effectively has eliminated state reviewing courts from the fight against discrimination in an entire class of cases. Consequently, the state courts will not have a chance to correct state agency errors when the agencies rule against discrimination victims, and the quality of state agency decisionmaking can only deteriorate. It is a perverse sort of comity that eliminates the reviewing function of state courts in the name of giving their decisions due respect.

* * *

And no drastic consequences would flow from a decision finding § 1738 inapplicable in this case. The Court would not be forced to permit a subsequent Title VII suit in federal court if the complainant already had lost a trial on the merits in state court. [cit.] Furthermore, the state court affirmance of the state agency's decision would not be discarded. The state decision could be "admitted as evidence and accorded such weight as the court deems appropriate," [cit.] that is, "substantial weight," see § 706(b).

But despite the reasonableness of the rule followed by other Courts of Appeals, [cit.], the Court improperly applies § 1738 to bar petitioner from bringing a Title VII suit in federal court. I dissent.

JUSTICE STEVENS, dissenting. The issue that divides the Court is fairly narrow. The majority concedes that state agency proceedings will not bar a federal claim under Title VII, [cit.] and Justice Blackmun assumes, arguendo, that a state court decision on the merits of a discrimination claim would create such a bar [cit.]. Thus, the area of dispute is limited to cases in which an adverse agency decision has been reviewed and upheld by a state court.

The proper resolution of the dispute depends, I believe, on the character of the judicial review to which the agency decision is subjected. If it is the equivalent of a de novo trial on the merits, then I would agree that the analysis in the Court's opinion leads to the conclusion that 28 U.S.C. § 1738 forecloses a second lawsuit in a federal court. But as Justice Blackmun has demonstrated, [cit.] that is not the character of the relevant judicial review in New York. The New York court's holding that the agency decision was not arbitrary or capricious merely establishes as a matter of law that a rational adjudicator might have resolved the discrimination issue either way. It is therefore entirely consistent with § 1738 for a federal district court to accept the New York judgment as having settled that proposition, and then to proceed to resolve the discrimination issue in a *de novo* trial.

Both the text of Title VII and its legislative history indicate that Congress intended the claimant to have at least one opportunity to prove his case in a *de novo* trial in court. Thus, while I agree with the Court that Title VII did not impliedly repeal § 1738, I cannot accept the Court's construction of § 1738 in this case. In New York, as Justice Blackmun demonstrates, the judicial review is simply a part of the "proceedings" that are entitled to "substantial weight" under Title VII.

Accordingly, I respectfully dissent.

Notes and Questions

1. The Court in *Kremer* states that the issue is whether Congress implicitly "repealed" § 1738. Is that really the issue? Suppose Congress had specified the preclusive effect of all Title VII adjudications. Would not these federal preclusion rules apply to a New York state court enforcement of a prior New York state court Title VII judgment? Yet in such a case, the reason federal preclusion law would apply would have nothing to do with § 1738 since that section is irrelevant to New York's enforcement of a New York judgment.

2. Compare *Kremer* with Kalb v. Feuerstein, 308 U.S. 433 (1940), supra at 744.

In *Kalb*, the Court allowed a debtor in bankruptcy to attack collaterally a prior state court foreclosure judgment on the grounds that "Congress manifested its intention that the issue of jurisdiction in the foreclosing court need not be contested or even raised by the distressed farmer-debtor." Id. at 444. The *Kalb* Court does not even cite § 1738.

3. Reconsider why federal preclusion rules apply to *federal* judgments involving federal rights. If the reason is that preclusion rules can significantly affect a federal right, then should not federal preclusion rules apply regardless of whether the federal right is adjudicated in federal court or in state court?

4. Professor Burbank argues that § 1738 does not require enforcing courts to apply the rendering state's domestic preclusion law, but instead requires the court to apply the preclusion law that the rendering state's courts would apply. The state court may and probably will apply domestic preclusion law unless federal law preempts that option. According to Professor Burbank, where preclusion rules significantly affect federal substantive rights, then under ordinary principles of preemption, federal common law should control. Burbank, *Interjurisdictional Preclusion*, at 810–11.

5. In Allen v. McCurry, 449 U.S. 90 (1980), McCurry was convicted in a state criminal proceeding. In the criminal trial McCurry had sought unsuccessfully to suppress certain evidence that he alleged was seized in violation of the Fourth Amendment. Later, McCurry filed a § 1983 suit in federal court against the officers who had seized the evidence. The Supreme Court held that all issues actually litigated in the state court proceeding were entitled to the same preclusive effect in federal court that they would receive in state court.

In Migra v. Warren City Sch. Dist., 465 U.S. 75 (1984), the Court extended this principle to claim preclusion. There, Dr. Migra brought a successful breach of contact case in state court. She later brought a § 1983 case in federal court based on the same events. The Court held that the federal court must apply the claim preclusion law of the rendering state. Dr. Migra had argued that "to give state-court judgments full issue preclusive effect but not claim preclusive effect would enable litigants to bring their state claims in state court and their federal claims in federal court, thereby taking advantage of the relative expertise of both forums." 465 U.S. at 84. The Court rejected this argument explaining:

> Although such a division may seem attractive from a plaintiff's perspective, it is not the system established by § 1738. That statute embodies the view that it is more important to give full faith and credit to state-court judgments than to ensure separate forums for federal and state claims. This reflects a variety of concerns, including notions of comity, the need to prevent vexatious litigation, and a desire to conserve judicial resources.

Id.

6. The holdings of *Allen* and *Migra* seem somewhat inconsistent with the language in Haring v. Prosise, 462 U.S. 306 (1983). In *Haring*, the Court held a defendant's guilty plea in a state criminal prosecution did not preclude him from filing a subsequent § 1983 damage action in federal court against the police officers who searched his apartment. In reaching this conclusion, the Court suggested that the federal court might not have to give preclusive effect even if the state court would.

The Court stated that "a state-court judgment will not be given collateral-estoppel effect * * * where 'the party against whom an earlier court decision is asserted did not have a full and fair opportunity to litigate the claim or issue decided by the first court.'" 462 U.S. at 313. The Court added:

> We have recognized various other conditions that must also be satisfied before giving preclusive effect to a state-court judgment. [cit.] For example, collateral-estoppel effect is not appropriate when "controlling facts or legal principles have changed significantly since the state-court judgment," [cit.] or when "special circumstances warrant an exception to the normal rules of preclusion." [cit.]

Id. at 313 n.7. What is the source of these "conditions?" Could a *state* court take these conditions into account in deciding whether to give preclusive effect to another state's judgment? Would the state be *required* to take them into account?

7. In University of Tenn. v. Elliott, 478 U.S. 788 (1986), the Court held that § 1738 does not require federal courts to give preclusive effect to unreviewed state administrative determinations. The Court noted, however, that "all of the opinions in *Thomas v. Washington Gas Light Co.* express the view that the Full Faith and Credit Clause compels the States to give preclusive effect to the factfindings of an administrative tribunal in a sister State." Id. at 798. Even though § 1738 did not require preclusion, the Court went on to consider whether to "fashion[ ] federal common-law rules of preclusion in the absence of a governing statute." Id. at 794. After reviewing the case law and legislative history of Title VII, the Court concluded that "Congress did not intend unreviewed state administrative proceedings to have preclusive effect on Title VII claims." Id. at 796. Given this conclusion, could a state court give preclusive effect to a sister state's unreviewed administrative determination of a Title VII claim? Even if Congress explicitly prohibited states from giving preclusive effect to unreviewed administrative determinations, can Congress override the Full Faith and Credit Clause? The *Elliott* Court then turned its attention to § 1983 and found that Congress "did not intend [that statute] to create an exception to the general rules of preclusion." Id. at 797. The Court noted that "'[w]hen an administrative agency is acting in a judicial capacity and resolves disputed issues of fact properly before it which the parties have had an adequate opportunity to litigate, the courts have not hesitated to apply *res judicata* to enforce repose.'" Id. at 797-98. The Court held that "federal courts must give the agency's factfinding the same preclusive effect to which it would be entitled in the State's courts." Id. at 799.

As in *Elliott* itself, Title VII claims are sometimes combined with § 1983 claims. Does it make sense to give preclusive effect to factual findings as they relate to one claim, but not give effect to those same factual findings as they relate to a different claim?

8. In Astoria Fed. Savings & Loan Ass'n v. Solimino, 501 U.S. 104 (1991), the Court followed the Title VII analysis in *Elliott* and held that in suits under the federal age discrimination act, judicially unreviewed state administrative findings have no preclusive effect on subsequent proceedings in federal court.

Marrese v. American Academy of Orthopaedic Surgeons
Supreme Court of the United States, 1985.
470 U.S. 373, 105 S.Ct. 1327, 84 L.Ed.2d 274.

JUSTICE O'CONNOR delivered the opinion of the Court. * * *

I. Petitioners are board-certified orthopaedic surgeons who applied for membership in respondent American Academy of Orthopaedic Surgeons (Academy). Respondent denied the membership applications without providing a hearing or a statement of reasons. In November 1976, petitioner Dr. Treister filed suit in the Circuit Court of Cook County, State of Illinois, alleging that the denial of membership in the Academy violated associational rights protected by Illinois common law. Petitioner Dr. Marrese separately filed a similar action in state court. Neither petitioner alleged a violation of state antitrust law in his state court action; nor did either petitioner contemporaneously file a federal antitrust suit. The Illinois Appellate Court ultimately held that Dr. Treister's complaint failed to state a cause of action, [cit.] and the Illinois Supreme Court denied leave to appeal. [cit.] After the Appellate Court ruled against Dr. Treister, the Circuit Court dismissed Dr. Marrese's complaint.

In March 1980, petitioners filed a federal antitrust suit in the United States District Court for the Northern District of Illinois based on the same events underlying their unsuccessful state court actions. As amended, the complaint alleged that respondent Academy possesses monopoly power, that petitioners were denied membership in order to discourage competition, and that their exclusion constituted a boycott in violation of § 1 of the Sherman Act, 15 U.S.C. § 1. [cit.] Respondent filed a motion to dismiss arguing that claim preclusion barred the federal antitrust claim because the earlier state court actions concerned the same facts and were dismissed with prejudice.[1] In denying this motion, the District Court reasoned that state courts lack jurisdiction over federal antitrust claims, and therefore a state court judgment cannot have claim preclusive effect in a subsequent federal antitrust suit. [cit.] Discovery began and respondent refused to allow petitioners access to certain files relating to membership applications. After respondent persisted in this refusal despite a discovery order, the District Court held respondent in criminal contempt. [cit.]

The judgment of contempt was reversed by a divided panel of the Court of Appeals in an opinion holding that the District Judge had abused his discretion by authorizing discovery of the membership files and also suggesting that the federal action was barred by claim preclusion and that the antitrust claims were groundless. [cit.] This opinion was vacated by an en banc vote, and the original panel issued a narrower opinion that did not discuss claim preclusion. [cit.] The Court of Appeals then vacated the second opinion and ordered rehearing en banc. In a divided vote, the Court of Appeals held that claim preclusion barred the federal antitrust suit and

---

1. In this opinion we use the term "claim preclusion" to refer to "res judicata" in a narrow sense, i.e., the preclusive effect of a judgment in foreclosing litigation of matters that should have been raised in an earlier suit. In contrast, we use the term "issue preclusion" to refer to the effect of a judgment in foreclosing relitigation of a matter that has been litigated and decided. [cit.]

reversed the contempt order because the discovery order was invalid. [cit.]

* * *

We granted certiorari limited to the question whether the Court of Appeals correctly held that claim preclusion requires dismissal of the federal antitrust action, [cit.] and we now reverse.

* * *

III. The issue presented by this case is whether a state court judgment may have preclusive effect on a federal antitrust claim that could not have been raised in the state proceeding. Although federal antitrust claims are within the exclusive jurisdiction of the federal courts, [cit.] the Court of Appeals ruled that the dismissal of petitioners' complaints in state court barred them from bringing a claim based on the same facts under the Sherman Act. The Court of Appeals erred by suggesting that in these circumstances a federal court should determine the preclusive effect of a state court judgment without regard to the law of the State in which judgment was rendered.

The preclusive effect of a state court judgment in a subsequent federal lawsuit generally is determined by the full faith and credit statute, which provides that state judicial proceedings "shall have the same full faith and credit in every court within the United States ... as they have by law or usage in the courts of such State ... from which they are taken." 28 U.S.C. § 1738. This statute directs a federal court to refer to the preclusion law of the State in which judgment was rendered. "It has long been established that § 1738 does not allow federal courts to employ their own rules of res judicata in determining the effect of state judgments. Rather, it goes beyond the common law and commands a federal court to accept the rules chosen by the State from which the judgment is taken." *Kremer v. Chemical Construction Corp.*; [cit.]. Section 1738 embodies concerns of comity and federalism that allow the States to determine, subject to the requirements of the statute and the Due Process Clause, the preclusive effect of judgments in their own courts. [cit.]

The fact that petitioners' antitrust claim is within the exclusive jurisdiction of the federal courts does not necessarily make § 1738 inapplicable to this case. Our decisions indicate that a state court judgment may in some circumstances have preclusive effect in a subsequent action within the exclusive jurisdiction of the federal courts. Without discussing § 1738, this Court has held that the issue preclusive effect of a state court judgment barred a subsequent patent suit that could not have been brought in state court. [cit.] Moreover, *Kremer* held that § 1738 applies to a claim of employment discrimination under Title VII of the Civil Rights Act of 1964, [cit.] although the Court expressly declined to decide whether Title VII claims can be brought only in federal courts. [cit.] *Kremer* implies that absent an exception to § 1738, state law determines at least the issue preclusive effect of a prior state judgment in a subsequent action involving a claim within the exclusive jurisdiction of the federal courts.

More generally, *Kremer* indicates that § 1738 requires a federal court to look first to state preclusion law in determining the preclusive effects of a state court judgment. [cit.] The Court's analysis in *Kremer* began with the finding that state law would in fact bar relitigation of the discrimination issue decided in the earlier state proceedings. [cit.] That finding implied that the plaintiff could not relitigate the same issue in federal court unless some exception to § 1738 applied. [cit.] *Kremer* observed that "an exception to § 1738 will not be recognized unless a later statute contains an express or implied repeal." [cit.] Title VII does not expressly repeal § 1738, and the Court concluded that the statutory provisions and legislative history do not support a finding of implied repeal. [cit.] We conclude that the basic approach adopted in *Kremer* applies in a lawsuit involving a claim within the exclusive jurisdiction of the federal courts.

To be sure, a state court will not have occasion to address the specific question whether a state judgment has issue or claim preclusive effect in a later action that can be brought only in federal court. Nevertheless, a federal court may rely in the first instance on state preclusion principles to determine the extent to which an earlier state judgment bars subsequent litigation. [cit.] *Kremer* illustrates that a federal court can apply state rules of issue preclusion to determine if a matter actually litigated in state court may be relitigated in a subsequent federal proceeding. [cit.]

With respect to matters that were not decided in the state proceedings, we note that claim preclusion generally does not apply where "[t]he plaintiff was unable to rely on a certain theory of the case or to seek a certain remedy because of the limitations on the subject matter jurisdiction of the courts...." Restatement (Second) of Judgments § 26(1)(c) (1982). If state preclusion law includes this requirement of prior jurisdictional competency, which is generally true, a state judgment will *not* have claim preclusive effect on a cause of action within the exclusive jurisdiction of the federal courts. Even in the event that a party asserting the affirmative defense of claim preclusion can show that state preclusion rules in some circumstances bar a claim outside the jurisdiction of the court that rendered the initial judgment, the federal court should first consider whether application of the state rules would bar the particular federal claim.

Reference to state preclusion law may make it unnecessary to determine if the federal court, as an exception to § 1738, should refuse to give preclusive effect to a state court judgment. The issue whether there is an exception to § 1738 arises only if state law indicates that litigation of a particular claim or issue should be barred in the subsequent federal proceeding. To the extent that state preclusion law indicates that a judgment normally does not have claim preclusive effect as to matters that the court lacked jurisdiction to entertain, lower courts and commentators have correctly concluded that a state court judgment does not bar a subsequent federal antitrust claim. [cit.] Unless application of Illinois preclusion law suggests, contrary to the usual view, that petitioners' federal antitrust claim is somehow barred, there will be no need to decide in this case if there is an exception to § 1738.[3]

---

3. The Chief Justice notes that preclusion rules bar the splitting of a cause of action between a court of limited jurisdiction and one of general jurisdiction, and suggests that state requirements of jurisdictional competency may leave unclear whether a state court action precludes a subsequent federal antitrust claim. [cit.] The rule that the judgment of a court of limited jurisdiction concludes the entire claim assumes that the plaintiff might have commenced his action in a court *in the same system of courts* that was competent to give full relief. See Restatement (Second) of Judgments § 24, Comment g (1982). Moreover, the jurisdictional competency requirement generally is understood to imply that state court litigation based on a state statute analogous to a federal statute, e.g., a state antitrust law, does not bar subsequent attempts to

(continued...)

The Court of Appeals did not apply the approach to § 1738 that we have outlined. Both the plurality opinion, [cit.] and an opinion concurring in part, [cit.] express the view that § 1738 allows a federal court to give a state court judgment greater preclusive effect than the state courts themselves would give to it. This proposition, however, was rejected by Migra v. Warren City School Dist. Bd. of Ed., 465 U.S. 75 (1984), a case decided shortly after the Court of Appeals announced its decision in the instant case. In *Migra*, a discharged school-teacher filed suit under 42 U.S.C. § 1983 in federal court after she prevailed in state court on a contract claim involving the same underlying events. The Federal District Court dismissed the § 1983 action as barred by claim preclusion. The opinion of this Court emphasized that under § 1738, state law determined the preclusive effect of the state judgment. [cit.] Because it was unclear from the record whether the District Court's ruling was based on state preclusion law, we remanded for clarification on this point. [cit.] Such a remand obviously would have been unnecessary were a federal court free to give greater preclusive effect to a state court judgment than would the judgment-rendering State. [cit.]

We are unwilling to create a special exception to § 1738 for federal antitrust claims that would give state court judgments greater preclusive effect than would the courts of the State rendering the judgment. Cf. Haring v. Prosise, 462 U.S. at 317–318 (refusing to create special preclusion rule for § 1983 claim subsequent to plaintiff's guilty plea). The plurality opinion for the Court of Appeals relied on Federated Department Stores, Inc. v. Moitie, 452 U.S. 394 (1981), to observe that the doctrine of claim preclusion protects defendants from repetitive lawsuits based on the same conduct, [cit.] and that there is a practical need to require plaintiffs "to litigate their claims in an economical and parsimonious fashion." [cit.] We agree that these are valid and important concerns, and we note that under § 1738 state issue preclusion law may promote the goals of repose and conservation of judicial resources by preventing the relitigation of certain issues in a subsequent federal proceeding. [cit.]

If we had a single system of courts and our only concerns were efficiency and finality, it might be desirable to fashion claim preclusion rules that would require a plaintiff to bring suit initially in the forum of most general jurisdiction, thereby resolving as many issues as possible in one proceeding. [cit.] The decision of the Court of Appeals approximates such a rule inasmuch as it encourages plaintiffs to file suit initially in federal district court and to attempt to bring any state law claims pendent to their federal antitrust claims. Whether this result would reduce the overall burden of litigation is debatable, [cit.] and we decline to base our interpretation of § 1738 on our opinion on this question.

More importantly, we have parallel systems of state and federal courts, and the concerns of comity reflected in § 1738 generally allow States to determine the

---

3. (...continued)
secure relief in federal court if the state court lacked jurisdiction over the federal statutory claim. Id. § 26(1)(c), Illustration 2. Although a particular State's preclusion principles conceivably could support a rule similar to that proposed by The Chief Justice, [cit.] where state preclusion rules do not indicate that a claim is barred, we do not believe that federal courts should fashion a federal rule to preclude a claim that could not have been raised in the state proceedings.

preclusive scope of their own courts' judgments. [cit.] These concerns certainly are not made less compelling because state courts lack jurisdiction over federal antitrust claims. We therefore reject a judicially created exception to § 1738 that effectively holds as a matter of federal law that a plaintiff can bring state law claims initially in state court only at the cost of forgoing subsequent federal antitrust claims. *Federated Department Stores, Inc. v. Moitie* does not suggest a contrary conclusion. That case did not involve § 1738; rather it held that "accepted principles of res judicata" determine the preclusive effect of a federal court judgment. [cit.]

In this case the Court of Appeals should have first referred to Illinois law to determine the preclusive effect of the state judgment. Only if state law indicates that a particular claim or issue would be barred, is it necessary to determine if an exception to § 1738 should apply. Although for purposes of this case, we need not decide if such an exception exists for federal antitrust claims, we observe that the more general question is whether the concerns underlying a particular grant of exclusive jurisdiction justify a finding of an implied partial repeal of § 1738. Resolution of this question will depend on the particular federal statute as well as the nature of the claim or issue involved in the subsequent federal action. Our previous decisions indicate that the primary consideration must be the intent of Congress. [cit.]

IV. The decisions below did not consider Illinois preclusion law in their discussion of the claim preclusion issue. * * * Before this Court, the parties have continued to disagree about the content of Illinois preclusion law. We believe that this dispute is best resolved in the first instance by the District Court. [cit.]

* * *

The judgment of the Court of Appeals is reversed, and the case is remanded for further proceedings consistent with this opinion.

It is so ordered.

JUSTICE BLACKMUN and JUSTICE STEVENS took no part in the consideration or decision of this case.

CHIEF JUSTICE BURGER, concurring in the judgment. I agree with the Court's implicit conclusion that the Court of Appeals approached 28 U.S.C. § 1738 too narrowly and technically by holding it irrelevant on the ground that Illinois law does not address the preclusive effect of a state court judgment on a federal antitrust suit [cit.]. In the circumstances presented by this case, a fair reading of § 1738 requires federal courts to look first to general principles of state preclusion law. Those principles control if they clearly establish that the state court judgment does not bar the later federal action: Only recently, we reaffirmed in Migra v. Warren City School District Board of Education, 465 U.S. 75 (1984), that a federal court is not free to accord greater preclusive effect to a state court judgment than the state courts themselves would give to it.

The Court now remands with directions for the District Court to consider Illinois claim preclusion law, but no guidance is given as to how the District Court should proceed if it finds state law silent or indeterminate on the claim preclusion question. The Court's refusal to acknowledge this potential problem appears to stem from a belief that the jurisdictional competency requirement of res judicata doctrine will dispose of most cases like this. [cit.]

I cannot agree with the Court's interpretation of the jurisdictional competency requirement. If state law provides a cause of action that is virtually identical with a federal statutory cause of action, a plaintiff suing in state court is able to rely on the same theory of the case and obtain the same remedy as would be available in federal court, even when the plaintiff cannot expressly invoke the federal statute because it is within the exclusive jurisdiction of the federal courts. In this situation, the jurisdictional competency requirement is effectively satisfied. Therefore, the fact that state law recognizes the jurisdictional competency requirement does not necessarily imply that a state court judgment has no claim preclusive effect on a cause of action within exclusive federal jurisdiction.

The states that recognize the jurisdictional competency requirement do not all define it in the same terms. Illinois courts have expressed the doctrine in the following manner: "The principle [of res judicata] extends not only to questions which were actually litigated but also to all *questions* which *could have been raised* or determined." [cit.] In the present case, each petitioner could have alleged a cause of action under the Illinois Antitrust Act, Ill. Rev. Stat., ch. 38, ¶ 60–1 et seq. (1981), in his prior state court lawsuit against respondent. The principles of Illinois res judicata doctrine appear to be indeterminate as to whether petitioners' ability to raise state antitrust claims in their prior state court suits should preclude their assertion of essentially the same claims in the present federal action. This indeterminacy arises from the fact that the Illinois courts have not addressed whether the notion of "questions which could have been raised" should be applied narrowly or broadly. No Illinois court has considered how the jurisdictional competency requirement should apply in the type of situation presented by this case, where the same theory of recovery may be asserted under different statutes. Nor has any Illinois court considered whether res judicata precludes splitting a cause of action between a court of limited jurisdiction and one of general jurisdiction.[3]

Hence it is likely that the principles of Illinois claim preclusion law do not speak to the preclusive effect that petitioners' state court judgments should have on the present action. In this situation, it may be consistent with § 1738 for a federal court to formulate a federal rule to resolve the matter. If state law is simply indeterminate, the concerns of comity and federalism underlying § 1738 do not come into play. At the same time, the federal courts have direct interests in ensuring that their resources are used efficiently and not as a means of harassing defendants with repetitive lawsuits, as well as in ensuring that parties asserting federal rights have an adequate opportunity to litigate those rights. Given the insubstantiality of the state interests and the weight of the federal interests, a strong argument could be made that a federal rule would be more appropriate than a creative interpretation of ambiguous state

---

3. Compare Restatement (Second) of Judgments § 24, Comment *g*, Illustration 14, pp. 204–205 (1982): "In an automobile collision, A is injured and his car damaged as a result of the negligence of B. Instead of suing in a court of general jurisdiction of the state, A brings his action for the damage to his car in a justice's court, which has jurisdiction in actions for damage to property but has no jurisdiction in actions for injury to the person.
Judgment is rendered for A for the damage to the car. A cannot thereafter maintain an action against B to recover for the injury to his person arising out of the same collision." * * *

law.[4] When state law is indeterminate or ambiguous, a clear federal rule would promote substantive interests as well: "Uncertainty intrinsically works to defeat the opportunities for repose and reliance sought by the rules of preclusion, and confounds the desire for efficiency by inviting repetitious litigation to test the preclusive effects of the first effort." [cit.]

A federal rule might be fashioned from the test, which this Court has applied in other contexts, that a party is precluded from asserting a claim that he had a "full and fair opportunity" to litigate in a prior action. [cit.] Thus, if a state statute is identical in all material respects with a federal statute within exclusive federal jurisdiction, a party's ability to assert a claim under the state statute in a prior state court action might be said to have provided, in effect, a "full and fair opportunity" to litigate his rights under the federal statute. [cit.]

The Court will eventually have to face these questions; I would resolve them now.

Notes and Questions

1. Section 1738 requires an enforcing court to give judgments "the same full faith and credit * * * as they have by law or usage." However, the Court itself notes, Illinois will never have occasion to decide whether a state judgment has issue or claim preclusion effect in a later action that can be brought only in federal court. Should the Court have decided that the § 1738 requirement of "the *same* full faith and credit" is simply inapplicable in this situation?

2. On the remand of *Marrese*, the district court held that under Illinois law, a state court dismissal of the antitrust action would not bar a subsequent federal antitrust action. Marrese v. American Acad. of Orthopaedic Surgeons, 628 F.Supp. 918 (N.D.Ill.1986). The judge began his analysis by characterizing the issue as a "nearly metaphysical question" and noted that his task was "an exercise in extrapolation because, of course, the Illinois courts never address issues pertaining to exclusively federal lawsuits." Id. at 919. The court then quoted the basic rule of Illinois claim preclusion:

> [A] final judgment rendered by a court of competent jurisdiction on the merits is conclusive as to the rights of the parties and their privies * * * [in] a subsequent action involving the same claim * * *. The doctrine of *res judicata* * * * extends not only to the questions actually litigated and decided, but to all grounds of recovery or defenses which might have been presented.

Id. at 920 (quoting People v. Kidd, 75 N.E.2d 851, 853 (Ill. 1947)). The court concluded that Illinois would bar a subsequent *state* antitrust action and then turned to "the more abstract question" of whether it would bar a federal antitrust action. The court declined to rely on the "court of competent jurisdiction" or the "might have been presented" language of the Illinois rule. It relied instead on Restatement (Second) § 26(1) and comment c(1) which indicates that state proceedings do not bar

---

4. By contrast, when a federal court construes substantive rights and obligations under state law in the context of a diversity action, the federal interest is insignificant and the state's interest is much more direct than it is in the present situation, even if the relevant state law is ambiguous.

subsequent lawsuits within the exclusive jurisdiction of the federal courts. The court acknowledged that the Illinois courts have never cited this section of the Restatement, but noted that they "have widely relied on portions of the Restatement concerning other aspects of *res judicata* law." 628 F.Supp. at 924.

3. The *Marrese* Court does not decide what happens if state law *would* preclude the subsequent federal claim. The Court states that in such a case, the issue would be "whether the concerns underlying a particular grant of exclusive jurisdiction justify a finding of an implied partial repeal of § 1738." What factors should the Court consider in determining whether to override a state preclusion rule?

4. Compare *Marrese* with *Thomas v. Washington Gas Light Co.*, supra at 724. In *Thomas*, an injured worker received a workers' compensation award in Virginia and was allowed to seek a second award in the District of Columbia. Justice Stevens' plurality opinion noted that a final judgment "normally establishes not only the measure of the plaintiff's rights but also the limits the defendant's liability." 448 U.S. at 282. However, the Virginia workers' compensation tribunal was only permitted to apply its own laws and therefore "it neither could nor purported to determine [the worker's] rights under the law of the District of Columbia." Id. at 282. Is not the same true with respect to the state court in *Marrese*? Given exclusive federal jurisdiction, the state court did not and could not determine rights under the federal antitrust laws.

5. In *Marrese* the Court suggests that § 1738 prohibits a federal court from granting greater preclusive effect to a state judgment than the rendering state would give. Justice White, in a concurring opinion in *Migra*, wrote:

> In Union & Planters' Bank v. Memphis, 189 U.S. 71, 75 (1903), this Court held that a federal court "can accord [a state judgment] no greater efficacy" than would the judgment-rendering State. That holding has been adhered to on at least three occasions since that time. [cit.] The Court has also indicated that the States are bound by a similar rule under the Full Faith and Credit Clause. [cit.] The Court is thus justified in this case to rule that preclusion must be determined under state law, even if there would be preclusion under federal standards.
>
> This construction of 28 U.S.C. § 1738 and its predecessors is unfortunate. In terms of the purpose of that section, which is to require federal courts to give effect to state-court judgments, there is no reason to hold that a federal court may not give preclusive effect to a state judgment simply because the judgment would not bar relitigation in the state courts. If the federal courts have developed rules of res judicata and collateral estoppel that prevent relitigation in circumstances that would not be preclusive in state courts, the federal courts should be free to apply them, the parties then being free to relitigate in the state courts. The contrary construction of § 1738 is nevertheless one of long standing, and Congress has not seen fit to disturb it, however justified such an action might have been.

465 U.S. at 88.

In Haring v. Prosise, 462 U.S. 306 (1983), discussed supra at 794, the Court suggested that a federal court could give greater effect to a judgment than the rendering state would give. There, the Court concluded that the law of the rendering state would not preclude subsequent litigation on an issue. Thus, the Court said, "the issue is not foreclosed under 28 U.S.C. § 1738." 462 U.S. at 317. Nonetheless, the opinion went on to analyze whether even if the "claim is not precluded under § 1738, this Court should create a special rule of preclusion which nevertheless would bar litigation" of the § 1983 claim. Id. The Court concluded that such a special rule of preclusion "would threaten important interests in preserving federal courts as an available forum for the vindication of constitutional rights." Id. at 322. But in reaching this conclusion, the Court did not even consider the possibility that § 1738 required federal courts to give state judgments the *same* effect as the rendering state would give. Can *Haring* be reconciled with *Marrese* and *Migra*?

6. Should courts interpret § 1738 to require application of the rendering state's law on all aspects of preclusion? In other words, maybe some aspects of preclusion doctrine are not encompassed by the Full Faith and Credit statute. Professor Shreve has argued that a type of interest analysis should be used in deciding whether a second forum can give greater effect to a judgment than the rendering forum would give. Shreve, *Preclusion and Federal Choice of Law*, 1209. "When the state rule of lesser preclusion is intended to facilitate a substantive policy," then that rule must be honored by other courts. Id. at 1256. However, where the rendering court would be uninterested in the preclusion rule applied by a different enforcing court, the enforcing court should be free to apply its own rule. Professor Shreve argues that under this approach, the mutuality doctrine is one that enforcing courts can ignore even if the rendering state would require mutuality. What would be the argument that the rendering court has no interest in whether a subsequent court enforces or abandons mutuality? What might be the counter-argument?

7. In Rooker v. Fidelity Trust Co., 263 U.S. 413 (1923), and District of Columbia Court of Appeals v. Feldman, 460 U.S. 462 (1983), the Supreme Court held that the United States Supreme Court is the only federal court authorized to exercise appellate review of state court judgments. Relying on this limit on appellate review, some courts have "cast[ ] in jurisdictional terms a rule that is very close if not identical to the more familiar principle that a federal court must give full faith and credit to a state court judgment." Gauthier v. Continental Diving Services, 831 F.2d 559, 561 (5th Cir.1987). See 18B Wright, Miller & Cooper, *Federal Practice* § 4469. The doctrine was applied in connection with one of the more notorious class actions. A class action was brought in Alabama state court on behalf of a nationwide class of escrow account holders. The suit was settled and attorneys fees awarded to the plaintiffs' lawyers with fees divided up among all class members. Some class members ended up losing money because their share of the attorneys fees was greater than their share of the award. These unhappy class members brought suit in federal court against the lawyers for both sides, alleging fraud and malpractice. The Seventh Circuit dismissed for lack of jurisdiction without considering whether such a suit would be barred under Alabama's preclusion rules. Kamilewicz v. Bank of Boston Corp., 92 F.3d 506 (7th Cir.1996) *cert. denied*, 520 U.S. 1204 (1997). For a symposium on the Rooker-Feldman Doctrine, see 74 Notre Dame L. Rev. 1081 (1999).

Parsons Steel, Inc. v. First Alabama Bank

Supreme Court of the United States, 1986.
474 U.S. 518, 106 S.Ct. 768, 88 L. Ed. 2d 877.

JUSTICE REHNQUIST delivered the opinion of the Court. The Full Faith and Credit Act, 28 U.S.C. § 1738, requires federal courts as well as state courts to give state judicial proceedings "the same full faith and credit ... as they have by law or usage in the courts of such State ... from which they are taken." The Anti–Injunction Act, 28 U.S.C. § 2283, generally prohibits a federal court from granting an injunction to stay proceedings in a state court, but excepts from that prohibition the issuance of an injunction by a federal court "where necessary ... to protect or effectuate its judgments." In the present case the Court of Appeals for the Eleventh Circuit held that the quoted exception to the latter Act worked a *pro tanto* amendment to the former, so that a federal court might issue an injunction against state-court proceedings even though the prevailing party in the federal suit had litigated in the state court and lost on the res judicata effect of the federal judgment. We * * * now reverse the judgment of the Court of Appeals.

Petitioners Parsons Steel, Inc., and Jim and Melba Parsons sued respondents First Alabama Bank of Montgomery and Edward Herbert, a bank officer, in Alabama state court in February 1979, essentially alleging that the bank had fraudulently induced the Parsonses to permit a third person to take control of a subsidiary of Parsons Steel and eventually to obtain complete ownership of the subsidiary. The subsidiary was adjudicated an involuntary bankrupt in April 1979, and the trustee in bankruptcy was added as a party plaintiff in the state action. In May 1979 Parsons Steel and the Parsonses sued the bank in the United States District Court for the District of Alabama, alleging that the same conduct on the part of the bank that was the subject of the state-court suit also violated the Bank Holding Company Act (BHCA) amendments, 12 U.S.C. §§ 1971-1978. The trustee in bankruptcy chose not to participate in the federal action.

The parties conducted joint discovery in the federal and state actions. The federal action proceeded to trial on the issue of liability before the state action went to trial. A jury returned a verdict in favor of petitioners, but the District Court granted judgment n.o.v. to the bank. That judgment was affirmed on appeal. [cit.] After the federal judgment was entered, respondents pleaded in the state action the defenses of res judicata and collateral estoppel based on that judgment. The Alabama court, however, ruled that res judicata did not bar the state action. Almost a year after the federal judgment was entered, the state complaint was amended to include a Uniform Commercial Code (UCC) claim that the bank's foreclosure sale of the subsidiary's assets was commercially unreasonable. A jury returned a general verdict in favor of petitioners, awarding a total of four million and one dollars in damages.

Having lost in state court, respondents returned to the District Court that had previously entered judgment in the bank's favor and filed the present injunctive action against petitioners, the plaintiffs in the state action. The District Court found that the federal BHCA suit and the state action were based on the same factual allegations and claimed substantially the same damages. The court held that the state claims should have been raised in the federal action as pendent to the BHCA claim and accordingly that the BHCA judgment barred the state claims under res judicata. Determining that the Alabama judgment in effect nullified the earlier federal-court judgment in favor of the bank, the District Court enjoined petitioners from further prosecuting the state action.

A divided panel of the Court of Appeals affirmed in relevant part, holding that the issuance of the injunction was not "an abuse of discretion" by the District Court. [cit.] The majority first agreed with the District Court that the fraud and UCC claims presented issues of fact and law that could have been and should have been raised in the same action as the BHCA claim. Thus the parties to the BHCA action and their privies, including the trustee in bankruptcy, were barred by res judicata from raising these claims in state court after the entry of the federal judgment.

The majority then held that the injunction was proper under the so-called "relitigation exception" to the Anti-Injunction Act, 28 U.S.C. § 2283, which provides:

> "A court of the United States may not grant an injunction to stay proceedings in a State court except as expressly authorized by Act of Congress, or where necessary in aid of its jurisdiction, or *to protect or effectuate its judgments*" (emphasis added).

In reaching this holding, the majority explicitly declined to consider the possible preclusive effect, pursuant to the Full Faith and Credit Act, 28 U.S.C. § 1738, of the state court's determination after full litigation by the parties that the earlier federal-court judgment did not bar the state action. According to the majority, "while a federal court is generally bound by other state court determinations, the relitigation exception empowers a federal court to be the final adjudicator as to the res judicata effects of its prior judgments on a subsequent state action." [cit.]

Finally, the majority ruled that respondents had not waived their right to an injunction by waiting until after the trial in the state action was completed. The majority concluded that the state-court pleadings were so vague that it was not clear until after trial that essentially the same cause of action was involved as the BHCA claim and that the earlier federal judgment was in danger of being nullified. According to the majority, the Anti-Injunction Act does not limit the power of a federal court to protect its judgment "to specific points in time in state court trials or appellate procedure." [cit.][3]

* * *

In our view, the majority of the Court of Appeals gave unwarrantedly short shrift to the important values of federalism and comity embodied in the Full Faith and Credit Act. As recently as last March, in *Marrese v. American Academy of Orthopaedic Surgeons*, we reaffirmed our holding in *Migra v. Warren City School Dist. Bd. of Education*, that under the Full Faith and Credit Act a federal court must give the same preclusive effect to a state-court judgment as another court of that

---

3. The Court of Appeals remanded the case to the District Court for a determination whether the trustee in bankruptcy should be allowed to litigate his UCC claim in state court because the trustee was not a party to the federal suit and the UCC claim might have been based on facts other than those that formed the basis for the federal action.

State would give. "It has long been established that § 1738 does not allow federal courts to employ their own rules of res judicata in determining the effect of state judgments. Rather, it goes beyond the common law and commands a federal court to accept the rules chosen by the State from which the judgment is taken." *Kremer v. Chemical Construction Corp.* The Full Faith and Credit Act thus "allow[s] the States to determine, subject to the requirements of the statute and the Due Process Clause, the preclusive effect of judgments in their own courts." *Marrese.*

In the instant case, however, the Court of Appeals did not consider the possible preclusive effect under Alabama law of the state-court judgment, and particularly of the state court's resolution of the res judicata issue, concluding instead that the relitigation exception to the Anti-Injunction Act limits the Full Faith and Credit Act. We do not agree. "[A]n exception to § 1738 will not be recognized unless a later statute contains an express or implied partial repeal." *Kremer*; [cit.]. Here, as in *Kremer*, there is no claim of an express repeal; rather, the Court of Appeals found an implied repeal. "'It is, of course, a cardinal principle of statutory construction that repeals by implication are not favored,' [cit.] and whenever possible, statutes should be read consistently." [cit.] We believe that the Anti–Injunction Act and the Full Faith and Credit Act can be construed consistently, simply by limiting the relitigation exception of the Anti-Injunction Act to those situations in which the state court has not yet ruled on the merits of the res judicata issue. Once the state court has finally rejected a claim of res judicata, then the Full Faith and Credit Act becomes applicable and federal courts must turn to state law to determine the preclusive effect of the state court's decision.

The contrary holding of the Court of Appeals apparently was based on the fact that Congress in 1948 amended the Anti-Injunction Act to overrule this Court's decision in Toucey v. New York Life Insurance Co., 314 U.S. 118 (1941), in favor of the understanding of prior law expressed in Justice Reed's dissenting opinion. [cit.] But the instant case is a far cry from *Toucey*, and one may fully accept the logic of Justice Reed's dissent without concluding that it sanctions the result reached by the Court of Appeals here. In each of the several cases involved in *Toucey*, the prevailing party in the federal action sought an injunction against relitigation in state court as soon as the opposing party commenced the state action, and before there was any resolution of the res judicata issue by the state court. In the instant case, on the other hand, respondents chose to fight out the res judicata issue in state court first, and only after losing there did they return to federal court for another try.

The Court of Appeals also felt that the District Court's injunction would discourage inefficient simultaneous litigation in state and federal courts on the same issue—that is, the res judicata effect of the prior federal judgment. But this is one of the costs of our dual court system:

> "In short, the state and federal courts had concurrent jurisdiction in this case, and neither court was free to prevent either party from simultaneously pursuing claims in both courts." Atlantic Coast Line R. Co. v. Locomotive Engineers, 398 U.S. 281, 295 (1970).

Indeed, this case is similar to *Atlantic Coast Line*, in which we held that the various exceptions to the Anti–Injunction Act did not permit a federal court to enjoin state proceedings in circumstances more threatening to federal jurisdiction than the circumstances of this case. There we stated that the phrase "to protect or effectuate its judgments" authorized a federal injunction of state proceedings only "to prevent a state court from so interfering with a federal court's consideration or disposition of a case as to seriously impair the federal court's flexibility and authority to decide that case." [cit.]

We hold, therefore, that the Court of Appeals erred by refusing to consider the possible preclusive effect, under Alabama law, of the state-court judgment. Even if the state court mistakenly rejected respondents' claim of res judicata, this does not justify the highly intrusive remedy of a federal-court injunction against the enforcement of the state-court judgment. Rather, the Full Faith and Credit Act requires that federal courts give the state-court judgment, and particularly the state court's resolution of the res judicata issue, the same preclusive effect it would have had in another court of the same State. Challenges to the correctness of a state court's determination as to the conclusive effect of a federal judgment must be pursued by way of appeal through the state-court system and certiorari from this Court. [cit.]

We think the District Court is best situated to determine and apply Alabama preclusion law in the first instance. See *Marrese v. American Academy of Orthopaedic Surgeons*; *Migra v. Warren City School Dist. Bd. of Education*. Should the District Court conclude that the state-court judgment is not entitled to preclusive effect under Alabama law and the Full Faith and Credit Act, it would then be in the best position to decide the propriety of a federal-court injunction under the general principles of equity, comity, and federalism discussed in Mitchum v. Foster, 407 U.S. 225 (1972).

The judgment of the Court of Appeals is reversed, and the case is remanded for further proceedings consistent with this opinion.

It is so ordered.

Notes and Questions

1. The Court in *Parsons Steel* holds that the federal court should give the Alabama judgment the same effect it would have had under Alabama law. Would Alabama have enforced an Alabama judgment that improperly ignored a prior federal judgment? The Restatement (Second) of Judgments suggests that the last in time rule may not apply where the second court erroneously denies "full faith and credit to the judgment of a sister state." Restatement (Second) of Judgments § 15, cmt. e (1982). Could Alabama recognize this exception but still enforce a state judgment that ignores a prior federal judgment?

2. Does the holding of *Parsons Steel* increase the likelihood that federal courts will enjoin state proceedings? Consider the following analysis:

> [T]he *Parsons Steel* decision will have the effect of increasing the frequency of federal court injunctions of state proceedings. Usually, if someone is sued in state court after prevailing on the same issues in federal court, he or she will raise res judicata as a defense to the state judicial proceedings. In most cases, the

state court will accord preclusive effect to the earlier federal judgment and that will end the state proceedings. In such instances, the federal courts need not enjoin the state court litigation; the state, on its own, will dismiss the matter because of claim and issue preclusion.

However, *Parsons Steel* creates a strong incentive to not litigate the preclusion issue in state court. If the question is presented there and lost, it will bar a subsequent federal injunction. Hence, after *Parsons Steel*, the person subjected to a repetitive suit in state court should immediately seek a federal court injunction. The result will be federal court injunctions in many instances where the state court would have dismissed the case anyway on preclusion grounds. This seems inconsistent with the Supreme Court's general preference that matters be litigated in state court where possible and its general desire to avoid injunctions of state judicial proceedings.

Chemerinsky, *Federal Jurisdiction* 657.

3. Whose preclusion law should the Alabama state court have applied in determining what effect to give the federal judgment? Since the federal judgment dealt solely with a federal claim, should the court have applied federal preclusion law? Does it matter that the claims that arguably were precluded were state law claims?

4. The original federal court judgment did not include the state claims. Because the parties were not diverse, the federal court could have adjudicated those claims only if the federal court had had and chosen to exercise supplemental jurisdiction. If the federal court did not have supplemental jurisdiction, then would *Parsons Steel* be the converse for *Marrese*?

5. Compare *Parsons* with *Treinies*, discussed supra at 762.

Chapter 12

RECOGNITION OF
FOREIGN-COUNTRY JUDGMENTS

A. INTRODUCTION

In Chapter 10, supra, we studied the principles governing the recognition and enforcement in one state of judgments rendered in another state of the United States. In this chapter, we explore the principles that govern the recognition of judgments rendered in foreign countries.

One of the basic questions explored in this chapter is to what extent the differences between sister-state judgments and foreign-country judgments require or justify a different approach. The fact that the Full Faith and Credit clause of the Constitution (which plays such an omnipotent role in recognition of sister-state judgments) is inapplicable to foreign-country judgments, answers only a small part of this question. It means that recognition of the latter judgments is a matter of state choice and discretion rather than federal compulsion. While this makes the study of recognition of foreign-country judgments more interesting, it leaves unanswered the question of what criteria should guide the proper exercise of this discretion. In this chapter, we shall search for those criteria through a critical study of the experience of American courts and legislatures. We begin with *Hilton v. Guyot*, a 19th century case that, although superseded in some respects, is generally viewed as the starting point of the American effort to develop a coherent approach to recognition of foreign-country judgments.

B. THE STARTING POINT

Hilton v. Guyot
Supreme Court of the United States, 1895.
159 U.S. 113, 16 S.Ct. 139, 40 L.Ed. 95.

[Hilton and Libbey, New York citizens trading in Paris, were sued in France by Guyot, the administrator of a French firm, for sums allegedly owed to that firm. Hilton and Libbey appeared in the French proceeding and litigated the merits. The French court rendered a judgment against them which was affirmed by a higher court and became final. Guyot then sought to enforce that judgment in federal district court

811

in New York. That court held the judgment enforceable without retrial on the merits. The Supreme Court reversed in an extremely lengthy opinion excerpted below.]

MR. JUSTICE GRAY, after stating the case, delivered the opinion of the court. * * * No law has any effect, of its own force, beyond the limits of the sovereignty from which its authority is derived. The extent to which the law of one nation, as put in force within its territory, whether by executive order, by legislative act, or by judicial decree, shall be allowed to operate within the dominion of another nation, depends upon what our greatest jurists have been content to call "the comity of nations." Although the phrase has been often criticized, no satisfactory substitute has been suggested.

"Comity," in the legal sense, is neither a matter of absolute obligation, on the one hand, nor of mere courtesy and good will, upon the other. But it is the recognition which one nation allows within its territory to the legislative, executive or judicial acts of another nation, having due regard both to international duty and convenience, and to the rights of its own citizens or of other persons who are under the protection of its laws. * * *

Mr. Wheaton says: "* * * No sovereign is bound, unless by special compact, to execute within his dominions a judgment rendered by the tribunals of another State; and if execution be sought by suit upon the judgment, or otherwise, the tribunal in which the suit is brought, or from which execution is sought, is, on principle, at liberty to examine into the merits of such judgment, and to give effect to it or not, as may be found just and equitable. The general comity, utility and convenience of nations have, however, established a usage among most civilized States, by which the final judgments of foreign courts of competent jurisdiction are reciprocally carried into execution, under certain regulations and restrictions, which differ in different countries." [Wheaton's International Law, (8th ed.) § 147.] * * *

* * * [I]t is important to distinguish different kinds of judgments. Every foreign judgment, of whatever nature, in order to be entitled to any effect, must have been rendered by a court having jurisdiction of the cause, and upon regular proceedings and due notice. In alluding to different kinds of judgments, therefore, such jurisdiction, proceedings and notice will be assumed. It will also be assumed that they are untainted by fraud, the effect of which will be considered later.

A judgment *in rem*, adjudicating the title to a ship or other movable property within the custody of the court, is treated as valid everywhere. * * * A judgment affecting the status of persons, such as a decree confirming or dissolving a marriage, is recognized as valid in every country, unless contrary to the policy of its own law. * * * Other judgments, not strictly *in rem*, under which a person has been compelled to pay money, are so far conclusive that the justice of the payment cannot be impeached in another country, so as to compel him to pay it again. For instance, a judgment in foreign attachment is conclusive, as between the parties, of the right to the property or money attached. Story on Conflict of Laws, (2d ed.) § 592 a. * * *

The extraterritorial effect of judgments *in personam*, at law or in equity, may differ, according to the parties to the cause. A judgment of that kind between two citizens or residents of the country, and thereby subject to the jurisdiction, in which it is rendered, may be held conclusive as between them everywhere. So, if a foreigner invokes the jurisdiction by bringing an action against a citizen, both may be held bound by a judgment in favor of either. And if a citizen sues a foreigner, and judgment is rendered in favor of the latter, both may be held equally bound. [cit.]

The effect to which a judgment, purely executory, rendered in favor of a citizen or resident of the country, in a suit there brought by him against a foreigner, may be entitled in an action thereon against the latter in his own country—as is the case now before us—presents a more difficult question, upon which there has been some diversity of opinion. * * *

In view of all the authorities upon the subject, and of the trend of judicial opinion in this country and in England, following the lead of Kent and Story, we are satisfied that, where there has been opportunity for a full and fair trial abroad before a court of competent jurisdiction, conducting the trial upon regular proceedings, after due citation or voluntary appearance of the defendant, and under a system of jurisprudence likely to secure an impartial administration of justice between the citizens of its own country and those of other countries, and there is nothing to show either prejudice in the court, or in the system of laws under which it was sitting, or fraud in procuring the judgment, or any other special reason why the comity of this nation should not allow it full effect, the merits of the case should not, in an action brought in this country upon the judgment, be tried afresh, as on a new trial or an appeal, upon the mere assertion of the party that the judgment was erroneous in law or in fact. The defendants, therefore, cannot be permitted, upon that general ground, to contest the validity or the effect of the judgment sued on. * * *

When an action is brought in a court of this country, by a citizen of a foreign country against one of our own citizens, to recover a sum of money adjudged by a court of that country to be due from the defendant to the plaintiff, and the foreign judgment appears to have been rendered by a competent court, having jurisdiction of the cause and of the parties, and upon due allegations and proofs, and opportunity to defend against them, and its proceedings are according to the course of a civilized jurisprudence, and are stated in a clear and formal record, the judgment is *prima facie* evidence, at least, of the truth of the matter adjudged; and it should be held conclusive upon the merits tried in the foreign court, unless some special ground is shown for impeaching the judgment, as by showing that it was affected by fraud or prejudice, or that, by the principles of international law, and by the comity of our own country, it should not be given full credit and effect.

There is no doubt that both in this country, as appears by the authorities already cited, and in England, a foreign judgment may be impeached for fraud. * * * Under what circumstances this may be done does not appear to have ever been the subject of judicial investigation in this country. * * *

In the case at bar, the defendants offered to prove, in much detail, that the plaintiffs presented to the French court of first instance and to the arbitrator appointed by that court, and upon whose report its judgment was largely based, false and fraudulent statements and accounts against the defendants, by which the arbitrator and the French courts were deceived and misled, and their judgments were based upon such false and fraudulent statements and accounts. This offer, if satisfactorily proved, would, according to the decisions of the English Court of

Appeal [cit.], be a sufficient ground for impeaching the foreign judgment, and examining into the merits of the original claim.

But whether those decisions can be followed in regard to foreign judgments, consistently with our own decisions as to impeaching domestic judgments for fraud, it is unnecessary in this case to determine, because there is a distinct and independent ground upon which we are satisfied that the comity of our nation does not require us to give conclusive effect to the judgments of the courts of France; and that ground is, the want of reciprocity, on the part of France, as to the effect to be given to the judgments of this and other foreign countries.

In France, the Royal Ordinance of June 15, 1629, art. 121, provided as follows: "Judgments rendered * * * in foreign kingdoms and sovereignties, for any cause whatever, shall have no lien or execution in our kingdom. Thus * * *, notwithstanding the judgments, our subjects against whom they have been rendered may contest their rights anew before our judges." Touillier, Droit Civil, lib. 3, tit. 3, c. 6, sect. 3, no. 77. * * * [T]he French Code of Civil Procedure [also provides to the same effect]. * * *

The defendants, in their answer, cited the above provisions of the statutes of France, and alleged, and at the trial offered to prove, that, by the construction given to these statutes by the judicial tribunals of France, when the judgments of tribunals of foreign countries against the citizens of France are sued upon in the courts of France, the merits of the controversies upon which those judgments are based are examined anew, unless a treaty to the contrary effect exists between the Republic of France and the country in which such judgment is obtained, (which is not the case between the Republic of France and the United States,) and that the tribunals of the Republic of France give no force and effect, within the jurisdiction of that country, to the judgments duly rendered by courts of competent jurisdiction of the United States against citizens of France after proper personal service of the process of those courts has been made thereon in this country. We are of opinion that this evidence should have been admitted.

* * * [The Court discusses several authorities, including the following.]

Mr. Justice Story said: "If a civilized nation seeks to have the sentences of its own courts held of any validity elsewhere, they ought to have a just regard to the rights and usages of other civilized nations, and the principles of public and national law in the administration of justice," Bradstreet v. Neptune Ins. Co., 3 Sumner, 600, 608.

Mr. Justice Woodbury said that judgments *in personam*, rendered under a foreign government, "are, *ex comitate*, treated with respect, according to the nature of the judgment, and the character of the tribunal which rendered it, and the reciprocal mode, if any, in which that government treats our judgments;" and added, "Nor can much comity be asked for the judgments of another nation, which, like France, pays no respect to those of other countries." Burnham v. Webster, 1 Woodb. & Min. 172, 175, 179.

Mr. Justice Cooley said, "True comity is equality; we should demand nothing more, and concede nothing less." McEwan v. Zimmer, 38 Michigan, 765, 769. * * *

By the law of France, settled by a series of uniform decisions of the Court of Cassation, the highest judicial tribunal, for more than half a century, no foreign judgment can be rendered executory in France without a review of the judgment *au fond*--to the bottom, including the whole merits of the cause of action on which the judgment rests. Pardessus, Droit Commercial, § 1488; Bard, Precis de Droit International, (1883) nos. 234-239; Story's Conflict of Laws, §§ 615-617; [cit.] * * * [The Court discusses a French decision which denied enforcement to an American judgment, and then, after reviewing the recognition laws of twenty foreign countries, concludes that] the rule of reciprocity has worked itself firmly into the structure of international jurisprudence.

The reasonable, if not the necessary, conclusion appears to us to be that judgments rendered in France, or in any other foreign country, by the laws of which our own judgments are reviewable upon the merits, are not entitled to full credit and conclusive effect when sued upon in this country, but are *prima facie* evidence only of the justice of the plaintiffs' claim.

In holding such a judgment, for want of reciprocity, not to be conclusive evidence of the merits of the claim, we do not proceed upon any theory of retaliation upon one person by reason of injustice done to another; but upon the broad ground that international law is founded upon mutuality and reciprocity, and that by the principles of international law recognized in most civilized nations, and by the comity of our own country, which it is our judicial duty to know and to declare, the judgment is not entitled to be considered conclusive.

By our law, at the time of the adoption of the Constitution, a foreign judgment was considered as *prima facie* evidence, and not conclusive. There is no statute of the United States, and no treaty of the United States with France, or with any other nation, which has changed that law, or has made any provision upon the subject. It is not to be supposed that, if any statute or treaty had been or should be made, it would recognize as conclusive the judgments of any country, which did not give like effect to our own judgments. In the absence of statute or treaty, it appears to us equally unwarrantable to assume that the comity of the United States requires anything more.

* * * If the judgment had been rendered in this country, or in any other outside of the jurisdiction of France, the French courts would not have executed or enforced it, except after examining into its merits. The very judgment now sued on would be held inconclusive in almost any other country than France. * * *

For these reasons, * * * the Judgment is reversed, and the cause remanded to the Circuit Court with directions to set aside the verdict and to order a new trial. * * *

MR. CHIEF JUSTICE FULLER, with whom concurred Mr. Justice HARLAN, Mr. Justice BREWER, and Mr. Justice JACKSON, dissenting. * * * [T]he doctrine of *res judicata* applicable to domestic judgments should be applied to foreign judgments as well, and rests on the same general ground of public policy that there should be an end of litigation.

This application of the doctrine is in accordance with our own jurisprudence, and it is not necessary that we should hold it to be required by some rule of international law. The fundamental principle concerning judgments is that disputes are finally determined by them, and I am unable to perceive why a judgment *in personam* which is not open to question on the ground of want of jurisdiction, either intrinsically or over the parties, or of fraud, or on any other recognized ground of impeachment, should not be held inter partes, though recovered abroad, conclusive on the merits.

* * * If plaintiffs in error had succeeded in their cross suit and recovered judgment against defendants in error, and had sued them here on that judgment, defendants in error would not have been permitted to say that the judgment in France was not conclusive against them. As it was, defendants in error recovered, and I think plaintiffs in error are not entitled to try their fortune anew before the courts of this country on the same matters voluntarily submitted by them to the decision of the foreign tribunal. We are dealing with the judgment of a court of a civilized country, whose laws and system of justice recognize the general rules in respect to property and rights between man and man prevailing among all civilized peoples. Obviously the last persons who should be heard to complain are those who identified themselves with the business of that country, knowing that all their transactions there would be subject to the local laws and modes of doing business. The French courts appear to have acted "judicially, honestly, and with the intention to arrive at the right conclusion;" and a result thus reached ought not to be disturbed. * * *

I cannot yield my assent to the proposition that because by legislation and judicial decision in France that effect is not there given to judgments recovered in this country which, according to our jurisprudence, we think should be given to judgments wherever recovered, (subject, of course, to the recognized exceptions,) therefore we should pursue the same line of conduct as respects the judgments of French tribunals. The application of the doctrine of *res judicata* does not rest in discretion; and it is for the government, and not for its courts, to adopt the principle of retorsion, if deemed under any circumstances desirable or necessary. * * *

Notes and Questions

1. *To Recognize or not to Recognize?: The Two Extremes.* The inapplicability of the Full Faith and Credit clause to foreign-country judgments leaves room for several possible approaches to the question of the conditions under which and the extent to which such judgments are to be recognized. At least theoretically, the alternatives range from the one extreme of total non-recognition to the other extreme of total full recognition under the same standards governing sister-state judgments.

Let us consider the first extreme. If it is true that "[n]o sovereign is bound * * * to execute within his dominions a judgment rendered by the tribunals of another State," *Hilton*, supra, then why should an American court ever recognize a foreign country-judgment? For example, Sweden and the Netherlands apparently do not recognize foreign judgments in the absence of a treaty. Professors von Mehren and Trautman believe that "[t]he ultimate justification for according some degree of recognition is that, if in our highly complex and interrelated world each community exhausted every possibility of insisting on its parochial interests, injustice would result and the normal patterns of life would be disrupted." von Mehren & Trautman, *Recognition of Foreign Adjudications*, 1603. Then they advance five specific reasons for which a regime of total non-recognition should be rejected:

> a desire to avoid duplication of effort and consequent waste involved in reconsidering a matter that has already been litigated; a related concern to protect the successful litigant * * * from harassing or evasive tactics on the part of the previously unsuccessful opponent; a policy against making the availability of local enforcement the decisive element * * * in the plaintiff's choice of forum; an interest in fostering stability and unity in [the] international order * * *; and, in certain classes of cases, a belief that the rendering jurisdiction is a more appropriate forum than the recognizing jurisdiction * * *.

Id. at 1603–04. Do you disagree with any of these reasons? What other reasons can you add?

Now let us consider the other extreme of automatic recognition. In his dissenting opinion in *Hilton*, Chief Justice Fuller seems to come very close to this extreme when he declares that "the doctrine of *res judicata* applicable to domestic judgments should be applied to foreign judgments as well, [because it] rests on the same general ground of public policy that there should be an end of litigation." Is this thesis not unduly generous towards foreign judgments? If so, what is wrong with that? To the extent that the domestic doctrine of res judicata is based on the need to avoid duplication of effort and conserve judicial resources, is it not true that, in foreign judgments, no prior *American* resources have been expended? To the extent that the domestic res judicata doctrine is motivated by other policies, are those policies equally strong when the judgment sought to be recognized was rendered in another country? Even if Chief Justice Fuller was using the term "domestic judgments" in the sense of sister-state (rather than forum) judgments, are those judgments not significantly different from foreign-country judgments? In what ways? Are these differences such as to make Fuller's thesis unacceptable? Why, or why not? For a comprehensive discussion of the differences between local and foreign adjudications, see von Mehren, *Foreign Judgments*, 32–54.

2. *The Middle Ground*. *Hilton* adopts an approach that lies somewhere between the two extremes described above. But where exactly does *Hilton* fit in the rather long spectrum between those extremes? Despite its holding on reciprocity, does *Hilton* attach a presumption of "conclusiveness" or "enforceability" to the foreign judgment? If so, what are the elements that make this presumption operable? How different are they from those that make a sister-state judgment enforceable under the Full Faith and Credit clause? Apart from reciprocity and public policy (see infra), what other grounds can rebut the above presumption? Are these grounds different from those that can prevent recognition of a sister-state judgment? All in all, is it true that, although it rejects Fuller's advocacy of the almost automatic recognition of foreign judgment, *Hilton* is still unnecessarily generous to foreign judgments? For example, subject to certain limited defenses specified therein, *Hilton* precludes a review of the merits of the foreign judgment, except when, as in *Hilton* itself, the foreign country subjects American judgments to such a review. Is this a good idea? Some countries deny recognition to foreign judgments unless the rendering court has

applied the substantive law that would have been applied by the recognizing court. See infra at 824. Does *Hilton* permit such a choice-of-law inquiry? Is this inquiry more justified in the case of foreign-country judgments than in the case of sister-state judgments? We shall revisit this question later. For now, try to identify those differences between the two categories of judgments that would justify a different treatment. Consider the following comparison by Judge Patrick Higginbotham:

> Many of the reasons for recognition and enforcement of foreign country judgments are the same as for giving conclusive effect to domestic judgments: prevention of harassment of the successful party, elimination of duplicative judicial proceedings, and providing some measure of settled expectations to the parties. [cit.] In a domestic context, the benefits of preclusion are palpable. In our Union, since courts in each state are subject to due process limitations * * * [and] to the same overlap of federal laws and the Constitution, * * * [and] shar[e] to a large extent the same body of court precedents and socio-economic ideas and are presumptively fair and competent, the benefits of giving conclusive effect are not balanced by any recognizable costs. Giving an automatically conclusive * * * full faith and credit [effect] to sister state judgments could be fully justified on the grounds of fairness to litigants and judicial economy; there is no reason for a second trial[;] the rendering forum had at least the constitutionally requisite contacts with the litigant[; and] there is little possibility of an error in the rendering forum * * *.

> The benefit-cost calculation for giving an automatically conclusive effect to foreign country judgments is far less favorable. There is less expectation that the courts of a foreign country will follow procedures which would comport with our notions of due process and jurisdiction and that they will apply substantively tolerable laws. Moreover, especially if the loser in the initial litigation is American, there will be suspicions here of unfairness or fraud.

Hunt v. BP Exploration Company, 492 F.Supp. 885 at 905 (N.D.Tex.1980). Judge Higginbotham then describes the current American approach to this subject as a "halfway house" of "neither pretending that the initial litigation never occurred, nor giving [it] an automatic conclusive effect." Id. at 905–06. He concludes that this "tempered" approach has the advantage of enabling courts to "deny effect to foreign country judgments when the rendering court has acted * * * in ways intolerable by our country's * * * ideal of fundamental fairness." Id. What do you think of the above comparison and the conclusion? For another comparison, see von Mehren & Trautman, *Recognition of Foreign Adjudications*, 1605–06, *et passim*.

3. *Reciprocity*. Ultimately, *Hilton* refused to recognize the French judgment because a French court in the reverse situation would not have recognized an American judgment without re-examining its merits (*revision au fond*). But what are the precise parameters of this reciprocity requirement under *Hilton*? For example, would *Hilton* have refused to recognize the French judgment if: (a) the French court had held for, rather than against, the American litigants; (b) if the successful litigant was not a French national but rather a national of another country, including the United States; (c) regardless of the litigants' nationality, the judgment was one *in rem* or over status; or, (d) regardless of the nature of the judgment or the litigants'

nationality, the judgment had been satisfied?

Regardless of the precise scope of the reciprocity requirement, is it a good idea to penalize private litigants for the positions taken by their governments? Should "courts [be] required to do, not as justice and reason require, but as they are done by"? MacDonald v. Grand Trunk Railway Co., 456, 52 A. 982 (N.H.1902).

Is reciprocity effective in changing the attitudes of foreign countries on matters such as the recognition of judgments? Could one expect Mr. Guyot, and similarly situated French-judgment creditors, to bring pressure on the French legislature to change its stance vis a vis foreign judgments? Eventually, 69 years after *Hilton*, the French *Cour de Cassation* abandoned its practice of subjecting foreign judgments to a *revision au fond* (see Munzer v. Munzer-Jacoby, Cass. Jan. 7, 1964, [1964] Semaine Juridique II, 13590), in part because of Germany's refusal, under the German reciprocity requirement, to recognize French judgments. See von Mehren, *Foreign Judgments*, 49. Does this suggest that reciprocity works, or that it works only as between certain countries?

Does reciprocity serve or harm American interests? Would it help to know if more American judgment-creditors seek recognition of American judgments in France than French judgment-creditors seek recognition of French judgments in the United States? Would it also help to know the approximate dollar amounts of unsatisfied judgments from each side?

Even if, as a general matter, reciprocity is an appropriate weapon with none of the drawbacks alluded to by the above questions, does this weapon belong in the hands of judges or of foreign-policy makers? Notice Chief Justice Fuller's statement that "it is for the government, and not for its courts, to adopt the principle of retorsion, if deemed under any circumstances desirable or necessary." Do you disagree? Furthermore, if the judges who use this "principle of retorsion" are state rather than federal judges, is there the additional problem of impermissible state intrusion into federal government's conduct of foreign affairs? See *American Ins. Ass'n v. Garamendi*, supra at 557.

Be that as it may, to date most courts in the United States have rejected the requirement of reciprocity. See infra at 821 (Uniform Act); Chabert v. Bacquie, 694 So.2d 8052 (Fla.Ct.App.1997); Bank of Montreal v. Kough, 612 F.2d 467 (9th Cir.1980); Nicol v. Tanner, 310 Minn. 68, 256 N.W.2d 796 (1976); Somportex Ltd. v. Philadelphia Chewing Gum Corp., 453 F.2d 435 (3d Cir.1971), *cert. denied*, 405 U.S. 1017 (1972); Johnston v. Compagnie Generale Transatlantique, 242 N.Y. 381, 152 N.E. 121 (1926). The Restatement (Second) of Conflicts and the Restatement (Third) of Foreign Relations also disapprove of this requirement. However, a *Project on International Jurisdiction and Judgments* (IJJ) currently under consideration by the American Law Institute would make reciprocity a mandatory basis for non-recognition, in both state and federal courts. See *IJJ Project*, § 7 (Tent. Draft 4/14/2003). The IJJ Project is drafted as a federal act that, if enacted by Congress, will preempt state law.

4. *Federal versus State Law*. *Hilton* was a diversity jurisdiction case and was decided well before Erie R. Co. v. Tompkins, 304 U.S. 64 (1938) and Klaxon Co. v. Stentor Electric Mfg. Co., 313 U.S. 487 (1941), which require federal courts

sitting in diversity to follow the substantive and conflicts law of the forum state. Is recognition of foreign judgments one of the questions that, under *Erie* and *Klaxon*, must be governed by state law? Most federal courts have held that, in the absence of a federal statute or treaty or some other basis for federal jurisdiction (such as admiralty), recognition of foreign-country judgments is a matter of state law. See, e.g., British Midland Airways Ltd. v. International Travel, Inc., 497 F.2d 869 (9th Cir.1974); *Somportex Ltd. v. Philadelphia Chewing Gum Corp.*, supra; Fairchild, Arabatzis & Smith v. Prometco, 470 F.Supp. 610 (S.D.N.Y.1979). Many state courts have also assumed or held that *Hilton*, having enunciated a rule of federal common law, is not binding on the states. See, e.g., Johnston v. Compagnie Generale Transatlantique, 152 N.E. 121 (N.Y.1926). In addition, thirty-one jurisdictions have adopted the Uniform Foreign Money-Judgments Recognitions Act, discussed below, which differs in some respects from *Hilton*. As a result of these developments, *Hilton*, though often cited, is rarely dispositive, especially on the issue of reciprocity. See infra 821. Nevertheless, many courts continue to find *Hilton*'s general approach to be persuasive.

What problems do you see with a regime that entrusts the recognition of foreign country judgments to the individual states? We have already alluded to the potential intrusion into the field of foreign affairs in discussing reciprocity. See supra. However, problems may exist even with regard to issues not involving reciprocity. Suppose, for example, that a state refuses to recognize any foreign judgment that is rendered: (a) against an American litigant; or (b) in non-English speaking countries; or (c) in "totalitarian" countries; or (d) countries whose judges are not popularly elected. What then? Aside from such unlikely scenarios, is there a danger that a hodgepodge of state approaches on this matter would confuse foreign courts trying to determine whether to recognize an American judgment? Would it not be preferable if, on this uniquely international problem, we were to develop a uniform solution within the United States and to speak with a single voice internationally? Assuming that such a development were desirable, what constitutional means are available to that end? For an exploration of these issues see Brand, *Uniformity and International Acceptance*, 253 ff. As noted above, the ALI's IJJ Project would federalize this whole area of the law and would grant concurrent jurisdiction to federal and state courts for the recognition of foreign judgments. See IJJ Project § 8.

THE UNIFORM ACT

1. In 1962, the National Conference of Commissioners on Uniform State Laws promulgated the Uniform Foreign Money-Judgments Recognition Act ("UFMJRA," or the "Act") which aspired to "increase the likelihood that American judgments will be recognized in foreign countries," and to "[re]state rules that have long been applied by the majority of courts in this country." Pref. Note, 13 U.L.A. 261–62

(2002). As of 2003, thirty-one jurisdictions have adopted this Act,[1] with slight variations from state to state. Although the Act abandons the reciprocity requirement, eight of the adopting states have added this requirement.[2] The Act applies to judgments for the recovery of money "other than a judgment for taxes, a fine or other penalty, or a judgment for support in matrimonial or family matters." (§ 1.)

2. ***Grounds for Non-Recognition***. The Act distinguishes between mandatory and discretionary grounds for non-recognition.

a. *Mandatory Grounds*. Section 4(a) provides that a foreign judgment *shall not* be recognized, if:

(1) the judgment was rendered under a system which does not provide impartial tribunals or procedures compatible with the requirements of due process of law; (2) the foreign court did not have personal jurisdiction over the defendant; or (3) the foreign court did not have jurisdiction over the subject matter.

b. *Discretionary Grounds*. Section 4(b) provides that a foreign judgment *need not* be recognized if:

(1) the defendant in the proceedings in the foreign court did not receive notice of the proceedings in sufficient time to enable him to defend; (2) the judgment was obtained by fraud; (3) the cause of action on which the judgment is based is repugnant to the public policy of this state; (4) the judgment conflicts with another final and conclusive judgment; (5) the proceeding in the foreign court was contrary to an agreement between the parties under which the dispute in question was to be settled otherwise than by proceedings in that court; or (6) in the case of jurisdiction based only on personal service, the foreign court was a seriously inconvenient forum for the trial of the action.

3. ***Jurisdiction of the Foreign Court:*** *a. Sufficient Bases of Jurisdiction*. Section 5(a) addresses the question of the foreign court's jurisdiction and provides that the foreign judgment shall not be refused recognition on this ground, if:

(1) the defendant was served personally in the foreign state; (2) the defendant voluntarily appeared in the proceedings, other than for the purpose of protecting property seized or threatened with seizure in the proceedings or of contesting the jurisdiction of the court over him; (3) the defendant prior to the commencement of the proceedings had agreed to submit to the jurisdiction of the foreign court with respect to the subject matter involved; (4) the defendant was domiciled in the foreign state when the proceedings were instituted, or, being a body corporate had its principal place of business, was incorporated, or had otherwise acquired corporate status, in the foreign state; (5) the defendant had a business office in the foreign state and the proceedings in the foreign court involved a

---

1. These jurisdictions are: Alaska, California, Colorado, Connecticut, Delaware, District of Columbia, Florida, Georgia, Hawaii, Idaho, Illinois, Iowa, Maine, Maryland, Massachusetts, Michigan, Minnesota, Missouri, Montana, New Jersey, New Mexico, New York, North Carolina, Ohio, Oklahoma, Oregon, Pennsylvania, Texas, Virgin Islands, Virginia, and Washington. See 13 U.L.A. 261 (2003).

2. These states are Florida, Georgia, Idaho, Massachusetts, North Carolina, Ohio and Texas. In Georgia and Massachusetts, reciprocity is a mandatory ground for non-recognition, while in the other states it is discretionary. New Hampshire has a reciprocity provision that is confined to Canadian judgments. See. N.H.Rev.Stat.Ann. §524:11.

cause of action arising out of business done by the defendant through that office in the foreign state; or (6) the defendant operated a motor vehicle or airplane in the foreign state and the proceedings involved a cause of action arising out of such operation.

b. Additional Bases for Jurisdiction. Section 5(b) expressly permits recognition of a judgment rendered on jurisdictional bases other than those listed above.

4. ***Additional Grounds for Recognition.*** Finally, section 7 provides that the Act "does not prevent the recognition of a foreign judgment in situations not covered by th[e] Act."

We shall discuss the provisions of the Act after reviewing the cases that apply them.

THE ALI'S RESTATEMENTS AND IJJ PROJECT

1. ***The Restatement (Second) of Conflict of Laws.*** This Restatement devotes only one section to foreign-country judgments. It is § 98, which states laconically that "[a] valid judgment rendered in a foreign nation after a fair trial in a contested proceeding will be recognized in the United States." A foreign trial is considered fair if it meets the standards enunciated in *Hilton*. See § 98 cmt. c. A foreign judgment is considered "valid" if it "meet[s] the requirements of § 92" (id. cmt. a.), which defines the validity of sister-state judgments. (§ 92 requires in personam and subject-matter jurisdiction, reasonable notice and opportunity to be heard, and "compliance with such requirements of the state of rendition as are necessary for the valid exercise of power by the court.") Indeed, the Restatement (Second) subscribes to the view that, "[i]n most respects," foreign judgments that are valid under § 92 "will be accorded the same degree of recognition to which sister State judgments are entitled * * * because the public interest requires that there be an end to litigation." § 98 cmt. b. However, this statement is modified by subsequent comments, such as comment g, which provides that foreign judgments "can be resisted, in among other ways, on the ground that * * * the underlying cause was contrary to the public policy of the State of the forum (§ 117) or that the judgment was on a governmental claim (§ 120)." § 98 cmt. g. Another comment also modifies the statement in the text of § 98, supra, regarding a "contested proceeding" and allows recognition of certain default judgments. See § 98 cmt. d. For a discussion of the Restatement (Second)'s approach, see Peterson, *Foreign Country Judgments*, 220.

2. ***The Restatement (Third), Foreign Relations.*** This Restatement parallels in most respects the UFMJRA, except that: (a) it is not limited to money judgments; and (b) it treats lack of subject matter jurisdiction as a discretionary ground for non-recognition. See §§ 481-86. However, section 482 of the Restatement (Third) is more explicit as to the standards by which to judge the existence of the rendering court's jurisdiction over the defendant: the court must have had jurisdiction "in accordance with the law of the rendering state *and* with the rules set forth in § 421." (Emphasis added.) Section 421 purports to restate or to enunciate standards of jurisdiction that are "similar to those developed under the due process clause of the United States Constitution." Restatement (Third) § 421 Reporter's note 1. However,

having been drafted before Burnham v. Superior Court of California, 495 U.S. 604 (1990) (supra at 648), section 421 specifically disapproves of "tag jurisdiction," i.e., jurisdiction based exclusively on service of process on a person only transitorily present in the forum state. See Restatement (Third) § 241(2)(a); Id. cmt. e.

3. **THE ALI'S IJJ PROJECT.** Although this Project is a work in progress, it represents the American Law Institute's current thinking on recognition of foreign judgments. It is far more detailed and comprehensive than either the UFMJRA or the two Restatements.

a. *Mandatory Grounds for Non-Recognition.* Besides making lack of reciprocity a mandatory ground of non-recognition (§ 7), the IJJ provides in § 5(a) that a foreign judgment *shall not* be recognized if it was rendered:

(1) under a system that "does not provide impartial tribunals or procedures compatible with fundamental principles of fairness;" (2) in circumstances that "cast justifiable doubt about the integrity of the rendering court;" (3) on a basis of jurisdiction over the defendant that is "unacceptable under §6" (described below); or (4) without reasonable notice to the defendant or in violation of a valid choice-of-forum agreement; or (5) if "the judgment or the claim on which the judgment is based is repugnant to the public policy of the United States." Section 6 lists the following as "unacceptable" bases of jurisdiction:

(1) (except in admiralty cases) the presence in the forum state of property belonging to the defendant, when the claim does not involve a direct right in the property; (2) the plaintiff's nationality, domicile, residence or incorporation; (3) tag jurisdiction, unless the defendant was a fugitive from justice. or the claim was based on a "gross violation of human rights under international law and the defendant could not have been sued in a more appropriate forum"; and (4) any other basis that is regarded as "unreasonable or unfair given the nature of the claim or the identity of the parties."

b. *Discretionary Grounds for Non-Recognition.* Section 5(b) provides that a foreign judgment *need not* be recognized if the judgment (1) was rendered by a court that did not have subject matter jurisdiction; (2) was obtained by fraud; (3) is irreconcilable with another judgment between the same parties rendered in the United States or a recognizable foreign judgment; or (4) it resulted from a proceeding initiated after a proceeding in the United States, or in order to frustrate the claimant's right to have the claim adjudicated in a more appropriate court in the United States.

FOREIGN RECOGNITION PRACTICES

How do foreign countries treat judgments rendered in the United States? This is a huge question that cannot be answered here, but the following summary of the recognition rules of four foreign countries and an international convention may provide a starting point.[1] In reading these summaries, try to identify the differences from and similarities to the UFMJRA and determine whether these countries are more or less "generous" to American judgments than American courts are to foreign judgments.

1. *France*. Foreign judgments are recognized in France if: (a) *under French law*, the rendering court had jurisdiction and French courts did not have exclusive jurisdiction; (b) the foreign procedure was "regular"; (c) the rendering court applied the law that would be applicable under French choice-of-law rules, or reached a substantially equivalent result; (d) the judgment is not repugnant to the French *ordre public*; and (e) did not violate certain "mandatory rules," (e.g., exchange controls). See Delaume, *Transnational Contracts*, 200-14; von Mehren, *Foreign Judgments*: 35, 40, 49-50, 56-57, 80.

2. *Germany*. Article 328 of the German Code of Civil Procedure prohibits recognition of a foreign judgment in the following cases: (a) if the foreign court did not have jurisdiction *under German law*; (b) if the defendant was not properly or timely served and did not appear in the foreign proceeding; (c) if the judgment is inconsistent with a German judgment, or with a prior foreign judgment that is sought to be recognized in Germany, or with a pending proceeding concerning the same facts; (d) if recognition would produce a result that is manifestly incompatible with German constitutional principles or with the German *ordre public*; or (e) if the foreign country does not accord reciprocity. See Hay, *American Money-Judgments in Germany*, 729; Martiny, *Foreign Judgments in Germany*, 721; von Mehren, *Adjudicatory Authority*, 74, 82-86, 142-78, 211-13, 232-37; Zekoll, *A Landmark Decision of the German Federal Court*, 30.

3. *Switzerland*. Under Arts. 25-26 of the Swiss conflicts codification, a foreign judgment is recognized in Switzerland: (a) if the foreign court had jurisdiction *under Swiss law*; or (b) if the defendant was domiciled in the rendering state; or (c) in certain "patrimonial" matters, if the defendant had submitted to the jurisdiction of the rendering court through a contract valid under Swiss conflicts law or had litigated the merits without protesting jurisdiction. Article 27 provides that the foreign judgment will not be recognized: (a) if the defendant was not properly served in accordance with the law of his domicile or habitual residence, unless the defendant proceeded to the merits without reservations: (b) if recognition would be "manifestly incompatible with the Swiss *ordre public*;" (c) if the judgment was rendered "in violation of fundamental principles derived from the Swiss conception of procedural law and, in particular, [if the affected] party did not have an opportunity to present his arguments;" or (d) if "litigation between the same parties and on the same object already has been initiated in Switzerland or already has been decided there, or [if] such a dispute previously has been decided in a third state, provided that the latter judgment satisfies the requirements for its recognition." For a discussion of Swiss recognition practices, see Bernet & Ulmer, *Foreign Civil Judgments in Switzerland*,

---

1. In addition to the countries discussed below, see Amado, *Foreign Judgments in Latin American Countries* 99 ff.; Kerameus, *Enforcement in the International Context*, 179; Kerameus, *Enforcement Proceedings*.

317 ff; Dutoit, *Commentaire*, 75-97.

4. *Japan*. Article 200 of the Japanese Code of Civil Procedure provides that a foreign judgment will be recognized in Japan: (a) if the foreign court's jurisdiction was "consistent with" Japanese law; (b) the judgment-debtor, "if a Japanese national," received proper service or appeared in the foreign proceeding; (c) the foreign judgment is not "contrary to the public order or good morals of Japan;" and (d) the rendering state recognizes Japanese judgments. For a discussion of Japanese recognition practices, see Sawaki, *Foreign Judgments in Japan*, 29 ff.

5. *The Brussels/Lugano Conventions and the Brussels Regulation*. In 1968, the then six member-states of the European Economic Community concluded the Brussels Convention on Jurisdiction and the Recognition and Enforcement of Judgments ("Brussels I"),[2] which was the first multilateral attempt on the European continent to establish a comprehensive regime for jurisdiction and recognition of civil and commercial judgments rendered in the member states.[3] The convention entered into force in 1973 and has since been amended four times as nine new countries joined the Community, later renamed the European Union (EU). In 1988, the convention was supplemented by a "parallel Convention" known as the "Lugano Convention" between the EU and the member states of the European Free Trade Association (EFTA).[4] On March 1, 2002 the Brussels-Lugano conventions were replaced by a virtually identical EU Regulation known as "Brussels II,[5] which is directly binding on the courts of the EU member states.

The Brussels Regulation (reproduced supra at 704) makes an important distinction between defendants who are domiciled in a member state (Arts. 2-3) and defendants not so domiciled (Art.4, id.). With regard to the former defendants, the Regulation preempts the laws of the member states and defines the permissible bases of jurisdiction in a manner that, in some important respects, is less expansive than the laws of most member states. The Regulation defines the permissible bases of jurisdiction through a detailed list (Arts. 2-3, 5-24) that specifically outlaws certain exorbitant jurisdictional bases found in the domestic rules of some member states (Art. 3, Annex I). Among these bases are tag jurisdiction as allowed in the United Kingdom; Article 14 of the French Civil Code (reproduced supra at 696) which authorizes unlimited general jurisdiction over any defendant when the plaintiff is a French national; and Article 23 of the German Code of Civil Procedure (reproduced supra at 694) and similar provisions in other EU countries, which authorize unlimited general jurisdiction based on the presence in the forum of any assets of the defendant. In contrast, with regard to defendants not domiciled in a member state, the Regulation permits a member state to assert jurisdiction on any basis authorized by its domestic law, even if that basis is among the exorbitant bases mentioned above. See Art. 4.

---

2. See [1990] O.J. C 189.

3. For another attempt for a potentially worldwide scope, see the discussion of the Hague Conventions, supra at 706, and infra at 848.

4. See [1988] O.J. L 319, 9. The EFTA includes Austria, Finland, Iceland, Norway, Sweden, and Switzerland. In the meantime, Austria, Finland, and Sweden, have joined the EU.

5. See [2001] O.J. L.12/1.

This differentiation between the two classes of defendants might have been defensible had the Regulation provided different standards for recognizing the judgments rendered in the two categories of cases. Unfortunately, this is not the case. For recognition purposes, the Regulation abandons the above differentiation and treats in the same manner all judgments rendered in a member state on any of the jurisdictional bases the Regulation allows. (See Arts. 32-52.) These judgments are automatically entitled to recognition without review of the merits (Art. 36) and subject to only limited exceptions, such as public policy, lack of proper and timely notice, or conflict with a judgment of the recognizing state or a prior judgment of a third state that is recognizable under the Regulation. (See Art. 34). Thus, if a French or German court asserts jurisdiction against a United States citizen not domiciled in any EU/EFTA country on the basis of French Civil Code Article 14 or German Civil Procedure Article 23, the resulting judgment will be entitled to recognition throughout the EU/EFTA, without any review of the jurisdictional basis of the French or German judgment. Article 35 of the Regulation provides that "the jurisdiction of the court of the Member State of origin may not be reviewed[, and] the test of public policy * * * may not be applied to the rules relating to jurisdiction."[6]

Despite some regressive elements such the one just described, the Brussels/Lugano convention is one of the most successful private international law conventions in history and has brought to the ET/EFTA countries a regime that approximates the unity and cohesion that is only possible among state members of a federal union.[7]

C. JURISDICTION

Hilton v. Guyot
Supreme Court of the United States, 1895.
159 U.S. 113, 16 S.Ct. 139, 40 L.Ed. 95.

GRAY, J. * * * Every foreign judgment, of whatever nature, in order to be entitled to any effect, must have been rendered by a court having jurisdiction of the cause[.] * * *

When an action is brought in a court of this country * * * to recover a sum of money adjudged by a court of [another] country * * * and the foreign judgment appears to have been rendered by a competent court, having jurisdiction of the cause and of the parties, and upon due allegations and proofs, and opportunity to defend against them, and its proceedings are according to the course of a civilized jurisprudence, and are stated in a clear and formal record, the judgment * * * should

---

6. For a critical review of this and other features of the Regulation, see von Mehren, *Sister-State Judgments*, at 1060 (concluding that this feature is "the single most regressive step that has occurred in international recognition and enforcement practice in this century.")

7. From the extensive literature on the Brussels Convention, see von Mehren, *Adjudicatory Authority*, 86-94, 224-25, 237-49, 263-68, 348-52, 362-97, 407; Herzog, P., *International Recognition*, 83 ff.; Kohler, *Practical Experience of the Brussels Convention*, 563 ff.; Moura Ramos, *The New EC Rules on Jurisdiction*, 199 ff.; Reuland, *The Twenty-Fifth Anniversary of the Brussels Convention*, 559 ff.

be held conclusive upon the merits tried in the foreign court, unless some special ground is shown for impeaching the judgment[.] * * *

It is objected that the appearance and litigation of the defendants in the French tribunals were not voluntary, but by legal compulsion, and therefore that the French courts never acquired such jurisdiction over the defendants, that they should be held bound by the judgment. * * *

The present case is not one of a person travelling through or casually found in a foreign country. The defendants, although they were not citizens or residents of France, but were citizens and residents of the State of New York, and their principal place of business was in the city of New York, yet had a storehouse and an agent in Paris, and were accustomed to purchase large quantities of goods there, although they did not make sales in France. Under such circumstances, evidence that their sole object in appearing and carrying on the litigation in the French courts was to prevent property, in their storehouse at Paris, belonging to them, and within the jurisdiction, but not in the custody, of those courts, from being taken in satisfaction of any judgment that might be recovered against them, would not, according to our law, show that those courts did not acquire jurisdiction of the persons of the defendants. * * *

Nippon Emo-Trans Co., Ltd. v. Emo-Trans, Inc.
United States District Court, E.D. New York, 1990.
744 F.Supp. 1215

DEARIE, J. In this action, plaintiff, Nippon Emo–Trans Co., Ltd. ("NET"), seeks recognition of a judgment it obtained against defendant, Emo–Trans, Inc. ("ETI"), in the Tokyo District Court of Japan. * * * NET is a Japanese corporation with its principal operations in Japan; ETI is a New York corporation with its principal place of business in New York City. Since the Court's jurisdiction is based on diversity of citizenship, this action is governed by New York law, including New York principles of conflict of laws. [cit.]

NET and ETI are freight forwarders; their business involves assembling goods from various sources for shipment, arranging shipment, and arranging to have the shipments broken down and delivered to the ultimate recipient. Between August 1982 and February 1986, NET and ETI had a contractual relationship pursuant to which each would act as the receiving end for shipments assembled by the other. At some point in 1985, a dispute arose as to the allocation of profits between the two companies in connection with freight charges collected from consignees. NET claimed that ETI had failed to remit approximately $354,000 due to NET. ETI claimed that NET's calculation was based on a misinterpretation of the contract.

In June 1986, NET filed an action (the "Japanese Action") in the District Court of Tokyo (the "Tokyo Court"), seeking to recover the money it claimed was owing from ETI. * * * In the Japanese Action, ETI initially contested the Tokyo Court's jurisdiction over it; that Court ruled on December 8, 1988, that it had personal jurisdiction over ETI. Thereafter, ETI appeared and defended in Japan. A trial was conducted, and on November 14, 1989, the Tokyo Court issued a decision awarding

NET * * * approximately $354,000 plus interest and costs (the "Japanese Judgment"). On November 28, 1989, ETI filed an appeal with the Tokyo High Court; that appeal is pending.

On February 1, 1990, NET commenced the present action by filing an application for an ex parte order of attachment which would permit it to attach any property of ETI found in New York, up to a limit of $400,000. The application was granted and the order of attachment was signed on February 2, 1990. * * *

JURISDICTION OF THE TOKYO COURT. ETI asserts that the Tokyo Court did not have in personam jurisdiction over it, and that as a result, [N.Y. CPLR] Section 5304(a)(2) [which corresponds with UFMJRA § 4(a)(2) reproduced supra] precludes recognition of the Japanese Judgment. ETI argues that (i) because it has preserved its jurisdictional objection in Japan, it did not "voluntarily appear" in Japan within the meaning of Section 5305(a)(2) [UFMJRA § 5(a)(2)]; (ii) none of the other bases of jurisdiction described in Article 53 [UFMJRA] is applicable in this case; and (iii) the Tokyo Court found that it had jurisdiction on the basis of principles which do not warrant recognition under Article 53. * * *

B. *"Voluntary Appearance".* [The court concludes that the question of whether ETI is deemed to have "voluntarily appeared" in the Tokyo proceeding is to be judged by New York standards; that, under those standards, ETI's appearance was voluntary; and thus, under New York's § 5305(a)(2) (which is the same as UFMJRA § 5(a)(2), supra), ETI was precluded from contesting the jurisdiction of the Tokyo court.] * * * Even if it were possible to conclude that Section 5305(a)(2) does not preclude ETI from challenging the jurisdiction of the Tokyo Court, Section 5305(b) makes it clear that a New York court may recognize a judgment based on grounds other than those articulated in Article 53. * * * [T]he Court * * * concludes, on the present state of the record, that jurisdiction could properly have been asserted in Japan, albeit not on the grounds articulated by the Tokyo Court.

(1) Recognition of Foreign Judgments at Common Law. As a general matter, New York courts have long maintained a strong policy of giving preclusive effect to foreign country judgments. [cit.]; indeed, at a time when the leading Supreme Court case, *Hilton v. Guyot*, [supra], conditioned recognition of a foreign judgment on reciprocity, the New York Court of Appeals rejected such a limitation. Johnston v. Compagnie Generale Transatlantique, 242 N.Y. 381 (1926). * * *

Notwithstanding New York's general rule favoring preclusive effect, courts have consistently recognized that under certain conditions, a foreign country judgment will be accorded significantly less weight than a sister-state judgment. [cit.] And it is clear, even in the earliest caselaw, that the determination of a foreign court as to jurisdiction is to be treated with circumspection. * * *

New York courts have not always been willing to recognize judgments based on foreign countries' long-arm statutes, even when the facts would have supported jurisdiction under New York's long-arm statute[.] * * * More recently [however], in Porisini v. Petricca, 90 A.D.2d 949, 456 N.Y.S.2d 888 (4th Dept.1982), the court asserted that "New York may, and appropriately should, recognize a foreign judgment predicated on any jurisdictional basis it recognizes in its internal law." 456 N.Y.S.2d at 890. Whether a New York court would recognize a judgment in a case where New York law would not authorize personal jurisdiction but where the requirements of due process were satisfied remains to be seen.

NET argues that cases such as Vander v. Casperson, 12 N.Y.2d 56, 58-60 (1962), and Dieter v. Dieter, 446 N.Y.S.2d 630 (4th Dept.1981), aff'd, 56 N.Y.2d 578 (1982) demonstrate that, unlike the case of default judgments, where a defendant litigates the question of jurisdiction in the foreign court, New York's common-law principles require that the decision of that court will be given preclusive effect. These cases, however, involved judgments rendered by Florida and Texas, respectively; the result in any such case will usually be dictated by the Full Faith and Credit Clause, unless the state rendering the judgment has unusual principles regarding the res judicata effect of its judgments. This by no means leads to the conclusion that foreign country judgments should be given the same treatment. In the case of sister-state judgments, a New York court can safely assume that minimum requirements of due process have been met, or that the defendant has foregone an opportunity to raise the issue. No such comparable assurances are available with regard to the judgment of a foreign country, particularly if the legal system of the country in question is not within the common-law tradition. Nor are the federal cases cited by NET controlling, as a matter of New York law. Baldwin v. Iowa State Traveling Men's Ass'n, 283 U.S. 522 (1931) held, in essence, that within the federal system, one court will treat the jurisdictional findings of another court as res judicata. * * * Unlike the federal cases cited above, New York courts have consistently distinguished between judgments of sister states, which must be accorded full faith and credit as a matter of constitutional law, and judgments of foreign countries, for which full faith and credit is not constitutionally mandated. [cit.] The Court is of the view that a New York court would not view *Baldwin* or cases relying on it as controlling under the circumstances presented here.

While it appears that neither Article 53 nor New York's common-law principles of recognition would prevent a court from reexamining a foreign court's determination of a jurisdictional issue, in appropriate circumstances such an examination might be cabined within narrow limits. The Restatement (Third) of the Foreign Relations Law of the United States suggests an approach which takes into account both the grounds of the foreign court's jurisdiction and the nature of the determination made by the foreign court:

> If the defendant appeared in the foreign court to challenge the jurisdiction of the court and failed to prevail, it is not clear whether such determination will be considered res judicata by a court in the United States asked to recognize the resulting judgment. If the determination of jurisdiction depended on a finding of fact to support an otherwise unobjectionable basis of jurisdiction--for example, whether X was an agent through whom the defendant did business in the forum state--he determination after contest ordinarily will be respected.... If the determination depended on a question of law or a mixed law/fact question-- for example, whether a nonresident corporation is present in the forum state by virtue of having an "alter ego" subsidiary there--he court asked to recognize the resulting judgment will scrutinize the jurisdictional determination on its merits.... If the judgment of the foreign court is founded on a basis of

jurisdiction not meeting the standards of § 421--for instance, the plaintiff's nationality under Article 14 of the French Civil Code--but another basis of jurisdiction would have supported the action--for instance, that the action grew out of an activity of the defendant conducted in the territory of the forum, § 421(i), a court in the United States may recognize and enforce the judgment. Restatement (Third) of the Foreign Relations Law of the United States § 482 comment c (1986).

The Court is of the view that such an approach would generally be consistent with the goals of New York's statutory and common law principles of recognition, and that a New York court, faced with this issue, would be likely to follow this approach.

(3) The Tokyo Court's Jurisdictional Ruling. The Tokyo Court based its assertion of jurisdiction on two factors: first, it found that ETI's duty to remit payments to NET constituted an obligation which was to be performed in Japan; second, it found that ETI had an affiliate in Japan, from which it received assistance in pursuing the lawsuit. The questions of the "place of performance" of ETI's obligation to make payments and the relationship between ETI and its Japanese affiliate are, at best, mixed questions of fact and law. Under these circumstances, the approach outlined above would require a court to look behind the judgment to see if the facts supported the exercise of jurisdiction.

It is clear that neither of the bases of jurisdiction articulated by the Tokyo Court would support jurisdiction under New York law. * * *

Simply because the articulated bases of jurisdiction would have been deemed insufficient under New York law does not lead to the conclusion that the Tokyo Court improperly asserted jurisdiction, however; if ETI's contacts with Japan were sufficiently well-developed to support jurisdiction, there would be little reason to deny recognition to the Japanese Judgment just because the Tokyo Court's stated rationale differed from that which a New York court would follow. In this case, uncontested facts readily lead to the conclusion that, judged by the standards of New York and federal constitutional law, jurisdiction could properly have been asserted in Japan.

(4) Jurisdiction Under New York Law. New York's general jurisdictional statute, Section 301 of the Civil Practice Law & Rules, [cit.], incorporates all bases of jurisdiction recognized at common law. Of cardinal importance at common law and under Section 301 is jurisdiction based on a finding that a foreign corporation is doing business within the state; so long as a corporation does business "not occasionally or casually, but with a fair measure of permanence and continuity," Tauza Susquehanna Coal Co., 220 N.Y. 259, 267 (1917), then it is deemed to be "present" within the state, and subject to suit on any cause of action, not merely those arising out of business transacted in the state. Id. * * * One of the traditional indicia of "doing business" is "substantial, regular and continuous sales or shipment of goods in the state." [cit.] * * *

There can be no question but that the value of shipments sent by ETI to Japan is "substantial". * * * In this context, the "substantiality" requirement is satisfied by the gross value of business transacted by ETI in Japan, in excess of half a million dollars annually. Further, ETI has engaged in "continuous" activity directed at Japan, as evidenced by its maintaining relationships first with NET and then with EJL, over a period of eight years. Thus, * * * it could be said that ETI had directed its activity at Japan with a "fair measure of permanence and continuity." * * *

In view of the volume and continuity of activity initiated by ETI and directed toward Japan, the Court concludes that, were it necessary to reexamine the facts to determine whether ETI is amenable to suit in Japan, it would find that, judged by the standards of Section 301, a New York court would conclude that ETI was doing business in Japan on a substantial, continuous and permanent basis, and that as a result the Tokyo Court could properly have asserted jurisdiction over it. * * *

Subject to the conditions described herein, (i) the motion for an order confirming the attachment is Denied, and (ii) the proceedings in this action are hereby Stayed pending the outcome of ETI's appeal of the Japanese Judgment. So Ordered.

Notes and Questions

1. **In personam** *jurisdiction*. "Every foreign judgment, of whatever nature, in order to be entitled to any effect, must have been rendered by a court having jurisdiction of the cause," proclaimed *Hilton*. Indeed, this is a universal principle. No country will recognize a judgment rendered in a country whose courts did not have jurisdiction over the judgment debtor. However, according to which country's standard should we judge the jurisdiction of the rendering court? With regard to sister-state judgments, this question is answered under the standards of the rendering state. Since that state is a member of the Union, those standards necessarily incorporate the federal due process standards. The fact that this is not true with regard to foreign countries makes the answer to this question somewhat more difficult. Should the foreign court's jurisdiction be judged by: (a) the foreign court's standards; (b) American state and/or federal standards; (c) a combination of the foreign and American standards; or (d) some supranational standard? Did *Hilton* answer this question? How? How do the *Nippon Emo-Trans* court, the UFMJRA, the two Restatements, and the IJJ Project answer this question? How do France, Germany, Switzerland, and Japan answer this question? See supra 824-25.

Nippon Emo-Trans is a relatively easy case in that the Tokyo court's assertion of jurisdiction satisfied the standards of both Japanese and New York law. Suppose, however, that the foreign judgment did not satisfy the American standards for jurisdiction. For example, suppose that in *Hilton* the American defendants did not have any of the connections described in the opinion, and that the French court's jurisdiction was grounded exclusively on the French plaintiff's nationality as authorized by the infamous Article 14 of the French Civil Code. (This article provides that "[a]n alien, even one not residing in France," is subject to the jurisdiction of French courts "for the fulfillment of obligations contracted by him," either in or outside France, "toward a French person.") Or suppose that a German court, relying on article 23 of the German Code of Civil Procedure, has asserted in personam jurisdiction over an American defendant on the basis of the presence in

Germany of the defendant's forgotten umbrella and has rendered against him a multimillion dollar judgment on an unrelated cause of action. (Article 23 authorizes unlimited general jurisdiction on the presence in Germany of any asset, however small its value, belonging to the defendant.) *May* an American court recognize the French or German judgment respectively in these two cases? Why, or why not?

Suppose now that the foreign court's assertion of jurisdiction would conform with American due process standards but not with the standards of the long-arm statute of the American state in which recognition is sought (because that statute does not exhaust the limits of due process). *Should* recognition be granted in such a case?

2. *Subject Matter Jurisdiction.* Under *Hilton,* which law determines the foreign court's "competence" or subject-matter jurisdiction? If the foreign court lacked subject-matter jurisdiction under the foreign law, may the judgment be recognized in the United States? Compare the UFMJRA, the two Restatements, and the IJJ Project, supra. Which approach produces the best result? Why?

3. *Effect of Defendant's Appearance in the Foreign Proceeding.* (a) *Default Judgments*: As with regard to sister-state judgments, if the defendant did not appear in the foreign proceeding (and did not otherwise waive his right to contest the foreign court's jurisdiction), then the defendant may challenge the rendering court's jurisdiction in the recognition proceeding.

If the recognizing court, using appropriate "circumspection," *Nippon Emo-Trans,* supra, determines that the rendering court had jurisdiction under American standards, may the court then recognize the foreign default judgment? Suppose, for example, that in *Nippon Emo-Trans* the defendant ETI had not appeared in the Tokyo proceeding. Would the resulting judgment be entitled to recognition in New York? If this were a sister-state judgment, the answer to this question would be "yes." Should the same answer be extended to foreign-country judgments? Some courts have done precisely that. See, e.g., Chabert v. Bacquie, 694 So.2d 805 (Fla.Ct.App.1997); John Sanderson & Co. (Wool) Pty. Ltd. v. Ludlow Jute Co., Ltd., 569 F.2d 696 (1st Cir.1978); Bank of Montreal v. Kough, 612 F.2d 467 (9th Cir.1980); Tahan v. Hodgson, 662 F.2d 862 (D.C.Cir.1981); Porisini v. Petricca, 90 A.D.2d 949, 456 N.Y.S.2d 888 (4th Dept.1982). The Restatement (Third) endorses this practice. See § 481 Rptr's n. 4 ("If jurisdiction of the foreign court over a resident of the United States was based on concepts similar to those of longarm jurisdiction in the United States * * *, a default judgment so rendered will be recognized in the United States--provided defendant received adequate notice.") Is this a good idea? Why, or why not? The IJJ Project provides in § 3(b) that a foreign default judgment is entitled to recognition if the foreign court had jurisdiction on a basis that the foreign law permits and which is not one of the "unacceptable" bases as defined in § 6 (described supra at 823). Is this standard more or less liberal than that of the Restatement (Third)?

(b) *Contested Proceedings.* When, as in *Hilton* and *Nippon Emo-Trans,* the defendant appears in the foreign proceeding and unsuccessfully challenges the foreign court's jurisdiction, then the defendant's chances of successfully renewing this challenge in the recognition proceeding are significantly reduced. Some courts have assumed or held that the defendant is precluded from challenging the jurisdiction of the foreign court in such circumstances. See, e.g., Sprague & Rhodes Commodity Corp. v. Instituto Mexicano Del Cafe, 566 F.2d 861 (2d Cir.1977); Somportex Ltd. v. Philadelphia Chewing Gum Corp., 453 F.2d 435 (3d Cir.1971), *cert. denied*, 405 U.S. 1017(1972). Is this a good idea? Suppose that the foreign country's jurisdictional bases are as exorbitant as the French or German bases described above. Should the defendant's appearance in the French or German proceeding automatically preclude a due process challenge in the American recognition proceeding? See Restatement (Third) § 481 cmt. i ("If the judgment debtor appeared in the rendering court for the purpose of challenging its jurisdiction and that jurisdiction was upheld, he is generally precluded from renewing the challenge in the state where recognition is sought, *unless the proceeding in the foreign court was manifestly unfair or the asserted basis for jurisdiction clearly untenable.*") (emphasis added); IJJ Project § 6(c) ("An appearance by the defendant in the state of origin, or an unsuccessful objection to the jurisdiction of the rendering court, does not deprive the defendant of the right to resist recognition under this section [which lists the "unacceptable bases], but factual determinations by the rendering court concerning jurisdiction are binding on the defendant.") Was the *Nippon Emo–Trans* court not correct to distinguish between sister-state and foreign-country judgments and to refuse to automatically extend the *Baldwin* principle (Baldwin v. Iowa State Traveling Men's Ass'n, 283 U.S. 522 (1931)) to foreign-country judgments?

D. PROCEDURAL FAIRNESS

Hilton v. Guyot
Supreme Court of the United States, 1895.
159 U.S. 113, 16 S.Ct. 139, 40 L.Ed. 95.

GRAY, J. * * * [W]here there has been opportunity for a full and fair trial abroad before a court of competent jurisdiction, conducting the trial upon regular proceedings, after due citation or voluntary appearance of the defendant, and under a system of jurisprudence likely to secure an impartial administration of justice between the citizens of its own country and those of other countries, and there is nothing to show either prejudice in the court, or in the system of laws under which it was sitting, or fraud in procuring the judgment, or any other special reason why the comity of this nation should not allow it full effect, the merits of the case should not, in an action brought in this country upon the judgment, be tried afresh, as on a new trial or an appeal, upon the mere assertion of the party that the judgment was erroneous in law or in fact. * * *

It is next objected that in th[e French] courts one of the plaintiffs was permitted to testify not under oath, and was not subjected to cross-examination by the opposite party, and that the defendants were, therefore, deprived of safeguards which are by our law considered essential to secure honesty and to detect fraud in a witness; and also that documents and papers were admitted in evidence, with which the defendants had no connection, and which would not be admissible under our own system of jurisprudence. But it having been shown by the plaintiffs, and hardly denied by the defendants, that the practice followed and the method of examining witnesses were according to the laws of France, we are not prepared to hold that the fact that the procedure in these respects differed from that of our own courts is, of itself, a sufficient ground for impeaching the foreign judgment. * * *

Cooley v. Weinberger
United States Court of Appeals, Tenth Circuit, 1975.
518 F.2d 1151.

McWILLIAMS, J.. This case concerns a claim for mother's insurance benefits under the Social Security Act. 42 U.S.C. § 402(g). Doris Cooley, the claimant, filed an application for the benefits resulting from the death of her husband, Melvin K. Cooley, the wage earner. * * * The administrative law judge, after hearing, denied the claim on the ground that the claimant, Doris Cooley, had herself feloniously and intentionally killed her husband, Melvin Cooley, and accordingly was not entitled to benefits by virtue of 20 C.F.R. § 404.364 (1971). That regulation reads as follows:

"A person who has been finally convicted by a court of competent jurisdiction of the felonious and intentional homicide of an insured individual shall not be entitled to * * * benefits * * * on the earnings of such deceased individual and such felon shall be considered nonexistent in determining the entitlement of other persons to * * * benefits * * *."

Claimant requested review of the decision of the administrative law judge, and on such review the decision was upheld by the Appeals Council. Claimant then sought judicial review of this administrative action, and the trial court upheld the denial of the claim. Claimant now seeks our review of the matter.

The real root of the present controversy is the fact that the claimant killed her husband in Iran. Melvin Cooley obtained employment with an oil company having drilling operations in Iran. Mrs. Cooley soon followed her husband to Iran. In a marital dispute, the details of which will be briefly alluded to, Doris Cooley shot her husband three times with a gun. She was arrested by the Iranian authorities and charged with "willful homicide" under Article 170 of the Iran Penal Code. This section reads as follows: "The penalty prescribed for an offender who commits *willful homicide* shall be death, except if otherwise provided by law." (Emphasis added.)

* * * Mrs. Cooley was convicted by a five-judge Iranian court of having committed "willful homicide" in violation of Article 170 of the Iran Penal Code, with the death sentence being commuted to ten years' imprisonment. On appeal, Mrs. Cooley's conviction was affirmed by an Iranian appellate tribunal. After she had been imprisoned for several years, she was released under a Royal Amnesty granted by the Shah which reduced her sentence to two years of solitary confinement. * * *

Mrs. Cooley was permitted to testify at length before the administrative law judge. She related all the details of her stormy marital life with Melvin Cooley. It was her position before the administrative law judge, as it was before the Iranian courts, that her husband was shot with his own gun as he assaulted her in a drunken rage. Mrs. Cooley testified that she and her husband fought over the gun and in so doing it discharged and killed him. Her defense at trial had been self-defense and accidental killing.

Mrs. Cooley was also permitted to testify as to the condition of the jail in which she was confined prior to trial, which trial occurred nearly a year after her arrest for the killing. She indicated that she was repeatedly questioned by the authorities, and that she was never given any *Miranda* warnings. She agreed that she had appointed counsel to represent her, but said they had a language difficulty. She also stated that she was subjected to continual torture and abuse, including the "water treatment," which consisted of letting a drop of water fall on her forehead as she lay on a shower floor. It was on this general state of the record that the administrative law judge found that Mrs. Cooley had been convicted of a "felonious and intentional" homicide in Iran and that such conviction should be recognized by the Secretary of Health, Education and Welfare. Our study of the record convinces us that there is substantial evidence to support the critical findings of the administrative law judge, which were adopted by the Appeals Council, and that the denial of Mrs. Cooley's claim must be upheld. [cit.]

The applicable regulation bars a person from receiving Social Security benefits if the claimant has "feloniously and intentionally" killed the wage earner, and the conviction therefor has become final. One guilty of a lesser degree of homicide is not barred by the regulation from receiving benefits. * * * [A] conviction of "willful homicide" under Article 170 is the equivalent of a "felonious and intentional homicide" as that phrase is used in the agency regulation. [cit.]

Perhaps the principal matter raised by the claimant in this appeal is whether the Iranian conviction should be recognized in the United States. In this regard claimant argues that her conviction was obtained by methods which not only did not comport with due process, but were so shocking in nature that the conviction should not be recognized by administrative agencies or courts in the United States.

It should be noted at the outset that the administrative judge did not accept the Iranian conviction at face value, but did inquire into the facts and circumstances giving rise to the conviction. * * * [T]he administrative law judge summarized as follows:

"The claimant presents a myriad of contentions that her rights under the United States Constitution were violated. The violation of the 'due process' clause of the United States Constitution seems to be the principal contention relied upon by the claimant for relief. In this connection the claimant contends: (1) she was not allowed to consult with her attorney; (2) that she was not advised of her rights; (3) that she was denied the right to post bail; (4) that an indictment was not issued in her case; (5) that she did not have the right to cross-examine witnesses; and (6) that the prosecution did not prove her guilty beyond a reasonable doubt. The evidence establishes that claimant had the right to be represented by an attorney; that she chose Dr. E. Paad, Attorney-at-Law, Tehran, Iran to represent her; that her legal rights were explained to her by her attorney; that he represented her at her trial; that the witnesses against her were cross-examined by the Judges and she was filed on pursuant to Article 170 of the Iranian Penal Code, and thereafter arraigned and held for trial pursuant thereto. In addition, an interpreter was appointed for her benefit during the trial. This evidence overturns the contentions of claimant and reveals a criminal process in Iran similar to that in the United States. * * *.

"It is not the duty or place of the Administrative Law Judge to become the judge and jury in a foreign land and re-try the criminal case based on facts from one side only for purposes of Social Security benefits; however, if the facts revealed that the procedural steps followed in the foreign legal system were bizarre, arbitrary, or capricious, and lacking in continuity, then the case might be different, but these are not the facts in this case. The fact that customs and mores of Iran are different from those in the United States should not act to overturn a decision of that sovereignty for Social Security purposes when the evidence reflects a legitimate legal process, although procedurally and substantially different from the United States federal system."

Brennan v. University of Kansas, 451 F.2d 1287 (10th Cir. 1971), sheds light on the question as to whether the Iranian conviction should be recognized by us. In *Brennan*, a search and seizure made in Italy according to Italian procedures was thereafter involved in a subsequent civil action brought in the United States by the one whose premises had been thus searched. In the proceeding brought in the United States it was contended that the search and seizure conducted in Italy violated Fourth and Fourteenth Amendment rights under the United States Constitution and accordingly should not be recognized by United States courts. In rejecting this argument, we commented at page 1289 as follows:

"* * * It is a firmly established principle of American jurisprudence that the laws of one state have no extra-territorial effect in another state. The forum state will give effect to foreign law as long as the foreign law is not repugnant to the moral sense of the community. The mere fact that the law of the foreign state differs from the law of the state in which recognition is sought is not enough to make the foreign law inapplicable. No attempt was made to show that the search was conducted in any manner but a lawful one in accord with the applicable Italian law. This Court cannot hold that the procedure followed in executing this search is so shocking to the forum community that it cannot be countenanced. * * * "

In the instant case, after listening to Mrs. Cooley's version of events, and after consideration of the opinion of the Iranian appellate tribunal, the statements made by Mrs. Cooley's Iranian lawyer, and other documentary evidence before him, the administrative law judge found, in effect, that the procedure followed in Iran was not "so shocking to the forum community that it cannot be countenanced." We think there is substantial evidence to support this finding and we are not inclined to disturb it. [cit.] The fact that Iranian procedures may not be consistent with due process protections guaranteed in United States criminal proceedings will not in itself prevent effect being given a judgment rendered in Iran in accord with Iranian law. [cit.]

* * * Judgment affirmed.

Bank Melli Iran v. Pahlavi

United States Court of Appeals, Ninth Circuit, 1995.
58 F.3d 1406.

FERNANDEZ, J.: Bank Melli Iran and Bank Mellat (the Banks) filed this action for the purpose of enforcing certain judgments, which they had obtained against Shams Pahlavi in the tribunals of Iran. She is a resident of California and is the sister of the former Shah of Iran. The district court determined that at the times that the judgments were obtained Pahlavi could not have obtained due process of law in the courts of Iran. It, therefore, granted summary judgment in her favor. The Banks appeal and we affirm.

* * * In January of 1979, the Shah of Iran fled the country in the midst of the series of events that ultimately resulted in the creation of the Islamic Republic of Iran. Prior to that time, Pahlavi, the Shah's older sister, had signed a number of promissory notes.

The Banks, which were the holders of those notes and which are at the very least closely associated with the government, brought collection actions against Pahlavi in the courts of Iran. They served her by publication and in 1982 and 1986 obtained default judgments in the total amount of $32,000,000. They now seek to enforce those judgments pursuant to * * * the California Uniform Foreign Money–Judgments Recognition Act. Cal.Civ.Proc.Code §§ 1713-1713.8 ("Foreign Money-Judgments Act" or the "Act"). * * *

It has long been the law of the United States that a foreign judgment cannot be enforced if it was obtained in a manner that did not accord with the basics of due process. *See Hilton*, [supra]. As the Restatement of the Foreign Relations Law of the United States succinctly puts it: "A court in the United States may not recognize a judgment of a court of a foreign state if: (a) the judgment was rendered under a judicial system that does not provide impartial tribunals or procedures compatible with due process of law...." § 482(1)(a) (1987).

We are aware of no deviation from that principle. In fact, as we have already shown, it was expressly incorporated into the Foreign Money-Judgments Act. Cal.Civ.Proc.Code § 1713.4; [cit.] It can hardly be gainsaid that enforcement will not be permitted under California law if due process was lacking when the foreign judgment was obtained. * * *

* * * [D]id [Pahlavi] show that she could not get due process in Iran? On this record, the answer is yes, as a précis of the evidence will show.

Pahlavi attached various reports to her motion to dismiss. Those included consular information sheets which gave travel warnings from 1981 through 1993 and noted that anti-American sentiment could make it dangerous to travel in Iran. In particular, the State Department noted that "U.S./Iranian dual nationals have often had their U.S. passports confiscated upon arrival and have been denied permission to depart the country documented as U.S. citizens." While those advisories apply to American nationals, there is no reason to believe that the Shah's sister would have fared any better. Further, a 1991 report on terrorism was attached. That report stated that even then Iran was a continuing state sponsor of terrorism. The report recounted the assassination of a former Iranian prime minister and his aide in Paris, France. [cit.] Again, one would anticipate that the Shah's sister would encounter great danger should she try to enter Iran.

In addition, other materials from the Department of State were obtained, pursuant to the request of the district court. One of those documents is the portion of the Country Report on Human Rights Practices for 1982 regarding Iran. [cit.] That report indicates that trials are rarely held in public, that they are highly politicized, and that the regime does not believe in the independence of the judiciary. See also Country Report for 1986 at 1159 (report detailing denials of fair public trial and discussing the purchase of verdicts in civil trials); [cit.] In addition, a 1990 declaration from Laurence Pope, a State Department official, was submitted. Pope declared that under the post-Shah regime "judges are subject to continuing scrutiny and threat of sanction and cannot be expected to be completely impartial toward U.S. citizens," and that "U.S. claimants can have little reasonable expectation of justice." The declaration also pointed out the fact that attorneys in Iran "have been officially discouraged from representing politically undesirable interests," and, "[w]itnesses to events living in Iran ... are likely to be subject to the same risks as lawyers." Those observations concentrated on the effect upon American citizens, but it can hardly be doubted that they would apply equally to Pahlavi. Further, the Country Report for 1986 suggested that people like Pahlavi (those with close ties to the Shah's regime) could not return to Iran without reprisals. * * * After all, much of the hostility to United States citizens stemmed from this country's connection to the Shah's regime, and it is hardly necessary to say that Pahlavi's connection was, if anything, closer. * * *

Of course, had the Banks put in any evidence of substance, summary judgment might have been averted. But the Banks' response to Pahlavi's evidence was information and belief declarations from their counsel. Those were entitled to no weight because the declarant did not have personal knowledge. [cit.] In addition, even if the material had been in proper form, the matters addressed by the declaration and the exhibits did not directly come to grips with the question placed at issue: whether Pahlavi could receive a fair trial in Iran. Instead, the information submitted merely indicated that service was made by publication, that Pahlavi should have received notice, and that Iranian experts had considered the claims against Pahlavi. Portions of the written law of Iran were also included.

The Banks did submit information to the effect that Pahlavi had argued in an earlier unrelated action that a claim against her would more properly be tried in Iran. Perhaps in so doing the Banks hoped for a kind of judicial estoppel, which would preclude Pahlavi from taking a different position in this case. [cit.]. At any rate, a review of that information reveals that even in the former proceeding Pahlavi had complained that the Iranian government "has seen fit to nullify fundamental fairness and due process." Her actual argument was that the case should be dismissed on *forum non conveniens* grounds because Iran would be the proper place for trial. She then added that the fact that Iran would not give her a fair trial should not allow it to argue against her position that it was the most convenient forum. The result, therefore, would have been that Iran could not effectively take action against her here or there. That is not truly inconsistent with her present position.

In short, the Banks failed to show that there was a material issue of fact on the question of whether Pahlavi could receive a trial in Iran that would be characterized by a "system of jurisprudence likely to secure an impartial administration of justice." *Hilton*, [supra]. Thus, summary judgment was properly granted in her favor. * * * The evidence in this case indicated that Pahlavi could not expect fair treatment from the courts of Iran, could not personally appear before those courts, could not obtain proper legal representation in Iran, and could not even obtain local witnesses on her behalf. Those are not mere niceties of American jurisprudence. [cit.] They are ingredients of "civilized jurisprudence." *Hilton*, [supra.] They are ingredients of basic due process. * * *

Affirmed.

Notes and Questions

1. *Fairness of Foreign Proceeding*: One of the essential requirements for recognition of foreign judgments that is taken for granted in sister-state judgment recognition practice is the requirement for a "fair trial," a "regular proceeding," conducted "under a system of jurisprudence likely to secure an impartial administration of justice." *Hilton*. Under which state's standards did *Hilton* and *Cooley* judge the fairness and impartiality of the foreign tribunal? The UFMJRA and the Restatement (Third) both speak of "procedures compatible with the requirements of due process of law." "Due process" of course, implies use of United States standards,[1] but does the word "compatible" imply that we do not expect one hundred percent compliance with those standards? Even so, did *Cooley* exact even a fifty percent compliance? Or did *Cooley* hold that due process is not exportable? What then of *Pahlavi*? Can *Cooley* and *Pahlavi* be reconciled? Might one explain the difference between these two cases, at least in part, in terms of our relations with Iran at the time the two decision were rendered? If so, is this appropriate? What non-political reasons might explain the difference between the two cases? For example, if, under social security law, a finding that Mrs. Cooley was eligible for social security benefits would preclude a child or dependent parent of the deceased from receiving those benefits, would the *Cooley* result be more defensible?

Notice that Mrs. Pahlavi had argued in an earlier unrelated action that a claim against her "would more properly be tried in Iran," rather than in the United States. In this case, in which the claim was tried in Iran, Mrs. Pahlavi argued strenuously against recognition of the resulting judgment. Do you agree with the court that the two arguments are "not truly inconsistent"? Why, or why not? Regardless of the answer, is it true that if both of Mrs. Pahlavi's arguments prevail, the Iranian banks

---

1. In Society of Lloyd's v. Aschenden, 233 F.3d 473 (7th Cir.2000), Judge Posner said "We'll call this the 'international concept of due process' to distinguish it from the complex concept that has emerged from American case law" Id. at 477. The IJJ Project avoids using the due process term and speaks of "procedures compatible with fundamental principles of fairness." § 5(a)(i). The Project also provides an additional ground for attacking the foreign judgment--if the judgment was rendered "in circumstances that cast justifiable doubt about the integrity of the rendering court *with respect to the judgment in question*." Project § 5(a)(ii) (emphasis added).

are effectively left without a remedy? The banks cannot sue in the United States (because of forum non conveniens), and they cannot enforce an Iranian judgment in the United States (because Mrs. Pahlavi could not have received a fair trial in Iran).

Be that as it may, cases that find the foreign tribunal to be partial or the foreign proceeding to be unacceptably irregular are rare. The majority of cases seem to apply a lenient [sub]standard in judging the fairness of foreign proceedings. For example, one court declared that only an "outrageous departure" from due process standards would prevent recognition. British Midland Airways Ltd. v. International Travel, Inc., 497 F.2d 869, 871 (9th Cir.1974). In Panama Processes S.A. v. Cities Service Co., 796 P.2d 276 (Okl.1990), the judgment-debtor complained that "in Brazil: (1) no witnesses of any party may be subpoenaed, (2) testimony of corporate employees is inadmissible, (3) there is no available process for requiring testimony of indispensable U.S. witnesses; (4) there is no right of cross-examination, and (5) the parties may neither conduct pre-trial discovery nor subpoena documents." Id. at 285. The court retorted:

> This argument, rather than having its basis in a denial of due process, actually rests on the procedural differences between United States and Brazilian courts. Although Brazilian norms of procedure differ from ours, that is not a basis for their condemnation as falling short of the minimum due process standards in the Anglo-American sense.

Id. at. 286. As another court observed:

> [T]he public policy of the state of Washington is not violated simply because there is a difference between the laws of a foreign state and this state. The laws and legal systems of different nations reflect historic and cultural diversity of their people. These laws and systems are designed to meet the needs of those people. Accordingly, differences of systems and of issues addressed by laws rationally exist between nations.

Tonga Air Services, Ltd. v. Fowler, 826 P.2d 204, 214 (Wash.1992). The court held, inter alia, that certain "irregularities" in the foreign proceeding, such as the lack of a verbatim record of the trial and the fact the judgment-debtor had not been allowed to present certain documentary evidence, were inconsequential. See also Ingersoll Mill. Mach. Co. v. Granger, 631 F.Supp. 314 (N.D.Ill.1986), aff'd 833 F.2d 680 (7th Cir.1987); von Mehren, *Foreign Judgments*, 38 ("In principle, all procedural systems should be viewed as a whole; weakness in one department may well be offset by strength in another. Furthermore, one must be cautious in evaluating other systems: too often the unfamiliar is equated with the unjust.")

2. ***Judgment obtained by fraud.*** As with regard to sister-state judgments, a foreign-country judgment will be denied recognition if it was obtained by fraud. The prevailing view is that only so-called "extrinsic fraud," as distinguished from "intrinsic fraud," can defeat recognition. Although the distinction is less than clear, "extrinsic fraud" is usually defined as fraud that prevented the judgment debtor from the opportunity to present his case fully to the foreign court (such as a default judgment based on a false affidavit that the defendant had been duly served). In contrast, "intrinsic fraud" is defined as fraud committed in the proceeding, such as the use of perjured testimony or falsified documents, which could have been

addressed by the foreign court. See John Sanderson & Co. v. Ludlow Jute Co., 569 F.2d 696 (1st Cir.1978); Fairchild, Arabatzis & Smith, Inc. v. Prometco (Produce & Metals) Co., 470 F.Supp. 610, 615 (S.D.N.Y.1979). What do you think is the rationale for this distinction? Did *Hilton* contemplate this distinction? Recall that the judgment debtors in that case had claimed that the French proceeding was tainted by fraud. Would that fraud, if proven, qualify as extrinsic or intrinsic? Because of its holding on the reciprocity issue, the *Hilton* court found it unnecessary to rule on the fraud issue, but one court opined that *Hilton* could have denied recognition on the basis of fraud, and hence *Hilton*'s statements regarding reciprocity were no more than a "magnificent dictum." Johnston v. Compagnie Generale Transatlantique, 152 N.E. 121 (N.Y.1926). Is this a correct reading of *Hilton*? Is it not more accurate to say that *Hilton*'s statements regarding fraud were plain dicta?

Some courts have abandoned the distinction between extrinsic and intrinsic fraud and have held that fraud of either type will defeat a foreign judgment. See, e.g., Bandai America, Inc. v. Bally Midway Mfg. Co., 775 F.2d 70, 73 (3d Cir.1985), *cert. denied*, 475 U.S. 1047 (1986). For a case denying recognition to a Bolivian judgment on the basis of fraud that was probably more intrinsic than extrinsic (failure to reveal the existence of a critical document that would be fatal to the judgment creditor's claim), see de la Mata v. American Life Ins. Co., 771 F.Supp. 1375 (D.Del.1991).

Suppose that the recognizing court found that the foreign proceeding was tainted by fraud (extrinsic or intrinsic), but also found that the judgment could not be impeached on that ground in the state of rendition. Should the court deny recognition in such a case?

3. *Notice Requirements.* Under both the UFMJRA and the Restatement (Third), failure to give notice to the defendant "in sufficient time to enable him to defend" is a discretionary ground of non-recognition of the foreign judgment. In contrast, the IJJ Project makes this a mandatory ground for non-recognition. See § 5(a)(iv)). Which of the two positions is more appropriate? Suppose that the foreign service of process does not meet due process requirements. *May* an American court grant recognition? For cases denying recognition on this ground, see Koster v. Automark Industries, 640 F.2d 77 (7th Cir.1981); Ma v. Continental Bank, N.A., 905 F.2d 1073, 1076 (7th Cir.), *cert. denied*, 498 U.S. 967 (1990); de la Mata v. American Life Ins. Co., 771 F.Supp. 1375 (D.Del.1991); *Bank of Montreal*, supra, at 470–71; Boivin v. Talcott, 102 F.Supp. 979 (N.D.Ohio 1951). Besides timeliness, what about the adequacy of notice? Recall *Hilton*'s reference to "adequate notice" and "due citation." Compare Julen v. Larson, 101 Cal.Rptr. 796 (Cal.App.1972) (denying recognition to German judgment because notice served on defendant in Germany and written in German was inadequate) with Tahan v. Hodgson, 662 F.2d 862 (D.C.Cir.1981) (recognizing an Israeli judgment even though the notice served on an American in Israel was written in Hebrew: "[e]ven if defendant were unable to read Hebrew, he should have surmised that the papers being served on him were legal in nature, and that he could ignore them only at his peril." Id. at 865.)

E. SUBSTANTIVE DEFENSES

Bachchan v. India Abroad Publications Inc.

Supreme Court, New York County, 1992.
154 Misc.2d 228, 585 N.Y.S.2d 661.

FINGERHOOD, J. Although the cases interpreting constitutional limitations on libel actions are legion, this is apparently the first time that a New York court has been asked to apply those limitations to bar the enforcement of a foreign judgment.

The judgment was granted in an action brought in the High Court of Justice in London, England by an Indian national against the New York operator of a news service which transmits reports only to a news service in India. The story held to be defamatory was written by a reporter in London, wired by defendant to the news service in India which sent it to newspapers there. It was reported in two Indian newspapers copies of which were distributed in the United Kingdom.

The story was also reported in an issue of "India Abroad," defendant's New York newspaper. An edition of "India Abroad" was printed and distributed in the United Kingdom by defendant's English subsidiary, India Abroad (U.K.) and a claim based on that distribution was asserted in the lawsuit approximately a year after its commencement.

The wire service story transmitted by defendant on January 31, 1990 stated that Dagens Nyjeter, a Swedish daily newspaper, (hereafter "DN") had reported that Swiss authorities had frozen an account belonging to plaintiff to which money was transferred from a coded account into which commissions paid by Bofars were deposited. Bofars is a Swedish arms company, which some time before had been charged with paying kickbacks to obtain a large munitions contract with the Indian government. Plaintiff's name had previously been mentioned in connection with the scandal in a variety of Indian and other publications. On February 3, 1990, defendant's wire service transmitted plaintiff's denial that he was the holder of such a bank account or that he or any member of his family had any connection with the Bofars contract.

Plaintiff brought an action against DN in London at the same time as it sued India Abroad. DN settled the claim against it by paying a sum of money and issuing an apology saying that it had been misled by Indian government sources. India Abroad did not apologize but did report DN's settlement and apology.

The jury assessed 40,000 pounds in damages for the wire service story together with attorney's fees against India Abroad, Inc. and its reporter, Rahul Bedi. As authorized by Section 5303 of New York's Civil Practice Law and Rules (CPLR) plaintiff seeks to enforce that judgment by motion for summary judgment in lieu of complaint. * * *

Entry of the judgment is opposed on the ground that it was imposed without the safeguards for freedom of speech and the press required by the First Amendment to the United States Constitution and Article I, Section 8 of the Constitution of the State of New York. Defendant asks this court to reject the judgment as repugnant to public policy, a ground for nonrecognition of foreign judgments under CPLR 5304(b)(4).

CPLR § 5304 is comprised of two parts: section (a) which is explicitly mandatory and precludes recognition of foreign judgments on certain constitutional grounds, i.e. if the procedures pursuant to which a foreign judgment was rendered are not compatible with the requirements of due process of law or when the foreign court did not have personal jurisdiction over the defendant; and section (b) which provides that a foreign judgment "need not be recognized if," inter alia, "the cause of action on which the judgment is based is repugnant to the public policy of this state." (Subsection 4)

It is plaintiff's position that the public policy exception to the rule that foreign judgments are afforded comity is narrow and inapplicable here. He asserts that this court should not reexamine the claim for which the judgment was awarded to determine whether it would be culpable under United States precedents. Pointing to CPLR 5304(b)(4)'s reference to "causes of action" rather than judgments, he argues that libel causes of action are cognizable in New York. If that subsection is deemed to refer to judgments as well as causes of action, plaintiff asks this court to exercise its discretion to recognize the judgment in view of the common antecedents of the law of Great Britain and that of the United States.

It is doubtful whether this court has discretion to enforce the judgment if the action in which it was rendered failed to comport with the constitutional standards for adjudicating libel claims. * * * [I]f, as claimed by defendant, the public policy to which the foreign judgment is repugnant is embodied in the First Amendment to the United States Constitution or the free speech guaranty of the Constitution of this State, the refusal to recognize the judgment should be, and it is deemed to be, "constitutionally mandatory." Accordingly, the libel law applied by the High Court of Justice in London in granting judgment to plaintiff will be reviewed to ascertain whether its provisions meet the safeguards for the press which have been enunciated by the courts of this country. * * *

Under English law, any published statement which adversely affects a person's reputation, or the respect in which that person is held, is prima facie defamatory. (See Justice Otten's instructions to the jury deciding Bachchan's action.) Plaintiffs' only burden is to establish that the words complained of refer to them, were published by the defendant, and bear a defamatory meaning. If, as in the present case, statements of fact are concerned, they are presumed to be false and the defendant must plead justification for the issue of truth to be brought before the jury. * * *

English law does not distinguish between private persons and those who are public figures or are involved in matters of public concern. None are required to prove falsity of the libel or fault on the part of the defendant. No plaintiff is required to prove that a media defendant intentionally or negligently disregarded proper journalistic standards in order to prevail.

The defendant has the burden of proving not only truth but also of establishing entitlement to the qualified privilege for newspaper publications and broadcasters provided by the [U.K.] 1952 Defamation Act Section 7(3) where "the matter published is ... of public concern and ... its publication ... is ... for the public benefit."

As stated by Mr. Gray, plaintiff's barrister, "[t]he difference between the

American and English jurisdictions essentially comes down to where the burden of proof lies...." (Gray aff. pp. 15-16)

Defendant argues that the defamation law of England fails to meet the constitutional standards required in the United States because plaintiff, a friend of the late prime minister of India Rajiv Ghandi and the brother and manager of a movie star and former member of Parliament, is a public figure. In New York Times Co. v. Sullivan, 376 U.S. 254, 279-280 (1964), the Supreme Court of the United States ruled that in order to recover damages for defamation a public official must prove by clear and convincing evidence that the defendant published the allegedly defamatory statement with "'actual malice'—that is, with knowledge that it was false or with reckless disregard of whether it was false or not." That burden of proof was placed on public figures who sued media defendants in Curtis Publishing Co. v. Butts, 388 U.S. 130 (1967).

However, it seems neither necessary nor appropriate to decide whether plaintiff, an Indian national residing in England or Switzerland, is a public figure. Instead, the procedures of the English Court will be compared to those which according to decisions of the United States Supreme Court are constitutionally mandated for suits by private persons complaining of press publications of public concern.

In Gertz v. Robert Welch, Inc., 418 U.S. 323, 347 (1974) the Court held that a private figure could not recover damages for defamation without showing that a media defendant was at fault, leaving the individual States to "define for themselves the appropriate standard of liability for a publisher or broadcaster of defamatory falsehood injurious to a private individual."

Reviewing the Supreme Court's decisions enunciating constitutional limitations on suits for defamation, Justice O'Connor stated in Philadelphia Newspapers v. Hepps, 475 U.S. 767, 775:

One can discern in these decisions two forces that may reshape the common-law landscape to conform to the First Amendment. The first is whether the plaintiff is a public official or figure, or is instead a private figure. The second is whether the speech at issue is of public concern. When the speech is of public concern and the plaintiff is a public official or public figure, the Constitution clearly requires the plaintiff to surmount a much higher barrier before recovering damages from a media defendant than is raised by the common law. When the speech is of public concern but the plaintiff is a private figure, as in *Gertz*, the Constitution still supplants the standards of the common law, but the constitutional requirements are, in at least some of their range, less forbidding than when the plaintiff is a public figure and the speech is of public concern.

The issue in *Hepps* was the validity under the First Amendment of the common-law presumption that a defamatory statement is false, pursuant to which the burden of proving truth is on the defendant. Finding plaintiff to be a private figure and the subject of the newspaper articles in issue to be of public concern, the Court held that, "the common-law's rule on falsity—that the defendant must bear the burden of proving truth—must ... fall here to a constitutional requirement that the plaintiff bear the burden of showing falsity, as well as fault, before recovering damages." (475 U.S. at 776)

It is obvious that defendant's publication relates to a matter of public concern. The affidavits and documents submitted by both parties reveal that the wire service report was related to an international scandal which touched major players in Indian politics and was reported in India, Sweden, the United States, England and elsewhere in the world. Consider the revelation of Mr. Zaiwalla, who had the conduct of the action resulting in the English judgment, that it was given priority over other defamation actions waiting to be tried because "the Indian General Election was imminent and the Bofars affairs and the plaintiff's long-time family friendship with Mr. Rajiv Gandhi, the former prime minister of India.... and leader of the main opposition party.... were being used as electoral weapons in India." (Zaiwalla aff. pp. 4-5) Mr. Justice Otten, in his instructions, referred to the political context of the story by suggesting to the jury that it "ignore the complexities" of the Indian politics and political parties which were the background of the news stories. (Transcript, p. 6, Exhibit B, Handman further aff.)

Placing the burden of proving truth upon media defendants who publish speech of public concern has been held unconstitutional because fear of liability may deter such speech.

Because such a "chilling" effect would be antithetical to the First Amendment's protection of true speech on matters of public concern, we believe that a private-figure plaintiff must bear the burden of showing that the speech at issue is false before recovering damages for defamation from a media defendant. To do otherwise could "only result in a deterrence of speech which the Constitution makes free." *Hepps*, supra at 777.

The "chilling" effect is no different where liability results from enforcement in the United States of a foreign judgment obtained where the burden of proving truth is upon media defendants. Accordingly, the failure of Bachchan to prove falsity in the High Court of Justice in England makes his judgment unenforceable here.

There is, of course, another reason why enforcement of the English judgment would violate the First Amendment: in England, plaintiff was not required to and did not meet the "less forbidding" constitutional requirement that a private figure show that a media defendant was at fault.

New York's standard for liability in actions brought by private persons against the press is set forth in Chapadeau v. Utica Observer-Dispatch, 38 N.Y.2d 196, 199 (1975): "[W]here the content of the article is arguably within the sphere of legitimate public concern, which is reasonably related to matters warranting public exposition, the party defamed may recover; however, to warrant such recovery he must establish, by a preponderance of the evidence, that the publisher acted in a grossly irresponsible manner without due consideration for the standards of information gathering and dissemination ordinarily followed by responsible parties."

As stated above, the English courts do not require plaintiff to prove that a press defendant was at fault in any degree. Bachchan certainly did not establish, as required by *Chapadeau*, that defendant was grossly irresponsible, a difficult task, where defendant disseminates another's news report. [cit.]

It is true that England and the United States share many common law principles of law. Nevertheless, a significant difference between the two jurisdictions lies in

England's lack of an equivalent to the First Amendment to the United States Constitution. The protection to free speech and the press embodied in that amendment would be seriously jeopardized by the entry of foreign libel judgments granted pursuant to standards deemed appropriate in England but considered antithetical to the protections afforded the press by the U.S. Constitution.

For the above stated reasons, the motion for summary judgment in lieu of complaint is denied.

Notes and Questions

1. *The Public Policy Exception.* As you recall from *Fauntleroy* and *Yarborough*, supra at 713, 717, public policy is not a ground for denying recognition to a sister-state judgment. In contrast, for reasons too obvious to need elaboration, public policy is a major and frequently invoked defense to recognition of foreign-country judgments. This is true not only in the United States but also in virtually any other country in the world, although of course the precise parameters of public policy differ from country to country. In this country, "[t]he public policy exception operates only in those unusual cases where the foreign judgment is 'repugnant to fundamental notions of what is decent and just in the State where enforcement is sought.'" McCord v. Jet Spray Intern. Corp., 874 F.Supp. 436 (D.Mass.1994) (quoting Tahan v. Hodgson, 662 F.2d 862 at 864 (D.C.Cir.1981), or when the judgment "'tends clearly' to undermine the public interest, the public confidence in the administration of the law, or security for individual rights of personal liberty or of private property." Ackermann v. Levine, 788 F.2d 830, 841 (2d Cir.1986) (quoting Somportex v. Philadelphia Chewing Gum, 453 F.2d 435, 443 (3d Cir.1971), *cert. denied*, 405 U.S. 1017 (1972)).

2. Did *Bachchan* meet the above standards? Why, or why not? For other cases involving English libel judgments and decided exactly like *Bachchan*, see Telnikoff v. Matusevitch, 702 A.2d 230 (Md.1997); Matusevitch v. Telnikoff, 877 F.Supp. 1 (D.D.C.1995); Abdullah v. Sheridan Square Press, Inc., 1994 WL 419847 (S.D.N.Y. 1994). If, as *Bachchan* concedes, the difference between American and English libel law "essentially comes down to where the burden of proof lies," how can such a difference be so repugnant to our sense of justice and decency? What distinguishes this case from cases like *Hilton* or *Panama Processes*, supra 840? The *Hilton* Court took note of defendant's assertions that "the plaintiff was permitted to testify not under oath, and was not subjected to cross-examination by the opposite party, * * * that documents and papers were admitted in evidence * * * which would not be admissible under our own system of jurisprudence." However, the Court found these to be inconsequential because "the practice followed and the method of examining witnesses were *according to the laws of France*," (emphasis added), and such differences in "procedure * * * [were not] a sufficient ground for impeaching the foreign judgment." Similarly, *Panama Processes* held that the fact that the parties were not allowed to cross-examine or subpoena witnesses, conduct pre-trial discovery, or subpoena documents were equally inconsequential. Can these two cases be explained by the fact that both cases involved civil-law countries in which

the judge plays a more active role in the presentation and evaluation of evidence than does a judge who sits in a state that follows the purely adversary model of procedure? If the difference between *Bachchan* and the above two cases can be explained by the elementary proposition that a state feels more strongly about constitutional safeguards than about statutory or common-law standards, then can *Bachchan* and *Cooley* be reconciled?

3. ***Judgment or Claim?*** Both the UFMJRA and New York's version of it embodied in CPLR 5304(b)(4) speak of the foreign "cause of action," but not the resulting foreign judgment, as being repugnant to the forum's public policy. Is this deliberate or simply the result of poor drafting? In *Bachchan* was the English libel *action* repugnant to New York's public policy? How did the New York court handle this issue? In contrast, the Restatement (Third) allows this defense if *either* the judgment or the claim on which the judgment is based are repugnant to the forum's public policy (see § 482(2)(d)). Finally, the IJJ Project follows the Restatement and, in addition, makes this a mandatory ground for non-recognition (see § 5(a)(vi)). Which of the three formulations is preferable? Why? For cases that upheld the foreign judgment because the *cause of action* did not offend the forum's public policy (even though the judgment itself arguably might), see The Society of Lloyd's v. Turner, 3003 F.3d 325 (5th Cir. 2002); Southwest Livestock & Trucking Co. v. Hargrove, 169 F.3d 317 (5th Cir. 1999).

4. ***State or National Policy?*** The UFMJRA and New York's CPLR 5304(b)(4) speak of repugnance to the public policy of "this state," i.e. the forum. In contrast, the Restatement (Third) speaks of repugnance to the public policy of "the *United States or* of the State where recognition is sought." § 482(2)(d), (emphasis added). Finally, the IJJ Project, which will federalize the whole subject, speaks of repugnance to "the public policy of the United States." Although the difference between these formulations would not affect the outcome in *Bachchan* can it affect the outcome in other cases? Which? For a discussion of these issues, see IJJ Project, § 5, Rptrs' Note 5(a).

5. ***Territorial Scope.*** In *Bachchan*, where was the wrongful act committed and by whom? Is the answer to this question helpful for delineating the territorial range of the public policy exception? Suppose that Dagens Nyjeter, the Swedish newspaper that reported the original story involving Mr. Bachchan, was also cast in judgment in the same English proceeding, and that Mr. Bachchan sought recognition of that judgment in New York. Would recognition of that judgment be as repugnant to New York's public policy as recognition of the judgment against defendant India Abroad? Why, or why not? Would the court's statements regarding the "'chilling' effect" on freedom of speech be as pertinent in that case? Why should a New York court be concerned about protecting a Swedish newspaper's freedom of speech in Sweden? In Telnikoff v. Matusevitch, 702 A.2d 230 (Md.1997), which also refused on public policy grounds to enforce an English libel judgment, neither the parties nor the publication had any pertinent connection with the United States. Are there no territorial limits to the policy embodied in the First Amendment? On the other hand, suppose that the foreign libel judgment was based on a law that prohibits any criticism against that country's government. In such a case, should the

lack of connections with the United States make any difference in determining whether to recognize that judgment in the United States?

6. *Penal and Tax Judgments.* American courts are not required to enforce penal or tax judgments rendered in other countries. See Restatement (Third), § 483 and authorities cited there. A judgment is penal in this sense only when it is "in favor of a foreign state or one of its subdivisions, and [is] primarily punitive rather than compensatory in character." Id., cmt. b. Was *Cooley* a penal judgment in this sense? Did the court *enforce* the Iranian judgment in that case or simply *recognize* it? What is the difference between enforcement and recognition?

7. *No Choice-of-Law Scrutiny.* Recall that many foreign countries, see supra 823-25, reserve the right to deny recognition to a foreign judgment if the rendering court failed to apply the substantive law that would be applicable under the conflicts rules of the recognizing court. For an evaluation and critique of this practice, see von Mehren, *Foreign Judgments*, 39-46. In the United States, the Full Faith and Credit clause forbids such a choice-of-law inquiry in the case of sister-state judgments (see *Fauntleroy* and *Yarborough*, supra 713, 717), but not in the case of foreign-country judgments. Yet, American courts have failed to take advantage of this freedom and have not subjected foreign judgments to a choice-of-law scrutiny. What do you think accounts for this stance? Could it be: (a) that these courts are too conditioned by the peculiarities of sister-state recognition practice and do not find it cost-efficient to develop a separate approach for the relatively few foreign country judgments? or (b) that the lack of clear cut choice-of-law "rules" in most American states makes a choice-of-law inquiry uncertain and thus unattractive? Is a choice-of-law scrutiny of foreign judgments necessary, at least in principle, or do the public policy and other defenses to recognition provide sufficient safeguards against objectionable foreign judgments?

F. THE HAGUE CONVENTIONS

The Hague Conference on Private International Law is an intergovernmental organization that today encompasses 62 countries and whose purpose is "to work for the progressive unification of the rules of private international law." (Statute, Art. 1). Since 1955, the Conference has produced 36 conventions, of which 25 are now in force.[1] The United States joined the Conference in 1964 and actively participated in the drafting of the 24 conventions produced since that year, but it has signed only six conventions and has ratified only four of them.[2]

In the 1960s, the Hague Conference undertook the drafting of a convention on the subject of this chapter, which produced the Convention on the Recognition and Enforcement of Foreign Judgments in Civil and Commercial Matters of 1 February

---

1. All of these conventions are posted on the official web site of the Conference, which also contains useful information on all aspects of this organization. See http://www.hcch.net/e.

2. These conventions, which are now in force, are: (1) the 1961 Convention Abolishing the Requirement of Legalisation for Foreign Public Documents; (2) the 1965 Convention on the Service Abroad of Judicial and Extrajudicial Documents in Civil or Commercial Matters; (3) the 1970 Convention on the Taking of Evidence Abroad in Civil and Commercial Matters; and (4) the 1980 Convention on the Civil Aspects of International Child Abduction.

1971. However, three decades later, only three countries had ratified this convention (Cyprus, The Netherlands, and Portugal), and this was one of the reasons for which in 1996 the Hague Conference began work for a new convention.

Unlike the 1971 convention, which regulated only the requirements for recognition ("single convention"), the new convention was to regulate both the rendering court's jurisdiction and the requirements for recognition and enforcement of the resulting judgment in other countries ("double convention"). Anticipating that it would be unlikely to attain consensus on both the required ("white list") and the prohibited ("black list") bases of jurisdiction, the United States delegation proposed the addition of a third list ("grey list") of jurisdictional bases that the Convention would permit but not regulate further. Under this scheme of a "mixed convention," recognition would be: (a) required, if the rendering court's jurisdiction was grounded on one of the bases on the white list; (b) prohibited, if it was grounded on one of the bases on the black list; and (c) left to the recognizing court's discretion, if it was grounded on a basis on the grey list. After intense negotiations in the course of seven years, even this proposal proved too optimistic. By the turn of the century, it was obvious that efforts to reach a consensus had reached an impasse. At the time of this writing (2003), this Convention remains on the agenda of the Hague Conference,[3] but the prospects of reaching a consensus in the foreseeable future are uncertain at best.

In a book published in 2003, Professor Arthur von Mehren, a member of the United States delegation and the proponent of the "mixed" convention concept, discussed in detail the reasons for this proposal and its prospects for adoption.[4] In the following excerpt, von Mehren reflects more generally on the current state of international efforts to harmonize private international law.

SOME CONCLUDING THOUGHTS[5]

1. *Legal cultures and their interpenetration*. Comparative study of any, or all, of private international law's branches--jurisdiction, choice of law, and recognition and enforcement of foreign judgements--requires consideration of the cultural, moral, economic, political, and social contexts that, as they change over time, shape--and reshape--a society and its legal order. Change may occur rapidly or slowly; it may reinforce a society's elements of uniqueness or cause diverse societies to converge. Seen in a broad perspective, the civil-law and common-law traditions have each

---

3. For all the official working documents and drafts produced so far for this convention, see http://www.hcch.net/e/workprog/jdgm.html.

4. See von Mehren, *Adjudicatory Authority*, 408-25. See also von Mehren, *Design of Recognition Conventions*, 17; von Mehren, *The Case for a Convention-mixte Approach*, 86. For an account of the Hague negotiations from another member of the US delegation, see Brand, *In Search of a Global Convention*, 11. For the perspectives of the two Hague co-reporters, see Nygh, *Arthur's Baby*, 151; Pocar, *World-Wide Convention*, 191. For the perspectives of the co-reporters of the IJJ Project, see Lowenfeld & Silberman, *The Hague Judgments Convention*, 121.

5. Excerpted from A. T. von Mehren, Theory and Practice of Adjudicatory Authority in Private International Law: A Comparative Study of the Doctrine, Policies and Practices of Common- and Civil Law Systems, 295 *Recueil des Cours* 9, 402-04, 417-19, 424-25 (2003) (footnotes omitted), copyright by the Hague Academy of International Law.

maintained their integrity for a period roughly corresponding to the second millennium of the Christian era. In the course of the third millennium, however, these two traditions may well interpenetrate and create one--or several--new legal traditions.

During the second millennium, system interpenetration has, of course, occurred on many occasions and in many respects. The rise of a *lex mercatoria,* resting not on local laws, but on shared practices and usages of merchants, was an early form of interpenetration. Anational international commercial arbitration, based on the United Nations Convention on the Recognition and Enforcement of Foreign Arbitral Awards of 1958, provides a late 20th century example of a not altogether different phenomenon.

Greater interpenetration clearly must result from the enormous increase in cross-border and inter-system activity that has occurred in the last half century as well as the related willingness of most legal systems to give increasing recognition to private autonomy by both tempering mandatory rules of law and allowing parties greater freedom to choose the forum in which to litigate and the law to be applied. New technology in the form of the Internet has created strong incentives for harmonization to promote economic efficiency. Indeed, convergence in many areas of law will come about through the working of the market place if the philosophy of a free, unregulated market prospers globally.

Convergence between case-law and codified systems could take place as well because of the tension between the claims of system and structure, on the one hand, and of just, fact-specific solutions, on the other. Each perspective has a contribution to make to a wise and humane system of justice. As the values in tension are incommensurate, no permanent balance is likely to be struck; accordingly, an element of instability exists on both sides of the equation that can cause one system to move closer to--or retreat from--another system's position.

The experience of the 20th century strongly suggests that, as societies and economies become increasingly complex and interrelated, legal orders will draw more than in the past on both the civil-law and the common-law traditions in thinking about law and its administration. At the level of method and style, the number of legal orders no longer squarely in either the codification- or the case-law tradition has increased; at the same time, these systems have become more complex. The 21st century may well witness a continuation of these developments. The European Union has brought about a confrontation of the civil law, the common law, and the mixed Scottish and Scandinavian systems. Will this combination result in a new system that blends in an original fashion these disparate legal traditions?

2. *The 20th century and globalization.* In the course of the 20th century, cross-border activity in most, if not all, areas of social, intellectual, and commercial activity increased significantly in both volume and intensity. Our lives as individuals, as members of groups and associations economic, political, and social in nature, as citizens of nations, and as members of the human race have become increasingly "delocalized." In many respects, we lead far more globalized lives than our forefathers did when the 19th century ended.

These changes in our world's infrastructure and conditions of living have profoundly affected almost every aspect of our existence. The problems created and the forces released have many consequences, some profound--others trivial, some conflicting--others harmonious or convergent. These developments have led to international efforts to regulate various aspects of the rules and practices of private international law including those that address jurisdiction to adjudicate and recognition and enforcement of foreign judgments.

In its nature, private international law is concerned with contexts in which two or more legal orders have a significant stake. Efforts to provide mechanisms for handling controversies regulating such matters began in ancient times and have continued ever since. Interest in regulating through multilateral international instruments various rules and practices of private international law increased in the last half of the 19th century. One consequence was the creation in 1893 of the Hague Conference on Private International Law. Efforts to "conventionalize" areas of private international law continued throughout the 20th century; its closing decades saw the entrance into force of the United Nations Convention on the Recognition and Enforcement of Foreign Arbitral Awards of 1958, the European Union's Brussels Convention on jurisdiction and the enforcement of judgments in civil and commercial matters of 1968, and the Lugano Convention of 1988. In the century's last decade, the Hague Conference began work on a world-wide convention on jurisdiction and the recognition and enforcement of foreign judgments.

* * *

[In the meantime], an unprecedented cascade of technological, sociological, political, and commercial changes began. Of these, the most profound and perplexing resulted from the new technology of the internet and the rise of internet commerce. Technical and economic assumptions on which rested many aspects of the theory and practice of adjudicatory authority in international controversies were not valid for this new sector of the economy; novel issues and new dilemmas were posed. Ever more protean, e-communications and e-commerce now pose intractable problems for all branches of private international law. The Hague Conference, endeavoring to draft a jurisdiction and judgments convention, finds itself adrift between the Scylla of "undermin[ing] the goal of encouraging the nascent e-commerce industry" and the Charybdis of "exclud[ing] e-commerce from the scope of the [Hague] project as a way of moving forward." For the next several decades, it seems likely that at least broad agreement will be possible on only two propositions: Consensus on how the Convention should deal with e-commerce cannot be achieved; the Convention *must* address e-commerce.

The political scene has also seen changes--in particular, the emergence of the European Union--that emphasize *regional* harmonization of the law respecting the assumption of adjudicatory authority and the recognition of non-local judgments. Once such harmonization is well under way, the national governments involved have a large stake in the new *status quo*; the region's interest in negotiating a world-wide convention on different terms and with other solutions inevitably declines.

The increased complexity and specialization of modern technology, of commercial and corporate structures and procedures, and of government regulation have also contributed to making the task undertaken in the late 1990s by the Hague Conference far more difficult than it would otherwise have been. For many areas of private international law, one now must be a specialist in the structure and economy of each area of activity that will be significantly affected in order to understand the considerations to be taken into account in drafting a jurisdiction and recognition convention.

Driven in part by the negotiators' need to understand an increasingly complex world, interest groups have been consulted far more than in the past. Where these groups disagree, as is often the case, on the positions to be taken, national delegations must seek to harmonize the views of their own constituencies or, at least, to strike acceptable compromises. To a degree, delegations thus face internally the perplexing and intractable problems of harmonization and compromise that the Hague Conference has collectively encountered.

* * *

3. *Universal conventions in matters of private international law: 21st Century prospects*. * * * Universal instruments harmonizing broad areas of the law of jurisdiction and enforcement of judgments do not have a bright future. Efforts to harmonize the law respecting topics for which a consensus is attainable can well be fruitful, however. This approach would seek universal harmonizations compatible with the regional harmonizations in force. The required degree of compatibility may exist with respect to jurisdiction and enforcement in several areas of considerable importance. These include exclusive choice-of-forum clauses in business-to-business contracts, place-of-injury jurisdiction for *physical* injury in products liability cases, and jurisdiction in the defendant's home-forum for most claims.

More problematic specific provisions that deserve consideration include, for litigation between businesses or professionals, jurisdiction based on the place of performance of a contract or on activity respecting its conclusion and performance. To the extent that consensus was reached on discrete solutions, a universal international instrument could displace regional harmonizations for controversies that were not entirely intraregional.

There are also areas of the law for which world-wide regulation is preferable to regional regulation because the controversies that arise are widely and randomly dispersed. For such matters, a universal convention has advantages that regional conventions lack. The most striking example of such a convention is the New York Convention on the Recognition and Enforcement of Foreign Arbitral Awards of 1958. Because under the New York Convention arbitration has become a "movable feast," the universal convention has largely displaced regional conventions addressing the same subject matters.

Two recent Hague Conventions, the Convention of October 1980 on the Civil Aspects of International Child Abduction and that of 22 May 1993 on Protection of Children and Co-Operation in Respect of Intercountry Adoption, illustrate another context in which a universal convention offers advantages that regional conventions cannot. In the nature of things, abductors will seek out safe havens; regional conventions will, in practice, be evaded. Most abductions from a member state of the European Union would, were the Union to have only a Brussels abduction convention, be to states not party to the regional convention. Furthermore, in areas such as child abduction and adoption, where national agencies are charged with supervising responsibilities, the attraction of a universal convention is clear.

D. ***The Future.*** As of 2003, the myriad of forces--*inter alia*, historical, economic, political, intellectual, and cultural--that affect the Hague experiment have become more complex and less stable. What was thought to be the playing field when the project was undertaken has changed dramatically. The vast river of history is now swifter and more turbulent than it was when the work began. In particular, the struggle of uniformity versus diversity has become more intense. Will efficiency and administrability concerns result in legal orders generally according less weight to concerns for justice in specific cases? Striking a proper balance between proportionality and subsidiarity, on the one hand, and efficiency and administrability, on the other, become ever more difficult and contentious.

These issues will be played out on many stages and over many years. What the Hague Conference can accomplish will depend on broader developments. Several decades may pass before the scene is clarified; until that has occurred, efforts at The Hague can hardly produce results except where consensus can be reached. What transpires will tell us much about how thinking and practice are likely to develop in the 21st century respecting adjudicatory authority and recognition and enforcement of foreign judgements.

Part IV

A FINAL LOOK AT CONFLICT

Chapter 13

A FINAL LOOK
AT CONFLICT OF LAWS:
CYBERSPACE AND INDIAN TRIBES

A. INTRODUCTION AND OVERVIEW

You have now examined choice of law, jurisdiction and enforcement of judgments in the state, federal, and international arenas. This concluding chapter offers a reexamination of these issues in two areas of law—cyberspace and Indian Tribes. Though these areas may seem very different, they both present issues concerning the nature of sovereignty and the role of territoriality.

B. CYBERSPACE–LAW AND SOVEREIGNTY IN THE VIRTUAL REALM

The Internet is a world-wide network of computer networks, all sharing a common communications technology. It is highly decentralized and there is no central hub through which information is routed and no central governing body. It has been estimated that there are over 500 million Internet users world-wide.

The Internet presents some unique difficulties for both jurisdiction and choice of law doctrine because it transcends physical boundaries. In traditional transactions, participants know with whom they are dealing and where events are located. On the Internet, participants may know neither. Users of the Internet have "addresses" but these are not tied to physical locations. As a result, some have argued that the Internet and cyberspace are so unique that we must create entirely new rules for this area.

> Because events on the Net occur everywhere but nowhere in particular, are engaged in by online personae who are both "real" (possessing reputations, able to perform services, and deploy intellectual assets) and "intangible" (not necessarily or traceably tied to any particular person in the physical sense), and concern "things" (messages, databases, standing relationships) that are not necessarily separated from one another by any physical boundaries, no physical jurisdiction has a more compelling claim than any other to subject these events exclusively to its laws.

Johnson & Post, *Law in Cyberspace*, at 1376. Others have disputed the uniqueness of cyberspace or Internet transactions. "The Internet is not, as many suggest, a separate place removed from our world. Like the telephone, the telegraph, and the smoke signal, the Internet is a medium through which people in real space in one jurisdiction communicate with people in real space in another jurisdiction." Goldsmith, *Territorial Sovereignty*, at 476.

Earlier we considered jurisdiction issues involving cyberspace, see supra at 664-71. As we saw, the Internet presents challenges to current doctrine. A single person who never leaves home can inflict significant harm on other people around the world. Standard jurisdiction doctrine requires that a defendant have "purposeful" contacts with the forum – effects alone is not sufficient. See *World-Wide Volkswagen v. Woodson*, supra at 593. Courts have struggled to articulate a test for when posting material on the Internet constitutes purposeful availment. One early effort was Zippo Mfg. Co. v. Zippo Dot Com, Inc., 952 F. Supp. 1119 (W.D. Pa. 1997), which attempted to differentiate among cases based on how interactive a web site is. See *Cybersell, Inc. v. Cybersell, Inc.*, supra at 664. However, with technological advances, the line between active and passive sites has become harder to draw. See Geist, *Toward Greater Certainty*, at 1379-80. More recently, other courts have focused on whether conduct was "targeted" at the forum. See, e.g., Young v. New Haven Advocate, 315 F.3d 256 (4th Cir. 2002), *cert. denied*, 123 S.Ct. 2092 (2003); Pavlovich v. Superior Court, 58 P.3d 2 (Cal. 2002).

Some have argued that the efforts to fit Internet cases into current doctrine simply highlight the inappropriateness of the purposeful availment standard and have urged its abandonment, at least in Internet cases. See Redish, *New Wine in Old Bottles*. Do you agree that current doctrine is ill-suited to the Internet? Other countries allow jurisdiction without requiring purposeful contact. For example, within the European Union, tort claims can be brought in the place where the harm occurs and consumer suits can be brought in the consumer's domicile. See Brussels II, Art. 5(3), Art. 16. France asserted jurisdiction over the U.S. based Yahoo! company based on the fact that French residents were able to access sites on Yahoo! that offered Nazi memorabilia for sale. See County Court of Paris, Interim Court Order, League Against Racism & Antisemitism – LICRA v. Yahoo! Inc., No. RG 00/05308 (Nov. 20, 2000). Similarly, Australia upheld jurisdiction based solely on an injury to reputation suffered by an Australian plaintiff in Australia from material posted on a web site in the U.S. by a U.S. company. See Dow Jones & Co., Inc. v. Gutnick, [2002] HCA 56 (10 December 2002) (High Court of Australia). Should U.S. courts rethink the requirement of purposeful availment and focus instead on effects?

What about choice of law? Do we need special choice of law rules for cyberspace? Cyberspace transactions may involve multiple jurisdictions and may also raise difficult issues of situs. Are these problems conceptually different from those we encountered in choice of law? Are some choice of law methodologies better suited than others to the problems of cyberspace? Consider the following:

Nor are the effects of online activities tied to geographically proximate locations. * * * A web site physically located in Brazil * * * has no more of an effect on individuals in Brazil than does a Web site physically located in Belgium or Belize that is accessible in Brazil. Usenet discussion groups, to take another example, consist of continuously changing collections of messages that are routed from one network to another, with no centralized location at all. They exist, in effect, everywhere, nowhere in particular, and only on the Net.

Nor can the legitimacy of any rules governing online activities be naturally traced to a geographically situated polity. There is no geographically localized set of constituents with a stronger claim to regulate it than any other local group. The strongest claim to control comes from the participants themselves, and they could be anywhere. And in Cyberspace physical borders no longer function as signposts informing individuals of the obligations assumed by entering into a new, legally significant place. Individuals are unaware of the existence of those borders as they move through virtual space.[1]

Johnson & Post, *Law in Cyberspace,* 1375. The authors go on to argue that because cyberspace is so disconnected from physical geography we should abandon altogether standard choice of law and instead treat cyberspace as a distinct "place" with its own laws and customs that are not tied to those of any particular sovereign. They point pointed to the medieval *lex mercatoria*--Law Merchant--as a possible model for law in cyberspace.

The Law Merchant first developed in medieval Europe and consisted of an "enforceable set of customary practices that inured to the benefit of merchants, and that was reasonably uniform across all the jurisdictions involved in the [medieval] trade fairs." Hardy, *Legal Regime for "Cyberspace,"* 1020. A modern version of the Law Merchant has developed and is used in some international transactions. See Draetta, Tabe & Nanda, *International Contracts*, 13. What do you think of the suggestion that transactions involving the Internet might be governed by a cyberspace version of the Law Merchant? Should the Law Merchant also control in non-consensual interactions such as torts? What about reviving *Swift v. Tyson* or using some version of Judge Weinstein's "national consensus law"? In re "Agent Orange" Product Liability Litigation, 580 F.Supp. 690 (E.D.N.Y.1984) (supra at 525).

Others disagree that cyberspace requires any unique approach for choice of law:

[Those who argue that current choice of law methodologies are ill-suited for cyberspace] are further mistaken to the extent that their arguments assume that all choice-of-law problems must be resolved by multilateral choice-of-law methodologies. A multilateral methodology asks which of several possible laws governs a transaction, and selects one of these laws on the basis of specified criteria. Multilateral methods accentuate the situs and complexity problems. But the regulatory issues that are most relevant to the cyberspace governance debate almost always involve unilateral choice-of-law methods that alleviate these problems. A unilateral method considers only whether the dispute at issue has close enough connections to the forum to justify the application of local law. If so, local law applies; if not, the case is dismissed and the potential applicability of foreign law is not considered. * * *

Unilateral choice-of-law methods make the complexity and situs problems

---

1. ©[1996] by the Board of Trustees of the Leland Stanford Junior University.

less significant. They do not require a determination of which of a number of possible laws apply. Nor do they require a court to identify where certain events occurred. What matters is simply whether the activity has local effects that are significant enough to implicate local law. By failing to recognize that courts can and will use unilateral rather than multilateral choice-of-law methods to resolve cyberspace conflicts, the skeptics again exaggerate the challenge of cyberspace regulation.[1]

Goldsmith, *Against Cyberanarchy*, at 1243, 1235, 1237. Do you agree that unilateral choice of law methods are preferable for Internet cases?

Other countries have confronted many of these same issues. For example, the High Court of Australia has explicitly rejected the argument that it should develop special choice of law rules for the Internet. See Dow Jones & Co., Inc. v. Gutnick, [2002] HCA 56 (10 December 2002) (High Court of Australia). In that case, an Australian plaintiff brought a defamation claim against a U.S. company for information it had posted in the U.S. on its website. The court applied the traditional lex loci delicti rule, holding that Australia was the place where the wrong occurred because it was the place where the plaintiff's reputation was damaged. Similarly, France applied its law in the *Yahoo!* case, and Germany applied its laws to an Australian who posted material on an Australian web site denying that the Nazis perpetrated the Holocaust. See Ray August, *International Cyber-Jurisdiction: A Comparative Analysis*, 39 Am. Bus. L. J. 531, 541 (2002).

An entity doing business over the Internet, indeed, anyone posting material on a web site, may find himself subject to the laws of a number of jurisdictions. The fact of multiple and potentially inconsistent regulation can impose significant burdens on business and raises questions about the extent to which one state ought to be able to impose costs and burdens on those using the Internet. Indeed, several courts have struck down on Commerce Clause grounds a state's efforts to apply its own laws to the Internet. As one court has explained:

> The unique nature of the Internet highlights the likelihood that a single actor might be subject to haphazard, uncoordinated, and even outright inconsistent regulation by states that the actor never intended to reach and possibly was unaware were being accessed. Typically, states' jurisdictional limits are related to geography; geography, however, is a virtually meaningless construct on the Internet. The menace of inconsistent state regulation invites analysis under the Commerce Clause of the Constitution, because that clause represented the framers' reaction to overreaching by the individual states that might jeopardize the growth of the nation -- and in particular, the national infrastructure of communications and trade -- as a whole.

American Libraries Ass'n v. Pataki, 969 F. Supp. 168-69 (S.D.N.Y. 1997). See American Civil Liberties Union v. Johnson, 194 F.3d 1149 (10th Cir, 1999). On the other hand, Washington and California have rejected Commerce Clause challenges to their "Anti-Spam" statutes on the grounds that the cost of compliance was modest. See Washington v. Heckel, 24 P.3d 404 (Wash. 2001); Ferguson v. Friendfinders, Inc.,115 Cal. Rptr.2d 258 (Cal. App. 2002). In both cases, the defendants argued that as a practical matter, they would have to comply with the anti-spam laws with

---

1. @ [1998] by The University of Chicago.

respect to all of their emails, not just those sent to Washington or California residents. The courts rejected the argument noting that the focus should be on the cost of compliance not on the burden of non-compliance. *Heckel*, 24 P.3d at 411; *Ferguson*, 115 Cal. Rptr.2d at 265-66. Of course, unless a business is able to screen out emails to residents of Washington and California, it will need to conform all its emails to the requirement of those states. Does this permit one state to inappropriately control business nationwide? See generally Goldsmith & Sykes, *Dormant Commerce Clause*; Loudenslager, *Policeman on the Information Superhighway*.

One solution might be screening technologies that allow a company easily to identify where its email or other information in being sent. In the *Yahoo!* case, the French court concluded that such technology was available and ordered the American company to use the technology in order to prevent French residents from having access to the offending site. But who should bear the cost of the screening technology? Should France be able to impose on a foreign company the obligation (and cost) of screening?

In response to these problems, there has been an effort to create uniform safe harbor rules for at least some categories of Internet transactions. For example, securities or franchise offerings made by Internet would be exempt from regulations of a state if the offer clearly indicates it does not extend to residents of that state and there are no other solicitations in the state. See North American Securities Administrators Association, "Statement of Policy Regarding Offers of Franchises on the Internet," May 3, 1998. Similarly, the European Union's Electronic Commerce Directive combines some harmonization of laws with a cyberspace choice of law rule--the "State where the [Internet] services originate" (except for consumer transactions). See Directive 2000/31/EC of the European Parliament and the Council of 8 June 2000.

Some of the most significant issues with respect to cyberspace may not be problems of jurisdiction or choice of law but the problem of enforcement of judgments. See Perritt, *Will the Judgment-Proof Own Cyberspace.* Enforcement problems may be particularly acute in the international arena. For example, after the French court entered a temporary judgment in the *Yahoo!* case, Yahoo! sought and was granted a declaratory judgment in federal court in California that the French judgment was unenforceable in the United States. See Yahoo! Inc. v. La Ligue Contre Le Racisme et L'Antisemitisme,145 F. Supp. 2d 1168 (N.D. Ca. 2001). See also Braintech Inc. v. Kostiuk, [1999] 171 D.L.R. (4th) 46 (B.C.C.A.) (Canadian court refused to enforce Texas default judgment against Canadian resident finding that the defendant posted defamatory material on an Internet bulletin board). Some may argue that a case such as *Yahoo!* highlights the need for international agreements on enforcement. On the other hand, *Yahoo!* may also highlight that so long as countries disagree about fundamental values as reflected in their substantive law (e.g., free speech versus hate speech), they are unlikely to reach agreement on enforcement of judgments.

C. INDIAN TRIBES—ADDING A THIRD SOVEREIGN

The federal and state governments are not the only sovereigns that reign within the territory of the United States. There is a third category of sovereign in this country—Indian tribes. The interrelationship among the federal government and state and tribal governments is complex, but provides rich material for exploring the meaning and limits of sovereignty.

Native Americans were not participants in the Constitutional Convention and did not ratify the Constitution. Even the Fourteenth Amendment did not make them citizens of the United States. See Elk v. Wilkins, 112 U.S. 94 (1884). Not until the 1924 passage of the Citizenship Act, now codified at 8 U.S.C. § 1401(a)(2), were they granted United States and state citizenship.

The Constitution refers to Indians and Indian tribes in several places, but does so in a way that suggests Native Americans were viewed as being outside of the constitutional compact. See U.S. Const. art. I, § 2, cl. 3 (in apportioning representatives of the House of Representatives, "Indians not taxed" are excluded); U.S. Const. amend. XIV, § 2 (same); U.S. Const. art. I, § 8, cl. 3 (giving Congress power to regulate commerce with "the Indian Tribes"). As one commentator has observed, the relationship between Indian tribes and the federal government is "both pre-constitutional and extra-constitutional." Resnik, *Dependent Sovereigns*, 696 (quoting Charles F. Wilkinson).

United States law treats Indian tribes as a unique type of entity—sovereign nations in some respects, but not wholly independent. The landmark case is Cherokee Nation v. Georgia, 30 U.S. (5 Pet.) 1 (1831), in which the Court held that Indian tribes are not "foreign nations" within the meaning of Article III § 2 of the Constitution. Chief Justice Marshall explained:

> Though the Indians are acknowledged to have an unquestionable, and heretofore unquestioned, right to the lands they occupy, until that right shall be extinguished by a voluntary cession to our government; yet it may well be doubted, whether those tribes which reside within the acknowledged boundaries of the United States can, with strict accuracy, be denominated foreign nations. They may, more correctly, perhaps, be denominated domestic dependent nations. They occupy a territory to which we assert a title independent of their will, which must take effect in point of possession, when their right of possession ceases. Meanwhile they are in a state of pupilage; their relation to the United States resembles that of a ward to his guardian.

Id. at 17.

Inherent in the Court's description of tribes as "domestic dependent nations," is a recognition of at least some sovereignty. The following term, in Worcester v. Georgia, 31 U.S. (6 Pet.) 515 (1832), the Court began to delineate the scope of this sovereignty. Georgia had enacted a series of laws that purported to divide Cherokee land among several Georgia counties. Along with these laws, Georgia also required all non-Indians residing in Cherokee territory to obtain a state license. Several missionaries were arrested and convicted for violating the state law. The Supreme

Court reversed.[1] Chief Justice Marshall explained that "[t]he Cherokee nation * * * is a distinct community, occupying its own territory, with boundaries accurately described, in which the laws of Georgia can have no force." Id. at 561.

The Supreme Court has frequently held that Congress has "plenary authority to limit, modify or eliminate the powers of local self-government which the tribes otherwise possess." Santa Clara Pueblo v. Martinez, 436 U.S. 49, 56 (1978). It has been suggested that this power can be traced to the Commerce Clause, the treaty, war, and other foreign affairs powers, and to the property power. See Newton, *Federal Power over Indians*, 199. How satisfactory are these as sources of authority to eliminate local self-government? Does not the Indian Commerce Clause equate Indian tribes with states and foreign nations? Is the real source of the federal authority simply "conquest, violence, [and] force?" Resnik, *Dependent Sovereigns*, 696. See, e.g., Tee-Hit-Ton Indians v. United States, 348 U.S. 272, 279–80 (1955) (Indian aboriginal lands are not property for purposes of the Takings Clause of the Fifth Amendment because the government acquired this land by "conquest;" this rule was applied to lands of a tribe with which the government had never gone to war).

Many of the disputes among tribes, states and the federal government turn on questions of jurisdiction. The following cases explore some of these jurisdictional issues.

1. Limits on Adjudicatory Authority of States and Tribes

Williams v. Lee
Supreme Court of the United States, 1959.
358 U.S. 217, 79 S.Ct. 269, 3 L.Ed.2d 251.

JUSTICE BLACK delivered the opinion of the Court. Respondent, who is not an Indian, operates a general store in Arizona on the Navajo Indian Reservation under a license required by federal statute. He brought this action in the Superior Court of Arizona against petitioners, a Navajo Indian and his wife who live on the Reservation, to collect for goods sold them there on credit. Over petitioners' motion to dismiss on the ground that jurisdiction lay in the tribal court rather than in the state court, judgment was entered in favor of respondent. The Supreme Court of Arizona affirmed, holding that since no Act of Congress expressly forbids their doing so Arizona courts are free to exercise jurisdiction over civil suits by non-Indians against Indians though the action arises on an Indian reservation. [cit.] Because this was a doubtful determination of the important question of state power over Indian affairs, we granted certiorari. [cit.]

Originally the Indian tribes were separate nations within what is now the United States. Through conquest and treaties they were induced to give up complete independence and the right to go to war in exchange for federal protection, aid, and grants of land. When the lands granted lay within States these governments

---

1. The *Worcester* decision supposedly prompted President Jackson to say: "John Marshall has made his decision; now let him enforce it." In fact, no one did enforce the decision. Notwithstanding the reversal of the conviction, Georgia refused to release the missionaries, and they served 16 months doing hard labor. In 1992, the state of Georgia admitted that the continued incarceration of the missionaries had been illegal and apologized to their descendants. See Associated Press, *Georgia to Pardon Missionaries Jailed in 1830s*, Wash. Post., Nov. 23, 1992, at A5.

sometimes sought to impose their laws and courts on the Indians. Around 1830 the Georgia Legislature extended its laws to the Cherokee Reservation despite federal treaties with the Indians which set aside this land for them. The Georgia statutes forbade the Cherokees from enacting laws or holding courts and prohibited outsiders from being on the Reservation except with permission of the State Governor. The constitutionality of these laws was tested in *Worcester v. Georgia*, when the State sought to punish a white man, licensed by the Federal Government to practice as a missionary among the Cherokees, for his refusal to leave the Reservation. Rendering one of his most courageous and eloquent opinions, Chief Justice Marshall held that Georgia's assertion of power was invalid. "The Cherokee nation ... is a distinct community, occupying its own territory ... in which the laws of Georgia can have no force, and which the citizens of Georgia have no right to enter, but with the assent of the Cherokees themselves, or in conformity with treaties, and with the acts of congress. The whole intercourse between the United States and this nation, is, by our constitution and laws, vested in the government of the United States." [cit.]

Despite bitter criticism and the defiance of Georgia which refused to obey this Court's mandate in *Worcester* the broad principles of that decision came to be accepted as law. Over the years this Court has modified these principles in cases where essential tribal relations were not involved and where the rights of Indians would not be jeopardized, but the basic policy of *Worcester* has remained. Thus, suits by Indians against outsiders in state courts have been sanctioned. [cit.] And state courts have been allowed to try non-Indians who committed crimes against each other on a reservation. [cit.] But if the crime was by or against an Indian, tribal jurisdiction or that expressly conferred on other courts by Congress has remained exclusive. [cit.] Essentially, absent governing Acts of Congress, the question has always been whether the state action infringed on the right of reservation Indians to make their own laws and be ruled by them. [cit.]

Congress has also acted consistently upon the assumption that the States have no power to regulate the affairs of Indians on a reservation. To assure adequate government of the Indian tribes it enacted comprehensive statutes in 1834 regulating trade with Indians and organizing a Department of Indian Affairs. [cit.] Not satisfied solely with centralized government of Indians, it encouraged tribal governments and courts to become stronger and more highly organized. [cit.] Congress has followed a policy calculated eventually to make all Indians full-fledged participants in American society. This policy contemplates criminal and civil jurisdiction over Indians by any State ready to assume the burdens that go with it as soon as the educational and economic status of the Indians permits the change without disadvantage to them. [cit.] Significantly, when Congress has wished the States to exercise this power it has expressly granted them the jurisdiction which *Worcester v. Georgia* had denied.

No departure from the policies which have been applied to other Indians is apparent in the relationship between the United States and the Navajos. On June 1, 1868, a treaty was signed between General William T. Sherman, for the United

States, and numerous chiefs and headmen of the "Navajo nation or tribe of Indians."[7] At the time this document was signed the Navajos were an exiled people, forced by the United States to live crowded together on a small piece of land on the Pecos River in eastern New Mexico, some 300 miles east of the area they had occupied before the coming of the white man. In return for their promises to keep peace, this treaty "set apart" for "their permanent home" a portion of what had been their native country, and provided that no one, except United States Government personnel, was to enter the reserved area. Implicit in these treaty terms, as it was in the treaties with the Cherokees involved in *Worcester v. Georgia*, was the understanding that the internal affairs of the Indians remained exclusively within the jurisdiction of whatever tribal government existed. Since then, Congress and the Bureau of Indian Affairs have assisted in strengthening the Navajo tribal government and its courts. [cit.] The Tribe itself has in recent years greatly improved its legal system through increased expenditures and better-trained personnel. Today the Navajo Courts of Indian Offenses exercise broad criminal and civil jurisdiction which covers suits by outsiders against Indian defendants. No Federal Act has given state courts jurisdiction over such controversies. In a general statute Congress did express its willingness to have any State assume jurisdiction over reservation Indians if the State Legislature or the people vote affirmatively to accept such responsibility. To date, Arizona has not accepted jurisdiction, possibly because the people of the State anticipate that the burdens accompanying such power might be considerable.

There can be no doubt that to allow the exercise of state jurisdiction here would undermine the authority of the tribal courts over Reservation affairs and hence would infringe on the right of the Indians to govern themselves. It is immaterial that respondent is not an Indian. He was on the Reservation and the transaction with an Indian took place there. [cit.] The cases in this Court have consistently guarded the authority of Indian governments over their reservations. Congress recognized this authority in the Navajos in the Treaty of 1868, and has done so ever since. If this power is to be taken away from them, it is for Congress to do it. [cit.]
Reversed.

Notes and Questions

1. According to the Court, why does Arizona lack authority? Does tribal sovereignty by its own force limit state power, or is it congressional actions that have limited state power?

2. Why would the exercise of state jurisdiction undermine the authority of tribal courts? Could not Arizona adjudicate the case but apply Navajo law? There may, of course, be difficulties establishing the precise content of tribal law, particularly tribal common law based on tribal tradition and custom. See generally Wallingford, *Navajo Judiciary*, 141. Are these problems any greater than those encountered with respect to establishing the content of any foreign law? See supra at 103.

3. In civil litigation in tribal courts, what law should the tribal court apply?

---

7. [cit.] In 16 Stat. 566 (1871), Congress declared that no Indian tribe or nation within the United States should thereafter be recognized as an independent power with whom the United States could execute a treaty but provided that this should not impair the obligations of any treaty previously ratified. Thus the 1868 treaty with the Navajos survived this Act.

Consider the Sisseton-Wahpeton Tribal Code ch. 33, § 1 (1982):

[c]ivil matters shall be governed by the laws, customs and usage of the tribe not prohibited by the laws of the United States, applicable federal laws and regulations and decisions of the Department of Interior. The laws of the State of South Dakota may be employed as a guide. Where doubt arises as to the customs and usage of the Tribe, the court shall request the address of tribal elders familiar with tribal customs and usages. Where appropriate, the laws of the State of South Dakota may be employed to determine civil matters. The laws of the State of South Dakota shall not be used as a substitute for existing tribal law.

(quoted in Pommersheim, *The Crucible of Sovereignty*, 337 n. 61.)

4. In *Williams*, the plaintiff was non-Indian and the defendant an Indian. If the parties were reversed, would that change the result? See Paiz v. Hughes, 417 P.2d 51, 53-54 (N.M.1966) (allowing Indian plaintiff to sue non-Indian defendant in state court for personal injuries occurring on a reservation; court notes that suit will not affect the rights of the Indians "to make their own laws and be ruled by them, will not affect their tribal relations, and will not affect the rights of the Federal Government"). If the states do not have jurisdiction, there may be no court with jurisdiction because many tribal codes limit the civil jurisdiction of tribal courts to cases "in which the defendant is an Indian" and cases "between Indians and non-Indians which are brought before the court by stipulation of the parties." 25 C.F.R. § 11.103 (1994). See Cohen, *Federal Indian Law*, 355.

5. In *Williams*, the transaction in question occurred on a Navajo reservation. Would the result have been different if the Indian defendant had been a member of a different tribe? See Washington v. Confederated Tribes, 447 U.S. 134, 161 (1980) (permitting state to impose sales tax on nonmember Indians on an Indian reservation; Court explains that the tax would not "contravene the principle of tribal self-government, for the simple reason that nonmembers are not constituents of the governing Tribe").

6. In *Williams*, suppose the non-Indian plaintiff had been from a different state than the Indian defendant and had brought a diversity action in federal court. Under *Erie*, should the federal court dismiss the case? Should the answer depend on why the Arizona state courts have no jurisdiction? Compare Poitra v. Demarrias, 502 F.2d 23 (8th Cir.1974), *cert. denied*, 421 U.S. 934 (1975) (federal court sitting in diversity has jurisdiction even though state court had no jurisdiction), with Hot Oil Service, Inc. v. Hall, 366 F.2d 295 (9th Cir.1966) (contra).

7. The Indian Child Welfare Act of 1978 (ICWA), 25 U.S.C. §§ 1901–1963, grants exclusive jurisdiction to tribal courts for custody proceedings involving any Indian child "who resides or is domiciled within the reservation of such tribe." In Mississippi Band of Choctaw Indians v. Holyfield, 490 U.S. 30 (1989), the Supreme Court held that this statute invalidated a state adoption decree. The birth parents of the adopted children were Indians and domiciliaries of the Choctaw Reservation. The children were born off the reservation and the parents signed consent to adoption forms off the reservation. The Court held that the children were domiciliaries of the reservation although they had never resided there, rejecting the argument that the children were abandoned by their parents and therefore should not be deemed to have the domicile of their parents. The Court explained that such an interpretation weakens considerably the tribe's ability to assert its interest in its children. The

> protection of this tribal interest is at the core of the ICWA, which recognizes that the tribe has an interest in the child which is distinct from but on a parity with the interest of the parents. This relationship between Indian tribes and Indian children domiciled on the reservation finds no parallel in other ethnic cultures found in the United States. It is a relationship that many non-Indians find difficult to understand and that non-Indian courts are slow to recognize.

Id. at 52 (quoting from In re Adoption of Halloway, 732 P.2d 962, 969-70 (Utah 1986)). What is it that gives the tribe an interest in these children? Is it genetics? Is it the fact that they were born to parents who were domiciliaries? Would these connections be a proper basis for giving state courts exclusive custody jurisdiction vis-a-vis other states? Compare the ICWA with the definition of "home state" the Parental Kidnapping Protection Act, 28 U.S.C. § 1738A(b)(4). See generally Atwood, *Fighting Over Indian Children*, 1051 (1989); Dale, *Indian Child Welfare Act*, 353.

8. Courts are split on whether a state can acquire personal jurisdiction over a defendant based solely on service of process made in Indian country that is located within the state's boundaries. Compare Francisco v. State, 556 P.2d 1 (Ariz.1976) (not valid), with State Securities, Inc. v. Anderson, 506 P.2d 786 (N.M. 1973) (service is valid). Courts are also split on whether a state court may enforce its judgments by attaching property located in Indian country. Compare Joe v. Marcum, 621 F.2d 358 (10th Cir.1980) (state cannot execute a judgment by garnishing the wages of an Indian earned on a reservation) with Little Horn State Bank v. Stops, 555 P.2d 211, 212 (Mont. 1976), *cert. denied*, 431 U.S. 924 (1977), ("any court having jurisdiction to render a judgment also has the power to enforce that judgment through any order or writ necessary to carry its judgment into effect").

9. Indian tribes have sovereign immunity and cannot be sued without their consent in state or federal court except where Congress has clearly removed immunity. See Santa Clara Pueblo v. Martinez, 436 U.S. 49, 58–59 (1978). Thus, if a customer is injured while gambling at an Indian casino, she may not sue the Tribe in state or federal court without the Tribe's consent. See Cohen v. Little Six, Inc., 543 N.W.2d 376 (Minn. App. 1996), *aff'd without opinion*, 561 N.W.2d 889 (Minn.1997). Compare this with *Nevada v. Hall*, supra at 498. Why can states be sued in the courts of another state but not Indian tribes?

Iowa Mutual Insurance Co. v. LaPlante

Supreme Court of the United States, 1987.
480 U.S. 9, 107 S.Ct. 971, 94 L.Ed.2d 10.

JUSTICE MARSHALL delivered the opinion of the Court. Petitioner, an Iowa insurance company, brought this action in Federal District Court against members of the Blackfeet Indian Tribe resident on the Tribe's reservation in Montana. The asserted basis for federal jurisdiction was diversity of citizenship. At the time the action was initiated, proceedings involving the same parties and based on the same dispute were pending before the Blackfeet Tribal Court. The question before us is whether a federal court may exercise diversity jurisdiction before the tribal court system has an opportunity to determine its own jurisdiction.

I. Respondent Edward LaPlante, a member of the Blackfeet Indian Tribe, was employed by the Wellman Ranch Company, a Montana corporation. The Wellman Ranch is located on the Blackfeet Indian Reservation and is owned by members of the Wellman family, who are also Blackfeet Indians residing on the Reservation. Petitioner Iowa Mutual Insurance Company was the insurer of the Wellman Ranch and its individual owners.

On May 3, 1982, LaPlante was driving a cattle truck within the boundaries of the Reservation. While proceeding up a hill, he lost control of the vehicle and was injured when the truck "jackknifed." Agents of Midland Claims Service, Inc., an independent insurance adjuster which represented Iowa Mutual in this matter, attempted unsuccessfully to settle LaPlante's claim. In May 1983, LaPlante and his wife Verla, also a Blackfeet Indian, filed a complaint in the Blackfeet Tribal Court. The complaint stated two causes of action: the first named the Wellman Ranch and its individual owners as defendants and sought compensation for LaPlante's personal injuries and his wife's loss of consortium; the second alleged a claim for compensatory and punitive damages against Iowa Mutual and Midland Claims for bad-faith refusal to settle.

Iowa Mutual and Midland Claims moved to dismiss for failure properly to allege Tribal Court jurisdiction and for lack of jurisdiction over the subject matter of the suit. The Tribal Court dismissed the complaint for failure to allege the factual basis of the court's jurisdiction, but it allowed the LaPlantes to amend their complaint to allege facts from which jurisdiction could be determined. The Tribal Court also addressed the issue of subject-matter jurisdiction, holding that the Tribe could regulate the conduct of non-Indians engaged in commercial relations with Indians on the reservation. Since the Tribe's adjudicative jurisdiction was coextensive with its legislative jurisdiction, the court concluded that it would have jurisdiction over the suit. Although the Blackfeet Tribal Code establishes a Court of Appeals, [cit.] it does not allow interlocutory appeals from jurisdictional rulings. Accordingly, appellate review of the Tribal Court's jurisdiction can occur only after a decision on the merits.

Subsequent to the Tribal Court's jurisdictional ruling, Iowa Mutual filed the instant action in Federal District Court against the LaPlantes, the Wellmans, and the Wellman Ranch Company, alleging diversity of citizenship under 28 U.S.C. § 1332 as the basis for federal jurisdiction. Iowa Mutual sought a declaration that it had no duty to defend or indemnify the Wellmans or the Ranch because the injuries sustained by the LaPlantes fell outside the coverage of the applicable insurance policies. The LaPlantes moved to dismiss the action for lack of subject-matter jurisdiction and the District Court granted the motion. * * * The District Court noted that the Montana state courts lack jurisdiction over comparable suits filed by Montana insurance companies;[4] it indicated that its jurisdiction was similarly precluded because, based on its reading of Woods v. Interstate Realty Co., 337 U.S. 535, 538 (1949), federal courts sitting in diversity operate solely as adjuncts to the state court system. The District Court held that "[o]nly if the Blackfeet Tribe decides not to exercise its exclusive jurisdiction ... would this court be free to entertain" the

---

4. A federal statute, [cit.] originally allowed States to assume civil jurisdiction over reservation Indians without tribal consent, but Montana did not take such action with respect to the Blackfeet Tribe. [cit.] Tribal consent is now a prerequisite to the assumption of jurisdiction, see 25 U.S.C. § 1326, and the Blackfeet Tribe has not consented to state jurisdiction. Petitioner does not contend that the Montana state courts would have jurisdiction over the dispute. [cit.]

case under 28 U.S.C. § 1332.

The Court of Appeals for the Ninth Circuit affirmed the District Court's order. [cit.] It found [cit.] [the district court's holding] to be consistent with this Court's intervening decision in National Farmers Union Ins. Cos. v. Crow Tribe, 471 U.S. 845 (1985). * * * We granted certiorari. [cit.]

II. We have repeatedly recognized the Federal Government's longstanding policy of encouraging tribal self-government. [cit.] This policy reflects the fact that Indian tribes retain "attributes of sovereignty over both their members and their territory," [cit.] to the extent that sovereignty has not been withdrawn by federal statute or treaty. The federal policy favoring tribal self-government operates even in areas where state control has not been affirmatively pre-empted by federal statute. "[A]bsent governing Acts of Congress, the question has always been whether the state action infringed on the right of reservation Indians to make their own laws and be ruled by them." *Williams v. Lee.*

Tribal courts play a vital role in tribal self-government, [cit.] and the Federal Government has consistently encouraged their development. Although the criminal jurisdiction of the tribal courts is subject to substantial federal limitation, see Oliphant v. Suquamish Indian Tribe, 435 U.S. 191 (1978), their civil jurisdiction is not similarly restricted. [cit.] If state-court jurisdiction over Indians or activities on Indian lands would interfere with tribal sovereignty and self-government, the state courts are generally divested of jurisdiction as a matter of federal law. [cit.]

A federal court's exercise of jurisdiction over matters relating to reservation affairs can also impair the authority of tribal courts, as we recognized in *National Farmers Union*.[7] In that case, a Tribal Court had entered a default judgment against a school district for injuries suffered by an Indian child on school property. The school district and its insurer sought injunctive relief in District Court, invoking 28 U.S.C. § 1331 as the basis for federal jurisdiction and claiming that the Tribal Court lacked jurisdiction over non-Indians. The District Court agreed and entered an injunction against execution of the Tribal Court's judgment, but the Court of Appeals reversed, holding that the District Court lacked jurisdiction. We refused to foreclose tribal court jurisdiction over a civil dispute involving a non-Indian. [cit.] We concluded that, although the existence of tribal court jurisdiction presented a federal question within the scope of 28 U.S.C. § 1331, considerations of comity direct that tribal remedies be exhausted before the question is addressed by the District Court. [cit.] Promotion of tribal self-government and self-determination required that the Tribal Court have "the first opportunity to evaluate the factual and legal bases for the challenge" to its jurisdiction. [cit.] We remanded the case to the District Court to determine whether the federal action should be dismissed or stayed pending exhaustion of the remedies available in the tribal court system.[8] [cit.]

---

7. See also Santa Clara Pueblo v. Martinez, 436 U.S. 49, 60 (1978) (providing a federal forum for claims arising under the Indian Civil Rights Act interferes with tribal autonomy and self-government).

8. As the Court's directions on remand in *National Farmers Union* indicate, the exhaustion rule enunciated in *National Farmers Union* did not deprive the federal courts of subject-matter jurisdiction. Exhaustion is required as a matter of comity, not as a jurisdictional prerequisite. In this respect, the rule is analogous to principles of abstention articulated in Colorado River Water Conservation Dist. v. United States, 424 U.S. 800 (1976): even where there is concurrent jurisdiction in both the state and federal courts, deference to state proceedings renders it appropriate for the federal courts to decline jurisdiction in certain circumstances. In *Colorado River*, as here, strong federal policy concerns favored resolution in the nonfederal forum. [cit.]

Although petitioner alleges that federal jurisdiction in this case is based on diversity of citizenship, rather than the existence of a federal question, the exhaustion rule announced in *National Farmers Union* applies here as well. Regardless of the basis for jurisdiction, the federal policy supporting tribal self-government directs a federal court to stay its hand in order to give the tribal court a "full opportunity to determine its own jurisdiction." [cit.] In diversity cases, as well as federal-question cases, unconditional access to the federal forum would place it in direct competition with the tribal courts, thereby impairing the latter's authority over reservation affairs. [cit.] Adjudication of such matters by any nontribal court also infringes upon tribal lawmaking authority, because tribal courts are best qualified to interpret and apply tribal law.

As *National Farmers Union* indicates, proper respect for tribal legal institutions requires that they be given a "full opportunity" to consider the issues before them and "to rectify any errors." [cit.] The federal policy of promoting tribal self-government encompasses the development of the entire tribal court system, including appellate courts. At a minimum, exhaustion of tribal remedies means that tribal appellate courts must have the opportunity to review the determinations of the lower tribal courts. In this case, the Tribal Court has made an initial determination that it has jurisdiction over the insurance dispute, but Iowa Mutual has not yet obtained appellate review, as provided by the Tribal Code, ch. 1, § 5. Until appellate review is complete, the Blackfeet Tribal Courts have not had a full opportunity to evaluate the claim and federal courts should not intervene.

Petitioner argues that the statutory grant of diversity jurisdiction overrides the federal policy of deference to tribal courts. We do not agree. Although Congress undoubtedly has the power to limit tribal court jurisdiction,[9] we do not read the general grant of diversity jurisdiction to have implemented such a significant intrusion on tribal sovereignty, any more than we view the grant of federal-question jurisdiction, the statutory basis for the intrusion on tribal jurisdiction at issue in *National Farmers Union*, to have done so. The diversity statute, 28 U.S.C. § 1332, makes no reference to Indians and nothing in the legislative history suggests any intent to render inoperative the established federal policy promoting tribal self-government. Tribal courts in the Anglo-American mold were virtually unknown in 1789 when Congress first authorized diversity jurisdiction, see Judiciary Act of 1789, § 11, 1 Stat. 78-79; and the original statute did not manifest a congressional intent to limit tribal sovereignty. Moreover, until the late 19th century, most Indians were neither considered citizens of the States in which their reservation was located, nor regarded as citizens of a foreign State, see, e.g., [cit.]; Elk v. Wilkins, 112 U.S. 94, 102-103 (1884), so a suit to which Indians were parties would not have satisfied the statutory requirements for diversity jurisdiction.[10] Congress has amended the diversity statute several times since the development of tribal judicial systems, but it has never expressed any intent to limit the civil jurisdiction of the tribal courts.

---

9. "Congress has plenary authority to limit, modify or eliminate the powers of local self-government which the tribes otherwise possess." *Santa Clara Pueblo v. Martinez*, supra, at 56. See generally F. Cohen, Handbook of Federal Indian Law 207–216 (1982).

10. In 1924, Congress declared that all Indians born in the United States are United States citizens, see Act of June 2, 1924, ch. 233, 43 Stat. 253, now codified at 8 U.S.C. § 1401, and, therefore, under the Fourteenth Amendment, Indians are citizens of the States in which they reside. There is no indication that this grant of citizenship was intended to affect federal protection of tribal self-government.

Tribal authority over the activities of non-Indians on reservation lands is an important part of tribal sovereignty. See Montana v. United States, 450 U.S. 544, 565–566 (1981); Washington v. Confederated Tribes of Colville Indian Reservation, 447 U.S. 134, 152-153 (1980); [cit.]. Civil jurisdiction over such activities presumptively lies in the tribal courts unless affirmatively limited by a specific treaty provision or federal statute. "Because the Tribe retains all inherent attributes of sovereignty that have not been divested by the Federal Government, the proper inference from silence ... is that the sovereign power ... remains intact." [cit.] In the absence of any indication that Congress intended the diversity statute to limit the jurisdiction of the tribal courts, we decline petitioner's invitation to hold that tribal sovereignty can be impaired in this fashion.

Petitioner also contends that the policies underlying the grant of diversity jurisdiction—protection against local bias and incompetence—justify the exercise of federal jurisdiction in this case. We have rejected similar attacks on tribal court jurisdiction in the past. See, e.g., *Santa Clara Pueblo v. Martinez*. The alleged incompetence of tribal courts is not among the exceptions to the exhaustion requirement established in *National Farmers Union*,[12] and would be contrary to the congressional policy promoting the development of tribal courts. Moreover, the Indian Civil Rights Act, 25 U.S.C. § 1302, provides non-Indians with various protections against unfair treatment in the tribal courts.

Although petitioner must exhaust available tribal remedies before instituting suit in federal court, the Blackfeet Tribal Courts' determination of tribal jurisdiction is ultimately subject to review. If the Tribal Appeals Court upholds the lower court's determination that the tribal courts have jurisdiction, petitioner may challenge that ruling in the District Court. See *National Farmers Union*. Unless a federal court determines that the Tribal Court lacked jurisdiction, however, proper deference to the tribal court system precludes relitigation of issues raised by the LaPlantes' bad-faith claim and resolved in the Tribal Courts.

III. The Court of Appeals correctly recognized that *National Farmers Union* requires that the issue of jurisdiction be resolved by the Tribal Courts in the first instance. However, the court should not have affirmed the District Court's dismissal for lack of subject-matter jurisdiction. Accordingly, we reverse and remand for further proceedings consistent with this opinion.[14]

It is so ordered.

JUSTICE STEVENS, concurring in part and dissenting in part.

* * *

* * * I see no reason why tribal courts should receive more deference on the merits than state courts. It is not unusual for a state court and a federal court to have concurrent jurisdiction over the same dispute. In some such cases it is appropriate

---

12. In *National Farmers Union*, we indicated that exhaustion would not be required where "an assertion of tribal jurisdiction 'is motivated by a desire to harass or is conducted in bad faith,' or where the action is patently violative of express jurisdictional prohibitions, or where exhaustion would be futile because of the lack of adequate opportunity to challenge the court's jurisdiction." [cit.] While petitioner contends that tribal court jurisdiction over outsiders "is questionable at best," [cit.] it does not argue that the present action is "patently violative of express jurisdictional prohibitions," nor do we understand it to invoke any of the other exceptions enumerated in *National Farmers Union*.

14. On remand, the District Court should consider whether, on the facts of this case, the federal action should be stayed pending further Tribal Court proceedings or dismissed under the prudential rule announced in *National Farmers Union*.

for the federal court to stay its hand until the state-court litigation has terminated, see, e.g., Colorado River Water Conservation District v. United States, 424 U.S. 800, 813-816 (1976), but as we have consistently held, "[a]bstention from the exercise of federal jurisdiction is the exception, not the rule." Id. The mere fact that a case involving the same issue is pending in another court has never been considered a sufficient reason to excuse a federal court from performing its duty "to adjudicate a controversy properly before it." [cit.] On the contrary, as between state and federal courts, the general rule is that "the pendency of an action in the state court is no bar to proceedings concerning the same matter in the Federal court having jurisdiction...." [cit.] In this case a controversy concerning the coverage of the insurance policy issued to respondents Wellman Ranch Co. and its owners by petitioner is properly before the Federal District Court.[1] That controversy raises no question concerning the jurisdiction of the Blackfeet Tribal Court.

Adherence to this doctrine, by allowing the declaratory judgment action to proceed in District Court, would imply no disrespect for the Blackfeet Tribe or for its judiciary. It would merely avoid what I regard as the anomalous suggestion that the sovereignty of an Indian tribe is in some respects greater than that of the State of Montana, for example.

Until today, we have never suggested that an Indian tribe's judicial system is entitled to a greater degree of deference than the judicial system of a sovereign State. Today's opinion, however, requires the federal court to avoid adjudicating the merits of a controversy also pending in Tribal Court although it could reach those merits if the case instead were pending in state court. Thus, although I of course agree with the Court's conclusion that the Federal District Court had subject-matter jurisdiction over the case, I respectfully dissent from its exhaustion holding.

Notes and Questions

1. In *Colorado River*, (discussed in n.8 of *Iowa Mutual*), the Court held that where parallel cases are pending in both state and federal courts, the federal court may abstain to avoid duplication only in "exceptional circumstances." See also Moses H. Cone Memorial Hospital v. Mercury Construction Corp., 460 U.S. 1, 14-16 (1983). Should the rule be different when the overlapping case is pending in a tribal court?

2. The exhaustion requirement does not apply in all cases. As the Court explained in *National Farmers Union*:

We do not suggest that exhaustion would be required where an assertion of tribal jurisdiction "is motivated by a desire to harass or is conducted in bad faith," [cit.] or where the action is patently violative of express jurisdictional prohibitions, or where exhaustion would be futile because of the lack of adequate opportunity to challenge the court's jurisdiction.

471 U.S. at 856 n.21. For example, in Nevada v. Hicks, 533 U.S. 353 (2001), the Court held a state official who was sued in tribal court was not required to exhaust tribal remedies before seeking relief in federal court. The Court acknowledged that the case did not fall within the exceptions to exhaustion set out in National Farmers

---

1. The Court seems to assume that the merits of this controversy are governed by "tribal law." [cit.] I express no opinion on this choice-of-law question.

Union but held that "[s]ince it is clear * * * that tribal courts lack jurisdiction over state officials for causes of action relating to their performance of official duties, adherence to the tribal exhaustion requirement in such cases 'would serve no purpose other than delay,' and is therefore unnecessary." Id. at 414.

3. Does the exhaustion requirement apply where the issue is solely a question of federal law (e.g., whether the federal Age Discrimination in Employment Act applies on Indian reservations)? Several courts have held that the exhaustion requirement does not apply to pure questions of federal law. See, e.g., Burlington Northern R.R. v. Blackfeet Tribe, 924 F.2d 899, 901 n.2 (9th Cir.1991), *cert. denied*, 505 U.S. 1212 (1992); Myrick v. Devils Lake Sioux Mfg. Corp., 718 F.Supp. 753 (D.N.D.1989). But is not there value in jurisdictional redundancy even as to questions of federal law? Consider the argument of Professor Pommersheim:

> Constitutional decision making in tribal courts can also potentially perform other important functions, in addition to its central task of illuminating the distinctive markers of tribal sovereignty. These functions include delineating the relationship of tribal courts to federal courts, providing tribal interpretations of federal standards, and incorporating international legal norms into tribal jurisprudence.

Pommersheim, *A Path Near the Clearing*, 410.

4. In *Iowa Mutual*, the Court required exhaustion of tribal remedies, but it also made clear that a federal forum would ultimately be available. However, in some contexts the Court has suggested that the availability of any federal forum may unduly interfere with tribal sovereignty. The Indian Civil Rights Act of 1968 (ICRA), 25 U.S.C. § 1302(8) provides that "[n]o Indian tribe in exercising powers of self-government shall * * * deny to any person within its jurisdiction the equal protection of its laws." In Santa Clara Pueblo v. Martinez, 436 U.S. 49 (1978), a female member of the Santa Clara Pueblo brought suit in federal court seeking declaratory and injunctive relief against enforcement of a tribal ordinance denying tribal membership to children of female members who marry outside the tribe, while extending membership to children of male members who marry outside the tribe. The Supreme Court dismissed the claim holding there was no private cause of action in federal court to secure enforcement of the ICRA. The Court expressed concern that "providing a federal forum for issues arising under [the ICRA] constitutes an interference with tribal autonomy and self-government beyond that created by the change in substantive law itself. * * * [R]esolution in a foreign forum of intratribal disputes of a * * * 'public' character, such as the one in this case, cannot help but unsettle a tribal government's ability to maintain authority." Id. at 59-60. The Court further noted:

> By not exposing tribal officials to the full array of federal remedies available to redress actions of federal and state officials, Congress may also have considered that resolution of statutory issues under § 1302 [of the ICRA], and particularly those issues likely to arise in a civil context, will frequently depend on questions of tribal tradition and custom which tribal forums may be in a better position to evaluate than federal courts.

Id. at 71.

5. In Martin v. Hunter's Lessee, 14 U.S. (1 Wheat.) 304 (1816), the Supreme Court held that the United States Supreme Court has authority to review state court decisions concerning federal law. The Court rejected the argument that no federal

review was necessary because the states were bound by federal law under the Supremacy Clause. The Court also noted that since Congress had legislative authority over the states, review of judicial decisions "is not a higher or more dangerous act of sovereign power." Id. at 344. Should Indian tribes be treated differently than states in this regard?

Martin, involved direct review by means of an appeal. *Iowa Mutual* in contrast involved a new action brought in federal court. Should tribal court decisions involving matters of federal law be appealable to the United States Supreme Court? Would such cases fall within the Supreme Court's Art. III jurisdiction? Is a decision of a tribal court interpreting United States federal law any different than the decision of a Finnish court on such a matter?

6. The Court in *Iowa Mutual* notes that tribes' criminal jurisdiction is narrower than tribes' civil jurisdiction. In Oliphant v. Suquamish Indian Tribe, 435 U.S. 191 (1978), the Court held that the Suquamish Tribe did not have criminal jurisdiction over a non-Indian for conduct that occurred on the tribe's reservation. The Court held that "Indians do not have criminal jurisdiction over non-Indians absent affirmative delegation of such power by Congress." Id. at 208. The Court explained that although Indian tribes "retain elements of 'quasi-sovereign' authority," they "are prohibited from exercising both those powers of autonomous states that are expressly terminated by Congress *and* those powers '*inconsistent with their status.*'" Id. (emphasis in original). Congress had not expressly revoked criminal jurisdiction over non-Indians, but the Court found that such power did not exist, explaining:

> But from the formation of the Union and the adoption of the Bill of Rights, the United States has manifested an equally great solicitude that its citizens be protected by the United States from unwarranted intrusions on their personal liberty. The power of the United States to try and criminally punish is an important manifestation of the power to restrict personal liberty. By submitting to the overriding sovereignty of the United States, Indian tribes therefore necessarily give up their power to try non-Indian citizens of the United States except in a manner acceptable to Congress. This principle would have been obvious a century ago when most Indian tribes were characterized by a "want of fixed laws [and] of competent tribunals of justice." [cit.] It should be no less obvious today, even though present-day Indian tribal courts embody dramatic advances over their historical antecedents.

Id. at 210. Why does it follow that by submitting to the overriding sovereignty of the United States, tribes "necessarily" gave up criminal jurisdiction? The same is not true of states. How is the sovereignty of states different from the sovereignty of tribes?

7. In Duro v. Reina, 495 U.S. 676 (1990), the Supreme Court held that an Indian tribe may not assert criminal jurisdiction over an Indian who is a member of a different tribe. The Court noted that the Indian non-member's "relations with this Tribe are the same as the non-Indian's in *Oliphant*." Id. at 688. The Court then stated:

> We hesitate to adopt a view of tribal sovereignty that would single out another group of citizens, nonmember Indians, for trial by political bodies that do not include them. As full citizens, Indians share in the territorial and political sovereignty of the United States. The retained sovereignty of the tribe is but a recognition of certain additional authority the tribes maintain over Indians who

consent to be tribal members.

Id. at 693. Following *Duro*, Congress statutorily granted Indian tribes criminal jurisdiction over Indians who are not members of the tribe. 25 U.S.C. § 1301. It did not grant criminal jurisdiction over non-Indians. Is this statute constitutional? Can Congress discriminate between Indians and non-Indians in this context? Cf. Morton v. Mancari, 417 U.S. 535, 553 n.24 (1974) (upholding employment preferences for Indians at Bureau of Indian Affairs because the preference "is political rather than racial in nature").

2. Tribal Legislative Jurisdiction

Strate v. A–1 Contractors
Supreme Court of the United States, 1997.
520 U.S. 438, 117 S.Ct. 1404, 137 L.Ed.2d 661.

JUSTICE GINSBURG delivered the opinion of the Court. This case concerns the adjudicatory authority of tribal courts over personal injury actions against defendants who are not tribal members. Specifically, we confront this question: When an accident occurs on a portion of a public highway maintained by the State under a federally granted right-of-way over Indian reservation land, may tribal courts entertain a civil action against an allegedly negligent driver and the driver's employer, neither of whom is a member of the tribe?

Such cases, we hold, fall within state or federal regulatory and adjudicatory governance; tribal courts may not entertain claims against nonmembers arising out of accidents on state highways, absent a statute or treaty authorizing the tribe to govern the conduct of nonmembers on the highway in question. We express no view on the governing law or proper forum when an accident occurs on a tribal road within a reservation.

I. In November 1990, petitioner Gisela Fredericks and respondent Lyle Stockert were involved in a traffic accident on a portion of a North Dakota state highway running through the Fort Berthold Indian Reservation. The highway strip crossing the reservation is a 6.59-mile stretch of road, open to the public, affording access to a federal water resource project. North Dakota maintains the road under a right-of-way granted by the United States to the State's Highway Department; the right-of-way lies on land held by the United States in trust for the Three Affiliated Tribes (Mandan, Hidatsa, and Arikara) and their members.

The accident occurred when Fredericks' automobile collided with a gravel truck driven by Stockert and owned by respondent A–1 Contractors, Stockert's employer. A–1 Contractors, a non-Indian-owned enterprise with its principal place of business outside the reservation, was at the time under a subcontract with LCM Corporation, a corporation wholly owned by the Tribes, to do landscaping work related to the construction of a tribal community building. A–1 Contractors performed all work under the subcontract within the boundaries of the reservation. The record does not show whether Stockert was engaged in subcontract work at the time of the accident. Neither Stockert nor Fredericks is a member of the Three Affiliated Tribes or an Indian. Fredericks, however, is the widow of a deceased member of the Tribes and has five adult children who are tribal members.

Fredericks sustained serious injuries in the accident and was hospitalized for 24 days. In May 1991, she sued respondents A–1 Contractors and Stockert, as well as A–1 Contractors' insurer, in the Tribal Court for the Three Affiliated Tribes of the Fort Berthold Reservation. In the same lawsuit, Fredericks' five adult children filed a loss-of-consortium claim. Together, Fredericks and her children sought damages exceeding $13 million. [cit.]

Respondents and the insurer made a special appearance in the Tribal Court to contest that court's personal and subject-matter jurisdiction. The Tribal Court ruled that it had authority to adjudicate Gisela Fredericks' case, and therefore denied respondents' motion to dismiss the action. [cit.] Respondents appealed the Tribal Court's jurisdictional ruling to the Northern Plains Intertribal Court of Appeals, which affirmed. [cit.] Thereafter, pursuant to the parties' stipulation, the Tribal Court dismissed the insurer from the suit. [cit.]

Before Tribal Court proceedings resumed, respondents commenced this action in the United States District Court for the District of North Dakota. Naming as defendants Fredericks, her adult children, the Tribal Court, and Tribal Judge William Strate, respondents sought a declaratory judgment that, as a matter of federal law, the Tribal Court lacked jurisdiction to adjudicate Fredericks' claims. The respondents also sought an injunction against further proceedings in the Tribal Court. [cit.]

Relying particularly on this Court's decisions in *National Farmers Union Ins. Cos.* v. *Crow Tribe*, and *Iowa Mut. Ins. Co.* v. *LaPlante*, the District Court determined that the Tribal Court had civil jurisdiction over Fredericks' complaint against A–1 Contractors and Stockert; accordingly, on cross-motions for summary judgment, the District Court dismissed the action. [cit.] On appeal, a divided panel of the United States Court of Appeals for the Eighth Circuit affirmed. [cit.] The Eighth Circuit granted rehearing en banc and, in an 8-to-4 decision, reversed the District Court's judgment. [cit.] The Court of Appeals concluded that our decision in Montana v. United States, 450 U.S. 544 (1981), was the controlling precedent, and that, under *Montana*, the Tribal Court lacked subject-matter jurisdiction over the dispute.[4]

We granted certiorari, [cit.], and now affirm.

II. Our case law establishes that, absent express authorization by federal statute or treaty, tribal jurisdiction over the conduct of nonmembers exists only in limited circumstances. In Oliphant v. Suquamish Tribe, 435 U.S. 191 (1978), the Court held that Indian tribes lack criminal jurisdiction over non-Indians.[5] *Montana v. United States*, decided three years later, is the pathmarking case concerning tribal civil authority over nonmembers. *Montana* concerned the authority of the Crow Tribe to regulate hunting and fishing by non-Indians on lands within the Tribe's reservation owned in fee simple by non-Indians. The Court said in *Montana* that the restriction on tribal criminal jurisdiction recognized in *Oliphant* rested on principles that

---

4. Petitioner Fredericks has commenced a similar lawsuit in a North Dakota state court "to protect her rights against the running of the State's six-year statute of limitations." [cit.] Respondents assert that they have answered the complaint and "are prepared to proceed in that forum." Respondents also note, without contradiction, that the state forum "is physically much closer by road to the accident scene ... than [is] the tribal courthouse." [cit.]

5. In Duro v. Reina, 495 U.S. 676, 684–685 (1990), we held that Indian tribes also lack criminal jurisdiction over nonmember Indians. Shortly after our decision in *Duro*, Congress provided for tribal criminal jurisdiction over nonmember Indians. See 25 U.S.C. § 1301(2).

support a more "general proposition." [cit.] In the main, the Court explained, "the inherent sovereign powers of an Indian tribe"—those powers a tribe enjoys apart from express provision by treaty or statute—"do not extend to the activities of nonmembers of the tribe." [cit.] The *Montana* opinion added, however, that in certain circumstances, even where Congress has not expressly authorized it, tribal civil jurisdiction may encompass nonmembers:

> To be sure, Indian tribes retain inherent sovereign power to exercise some forms of civil jurisdiction over non-Indians on their reservations, even on non-Indian fee lands. A tribe may regulate, through taxation, licensing, or other means, the activities of nonmembers who enter consensual relationships with the tribe or its members, through commercial dealing, contracts, leases, or other arrangements. A tribe may also retain inherent power to exercise civil authority over the conduct of non-Indians on fee lands within its reservation when that conduct threatens or has some direct effect on the political integrity, the economic security, or the health or welfare of the tribe. [cit.]

The term "non-Indian fee lands," as used in this passage and throughout the *Montana* opinion, refers to reservation land acquired in fee simple by non-Indian owners. [cit.]

Montana thus described a general rule that, absent a different congressional direction, Indian tribes lack civil authority over the conduct of nonmembers on non-Indian land within a reservation, subject to two exceptions: The first exception relates to nonmembers who enter consensual relationships with the tribe or its members; the second concerns activity that directly affects the tribe's political integrity, economic security, health, or welfare. The *Montana* Court recognized that the Crow Tribe retained power to limit or forbid hunting or fishing by nonmembers on land still owned by or held in trust for the Tribe. [cit.] The Court held, however, that the Tribe lacked authority to regulate hunting and fishing by non-Indians on land within the Tribe's reservation owned in fee simple by non-Indians.[6] [cit.]

Petitioners and the United States as *amicus curiae* urge that *Montana* does not control this case. They maintain that the guiding precedents are *National Farmers* and *Iowa Mutual*, and that those decisions establish a rule converse to *Montana's*. Whatever *Montana* may instruct regarding *regulatory* authority, they insist, tribal courts retain *adjudicatory* authority in disputes over occurrences inside a reservation, even when the episode-in-suit involves nonmembers, unless a treaty or federal statute directs otherwise. Petitioners, further supported by the United States, argue, alternately, that *Montana* does not cover lands owned by, or held in trust for, a tribe

---

6. Montana's statement of the governing law figured prominently in Brendale v. Confederated Tribes and Bands of Yakima Nation, 492 U.S. 408 (1989), and in South Dakota v. Bourland, 508 U.S. 679 (1993). The Court held in *Brendale*, 6 to 3, that the Yakima Indian Nation lacked authority to zone nonmembers' land within an area of the Tribe's reservation open to the general public; almost half the land in the area was owned in fee by nonmembers. The Court also held, 5 to 4, that the Tribe retained authority to zone fee land in an area of the reservation closed to the general public. No opinion garnered a majority. Justice White, writing for four Members of the Court, concluded that, under *Montana*, the Tribe lacked authority to zone fee land in both the open and closed areas of the reservation. [cit.] Justice Stevens, writing for two Justices, concluded that the Tribe retained zoning authority over nonmember land only in the closed area. [cit.] Justice Blackmun, writing for three Justices, concluded that, under *Montana's* second exception, the Tribe retained authority to zone fee land in both the open and the closed areas. [cit.]

In *Bourland*, the Court considered whether the Cheyenne River Sioux Tribe could regulate hunting and fishing by non-Indians in an area within the Tribe's reservation, but acquired by the United States for the operation of a dam and a reservoir. We determined, dominantly, that no treaty or statute reserved to the Tribe regulatory authority over the area [cit.] and we left for resolution on remand the question whether either *Montana* exception applied. [cit.]

or its members. *Montana* holds sway, petitioners say, only with respect to alienated reservation land owned in fee simple by non-Indians. We address these arguments in turn.

A. We begin with petitioners' contention that *National Farmers* and *Iowa Mutual* broadly confirm tribal-court civil jurisdiction over claims against nonmembers arising from occurrences on any land within a reservation. We read our precedent differently. *National Farmers* and *Iowa Mutual*, we conclude, are not at odds with, and do not displace, *Montana*. Both decisions describe an exhaustion rule allowing tribal courts initially to respond to an invocation of their jurisdiction; neither establishes tribal-court adjudicatory authority, even over the lawsuits involved in those cases. [cit.]

National Farmers involved a federal-court challenge to a tribal court's jurisdiction over a personal injury action initiated on behalf of a Crow Indian minor against a Montana School District. The accident-in-suit occurred when the minor was struck by a motorcycle in an elementary school parking lot. The school occupied land owned by the State within the Crow Indian Reservation. [cit.] The School District and its insurer sought a federal-court injunction to stop proceedings in the Crow Tribal Court. [cit.] The District Court granted the injunction, but the Court of Appeals reversed, concluding that federal courts lacked subject-matter jurisdiction to entertain such a case. [cit.]

We reversed the Court of Appeals' judgment and held that federal courts have authority to determine, as a matter "arising under" federal law, see 28 U.S.C. § 1331, whether a tribal court has exceeded the limits of its jurisdiction. [cit.] We further held, however, that the federal suit was premature. Ordinarily, we explained, a federal court should stay its hand "until after the Tribal Court has had a full opportunity to determine its own jurisdiction." [cit.] Finding no cause for immediate federal court intervention,[7] we remanded the case, leaving initially to the District Court the question "[w]hether the federal action should be dismissed, or merely held in abeyance pending ... further Tribal Court proceedings." [cit.]

Petitioners underscore the principal reason we gave in *National Farmers* for the exhaustion requirement there stated. Tribal-court jurisdiction over non-Indians in criminal cases is categorically restricted under *Oliphant*, we observed, while in civil matters "the existence and extent of a tribal court's jurisdiction will require a careful examination of tribal sovereignty, the extent to which that sovereignty has been altered, divested, or diminished, as well as a detailed study of relevant statutes, Executive Branch policy as embodied in treaties and elsewhere, and administrative or judicial decisions." [cit.]

The Court's recognition in *National Farmers* that tribal courts have more extensive jurisdiction in civil cases than in criminal proceedings, and of the need to inspect relevant statutes, treaties, and other materials, does not limit *Montana*'s instruction. As the Court made plain in *Montana*, the general rule and exceptions there announced govern only in the absence of a delegation of tribal authority by treaty or statute. In *Montana* itself, the Court examined the treaties and legislation

---

7. The Court indicated in National Farmers that exhaustion is not an unyielding requirement: "We do not suggest that exhaustion would be required where an assertion of tribal jurisdiction 'is motivated by a desire to harass or is conducted in bad faith,' or where the action is patently violative of express jurisdictional prohibitions, or where exhaustion would be futile because of the lack of an adequate opportunity to challenge the court's jurisdiction." [cit.]

relied upon by the Tribe and explained why those measures did not aid the Tribe's case. [cit.] Only after and in light of that examination did the Court address the Tribe's assertion of "inherent sovereignty," and formulate, in response to that assertion, *Montana's* general rule and exceptions to it. In sum, we do not extract from *National Farmers* anything more than a prudential exhaustion rule, in deference to the capacity of tribal courts "to explain to the parties the precise basis for accepting [or rejecting] jurisdiction." [cit.]

Iowa Mutual involved an accident in which a member of the Blackfeet Indian Tribe was injured while driving a cattle truck within the boundaries of the reservation. [cit.] The injured member was employed by a Montana corporation that operated a ranch on reservation land owned by Blackfeet Indians residing on the reservation. [cit.] The driver and his wife, also a Tribe member, sued in the Blackfeet Tribal Court, naming several defendants: the Montana corporation that employed the driver; the individual owners of the ranch; the insurer of the ranch; and an independent insurance adjuster representing the insurer. [cit.] Over the objection of the insurer and the insurance adjuster—both companies not owned by members of the Tribe—the Tribal Court determined that it had jurisdiction to adjudicate the case. [cit.]

Thereafter, the insurer commenced a federal-court action against the driver, his wife, the Montana corporation, and the ranch owners. [cit.] Invoking federal jurisdiction based on the parties' diverse citizenship, see 28 U.S.C. § 1332, the insurer alleged that it had no duty to defend or indemnify the Montana corporation or the ranch owners because the injuries asserted by the driver and his wife fell outside the coverage of the applicable insurance policies. [cit.] The Federal District Court dismissed the insurer's action for lack of subject-matter jurisdiction, and the Court of Appeals affirmed. [cit.]

We reversed. Holding that the District Court had diversity-of-citizenship jurisdiction over the insurer's complaint, we remanded, as in *National Farmers*, for a determination whether "the federal action should be stayed pending further Tribal Court proceedings or dismissed." [cit.] The Court recognized in *Iowa Mutual* that the exhaustion rule stated in *National Farmers* was "prudential," not jurisdictional. [cit.] Respect for tribal self-government made it appropriate "to give the tribal court a 'full opportunity to determine its own jurisdiction.'" [cit.] That respect, the Court reasoned, was equally in order whether federal-court jurisdiction rested on § 1331 (federal question) or on § 1332 (diversity of citizenship). [cit.] Elaborating on the point, the Court stated:

> Tribal authority over the activities of non-Indians on reservation lands is an important part of tribal sovereignty. See Montana v. United States, 450 U.S. 544, 565-66 (1981); Washington v. Confederated Tribes of Colville Indian Reservation, 447 U.S. 134, 152-53 (1980); Fisher v. District Court [of Sixteenth Judicial Dist. of Mont.], 424 U.S. [382,] 387-89 (1976). Civil jurisdiction over such activities presumptively lies in the tribal courts unless affirmatively limited by a specific treaty provision or federal statute.... In the absence of any indication that Congress intended the diversity statute to limit the jurisdiction of the tribal courts, we decline petitioner's invitation to hold that tribal sovereignty can be impaired in this fashion. [cit.]

Petitioners and the United States fasten upon the Court's statement that "[c]ivil jurisdiction over such activities presumptively lies in the tribal courts." Read in context, however, this language scarcely supports the view that the *Montana* rule does not bear on tribal-court adjudicatory authority in cases involving nonmember defendants.

The statement stressed by petitioners and the United States was made in refutation of the argument that "Congress intended the diversity statute to limit the jurisdiction of the tribal courts." [cit.] The statement is preceded by three informative citations. The first citation points to the passage in *Montana* in which the Court advanced "the general proposition that the inherent sovereign powers of an Indian tribe do not extend to the activities of nonmembers of the tribe" [cit.] with two prime exceptions. [cit.] The case cited second is *Colville*, a decision the *Montana* Court listed as illustrative of the first *Montana* exception, applicable to "nonmembers who enter consensual relationships with the tribe or its members," [cit.]; the Court in *Colville* acknowledged inherent tribal authority to tax "non-Indians entering the reservation to engage in economic activity," [cit.]. The third case noted in conjunction with the *Iowa Mutual* statement is a decision the *Montana* Court cited in support of the second *Montana* exception, covering on-reservation activity of nonmembers bearing directly "on the political integrity, the economic security, or the health or welfare of the tribe." [cit.] The Court held in *Fisher* that a tribal court had exclusive jurisdiction over an adoption proceeding when all parties were members of the tribe and resided on its reservation. [cit.] State-court jurisdiction over such matters, the Court said, "plainly would interfere with the powers of self-government conferred upon the ... Tribe and exercised through the Tribal Court." [cit.] The Court observed in *Fisher* that state courts may not exercise jurisdiction over disputes arising out of on-reservation conduct--even over matters involving non-Indians--if doing so would "'infring[e] on the right of reservation Indians to make their own laws and be ruled by them.'" [cit.]

In light of the citation of *Montana*, *Colville*, and *Fisher*, the *Iowa Mutual* statement emphasized by petitioners does not limit the *Montana* rule. In keeping with the precedent to which *Iowa Mutual* refers, the statement stands for nothing more than the unremarkable proposition that, where tribes possess authority to regulate the activities of nonmembers, "[c]ivil jurisdiction over [disputes arising out of] such activities presumptively lies in the tribal courts." [cit.]

Recognizing that our precedent has been variously interpreted, we reiterate that *National Farmers* and *Iowa Mutual* enunciate only an exhaustion requirement, a "prudential rule," [cit.] based on comity [cit.]. These decisions do not expand or stand apart from *Montana's* instruction on "the inherent sovereign powers of an Indian tribe." [cit.] While *Montana* immediately involved regulatory authority, the Court broadly addressed the concept of "inherent sovereignty." [cit.] Regarding activity on non-Indian fee land within a reservation, *Montana* delineated—in a main rule and exceptions—the bounds of the power tribes retain to exercise "forms of civil jurisdiction over non-Indians." [cit.] As to nonmembers, we hold, a tribe's adjudicative jurisdiction does not exceed its legislative jurisdiction. Absent congressional direction enlarging tribal-court jurisdiction, we adhere to that understanding. Subject to controlling provisions in treaties and statutes, and the two exceptions identified in *Montana*, the civil authority of Indian tribes and their courts with respect to non-Indian fee lands generally "do[es] not extend to the activities of nonmembers of the tribe." [cit.]

B. We consider next the argument that *Montana* does not govern this case because the land underlying the scene of the accident is held in trust for the Three Affiliated Tribes and their members. Petitioners and the United States point out that in *Montana,* as in later cases following *Montana's* instruction—*Brendale v. Confederated Tribes* and *Bands of Yakima Nation,* and South Dakota v. Bourland, 508 U.S. 679 (1993) * * *—the challenged tribal authority related to nonmember activity on alienated, non-Indian reservation land. We "can readily agree," in accord with *Montana,* [cit.] that tribes retain considerable control over nonmember conduct on tribal land. On the particular matter before us, however, we agree with respondents: The right-of-way North Dakota acquired for the State's highway renders the 6.59-mile stretch equivalent, for nonmember governance purposes, to alienated, non-Indian land.

Congress authorized grants of rights-of-way over Indian lands in 1948 legislation. [cit.] A grant over land belonging to a tribe requires "consent of the proper tribal officials," § 324, and the payment of just compensation, § 325. The grant involved in this case was made, pursuant to the federal statute, in 1970. Its purpose was to facilitate public access to Lake Sakakawea, a federal water resource project under the control of the Army Corps of Engineers.

In the granting instrument, the United States conveyed to North Dakota "an easement for a right-of-way for the realignment and improvement of North Dakota State Highway No. 8 over, across and upon [specified] lands." [cit.] The grant provides that the State's "easement is subject to any valid existing right or adverse claim and is without limitation as to tenure, so long as said easement shall be actually used for the purpose ... specified." [cit.] The granting instrument details only one specific reservation to Indian landowners:

> The right is reserved to the Indian land owners, their lessees, successors, and assigns to construct crossings of the right-of-way at all points reasonably necessary to the undisturbed use and occupan[cy] of the premises affected by the right-of-way; such crossings to be constructed and maintained by the owners or lawful occupants and users of said lands at their own risk and said occupants and users to assume full responsibility for avoiding, or repairing any damage to the right-of-way, which may be occasioned by such crossings. [cit.]

Apart from this specification, the Three Affiliated Tribes expressly reserved no right to exercise dominion or control over the right-of-way.

Forming part of the State's highway, the right-of-way is open to the public, and traffic on it is subject to the State's control.[11] The Tribes have consented to, and received payment for, the State's use of the 6.59-mile stretch for a public highway. They have retained no gatekeeping right. So long as the stretch is maintained as part of the State's highway, the Tribes cannot assert a landowner's right to occupy and exclude. Cf. *Bourland* (regarding reservation land acquired by the United States for operation of a dam and a reservoir, Tribe's loss of "right of absolute and exclusive use and occupation ... implies the loss of regulatory jurisdiction over the use of the land by others"). We therefore align the right-of-way, for the purpose at hand, with land alienated to non-Indians. Our decision in *Montana,* accordingly, governs this case.

---

11. We do not here question the authority of tribal police to patrol roads within a reservation, including rights-of-way made part of a state highway, and to detain and turn over to state officers nonmembers stopped on the highway for conduct violating state law. [cit.]

III. Petitioners and the United States refer to no treaty or statute authorizing the Three Affiliated Tribes to entertain highway-accident tort suits of the kind Fredericks commenced against A–1 Contractors and Stockert. Rather, petitioners and the United States ground their defense of tribal-court jurisdiction exclusively on the concept of retained or inherent sovereignty. *Montana*, we have explained, is the controlling decision for this case. To prevail here, petitioners must show that Fredericks' tribal-court action against nonmembers qualifies under one of *Montana's* two exceptions.

The first exception to the *Montana* rule covers "activities of nonmembers who enter consensual relationships with the tribe or its members, through commercial dealing, contracts, leases, or other arrangements." [cit.] The tortious conduct alleged in Fredericks' complaint does not fit that description. The dispute, as the Court of Appeals said, is "distinctly non-tribal in nature." [cit.] It "arose between two non-Indians involved in [a] run-of-the-mill [highway] accident." [cit.] Although A–1 was engaged in subcontract work on the Fort Berthold Reservation, and therefore had a "consensual relationship" with the Tribes, "Gisela Fredericks was not a party to the subcontract, and the [T]ribes were strangers to the accident." [cit.]

Montana's list of cases fitting within the first exception, [cit.], indicates the type of activities the Court had in mind: *Williams v. Lee,* (declaring tribal jurisdiction exclusive over lawsuit arising out of on-reservation sales transaction between nonmember plaintiff and member defendants); Morris v. Hitchcock, 194 U.S. 384 (1904) (upholding tribal permit tax on nonmember-owned livestock within boundaries of the Chickasaw Nation); Buster v. Wright, 135 F. 947, 950 (C.A.8 1905) (upholding Tribe's permit tax on nonmembers for the privilege of conducting business within Tribe's borders; court characterized as "inherent" the Tribe's "authority ... to prescribe the terms upon which noncitizens may transact business within its borders"); *Colville* (tribal authority to tax on-reservation cigarette sales to nonmembers "is a fundamental attribute of sovereignty which the tribes retain unless divested of it by federal law or necessary implication of their dependent status"). Measured against these cases, the Fredericks-Stockert highway accident presents no "consensual relationship" of the qualifying kind.

The second exception to *Montana's* general rule concerns conduct that "threatens or has some direct effect on the political integrity, the economic security, or the health or welfare of the tribe." [cit.] Undoubtedly, those who drive carelessly on a public highway running through a reservation endanger all in the vicinity, and surely jeopardize the safety of tribal members. But if *Montana's* second exception requires no more, the exception would severely shrink the rule. Again, cases cited in *Montana* indicate the character of the tribal interest the Court envisioned.

The Court's statement of *Montana's* second exceptional category is followed by citation of four cases, [cit.]; each of those cases raised the question whether a State's (or Territory's) exercise of authority would trench unduly on tribal self-government. In two of the cases, the Court held that a State's exercise of authority would so intrude, and in two, the Court saw no impermissible intrusion.

The Court referred first to the decision recognizing the exclusive competence of a tribal court over an adoption proceeding when all parties belonged to the Tribe and resided on its reservation. See *Fisher.* Next, the Court listed a decision holding a tribal court exclusively competent to adjudicate a claim by a non-Indian merchant seeking payment from tribe members for goods bought on credit at an on-reservation store. See *Williams*. ("[A]bsent governing Acts of Congress, the question [of state-court jurisdiction over on-reservation conduct] has always been whether the state action infringed on the right of reservation Indians to make their own laws and be ruled by them."). Thereafter, the Court referred to two decisions dealing with objections to a county or territorial government's imposition of a property tax on non-Indian-owned livestock that grazed on reservation land; in neither case did the Court find a significant tribal interest at stake. See Montana Catholic Missions v. Missoula County, 200 U.S. 118, 128-29 (1906) ("the Indians' interest in this kind of property [livestock], situated on their reservations, was not sufficient to exempt such property, when owned by private individuals, from [state or territorial] taxation"); Thomas v. Gay, 169 U.S. 264, 273 (1898) ("[territorial] tax put upon the cattle of [non-Indian] lessees is too remote and indirect to be deemed a tax upon the lands or privileges of the Indians").

Read in isolation, the *Montana* rule's second exception can be misperceived. Key to its proper application, however, is the Court's preface: "Indian tribes retain their inherent power [to punish tribal offenders,] to determine tribal membership, to regulate domestic relations among members, and to prescribe rules of inheritance for members.... But [a tribe's inherent power does not reach] beyond what is necessary to protect tribal self-government or to control internal relations." [cit.] Neither regulatory nor adjudicatory authority over the state highway accident at issue is needed to preserve "the right of reservation Indians to make their own laws and be ruled by them." [cit.] The *Montana* rule, therefore, and not its exceptions, applies to this case.

Gisela Fredericks may pursue her case against A–1 Contractors and Stockert in the state forum open to all who sustain injuries on North Dakota's highway. Opening the Tribal Court for her optional use is not necessary to protect tribal self-government; and requiring A–1 and Stockert to defend against this common-place state highway accident claim in an unfamiliar court[13] is not crucial to "the political integrity, the economic security, or the health or welfare of the [Three Affiliated Tribes]." *Montana*.[14] [cit.]

For the reasons stated, the judgment of the Court of Appeals for the Eighth Circuit is

Affirmed.

Notes and Questions

1. In *A–1 Contractors*, the Court assumes that the Tribe's adjudicative jurisdiction does not exceed its legislative jurisdiction. Is the same true for states? Should tribes be treated differently than states in this regard?

2. The Court notes that "the inherent sovereign powers of an Indian tribe * * *

---

13. Within the federal system, when nonresidents are the sole defendants in a suit filed in state court, the defendants ordinarily may remove the case to federal court. See 28 U.S.C. § 1441.

14. When, as in this case, it is plain that no federal grant provides for tribal governance of nonmembers' conduct on land covered by *Montana's* main rule, it will be equally evident that tribal courts lack adjudicatory authority over disputes arising from such conduct. As in criminal proceedings, state or federal courts will be the only forums competent to adjudicate those disputes. See *National Farmers Union Ins. Cos. v. Crow Tribe*. Therefore, when tribal-court jurisdiction over an action such as this one is challenged in federal court, the otherwise applicable exhaustion requirement, [cit.] must give way, for it would serve no purpose other than delay. [cit.]

do not extend to the activities of nonmembers of the tribe." Why should this be so? Professor Frickey has observed that the Court's "baseline assumption seems to be that state jurisdiction over Indian and non-Indian alike is customary, fair, and efficient, while tribal responsibility concerning non-Indians is bizarre, unfair, and inefficiently overlapping with state authority." Frickey, *Age of Colonialism*, at 26.

3. The Court observes that after granting the state a right-of-way, the Tribe could no longer assert a landowner's right to "occupy and exclude." Why is this relevant in determining whether the Tribe can apply its laws to conduct occurring on the land? States can regulate conduct occurring within their borders regardless of who owns the land.

4. In Nevada v. Hicks, 533 U.S. 353 (2001), a state warden executed a search warrant at the home of a tribal member located on tribe-owned land within the reservation. The tribe member sued the warden in tribal court alleging tortious conduct as well as violations of 42 U.S.C. § 1983. After the tribal court upheld jurisdiction, the defendant brought a declaratory judgment in federal court. The Supreme Court held that the tribal court lacked jurisdiction over either claim. The Court reiterated that as to non-members, tribal adjudicatory jurisdiction does not exceed its legislative jurisdiction. It then held that although the conduct occurred on tribal land, regulatory authority was "not essential to tribal self-government or to internal relations." 533 U.S. at 364. In reaching this conclusion, the Court stressed the "State's inherent jurisdiction on reservations," noting that "State sovereignty does not end at a reservation's border." Id. at 361.

As to the § 1983 claim, the Court explained that tribal courts are not courts of general jurisdiction and that no provision of federal law specifically grants tribal courts jurisdiction over such claims. The Court further explained that tribal jurisdiction would create "anomalies" because a defendant could not remove the suit to federal courts. Would it be permissible for the courts of Canada to entertain a claim based on U.S. federal law. If so, why are tribal courts different?

5. Tribes may tax the commercial activities of both members and nonmembers conducted on tribal lands. See Merrion v. Jicarilla Apache Tribe, 455 U.S. 130 (1982); Washington v. Confederated Tribes of the Colville Indian Reservation, 447 U.S. 134, 152-54 (1980). However, tribal taxing authority is more limited on land located within a reservation but owned in fee by non-Indians. In Atkinson Trading Co. v. Shirley, 532 U.S. 645 (2001), the Supreme Court held that as to non-members on non-Indian fee land, a Tribe's taxing authority is limited to the exceptions set forth in Montana. The Tribe had argued that because it provided police, fire, and medical emergency services to hotel guests staying on non-Indian fee land the Tribe had a commercial relationship with the guests that allowed the Tribe to impose a room tax. The Court rejected this argument holding that "a nonmember's actual or potential receipt of tribal police, fire, and medical services does not create the requisite connection." Id. at 655. The Court noted that in Strate "we held that the nonmembers had not consented to the Tribes' adjudicating authority by availing themselves of the benefits of tribal police protection while traveling within the reservation." Id. Compare this with Justice Brennan's opinion in *Burnham* in which he notes that "[b]y visiting the forum state, a transient defendant actually 'avail[s]' himself, of significant benefits provided by the State. His health and safety are guaranteed by the State's police, fire, and emergency medical services ***." Supra at 657.

States may also tax nonmembers on tribal land, see Cotton Petroleum Corp. v. New Mexico, 490 U.S. 163 (1989), but they cannot ordinarily tax member Indians on tribal lands. See Oklahoma Tax Commission v. Sac & Fox Nation, 508 U.S. 114 (1993); McClanahan v. Arizona State Tax Comm'n, 411 U.S. 164 (1973). In *Cotton Petroleum*, the Court upheld state power to tax oil and gas extracted by a non-Indian lessee of wells located on a reservation. The Court explained: "In this case * * *, all of Cotton's leases are located entirely within the borders of the State of New Mexico and also within the borders of the Jicarilla Apache Reservation." 490 U.S. at 188. Does the fact that land is located "within the borders" of the state mean that the state has sovereignty over the land? If New Mexico does have sovereignty over the land, why can it not tax Indians on the land?

6. The Federal Tort Claims Act provides that the government can be sued in federal court for certain claims "under circumstances where the limited States, if a private person, would be liable to the claimant in accordance with the law of the place where the act or omission occurred." 28 U.S.C. § 1346(b)(1). Suppose a claimant sues the federal government for an injury that occurs on an Indian reservation. Is tribal law "the law of the place" that should be applied? Compare Cheromiah v. United States, 55 F. Supp. 2d 1295 (D.N.M. 1999) (applying tribal law) with Louis v. United States, 54 F. Supp. 2d 1207, 1209-10 (D.N.M. 1999) (applying state law).

3. *Tribal Courts and Recognition of Judgments*

Section 1738 requires full faith and credit to the judgments of a "court of any * * * State, Territory or Possession." Under this language, must state and federal courts give full faith and credit to the judgments of tribal courts? Similarly, § 1738's obligations apply to all courts "within the United States and its Territories and Possessions." Does the language require tribal courts to give full faith and credit to state judgments?

The Supreme Court has never squarely addressed these questions. In Santa Clara Pueblo v. Martinez, 436 U.S. 49 (1978), the Supreme Court observed in dicta, "Judgments of tribal courts, as to matters properly within their jurisdiction, have been regarded in some circumstances as entitled to full faith and credit in other courts." Id. at 66 n.21. Does this statement suggest that tribal courts do fall within § 1738, or does the use of the other phrase "in some circumstances" imply that tribal judgments are subject to different standards than state court judgments? Lower courts have split on whether they are required to give full faith and credit to judgments of tribal courts. Some courts have accorded tribal judgments full faith and credit, see Jim v. CIT Financial Services Corp., 533 P.2d 751 (N.M. 1975); Sheppard v. Sheppard, 655 P.2d 895 (Idaho,1982), while others have treated them as they would a judgment from another country and entitled only to comity. See Wilson v. Marchington, 127 F.3d 805, 807-808 (9th Cir. 1997), *cert. denied*, 523 U.S. 1074 (1998). Several states have enacted legislation requiring that their state courts give full faith and credit to tribal judgments, see, e.g., Wis.Stat. 806.245(1)(e)(1997 supp.); Wyo.Stat.Ann. 5-1-111(a)(iv) (Michie 1997), and the Indian Child Welfare Act, 25 U.S.C. § 1911(d), requires tribal, state and local courts to give full faith and credit to tribal judgments in Indian child custody proceedings. See generally Clinton, *Tribal Courts*, 897-921; Laurence, *The Enforcement of Judgments Across Indian Reservation Boundaries*,

589; Ragsdale, *Full Faith and Credit for Indian Tribes*, 133.

Regardless of how the current § 1738 is interpreted, Congress could amend that statute to bring tribal courts within its ambit. Would that be a good idea? Consider the following analysis:

A conclusion that tribal court judgments are entitled to full faith and credit under section 1738 may outwardly support the current theory of Indian self-determination. However, the court or commentator wishing to reach that result, for that reason, faces a dilemma. A conclusion that section 1738 includes Indian tribes must be based on the proposition that they are part of the United States' federal polity, while Indian self-determination is based on the proposition that they are *not* a part of that polity. In addition, the reciprocity required by section 1738 would tend to limit tribal flexibility which is an important part of the concept of self-determination and which may be needed to adequately protect the tribes' interests or those of its members.

Excluding Indian tribes from the operation of section 1738 does not mean that tribal judgments will be unenforceable in state or federal courts. A number of non-Indian court decisions have, directly or indirectly, enforced tribal court decisions despite an unwillingness to find that section 1738 requires that result. Application of principles of comity have resulted in numerous favorable decisions. Employing comity, rather than full faith and credit, should not be seen as somehow derogatory. Except where controlled by treaty, judgments of all truly foreign nations are subject to comity considerations. It would not seem that tribes, which claim sovereignty antecedent to and independent of that of the United States, should object to being treated on an equal footing with European or Asian nations which antedate and are independent of the United States.

Perhaps unfortunately, some non-Indian courts applying comity considerations may decline to enforce judgments of some tribal courts because of perceived inadequacies in those courts. Those inadequacies may be of two types: (1) use of a traditional tribal remedy not available in an "Anglo" court; or (2) procedural or qualitative deficiencies. Since state and federal courts may not have the powers or facilities to enforce the more traditional tribal remedies (which, in any event, may be ineffectual in non-Indian society), tribal judges and litigants will undoubtedly recognize the limited effect of such remedies and avoid them in situations which might require off-reservation enforcement. The perceived procedural and qualitative inadequacies of tribal courts can be overcome, but only by the tribes themselves and perhaps only with the surrender of some of the attributes which distinguish tribal courts from state courts.

If tribal courts continue to exercise jurisdiction only over those subject matters over which tribal jurisdiction has been historically supported, that is, actions between tribal members or concerning tribal benefits or property rights, the lack of enforceable full faith and credit for tribal court judgments does not create a significant problem. It is only when tribes and tribal courts act like non-Indian governments and courts and attempt to involuntarily affect the rights of nonmembers that problems arise.

Thus, as is usual in Indian law matters, the problem comes full circle-back to the fundamental question of the proper political, social and ideological relationship between Indian tribes and the other peoples and governments of the United States. That, of course, is not a justiciable issue.

Vetter, *Of Tribal Courts and "Territories"*, 269–70.

Question

The native population of the Hawaiian Islands has not been recognized by the federal government as an Indian tribe. There is a growing "sovereignty movement" among this native population. See generally Levy, *Native Hawaiian Land Rights*, 848; Nalcashima, *Native Hawaiians Consider Asking for Their Islands Back*, WASH. POST, Aug. 27, 1996, at A1.

Assume that some autonomy or self-governance is to be granted to this group. Consider what mechanisms might be used to recognize that autonomy. Could the group be granted some type of sovereign status without control over a delineated portion of land? If land is necessary, would it matter whether any or all of the governed population lived on that land? Would it be sufficient that the group owned an office building in Honolulu?

If the native group is granted some form of autonomy short of complete international independence, it will be necessary to allocate authority among the native group, the state and the federal governments. Should the primary allocational mechanism be choice of law, jurisdictional restrictions, or a combination of both? Are there cultural or social factors that may influence your analysis of any of these issues?

Table of Cases

The principal cases are in bold type.
Cases cited or discussed in the text are in roman type.
References are to pages.
Cases cited in principal cases or within quoted material are not included

Bibliography and Abbreviations

Restatements and ALI Projects; Conflicts Codifications;
International Conventions; and Academic Commentaries

(The use of *italics* denotes the abbreviations used in the text)

A. Restatements and ALI Projects

Complex Litigation Project: American Law Institute, Complex Litigation: Statutory Recommendations and Analysis (1994)

IJJ Project: American Law Institute, Project on International Jurisdiction and Judgments (Tent. Draft 4/14/2003)

Restatement: American Law Institute, Restatement of the Law: Conflict of Laws (1934)

Restatement (Second): American Law Institute, Restatement of the Law Second: Conflict of Laws 2d (1971)

Restatement of Judgments: American Law Institute, Restatement of the Law Second: Judgments 2d (1980)

Restatement (Third): American Law Institute, Restatement (Third) of Foreign Relations Law of the United States (1986)

B. Conflicts Codifications

Austrian codification: Federal Law of 15 June 1978 on Private International Law (Transl. by Palmer, 28 Am.J. Comp. L. 222, 234 (1980))

Benelux Convention: Uniform Law on Private International Law of 1969 (Transl. by Nadelmann, 18 Am. J. Comp. L. 407 (1970))

Bustamante Code: Convention on Private International Law of February 20, 1928

German codification: Federal Acts of 1986 and 1999 for the Revision of Private International Law (amending the Introductory Law to the Civil Code (EGBGB)) (Transl. by Wegen, 27 I.L.M. 1, 18 (1988), and Hay, 47 Am. J. Comp. L. 650 (1999))

Greek Civ. Code: Civil Code of 1940

Hungarian codification: Decree N. 3 on Private International Law of 1979 (Transl. by F. Gabor, 55 Tul. L. Rev. 63 (1980))

Italian codification: Law No. 218 of May 31, 1995, Reforming the Italian System of Private International Law (Transl. by Italian Ministry of Justice, 35 I.L.M. 760 (1996))

Louisiana codification: Louisiana Civil Code, arts. 3515-49 as amended by La. Act 923 of 1991

Oregon codification: O.R.S §§ 81-100 to 81-135, effective January 1, 2002.

Peruvian codification: Civil Code as Amended in 1984 (Transl. by Garro, 24 I.L.M. 997 (1985))

Polish codification: Act of Nov. 12, 1965 on Private International Law

Portuguese codification: Civil Code as Amended in 1966

Puerto Rico Draft Code: Puerto Rican Academy of Legislation and Jurisprudence, A Projet for the Codification of Puerto Rican Private International Law (Symeonides & von Mehren, Reporters, 1991)

Quebec codification: Quebec Civil Code as Amended in 1994

Spanish Civ. Code: Preliminary Title of the Civil Code as amended 9 July 1974 (Transl. in 21 Neth. Int'l. L. Rev. 367 (1974))

Swiss codification: Federal Statute of December 18, 1987 on Private International Law (Transl. by Cornu, Hankins & Symeonides, 37 Am. J. Comp. L. 193 (1989))

U.K. codification Private International Law (Miscellaneous Provisions Act) (c. 42), 8 Nov. 1995

Venezuelan codification: Private International Law Act of 6 August 1998, Gaceta Oficial N. 36.511 de 6 de agosto de 1998 (Transl. in 1 Ybk. Priv. Int'l L., 341 (1999))

C. International Conventions

1. Hague Conventions

Adoption: Hague Convention of 15 November 1965 on Jurisdiction, Applicable Law and Recognition of Decrees Relating to Adoptions

Agency: Hague Convention of 14 March 1978 on the Law Applicable to Agency

Child Abduction: Hague Convention of 25 October on the Civil Aspects of International Child Abduction

Divorce: Hague Convention of 1 June 1970 on the Recognition of Divorces and Legal Separations

Estates: Hague Convention of 1 August 1989 on the Law Applicable to the Estates of Deceased Persons

Evidence: Hague Convention of 18 March 1970 on the Taking of Evidence Abroad in Civil or Commercial Matters

Judgments: Hague Convention of 1 February 1971 on the Recognition and Enforcement of Foreign Judgments in Civil and Commercial Matters

Marriage: Hague Convention of 14 March 1978 on Celebration and Recognition of the Validity of Marriages

Matrimonial Regimes: Hague Convention of 14 March 1978 on the Law Applicable to Matrimonial Property Regimes

Products Liability: Hague Convention of 2 October

1973 on the Law Applicable to Products Liability

Sales: Hague Convention of 22 December 1986 on the Law Applicable to Contracts for the International Sale of Goods

Service of Process: Hague Convention of 15 November 1965 on the Service Abroad of Judicial and Extrajudicial Documents in Civil or Commercial Matters

Testaments: Hague Convention of 5 October 1961 on the Conflicts of Laws Relating to the Form of Testamentary Dispositions

Traffic Accidents: Hague Convention of 4 May 1971 on the Law Applicable to Traffic Accidents

Trust: Hague Convention of 1 July 1985 on the Law Applicable to Trusts and their Recognition

2. Other Conventions

Benelux: Benelux Treaty Concerning A Uniform Law on Private International Law (1969)

Brussels: Convention on Jurisdiction and the Enforcement of Judgments in Civil and Commercial Matters (1968)

Brussels II: Council Regulation (EC) No. 44/2001 of 22 Dec. 2000 on Jurisdiction and the Recognition and Enforcement of Judgments in Civil and Commercial Matters, [2001] O.J. L.12/1.

Lugano Convention: Convention on Jurisdiction and the Enforcement of Judgments in Civil and Commercial Matters (1988)

Rome Convention: [European Community] Convention on the Law Applicable to Contractual Obligations (1980)

Rome II: [European Union] Proposal for a Regulation of the European Parliament and the Council on the Law Applicable to Non-Contractual Obligations, 2003/0168(COD) (22.7.203)

D. Academic Commentaries

(The abbreviations used in the text consist of the author's surname and the part of the title that appears below in italics.)

ACKER, R.H., Choice-of-Law Questions in Cyberfraud, 1996 U.Chi. Legal F. 437

ADAMS, C., World-Wide Volkswagen v. Woodson --*The Rest of the Story*, 72 Neb. L. Rev. 1122, (1993)

ADLER, M.H., *If We Build it, Will They Come?*--The Need for a Multilateral Convention on the Recognition and Enforcement of Civil Monetary Judgments, 26 Law & Pol'y Int'l Bus. 79 (1994)

ALLEN, W. & O'HARA, E., Second Generation Law and Economics of Conflict of Laws: Baxter's Comparative Impairment and Beyond, 51 Stan. L. Rev. 1011 (1999)

ALTHOUSE, A., The Use of *Conspiracy Theory* to Establish In Personam Jurisdiction: A Due Process Analysis, 52 Fordham L. Rev. 234 (1983)

AMADO, J.D., Recognition and Enforcement of *Foreign Judgments in Latin American Countries*: An Overview and Update, 31 Va. J. Int'l L. 99 (1990)

AMERICAN BAR ASSOCIATION, *Global Cyberspace Jurisdiction* Project, 55 Bus. Law. 1801 (2000)

ARNOLD, R.S., *The Power of State Courts* to Enjoin Federal Officers, 73 Yale L. J. 1385 (1964)

ATWOOD, B., *Fighting Over Indian Children:* The Uses and Abuses of Jurisdictional Ambiguity, 36 U.C.L.A. L. Rev. 1051 (1989)

AUDIT, B., *Droit international privé*, 2d ed. (1997)

AUDIT, B., Le droit international privé français à la fin du vingtième siècle: Progrès ou recul? in Symeonides, "Private International Law at the End of the 20th Century: Progress or Regress?" 191 (2000)

AUDIT, B., Le caractère fonctionnel de la règle de conflit, 186 Recueil des Cours 219 (1985)

AUDIT, B., A Continental Lawyer Looks at Contemporary American Choice–of–Law Principles, 27 Am. J. Comp. L. 589 (1979)

BAADE, H.W., The Operation of Foreign Public Law, 30 Tex. Int'l L. J. 429 (1995)

BAADE, H.W., *Counter-Revolution* or Alliance for Progress? Reflections on Reading Cavers, The Choice-of-Law Process, 46 Tex. L. Rev. 141 (1967)

BAKER, G. B., Interstate Choice of Law and Early-American Constitutional Nationalism. An Essay on Joseph Story and the Comity of Errors: A Case Study in Conflict of Laws, 38 McGill L. J. 454 (1993)

BAKER, J., Respecting a State's Tort Law, while Continuing its Reach to that State, 31 Seton Hall L. Rev. 698 (2001)

BALLARINO, T., Diritto internazionale Privato (1996)

BALLARINO, T. Questions de droit international privé et dommages catastrophiques, 220 Recueil des Cours 289 (1990)

BASEDOW, J., International Antitrust: From Extraterritorial Application to Harmonization, 60 La. L. Rev. 1037 (2000)

BATIFFOL, H. & LAGARDE, P., Droit international privé (8th ed.1983) [*DIP*]

BATIFFOL, H., Le pluralisme des méthodes en droit international privé, 139 Recueil des Cours 75 (1973)

BATIFFOL, H., La loi applicable a la responsabilité du fait des produits, 62 Rev. critique 252 (1973)

BAXTER, W. F., *Choice of Law* and the Federal System, 16 Stan. L. Rev. 1 (1963)

BEALE, J.H., A Treatise on the *Conflict of Laws* (3 vols. 1935)

BEHR, V., *Punitive Damages in American and German Law*–Tendencies Towards Approximation of Apparently Irreconcilable Concepts. 78 Chi.-Kent L. Rev. 105 (2003).

BERNET, M. & ULMER, N.C., Recognition and Enforcement of *Foreign Civil Judgments in Switzerland*, 27 Int'l Law. 317 (1993)

BEITZKE, G., Les obligations delictuelles en droit international privé, 115 Recueil des Cours 67 (1965)

BLAIKIE, J., Foreign Torts and Choice of Law Flexibility, 1995 S.L.T. 23

BLIESENER, D.H., Fairness and Choice of Law: A Critique of the Political Rights-Based Approach to the Conflict of Laws, 42 Am. J. Comp. L. 687 (1994)

BODENHEIMER, E., The Need for a *Reorientation* in American Conflicts Law, 19 Hastings L. J. 731 (1978)

BODENHEIMER, B. & NEELEY-KVARME, J., *Jurisdiction Over Child Custody* and Adoption After Shaffer and Kulko, 12 U.C. Davis L. Rev. 229 (1979)

BOELE-WOELKI, K., Unification and Harmonization of Private International Law in Europe, in Private Law in the International Arena--Liber Amicorum Kurt Siehr 61 (J. Basedow, e.o., eds. 2000)

BOELE-WOELKI, K., JOUSTRA, C., & STEENHOFF, G., Dutch Private International Law at the End of the 20ᵗʰ Century: Progress or Regress? in Symeonides, "Private International Law at the End of the 20th Century: Progress or Regress?" 295 (2000)

BOLARD, Universalisme ou nationalisme: l'hésitation française, Ann.Suiss.d.i.p. 83 (1977)

BORCHERS, P., Jurisdiction to Adjudicate Revisited, in "Law and Justice in a Multistate World: Essays in Honor of Arthur T. von Mehren," 3 (Nafziger & Symeonides, eds. 2002)

BORCHERS, P., The Problem of General Jurisdiction, 2001 U.Chi. Legal F. 119

BORCHERS, P., Louisiana's Conflicts Codification: Some Empirical Observations Regarding Decisional Predictability, 60 La. L. Rev. 1061 (2000)

BORCHERS, P., Empiricism and Theory in Conflicts Law, 75 Ind. L. J. 509 (2000)

BORCHERS, P., Baker v. General Motors: Implications for Interjurisdictional Recognition of Non-Traditional Marriages, 32 Creighton L. Rev. 147 (1998)

BORCHERS, P., Back to the Past: Anti-Pragmatism in American Conflicts Law, 48 Mercer L. Rev. 721 (1997)

BORCHERS, P., Choice of Law in the American Courts in 1992: Observations and Reflections, 42 Am. J. Comp. L. 125 (1994)

BORCHERS, P., *Conflicts Pragmatism*, 56 Alb. L. Rev. 883 (1993)

BORCHERS, P., *Forum Selection* Agreements in the Federal Courts After Carnival Cruise: A Proposal for Congressional Reform, 67 Wash. L. Rev. 55 (1992)

BORN, G., *International Civil Litigation* in United States Courts (3d ed. 1996)

BORN, G., *Reflections on Judicial Jurisdiction* in International Cases, 17 Ga.J.Int'l & Comp. L.1 (1987)

BRAND, R.A., Jurisdictional Common Ground: *In Search of a Global Convention*, in "Law and Justice in a Multistate World: Essays in Honor of Arthur T. von Mehren," 11 (Nafziger & Symeonides, eds. 2002)

BRAND, R.A.., *Forum Selection* and Judgment Recognition in US Courts: One Rationale for a Global Choice of Court Convention, in Reform and Development of Private International Law Essays in Honour of Sir Peter North 86 (ed. J. Fancett, 2002).

BRAND, R.A., Enforcement of Foreign Money-Judgments in the United States: In Search of *Uniformity and International Acceptance*, 67 Notre Dame L. Rev. 253 (1991)

BRIGGS, A., Choice of Law in Tort and Delict, 1995 L.M.C.L.Q. 519

BRILMAYER, L.R., *Conflict of Laws* (2d ed. 1995)

BRILMAYER, L.R., The Role of Substantive and Choice of Law Policies in the Formation and Application of Choice of Law Rules, 252 Recueil des Cours 9 (1995)

BRILMAYER, L., Interstate Preemption: The Right to Travel, the Right to Life, and the Right to Die, 91 Mich. L. Rev. 873 (1993)

BRILMAYER, L.R., The Other State's Interests, 24 Cornell Int'l L. J. 233 (1991)

BRILMAYER, L.R., Rights, Fairness, and Choice of Law, 98 Yale L. J. 127 (1989)

BRILMAYER, L.R., *Shaping and Sharing* in Democratic Theory: Towards a Political Philosophy of Interstate Equality, 15 Fla.St. L. Rev., 389 (1987)

BRILMAYER, L.R., *Methods and Objectives* in the Conflict of Laws: A Challenge, 35 Mercer L. Rev. 556 (1984)

BRILMAYER, L.R., Interest Analysis and *The Myth* of Legislative Intent, 78 Mich. L. Rev. 392 (1980)

BRILMAYER, L.R., *How Contacts Count*: Due Process Limitations on State Court Jurisdiction, 1980 Sup. Ct. Rev. 77

BRILMAYER, L. & PAISLEY K., *Personal Jurisdiction and Substantive Legal Relations*: Corporations, Conspiracies, and Agency, 74 Calif. L. Rev. 1 (1986)

BRUCH, C.S., The Hague Convention on the Law Applicable to Succession to the Estates of Deceased Persons: Do Quasi-Community Property and Mandatory Survivorship Laws Need Protection?, 56 Law & Contemp.Probs. 309 (1993)

BUCHER, A., Sur les règles de rattachement à charactère substantiel, Liber Amicorum Adolf Schnitzer, 37 (1979)

BUCHER, A., L'Ordre public et le but social des lois en droit international privé, 239 Recueil des Cours 9 (1993)

BURBANK, S., Jurisdictional Conflict and Jurisdictional Equilibration: *Paths to a Via Media*, __ Houston J.Int'l L. ___ (2004)

BURBANK, S., Reason, Rigor and Regret: An Essay for Arthur von Mehren, in "Law and Justice in a Multistate World: Essays in Honor of Arthur T. von Mehren," 33 (Nafziger & Symeonides, eds. 2002)

BURBANK, S., Semtek, Forum Shopping, and Federal Common Law, 77 Notre Dame L. Rev. 1027 (2002)

BURBANK, S., *Interjurisdictional Preclusion*, Full Faith and Credit and Federal Common Law: A General Approach, 71 Cornell L. Rev. 733 (1986)

BURBANK, S., *Where's the Beef?* The Interjurisdictional Effects of New Jersey's Entire Controversy Doctrine, 28 Rutgers L. J. 87 (1996)

BURIÁN, L., Hungarian Private International Law at the End of the 20th Century: Progress or Regress? in Symeonides, "Private International Law at the End of the 20th Century: Progress or Regress?" 263 (2000)

BURNSTEIN, M.R., Conflicts on the Net: Choice of Law in Transnational Cyberspace, 29 Vand. J. Transn'l L. 75 (1996)

CABRASER, E., *Products Liability Class Actions*: Essential Jurisprudence, 30 ALI-ABA 61, 77

(2001)

CAMERON, C. & JOHNSON, K., *Death of a Salesman?* Forum Shopping and Outcome Determination Under International Shoe, 28 U.C. Davis 769 (1995)

CARRILLO SALCEDO, A., Le renouveau du particularism en droit international privé, 160 Recueil des Cours 181 (1978)

CARRINGTON, P., *Collateral Estoppel* and Foreign Judgments, 24 Ohio St. L. J. 381 (1963)

CARTER, P., Choice of Law in Tort: The Role of the Lex Fori, 54 Cambridge L. J. 38 (1995)

CASAD, R., *Jurisdiction* in Civil Actions (2d ed. 1991)

CASTEL, J.-G., Canadian Conflict of Laws (4th ed. 1997)

CASTEL, J.-G., The Erosion of the Foreign Public Law Exception: Recent Canadian Developments, in "Law and Justice in a Multistate World: Essays in Honor of Arthur T. von Mehren," 243 (Nafziger & Symeonides, eds. 2002)

CASTEL, J.-G., Back to the Future! Is the 'New' Rigid Choice of Law Rule for Interprovincial Torts Constitutionally Mandated? 33 Osgoode Hall L. J. 35 (1995)

CAUST-ELLENBOGEN, S., False Conflicts and *Interstate Preclusion*: Moving Beyond a Wooden Reading of the Full Faith and Credit Statute, 58 Fordham L. Rev. 593 (1990)

CAVERS, D.F., The Choice-of-Law *Process* (1965)

CAVERS, D.F., A *Correspondence with* Brainerd *Currie*, 1957-58, 34 Mercer L. Rev. 471 (1983)

CAVERS, D.F., The Proper Law of *Producer's Liability*, 26 Int'l & Comp. L.Q. 703 (1977)

CAVERS, D.F., The *Value of Principled Preferences*, 49 Tex. L. Rev. 211 (1971)

CAVERS, D.F., Cipolla and *Conflicts Justice*, 9 Duq. L. Rev. 360 (1971)

CAVERS, D.F., Legislative Choice of Law: Some European Examples, 44 S. Cal. L. Rev. 340 (1971)

CAVERS, D.F., *Contemporary Conflicts* in American Perspective, 131 Recueil des Cours 75 (1970)

CAVERS, D.F., Comments on Reich v. Purcell, 15 U.C.L.A. L. Rev. 467 (1968)

CAVERS, D.F., Some of Ehrenzweig's Choice-of-Law Generalizations, 18 Okla. L. Rev. 357 (1965)

CAVERS, D.F., The Changing Choice-of-Law Process and the Federal Courts, 28 Law & Contemp. Probs. 732 (1963)

CAVERS, D.F., Comments on Babcock v. Jackson, 63 Colum. L. Rev. 1219 (1963)

CAVERS, D.F., A *Critique* of the Choice-of-Law Problem, 47 Harv. L. Rev. 173 (1933)

CHEATHAM, E., Conflict of Laws: Some Developments and Some Questions, 25 Ark. L. Rev. 9 (1971)

CHEATHAM, E. & MAIER, H., Private International Law and Its Sources, 22 Vand. L. Rev. (1968)

CHEATHAM, E. & REESE, W., Choice of the Applicable Law, 52 Colum. L. Rev. 959 (1952)

CHEMERINSKY, E., *Federal Jurisdiction* (2d ed. 1994)

CHEN, J., Australian Private International Law at the End of the 20th Century: Progress or Regress? in

Symeonides, "Private International Law at the End of the 20th Century: Progress or Regress?" 83 (2000)

CLINTON, R., *Tribal Courts* and the Federal Union, 26 Willamette L. Rev. 841 (1990)

COHEN, F.S., Handbook of *Federal Indian Law* (1982)

COMMENT, (Westen, P.), *False Conflicts*, 55 Cal. L. Rev. 74 (1976)

COOK, W. W., The *Logical* and Legal *Bases* of the Conflict of Laws (1942)

COOK, W.W., *An Unpublished Chapter* of the Logical and Legal Bases of the Conflict of Laws, 37 U.Ill. L. Rev. 418 (1943)

COOMBS, R., Child Custody and Visitation by Non-Parents Under the New Uniform Child Custody Jurisdiction and Enforcement Act: A *Rerun of Seize-and-Run*, 16 J. Am. Acad. Matrim. Law. 1 (1999)

COOMBS, R., *Interstate Child Custody:* Jurisdiction, Recognition, and Enforcement, 66 Minn. L. Rev. 711 (1982)

COX, B., *Same-Sex Marriage and Choice of Law:* If We Marry in Hawaii, Are We Still Married When We Return Home?, 1994 Wis. L. Rev. 1033 (1994)

COX, S., Substantive Multilateral, and Unilateral Choice of Law Approaches, 37 Willamette L. Rev. 171 (2000)

COX, S., Razing Conflicts Facade to Build Better Jurisdiction Theory: The Foundation: *There Is No Law But Forum Law*, 28 Val.U. L. Rev. 1 (1993)

CROSS, John, *The Conduct-Regulating Exception* in Modern United States Choice-of-Law, 36 Creighton L. Rev. 425 (2003)

CURRIE, B., *Selected Essays* on the Conflict of Laws (1963)

CURRIE, B., The *Disinterested Third State*, 28 Law & Contemp. Probs. 754 (1963)

CURRIE, B., Notes on *Methods and Objectives* in the Conflict of Laws, 1959 Duke L. J. 171 (1959)

CURRIE, B., *Married Women's Contracts:* A Study in Conflict-of-Laws Method, 25 U.Chi. L. Rev. 227 (1958)

CURRIE, B., *Full Faith and Credit* to Foreign Land Decrees, 21 U.Chi. L. Rev. 620 (1954)

CURRIE, B. & SCHRETER, H.H., Unconstitutional Discrimination in the Conflict of Laws: *Privileges and Immunities*, 69 Yale L. J. 1323 (1960)

CURRIE, B.) & SCHRETER, H.H., Unconstitutional Discrimination in the Conflict of Laws: *Equal Protection*, 28 U.Chi. L. Rev. 1 (1960)

DALE, M., State Court Jurisdiction Under the *Indian Child Welfare Act* and the Unstated Best Interest of the Child Test, 27 Gonzaga L. Rev. 353 (1991/92)

DANE, P., Whereof One Cannot Speak: Legal Diversity and the Limits of a Restatement of Conflict of Laws, 75 Ind. L. J. 511 (2000)

DANE, P., *Sovereign Dignity and Glorious Chaos:* A Comment on the Interjurisdictional Implications of the Entire Controversy Doctrine, 28 Rutgers L. Rev. 173 (1996)

DANE, P., Vested Rights, "Vestedness," and Choice of Law, 96 Yale L. J. 1191 (1987)

DAVIS, G., Choice of Law in Tort at the Dawning of

the 21st Century, 24 Melb.U. L. Rev. 982 (2000)

DE BOER, T.M., Beyond Lex Loci Delicti: Conflicts Methodology and Multistate Torts in American Case Law (1987)

DE BOER, T.M., Facultative Choice of Law: The Procedural Status of Choice-of-Law Rules and Foreign Law, 257 Recueil des Cours 223 (1996)

DEBY-GÉRARD, F., Le rôle de la règle de conflict dans le règlement des rapports internationaux (1973)

DE MAEKELT, T., Venezuelan Private International Law at the End of the 20th Century: Progress or Regress? in Symeonides, "Private International Law at the End of the 20th Century: Progress or Regress?" 445 (2000)

DE NOVA, R., Glancing at the Content of Substantive Rules under the Jurisdiction-Selecting Approach, 41 Law & Contemp. Prob. 1 (1977)

DE NOVA, R., Historical and *Comparative Introduction* to Conflict of Laws, 118 Recueil des Cours 441 (1966)

DE NOVA, R. The First American Book on Conflict of Laws, 8 Am. J. Leg. Hist. 136 (1964)

DE VRIES, H. & LOWENFELD, A., *Jurisdiction in Personal Actions*—A Comparison of Civil Law Views, 44 Iowa L. Rev. 306 (1959)

DEGNAN, R., *Federalize Res Judicata*, 85 Yale L. J. 741 (1976)

DOBBS, D., The Validation of Void Judgments: *The Bootstrap Principle*, 53 Va. L. Rev. 1003, 1241 (Parts I & II, 1967)

DOLINGER, J., Evolution of Principles for Resolving Conflicts in the Field of Contracts and Torts, 283 Recueil des Cours 189 (2000)

DRAETTA, U., TABE, R. & NANDA, V., Breach and Adaptation of *International Contracts:* An Introduction to Lex Mercatoria (1992)

DREYFUSS, R.C. & SILBERMAN, L., Interjurisdictional Implications of the *Entire Controversy Doctrine*, 28 Rutgers L. Rev. 123 (1996)

DROZ, G., Regards sur le droit international privé comparé, 229 Recueil des Cours 9 (1991)

DRUM, S.M., DeWeerth v. Baldinger: Making New York a *Haven for Stolen Art?* 64 N.Y.U. L. Rev. 909 (1989)

DUBLER, C., Les clauses d'exception en droit international privé (1983)

DUTOIT, B., *Commentaire* de la loi fédérale du 18 décembre 1987 (1997)

DUTSON, S., Product Liability and Private International Law: Choice of Law in Tort in England, 47 Am. J. Comp. L. 129 (1999)

DUTSON, S. Choice of Law in Tort in Domestic and International Litigation, 26 Austl.Bus. L. Rev. 238 (1998)

EADES, R., Attempts to Federalize and Codify Tort Law, 36 Tort & Ins. L. J. 1 (2000)

EHRENZWEIG, A.A., Private International Law (v. 1 1967) [*PIL*]

EHRENZWEIG, A.A., A *Treatise* on the Conflict of Laws (1963)

EHRENZWEIG, A.A., Choice of Law in California--A 'Prestatement,' 21 U.C.L.A. L. Rev. 781 (1974)

EHRENZWEIG, A.A., Conflict, Crisis and Confusion in Pennsylvania, 9 Duquesne L. Rev. 459 (1971)

EHRENZWEIG, A.A., The Value of Principled Preferences, 49 Tex. L. Rev. 236 (1971)

EHRENZWEIG, A.A., Specific Principles of Private Transnational Law, 124 Recueil des Cours 167 (1968-II)

EHRENZWEIG, A.A., A Counter-Revolution in Conflicts Law? From Beale to Cavers, 80 Harv. L. Rev. 377 (1966)

EHRENZWEIG, A.A., *A Proper Law in a Proper Forum*: A "Restatement" of the "Lex Fori Approach," 18 Okla. L. Rev. 340 (1965)

EHRENZWEIG, A.A., *The Second Conflicts Restatement:* A Last Appeal for Its Withdrawal, 113 U.Pa. L. Rev. 1230 (1965)

EHRENZWEIG, A.A., Choice of Law: Current Doctrine and "True Rules," 49 Calif. L. Rev. 240 (1961)

EHRENZWEIG, A.A., *The Lex Fori*-Basic Rule in the Conflict of Laws, 58 Mich. L. Rev. 637 (1960)

ELLIS, D., Projecting the Long Arm of the Law: *Extraterritorial Criminal Enforcement of U.S. Antitrust Laws* in the Global Economy, 1 Wash.U. Global Stud. L. Rev. 477 (2002)

ELY, J., Choice of Law and *the State's Interest* in Protecting its Own, 23 Wm. & Mary L. Rev. 173 (1981)

ELY, J., *The Irrepressible Myth of Erie*, 87 Harv. L. Rev. 693 (1974)

EPSTEIN, R., *Consent, Not Power*, as the Basis of Jurisdiction, 2001 U.Chi. Legal F. 1

ERICHSON, H., Interjurisdictional Preclusion, 96 Mich. L. Rev. 945 (1998)

EVRIGENIS, D., Idiotikon Diethnes Dikaion (1968) [*PIL*]

EVRIGENIS, D., *Tendances Doctrinales* Actuelles en Droit International Privé, 118 Recueil des Cours 313 (1966)

FALLON, M. & MEEUSEN, J., Belgian Private International Law at the End of the 20th Century: Progress or Regress? in Symeonides, "Private International Law at the End of the 20th Century: Progress or Regress?" 109 (2000)

FAUVARQUE-COSSON, B., Libre disponibilité des droits et conflits de lois (1996)

FAUVARQUE-COSSON, B., Comparative Law and Conflict of Laws: Allies or Enemies? New Perspectives on an Old Couple, 49 Am. J. Comp. L. 407 (2001)

FAWCETT, J., Cross-Fertilization in Private International Law, 53 Current Leg.Prob. 303 (2000)

FAWCETT, J., Products Liability in Private International Law: A European Perspective, 238 Recueil des Cours 9 (1993)

FAWCETT, J., Is American Governmental Interest Analysis the Solution to English Tort Choice of Law Problems? 31 Int'l & Comp. L.Q. 31 (1982)

FELIX, R., Leflar in the Courts: Judicial Adoptions of Choice-Influencing Considerations, 52 Ark. L. Rev. 35 (1999)

FENTIMAN, R., Foreign Law and Forum Conveniens, in "Law and Justice in a Multistate World: Essays in Honor of Arthur T. von Mehren," 275 (Nafziger & Symeonides, eds. 2002)

FENTIMAN, R., English Private International Law at the End of the 20th Century: Progress or Regress?

in Symeonides, "Private International Law at the End of the 20th Century: Progress or Regress?" 165 (2000)

FERNÁNDEZ ARROYO, D., La codificación del derecho internacional privado en América Latina (1994)

FERRER-CORREIA, A., Les problèmes de codification en droit international privé, 145 Recueil des Cours (1975)

FETTIG, K., Criminal and Civil Remedies for Transboundary Water Pollution, 15 Transnat'l Law. 117 (2002)

FINCH, M., Giving Full Faith and Credit to Punitive Damages Awards: Will Florida Rule the Nation? 86 Minn. L. Rev. 497 (2002)

FLESSNER, A., Interessenjurisprudenz im internationnalen Privatrecht (1990)

FORGET, L. Les conflits de lois en matière d'accidents de la circulation routière (1973)

FRANCESCAKIS, P., La théorie du renvoi et les conflit des systèmes en droit international privé (1958)

FRANCESCAKIS, P., Lois d'application immédiate' et règles de conflits, 3 Riv. dir. int'le priv. proces. 699 (1966)

FRANCESCAKIS, P., Quelques précisions sue les 'lois d'application immédiate' et leur rapports avec les règles de conflit de lois, 55 Rev. critique 1 (1955)

FREED, D.J & WALKER, T.B., Family Law in the Fifty States: An Overview, 18 Fam. L.Q. 369 (1985)

FREER, R., Erie's Mid-Life Crisis, 63 Tul. L. Rev. 1087 (1989)

FRICKEY, P., A Common Law for Our Age of Colonialism: The Judicial Divestiture of Indian Tribal Authority over Nonmembers, 109 Yale L. J. 1 (1999)

GARFIELD, H., The Transitory Divorce Action: Jurisdiction in the No-Fault Era, 58 Tex. L. Rev. 501 (1980)

GELLER, P.E., Conflicts of Laws in Cyberspace: Rethinking International Copyright in a Digitally Networked World, 20 Colum.-VLA J. L. & Arts 571 (1996)

GEIST, M., Is There a There There? Toward Greater Certainty for Internet Jurisdiction, 16 Berkeley Tech. L. J. 1345 (2001)

GERGEN, M., Equality and the Conflict of Laws, 73 Iowa L. Rev. 893 (1988)

GINSBURG, R., Judgments in Search of Full Faith and Credit: The Last-in-Time Rule for Conflicting Judgments, 82 Harv. L. Rev. 798 (1969)

GLENN, H. P., Codification of Private International Law in Quebec, 60 RabelsZ 231 (1996)

GOLDSMITH, J., Against Cyberanarchy, 65 U.Chi. L. Rev. 1199 (1998)

GOLDSMITH, J. & SYKES, A., The Internet and the Dormant Commerce Clause, 110 Yale L. J. 785 (2201)

GONZÁLEZ CAMPOS, J., Diversification, spécialisation et matérialisation des règles de droit international privé, 287 Recueil des Cours 9 (2000)

GOTHOT, Le renouveau de la tendance unilatérale en droit international privé, 60 Rev. critique 1, 209, 415 (1971)

GOTTESMAN, M., Draining the Dismal Swamp: The

Case for Federal Choice of Law Statutes, 80 Geo. L. J. 1 (1991)

GOTTESMAN, M., Adrift in the Sea of Indeterminacy, 75 Ind. L. J. 527 (2000)

GRAMMATIKAKI-ALEXIOU, A., Delictual Obligations in Private International Law (1987)

GRAMMATIKAKI-ALEXIOU, A., Substantive Conflicts Rules and Connecting Factors of a Substantive Character: Two Versions of Methodological Pluralism, Rev. Hellenique Droit Europ. 299 (1986)

GRAMMATIKAKI-ALEXIOU, A., PAPASSIOPI-PASSIA, Z. & VASSILAKAKIS, E., Idiotikon Diethnes Dikaion (1997)

GRAULICH, P., Principes de Droit International Privé (1961)

GREEN, M.S., Legal Realism, Lex Fori, and the Choice-of-Law Revolution, 104 Yale L. J. 967 (1995)

GREENE, J., Choice of Law in Tort-The Song that Never Ends, 26 Fed. L. Rev. 349 (1998)

GUZMAN, A., Choice of Law: New Foundations, 90 Geo. L. J. 883 (2002)

GUTZWILLER, P., Von Ziel und Methode des IPR, Ann. Suisse droit int'l 161 (1968)

HANOTIAU, B., Le droit international privé américain (1979)

HARDY, I.T., The Proper Legal Regime for "Cyberspace", 55 U. Pitt. L. Rev. 993 (1994)

HARRIS, J., Choice of Law in Tort - Blending in With the Landscape of the Conflict of Laws? 61 Mod. L. Rev. 33 (1998)

HAY, P., From Rule-Orientation to "Approach" in German Conflicts Law: The Effect of the 1986 and 1999 Codifications, 47 Am. J. Comp. L. 633 (1999)

HAY, P., The Recognition and Enforcement of American Money-Judgments in Germany: The 1992 Decision of the German Supreme Court, 40 Am. J. Comp. L. 729 (1992)

HAY, P., Flexibility Versus Predictability and Uniformity in Choice of Law: Reflections on Current European and United States Conflicts Law, 226 Recueil des Cours 281 (1991)

HAY, P., Transient Jurisdiction, Especially Over International Defendants: Critical Comments on Burnham v. Superior Court of California, 1990 U. Ill. L. Rev. 593

HAY, P., Judicial Jurisdiction and Choice of Law: Constitutional Limitations, 59 U. Colo. L. Rev. 9 (1988)

HAY, P., Full Faith and Federalism in Choice of Law, 1983 Mercer L. Rev. 709 (1983)

HAY, P., Reflections on Conflict-of-Laws Methodology: A Dialogue, 32 Hastings L. J. 1644 (1981)

HAY, P. & ELLIS, R.B., Bridging the Gap Between Rules and Approaches in Tort Choice of Law in the United States: A Survey of Current Case Law, 27 Int'l Law. 369, 1993)

HENSON, D., Will Same-Sex Marriages Be Recognized in Sister States: Full Faith and Credit and Due Process Limitations on States: Choice of Law Regarding the Status and Incidents of Homosexual Marriages Following Hawaii's Baehr v. Lewin, 32 U. Louisville J. Fam. L. 551 (1994)

HERZOG, P., Rules on the International Recognition

of Judgments (and on International Jurisdiction) by Enactments of an International Organization: European Community Regulations 1347/2000 and 44/2001, in "Law and Justice in a Multistate World: Essays in Honor of Arthur T. von Mehren," 83 (Nafziger & Symeonides, eds. 2002)

HERZOG, P., The 'Conflict of Laws Revolution' in New York, and Where Did it Leave Us, 50 Syr. L. Rev. 1279 (2000)

HERZOG, P., *Brussels and Lugano*, Should You Race to the Courthouse or Race for a Judgment?, 43 Am. J. Comp. L. 379 (1995)

HILL, A., For a Third Conflicts Restatement—But Stop Trying to Reinvent the Wheel, 75 Ind. L. J. 535 (2000)

HILL, A., After the *Big Bang*: Professor Sedler's Remaining Dilemma, 38 Wayne L. Rev. 1471 (1992)

HILL, A., *Choice of Law and Jurisdiction* in the Supreme Court, 81 Colum. L. Rev. 960 (1981)

HILL, A., Governmental Interest and the Conflict of Laws--A *Reply to* Professor *Currie*, 27 U.Chi. L. Rev. 463 (1960)

HILL, A., *The Erie Doctrine* and the Constitution, 53 Nw.U. L. Rev. 427 (1958)

HILLER, L., The 'Most Significant Relationship' Test of the Second Restatement of Conflicts and its Effect Outside the United States in the Area of Torts, 12 N.Y. Int'l L. Rev. 55, 1999)

HOROWITZ, H., The Law of *Choice of Law in California*—A Restatement, 21 UCLA L. Rev. 719, 1974)

HOROWITZ, H., *The Commerce Clause* as a Limitation on State Choice-of-Law Doctrine, 84 Harv. L. Rev. 806 (1971)

HOROWITZ, H., Toward a *Federal Common Law of Choice of Law*, 14 U.C.L.A. L. Rev. 1191 (1967)

HOVERMILL, J., *A Conflict of Laws and Morals:* The Choice of Law Implications of Hawaii's Recognition of Same-Sex Marriage, 53 Md. L. Rev. 450 (1994)

JAFFEY, A., Topics in Choice of Law (1996)

JAYME, E., Ein Internationales Privatrecht für Europa (1991)

JAYME, E., Methoden der Konkretisierung des ordre public im Internationalen Privatrecht (1989)

JAYME, E., Le droit international privé du nouveau millénaire: La protection de la personne humaine face à la globalisation, 282 Recueil des Cours 9 (2000)

JAYME, E. Identité culturelle et intégration: Le droit international privé postmoderne, 251 Recueil des Cours 9 (1995)

JAYME, E., The American Conflicts Revolution and its Impact on European Private International Law, in "Forty Years On: The Evolution of Postwar Private International Law in Europe," Cent. v. Buitenlands Recht en Int'l Priv. U. Amsterdam, 15 (1992)

JAYME, E. Considerations historiques et actuelles sur la codification du droit international privé, 177 Recueil des Cours 9 (1982)

JAYME, E., Neue Kodifikation des Internationalen Privatrechts in Louisiana, IPRax. 1993, 80

JOHNSON, D. & POST, D., Law and Borders--The Rise of *Law in Cyberspace*, 48 Stan. L. Rev.

1367 (1996)

JOERGES, C., Zum Functionswandel des Kollisionsrecht, Die 'Governmental Interest Analysis' und die 'Krise des Internationalen Privatrechts (1971)

JUENGER, F., Selected Essays on the Conflict of Laws, (2001)

JUENGER, F., Choice of Law and *Multistate Justice* (1993)

JUENGER, F., The American Law of General Jurisdiction, 2001 U.Chi. Legal F. 141

JUENGER, F., How Do you Rate a Century? 37 Willamette L. Rev. 89 (2000)

JUENGER, F., A Third Conflicts Restatement? 75 Ind. L. J. 403 (2000)

JUENGER, F., Choice of Law: How it Ought Not to Be, 48 Mercer L. Rev. 757 (1997)

JUENGER, F., Contract Choice of Law in the Americas, 45 Am. J. Comp. L. 195, 1997)

JUENGER, F., *The Complex Litigation Project*'s Tort Choice-of-Law Rules, 54 La. L. Rev. 907 (1994)

JUENGER, F., *What's Wrong with Forum Shopping?*, 16 Sydney L. Rev. 5 (1994)

JUENGER, F., *Forum Shopping*: A *Rejoinder*, 16 Sydney L. Rev. 28 (1994)

JUENGER, F., *Babcock v. Jackson Revisited*: Judge Fuld's Contribution to American Conflicts Law, 56 Alb. L. Rev. 727 (1993)

JUENGER, F., American Jurisdiction: A Story of Comparative Neglect, 65 U.Colo. L. Rev. 1 (1993)

JUENGER, F., Governmental Interests and Multistate Justice: A *Reply to* Professor *Sedler*, 24 U.C. Davis L. Rev. 227 (1990)

JUENGER, F., *Mass Disasters* and the Conflict of Laws, 1989 U.Ill. L. Rev. 105 (1989)

JUENGER, F., Conflict of Laws: A *Critique* of Interest Analysis, 32 Am. J. Comp. L. 1 (1984)

JUENGER, F., *Marital Property* and the Conflict of Laws: A Tale of Two Countries, 81 Colum. L. Rev. 1061 (1981)

JUENGER, F., Robert A. *Leflar's Contribution* to American Conflicts Law, 31 S.C. L. Rev. 413 (1980)

JUENGER, F., Choice of Law in *Interstate Torts*, 118 U.Pa. L. Rev. 202 (1969)

JOSEPHS, H., Book Review--Conflict of Laws: American, Comparative, International: Cases and Materials, 60 La. L. Rev. 1123 (2000)

KAHN-FREUND, O., General Problems of Private International Law (1976)

KAHN-FREUND, O., Delictual Liability and the Conflict of Laws, 124 Recueil des Cours 1 (1968)

KALIS, P.J., SEGERDAHL, J.R., & WALDRON, J.T., The Choice-of-Law Dispute in Comprehensive Environmental Coverage Litigation: Has Help Arrived from the American Law Institute Complex Litigation Project?, 54 La. L. Rev. 925 (1994)

KANOWITZ, L., *Comparative Impairment* and Better Law: Grand Illusions in the Conflict of Laws, 30 Hastings L. J. 255 (1978)

KAY, H.H., Currie's Interest Analysis in the 21st Century: Losing the Battle, But Winning the War, 37 Willamette L. Rev 123 (2001)

KAY, H.H., *A Defense* of Currie's Governmental Interest Analysis, 215 Recueil des Cours 9 (1989)

KAY, H.H., Chief Justice Traynor and Choice of Law Theory, 35 Hastings L. J. 747 (1984)

KAY, H.H., Theory into Practice: Choice of Law in the Courts, 34 Mercer L. Rev. 521 (1983)

KAYE, P., Private International Law of Tort and Product Liability (1991)

KEGEL, G., Paternal Home and Dream Home: Traditional Conflict of Laws and the American Reformers, 27 Am. J. Comp. L. 615 (1979)

KEGEL, G., The *Crisis* of Conflict of Laws, 112 Recueil des Cours 91 (1964)

KERAMEUS, K., *Enforcement Proceedings*, in 10 Int'l Encyc. Comp. L. ch. 10 (2003)

KERAMEUS, K., Enforcement of Non-Money Judgments and Orders in a Comparative Perspective, in "Law and Justice in a Multistate World: Essays in Honor of Arthur T. von Mehren," 107 (Nafziger & Symeonides, eds. 2002)

KERAMEUS, K., *Enforcement in the International Context*, 264 Recueil des cours 179 (1997)

KIRGIS, F., *The Roles of Due Process and Full Faith and Credit* in Choice of Law, 62 Cornell L. Rev. 94 (1976)

KOHLER, C., *Practical Experience of the Brussels* Jurisdiction and Judgments *Convention* in the Six Original Contracting States, 34 Int'l & Comp. L.Q. 563 (1985)

KOGAN, T.S., Toward a Jurisprudence of Choice of Law: The Priority of Fairness over Comity, 62 N.Y.U. L. Rev. 651 (1987)

KOKKINI-IATRIDOU, D., Les Clauses d'Exception en matière de Conflits de Lois et de Conflits de Juridictions --ou le principe de proximité (1994)

KORN, H., Big Cases and Little Cases: Babcock in Perspective, 56 Alb. L. Rev. 933 (1993)

KORN, H., The Choice-of-Law Revolution: A *Critique*, 83 Colum. L. Rev. 772 (1983)

KOZYRIS, P.J., Conflict of Laws for Corporate Shareholdings: Predicaments and Prospects, in "Law and Justice in a Multistate World: Essays in Honor of Arthur T. von Mehren," 295 (Nafziger & Symeonides eds. 2002)

KOZYRIS, P.J., Conflicts Theory for Dummies: Après le Deluge, Where Are We on Producers Liability?, 60 La. L.Rev 1161 (2000)

KOZYRIS, P.J., The Conflicts Provisions of the ALI's Complex Litigation Project: A Glass Half Full?, 54 La. L. Rev. 953 (1994)

KOZYRIS, P.J., *Values and Methods* in Choice of Law For Products Liability: A Comparative Comment on Statutory Solutions, 38 Am. J. Comp. L. 475 (1990)

KOZYRIS, P.J., *Corporate Wars* and Choice of Law, 85 Duke L. J. 1 (1985)

KOZYRIS, P.J., *Corporate Takeovers* at the Jurisdictional Crossroads: Preserving State Authority Over Internal Affairs While Protecting the Transferability of Interstate Stock Through Federal Law, 36 UCLA L. Rev. 1109 (1989)

KOZYRIS, P.J., Interest Analysis Facing its *Critics*, 46 Ohio St. L. J. 569 (1985)

KOZYRIS, P.J., Justified Party Expectations in Choice of Law and Jurisdiction: Constitutional Significance or Bootstrapping?, 19 San Diego L.

Rev. 313 (1982)

KOZYRIS, P.J., Reflections in Allstate—The Lessening of Due Process in Choice of Law, 14 U.C. Davis L. Rev. 887 (1981)

KOZYRIS, P.J. & Symeonides, S.C., *Choice of Law* in the American Courts *in 1989*: An Overview, 38 Am. J. Comp. L. 601 (1990)

KRAMER, L., Same-Sex Marriage, Conflict of Laws, and the Unconstitutional Public Policy Exception, 106 Yale L. J. 1965 (1997)

KRAMER, L., Choice of Law in Complex Litigation, 71 N.Y.U. L. Rev. 547 (1996)

KRAMER, L., On the Need for a Uniform Choice of Law Code, 89 Mich. L. Rev. 2134 (1991)

KRAMER, L., More Notes on *Methods and Objectives* in the Conflict of Laws, 24 Cornell Int'l L. J. 245 (1991)

KRAMER, L., Return of the *Renvoi*, 66 N.Y.U. L. Rev. 979 (1991)

KRAMER, L., *Rethinking* Choice of Law, 90 Colum. L. Rev. 277 (1990)

KRAMER, L., *The Myth of the "Unprovided For" Case*, 75 Va. L. Rev. 1045 (1989)

KRAMER, L., Interest Analysis and *the Presumption of Forum Law*, 56 U.Chi. L. Rev. 1301 (1989)

KREIMER, S., *The Law of Choice* and Choice of Law: Abortion, the Right to Travel, and Extraterritorial Regulation in American Federalism, 67 N.Y.U. L. Rev. 451 (1992)

KROPHOLLER, J., Internationales Privatrecht (3rd ed.1997)

KROPHOLLER, J. &. VON HEIN, J., From Approach to Rule-Orientation in American Tort Conflicts in "Law and Justice in a Multistate World: Essays in Honor of Arthur T. von Mehren," 317 (Nafziger & Symeonides, eds. 2002)

LALIVE, P., Tendances et méthodes en droit international privé, 155 Recueil des Cours 1 (1977)

LAGARDE, P., Le principe de proximité dans le droit international privé, 196 Recueil des Cours 9 (1986)

LAURENCE, R., *The Enforcement of Judgments Across Indian Reservation Boundaries:* Full Faith and Credit, Comity, and the Indian Civil Rights Act, 69 Oreg. L. Rev. 589 (1990)

LAYCOCK, Douglas, *Equal Citizens* of Equal and Territorial States: The Constitutional Foundations of Choice of Law, 92 Colum. L. Rev. 249 (1992)

LEE, T., *In Rem Jurisdiction in Cyberspace*, 75 Wash. L. Rev. 97 (2000)

LEFLAR, R.A., *The New Conflicts-Limitations Act*, 35 Mercer L. Rev. 461 (1984)

LEFLAR, R.A., *Choice-Influencing Considerations* in Conflicts Law, 41 N.Y.U. L. Rev. 367 (1966)

LEFLAR, R.A., Conflicts of Law: *More on Choice Influencing Considerations*, 54 Calif. L. Rev. 1584 (1966)

LEFLAR, R.A., Extrastate Enforcement of *Penal and Governmental Claims*, 46 Harv. L. Rev. 193 (1932)

LEFLAR, R.A., The Nature of Conflicts Law, 81 Colum. L. Rev. 1080 (1981)

LEFLAR, R.A., Choice of Law: A Well-Watered Plateau, 41 Law & Contemp. Prob. 10 (1977)

LEFLAR, R.A., The "New" Choice of Law, 21 Am.U. L. Rev. 457 (1972)

LEFLAR, R., MCDOUGAL, L. & FELIX, R., *American Conflicts* Law (4th ed. 1986)

LEVY, D. & MCCARTHY, N., A *Critique* of the Proposed Uniform Child Custody Jurisdiction and Enforcement Act, 15 J.Am.Acad. Matrimonial Law. 149 (1998)

LEVY, N., *Native Hawaiian Land Rights*, 63 Cal. L. Rev. 848 (1975)

LEWIS, D., Jurisdiction over Foreign Corporations Based on Registration and Appointment of an Agent: *An Unconstitutional Condition Perpetuated*, 15 Del.J.Corp. L. 1 (1990)

LINDE, H., A New Foreign-Relations Restraint on American States: Zschernig v. Miller, 28 RabelsZ 594 (1968)

LIVERMORE, S., Dissertations on the Questions Which Arise from the Contrariety of the Positive Laws of Different States and Nations (1828)

Lookofsky, J., Danish Private International Law at the End of the 20th Century: Progress or Regress? in Symeonides, "Private International Law at the End of the 20th Century: Progress or Regress 147" (2000)

LORENZEN, E., *Selected Articles on the Conflict of Laws* (1947)

LOUDENSLAGER, M., Allowing Another *Policeman on the Information Superhighway*: State Interests and Federalism on the Internet in the Face of the Dormant Commerce Clause, 17 B.Y.U. J.Pub. L. 191 (2003)

LOUSSOUARN, Y. & BOUREL, P., *Droit international privé* (7th ed. 2001)

LOWENFELD, A.F., Conflict, Balancing of Interests, and the Exercise of Jurisdiction to Prescribe: *Reflections on the Insurance Antitrust Case*, 89 Am.J.Int'l L. 42 (1995)

LOWENFELD, A., Thoughts About a Multinational Judgments Convention: A *Reaction to the von Mehren Report*, 57 Law & Contemp. Probs. 289 (1994)

LOWENFELD, A., *Lex Mercatoria*: An Arbitrator's View, in Lex Mercatoria and Arbitration 56 (T. Carbonneau, ed. 1990)

LOWENFELD, A. & SILBERMAN, L., *The Hague Judgments Convention*—and Perhaps Beyond, in "Law and Justice in a Multistate World: Essays in Honor of Arthur T. von Mehren," 121 (Nafziger & Symeonides, eds. 2002)

LOWRY, L. & FRANK, A., *Exporting* DBCP and Other *Banned Pesticides*: Consideration of Ethical Issues, 5 Int'l J.Occup.Envtl. Health 135 (1999,

MAIER, H.G., The Utilitarian Role of a Restatement of Conflicts in a Common Law System: How Much Judicial Deference is Due to the Restaters or 'Who Are These Guys, Anyway?', 75 Ind. L. J. 541 (2000)

MAIER, H.G., Finding the Trees in Spite of the Metaphorist: *The Problem of State Interests* in Choice of Law, 56 Alb. L. Rev. 753 (1993)

MAIER, H.G., *Preemption of State Law*: A Recommended Analysis, 83 Am.J.Int'l L. 832, 1989)

MAIER, H.G., *The Three Faces of Zapata*: Maritime Law, Federal Common Law, Federal Courts Law, 6 Van.J.Trans. L. 387 (1973)

MAIER, H.G. & MCCOY, T., *A Unifying Theory* for Judicial Jurisdiction and Choice of Law, 39 Am. J. Comp. L. 249 (1991)

MALTZ, E., The Full Faith and Credit Clause and the First Restatement: The Place of Baker v. General Motors Corp. in Choice of Law Theory, 73 Tul. L. Rev. 305 (1998)

MARTIN, J., *Statutes of Limitations* and Rationality in the Conflict of Laws, 19 Washburn L. J. 405 (1980)

MARTIN, J., *Constitutional Limitations* on Choice of Law, 61 Cornell L. Rev. 185 (1976)

MARTINY, D., Recognition and Enforcement of *Foreign* Money *Judgments in* the Federal Republic of *Germany*, 35 Am. J. Comp. L. 721 (1987)

MAYER, P., *Droit international privé* (5th ed. 1994)

MCCLEAN, D., Perspectives on Private International Law at the Turn of the Century, 282 Recueil des Cours 41 (2000)

MCDOUGAL, L.L., Leflar's Choice-Influencing Considerations: Revisited, Refined and Reaffirmed, 52 Ark.L. Rev. 105 (1999)

MCDOUGAL, L.L., Toward the Increased Use of Interstate and International Policies in Choice-of-Law Analysis in Tort Cases under the Second Restatement and Leflar's Choice-Influencing Considerations, 70 Tul. L. Rev. 2465 (1996)

MCDOUGAL, L.L., The Real Legacy of Babcock v. Jackson: Lex Fori Instead of Lex Loci Delicti and Now it's Time for a Real Choice-of-Law Revolution, 56 Alb. L. Rev. 795 (1993)

MCDOUGAL, L.L., Private International Law: Jus Gentium Versus Choice of Law Rules or Approaches, 38 Am. J. Comp. L. 521 (1990)

MCDOUGAL, L.L., Toward Application of the *Best Rule of Law* in Choice of Law Cases, 35 Mercer L. Rev. 483 (1984)

MCDOUGAL, L.L., Comprehensive Interest Analysis Versus Reformulated Governmental Interest Analysis: An Appraisal in the Context of Choice-of-Law Problems Concerning Contributory and Comparative Negligence, 26 U.C.L.A. L. Rev. 439 (1979)

MCDOUGAL, L.L., New Frontier in Choice of Law--Trans-state Laws: The Need Demonstrated in Theory and in the Context of Motor Vehicle Guest-Host Controversies, 53 Tul. L. Rev. 731 (1979)

MCDOUGAL, L.L., Choice of Law--Prologue to a Viable Interest-Analysis Theory, 51 Tul. L. Rev. 207 (1977)

MCLELLAN, G.D., *Equitable Distribution* Law and Practice (1985)

MERRILL, T., *The Common Law Powers* of the Federal Courts, 52 U.Chi. L. Rev. 1 (1985)

MISHKIN, P., Some Further *Last Words on Erie*-- The Thread, 87 Harv. L. Rev. 1682 (1974)

MOORE, K., *Collateral Attack on Subject Matter Jurisdiction: A Critique of the* Restatement (Second) of Judgments, 66 Cornell L. Rev. 534 (1981)

MOORE, Enforcing Foreign Ownership Claims in the *Antiquities Market*, 97 Yale L. J. 466 (1988)

MORRIS, J.H., The *Conflict of Laws* (1971)

MORSE, C., Torts in Private International Law (1978)

MORSE, C., Torts in Private International Law: A

New Statutory Framework, 45 Int'l & Comp. L.Q. 888 (1996)

MOSCONI, F., Exceptions to the Operation of Choice of Law Rules, 217 Recueil des Cours 9 (1989)

MOURA RAMOS, R., Das relaçoes privadas internacionais (1995)

MOURA RAMOS, R., *The New EC Rules on Jurisdiction* and the Recognition and Enforcement of Judgments, in "Law and Justice in a Multistate World: Essays in Honor of Arthur T. von Mehren," 199 (Nafziger & Symeonides, eds. 2002)

MOURA RAMOS, R., Le droit international privé portugais à la fin du vingtième siècle: Progrès ou recul? in Symeonides, "Private International Law at the End of the 20th Century: Progress or Regress?" 349 (2000)

MOUSTAIRA, A., The Evolution of Private International Law in the United States: Tradition, Revolution, Counter-Revolution (1996)

MULLENIX, L.S., Mass Tort Litigation and the Dilemma of Federalization, 44 De Paul L. Rev. 755 (1995)

MULLENIX, L.S., Federalizing Choice of Law for *Mass-Tort Litigation*, 70 Tex. L. Rev. 1623 (1992)

MUSHLIN, M., *The New Quasi in Rem Jurisdiction*: New York's Revival of a Doctrine Whose Time Has Passed, 55 Brooklyn L. Rev. 1059 (1990)

NADELMANN, K.H., *Wächter's Essay* on the Collision of Private Laws of Different States, 13 Am. J. Comp. L. 414 (1963)

NADELMANN, K.H., *Jurisdictionally Improper Fora*, in XXth Century Comparative and Conflicts Laws: Legal Essays in Honor of Hessel E. Yntema (Nadelmann, von Mehren & Hazard, eds. 1961)

NADELMANN, K.H., *Full Faith and Credit to Judgments* and Public Acts, 56 Mich. L. Rev. 33 (1957)

NADELMANN, K.H. & VON MEHREN, A.T.. Some *Remarks on the Proposed Codification*: The Draft of the Commission for the Reform of the Civil Code, 1 Am. J. Comp. L. 407 (1952).

NAFZIGER, J., Oregon's Conflicts Law Applicable to Contracts, 38 Willamette L. Rev. 397 (2002)

NAFZIGER, J., Avoiding Courtroom 'Conflicts' Whenever Possible, in "Law and Justice in a Multistate World: Essays in Honor of Arthur T. von Mehren," 341 (Nafziger & Symeonides, eds. 2002)

NAFZIGER, J., Making Choices of Law Together, 37 Willamette L. Rev. 209 (2000)

NAFZIGER, J., Choice of Law in Air Disaster Cases: Complex Litigation Rules and the Common Law, 54 La. L. Rev. 1001 (1994)

NAFZIGER, J. & SYMEONIDES, S., Law and Justice in a Multistate World: Essays in Honor of Arthur T. von Mehren (2002)

NEWTON, N.J., *Federal Power Over Indians:* Its Sources, Scope and Limitations, 132 U. Pa. L. Rev. 195 (1984)

NORTH, P., Essays in Private International Law (1993)

NORTH, P., Private International Law: Change or Decay?, 50 Int'l & Comp. L.Q. 477 (2001)

NOTE, *Jurisdiction over a Parent Corporation* in its Subsidiaries State of Incorporation, 141 U.Pa. L. Rev. 327 (1992)

NOTE, *Interstate Child Custody* and the Parental Kidnapping Prevention Act: The Continuing Search for a National Standard, 45 Hastings L. J. 1329 (1994)

NOTE, Choice of Law for *Land Transactions*, 38 Colum. L. Rev. 1049 (1938)

NYGH, P., Conflict of Laws in Australia (6th ed. 1995)

NYGH, P., *Arthur's Baby*: The Hague Negotiations for a World-Wide Judgements Convention, in "Law and Justice in a Multistate World: Essays in Honor of Arthur T. von Mehren," 151 (Nafziger & Symeonides, eds. 2002)

NYGH, P., The Reasonable Expectations of the Parties as a Guide to the Choice of Law in Contract and Tort, 251 Recueil des Cours 269 (1995)

NYGH, P., Conflict of Laws in Australia (6th ed. 1995)

O'HARA, E., Economics, Public Choice, and the Perennial Conflict of Laws, 90 Geo. L. J. 941 (2002)

O'HARA, E., & RIBSTEIN, L., From Politics to Efficiency in Choice of Law, 67 U.Chi. L. Rev. 1151 (2000)

OLDHAM, J.T., Conflict of Laws and *Marital Property* Rights, 39 Baylor L. Rev. 1255 (1987)

OLIVER, C.T., FIRMAGE, E.B., BLAKESLEY, C.L., SCOTT, R.F., & WILLIAMS, S.A., Cases and Materials on *The International Legal System* (4th ed.1995)

OPESKIN, B., The *Price of Forum Shopping*: A Reply, 16 Sydney L. Rev. 14 (1994)

PAJOR, T., Polish Private International Law at the End of the 20th Century: Progress or Regress? in Symeonides, "Private International Law at the End of the 20th Century: Progress or Regress? 329" (2000)

PAMBOUKIS C., Les clauses d' exception en matière de conflits de lois et de conflits de juridictions – Grèce, in Les Clauses d'Exception en matière de Conflits de Lois et de Conflits de Juridictions -- ou le principe de proximité (Kokkini-Iatridou, ed. 1994)

PAPADOPOULOU, T., The Role of the Judge in Private International Law (2000)

PAPASSIOPI-PASSIA, Z., Rules of Immediate Application and Substantive Choice of Law Rules (1989)

PAPASSIOPI-PASSIA, Z., New Trends in the Private International Law of Conventional Obligations, (1985)

PARRA-ARANGUREN, G., Codificacion del derecho internacional privado en America (1998)

PARRA-ARANGUREN, G., Monografias selectas de derecho internacional privado (1984)

PARRA-ARANGUREN, G., The Venezuelan Act of Private International Law of 1998, 1 Ybk.Priv.Int'l L., 103 (1999)

PARRA-ARANGUREN, G., General Course of Private International Law: Selected Problems, 210 Recueil des Cours 9 (1988)

PATOCCHI, P., Règles de rattachement localisatrices et règles de rattachement à caractère substantiel: De quelques aspects récents de la diversification de la méthode conflictuelle en Europe (1985)

PERDUE, W.C., *A Reexamination of the Distinction* between 'Loss Allocating' and 'Conduct-Regulating' Rules, 60 La. L. Rev. 1251 (2000)

PERDUE, W.C., *Personal Jurisdiction and the Beetle in the Box*, 32 B.C.L. Rev. 529 (1991)

PERRITT, H., *Will the Judgment-Proof Own Cyberspace?* 32 Int'l Law. 1121 (1998)

PERRITT, H., *Jurisdiction in Cyberspace*, 41 Vill. L. Rev. 1 (1996)

PETERSON, C.H., Limits on the Enforcement of Foreign Country Judgments and Choice of Law and Forum Clauses, in "Law and Justice in a Multistate World: Essays in Honor of Arthur T. von Mehren," 173 (Nafziger & Symeonides, eds. 2002)

PETERSON, C.H., Restating Conflicts Again: A Cure for Schizophrenia? 75 Ind. L. J. 549 (2000)

PETERSON, C.H., American Private International Law at the End of the 20th Century: Progress or Regress? in Symeonides, "Private International Law at the End of the 20th Century: Progress or Regress?" 430 (2000)

PETERSON, C.H., New Openness to Statutory Choice of Law Solutions, 38 Am. J. Comp. L. 423 (1990)

PETERSON, C.H., Particularism in the Conflict of Laws, 10 Hofstra L. Rev. 973 (1982)

PETERSON, C.H., Proposals of Marriage Between Jurisdiction and Choice of Law, 14 U.C. Davis L. Rev. 869 (1981)

PETERSON, C.H., *Foreign Country Judgments* and the Second Restatement of Conflict Laws, 72 Colum. L. Rev. 220 (1972)

PHAIR, R., Resolving the 'Choice-of-Law Problem' in Rule 23(b)(3) *Nationwide Class Actions*, 67 U.Chi. L. Rev. 835 (2000)

PICONE, P., La riforma italiana del diritto internazionale privato (1998)

PICONE, P., Les méthodes de coordination entre ordres juridiques en droit international privé, 276 Recueil des Cours 9 (1999)

PICONE, P., Caratteri ed evoluzione del methodo tradizionale dei conflitti di leggi, Riv.dir.int'le 5 (1990)

POCAR, F., The Drafting of a *World-Wide Convention* on Jurisdiction and the Enforcement of Judgements: Which Format for the Negotiations in The Hague? in "Law and Justice in a Multistate World: Essays in Honor of Arthur T. von Mehren," 191 (Nafziger & Symeonides, eds. 2002)

POCAR, F., La protection de la partie faible en droit international privé, 188 Recueil des Cours 340 (1984)

POCAR, F. & HONORATI, C., Italian Private International Law at the End of the 20th Century: Progress or Regress? in Symeonides, "Private International Law at the End of the 20th Century: Progress or Regress?" 279 (2000)

POMMERSHEIM, F., *A Path Near the Clearing:* An Essay on Constitutional Adjudication in Tribal Courts, 27 Gonz. L. Rev. 393 (1991-92)

POMMERSHEIM, F., *The Crucible of Sovereignty:* Analyzing Issues of Tribal Jurisdiction, 31 Ariz. L. Rev. 329 (1989)

POSCH, W. *Resolving Business Disputes* Through Litigation or Alternatives: The Effects of Jurisdictional Rules and Recognition Practice, ___Houston J.Int'l L. ___ (2004).

POSNAK, B., The Restatement (Second): Some Not so Fine Tuning for a Restatement, Third): A Very Well-Curried Leflar over Reese with Korn on the Side (or is it Cob?, 75 Ind. L. J. 561 (2000)

POSNAK, B., Choice of Law--Interest Analysis: *They Still Don't Get It*, 40 Wayne L. Rev. 1121 (1994)

POSNAK, B., Choice of Law: Interest Analysis and Its *"New Crits,"* 36 Am. J. Comp. L. 681 (1988)

POSNAK, B., Choice of Law: *A Very Well-Curried Leflar Approach*, 34 Mercer L. Rev. 731 (1983)

POSNER, K.B., Coverage for Punitive Damages: Choice of Law Shell Game, 60 Def. Couns. J. 399 (1993)

POWELL, T., *And Repent at Leisure*, 58 Harv. L. Rev. 930 (1945)

PRICE, P., Full Faith and Credit and the *Equity Conflict*, 84 Va. L. Rev. 747 (1998)

PRUJINER, A., Canadian Private International Law at the End of the 20th Century: Progress or Regress? in Symeonides, "Private International Law at the End of the 20th Century: Progress or Regress?" 127 (2000)

RABEL, E., The *Conflict of Laws*: A Comparative Study (v. IV) (1958)

RAGSDALE, F., Problems in the Application of *Full Faith and Credit for Indian Tribes*, 7 N.M. L. Rev. 133 (1977)

REAVLEY, T.M. & WESEVICH, J.W., An Old Rule for New Reasons: Place of Injury as a Federal Solution to Choice of Law in Single-Accident Mass-Tort Cases, 71 Tex. L. Rev. 1 (1992)

REDISH, M., *Federal Jurisdiction:* Tensions in the Allocation of Judicial Power (2d ed. 1990)

REDISH, M., Of *New Wine and Old Bottles*: Personal Jurisdiction, the Internet, and the Nature of Constitutional Evolution, 38 Jurimetrics J. 575 (1998)

REDISH, M., *Due Process, Federalism, and Personal Jurisdiction*: A Theoretical Evaluation, 75 Nw.U. L. Rev. 1112 (1981)

REDISH, M., & WOODS, C., *Congressional Power* to Control the Jurisdiction of Lower Federal Courts: A Critical Review and a New Synthesis, 124 U.Pa. L. Rev. 45 (1975)

REED, A., The Anglo-American Revolution in Tort Choice of Law Principles: Paradigm Shift or Pandora's Box? 18 Ariz.J.Int'l & Comp. L. 867 (2001)

REED, A., The Private International Law (Miscellaneous Provisions) Act 1995 and the Need for Escape Devices, 15 Civ.Just.Q. 305 (1996)

REES, J., *Choice of Law in Georgia:* Time to Consider a Change?, 34 Mercer L. Rev. 787 (1983)

REESE, W.L., The Second Restatement of Conflict of Laws Revisited, 34 Mercer L. Rev. 501 (1983)

REESE, W.L., American Choice of Law, 30 Am. J. Comp. L. 135 (1982)

REESE, W.L., American Trends in Private International Law: Academic and Judicial Manipulation of Choice of Law Rules in Tort Cases, 33 Vand. L. Rev. 717 (1980)

REESE, W.L., Choice of Law in Torts and Contracts and Directions for the Future, 16

Colum.J.Transnat'l L. 1 (1977)

REESE, W.L., *Dépeçage*: A Common Phenomenon in Choice of Law, 73 Colum. L. Rev. 58 (1973)

REESE, W.L., Choice of Law: Rules or Approach, 57 Cornell L.Q. 315 (1972)

REESE, W.L., *Choice of Law*, 71 Colum. L. Rev. 548 (1971)

REESE, W.L., Chief *Judge Fuld* and Choice of Law, 71 Colum. L. Rev. 548 (1971)

REESE, W.L., *General Course* on Private International Law, 150 Recueil des Cours 1 (1976)

REESE, W.L., Full Faith and Credit to *Foreign Equity Decrees*, 42 Iowa L. Rev. 183 (1957)

REESE, W.L. & JOHNSON, V., The Scope of *Full Faith and Credit to Judgments*, 49 Colum. L. Rev. 153 (1949)

REIMANN, M., *Liability for Defective Products* and Services: Emergence of a Worldwide Standard? General Report to the XVIth International Congress of Comparative Law, Brisbane (2002)

REIMANN, M., Parochialism in American Conflict Law, 49 Am. J. Comp. L., 369 (2001)

REIMANN, M., Codifying Torts Conflicts: The 1999 German Legislation in Comparative Perspective, 60 La. L. Rev. 1297 (2000)

REIMANN, M., A New Restatement-for the International Age, 75 Ind. L. J. 575 (2000)

REPPY, W., *Codifying Interest Analysis* in the Torts Chapter of a New Conflicts Restatement, 75 Ind. L. J. 591 (2000)

REPPY, W., *Louisiana's* Proposed *Hybrid* Quasi-Community Property Approach Could Cause Unfairness, 13 Com.Prop.J. 1 (1986)

REPPY, W., Eclecticism in Choice of Law: Hybrid Method or Mishmash?, 34 Mercer L. Rev. 645 (1983)

RESNIK, J., *Dependent Sovereigns:* Indian Tribes, States, and the Federal Courts, 56 U.Chi. L. Rev. 671 (1989)

REULAND, R.C., The Recognition of Judgments in the European Community: *The Twenty-Fifth Anniversary of the Brussels Convention*, 14 Mich.J.Int'l L. 559 (1993)

REYNOLDS, W., Robert Leflar, Judicial Process and Choice of Law, 52 Ark. L. Rev. 123 (1999)

REYNOLDS, W., Legal Process and Choice of Law, 56 Md. L. Rev. 1371, 1997)

RHEINSTEIN, M., How to Review a *Festschrift*, 11 Am. J. Comp. L. 632, 1962)

RICHMAN, W.M., Graphic Forms in Conflict of Laws, 27 U.Tol. L. Rev. 631 (1996)

RICHMAN, W.M., Carnival Cruise Lines: Forum Selection Clauses in Adhesion Contracts, 40 Am. J. Comp. L. 977 (1992)

RICHMAN, W.M., Review Essay: Part I: Casad's Jurisdiction in Civil Actions; Part II: *A Sliding Scale* to Supplement the Distinction Between General and Specific Jurisdiction, 72 Cal. L. Rev. 1328 (1984)

RICHMAN, W.M., Diagramming Conflicts: A Graphic Understanding of Interest Analysis, 43 Ohio St. L. J. 317 (1982)

RICHMAN, W.M. & REYNOLDS, W., Understanding Conflict of Laws, 2d ed. 1992

RICHMAN, W.M. & REYNOLDS, W., Prologomenon to an Empirical Restatement of Conflicts, 75 Ind.

L. J. 417 (2000)

RICHMAN, W.M. & RILEY, D., The First Restatement of Conflict of Laws on the Twenty-Fifth Anniversary of Its Successor: Contemporary Practice in Traditional Courts, 56 Md. L. Rev. 1196 (1997)

RIGAUX, F., *La théorie des qualifications* en droit international privé (1956)

RIGAUX, F., Codification of Private International Law: Pros and Cons, 60 La. L. Rev. 1321 (2000)

RIGAUX, F., Droit privé matériel et règles de conflit de lois, Rev.Belge dr.int'l 385 (1991)

RITZ, W., Rewriting the *History of the Judiciary Act* of 1789 (1990)

ROBERTSON, A.H., *Characterization* in the Conflict of Laws (1940)

ROGERS, J., Applying the International Law of *Sovereign Immunity* to the States of the Union, 1981 Duke L. J. 449

ROGERSON, P., Choice of Law in Tort: A Missed Opportunity? 44 Int'l Comp. L. Q. 650 (1995)

ROSEN, M., Extraterritoriality and Political Heterogeneity in American Federalism, 150 U.Pa. L. Rev. 855 (2002)

ROSENBERG, M., *The Comeback* of Choice-of-Law Rules, 81 Colum. L. Rev. 946 (1981)

ROSENBERG, M., *Comments on Reich* v. Purcell, 15 UCLA L. Rev. 641 (1968)

ROSENBERG, M., *Two Views on Kell* v. Henderson: An Opinion for the New York Court of Appeals, 67 Colum. L. Rev. 459 (1967)

ROOSEVELT, K., The Myth of Choice of Law: Rethinking Conflicts, 97 Mich. L. Rev. 2448 (1999)

ROSS, G.W.C., *"Full Faith and Credit"* in a Federal System, 20 Minn. L. Rev. 140 (1936)

RYAN, R., *Uncertifiable?*: The Current Status of Nationwide State-Law Class Actions, 54 Baylor L. Rev. 467 (2002)

SAVIGNY, F.K. von, *System* des heutigen Römischen Rechts (v. 8) (1849)

SAVIGNY, F.K. von, *Private International Law*, A Treatise on the Conflict of Laws and the Limits of their Operation in Respect of Place and Time (Transl. by W. Guthrie (1869))

SAWAKI, T., Recognition and Enforcement of *Foreign Judgments in Japan*, 23 Int'l Law. 29 (1989)

SCHOENBLUM, J., Choice of Law and Succession to Wealth: A Critical Analysis of the Ramifications of the Hague Convention on Succession to Decedents' Estates, 32 Va.J.Int'l L. 83 (1991)

SCOLES, E., *The Hague Convention on Succession*, 42 Am. J. Comp. L. 85 (1994)

SCOLES, E., HAY, P., BORCHERS, P. & SYMEONIDES, S. *Conflict of Laws* (3rd ed. 2000)

SEDLER, R., American Federalism, State Sovereignty, and the Interest Analysis Approach to Choice of Law, in "Law and Justice in a Multistate World:Essays in Honor of Arthur T. von Mehren," 369 (Nafziger & Symeonides, eds. 2002)

SEDLER, R., The Louisiana Codification and Tort Rules of Choice of Law, 60 La. L. Rev. 1331 (2000)

SEDLER, R., Choice of Law in Conflicts Torts Cases: A Third Restatement or Rules of Choice of Law?

75 Ind. L. J. 615 (2000)

SEDLER, R., A Real World Perspective on Choice of Law, 48 Mercer L. Rev. 781 (1997)

SEDLER, R., The Complex Litigation Project's Proposal for Federally-Mandated Choice of Law in Mass Torts Cases: Another Assault on State Sovereignty, 54 La. L. Rev. 1085 (1994)

SEDLER, R., Interest Analysis, Party Expectations and Judicial Method in Conflicts Torts Cases: Reflections on Cooney v. Osgood Machinery, Inc., 59 Brook. L. Rev. 1323 (1994)

SEDLER, R., Interest Analysis, State Sovereignty, and Federally-Mandated Choice of Law in "Mass Tort" Cases, 56 Alb. L. Rev. 855 (1993)

SEDLER, R., Continuity, Precedent, and Choice of Law: A Reflective Response to Professor Hill, 38 Wayne L. Rev. 1419 (1992)

SEDLER, R., Professor Juenger's Challenge to the Interest Analysis Approach to Choice-of-Law: An Appreciation and a Response, 23 U.C. Davis L. Rev. 865 (1990)

SEDLER, R., Interest Analysis as the Preferred Approach to Choice of Law : A Response to Professor Brilmayer's "Foundational Attack," 46 Ohio St. L. J. 483 (1985)

SEDLER, R., Interest Analysis and Forum Preference in the Conflict of Laws: A Response to the "New Crits," 34 Mercer L. Rev. 593 (1983)

SEDLER, R., Reflections on Conflict-of-Laws Methodology, 32 Hastings L. J. 1628 (1981)

SEDLER, R., Rules of Choice of Law Versus Choice-of-Law Rules: Judicial Method in Conflicts Torts Cases, 44 Tenn. L. Rev. 975 (1977)

SEDLER, R., The Governmental Interest Analysis to Choice of Law: An Analysis and a Reformulation, 25 UCLA L. Rev. 181 (1977)

SEDLER, R., On Choice of Law and the Great Quest: A Critique of Special Multistate Solutions to Choice-of-Law Problems, 7 Hofstra L. Rev. 807 (1979)

SEDLER, R., Interstate Accidents and the Unprovided-for Case: Reflections on Neumeier v. Kuehner, 1 Hofstra L. Rev. 125 (1973)

SEDLER, R., The Truly Disinterested Forum in the Conflict of Laws, 25 S.C. L. Rev. 185 (1973)

SEIDELSON, D.E., Section 6.01 of the ALI's Complex Litigation Project: Function Follows Form, 54 La. L. Rev. 1111 (1994)

SEIDELSON, D.E., Resolving Choice-of-Law Problems Through Interest Analysis in Personal Injury Actions: A Suggested Order of Priority Among Competing State Interests and Among Available Techniques for Weighing those Interests, 30 Duq. L. Rev. 869 (1992)

SEIDELSON, D.E., Interest Analysis: The Quest for Perfection and the Frailties of Man, 19 Duq. L. Rev. 207 (1981)

SHAPIRA, A., The Interest Approach to Choice of Law (1970)

SHAPIRA, A., Foreign Same-Sex Adoption and Domestic Public Policy: Recognition of Foreign Decrees as a Playground for Domestic Timid Reformers, in "Law and Justice in a Multistate World: Essays in Honor of Arthur T. von Mehren," 219 (Nafziger & Symeonides, eds. 2002)

SHAPIRA, A., Territorialism, National Parochialism, Universalism and Party Autonomy: How does One Square the Choice of Law Circle? 26 Brooklyn J.Int'l L. 199 (2000)

SHAPIRA, A., Torts Choice of Law in Israel: Putting Order in a Methodological Chaos, in Private Law in the International Arena -- Liber Amicorum Kurt Siehr 685 (J. Basedow, e.o., eds. 2000)

SHERMAN, S.B., Child Custody Jurisdiction and the Parental Kidnapping Prevention Act—A Due Process Dilemma?, 17 Tulsa L. J. 713 (1982)

SHREVE, G.R., A Conflict-of-Laws Anthology (1997)

SHREVE, G.R., Conflicts Altruism, in "Law and Justice in a Multistate World: Essays in Honor of Arthur T. von Mehren," 383 (Nafziger & Symeonides, eds. 2002)

SHREVE, G.R., Every Conflicts Decision is a Promise Broken, 60 La. L. Rev. 1345 (2000)

SHREVE, G.R., Notes from the Eye of the Storm, 48 Mercer L. Rev. 823 (1997)

SHREVE, G.R., Choice of Law and the Forgiving Constitution, 71 Ind. L. J. 271 (1996)

SHREVE, G.R., Conflicts Law—State or Federal?, 68 Ind. L. J. 907 (1993)

SHREVE, G.R., Judgments from a Choice-of-Law Perspective, 40 Am. J. Comp. L. 985 (1992)

SHREVE, G.R., Preclusion and Federal Choice of Law, 64 Tex. L. Rev. 1209 (1986)

SHREVE, G.R. & RAVEN-HANSON, P., Understanding Civil Procedure, 2d ed. 1994)

SIEGEL, D.D., A Retrospective on Babcock v. Jackson: A Personal View, 56 Alb. L. Rev. 693 (1993)

SIEGEL, D.D., Case and Comment, In Vagrant Verse, 76 Case Comment 56 (Sept.-Oct. 1971)

SIEHR, K., Internationales Privatrecht, Heidelberg (2001)

SIEHR, K., Revolution and Evolution in Conflicts Law, 60 La. L. Rev. 1353 (2000)

SIEHR, K., Swiss Private International Law at the End of the 20th Century: Progress or Regress? in Symeonides, "Private International Law at the End of the 20th Century: Progress or Regress?" 389 (2000)

SIEHR, K., International Art Trade and the Law, 243 Recueil des Cours 9 (1993)

SIEHR, K., Ehrenzweigs lex-fori-Theorie und ihre Bedeutung für das amerikanische und deutsche Kollisionsrecht, 34 RabelsZ 583, 1970)

SILBERMAN, L., Judicial Jurisdiction in the Conflict of Laws Course: Adding a Comparative Dimension, 28 Vand. J. Transn'l L. 389 (1995)

SILBERMAN, L., Cooney v. Osgood Machinery, Inc.: A Less than Complete "Contribution", 59 Brooklyn L. Rev. 1367 (1994)

SILBERMAN, L., Shaffer v. Heitner: The End of an Era, 53 N.Y.U.L. Rev. 33, 88 (1978)

SIMON-DÉPITRE, Les règles matérielles dans le conflit de lois, 63 Rev. critique 591 (1974)

SIMSON, G., State Interests, State Autonomy, and the Quest for Uniformity in Choice of Law, in "Law and Justice in a Multistate World: Essays in Honor of Arthur T. von Mehren," 391 (Nafziger & Symeonides, eds. 2002)

SIMSON, G., Leave Bad Enough Alone, 75 Ind. L.

J. 649 (2000)

SIMSON, G., Resisting the Allure of Better Rule of Law, 52 Ark. L. Rev. 141 (1999)

SIMSON, G., The Neumeier-Schultz Rules: How Logical a "Next State in the Evolution of the Law" After Babcock?, 56 Alb. L. Rev. 913 (1993)

SIMSON, G., Plotting the Next "Revolution" in Choice of Law: A Proposed Approach, 24 Cornell Int'l L. J. 279 (1991)

SINGER, J.W., Pay No Attention to that Man behind the Curtain: The Place of Better Law in a Third Restatement of Conflicts, 75 Ind. L. J. 659 (2000)

SINGER, J.W., Justice and the Conflict of Laws, 48 Mercer L. Rev. 831 (1997)

SINGER, J.W., A Pragmatic Guide to Conflicts, 70 B.U. L. Rev. 731 (1990)

SINGER, J.W., Facing Real Conflicts, 24 Cornell Int'l L. J. 197 (1991)

SOLIMINE, M.E., The Impact of Babcock v. Jackson: An Empirical Note, 56 Alb. L. Rev. 773 (1993)

SOLIMINE, M.E., Choice of Law in the American Courts in 1991, 40 Am. J. Comp. L. 951 (1992)

SOLIMINE, M.E., An Economic and Empirical Analysis of Choice of Law, 24 Ga. L. Rev. 49 (1989)

SONNENBERGER, H., Le droit international privé allemand à la fin du vingtième siècle: Progrès ou recul? in Symeonides, "Private International Law at the End of the 20th Century: Progress or Regress?" 221 (2000)

SOUTHERLAND, H., Sovereignty, Value Judgments, and Choice of Law, 38 Brandeis L. J. 451 (2000)

SPAHT, K. & SYMEONIDES, S., Covenant Marriage and the Conflict of Laws, 32 Creighton L. Rev. 1085 (1999)

STANIVUKOVIĆ, M., Yugoslavian Private International Law at the End of the 20th Century: Progress or Regress? in Symeonides, "Private International Law at the End of the 20th Century: Progress or Regress?" 461 (2000)

STEIN, A., The Unexceptional Problem of Jurisdiction in Cyberspace, 32 Int'l Law. 1167 (1998)

STEIN, A., Erie and Court Access, 100 Yale L. J. 1935 (1991)

STEIN, A., Symposium: Entire Controversy Doctrine: Forward, 28 Rutgers L. Rev. 1 (1996)

STEPHAN, P., The Political Economics of Choice of Law, 90 Geo. L. J. 957 (2002)

STERK, S.E., The New York Court of Appeals: 150 Years of Leading Decisions, 48 Syr. L. Rev. 1391 (1998)

STERK, S.E., The Marginal Relevance of Choice of Law Theory, 142 U.Pa. L. Rev. 949 (1994)

STERK, S.E., Full Faith and Credit, More or Less, to Judgments: Doubts About Thomas v. Washington Gas Light Co., 69 Geo. L. Rev. 1329 (1981)

STEVENS, B., Translating Filartiga: A Comparative and International Law Analysis of Domestic Remedies for International Human Rights Violations, 27 Yale J. Int'l L. 1 (2002)

STEWART, M., A New Litany of Personal Jurisdiction, 60 U. Colo. L. Rev. 5 (1989)

STOFFEL, W., Corporate Autonomy and Market Regulations, in "Law and Justice in a Multistate World: Essays in Honor of Arthur T. von Mehren," 399 (Nafziger & Symeonides, eds. 2002)

STORY, J., Commentaries on the Conflict of Laws (1834)

STRUVE, C. & WAGNER, R.P., Realspace Sovereigns in Cyberspace: Problems with the Anticybersquatting Consumer Protection Act, 17 Berkeley Tech. L. J. 989 (2002)

SYMEONIDES, S., Private International Law at the End of the 20th Century: Progress or Regress? (2000)

SYMEONIDES, S., An Outsider's View of the American Approach to Choice of Law: Comparative Observations on Current American and Continental Conflicts Doctrine (1980)

SYMEONIDES, S., The American Choice-of-Law Revolution in the Courts: Today and Tomorrow, 298 Recueil des Cours ___ (2003)

SYMEONIDES, S., Tort Conflicts and Rome II: A View from Across, in Festschrift für Erik Jayme ___ (2003)

SYMEONIDES, S., Resolving Punitive Damages Conflicts, 5 Swiss Ybk.Priv.Int'l L., ___ (2003)

SYMEONIDES, S., Territoriality and Personality in Tort Conflicts, in "Intercontinental Cooperation Through Private International Law: Essays in Memory of Peter Nygh" (T.Einhorn & P. Siehr eds) 405 (2003)

SYMEONIDES, S., Codifying Choice of Law for Contracts: The Oregon Experience, 67 RabelsZ ___ (2003)

SYMEONIDES, S., Choice of Law in the American Courts in 2002: Sixteenth Annual Survey, 51 Am. J. Comp. L. 1 (2003)

SYMEONIDES, S., Choice of Law in the American Courts in 2001: Fifteenth Annual Survey, 50 Am. J. Comp. L. 1 (2002)

SYMEONIDES, S., Codifying Puerto Rico's Choice-of-Law for Contracts, in "Law and Justice in a Multistate World: Essays in Honor of Arthur T. von Mehren," 419 (Nafziger & Symeonides eds. 2002)

SYMEONIDES, S., Choice of Law in the American Courts in 2000: As the Century Turns, 49 Am. J. Comp. L. 1 (2001)

SYMEONIDES, S., American Choice of Law at the Dawn of the 21st Century, 37 Willamette L. Rev. 1 (2000)

SYMEONIDES, S., Material Justice and Conflicts Justice in Choice of Law, in "International Conflict of Laws for the Third Millennium: Essays in Honor of Friedrich K. Juenger," 125 (Borchers & Zekoll, eds. 2000)

SYMEONIDES, S., On the Side of the Angels: Choice of Law and Stolen Cultural Property, in "Private Law in the International Arena -- Liber Amicorum Kurt Siehr," 649 (J. Basedow, e.o., eds. 2000)

SYMEONIDES, S., The Need for a Third Conflicts Restatement (And a Proposal for Tort Conflicts, 75 Ind. L. J. 437-74, 2000)

SYMEONIDES, S., Choice of Law in the American Courts in 1999: One More Year, 48 Am. J. Comp. L. 143 (2000)

SYMEONIDES, S., Choice of Law in the American Courts in 1998: Twelfth Annual Survey, 47 Am.

J. Comp. L. 327 (1999)

SYMEONIDES, S., *Choice of Law in* the American Courts in *1997*, 46 Am. J. Comp. L. 233 (1998)

SYMEONIDES, S., The Judicial Acceptance of *the Second Conflicts Restatement*: A Mixed Blessing, 56 Md. L. Rev. 1246 (1997)

SYMEONIDES, S., Resolving *Six Celebrated Conflicts Cases* Through Statutory Choice-of-Law Rules, 48 Mercer L. Rev. 837 (1997)

SYMEONIDES, S., *Choice of Law* in the American Courts *in 1996*: Tenth Annual Survey, 45 Am. J. Comp. L. 447 (1997)

SYMEONIDES, S., *Choice of Law* in the American Courts *in 1995*: A Year in Review, 44 Am. J. Comp. L. 181 (1996)

SYMEONIDES, S., Choice of Law in the American Courts in 1994: *A View "From the Trenches,"* 43 Am. J. Comp. L. 1 (1995)

SYMEONIDES, S., *Choice of Law* in the American Courts *in 1993* (and in the Six Previous Years, 42 Am. J. Comp. L. 599 (1994)

SYMEONIDES, S., Louisiana Conflicts Law: *Two "Surprises,"* 54 La. L. Rev. 497 (1994)

SYMEONIDES, S., The ALI's Complex Litigation Project: *Commencing the National Debate*, 54 La. L. Rev. 843 (1994)

SYMEONIDES, S., *Exception Clauses* in American Conflicts Law, 42 Am. J. Comp. L. 813 (1994) (Suppl.)

SYMEONIDES, S., Private International Law Codification in a Mixed Jurisdiction: The *Louisiana Experience*, 57 RabelsZ 460 (1993)

SYMEONIDES, S., Louisiana's New Law of Choice of Law for Tort Conflicts: An *Exegesis*, 66 Tul. L. Rev. 677 (1992)

SYMEONIDES, S., *Revising Puerto Rico's Conflicts Law*: A Preview, 28 Colum.J.Transn'l L. 413 (1990)

SYMEONIDES, S., *Choice of Law* in the American Courts *in 1988*, 37 Am. J. Comp. L. 457 (1989)

SYMEONIDES, S., *Exploring the "Dismal Swamp"*: Revising Louisiana's Conflicts Law on Successions, 47 La. L. Rev. 1029 (1987)

SYMEONIDES, S., In Search of New Choice-of-Law Solutions to Some Marital Property Problems of *Migrant Spouses*: A Response to the Critics, 13 Com.Prop.J. 11 (1986)

SYMEONIDES, S., Revolution and Counter-Revolution in American Conflicts Law: Is there a *Middle Ground?*, 46 Ohio St. L. J. 549 (1985)

SYMEONIDES, S., *Maritime Conflicts* Law from the Perspective of Modern Choice of Law Methodology, 7 Mar. Law. 223 (1982)

TETTLEY, W., A Canadian Looks at American Conflict of Law Theory and Practice, Especially in Light of the American Legal and Social Systems (Corrective vs. Distributive Justice), 38 Colum.J.Transn'l L. 299 (1999)

THUE, H., Norwegian Private International Law at the End of the 20th Century: Progress or Regress? in Symeonides, "Private International Law at the End of the 20th Century: Progress or Regress?" 319 (2000)

TODD, J.J., *A Judge's View*, 31 S.C. L. Rev. 435 (1980)

TRAUTMAN, D.T., Toward *Federalizing Choice of Law*, 70 Tex. L. Rev. 1715 (1992)

TRAUTMAN, D.T., A Comment on Twerski and Mayer: A Pragmatic Step Towards Consensus as a Basis for Choice-of-Law Solutions, 7 Hofstra L. Rev. 833 (1979)

TRAUTMAN, D.T., The Relation Between American Choice of Law and *Federal Common Law*, 41 Law & Contemp. Prob. 105 (1977)

TRAUTMAN, D.T., *Two Views on Kell* v. Henderson: A Comment, 67 Colum. L. Rev. 465 (1967)

TRAYNOR, M., Conflict of Laws, Comparative Law, and the American Law Institute, 49 Am. J. Comp. L. 391 (2001)

TRAYNOR, R., *Is this Conflict Really Necessary?*, 37 Tex. L. Rev. 658, 670 (1959)

TWERSKI, A., One Size Does not Fit All: The Third Multi-Track Restatement of Conflict of Laws, 75 Ind. L. J. 667 (2000)

TWERSKI, A., A Sheep in Wolf's Clothing: Territorialism in the Guise of Interest Analysis in Cooney v. Osgood Machinery, Inc., 59 Brook. L. Rev. 1351 (1994)

TWERSKI, A., With Liberty and Justice for All: An Essay on Agent Orange and Choice of Law, 52 Brook. L. Rev. 341 (1986)

TWERSKI, A., On Territoriality and Sovereignty: System Shock and Constitutional Choice of Law, 10 Hofstra L. Rev. 149 (1981)

TWERSKI, A., Neumeier v. Kuhner: Where Are the *Emperor's Clothes?*, 1 Hofstra L. Rev. 93 (1973)

TWERSKI, A., Enlightened Territorialism and Prof. Cavers: The Pennsylvania Method, 9 Duq. L. Rev. 373 (1971)

TWERSKI, A. & MAYER, R., Toward a *Pragmatic Solution* of Choice-of-Law Problems: At the Interface of Substance and Procedure, 74 N.W.U. L. Rev. 781 (1979)

TWITCHELL, M., Why We Keep Doing Business with Doing-Business Jurisdiction, 2001 U.Chi. Legal F. 171

TWITCHELL, M., *The Myth of General Jurisdiction*, 101 Harv. L. Rev. 610 (1988)

VAN BOESCHOTEN, C.D., Hague Conference Conventions and the United States: *A European View*, 57 Law & Contemp. Probs. 47 (1994)

VASSILAKAKIS, E., Orientations méthologiques dans les codifications récentes du droit international privé en Europe (1987)

VETTER, W., *Of Tribal Courts and "Territories"*: Is Full Faith and Credit Required, 23 Cal W. L. Rev. 219 (1987)

VISCHER, F., New Tendencies in European Conflict of Laws and the Influence of the US-Doctrine--A Short Survey, in "Law and Justice in a Multistate World: Essays in Honor of Arthur T. von Mehren," 459 (Nafziger & Symeonides, eds. 2002)

VISCHER, F., General Course on Private International Law, 232 Recueil des Cours 9 (1992)

VISCHER, F., Drafting National Legislation on Conflict of Laws: The Swiss Experience, 41 Law & Contemp. Prob. 131 (1977)

VITTA, E., The Impact in Europe of the American 'Conflicts Revolution', 30 Am. J. Comp. L. 1 (1982)

VITTA, E., Cours general de droit international privé,

162 Recueil des Cours 9 (1979)

VOLKEN, P., Wenn Wächter mit Story, in "Private Law in the International Arena -- Liber Amicorum Kurt Siehr," 815 (J. Basedow, e.o., eds. 2000)

VON BAR, C., Environmental Damage in Private International Law, 268 Recueil des Cours 291 (1997)

VON MEHREN, A.T., Theory and Practice of *Adjudicatory Authority* in Private International Law: A Comparative Study of the Doctrine, Policies and Practices of Common- and Civil Law Systems, 295 Recueil des Cours 9 (2003)

VON MEHREN, A.T., American Conflicts Law at the Dawn of the 21st Century, 37 Willamette L. Rev. 133 (2000)

VON MEHREN, A.T., Enforcing Judgments Abroad: Reflections on the *Design of Recognition Conventions*, 24 Brooklyn J.Int'l L. 17 (1998)

VON MEHREN, A.T., *The Case for a Convention-mixte Approach* to Jurisdiction to Adjudicate and Recognition and Enforcement of Foreign Judgments, 61 RabelsZ 86 (1997)

VON MEHREN, A.T., Recognition and Enforcement of Foreign Judgments: *A New Approach* for the Hague Conference?, 57 Law & Contemp. Probs. 271 (1994)

VON MEHREN, A.T., Recognition of United States Judgments Abroad and Foreign Judgments in the United States, 57 RabelsZ 449 (1993)

VON MEHREN, A.T., *Adjudicatory Jurisdiction*: General Theories Compared and Evaluated, 63 Boston U.L.Rev. 279 (1983)

VON MEHREN, A.T., Recognition and Enforcement of *Sister-State Judgments*: Reflections on General Theory and Current Practice in the European Economic Community and the United States, 81 Colum. L. Rev. 1044 (1981)

VON MEHREN, A.T., Recognition and Enforcement of *Foreign Judgments*: General Theory and the Role of Jurisdictional Requirements, 167 Recueil des Cours 9 (1980)

VON MEHREN, A.T., Choice of Law and the Problem of Justice, 41 Law & Contemp. Probs. 27 (1977)

VON MEHREN, A.T., *Recent Trends* in Choice-of-Law Methodology, 60 Cornell L. Rev. 927 (1975)

VON MEHREN, A.T., *Special Substantive Rules* for Multistate Problems: Their Role and Significance in Contemporary Choice of Law Methodology, 88 Harv. L. Rev. 298 (1974)

VON MEHREN, A.T., Conflict of Laws in a Federal System: Some Perspectives, 18 Int. & Comp. L. Q. 681 (1969)

VON MEHREN, A.T., *Book Review*, 17 J. Legal Ed. 91 (1964) (reviewing Brainerd Currie, Selected Essays on the Conflict of Laws (1963))

VON MEHREN, A.T., The *Renvoi* and its Relation to Various Approaches to the Choice-of-Law Problem, XXth Century Comparative and Conflicts Law 380 (1961)

VON MEHREN, A.T. & TRAUTMAN, D.T., The Law of *Multistate Problems* 76 (1965)

VON MEHREN, A.T. & TRAUTMAN, D.T., Constitutional Control of Choice of Law: Some Reflections on Hague, 10 Hofstra L. Rev. 35 (1981)

VON MEHREN, A.T. & TRAUTMAN, D.T., *Recognition of Foreign Adjudications*: A Survey and a Suggested Approach, 81 Harv. L. Rev. 1601 (1968)

VON MEHREN, A.T. & TRAUTMAN, D.T, *Jurisdiction to Adjudicate*: A Suggested Analysis, 79 Harv. L. Rev. 1121 (1966)

VON MEHREN, R.B., *International Control of Civil Procedure*: Who Benefits? 57 Law & Contemp. Probs. 13 (1994)

VON OVERBECK, A., De quelques règles générales de conflit de lois dans les codifications récentes, in "Private Law in the International Arena -- Liber Amicorum Kurt Siehr" 545 (J. Basedow, e.o., eds. 2000)

VON OVERBECK, A., The Fate of Two Remarkable Provisions of the Swiss Statute on Private International Law, 1 Ybk. Priv. Int'l L. 119 (1999)

VON OVERBECK, A., Les questions generales du droit international privé a la lumière des codifications et projets recents, 176 Recueil des Cours 9 (1982)

VRELLIS, S., Le droit international privé grec vers la fin du vingtième siècle: Progrès ou recul? in Symeonides, "Private International Law at the End of the 20th Century: Progress or Regress?" 243 (2000)

VRELLIS, S., La justice 'matérielle' dans une codification du droit international privé, in "E Pluribus Unum, Liber Amicorum Georges Droz," 541 (1996)

WALKER, J., 'Are We There Yet?': Towards a New Rule for Choice of Law in Tort, 38 Osgoode Hall L. J. 331 (2000)

WALKER J., Choice of Law in Tort: the Supreme Court of Canada Enters the Fray, 111 Law Q. Rev. 397 (1995)

WALLINGFORD, J., The Role of Tradition in the *Navajo Judiciary:* Reemergence and Revival, 19 Okla. City U. L. Rev. 141 (1994)

WEINBERG, L., Of Theory and Theodicy: The Problem of Immoral Law, in "Law and Justice in a Multistate World: Essays in Honor of Arthur T. von Mehren," 473 (Nafziger & Symeonides, eds. 2002)

WEINBERG, L., A Structural Revision of the Conflicts Restatement, 75 Ind. L. J. 475 (2000)

WEINBERG, L., Choosing Law and Giving Justice, 60 La. L. Rev. 1361 (2000)

WEINBERG, L., *Mass Torts* at the Neutral Forum: A Critical Analysis of the ALI's Proposed Choice Rule, 56 Alb. L. Rev. 807 (1993)

WEINBERG, L., Choosing Law: *The Limitations Debates*, 1991 U. Ill. L. Rev. 683 (1991)

WEINBERG, L., *The Place of Trial* and the Law Applied: Overhauling Constitutional Theory, 59 U.Colo. L. Rev. 67 (1988)

WEINBERG, L., *On Departing from Forum Law*, 35 Mercer L. Rev. 595 (1984)

WEINBERG, L., Choice of Law and Minimal Scrutiny, 49 U.Chi. L. Rev. 440 (1982)

WEINBERG, L., Conflicts Cases and the Problem of Relevant Time: A Response to the Hague Symposium, 10 Hofstra L. Rev. 1023 (1981)

WEINSTEIN, J., *Mass Tort Jurisdiction and Choice*

of Law In a Multinational World Communicating by Extra-Terrestrial Satellites, 37 Willamette L. Rev. 145 (2000)

WEINSTEIN, J., *Ethical Dilemmas in Mass Tort Litigation,* 88 Nw. U. L. Rev. 469 (1994)

WEINTRAUB, R., *Commentary on the Conflict of Laws* (4th ed. 2001)

WEINTRAUB, R., Parallel Litigation and Forum-Selection Agreements, in "Law and Justice in a Multistate World: Essays in Honor of Arthur T. von Mehren," 229 (Nafziger & Symeonides, eds. 2002)

WEINTRAUB, R., Getting the Conflict of Laws Y2K Ready, 37 Willamette L. Rev. 157 (2000)

WEINTRAUB, R., The Restatement Third of Conflict of Laws: An Idea whose Time has not Come, 75 Ind. L. J. 679 (2000)

WEINTRAUB, R., Flailing in the Waters of the Louisiana Conflicts Code: Not Waving but Drowning, 60 La. L. Rev. 1365 (2000)

WEINTRAUB, R., Choice of Law for Products Liability: Demagnetizing the United States Forum, 52 Ark. L. Rev. 157 (1999)

WEINTRAUB, R., 'At Least to Do no Harm': Does the Second Restatement of Conflicts Meet the Hippocratic Standard?, 56 Md. L. Rev. 1284 (1997)

WEINTRAUB, R., International Litigation and *Forum Non Conveniens,* 29 Tex.Int'l L. J. 321 (1994)

WEINTRAUB, R., An Approach to Choice of Law That Focuses on *Consequences,* 56 Alb. L. Rev. 701 (1993)

WEINTRAUB, R., The Extraterritorial Application of Antitrust and Securities Laws: An Inquiry into the Utility of a "Choice-of-Law" Approach, 70 Tex. L. Rev. 1799 (1992)

WEINTRAUB, R., An Objective Basis for *Rejecting Transient Jurisdiction,* 22 Rutgers L. J. 611, 622 (1991)

WEINTRAUB, R., *The Contributions of Symeonides and Kozyris* to Making Choice of Law Predictable and Just: An Appreciation and Critique, 38 Am. J. Comp. L. 511 (1990)

WEINTRAUB, R., A Proposed Choice-of Law Standard for International Products Liability Disputes, 16 Brook.J.Int'l L. 225 (1990)

WEINTRAUB, R., Methods For Resolving Conflict-of-Laws Problems in *Mass Tort Litigation,* 1989 U.Ill. L. Rev. 129 (1989)

WEINTRAUB, R., *Asahi* Sends Personal Jurisdiction Down the Tubes, 23 Tex. Int'l L. J. 55 (1988)

WEINTRAUB, R., *Interest Analysis* in the Conflict of Laws as an Application of Sound Legal Reasoning, 35 Mercer L. Rev. 629 (1984)

WEINTRAUB, R., Functional Developments in *Choice of Law for Contracts,* 187 Recueil des Cours 239 (1984)

WESER, M., *Bases of Judicial Jurisdiction* in the Common Market Countries, 10 Am. J. Comp. L. 323 (1961)

WHINCOP, M., The Market Tort in Private International Law, 19 Nw. J. Int'l L. & Bus. 215 (1999)

WHITTEN, R., Curing the Deficiencies of the Conflicts Revolution: A Proposal for National Legislation on Choice of Law, Jurisdiction, and Judgments, 37 Willamette L. Rev. 259 (2000)

WHITTEN, R., Improving the Better Law System: Some Impudent Suggestions for Reordering and Reformulating Leflar's Choice-influencing Considerations, 52 Ark. L. Rev. 177 (1999)

WHITTEN, R., The Constitutional Limitations on State Choice of Law: *Full Faith and Credit,* 12 Mem.St. U. L. Rev. 1 (1981)

WHITTEN, R., The *Constitutional Limitations on State-Court Jurisdiction*: A Historical-Interpretative Reexamination of the Full Faith and Credit and Due Process Clauses (Part Two), 14 Creighton L. Rev. 735 (1981)

WHITTEN, R., The Constitutional Limits on State Choice of Law: *Due Process,* 9 Hast. Con. L. Q. 851 (1982)

WILDE, *Dépeçage* in the Choice of Tort Law, 41 S. Cal. L. Rev. 329 (1968)

WILLIAMS, F.I., The Complex Litigation Project's Choice of Law Rules for Mass Torts and How to Escape them (1995) B.Y.U. L. Rev. 1081

WOLFF, M., Private International Law (2d ed. 1950) [*PIL*]

WRIGHT, C.A., MILLER, A., & COOPER, E., *Federal Practice* and Procedure (1986)

WRIGHT, J.S., The *Federal Courts* and the Nature and Quality of State Law, 13 Wayne L.R. 317 (1967)

YNTEMA, H., The Hornbook Method and the Conflict of Laws, 37 Yale L. J. 468 (1928)

ZEKOLL, J., Liability for Defective Products and Services, in "American Law in a Time of Global Interdependence: U.S. National Reports to the XVIth International Congress of Comparative Law," 121 (Symeonides & Reitz, eds. 2002)

ZWEIGERT, K., Zur Armut des internationalen Privatrechts an socialen Werten, 37 RabelsZ 435 (1973)

ZWEIGERT, K., Some Reflections on the Sociological Dimensions of Private International Law or: What Is Justice in the Conflict of Laws?, 44 U. Colo. L. Rev. 283 (1973)

ISBN 0–314–26473–6

90000

9 780314 264732